INTRODUCTION TO TAXATION
Sixth Edition

INTRODUCTION TO TAXATION

SIXTH EDITION

WILLIAM D. POPKIN
Walter D. Foskett Professor Emeritus of Law
Indiana University Maurer School of Law

Casebook ISBN: 978-0-7698-8198-0
Looseleaf ISBN: 978-0-7698-8199-7
eBook ISBN: 978-0-7698-8200-0

Library of Congress Cataloging-in-Publication Data
Popkin, William D., author.
Introduction to taxation / William D. Popkin, Walter D. Foskett Professor Emeritus of Law, Indiana University Maurer School of Law. -- Sixth edition.
pages cm
Includes index.
ISBN 978-0-7698-8198-0
1. Income tax--Law and legislation--United States--Cases. I. Title.
KF6369.P668 2013
343.7305'2--dc23
2013041280

NOTE TO USERS
To ensure that you are using the latest materials available in this area, please be sure to periodically check the LexisNexis Law School web site for downloadable updates and supplements at www.lexisnexis.com/lawschool.

Editorial Offices
121 Chanlon Rd., New Providence, NJ 07974 (908) 464-6800
201 Mission St., San Francisco, CA 94105-1831 (415) 908-3200
www.lexisnexis.com

MATTHEW BENDER

To my children

Carol, Meera, and Lionel

Preface to the Sixth Edition

Incorporation of the 2013 tax law. This sixth edition includes updates to the income tax law that were contained in the American Taxpayer Relief Act of 2012 (ATRA). ATRA was passed to prevent the expiration of the Bush Tax Cuts that were part of the 2001 Tax Law (and later laws) and the sequestering of government expenditures that were scheduled to take effect on January 1, 2013.

Introduction to (not just income) taxation. When I started out teaching at Harvard's International Tax Program, it was obvious that the subject of taxation was much broader than the income tax. But when I suggested that the basic tax course should reflect the variety of available taxes, it aroused only skepticism. This edition includes my efforts — after some four decades of teaching — to overcome that skepticism. To that end, Part II of the coursebook deals with property taxes, the estate and gift tax, the Social Security (payroll) tax, the taxation of trusts and estates, corporate taxation, international tax issues, and multistate taxation. The treatment (necessarily) provides only a preliminary introduction but it should give the student a sense of the breadth of available taxes and their structure. It should also lay a useful foundation for advanced courses in those subjects. It can be taught at the end of the basic tax course or as a separate two-hour introductory course (or seminar).

Statutory interpretation. The bulk of the material in the coursebook continues to dwell on the income tax, with an emphasis on statutory interpretation. Tax law is the quintessential statutory course, originating solely from the legislative process and unencumbered by a common law tradition. In this respect, it differs from commercial law and criminal law. It is therefore an ideal vehicle for teaching statutory interpretation — either in the first year or in later years of law school.

I have drawn heavily on my own background as a legislation teacher and author of a Legislation casebook to provide the material on statutory interpretation. I do not mean to suggest that a study of tax law should be a substitute for a course in statutory interpretation; only that an understanding of the Internal Revenue Code and its application is vastly enhanced by an awareness of the statutory interpretation issues that recur in the case law. To that end, there are more than 25 separate statutory interpretation notes.

Lawmaking process. I have also tried to present the material in a way that makes the student aware of the lawmaking process in two major respects. First, the code is a document that is constantly changing. Students who are anxious to find some anchor amid the complexity are likely to look at the tax law as a still snapshot rather than as a moving picture and thereby overlook the fact that whatever they learn could become obsolete in the near future. The detail in the book is presented, not so that students can memorize the rules, but to give a rich sense of how Congress is constantly tinkering with the law. The Introduction, as well as subsequent chapters, describes the constant amendment process that has been typical of the income tax law. Second, income tax law is not only made by legislation. It also emerges from a variety of administrative and judicial sources. The book presents this avalanche of legal materials in a way that should make the student aware of their varying persuasive authority.

Pedagogy. This edition straddles the two approaches to teaching tax law. First, it includes many problems that force the student to work out an answer, usually when the answer is clear but the rules are not easy to read. Even though this is unlikely to involve work that will be done by lawyers, it is still a useful way to provide a window on how the law is structured and how it attempts to solve important policy issues. The phantom tax rates, the earned income credit, and the "child care" credit are illustrations. Second, it presents material that forces the student to worry about the uncertainties in the law — often involving statutory interpretation — that is the traditional stuff of legal work.

This edition also straddles another pedagogical divide. This edition tries to reduce some of the complexity that appeared in earlier editions without oversimplifying the material. Too much complexity can get in the way of a useful introduction to tax law. Too little complexity can give a misleading picture of the challenges and the richness that tax law presents.

Finally, Chapter 6 (dealing with the processes by which income tax law is made) can be taken up as a unit or split into sections. The material discusses the legislative process, administrative rulemaking, adjudication, and the ethical responsibilities of tax practitioners. It follows Chapters 1-5, because the Chapter 6 material makes more sense after the student is exposed to the various sources of income tax law. But it also makes sense to consider a selection of this material immediately after a particular source of law is referenced — e.g., right after Treasury Regulations or Revenue Rulings are cited as legal authority. Either way works.

TABLE OF CONTENTS

TABLE OF CONTENTS

TABLE OF CONTENTS

TABLE OF CONTENTS

TABLE OF CONTENTS

TABLE OF CONTENTS

TABLE OF CONTENTS

TABLE OF CONTENTS

TABLE OF CONTENTS

TABLE OF CONTENTS

TABLE OF CONTENTS

TABLE OF CONTENTS

TABLE OF CONTENTS

TABLE OF CONTENTS

TABLE OF CONTENTS

TABLE OF CONTENTS

TABLE OF CONTENTS

TABLE OF CONTENTS

TABLE OF CONTENTS

TABLE OF CONTENTS

TABLE OF CONTENTS

TABLE OF CONTENTS

TABLE OF CONTENTS

TABLE OF CONTENTS

TABLE OF CONTENTS

TABLE OF CONTENTS

TABLE OF CONTENTS

TABLE OF CONTENTS

TABLE OF CONTENTS

TABLE OF CONTENTS

TABLE OF CONTENTS

TABLE OF CONTENTS

TABLE OF CONTENTS

INTRODUCTION

[A] A BRIEF HISTORY OF U.S. TAXATION[1]

[1] Federal Taxation

The federal government does not have to depend solely on taxes to raise revenue. It can borrow funds and print money. It can sell public land. It can also charge customers for buying or using government property, in which case the payment is for a benefit received, not a tax; for example, federal lands are sometimes leased for oil and gas exploration; and charges are imposed for entry into national parks and for use of toll roads. This introduction (and the course book) deal only with taxes.

[a] Before the Civil War

Until 1863 (when the Civil War changed the fiscal landscape), more than 90% of federal revenue came from customs duties — that is, tariffs imposed on imported goods. In other words, the revenue source was "external," not "internal." Sale of public lands contributed a significant percentage of the remaining federal revenue.

A few other federal taxes — primarily excise taxes on specific goods — produced a small amount of revenue before the Civil War, but gained a lot of attention. First, an excise tax on liquor in the 1790s led to the Whiskey Rebellion, during which a tax collector's home was burned. The rebellion was suppressed with federal troops sent by President Washington. (Other excise and stamp taxes, such as those on legal instruments and bonds, did not produce a similar reaction.)

Second, a 1791 tax on carriages led to an important Supreme Court decision. *Hylton v. United States*, 3 U.S. 171 (1796), held that the carriage tax was not a direct tax. This holding was important because the U.S. Constitution (in Article I, sec. 2, cl. 3) requires "direct" taxes to be apportioned among the states according to population. This requirement prevents populous states from voting in favor of a federal tax on real estate, which will fall mostly on people living in property-rich, low-population states.

As is often the case in the history of taxation, the need for military expenditures produced an expansion of the tax base. The undeclared naval war with France led (in 1798) to a direct tax apportioned among the states by population on houses, land, and slaves. And a death tax was imposed by the Stamp Act of 1797. Neither of these taxes survived the end of the military confrontation and was repealed at the beginning of the nineteenth Century.

[b] From the Civil War to the Sixteenth Amendment

---

[1] The data regarding federal, state, and local revenue is based on the following: Historical Statistics of the United States, Millennial Edition On Line (Cambridge University Press 2006) — Federal government revenue, by source, 1789–1939, 1934–1999 [OMB]; Federal government internal tax revenue, by source, 1863–1940 & 1940–1999; Federal, State, and Local Government Finances — Census of Governments, Total government revenue and expenditure, by level & by source, 1902–1995; State and Local government revenue, by source, 1902–1995; State government revenue, by source, 1902–1996; Local government revenue, by source, 1902–1995. In addition, some of the discussion relies on Brownlee, Federal Taxation in America (2d ed. 2004); Teaford, The Rise of the States (2002).

INTRODUCTION

The Civil War also spawned a new tax — the first income tax, which became effective in 1862. An early version of the law imposed progressive tax rates in the 3%-5% range with a $600 exemption; these rates rose to 5%-10% by the end of the War. An inheritance and a gift tax were also adopted at this time. However, by 1872, these taxes had expired and would not be revived for many decades.

After the Civil War and until the first modern income tax in 1913, customs duties continued to be the major source of federal revenue. Internal revenue, primarily in the form of excise taxes on alcohol and tobacco, usually produced between 40-50% of federal revenue and occasionally exceeded customs duties.

In 1894, political pressure from labor, farmers, and small businesses led to adoption of the first modern income tax, but it was vigorously opposed by Eastern financial interests (whose income from intangibles, such as stocks and bonds, would now be taxed). They insisted that the 2% tax on income amounted to "socialism" and "communism." And, in *Pollock v. Farmers' Loan & Trust Co.*, 157 U.S. 429 (1895), they won a judicial victory after losing in Congress. The tax on income from property was deemed an unconstitutional unapportioned direct tax, despite a number of judicial precedents to the contrary. The constitutional part of the tax on personal service income was found to be inseverable from the unapportioned direct tax, and it fell along with the unconstitutional tax on property income. An estate tax, which was adopted by the War Revenue Act of 1898 and lasted until 1902, did better in the courts; the tax was deemed an indirect tax on the transfer of property in *Knowlton v. Moore*, 178 U.S. 41 (1900). Similarly, the corporate income tax (adopted in 1909) was upheld as an indirect tax on doing business in *Flint v. Stone Tracy Co.*, 220 U.S. 107 (1911).

[c] The Modern Era

[i] New Taxes

But the political forces favoring an income tax proved too strong to resist. The Sixteenth Amendment to the Constitution, adopted in 1913, removed the apportionment obstacle for taxes on income from property. Although you sometimes hear statements that this Amendment permitted taxes on income, an income tax is authorized elsewhere in the Constitution, by Article I, sec. 8, cl. 1: "The Congress shall have Power To lay and collect Taxes, Duties, Imposts and Excises, to pay the Debts and provide for the common Defence and general Welfare of the United States; but all Duties, Imposts and Excises shall be uniform throughout the United States." The 16th Amendment only removed the apportionment requirement.

In 1913, Congress took advantage of its new power and passed an income tax, with progressive rates ranging from 1%-6% on individuals (with a $1,000 exemption), as well as a 1% tax on corporate income. The income tax fell primarily on the wealthy, reaching only about 5% of the population in 1920. On the judicial front, the Court turned back an objection that the tax was not uniform, relying on precedent which established that the U.S. Constitution's Uniformity Clause (Art. I, sec. 8, cl. 1, quoted above) required only geographic uniformity; *Brushaber v. Union Pacific Railroad Co.*, 240 U.S. 1 (1916).

An estate tax was adopted in 1916, which also fell mainly on the wealthy. It left open a major loophole — which was the taxpayer's ability to make lifetime gifts free of tax. Consequently, a gift tax was adopted temporarily from 1924-1926, and became permanent in 1932.

INTRODUCTION

The next important fiscal development occurred during the Depression — to finance new social insurance programs: specifically, Social Security for the aged and Unemployment Insurance. These programs were financed through payroll taxes on personal service income. In the case of Social Security, employers and employees each paid one half of the Social Security tax, but most economists assume that the employer's tax is shifted to employees in the form of lower wages. (The only prior federal experience with a social insurance program provided retirement and disability benefits for Civil War Union veterans.) At present, the Social Security tax exceeds the income tax for many lower-income workers, although a refundable earned income credit provided by the income tax reduces the impact of this burden.

Despite the importance of the income tax after passage of the 16th Amendment, this tax did not become a mass tax until World War II (no longer falling primarily on the wealthy). Exemptions were reduced to $500, top tax rates rose to a high of 50%, and taxes on wages were collected through withholding. Rates decreased after the end of World War II and increased during the Korean War in the early 1950s. Top individual tax rates went as high as 91%, but they have been steadily lowered in the past few decades. At one time, when the top rate was 70%, the maximum rate on personal service income was limited to 50%.

An interesting feature of federal taxation is the absence of a general sales tax (which falls on the sale of most tangible personal property and not just on selected items, such as a federal tax on alcohol and gasoline). Occasional suggestions that the U.S. adopt such a tax have failed, in part because it is viewed as regressive (falling disproportionately on those with lower incomes); and, since the 1930s, because the general sales tax has been adopted by many states which fear that federal use of this tax base would displace state reliance on this revenue source.

[ii] Data

The adoption of the income tax in 1913 began a major shift in the sources of federal revenue. Customs duties, which had been the mainstay of nineteenth-century federal taxation, hovered around 10-20% of federal revenue in the 1920s and dipped below 10% during most of the 1930s; thereafter, it produced only around 1-2% of federal revenue. Tariffs are now important only for trade policy.

The contribution of excise taxes — the other significant source of federal revenue in the nineteenth century — has also declined. These taxes sometimes equaled or exceeded that of the income tax during the Depression — for example, the contributions to federal revenue of excise taxes and income taxes in 1934 were 46% and 26% respectively, but the balance shifted in 1937 to 35% and 39%. With the end of the Depression and the expansion of the income tax during World War II, excise taxes produced an increasingly insignificant percentage of federal revenue. The dollar amounts of excise taxes on selected goods and services, such as alcohol, tobacco, gasoline and diesel fuel, and airplane travel, are still significant (about $88 billion in 2013), but only about 3-4% of federal revenue.

Estate and gift taxes, despite being politically important, have been a small contributor to federal taxes throughout their history — in recent years, contributing less than 2% of federal revenue, declining to less than 1% with recently adopted high exemptions.

The individual income tax began to be a significant source of federal revenue in the 1920s, but its contribution to federal revenue was cut almost in half during the

INTRODUCTION

Depression. Since becoming a mass tax during World War II, and despite fluctuations in legislatively enacted tax rates, the individual income tax has annually produced between 45-48% of federal revenue.

The percentage contribution of the corporate income tax to federal revenue has gradually declined from around 30% just after World War II to about 10-12% or less today — in part, because business tax breaks are more pervasively available to corporations and because foreign corporate income (which has become more important with globalization) is not usually taxed until it is brought back to the United States.

The other major contributor to federal revenue is Social Security taxes. These taxes (expanded to include Medicare in 1965) now raise a significant percentage of federal revenue — gradually rising from less than 10% prior to 1958 to about 33% today.

[d] The Contemporary Income Tax

The pattern of wartime increases and peacetime decreases in income tax rates continued until recently. Despite the need to finance military actions in the first decade of the twenty-first century, the President and Congress have agreed on income tax reductions, primarily on the theory that this would provide economic incentives and, eventually, increase revenue. Lower taxes resulted not only from lower progressive tax rates, but also from a maximum 15% tax rate on long-term capital gains and dividends and the provision of numerous deductions and credits that lower the effective tax rate on a broad-based definition of income.

The other major feature of the current income tax — which has exploded since the 1960s — has been its use to address nearly every major economic and social problem. Tax breaks for all sorts of activities — from investing in machinery and environmental clean-up to social programs such as child care, education, retirement, and medical expenditures — have proliferated in the tax code. This has resulted in large part from the political difficulty that Congress encounters in spending money directly, with a resulting reliance on tax breaks to achieve specific goals. Legislators are able to say that they did something about a problem, without worrying too much about whether it is the best way to achieve their objectives.

The result of using the tax law for many nontax purposes has been an immensely complex income tax law, which contains provisions that have nothing to do with raising revenue. The complexity of the current legislation has deprived the income tax of whatever clarity it might once have had and, incidentally, created a pedagogical nightmare. It is fair to say that there are very few income tax specialists any more. Instead there are practitioners who specialize in the taxation of particular industries and activities — natural resources, real estate, the entertainment industry, retirement planning, etc. Moreover, tax law practice has yielded significant ground to accountants, who are better trained to deal with the kind of jigsaw-puzzle complexity that yields a clear answer after negotiating the statutory maze. Lawyers are better able to deal with the application of general and uncertain principles to complex fact situations than they are with rules for which complex algorithms provide answers. Indeed, tax preparers using computer programs are often better able to provide answers to complex tax problems than tax practitioners.

Among the most distracting features of current law, which results in part from the need to make federal deficits less daunting, is the adoption of some tax breaks with a statutory expiration date. The 2001 Tax Law (Economic Growth and Tax Relief Reconciliation

INTRODUCTION

Act of 2001) contained numerous such provisions and a series of subsequent statutes dealt, among other things, with the need to revisit these provisions. The following partial list of these laws suggests how much legislative time was taken in addressing these issues: Job Creation and Worker Assistance Act of 2002; Jobs and Growth Tax Relief Reconciliation Act of 2003; Working Families Tax Relief Act of 2004; American Jobs Creation Act of 2004; Katrina Emergency Tax Relief Act of 2005; Tax Increase Prevention and Reconciliation Act of 2005; Small Business and Work Opportunity Tax Act of 2007 (a subtitle of Pub. L. 110-28); and Tax Relief, Unemployment Insurance Reauthorization and Job Creation Act of 2010. Finally, the American Taxpayer Relief Act of 2012 (Public Law 112-240) (ATRA) made many (but not all) of these tax breaks permanent. Some tax breaks are extended only through 2013, requiring Congress to revisit these rules periodically. This political process makes it very difficult to say what the law is or will be in the near future.

The complexity of the modern income tax — riddled as it is with special tax breaks — has also called into question its status as the fairest tax. Polling data show that the percentage of people ranking the income tax as the fairest way to raise revenue has sharply declined. Feeding this view has been a loss of confidence in the tax administration from two diverse perspectives. Anecdotes about an overbearing agency lead many to believe that the tax falls unfairly on the "little" individual. At the same time, expensive tax advisors are able to exploit weaknesses in the tax law and an overburdened agency is unable to successfully catch tax evasion or litigate whether tax avoidance schemes are legal, leading to the view that the law benefits the rich.

[2] State and Local Taxation

Our knowledge of nineteenth-century state and local taxation is hampered by inadequate data. We know that states borrowed heavily until the depression in the early 1840s; and that, thereafter, property taxes increasingly dominated state and local tax sources. Data for the twentieth century are more reliable and they provide us with an insight into the shifting role of different revenue sources at the state and local level. Keep in mind that the following discussion aggregates data for all state and local jurisdictions and that there are significant variations among states and localities. In addition, the percentages are of government revenue from its own sources, not intergovernmental (especially federal) grants.

[a] State Taxes

Around 1900, property taxes were the major source of state tax revenue, but the property tax was in trouble. Taxpayers did not report intangible property (such as stocks and bonds), which had become a significant source of wealth; in addition, few taxpayers reported their tangible personal property, such as furniture, watches, etc. States therefore began to leave the property tax to local governments and to rely on other sources of revenue. Consequently, property taxes lost their importance at the state level during the twentieth century. In 1902, property taxes produced a little more than 50% of total state tax revenue, after which this percentage declined, as follows: 1922 (37%); 1934 (14%); 1950 (4%). Since 1969, property taxes produce less than 2% of state revenues.

In the first few decades of the twentieth century, a significant minority of states adopted income taxes, influenced by federal precedent and by the fact that a tax on income could reach interest and dividends accruing to intangible wealth. Wisconsin led the way by demonstrating that the tax could be effectively administered by professional civil servants and through the reporting of wages paid by employers and dividends and interest paid by businesses. As of 1922, 13 states had adopted an income tax, producing around 11% of state revenue.

However, during the Depression, the income tax became unreliable as a revenue source despite its widespread adoption. By the end of the 1930s, two-thirds of the states had adopted an income tax, but that tax still produced only about 11% of state tax revenue. States therefore turned increasingly to sales taxes, imposed both on sales generally and on selected items (such as gasoline). By the end of the 1930s, 23 states had adopted general sales tax (fewer than the income tax), but this tax accounted for more state revenue than the income tax. Sales taxes (both general and selective) continued to dominate as a revenue source during and after World War II, although the percentage contribution declined — 1950 (59%); 1964 (57%); 1969 (57%). Since 1966, the percentage has been about 48-49%. In 1969, revenue from general sales taxes exceeded excise taxes on selected items for the first time, and that pattern has continued ever since.

Income taxes on individuals and corporations also became a more important source of state tax revenue after the Depression, although the percentage contribution was at first much less than sales taxes — 1934 (7%); 1950 (17%); 1964 (21%); 1969 (26%). Since 1996, the percentage has been about 39%. In 1973, for the first time, income tax revenue exceeded *general* sales tax revenue (but not general sales taxes and excise taxes on selected items combined), and that remains the contemporary pattern. The vast majority of states now rely on both income and sales taxes.

[b] Local Taxes

At the beginning of the twentieth century (and unlike today), local tax revenues greatly exceeded state tax revenues — by approximately a five-to-one ratio. About 90% of local taxes came from the property tax (which was rapidly becoming just a tax on real property).

Today, the mix of local revenue has changed, but the property tax still produces well over 50% of local tax revenue. The change has been in the increase in local government use of sales and income taxes.

[B] CRITERIA FOR A SUCCESSFUL TAX

A successful tax must satisfy a number of criteria. First, the tax base must be broad enough to provide significant revenue. That is one reason why wars and economic depressions are usually the occasion for significant changes in the tax laws.

Second, a tax must be administrable without too much difficulty. Concerns about administration shape the tax law — for example: in limiting the current property tax base to real property; in relying on withholding from wages to support an income tax; and in deciding whether a sales tax can be reliably collected. The current global economy places tremendous strains on tax administration, as businesses are able to shift income around among geographic locations (either legally or illegally), and governments are hard-pressed to keep up with astute tax planners.

Third, the impact of a tax on behavior must be considered. No tax is ever completely neutral. For example, an income tax burdens wage work more than untaxed "leisure" and self-performed services (such as housework). It also burdens savings by taxing the income that generates the savings and the income from savings (such as dividends and interest). This burden is one reason that some people advocate greater reliance on taxes that fall on consumption (such as a sales tax). However, sales taxes have their own imperfections — some sales tax regimes do not tax services, which is a major omission in our service economy; and sales taxation sometimes burdens purchases by businesses as well as personal consumption, which can distort both business and personal consumption.

Moreover, within the boundaries of any tax base, there is an opportunity to influence behavior. Particular industries and specific expenditures can be encouraged — for example, through special depreciation deductions under the income tax or by property tax holidays. Social values can also be advanced — for example, the income tax law provides incentives for retirement, education, and medical expenditures; and taxes on personal consumption typically exempt education and hospital services and some food.

Fourth, the tax must satisfy some notion of fairness, at least in a political democracy. Tax fairness is often measured by something referred to as "ability to pay," a criterion that is remarkably fuzzy when examined closely but which remains clear enough in its popular conception. The idea is that taxation should treat equals equally with respect to their economic well-being (horizontal equity).

Another and more controversial notion of equity taxes people with more of the tax base at progressively higher tax rates (vertical equity). For example, in an income tax, it is not just that some people with $100,000 income pay more taxes than someone with $50,000 income; a flat rate tax would do that. Vertical equity calls for taxing someone with higher income at a higher tax rate. Thus, the first $50,000 of income might be taxed at 15%, but the next $50,000 at 25%. If only consumption were taxed, vertical equity calls for taxing higher consumption at higher tax rates.

[C] CONTEMPORARY POLICY ISSUES

This review of the evolution of taxation in the United States focuses attention on several contemporary policy issues. A law course is not going to make any serious attempt to address questions of public finance, such as whether taxes should or should not be raised to deal with future budget deficits. But there are a number of important policy issues that shape current debates about taxation that we will consider in this course.

[1] Progressivity

Progressive tax rates have long been an intrinsic part of United States taxation — sometimes praised as a positive "equity" feature or vilified as evidence of socialism or a threat to economic expansion.

Progressive income taxation is sometimes defended on the "scientific" notion that people with more income have a lesser preference for higher amounts of income than for lower amounts of income, but such psychological observations give progressive income taxation a scientific veneer that cannot be sustained. (Who knows how badly someone craves their particular lifestyle? It often depends on their social and economic background and on whether they are going up or down the income scale.) *See generally* Blum & Kalven, THE UNEASY CASE FOR PROGRESSIVE TAXATION (1952).

The best defense of progressive tax rates rests on the "political" value of wealth. As people have more and more wealth, the relative value of that extra wealth to society as a whole goes up in relation to its private value — or at least that is one political point of view. When the argument is made that progressive taxes are bad because they take an individual's wealth, that is an indirect way of asserting that the relative value of public and private expenditures disfavors public over private spending. Put differently, instead of taxes being the price we pay for civilization, as Oliver Wendell Holmes, Jr. once put it, the argument is that progressive taxes undermine the economic initiatives and political freedoms that are valuable in our society. An electorate that has lost faith in the government's public spending is not likely to embrace Holmes's aphorism.

The debate over the political value of wealth is not limited to the income tax. It also underlies disputes over whether an estate tax is a good idea. Proponents of the estate tax argue that inherited wealth lacks social value in the hands of those who inherit it. Opponents of the tax label it a "death" tax and describe it as an unfair burden on the wealth that someone has struggled to acquire.

Taxes on personal consumption can also be tailored to fall more heavily on those with higher income or consumption — by fiddling with the tax rates (higher rates on luxury goods) and exemptions (no tax on groceries).

[2] Flat Tax

In recent years, proposals have been floated for a flat tax, usually around the low 20% range. These proposals might seem to derive much of their impetus from objections to progressive tax rates, but that would misread their political attraction. The most important feature of a flat tax is that it would fall on a greatly simplified tax base — an income tax without many of the tax breaks that now dot the tax code. In other words, the flat tax is defended primarily as economically efficient (because the tax would fall neutrally on different types of economic activities) and as administratively simple (making it easier for taxpayers to fill out returns and for the agency to audit those returns).

Although a flat tax has had some political traction, its lack of success may result from the fact that the tax rate on lower income taxpayers would have to be higher than the current rate to raise enough revenue to replace the current income tax. In addition, many taxpayers benefit from the tax breaks in the current law (such as the deduction of interest on some home loans, retirement savings, some state and local taxes, and charitable contributions), some of which would have to be eliminated by a flat tax rate on a simplified tax base.

[3] Greater Reliance on Consumption Taxes?

Within the boundaries of some general notion of ability to pay, there is a modern debate about whether the tax base should be income and/or consumption. There are several types of consumption taxes. First, there is a sales tax imposed (usually) at a single point — retail sales. Second, a value-added tax is imposed at each step of the production and distribution chain, which (in theory) adds up to the same total as a single-point retail sales tax. Third, a consumption tax is imposed on income minus savings; it would be administered like an income tax but with a deduction for all savings. A consumption tax is likely to have a broader tax base than other taxes on consumption. For example, unlike typical retail sales taxes, it would not exempt most services.

The debate about income and consumption taxes is usually about the proper mix of these tax bases, not replacement of the income tax with a tax on consumption. Some observers suggest use of consumption taxes, supplemented by an income tax on those with higher incomes to preserve a measure of progressivity. Lower income taxpayers would be subject to a flat consumption tax, which would amount to a flat tax on income if they consumed all of their income.

Consumption taxes are sometimes defended on the ground that they tax what someone takes out of the economy rather than what they earn. Income equals consumption plus savings and (so the argument goes) people should not be taxed on the savings they leave in the economy. Moreover, a better measure of ability to pay is lifetime consumption, which tends to smooth out fluctuations in income — because taxpayers save when they are young and consume their savings when they retire. A consumption tax is neutral regarding when consumption occurs but an income tax favors earlier consumption because current savings and the return on those savings (such as interest) are included in the tax base.

Taxes on consumption are also said to encourage savings, which many observers think is inadequate in the United States. And some taxes on consumption — specifically, retail sales and value added taxes — are easier to rebate to the seller than income taxes when sales occur outside the country, thereby encouraging exports.

Consumption taxes have attracted support from such varied political philosophers as Adam Smith, Thomas Hobbes, and John Stuart Mill. A recent discussion in the legal literature rejects arguments that the consumption tax is regressive and inefficient, and concludes that its Achilles' heel is its implementation; *see* Bankman & Weisbach, *The Superiority of an Ideal Consumption Tax* over an Ideal Income Tax, 58 STAN. L. REV. 1413 (2006).

[4] Tax Levels

Underlying the discussion of tax policy is the fundamental question of the overall tax level, regardless of the tax base. When taxpayers are suspicious of government, they do not trust public sector spending and are more reluctant to permit the purchase of goods and services by the government — leading to objections to taxes in general. When a bridge collapses, there is a public outcry for more spending on infrastructure, but the enthusiasm fades when the legislature considers whether or not to raise taxes for this purpose. We seem especially unwilling to tax ourselves to help others — viz., medical insurance — even if the benefits are financed by payroll taxes. An economic reason for this reluctance may be that taxes (especially payroll taxes, which increase the cost of labor) might encourage taxpayers to move their operations abroad in our global economy.

[D] OUTLINE OF THE BOOK

Although there is now serious doubt about whether the federal income tax is the fairest tax, it continues to be the primary source of federal revenue. My guess is that a "better" income tax would still pass muster as our best tax. Consequently, Part I of this book follows the usual practice in law school courses of emphasizing the income tax on individuals.

Nonetheless, because of doubts about the current individual income tax, it is appropriate for an introductory tax course to include material about other taxes as well — including the following:

— state and local taxes — especially property and sales taxes;

— payroll taxes — especially Social Security taxes, which have increased considerably in recent years;

— taxes on consumption — including not only the sales tax but also the tax on value added (used widely in Europe), and proposals for a consumption tax (much talked about but rarely adopted);

INTRODUCTION

- the estate and gift tax — which is a flash point for liberal and conservative politics (the estate tax actually expired in 2010 but was later revived with high exemption levels);

- entity taxation — the income tax rules regarding partnerships, trusts, estates, and corporations; and

- inter-jurisdictional issues — international taxation and the problems of allocating the tax base to different states.

To that end, Part II of the book deals with the following taxes.

- Taxation of property
  - Property tax
  - Estate and gift tax
- Payroll taxes
  - Social Security tax
- Taxes on consumption
  - Sales tax
  - Value added tax
  - Consumption tax
- Entity taxation
  - Pass-thru entities; Partnerships, Trusts, and Estates
  - Corporate income tax
- Multi-jurisdictional issues
  - International taxation
  - Interstate taxation

INCOME TAX

Part I deals with the income tax on individuals. Part I-A explains the basic concepts underlying taxation of income, and subsequent Parts deal with specifics under the following headings — taxation of personal consumption (Part I-B), taxation of savings (Part I-C), limits on deductions (Part I-D), the Alternative Minimum Tax (Part I-E), taxation of appreciation (Part I-F), and timing issues (Part I-G).

Part I-A

BASIC CONCEPTS

Outline of Part I-A

Part I-A explains the basic concepts underlying the income tax on individuals:

— Chapter 1: the tax base, tax rates, and taxable units

— Chapter 2: who is the taxpayer

— Chapter 3: the definition of income

— Chapter 4: the taxation of gifts

— Chapter 5: the concept of the taxable year

— Chapter 6: the process by which tax law is made (legislative, administrative, and judicial; and the tax adviser's ethical role)

You will be working with the Internal Revenue Code, which is published in Volume 26 of the U.S. Code. Before 1939, most income tax law was adopted by a Revenue Act of a particular year. These Acts usually reenacted the entire tax law, along with any modifications made by the reenacting statute. Beginning in 1939, the income tax was placed in the Internal Revenue Code of 1939, which was then periodically amended. Since then, there have been two major reworkings of the income tax law that Congress decided to label with a new Internal Revenue Code year — once in 1954 and then in 1986. You are now dealing with the Internal Revenue Code of 1986.

Chapter 1

TAX BASE, TAX RATES, AND TAXABLE UNITS

§ 1.01 TAX BASE

[A] Taxable Income

The "tax base" for any tax is the amount by which the tax rate is multiplied to compute the tax. For the income tax, the tax base is "income." More precisely, it is something that the statute defines as "taxable income." That figure is computed by first identifying "gross income," and then subtracting deductions to arrive at taxable income. The deductions come in two categories. First, you subtract certain deductions to reduce gross income to "adjusted gross income" (AGI). (These are often called "above the line deductions.") Second, you subtract additional deductions to reduce adjusted gross income to "taxable income." (Most of these are called "below the line deductions," or "itemized deductions." § 63(d).)

The relevant statutory sections are § 61 (gross income); § 62 (adjusted gross income); and § 63 (taxable income).

[1] Standard Deduction

Why does it matter whether a deduction reduces gross to adjusted gross income or reduces adjusted gross to taxable income? One reason is that taxpayers can elect not to itemize deductions and instead take a standard deduction. § 63(b), (c). A taxpayer *cannot* take *both* the itemized deductions and the standard deduction. If, however, the deduction is "above the line" (if it reduces gross to adjusted gross income), the deduction *and* the standard deduction are both available.

[2] Itemized Deductions

Itemized deductions come in two categories. Some itemized deductions must be added together and only the total over 2% of adjusted gross income is deductible. § 67. Other itemized deductions are deductible without regard to the 2% floor. The idea is that the deductions subject to the 2% floor tend to be small and the requirement that their total exceed a specified floor eliminates some difficult administrative problems. This makes some sense in the context of unreimbursed employee business expenses, which are subject to the floor.

[3]   Horizontal Equity

These rules sound very mechanical, but they have a serious impact on different groups of taxpayers. The significant policy issue is one of "horizontal equity" — who is like someone else, so that they should pay the same tax. Exclusions or deductions available to one taxpayer but not to another treat taxpayers differently. Do these taxpayers deserve "different" treatment? If not, horizontal equity is violated.

[B]   Types of Deductions

Here is a short (and very incomplete) list of typical above the line deductions; and itemized (below the line) deductions. Note carefully that neither § 62 nor § 63 allows deductions — these sections only tell you how to compute taxable income based on deductions allowed by some other section. The basic sections *allowing* deductions are § 162 (business expenses) and § 212 (investment expenses). Numerous personal expenses are deductible as well (see citations in § 67(b)(1–5)).

Typical below the line deductions are small deductions that the IRS has difficulty auditing (usually subject to the 2% floor), and nonbusiness expenses that the tax law wants to encourage (usually *not* subject to the 2% floor).

EXPENSES

Above the line	Below the line 2% floor	Below the line No 2% floor
(§ 62)	(§ 67(a))	(§ 67(b))
Business, except by employees Employees, if reimbursed	Employees, if not reimbursed Investment (other than interest)	Charitable Medical Some state/local taxes Some investment interest Some home loan interest

Some basic themes should emerge from the list. Typical above the line deductions are business deductions, except those incurred by employees. Business deductions incurred by employees are usually below the line, except for reimbursed expenses, which are above the line. Do you see why the teacher of this course might prefer to have her employer reimburse expenses, rather than have her employer pay the reimbursement as a taxable wage, followed by the employee taking a deduction for the expense?

The below the line deduction for state and local taxes has been modified over the years. For a long time, state and local income, property, and sales taxes were deductible. In 1986, the deduction for sales taxes was repealed. Then, a 2004 tax law permitted a taxpayer to elect to deduct either state and local income taxes or state and local general sales taxes. § 164(b)(5). This election was extended through 2014 by ATRA. (ATRA refers here and throughout the book to the American Taxpayer Relief Act of 2012.) Sales tax payments can be proven either by receipts showing amounts paid or by using tables issued by the IRS that reflect average taxpayer consumption and that vary with family size and income. In addition to the amount in the IRS table, a taxpayer can deduct actual sales taxes paid on cars, boats, and some other items identified by the IRS.

[C] Deduction for Personal Exemptions

The discussion has not mentioned one important deduction — the deduction for personal exemptions. Generally speaking, each individual is entitled to one such deduction for himself or herself, and for certain dependents (we will explain "dependents" later — typically, a child in the household will be a dependent). The personal exemption deduction is available to all individual taxpayers, whether or not they take the standard deduction. §§ 151, 63(a), 63(b)(2). It is a below the line deduction, but is not replaced by the standard deduction and is not subject to the 2% floor.

[D] Inflation Adjustments

The dollar figures in the code are sometimes adjusted for inflation — for example, § 63(c)(4) (standard deduction) (tax year 2013 — $12,200 for a married couple filing joint returns; $6,100 for a single taxpayer; $8,950 for a head of household); § 151(d)(4) (personal exemption deduction) (tax year 2013 — $3,900 per deduction).

A marriage tax penalty is avoided by providing a married couple with a standard deduction that is twice that of a single taxpayer. This doubling of the standard deduction for married taxpayers has been made permanent by ATRA.

§ 1.02 TAX RATES

[A] Progressivity; Marginal Tax Rates

The income tax is taxable income times the tax rate — that is:

$$\text{TAX BASE * TAX RATE = TAX}$$

Income tax rates are progressive — meaning that the tax rate increases on *additional* amounts of income. I did not say that taxpayers with higher income pay tax at a higher rate on *all* their income, only that the tax rate increases on additional income. Another way of saying the same thing is that the "marginal" tax rate increases with additional income.

A progressive rate ladder, illustrated below, helps you understand the concept of progressivity. Each rung of the ladder represents additional income. There are now seven rungs to the ladder. The following Table sets forth the tax rates in § 1(a) on married couples (filing joint returns) and single individuals. The dollar figures in § 1 are adjusted for inflation so that an increase in taxable income that does not increase purchasing power will not push a taxpayer into a higher bracket. § 1(f).

Progressive Rate Ladder (§ 1(a), (c))

Tax Year 2013

Taxable income		Tax rates
Married — file jointly	**Single**	
> 450,000	> 400,000	39.6%
> 398,350 but not over 450,000	> 398,350 but not over 400,000	35%
> 223,050 but not over 398,350	> 183,250 but not over 398,350	33%
> 146,400 but not over 223,050	> 87,850 but not over 183,250	28%
> 72,500 but not over 146,400	> 36,250 but not over 87,850	25%
> 17,850 but not over 72,500	> 8,925 but not over 36,250	15%
Not over $17,850	Not over $8,925	10%

The top tax rate to which a taxpayer is subject is usually referred to as the taxpayer's marginal tax rate. In the above chart, a married taxpayer with more than $450,000 of taxable income is subject to a 39.6% marginal tax rate. That is different from the average tax rate on all taxable income. The average tax rate is the total tax divided by taxable income. It is lower than the marginal tax rate, when the tax rate on lower rungs of the ladder is less than the tax rate on the top rung.

The marginal tax rate is critical for tax planning. For example, a taxpayer who can shift income subject to the top rate to other lower-rate taxpayers in the family can reduce the total family tax. The marginal tax rate is also critical for deciding whether to earn more money.

Relief from the marriage tax penalty for the three lowest tax brackets has been provided by making the top of the brackets for a married couple twice the top of the brackets for a single taxpayer (for example, 72,500 = 2 times 36,250, for the 25% bracket). Absent this provision, the inflation-adjusted top of the bracket for a married couple would be less than twice the top of the bracket for a single taxpayer. ATRA made this provision permanent.

PROBLEM: COMPUTING TAXABLE INCOME

Work out this problem. Be sure to use the tax rates for married couples. The reasons for the different rate structures are explained later in this chapter.

Husband earns $70,000 salary income as an employee. Wife earns $75,000 as a freelance (non-employee) author. The husband has, in addition, $4,000 employer-reimbursed business expenses while traveling; and $2,500 unreimbursed employee business expenses. The wife has $5,000 of her own business expenses for equipment and supplies. The couple pays $8,500 state and local property and income taxes, and $6,000 interest on a home loan, both of which are below the line deductions, not subject to the 2% floor. They have two children, ages 5 and 8, who live in their household and receive all of their support from their parents. *What are the couple's gross income, adjusted gross income, and taxable income? What are their average and marginal tax rates?*

[B] Effect of Deductions and Credits in a Progressive Tax

One of the effects of progressive tax rates is that the value of a deduction increases as the marginal tax rate increases. You can see this by redoing the above problem on the assumption that the couple has only one child — that is, one less deduction for personal exemptions. What is the value of the deduction for the second child? What is the value of a $1,000 deduction for someone in the top bracket?

A tax "credit" reduces the tax, not taxable income. A credit expressed as a percentage of a dollar figure reduces tax by the same amount regardless of the marginal tax rate. For example, a credit for a dependent child equal to 20% of $2,000 per child would reduce tax by $400 per child in all cases, even for a taxpayer in the 15% marginal tax bracket.

Is this last statement entirely accurate? Suppose a couple with two children has $8,000 total earnings. Would this taxpayer benefit by substituting a $400 credit for a deduction for personal exemptions? How could you change the law to give this couple the benefit of the credit?

[C] "Phantom" Marginal Tax Rates

[1] In General

The earlier problem of the couple with $145,000 earnings raises an important policy issue — should people with higher income enjoy: (1) the benefit of lower tax rates on lower amounts of income; (2) the benefit of the personal exemption deductions; and (3) the benefit of itemized deductions? Suppose you said "no" — those with higher income should *not* enjoy these benefits. The tax code has sometimes said "no."

That sounds easy enough. Just tell those with higher incomes that they cannot be taxed at lower rates on their "lower-bracket" income; and that they cannot take personal exemptions or itemized deductions when their income rises above a certain threshold. Well, it is not so easy. A policy that sounds simple may be mechanically difficult to implement.

First, define "higher income." Above what income should tax benefits be lost?

Second, how should the benefit be reduced? Can you say, for example, that everyone with adjusted gross income over $300,000 loses the benefit of tax rates below the top rate? No, you can't. Do you see why? Suppose the tax law said that. Assume you have $300,000 adjusted gross income from earnings and are offered an additional $10,000 compensation. Would the marginal tax rate on that added $10,000 be more than 100% (that is, would you lose more in higher taxes than you earned from the income increase)?

Under current law, the benefit of the lower tax rate on lower amounts of income is *not* lost by individuals with higher income. Corporations, however, do lose the benefit of the lower rates as their incomes rise above certain thresholds. **§ 11(b)(1) (flush paragraph)**.

But taxpayers do gradually lose some of the deduction for personal exemptions and itemized deductions as income rises above a threshold so that the burden is nowhere near the equivalent of a 100% marginal tax rate. This burden is called a phantom tax rate because it is not explicitly set forth in the rate structure.

You may be puzzled by the idea of a phantom tax rate because the arithmetic can seem complex, but the idea is not difficult to grasp. It may be easiest to understand in the context of welfare law. Assume someone is receiving money as welfare assistance from the government. As income rises, the benefits may be reduced. This confronts the beneficiary with a difficult choice if every dollar earned reduces welfare by one dollar — a 100% tax (or even higher if child care and transportation expenses are considered, so that $1 of earnings yields only 80 cents in available income after expenses). The welfare law has often dealt with this problem by disregarding some of the earnings. For example, only two-thirds of the earnings might be counted. Consequently, $1 dollar of earnings results in a loss of 66⅔ cents in welfare benefits — still a steep 66⅔% "tax," when viewed from the beneficiary's perspective.

[2]   Phase-out of Personal Exemption Deductions

PROBLEM: DISAPPEARING PERSONAL EXEMPTION DEDUCTIONS

A phantom tax rate, like any marginal tax rate, identifies the increase in tax that results from additional income. The numerator is the added tax; the denominator is the added income. For example, if a taxpayer in the 35% tax bracket has an additional $1,000 of real income that results in $1,100 of additional *taxable* income, the $1,000 leads to an increased tax of 35% times $100 (or $35), over and above the 35% times $1,000 of actual income. That results in a phantom tax rate of 35/1000, which equals 3.5%. The effective marginal tax rate in this example is 38.5%, not the 35% that appears explicitly in the tax law.

How can an added $1,000 of income result in an even greater amount of taxable income? That is easy. Take away some deductions as income rises. And that is what happens with the deduction for personal exemptions. In the following problem illustrating the disappearing deduction for personal exemptions, the added tax in the numerator is the tax rate times the reduction in the amount of the deduction. *See* § 151(d)(3).

The rationale for phasing out the deduction for personal exemptions with rising income is that these deductions are primarily aimed at getting low-income people off the tax rolls, both to lower their taxes (although they still pay Social Security taxes), and to reduce administrative burdens. The effect of the rule is to raise the *marginal* tax rate when adjusted gross income exceeds the "threshold amount" ATRA defines the threshold amount as $300,000 for a married taxpayer and $250,000 for a single individual, adjusted for inflation beginning in 2014.

The formula for working out the increase in marginal tax rates from disappearing personal exemption deductions is complex, even though the idea is simple. Each $2,500 of adjusted gross income (or fraction thereof) over the threshold amount results in a loss of 2% of the personal exemption deductions. The formula for the phantom tax rate is:

$$\text{phantom tax rate} \quad = \quad \frac{0.02 * p * n * \text{marginal tax rate}}{\$2,500}$$

where p = the personal exemption deduction amount; and n = the number of personal exemptions. (We disregard the "fractional thereof" feature in the following explanation.)

This phantom tax rate (like all such rates) has a phase-out range — a range of income over which the phantom tax rate begins and ends. Somewhat simplified, the phantom tax rate applies over a $125,000 income range, because the taxpayer loses 2% of the deductions for each $2,500; 50 times 2% is 100%; and 50 times $2,500 = $125,000. Thus, the phase-out range for the phantom tax rate applicable to the personal exemption deduction of a married couple in tax year 2013 is $300,000 to $425,000. Once income rises beyond the end of the phase-out range, marginal tax rates revert to those in § 1, unless there is another phantom tax rate resulting from the loss of another tax benefit.

The phase-out for the personal exemption deductions had been eliminated, as of 2010, but was reinstated by ATRA.The arguments for elimination of the phase-out are that it adds immense complexity to the tax law and that the concerns that led to its adoption — that higher income taxpayers should not benefit from the deduction — are better addressed through the income tax rate structure. Of course, the tax law that eliminates the phantom tax rate relating to personal exemption deductions also lowers the tax rates, so it is hard to argue that the problem of higher income taxpayers enjoying the deduction was, in fact, addressed through the rate structure. There are, however, political obstacles to explicit rate increases and a disappearing tax break is an indirect way of achieving the same result.

[3]　Itemized Deductions Phase-out

Another phantom tax rate occurs because the deduction of *certain* itemized deductions (after applying the 2% floor) is reduced as an individual's adjusted gross income rises above the "applicable amount" which is the same threshold as for the disappearance of the personal exemption deduction ($300,000 for a married couple and $250,000 for a single individual, adjusted for inflation beginning in 2014). The effect, again, is to raise marginal tax rates over the rates stated in § 1. *Certain* itemized deductions are reduced by 3% of adjusted gross income over the "applicable amount," except that the reduction cannot exceed 80% of the itemized deductions subject to the reduction. § 68. There is no point in memorizing this complexity, but there is a point in reading about it.

You should also keep in mind that there are other ways to limit deductions — e.g., allow the deduction only if it exceeds a percentage of AGI (currently true of medical expense deductions); allow only a percentage of the deduction (currently true of some entertainment expenses); and provide that the value of the deduction is capped at its value to a 15% (or other) bracket taxpayer (so that a deduction of $100 could not reduce taxes by more than $15).

[D] Medicare Tax on "Unearned" Income

Social Security taxes to fund benefits for the aged and disabled and to pay for Medicare are discussed in Chapter 28. But it is important to note one tax added by the Patient Protection and Affordable Health Care Act (Obamacare) (Public Law 111-148) to help fund Medicare. This tax, which goes into effect in 2013, applies to "unearned income." The term "unearned income" refers to investment income, such as interest (not counting the tax exempt interest on state and local bonds), dividends, capital gains, royalties, and rents, unless any of these items is derived from a trade or business. ("Unearned" contrasts with "earned" income; the latter refers to employee wages and self-employment income.)

The tax is 3.8% on the lesser of (1) net investment income or (2) modified adjusted gross income in excess of $200,000 for an individual and $250,000 for a married couple. Assume an individual has $180,000 of wages, $45,000 of unearned income, and modified adjusted gross income of $215,000. The 3.8% tax would be imposed on $15,000 (the lesser of $215,000 minus $200,000; and $45,000).[1]

This tax raises the tax rate on capital gains and dividends above the explicit tax rate provided by § 1(h) (discussed later in the book).

§ 1.03 DEDUCTION FOR DEPENDENTS

In the problem we discussed in Chapter 1.02[A], the children had no income and were supported by their parents. They were obviously "dependents" within § 152. The category of dependents is not limited to children, but includes all of the individuals listed in § 152(a), if the taxpayer provides more than one-half of their support. For some purposes, being a dependent is sufficient to provide a tax break — e.g., to permit someone to deduct a dependent's medical expenses (discussed in Chapter 9.02[B][1]). However, being a dependent is necessary but not sufficient to permit the person providing support to obtain the personal exemption deduction.

The personal exemption deduction is permitted for a dependent if the dependent's gross income is less than the "exemption amount," which is the amount allowed as a personal exemption deduction in the relevant tax year. There are a few exceptions to the income ceiling. The most important exception permits parents to take the personal exemption deduction for a dependent child even if the child's income is over the ceiling, if the child is under age 19, or is a full-time student and is not age 24 or older.

---

[1] "Modified" adjusted gross income refers in general to the addition to adjusted gross income of various tax exempt items (such as state and local bond interest) and some deductions. References throughout this book to adjusted gross income do *not* specify whether or not some modification is required. Sometimes it is and sometimes not; and the modifications are not uniform. These are complications that must be addressed for each statutory provision.

[A] Dependent Children and the Taxable Unit

The income of parents and children is generally not combined into one taxable unit, but there are code provisions that move in that direction. Before the Tax Reform Act of 1986, a parent could take a personal exemption deduction for a child *and* the child could also take a personal exemption deduction for herself. That is no longer true. If a child is *eligible* to be taken by a parent as a personal exemption deduction, the child cannot also take the deduction. This is not elective. Thus, a full-time college student (age 20) who receives more than one-half of his support from his parents cannot take a personal exemption deduction.

Of course, the child can still take the standard deduction, but there are limits. The statute says that a dependent child's standard deduction cannot exceed the *greater* of (1) earned income (typically, income from personal services) plus $250; or (2) $750. (The "plus $250" provision was added in 1997, probably aimed at children with small bank accounts?) The $250 and $750 amounts are adjusted for inflation. For tax year 2013, these figures are $350 and $1,000, respectively. The purpose of this limit on the standard deduction is to prevent higher income parents from shifting investment income (such as dividends and interest) to a child, which could be sheltered by a high standard deduction. The rule is not, however, limited to investment income from property received from a parent. § 63(c)(5).

Yet another provision prevents shifting investment income to a child under age 18; or to a child who is under age 24 and is a student who can be claimed as the parent's dependent. This so-called "kiddie tax" taxes the child *at the parent's tax rate* (if higher than the child's rate) on investment income that *exceeds* twice the standard deduction available to offset the dependent child's investment income (for tax year 2013 — two times $1,000, or $2,000). § 1(g). The child continues to be taxed on the $2,000, taking a $1,000 standard deduction, and paying a 10% tax on the remaining $1,000. (There is no kiddie tax if parents elect to be taxed on their children's unearned income under detailed conditions described in the statute.)

[B] Defining Support

Providing enough support is a necessary condition for someone to be another's dependent. But what does "support" mean? "Support" is not limited to items included in gross income. The rental value of a home is "support" but is not gross income.

The following case is concerned with defining support, not only because of the deduction for dependents, but also because of "head of household" status under §§ 1(b), 2(b)(1)(A)(ii) (which is conditioned on having a dependent in the household). In a later section, you will read about the favorable tax rates for married couples, as compared to a single individual with the same income as the married couple. Head of household rates fall in between the rates for single and married couples.

BARTSCH v. COMMISSIONER
United States Tax Court
41 T.C. 883 (1964)

TIETJENS, JUDGE: . . .

Section 152(a) defines a dependent as any of enumerated individuals (including the mother of the petitioner) over half of whose support, for the calendar year in which the taxable year of the taxpayer begins, was received from the taxpayer.

The problem here is whether petitioner is entitled to add the value of her "services" to her mother to her out-of-pocket expenses in that regard. If she can do so under the statute, then the claimed mother dependent can be held to have received over half of her support from petitioner and petitioner can have the dependency exemption, and the head of a household status, as well.

We think this cannot be done and accordingly hold that Anna did not receive over half her support in the taxable year from the taxpayer, her daughter.

. . . [T]he Treasury promulgated section 1.152-1 of the Income Tax Regulations which provided in part: The term "support includes food, shelter, clothing, medical and dental care, education, and the like. Generally, these items of support are measured in terms of the amount of expense incurred by the one furnishing such items. However, if the item of support furnished an individual (either by himself or others) is in the form of goods, services, or other benefits, it will be necessary to measure the amount of such items of support in terms of its fair market value."

However, . . . the Treasury amended the above regulation by substituting for the last two sentences in the above quotation the following: Generally, the amount of an item of support will be the amount of expense incurred by the one furnishing such item. If the item of support furnished an individual is in the form of property or lodging, it will be necessary to measure the amount of such item of support in terms of its fair market value.

Thus, the reference to valuing services in determining the amount of support was deliberately deleted from the regulations. . . .

To use what has become a cliche: taxation is a practical matter. . . . Taxpayer and her mother lived together in a home owned by the mother. Each performed household tasks commensurate with her physical capacities. Neither charged nor collected from the other for such tasks on a monetary basis. Yet our taxpayer would have us place a value on what she "did" for her mother in order to claim her as a dependent. We attach no opprobrium to her claim; but we are reluctant to say, in the absence of specific statutory direction, and in the face of the equivocal regulatory history, that the taxpayer is entitled to her claim.

We find nothing in the statute requiring that such services as taxpayer rendered to her mother are to be "valued" in computing the "support" which she furnished her mother for dependency exemption purposes. Without clear statutory direction, it is beyond our comprehension why or how such services must be measured in the market place, or anywhere. How can a quantum meruit be put upon a daughter's care for an aged mother? . . . The term "support" in the Code must mean something more than furnishing the ordinary kindnesses and helpfulness and the cooking and the cleaning and the dishwashing that one able member of the household furnished another less able. These things are not to be valued in the market for tax purposes. Support, as defined in the regulation, includes items such as food, shelter, etc., of which the amount will be "the amount of expense incurred by the one furnishing such item." Petitioner in this case has incurred no expense for furnishing the care ordinarily expected of a daughter for an aged mother (and that is all that is here involved) and we hold she cannot count the value of her personal services in computing whether she furnished "over half" of her mother's support.

FISHER, J., DISSENTING: The question here is whether the value of personal service rendered to a dependent is to be considered as support under Internal Revenue Code section 152.

. . . I disagree with the construction the majority places upon the present form of respondent's regulations. The fact that reference to valuing services in determining the amount of support was deliberately deleted by the respondent from his original regulations in no way forecloses the conclusion that such services are proper considerations in determining the support provided a dependent.

To my mind, it is inconsistent in principle to allow the fair market value of lodging furnished an individual (as the regulations clearly do) but not the fair market value of related household services in determining the support provided the same individual. Why not include only the additional "cost" of such lodging?

In addition, I feel that the majority view tends to discriminate in favor of those who can afford to hire the services of others over the not-so-fortunate who can only provide time and effort and thereby forced personally to provide the needed services.

QUESTIONS AND COMMENTS

1. What do the majority and dissent disagree about in the *Bartsch* case? Do they differ regarding administrative concerns (that is, how easy is it for the agency to administer a rule)? Do they have different policy concerns?

2. How should payment of medical expenses and medical insurance premiums enter into computing who provides more than half the support? Payment of medical bills is support. However, if a person is insured (either by private insurance or Medicare), courts have held that payments made by the insurance company do not count as support; only the insurance premiums count. *Turecamo v. Commissioner*, 554 F.2d 564 (2d Cir. 1977). This makes it easier for an aged parent to be the dependent of an adult child.

3. Should Medicaid benefits be considered government support or disregarded, like Medicare? Medicaid consists of government payments for the poor, which (unlike Medicare) are not tied to prior "insurance-like" tax payments. *Archer v. Commissioner*, 73 T.C. 963 (1980) (Medicaid benefits excluded to avoid "sharp horizontal inequities"; four dissents).

4. *Williams v. Commissioner*, 71 T.C.M. (CCH) 2423 (1996), holds that welfare payments (AFDC) and Food Stamps count as government support, making it more

difficult for parents to take a dependent's deduction for a child (or to obtain head of household status).

[C] Divorced or Separated Parents

The income tax law is concerned not only with defining support but also with determining who provides more than one-half the support for a child. This is very difficult to determine in the case of divorced or separated parents. Responding to the fact that about 5% of all lower-level agency disputes involved this issue, Congress passed § 152(e) to reduce controversy. That section gave the dependency deduction to the custodial parent except in certain specified circumstances.

In *Prophit v. Commissioner*, 57 T.C. 507 (1972), *affirmed per curiam*, 470 F.2d 1370 (5th Cir. 1973), a father provided more than half the support for a child, who was in the custody of a nonresident alien German mother. There was no dispute over these facts, which would qualify the father for the dependency deduction, in the absence of any special rules applicable to divorced or separated parents. The custodial mother did not in fact claim the deduction and was prohibited from doing so as a nonresident alien. The court held that the reason for the passage of § 152(e) was absent in this case, because there was no controversy between the parents. The father asked the court to consider "the intent of the law and not the 'letter' of it." The court agreed, allowing the father the deduction. It cited the Apostle Paul: "Not of the letter, but of the spirit; for the letter killeth, but the spirit giveth life." The concurring opinion held, more narrowly than the majority, that the taxpayer should win *because* there was only one potential claimant — because the mother was a nonresident alien.

Do you agree with the following dissent?

> TANNENWALD, J., DISSENTING: I think the majority decision flies in the face of section 152(e). That language expressly states that where a child receives over one-half of his support from his parents, who are legally divorced or separated under a decree or written separation agreement, and such child is in the custody of one or both parents "such child shall be treated, for purposes of subsection (a), as receiving over half of his support during the calendar year," unless the other parent meets certain specified conditions. It is undisputed that petitioner did not satisfy those conditions. I do not think it is possible to deal with this case under section 152(a) without regard to the express language of section 152(e). Granted that the difficulties stemming from conflicting claims between parents for dependency exemptions were the generating force for legislative action, the clear mandate of section 152(e) is not limited in application to situations where a conflict exists. The fact that the [taxpayer and government] have agreed on the amounts of support involved is beside the point. A third party, namely, the other spouse, is usually involved in this type of situation, albeit, in this particular case, the petitioner's former wife was a nonresident alien during the taxable year and therefore not subject to United States tax.

[D]   Note on Statutory Interpretation — Statutory Purpose vs. Statutory Text

Was the court in *Prophit* correct in disregarding the letter of the law for the spirit? Spirit is another word for "purpose," so it is crucial to define the legislative purpose accurately. The court chose to define purpose in general terms, which was to reduce the number of cases in which there was controversy about who provided support. The statutory mechanism was reduced to the minor status of a means to implement that purpose. But can means and ends be so easily separated? Wasn't the congressional purpose to eliminate disputes by the particular means set forth in § 152(e)?

In resolving the broader interpretive question of whether statutory purpose should prevail over the text, the substantive area of the law might matter. Some interpreters might adopt a bias against relying on purpose over text in the *tax* law, whatever their general approach to statutory interpretation might be. Textualism might produce more certainty, thereby enabling tax planning and reducing agency discretion.

Even if tax law can sometimes be read in light of purpose over letter, when is that appropriate? The strongest case for going behind the letter of the law is a case in which Congress appears to have overlooked the particular situation in the case. What was that situation in *Prophit*? Was it the absence of a dispute between the taxpayer and his spouse about how much support each provided? Or was it the special case of one spouse not being allowed to take a personal exemption deduction because she was a nonresident alien? Is there any evidence in the statute that the taxpayer's situation was *not* entirely overlooked?

§ 1.04   MARRIED UNITS

[A]   History of Taxing Marital Units; Tax on Marriage

Assume that two taxpayers each earn $87,850 salary. Why do their taxes rise if they marry? Compare the rate structures for married couples (§ 1(a)) and single individuals (§ 1(c)), set forth in the following Table in Chapter 1.02[A]. The top of the 25% tax rate for married couples ($146,400 in 2013) applies to *less* than twice the taxable income to which the top of the 25% tax rate applies for a single individual (for 2013, that is 2 * 87,850 = $175,700). Some income is therefore subject to the 28% tax rate after marriage which was not true before marriage when each single taxpayer has $87,850 income. Notice that married couples cannot avoid this result by filing separate tax returns because of the higher tax rates provided for such filers by § 1(d).

This result is a product of history. Before 1948, individuals, whether married or not, were taxed on their own income. If a husband and wife each earned $87,850, they paid the same tax as two single individuals with $87,850 income. If a husband earned $175,700, and was married to a wife without income, he paid taxes on $175,700.

However, states with Spanish law background (like California) had "community property" laws, which allocated one half of each spouse's earnings to the other; in such states, the marital unit with $175,700 earnings was therefore taxed like two $87,850 single individuals. Because tax rates were progressive, the California married couple was taxed lower than a New York couple with a $175,700/$0 earnings pattern. The Supreme Court recognized state property law for tax purposes; *Poe v. Seaborn*, 282 U.S. 101 (1930). However, the Court refused to recognize an income split between husband and wife when it was elected voluntarily under state legislation giving residents the same tax break as taxpayers living in community property states; *Commissioner v. Harmon*, 323 U.S. 44 (1944).

In 1948, a Republican Congress was in a mood to cut taxes and provided that *all* married couples would be taxed *as though* their total income was split in half, with each half subject to the single individual's tax rate. That brought the tax on a New York couple down to the California couple's level. It also equalized the tax on married units with the same total income (whether the actual earnings followed a $175,700/$0, $100,000/$75,700, or $87,850/87,850 pattern).

By 1969, however, one dramatic effect of the split income approach seemed intolerable. A married couple (for example, with $150,000 total income) paid much lower taxes than a single individual with the same $150,000 total income. As marriage was viewed more as an individual preference, the lower tax on married couples seemed to be a tax preference for people who chose a particular lifestyle. Therefore, in 1969, income-splitting was repealed. **Section 1(c)** *lowered* the tax rates on single individuals. However, a new § **1(a)** was passed for married units. It provided married units with their own rate structure, based on the tax they would have paid if they had split their income under the *higher* pre-1969 rates.

This "solution" continued to treat all married units with the same total income equally. However, by building the old higher pre-1969 rates on single individuals into the 1969 rates on marital units, two single individuals with approximately equal incomes (for example, $87,850 each) increased their taxes by marrying. Marriage deprived these single individuals of the new lower 1969 tax rates on single individuals. Individuals could still lower tax by marrying, *if* one taxpayer earned all of the income; for example, two individuals with $175,700 and $0 income respectively could still lower taxes by getting married, even though the size of the advantage for married couples was reduced beginning in 1969. Whether marriage raises the total taxes on a two-income couple depended on the relative contributions of each spouse to the total income of the marital unit.

There have been complaints about the tax on marriage for years, in part on the ground that it undermined family values. These objections bore fruit in the 2001 Tax Bill, as noted above, by making the top income figure for the three lowest tax brackets for married taxpayers filing jointly equal to double the top income figure for the three lowest tax brackets for single taxpayers. ATRA makes this result permanent. As noted earlier, another source of a tax on marriage has been eliminated — by providing that the standard deduction for a married couple is twice that of a single taxpayer (also made permanent by ATRA).

QUESTIONS

1. Would you favor a repeal of § 1(a) to achieve a total elimination of the tax on marriage for all taxpayers and letting a husband and wife file as single individuals under § 1(c)? Is there a feminist answer to this question?

2. Should all married units with the same total income be taxed the same, because the income tax should be concerned with consumption units rather than who earns income? If consumption units are the appropriate way to think about tax equity, are married couples a consumption unit or do the husband and wife make separate spending decisions?

3. Is the "tax on marriage" fair tax policy because it takes account of the economies of living together. For example, a couple, each of whom earns $30,000, has lower living expenses than two single people who live apart and each earn $30,000. If that is the right way to think about the tax law, should roommates be taxed like married couples, because they enjoy the same economies in living expenses?

4. Does the higher tax on marriage actually dissuade people from marrying?

[B] Untaxed Housework

Another tax rule has a potential impact on married units. The tax law does not tax the value of services performed for oneself — that is called "imputed income." Carried to an extreme, the prospect of taxing such services seems silly and offensive. Would we tax the value of grooming oneself, walking to work, etc.? Why not? Is it hard to value? Would detecting and valuing these services intrude the IRS into private life? How would the taxpayer get cash to pay the tax?

Housework presents a special problem. The value of wagework is taxed but the value of housework is not. This means that one spouse can stay home and produce housework tax free, but would have to pay tax on wages earned to pay someone else to do the work. This provides an incentive not to take wagework. The incentive to provide services for oneself always exists, but the social implications are more severe in the case of housework.

At one time, the problem of untaxed housework was dealt with by giving a married unit a deduction for 10% of the earned income of the lesser-earning spouse, but this provision was repealed. This deduction also had some impact in reducing the tax on marriage. With the reduction in the tax on marriage, there is unlikely to be any political pressure for dealing with the discrepancy between untaxed housework and taxed wagework by allowing a deduction for the lesser-earning spouse.

[C] Defining "Marriage" for Tax Purposes

In an effort to avoid the tax on marriage, some taxpayers got divorced and quickly remarried. The IRS's position challenging this practice is discussed in the following Revenue Ruling and case.

REVENUE RULING 76-255
1976-2 C.B. 40

Advice has been requested concerning the marital status of certain taxpayers for Federal income tax purposes under the circumstances described below. . . .

C and D were married in 1964 and filed joint Federal income tax returns for the years 1964 throughout 1974. In 1975, C and D determined that for Federal income tax purposes it would be advantageous for them to be unmarried so that each of them could file a separate Federal income tax return as an unmarried individual.

On December 30, 1975, C and D secured a divorce under the laws of a foreign jurisdiction. For purposes of this ruling, it is assumed that such divorce was valid. However, at the time of the divorce, they intended to remarry each other and did so in January 1976.

Section 143(a)(1) of the Internal Revenue Code of 1954 [Editor — now § 7703] provides generally that the determination of whether an individual is married shall be made as of the close of the taxable year. . . .

Rev. Rul. 67-442, 1967-2 C.B. 65, provides that the Internal Revenue Service generally will not question for Federal income tax purposes the validity of any divorce decree until a court of competent jurisdiction declares the divorce to be invalid. . . .

[A]lthough C and D were divorced under the laws of the foreign jurisdiction, the divorce was not intended by them to have effect except to enable them to qualify as unmarried individuals who would be eligible to file separate returns. In addition, C and D intended to and did remarry each other early in the succeeding taxable year.

The true nature of a transaction must be considered in light of the plain intent and purpose of the statute. Such transaction should not be given any effect for Federal income tax purposes if it merely serves the purpose of tax avoidance. In determining whether it serves the purpose of tax avoidance all of the surrounding facts and circumstances are to be considered. [The statute does not] contemplate[] a "sham transaction" designed to manipulate for Federal income tax purposes an individual's marital status as of the close of a taxable year.

[Editor — The Ruling concludes that C and D were married for tax purposes as of the close of tax year 1975.]

BOYTER v. COMMISSIONER
United States Tax Court
74 T.C. 989 (1980), *remanded*, 668 F.2d 1382 (4th Cir. 1981)

WILBUR, JUDGE . . .

[Editor – This case concerns the validity of a divorce obtained for tax purposes.]

We . . . agree with the assertion emphatically made by [taxpayer] on brief that "the Tax Court is bound by state law rather than federal law when attempting to construe marital status." Except in a few specific situations, the definition of "husband and wife," or "marriage" is not addressed in the Internal Revenue Code, even though the application of many provisions of the statute turns on the marital status of the taxpayer. It has consistently been held that for Federal income tax purposes, the determination of the marital status of the parties must be made in accordance with the law of the State of their domicile. . . . The rationale for deferring to State law is that domestic relations is "an area that has long been regarded as a virtually exclusive province of the States." . . .

With regard to the provisions for filing a joint return or filing as an unmarried individual, it has been held that State law is determinative on the question of the recognition of common law marriage; the effect of an invalidated Mexican divorce decree; the effect of an interlocutory divorce decree; and whether the taxpayer is legally separated under a decree of separate maintenance. . . . These decisions reflect a consensus that marriage and divorce generally relate to the most intimate and personal of human interaction and are thus better defined by the one entity which has traditionally exercised exclusive regulation and control over these matters.

[Editor — The Tax Court then holds that Maryland courts would not recognize the foreign divorce as effective to terminate the marriage. Thus, petitioners were still married under the tax law. The Court of Appeals reversed the Tax Court decision, holding that the couple was *not* married under Maryland law. The appellate court was, however, willing to apply the "sham transaction" doctrine to supersede state law and treat the couples as married for tax law purposes. It remanded the case to determine how to apply that doctrine. The case then disappears from the reports, presumably because it was settled. As for the Boyters, they became the political poster-family for repeal of the tax on marriage and, eventually, divorced for real. They claimed that their divorce made no change in their lifestyle.]

[D] Note on Statutory Interpretation — Technical Tax Meaning vs. Meaning Borrowed from Family Law

Must the word "married" in the tax law have the same meaning as in state family law, as the Tax Court in *Boyter* held?

The statutory interpretation issue here is a version of the spirit over letter (or purpose over text) issue encountered in the *Prophit* case, except now the text of the tax law uses language borrowed from nontax law rather than from ordinary everyday language. The issue is whether the structure or policy of the tax law requires giving the text a meaning different from the usage familiar in the nontax area of law.

The word "sham" is often used to identify when a transaction will not be recognized for tax purposes. One meaning of this term is uncontroversial — if the *nontax* law does not recognize the transaction (that is, if the couple is still married under state law), the tax law will treat the divorce as a sham and disregard the divorce. You could call this a "legal sham." But this approach makes no effort to interpret a nontax term differently from the usage in the nontax area of law from which it is borrowed.

It is often unclear whether a court uses the word "sham" to mean "legal sham," or whether it is a synonym for any of the other approaches to depriving the taxpayer of a tax break — that is: (1) whether the taxpayer intends to avoid taxes or (2) whether the intent or purpose of the statute does not permit the taxpayer to engage in the activity with favorable tax consequences.

Is the intent to avoid taxes a useful legal test? Doesn't the tax law often allow people to "avoid" taxes. ("Evasion" is a different term — it refers to illegal activity, or cheating.) For example, tax avoidance is no reason to deny an investor the benefit of tax exempt bonds (§ 103). Even if tax avoidance is not *the* legal test, is it useful as a red flag, inviting close scrutiny of the transaction?

Does this discussion suggest that you must always ask whether the "intent or purpose" of the statute is to allow the taxpayer to reduce (avoid) taxes in the manner attempted? If that is so, can you do any better in stating the statutory standard than to say: tax avoidance is not allowed except when it is? That is the way I like to put it, because it forces you to accept the fact that tax avoidance always raises difficult questions of statutory interpretation.

In deciding whether the Boyters should be allowed to avoid tax by divorcing and then remarrying, consider the following more specific questions:

1. Should a court decide whether two individuals, never married, are living so much like a married unit, that they should be taxed as "married?"

2. Should the agency question whether two single people who marry on December 30 and divorce on January 2 are really married (they want the tax reduction that results when one of the individuals has no income)? Is the single-married-single case different from the married-divorced-married case?

3. Should the agency inquire into the marital status for tax purposes of a couple married in name only? The statute is not entirely silent regarding the marital status of separated married couples. *See* § 6013(d)(2); § 7703(a)(2), (b) (individuals legally separated under a decree of divorce or separate maintenance are not considered married; and a married individual who files a separate return, who maintains a household which is the child's principal place of abode, who furnishes more than one-half of the cost of the household, and who lives apart from his spouse for the last 6 months of the year, is not considered married for tax purposes).

4. One of the significant institutional consequences of not automatically incorporating state family law into the tax law is that the agency administering the tax law has some discretion in determining marital status. Why might you want to deny that discretion? Do your reasons apply to couples (like the Boyters) who divorce and remarry quickly?

[E] Spousal Relief from Tax Liability

One of the potential disadvantages for taxpayers who file and sign joint returns, aside from the possible tax on marriage, is joint and several liability for the tax obligation. Absent some statutory relief (described below), both signers are obligated to pay any tax deficiency later assessed, along with any interest and penalties, whether or not the spouse signing the return enjoyed the benefit of the income or deduction giving rise to the deficiency.

The latest version of "innocent spouse" statutory relief was adopted in 1998 and appears in § 6015. It sets forth three statutory provisions allowing a spouse to obtain relief from liability so as to avoid paying a portion of an understatement of tax attributable to the other spouse. The rules, with some detail omitted, are as follows. (1) **Section 6015(b)** allows a taxpayer to elect innocent spouse relief, whether or not divorced or separated at the time of the election, if he or she did not know *or* have reason to know of the understatement and it would be inequitable to hold the taxpayer liable. The taxpayer has the burden of proof regarding state of mind. The "inequitable" standard refers to situations in which the taxpayer did not enjoy a substantial financial benefit from the understatement on the tax return. (2) **Section 6015(c)** allows a taxpayer to elect innocent spouse relief, if the election occurs after divorce or separation, if he or she did not know of the item giving rise to an understatement of tax, except that knowledge is not a bar to relief if the spouse seeking relief signed the return under duress. (3) Finally, **§ 6015(f)** is a catch-all provision allowing the IRS to provide relief to an individual if neither of the above provisions applies and it would be "inequitable" to hold the person liable for all or part of the tax.

Section 6015(f) gave rise to an interesting statutory interpretation issue in *Lantz v. Commissioner*, 607 F.3d 479 (7th Cir. 2010), *reversing*, 132 T.C. 131 (2009). The statute — in § 6015(b) & (c) — explicitly required filing for innocent spouse relief within two years of the IRS's first collection action, but § 6015(f) was silent on a filing date. Nonetheless, a Treasury regulation implementing § 6015(f) stated that the taxpayer had to file for innocent spouse relief within two years. The Tax Court refused to follow the Regulation because of the contrast between the explicit statutory limitation periods in § 6015(b) & (c) and silence in § 6015(f). On appeal, Judge Posner held for the government.

> [We do] not accept "audible silence" as a reliable guide to congressional meaning. "Audible silence," like Milton's "darkness visible" or the Zen *koan* "the sound of one hand clapping," requires rather than guides interpretation. Lantz's brief translates "audible silence" as "plain language," and adds (mysticism must be catching) that "Congress intended the plain language of the language used in the statute." . . .

> Agencies, [] being legislative as well as adjudicatory bodies, are not bashful about making up their own deadlines. And because they are not bashful, and because it is as likely that Congress knows this as that it knows that courts like to borrow a statute of limitations when Congress doesn't specify one, the fact that Congress designated a deadline in two provisions of the same statute and not in a third is not a compelling argument that Congress meant to preclude the Treasury Department from imposing a deadline applicable to cases governed by that third provision. Whether the Treasury borrowed the two-year limitations period from subsections (b) and (c) or simply decided that two years was the right deadline is thus of no consequence; either way it was doing nothing unusual.

Judge Posner added a policy argument: "[I]f there is no deadline in subsection (f), the two-year deadlines in subsections (b) and (c) will be set largely at naught because the substantive criteria of those sections are virtually the same as those of (f)."

Despite the government victory in *Lantz*, the Treasury and IRS have decided "that individuals who request equitable relief under § 6015(f) will no longer be required to submit a request for equitable relief within two years of the IRS's first collection activity against the requesting spouse with respect to the joint tax liability." IRS Notice 2011-70.

[F]   Constitutional Issues

The current rate structure helps married couples when one spouse earns much more than the other spouse but hurts them when each spouse contributes more or less equally to the total income of the married unit. The federal Defense of Marriage Act (DOMA) (1 U.S.C. sec. 7) states: "In determining the meaning of any Act of Congress, or of any ruling, regulation, or interpretation of the various administrative bureaus and agencies of the United States, the word 'marriage' means only a legal union between one man and one woman as husband and wife, and the word 'spouse' refers only to a person of the opposite sex who is a husband or a wife." DOMA therefore prevented a same-sex couple who were legally married under state law from obtaining the advantages (or suffering the disadvantages) of the rate structure applicable to married units.

In *United States v. Windsor*, 133 S.Ct. 2675 (2013), the Supreme Court held (in a 5-4 decision) that DOMA was an unconstitutional deprivation of equal liberty protected by the 5th Amendment. The Court stressed that the regulation of domestic relations had long been the province of state law and that federal efforts to override state law visited injury and indignity on a class of people that the state sought to protect. This amounted to an unconstitutional effort to harm a politically unpopular group. The Court claimed to rest its decision on federal considerations, without reaching the broader question of whether a state was constitutionally required to recognize same-sex marriages.

The Court did not discuss the status of a couple married in a state that recognized same-sex marriages who later moved to a state that does not recognize such marriages. In IR 2013-72, the IRS stated that the same-sex couple would be married for federal income tax purposes as long as they were legally married in one state, even though they moved to a state that did not recognize such marriages.

Chief Justice Roberts' dissent in *Windsor* embraced the majority's claim that the decision rested on federalism considerations, leaving open the issue whether same-sex couples had a constitutional right to marry. Justice Scalia's dissent argued that the Court's decision unmistakably foreshadowed a decision that same-sex couples had a constitutional right to marry.

§ 1.05   EARNED INCOME CREDIT

The earned income credit (EIC) (§ 32) allows taxpayers with (1) earned income and (2) a "qualifying child" (§ 32(c)(3)) to lower their taxes by a percentage of the earned income. It does more. If the credit exceeds taxes otherwise due, the taxpayer gets a payment from the government. That is, the credit is refundable. For example, a taxpayer with only $3,000 of earnings (and therefore no tax after the personal exemption and standard deduction) fills out the tax form and computes the credit as though it equaled taxes that had been withheld from wages. The idea is to compensate for the burden of Social Security taxes on lower income earners.

The percentage used to compute the credit varies, depending on whether the taxpayer has one, two, or three or more children. In addition, the 1993 tax law introduced one further EIC wrinkle. For the first time, workers without children became eligible — if they are at least age 25 and under age 65, and if they cannot be deducted as another's dependent. The credit percentages are as follows:

Earned income credit percentage:
No children	7.65%
One child	34%
Two children	40%
Three or more children	45% (scheduled to expire after 2017)

The earned income credit is designed to help lower income earners. Consequently, the law provides for a maximum amount of earned income (referred to as the "earned income amount") eligible for the credit; and the credit phases out by a percentage of the excess of AGI over a specified threshold. The earned income amount and the phase-out threshold (inflation-adjusted) for 2013 are as follows:

Earned income amount:
No children	$6,370
One child	$9,560
More than one child	$13,430

Phase-out thresholds:
Married, filing jointly:	
No children	$13,310
One or more children	$22,870
Other taxpayers:	
No children	$7,970
One or more children	$17,530

The phase-out percentage varies with the number of children, as follows:

Phase-out percentage:
No children	7.65%

| One child | 15.98% |
| More than one child | 21.06% |

The phase-out has the impact of an increased (phantom) marginal tax rate on lower income earners, counteracting the incentive effects of the credit itself.

Marriage between two workers might also be discouraged, if increased total earnings cost the couple some or all of the earned income credit. In an effort to offset the tax on marriage, the law now provides an upward adjustment of the phase-out threshold for married couples. However, there is still a potential marriage tax penalty because the phase-out threshold for a married couple is less than double the phase-out threshold for a single taxpayer.

An additional provision prevents well-off taxpayers from taking advantage of the earned income credit. It denies the credit to individuals with "disqualified income" in excess of an inflation-adjusted threshold. For tax year 2013, the threshold is $3,300. "Disqualified income" is, in general terms, investment income, such as interest and dividends. An important feature of the definition of disqualified income is that it includes otherwise tax exempt interest income (that is, the interest on state and local bonds, discussed later in the course). *See* § 32(i).

Notice that the income reporting incentives created by the EIC may be perverse. If you have one eligible child and are eligible for a 34% EIC credit, would you overreport your earnings (for example, report earnings of $6,000 instead of $5,000)? (Don't forget that you have to pay social security taxes on earnings.)

There have been considerable compliance problems associated with the earned income credit. The 1997 Tax Act adds several penalty provisions, one of which prohibits claiming the EIC for ten years after a fraudulent EIC claim.

§ 1.06 CHILD TAX CREDIT

The 1997 tax law added a child tax credit, found in § 24.

a. The credit amount was $400 per child in tax year 1998; $500 thereafter. Then, the 2001 Tax Bill increased the credit further, spurred on by the same "family values" concerns that led to the substantial modification of the tax on marriage. Originally, the increase was to be gradually phased in until it reached $1,000 in 2010 (thereby backloading the increase to reduce the budget impact in the early years), but the 2003 Tax Law set the figure at $1,000. ATRA makes the $1,000 figure permanent.

b. The credit is available for a dependent of the taxpayer — who is also a child, a direct descendant of a child, a stepchild, or a foster child. The dependent must be under age 17. Why do you think this tax break was preferred to a rate reduction for low- and middle-income taxpayers? Politically, the child tax credit (unlike a rate reduction) can be billed as a benefit for families with children, with strong "conservative" family values overtones.

c. The child tax credit is phased out at the rate of $50 for every $1,000 of *modified* AGI (or part thereof) above a threshold. The threshold is $110,000 for married taxpayers filing joint returns and $75,000 for single taxpayers.

If there is more than one dependent child eligible for the credit, the phase out applies to the credit for one child first and then the next child, and so on. **§ 24(b)(1)**. Thus, if there are three dependent children of married taxpayers, the $1,000 credit per child phases out at $170,000 of income. ($20,000 of income results in the full loss of the $1,000 credit per child.) This is different from the phase out of personal exemption deductions, where the 2% reduction of the deduction applies to *total* personal exemption deductions for each $2,500 of "excess" income. **§ 151(d)(3)(A–B)**.

The phantom tax rate that results from phasing out the child tax credit is 5%, because there is a lost benefit of $50 for every $1,000 of income (that is 50/1000).

Note where in the income scale this phantom tax rate operates — that is, the phase-out range. You have seen some phantom tax rates and will see others in the tax code (e.g., educational and retirement savings tax breaks). Is there any effort to make sure that they do not cumulate at certain income levels to raise effective marginal tax rates too much? Hint: Look at the phase-out threshold in each instance.

d. The child tax credit is refundable, in an amount equal to 15% of the excess of earned income of more than $3,000 (*not* inflation-adjusted). This $3,000 amount is a reduction from prior law and will expire after 2017. For families with three or more children, the refund rule is a little different and more complex. **§ 24(d)(1)**.

e. The credit amount and the phase-out threshold are *not* indexed for inflation.

§ 1.07 COMPLEXITY

One complaint about the earned income and child tax credits is an increase in tax complexity. Actually, tax complexity is itself a complex idea.

Tax complexity is sometimes equated with excessive statutory detail, which produces *jigsaw* puzzle complexity, in the sense that the answer is there but cannot be determined without a great deal of effort — often with the aid of a committee report or a summary explanation published by a private publisher.

Another type of complexity is *legal* complexity, which leads to divergent legal authorities and uncertainty. Recall the problem of whether married taxpayers can divorce and remarry soon thereafter to avoid the tax on marriage (divergent Tax Court, Court of Appeals, and IRS authority). Legal complexity can result from the simplest of statutory texts. Indeed, the right amount of statutory detail can reduce legal complexity, without making the jigsaw puzzle too complex.

In most public conversations of tax complexity, the reference to complexity is to *tax form* complexity. This type of complexity is of greatest concern when it forces taxpayers to hire outside tax return preparers. Both the earned income credit and child tax credit are likely examples of this problem. Tax form complexity often results from jigsaw puzzle complexity.

The political problem of tax complexity is most acute for low income taxpayers (who must pay a tax preparer), and for small businesses (who must pay for tax advisors and preparers). Consequently, reduction in tax complexity often takes the form of exempting these taxpayers from rules that produce the complexity, rather than changing the underlying rules. The standard deduction is a classic example of reducing tax complexity for low income taxpayers.

All three types of tax complexity can also complicate tax administration and, therefore, indirectly cause problems for taxpayers, either as a result of administrative errors or excessive agency discretion, as the agency itself struggles to comprehend the law.

In some situations, all three types of complexity can so befuddle the IRS that taxpayers with good tax advisers can avoid taxes, either because government auditors are no match for taxpayer counsel or there is no audit in the first place. The result is tax inequity, as the rules are avoided by some but not all taxpayers.

Congress is certainly aware of the problem(s) of tax complexity and constantly complains about it, even as it legislates more and more complex rules in response to the political dynamics underlying tax law. Those dynamics include: helping taxpayers know exactly what their tax obligations are (e.g., which divorced parent can take the personal exemption deduction for the child); providing precisely tailored tax breaks (e.g., earned income and child tax credits); selectively closing off tax breaks that taxpayers have uncovered (*see* Chapter 6.01[C][4], discussing the Industrial Revenue Bond loophole). Some recent tax bills are referred to colloquially as Lawyers and Accountants Relief Act of [some year], because complexity increases the demand for tax advisers. The Report of the National Commission on Restructuring the IRS (Kerrey-Portman Report), published in 75 TAX NOTES 1683 (June 30, 1997), called for Congress to consider a Tax Complexity Analysis for each tax proposal, but it has not been effective. *See also* Study of the Overall State of the Federal Tax System and Recommendations for Tax Simplification, Prepared by the Staff of the Joint Committee on Taxation (April 2001) (3 volumes); and Special Supplement to Tax Notes (May 28, 2001) (five reports on tax simplification).

As you reflect on tax complexity discussed in this and later chapters, consider (1) whether Congress gave adequate attention to any of the above sources of complexity; (2) what kind of tax complexity the law causes; and (3) whether the complexity is warranted in achieving the appropriate goals of the income tax law.

§ 1.08 STATE INCOME TAXES

Most states impose a tax on personal income. Most of these laws use some or all of the federal income tax computations to compute the state tax (either AGI or taxable income, with adjustments), which greatly eases tax administration. Some adjustments are considered constitutionally mandatory, such as permitting a deduction of interest on federal debt. Others reflect state policy, such as their own personal exemption deductions, credits for educational or environmental expenditures, and different itemized deductions.

Whenever federal law changes the income tax base, state income taxation can be affected. Broadening the federal tax base (for example, by closing loopholes) can increase state revenue, but adding federal tax breaks can lower the state income tax base. (When Congress recently provided bonus depreciation deductions, about 35 states denied the deduction for computing the state income tax base.) If the federal income tax is changed by raising or lowering tax credits or lowering progressive tax rates, this will not affect state income taxes tied to federal income definitions. However, it will affect state income tax collections in those few states whose income tax is a percentage of the federal tax.

State constitutions usually prohibit incorporation of a law by reference when it is the law of another jurisdiction and the incorporation includes future amendments to the incorporated law. The idea is that this would improperly delegate lawmaking authority to another government. However, some states accept incorporation of federal income tax law as a legitimate means of simplifying tax administration; *see, e.g.*, *Alaska Steamship Co. v. Mullaney*, 180 F.2d 805 (9th Cir. 1950).

If state law depends on federal law, how is federal law determined. This is the reverse of the *Erie* problem, where federal courts have to decide how to determine state law. In *Calhoun v. Franchise Tax Bd.*, 574 P.2d 763 (Cal. 1978), a federal Tax Court decision estopped the state taxpayers from relitigating the amount of gross income determined in the Tax Court.

Chapter 2

WHOSE INCOME IS IT

§ 2.01 INTRODUCTION

Rate differences create an incentive to shift income to different taxpayers to achieve the lowest total tax. A taxpayer wants to do this, however, only if there is a close relationship with the transferee (for example, a family member or a wholly owned corporation). Many income shifting efforts therefore occur within the family or between a taxpayer and a controlled corporation. The "kiddie tax" is one complex and explicit effort by the statute to discourage intra-family income shifting; *see* Chapter 1.03[A].

This area of the law has special interest for lawyers interested in how tax law is made. Historically, the"law" responding to income shifting was first developed by the courts. The statute (§ 61) simply taxed income without saying anything about whose income it was. The seminal case dealing with assignment of income is *Lucas v. Earl*, set forth below. Thereafter, Congress responded with *specific* statutory rules dealing with income shifting in certain areas of the law (for example, setting up family trusts). Still other areas of law are dealt with by detailed Regulations (such as family partnerships).

These various sources of law suggest two questions about the evolution of tax law. First, what is the role of courts in initiating efforts to close potential loopholes? The *Lucas v. Earl* decision was in 1930, at the height of the U.S. judiciary's willingness to read purpose into a statute that might otherwise permit a loophole. Once launched, the assignment of income doctrine became part of the law, but it is not clear that a modern court would have taken that step if the issue had arisen for the first time today. Second, who does a better job of addressing the assignment of income problem: courts, agency, or legislature?

§ 2.02 PERSONAL SERVICES

LUCAS v. EARL
United States Supreme Court
281 U.S. 111 (1930)

MR. JUSTICE HOLMES delivered the opinion of the Court.

This case presents the question whether the respondent, Earl, could be taxed for the whole of the salary and attorney's fees earned by him in the years 1920 and 1921, or should be taxed for only a half of them in view of a contract with his wife which we shall mention. . . .

By the contract, made in 1901, Earl and his wife agreed "that any property either of us now has or may hereafter acquire . . . in any way, either by earnings (including salaries, fees, etc.), or any rights by contract or otherwise, during the existence of our marriage, or which we or either of us may receive by gift, bequest, devise, or inheritance, and all the proceeds, issues, and profits of any and all such property shall be treated and considered, and hereby is declared to be received, held, taken, and owned by us as joint tenants, and not otherwise, with the right of survivorship." The validity of the contract is not questioned, and we assume it to be unquestionable under the law of the State of California, in which the parties lived. . . .

The Revenue Act of 1918 . . . imposes a tax upon the net income of every individual including 'income derived from salaries, wages, or compensation for personal service . . . of whatever kind and in whatever form paid.' . . . A very forcible argument is presented to the effect that the statute seeks to tax only income beneficially received, and that taking the question more technically the salary and fees became the joint property of Earl and his wife on the very first instant on which they were received. We well might hesitate upon the latter proposition, because however the matter might stand between husband and wife he was the only party to the contracts by which the salary and fees were earned, and it is somewhat hard to say that the last step in the performance of those contracts could be taken by anyone but himself alone. But this case is not to be decided by attenuated subtleties. It turns on the import and reasonable construction of the taxing act. There is no doubt that the statute could tax salaries to those who earned them and provide that the tax could not be escaped by anticipatory arrangements and contracts however skillfully devised to prevent the salary when paid from vesting even for a second in the man who earned it. That seems to us the import of the statute before us and we think that no distinction can be taken according to the motives leading to the arrangement by which the fruits are attributed to a different tree from that on which they grew.

Judgment reversed.

COMMENTS AND QUESTIONS

1. **Impact of attribution to transferor — Recast transaction.** *Lucas v. Earl* is an example of a situation in which a transaction in the real world is recast for tax purposes so that it is taxed more in accordance with its economic reality. As such, it is a precursor to cases dealt with later in the book concerning tax avoidance (e.g., recasting a sale and lease-back of property as a loan; Chapter 19.03[F][2]).

Mechanically, all *Lucas v. Earl* does is to recast the transaction so that the income collected by the transferee is taxed as though it had first been received by the transferor and then transferred to the transferee. How this recast transaction is taxed depends on the tax rules applicable to the relationship between the various parties. In *Lucas*, the assigned income was salary so the transferor is treated as though he received taxable salary. The transferee is a family member, so the subsequent transfer is a gift to the transferee (gifts are tax free, (§ 102), as explained in Chapter 4).

In other cases, the receipt of the amount assigned by the transferor might not result in taxable income (e.g., some foreign personal service income is not taxed), and the relationship between the transferor and transferee might result in taxation of the transferee (e.g., if the transferee works for the transferor).

2. **Income earner vs. beneficially received.** Why doesn't the court in *Lucas v. Earl* adopt the "beneficially received" rather than the "income earner" approach to identifying the taxpayer? Perhaps the point is that the income is likely to be transferred around within the family, which is a consumption unit that enjoys the benefit of the income. In other words, despite the emphasis on earning income, *Lucas v. Earl* used the "income earner" approach to implement a broad conception of the taxable consumption unit that enjoyed the benefit. The holding of the case meant that income earned by the husband and given to the wife would be taxed at the husband's rates, which are arguably the correct rates to apply to the income earned by the marital unit. (Remember that the case was decided before a husband and wife were taxed as one taxable unit.)

3. **Transfers outside family.** Whatever you think might be the best reading of the *Lucas v. Earl* decision, it has come to stand for the broad proposition that income is taxed to the earner, even if it is assigned outside of the family unit — *e.g.*, to charity. Moreover, the use of the assignment of income doctrine to indirectly tax the marital unit on its total income has never developed so that the assignment of property by one family member to another necessarily results in taxing the transferor on *investment* income. That is the holding in the following case of *Blair v. Commissioner.*

§ 2.03   PROPERTY TRANSFERS

[A]   Transfer of Entire Interest

BLAIR v. COMMISSIONER
United States Supreme Court
300 U.S. 5 (1937)

Mr. Chief Justice Hughes delivered the opinion of the Court.

[Editor — The taxpayer was a beneficiary under a trust. He assigned all of his trust interest to his children prior to the tax years in which the trust income arose, so the income was paid to the children. The issue was whether the assignor or the assignee-children should be taxed on the income. The Court first held that a valid assignment of property had been made under state law and then discussed its tax consequences, distinguishing *Lucas v. Earl.*]

Our decision . . . in *Lucas v. Earl,* 281 U.S. 111 [is] cited. In the *Lucas* Case the question was whether an attorney was taxable for the whole of his salary and fees earned by him in the tax years or only upon one-half by reason of an agreement with his wife by which his earnings were to be received and owned by them jointly. We were of the opinion that the case turned upon the construction of the taxing act. We said that 'the statute could tax salaries to those who earned them and provide that the tax could not be escaped by anticipatory arrangements and contracts however skillfully devised to prevent the salary when paid from vesting even for a second in the man who earned it.' That was deemed to be the meaning of the statute as to compensation for personal service and the one who earned the income was held to be subject to the tax. . . . [*Lucas* is] not in point. The tax here is not upon earnings which are taxed to the one who earns them. . . .

In the instant case, the tax is upon income as to which, in the general application of the revenue acts, the tax liability attaches to ownership.

The Government points to the provisions of the revenue acts imposing upon the beneficiary of a trust the liability for the tax upon the income distributable to the beneficiary. But the term is merely descriptive of the one entitled to the beneficial interest. These provisions cannot be taken to preclude valid assignments of the beneficial interest, or to affect the duty of the trustee to distribute income to the owner of the beneficial interest, whether he was such initially or becomes such by valid assignment. The one who is to receive the income as the owner of the beneficial interest is to pay the tax. If under the law governing the trust the beneficial interest is assignable, and if it has been assigned without reservation, the assignee thus becomes the beneficiary and is entitled to rights and remedies accordingly. We find nothing in the revenue acts which denies him that status.

The will creating the trust entitled the petitioner during his life to the net income of the property held in trust. He thus became the owner of an equitable interest in the corpus of the property. By virtue of that interest he was entitled to enforce the trust, to have a breach of trust enjoined and to obtain redress in case of breach. The interest was present property alienable like any other, in the absence of a valid restraint upon alienation. The beneficiary may thus transfer . . . his interest. . . .

We conclude that the assignments were valid, that the assignees thereby became the owners of the specified beneficial interests in the income, and that as to these interests they and not the petitioner were taxable for the tax years in question. The judgment of the Circuit Court of Appeals is reversed and the cause is remanded with direction to affirm the decision of the Board of Tax Appeals.

[Editor — The import of *Blair* is that anyone can assign his entire interest in property (e.g., land, shares of stock, or a bond) and deflect the rent, dividends or interest to the assignee, even if it is to a family member. Why is there a distinction between taxpayers who assign personal service income and those who assign property?]

[B]   Retained Control Over Property

You have not yet finished with the permutations of the assignment of income doctrine in connection with property transfers. The concept of "earning" income, which resulted in taxing someone who earns personal service income under *Lucas v. Earl*, has evolved to include "control over transferred property." It turns out that what leads to taxing the income earner on transferred personal service income is his control over income production, and that idea has developed so that a transferor who retains control over transferred *investment* property is also unable to deflect income to a transferee.

It is not clear why this should be so. If transfers of property occur within the family, it might make sense to prevent assignment of income. But why does it make sense to limit taxing the transferor on income from transferred property to a case where the transferor retains control over the transferred property?

The "control over transferred property" idea is applied to both trusts and partnerships, as explained below.

[1]　Trusts

The Supreme Court originally decided that retention of "too much" control over a trust could result in taxing the trust grantor on trust income. Thereafter, detailed Regulations explained when the grantor could not shift income to the trust or the trust beneficiaries. Finally, the Code was amended to provide very detailed rules specifying when the trust grantor was taxed because of retained control. In this corner of "assignment of income" doctrine, the statutory rules are exclusive. Case law is no longer relevant. § 671 (last sentence).

In general, if the trust grantor does not have too much control, either the trust or its beneficiaries are taxed on the income. The usual pattern is for the beneficiaries to be taxed on income distributed to them, and for the trust to be taxed on retained income. (Trust taxation is discussed in Part II-D, Chapter 32.02.)

The use of trusts for tax planning purposes has been substantially reduced by the elegant "solution" of raising the tax rates on trusts. *See* § 1(e). For tax year 2013, the tax rates and brackets are as follows: 15% ($0to $2,450); 25% (over $2,450 to $5,700); 28% (over $5,700 to $8,750); 33% (over $8,750 to $11,950); 39.6% (over $11,950). Assigning property to a trust has therefore become a very unattractive tax planning technique.

[2]　Partnerships

Another situation in which retained control over property might prevent transfer of income to a transferee is the assignment of a partnership income interest to a family member. The Regulations specify the conditions under which the transfer will be effective, one of which is that the transferor shall not retain too much control over income distribution or over management beyond the reasonable needs of the business. A transfer to a minor child who is not competent to manage his own affairs is generally not effective for tax purposes, unless the child's interests are protected by a judicially-supervised fiduciary. **Treas. Reg. § 1.704-1(e)(1), (2).**

In addition, the statute says that a donor of a partnership interest is taxed on a reasonable amount attributable to his personal services. The donor-transferor cannot work for nothing. § 704(e)(2).

Finally, these partnership rules apply only to partnerships in which capital is a material income-producing factor. A partner in a personal service partnership cannot transfer the income to a transferee under the general principles of *Lucas v. Earl.*

§ 2.04 DOMESTIC PARTNERS?

In a 2010 Private Letter Ruling (201021048), the IRS dealt with the federal income tax treatment of earned income under California community property law, as follows:

> In 2005, California law significantly expanded the rights and obligations of persons entering into a California domestic partnership for state property law purposes, but not for state income tax purposes. Specifically, the California Domestic Partner Rights and Responsibilities Act of 2003 (the California Act), effective on January 1, 2005, provided that "Registered domestic partners shall have the same rights, protections, and benefits, and shall be subject to the same responsibilities, obligations, and duties under law . . . as are granted to and imposed upon spouses." However, the California Act provided that "earned income may not be treated as community property for state income tax purposes."

> On September 29, 2006, California enacted Senate Bill 1827. Senate Bill 1827 repealed the language of the California Act providing that earned income was not to be treated as community property for state income tax purposes. Thus, effective January 1, 2007, the earned income of a registered domestic partner (RDP) must be treated as community property for state income tax purposes (unless the RDPs execute an agreement opting out of community property treatment). As a result of the legislation, California, as of January 1, 2007, treats the earned income of registered domestic partners as community property for both property law purposes and state income tax purposes.

The ruling then applies California property law to determine federal income tax consequences without regard to whether the law deals with traditional marriage relationships.

> California community property law developed in the context of marriage and originally applied only to the property rights and obligations of spouses. The law operated to give each spouse an equal interest in each community asset, regardless of which spouse is the holder of record.

> By 2007, California had extended *full community property treatment* to registered domestic partners. Applying the principle that federal law respects state law property characterizations, the federal tax treatment of community property should apply to California registered domestic partners. Consequently, for tax years beginning after December 31, 2006, a California registered domestic partner must report one half of the community income, whether received in the form of compensation for personal services or income from property, on his or her federal income tax return.

The Ruling does not cite *Commissioner v. Harmon*, 323 U.S. 44 (1944), which had denied community property status for federal income tax purposes when state law allowed taxpayers to elect community property status. Presumably, the California law dealing with domestic partnerships is not analogous to electing community property status, even though a domestic partnership can elect out of community property treatment.

The Ruling also does not cite the federal Defense of Marriage Act (DOMA) (1 U.S.C. sec. 7). Now that DOMA has been held unconstitutional, a same-sex couple that wants to obtain community property treatment can simply marry if they live in a state that recognizes same-sex marriage. The Ruling is still important, however, for same-sex couples who do not live in a state that recognizes same-sex marriage but does extend community property treatment to unmarried domestic partners.

§ 2.05 TRANSFERRING INCOME TO A CORPORATION

Suppose a taxpayer is an athlete or movie actor who owns all of the stock of a corporation. The taxpayer-shareholder has a contract with the corporation so that, on paper, the taxpayer-shareholder's services are loaned out by the corporation to the sports team or movie company. Payment for the taxpayer's personal services is made to the corporation. The taxpayer-shareholder receives a salary from her corporation as an employee, which is less than the total personal service income. Who is taxed on the personal service income collected by the corporation?

The following cases reveal a sharp split among the courts in deciding whether to apply assignment of income doctrine to prevent deflection of income to the corporation. You should take note of the fact that the incentive to deflect income to a corporation is much diminished under the current rate structure, in which the top individual and corporate tax rates are close together, disregarding phantom tax rates (the top corporate rate is 35% — § 11). At various times, the top corporate rate has been 20% or more below the top individual tax rate. There are still other reasons to deflect income to a corporation, however. As we will see later, the cost of tax-free fringe benefits can sometimes be paid out of corporate income — deductible by the corporation and tax free to the recipient — under circumstances where the individual could not deduct the expenditures if incurred out of his own income.

Several Courts of Appeals have been very reluctant to apply assignment of income doctrine in the corporate-shareholder context to tax the taxpayer-shareholder on the total personal service income. *Foglesong v. Commissioner*, 691 F.2d 848 (7th Cir. 1982), *reversing* 77 T.C. 1102 (1981); *Sargent v. Commissioner*, 929 F.2d 1252 (8th Cir. 1991), *reversing* 93 T.C. 572 (1989). In both cases, the Tax Court had applied assignment of income doctrine to tax the shareholder-employee on all of the corporation's income, when the shareholder was the employee of the person for whom the services were performed (e.g., an employee of a sports team which "borrowed" the taxpayer's services from the taxpayer's corporation). The Courts of Appeals reversed, stressing that a corporation is a separate tax entity, a separation that was contradicted by taxing the shareholder on personal service income deflected to the corporation. Of course, the family member to whom personal service income is transferred is also a separate tax "entity," and yet, the transferor is taxed (under *Lucas v. Earl*) on the personal service income.

The Tax Court stuck to its guns in *Leavell v. Commissioner*, 104 T.C. 140 (1995). A professional basketball player organized and owned a personal service corporation and agreed to furnish his services to his own corporation. The corporation then executed a contract with an NBA professional basketball team to furnish the player's services to the NBA team. As a condition of executing the player contract, the team required the player to execute a written agreement personally agreeing to perform the individual services called for by the player contract. The team paid the corporation for the player's services, only part of which amount was paid as compensation by the corporation to the player. The government asserted that the *entire* amount paid to the corporation was the player's personal service income and could not be deflected to the corporation. The Tax Court held that, because the team had the power to control the performance of the services, the player was an employee of the team and could not therefore deflect the personal service income to his corporation, based on the principles of *Lucas v. Earl*. The Tax Court followed its earlier decision in *Sargent*, which had been reversed by the Eighth Circuit.

COMMENTS AND QUESTIONS

1. **Double tax on corporate profits.** Is there some explanation for the division of opinion between the Tax Court, which is inclined to tax the individual, and the Court of Appeals decisions, which do not tax the individual? The deeper reason for the Court of Appeals decisions may be the double tax on corporate profits (discussed further in Part II-D, Chapter 33.02). Corporate profits can be provided to shareholders only by suffering both a tax on the corporate profits at the corporate level and again at the shareholder level on dividend distributions. This double tax on corporate profits will usually exceed the tax on personal service income received directly by the shareholder, depending on the corporate and individual tax rates and how long a delay there is before the dividend distribution. Therefore, preventing assignment of income to a corporation might seem unnecessary. In other words, the rationale for the assignment of income doctrine really is that the taxpayer's tax rate is the proper tax rate to apply when the income earner could have obtained the income for personal consumption and, if the assignment of income doctrine is not needed to protect that tax rate, there is no need to invoke the doctrine.

2. **Taxpayer as employee of the team.** The Tax Court in *Leavell* (taxing the athlete on the entire income) stressed that the shareholder-employee was an employee of the team. Why is that important? There are two possible reasons. First, the team's control over the player, which is implicit in the employment relationship with the team, negates control by the player's personal service corporation. And it might appear that the player should avoid tax only when the player's corporation is in control. Control by the player's corporation instead of the team would make the corporation look more like the following situation in which the corporation is clearly the income recipient rather than the person who performs the personal services: a music talent corporation sends out performers to do gigs at various locations during the year and pays the performer a salary, which is less than the corporation collects for lending out the performer's services.

Second, control by the team distinguishes the actor or athlete from the typical family corporation situation in which there is a capital investment and in which owner-employees do not always draw down a salary equal to the full value of their services. Courts are reluctant to impute a reasonable salary to the owner-employee of a family business and the Tax Court might therefore be reluctant to open the door to that possibility by invoking the assignment of income doctrine in the corporate context.

Query. Do either of these reasons for not taxing players or actors on the income of their personal service corporations make sense? The talent corporation with multiple performers under contract and the typical family business are not like a one-person personal service corporation.

3. § 482. When the government seeks to tax the shareholder-employee, it has another string to its bow besides the assignment of income doctrine. **Section 482** permits income to be reallocated among businesses to "clearly reflect income." **Section 482** has its major impact on relationships between foreign and domestic corporations with common ownership, discussed in Part II-E, Chapter 34.03[B]. These corporations fix prices between their respective businesses to deflect income to the country with the lowest tax rate.

The Court of Appeals in *Foglesong, supra*, held that § 482 could not be used to rearrange personal service income between an individual shareholder and a controlled corporation unless the shareholder has a business separate from the corporation. When a shareholder-employee has no business other than performing the services loaned out by his or her corporation, the court held that § 482 did not apply.

Chapter 3

DEFINING INCOME

§ 3.01 GROSS INCOME

When we did a problem computing taxable income in Chapter 1.02[A], we identified gross income in the form of personal service income and then reduced the gross income by various deductions to determine taxable income. Sometimes, gross income is itself the result of a deduction from a larger figure. That occurs when a taxpayer disposes of property, of which a sale or exchange is the most common example. The sales price is technically an "amount realized," or, in more conventional terms, gross receipts; and the gross income is the result of reducing the sales price by the property's cost. The code refers to as "basis." But gross income also results from reducing the amount realized by basis whenever the taxpayer disposes of property, even if not by a sale or exchange, as when insurance proceeds are collected after property is destroyed.

Technically, the reduction of gross receipts by cost is not called a deduction in the tax code; the reduction of gross receipts by cost is simply part of the definition of "gross income." You can usually get this result from the following sections in the code. First, look at § 1001(a), which defines "gain" as "amount realized" minus "adjusted basis" (adjusted basis is original cost, minus any of the original cost previously deducted); then look at § 61(a)(3), along with the introductory language to § 61(a), which says that gross income includes "gain derived from dealings in property." In combination, these sections say that gross income included in the tax base is amount realized minus cost.

For example, if a taxpayer buys a residence for $60,000 and sells it for $100,000, only $40,000 is included in gross income. The function of the $60,000 cost figure in computing the tax base is to prevent imposing tax twice. For example, suppose a taxpayer in the 28% tax bracket earns $83,333 and pays $23,333 tax, and uses the remaining $60,000 to buy a residence. If he later sells the building for $100,000, he should be taxed on $40,000 gain, not $100,000, because $60,000 is a recovery of after tax income invested in the residence. *Cost is a record of previously taxed income that should not be taxed again.*

Or, more precisely, cost is a record of an amount previously reported as an "amount realized," including an amount that the code exempts from taxation. This refinement in the definition of cost reflects the fact that the taxpayer should not pay tax on an amount that the code explicitly exempts from taxation when it is received. Cost must include an exempt amount in basis or else the taxpayer will be taxed on such amount when property purchased with the exempt income is later sold, thereby undermining the exemption. For example, if a taxpayer used $60,000 of tax exempt income to buy a house, the house has a $60,000 basis.

The idea that gross income is amount realized minus cost is so fundamental that it is hard-wired into the definition of "gross income," even without the reference in § 61(a)(3) to gains derived from dealings in property. For example, what statutory language determines how much gross income a taxpayer has if a residence costing $60,000 burns down (rather than being sold) and the owner collects $100,000 insurance? Do not concern yourself with whether the taxpayer can avoid tax on the income by reinvesting the proceeds (§ 1033 provides this opportunity in some cases), or whether the gain is capital gain. That comes later. Focus solely on the question of computing the amount of gross income.

In the insurance example, it might be hard to say that the gain is from "dealings in property," and yet the answer is clear — gross income is amount realized minus cost ($100,000 minus 60,000). This result comes from the reference to "gross income" in the introductory text of § 61(a), which is understood to mean amount realized (gross receipts) minus cost, even without further language.

Section 1001(c), which says that gain on the sale or exchange of property shall be recognized, is also superfluous. It would probably not apply to the collection of insurance because collection of insurance is not a sale or exchange. And yet the gain on collecting insurance is taxed because it is gross income and this income is taxed by § 1. So much for the canon of statutory interpretation that a statute is presumed not to contain superfluous language.

What is happening here is that the general concept of taxable gain is so fundamental that it does not require the more specific provisions in the code. Examples not dealt with by these specific provisions are still covered by the safety net of the introductory text of § 61(a) referring to gross income.

§ 3.02 BASIS

[A] Defining Basis — Basis of Property Received

As you worked out the meaning of gross income, you encountered the statutory term "basis" as the technical term for cost. That is what § 1012 says — it defines basis as cost. Moreover, you had no trouble determining the basis of purchased property — it is the purchase price, which is the colloquial meaning of "cost."

What is the basis of property *received* in a taxable transaction? For example, suppose the taxpayer receives (rather than purchases) $60,000 worth of land as salary. The basis of property received is its fair market value — $60,000 in this example. The reason is that the taxpayer who receives $60,000 worth of property is in the same position as the taxpayer who buys the property for $60,000 and should, therefore, have the same $60,000 basis, as the following paragraphs explain.

The purchaser. How much income must the taxpayer receive to be able to buy $60,000 worth of property? Assume the taxpayer pays 28% of income in taxes. She must receive $83,333; tax = 0.28 * $83,333 = $23,333; subtracting the tax from $83,333 leaves $60,000 to buy the land.

The land recipient. The 28% bracket taxpayer receiving $60,000 of land as salary must pay $16,800 tax (0.28 * $60,000 = $16,800). To pay that tax and still have $60,000 of land left, she must have additional income to pay the tax. How much income does she need to pay $16,800 in tax? The answer is $23,333. A 28% tax on $23,333 is $6,533; after tax, she has $16,800, which she pays to the government as the tax on the receipt of the $60,000 land.

Therefore, both the land purchaser and land recipient need $83,333 income to acquire $60,000 worth of land. They should both have the same $60,000 basis, reflecting after tax income invested in the land. In both cases, the $60,000 basis is a record of previously taxed income that should not be taxed again.

[B] Note on Statutory Interpretation — Plain Meaning vs. Tax Term of Art

Notice that the statute defines basis as "cost." Ordinary usage of the term "cost" easily fits the purchaser. But the "cost" for the land recipient is not "cost" in any ordinary sense. The statute departs from ordinary usage to implement the statute's underlying structure — basis is after tax income on which no further tax should be paid, whether the taxpayer buys the property or receives it in a taxable event.

This is an approach to statutory interpretation similar to giving "marriage" a special tax law meaning to implement the underlying structure of the tax law. However, in the "cost" example, the result is much less controversial because there are no adverse policy implications of letting the government apply the specialized tax law meaning.

[C] Recovery of Basis

Basis is "deductible" under certain circumstances. For introductory purposes, the following explanation suffices. As noted above, the basis of an asset is "deductible" when the asset is disposed of at a gain. This is provided by § 61(a). This rule applies to both income-producing and personal use property (such as a home).

Loss is computed in the same way as gain — amount realized minus basis — except that the amount realized is less than cost when there is a loss. The rules dealing with deduction of losses differ depending on whether the property is used for income-production or personal use. A loss can occur for any reason — e.g., sale, casualty, or abandonment. If the property is used for income production, the loss is deductible whatever the cause of the loss. If the property is used for personal purposes, only a casualty loss results in a deduction. § 165(a–c); *see* Chapter 12.02[A].

Basis of income-producing assets is deductible *prior* to disposition if the asset is a wasting asset — that is, an asset with a determinable useful life, such as a machine or building. In such cases, the deduction is called a depreciation deduction or, sometimes, an amortization deduction. **Section 167(a)** allows the depreciation deduction and other sections expand on what § **167(a)** allows — e.g., § **168** provides an accelerated cost recovery system and § **197** provides special rules for intangible property. No depreciation deductions are allowed for personal use property.

The amount of the depreciation deduction depends on the method of deprecation, discussed in Chapter 11. The simplest method is *straight line depreciation*, which is basis divided by the expected life of the asset. For example: $60 cost; five-year life; $12 per year straight line depreciation. That is:

$$\frac{\text{cost}}{\text{useful life}} \quad = \quad \text{depreciation deduction}$$

This discussion of the recovery of basis can be summarized as follows:

	Income producing property	**Personal use property**
Disposition — gain	Deduct to compute taxable gain	Deduct to compute taxable gain
Disposition — loss	Deduct	Deduct only if casualty
Wasting asset	Depreciation deduction	No depreciation deduction

QUESTIONS: SALE OF PART OF THE ENTIRE PROPERTY

Suppose a taxpayer owns a 10-acre plot of land and sells an easement permitting the buyer to cross the land to transport goods to a destination. The 10-acre plot has a $60 basis. The sales price for the easement is $10.

1. Does the taxpayer have taxable gain on the sale? That requires you to determine the basis of the easement. What administrative problems do you encounter in answering that question? How can you avoid administrative problems when deciding what the basis of the easement should be? *Inaja Land Co., Ltd. v. Commissioner*, 9 T.C. 727 (1947), solves the problem by following the principles discussed in the following *Raytheon* case.

In *Raytheon Production Corp. v. Commissioner*, 144 F.2d 110 (1st Cir. 1944) the court held that the amount received in settlement of a lawsuit for destruction of goodwill was income in an amount equal to the amount received minus the taxpayer's basis in the goodwill. Because the taxpayer was unable to prove any basis, the entire proceeds were taxable. The court distinguished other cases in which the amount received for *part* of the property was less than the basis in the entire property, as follows:

> Where the cost basis that may be assigned to property has been wholly speculative, the gain has been held to be entirely conjectural and not taxable. In *Strother v. Commissioner*, 4th Cir., 1932, 55 F.2d 626, a trespasser had taken coal and then destroyed the entries so that the amount of coal taken could not be determined. Since there was no way of knowing whether the recovery was greater than the basis for the coal taken, the gain was purely conjectural and not taxed. Magill explains the result as follows: "as the amount of coal removed could not be determined

until a final disposition of the property, the computation of gain or loss on the damages must await that disposition." Taxable Income, pp. 339-340. The same explanation may be applied to *Farmers' & Merchants' Bank v. Commissioner*, 6th Cir., 1932, 59 F.2d 912, which relied on the *Strother* case in finding no gain. The recovery in that case had been to compensate for the injury to good will and business reputation of the plaintiff bank inflicted by defendant reserve banks' wrongful conduct in collecting checks drawn on the plaintiff bank by employing agents who would appear daily at the bank with checks and demand payment thereof in cash in such a manner as to attract unfavorable public comment. Since the plaintiff bank' business was not destroyed but only injured and since it continued in business, it would have been difficult to require the taxpayer to prove what part of the basis of its good will should be attributed to the recovery. In the case at bar, on the contrary, the entire business and good will were destroyed so that to require the taxpayer to prove the cost of the good will is not more impractical than if the business had been sold.

2. Suppose the taxpayer sold one-tenth of the land (for example, one acre) for $10. Would your answer in the case of the one-acre sale differ from the sale of the easement?

3. What is the basis of the remaining property after the sale of the easement? After the sale of one-acre? Use your answer to this question to determine the gain on the sale of the remaining property for $54 — either the land without the easement or the remaining nine acres of property.

[D] Inflation

Suppose the taxpayer who purchases land for $60,000 sells it in a later year for $120,000 after consumer prices have doubled. If basis records the amount on which the taxpayer should not pay tax again, so that he can buy personal consumption equal to that amount, it is a short step to the conclusion that the basis should be adjusted for inflation. If consumer prices double, the basis should be $120,000. That adjustment will produce no gain on the $120,000 sale and allow the taxpayer to use $120,000 for personal consumption. Because of inflation, $120,000 buys what $60,000 would have bought in the earlier year when the land was bought.

Our tax system has not so far adjusted basis for inflation, despite proposals to do so. One reason is the lack of symmetry it would create between owners and debtors. If a debtor borrows $60,000 in year 1 and pays it back in year 5 when consumer prices have doubled to $120,000, the debtor arguably has $60,000 of income in year 5. Here is why. The $60,000 paid back in year 5 is the equivalent of $30,000 purchasing power in the earlier year 1 when the taxpayer borrowed $60,000. Borrowing $60,000 in year 1 therefore gave the borrower access to double the amount of personal consumption given up in year 5 when repaying the $60,000 loan. The mechanism for taxing the debtor in year 5 would be to increase the debt by the inflation factor (100% in this example — so the loan would be treated as $120,000), and to tax the difference between the $120,000 and the amount repaid ($60,000) in year 5. Taxing cancellation of indebtedness is discussed in Chapter 3.06[C]. Reluctance to implement such complexity for debtors is one reason why owners have not been allowed to adjust basis upward for inflation.

§ 3.03 WHAT IS INCOME — REALIZATION, DEFERRAL, AND TIMING

[A] Income as "Realized" Income

The Constitution states that direct taxes must be apportioned among the states according to population. U.S. CONST., Art. I, sec. 2, cl. 3. The classic case of a direct tax is a property tax; the classic example of an indirect tax is a sales or excise tax. As explained in the Introduction, the apportionment requirement discourages populous states from voting for a federal property tax. The Court, in *Pollock v. Farmers' Loan & Trust Co.*, 158 U.S. 601 (1895), held that a tax on *income from* property was a direct tax, thereby making it politically impossible to adopt income taxes. A tax on personal service (non-property) income was not a direct tax, but it was politically impossible to tax personal service income and not tax income from property. The Sixteenth Amendment to the Constitution was then adopted to override the *Pollock* decision, stating that "Congress shall have power to lay and collect taxes on incomes, from whatever source derived, without apportionment . . . " There was no definition of income in the constitutional provision.

Eisner v. Macomber, 252 U.S. 189 (1920), supplied a definition. The case dealt with common stock dividends, which are pieces of paper embodying ownership interests in a business carried on in corporate form. The corporation issued one share of common stock as a dividend for every two shares of common stock owned in the corporation. The statute taxed the shareholder on the receipt of the stock dividend. The case held that the tax was unconstitutional, because the stock dividend was not "income" and was not apportioned among the states by population.

Although the decision rests on constitutional grounds, the language the Court used to define income has had a major impact on how the statute has been interpreted after the decision. For example, the terms "derived" and "realized," used in the *Eisner v. Macomber* opinion to define "income," also appear in §§ 61(a)(2)–(3), 1001(a), (b).

The point about statutory interpretation is important because no one thinks the Court's interpretation of the Constitution is still good law. Therefore, Congress could tax *unrealized* gain if it wanted to. The issues the Court addresses continue to be relevant, however, in deciding whether Congress *has* imposed tax. "Unrealized" gain is still usually (though not always) excluded from the income tax base under the statute, because it is not "income," as defined in § 61.

Here are portions of the Court's opinion in Macomber.

EISNER v. MACOMBER
United States Supreme Court
252 U.S. 189 (1920)

MR. JUSTICE PITNEY delivered the opinion of the Court.

The fundamental relation of "capital" to "income" has been much discussed by economists, the former being likened to the tree or the land, the latter to the fruit or the crop; the former depicted as a reservoir supplied from springs, the latter as the outlet stream, to be measured by its flow during a period of time. For the present purpose we require only a clear definition of the term "income," as used in common speech, in order to determine its meaning in the amendment, and, having formed also a correct judgment as to the nature of a stock dividend, we shall find it easy to decide the matter at issue.

After examining dictionaries in common use, we find little to add to the succinct definition adopted in two cases arising under the Corporation Tax Act of 1909 – "Income may be defined as the gain derived from capital, from labor, or from both combined," provided it be understood to include profit gained through a sale or conversion of capital assets.

Brief as it is, it indicates the characteristic and distinguishing attribute of income essential for a correct solution of the present controversy. The government, although basing its argument upon the definition as quoted, placed chief emphasis upon the word "gain," which was extended to include a variety of meanings; while the significance of the next three words was either overlooked or misconceived. "*Derived — from — capital*"; "*the gain – derived – from – capital*," etc. Here we have the essential matter: *not* a gain *accruing* to capital; not a *growth* or *increment* of value *in* the investment; but a gain, a profit, something of exchangeable value, *proceeding from* the property, *severed from* the capital, however invested or employed, and *coming in*, being "*derived*" – that is, *received* or *drawn by* the recipient (the taxpayer) for his *separate* use, benefit and disposal – *that* is income derived from property. Nothing else answers the description. The same fundamental conception is clearly set forth in the Sixteenth Amendment – "incomes, *from* whatever *source derived*" – the essential thought being expressed with a conciseness and lucidity entirely in harmony with the form and style of the Constitution.

Can a stock dividend, considering its essential character, be brought within the definition? To answer this, regard must be had to the nature of a corporation and the stockholder's relation to it. We refer, of course, to a corporation such as the one in the case at bar, organized for profit, and having a capital stock divided into shares to which a nominal or par value is attributed. . . .

A "stock dividend" shows that the company's accumulated profits have been capitalized, instead of distributed to the stockholders or retained as surplus available for distribution in money or in kind should opportunity offer. Far from being a realization of profits of the stockholder, it tends rather to postpone such realization, in that the fund represented by the new stock has been transferred from surplus to capital, and no longer is available for actual distribution.

The essential and controlling fact is that the stockholder has received nothing out of the company's assets for his separate use and benefit; on the contrary, every dollar of his original investment, together with whatever accretions and accumulations have resulted from employment of his money and that of the other stockholders in the business of the company, still remains the property of the company, and subject to business risks which may result in wiping out the entire investment. Having regard to the very truth of the matter, to substance and not to form, he has received nothing that answers the definition of income within the meaning of the Sixteenth Amendment. . . .

We have no doubt of the power or duty of a court to look through the form of the corporation and determine the question of the stockholder's right, in order to ascertain whether he has received income taxable by Congress without apportionment. But, looking through the form, we cannot disregard the essential truth disclosed, ignore the substantial difference between corporation and stockholder, treat the entire organization as unreal, look upon stockholders as partners, when they are not such, treat them as having in equity a right to a partition of the corporate assets, when they have none, and indulge the fiction that they have received and realized a share of the profits of the company which in truth they have neither received nor realized. . . .

Conceding that the mere issue of a stock dividend makes the recipient no richer than before, the government nevertheless contends that the new certificates measure the extent to which the gains accumulated by the corporation have made him the richer. There are two insuperable difficulties with this: In the first place, it would depend upon how long he had held the stock whether the stock dividend indicated the extent to which he had been enriched by the operations of the company; unless he had held it throughout such operations the measure would not hold true. Secondly, and more important for present purposes, enrichment through increase in value of capital investment is not income in any proper meaning of the term. . . .

Thus, from every point of view we are brought irresistibly to the conclusion that neither under the Sixteenth Amendment nor otherwise has Congress power to tax without apportionment a true stock dividend made lawfully and in good faith, or the accumulated profits behind it, as income of the stockholder. The Revenue Act of 1916, in so far as it imposes a tax upon the stockholder because of such dividend, contravenes the . . . Constitution, and to this extent is invalid, notwithstanding the Sixteenth Amendment.

COMMENTS

1. **No richer than before.** The Court in *Macomber* says that the taxpayer who receives the stock dividend is "no richer than before." But an income tax is often imposed when the taxpayer is no richer than before. Sale of property worth $100 for $100 does not enrich the seller. Prior gain is all that is needed to support the tax.

Indeed, prior gain is not always necessary. If a taxpayer buys stock for $100 and then immediately receives a $20 cash dividend out of corporate profits, the $20 is taxable. § 301(a), (b)(1), (c)(1). The value of the stock probably declines to $80 so the investor has a $20 loss in the stock (offsetting the $20 dividend), but that loss is not recognized until sale.

2. **Ideas behind "realization."** A taxpayer who retains appreciating property does not (under the statute) "realize" gain as the property appreciates. This paradigm suggests the following policies requiring realization as a statutory condition for imposing tax: (1) Appreciation generates no cash to pay the tax. (Couldn't the taxpayer borrow on the property?) (2) The taxpayer has not changed his investment. (3) Valuation will be administratively difficult. All three ideas cluster together to make up the theme of realization, but no one idea by itself is sufficient to prevent taxing gain. For example, a taxpayer who exchanges a farm for a residence pays tax, even though it is difficult to value the assets and there is no cash received. Realization does not usually occur, however, if the taxpayer retains the investment. This suggests that the strongest of the policies which make up the realization requirement is the idea that it is economically undesirable or in some sense, unfair to disturb ownership by taxing it, if the taxpayer doesn't want to change ownership.

[B]   Value of Deferral

You should carefully note that the realization requirement provides the taxpayer with tax deferral, not tax exemption. It is expected that, eventually, the taxpayer will realize and pay tax on the deferred gain. Nonetheless, the value of deferral is significant. In effect, the government is lending the taxpayer the deferred tax without interest. The value of that loan to the taxpayer depends on three things: how long the tax is deferred, the tax rate, and the rate of return the taxpayer can obtain by investing the deferred tax.

To illustrate the value of deferral, assume that the taxpayer paid $60 for a share of stock that increases in value to $100 in year 1. The taxpayer is in the 30% bracket (to simplify arithmetic). If there were no tax deferral on the $40 gain, the government takes $12 tax in year 1 (30% times $40). With deferral of tax on the $40 gain, the taxpayer keeps the full $100.

Now assume that the taxpayer can invest the $100, which includes the $40 gain on which tax is deferred, at a 20% annual rate of return. The stock will rise to $120 in year 2. Now the taxpayer sells the stock, paying a 30% tax (no change in tax rate) on the $40 previously unrealized gain (tax deferral has ended) and on the $20 year 2 appreciation. The total tax on the $60 gain is $18, and the taxpayer retains $102 (120 minus 18). How much better off is the taxpayer as a result of deferring tax on the $40 gain?

1. *Mechanical computation.* You can do the arithmetic mechanically — just assume the $40 gain was taxed in year 1 (tax = $12, which is 30% of $40), leaving the taxpayer with $88. The $88 appreciates 20% (17.60) to $105.60 in year 2. A sale in year 2, produces gain of $17.60. (Be sure you see why — what is the basis of the property after the $40 is taxed? Subtract that basis from the $105.60 amount realized to get the gain.) A 30% tax on $17.60 is $5.28. That leaves the taxpayer with $100.32 ($105.60 minus $5.28). *So the taxpayer is better off, with deferral, by $1.68 (102 minus 100.32).*

2. *After-tax return on deferred tax.* Is there a way to generalize the $1.68 advantage, without doing all the arithmetic? Sure. If the government allowed the taxpayer to use $40 as an investment for one year without tax (and without interest), the government has allowed the taxpayer to invest the tax that otherwise would have been paid — that is, $12 (30% of $40). For one year, the taxpayer can invest $12 at 20%, which equals $2.40. But when tax deferral ends, after one year, the taxpayer must pay tax on that $2.40. If the taxpayer is still in the 30% bracket, he keeps 70% of $2.40, which equals $1.68. *So tax deferral gives the taxpayer the after-tax rate of return on the investment of the deferred tax.*

3. *Exemption of income on after-tax savings.* The value of tax deferral can be quantified in another way, with significant policy implications. Focus on the $40 gain that is deferred in the above example. Suppose there is *no* deferral, so the taxpayer has only $28 to invest ($40 minus the 30% tax of $12). Now assume that the taxpayer invests the after-tax savings of $28 in a bank or stock, just as any saver might. Still assuming a 20% rate of return, the taxpayer earns $5.60 in interest or dividends (20% of $28). The government exempts the investment income from tax. What is the value of the exemption? It is the tax that would have been paid on $5.60; for a taxpayer in the 30% bracket, that is $1.68 (30% of $5.60). *The value of deferring tax on savings equals the exemption of the investment income earned on after-tax savings.*

Notice that these computations assume that the tax rates are the same in all tax years and that the rate of return is the same, regardless of the size of the investment. If tax rates rise after an investment is made, tax deferral may not be the good deal it appears to be. Moreover, the value of deferral alsos depends on how long the deferral lasts and what the rate of return is.

You will encounter numerous examples of tax deferral on savings throughout the course. You should see now why this is so politically popular. Congress would have trouble passing a tax break exempting investment income on after-tax savings. But how well does the public understand that deferring tax can provide the equivalent of exempting investment income?

[C] Demise of the Constitutional Realization Requirement

[1] Expansion of Definition of "Realization"

It is important to keep in mind that the precise holding of *Eisner v. Macomber* is probably not good law any more. There are probably no constitutional barriers to taxing unrealized appreciated gain and undistributed corporate earnings to the shareholders. One case that is thought to overrule *Eisner v. Macomber* is *Helvering v. Bruun*, 309 U.S. 461 (1940). The taxpayer was a landlord who had leased land to a tenant. The tenant had erected a new building on the premises. On July 1, 1933, the lease was cancelled for default in payment of rent and taxes and the taxpayer gained possession of both the land and building. The government taxed the landlord on the value of the building. The taxpayer argued that "improvements affixed to the soil became part of the realty indistinguishably blended in the capital asset; . . . that they are, therefore, in the same category as improvements added by the [taxpayer] to his land, or accruals of value due to extraneous and adventitious circumstances. Such added value, it is argued, can be considered capital gain only upon the owner's disposition of the asset. The position is that the economic gain consequent upon the enhanced value of the recaptured asset is not gain derived from capital or realized within the meaning of the Sixteenth Amendment and may not, therefore, be taxed without apportionment."

The Court in *Bruun* rejected the taxpayer's argument, as follows (309 U.S. at 468–69):

> Essentially the respondent's position is that the Amendment does not permit the taxation of such gain without apportionment amongst the states. He relies upon what was said in . . . the decisions of this court dealing with the taxability of stock dividends to the effect that gain derived from capital must be something of exchangeable value proceeding from property, severed from the capital, however invested or employed, and received by the recipient for his separate use, benefit, and disposal. He emphasizes the necessity that the gain be separate from the capital and separately disposable. These expressions, however, were used to clarify the distinction between an ordinary dividend and a stock dividend. They were meant to show that in the case of a stock dividend, the stockholder's interest in the corporate assets after receipt of the dividend was the same as and inseverable from that which he owned before the dividend was declared. We think they are not controlling here.

> While it is true that economic gain is not always taxable as income, it is settled that the realization of gain need not be in cash derived from the sale of an asset. Gain may occur as a result of exchange of property, payment of the taxpayer's indebtedness, relief from a liability, or other profit realized from the completion of a transaction. The fact that the gain is a portion of the value of property received by the taxpayer in the transaction does not negative its realization.

> Here, as a result of a business transaction, the respondent received back his land with a new building on it, which added an ascertainable amount to its value. It is not necessary to recognition of taxable gain that he should be able to sever the improvement begetting the gain from his original capital. If that were necessary, no income could arise from the exchange of property; whereas such gain has always been recognized as realized taxable gain.

[2]   Statutory Deferral of Realized Income

Just because income is realized under § 61 does not mean that it is a good idea to tax it. After *Bruun*, Congress decided that the government's victory should not stand. It adopted §§ 109, 1019. These sections are typical in the following respect. They accept the Court's more expansive definition of "realization" under the statute. They do not amend § 61 to state that the income is not "realized." But the statute *is* amended to exclude realized income from the tax base. Realization remains a core *statutory* concept (although its contours are expanded), but realized income is not always taxed.

Look at § 109 and § 1019 and make sure you understand that they only defer income, not exempt it, even though the statute uses the language of "exclusion." For example, suppose the landlord recovers land with a building worth $20,000 after termination of a lease. The landlord's prior investment in the land is $15,000. He holds the land and building for 10 years and then sells them both for $35,000. What is the landlord's taxable gain, assuming that the values of the land and building do not change?

[3] Taxing Unrealized Income in the Form of Undistributed Corporate Profits, Stock Dividends, and Unrealized Gain

Bruun does not technically eliminate the realization requirement; it simply interprets "realization" very broadly. But there are statutory provisions that explicitly tax what is still considered unrealized income under § 61. For example, one section taxes undistributed corporate profits to the shareholder when there are only a small number of shareholders who control the corporation and the shareholders are attempting to avoid United States taxes through use of foreign corporations. § 951. In addition, stock dividends that rearrange stock ownership are taxable. § 305(b)(2–4). Finally, several provisions explicitly tax unrealized gain or loss. *See, e.g.*, § 475 (securities dealers taxed on unrealized gain or loss on certain securities); § 1256 (unrealized gain or loss taxed on certain option and option-like assets).

[D] Losses

Do not assume that the taxpayer always wants an event to be *unrealized* for tax purposes. In *Cottage Savings Association v. Commissioner*, 499 U.S. 554 (1991), the taxpayer was a savings and loan association (S&L) regulated by the Federal Home Loan Bank Board (FHLBB). It wanted to realize tax-deductible losses by exchanging its interests in one group of residential mortgage loans for a different group of residential mortgage loans. Like many S&Ls, it held numerous long-term, low-interest mortgages that declined in value when interest rates surged in the late 1970s. If they sold their devalued mortgages to realize tax-deductible losses, FHLBB accounting regulations required them to record those losses on their books. Reporting these losses for banking regulation purposes would have placed many S&Ls at risk of closure by the FHLBB.

FHLBB, therefore, relaxed its requirements for the reporting of losses. It determined that S&Ls need not report losses associated with mortgages that are exchanged for "substantially identical" mortgages held by other lenders. The FHLBB's acknowledged purpose was to facilitate transactions generating tax losses that would not substantially affect the economic position of the S&Ls.

Responding to this opportunity, Cottage Savings transferred "90% participation interests" in 252 mortgages to four S&Ls and received "90% participation interests" in 305 mortgages held by these S&Ls. All of the loans involved in the transaction were secured by single-family homes, most in the Cincinnati area. The fair market value of the package of participation interests exchanged by each side was approximately $4.5 million. The basis of the participation interests Cottage Savings relinquished in the transaction was approximately $6.9 million. Cottage Savings claimed a deduction for $2,447,091, which represented the difference between the basis of the participation interests that it traded and the fair market value of the participation interests that it received. It did not report this loss to the FHLBB. The Court held that the loss was realized for tax purposes.

The Court first noted that a disposition of property under § 1001(a) required that the properties exchanged be "materially different." The government argued that material difference required a difference in "economic substance," but the Court held that the Regulation imposed "a much less demanding and less complex test." It concluded as follows:

> [P]roperties are "different" in the sense that is "material" to the Internal Revenue Code so long as their respective possessors enjoy legal entitlements that are different in kind or extent. . . . No more demanding a standard than this is necessary in order to satisfy the administrative purposes underlying the realization requirement in 1001(a). For, as long as the property entitlements are not identical, their exchange will allow both the Commissioner and the transacting taxpayer easily to fix the appreciated or depreciated values of the property relative to their tax bases.

The Court relied on an earlier case dealing with the reorganization of a corporation into a new corporation that carried on the business of the old corporation. No gain was realized on the exchange of shares in the old corporation for shares of the new corporation as long as the reincorporation occurred in the same state, because the legal entitlements did not change. The use of a legal entitlement test had the advantage of administrative convenience, when compared to the government's economic substance test.

Using this standard, the Court concluded that the exchange of properties in *Cottage Industries* was clearly a disposition resulting in a realized loss, because the legal entitlements were different. You should recognize that this approach opted for administrative simplicity over economic substance and that this tension between these two ways of analyzing a transaction are not always resolved in favor of administrative simplicity in other contexts.

As for the fact that the regulatory agency (FHLBB) did not treat the exchange as a loss for banking purposes, the Court noted that banking and income tax law are not necessarily the same.

§ 3.04   CAPITAL GAINS PREFERENCE

The realization requirement that survives in § 61 reverberates throughout the tax law because it creates a sharp distinction between untaxed unrealized gain and taxable realized gain. The economic impact is often referred to as the "lock-in" effect. A taxpayer might not dispose of an asset because realized gain is taxed (that is, the taxpayer is "locked-in"), even though the amount equal to the asset's value could be more efficiently invested elsewhere or the taxpayer might prefer to use that value for personal consumption. The economic implications seem more serious when the taxpayer forgoes an alternative investment.

The tax law responds to the lock-in problem with several provisions. First, it sometimes lowers the tax on gain from selling the investment (the capital gains preference). (Recall that *Eisner v. Macomber* conceded that income included "profit gained through the conversion of capital assets.") Second, it sometimes defers tax on gain if the taxpayer reinvests the proceeds in certain types of property. None of these rules would be necessary if unrealized gain were taxed annually.

These two statutory responses are discussed in detail later in the book — in Part I-F (deferral after reinvestment — Chapter 19; capital gains — Chapter 20). However, the capital gains preference is introduced here because it is hard to understand why taxpayers engage in certain activities and why the statute responds in certain ways unless the capital gains preference is taken into account.

[A] Statutory Rules

The core example of a capital gain is the gain recognized on the sale of corporate stock, which is not held as inventory by the seller. It is helpful to remember why this is the core case as you try to understand capital gains. The asset is a risky investment whose value has increased due to a favorable change in the future income anticipated from the investment; that is the type of activity that the capital gains preference is meant to encourage.

The capital gains provisions have the following statutory structure. A capital gain or loss arises on the "sale or exchange of a capital asset." § 1222. This definition has two components: (1) sale or exchange; and (2) capital asset.

The definition of a capital asset appears in § 1221. The statute says that a capital asset means "property," but then excludes certain property from the definition. The most important exclusion is property that is held primarily for sale in the ordinary course of business, such as inventory (§ 1221(a)(1)). Usually, property eligible for the capital gains preference is the "tree" and inventory is the "fruit."

Section 1222 distinguishes between long- and short-term capital gains and losses. Long-term capital gains and losses arise on the sale or exchange of capital assets held for *more than one year*. Short-term capital gains and losses arise on the sale or exchange of a capital asset held for one year or less.

The preferential tax rate on capital gains is provided in § 1(h). More precisely, the preference is for net capital gains, which is net long-term capital gain ("net" means the excess of long-term capital gains over long-term capital losses), over net short-term capital losses (the excess of short-term capital losses over short-term capital gains). § 1222(11). The idea behind not favoring short-term capital gain is to deny a tax preference for short-term speculation.

[B] History of Preferential Treatment

Prior to 1921, there was concern about the effect of high progressive tax rates imposed during World War I on the realization of gain accruing over more than one year. The problem was serious for both personal service income earned over a period of time and appreciated gain on capital assets. In both cases, it was feared that the progressive tax rate on accrued income bunched into one year would be higher than the lower tax rate on the income as it accrued annually. In 1920, the House of Representatives considered allowing taxpayers to spread such income back over the years it was earned or the asset was held, but the provision failed because it appeared too complex.

In 1921, Congress became more concerned with the impact of progressive tax rates on an investor's willingness to shift investment — that is, the lock-in effect. Economically, desirable shifts of investments were thought to be discouraged by the difference between taxing sales and not taxing unrealized gain. This resulted in adoption of a tax preference for capital gains for individuals. The mechanism for helping the taxpayer was to limit the tax to 12.5% of the gain, if that produced a lower tax than including the gain in ordinary income. Only assets held for more than two years were eligible for preferential treatment. Corporate capital gains were not preferentially treated, because the top corporate tax on ordinary income was already 12.5%.

This general pattern persisted until 1934. At that time, there was criticism of the capital gains tax rate for two reasons. First, it did not help individual taxpayers in tax brackets below the capital gains rate. Second, it did not differentiate among taxpayers who held capital assets for different periods of time and who were therefore affected differently by the bunching of gain into the year of sale. The statute was therefore amended to tax a declining percentage of capital gain as the asset's holding period lengthened. The declining percentage approach created a bias in favor of holding an asset, however, which was one of the problems that the preferential rates were supposed to alleviate. The declining percentage approach was modified in 1938 and eliminated in 1942.

In 1942, long-term capital gain was defined as gain arising from the sale or exchange of a capital asset held for more than six months. The mechanism for favoring these gains was to allow individuals a deduction of 50% of the gain or to impose a 25% tax on the entire gain, whichever produced a lower tax.

In 1969, the rules were again changed to eliminate the 25% ceiling, except for the first $50,000 of gain. Later, the 25% ceiling was totally eliminated and a deduction became the only preference for an individual's long-term capital gains. By 1986, the deduction was 60% of long-term capital gain. That produced a maximum 20% effective tax rate on an individual's long-term capital gain, because the top marginal tax rate was 50%, and 40% of the gain was taxed.

In 1986, Congress eliminated the preferential tax rate on long-term capital gains for a brief period (the top rate on all income was 28%). Later, when the top individual tax rate was increased (first, to 31% and, then, to 36% and 39.6%), the preferential tax rate on long-term capital gains was capped at 28%.

By 1997, the political pressure to lower the preferential rate on long-term capital gains led to further significant reductions. The issue was politically contentious, which therefore produced a very complex statute. The pattern of the 1997 law was to create two categories of preferentially taxed long-term capital gain — gain on property held more than 18 months (maximum tax of 20%) and gain on property held more than 12 months but not more than 18 months (maximum tax of 28%).

However, the complexity of having two preferentially taxed types of long-term capital gain was soon eliminated. The maximum tax rate on "long-term" capital gains (gain on property held more than 12 months) was capped at 20%, except that for people in a less-than-20% bracket, the cap was 10%.

The 2003 Tax Law provided a further rate reduction for long-term capital gains. It lowered the top rate to 15%. The 10% rate, which was applicable to those for whom the regular tax rate was 15% or less, was lowered to 5% (and lowered further to 0% in 2008). The mechanics of computing this preference are daunting and make the Form 1040-Schedule D used to make the computations beyond comprehension (except by a computer).

The 2003 Tax Law also lowered the tax on dividends to the same maximum 15% rate applicable to long-term capital gains. This provision was adopted as a compromise when Congress refused to go along with President Bush's proposal to eliminate the double tax on corporate dividends by completely exempting dividends from tax, leaving only the corporate tax on corporate profits. However, the reduction in the tax rate on dividends that was enacted into law is more generous than the Bush proposal in one respect. The Bush proposal applied only to dividends paid out of corporate income that had already been taxed, but that provision was dropped, in part because it is administratively difficult to identify the source of dividends when some corporate income is taxable and some is exempt. (For example, if a corporation has $50 tax exempt interest and $50 taxable income, is a $50 dividend paid out of exempt or taxable income or perhaps half and half?)

The idea behind the rate reduction on dividends can be illustrated by the following example. A taxpayer who confronts a 15% tax rate on gain attributed to the sale of corporate stock should not be taxed at a higher rate if, instead of selling and realizing gain, he instead receives dividends (which are paid out of profits that were, in part, responsible for the gain).

The mechanism used to reduce the tax rate on dividends is to increase "net capital gain" by the amount of such dividends, but only for the "purposes of this subsection" — referring to § 1(h)(11)(A)), which identifies the tax rates. This means that dividends are *not* included in the computation of "net capital gain" under § 1222 and are therefore not offset by capital losses. (The deduction of capital losses is discussed below.) Consequently, although the tax rates on dividends and preferentially taxed capital gains have converged, the distinctive character of dividends as ordinary income remains important.

Post-2003 laws extended the tax break for both dividends and net capital gains through 2012. Then, ATRA made permanent the lower tax rates on net capital gains and dividends but increased the maximum tax rate for higher-income individuals to 20%. Beginning in 2013, the maximum rates on capital gains and dividends received by individuals are: 0% if gain would otherwise be subject to the 10% or 15% regular tax rate; 15% if gain would otherwise be subject to regular rates between 25% and 35%; and 20% if regular rates would be 39.6%.

Remember that capital gains and dividends are also now subject to a 3.8% tax on certain higher-income taxpayers. *See* Chapter 1.02[D].

The rules for "collectibles" (defined in § 408(m) — e.g., works of art, antiques, etc.) are different. If they are capital assets held for more than 12 months, the tax rate is capped at 28%.

Finally, *corporations* are *not* eligible for the preferential tax rate on long-term capital gains.

[C] Capital Losses

[1] History

Capital losses have a more complicated history. The basic pattern today (with exceptions) is to limit the deduction of capital losses to capital gains. § 1211(a), (b). It is tempting to think that this symmetry depends on gains being preferentially taxed, but that is historically inaccurate. Several times — both before 1921 when the tax rate preference was introduced and for a brief period after 1986 when there was no preferential tax rate on capital gains — the deduction of capital losses was limited to capital gains. Moreover, capital loss limits apply to corporations, whose capital gains are not preferentially taxed.

[2] Rationale

Why should capital losses not be deductible against ordinary income, even when capital gains are taxed at ordinary rates? The reason is that taxpayers have too much control over the timing of capital gains and losses. Assume the taxpayer has two assets, one with an unrealized capital gain and one with an unrealized capital loss equal to the capital gain. The taxpayer has no economic gain or loss. Should the taxpayer be able to realize *only* the capital loss and reduce ordinary income by selling the loss asset? That potential would be aggravated when progressive tax rates were high in the capital loss year.

[3] Current Law

Capital losses are now deductible up to capital gains, plus (in the case of individuals) $3,000 ordinary income. (Remember, for this purpose, dividends are ordinary income.) The losses are deductible in computing adjusted gross income; they are not an itemized deduction. § 62(a)(3).

Unused capital losses are carried over to other years. An individual's unused capital losses are carried forward forever as whichever category of loss they are (short- or long-term). § 1212(b). A corporation's unused capital losses are carried back three years and forward five years as short-term capital losses. § 1212(a).

PROBLEMS

Assume that the following assets are owned by an individual, are nondepreciable, and are capital assets held for investment.

	Basis	Sales Price	Holding Period (in months)
Asset 1	$80,000	$100,000	12½
Asset 2	$80,000	$100,000	4
Asset 3	$90,000	$60,000	12½
Asset 4	$20,000	$50,000	12½

The problems call for the sale of different combinations of these assets. If there is a deductible capital loss, assume the taxpayer has another $70,000 taxable business income.

Problem 1.   Sell assets 1 & 2.
Problem 2.   Sell assets 2 & 3. Would it matter whether the sale of asset 2 produced ordinary income, rather than short-term capital gain?
Problem 3.   Sell assets 2 & 3 in January. What is the tax impact of selling asset 4 in December of the same year?

[D] Reasons for Preferential Rate on Capital Gains

Two reasons for the capital gains preference have already been noted in discussing the history of the provision — to prevent bunching of past accrued gain in the year of sale and to reduce the lock-in effect.

[1] Bunching Past Income

Is bunching of past accrued gain a sound reason for the tax preference? If so, why is there no requirement that the taxpayer be in a higher bracket in the year of sale than in the years when the gains accrued? Moreover, gain has sometimes been preferentially taxed even when the asset's holding period was entirely in one tax year (that is, more than six months).

[2] Lock-In

If the lock-in effect is a problem and the code is intended to encourage shifts of investments by lowering the tax on sale, why isn't there a requirement that the sales proceeds be reinvested? Under current law, sales proceeds producing capital gain can be used for personal consumption.

[3] Inflation

Inflation is sometimes given as a reason for the long-term capital gains preference. The idea is that the gain is not real income. For example, if a taxpayer earns $100 in year 0, pays a $30 tax, and invests the remaining $70, he has paid the tax necessary to entitle him to $70 of consumption whenever he wants to consume. If prices and value rise 100% by year 5, however, it will take him $140 to buy the same basket of goods in year 5 which he could have bought in year 0 for $70. The capital gains tax break might relieve the taxpayer of some of the burden of an ordinary tax on the $70 gain ($140 minus $70). But the present rule gives the same benefit to the taxpayer whose investment doubles after two, rather than five years, even though the inflation during the two-year period is less than 100%. The tax break is the same regardless of the differential impact of inflation on different assets. Moreover, the present rules give no benefit to the taxpayer who paid $70 in year 0 and then sells for $70 in year 5; or to the creditor who lends $70 in year 0 and collects the $70 debt in depreciated currency in year 5. The correct adjustment for inflation is a basis adjustment for the inflation rate. The $70 investment should result in a $140 basis if there is 100% inflation, for purposes of computing both gain and loss.

[4]   Incentive

Another reason for the capital gains preference is to encourage investments. But why not exempt interest, rents, and other periodic returns on investments, not just the return in the form of capital gains? Or perhaps a tax credit for investment would be a more effective incentive to invest. Is there some way to distinguish between very desirable high risk venture capital and other investments for preferential rate purposes, other than by reference to the holding period?

[5]   Bunching Future Income

There is one fairness argument for the capital gains preference. The amount realized is the present value of future income. If the taxpayer waits for the future income, he defers tax. If he sells the asset, the government collects tax in the year of sale. In effect, the taxpayer has helped the government by eliminating tax deferral. Perhaps a lower rate should compensate the taxpayer for paying taxes early and giving up tax deferral.

§ 3.05   WHEN IS IT INCOME — TIMING AND ACCOUNTING METHODS

Realization, technically, determines whether there is "income." The fundamental issue, however, is one of timing — when to report an item as income — because unrealized income is simply deferred until the time of realization. The "when" question is also addressed by accounting methods. Even if an item is technically realized income under § 61, the tax accounting method must be consulted to determine whether it is reported as income in a particular year.

[A]   Introduction to Accounting Methods

The primary code section that addresses accounting issues is § 446(a–c), but it does not say much. Basically, it authorizes the cash or accrual method, *but only* if the method chosen clearly reflects income. § 446(b). The following paragraphs give you an introduction to these concepts, which are revisited in Part I-G of the book.

There are two fundamental questions — (1) defining "cash" and "accrual," so that someone using the cash or accrual method knows what to report; and (2) determining when a taxpayer is allowed to use one or the other method. These paragraphs address the definitional questions, leaving until Part I-G the question of when a taxpayer can or must use a particular accounting method.

[1]   Cash Method

"Cash" includes more than cash. It includes the fair market value of anything that is the "equivalent of cash." The idea is this — if you earn $10,000 of salary, you should not be able to avoid tax by receiving property worth $10,000. The property has a taxable cash equivalent. But what is the cash equivalent?

(1) When property is used for personal consumption, its cash equivalent may be impaired by limits on transferability and doubts about the subjective value of the asset to the recipient (as when an employer gives a meal to an employee). (2) When the received property is investment property (such as stock), restrictions on transferability and the potential for forfeiting the property may seriously impair its cash equivalence. (3) There is also doubt about whether receipt of a nonnegotiable note should be taxed to a cash method taxpayer, if the note is not likely to sell for anything near its face value. We return to these issues in later material. In each of these situations, the taxable value may be reduced below what would be its normal objective fair market value or the value may be so impaired that it is not taxable at all or not until the impairment is removed.

[2]   Accrual Method

"Accrual" occurs when all events have occurred to entitle a taxpayer to income, except for the passage of time, if the promisor is solvent. For example, once the promisee has performed under a contract in year 1, entitling her to $100 in year 2, the right has ripened (that is, it is not subject to any conditions except the passage of time), and the amount of the $100 claim accrues in year 1. **Treas. Reg. § 1.451-1(a)**. It does not matter that the $100 payment occurs in year 2. In some situations, discussed later in the book, something less than the $100 debt is accrued, if the interest on the debt is inadequate, thereby reducing the value of the claim below $100.

[3]   Difference Between Methods

This discussion highlights the essential difference between cash and accrual taxpayers — a promise not embodied in a note or other instrument of commerce is not itself the equivalent of cash. A cash method taxpayer (unless there is a statutory exception) is therefore able to defer tax on value embodied in a mere promise, until cash is received.

An accrual method taxpayer, however, must accrue a solvent debtor's promise at its face amount. This eliminates the deferral opportunity enjoyed by cash method taxpayers. The accrual method taxpayer, however, is forced to accrue a promise based on its face amount, not its actual value. Thus, a promise to pay $100 results in accrual of $100 income to the promisee, even though sale of the right to collect the $100 might not produce more than $80. As noted earlier, however, the accrued amount might be discounted if the interest charge on the deferred payment is inadequate.

[4]   Assignment of Income Issues

In one situation, it is very important for cash method taxpayers to know about accrual accounting rules. The assignment of income rules prevents a cash method taxpayer from shifting accrued income to a transferee. For example, assume that a cash method creditor lends $100,000 at 10% interest payable annually ($10,000 interest per year) on December 31. In the middle of the year, the creditor gives the entire bond, with one-half year's accrued interest, to a relative. The $5,000 accrued interest will be taxed to the *transferor* when it is collected by the relative.

The interaction between the concept of accrual and assignment of income doctrine also extends to gains on the sale of property. Moreover, the sale cases illustrate that the concept of "accrual" for assignment of income purposes may be a little broader than the concept of accrual for purposes of reporting income. For example, in *Ferguson v. Commissioner*, 174 F.3d 997 (9th Cir. 1999), the taxpayer owned stock in AHC Corporation. Another corporation (DC Acquisition) wanted to acquire control of AHC and made a tender offer to purchase AHC stock. The expiration date for the tender offer was September 9, 1988. DC Acquisition wanted control of AHC and had the right to abandon its tender offer if it did not acquire at least 85% of the AHC stock by the expiration date.

The taxpayer transferred its shares to a charity after August 31, 1988 and before September 12, 1988. The court held that August 31 was the date on which the right to cash had ripened for purposes of the assignment of income doctrine. Here is some of what the court said:

> Under the anticipatory assignment of income doctrine, once a right to receive income has "ripened" for tax purposes, the taxpayer who earned or otherwise created that right, will be taxed on any gain realized from it, notwithstanding the fact that the taxpayer has transferred the right before actually receiving the income. . . .

> To determine whether a right has "ripened" for tax purposes, a court must consider the realities and substance of events to determine whether the receipt of income was practically certain to occur (i.e., whether the right basically had become a fixed right). While the finding of a mere anticipation or expectation of the receipt of income has been deemed insufficient to conclude that a fixed right to income existed, courts also have made it quite clear that the overall determination must not be based on a consideration of mere formalities and remote hypothetical possibilities.

> In the present case, the Tax Court determined that the realities and substance of the ongoing tender offer and the pending merger agreement indicated that the AHC stock already had ripened from an interest in a viable corporation into a fixed right to receive cash, by August 31, 1988 — the first date by which over 50% of the AHC share had been tendered. To wit, the Tax Court determined that by August 31, 1988, it was practically certain that the tender offer and the merger would be completed successfully and that all AHC stock, even untendered stock, either already had been converted into cash (via the tender offer) or imminently would be converted into cash (via the merger).

The [taxpayers] contend that until September 12, 1988, the date when DC Acquisition formally announced its acceptance of over 95% of the outstanding AHC shares, the tender offer and the merger still could have been derailed and their AHC stock thus had not ripened. However, in support of their many contentions, the [taxpayers] raise only possibilities that the Tax Court correctly considered to be remote and hypothetical and therefore irrelevant.

COMMENTS

1. In *Braunstein v. Commissioner*, 21 T.C.M. (CCH) 1132 (1962), the taxpayer held an Irish Sweepstakes (horse race) ticket, which he assigned to a trust for his children's future education *before* the horse race was run. At the time of the assignment, the taxpayer was guaranteed proceeds of $2,147. After the assignment, the taxpayer's horse won the race. The court held that the taxpayer did not successfully assign income equal to $2,147. However, the additional proceeds arising because the taxpayer's horse won the race was successfully assigned.

2. In *Teschner v. Commissioner*, 38 T.C. 1003 (1962), the taxpayer entered a contest but he could not receive the prize. He had to designate, at the time of entry, a recipient under the age of 17 years and one month. Taxpayer designated his seven-year-old daughter. The prize was awarded to the entrant who best completed the following sentence in 50 words or less: "A good education is important because. . . . " The taxpayer won the contest and was not taxed on the dollar benefit provided to his minor child. Even if no value had accrued to the taxpayer, did he earn the income (as in *Lucas v. Earl*)?

[5] Deductions

Cash and accrual rules also apply to deductions. A deduction accrues when the obligation to pay is fixed (e.g., wage deductions accrue to the employer when an employee has performed personal services and the obligation to pay a fixed sum arises).

Under the cash method, the deduction is allowed only when cash is paid. "Payment" for deduction purposes, however, is not exactly the same as for receipt purposes. Giving a note, for example, is not "payment" for a cash method taxpayer (even though its receipt is often the equivalent of cash), because that would allow a cash method taxpayer to control the deduction year too easily.

[6] Other Accounting Methods

There are other accounting methods besides cash and accrual.

[a] Percentage of Completion Method

The percentage of completion method taxes income from performing a contract (such as building an airplane) while the job is being performed. When one half is completed, one half the anticipated net income from the job is taxed. At one time, gain on contract performance could be deferred until completion of the contract; but now, the percentage completion of contract method must usually be used, eliminating the opportunity to defer tax until contract completion. § 460(a). Certain shipbuilding contracts enjoy a limited exception from using the percentage-of-completion method, requiring that only 40% of the income has to be accounted for by the percentage-of-completion method.

[b]   Installment Method

The installment method allows a taxpayer to spread out the recognition of gain from the sale of certain property. Generally, the gain is taxed as and when the sales price is received in cash. For example, if property with a $60,000 cost is sold for $100,000 (plus interest), payable in four equal cash installments in years 1–4, $10,000 of sales gain would be reported each payment year. § 453. Chapter 21 discusses when the installment method can be used.

[7]   Clearly Reflect Income

The taxpayer's choice of accounting methods is subject to the overriding requirement that it must clearly reflect income. One example here will suffice. Suppose a cash method taxpayer buys a machine with cash. Can the taxpayer deduct the cost when the cash is paid? Of course not, absent some special tax incentive provision. Income must include both consumption and savings and a deduction for the cost of a long-lived asset would permit a deduction for savings — it would not clearly reflect income.

[B]   Original Issue Discount; Putting Some Transactions on the Accrual Method

This section discusses original issue discount. It introduces you to the time value of money — an important and pervasive idea throughout the income tax law. It also provides an example of forcing cash method taxpayers to report accrued income prior to receipt of cash.

Original issue discount is interest. Normally, interest is earned on money loaned to a debtor. For example, if you lend $16.15 to someone at 20% interest (for example, deposit it in a bank), the interest income in the first year is $3.23. The next year, interest is $3.88, assuming you left both the $16.15 and the $3.23 in the bank. Interest is compounding because you get interest on the interest. In ten years, total interest will equal $83.85.

The interest accruing each year on the $16.15 loan is as follows:

Year	1	2	3	4	5	6	7	8	9	10
Interest	3.23	3.88	4.65	5.58	6.70	8.04	9.65	11.57	13.89	16.67

Suppose a taxpayer does not want to pay tax on the interest until some later date — say, 10 years from now. The taxpayer tries this scheme. She lends $16.15 to a debtor (for example, she buys a corporate bond), and the debtor agrees to pay the creditor $100 in 10 years. No interest is paid before then. The difference between the $100 repayment and the $16.15 loan is called original issue discount. It is "original" because it arises when the obligation is originally issued by the debtor. It is "discount" because it is computed by discounting the $100 back to its "present value" in the year of the loan.

The formula for computing present value is:

$$\text{present value} \quad = \quad \frac{x}{(1 + i)^p}$$

where x is the amount paid in the future ($100 in the example), '$i$ is the interest (or discount) rate (20% in the example), and p is the number of time periods during which the interest is paid.

If interest had been earned from a bank in the typical savings deposit, the interest would be taxed annually. The question is whether the loan to a corporation creating original issue discount should be taxed any differently. Obviously, the answer should be "no," if the tax law is to remain neutral between different kinds of investments. The tax law forces the lender to accrue original issue discount annually as identified in accordance with the above principles, whether or not the lender is a cash method taxpayer. The basic statutory sections are §§ **1272(a)(1), 1273(a)**. For example, assume that the taxpayer lends $1,615 in year 0 in exchange for the borrower's promise to pay $10,000 in year 10. The lender (whether or not a cash or accrual method taxpayer) must report $323 interest income in year 1, etc. The reported income is then added to the lender's basis in the claim against the debtor.

The above example simplifies current law. The tax law has to make certain decisions — should the interest be computed as though it compounds annually or semi-annually or more often? What should lenders do if the accrual period straddles the end of a tax year (for example interest compounds semi-annually but the loan occurs on October 1, so that the six-month period is from October to March)? These complexities must be addressed by the tax law but there is no need for you to do so now.

[C]   More on Present Value

You will find it useful as you go through the course to apply present value concepts. The following chart sets forth the present value of $1 for different interest rates and future time periods. It in effect specifies how much someone would lend you today in exchange for a promise by you to repay $1 at a specified future date and at a specified annual compound interest rate. Notice how little $1, to be received 20 years from now, is worth today when interest rates are 6% or higher. If interest is compounded semi-annually, the present value figures would be different.

Present Value of $1 Interest (Discount) Rate

Year in Future Paid	1%	6%	10%	12%	20%	30%
1	.99	.943	.909	.892	.833	.769

Year in Future Paid	1%	6%	10%	12%	20%	30%
5	.951	.747	.62	.567	.401	.269
10	.905	.558	.385	.321	.161	.072
20	.819	.311	.148	.103	.026	.005

§ 3.06   WHAT IS INCOME — ACCESSION TO WEALTH

[A]   From "Sources" to "Accession to Wealth"

[1]   Judicial Revisions of the "Income" Definition

We saw earlier that the holding of *Eisner v. Macomber* is no longer considered good constitutional law. In *Glenshaw Glass*, the Court revisited the case law interpretation of the *statutory* term "income." The case considered whether punitive damages were income. The punitive damages arose out of an anti-trust lawsuit in which the plaintiff also recovered compensatory damages replacing lost profits. Everyone agreed that the compensatory damages were taxable income.

The Court of Appeals held that the punitive damages did not fall within the *Eisner v. Macomber* definition of income, because they "are not compensatory. They certainly possess no periodicity. They are not derived from capital, from labor or from both combined and assuredly are not profit gained through the sale or conversion of capital assets." The court stated that "the ordinary man regards income as something which comes to him from what he has done, not from something that is done to him. . . . [T]he ordinary man using terms of common speech would not regard punitive damages as 'income.'" The Supreme Court reversed, as follows.

COMMISSIONER v. GLENSHAW GLASS CO.
United States Supreme Court
348 U.S. 426 (1955)

MR. CHIEF JUSTICE WARREN delivered the opinion of the Court.

It is conceded by the respondents that there is no constitutional barrier to the imposition of a tax on punitive damages. Our question is one of statutory construction: are these payments comprehended by 22(a) [Editor — now § 61]?

The sweeping scope of the controverted statute is readily apparent:

SEC. 22. GROSS INCOME.

(a) General definition. "Gross income" includes gains, profits, and income derived from salaries, wages, or compensation for personal service . . . whatever kind and in whatever form paid, or from professions, vocations, trades, businesses, commerce, or sales, or dealings in property, whether real or personal, growing out of the ownership or use of or interest in such property; also from interest, rent, dividends, securities, or the transaction of any business carried on for gain or profit, *or gains or profits and income derived from any source whatever.* . . . (Emphasis added.)

This Court has frequently stated that this language was used by Congress to exert in this field " 'the full measure of its taxing power." Respondents contend that punitive damages, characterized as "windfalls" flowing from the culpable conduct of third parties, are not within the scope of the section. But Congress applied no limitations as to the source of taxable receipts, nor restrictive labels as to their nature. And the Court has given a liberal construction to this broad phraseology in recognition of the intention of Congress to tax all gains except those specifically exempted. Thus, the fortuitous gain accruing to a lessor by reason of the forfeiture of a lessee's improvements on the rented property was taxed in *Helvering v. Bruun*, 309 U.S. 461. Cf. *United States v. Kirby Lumber Co.*, 284 U.S. 1. Such decisions demonstrate that we cannot but ascribe content to the catchall provision of sec. 22(a), "gains or profits and income derived from any source whatever." The importance of that phrase has been too frequently recognized since its first appearance in the Revenue Act of 1913 to say now that it adds nothing to the meaning of "gross income."

Nor can we accept respondents' contention that a narrower reading of § 22(a) is required by the Court's characterization of income in *Eisner v. Macomber*, 252 U.S. 189, 207, as "the gain derived from capital, from labor, or from both combined." The Court was there endeavoring to determine whether the distribution of a corporate stock dividend constituted a realized gain to the shareholder, or changed "only the form, not the essence," of his capital investment. It was held that the taxpayer had "received nothing out of the company's assets for his separate use and benefit." The distribution, therefore, was held not a taxable event. In that context — distinguishing gain from capital — the definition served a useful purpose. But it was not meant to provide a touchstone to all future gross income questions.

Here we have instances of undeniable accessions to wealth, clearly realized, and over which the taxpayers have complete dominion. The mere fact that the payments were extracted from the wrongdoers as punishment for unlawful conduct cannot detract from their character as taxable income to the recipients. Respondents concede, as they must, that the recoveries are taxable to the extent that they compensate for damages actually incurred. It would be an anomaly that could not be justified in the absence of clear congressional intent to say that a recovery for actual damages is taxable but not the additional amount extracted as punishment for the same conduct which caused the injury. And we find no such evidence of intent to exempt these payments.

It is urged that re-enactment of § 22(a) without change since the Board of Tax Appeals held punitive damages nontaxable in *Highland Farms Corp.*, 42 B.T.A. 1314(1940) indicates congressional satisfaction with that holding. Re-enactment — particularly without the slightest affirmative indication that Congress ever had the *Highland Farms* decision before it — is an unreliable indicium at best. Moreover, the Commissioner promptly published his non-acquiescence in this portion of the *Highland Farms* holding and has, before and since, consistently maintained the position that these receipts are taxable. It therefore cannot be said with certitude that Congress intended to carve an exception out of § 22(a)'s pervasive coverage.

Nor does the 1954 Code's legislative history, with its reiteration of the proposition that statutory gross income is "all-inclusive," give support to respondents' position. The definition of gross income has been simplified, but no effect upon its present broad scope was intended. Certainly punitive damages cannot reasonably be classified as gifts, nor do they come under any other exemption provision in the Code. We would do violence to the plain meaning of the statute and restrict a clear legislative attempt to bring the taxing power to bear upon all receipts constitutionally taxable were we to say that the payments in question here are not gross income.

COMMENTS

1. **Income definitions — Sources and uses**. It is not unusual for a court to refer to plain or common meaning, as both the Court of Appeals and Supreme Court did, but then add other reasons for the decision. Both decisions in *Glenshaw Glass* elaborate conceptions of income that flesh out the bare statutory language. The Court of Appeals followed the *Eisner v. Macomber* definition of income, stressing gain from particular sources. The Supreme Court stressed "realized accessions to wealth," and "complete dominion," rejecting limitations on the definition of income that depend on the particular source of income.

The shift from sources to accessions to wealth is also apparent in the following definition of income, which focuses on the uses to which income can be put. This is usually referred to as the Haig-Simons definition of income. The quote comes from Simons, *Personal Income Taxation* 50 (1938).

> Personal income may be defined as the algebraic sum of (1) the market value of rights exercised in consumption and (2) the change in the value of the store of property rights between the beginning and end of the period in question. In other words, it is merely the result obtained by adding consumption during the period to "wealth" at the end of the period and then subtracting "wealth" at the beginning. The *sine qua non* of income is *gain* as our courts have recognized in their more lucid moments — and gain *to* someone during a specified time interval. Moreover, this gain may be measured and defined most easily by positing a dual objective or purpose, consumption and accumulation, each of which may be estimated in a common unit by appeal to market prices.

The point of the Haig-Simons definition is that accession to wealth is identified by its uses. Any accountant will tell you that every credit has a debit. Income sources can be used in two ways. They can be used for personal consumption, such as food, clothing, or vacations; or for savings, such as a deposit in a bank account or purchase of land. That is what the Haig-Simons definition of income, quoted above, explicitly says.

If you think of income as a proxy for the uses to which income is put, a significant legal question in defining income remains, which is whether an item that is allegedly income is really available for personal consumption or savings — an issue to which we return later in this chapter and in Chapter 7 (dealing with employee fringe benefits). From this perspective, *Glenshaw Glass* is an easy case because unrestricted cash (in the form of punitive damages) is available for consumption and savings.

Focusing on uses also helps to explain why the *Eisner v. Macomber* definition might have been so attractive at one time, especially with the "periodicity" gloss mentioned by the Court of Appeals in *Glenshaw Glass*. In an agricultural era, people lived on the periodic gain from rent and crop production, derived from capital and labor. No one would have dreamed of drawing down capital for their own use, and nonperiodic lump sums were regarded as capital that could produce income, contrasted with the income itself — tree vs. fruit. In earlier times, therefore, many people would have felt comfortable saying that some receipts were inherently capital and therefore not income, because they were not available for consumption. This can be restated in the language of *Glenshaw Glass* as follows: even if the taxpayer might have legal and effective dominion over certain resources, social practice did not contemplate exercise of that dominion in all cases. As time passed, however, this pastoral image of the economy became obsolete. People used increases in capital and lump sum receipts for consumption, if they wanted to, and the decision to save or consume became discretionary rather than a more or less automatic practice when certain items were received. Today, we do not associate the availability or lack of availability of wealth for consumption purposes with the source of that wealth. That explains why *Glenshaw Glass* rejects a definition of income based on sources of income.

2. **Treasure trove.** One example of a fact situation that might come out differently under an *Eisner v. Macomber* "gains based on sources" approach and a *Glenshaw Glass* "accession to wealth" approach is "treasure trove" — such as an asset found on the street and kept by the taxpayer. *See* **Treas. Reg. § 1.61-14**; Rev. Rul. 61, 1953-1 C.B. 17 (treasure trove taxed when "reduced to undisputed possession"). The best known example in the case law is *Cesarini v. United States*, 296 F. Supp. 3 (N.D. Ohio 1969), *aff'd per curiam*, 428 F.2d 812 (6th Cir. 1970). In 1964, the taxpayer discovered $4,500 in a piano purchased in 1957. The statute of limitations on tax assessment for 1964 had not run and the found money was taxed in 1964.

3. **Personal injuries.** The tax rules dealing with compensatory and punitive damages arising from personal injury claims are discussed in Chapter 9.03.

[2]   Note on Statutory Interpretation

[a]   Internal Context — Whole Text

Both the Court of Appeals and the Supreme Court claim to be relying on the ordinary or plain meaning of the statutory text. And yet they reach different results. What exactly do they disagree about?

Two interpreters can appeal to plain meaning and come out differently when they focus on different parts of the text. The Court of Appeals seems to have looked at only one word — "income." That is not good textualism, because writers and readers routinely understand language by looking at the entire text in which one or two words are embedded. That is what the Supreme Court did in the case —

looking at the phrase "derived from any source whatever" along with the word "income" to support an expansive definition. In effect, the Supreme Court identified the old *Eisner v. Macomber* definition of income as one focused on a limited set of sources — that is, derived from capital or labor — rather than on the receipt of anything producing an accession to wealth, "derived from any source whatever."

[b] Legislative Reenactment

The Court of Appeals in *Glenshaw Glass*, in holding for the taxpayer, had emphasized congressional reenactment of the identical statutory language after an intervening interpretation of that language by a court. The reenactment doctrine is a favorite among judges, but its use is usually implausible on its own terms. The doctrine states that reenactment ratifies an intervening interpretation of a statute by an agency or a court. For this to make any sense, however, it is essential that there be some evidence that the reenacting Congress was aware of the intervening interpretation. In *Glenshaw Glass*, the Supreme Court found no such evidence.

Moreover, awareness without more is still weak evidence that the legislature approved of the intervening interpretation. Congress has lots to do besides going around rejecting intervening interpretations every time it reenacts a statutory text. Approval *might* be inferred, however, if Congress was aware of an interpretation of part of a statutory text and amended other nearby language of the statute without changing the previously interpreted text. That might suggest that the legislature meant to approve the text it left unamended while focusing on the surrounding language. Or a statement in the legislative history might indicate approval. These are controversial claims, however, and there is widespread suspicion that the reenactment doctrine is invoked when there is some other ground of decision that is too controversial for the court to explain.

[c] Change

The most striking aspect of the decision in *Glenshaw Glass* is that it changed the definition of income, which is obviously the most basic concept in an income tax statute.

The common law has always adapted to change. The common law text — contained in cases — is always understood to be a statement of principle that can grow or decline in influence as it is applied to new facts. But it is less easy to view statutory texts in this way.

However, when the statutory text is itself open-ended, it is easier to view the language as a delegation of authority to a court to adjust meaning over time. A typical example is the use of the word "reasonable" in a statute. But is "income" an open-ended text, so that a court should be able to shift meaning from a "source" to an "accession to wealth" approach?

[d]   General Welfare Exclusion

The government has long interpreted § 61 to exclude certain "general welfare" benefits from income. The exclusion typically applied to needs-tested programs, but was also applied to Social Security and Unemployment Insurance benefits. *See*, for example, Rev. Rul. 70-217, 1970-1 C.B. 13 (Social Security benefits are not taxable). Today, the statute explicitly taxes Social Security and Unemployment Insurance benefits — *see* § 86 (a percentage of Social Security is taxed if income exceeds a certain amount); § 85 (full amount of Unemployment Insurance is taxed). However, the general welfare exclusion remains intact, even though its statutory basis has never been entirely clear. (Perhaps the gift exclusion, discussed in Chapter 4.01, might be invoked, except that the payments are not intra-family.)

1. In Rev. Rul. 2003-12, 2003-1 C.B. 283, the government considered whether payments to reimburse individuals for certain expenses incurred as a result of a Presidentially declared disaster are excluded from § 61 income. The ruling states:

> Section 61(a) provides that, except as otherwise provided by law, gross income means all income from whatever source derived. . . .

> The Internal Revenue Service has concluded that payments made by governmental units under legislatively provided social benefit programs for the promotion of the general welfare (i.e., based on need) are not includible in the gross income of the recipients of the payments ("general welfare exclusion"). For example, Rev. Rul. 98-19, 1998-1 C.B. 840, concludes that a relocation payment, authorized by the Housing and Community Development Act of 1974 and funded under the 1997 Emergency Supplemental Appropriations Act for Recovery from Natural Disasters, made by a local jurisdiction to an individual moving from a flood-damaged residence to another residence, is not includible in the individual's gross income. Likewise, Rev. Rul. 76-144, 1976-1 C.B. 17, concludes that grants received under the Disaster Relief Act of 1974 by individuals unable to meet necessary expenses or serious needs as a result of a disaster are in the interest of general welfare and are not includible in the recipients' gross income. . . .

The ruling held that these "grants are in the nature of general welfare and are, therefore, excluded from the recipients' gross income under the general welfare exclusion," as well as being excluded from income under § 139, dealing with disaster relief payments.

2. In Rev. Rul. 85-39, 1985-1 C.B. 21, the government dealt with payments by the State of Alaska to its residents, as follows:

> Alaska adopted a constitutional amendment in 1976 that established a permanent fund into which the State must deposit at least 25 percent of its mineral income each year. ALASKA CONST., Art. IX, section 15. In 1980, the Alaska State legislature enacted a statute establishing a dividend program to distribute annually a portion of the fund's earnings directly to the State's adult residents. As stated in section 1 of the 1980 statute, the purposes of the statute are threefold. The statute is to provide a mechanism for equitably distributing to the people of Alaska a portion of the State's

energy wealth, to encourage increased awareness and involvement by the residents of the State in the management and expenditure of the fund, and to encourage persons to maintain their residence in Alaska and to reduce population turnover. The Alaska legislature found that the constant turnover in the population led to political, economic, and social instability and was harmful to the State. They also found that it was in the public interest of the State to promote a stable population by providing an incentive to encourage Alaskans to maintain their residency in the State.

The dividend payments made by the State of Alaska . . . are not general welfare program payments. The payments are not restricted to those in need. There is no indication of a legislative intent that would support their characterization as gifts. As stated expressly in the statute, the State anticipates a benefit from making the payment, namely a reduced population turnover resulting in a more stable political, economic, and social environment.

[3] Dominion and Control

Glenshaw Glass interprets § 61 to require "complete dominion" as a necessary factor in defining income. For example, in *Bailey v. Commissioner*, 88 T.C. 1293 (1987),the court dealt with facade grants. A facade grant was payable pursuant to a program conducted by an urban renewal agency (URA). It provided facade grants to purchasers of property to provide historic rehabilitation for the facades of the purchased property. In exchange for the purchaser's agreement to remodel the interior of the structure, the URA agreed to rehabilitate the facade.

The court held that the facade grants were not income to the property owner because of lack of dominion and control, based on the following facts: the purchaser signed a facade rehabilitation agreement granting an easement, or right to enter the property, to the URA; the URA secured a contractor to perform the required rehabilitation of the facade before obtaining the easement so that the facade would be rehabilitated in a manner consistent with the historic classification of the district; the amount of the facade grant for any particular property was established in advance and known to the URA at the time the facade rehabilitation agreement was secured, but was not made known to the purchaser of the property; and the property owner had no control over the rehabilitation work performed on the facade of his property.

[4] Nontaxable Compensation for Loss

The punitive damages in *Glenshaw Glass* obviously provided an accession to wealth. The cash could be spent for any purpose and it did not compensate for any loss incurred by the taxpayer. In the following decisions, the taxpayer suffered a loss for which he is compensated and the question is whether the compensation is taxable. Try to figure out a principle that can reconcile the decisions.

It is important in thinking about these decisions to contrast another situation where there is a compensation for loss and the answer is clear. Assume a taxpayer with a $20,000 basis in business property that burns down, for which he receives

$20,000 insurance compensation. There is no gross income, but that is because it is obvious that the loss of the property provided no personal consumption or savings — as confirmed by the fact that the *uncompensated* loss would have resulted in a $20,000 loss deduction. Therefore, the $20,000 compensation is reduced by the $20,000 loss (reflected in the asset's basis), resulting in no gross income.

By contrast, in the following cases, the taxpayer who did *not* receive compensation would *not* be able to deduct the loss, and yet sometimes the compensation is not taxable. How come? Can there be a loss that provides no personal consumption or savings, which is *not* deductible in the absence of compensation, but for which the compensation is still excluded? Try to figure out why a deduction for an *uncompensated* loss might be denied in all of the following cases, and you may have a clue as to why the compensation can sometimes be tax free despite the absence of a deduction for uncompensated losses.

1. A taxpayer got *erroneous* advice from tax counsel about making an election on the income tax form. As a result of the advice, the taxpayer made an election that resulted in paying $20,000 more tax than would have been due if no election had been made. Sometime later, tax counsel paid taxpayer $20,000 to compensate for the error. The payment was *not* taxed because there was no "accession to wealth," even though there would have been no deduction for the "extra" $20,000. *Clark v. Commissioner*, 40 B.T.A. 333 (1939).

2. In *Concord Instruments Corp. v. Commissioner*, 67 T.C.M. (CCH) 3036 (1994), the Tax Court had held in an earlier case that the taxpayer (Concord) owed back taxes. The taxpayer's lawyer negligently failed to file an appeal. Taxpayer then made a claim against the lawyer's malpractice insurer, which was settled for $125,000. In this case, the taxpayer wanted to exclude the $125,000 recovery, based on *Clark*, and the court agreed. The court stated as follows:

> *Clark v. Commissioner*, 40 B.T.A. 333 (1939), is instructive in deciding this case, and is closer to this situation than any other decided case either party has cited. We recognize that in *Clark*, unlike the instant case, there was no dispute that Clark was injured by his counsel's error, and that the amount of the injury was known. In contrast here, there is no certainty whether, or by how much, petitioner was injured by its counsel's conduct. Nevertheless, the fact remains that American Home [the lawyer's insurance company] paid petitioner $125,000 to settle the latter's claim against its counsel for malpractice in the handling of the tax case.
>
> . . . The essence of respondent's argument is that any error by petitioner's counsel was harmless because petitioner's case was correctly decided by the Tax Court. Under that assumption, any funds petitioner received were an economic benefit and not compensation for injury. . . . [The government] does not argue that American Home paid petitioner the $125,000 for any reason other than petitioner's claim. We conclude that American Home paid the $125,000 because of petitioner's claim. Thus, petitioner's claim and American Home's payment was to compensate petitioner for a loss similar to that in *Clark*.

Suppose there was evidence in *Concord Instruments* that the taxpayer's claim was frivolous and the lawyer and his insurance company settled to avoid the nuisance and bad publicity. Can the government go behind the surface of the taxpayer's claim to recharacterize the recovery, so that it would be a taxable accession to wealth, rather than a tax-free loss recovery? In answering this question, put yourself in the position of a trial judge who must adjudicate such claims. Should you adopt a rule that distinguishes real from frivolous claims?

3. In Letter Ruling 200328033, taxpayer-employees received nontaxable disability payments that were converted by the employer to taxable retirement payments on a certain date. The employees sued the employer, claiming that the conversion occurred too early. The employees won their lawsuit and, as a result, the conversion date occurred later and some earlier-taxed retirement benefits turned out to be exempt disability benefits. For those earlier tax years on which the statute of limitations to file for a refund had expired, the employer paid the employees the excess income taxes that the employees had paid because they had reported taxable instead of exempt benefits. The letter ruling held that the employer's payment to the employees of the excess taxes was exempt from taxation under the *Clark* case.

4. In Letter Ruling 9728052, Taxpayer A argued that receipt of a tax indemnity payment should not be includible in A's gross income. The ruling set forth the facts and its conclusion rejecting the taxpayer's position, as follows:

> A executed an agreement (the "Agreement") to pay his former spouse annually for [some] years. The Agreement also provides that if the former spouse dies, the payments will be made to her estate. A's attorney informed A that payments under the Agreement would qualify as deductible alimony payments under section 215 of the Internal Revenue Code.

> The Internal Revenue Service subsequently examined A's federal income tax returns and disallowed the alimony deduction. . . . The payments under the Agreement are not deductible as alimony because A's obligation to make the payments continues after the death of his former spouse. See section 71(b)(1)(D). A is now negotiating with his attorney's malpractice insurer for an indemnification payment. This payment will recompense A for the additional federal income taxes . . . he has paid and the additional federal income taxes he expects to pay over the term of the Agreement arising from the nondeductibility of payments made under the Agreement. . . .

> The indemnity payment that A will receive as reimbursement for the additional federal income taxes A has paid or will pay are distinguishable from the indemnity payments in Clark. . . . In Clark . . . the preparers' errors in filing returns . . . caused the taxpayers to pay more than their minimum proper federal income tax liabilities based on the underlying transactions for the years in question. In this case, however, the error of A's attorney related to the underlying transaction, that is, the terms of the Agreement. As a result of that error, A's payments under the Agreement are properly not deductible. Thus, unlike the situations in Clark . . . A is not paying more than his minimum proper federal income tax liability based on A's transactions for the tax years to which the tax reimburse-

ments relate. Therefore, under section 1.61-14(a) the reimbursement of prior and future years federal income taxes that A receives represents a gain that is includible in A's gross income. . . .

Accordingly, we conclude that A must include in gross income the indemnity payment A will receive as compensation for additional federal income taxes . . . arising from A's attorney's misrepresentation that payments under the Agreement are deductible under section 215.

QUESTIONS AND COMMENTS

1. If the taxpayer had gotten correct tax advice in the "alimony" private ruling — that the payments were not deductible — what would he have done? Would he have lowered his payments to the wife by the amount of the tax that he would have saved if the payments had been deductible? If he would not have lowered the payments by the additional tax he had to pay, how much loss did he suffer from the bad tax advice? In other words, when someone gets bad tax planning advice, can we be sure about how much loss he suffers from the bad advice?

2. Is the following example like getting bad tax advice about deducting alimony? Assume the taxpayer owed the government an additional $20,000 after receiving erroneous tax advice that some income was tax exempt. Because the income was taxable, the taxpayer owed $20,000 more in taxes than he expected. If a taxpayer erroneously thinks that some income is exempt, how do we know what he would have done with correct tax advice? Maybe there is no better investment for him to make other than the taxable investment that he actually made, so the wrong tax advice costs him nothing.

3. Now think again about why compensation for a loss might be tax free even though uncompensated losses related to the same loss might not be deductible. Assume that the cases excluding compensation were correctly decided — the compensation was not income. If there had been no compensation, what issues would a lawsuit claiming a deduction have involved? The taxpayer would claim that he overpaid taxes, even though no neutral third party paid anything to the taxpayer to verify that claim. And litigation about the correct tax amount would arise, not through the procedures established for challenging a tax obligation (*see* Chapter 6.03), but as a loss deduction claim.

[B]   Accessions to Wealth — Loans and Debts

[1]   Why Aren't Loans Income?

[a]   The Explanation

Loans are not taxable. Why not? The simple answer is that the receipts are offset by debt so the taxpayer has no gain. The receipts are a plus but the debt is an equivalent minus.

This observation — that the value of the offsetting debt equals the amount of the loan — suggests the following question. Suppose the value of the debt is less than the loan because the interest rate does not make up for the financial risk that the debtor might not repay the loan. In theory, the loan should be income in an amount equal to the loan minus the value of the debt obligation; that difference is an accession to wealth in the year of the loan. In *Illinois Power Co. v. Commissioner*, 792 F.2d 683 (7th Cir. 1986), Judge Posner noted the theoretically correct approach, but explained that this was too difficult to compute on a case-by-case basis. Consequently, the nontaxability of the usual loan was an example of an all-or-nothing approach to defining income. Either it is all income or all of it is excluded. (We will see this approach later in connection with the taxation of fringe benefits and the deduction of travel and entertainment expenses in Chapters 7 and 8.) Moreover, can you imagine telling a typical consumer that some of the loan to buy an asset for personal use is income?

[b]   Nontaxation of Loans and the Nondeductibility of Interest

Before you assume too readily that the code does not tax loans, consider the following. Suppose loans were taxed. If that were true, the repayment and interest would have to be deductible, to reflect the fact that the taxpayer has no gain over time. For example, assume a taxpayer wants $100 of personal consumption in year 1. To simplify the arithmetic, assume a 50% tax rate. If loans are taxable, the taxpayer must borrow $200, to get $100 after tax. Assume further that interest rates are 10% and the loan with interest is paid back in year 2. The taxpayer would need $220 gross income to pay back the loan with interest. Taxable income in year 2 would be zero ($220 – $220 = $0), and the entire $220 would be used to repay the $200 loan and $20 (10%) interest.

LOANS TAXABLE
$100 PERSONAL CONSUMPTION IN YEAR 1;
10% INTEREST DEDUCTIBLE

YEAR 1	YEAR 2
$200 LOAN	$220 INCOME [TO PAY $200 LOAN AND $20 INTEREST; BOTH DEDUCTIBLE]

If loans are *not* taxed, the taxpayer has to borrow only $100 in year 1 to get $100 personal consumption. How much gross income does the taxpayer need in year 2 to repay the debt? Because loans were not taxed, repayment is not deductible. The taxpayer needs $200 to get the $100 to repay the loan. What about the interest? The taxpayer owes $10 interest (10% of $100). How much gross income does she need to get $10 to pay the interest? That depends on whether interest is deductible. In fact, interest on loans for personal purposes may or may not be deductible, depending on the use of the loan (discussed in Chapter 16.01). At this point, it is enough to know that interest on some personal loans is not deductible. If interest is *not* deductible, the taxpayer needs $20 gross income to get the $10 after tax to pay the interest, plus $200 gross income to pay back the $100 loan.

LOANS NOT TAXABLE
$100 PERSONAL CONSUMPTION IN YEAR 1;
10% INTEREST NOT DEDUCTIBLE

YEAR 1	YEAR 2
$100 LOAN	$220 INCOME [TO PAY $100 LOAN AND $10 INTEREST; BOTH NOT DEDUCTIBLE]

In other words, if loans are not taxable, *but* interest is not deductible, the taxpayer needs $220 income in year 2 to repay the $100 loan with interest. But that is the same amount she needed if loans were taxable and the interest and loan repayments were deductible. Disallowing the interest deduction when loans were not taxable produced the equivalent of taxing the loan. In both cases, the taxpayer needs $220 gross income in year 2 to repay the loan and interest. Why don't taxpayers object to disallowing interest deductions, when they would object vehemently to taxing loans?

[2]   Obligations to Repay, But Not Loans

[a]   Typical Embezzler

What happens if someone embezzles income? How can there be any income? There is an obligation to repay that offsets the receipts. Or is there? Put technically, what is the present value of the debt obligation? Put colloquially, what are the chances of repayment?

For some time, the Supreme Court did not tax the embezzler. Specifically, it relied on an early case dealing with the taxation of someone whose possession of money was the subject of litigation. The Court established the "claim of right" rule, which stated:

> If a taxpayer receives earnings under a claim of right and without restriction as to its disposition, he has received income . . . , even though it may still be claimed that he is not entitled to retain the money, and even though he may still be adjudged liable to restore its equivalent.

The Court then went on to view a "claim of right" as a *necessary*, not just a sufficient reason to tax. Embezzled funds were therefore not taxable, because the embezzler laid no claim of right to the income.

This approach was reversed in *James v. United States*, 366 U.S. 213 (1961). The Court held that a taxpayer has income "when [the taxpayer] acquires earnings, lawfully or unlawfully, without the consensual recognition, express or implied, of an obligation to repay and without restriction as to their disposition . . . ." Claim of right is now a *sufficient* but not a necessary condition for having taxable income. When there is a claim of right, there is no consensual recognition of the obligation to repay, but there are other situations where there is typically no consensual recognition of the obligation to repay (unlike a loan), and that therefore result in the receipt of taxable income (e.g., the embezzler).

[b]   White Collar Embezzler

There are borderline cases, of which the following is an example. Read the opinion in *Gilbert* carefully to identify the crucial fact(s) that determine why Gilbert was not taxed.

GILBERT v. COMMISSIONER
United States Court of Appeals, Second Circuit
552 F.2d 478 (2d Cir. 1977)

LUMBARD, CIRCUIT JUDGE:

Until June 12, 1962, Gilbert [the taxpayer] was president, principal stockholder, and a director of the E. L. Bruce Company, Inc., a New York corporation which was engaged in the lumber supply business. In 1961 and early 1962 Gilbert acquired on margin substantial personal and beneficial ownership of stock in another lumber supply company, the Celotex Corporation, intending ultimately to bring about a merger of Celotex into Bruce. . . . [He] also induced Bruce itself to purchase a substantial number of Celotex shares. In addition, on March 5, 1962, Gilbert granted Bruce an option to purchase his Celotex shares from him at cost. By the end of May 1962, 56% of Celotex was thus controlled by Gilbert and Bruce, and negotiations for the merger were proceeding; agreement had been reached that three of the directors of Bruce would be placed on the board of Celotex. It is undisputed that this merger would have been in Bruce's interest.

The stock market declined on May 28, 1962, however, and Gilbert was called upon to furnish additional margin for the Celotex shares purchased by him . . . . Lacking sufficient cash of his own to meet this margin call, Gilbert instructed the secretary of Bruce to use corporate funds to supply the necessary margin. Between May 28 and June 6 a series of checks totaling $1,958,000 were withdrawn from Bruce's accounts and used to meet the margin call. $5,000 was repaid to Bruce on June 5. According to his testimony in the tax court, Gilbert from the outset intended to repay all the money and at all times thought he was acting in the corporation's best interests as well as his own. He promptly informed several other Bruce officers and directors of the withdrawals; however, some were not notified until June 11 or 12.

On about June 1, Gilbert returned to New York from Nevada, where he had been attending to a personal matter. . . . On June 8, Gilbert went to the law offices of Shearman, Sterling & Wright and executed interest-bearing promissory notes to Bruce for $1,953,000 secured by an assignment of most of his property. The notes were callable by Bruce on demand, with presentment and notice of demand waived by Gilbert. The tax court found that up through June 12 the net value of the assets assigned for security by Gilbert substantially exceeded the amount owed.

After Gilbert informed other members of the Bruce board of directors of his actions, a meeting of the board was scheduled for the morning of June 12. At the meeting the board accepted the note and assignment but refused to ratify Gilbert's unauthorized withdrawals. During the meeting, word came that the board of directors of the Ruberoid Company had rejected the price offered for sale of the Celotex stock. Thereupon, the Bruce board demanded and received Gilbert's resignation and decided to issue a public announcement the next day regarding his unauthorized withdrawals. All further attempts on June 12 to arrange a sale of the Celotex stock fell through and in the evening Gilbert flew to Brazil, where he stayed for several months. On June 13 the market price of Bruce and Celotex stock plummeted, and trading in those shares was suspended by the Securities and Exchanges Commission.

On June 22 the Internal Revenue Service filed tax liens against Gilbert . . . . Several years later Gilbert pled guilty to federal and state charges of having unlawfully withdrawn the funds from Bruce. . . .

The Commissioner contends that there can never be "consensual recognition . . . of an obligation to repay" in an embezzlement case. He reasons that because the corporation as represented by a majority of the board of directors was unaware of the withdrawals, there cannot have been *consensual* recognition of the obligation to repay at the time the taxpayer Gilbert acquired the funds. Since the withdrawals were not authorized and the directors refused to treat them as a loan to Gilbert, the Commissioner concludes that Gilbert should be taxed like a thief rather than a borrower. . . .

This is not a typical embezzlement case, however, and we do not interpret James as requiring income realization in every case of unlawful withdrawals by a taxpayer. . . . When Gilbert withdrew the corporate funds, he recognized his obligation to repay and intended to do so. The funds were to be used not only for his benefit but also for the benefit of the corporation; meeting the margin calls was necessary to maintain the possibility of the highly favorable merger. Although Gilbert undoubtedly realized that he lacked the necessary authorization, he thought he was serving the best interests of the corporation and he expected his decision to be ratified shortly thereafter. That Gilbert at no time intended to retain the corporation's funds is clear from his actions. He immediately informed several of the corporation's officers and directors, and he made a complete accounting to all of them within two weeks. He also disclosed his actions to the corporation's outside counsel, a reputable law firm, and followed its instructions regarding repayment. In signing immediately payable promissory notes secured by most of his assets, Gilbert's clear intent was to ensure that Bruce would obtain full restitution. In addition, he attempted to sell his shares of Celotex stock in order to raise cash to pay Bruce back immediately.

When Gilbert executed the assignment to Bruce of his assets on June 8 and when this assignment for security was accepted by the Bruce board on June 12, the net market value of these assets was substantially more than the amount owed. The Bruce board did not release Gilbert from his underlying obligation to repay, but the assignment was nonetheless valid and Bruce's failure to make an appropriate filing to protect itself against the claims of third parties, such as the IRS, did not relieve Gilbert of the binding effect of the assignment. Since the assignment secured an immediate payable note, Gilbert had as of June 12 granted Bruce full discretion to liquidate any of his assets in order to recoup on the $1,953,000 withdrawal. Thus, Gilbert's net accretion in real wealth on the overall transaction was zero: he had for his own use withdrawn $1,953,000 in corporate funds but he had now granted the corporation control over at least $1,953,000 worth of his assets.

We conclude that where a taxpayer withdraws funds from a corporation which he fully intends to repay and which he expects with reasonable certainty he will be able to repay, where he believes that his withdrawals will be approved by the corporation, and where he makes a prompt assignment of assets sufficient to secure the amount owed, he does not realize income on the withdrawals under the James test. When Gilbert acquired the money, there was an express consensual recognition of his obligation to repay: the secretary of the corporation, who signed the checks, the officers and directors to whom Gilbert gave contemporaneous notification, and Gilbert himself were all aware that the transaction was in the nature of a loan. Moreover, the funds were certainly not received by Gilbert "without restriction as to their disposition" as is required for taxability under James; the money was to be used solely for the temporary purpose of meeting certain margin calls and it was so used. For these reasons, we reverse the decision of the tax court.

QUESTIONS

1. Why wasn't there an accession to wealth in *Gilbert*? Was there the kind of "consensual recognition" that typically occurs when people borrow money? When did the taxpayer acknowledge the debt; did the creditor acquiesce in the "loan"? Was the debtor able to pay back the debt when he obtained the money?

2. In *Gilbert*, did the debtor think he was helping the creditor? Was that relevant?

3. Compare *Gilbert* to *Buff*. In *Buff*, a bookkeeper embezzled $22,000 between January and June 1965. The crime was discovered in June. The employee confessed and agreed to repay $25 per week out of his paycheck; he also borrowed $1,000 from a bank to make a repayment. In July 1965, the employee was fired. Is *Buff* a stronger or weaker case for the taxpayer than *Gilbert*? *Buff v. Commissioner*, 58 T.C. 224 (1972) (not tax), *reversed*, 496 F.2d 847 (2d Cir. 1974) (tax).

4. Why is the government so anxious to tax illegally acquired funds? Why not wait until a later date when repayment is clearly unlikely and impose tax at that time? One answer is that the government has a lien on a taxpayer's property for unpaid taxes and that lien might have priority over another creditor's rights (in *Gilbert*, the corporate creditor had failed to protect its security interest). If the government waits too long to establish its lien, the taxpayer's property may be gone.

[C] Discharge of Indebtedness

The following case discusses whether a debtor has income when a debt is forgiven.

UNITED STATES v. KIRBY LUMBER CO.
United States Supreme Court
284 U.S. 1 (1931)

MR. JUSTICE HOLMES delivered the opinion of the court.

In July, 1923, the plaintiff, the Kirby Lumber Company, issued its own bonds for $12,126,800 for which it received their par value. Later in the same year it purchased in the open market some of the same bonds at less than par, the difference of price being $137,521.30. The question is whether this difference is a taxable gain or income of the plaintiff for the year 1923. . . . [G]ross income includes "gains or profits and income derived from any source whatever," and by the Treasury Regulations [] that have been in force through repeated re-enactments, "If the corporation purchases and retires any of such bonds at a price less than the issuing price or face value, the excess of the issuing price or face value over the purchase price is gain or income for the taxable year." We see no reason why the Regulations should not be accepted as a correct statement of the law.

. . . Here there was no shrinkage of assets and the taxpayer made a clear gain. As a result of its dealings it made available $137,521.30 assets previously offset by the obligation of bonds now extinct. We see nothing to be gained by the discussion of judicial definitions. The defendant in error has realized within the year an accession to income, if we take words in their plain popular meaning, as they should be taken here. *Burnet v. Sanford & Brooks Co.*, 282 U.S. 359, 364, 51 S. Ct. 150, 75 L. Ed. 383.

Judgment reversed.

[1]   Defer Taxation of Income; Basis Adjustment

Kirby, like *Bruun*, evoked a congressional reaction. Even though there was income under § 61, the taxable event was an inopportune time to impose tax. Debts are often forgiven when taxpayers are in financial trouble and, moreover, the act of forgiveness provides no cash with which to repay the debt. For this reason, immediately after *Kirby Lumber* was decided, Congress passed the predecessor of §§ 108, 1017. These sections provided that taxpayers who otherwise had taxable income when a debt was forgiven could usually defer tax on the discharge of indebtedness income.

[a]   Bankrupt and Insolvent Debtors

The current § 108 is not as generous and the taxpayer in *Kirby* would probably be taxed under current law when the debt was discharged. The core of the current section allows bankrupt or insolvent taxpayers to avoid paying tax when a debt is forgiven, but only at a price. They must reduce various tax benefits in the order specified in § 108(b)(2), unless they elect to reduce the basis of depreciable property. § 108(b)(5). Under this provision, insolvent taxpayers cannot exclude from income any more than the amount by which they are insolvent before the forgiveness (e.g., $100 debt, $80 assets, $20 insolvency). § 108(a)(3).

[b]　Solvent Debtors

What about the solvent debtor? Under current law, there are several situations in which a solvent debtor can defer tax when a debt is discharged. First, solvent farmers can exclude discharge of indebtedness income and defer tax by reducing future tax benefits, if the debt is owed to certain types of creditors (usually, a typical business lender), and if the debt is related to the farming business. **§ 108(a)(1)(C), (g).**

Second, an individual who borrows to acquire, construct, or substantially improve business real property (secured by the debt) can exclude forgiven debt from income. The maximum exclusion is the amount of such debt outstanding before the discharge over the value of the business real property (minus any other qualified real property business indebtedness secured by the property — e.g., a second mortgage). The taxpayer must reduce the basis of the property in an amount equal to the forgiven debt excluded from income. **§ 108(a)(1)(D), (c), § 1017(b)(3)(F).** For example, assume that a bank lends a taxpayer $100,000 towards the $150,000 purchase price of land used in the business, taking back a first mortgage on the property; and assume further that there is a $15,000 second mortgage on the property. Thereafter, the property declines in value to $70,000. The taxpayer then negotiates a $45,000 reduction in the first mortgage debt — down to $55,000 from $100,000. In that case, the taxpayer does not pay tax on the $45,000 of debt forgiveness. ($45,000 is the maximum amount that could be excluded — $100,000 minus $55,000, which is the property's $70,000 value minus the outstanding $15,000 second mortgage.)

Third, current law also allows a debtor to reduce basis on purchased property if the *seller* forgives all or part of the purchase price, without regard to the debtor's solvency. **§ 108(e)(5).** This might help the purchaser of a home bought on credit from the seller. It does not apply to forgiveness by a third party, such as a lender-bank. This section is designed for situations in which a buyer disputes the debt (perhaps because of a discovered defect in the purchased property), but the section is applied without inquiring into the circumstances that give rise to the discharge of the debt. For example, if a home buyer promises to pay the seller $100,000 but demands and receives a reduction in debt to $95,000 because the roof leaks, the buyer does not have income but adjusts his purchase price (basis) to $95,000.

Fourth, the Mortgage Forgiveness Debt Relief Act of 2007, amends the code to exclude from gross income amounts attributable to a discharge of indebtedness incurred to acquire a principal residence, as long as the discharge is "directly related to a decline in the value of the residence or to the financial condition of the taxpayer"; the exclusion is limited to $2 million. In addition, the basis of the principal residence is reduced by the amount of the discharged indebtedness excluded from gross income. **§ 108(a)(1)(E), (h).** This amendment was a response to the foreclosures and the renegotiation of home loans that resulted from the mortgage lending crisis in 2007. ATRA extends this tax break through 2013.

[c]   Student Loans

Another example of a forgiven debt that would typically be included in § 61 income is the forgiveness of a student loan when the student is solvent. Rev. Rul. 73-256, 1973-1 C.B. 56. After this ruling, Congress exempted student loans if the borrower "serves in occupations with unmet needs or in areas with unmet needs" and is under the direction of a government or exempt organization. A loan forgiveness program for law students who work in a Legal Services Office or legal aid office would be covered by this provision. § 108(f).

[2]   Discharge of Debt Other Than by a Creditor

In *Kirby*, the creditor released the debtor from his obligation. In other situations, a debtor may have a relationship to a third party and the debt is discharged because the third party pays off the creditor. In such cases, the debtor's relationship to the third party determines whether there is taxable income or not; the "discharge of indebtedness" rules are inapplicable. For example, in *Old Colony Trust Co. v. Commissioner*, 279 U.S. 716 (1929), the third party was the debtor's employer. The employer paid salary to the debtor by paying off the debtor's tax obligation. Payment of the tax debt was taxable income to the debtor because it was additional compensation.

In other cases, the third party may have some other relationship with the debtor, so that payment of the debtor's obligation might or might not produce taxable income. If the third party was the debtor's relative, payment of the debt might be a tax exempt gift to the debtor (discussed in Chapter 4). Or the third party might owe the debtor money because he bought property from the debtor; payment of the debtor's debt might then be additional sales proceeds, taxable as capital gain.

The rules applicable to a discharge of indebtedness are also inapplicable if the creditor who forgives the debt is acting in some capacity other than as a creditor — that is, when the creditor is acting like a third party. For example, sometimes debt forgiveness can be a tax-free gift; for example, if the creditor is the debtor's parent who had loaned money to a child. Or, suppose a creditor forgives a debt but only because the creditor owes the debtor money — as when an employer lends money to an employee, but is later obligated to pay the employee wages. The employer-creditor forgives the original loan to the employee to discharge *his* debt to pay wages. In such a case, the employee has wage income, not discharge of indebtedness income. Do you see why it matters which kind of income it is? Hint: suppose the employee is insolvent?

[3]   Distinguishing Sales Proceeds from Discharge of Indebtedness

1. In *Gehl v. Commissioner*, 102 T.C. 784 (1994), *aff'd*, 1995 U.S. App. LEXIS 5482 (8th Cir. Mar. 20, 1995) (unpublished opinion), an insolvent farmer conveyed property to his creditor in partial discharge of an (approximately) $152,000 debt, for which the farmer was personally liable. The property's basis was about $48,000 and its value about $116,000. After this conveyance, the farmer was still insolvent. The bank also forgave the remainder of the loan (about $36,000). The government

argued that this conveyance produced taxable gain to the farmer as a sale of the property in an amount equal to the fair market value of the property minus basis ($68,000 = $116,000 minus $48,000). Both sides agreed that the $36,000 forgiveness of debt ($152,000 minus $116,000) was eligible for § 108 treatment. The farmer argued that the $68,000 gain on the land was also eligible for § 108 treatment, but the court disagreed. The gain on the property was taxable as gain from dealings in property under § 61(a)(3), not income from discharge of indebtedness. The transaction had to be bifurcated into the gain from the disposition of the property (value over basis) and gain from debt discharge (debt over value), and only the latter was eligible for § 108 treatment. The court relied on **Treas. Reg. § 1.1001-2(c) (example 8)** to support its conclusion.

2. In *Frazier v. Commissioner*, 111 T.C. 243 (1998), a creditor-lender bid on property owned by the taxpayer at a foreclosure sale. The court held that the amount realized on the disposition of property to repay the debt is its fair market value, when the debtor is personally liable. However, the fair market value was not the same as the amount that the creditor-lender bid for the property. The court stated that the lender might bid more than fair market value because the debtor was insolvent and because the lender might want to remove the debt from its books. Consequently, the amount realized on the sale was only $375,000 (its fair market value), not the $571,179 price at which the lender bid in the property. Because the debtor's basis was $495,544, the debtor had a loss on the sale portion of the transaction. The difference between the debt and the $375,000 was discharge of indebtedness income, but was not taxed in the year of the sale because the taxpayer was insolvent.

QUESTIONS

1. If a taxpayer gives property to a relative but requires the donee to pay the gift tax (for which the donor is liable), is the donee's payment of the tax considered sales proceeds to the donor? The Supreme Court in *Diedrich v. Commissioner*, 457 U.S. 191 (1982), treated the gift tax paid by the donee as sales proceeds. Because the gift tax exceeded the taxpayer's basis, the taxpayer had taxable gain on the transaction.

2. Suppose a taxpayer owes $100,000 to a tort plaintiff resulting from a car accident on the taxpayer's vacation, which was the taxpayer's fault. The $100,000 is paid by an insurance company from whom the taxpayer had purchased liability insurance. The taxpayer does not have $100,000 income from this discharge of liability, but why not?

§ 3.07   ACCESSION TO WEALTH — PERSONAL CONSUMPTION

[A]   In-Kind Benefits; Subjective vs. Objective Value

The *Glenshaw Glass* definition of income invites looking at the definition of income from the point of view of the uses to which income is put (personal consumption and savings). The discussion of loans focused on whether the taxpayer had any increase in net worth — that is, savings. Now let us focus on whether a taxpayer has taxable personal consumption.

At least some itemized deductions may be permitted by the code on the theory that the expenditures do not provide personal consumption (for example, the medical expense deduction — discussed in Chapter 9.02[B][1]). Another setting in which this question arises is when a taxpayer receives something other than cash for personal consumption (income in-kind rather than in-cash). This often occurs when an employee receives fringe benefits from an employer (discussed in Chapter 7.01-.02). Here, we look at a benefit received in a non-employment setting — a prize. We want to know whether the subjective benefit enjoyed by a particular taxpayer discounts the taxable benefit below the objective market value of an item.

[1]   Prizes

The statute taxes prizes unless (1) they are provided in recognition of religious, charitable, scientific, educational, artistic, literary, or civic achievement, and (2) if the recipient was selected without any action on his part to enter the contest, and (3) the recipient is not required to perform "substantial future services" as a condition of receiving the award, and (4) the prize is transferred by the payor to a charitable organization. § 74. In addition, if the taxpayer refuses to accept a prize, it is not includible in income; Rev. Rul. 57-374, 1957-2 C.B. 69.

In *Turner v. Commissioner*, 13 T.C.M. (CCH) 462 (1954), the taxpayer won a prize of two nontransferable first-class steamship tickets for a cruise to Buenos Aires for himself and his wife. His income was otherwise quite low and his lifestyle did not include cruises. His wife was from Rio de Janeiro and he was able to turn in the two tickets and $12.50 for four tourist class tickets to Rio for himself, his wife and two children. The taxpayer valued the tickets on the tax return at $520, but the government argued that the retail market value of the tickets, which was $2,220, should be taxed. The court included $1,400 in taxable income.

If the steamship tickets had been transferable for, say, $1,800, would the decision be different? Would transferability for $1,800 eliminate any dispute about whether the taxpayer should be taxed on the retail market value ($2,220)? Suppose a taxpayer receives a new car, with a retail value of $10,000 and a resale value of $8,900. How would you decide what taxable income to report?

Turner is a rare case in which the taxpayer could discount objective retail market value because of lower subjective value. The fact that the court virtually split the difference between taxable value conceded by the taxpayer and retail value suggests that a subjective standard is not administrable. But subjective criteria may still be relevant for rulemaking purposes. The courts, the agency, and the statute usually take an all-or-nothing approach to devising rules about including or excluding an in-kind benefit (as with employee fringe benefits, discussed in Chapter 7). In doing this, however, they consider whether taxpayers would derive significant subjective value from the benefit. Subjective value is therefore relevant for framing general rules, even if it is not generally useful on a case-by-case basis.

Another context in which someone can receive an in-kind benefit whose subjective value does not equal retail price is the provision of "goodie bags" to celebrity attendees at the Oscar ceremonies, some of which are reputed to have significant retail value. The government recently reminded the celebrities that the benefits are taxable to the recipients (posted at www.irs.gov/newsroom, March 5, 2006). Should these benefits be discounted for subjective value?

[2] Employees and Other Business Contexts

1. In *McDonald v. Commissioner*, 66 T.C. 223 (1976), a United States executive in Japan was provided Western-style housing by his employer, who had rented a house for the employee. Somewhat simplified, the facts were that the employer paid about $1,000 per month to rent the house for the employee. The employee was willing to include $350 per month in income because that was what "a study indicated an average American Businessman with a position and salary comparable to petitioner's would spend for lodgings in the United States." The court included the employer's $1,000 cost in the employee's income. (Note that Congress has come to the rescue of U.S. workers abroad by giving them a deduction for "excessive" housing costs. §§ 911(a)(2), 911(c).)

The employment context in *McDonald* makes the case stronger for taxing the benefit at "full" value? Unless employment income is effectively taxed, the income tax will fail as a major source of revenue. It is therefore not surprising that the value was discounted in the prize case, not involving an employee, or that the employee was taxed on the objective cost of the housing in *McDonald*. In addition, the *McDonald* case involved a core consumption item — housing — and it might seem especially unfair if such items are taxed at a discount for selected taxpayers.

2. In *Rooney v. Commissioner*, 88 T.C. 523 (1987), the value of goods and services received by an accounting firm from clients who were unable to pay their bills in cash was measured by the retail price of those goods and services, not some lower discounted value. And, in *Koons v. United States*, 315 F.2d 542 (9th Cir. 1963), the court taxed an employee on the full amount of the employee's moving expenses paid by the employer. It rejected the taxpayers' argument that the amount should be discounted because "the services were of little or no value to them. . . . We think that the use of any such measure of value [] is contrary to the usual way of valuing either services or property, and would make the administration of the tax laws in this area depend upon a knowledge by the Commissioner of the state of mind of the individual taxpayer. We do not think that tax administration should be based upon anything so whimsical."

3. In *McCoy v. Commissioner*, 38 T.C. 841 (1962), an employee received a car from his employer as an award in a sales contest. The employer had bought the car for $4,452.54 about one month before transferring it to the employee, and had not

used it prior to the transfer. The car was a Lincoln and the employee had never owned that luxurious a car, although he did not own a car when he received the Lincoln. The employee drove the car for 10 days and then sold it for $1,000 cash and a Ford car worth $2,600. The employee reported $3,600 income. The government argued for $4,452.54 income (the employer's cost). The court held that the value to the employee should be reduced to reflect the fact that the employer could not have sold the car it had bought for the $4,452.54 that it paid, but that there should be no further reduction. The court hit on a $3,900 value. Does that reflect the objective market value of a "used" car or a discount for subjective value?

[3] Trophies; Conversion to an Economic Asset

Suppose the taxpayer obtains something with value on the market but retains it for its noneconomic value — as a trophy. In *Wills v. Commissioner*, 48 T.C. 308 (1967), the taxpayer was awarded the Hickok belt for being the "outstanding professional athlete" in 1962. The value of the belt was included in his income, which makes it sound as though receipt of a trophy would also be taxed. Indeed, the taxpayer had argued that it was not taxable because it was a "trophy." (The case of the Oscar might be different because recipients must sign an agreement that, if they want to sell the trophy, they must sell it to the award-granting Academy for $1.)

Does the following finding of fact distinguish the Hickok belt from the typical trophy? "The S. Rae Hickok belt was jewel-studded, contained 27 one and one-half carat diamonds, simulated stones, and had a 3 1/2-pound gold belt buckle. It is stipulated that the value of the belt at the time of receipt was $6,038.19. One of the gems in the belt was subsequently removed by and used in a ring for petitioner's wife."

How would the following situation, discussed in the newspapers and on the Internet, be taxed? A baseball fan in the stands catches a home run ball that is hit by someone who has just set a record for the most home runs in a year, or some similar accomplishment. In a 1998 News Release (IR-98-56), the government stated that the fan would not be taxed if he immediately returned the ball, by analogy to the nontaxation of a prizewinner who declines the prize. (1) But what if he keeps the ball and does not sell it? Treasure trove is normally taxed when it is reduced to undisputed possession, without waiting for a sale. (2) Does it matter whether (a) the player has offered to buy the ball for a specific sum, or (b) the ball could be sold on eBay for a significant sum? These facts make valuation easier but do not eliminate the character of the baseball as a "trophy." (3) Does the baseball player have income if he gets the ball back from the fan and keeps it, without planning to sell it? Of course, if the ball is sold, the sales price would be included in gross income.

The recipient of an Oscar is required to sell the trophy for $1 to the motion picture organization that gives the prize, if the recipient puts the Oscar up for sale. Does that avoid the problem of taxing the Oscar recipient?

[B]   Imputed Income

Section 61 has never been interpreted to include "imputed income" — which is value generated by a taxpayer for his or her own use. The best examples are the following: the rental value of the residence owned by the taxpayer; the consumption of inventory produced by the taxpayer; the value of self-performed services (e.g., mowing the lawn; filling out one's own tax returns; etc.).

There are several rationales for this result. First, it would be administratively difficult to identify and value many of these items. Second, the government might seem to be intruding improperly into the taxpayer's private life if it tried to tax these items that have not been realized in an economic transaction.

These rationales are strongest in the case of personal services performed for oneself; and weakest when the item is rental value of property owned by the taxpayer. Rental value of many personal assets, such as a home or car, could be estimated with some accuracy (perhaps as a percentage of cost), and their ownership identified from state and local property and excise tax records. Moreover, such property has been purchased on the market, even if the rental value has not been realized in an economic transaction.

[C]   Barter Clubs

Gains from barter have been the subject of several rulings, aimed at barter clubs. Barter transactions allow club members to exchange property and services for value in an economic transaction and are therefore not imputed income. In Rev. Rul. 79-24, 1979-1 C.B. 60, the members exchanged the property and/or services directly (for example, legal services for house painting); each member was taxed on value received. In Rev. Rul. 80-52, 1980-1 C.B. 100, a member who engaged in a barter transaction received credit units, valued at $1 per unit, based on the normal retail value charged by the member for providing the property or services; the member was taxed on the receipt of the credits.

[D]   Homeowners' Insurance for Meals and Lodging

[1]   Section 123

Suppose a taxpayer's principal residence burns down and the family lives in a motel and eats at restaurants for a month. The home mortgage, still being paid, is $500 per month. Motel charges are $750 for the month. Food costs are $700, instead of the usual $400. The insurance company pays the taxpayer for the $750 motel and $700 food expenses. Is this insurance reimbursement income? How does § 123 answer these questions?

QUESTIONS

1. What is the strongest argument for not taxing at least some of the meals and lodging expenses when reimbursed by homeowner's insurance? How is the taxpayer who receives reimbursement from the insurance company similar to Mr.

Turner receiving a steamship ticket as a prize?

2. Why are such expenses not deductible if there is no insurance?

[2] Note on Statutory Interpretation and the Political Process

[a] Judicial Interpretation Heading Off Legislation

Could the courts have excluded homeowner's insurance for meals and lodging from gross income under § 61 without specific statutory authority? Recall the *Clark* case in Chapter 3.06[A][4], excluding some payments from income because they were not an accession to wealth. Should a court have reached a similar conclusion with homeowner's insurance?

One way to think about this question is to ask whether a judicial decision is desirable because it might head off the pressure for a legislative amendment, with all the attendant statutory detail that often follows from congressional resolution of a problem. More generally, it is fair to ask how many of the detailed statutory provisions in the code are the result of courts not making decisions that would have avoided the need for a statute.

But perhaps, complex legislation is exactly what is needed, because the solution to a problem is politically or technically complex. A court should not try to resolve at least some issues because of such complexity, leaving the solution to the legislature. Was the homeowner's insurance situation better left to Congress or not?

[b] Prospective Statute and Interpreting Prior Law

The homeowner's insurance statute gave rise to another statutory interpretation issue — whether a prospective amendment precludes a court from revisiting an issue under prior law. Most legislation is prospective and that was true of § 123. After this law was passed, the Tax Court was asked to revisit the issue of not taxing the insurance under § 61 for a tax year prior to the effective date of the new § 123. The argument against doing so is the expressio unius argument — that the expressly prospective legislation providing an exemption excluded the same result for a period predating the new law, because the new law would have been unnecessary if prior law had already provided an exclusion from income.

In *McCabe v. Commissioner*, 54 T.C. 1745 (1970), the Tax Court thought itself free to revisit the prior law, despite the prospective change in the law. That seems to be the correct result. Like most explicit legislation, § 123 did not mean to address situations it did not cover, only to resolve the law for those situations it did cover. Though free to revisit prior law, the Tax Court nonetheless refused to exclude the insurance from income, analogizing the insurance payment to taxable rent, rather than tax-free enjoyment of the rental value of one's own home.

[E] Compulsive Gambler

In *Zarin v. Commissioner*, 92 T.C. 1084 (1989), *rev'd*, 916 F.2d 110 (3d Cir. 1990), a taxpayer, who was a professional engineer, was also a compulsive gambler. In 1980, he ran up a $3,435,000 debt to a gambling establishment in New Jersey named Resorts. He obtained a line of credit by giving his "marker" (like a promissory note) to obtain chips. Currency could not be used to gamble in New Jersey. Resorts had violated state law in various respects, which made its claim against Zarin legally unenforceable. In 1981, a lawsuit to collect the debt was settled for $500,000. The government claimed that the difference between $3,435,000 and $500,000 was discharge of indebtedness income. The 1980 gambling losses could not offset any 1981 gain because **Treas. Reg. § 1.165-10** interprets the rule in **§ 165(d)** (limiting the deduction of gambling losses to gambling gains) to mean that loss deductions can only offset gains arising in the *same* year as the losses.

Zarin involves the following issues: (1) Is there **§ 61** income on the discharge of indebtedness in the first place? If there is no **§ 61** income in the first place, there is no need to rely on **§ 108** to prevent taxation. (2) If there is **§ 61** income, does **§ 108** apply to provide taxpayer relief?

The Tax Court held against the taxpayer, with a dissent. The Court of Appeals reversed, holding for the taxpayer, with a dissent.

The Tax Court held that the taxpayer received value when he incurred the debt and only the promise to repay prevented taxation when credit was extended. Legal enforceability of the debt was not a prerequisite to taxing its forgiveness. Moreover, the court refused to treat the debt like a disputed debt, whose renegotiation to settle the amount results in a purchase price adjustment rather than gross income, on the theory that a dispute casts doubt on the value of the original purchase; here, the debt was liquidated so there was no dispute about its amount.

As for the statutory provision in **§ 108(e)(5)**, which prevents taxation of a purchase price adjustment, that section only applies to "property" and the opportunity to gamble was not "property." A dissent in the Tax Court concluded that the chips were "property" and that, if they were of sufficient value to support discharge of indebtedness income under **§ 61**, their discharge was a purchase price adjustment regarding the purchase of property.

The Tax Court majority also stated that the chips were not normal commercial property, which hints that there might have been a public policy argument disfavoring the use of **§ 108** by gamblers.

The difficulty the judges had in *Zarin* agreeing on the right analysis and the right result probably conceals a deep unease about something they did not discuss. We usually accept purchase price as a proxy for valuing taxable personal consumption. Is that assumption valid in the case of gamblers? Perhaps it is, if they engage in a lot of recreational gambling, in which case total costs are likely to average out over the years and the losses will approximate personal consumption. Or perhaps the purchase price produces satisfaction when engaged in by a very rich person who enjoys the occasional "fling," by dropping more than $3 million in a short time. But what if the gambler is compulsive about his habit? Do the losses represent "personal consumption" that should be taxed?

One way to conclude that the losses are not personal consumption is to emphasize the relationship in this case between unenforceability of the gambling debt and value to the taxpayer, relying on how the theory behind the disputed debt doctrine might apply to an unenforceable debt. Indeed, the Court of Appeals reversed the Tax Court and held for the taxpayer on the ground that there was no § 61 income because an unenforceable debt is like a disputed debt. Normally, unenforceability would not mean that value had not been received for the face amount of the debt. But if it always led to renegotiation of the debt, as is likely with a compulsive gambler, that suggests that the initial value received for the loan was not equal to the face amount of the loan. The disputed debt doctrine becomes a subset of a broader principle — that value has to be received for the loan — and unenforceability in the case of a compulsive gambler becomes another example of that principle.

Chapter 4

GIFTS

§ 4.01 CASH GIFTS

Look at § 102. It excludes gifts from the donee's income. A typical case is a cash gift from parent to child. The result of this statutory pattern is that the donor pays tax on income necessary to pay the gift, but there is only one tax on that income because the donee is not taxed. What is the rationale for that pattern?

A gift is not periodic income, derived from labor or capital. After *Glenshaw Glass*, however, that should not matter.

Is there another reason for excluding gifts from the donee's income? Should there be two taxes, one on the donor and another on the donee? Are there two items of income when cash flows from person to person? Sometimes there are, as when income is used by a homeowner to pay someone to paint the house — in that case, both owner and painter have income. But are there two items of income in the gift case? Isn't the donee (who gets cash) the real recipient of income, rather than the donor (who just has the satisfaction of giving)? This suggests that a gift might produce only one item of income, but why is the *donor* taxed but the donee exempt?

Suppose the donor is a wealthy head of a family. What is the proper tax rate on income shifted around within the family by gift? If you think the donor's rate is the proper rate, you have provided an explanation for the existing pattern of taxing gifts — one tax on the donor, not the donee. In effect, the gift exclusion treats the don*or* and donee as part of a taxable unit *to the extent of the gift property.* What other examples of treating the family as a taxable unit have you encountered?

Another reason for the gift exclusion is that support payments are not taxed and it is often hard to distinguish gift and support.

§ 4.02 DEFINITION OF GIFT

[A] Detached and Disinterested

Commissioner v. Duberstein, 363 U.S. 278 (1960), established the test for defining nontaxable gifts. In this case, a business associate had given the taxpayer a luxury automobile as thanks for client references. The Court stated that "the mere absence of a legal or moral obligation . . . does not establish that . . . [a voluntarily executed transfer of property, without any consideration or compensation therefor] is a gift." If "the payment proceeds primarily from 'the constraining force of any moral or legal duty,' or from 'the incentive of anticipated benefit' of an economic nature, it is not a gift." Duberstein established the test of an excludable gift as a transfer that proceeds from a "detached and disinterested generosity," "out of affection, respect, admiration, charity, or like impulses."

[1]   Strike Benefits

One setting that gives courts difficulty involves strike benefits paid by a union. On the same day that the opinion in *Duberstein* was handed down, the Court issued its opinion in *United States v. Kaiser*, 363 U.S. 299 (1960), involving strike benefits. But the Court provided little guidance. The jury had concluded that the benefits were gifts, but the District Court concluded that the benefits paid were not gifts as a matter of law. *Kaiser v. United States*, 158 F. Supp. 865 (E.D. Wis. 1958). The Court of Appeals reversed. *Kaiser v. United States*, 262 F.2d 367 (7th Cir. 1958). The Supreme Court affirmed the judgment of the Court of Appeals for the Seventh Circuit, concluding that there was evidence upon which the jury could have reasonably concluded that the benefits were gifts.

In *Osborne v. Commissioner*, 69 T.C.M. (CCH) 1895 (1995), a union, the Air Line Pilots Association International (ALPA), paid strike benefits of $2,400 per month. These payments were financed by assessments against the employees that were deductible in computing the employee's income.

The court listed six relevant factors in deciding whether the benefits were nontaxable gifts: (1) whether the union was under a moral or legal obligation to make the payments; (2) whether the payments were made upon a consideration of the recipient's financial status and need; (3) whether the benefits continued during the strike regardless of whether the recipient worked elsewhere; (4) whether the recipient was a member of the striking union; (5) whether the payments required the recipient to perform any strike duties such as picketing, and if not, whether or to what extent the recipient was under a moral obligation to participate in such strike activities; and (6) whether any restrictions were placed on the use of the payments, particularly in regard to whether the benefits were restricted to payment of basic necessities such as food and shelter or whether the recipient had unfettered control over use of the funds.

The court concluded that the amounts paid to the striking pilots were not gifts within the meaning of § 102(a), emphasizing: (1) that there was a moral if not legal obligation to pay strikers; (2) that the payments were not limited to basic necessities; and (3) that pilots could not receive benefits unless they were available for and performing any strike activities the union required.

[2]   Tips

One setting that provides little conceptual difficulty but a lot of administrative problems is tips. Tips are clearly income but recipients did not report them accurately. Current law authorizes a procedure by which the employer will withhold an amount from cash wages to cover at least some of the income taxes due from tips as well as cash wages. § 3402(k).

When someone wins at a gambling table, it is customary to give a tip in the form of a "toke." These are considered income; *Olk v. United States*, 536 F.2d 876 (9th Cir.

1976).

[B]   Preventing Double Tax Benefit

The government worries a lot about a double tax benefit in the form of excluded gifts being deducted by the payor. *Duberstein* had involved a gift in a business context. **Section 274(b)(1)** attempts to prevent the double benefit by disallowing the *payor's* deduction *if* the payee relies on the gift exclusion to exclude the payment. This is supposed to have the added effect of creating a conflict between payor and payee, because the facts providing a gift exclusion would cost the payor a deduction, and the facts providing the payor a deduction would cost the payee the exclusion by undermining a claim of detached and disinterested generosity. That would not happen, however, in the *Osborne* case because unions are tax exempt organizations and do not care whether a deduction is disallowed if the payments are excludable gifts.

§ 4.03   APPRECIATED PROPERTY

[A]   Gain Property

TAFT v. BOWERS
United States Supreme Court
278 U.S. 470 (1929)

Mr. Justice McReynolds delivered the opinion of the Court. . . .

During the calendar years 1921 and 1922, the father of petitioner, Elizabeth C. Taft, gave her certain shares of Nash Motors Company stock, then more valuable than when acquired by him. She sold them during 1923 for more than their market value when the gift was made.

The United States demanded an income tax reckoned upon the difference between cost to the donor and price received by the donee. She paid accordingly and sued to recover the portion imposed because of the advance in value while the donor owned the stock. The right to tax the increase in value after the gift is not denied.

Abstractly stated, this is the problem:

In 1916, A purchased 100 shares of stock for $1,000, which he held until 1923 when their fair market value had become $2,000. He then gave them to B who sold them during the year 1923 for $5,000. The United States claim that under the Revenue Act of 1921, B must pay income tax upon $4,000, as realized profits. B maintains that only $3,000 — the appreciation during her ownership — can be regarded as income; that the increase during the donor's ownership is not income assessable against her within intendment of the Sixteenth Amendment. . . .

The only question subject to serious controversy is whether Congress had power to authorize the exaction.

It is said that the gift became a capital asset of the donee to the extent of its value when received and, therefore, when disposed of by her no part of that value could be treated as taxable income in her hands. . . .

If, instead of giving the stock to petitioner, the donor had sold it at market value, the excess over the capital he invested (cost) would have been income therefrom and subject to taxation under the Sixteenth Amendment. He would have been obliged to share the realized gain with the United States. He held the stock — the investment — subject to the right of the sovereign to take part of any increase in its value when separated through sale or conversion and reduced to his possession. Could he, contrary to the express will of Congress, by mere gift enable another to hold this stock free from such right, deprive the sovereign of the possibility of taxing the appreciation when actually severed, and convert the entire property into a capital asset of the donee, who invested nothing, as though the latter had purchased at the market price? And after a still further enhancement of the property, could the donee make a second gift with like effect, etc.? We think not.

In truth, the stock represented only a single investment of capital-that made by the donor. And when through sale or conversion the increase was separated therefrom, it became income from that investment in the hands of the recipient subject to taxation according to the very words of the Sixteenth Amendment. By requiring the recipient of the entire increase to pay a part into the public treasury, Congress deprived her of no right and subjected her to no hardship. She accepted the gift with knowledge of the statute and, as to the property received, voluntarily assumed the position of her donor. When she sold the stock she actually got the original sum invested, plus the entire appreciation and out of the latter only was she called on to pay the tax demanded.

The provision of the statute under consideration seems entirely appropriate for enforcing a general scheme of lawful taxation. To accept the view urged in behalf of petitioner undoubtedly would defeat, to some extent, the purpose of Congress to take part of all gain derived from capital investments. To prevent that result and insure enforcement of its proper policy, Congress had power to require that for purposes of taxation the donee should accept the position of the donor in respect of the thing received. And in so doing, it acted neither unreasonably nor arbitrarily. . . .

There is nothing in the Constitution which lends support to the theory that gain actually resulting from the increased value of capital can be treated as taxable income in the hands of the recipient only so far as the increase occurred while he owned the property.

The judgment below is affirmed.

COMMENT

In other words, the donee does not realize income at the time of the gift, but the donee is taxed on the property's appreciated gain if and when she realizes it. This is accomplished by transferring the donor's basis to the donee. §§ 1015(a), 7701(a)(42)(A), (43).

[B] Loss Property

[1] Sale of Loss Property Received as Gift

Suppose the taxpayer has a loss in property and wants to shift the loss to someone in the family who can take better advantage of the deduction. Suppose, further, that Congress wants to prevent that loss from being shifted around in this manner. What solution would you adopt to prevent this type of tax avoidance?

You can see how Congress has addressed this by working out the following problem. Suppose property with a basis of $1,000 was worth $700 when given by a parent to a child-donee. The donee then sells the property for: (a) $600; (b) $800; or (c) $1,100. How much recognized gain or loss does the donee have? Be sure to read the portion of **§ 1015(a)** beginning with "except that."

[2] Note on Statutory Drafting

You will undoubtedly find **§ 1015(a)** hard to read. It is a good example of jigsaw puzzle complexity; the answer is there, but it is hard to find. This subsection uses an older form of statutory drafting — the run-on sentence. More recent statutes divide sections into subsections, paragraphs, subparagraphs, clauses, subclauses, etc. These divisions often look bewildering but are (in my judgment) a clearer way to draft than the run-on sentence. You might try your hand at rewriting **§ 1015(a)** to deal with the problem of a donor giving loss property to a donee so it is easier to understand.

Is the following redraft of the first sentence of **§ 1015(a)** easier to understand?

(a) *Gifts after December 31, 1920*

(i) Except as provided in paragraph (ii), if the property was acquired by gift after December 31, 1920, the basis shall be the same as it would be in the hands of the donor or the last preceding owner by whom it was not acquired by gift.

(ii) If the basis provided by paragraph (i) is greater than the fair market value of the property at the time of the gift, then —

(A) solely for the purpose of determining whether the acquirer has a loss,

(B) the basis shall be such fair market value.

[3] Sale of Loss Property to Family Member

Suppose the parent decides to sell the property to the child instead of giving it away, because the parent can put the deduction to better use than the child. Assume the basis is $1,000, and that the value and sales price are $700. The parent-taxpayer wants to recognize the $300 loss. Can she accomplish this by selling to her son, or only by selling to an "outsider"? How is the child taxed if he later sells the property for $600, $800, or $1,100? *See* **§ 267(a)(1), (d)**.

§ 4.04   DEATH

[A]   Date-of-death Value as Basis

Suppose a parent owns property worth $2,000, with a $1,000 basis. That person dies. The child inherits the property and sells it for $5,000. How is the child taxed? **Section 1014(a)** gives the child a date-of-death-value basis in the property (or, the value six months after death, if that value has instead been elected for estate tax purposes). This is usually called a stepped-up basis rule, because property is expected to appreciate. But the date-of-death-value rule applies whether or not the property has gone up or down in value.

What is the reason for the date-of-death-value rule? It does not merely defer gain, but exempts it altogether. If it is meant to compensate for estate tax, why not reduce the income tax by a credit for estate taxes attributable to the gain on the property? A credit for estate taxes against the income tax would, of course, not help taxpayers who do not owe estate tax and, perhaps, that is one reason why the credit mechanism has not been used.

Is it administratively difficult for people to keep track of historical basis? In 1976, the date-of-death-value basis rule was replaced by a transferred basis approach (like an inter vivos gift), but complaints about alleged administrative problems in identifying historical basis, especially for farmers and small businesses, prompted a return to the date-of-death-value basis in 1980, even for taxpayers with assets whose historical basis is less difficult to determine (e.g., publicly traded stock).

[B]   Diverging from Value Used for Estate Tax

Even though the date-of-death-value rule is usually tied to the estate tax value (*see* **Treas. Reg. § 1.1014-3(a)**), that is not necessarily the case. In TAM (Taxpayer Advice Memorandum) 199933001, the taxpayer had inherited a 1/6th interest in the stock of a family corporation in 1988. In 1995, this stock was purchased by the corporation and the taxpayer argued that the basis of the stock was equal to the sales price, producing no gain. The basis claimed by the taxpayer on the sale was higher than the value of the stock previously agreed upon for estate tax valuation purposes.

The TAM first cites the Treasury Regulation but then cites Rev. Rul. 54-97, 1954-1 C.B. 113, which provides that such value is only presumptive and that it may be rebutted by clear and convincing evidence, except where the taxpayer is estopped by his previous actions or statements. Estoppel usually applies when the taxpayer or the taxpayer's relative was the executor of the estate.

The TAM holds for the taxpayer, noting that he was not a personal representative of the estate and was not involved in preparing the estate tax return or in resolving the subsequent audit, and that there was no evidence that the taxpayer was consulted or provided assistance in settling the estate other than informal conversations with one or more of the other beneficiaries or personal representatives.

In *Janis v. Commissioner*, 469 F.3d 256 (2d Cir. 2006), the taxpayers sold assets inherited from a decedent, for whose estate the taxpayers had been co-executors. The taxpayers were not permitted to use a basis different from the low value that they had established for computing the taxable estate.

[C] Income in Respect of a Decedent

There is one important exception to the date-of-death-value basis rule. An item of "income in respect of a decedent" is inherited with a transferred basis from the decedent, just like a gift. §§ 691, 1014(c). Income in respect of a decedent is not defined in the statute, but the idea is very straightforward. Any income that could not be assigned for tax purposes to the donee is income in respect of a decedent.

For example, if a taxpayer dies having earned but not collected $20,000 salary, the $20,000 is fully taxed when collected (assuming, as would normally be the case, that a claim to personal service income has a zero basis). The value of the claim to $20,000 may be only $15,000 at date of death (due to the time value of money or a financially shaky debtor), but that is irrelevant for income tax purposes. The taxpayer could not have deflected taxation of that income to a donee by a lifetime gift, and it is therefore income in respect of a decedent, which does not enjoy a date-of-death-value basis.

[D] 2001, 2010, and ATRA

The 2001 Tax Bill phased in a reduction and, eventually (in 2010), the repeal of the estate tax. Before tax year 2010, basis of property inherited from a decedent continued to be the date-of-death value, because there was still the potential for an estate tax, despite the large exemptions. Upon the repeal of the estate tax in 2010, however, the basis of property held by the decedent at death was the lower of its fair market value at death or the decedent's basis (in other words, the inter vivos gift rule), with some complicated exceptions.

The 2010 Tax Relief Act did not extend the 2010 abolition of the estate tax but still modified the rules in a way favorable to taxpayers through 2012. The exemption was $5 million (indexed for inflation after 2011). ATRA continues the $5 million exemption, adjusted for inflation — it is $5.25 million for 2013. But it increases the maximum estate tax rate to 40%. Because there remains a potential estate tax, the date-of-death-value-as-basis rules still apply.

[E] Gift Tax

The gift tax is integrated with the estate tax, so that a lifetime gift is eligible for and uses up the $5 million (inflation-adjusted) amount.

The gift tax *exemption* should not be confused with the annual per donee gift tax *exclusion* — which is $14,000 in 2013 (adjusted for inflation). This exclusion applies to cash gifts of a present interest (not gifts in trust). Thus, a cash gift of $15,000 uses up the $14,000 exclusion, leaving $1,000 to be debited against the $5 million (inflation-adjusted) exemption. (The donor must file a return to claim an exemption, but not the exclusion.) The exclusion applies to each donor and donee, so that a husband and wife can give a total of $56,000 cash each year to their two children.

If a gift is subject to a gift tax, its basis is increased by the gift tax attributable to the appreciated gain on the gift. § 1015(d).

§ 4.05 CARVED OUT INCOME INTEREST

[A] Gift of Carved Out Income Interest, Remainder to Another

IRWIN v. GAVIT

United States Supreme Court

268 U.S. 161 (1925)

Mr. Justice Holmes delivered the opinion of the Court. . . .

[Editor — The facts of this case can be simplified as follows. A transferor sets up a trust under his will with a gift of income to one relative and remainder to another. Under state property law, the owner of the income interest had no property interest in the trust corpus, only the income.

Section 102(b)(2) now provides the same result as the following decision. The income is taxed to the income beneficiary, notwithstanding the exclusion of gifts, and § 273 prevents the owner of an income interest received by gift from taking depreciation deductions to offset income derived from the income interest. However, the case is still of interest for two reasons: (1) as a statement about statutory interpretation; and (2) as an effort to deal with the problem of carved out income interests, to which we return in Chapter 22.]

The statute in Section 2, A, subdivision 1, provides that there shall be levied a tax 'upon the entire net income arising or accruing from all sources in the preceding calendar year to every citizen of the United States.' If these payments properly may be called income by the common understanding of that word and the statute has failed to hit them it has missed so much of the general purpose that it expresses at the start. Congress intended to use its power to the full extent. By B, the net income is to include 'gains or profits and income derived from any source whatever, including the income from but not the value of property acquired by gift, bequest, devise, or descent.' By D, trustees are to make 'return of the net income of the person for whom they act, subject to this tax,' and by D trustees and others, having the control or payment of fixed or determinable gains, etc., of another person who are required to render a return on behalf of another are 'authorized to withhold enough to pay the normal tax.' The language quoted leaves no doubt in our minds that if a fund were given to trustees for A for life with remainder over, the income received by the trustees and paid over to A would be income of A under the statute. It seems to us hardly less clear that even if there were a specific provision that A should have no interest in the corpus, the payments would be income none the less, within the meaning of the statute and the Constitution, and by popular speech. In the first case, it is true that the bequest might be said to be of the corpus for life, in the second it might be said to be of the income. But we think that the provision of the act that exempts bequests assumes the gift of a corpus and contrasts it with the income arising from it, but was not intended to exempt income property so called simply because of a severance between it and the principal fund. . . . The money was income in the hands of the trustees and we know of nothing in the law that prevented its being paid and received as income by the donee.

The courts below went on the ground that the gift to the plaintiff was a bequest and carried no interest in the corpus of the fund. We do not regard those considerations as conclusive. . . . This is a gift from the income of a very large fund, as income. . . . We are of opinion that quarterly payments, which it was hoped would last for fifteen years, from the income of an estate intended for the plaintiff's child, must be regarded as income within the meaning of the Constitution and the law. It is said that the tax laws should be construed favorably for the taxpayers. But that is not a reason for creating a doubt or for exaggerating one when it is no greater than we can bring ourselves to feel in this case.

Judgment reversed.

Mr. Justice Sutherland, dissenting.

By the plain terms of the Revenue Act of 1913, the value of property acquired by gift, bequest, devise, or descent is not to be included in net income. Only the income derived from such property is subject to the tax. The question, as it seems to me, is really a very simple one. Money, of course, is property. The money here sought to be taxed as income was paid to respondent under the express provisions of a will. It was a gift by will — a bequest. It, therefore, fell within the precise letter of the statute; and, under well-settled principles, judicial inquiry may go no further. The taxpayer is entitled to the rigor of the law. There is no latitude in a taxing statute; you must adhere to the very words.

The property which respondent acquired being a bequest, there is no occasion to ask whether, before being handed over to him, it had been carved from the original corpus of, or from subsequent additions to, the estate. The corpus of the estate was not the legacy which respondent received, but merely the source which gave rise to it. The money here sought to be taxed was not the fruits of a legacy; it was the legacy itself.

With the utmost respect for the judgment of my brethren to the contrary, the opinion just rendered, I think without warrant, searches the field of argument and inference for a meaning which should be found only in the strict letter of the statute.

[B]   Carved Out Income Interest; Economic Reality

What is the economic reality of the gift in *Irwin v. Gavit*, where an income interest and remainder are owned by different people? Assume that the total value of the property left to both the income and remainder interests was $100. This is true if interest rates are 20% and the income from the property is $20 per year. At the testator's death, basis equals value. Using the 20% interest and $20 per year income assumptions, the income interest is worth (approximately) 60% of the total value of the property and the remainder is worth 40%. That means that the income interest has a basis equal to date-of-death value of $60; and the remainder interest's basis is $40.

Do not be troubled by the fact that the property is divided into parts over time. Temporal divisions are as possible as physical divisions. If the inherited property consisted of 10 acres, six acres might have a $60 basis and four acres a $40 basis. In the example we consider, the division is temporal rather than physical. The following depicts the temporal division.

ANNUAL INCOME = $20; TOTAL BASIS = $100

Five Year, carved out income interest; Basis = $60	Remainder income interest; Basis = $40	————→

It would appear that, absent a special statutory rule, the owner of the income interest could take depreciation deductions. Recall the earlier example of a depreciable asset with a $60 cost and a five-year life. Straight line depreciation permitted a $12 per year deduction. If the gross income paid to the trust income beneficiary is $20, the annual taxable income would be $8 ($20 minus $12 depreciation); $40 over five years. That seems to be an analytically airtight argument, but it poses a dilemma. If the property had not been given away, there would be $20 income each year; $100 over five years. Where is the other $60 of income over five years?

The answer is this. Look closely at the remainder's interest, worth $40 at the time of death. How much is the remainder's interest worth after five years, when the income interest has expired? Assuming no change in the underlying value of the property (for example, it is land in a stable neighborhood without zoning changes and interest rates do not change), it should be worth $100. You just found the other $60. The $60 accrues gradually over the five-year period as time passes and the remainder's interest gets closer to vesting in possession.

Why not just tax the owner of the remainder interest each year on the appreciation of the $40 investment? After five years, the owner of the *income* interest will have paid tax on $8 per year ($20 minus $12), or a total of $40; and the owner of the *remainder* interest will pay tax on the other $60. Do you think the owner of the remainder interest will ever report that income? The government usually keeps track of periodic income in the nature of interest by examining information returns filed by debtors, such as banks. The interest-like accession to the remainder's $40 investment will not, however, be reported by any independent party. Indeed, it is not technically similar to interest, because we cannot be sure that the property will be worth $100 after five years have passed.

If the owner of the remainder interest will not report this income, what is the easiest way to make sure that the full $20 is taxed each year; ($100 over five years)? Just tax the owner of the income interest on $20 per year. And that is exactly what the statute now does by taxing the owner of the income interest on all of the gross income ($20) and denying depreciation when the income interest is received by gift (§ 273). And that is exactly what the *Irwin* case did by case law, simply disregarding any possibility of a depreciation deduction.

QUESTION

What is the remainder interest's basis after five years have passed and he obtains possession of the land?

[C]   Note on Statutory Interpretation

[1]   Whole Text

Justices Holmes and Sutherland disagree about statutory interpretation. Both rely on the text, or at least say they do. Holmes refers to "common understanding" of "income." Sutherland appeals to "plain terms." What does each judge consider to determine the text's meaning?

Holmes looks at the whole text — both the provisions exempting gifts and taxing income — and concludes that the statutory structure dealing with gifts excludes from gross income only the income-producing property, not the income that this property produces (such as interest or dividends). Sutherland insists on reading the exemption for "property" in isolation from the rest of the statute. This is a form of textualism that is often described (pejoratively) as literalism — because it purports to rely on the text but does so in a literalist way that does not take account of how people write and read language. The whole text approach is more faithful to how authors and audiences understand statutory language.

[2]   Substantive Canons of Interpretation

Another interpretive issue in *Irwin v. Gavit* is the relevance of a presumption in favor of taxpayers, which Holmes describes this way: "It is said that the tax laws should be construed favorably for the taxpayers." Sutherland describes the presumption as follows: "The taxpayer is entitled to the rigor of the law. There is no latitude in a taxing statute; you must adhere to the very words."

This is an example of a substantive canon of construction that tilts interpretation in a particular direction. If you have studied criminal law, you probably encountered the rule of lenity, which is another substantive canon of interpretation.

One of the puzzles about substantive canons of interpretation is how much they affect interpretation. One use — the least aggressive — is as a tie-breaker. That is, the interpreter first relies on everything that is legitimate to interpret legislation and, if the answer is still unclear, the answer tilts in favor of the presumption embodied in the canon. That seems to be what Holmes means when he refuses to apply the presumption, stating: "But [the rule favoring taxpayers] is not a reason for creating a doubt or for exaggerating one when it is no greater than we can bring ourselves to feel in this case." Holmes, relying on the whole text, found no uncertainty to be resolved by the canon.

Other canons are applied as strong presumptions, requiring a clear statement in the statutory text to reach the specific result overriding the values embodied in the canon. If that approach applied to the statutory text dealing with the gift of an income interest, the interpreter might insist on something like the current § 102(b)(2) before taxing the income given to the donee. A strong presumption usually cannot be rebutted by legislative history, only by the statutory text. Perhaps Sutherland was being literal in order to implement a strong presumption when he said that "[t]he taxpayer is entitled to the rigor of the law."

Many canons are applied as in-between presumptions that play some unclear role in the interpretive mix of text, statutory structure, purpose, legislative history, and administrative rulings.

The canon favoring taxpayers, like many canons, has probably undergone change over time. As hostility to taxation has diminished with the rise of the modern welfare state, the canon has probably shifted to a weak presumption, although it is hard to be sure how state courts apply the canon to state tax laws.

For some reason, the canon favoring taxpayers is often applied only when the issue is defining gross income, but a canon *against* the taxpayer is applied when the issue is whether or not the taxpayer is entitled to a deduction. In this connection, courts sometimes say that deductions are a "matter of grace." When you study deductions in greater detail later on in this course, see whether that statement makes any sense.

Two Supreme Court Justices recently revisited the pro-taxpayer presumption, commenting both on its weight and the circumstances in which it applied. In *United Dominion Industries, Inc. v. United States,*, 532 U.S. 822 (2001), Justice Thomas (concurring) was willing to resolve an ambiguity in favor of a taxpayer when an income tax provision provided an exception from a general revenue duty for the benefit of some taxpayers." Justice Stevens' dissent argued that the tradition of construing the tax law in favor of the taxpayer only applied to an ambiguous provision *imposing* tax liability, not to a provision providing an exception to tax liability.

[D] Gift of Carved Out Income Interest, with Retained Remainder

[1] The *Horst* Decision

In *Helvering v. Horst*, 311 U.S. 112 (1940), the taxpayer separated the income and remainder interests and gave away the carved out income interest (as in *Irwin v. Gavit*), but retained the remainder interest. The asset was a bond with interest coupons and the taxpayer gave away the following year's interest by detaching the coupons and delivering them as a gift to his son. The Court held that the interest income received by the son was taxable at the time of the receipt to the father who had made the gift. The Court based its decision on some very questionable reasoning, stating:

> The power to dispose of income is the equivalent of ownership of it. The exercise of that power to procure the payment of income to another is the enjoyment and hence the realization of the income by him who exercises it. We have had no difficulty in applying that proposition where the assignment preceded the rendition of the services, Lucas v. Earl . . . . But it is the assignment by which the disposition of income is controlled when the service precedes the assignment and in both cases it is the exercise of the

power of disposition of the interest or compensation with the resulting payment to the donee which is the enjoyment by the donor of income derived from them. . . .

When, by the gift of the coupons, he has separated his right to interest payments from his investment and procured the payment of the interest to his donee, he has enjoyed the economic benefits of the income in the same manner and to the same extent as though the transfer were of earnings and in both cases the import of the statute is that the fruit is not to be attributed to a different tree from that on which it grew.

[2] *Horst v. Blair*

The *Horst* opinion keeps repeating that the exercise of control by gift is the "realization" of income, but that (of course) is not true. A donor is not taxed on the appreciated value of property at the time of the gift or on the income received by the donee of the gift at a later time (*see Blair v. Commissioner*, Chapter 2.03[A]). *Blair* can be distinguished from *Horst* on its facts, on the ground that the tree was given away, not just some of the fruit. Well, tax law is not botany. The question is why the gift of a carved out income interest cannot deflect income to a donee, but gift of the entire property can. Nothing in *Horst* really addresses that question, although the general principle adopted by the case is still good law — donors cannot deflect income from themselves by giving less than the entire time period that they own.

Horst does make sense if you think shifting income around within the family to lower total taxes is improper tax avoidance. But, again, why is that any worse when a carved out income interest is assigned than when the entire property is transferred?

Maybe this is why the gift of a carved out income interest is worse. *Some* of the income from the bond in *Horst* should be taxed to the transferor. Remember our discussion of the carved out income interest and remainder interest in connection with the *Irwin v. Gavit* case. Considering economic reality, *some* of the annual income really does accrue to the remainder interest after an income interest has been carved out. Horst, the transferor, retained the remainder interest, so some of the income from the bond accrues to him and it would be fair to tax him on that limited amount. But not all of the annual income accrues to the transferor with a retained remainder interest. We are still looking for a theory justifying taxation of the transferor on *all* of the annual interest income, when a carved out income interest is given away and a remainder interest retained.

Perhaps the easiest solution is to tax only one person on the income accruing to both the income and remainder interests. That avoids the administrative problems of trying to tax both the owner of the income and remainder interests. Given the fact that the donor is the owner of the remainder interest and the donee is likely to be a family member, the easiest thing to do is to tax the donor on the entire amount of the assigned income.

[3] Property vs. Personal Services

The sharp distinction between gifts of property (effective-for-tax-purposes) and assignments of personal service income (ineffective-for-tax-purposes) can produce some strange results. If the author who owns a copyright on property created by her services transfers the copyright to a relative, the relative is taxed on the income. A copyright is "property." *Meisner v. United States*, 133 F.3d 654 (8th Cir. 1998) (40% interest in copyright royalties assigned); Rev. Rul. 54-599, 1954-2 C.B. 52 (taxpayer can assign copyright interest in a specific medium, such as television); Rev. Rul. 71-33, 1971-1 C.B. 30 (assignment of manuscript of memoirs transfers income to assignee). Is this a case of property law concepts being incorporated unthinkingly into tax law, in the same way that corporate law concepts helped to decide *Eisner v. Macomber* (shareholders do not have income on undistributed corporate profits)?

Suppose an insurance salesman has a right to "renewal commissions," if people to whom he has sold insurance policies renew the policy, even without any further work by the salesman. Long before the renewals occur, the salesman assigns the future renewal commissions to his child. *Helvering v. Eubank*, 311 U.S. 122 (1940), taxed the salesman on the renewal commissions when they were later paid to the child. Does this decision make sense? First, this case differs from *Lucas v. Earl* because the assignment occurs *after* the services have been completed; the taxpayer retains no control over generating the personal service income. Second, the income from the renewal commissions does not seem to be accrued or to have "ripened" at the time of the transfer. The income assigned appears to be risky future income. Third, if the taxpayer in *Eubank* cannot transfer income to the donee, why can the copyright owner transfer income to the donee? In both instances, personal services generated *some* value but future income was speculative.

Compare the following two situations to *Eubank*. First, suppose an employee receives land from his employer as compensation and then gives the land away to his child. The rent on the land would be taxed to the child. Second, if the taxpayer in *Eubank* sold the right to the renewal commissions for its fair market value to his child, future income collected by the purchaser-child would be taxable to the purchaser. Does the result in these two situations shed any light on why Eubank might *not* be able to transfer income to the donee?

[4] Interest Free Loans

Suppose a taxpayer lends $200,000 to a child for one year without charging interest. This seems like a good way to avoid *Horst*. The child simply buys a $200,000 bond, collects the interest, and (after one year) sells the bond and returns the $200,000 to the lender. This seemed to work, as far as case law was concerned, to shift the interest income to the child. So the code was amended in § 7872(a) to impute taxable interest to the lender on the interest-free "gift" loan, by *pretending* that the borrower paid interest to the lender and the lender made a gift of the interest to the borrower — at a specified "federal rate." This produces a result similar to *Horst*, in the above example, assuming that the imputed federal interest rate approximates the rate earned by the donee on the bond and that the borrower can deduct the presumed-interest payment to the creditor. The result is not necessarily the same, however, because interest can sometimes be imputed from the debtor-child to the lender under § 7872, whether or not the borrower-child has any investment income. Moreover, the borrower might not be able to deduct the imputed interest — as explained in Chapter 16, dealing with the interest deduction.

Like so many tax statutes, this one has qualifications. First, if the gift loans between creditor and debtor do not aggregate to more than $100,000, the imputed interest cannot exceed the borrower's *actual* investment income. This helps a parent who lends a child money for education. Second, no interest is imputed if gift loans between individuals do not exceed $10,000. **§ 7872(c)(2), (d)(1).**

§ 4.06 SPLIT UNITS

[A] Splitting Income?

When a couple is married, there is only one item of income enjoyed by the marital unit, taxable under § 1(**a**). Suppose a marital unit has split (divorced or separated) and one member of the former marital unit pays money to the other. Should there still be one item of income and, if so, whose income is it?

It certainly makes sense to say that there is only one item of income. Someone who pays alimony, for example, is not likely to think of this amount as an accession to his or her wealth, but the recipient will view the amount received as an accession to her or his wealth.

The fact that there is only one item of income does not tell you whose tax rate should apply. After all, cash gifts are (in effect) taxed only once, but at the payor's tax rate. The taxation of gifts, however, is best explained on the theory that the payor's tax rate is the proper tax rate, to prevent shifting income around within a family. When a marital unit splits, the income should be taxed at the payee's rate.

The fact that the payment discharges a payor's obligation should not matter. It is true that taxpayers cannot usually deduct payments to creditors when the debt has a personal origin (a point we discuss in detail in Chapter 8.02). But payment by one former member of a split family unit to another former member is a special type of personal obligation. The property used to discharge that obligation can be thought of as flowing through the payor to the payee so as to enhance the payee's wealth, while reducing the payor's wealth.

[B] Old Case Law

[1] Alimony

Prior to the statutory law dealing explicitly with alimony, alimony was not deductible by the payor but was not taxed to the payee. *Gould v. Gould*, 245 U.S. 151 (1917). The *Gould* decision made sense because only one person should be taxed on alimony and there was no statutory basis for giving the payor a deduction. But the exclusion from § 61 income should strike you as strange, given the *Glenshaw Glass* "accession to wealth" approach to defining income. Perhaps the best explanation for the *Gould* decision, apart from the result-oriented one-tax conclusion, is that alimony did not fit the *Eisner v. Macomber* conception of income as a return to labor or capital. After all, the *Gould* case was decided well before the *Glenshaw Glass* decision in 1955.

[2] Property Transfers

Property transfers were dealt with in the case law in the context of pre-nuptial agreements. Case law reached the following result in a situation where the taxpayer transferred appreciated property in exchange for a release from the prospective spouse of any claims in the transferor's property. The transaction was treated as a realizable taxable event by the transferring property owner. *United States v. Davis*, 370 U.S. 65 (1962). Thus, assuming the property had a basis of $20 and a value of $100, the transferor recognized $80 gain.

This raised the question of how the transferee was treated. A Revenue Ruling concluded that there was no gain to the transferee as a result of relinquishing claims on the transferor's property. Rev. Rul. 67-221, 1967-2 C.B. 63. Moreover, the transferee's basis in the property was its fair market value. The conclusion about basis appears in *Farid-Es-Sultaneh v. Commissioner*, 160 F.2d 812 (2d Cir. 1947). In *Farid-Es-Sultaneh*, a prospective spouse received property from her future husband as protection for her welfare in case her future husband died before the marriage, in exchange for her release of dower and other marital rights (as set forth in a pre-nuptial agreement). Consequently (using the numbers in the prior example), the transferee acquired the property with a $100 basis and without recognizing gain.

The overall impact of these decisions was one tax on the gain, falling on the transferor. But the *Davis/Farid*/Rev. Rul. results raise these questions. First, why isn't the transferee in *Farid* taxed on the value of the property received, given the fact that the transaction is likened to an exchange of her dower and other marital rights for valuable property from her prospective husband? Second, if there is going to be only one tax on the gain inherent in the transferred property, why did the tax fall on the transferor rather than on the transferee? Third, what do these results say about the lawmaking process? One tax on the gain seems like the right result, but the analysis seems awkward, just as in the alimony situation.

[C] Statutory Rules

The code was amended in 1942, changing the results under the case law results. In general, the payor can deduct and the payee must include alimony in most situations when the marital unit is split, overriding *Gould v. Gould*. The statutory provisions are found in §§ 71(a), (b), 215(a), (b).

The payor deduction and payee inclusion approach under the current statute does not apply, however, if the payment obligation survives the payee's death. § 71(b)(1)(D). In practice, this means that payments made pursuant to many state laws that treat payments incident to a divorce as marital property splits (rather than alimony support payments) will not be subject to the deduction-inclusion approach, because the property split obligation usually survives the payee's death.

Like so many ideas in tax law, it is easier to state the general principle, but harder to decide when the principle should apply. Here are some of the complexities.

First, when is the unit split resulting in payor-deduction and payee-inclusion? Payments must be made under a "divorce or separation instrument," defined in § 71(b)(1)(A), (2). However, the unit is not split if the couple is legally separated under a decree of divorce or separate maintenance, and they are support or maintenance decrees and they are members of the same household. *See* § 71(b)(1)(c). This prevents a couple from divorcing, filing tax returns as single individuals under § 1(c), and avoiding any tax on marriage by splitting their income.

Second, only cash payments are subject to the rules shifting income from a payor to payee. § 71(b)(1).

Third, the shifting of taxable income from the payor to the payee is *elective*. § 71(b)(1)(B). If the payee is in a higher tax bracket than the payor, the parties can elect to have the payee exclude the payment from income and the payor is denied a deduction. One tax is imposed on the total income, but the parties can choose the lower of the two individual's tax rates and bargain over how to split the benefit of the lower tax rate. For example, assume the payor is in 25% bracket and the payee is in the 35% bracket. Because the payee is in the higher bracket, the parties will elect payor-nondeductibility and payor-noninclusion. They will bargain over who gets the 10% saved by using the lower 25% tax rate.

Fourth, property transferred between: (1) spouses; or (2) former spouses, if incident to a divorce, is treated like a gift, with the following exception. § 1041. The exception to "gift" treatment is that "loss property" (property worth less than basis at the time of gift) has a transferred basis for both gain *and* loss computations. There is no reduction in basis for computing loss, as there was under § 1015(a). Presumably, there is no tax avoidance potential from shifting losses around between members of a split family unit. However, this statutory provision does not apply to pre-marriage transfers incident to a pre-nuptial agreement; in those situations, the old case law applies to tax the transferor rather than the transferee, with the transferee taking a basis equal to the fair market value of the transferred property.

Fifth, how can you distinguish between a lump sum transfer (which should not be deductible by the payor and not taxed to the payee) and periodic payments (which should be deductible by the payor and taxed to the payee)? If a taxpayer gives a former spouse $1 million cash in a lump sum and nothing thereafter, it would distort income to permit that $1 million to be shifted from the payor to the payee. It makes more sense to tax the payee only on the income derived from the $1 million, such as interest or dividends. Again, the idea is simple but taxpayer ingenuity reaches for tax advantages, requiring a complex statutory response.

Suppose the payor pays a large amount in both years 1 and 2, after the divorce, and declining amounts thereafter. When is "front-loading" more like a lump sum paid in the first year than like periodic payments spread over a long time? The statute's answer is in § 71(f) (too complicated to be reviewed here). Essentially, the cash payments are deducted by the payor and taxed to the payee when made, but front-loading results in the payor taking back the prior deductions into income and the payee deducting previously included income *in a later year*, when it turns out that future payments decline rapidly from a large initial payment. However, the payor and the payee do not have to reverse the prior tax treatment, if the decline in payments is due to the payee's death or remarriage, or to the payee's right to share in the payor's business income.

Sixth, payments to support children are not deductible. They would not have been deductible if the marriage survived and do not become deductible after a marital split. Frequently, divorce decrees specify that a sum shall be paid to a former spouse, to be reduced when the child reaches a certain age or marries. Is the amount slated for future reduction a nondeductible child support payment? Yes. *See* § 71(c)(2).

PROBLEM

Suppose a taxpayer in the 30% tax bracket wins the lottery in 1985, payable in future annual installments of $100,000. In 1990, the state court orders him to pay one-half of the $100,000 to his divorced former spouse. Must he pay tax on the one-half paid to the former wife? How much does the former wife get; $50,000 or $35,000?.

In *Smith v. IRS*, 1994 U.S. Dist. Lexis 13294 (S.D.N.Y. Sept. 19, 1994), the taxpayer argued in a tax case that the one-half paid to the former wife for the *prior* tax year 1987 should *not* have been his income, but the court disagreed. The government agreed that the 1990 court order shifted taxable income to the former wife for *future* tax years. But the government contended and the court agreed that the 1990 court order did not shift income for pre-1990 years to the wife for federal income tax purposes. The former wife did not own a one-half interest in the property prior to the court order. The payment of the taxpayer's property to the former wife did not shift income to the payee-spouse for tax purposes. The court concluded:

> Plaintiff [the former husband] will have suffered an inequity if, but only if, the state court's award to his ex-wife failed to recognize appropriately the plaintiff's after-tax resources. If this occurred, plaintiff's recourse would be to the state court, not the Internal Revenue Service.

In other words, it was up to the state court to decide whether the former wife got $50,000 or only $35,000, to reflect the $15,000 tax obligation owed by the taxpayer.

Chapter 5

TAXABLE YEAR

§ 5.01 INTRODUCTION

Another major structural provision in an income tax is the taxable period. Even if you know the taxable income and the taxable unit, you still must decide what taxable period to use to measure the unit's income. The government and the taxpayer must close their books periodically, at least provisionally. The usual tax period is one year. § 441. Does that mean that events occurring in one tax year have *no* impact on the tax treatment of events in another tax year? Do you ever break down the accounting year barrier?

For example, the use of any taxable period is arbitrary and can make two taxpayers with equal total income over a long period look unequal. The obvious case is that of a taxpayer with a business loss in one year (say, $10,000) and a greater gain in the next year (say, $15,000). Total income is $5,000, which is similar to a taxpayer with two $2,500 years. But the former taxpayer will have a total of $15,000 taxable income, if the accounting year barrier is not broken down to account for losses in another tax year.

The obvious solution is to adopt a taxable year provisionally, but make adjustments in later years, much like a wage earner treats tax withholding during a pay period as a tentative tax payment. This chapter is about such adjustments. Some of the rules are from case law, others are statutory.

An early Supreme Court case refused to adopt a case law adjustment to the accounting year principle. The taxpayer in *Burnet v. Sanford & Brooks Co.*, 282 U.S. 359 (1931), was performing a river dredging contract. Early years produced losses and the taxpayer argued against inclusion of later contract profits until they exceeded earlier losses. The later profits arose from proceeds of a breach of warranty lawsuit by the taxpayer-dredger against the other contracting party. The Court of Appeals agreed with the taxpayer, stating that "a return of losses suffered in earlier years" was not income. The Supreme Court disagreed on the ground that profit and loss are specific to particular accounting year periods. The Court said that prior losses were not capital investments, producing a cost that must be recovered before there is taxable gain. By implication, the Court refused to analogize prior business losses to costs.

The Court made some very broad and unobjectionable comments about the need for annual accounting to provide the government with taxes at regular intervals. It noted that taxpayers may have income in one year and losses in another, and that this pattern would not preclude taxing the income in profitable years. That broad statement clearly applies to the case of a profitable shoe business in one year and a losing shirt business in another year, but the Court also applied the principle to taxing profits and losses on a single (dredging) contract. The Court therefore failed to treat the profits and losses on a single contract any differently from profits and losses from separate businesses.

§ 5.02   NET OPERATING LOSSES

The statute now overrides the *Sanford* and *Brooks* decision and allows business losses ("net operating losses") to be carried over to other tax years. § **172**. This invites a distinction between business and other income-producing activities that are not businesses. The distinction can be murky. A business is an activity carried on with continuity and regularity, to produce a livelihood. Investors in the stock market are rarely in business, unless they are short-term "traders" (people who get most of their income from high-volume sales of stocks and bonds, not dividends and interest). Typical investors, even those who buy and sell short-term, are not "in business." *See Groetzinger v. Commissioner*, 771 F.2d 269 (7th Cir. 1985), *affirmed*, 480 U.S. 23 (1987).

The common situation to which § **172** applies is illustrated by the following example. Assume that a corporation in year 8 has $100,000 business gross income and $400,000 of related deductions, for a $300,000 net loss. Suppose it has taxable income in years 3, 7, and 12. There is no income or loss in other tax years. Can it ever deduct its $300,000 loss?

The statute allows net operating business losses to be carried back two years and forward 20 years. Taxpayers must first deduct the loss in the earliest carryback year and work forward, except that they can waive use of the carryback period and start with the first carryforward year. Quick refunds (without interest) are paid if a carryback offsets prior taxable income. §§ **6611(e)(1), (f)(1), 6411**

There is another operating loss carry*forward* provision, in § **186**. It applies to losses from breaches of contract (as in *Sanford* and *Brooks*), competitive torts, and breaches of fiduciary duty. There is no time limit on these carryforwards.

The mechanics of the net operating loss carryover rules reflect their origin in economic policy: encourage new businesses with initial losses; cushion the impact of a recession; encourage risk taking by equating taxable income over multi-tax-year periods. Some of these policies might argue for a refundable tax credit when there are business losses, without regard to whether a taxpayer has income in another tax year. One problem with being too generous to taxpayers with tax losses is that the losses do not always reflect real economic loss. Many provisions (discussed in Chapter 11 on depreciation deductions and Chapter 17 on loans, basis, and tax shelters) allow taxpayers to take deductions in excess of economic loss.

§ 5.03   "TAX BENEFIT" RULE

[A]   Case Law

Despite the strong statements in *Sanford* and *Brooks* about separate accounting years, the Supreme Court affirmed one case law rule that broke down the accounting year barrier. In *Dobson v. Commissioner*, 320 U.S. 489 (1943), the taxpayer sold stock at a loss and deducted the loss. The loss resulted from fraud in the original stock purchase and the taxpayer sued the person committing the fraud to recover some of her losses. The recovery occurred in a year after the losses were deducted. In the year of the loss deduction, however, the taxpayer had so many other deductions that the loss deduction was useless; it provided her with "no tax benefit." She argued that recovery of the item should not be taxed because she received no tax benefit from the deduction. The Court affirmed a Tax Court decision agreeing with the taxpayer. This is known as the "tax benefit" rule, but it might better be called the "no tax benefit" rule.

The *Dobson* Court did not deal very effectively with the *Sanford* and *Brooks* case. It stated that the losses in *Sanford* and *Brooks* were "not capital investments, the cost of which . . . must first be restored from the proceeds before there is capital gain taxable as income." The trouble with this statement is that the losses in *Dobson* were not capital investments either; they were losses. Of course, it might make sense to treat the losses *like* capital investments, but it would also have made sense to do that in the dredging contract case as well.

[B]   The Statutory "Tax Benefit" Rule

The tax benefit rule has now been adopted by statute to cover a broad range of events, applying to any situation (including *Dobson*) in which income is received during a taxable year attributable to an amount deducted in a prior tax year.

You can see how the "tax benefit" rule works from the following example. Assume in year 1, a taxpayer has business losses and also has a $1,000 nonbusiness bad debt loss (on a loan made to a corporation). That is, even before the bad debt loss deduction, there is no tax. In year 2, the taxpayer recovers the $1,000 because the debtor suddenly has a reversal of economic fortune. How much of the $1,000 recovery is income in year 2? What would your answer be if the taxpayer's business income in year 1 had been $700 (not a loss). How much of the $1,000 bad debt deduction was useful in lowering the taxpayer's tax in year 1? Disregard personal exemptions and the standard deduction in answering these questions.

Notice carefully the limited scope of the "tax benefit" rule. First, it does not lower taxes if the earlier deduction was of some use to the taxpayer. For example, suppose a taxpayer itemized deductions in year 3, including $1,000 of state income taxes, and the deduction lowers taxes by $150, because the taxpayer is in the 15% bracket. In year 4, her income rises and she is in the 35% bracket. . In year 4, she obtains a $200 refund of year 3 state income taxes. She pays 35% tax on the $200, not 15%. Why? At one time, the Court of Claims limited the tax rate on a recovered item to the marginal tax rate in the year of the related deduction, but it reversed itself in *Alice Phelan Sullivan Corp. v. United States*, 381 F.2d 399 (Ct. Cl. 1967).

Second, assume that the taxpayer was in the high 35% bracket in the year of the deduction (year 3), and in the 15% bracket in the tax refund year (year 4). The government cannot force the taxpayer to pay tax equal to 35% of the $200 refund? Why not?

The point of the "why" and "why not" questions is to wonder what principle underlies the tax benefit rule and its limits. Without a clear idea of the policy supporting the law, its limits seem arbitrary.

[C]   Note on Statutory Interpretation — Linguistic Canons (Expressio Unius); Statutory Analogy

An interesting aspect of the *Dobson* decision is how it dealt with the statute, which provided an explicit tax benefit rule for bad debt recoveries and state tax refunds, when the taxpayer had previously deducted the bad debt or tax payment. The statutory text did *not* apply to the situation in *Dobson* at the time *Dobson* was decided, and the Court was asked by the government to interpret the law to preclude expansion of the tax benefit rule beyond what the statute explicitly provided.

The government's argument is referred to in Latin as the expressio unius est exclusio alterius doctrine, which is a linguistic canon of statutory construction. It means, in English, that the expression of one thing excludes another. It is based on the idea that the legislature, by listing certain things, means to exclude similar treatment for unlisted items. This inference is sometimes justified on the ground that there would be no need for specific legislation if there were an implicit case law rule reaching the same result.

The difficulty with the expressio unius canon is that it often lacks a secure foundation in fact. The canon is strongest when a legislature considers a universe of possibilities and selects only those it means to cover — as when you select vanilla ice cream from a choice of flavors. But legislatures usually legislate to solve the specific problems called to their attention by the government or lobbyists. They are often unaware of the broader set of analogous problems or, if they are aware, may decide that solving them is too controversial or complex, so they are left to case law for future resolution.

The Court in *Dobson* not only refused to apply the expressio canon, but also hinted at an approach to statutory interpretation that treats specific statutory provisions like the common law — arguing by analogy from specific provisions to an interpretation of the law. The Court stated:

> Government now argues that by extending legislative relief in bad debt cases, Congress recognized that in the absence of specific exemption recoveries are taxable as income. We do not find that significance in the amendment. A specific statutory exception was necessary in bad debt cases only because the courts reversed the Tax Court and established as a matter of law a "theoretically proper" rule which distorted the taxpayer's income. Congress would hardly expect the courts to repeat the same error in another class of cases.

§ 5.04   "TAX DETRIMENT" RULE

In the examples discussed so far, the taxpayer recovered a loss. What happens if the taxpayer repays income previously received? For example, if the taxpayer was taxed at 35% on receipt of income in year 1, but repays the item in year 5 when he is in the 15% bracket, should his tax be reduced by 35% or 15% of the repayment? If the tax accounting year barrier is inviolate, the deduction reduces his tax by only 15% of the deductible repayment.

Section 1341 identifies situations in which the accounting year barrier is broken down, allowing the taxpayer to elect (in effect) to take a deduction for the repayment in year 5 (the 15% tax rate year) as though he were still in the 35% tax bracket. The reduction in tax provided by § 1341(a)(5) can result in a refund for the deduction year, but not interest. **Treas. Reg. § 1.1341-1(I).**

The election provided by § 1341 is a one way street *for* the taxpayer. If the taxpayer is in a *higher* bracket in the *repayment* year, the government cannot prevent a deduction at the higher rates.

I call this the "tax detriment" rule simply because it is the opposite of the tax benefit rule discussed in *Dobson* and provided by § 111. Instead of limiting the inclusion of income after an earlier loss, it increases the value of a deduction to match the detriment from an earlier inclusion of income.

There is a disagreement between some courts and the IRS regarding what test to use when applying § 1341. In the following case, the court expressed its preference for a "substantive nexus" test, which permitted application of § 1341.

DOMINION RESOURCES, INC. v. U.S.
United States District Court, Eastern District of Virginia
48 F. Supp. 2d 527 (E.D. Va. 1999), *affirmed*, 219 F.3d 359 (4th Cir. 2000)

[Editor — The taxpayer (DRI) was a public utility that received income based on charges approved by the regulatory authorities. Part of its receipts were, however, subject to repayment if, in the future, corporate tax rates were reduced on the utility charges previously received. When these tax rates were reduced, the taxpayer paid refunds to its customers. The question was whether these refunds were eligible for § 1341 treatment.]

. . . [T]he IRS concluded that DRI did not meet the terms of Section 1341(a) because DRI had an "actual" unrestricted right to the deferred tax component in the years at issue and that, as a consequence, DRI could not have the "appearance" of an unrestricted right. The IRS finds support for this rather tortured reasoning in the opinion of the Tax Court in Blanton v. Commissioner, 46 T.C. 527 (1966). . . . In Blanton, the taxpayer received director's fees from a corporation and later entered into an agreement to return them if the IRS subsequently determined that the fees were excessive. The Tax Court interpreted Section 1341 to apply only where the refund or repayment event arises "out of the circumstances, terms, and conditions of the original payment of such item to the taxpayer and not out of circumstances, terms, and conditions imposed upon such payment by reason of some subsequent agreement between payor and payee." The Tax Court then determined that the repayment agreement was not in existence when the taxpayer received the income at issue, but was executed only after the taxpayer had received the director's fees. For that reason, the Tax Court concluded that the obligation to repay the director's fees arose from the subsequent agreement, not out of the "circumstances, terms, and conditions" of the original payment of the director's fees. Thereupon, the Tax Court denied the taxpayer relief under Section 1341.

The decision in Blanton gave rise to the so-called "subsequent event" test which has been applied by several courts in denying a taxpayer relief under Section 1341. . . .

[Editor — The court also cited *Pahl v. Commissioner*, 67 T.C. 286 (1976), which reached the same result as *Blanton*, rejecting application of § 1341 to repayments of compensation received before the taxpayer entered into an agreement to repay excess compensation. Repayment of excess compensation received *after* the agreement was signed was eligible for § 1341.]

The IRS reads *Blanton* . . . [and] *Pahl* . . . to articulate the principle that where, in the prior year, a taxpayer has an "actual unrestricted right" rather than the "appearance of an unrestricted right," Section 1341(a) does not apply. None of those decisions addressed or articulated that proposition and hence they simply cannot be stretched to support the construction of the statute here urged by the IRS. More importantly, contrary to the position taken by the IRS, neither the statute nor the controlling Treasury Regulation speak in terms of actual unrestricted rights annulled by subsequent events. Instead, both authorities use the language "appeared" and "unrestricted right" in the year of inclusion in gross income. And, both authorities make qualification for relief depend on the establishment in a later year that the right was not unrestricted. Thus, the temporal language in both the statute and the regulation addresses the subsequent determination that the earlier belief was wrong, not the subsequent occurrence of an event which annuls the previously perceived right. To the extent that *Blanton* and its progeny hold otherwise, they are flatly at odds with the statute. . . .

However, it does not appear that *Blanton* . . . [and] *Pahl* . . . create such a conflict. First, it is essential to keep in mind that Section 1341 requires that there be some substantive nexus between the appearance of the unrestricted right and the defeasance of the right in a subsequent year. Second, it is important to read *Blanton* and its progeny in perspective of the facts there at issue and to understand what *Blanton* actually held. In each case, the taxpayer voluntarily took some action after the receipt of apparently unrestricted income which required the taxpayer to thereafter return the remuneration. *Blanton* and its progeny simply hold that, although such consensual ex post facto arrangements might be contractually binding on the taxpayer, they are insufficient to trigger the benefits of Section 1341.

A careful examination of *Blanton* . . . [and] *Pahl* . . . discloses that, in each instance, there was no substantive nexus between the appearance of an unrestricted right which had produced the included income and the circumstances which defeated the apparently unrestricted right. Understood then, in perspective of their facts and actual holdings, those authorities do not support the interpretation on which the IRS bases its contention respecting how Section 1341 is to be applied in assessing the claim for refund in this action. . . .

[R]eliance on the term "subsequent event" tends to confuse, rather than inform, the appropriate analysis. In all situations involving Section 1341, there will be some event which occurs in a year after the filing of the original tax return which will prompt the taxpayer to request a refund. The true focus of the inquiry is whether there is a substantive nexus between the right to the income at the time of receipt and the subsequent circumstances necessitating a refund. . . .

[Editor — The court goes on to conclude that "there is a substantive nexus between DRI's refund of $10,058,336 and DRI's original receipt of that amount from its customers," stating that "DRI has satisfied the 'unrestricted right' requirement for Section 1341 application for the reason that DRI reported an item of income in a prior year because it 'appeared' it had an 'unrestricted right' to such item, and it was later established that the taxpayer, in fact, did not have such a claim of right."]

In *Cinergy Corp. v. United States*, 55 Fed. Cl. 489 (2003)), however, the court rejects the reasoning in *Dominion Resources*, stating:

. . . [T]he IURC [Indiana Utility Regulatory Commission] ordered PSI [a utility company] to return its customers a total of $134.4 million, which represented the amount that PSI's customers previously had paid to PSI to fund certain of PSI's deferred taxes. [Editor — The issue was whether these payments were eligible for § 1341.] . . .

Section 1341 of the Code was "enacted to alleviate some of the inequities which Congress felt" had been engendered by the so-called "claim of right" doctrine. Claim of right cases tend to coalesce around some dispute over the ownership of income or a mistake of fact, deriving, for example, from a quarrel over the ownership of income producing property, the misapplication of a contract provision, or the payment of funds under a contingency based upon business expectations that were thought to, but actually did not, materialize. . . .

[The government] initially argues that PSI is not entitled to section 1341 treatment [on these repayments] because it had an "actual" right to the amounts collected from its ratepayers and thus did not "appear" to have such a right within the meaning of section 1341(a)(1). . . .

Beginning, as we must, with the statute's language, the first thing evident is that the "plain language" of the statute does not contradict [the government's] position. To be sure, the primary definitions of the verb "appear," as well as the related adjective "apparent," both focus on that which is "in sight," "visible" or "plain." . . . Nonetheless, a second well-accepted meaning of "appear," and, its adjectival first cousin "apparent," is to describe a circumstance that seems true, but is not. For example, Webster's alternatively defines "appear" as "to have an outward aspect: seem." It likewise defines "apparent" as to "manifest to the senses or mind as real or true on the basis of evidence that may or may not be factually valid," further indicating that this word "suggests appearance to unaided senses that is not or may not be borne out by more rigorous examination or greater knowledge." In similar vein, the AMERICAN HERITAGE DICTIONARY defines "appear" as "[t]o seem or look to be," and "apparent" as "[a]ppearings as such but not necessarily so; seeming." These secondary definitions — summed up as that which seems to be true, but is at least questionable — linguistically fit [the government's] construction of section 1341(a)(1) like a glove of the finest leather; that is, the section applies only to one who seemed to, but did not, have an absolute right to a particular item of income.

At the least, these varied dictionary definitions suggest that the language of the statute is sufficiently ambiguous to warrant reference to its legislative history. That legislative history indicates that the statute was enacted to ameliorate the impact of the claim of right doctrine. . . . The purpose of section 1341 . . . was to place a taxpayer that had been impacted by the claim of right doctrine in no worse tax position than he would have been had he never recognized the income originally. . . .

Out of this realization emerges a limiting principle because the claim of right doctrine simply does not apply where an individual receives an item of income under an "absolute" right. Numerous cases so hold. [Editor — Discussion of cases omitted.]

Based on its analysis of the statute, its legislative history and the case law, this court, therefore, concludes that an entity which had an actual, rather than apparent, right to funds does not meet the threshold requirement of section 1341(a)(1). Those are the facts here. When PSI received the deferred tax income and other income in question, it clearly had an absolute right thereto under the rate schedules then in effect. Thus, this is not a case where a utility obtained funds in one year based upon a mistaken calculation or the seeming triggering of a condition precedent later found not to have occurred. Rather, plaintiff included the amounts in question in income not under the claim of right doctrine at all, but consistent with the broader notion that income is an "undeniable accession[ ]to wealth, clearly realized, and over which the taxpayers have complete dominion." *Comm'r v. Glenshaw Glass Co.*, 348 U.S. 426, 431 (1955). As such, PSI does not meet the first requirement of section 1341, rendering that section unavailable.

COMMENTS AND QUESTIONS

1. The problem with interpreting § 1341 is that it is hard to know what rationale justifies breaking down the accounting year barrier. Without knowing the statute's purpose, it is difficult to know how to apply the law when the result is not obvious. The *Cinergy* case makes an attempt at using statutory purpose gleaned from legislative history — specifically, relief from application of the claim of right doctrine. It therefore comes out differently from the *Dominion Resources* decision.

A recent Court of Federal Claims case agrees with *Dominion*, rather than *Cinergy Pennzoil-Quaker State Co. v. United States*, 62 Fed. Cl. 689 (2004). This case found the statute ambiguous and, like the court in *Cinergy* , also relied on legislative history. But it reached the opposite conclusion from *Cinergy* , as follows:

In the House and Senate Committee Reports, the legislature states that § 1341 will apply "[i]f the taxpayer included an item in gross income in one taxable year, and in a subsequent taxable year he becomes entitled to a deduction because the item or a portion thereof is no longer subject to his unrestricted use." H.R. REP. 83-1337, at A294; S. REP. No. 83-1662, at 451. The Dominion Resources court interpreted this passage to "strongly suggest[ ] that a taxpayer may enjoy the benefits of § 1341 even if his unrestricted right to use the income did not end until the 'subsequent taxable year.' " This Court agrees and therefore finds that an actual right is included in the definition of an apparent right for purposes of § 1341.

2. Are the following repayments eligible for § 1341 relief?

a. An embezzler reimburses his victim; or, a person who commits stock fraud returns the purchase price to the defrauded seller. *Wang v. Commissioner*, 76 T.C.M. (CCH) 753 (1998).

b. A judge returns a lecture fee after newspaper reporters suggested an impropriety in the judge accepting the lecture engagement and the judge was concerned with her reputation.

c. A seller repays someone who purchased goods that turn out, on closer inspection, to have a defect.

d. A person repays the price received for services because a mathematical error overstated the contract price. Rev. Rul. 68-153, 1968-1 C.B. 371.

e. An employee repays a corporation an amount of compensation that is so large that it is not deductible under § 162(a)(1). The agreement to repay excess compensation was signed *before* receipt of the excess compensation. The *Blanton* and *Pahl* cases, cited in the *Dominion* opinion, disallowed the application of § 1341 when the agreement was made *after* payment of the unreasonable compensation.

§ 5.05 INCOME AVERAGING

In general. Another example of breaking down the accounting year barrier is income averaging. The prior material in this chapter deals with situations in which there is income in one year and a deduction in another year. Income averaging deals with situations in which there is income in all the relevant years, but the income rises quickly, so that the taxpayer is pushed into a higher bracket. For example, assume that the taxpayer has no income in years 1 and 2, and $90,000 income in year 3. This taxpayer would pay much more in taxes under the current law compared to a situation in which the taxpayer had $30,000 income in years 1, 2, and 3. Income averaging provides relief to taxpayers with rising income.

A generally applicable income averaging provision was repealed in 1986 when tax rates were lowered. The technique used in the repealed law was to define a dramatic increase in income in a tax year, and then reduce the effective tax rate on the "excess income" in *that* tax year. For example, if income in years 1-4 averaged $80,000 and income in year 5 was $300,000, the year 5 income was eligible for income averaging. The year 5 income was "excessive" because, under the prior statute, it exceeded 5/4 of the average of the income in years 1–4 (that is, it exceeded $100,000; 5/4 times $80,000 = $100,000). The excess income of $200,000 was then eligible for tax relief. The relief was provided by imposing a tax on that $200,000 equal to five times the tax on $40,000, placed on top of the $100,000, and based on year 5 tax computations. In other words, the tax on $200,000 did not force the taxpayer all the way up the progressive rate ladder. Thus, if $40,000 would have been taxed at a 30% marginal tax rate and the top tax rate was 35%, the entire $200,000 was still subject to a 30% tax rate. This complexity produced a very complicated tax form but the idea underlying the rules was relatively simple — excess income would not be fully exposed to the progressive tax rate ladder. This income averaging technique did *not* spread year 5 income back over prior tax years.

Farmers. 1997 amendments to the tax law allow farmers to elect to income-average farm income over a three-year period. § **1301**. However, this provision uses a different technique from the law repealed in 1986. The technique used is to spread eligible farm income for one year evenly over the prior three years and pay only the tax that would have been due if these ⅓ amounts had been taxed in the prior three years. Thus, assume a taxpayer has $40,000 income in years 1-3; and $130,000 of income in year 4, $60,000 of which was farm income. This taxpayer can pay tax in year 4 in an amount equal to the tax on $70,000 (the nonfarm income in year 4), plus the additional tax that *would have been paid* if $20,000 (that is, one third of the $60,000 farm income in year 4) had been added to the $40,000 of income in years 1, 2, and 3.

Compensation paid to victims of the Exxon Valdez oil spill are also eligible for the three-year income averaging provision in § **1301**. This provision appears in § **504(a)** of the Emergency Economic Stabilization Act of 2008 (Public Law 110-343) and is not codified as part of the Internal Revenue Code of 1986.

Chapter 6

LEGISLATIVE PROCESS, ADMINISTRATIVE RULEMAKING, THE ADJUDICATION SYSTEM, AND PROFESSIONAL ETHICS

The material in prior chapters has called attention to various sources of tax law — legislation, administrative rules, and court decisions — but we have not explained in any detail how the law gets made and what weight these different sources have in the lawmaking process. Obviously, the statute that emerges from the legislative process sits on top of the lawmaking pyramid. The process by which tax legislation gets enacted is not a pretty sight, making the old saying that you should never watch sausage and legislation being made especially apt for tax statutes.

But this is also an administrative law course because a great deal of the law that is applied comes from agency rules. The precise weight given to these rules by the courts is far from clear. It is important that you have some idea about this issue because a lot of the material you read is found in various agency rules and some of these rules do not have anything like the force of law. You need to know when you can rely on an agency rule for your client and when such rules have more modest weight.

Moreover, the adjudication system is complex, largely as a result of history. We have three trial courts (four, if you count bankruptcy courts) and an inverted appellate process when the appeal lies from the Tax Court (fanning out to the different courts of appeal). The student's tendency to associate law with judicial law can be very misleading because a judicial decision in favor of the taxpayer means that the agency is fighting the taxpayer's position and the last thing a taxpayer might want is to be hauled into court by the IRS.

Finally, as a practical matter, law is "made" by tax advisors who tell clients what they can and cannot do. This means that the ethical rules applicable to tax practitioners are important in working out the interaction of the law and taxpayer behavior, at least if the ethical rules are enforced. The fact that so few tax returns are audited increases the relevance of ethical standards.

§ 6.01 LEGISLATIVE PROCESS

[A] The Origination Clause

The Constitution states that "[a]ll bills for raising revenue shall originate in the House of Representatives; but the Senate may propose or concur with amendments as on other bills." Article I, sec. 7, cl. 1. It is, however, very hard to prove a violation of this clause.

1. Challenges based on the Origination Clause often involve House bills whose language is completely replaced by the Senate — known as "bill stripping" — but the courts have permitted this practice. *Flint v. Stone Tracy Co.*, 220 U.S. 107 (1911) (Senate could substitute corporate tax for House-passed inheritance tax); *Texas Ass'n of Concerned Taxpayers, Inc. v. United States*, 772 F.2d 163 (5th Cir. 1985) (Senate can substitute tax increase for House-passed tax cut).

2. In *United States v. Munoz-Flores*, 495 U.S. 385 (1990), the Court held that the Constitution's reference to revenue raising in the Origination Clause refers only to a statute raising revenue to support government generally, not to legislation that imposes a tax for a particular government program. Justice Scalia would have gone further and held that the enrolled bill rule, adopted in *Field v. Clark*, 143 U.S. 649 (1892), meant that a statute with the designation "H.J. Res." should be conclusively presumed to originate in the House. The enrolled bill rule blocks judicial consideration of whether a law that has been enrolled after passage by Congress has violated rules applicable to the lawmaking process. The majority did not rely on the enrolled bill rule on the ground that *Field v. Clark* did not apply to a constitutionally mandated procedure.

[B] How Congress Legislates Tax Law

[1] The Legislative Process

Because tax bills originate in the House, the House Ways and Means Committee is one of the most powerful committees in Congress. (At one time, it was also the appropriations committee, but that ended in the mid-nineteenth century.) The Committee is usually a consensus builder rather than an advocate for a particular political point of view. Consequently, bills that emerge from the Committee usually have majority support. House passage of the committee's bill is even more likely because the House Rules Committee controls the voting procedure and will often limit debate on and amendments to committee-sponsored bills. In addition, the House (and the Senate) tax committees often allocate a fairly small sum (say, $5 billion!) to provide tax breaks to people located in geographical areas represented by legislators who might be wavering in their support of the proposed legislation. Many of these tax breaks take the form of transitional rules, preventing the application of a new law to transactions entered into before a certain date.

After passage by the House, the bill goes to the Senate, where it is likely to be subject to significant amendment. The Senate Finance Committee lacks the kind of control over tax legislation characteristic of the House Ways and Means Committee. Senate procedures are very generous in permitting floor amendment and pet projects may be added to the Senate version of the bill.

When the House and Senate disagree on the text of a bill, a conference committee of House and Senate members is usually established to resolve the differences. It is not unusual for a bill to pass in one chamber with the implicit understanding that one or more of its provisions (often those added on the Senate floor) will be conceded in the conference, allowing legislators to say that they supported one position, but knowing that it will fail. The conference is not, under legislative rules, supposed to add new measures outside the scope of what the House and Senate bills provided, but those rules are often breached. There is no judicial remedy for violation by the legislature of its own internal rules (in contrast to rules required by the Constitution).

The President is then free to veto the law. In such instances, a two-thirds vote in both House and Senate is required to override the veto. A 1996 law gave the President a line item veto, which allowed the President to veto selected items of spending and taxation. The Supreme Court struck this down as an effort to permit legislation — in this case to negate what the legislature had done — without going through the usual legislative process of passage by both chambers and presentment to the President; *Clinton v. City of New York*, 524 U.S. 417 (1998), discussed in Chapter 6.01[E].

The President's legislative role goes beyond the veto power. Although the tax bill technically originates in the House, major tax legislation is often proposed by the President. The Treasury Department plays the major role in developing executive branch proposals and the Assistant Secretary of the Treasury for Tax Policy is the primary tax advisor within the Treasury.

[2]   Legislative History; Committee Reports

Committee reports from each chamber (House and Senate) will explain how the law is supposed to work. A House-Senate conference will also produce a report setting forth the understanding of the law emerging from the conference. In addition, the staff of the Joint Committee on Taxation will write a report (known as the "Blue Book" because of the color of the pages) after passage of a tax law. The Joint Committee staff has a strong nonpartisan reputation.

The weight to which these reports are entitled when judges interpret legislation is a subject of intense debate. The still-dominant view is that reports can be considered when the text of the law is unclear, although there is often disagreement about how textual uncertainty is determined. Moreover, two Justices of the U.S. Supreme Court have stated that they would consider legislative history regardless of whether the statutory language is clear (Stevens and Breyer), and some will not consider legislative history under almost any circumstances (Scalia).

The Blue Book raises a special problem for interpretive theory because it is written after the voting on the statute. This means that the report could not have formed the basis of any legislator's understanding of the law. However, the audience for the tax law (a specialized bar) makes use of the Blue Book and the staff's expertise makes this report at least as useful as any treatise, interpretive theory to the contrary notwithstanding. *See generally* Livingston, *What's Blue and White and Not Quite as Good as a Committee Report: General Explanations and the Role of "Subsequent" Tax Legislative History*, 11 Am. J. Tax Pol'y 91 (1994). *See also Robinson v. Commissioner*, 119 T.C. 44 (2002) (reviewed by the court) (wide variety of opinions about the weight of the Blue Book); and the earlier case of *Redlark v. Commissioner*, 106 T.C. 31 (1996) (no reliance on Blue Book without corroboration in the regular legislative history), *rev'd*, 141 F.3d 936 (9th Cir. 1998).

[C] The Problem of Tax Expenditures

[1] Definition

In addition to raising revenue and distributing tax burdens fairly, the tax law contains numerous provisions intended to encourage certain behavior. These have come to be known as "tax expenditures" because they are similar to direct government appropriations of funds. The idea is that giving up revenue to achieve some objective can be compared to collecting revenue and appropriating government funds to achieve that objective.

The tax expenditure analysis was originally the brainchild of a tax academic, Professor Stanley Surrey. When he became Assistant Secretary of the Treasury for Tax Policy in the 1960s, his ideas about tax expenditures were adopted by the Treasury, and later by Congress. Since then, the executive branch has not always agreed with Congress' tax expenditure analysis. The published lists of tax expenditures by the Office of Management and Budget (OMB) (in the executive branch) and by the Congressional Budget Office (CBO) differ in certain particulars.

Surrey's definition of tax expenditures, which was embodied in the Budget Act of 1974, is as follows:

> Those revenue losses attributable to provisions of the Federal tax laws which allow a special exclusion, exemption, or deduction from gross income or which provide a special credit, a preferential rate of tax, or a deferral of tax liability. Surrey & McDaniel, *The Tax Expenditure Concept and the Budget Reform Act of 1974*, 17 B.C. Indus. & Com. L. Rev. 679 (1976).

This definition of tax expenditures assumed that the term "special" referred to a "deviation from the normal tax structure." The conception of a "normal" tax structure began with "widely-accepted definitions of income," based on the economist's conception of income as personal consumption plus changes in net wealth. The tax expenditure definition was tempered, however, by the "generally-accepted structure of an income tax," thereby excluding unrealized appreciation and imputed income (e.g., from the rental value of homes).

Surrey argued that identification of a tax expenditure was not a judgment about the wisdom of using the tax law to achieve social or economic policy. Defining an item as a tax expenditure was meant to serve a procedural or deliberative goal by calling attention to the use of the tax law for other than its core purpose of raising revenue fairly. The hope was that potential inefficiencies and unfairness from using the tax law to implement nontax purposes would be highlighted and, where appropriate, eliminated.

In the 1980s, the Reagan Administration became concerned about efforts to equate a "normal" tax base with some "ideal." Unable to identify the "ideal," the Reagan Administration had the Office of Management and Budget issue its own tax "subsidy" list (they preferred the term "subsidy" to "expenditure"), which used a slightly different approach. *See* Office of Management and Budget, The Budget of the United States Government, 1983, Special Analysis G, Tax Expenditures, 305 (1982). The OMB approach emphasized as the "norm" the "reference" provisions of the statute, which were "those which deal with the basic structural features of the income tax." The CBO, however, continued to lean toward reliance on an "ideal" tax base to identify tax expenditures.

The contrasting CBO and OMB general definitions of tax expenditures did not themselves compel obvious distinctions in application. And indeed, there was much agreement. For example, both tax expenditure lists agree that the personal exemption deduction, individual tax rates below the top rate, and different rate structures for married couples and single individuals are not tax expenditures. Both agree that the extra standard deduction for the aged and blind is a tax expenditure (§ 63(f)). But there were differences. Only CBO, not OMB, treats accelerated depreciation and the corporate tax rates below the top rate as tax expenditures. OMB argues that no particular depreciation system and no particular rate structure can be identified as a "reference" point and that, therefore, a depreciation rate and a tax rate structure cannot create "departures" that are tax expenditures.

Professor Bittker had a different objection to the tax expenditure approach. He argued that it would encourage the government to avoid tax rules that would show up adversely on the tax expenditure list, and that this would favor business and investment tax breaks rather than social welfare tax benefits. For example, deferral of tax on unrealized appreciation is not a tax expenditure, but tax free fringe benefits for employees are. *See* Bittker, *Accounting for Federal "Tax Subsidies" in the National Budget*, 22 Nat'l Tax J. 244 (1969).

It is fair to say that the current Internal Revenue Code has abandoned all qualms about using the tax law to achieve policy objectives. Indeed, Congress has expanded the use of tax expenditures beyond the traditional economic incentives (such as faster depreciation for business investments; exemption of some income from natural resources; etc.). Amendments to the tax code since the 1990s have used the tax law to provide middle-class tax breaks for families with children, and for education, retirement, and medical expenditures, far beyond what prior law had done. *See, e.g.* — the child tax credit (§ 24); education tax credits (§ 25A); pre-paid tuition plans which allow after-tax investments to earn tax-free income if used later for education (§ 529); new retirement income tax breaks (Roth IRAs) (§ 408A); and health savings accounts (§ 223).

An Appendix to a recent Tax Expenditure Budget presented by the Treasury introduces further uncertainty into efforts to measure departures in the tax law from some baseline. It notes that current tax expenditure budgets fail to include measures of over-taxation, what it calls "negative tax expenditures" (giving as an example the double tax of corporate profits). *See* Appendix, Treasury Review of the Tax Expenditure Presentation, Analytical Perspectives, Budget of the U.S. Government, Fiscal Year 2004, pp. 130–40. And a disagreement between the Joint

Committee on Taxation in the Congress and the Treasury illustrates the uncertainty that the idea of "over-taxation" introduces into tax expenditure analysis. The Treasury used an "integrated corporate-shareholder" system as its base from which to compare existing law (that is, there should be only one tax on corporate profits). This meant that the (then) current maximum 15% tax rate on dividends was a "negative tax expenditure" — the opposite of a tax break. By contrast, the Joint Committee used the double tax on corporate profits (at both the corporate and shareholder levels) as its normative base, which meant that the reduction to a 15% tax rate was a tax expenditure.

A publication prepared by the Congressional Research Service suggests that there might still be some political life in the idea of tax expenditures, although (in my judgment) the publication suggests lip service to an idea that no longer influences legislative behavior. *See* Tax Expenditures, Compendium of Background Material on Individual Provisions, Committee on the Budget, U.S. Senate (Dec. 2006). This compendium discusses about 150 tax expenditure items, providing a description of the item and its legal authority (whether statute, regulation, or ruling), an estimated revenue loss, an analysis of its impact and distribution of benefits (where data are available), a statement of rationale, an assessment of arguments for and against, and a selected bibliography.

A speech titled "Rethinking Tax Expenditures" by the Chief of Staff of the Joint Committee on Taxation (May 1, 2008, at the Chicago-Kent College of Law Federal Tax Institute) captures some of the criticism of efforts to identify tax expenditures:

> Surrey's original hope that tax expenditure analysis would have a salutary effect on budget transparency (and through that, on actual budget outlays) has not been realized, for several reasons. First, tax laws and appropriations follow completely different paths through Congress, and in particular are developed by different substantive committees. . . . Second, many tax expenditures have vaguely similar distributional effects to those achieved through spending programs, but the two delivery systems are so different that in many cases each is a highly imperfect economic substitute for the other. Third, many commentators believe that, as budget and other pressures have made it more difficult to advance policies through the appropriations process, policymakers have wholeheartedly embraced tax expenditures as a second best means of implementing their policy agendas.

The speech went on to note that tax expenditure analysis has proved "less helpful to policymakers in fashioning tax policy than might otherwise be the case, because the proponents of tax expenditure analysis generally have failed to respond convincingly to the important criticisms leveled against it." Of special concern was the reliance on the concept of a "normal" tax system as a "benchmark" and as a "reproach to the current tax system." Because "the 'normal' tax is largely a common sense extension (and cleansing) of current tax policies, not a rigorous tax framework developed from first principles . . . the 'normal' tax cannot be defended from criticism as a series of ultimately idiosyncratic or pragmatic choices. If tax expenditure analysis is to enjoy broad support, it must be seen as neutral and principled. . . ." At present, however, it "satisfies these requirements only in the eyes of those who already believe that the 'normal' tax accurately captures their personal ideal of an aspirational tax system."

[2]　Efficiency Problems and the Legislative Process

The use of tax law to implement nontax policy raises the same kinds of efficiency questions as any expenditure program: Should the government be encouraging the subsidized activity? Is it spending too much money or giving up too much revenue to achieve its goals? Are the right people getting the benefit? For example, when the tax law encourages investments by allowing the deduction of savings, is the loss of revenue carefully compared with the economic and social benefits that the nation will enjoy? The debate over lower taxes on capital gains is about the same question.

The principal question raised by tax expenditure analysis concerns whether the political process that produces the tax expenditure is more likely to produce inefficient results than other kinds of government decisions. The reason for suspecting that tax expenditures may receive less public and political scrutiny is the assumption that tax committees are an easier target for obtaining government benefits than appropriations committees dealing with specific substantive areas of legislation. First, the public fails to understand the impact of tax breaks, compared to attention given to specific dollar appropriations. Exempting one-half of an oil producer's income by excluding some income from the tax base or by raising deductions "feels" different from a $500,000,000 appropriation. Second, tax bills are massive statutes in which a tax break can be well hidden, or used to "purchase" a key supporting vote. Third, political influence operates very strongly through political contributions to tax committee members.

These are, of course, empirical claims that must be verified. Tax committees may in fact be *less* subject to special interest group pressure than appropriations committees dealing with specific areas of law. Tax committees may get campaign contributions from and represent a wide range of interest groups, which might offset each other, resulting in a perceived need to hold the line on tax breaks. By contrast, an appropriations subcommittee may be especially vulnerable to a single constituency. Moreover, publicity about tax expenditures may increase public scrutiny of tax breaks, but appropriations committee work may not be carefully scrutinized, except by the beneficiaries. *See* Zelinsky, *James Madison and Public Choice at Gucci Gulch: A Procedural Defense of Tax Expenditures and Tax Institutions*, 102 YALE L.J. 1165 (1993).

[3]　Efficiency and Progressive Rates

There is another efficiency problem applicable even to the most well-thought-out tax expenditure. The progressive tax rate system builds in a potential for excessive loss of revenue. The following discussion of tax exempt bonds for core governmental purposes illustrates this potential.

Everyone agrees that the exemption of interest on state and local bonds in § 103(a) is a tax expenditure.[1] The federal government gives up income tax on the

---

[1] The exemption for interest does not apply to state and local bonds guaranteed by the federal government. § 149(b)(1). This could have serious implications if financially shaky state and local

interest, which helps state and local governments by lowering interest rates on borrowing. It is not meant to help investors. However, the way interest rates are set results in some of the tax expenditure being enjoyed by high bracket taxpayers. The explanation of this process can be generalized to illustrate a pervasive problem with tax breaks. Whenever someone gets a tax break (such as the investor in tax exempt bonds or the recipient of a tax free fringe benefit), someone who deals with that person will try to capture some of the tax benefit. The state borrower will lower interest rates, or the employer will lower cash wages. Here is how this can happen with tax exempt bonds.

The recipient of interest on a tax exempt bond will accept an interest payment that equals the *after*-tax interest rate on taxable bonds. For example, if the risk associated with a particular borrower requires the borrower to pay 16% taxable interest (a GM bond, for example), how much interest would a state or local government borrower with the same risk have to pay to a taxpayer in the 35% bracket? Interest could fall to 10.4% (65% of 16%), and the tax exempt bond would be as good as a GM bond of equivalent risk. This works out well. The federal government loses 35% of the 16% interest in tax revenue (that is, 5.6%); and the state gets an equivalent benefit in the form of reduced interest rates (10.4% is 5.6% less than the 16% it would have to pay if its bonds were taxable).

Why can't the state or local government borrower capture all of the revenue lost by the federal government through tax exemption? Because there are not enough high bracket taxpayers to lend them money. Assume that some 25% bracket taxpayers must be attracted to finance state and local roads and schools. A tax exempt bond paying 10.4% will be shunned by the 25% bracket taxpayer. She can get 12% buying a taxable GM bond (75% of 16%). So the state must pay 12% tax exempt interest, instead of 10.4%. Some of the tax revenue lost by tax exemption goes to the top 35% bracket taxpayer.

More specifically, the federal government loses the 5.6% it would have collected from the 35% bracket taxpayer if the bond had been taxable. But that 5.6% does not all go to the state issuing the bond. The state issuing a bond paying 12% interest gets 4% (16 minus 12), and the 35% taxpayer gets an extra 1.6% (12% minus 10.4%). The 5.6% has been divided between the state and the 35% bracket taxpayer (4% plus 1.6%).

What is wrong with the following proposal to eliminate this problem? Every calendar quarter the federal government states that it will pay state and local governments issuing *taxable* bonds a subsidy equal to 26% of the interest. Because the bonds are taxable, the state pays 16% interest but gets back 26% of 16% from the federal government, for a net interest cost to the state or local government of 11.84% (74% of 16%). That 11.84% cost is less than the 12% in the prior example where interest rates were set to attract the 25% bracket investor. The state is better off, and the windfall for the 35% bracket taxpayer is eliminated (he must pay tax of 35% times the 16% interest on the taxable bond).

---

governments seek a federal guarantee for their obligations.

[4] "Loopholes" and the Political Process

Many tax expenditures do attract public attention, but Congress still consciously chooses to enact them. The political process is not always so self-conscious, however. Sometimes a tax break emerges more gradually as a result of tax planning by tax counsel, the acquiescence and even approval of the IRS, and an inattentive legislature. By the time the Treasury and Congress become aware of the implications of the tax break, it may be too late. Political forces coalescing around the tax benefit are too powerful for the IRS to interpret the law against the taxpayer, for the Treasury to adopt anti-taxpayer regulations, and even for Congress to revoke the prevailing interpretation. This is what happened to Industrial Revenue Bonds (IRBs).

IRBs are tax-exempt bonds in which a private industry is either the legal debtor or is the source of funds to pay the debt for all practical purposes. In the usual case, § 103 exempts the interest on state and local bonds issued to finance government projects (roads, schools, etc.) and the government borrower finances repayment with taxes. An IRB is different. The government lends its name to the bond and "borrows" the money; the government then either re-lends the money to private industry or arranges to construct a facility that is then rented to private industry. The government is either not liable to repay the loan or the lender does not in reality look to the government for repayment. The loan repayment is legally or in reality out of funds paid by the private industry beneficiary of the loan and funneled through the state or local government.

How could this arrangement be considered a state or local obligation, especially in the case where the government is not even technically liable? Contrary to the image you may have of an overbearing IRS, the agency actually issued private letter rulings in the 1930s and then published Rev. Rul. 54-106, 1954-1 C.B. 28–29, favoring tax exemption for the interest arising from such arrangements. The agency's acquiescence and approval occurred when the amounts involved with IRBs were small. In 1957, only $20 million of such bonds were issued. By 1963, only 23 states even authorized such bonds, although all but three of these had enacted enabling legislation since 1950. Trouble was coming.

The Advisory Commission on Intergovernmental Relations issued a warning in 1963. *See* ACIR, Industrial Development Bond Financing (1963). They saw one group of states pirating business from others (often Southern states attracting Northern business). Moreover, the tax breaks were often wasted, both because they were not really needed to attract the business and because multi-state competition to offer tax exempt IRBs simply lowered the cost of borrowing equally in all states.

Here, you have the classic case of a "loophole." That term is sometimes used casually to mean any tax break, but that is misleading. Some tax breaks are consciously adopted. A loophole is different. It is a tax scheme devised by astute tax counsel, which stretches the statute beyond its reasonable meaning or that exploits an unintended result of the law. Why doesn't the administrative process adequately address such efforts? Sometimes the administration is unaware of what is happening. Sometimes the authors of letter rulings issued at the lower administrative levels are not alert to the implications of what they are doing. Sometimes the implications are unclear — IRBs started small as an effort to build up rural manufacturing in the

South. Over time, the economic implications alter and grow.

By 1969, the Treasury became alarmed. Forty states now authorized such bonds and well over $1 billion were marketed annually. Politically, IRBs were too prominent for the agency to revoke a Revenue Ruling. The Regulation process was therefore invoked. The Treasury adopted a Proposed Regulation that such bonds were *not* an obligation of a state or local government, but the politics of IRBs overwhelmed even the Regulatory process. The Senate Finance Committee proposed an amendment to a pending tax bill *freezing* the tax law on IRBs to preserve the pro-exemption principles of specifically cited prior Revenue Rulings, including Rev. Rul. 54-106. Some in Congress, often from Northern states and with the backing of labor unions, proposed amendments explicitly withdrawing exemption for IRBs.

The end result was a complex statute allowing interest on some IRBs to be tax exempt (often relating to public purposes like pollution control or airports), while withdrawing exemption for most private industry IRBs. This type of legal evolution is one of the major causes of tax law complexity, as you can see by scanning §§ 141–147.

[D]   Tax Breaks, Equal Protection, and the Political Process

Sometimes tax breaks are provided to a narrow group of taxpayers with little pretense of advancing public goals. This can happen as part of regular tax legislation but often occurs in transition provisions when major tax reforms are passed. Law reform disrupts some expectations and taxpayers seek exceptions from retroactive impact. Only those with political clout, however, might get relief from the new law. For example, a real estate developer in New York might get relief from a new tax law ending favorable treatment of real estate investment, but a California developer might not. In the following case, a three-judge Fifth Circuit panel held that the selective tax breaks were constitutional. The plaintiffs were not competitors of the taxpayers who benefited from the relief provisions.

APACHE BEND APARTMENTS, LTD. v. UNITED STATES
United States Court of Appeals, Fifth Circuit
964 F.2d 1556 (5th Cir. 1992)

GOLDBERG, CIRCUIT JUDGE:

In an effort to dampen the impact of the radical changes brought about by the Tax Reform Act of 1986, Congress provided certain taxpayers exemptions from the new tax laws. In many instances, Congress designed these exemptions, known as "transition rules," to favor only one or a very few taxpayers. The method by which Congress selected those taxpayers that would enjoy the benefit of the transition rules is the subject of this lawsuit.

Plaintiffs are taxpayers that were not granted any relief under the transition rules. Claiming that they are similarly situated to those taxpayers to whom the transition rules do apply, they brought this lawsuit to challenge the constitutionality of the transition rules under the . . . equal protection component of the Due Process Clause of the United States Constitution. They argued that Congress exhibited favoritism to those taxpayers with strong congressional lobbies, and thus discriminated against those taxpayers, like plaintiffs, that "were not fortunate to have an ear in Congress." Plaintiffs . . . request[ed] the court [to] enjoin the enforcement of the transition rules so that no taxpayer could benefit from them. . . .

. . . A transition rule of general application, as opposed to these "rifle shot" transition rules, would have been far more costly in terms of tax revenue, albeit eminently fairer.

This method of doling out tax breaks raised more than a few eyebrows in Congress. Several members of Congress expressed concern that similarly situated taxpayers were not being treated equally. Others conceded their use of raw political power to obtain transition rules for favored constituents. Even in this court, the government acknowledges that "political considerations definitely played a significant role in the selection process . . . [and] the focus of the debate was on subjective factors [as opposed to objective factors]."

Plaintiffs contend that no rational basis exists for Congress' classification as between those taxpayers afforded relief under the transition rules and those who were not. They maintain that but for the fact that they did not have "the right people speaking for [them]" in Congress, they are similarly situated to those taxpayers who presently enjoy tax breaks accorded by the transition rules. In plaintiffs' view, this classification — providing benefits only to those taxpayers with connections in Congress and the political savvy to exploit those relationships — amounts to a violation of equal protection. . . .

. . . [T]he legislature has a legitimate governmental purpose in making exceptions from the general application of the Tax Reform Act to protect "substantial reliance interests." . . .

But that does not end our inquiry, for we must evaluate not only the purpose of the legislation, but the purpose and legitimacy of the classifications as well. To do that, we must first identify the classification. Plaintiffs take the position that:

> [w]hile assisting all taxpayers with general transition relief would be a valid and appropriate governmental purpose, the objective of providing selective exemptions to only a few, based upon their access to politicians, is an illegitimate and prohibited objective. . . . There can never be a legitimate public purpose served by the arbitrary selection of a favored few from the general applicability of a taxing statute.

Plaintiffs would have us define the "favored" class as those taxpayers with "access to influential members of Congress." Their argument is not without some foundation. . . . For example, the Chairman of the Senate Finance Committee confessed that:

> [i]t would be foolish of me to say that, on occasion, politics did not enter those judgments. If the Speaker of the House requested the chairman of the Ways and Means Committee a transition rule, my hunch is that [he] would give it reasonably high priority in his thinking.

If Senator Dole requested one of me, I would give it reasonably high priority in my thinking.

132 Cong. Rec. S 13,786 (daily ed. Sept. 26, 1986) (statement of Sen. Packwood). [Editor — Dole was Senate Majority Leader and Packwood was Chair of the Senate Finance Committee.] . . .

Moreover, it is quite plain that absent "access to the conference committee which enabled them to obtain a so-called transition rule so their activity could continue to be taxed under the old law," 132 Cong. Rec. S 13,810 (daily ed. Sept. 26, 1986) (statement of Sen. Levin), there was little, if any, chance that a taxpayer would receive transitional relief. As one Senator asked: "[W]hat about those who could not come to Washington and make their case? What about those who could not hire the lobbyists to present their appeal? Where is the fairness to them?"

While we recognize that politics played a part in determining to whom the transition rules would apply, we nevertheless believe that, in view of the great deference accorded by the Supreme Court to tax legislation, the classifications contain no constitutional malady. Congress sought to give transitional relief to those taxpayers who petitioned for relief and demonstrated, most convincingly, that they relied substantially on the old tax laws in making major investment decisions. Not every application for transitional relief was granted, however, political clout notwithstanding. Congressional staff members examined more than one thousand requests for rifle shot transition relief before recommending the inclusion of several hundred. As the Senate Finance Committee Chairman explained: . . . [We said] to the staff, "Here are the rules by which transitions are to be selected. Try to avoid violating those rules." . . . Congress could not grant every request for transitional relief, for that would have threatened the success of the Act, which, by design of the President and Congress, was to be revenue neutral, neither raising nor lowering the aggregate level of federal revenue collections.

. . . [A]s far as we can tell from the legislative history, Congress made their decisions based on the merits of the applications for transitional relief made to the Finance Committee. We realize that those taxpayers with political connections had better access to the Committee than others. Nevertheless, nothing suggests that Congress aimed to exclude others or that Congress designed the classifications with such a purpose in mind: "If the adverse impact on the disfavored class is an apparent aim of the legislature, its impartiality would be suspect. If, however, the adverse impact may reasonably be viewed as an acceptable cost of achieving a larger goal, an impartial lawmaker could rationally decide that that cost should be incurred." *U.S. Railroad Retirement Bd. v. Fritz*, 449 U.S. 166, 181 (1980) (Stevens, J., concurring in judgment).

Moreover, it appears that Plaintiffs never sought transitional relief from the Tax Reform Act. That places them in an especially difficult position to challenge the rifle shot rules. They did not ask for, and therefore did not receive, the congressional manna: Congress cannot be expected to search out on its own those taxpayers whose peculiar circumstances give them strong equitable arguments for special relief from general tax provisions; rather, such taxpayers must come to Congress. . . .

We hold that the classifications made by Congress were not arbitrary. It accorded transitional relief to those deserving taxpayers who applied for such relief and established most convincingly that they relied substantially on the old tax laws in making major investment decisions.

> The court's decision was later reversed *en banc* by the Fifth Circuit, 987 F.2d 1174 (5th Cir. 1993), on the ground that the plaintiffs lacked standing. The court noted that "[t]he transition rules apply only to a very, very few taxpayers who requested such relief from Congress. The plaintiffs, claiming to lack political access, did not request such relief. In this lawsuit, they do not seek transition relief for themselves, but ask only that transition relief be denied to the favored taxpayers." In addition, the *en banc* decision emphasized that the "injury of unequal treatment alleged by the plaintiffs is shared in substantially equal measure by a 'disfavored class' that includes all taxpayers who did not receive transition relief. Like myriad taxpayers who did not request transition relief, the plaintiffs have not suffered any direct injury in the sense that they personally asked for and were denied a benefit granted to others. . . . [T]he Supreme Court has made it clear that when the asserted harm is a 'generalized grievance' shared in substantially equal measure by all or a large class of citizens, that harm alone normally does not warrant exercise of jurisdiction."

QUESTIONS AND COMMENTS

1. **Stating a cause of action.** What does the original three-judge Fifth Circuit decision (not the *en banc* reversal) suggest that the taxpayer must prove to establish an equal protection claim?

    (a) Is it sufficient or just necessary to prove that the taxpayer sought relief from Congress? How would such relief be sought?

    (b) Must the taxpayer also prove that he/she/it is in all respects like those who got the tax break?

    (c) What else would you want to prove about those who *did* get a tax break?

    (d) Why might it be very important for the taxpayer to obtain standing (denied by the *en banc* decision), even if the taxpayer loses on the merits (as in the original three-judge decision)?

2. **Interpreting rifle shot tax breaks.** The legislation in *Apache Bend* is an example of what are called "rifle shot" provisions, usually aimed at a single taxpayer. In *Airborne Freight Corp. v. United States*, 153 F.3d 967 (9th Cir. 1998), the court dealt with such a provision intended to help Merrill Lynch; however, the statutory text was broader. The statute preserved a tax credit for businesses that were obligated to lease a building for its world headquarters before September 26, 1985. The statute did not say that the lease had to be *entered into after* September 26, 1985 pursuant to an obligation incurred prior to that date, although that was Merrill Lynch's situation and was the circumstance that Congress intended to cover (as the legislative history made clear). Another taxpayer claimed and the court allowed the tax credit even though the taxpayer had entered into the lease *prior* to September 26, 1985. The court "decline[d] . . . to write the government's

additional proposed restrictions into the statute in order to confine the exception virtually to a class of one."

[E]   Tax Breaks, the Political Process, and the Line Item Veto

Another way to deal with rifle shot tax breaks is to permit the President to line item veto such provisions. The usual line item veto (allowed in more than 40 states by state constitutions) gives the chief executive the power to strike out specific spending in an appropriations law, without vetoing the entire law. When Congress passed a statute giving the President a line item veto — in the 1996 Line Item Veto Act (**2 U.S.C. § 691** *et seq.*) — it was sensitive to the argument that tax breaks could substitute for expenditures of money. Consequently, it included tax expenditures in the President's line item veto power, subject to certain exceptions. The following excerpts from the statute (**2 U.S.C. § 691e(9)**) give you an idea of what Congress had in mind:

(A) The term 'limited tax benefit' means —

(i) any revenue-losing provision which provides a Federal tax deduction, credit, exclusion, or preference to 100 or fewer beneficiaries . . . ;

(ii) any Federal tax provision which provides temporary or permanent transitional relief for 10 or fewer beneficiaries in any fiscal year from a change to the Internal Revenue Code of 1986.

(B) A provision shall not be treated as described in subparagraph (A)(I) if the effect of that provision is that —

(i) all persons in the same industry or engaged in the same type of activity receive the same treatment;

. . . , or

(iii) any difference in the treatment of persons is based solely on —

(I) in the case of businesses and associations, the size or form of the business or association involved;

(II) in the case of individuals, general demographic conditions, such as income, marital status, number of dependents, or tax return filing status;

(III) the amount involved.

(C) A provision shall not be treated as described in subparagraph (A)(ii) if —

(i) it provides for the retention of prior law with respect to all binding contracts or other legally enforceable obligations in existence on a date contemporaneous with congressional action specifying such date. . . .

In the end, the Supreme Court held that the President's line item veto was unconstitutional because it gave the President the legislative authority to alter a law passed by Congress. *Clinton v. City of New York*, 524 U.S. 417 (1998). Under the statute, the President had the authority to "cancel" a provision of the law after he had signed it, rather than removing a selected provision and then signing what was left of the law. The Court held that this violated the constitutional rules about making law — which required passage by both houses of Congress, subject to Presidential veto. The cancellation of a provision that had been signed into law was itself a change in the law that had to go through the usual lawmaking procedures. The Court rejected the view that the line item veto simply delegated discretionary authority to the President, analogous to the type of authority routinely delegated to administrative agencies.

There are two other ways in which something like a line item veto might survive scrutiny. First, the Court might uphold a line item veto that was more explicitly a delegation of administrative authority to the President, constrained by legislative standards. Second, a recent proposal would authorize the President to propose to Congress that an item in the law be rescinded. The President's legislative proposal would be placed on a fast-track in the Congress, which would vote explicitly to accept or reject rescission. This would give the President the power to force an open political debate about legislating selected tax breaks.

§ 6.02 AGENCY RULEMAKING

[A] Regulations

Introduction. You always start with the statute to determine tax law, but agency rules play a significant role in determining what the statute means. In general, Regulations are at the top of the agency-rulemaking ladder, followed by Revenue Rulings. The quality of the procedures used in promulgating income tax regulations makes them the most authoritative agency interpretation of the tax law. They not only follow a public notice and comment procedure but are also signed by both administrative and tax policy officials (the Commissioner and the Assistant Secretary of the Treasury for Tax Policy). Other types of agency rulings do not usually follow these procedures.

An analysis of the weight accorded to tax regulations is a branch of administrative law, which has some quirks arising from the income tax statute. The issue is best approached by first considering regulations that have been issued after public notice and comment and then considering temporary regulations, which are not issued after public notice and comment.

Regulations issued with notice and comment; Chevron. Regulations issued after notice and comment are usually authoritative, but what does that mean? The conventional administrative law answer is given by Chevron U.S.A., Inc. v. Natural Resources Defense Council, Inc., 467 U.S. 837 (1984), which holds that the court should defer to a regulation if the statute has not resolved an issue and the agency interpretation is reasonable. There are two slightly different ways to describe when Congress has failed to resolve an issue — when the statute has left a gap for an agency to fill or Congress has delegated authority to the agency interpretation is reasonable. In United States v. Mead Corp., 533 U.S. 218 (2001), the Court made it clear that the gap can be created either expressly (by an express textual delegation of authority) or implicitly ("from the agency's generally conferred authority and other statutory circumstances [indicating] that Congress would expect the agency to be able to speak with the force of law").

In tax cases, there were doubts whether *Chevron* deference should be accorded to both substantive and interpretive tax regulations until the Court decided *Mayo Foundation* for *Medical Education and Research v. United States*, 131 S. Ct. 704 (2011). The doubts arose because substantive regulations have traditionally been understood as being issued pursuant to an explicit grant of regulatory authority in the governing statute — as is often found in specific sections of the Internal Revenue Code. In addition to specific grants of regulatory authority, a more general provision of the code gave the Secretary of the Treasury the authority to "prescribe all needful rules and regulations" to enforce the law; § 7805(a). Arguably, § 7805(a) provided authority for interpretive, not substantive regulations.

The *Mayo* case dealt with a Treasury Department rule interpreting the Social Security Act. That Act exempted from taxation "service performed in the employ of . . . a school, college, or university . . . if such service is performed by a student who is enrolled and regularly attending classes at such school, college, or university." The Treasury regulations exempted students whose work was "incident to and for the purposes of pursuing a course of study." In 2004, the Treasury replaced its case-by-case application of this standard with a rule that categorically excludes from the student exemption a "full-time employee," defined in all events as an employee "normally scheduled to work 40 hours or more per week." The issue was whether this regulation could be applied to deny an exemption for medical residents who have graduated from medical school and train for a specialty. These doctors are required to engage in formal educational activities but spend most of their time (50 to 80 hours per week) caring for patients. The Court concluded that Congress had not directly addressed this precise question because it did not define "student" or consider how to deal with medical residents.

The Court noted that it had sometimes relied in tax cases on the *National Muffler* case, 440 U.S. 472 (1979), which had been skeptical of regulations that were inconsistent over time, were issued long after the law was enacted, or were a response to litigation. Those of you familiar with administrative law will recognize *National Muffler* as an application of what is referred to as Skidmore deference, named after *Skidmore v. Swift & Co.*, 323 U.S. 134 (1944). Under *Skidmore*, the courts look at the agency's care in reasoning, its consistency in sticking to its rules, the longstanding nature of the rule, the formality of its rulemaking procedures (such as following notice and comment procedures), its expertise, and "all those factors which give power to persuade, if lacking power to control."

In *Mayo* the Court concluded that *Chevron* deference did not depend on the factors mentioned in *National Muffler* and it then deferred to the Treasury's Regulation. In reaching its conclusion, the Court made no distinction between rules issued pursuant to the Treasury Department's general authority to "prescribe all needful rules and regulations for the enforcement" of the tax law (that is, regulations that might be considered interpretive issued under § 7805(a)) and rules "issued under a specific grant of authority to define a statutory term or prescribe a method of executing a statutory provision" (that is, "substantive" regulations).

The Court also noted that the Treasury Department had "issued the [] rule only after [public] notice-and-comment procedures, again a consideration identified in our precedents as a 'significant' sign that a rule merits *Chevron* deference."

No notice and comment; Administrative Procedure Act. Regulations issued without public notice and comment raise questions, not only about *Chevron* deference, but also about the impact of the Administrative Procedure Act. Under the Administrative Procedure Act (APA), substantive (but not interpretive) regulations must be issued after notice to the public and an opportunity for public comment. Whatever the understanding of § 7805(a) under the tax code, regulations issued under § 7805(a) are probably substantive regulations under the APA — because they are intended to have the force of law. As a practical matter, the APA's requirement is often irrelevant under the income tax law because the Treasury usually relies on public notice and comment procedures for regulations, regardless of what the law requires.

However, a major exception to the practice of issuing tax regulations after public notice and comment is the practice regarding temporary regulations. These regulations are issued without public notice and comment. Under § 7805(e), temporary regulations must be accompanied by the issuance of proposed regulations with an opportunity for notice and comment, and the temporary regulations must expire in three years. Proposed Regulations are published in the Federal Register and final regulations appear in the Code of Federal Regulations (C.F.R.). The validity of temporary regulations under the APA was at issue in *Intermountain Insurance Service v. Commissioner*, 134 T.C. 211 (2010).

A *concurring* opinion in the Tax Court argued that a tax regulation is "substantive," subject to the APA requirements of public notice and comment, whenever "Congress has given the agency authority to issue rules with the force of law and the agency intended to use that authority." (It did not matter that, under tax law, these regulations might be considered "interpretive.") Consequently, the concurring opinion argued, the temporary regulation was invalid under the APA because of a failure to provide public notice and comment.

The Tax Court concurring opinion also dealt with the APA provision that permitted a later statute to override the APA requirements if it does so "expressly" — "no subsequent legislation shall be held to supersede or modify the provisions of this Act except to the extent that such legislation shall do so expressly"; **5 USC § 559.** The concurring opinion rejected the argument that § 7805(e) amounted to an "express" override of the APA requirement as follows:

> The legislative history of [sec. 7805(e)] shows that Congress was aware of the Secretary's procedures of issuing temporary regulations that were effective immediately but without notice and comment. [The Commissioner] says that Congress implicitly okayed that process by limiting the temporary regulations to 3 years and ensuring that the Secretary issued an

NPRM at the same time. Even though this violates the APA, he justifies it by arguing that section 7805(e) conflicts with the APA, and in the battle of the statutes, a specific statute trumps a general one.

We do not agree. First we note that nothing in the text of the statute suggests that the notice-and-comment requirement has been waived, nor does the legislative history state that it has. The legislative history does note that the Secretary commonly issued temporary regulations with immediate effect, but this alone hardly suggests Congress meant to waive notice and comment for all temporary regulations. The legislative history does not even mention the APA, and both the Supreme Court and the APA itself provide that exceptions to the APA's terms cannot be inferred — much less inferred from an absence in the legislative history. . . . [The Commissioner] may think that section 7805(e) makes him special when it comes to rulemaking, but the APA makes it clear that he is not.

There is an argument against applying the APA to at least some Temporary Regulations. 5 U.S.C. § 553(b)(B) provides an exemption from the APA for "good cause." In the tax context, this exemption might apply when a proposed regulation (not yet effective) would lead to undesirable behavior that tries to avoid the impact of any final regulation — for example, when a proposed regulation stated that preferential capital gains treatment would no longer be available for specified transactions, thereby leading to a flood of "capital gains" transactions.

Remember Skidmore. The impact of failing to satisfy the APA is unclear. Even if the rule is invalid under the APA for failure to meet notice and comment requirements and is, as a result, not entitled to *Chevron* deference, it might still be entitled to some weight under *Skidmore v. Swift & Co.*, 323 U.S. 134 (1944). (The same issue arises with Revenue Rulings, discussed below.) Those familiar with administrative law will probably tell you that the line between *Chevron* and *Skidmore* deference is less than clear.

Retroactive Regulations. **Section 7805(b)(1)** provides that no Regulation (relating to laws enacted on or after July 30, 1996) shall apply retroactively (with some exceptions). The statutory exceptions include regulations filed or issued within 18 months of enactment of the law to which the regulation relates; and any regulation that the Secretary of the Treasury provides is needed to prevent "abuse." However, this anti-retroactivity statute only applies to laws enacted on or after July 30, 1996 (Public Law 104-168, sec. 1101(b)). Whether or not the Treasury can adopt a Regulation retroactively when it is not subject to § 7805(b)(1) remains an open question.

Regulation that helps a taxpayer. If the Regulation *helps* the taxpayer, there is no need to invoke *Chevron*. The courts will not permit the agency to disavow the regulation retroactively, even if the government could not rely on the regulation to support the government's position. Retroactive revocation is an abuse of agency discretion. Consequently, the dispute over whether *Chevron* applies and what it means is relevant primarily when the government invokes the regulation.

[B]   Revenue Rulings

[1]   Can Taxpayers Rely on Revenue Rulings?

Revenue Rulings are usually published distillations of the contents of important letter rulings. (Letter rulings are discussed below.) They are almost always issued by the IRS without public notice and comment. They appear first in the Internal Revenue Bulletin and are then published semi-annually in the Cumulative Bulletin (C.B.).

The IRS says that taxpayers can generally rely on Revenue Rulings and that any new ruling will not generally be applied retroactively to the extent that it would have adverse effects on the taxpayer. Rev. Proc. 78-24, 1978-2 C.B. 502.

Courts have sometimes said that retroactive revocation of a Revenue Ruling is permitted, but there are strong hints that retroactive revocation might be disallowed as an abuse of agency discretion if the result would be unduly harsh. *Dunn v. United States*, 468 F. Supp. 991, 995 (S.D.N.Y. 1979). *See also Estate of McLendon v. Commissioner*, 135 F.3d 1017 (5th Cir. 1998) (the agency cannot depart from a Revenue Ruling in the taxpayer's favor, if the law interpreted by the ruling is unclear).

See also *Rauenhorst v. C.I.R.*, 119 T.C. 157 (2002), where the Tax Court forced the government to apply its own Revenue Ruling to benefit a taxpayer claiming a charitable contribution, stating:

> The Commissioner has neither revoked nor modified Rev. Rul. 78-197. . . . Indeed, the Commissioner has continued to rely on Rev. Rul. 78-197, in issuing his private letter rulings. . . . [W]e are not prepared to allow respondent's counsel to argue . . . against the principles and public guidance articulated in the Commissioner's currently outstanding revenue rulings. . . . [W]e cannot agree that the Commissioner is not bound to follow his revenue rulings in Tax Court proceedings. Indeed, we have on several occasions treated revenue rulings as concessions by the Commissioner where those rulings are relevant to our disposition of the case. . . . Respondent's counsel may not choose to litigate against the officially published rulings of the Commissioner without first withdrawing or modifying those rulings. The result of contrary action is capricious application of the law. . . . The Commissioner's revenue ruling has been in existence for nearly 25 years, and it has not been revoked or modified. No doubt taxpayers have referred to that ruling in planning their charitable contributions, and, indeed, petitioners submit that they relied upon that ruling in planning the charitable contributions at issue. Under the circumstances of this case, we treat the Commissioner's position in Rev. Rul. 78-197, 1978-1 C.B. 83, as a concession.

[2]   *Chevron* Deference?

When the government relies on a Revenue Ruling as legal authority, courts once said that they carry no weight as interpretations of law — they are just the opinion of one of the litigants. *Browne v. Commissioner*, 73 T.C. 723, 731 (1980) (Hall, J., concurring). More recently, some courts have applied *Chevron* deference to Revenue Rulings and there is considerable uncertainty as to whether that is appropriate and whether it is good law. *See, e.g.*, Bankers Life and Casualty Co. v. United States, 142 F.3d 973 (7th Cir. 1998), which states:

> Revenue rulings receive the lowest degree of deference — at least in this circuit. In First Chicago, we held that revenue rulings deserve "some weight," and are "entitled to respectful consideration, but not to the deference that the Chevron doctrine requires in its domain." In other circuits this question has generated inconsistent rulings ranging from Chevron deference to no deference.

In Ryan Lirette, *Giving* Chevron *Deference to Revenue Rulings and Procedures*, 129 TAX NOTES 1357 (2010), the author notes that there is now a lower court consensus that Revenue Rulings and Revenue Procedures are only eligible for *Skidmore* (not *Chevron*) deference. *See also In re Quality Stores, Inc.*, 693 F.3d 605 (6th Cir. 2012) (no *Chevron* deference for Revenue Rulings because they are not issued pursuant to the power to make law; however, the court will give substantial judicial deference to long-standing and reasonable revenue rulings in "appropriate circumstances"). But the author of the Tax Notes article advocates *Chevron* deference for these rulings if "Congress would have wanted [them] to receive *Chevron* deference," which (he argues) is often true. This would mean *Chevron* deference despite the absence of public notice and comment prior to issuing the rulings.

Supreme Court cases, dealing with nontax agencies, suggest some uncertainty about the level of deference to accord agency rules that do not go through a public notice and comment procedure (such as a Revenue Rulings): *Raymond B. Yates v. Hendon*, 541 U.S. 1 (2004) (*Skidmore* deference to a Department of Labor advisory opinion; Justice Scalia's concurrence argued for *Chevron* deference because the opinion was the agency's considered official view and was not "contrived for this litigation"); *Alaska Dept. of Environmental Conservation v. E.P.A.*, 540 U.S. 461 (2004) (refusing *Chevron* deference to an internal guidance memoranda, but nevertheless giving it "respect"; Kennedy's dissent argued that the "respect" had amounted to *Chevron* deference).

The Department of Justice (DOJ) once argued that Revenue Rulings had the force of law under *Mead* and were therefore entitled to Chevron deference, but the appellate section chief of the DOJ announced at a May 2011 meeting of the American Bar Association Section on Taxation that the DOJ would no longer argue that revenue rulings should receive *Chevron* deference (Tax Notes, May 16, 2011, p. 674). Presumably the IRS can take a different position in litigation than the DOJ, so the issue remains open. (The subsequent discussion of Tax Litigation distinguishes between Tax Court and U.S. District Court venues. The DOJ handles district court litigation; the IRS's Chief Counsel's Office is responsible for Tax Court litigation.)

In any event, the fact that Revenue Rulings are not issued with public notice and comment might make them invalid under the APA. Consequently, they might only be entitled to *Skidmore* deference on that account. *See* Leandra Lederman, *The*

Fight Over "Fighting Regulations" and Judicial Deference in Tax Litigation, 92 BOSTON UNIV. L. REV. 643 (2012).

For scholarly comment on this issue, *see* Ellen P. Aprill, *Muffled Chevron: Judicial Review of Tax Regulations*, 3 Fla. Tax Rev. 51 (1996); Paul L. Caron, *Tax Myopia Meets Tax Hyperopia: The Unproven Case of Increased Judicial Deference to Revenue Rulings*, 57 Ohio St. L.J. 637 (1996); John F. Coverdale, *Court Review of Tax Regulations and Revenue Rulings in the Chevron Era*, 64 Geo. Wash. L. Rev. 35 (1995); Linda Galler, *Judicial Deference to Revenue Rulings: Reconciling Divergent Standards*, 56 Ohio St. L.J. 1037 (1995).

[3] Revenue Rulings Interpreting Regulations

Yet another wrinkle is the weight accorded to Revenue Rulings that explicitly interpret Treasury Regulations. Courts sometimes say that an agency interpretation of its own regulations is entitled to substantial deference. A recent tax case — *United States v. Cleveland Indians Baseball Co.*, 532 U.S. 200 (2001) — is an example. The Court said:

> . . . [T]he Internal Revenue Service has consistently interpreted [the Regulations] to require taxation of back wages according to the year the wages are actually paid, regardless of when those wages were earned or should have been paid. Rev. Rul. 89-35, 1989-1 C.B. 280; Rev. Rul. 78-336, 1978-2 C.B. 255. We need not decide whether the Revenue Rulings themselves are entitled to deference. In this case, the Rulings simply reflect the agency's longstanding interpretation of its own regulations. Because that interpretation is reasonable, it attracts substantial judicial deference. Thomas Jefferson Univ. v. Shalala, 512 U.S. 504, 512 (1994). We do not resist according such deference in reviewing an agency's steady interpretation of its own 61-year-old regulation implementing a 62-year-old statute. "Treasury regulations and interpretations long continued without substantial change, applying to unamended or substantially reenacted statutes, are deemed to have received congressional approval and have the effect of law." Cottage Savings Ass'n v. Commissioner, 499 U.S. 554, 561 (1991) (citing *Correll*, 389 U.S. at 305–06).

Whether agency interpretations of its own regulations *should* receive substantial deference is not an easy question. If a court accords such deference, that could encourage the agency to adopt regulations in need of further interpretation, which is then provided by rulemaking procedures that do not provide the public with notice and an opportunity to comment. *See* Lars Noah, *Divining Regulatory Intent: The Place for a "Legislative History" of Agency Rules*, 51 Hastings L.J. 255, 284–90 (2000). Nonetheless, the Supreme Court has accorded agency interpretations of its own rules substantial deference; *Auer v. Robbins*, 519 U.S. 452 (1997).

In *Gonzales v. Oregon*, 546 U.S. 243 (2006), the Court imposed a qualification on the principle that an agency's interpretation of its own regulations deserves substantial deference. The Attorney General had issued an Interpretive Rule interpreting a Regulation. This Rule stated that assisted suicide was not a legitimate medical purpose and that prescribing a federally controlled substance for that purpose violated the federal Controlled Substances Act. The Court held that this Rule was not entitled to deference under *Auer v. Robbins* because the regulation that the Rule interpreted merely paraphrased the statutory language. See also *Talk America, Inc.* v. *Michigan Bell Telephone Co.*, 131 S. Ct. 2254, 2263 (2011), the Court explicitly noted that the agency's interpretation of its own regulation was not a "post-hoc rationalization [] of agency action under judicial review," rather than a "fair and considered agency judgment."

[4]   Other Agency Rulings

There are a few other agency statements about the law.

1. Revenue Procedures usually deal with (not surprisingly) procedure — such as how returns should be filed. But sometimes they provide substantive guidance — such as explaining the multiple factors that go into reaching a substantive decision. *See, e.g.*, Revenue Procedures discussed in later chapters — Rev. Proc. 72-18, 1972-1 C.B. 740 (Chapter 16.02[A]; allocating interest on debt incurred to purchase or carry tax exempt bonds); Rev. Proc. 71-21, 1971-2 C.B. 549; Rev. Proc. 2004-34, 2004-1 C.B. 991 (Chapter 25.01[B][2][c][i, ii]; deferring prepaid income). Presumably, they are entitled to the same deference as Revenue Rulings. Revenue Procedures also state those areas of tax law where the government will not issue letter rulings (discussed below) — usually involving fact-specific issues or tax avoidance potential.

In *Federal National Mortgage Ass'n v. United States*, 379 F.3d 1303 (Fed. 2004), the court discussed whether a Revenue Procedure was entitled to *Chevron* deference. The answer was "no," but with a lot of hemming and hawing. The court said: (1) although the agency asked for public comment (unusual for a Revenue Procedure), it did not ask for comment on the interpretive issue arising in this case; (2) even if Revenue Rulings might be eligible for *Chevron* deference, Revenue Procedures were different; and (3) the Revenue Procedure lacked any analysis of the relevant text or legislative history. This last observation also denied the Revenue Procedure any *Skidmore* deference.

2. The IRS will sometimes issue an acquiescence or nonacquiescence in a Tax Court decision (the Tax Court is discussed below). These statements tell taxpayers whether a decision will or will not be followed by the government. The government does not consider these statements to be precedent in other cases, so (presumably) they are entitled to little or no judicial deference.

[C]   Letter Rulings; TAMs

There are other forms of agency interpretations, which you will see cited throughout the course. A letter (or private) ruling is an administrative "declaratory judgment," which the National Office of the IRS will issue to a taxpayer for a fee. If the taxpayer has accurately described the facts and has relied on the ruling to plan future behavior, the agency promises that it will not revoke the ruling *as to that taxpayer*. Taxpayers cannot rely on a ruling issued to another taxpayer, although there are occasional cases holding that a taxpayer cannot be denied the benefit of a favorable ruling received by a competitor. *IBM v. United States*, 343 F.2d 914 (Ct. Cl. 1965). *But see Florida Power & Light Co. v. United States*, 56 Fed.

Cl. 328 (2003) (limiting IBM case to taxpayers who have asked for a ruling providing the benefit received by a competitor), *aff'd*, 375 F.3d 1119 (Fed. Cir. 2004). *See also Farmers' & Merchants' Bank v. United States*, 476 F.2d 406 (4th Cir. 1973) (taxpayer-bank should be allowed same tax benefit as other banks who benefitted from an exception to a retroactive revocation of a Revenue Ruling).

Another type of agency interpretation, specific to a particular taxpayer, is a Taxpayer Advice Memorandum (TAM). Like a letter ruling, it is issued by the National Office of the IRS, but is a response to a request for legal advice by an IRS field agent, not the taxpayer.

Letter rulings and TAMs are not officially published by the government but are available to the public under the Freedom of Information Act and § 6110 (with confidential information, including the taxpayer's identity, redacted). Because of the amount of money involved in taxation, private publishers (including Lexis and Westlaw) routinely publish most important letter rulings and TAMs, so that they are read by interested tax advisors.

The government's position is that letter rulings and TAMs are not precedent. Indeed, § 6110(k)(3) states that they "may not be used or cited as precedent," except as the government otherwise provides by Regulation. But the practice is more complex. *See* 88 Tax Notes 1035 (2000). A long-standing practice of issuing letter rulings is likely to carry some weight with a court, especially if the reasoning of the rulings seems persuasive. And, in a recent case, the government asked the court to purge a judicial opinion of references to TAMs, but the court refused. *Buckeye Power, Inc. v. United States*, 38 Fed. Cl. 283 (1997):

> [The government] does not agree with the reasoning of the TAM referenced by the court and requests that it be deleted from the record. Defendant presents no evidence that Congress intended I.R.C. § 6110(k)(3) to shield all non-precedential decisions from use by the outside world. [Editor — The court states in a footnote: "It is worth noting that the government cites TAMs when the TAMs support its position."] [T]he purpose for the non-precedential status of TAMs is that if all publicly disclosed written determinations were to have precedential value, the Service would be required to subject them to considerably greater review than as provided under current procedures. Congress believed that the resulting delays in the issuance of determinations would mean that many taxpayers could not obtain timely guidance from the Service and the ruling program would suffer accordingly.
>
> I.R.C. § 6110(k)(3) permits the IRS to provide expeditious guidance to a single taxpayer, while preserving the opportunity to revisit its reasoning at a future time. However, the mere fact that TAMs are not binding on the IRS does not insulate the IRS from persuasive reasoning contained in prior decisions. Stated differently, strong analytical reasoning does not lose its persuasive force simply because the reasoning does not bind the IRS or constitute authority to be cited in judicial opinions. As the Supreme Court has explained, "although the petitioners are not entitled to rely upon unpublished private rulings which were not issued specifically to them, such rulings do reveal the interpretation put upon the statute by the agency

charged with the responsibility of administering the revenue laws." Hanover Bank v. Commissioner, 369 U.S. 672, 686 (1962).

In the case at bar, the court expressly stated that the TAM did not bind [the government]. The court fully evaluated [the government's] argument, but found that the uncontroverted facts did not support [the government's] position. After reviewing the factual record, the court discussed and quoted the TAM to note that it reinforced plaintiff's independently viable position.

See also Merchant v. Kelly, Haglund, Garnsey & Kahn, 874 F. Supp. 300 (D. Colo. 1995), where the court held that the trier of fact in a malpractice lawsuit should consider the attorney's failure to take account of a prior letter ruling adverse to his client's position when planning a transaction.

A recent Federal Claims Court decision, *Amergen Energy Co., LLC ex rel. Exelon Generation Co., LLC v. United States*, 94 Fed. Cl. 413 (2010), also discussed the limited use of private letter rulings, as follows:

The parties clearly disagree as to the relevance of a private letter ruling, issued by the IRS to one taxpayer, to the litigation of a different tax claim brought by another taxpayer. Plaintiff's argument is founded on assumptions that the court cannot endorse. First, plaintiff states that "[t]he Court of Federal Claims . . . has ruled repeatedly that PLRs can be relevant to ongoing litigation, and many cases have explicitly considered PLRs as evidence." This statement does not give a full picture of this court's, or other courts', consideration of PLRs in tax cases.

[Editor — The court noted in footnote 6 that plaintiff relies extensively on *IBM v. United States*, 343 F.2d 914, 170 Ct. Cl. 357 (1965), a case with thirty negative citing references, and omits any reference to the precedential limitation of the holding of that case to its facts (citations omitted).]

Private letter rulings, like certain other written determinations issued by the IRS, "may not be used or cited as precedent." 26 U.S.C. § 6110(k)(3) (2006). Most courts, therefore, do not find private letter rulings, issued to other taxpayers, to be of precedential value in deciding the tax claims before them (citations omitted).

[D]   Other Agency Guidance

Various documents explain the basis for conclusions reached in various rulings. The detailed legal reasoning behind the issuance of a Revenue Ruling often appears in General Counsel Memorandums (GCMs); but GCMs are not used much today. They have been replaced by Chief Counsel Advisories (CCAs). Similarly, an Action on Decision (AOD) explains the decision to acquiesce or nonacquiesce in a Tax Court decision. Lawyers often find material discussed and cited in GCMs, CCAs, and AODs very useful as research tools. GCMs, CCAs, and AODs are available to the public (see § 6110(i)), and are published privately.

In *Nathel v. Commissioner*, 615 F.3d 83 (2d Cir. 2010), the court refused to give *Chevron* guidance to a GCM, as follows:

I.R.S. General Counsel Memoranda are informal documents written by the I.R.S. Chief Counsel's office. They provide the Chief Counsel's opinion on particular tax matters before other I.R.S. officials. The Memorandum at issue in this case includes a disclaimer that it is "not to be relied upon or otherwise cited as precedent by taxpayers." As a result, the Memorandum is not entitled to deference under *Chevron U.S.A. Inc. v. National Resources Defense Council, Inc.*, 467 U.S. 837 (1984), because it is an informal letter that itself renounces any force of law effect. See *United States v. Mead Corp.*, 533 U.S. 218, 226–27 (2001) (holding that Chevron deference is appropriate "when it appears that Congress delegated authority to the agency generally to make rules carrying the force of law, and that the agency interpretation claiming deference was promulgated in the exercise of that authority"); *Christensen v. Harris County*, 529 U.S. 576, 587–88 (2000) (holding that agency interpretations contained in informal opinion letters are not entitled to *Chevron* deference). Any "respect" afforded to the Memorandum would only be proportional to its "power to persuade" pursuant to *Skidmore v. Swift & Co.*, 323 U.S. 134, 140. In this case, we decline to rely on the Memorandum because it disclaims precedential effect and is not entitled to deference under *Chevron*.

§ 6.03   TAX LAW ADJUDICATION

[A]   Agency Level

Agency audits. Tax law adjudication usually begins with an agency audit of the taxpayer's return. In general, individuals are required to file returns if their gross income equals or exceeds the personal exemption amount (**§ 6012(a)(1)**) The return is due by April 15 following the end of the tax year. Most of the tax has already been collected through wage withholding and estimated tax payments made during the tax year.

All returns are checked for mathematical mistakes. Computers also match information returns (primarily regarding wages, interest, and dividends) against the taxpayer's return. Some taxpayer returns are selected for audit, although the percentage has been declining so that it is now well below 1% overall. Audit criteria are, of course, not public but higher income taxpayers have a higher percentage of their returns audited and certain types of taxpayers (with a lot of cash transactions) and certain return items are more likely to attract attention. The items that attract attention will vary over time — for example, charitable deduction of highly valued property; a lot of deductible travel expenses relative to income; earned income credit claims that might be fraudulent.

Audits fall into three general categories: a correspondence audit (with answers provided by mail); an office audit (where the taxpayer goes to the IRS office with records); and a field audit (where the agent visits the taxpayer's place of business, typically used for large corporations).

If the taxpayer and the IRS cannot agree, a 30-day letter is issued to the taxpayer explaining the opportunity for an "Appeals Office" conference. Appeals

Offices are located throughout the country and are administratively part of the Chief Counsel's office. Settlement of tax disputes is permitted. However, the IRS will not settle a case based on its nuisance value (sometimes said to involve less than a 20% chance of winning), on the theory that to do so would encourage frivolous litigating positions. Taxpayers do not have to exhaust their administrative remedies, but doing so is a prerequisite to recovering attorneys' fees (and some other costs) from the government under certain circumstances; § 7430(b–c).

If, after completion of the administrative appeals process, the government still asserts a tax deficiency, it issues a 90-day letter, giving the taxpayer 90 days to go to the Tax Court.

Statutes of limitations. The statute of limitations for issuing the 90-day letter is three years from the filing of the tax return (or the April 15 filing date, if later). § 6501(a). A six-year limitations period is provided if the taxpayer omits at least 25% of gross income from the return (one of the few times the gross income figure is critical); and there is no statute of limitations if the taxpayer fails to file a return or files a false or fraudulent return. § 6501(c)(1,3), (e). Taxpayers usually consent to extending the limitations period if there is an ongoing dispute with the IRS, in order to avoid an immediate issuance of a 90-day letter. If the taxpayer has paid the tax and seeks a refund, the limitations period for filing for a refund is the later of three years from filing the return or two years of payment. § 6511(a).

Is there an omission from gross income in the nonbusiness context when there is an overstatement of cost and, therefore, a six-year statute of limitations? For example, if a taxpayer claims a $10,000 cost on the sale of an investment asset for $10,000, but the correct cost is zero, there is a $10,000 understatement of gross income, but is there an "omission" from gross income? A Supreme Court case had interpreted an earlier version of the Code (the 1939 Code) to mean that an overstatement of cost did *not* constitute an omission from gross income (*Colony v. Commissioner*, 357 U.S. 28 (1958)), and the 1954 Code explicitly adopted that view with regard to business income. The Treasury issued a Regulation stating that, in the *nonbusiness* context, an overstatement of basis was an omission from gross income. **Treas. Reg. § 301.6501(e)-1(a)(iii).** Federal courts usually defer to reasonable regulations when the statute is unclear (under the *Chevron* case), and even uphold a regulation disagreeing with a prior judicial interpretation as long as the prior judicial interpretation resolved a statutory ambiguity. *National Cable & Telecommunications Assn. v. Brand X Internet Services*, 545 U.S. 967 (2005). However, in *United States v. Home Concrete & Supply, LLC*, 132 S. Ct. 1836 (2012), in an opinion by Justice Breyer, the Court followed the *Colony* case and rejected the Treasury Regulation — an overstatement of basis was not an omission from gross income under § 6501(e)(1)(A) in the nonbusiness context. It reached this conclusion even though the *Colony* case had acknowledged that the 1939 Code provision was ambiguous and even though the 1954 Code provision favorable to business income arguably left open the treatment of nonbusiness income. Apparently, the fact that the Colony case predated *Chevron* means that the concept of "ambiguity" for purposes of applying *Brand X* is different depending on when the court has interpreted the prior law that the agency wants to override by a regulation. If you have trouble wrapping your mind around this complication, do not be too disturbed. So did Justice Scalia, who refused to join the part of Justice

Breyer's opinion dealing with the *Brand X* case.

Interest; penalties. Interest is due on underpayments, running from the date the tax was due (usually the date for filing the return). The interest rate is generally the short-term federal rate plus 3%. Interest paid by the government on overpayments is the same figure. §§ **6601, 6611, 6621**. Civil penalties can also be imposed for failure to file or pay in a timely fashion and for inaccuracy rising to the level of fraud, negligence, substantial understatement of taxes, and various other "improper" activities. §§ **6651, 6662, 6663,** etc. In addition, § **6702** provides a penalty for filing a frivolous return, as that term is defined by the government (which cannot include a position for which there is a "reasonable basis").

[B]   Court Level

Here is an overview of the judicial process in tax cases. One constant among the different trial courts is the burden of proof, which is generally on the taxpayer. An exception is provided by § **162(c)(1,2)** (government has the burden of proof as to whether a deduction should be disallowed because a payment is illegal). *See also* § **7491(c)**, which provides that "the Secretary shall have the burden of production in any court proceeding with respect to the liability of any individual for any penalty, addition to tax, or additional amount imposed by this title." Burden of proof is discussed further in Chapter 8.08[B].

A taxpayer has three choices for a judicial trial — the Tax Court, the U.S. District Court, and the Court of Federal Claims. The oldest of these is the U.S. District Court, where an aggrieved taxpayer originally sued the tax collector for money had and received, long before there was an income tax. Today, the lawsuit is against the United States. As a condition of access to the District Court, the taxpayer must pay the entire disputed tax for the tax year. The taxpayer may want to do this to stop interest running. One "reward" for paying is the right to a jury trial in the District Court, not available in any other court. People without the cash to pay the tax are unable to sue for a refund, which means that they are denied practical access to a jury trial.

An alternative judicial remedy, again only by paying the disputed tax in full, is the Court of Federal Claims. This forum (under various names — previously the Court of Claims and the Claims Court) goes back to the second half of the nineteenth century. It is a Washington-based court but the judges travel throughout the country to hear cases.

The Tax Court began in 1924 (as the Board of Tax Appeals), specifically to give the taxpayer a forum to resolve disputes without first paying taxes. It began as an independent agency within the executive branch, but was designated as an Article I court in 1969. (Article I judges differ from Article III judges in not having life tenure.) There are 19 Tax Court judges, appointed for 15 years by the President.

The taxpayer invokes the Tax Court's jurisdiction by filing before expiration of the 90-day letter. The Tax Court is a national court but individual judges travel to local areas to conduct trials. Cases involving important legal issues are reviewed by all 19 Tax Court judges on the written record. Tax Court decisions that are primarily factual, not legal, are not officially published by the government (these are Tax Court Memorandum decisions — T.C.M.), but they are privately published. T.C.M. cases are not supposed to be cited as precedent, but (as the material in this book illustrates) many of T.C.M. decisions deal with important tax issues.

The Tax Court can also issue Summary Opinions in "small tax cases," involving no more than $50,000 in a tax year, if the taxpayer elects this procedure. These opinions (cited as "T.C. Summary Opinions") are usually written by a "special trial judge" appointed by the Chief Judge of the Tax Court. § 7463. Decisions in these cases are not appealable and cannot be cited as precedent.

Finally, tax cases can also be litigated in bankruptcy court, as part of the determination of an individual's debts. This is not usually listed as one of the three trial courts that can hear tax cases because the taxpayer does not usually choose whether to litigate a tax issue in that court. However, a large tax debt might lead an insolvent taxpayer to declare bankruptcy and, in that sense, the bankruptcy court becomes a fourth choice for a tax litigation forum. In any event, bankruptcy judges decide a lot of tax cases.

Judicial review of lower court decisions from the District Court and Bankruptcy Court is the same as for any nontax case arising in these courts — usually to the Court of Appeals of the taxpayer's residence. The taxpayer's residence also determines which Court of Appeals hears appeals from the Tax Court, which means that the national Tax Court's decisions fan out to divergent Courts of Appeals. The Tax Court conforms to Court of Appeals decisions in the region to which a taxpayer can appeal. *Golsen v. Commissioner*, 54 T.C. 742 (1970). The Tax Court does, however, stick to its own legal views if there is no specific holding in the relevant appellate court, even though other Courts of Appeals do not agree with the Tax Court.

Appeals from the Court of Federal Claims go to the Court of Appeals for the Federal Circuit, based in Washington, D.C. In the early 1980s, this court almost became the single Court of Tax Appeals for the entire nation, ending the multiple appellate court system. Efforts to establish a specialized appellate tax court have consistently failed, allegedly because of enthusiasm for generalist rather than specialist courts. Another reason is probably that the current system gives taxpayers great flexibility in choosing a forum and denies the government the power to control which cases to take to a single appellate court where precedent will be set.

The Supreme Court sits on top of this appellate structure but its docket is discretionary. Today, it rarely hears more than one or two income tax cases per year, and often the issue involves tax procedure rather than substantive law.

This is the judicial system to which the Supreme Court reacted in *Dobson v. Commissioner*, 320 U.S. 489 (1943) (applying the tax benefit rule). The Court deferred to an "expert" Tax Court to resolve tax disputes, but the statute was then amended to provide that appellate courts would give no greater deference to the Tax Court than to the District Courts. § 7482(a). More fundamentally, the reality of the trifurcated trial system made privileging Tax Court decisions difficult to sustain. For a renewed debate over whether deferring to the Tax Court is a good idea, *see* David F Shores, *Rethinking Deferential Review of Tax Court Decisions*,

53 TAX LAW. 35 (1999); Steve R Johnson, *The Phoenix and the Perils of the Second Best: Why Heightened Appellate Deference to Tax Court Decisions is Undesirable*, 77 OR. L. REV. 235 (1998). For an example of an appeals court still deferring to the Tax Court's expertise, *see California Federal Life Ins. v. Commissioner*, 680 F.2d 85 (9th Cir. 1982).

An intriguing question is whether different courts are disposed to take different approaches to interpreting the income tax code. In David F. Shores, *Textualism and Intentionalism in Tax Litigation*, 61 TAX LAW. 53 (2007), the author looked at how the Tax Court and the Courts of Appeals dealt with ten cases in which there was a clear difference in result depending on whether the court deferred to the plain meaning of the text or relied on other evidence of legislative intent. The finding was that the Tax Court relied on intent in every such case, but the Courts of Appeals relied on plain meaning. *Query*. If this finding holds up across a wide range of cases, why might it be true? Does the "expert" Tax Court believe it has better insight into the underlying meaning of the Code than generalist courts?

§ 6.04 ETHICAL RESPONSIBILITIES OF A REPRESENTATIVE

It is often said that the law is what the judge says it is, because the court's judgment is the operative event in the application of the law. An even more realistic way to describe what makes law is that the law is what the lawyer (or other representative) says it is, because most issues are not litigated in an administrative or judicial process. It is, therefore, useful in thinking about tax law to consider the tax advisor's ethical responsibilities, based on the American Bar Association interpretations of the Code of Professional Responsibility and the Treasury's rules appearing in Circular 230.

It will help you to focus on this material if you have some substantive issues in mind — for example: (1) If your client won a prize of a car on a quiz show, could you advise him to report a value based on his subjective value for the car? (2) Would your advice be different if your client received a car from his employer?

It will also help if you keep in mind the following questions: (1) Would it be ethical to consider the likelihood of an audit when you give tax advice? (2) To what extent would your advice be shaped by the risk of penalties? (3) When is disclosure of information to the IRS about a questionable position relevant?

In addition to the ethical rules, there are statutory penalties imposed on taxpayers and tax return preparers and these penalties rely on standards of behavior similar to the ethical standards imposed on tax advisors. The following discussion, therefore, provides some information about these penalties — both because they are important in their own right and because of the light they might shed on the ethical standards. Indeed, the rules dealing with penalties have had an impact on the evolution of the ethical standards.

It will help you to manage the detail in these rules if you keep in mind the following possible standards regarding the likelihood of success in a tax dispute:

• Reasonable basis of success for the taxpayer

- Realistic possibility of success for the taxpayer (the "one-third" standard)
- Substantial authority for the taxpayer's position
- More likely than not to succeed (the "greater than 50%" standard)

The discussion begins with the 1967 and 1985 ABA Formal Opinions; then considers statutory penalty provisions that postdate the 1985 ABA Opinion; and then moves on to the subsequently adopted Treasury rules.

[A] ABA Rules

A 1967 American Bar Association Formal Opinion 314 stated that a "lawyer who is asked to advise his client in the course of the preparation of the client's tax returns may freely urge the statement of positions most favorable to the client just as long as there is a *reasonable basis* for those positions." It goes on to insist that the "lawyer has no duty to advise that riders be attached to the client's tax return explaining the circumstances surrounding the transaction or the expenditures."

More recently, in 1985, the American Bar Association reconsidered the reasonable basis test in Formal Opinion 85-352. It adopted a *realistic possibility of success* standard, although it claimed that this was no different from reasonable basis. (This opinion did not deal with a lawyer's opinion on tax shelter investment offerings, which is specifically addressed in ABA Formal Opinion 346 and which is discussed in Chapter 17.06[1].) The 1985 Opinion also states that the "lawyer has no duty to require as a condition of his or her continued representation that riders be attached to the client's tax return explaining the circumstances surrounding the transaction or the expenditures." However, the lawyer should explain to the client the potential application of § **6662**. That section, discussed below, imposes a penalty when there is a substantial understatement of tax. The § **6662** penalty can be avoided if the facts are adequately disclosed and there is a reasonable basis for the taxpayer's position or if there is substantial authority for the position. The lawyer is expected to advise the client of the opportunity to avoid this penalty by adequately disclosing the facts in the return or in a statement attached to the return. But, the Opinion repeats, a lawyer is under no obligation to make a disclosure if the client decides to risk the penalty without disclosing the questionable item. The Opinion sums up:

> In summary, a lawyer may advise reporting a position on a return even where the lawyer believes the position probably will not prevail, there is no "substantial authority" in support of the position, and there will be no disclosure of the position in the return. However, the position to be asserted must be one which the lawyer in good faith believes is warranted in existing law or can be supported by a good faith argument for an extension, modification or reversal of existing law. This requires that there is some realistic possibility of success if the matter is litigated. In addition, in his role as advisor, the lawyer should refer to potential penalties and other legal consequences should the client take the position advised.

Note that, according to the ABA Opinion, there can be a reasonable possibility of success even though the "substantial authority" test is not satisfied. How can that be? Consider this question later when you read what counts as substantial authority.

[B]   Related Penalties

[1]   Substantial Understatement Penalty

No one pretends that it is easy to determine when there is a "realistic possibility of success," as it was understood in 1985 when the ABA adopted Formal Opinion 85-352. One possible clue is the concept of "substantial authority" as it relates to the 20% "substantial understatement" penalty in **§ 6662**. For individuals, an understatement is "substantial" if the tax required to be shown on the tax return minus the tax actually shown on the return (that is, the "understatement") exceeds the greater of 10% of the required tax or $5,000. Consequently, a lower income taxpayer whose underpayment is more than 10% of the required tax would probably not be subject to the penalty if the underpayment was less than $5,000.

The substantial understatement penalty is imposed when the taxpayer takes a position for which there is no *"substantial authority,"* unless the taxpayer "adequately discloses" the position on the return or attached statement and that position has a *reasonable basis.* **§ 6662(d)**. A "reasonable basis" test is "significantly higher than not frivolous or not patently improper" and is "not satisfied by a return position that is merely arguable." **Treas. Reg. 1.6662-3(b)(3)**. The Regulations authorize the government to permit disclosure in some instances by filing an accurate return instead of a supplemental form containing the disclosure information. *See* **Treas. Reg. § 1.6662-4(f)(1-2)**; Rev. Proc. 2011-13, 2011-3 I.R.B. 318; Form 8275.

In certain cases, referred to as tax shelters, adequate disclosure is insufficient and the taxpayer must also reasonably believe that his position is "more likely than not" correct, discussed in Chapter 17.06[B].

As noted above, the ABA Opinion assumes that there can be a realistic possibility of success without "substantial authority." However, the meaning of "substantial authority" has undergone some dilution since 1985, when the ABA Opinion was issued. The Treasury has complied with a 1989 Committee Report calling for the expansion of the authorities that can provide "substantial authority." Previously, "substantial authority" included cases, temporary and final Regulations, Revenue Rulings, and authoritative committee reports, but now also includes proposed regulations, post-October 31, 1976 letter rulings and taxpayer advice memoranda, post-March 12, 1981 General Counsel Memoranda and Actions on Decisions, Internal Revenue Service Notices, and the Blue Book (which is an explanation of the law written after its passage by the staff of the Joint Committee on Taxation). Treas. Reg. § 1.6662-4(d)(3)(iii). This expansion probably reflects the fact that courts place more weight on these aids to interpretation than was previously thought (especially letter rulings and taxpayer advice memorandums). It is unclear whether reliance on this broadened definition of "substantial authority" for penalty purposes will turn out to equate with the "reasonable possibility of success" as an ethical standard.

There is "substantial authority" "only if the weight of the authorities supporting the treatment is substantial in relation to the weight of authorities supporting contrary treatment." **Treas. Reg. § 1.6662-4(d)(3)(i-ii).** There is little guidance regarding what is meant by "weight," although the Regulations state that a Revenue Ruling is accorded greater weight than a letter ruling. Moreover, older letter rulings, technical advice memorandums, and general counsel memorandums are generally accorded less weight than more recent documents (with such documents that are more than 10 years old "generally . . . accorded very little weight"). The Regulations state that "[c]onclusions reached in treatises [and] legal periodicals . . . are not authority."

Whatever is meant by "realistic possibility of success" and "substantial author-ity," § 6662 assumes that "a reasonable basis" is a more lax standard — because a taxpayer who lacks substantial authority can still avoid the penalty with disclosure, if there is a "reasonable basis." Presumably, some more subtle calculation of the weight of the documents relevant for identifying substantial authority might result in satisfying a reasonable basis test even though the "substantial authority" standard is not met. (The same question should be asked about the ABA's "realistic possibility of success" standard.)

One more point about the § 6662 penalty. **Section 6664(c)** provides that there will be no penalty under § 6662 if "it is shown that there was a reasonable cause for [the substantial understatement] and that the taxpayer acted in good faith with respect to [that understatement]." In *Murfam Farms, LLC ex rel. Murphy v. United States*, 94 Fed. Cl. 235 (2010), the court noted that "[r]eliance on . . . the advice of a professional tax advisor . . . does not necessarily demonstrate reasonable cause and good faith." The court continued:

> In the circumstances presented here, reliance on [Ernst & Young's] advice was not reasonable. As the Federal Circuit stated in [another case]: "Reliance is not reasonable, for example, if the adviser has an inherent conflict of interest about which the taxpayer knew or should have known." The Murphys could not reasonably have expected to receive independent advice from the same firm that was selling them [a tax shelter]. Because Ernst & Young had a financial interest in having the Murphys participate in [the tax shelter], the firm had an inherent conflict of interest in advising on the legitimacy of that transaction.
>
> That conflict of interest was exacerbated by the fee structure. The Murphys have conceded that from the beginning they understood that Ernst & Young's fee would be a percentage of their desired tax loss. ("The Murphys believed initially that the fees for [tax shelter transaction] were to be 4.5% of the tax benefits or tax savings from the [] transaction."). In other words, the Murphys understood that the more taxes they avoided by following Ernst & Young's advice the more they would pay [] in fees. The Murphys knew that Ernst & Young stood to earn millions by advising them to participate in [the tax shelter], and they therefore knew or should have known that Ernst & Young's advice lacked the trustworthiness of an impartial opinion. Given Ernst & Young's obvious conflict of interest,

reliance on its advice does not demonstrate that Murfam acted with reasonable cause or in good faith.

[2] Return Preparer Penalty

Section 6694(a) imposes a penalty on a tax return preparers. For tax returns prepared after May 25, 2007, the standards for the return preparer penalty have been revised to conform to standards applicable to the substantial understatement penalty. First, for *undisclosed* positions, substantial authority will suffice (reduced from a higher "more likely than not" standard). In addition, there is another wrinkle: the penalty is avoided if there is *reasonable* cause for the understatement and the tax return preparer acted in good faith. Second, for *disclosed* positions, a lower "reasonable basis" standard applies.

The penalty is the greater of $1,000 or 50% of the income derived by the preparer from preparing the return; these figures are increased to $5,000 and 50% if the tax return preparer willfully understates tax liability or acts in reckless manner or with intentional disregard of rules and regulations.

[C] Treasury Rules

The Treasury has issued ethical rules applicable to those who practice before the Treasury. These rules apply not only to lawyers but also to certified public accountants and those who pass a qualifying examination to practice before the IRS. They are published in **Circular 230, 31 Code of Federal Regulations, Part 10**.

The latest version of **Circular 230, sec. 10.34**, issued on June 3, 2011, conforms the ethical standard imposed by the Treasury to the return preparer penalty rules (for the most part). The practitioner "may not willfully, recklessly, or through gross incompetence — (a)(1)(i) Sign a tax return or claim for refund that the practitioner knows or reasonably should know contains a position that — (A) Lacks a reasonable basis; [or] (B) Is an unreasonable position as described in § 6694(a)(2) of the Internal Revenue Code (Code) (including the related regulations and other published guidance). . . . " (The same standard applies to advising the client to take a position on the tax return.) The substantial authority standard for undisclosed positions results from the reference to "an unreasonable position as described in § 6694(a)(2)."

There are, however, two important differences between the Treasury's ethical rules and the preparer penalty. First, there is no reasonable cause/good faith exception under the ethical rules, as there is for avoiding the preparer penalty. Second, the Treasury's ethical rules apply only to "willful or reckless behavior or gross incompetence." The rules state that a "pattern of conduct is a factor that will be taken into account in determining whether a practitioner acted willfully, recklessly, or through gross negligence." Will the "pattern of conduct" criterion ease a practitioner's concern about application of the ethical rules?

Current law attempts to put more teeth into enforcement of Circular 230 by adding censure and monetary penalties to the existing disbarment and suspension sanctions available to the Treasury. 31 U.S.C. § 330(b). Presumably, these lesser sanctions are more likely to be used than disbarment or suspension.

There are two interesting differences between the Treasury and the ABA ethical standards. First, the ABA rejects any rule that favors disclosure by the practitioner. Under the ABA rules, the attorney only has to advise the client on the importance of disclosure to avoid understatement penalties. Under the Treasury rules, disclosure reduces the standard from substantial authority to reasonable basis. Second, the ABA requires only a realistic possibility of success (the one-third standard), but the Treasury requires substantial authority for undisclosed positions.

PERSONAL CONSUMPTION AND BUSINESS EXPENSES

Part I-A introduced all the basic themes in an income tax course — (1) tax base, (2) tax rates, (3) taxable units, (4) accounting methods, (5) accounting periods, and (6) the political, administrative, and judicial processes that shape tax law, as well as the ethical rules applicable to tax advisors. Parts I-B and I-C focus on the tax base. Recall that income is defined as an "accession to wealth," which equals personal consumption plus savings. Part I-B deals primarily with the personal consumption element of that definition.

Most of the issues in Chapters 7 and 8 arise in a business setting. Chapter 7 deals with the exclusion from income of business-financed employee fringe benefits. Chapter 8 deals with business deductions.

Chapter 9 has a broader reach. It deals with personal insurance protection and personal losses — which raise both fundamental questions about defining accession to wealth and the use of the tax law to encourage socially desirable expenditures. Chapter 9 concludes with a discussion of tort recoveries.

Chapter 10 deals with charities — where the tax rules are usually understood to provide a tax expenditure in the form of a deduction for charitable gifts.

Chapter 7

INCOME IN-KIND

§ 7.01   MEALS AND LODGING

[A]   Case Law Background and Statutory Amendment; § 119

In *Benaglia v. Commissioner*, 36 B.T.A. 838 (1937), the court held that meals and lodging were not taxable when they were provided to a hotel manager and his wife merely as a convenience to the employer. This case predates adoption of § 119 and interprets the definition of § 61 income. The court stated that "residence at the hotel was not by way of compensation for . . . services, not for his personal convenience, comfort, or pleasure, but solely because he could not otherwise perform the services required of him." It did not matter that the expense "relieve[d] him of an expense which he would otherwise bear." Much of the opinion discusses the facts that support the "convenience of the employer" conclusion. The government agreed with the legal test — that "convenience of the employer" justified an exclusion — but disagreed with its application in this case. The dissent stressed that the employment contract treated the meals and lodging as compensation. The dissent also disagreed fundamentally with the court's approach. Meals and lodging solely for the employer's convenience are still income because they are necessities the employee would otherwise have to purchase. The employer therefore "enriched" the employee.

The convenience of the employer test has more general application than just meals and lodging — which are now dealt with by § 119. For example, in *United States v. Gotcher*, 401 F.2d 118 (5th Cir. 1968), the Volkswagen company in Germany brought U.S. car dealers to Germany for a 12-day expense-paid trip. The court held that the cost of the trip was not income to the taxpayer, but was income to the taxpayer's wife, who had accompanied him. The court noted that the:

> trip was made in 1959 when VW was attempting to expand its local dealerships in the United States. The 'buy American' campaign and the fact that the VW people felt they had a 'very ugly product' prompted them to offer these tours of Germany to prospective dealers. . . . VW operations were at first so speculative that cars had to be consigned with a repurchase guarantee. In 1959, when VW began to push for its share of the American market, its officials determined that the best way to remove the apprehension about this foreign product was to take the dealer to Germany and have him see his investment first-hand. It was believed that once the dealer saw the manufacturing facilities and the stability of the 'new Germany,' he would be convinced that VW was for him. Furthermore, VW considered the

expenditure justified because the dealer was being asked to make a substantial investment of his time and money in a comparatively new product. . . . Apparently, these trips have paid off since VW's sales have skyrocketed and the dealers have made their facilities top-rate operations under the VW requirements for a standard dealership.

The court stressed that "a substantial amount of time [during the 12-day tour] was spent touring VW facilities and visiting local dealerships. VW had set up these tours with local dealers so that the travelers could discuss how the facilities were operated in Germany. Mr. Gotcher took full advantage of this opportunity and even used some of his 'free time' to visit various local dealerships. Moreover, at almost all of the evening meals VW officials gave talks about the organization and passed out literature and brochures on the VW story." Even though "[s]ome of the days were not related to touring VW facilities," the "dominant purpose of the trip is the critical inquiry and some pleasurable features will not negate the finding of an overall business purpose."

The court then cited the "convenience of the employer" cases that did not tax an employee in the meals and lodging context and stated that "when it has been shown that the expenses were paid to effectuate a legitimate corporate end and not to benefit the officer personally, the officer has not been taxed though he enjoyed and benefited from the activity. Thus, the rule is that the economic benefit will be taxable to the recipient only when the payment of expenses serves no legitimate corporate purpose. The decisions also indicate that the tax consequences are to be determined by looking to the primary purpose of the expenses and that the first consideration is the intention of the payor." On this record, the court concluded that the "primary purpose of the trip was to induce Mr. Gotcher to take out a VW dealership interest." As for the wife, however, the trip was just a taxable personal vacation.

Meals and lodging proved to be a constant source of litigation and the 1954 law codified the convenience of the employer test in § 119, with added statutory detail. This statutory exclusion of meals and lodging provided by the employer might strike you as anomalous — some taxpayers can enjoy meals and lodging tax-free while others finance these expenses out of after tax income.

One provision of the tax law might seem to limit this tax break *indirectly*, but it does not. **Section 274(n)** limits the employer's deduction of meals (but not lodging) to 50% of their cost. And the loss of a deduction by the employer often reduces the amount of tax-free personal consumption that an employee will receive from the employer. But the 1997 Tax Act has repealed the 50% limit on the employer's deduction for meal expenses that are excluded from the employee's income by § 119. It did this by amending § 132(e) (last sentence), so that meals excluded under § 119 are always treated as *de minimis* fringe benefits under § 274(n)(2)(B); and § 274(n)(2)(B) exempts *de minimis* fringe benefits from the limits on the employer's deduction. That is remarkably convoluted drafting. Why doesn't § 274(n) state directly that the 50% limit does not apply to meals excluded under § 119?

[B]   Business Premises

LINDEMAN v. COMMISSIONER
United States Tax Court
60 T.C. 609 (1973)

[Editor — The employer ran an oceanfront resort hotel in Fort Lauderdale. The employer also owned parking lots and a house across Oakland Park Boulevard, which was the southern boundary of the hotel property. The house, which was on Lot 18, was the residence for the hotel's general manager, the taxpayer in the case.]

These deceptively simple words — "on the business premises" of the employer — have been the subject of extended judicial opinions with varying results. We examine anew the legislative history of section 119 insofar as it bears on the issue presented for decision.

The requirement of section 119 that, to be excludable from gross income, lodging must be furnished and accepted "on the business premises" of the employer was first adopted as part of the 1954 Code. As passed by the House of Representatives, the section used the term "place of employment" rather than "business premises." H.R. REP. No. 1337, to accompany H.R. 3300 (Pub. L. No. 591), 83d Cong., 2d Sess., pp. 18, A39 (1954). The Senate changed the term to "business premises," but the accompanying report explained that "Under both bills meals and lodging are to be excluded from the employee's income if they are furnished at the place of employment and the employee is required to meet certain other conditions," S. REP. No. 1622, to accompany H.R. 8300 (Pub. L. No. 591), 83d Cong., 2d Sess., pp. 19, 190–191 (1954).

The Senate version was adopted with the following explanation in CONF. REP. No. 2548, 83d Cong., 2d Sess., p. 27 (1954):

> The term "business premises of the employer" is intended, in general, to have the same effect as the term "place of employment" in the House bill. For example, lodging furnished in the home to a domestic servant would be considered lodging furnished on the business premises of the employer. Similarly, meals furnished to a cowhand while herding his employer's cattle on leased lands, or on national forest lands used under a permit, would also be regarded as furnished on the business premises of the employer. . . .

As in the case of other exclusions from gross income, this one is subject to abuse, and the statutory language must be construed with this thought in mind. Accordingly, the term "on" in relation to the employer's business premises does not mean "in the vicinity of" or "nearby" or "close to" or "contiguous to" or similar language, but is to be read literally. If the lodging is furnished at a location some distance from the place where the employee works, the lodging is not furnished on his employer's business premises.

In determining what are the employer's "business premises," Congress quite obviously intended a commonsense approach. Read literally, the statutory language ordinarily would not permit any exclusion for lodging furnished a domestic servant, since a servant's lodging is rarely furnished on "the business premises of his employer"; yet the committee report, quoted above, shows a clear intention to allow the exclusion where the servant's lodging is furnished in the employer's home. Similarly, the section, as a condition to the exclusion, does not require that the meals or lodging be furnished at any particular location on the employer's property; thus, the same committee report clearly states that meals provided for a cowhand are excludable even though they are furnished on leased lands or on lands used under a permit.

These illustrations in the committee report, moreover, demonstrate that section 119 does not embody a requirement that the meals or lodging be furnished in the principal structure on the employer's business premises. Thus, the committee report makes it explicitly clear that a cowhand's meals and lodging need not be furnished at the ranch headquarters. And surely, the right of a domestic servant to the section 119 exclusion cannot be made to turn on whether his lodging is furnished in the family residence or in servants' quarters located elsewhere on the estate. Indeed, in *Boykin v. Commissioner*, 260 F.2d 249 (C.A. 8, 1958), *affirming in part and reversing in part*, 29 T.C. 813 (1958), the Commissioner at least implicitly conceded that a physician's living quarters, located on the grounds of a Veterans Administration Hospital, were on his employer's business premises even though he performed none of his employment services in his living quarters. Similarly, the Commissioner has ruled that meals furnished at branch offices of an employer, as well as at a central dining facility, meet the requirements of the section. Rev. Rul. 71-411, 1971-2 C.B. 103.

The issue as to the extent or the boundaries of the business premises in each case is a factual issue, and in resolving that question consideration must be given to the employee's duties as well as the nature of the employer's business. The section 119 exclusion applies where the lodging is furnished at a place where the employee conducts a significant portion of his business. *Commissioner v. Anderson*, 371 F.2d at 67. Or, in the words of this Court in *Gordon S. Dole*, 43 T.C. at 707, "the phrase should be construed to mean either: (1) living quarters that constitute an integral part of the business property; or (2) premises on which the company carries on some of its business activities."

We think petitioner has shown that the house which his employer furnished him during 1968 and 1969 was part and parcel of the "business premises" of Beach Club Hotel. In reaching this conclusion, we think it apparent that the business premises of the hotel are not limited to 3100 North Ocean Boulevard, where the hotel building is located, but include both parking lots and the house furnished to petitioner.

. . . [T]he nature of the Beach Club Hotel business is such as to require the general manager to live where he is immediately accessible at all hours, and the house on lot 18 meets this need. It is stipulated that:

> In 1963, after a cost study, Beach Hotel Corporation determined it should be more profitable to purchase or rent accommodations for . . . (petitioner) and his family as close to the hotel as possible and have the suite of four rooms he was occupying available to be rented.

Thereupon, [the employer] acquired lot 18, containing the house, and Beach Hotel Corp. leased it to provide housing for petitioner and his family. This was a business decision based on business considerations, and there is no suggestion in the record that it was prompted by any other factors or that it involves an abuse of the section 119 exclusion.

The house is so situated and so used that it is part of the hotel plant. While petitioner's office is located in the business area of the hotel building (as it was while he occupied the suite of rooms as his residence), he is subject to call 24 hours a day, and he is as readily accessible for the frequent calls by direct telephone as he was in the suite located in the hotel building. He often returns to the hotel building several times in an evening. People dealing with him through the direct telephone line have no way of knowing whether he is in the hotel building or his home. Moreover, from the house he can observe the entire south half of the building and can "tell if there is a disturbance of any kind, see if lights are on or off, if the night lights don't come on early enough," and the like.

While petitioner does most of his management work in his office in the hotel building, he also has an office in the house on lot 18. In this latter office in his home, he receives calls from the hotel personnel or guests on the direct telephone line from the hotel while he is not on regular duty. He also uses this office when he is working on new brochures or rate structures and when he is planning a program for future hotel activities, such as "cook-outs, games, picnics on the beach, cocktail parties, and this sort of thing." In addition, he occasionally entertains a guest of the hotel.

In our view, these facts demonstrate that the lodging furnished petitioner is, within the meaning of section 119, "on the business premises of his employer" or, within the meaning of the accompanying committee reports, "at the place of employment." The house in which he lives is an indispensable and inseparable part of the hotel plant, and it is within the perimeter of the hotel property. Since it is part of the premises where petitioner performs the duties required in his job and where his employer carries on its business, we hold that petitioner is entitled to the section 119 exclusion.

Commissioner v. Anderson, 371 F.2d 59 (C.A. 6, 1966), on which respondent relies, is factually distinguishable. In that case, the housing furnished the employee was "two short blocks" from the facility being managed by the taxpayer, and the Court of Appeals did not conclude, as we do here, that the living quarters of the employee-taxpayer were an integral part of the business property. Accordingly, the Court of Appeals held that the requirements of the statute were not met. In the instant case, the premises of the business managed by petitioner include the house in which his lodging was furnished.

Reviewed by the Court.

QUESTIONS

The following questions suggest some of the difficulty in interpreting the phrase "business premises." You will almost certainly find it difficult to apply the "plain meaning" of that phrase. There is a risk that it will be interpreted in a sterile manner, cut off from the structural principles which underlie the statute. But what structural principles would you use — (1) whether the employer's convenience is a dominant factor in making the employee live or eat somewhere; (2) how likely it is that the benefit is what the employee would have selected if he had made a free choice?

Is the taxpayer "on the business premises" in any of the following situations?

1. Meals and lodging are provided by the employer at an Alaskan campsite where an oil pipeline is being constructed. **Treas. Reg. § 1.119-1(f) (Example 7)**.

2. A factory manager responsible for labor relations lives in housing owned by the employer about one mile from the factory. The employee must live there to be close enough to get to the factory if labor trouble develops at any time. *Dole v. Commissioner*, 43 T.C. 697, *affirmed per curiam*, 351 F.2d 308 (1st Cir. 1965). Would it matter if the house was one block from the factory? *Erdelt v. United States*, 715 F. Supp. 278 (D.N.D. 1989), *affirmed without opinion*, 909 F.2d 510 (8th Cir. 1990).

3. A receptionist lives in an apartment above a doctor's office. The receptionist cleans up the office after hours and answers phone calls, and sometimes looks up a file in the office after hours if a patient calls the doctor at home for medical advice. *Nolen v. Commissioner*, 23 T.C.M. (CCH) 595 (1964).

4. A company executive lives in Japan in Western-style housing owned by the employer, in part so that he can entertain company clients. *Compare Adams v. United States*, 585 F.2d 1060 (Ct. Cl. 1978), *with McDonald v. Commissioner*, 66 T.C. 223 (1976).

5. A president of the state university lives in an official residence owned by the university, which is one mile from campus and is used as an office and to entertain university and state officials. Rev. Rul. 75-540, 1975-2 C.B. 53; Private Ruling 7823007. Is the President or Vice-President of the United States or a state Governor taxed on the value of the official residence in which he or she lives?

[C] Convenience of Employer

Section 119 echoes prior case law by requiring that the meals and lodging be for the convenience of the employer. The best argument for excluding benefits provided for the employer's convenience is the lack of choice that often accompanies these benefits. **Treas. Reg. § 1.119-1(a)(2)(i)** states that the presence of a substantial noncompensatory reason satisfies the statutory test. The statute disregards any provision *in the contract* specifying that the meals or lodging are or are not compensatory. **§ 119(b)(1)**. Presumably, it is too easy to manipulate the contract to omit reference to such compensation and, in any event, the marketplace will fix cash wages by taking into account the fringe benefit, regardless of whether the contract specifies that the benefits are compensatory.

COMMENTS AND QUESTIONS

1. In *McGinty v. Commissioner*, T.C. Summary Opinion 2003-74 2003 Tax Ct. Summary LEXIS 75 (2003), the taxpayer did not satisfy the convenience of the employer test. A student worked 15 hours per week in a professor's home

preparing meals, doing laundry, and answering the phone in exchange for free room and board. The court held that there was no business reason for the employer to provide room and board and the value of the meals and lodging was added to the student's taxable compensation. How does this student differ from the domestic servant whose meals and lodging are excluded under § 119?

2. If the rationale for exclusion is the likelihood that the benefits would not be freely chosen by the employee, should an employee who is a principal owner of a corporation for which he works ever be allowed to exclude meals and lodging under § 119? *Adolph Coors Co. v. Commissioner*, 27 T.C.M. (CCH) 1351 (1968), permitted a principal shareholder who was an employee of his corporation to rely on § 119. Does that provide a good reason to incorporate?

3. The "convenience of employer" test has been a prolific source of statutory amendments, to respond to decisions adverse to taxpayers that Congress wanted to reverse. First, the Regulations once provided that meals could not be "for the convenience of the employer" if the employee had discretion to buy the meal. Thus, if a company cafeteria served meals for which the employee paid one-half the normal price if he wanted to purchase the meal, the value in excess of the price paid by the employee was taxable. Congress overrode this IRS position in § 119(b)(2). This statutory provision does not entirely eliminate the "convenience of the employer" test. It only eliminates one element of the test (the no-employee-discretion element). It is still necessary to prove that the meal is provided for the convenience of the employer. *See, e.g.*, **Treas. Reg. § 1.119-1(f) (Example 3)** (the meal was provided for the employer's convenience where a bank teller's lunch hour was restricted to 30 minutes because that was the peak time for bank business; the employer required the employee to eat on the premises and provided a cafeteria for this purpose).

Second, the 1998 tax legislation adopted § 119(b)(4), which treats *all* meals on the business premises as for the convenience of the employer if more than half the employees receive meals for the convenience of the employer. It was reported that casino employees were the prime target of this new rule. But you should note that casino employers like this rule as well as employees, because it allows 100% of the cost of these meals to be deducted by the employers. This result is provided by the following chain of statutory sections: **§ 274(n)(2)(B); § 132(e) (last sentence); § 119(b)(4).**

[D] Condition of Employment

This phrase — "condition of employment" — applies only to housing, not meals. **§ 119(a)(2).** The Regulations specify that the test is an objective one. How does it differ from the "convenience of the employer" test? **Treas. Reg. § 1.119-1(b).** Does it make that test somewhat stricter for lodging in some unspecified way, perhaps because housing is a bigger item than food? If not, why is the statute redundant?

[E] Cash vs. In-kind

SIBLA v. COMMISSIONER
United States Court of Appeals, Ninth Circuit
611 F.2d 1260 (9th Cir. 1980)

CURTIS, DISTRICT JUDGE:

During the relevant period [1972 and 1973] the taxpayers were employed as firemen by the Los Angeles Fire Department and were assigned to Fire Station No. 89 in North Hollywood, California. They normally worked 24-hour shifts and were not permitted to leave the fire station on personal business while on duty.

In the late 1950's, a desegregation plan was implemented by the Fire Department. Previously segregated posts were consolidated in order to eliminate segregation within a post. The Board of Fire Commissioners adopted rules requiring all firemen at each fire station to participate in a nonexclusionary organized mess at the station house, unless officially excused. The only recognized grounds for nonparticipation was a physical ailment verified by the city's own examining physician.

The Fire Department provided kitchen facilities, but the firemen themselves generally organized the activities themselves. They provided dishes and pots, purchased and prepared the food, assessed members for the cost of the meals and collected the assessments. Meal expenses averaged about $3.00 per man for each 24-hour shift which the taxpayers were required to pay even though they were at times away from the station on fire department business during the mess period. . . .

In the light of all the circumstances in this case, the meals in question in a very real sense were "furnished in kind by the employer" upon the "business property" by means of a device conceived and established by the employer for its convenience. This being so, the taxpayers should be permitted to exclude from their gross income under the provisions of section 119 the value of these meals notwithstanding the fact that cash has been used as a simple method of implementing the plan.

We hold therefore that taxpayers may . . . exclude [the mess fees] from income under section 119.

KENNEDY, CIRCUIT JUDGE, dissenting:

I respectfully disagree with the majority's holding. . . .

. . . [T]he underlying principle [of exclusion] is the idea that forced consumption should in some cases be treated as a transaction that is not dependent on significant elements of personal choice. That is, if the convenience of the employer dictates a certain type of consumption that is likely to be different from that which a taxpayer would normally prefer, this restriction of the taxpayer's preferences is an occasion for an "accession to wealth" over which the taxpayer does not "have complete dominion." Cf. *Commissioner v. Glenshaw Glass Co.*, 348 U.S. 426, 431 (1955) (defining gross income in terms of quoted phrases). It appears from the record that such a restriction on the taxpayers' consumption preferences was not present in this case: the only aspect of the common dining arrangement that suited the employer was its location. The firemen were apparently free to suit their own tastes in the groceries purchased and the food prepared. This freedom points up the critical omission in the majority's hypothetical, which is the failure to specify the amount of the individual taxpayer's participation in either the choice of food or the decision of how much to spend on the meals.

The necessity in cases like these to focus on such minutiae to determine the degree of taxpayer control suggests the hair-splitting artificiality of isolating an otherwise clear type of personal expense which all taxpayers must incur in the ordinary course of living and labeling that expense "business" and therefore nontaxable for a particular, and to that extent special, class of taxpayers. Legislative exceptions such as section 119 should not be broadened beyond their explicit terms by judicial interpretation. . . .

QUESTIONS AND COMMENTS

1. Are the groceries in *Sibla* "meals furnished by the employer" under the statute? What criteria do you consider to answer that question? *Compare Tougher v. Commissioner*, 51 T.C. 737 (1969), *affirmed per curiam*, 441 F.2d 1148 (9th Cir. 1971), *with Jacob v. United States*, 493 F.2d 1294 (3d Cir. 1974).

2. Did you spot the legal error in *Sibla* — referring to the taxpayer's deduction rather than an exclusion under § 119? Why is it so important to make sure that any tax break for the firemen is an exclusion rather than a deduction?

[F] Note on Statutory Drafting and Interpretation

Now that you have read the original § 119 and its subsequent elaborations, you might make a judgment about whether we would have been better off leaving these issues to the case law and Regulations, as illustrated by the convenience of employer test in the *Benaglia* case discussed in Chapter 7.01.

The reason for the statutory detail was to provide greater legal certainty. But more precise statutes do not always work out that way, because the statutory text might add new language that is just as hard to interpret as the word "income." Simplicity proves elusive. For example, the new phrase "business premises" in § 119 raised a whole new set of interpretive problems. However, before you jump to the conclusion that the new language made matters worse, you should compare it with the old statutory text. It is possible that the new language is just as difficult to apply as the old but that it significantly reduces the number of situations in which there is a problem applying the law. Thus, the statute eliminates uncertainty about whether the meals and lodging are taxable when the taxpayer is clearly living off the business premises.

Another problem is that the statutory detail might obscure the basic principle underlying the statute. I think that the principle underlying § 119 (and many other exclusions from the tax base) is whether the presence or absence of personal choice suggests that the benefit is or is not taxable personal consumption. The more amendments you add to § 119, the less likely it is that a judge will be able to see the forest for the trees. For example, how did you decide whether the receptionist living above the doctor's office was taxed on the housing provided by her employer?

Another way of looking at the impact of statutory detail is that it leads the judge away from applying the purpose rather than the letter of the law. It is not always easy to discern and apply a statutory purpose. Consequently, the more detail there is in the statute, the more the judge is likely to say either that the legislature intends the letter to be applied strictly or that it is best to leave such difficult issues for further legislative elaboration.

§ 7.02 EMPLOYEE FRINGE BENEFITS

[A] Legislative Background

Another area of the law that used to be the domain of case law elaborating on the definition of § 61 income has now been taken over by statute. Meals and lodging are only one example of benefits provided by employers to employees. Employers provide a variety of other benefits, such as fancy offices, free flights on airlines, bargain discounts of retail merchandise, use of demonstrator cars, and free parking. As a general rule, many, if not most, of these benefits were not reported by the employees as income and employers were not withholding tax from their employees' income. Employers and employees in specific industries came to rely on the exclusion of many of these benefits, even though it was difficult to reconcile that result with the statute. Revenue agents, in the absence of clearer standards than the general language of § 61, were reaching diverse results in different parts of the country, if they were able to detect the benefits at all.

In 1975, the Treasury confronted this chaotic situation by issuing a Discussion Draft of proposed regulations as a trial balloon, but the draft was withdrawn when the political impact of taxing many fringe benefits became apparent. The Treasury did not stop worrying about the matter, however, and Congress decided to prohibit the issuance of regulations dealing with fringe benefits, in the expectation that Congress would address the issue. The expiration date of the prohibition was periodically renewed as Congress found it difficult to resolve the problem. Finally, in 1984, the code was amended by adopting § 132.

Once again, lobbying had a significant impact on the results. When you work out the answers to the following questions, consider which results might have been reached under Regulations. In general, Regulations can respond to arguments that the benefits are not income in the first place under § 61 or are administratively too difficult to tax, but the Treasury has trouble simply responding to a request by an industry for tax-free fringe benefits on other grounds.

For an example of a ruling that excludes an item from income on administrative grounds, see Rev. Proc. 2000-30, 2000-2 C.B. 113. The Revenue Procedure disregarded benefits received by bank depositors as incentives to open a deposit, if the bank's cost for the benefit was no more than $10 to open a bank account under $5,000 and no more than $20 for a larger bank account. The benefit to the depositor was neither interest income nor a reduction in the depositor's basis.

[B]   Valuation

If a fringe benefit is taxable, the amount included in the employee's income is its fair market value. But what is the value of a free plane ticket, or free use of a car? There are often many prices at which such services can be purchased. You can get some idea of the complexity of the rules by looking at the following portion of the Table of Contents to **Treas. Reg. § 1.61-21**:

(b)(4) fair market value of the availability of an employer-provided vehicle;

(b)(5) fair market value of chauffeur services;

(b)(6) fair market value of a flight on an employer-provided piloted aircraft;

(b)(7) fair market value of the use of an employer-provided aircraft for which the employer does not provide a pilot;

(d) automobile lease valuation rule;

(e) vehicle cents-per-mile valuation rule;

(f) commuting valuation rule;

(g) non-commercial flight valuation rule; and

(h) commercial flight valuation rule

[C]   The Statutory Exclusion Rules

[1]   No Additional Cost

Consumers frequently take advantage of discounts provided in the marketplace and no one thinks that this value ought to be taxed. Indeed, no one would try to tax the difference between what a consumer pays for an item and its value to the consumer (often referred to as "consumer surplus"). One reason for this result is that, absent an expenditure in the marketplace, it is hard to know whether the consumer really places much value on the "discount." Indeed, even a cash rebate from a seller to the buyer is treated as an adjustment of the purchase price rather than taxable income; Rev. Rul. 76-96, 1976-1 C.B. 23.

In the employer-employee setting, however, our intuition is that a discount has significant value to the consuming employee. The availability of such discounts may be one reason the employee took the job; and the failure to tax such value would result in a shift from taxable wages to tax-free discounts from an employer. When the IRS made an attempt to tax such discounts, certain industries (especially the airline and retail industries) objected. The legislative result is apparent from working out the following hypotheticals.

a) F, a flight attendant in the employ of A, an airline company, and F's spouse decide to spend their 1984 annual vacation in Europe. A has a policy whereby any of its employees, along with members of their immediate families, may take a number of personal flights annually for a nominal charge. F and F's spouse take advantage of this policy and fly to and from Europe. **§ 132(a)(1), (b), (h)(2), (j)(1).**

b) P is the president of C, a corporation that has its executive offices situated in New York City. P is planning a week-long business trip to Los Angeles and will fly there and back on C's corporate jet. P's spouse intends to accompany P on the round trip flight for personal reasons. **§ 132(a)(1), (b).**

What is the justification for the exclusion of "no additional cost" fringe benefits: the value to the employee should in any event be heavily discounted (as in the *Turner* steamship ticket case, *supra* Chapter 3.07[A][1]); the service would otherwise go to waste and that is bad economic policy; the airline industry had political clout?

[2] Working Conditions

The statutory provision about working condition fringe benefits contains a statement that anticipates the future discussion of deductions — the benefit provided by the employer must be one that would be deductible if paid for by the employee under either (1) **§ 162** or (2) **§ 167**.

The former provision — **§ 162** — is the general trade or business deduction section, allowing a deduction for the ordinary and necessary expenses of doing business. Although we do not discuss this section until the next chapter, the idea is intuitively obvious, once you remember that expenses that do not provide personal consumption are not part of the tax base. The deduction for business expenses implements that principle. And the exclusion for working condition fringes means that the exclusion occurs whether it is provided by the employer directly (so it is not income) or by the employee (so it is a deduction). Of course, it is better to exclude the benefit from income, because employee deductions are usually below the line and subject to limitations. The broader significance of the working condition fringe benefit rules is that they may signal what expenses can be deducted under **§ 162**. This is especially important for the safety-related example, presented in (d) below.

The latter provision — **§ 167** — allows depreciation deductions. The exclusion of a working condition fringe benefit that would be depreciable if paid for by the employee provides the employee with a substantial benefit, because expenditures to acquire depreciable assets are added to basis and their deduction is deferred until such time as the depreciation rules allow the deduction. The working condition fringe benefit rules therefore allow the current exclusion from the employee's tax base of an expenditure that would have been a capital expenditure added to basis and excluded from the employee's income only through future depreciation, if the expenditure had been financed directly by the employee.

a. E is an executive employed by C, an advertising company. E thinks that the office in which E works is inadequately decorated and C agrees to redecorate the office with more comfortable furniture, live plants, and a selection of artwork. The newly redecorated office has made E more comfortable and has created an office environment more conducive to carrying on the ordinary and necessary business activities of the company. **§ 132(a)(3), (d).**

There are a few cases in which an employee tried to deduct expenses for this type of benefit. Compare *Henderson v. Commissioner*, 46 T.C.M. (CCH) 566 (1983) (state assistant attorney general, who was provided with office and furnishings by the state, could not deduct costs of plant and framed print used in her office), with *Judge v. Commissioner*, 35 T.C.M. (CCH) 1264 (1976) (pediatrician could deduct costs of paintings used only in his office, where pictures were intended to be of interest to children).

b. S is a salesman employed by A, an automobile dealership. S is supplied with an automobile by A for use as a customer demonstrator during regular business hours. S also uses the automobile both before and after regular business hours for personal errands and for commuting between home and office. § 132(a)(3), (j)(3).

c. F, a financial vice-president employed by A (an automobile manufacturer) is regularly provided with a new automobile for F's personal use. A requires F to file a report describing F's reaction to each automobile. **Treas. Reg. § 1.132-5(n).**

d. E, an executive employed by M, a multinational corporation, has been promoted to president of S, one of M's foreign subsidiaries. The country in which S is located has been beset by violent terrorist activity. Major targets of such activity are Americans who are employed by American-owned corporations doing business in that country. In order to protect these employees, the American corporations have instituted a number of security measures. For example, a heavily guarded residential compound has been established within which all American employees and their families must live. Additionally, residents traveling outside the compound are always accompanied by armed security personnel. § 132(a)(3), (d); **Treas. Reg. § 1.132-5(m), –6(d)(2)(ii).**

e. IRS Notice 2011-72 provides as follows regarding employer-provided cell phones:

> Many employers provide their employees with cell phones primarily for noncompensatory business reasons. The value of the business use of an employer-provided cell phone is excludable from an employee's income as a working condition fringe to the extent that, if the employee paid for the use of the cell phone themselves, such payment would be allowable as a deduction under section 162 for the employee.

> An employer will be considered to have provided an employee with a cell phone primarily for noncompensatory business purposes if there are substantial reasons relating to the employer's business, other than providing compensation to the employee, for providing the employee with a cell phone. For example, the employer's need to contact the employee at all times for work-related emergencies, the employer's requirement that the employee be available to speak with clients at times when the employee is away from the office, and the employee's need to speak with clients located in other time zones at times outside of the employee's normal work day are possible substantial noncompensatory business reasons. A cell phone provided to promote the morale or good will of an employee, to attract a prospective employee or as a means of furnishing additional compensation to an employee is not provided primarily for noncompensatory business purposes.

> This notice provides that, when an employer provides an employee with a cell phone primarily for noncompensatory business reasons, the IRS will

treat the employee's use of the cell phone for reasons related to the employer's trade or business as a working condition fringe benefit, the value of which is excludable from the employee's income and, solely for purposes of determining whether the working condition fringe benefit provision in section 132(d) applies, the substantiation requirements that the employee would have to meet in order for a deduction under §162 to be allowable are deemed to be satisfied. In addition, the IRS will treat the value of any personal use of a cell phone provided by the employer primarily for noncompensatory business purposes as excludable from the employee's income as a de minimis fringe benefit. The rules of this notice apply to any use of an employer-provided cell phone occurring after December 31, 2009. The application of the working condition and de minimis fringe benefit exclusions under this notice apply solely to employer-provided cell phones and should not be interpreted as applying to other fringe benefits.

QUESTION

What facts explain why the following employee benefit was excluded from income as a working condition fringe? In *Townsend Indus., Inc. v. United States*, 342 F.3d 890 (8th Cir. 2003), an employer paid for a four-day fishing trip for corporate staff and some factory workers (none of which involved other family members). The government argued that the per-employee cost was a wage on which the employer was required to withhold taxes. The District Court agreed with the government but the Court of Appeals reversed, stating:

> . . . [T]he real crux of the matter for Townsend is the extent to which it could prove the trips were a reasonable and necessary business trip; whether they were directly related to, or associated with, the active conduct of Townsend's business; and whether the principal character of the events was the active conduct of business. Our review of the entire record convinces us that the business nature of the trip was well established by the witnesses who testified both for and against Townsend. . . . [Editor — The court then recounts testimony about actual business discussions during the fishing trip; and then distinguishes the *Danville Plywood* case.]

The Government urges that *Danville Plywood Corporation v. United States*, 899 F.2d 3 (Fed. Cir. 1990), governs the case at hand. We think that case, which concerned the deductibility of a corporate trip to the Super Bowl, is distinguishable from the case at hand. In *Danville*, the Federal Circuit held that the taxpayer was unable to demonstrate that its Super Bowl weekend trip was a reasonable and necessary business expense and was directly related to, or associated with, the active pursuit of its business. In so holding, the Federal Circuit emphasized that on the narrow facts presented to it, it was compelled to rule that "[t]he Super Bowl weekend," which involved spouses and children, "appears to have been little more than a group social excursion with business playing a subsidiary role." Here, in contrast, there was no lack of evidence concerning specific and general business discussions and the attendant benefits. Moreover, the absence of spouses and children in this case is important for, as more than one Townsend employee noted, the trip was not some sort of paid vacation because, logically enough, "I don't go on vacation with 60 people I work with. I go on vacation with my wife and kids."

[3] Parking

P, the President of the company, is provided with free parking in the corporate building's indoor parking lot in a big city. No one else enjoys this free privilege. §§ 132(a)(5); 132(f)(1)(C), (2)(B), (7). As you consider this example, you will observe that parking fringe benefits can be excluded up to $175 per month, adjusted for inflation beginning in 2000. The amount is $220 per month for tax year 2013. § 132(f)(2)(B).

The exclusion of parking fringe benefits is one of several "qualified transportation fringe benefits" eligible for a tax break. The most recent tax break is an exclusion of an employer reimbursement for bicycle expenses, not to exceed $20 per month during which the employee regularly bikes to work. The amount is small but is a triumph of political symbolism. The taxpayer cannot take advantage of the parking fringe benefit exclusion during any month for which the $20 bicycle expense exclusion is used.

[4] Cafeterias

E, an executive assistant in the employ of B, a bank, works at B's executive offices. B provides, for the use of all executive employees, a cafeteria near the business premises, which provides meals during regular business hours. The receipts from the cafeteria, on the average, approximately cover the direct costs of providing the meals. **Section 132(e)(2)** (certain eating facilities). Would the fringe benefit in this example be excluded under **§ 119**?

[5] Employer Discounts

S, a sales clerk in the employ of D, a retail department store, purchases the following from D at a 20% discount, which covers D's cost: (a) an appliance from the appliance department; (b) an expensive wedding ring from the jewelry department; and (c) auto repair from an auto service center department maintained solely for employees, not the general public. § 132(a)(2), (c).

[6] Retirement Planning Services

An employer with a retirement plan provides all of its employees with retirement planning advice. § 132(a)(7), (m). Why wouldn't these benefits be excluded from income under the rules applicable to employer discounts?

[7] *De Minimis* Benefits

De minimis fringe benefits are not taxed. The Regulations specify that the de minimis exclusion is based on whether, after considering the frequency of providing the benefit to employees, the value is so small as to make it unreasonable or administratively impracticable to account for the benefit. § 132(a)(4), (e)(1); **Treas. Reg § 1.132-6(a-c)**. Generally, the frequency test is applied on a per-employee basis.

American Airlines, Inc. v. United States, 204 F.3d 1103 (Fed. Cir. 2000), rejected a taxpayer's claim that an employee's benefits were *de minimis*. Employees were provided with vouchers for use in restaurants, consisting of blank American Express charge forms and bearing an American Airlines account number in an amount "not to exceed $50." The vouchers did not contain the employee's name or any transfer restrictions. The employer argued that because the vouchers did not contain the recipient employees' names, it was impossible for American Airlines to determine which employees used their vouchers. American Airlines also argued that while it may have been possible to create a system for tracking the employees' use of the vouchers for employment tax withholding purposes, to do so "would have been unreasonable and administratively impractical in light of the low value and infrequency of distribution." The court held that there was inadequate evidentiary support for an assertion of administrative impracticability.

"Occasional" supper money is dealt with in an unusual way. For example, an assistant manager in a department store is occasionally required to work overtime to help mark down merchandise for special sales. On those occasions, the employer pays for the actual cost of the manager's evening meal at a nearby restaurant. Such payment is pursuant to company policy whereby the employer will pay the actual, reasonable meal expense of a management-level employee when such an expense is incurred in connection with the performance of services either before or after such an employee's regular business hours. An example that will soon seem closer to home is the reimbursed expense of supper money at a restaurant for a law associate who must work long into the night to finish a project. The Committee Reports provide that occasional supper money is excluded from an employee's income under the de minimis rule, set forth in § 132(a)(4), (e)(1). Moreover, these reports also state that "Treasury Regulations are to be issued to implement the provisions of this bill. Such regulations must be consistent with the language of the bill and with the legislative history (as reflected in part, in the committee reports on the bill). Thus, any example of a fringe benefit which the reports state is excluded under the bill from income and wages must be so treated in the regulations." The regulation excluding occasional supper money is Treas. **Reg. § 1.132-6(d)(2)**.

[8]   Frequent Flyer Benefits

a. If a taxpayer earns frequent flyer miles by purchasing his own tickets and traveling for personal enjoyment, any eventual frequent flyer award will be treated as an adjustment of the purchase price of the tickets entitling the taxpayer to the award. Thus, if it costs $5,000 to buy 12 tickets, which entitles the taxpayer to a thirteenth free ticket, the taxpayer is treated as buying 13 tickets for $5,000. Consequently, there is no taxable income; it is as though the baker threw in a thirteenth roll for the price of 12.

b. But is a thirteenth ticket tax-free if the relationship between the person financing the ticket and the person who travels is a taxable relationship, such as employer and employee? There was much speculation about whether the IRS would tax the employee's frequent flyer benefit. There seemed to be no way to exclude the benefit from income, unless it was a de minimis benefit. Finally, in 2002, the IRS decided not to tax employer-provided benefits; Announcement 2002-18 (Feb. 21, 2002), appearing at 2002 IRB LEXIS 1203. The Announcement states:

> The IRS will not assert that any taxpayer has understated his federal tax liability by reason of the receipt or personal use of frequent flyer miles or other in-kind promotional benefits attributable to the taxpayer's business or official travel. Any future guidance on the taxability of these benefits will be applied prospectively. The relief provided by this announcement does not apply to travel or other promotional benefits that are converted to cash, to compensation that is paid in the form of travel or other promotional benefits, or in other circumstances where these benefits are used for tax avoidance purposes.

c. We will return to the issue of an employee's frequent flyer benefits when we consider the deduction of gifts to charities (Chapter 10.04[C]). The question is whether a taxpayer who does not report the value of frequent flyer benefits as income can nonetheless deduct that value as a gift to charity.

d. The tax treatment of free frequent flyer tickets has also arisen in another setting. In Letter Ruling 199920031, an investment company awarded the investor one frequent flyer mile for every dollar invested in the company's stock. The government concluded that the value of the miles would reduce the investor's basis in the stock. The result is that the taxpayer will have greater gain or lesser loss on sale of the stock than if there had been no frequent flyer benefit incident to the investment.

The letter ruling states that the provider of the frequent flyer points "will arrive at a fair market value . . . based on a comparison of the costs of purchasing frequent flyer miles and by taking into account the following additional factors: (1) estimates on the probabilities that the points will eventually be redeemed by shareholders; (2) the fact that points can be utilized only within the confines of Fund's program and cannot be combined with any other frequent flyer program; (3) the fact that the maximum value of one point cannot exceed one cent. . . . "

[D] Nondiscrimination Rules

Whenever the tax law provides a tax break to employees, you should always look to see whether it is conditioned on nondiscrimination in favor of highly compensated employees. Some of the fringe benefits dealt with by § 132 are subject to nondiscrimination rules, but some are not. Of the benefits discussed in this section, nondiscrimination rules apply to the following: "no additional cost," "employee discount," certain cafeteria eating facilities, and "qualified retirement planning services." § 132(e)(2)(last sentence), (j)(1), (m)(2).

The definition of highly compensated employees appears in § 132(j)(6). Do not expect that the definition of "highly compensated employees" will be exactly the same for all tax-preferred fringe benefits provided by the tax law.

Working condition fringes are not subject to nondiscrimination rules. Why not? Is it because the element of employer control deprives the employee of taxable personal consumption, as with § 119?

Why aren't parking fringe benefits required to be nondiscriminatory?

If the benefits covered by § 132 violate a nondiscrimination requirement, only the highly compensated employees are taxed on the fringe benefit. Other employees continue to receive the benefits tax-free. That is the usual statutory pattern, although it is possible for the tax law to condition everyone's tax break on the benefit being provided on a nondiscriminatory basis.

[E] Cafeteria Plans

One of the more unusual statutory provisions is § 125, which allows the taxpayer to elect between cash and certain tax-free fringe benefits without having to pay tax as long as the cash option is not elected. These are called cafeteria plans, not because they concern eating at a cafeteria, but because the taxpayer can select (cafeteria-like) from among benefits. The most important of the fringe benefits that can be included in a cafeteria plan are employer-financed medical insurance and medical payments, and employer-financed group-term life insurance and disability insurance, discussed in Chapter 9.01.

An almost complete list of fringe benefits that qualify for cafeteria plan treatment appears in § 125(f) and it does *not* generally include the employee fringe benefits made tax-free by § 132. However, there is one § 132 benefit that can be made part of a cafeteria plan — and that is parking (and some other transportation fringe benefits not discussed in the text). This rule is tucked away in § 132(f)(4). For example, the employer can offer the taxpayer either cash or up to $245 per month in tax-free parking (in 2013), and the taxpayer can elect the parking fringe benefit without having to pay tax.

One disadvantage of a cafeteria plan is that benefits unused at the end of the year expire. They cannot be carried over to a later year. **Treas. Reg. § 1.125-2 (Q.-5 & A.-5).**

The exclusion of fringe benefits from income, despite the cash option, will seem odd if the reason for not taxing the benefits is the difficulty of determining subjective value (as in the steamship ticket case). After all, the cash election assures that someone who prefers the fringe benefit must value it at least as highly as the cash. However, if the exclusion of the fringe benefit is based on social policy, then (perhaps) a cash option ought not to eliminate the tax break. Social policy helps to explain applying the cafeteria plan rules to medical, disability, and some life insurance, but why is parking included (especially if there is no nondiscrimination requirement)?

Tax breaks under cafeteria plans are available only if the benefits do not discriminate in favor of highly compensated employees or key employees. This requirement discouraged adoption of these plans in some instances, so the Patient Protection and Affordable Health Care Act (Obamacare) provides that (beginning in 2011) "small employers" will be deemed to meet nondiscrimination requirements if they adopt "simple cafeteria plans." In general, a small employer is one that employs an average of 100 or fewer employees during either of two preceding years. A "simple cafeteria plan" must meet certain minimum eligibility and participation requirements and the employer must make contributions to providing employees with plan benefits.

§ 7.03 INTEREST-FREE LOANS

Suppose an employer gives the employee an interest-free $100,000 loan in year 0, repayable in ten years. Does the employee have income? Look at this loan from the employee's point of view. The employee can deposit a small amount in the bank, earn interest for ten years to have enough to repay the $100,000, and pocket the rest of the $100,000 right now. If the interest rate is 20% per year, $16,150 could be deposited at 20% compounded annually, to produce $100,000 in ten years. The remaining $83,850 could be used by the employee for anything he wants; it was in effect salary. **Sections 7872(b), (c)(1)(B)** taxes this transaction in accordance with its economic reality. The salary element ($83,850) would usually be taxable salary to the employee and deductible by the employer. As time passes, original issue discount would accrue to the employer-lender on the $16,150 loan. The lender would be taxed and the employee-borrower would (probably) deduct annually the amount of that interest.

The problem in the real world is to know what interest rate to impute. The code settles on a semiannual interest rate on these transactions by reference to **§ 7872(f)(1)(B), (2); § 1274(d)**. That is the rate on federal government bonds, which have a maturity comparable to the interest-free loan. This will be a lower rate than would normally be charged. Thus, if the federal rate is 12% per year (6% per six months), the present value of the $100,000 ten-year loan is $31,180, computed as follows:

$$\frac{\$100,000}{(1 + 0.06)^{20}} \quad = \quad \$31,180$$

Salary in year 0 is therefore $68,820. Original issue discount is taxed semiannually on a $31,180 loan for ten years. The employer reports interest income and the employee (probably) deducts interest during the ten-year period. The first six months interest, for example, would be $1,870.

These rules do not usually apply — there is no bifurcation of the loan into both salary and an original issue discount loan — if there is no more than $10,000 in outstanding "inadequate-interest" loans during the tax year between employer and employee. **§ 7872(c)(3)**.

You might think that there is no need to bother with these computations because the employer's deduction for salary is offset by the employer's interest income; similarly, the employee's salary income is offset by an interest deduction. Moreover, the employer's salary deduction equals the employee's salary income; and, the employer's interest income equals the employee's interest deduction. The easiest thing to do, therefore, would be to pay no attention to the interest element in an interest-free loan. But that would be a mistake. First, the timing of the taxable and deductible items does not occur in the same year, unless it is a one-year loan repayable in the same year. In the example of the 10-year loan, the salary is reported in the year of the loan and interest accrues annually over the following 10-year period. Second, the employer's and employee's tax rates might be different, so the tax burdens of an equal amount of income and deductions in the same tax year do not cancel out. Third, it is not always true that salary and interest are deductible when paid. Salary might be a capital expenditure and interest is not always deductible, as Chapter 16 explains.

The tax complexities are indicated by the following chart:

	Employer	Employee
Year 0 (the loan year)	(probably deduct salary)	Include salary
Year 1-10 deduct	include interest	(probably) deduct interest

§ 7.04 PREPAID CONSUMPTION

[A] Prepayment for Fixed Dollar Value

Suppose the taxpayer prepays for a consumption item with a fixed dollar value. For example, assume that a prepayment in year 0 entitles the purchaser or designated family member to $1,000 tuition due in two years (in year 2). In effect, the taxpayer is lending money to the payee and would expect a discount in the price sufficient to give him a return on his prepayment at the going interest rate. If that rate is 10%, he would pay (lend) $826.45 ($1,000/1.1^2$) today (in year 0) and earn 10% interest each year. When he received the service in year 2, he would in effect be collecting in year 2 the $826.45 loan plus interest, totaling $1,000, and then pay that $1,000 for the service. The prepayment technique shortcuts the process, avoiding collection and repayment of the $1,000. In tabular form, the prepayment is equated with an interest-bearing loan as follows:

Year 0	Year 1	Year 2
– $826.45 (loan = prepayment)	+ $82.65 (interest)	+ $90.91 (interest) + $826.45 (repay loan) – $1,000 (pay for tuition)

The lender should pay tax on the interest just as he would if he had deposited the money in a bank. If he was in the 35% bracket, he would not have enough left to pay $1,000 for tuition, but no one in the 35% bracket should be able to get personal consumption of $173.56 (the interest total of $82.65 plus $90.91) by earning just $173.56. You are supposed to earn a greater amount of before-tax income to have $173.56 left. The problem in the above example is that the payor is enjoying a tax free 10% return equal to $173.56, which is the difference between the $1,000 personal consumption in year 2 and the $826.45 prepayment in year 0.

Would the statutory rules dealing with interest earned on loans apply to the above example? This is really two questions. First, do the original issue discount rules apply? I think not. *See* **§ 1273(b)(4)**. Second, is the gain on the difference between the value received and the amount prepaid considered interest, and therefore tax exempt under § 103, if the obligor is a state or local government?

Consolidated Edison of New York v. United States, 10 F.3d 68 (2d Cir. 1993), deals with the second issue. The taxpayer prepaid New York City property taxes to help the City during a financial crisis. In one instance it prepaid $50,000,000, and the City provided Consolidated Edison with a receipt for a tax payment of $50,937,814, calculated to provide an 8% discount. The taxpayer excluded the $937,814 from income on the ground that it was tax exempt § 103 interest and deducted the full $50,937,814 as an accrued tax debt. The court held that the $937,814 was income, but was not tax exempt interest. It attached controlling weight to the taxpayer's decision to avoid being a creditor, having refused to lend money explicitly to the City because of bankruptcy concerns. The court distinguished the discount in this case from original issue discount, where the discount is given in exchange for an extension of credit. In this case, the court said, the prepayment discount given by the City was not given in exchange for an extension of credit, but as consideration for the taxpayer's agreement to prepay its tax liability. The court also allowed the $50,937,814 to be deducted as accrued taxes under § 164(a)(1).

Is *Consolidated Edison* correct? Suppose the taxpayer had invested $50,000,000 in a tax exempt bond and used the proceeds of the bond ($50,937,814, which includes the tax exempt interest) to pay New York City property taxes. How does that situation differ from what Consolidated Edison did?

[B] Prepayment for Uncertain Dollar Value

A taxpayer might prepay for a future benefit that has no fixed dollar value; consequently, any gain would not be interest. But, in theory, there would be taxable gain equal to the value enjoyed in the future minus basis. However, in the common case of a prepayment for a short period of time (e.g., prepaying for a vacation), it would not be worth trying to tax this gain, even if it could be detected.

But suppose that the prepayment entitles the payor or his designee to free tuition, not fixed at any specific dollar value, sometime in the future. This could amount to a great deal of money. These prepayment plans have proliferated recently and elicited agency, judicial, and statutory responses. In some instances, the prepayment was directly to a university which promised the free tuition; in other cases, the prepayment was to a trust set up to fund future tuition benefits.

Prepayments to trusts have received the most attention. The IRS dealt with the Michigan prepaid tuition plan in Letter Ruling 8825027. The taxpayer (usually a parent or grandparent) made a payment to a trust that agreed to pay four years tuition at specified institutions for a designated beneficiary. The ruling treated the payment to the trust as a tax exempt gift, but taxed the child when the tuition benefits were provided in the future. Assuming a four-year pay-out, the child realized gross income equal to the value of each tuition payment minus one-fourth of the basis (which equaled the payment to the trust). For example, if the parent contributed $4,000 to the trust when the child was four years old, and the child received $6,000 in tuition benefits in each of four years beginning at age 18, the child's annual gross income would include $5,000 ($6,000 minus $1,000). In effect, the child received a gift of an asset with a four-year life, and reported the income from the asset minus straight-line depreciation.

The Letter Ruling dealt with an additional problem — whether the trust was itself tax free. This was of little tax interest to the parent or child, but was financially very important. If the trust was taxed, there might be insufficient assets to fund the future tuition obligations. The ruling held that the trust was *not* exempt under a little-known section (§ 115), which exempts income derived from the exercise of any essential government function that accrues to a state or any political subdivision of a state. The ruling held that the private benefit to individuals who made the investment prevented application of § 115.

The Sixth Circuit also held that the trust was *not* taxable, but did not rely on § 115. *State of Michigan v. United States*, 40 F.3d 817 (6th Cir. 1994), *reversing*, 802 F. Supp. 120 (D. Mich. 1992). The court relied on a principle of law that no one disputed — that no income tax is imposed, unless the law imposes tax on the entity in question. The relevant section is § 11, which taxes corporations, and (as the court noted) "this section has never been interpreted as imposing a tax on income earned directly by a state, a political subdivision of a state, or 'an integral part of a State.' " Examples included the following: Rev. Rul. 71-131, 1971-1 C.B. 28 (income derived from the operation of liquor stores by the State of Montana is not subject to federal income tax); Rev. Rul. 87-2, 1987-1 C.B. 18 (exempting income earned by a Lawyer Trust Account Fund created by a state supreme court using client funds held by attorneys in a fiduciary capacity; "Fund is an integral part of the state," when it is used for public purposes).

The court adopted a substantive canon of statutory construction "requiring that before a federal tax can be applied to activities carried on directly by the States . . . , the intention of Congress to tax them should be stated expressly and not drawn merely from general wording of the statute applicable ordinarily to private sources of revenue." *State of New York v. United States*, 326 U.S. at 585 (Rutledge, J., concurring). It gave as an example of an express taxing provision § 511(a)(2)(B), which taxes the unrelated business income "of any college or university which is an agency or instrumentality of any government or any political subdivision thereof, or which is owned or operated by a government or any political subdivision thereof, or by any agency or instrumentality of one or more governments or political subdivisions."

Although prepayments to trusts have received the most attention, a prepayment of future tuition directly to a university is still a possibility. In such cases, the problem of taxing the income accruing to the investment does not arise. The university itself is a tax-exempt organization and the investment income would therefore be exempt as it accrued to the university. The difficulty with such arrangements is that they do not provide the taxpayer with the flexibility in choosing among educational institutions that the trust plans provide.

[C]   Prepaid Tuition Plans; § 529

Further litigation about taxing a state educational trust will not occur. The entire subject matter of prepaid tuition has been taken over by an evolving series of statutory provisions, which accord significant tax breaks for investment in education. As a result, the prior rulings and case law dealing with prepayment for future consumption will only be relevant for situations not covered by these new provisions. It remains to be seen whether taxpayer ingenuity will spawn new prepayment arrangements that will attract government scrutiny.

In 1996, Congress adopted § 529, which explicitly made "qualified state tuition programs," such as the Michigan trust, tax exempt. In general, a qualified plan was one that covered tuition, books, and supplies and, for students attending at least half-time, room and board (up to a certain limit).

Later law made contributions to qualified tuition plans adopted under § 529 even more attractive. First, it expanded the "qualified tuition program" to include a program run by an educational institution, including private institutions or a consortium of private institutions, not just state-sponsored plans. Second, and most important, it exempted (not just deferred) the taxation of distributions from a qualified program for qualified higher education expenses.

These rules illustrate an interesting feature of the tax legislative process. What began as a creative effort by taxpayers and their tax advisers to defer tax on the interest-like element accruing to prepaid consumption has evolved into a major tax break for prepaid education expenses, exempting the income on investments used for these purposes. Significantly, this tax break is *not* phased out based on higher amounts of AGI.

Amounts not used for qualified education costs and not a return of the original capital investment are subject to a 10% penalty, unless an exception applies (e.g., if the distribution is made on account of the death or disability of the beneficiary). However, the beneficiary can be changed or amounts rolled over into an account for another beneficiary without tax consequences, as long as the new beneficiary is a member of the same family as the original beneficiary (including first cousins).

Chapter 8

DEDUCTIONS FROM INCOME

§ 8.01 INTRODUCTION

[A] Statutory Rules

Section 162. The other side of the income coin is a deduction. The most important section is § 162, authorizing a deduction for business expenses. If you think income equals personal consumption plus savings, then the deduction for business expenses is an essential feature of the law — business expenses do not provide personal consumption. **Sections 62, 63** deal with whether deductions otherwise allowable are deductible in computing adjusted gross income or taxable income.

Section 212. Another important section is § 212(1), (2). It was passed after the Supreme Court held that investors were not in business and was therefore not entitled to business deductions, even though they engaged in an income-producing activity. *Higgins v. Commissioner*, 312 U.S. 212 (1941). This section expands the kinds of activities taxed on a net income basis to include income-producing nonbusiness activities.

Most § 212 deductions are itemized deductions, below the line. In most cases, a § 212 expense is a below the line itemized deduction (replaceable by the standard deduction), and subject to the 2% floor. An exception is a § 212 expense attributable to rent and royalty income; this expense is an above the line deduction. § 62(a)(4).

Most business expenses are above the line, except for most employee expenses. By contrast, most business expenses are above the line, deductible in going from gross to adjusted gross income. An exception is unreimbursed employee business expenses, which are usually below the line and subject to the 2% floor. However, the 2002 Tax Law provided that kindergarten through grade 12 teachers could take an above the line deduction for up to $250 per year; § 62(a)(2)(D). This tax break has been extended through 2013 by ATRA.

The fact that most unreimbursed employee business expenses are itemized deductions creates enormous pressure to finds ways to decide in favor of the employee when the amounts are large. What do you think of the reasoning in *Beatty v. Commissioner*, 106 T.C. 268 (1996)? A sheriff received $31,000 salary and per diem prisoner meal allowances of $110,000. The sheriff could keep any amount of the per diem allowance not spent for prisoner meals. Is the amount spent on prisoner meals (1) a reduction in computing gross income, (2) a deduction in computing adjusted gross income, or (3) an itemized employee business expense deduction? The taxpayer argued that the provision of meals was a separate nonemployee trade or business, in which case the prisoner meal expenses were deductible in computing adjusted gross income, reducing the $110,000 per diem allowance included in his gross income.

The court took a different route in finding for the taxpayer. Recall that if a taxpayer has a cost in an asset (e.g., a house), that cost is deducted from the gross proceeds of a sale to determine gross income. The same principle applies to a taxpayer who sells inventory — the costs of the inventory (cost of goods sold) is a cost that reduces the gross proceeds from inventory sales to compute gross income. The Tax Court in Beatty held that the costs of the meals for prisoners was a cost of goods sold, reducing the $110,000 in computing gross income.

Notice that this result avoids opening the floodgates for employees to argue that some of their activities are nonemployee businesses, but still lets a huge expenditure be deducted by the employee. That seems fair, because the itemized deduction status for employee expenses was meant to prevent the deduction of small expenses. But how can the court seriously suggest that the meals were "goods sold." Who bought them?

A special rule for estates and trusts. Section 67(e)(1) permits trusts and estates to deduct expenses above the line (that is, not subject to the 2% floor) if (1) they are "paid or incurred in connection with the administration of the estate or trust"; and (2) they "would not have been incurred if the property were not held in such estate or trust."

In *Knight v. C.I.R.*, 552 U.S. 181 (2008), the Court held that investment advisory fees were not above the line deductions, unless the investment advisor imposed a "special, additional charge applicable only to its fiduciary accounts," or the trust had "an unusual investment objective" that required "a specialized balancing of the interests of various parties, such that a reasonable comparison with individual investors would be improper." In reaching this conclusion, the Court rejected an interpretation of the statute that required that an above the line deduction be an expense that "could" not have been incurred by an individual. That was not the plain meaning of the statute, which used the word "would," rather than "could" not have been incurred. Consequently, the Court concluded that "the word 'would' is best read as 'express[ing] concepts such as custom, habit, natural disposition, or probability.' *See* Webster's Third New International Dictionary 2637–2638 (1993); American Heritage Dictionary 2042, 2059 (3d ed. 1996)."

Business vs. nonbusiness activity. The result of this statutory pattern is that taxpayers generally want activities to be business rather than investment activities.

For example, in *Commissioner v. Groetzinger*, 480 U.S. 23 (1987), the Court held that a professional gambler was entitled to above the line deductions. And someone who makes his livelihood by trading a large amount of stocks and bonds to provide a livelihood is likely to be a "trader," rather than an investor, and therefore allowed to deduct expenses above the line. *Snyder v. Commissioner*, 295 U.S. 134, 138–39 (1935) (not a trader on the facts of the case); *Cameron v. Commissioner*, T.C. Memo. 2007-260, 94 T.C.M. (CCH) 245 (same).

But, in *Forrest v. Commissioner*, T.C. Memo. 2009-228, 98 T.C.M. (CCH) 316 (2009), the court held that the taxpayer's activities in 2003 in trying to earn money as a contract attorney were not "regular and continuous" and therefore did not amount to a trade or business. The court stated the facts as follows:

> Before 1988 petitioner worked as a contract attorney performing various legal services, e.g., researching legal issues, attending hearings, etc., on behalf of other attorneys. She represented her own clients on occasion, but this was rare. . . . From 1988 until her employment was terminated in 2000 she worked as a securities regulator for the California Department of Corporations (the department). Petitioner worked as a contract attorney again in 2000 but not at all during 2001 and 2002.
>
> In 2003 petitioner decided once again to try to work as a contract attorney. She attended the ABA 2003 Midyear Meeting in Seattle, Washington, on February 8-11. While there she attended a women's caucus luncheon, a solo and small firm lawyers breakfast caucus, and seminars on securities law. Petitioner networked with colleagues and informed them she was available as a contract attorney to perform various legal services on their behalf. Petitioner also purchased various supplies, including a computer, printer, paper products, etc., as well as telephone, fax, and Internet services between January and March 2003. Petitioner attempted to be reinstated as a securities regulator by the department and eventually filed suit against the department in 2003. She used some of the supplies she had purchased to assist in her reinstatement efforts. Before petitioner secured any clients or earned any income as a contract attorney in 2003, she was reinstated by the department and returned to work on or around March 25.

The court rejected the taxpayer's argument that her "activity was a continuation of a trade or business carried on previously; i.e., in the 1980s and in 2000. [E]ven if her activities in the past amounted to a trade or business, which we do not decide, there was a substantial lack of continuity between her prior work and her efforts in 2003. Petitioner did not work as a contract attorney between 1988 and 2000 while she worked for the department. She also did not work as a contract attorney in 2001 or 2002, and her activity in 2003 was sporadic. Accordingly, under the facts of this case petitioner's activity in 2003 was not a continuation of a trade or business carried on in any previous period."

As for the taxpayer's work as a contract attorney from mid-January of 2003 to around March 25, 2003, when she returned to her job as a securities regulator, this was not a "substantial time period." And, "[e]ven though [taxpayer] expended some time and effort in an attempt to find work as a contract attorney during this period, her involvement was not regular and continuous. Her only activity was her attendance at the ABA meeting for 4 days in February, at which petitioner marketed herself to other attorneys. She did not negotiate for or perform any legal services as a contract attorney for any party during this period. Finally, she abandoned her efforts upon returning to the department in late March. Accordingly, her activity was neither regular nor continuous."

Alternative minimum tax. Chapter 18 will discuss the alternative minimum tax. Deductions that are below the line are often not deductible in computing this tax, so the business/nonbusiness distinction is often very important to a taxpayer who might be subject to the alternative minimum tax.

Business activity supports NOL carryover. Another statutory context in which business status is important concerns the net operating loss carryover. Net operating business losses can be carried over under § 172. In *Yerkie v. Commissioner*, 67 T.C. 388 (1976), the court held that an employee's repayment of embezzled funds supported only a nonbusiness deduction, not a business deduction. Consequently, there was no net operating loss carryover to another year.

"Ordinary and necessary." In this chapter we pay no attention to the words "ordinary and necessary" in §§ 162(a), 212, because (as Chapter 14.01[A] explains) their statutory meaning is not their colloquial meaning and they rarely operate as a limitation on deductions.

[B] Exclusion vs. Deduction

The limits on itemized deductions highlight not only the difference between above the line and below the line deductions, but also the difference between exclusions from income and below the line deductions. For example, an exclusion from § 61 income is likely to be better than including the fringe benefit in income and deducting it as an itemized deduction, because the exclusion avoids the limits on itemized deductions.

Exclusions also raise a broader question. Is it ever sensible to allow an exclusion for benefits provided to a taxpayer (by an employer, for example) under circumstances where the taxpayer is *not* allowed to take the deduction as a § 162 business expense at all? That question is not about the mechanics of computing deductibility. It is about the underlying conception of income. Is something less deserving of inclusion in the tax base when it is provided as an in-kind benefit?

Sometimes the answer seems to be "yes." The exclusion of part of the cost of the steamship ticket prize in *Turner* (Chapter 3.07[A][1]) rested on the lack of complete dominion (or choice) that accompanies in-kind benefits. Certainly, the price of a freely purchased steamship ticket would not have been partially deductible. And many fringe benefits excluded under §§ 119 and 132 would not have been deductible if purchased by the employee. You should watch throughout this chapter for examples where a deduction might be disallowed (not just replaced by a standard deduction or subject to a 2% floor), but an in-kind benefit for the same item might be excluded. If that happens, ask yourself why. Is it because the benefit is less likely to be § 61 income; is the exclusion justified by social policy?

§ 8.02 DEFINING DEDUCTIBLE BUSINESS EXPENSES

Most deductible business-related expenditures are easy to identify — e.g., salary, rent, and the purchase price of raw materials used to produce inventory. Some of these outlays might be "costs" rather than "expenses," and their deduction deferred until a later year (*see* Chapter 13), but the business connection is obvious. That connection is not so obvious, however, when the expense might provide personal consumption. The line between business and personal expenses is therefore the focus of this chapter.

[A]   Two Cases: Child Care; Work Clothing

SMITH v. COMMISSIONER
United States Board of Tax Appeals
40 B.T.A. 1038 (1939), *affirmed per curiam*, 113 F.2d 114 (2d Cir. 1940)

JUDGE OPPER:

Respondent determined a deficiency of $23.62 in petitioner's 1937 income tax. This was due to the disallowance of a deduction claimed by petitioners, who are husband and wife, for sums spent by the wife in employing nursemaids to care for petitioners' young child, the wife, as well as the husband, being employed. The facts have all been stipulated and are hereby found accordingly.

Petitioners would have us apply the 'but for' test. They propose that but for the nurses the wife could not leave her child; but for the freedom so secured she could not pursue her gainful labors; and but for them there would be no income and no tax. This thought evokes an array of interesting possibilities. The fee to the doctor, but for whose healing service the earner of the family income could not leave his sickbed; the cost of the laborer's raiment, for how can the world proceed about its business unclothed; the very home which gives us shelter and rest and the food which provides energy, might all by an extension of the same proposition be construed as necessary to the operation of business and to the creation of income. Yet these are the very essence of those 'personal' expenses the deductibility of which is expressly denied.

We are told that the working wife is a new phenomenon. This is relied on to account for the apparent inconsistency that the expenses in issue are now a commonplace, yet have not been the subject of legislation, ruling, or adjudicated controversy. But if that is true it becomes all the more necessary to apply accepted principles to the novel facts. We are not prepared to say that the care of children, like similar aspects of family and household life, is other than a personal concern. The wife's services as custodian of the home and protector of its children are ordinarily rendered without monetary compensation. There results no taxable income from the performance of this service and the correlative expenditure is personal and not susceptible of deduction. IIere the wife has chosen to employ others to discharge her domestic function and the services she performs are rendered outside the home. They are a source of actual income and taxable as such. But that does not deprive the same work performed by others of its personal character nor furnish a reason why its cost should be treated as an offset in the guise of a deductible item.

[Editor — The statement that the expenses are not deductible *because* the services performed by the wife would not generate taxable income has it backwards. If self-performed services are not taxable income, that is an argument *for* a deduction when the services are paid for in cash.]

We are not unmindful that, as petitioners suggest, certain disbursements normally personal may become deductible by reason of their intimate connection with an occupation carried on for profit. In this category fall entertainment, and traveling expenses, and the cost of an actor's wardrobe. The line is not always an easy one to draw nor the test simple to apply. But we think its principle is clear. It may for practical purposes be said to constitute a distinction between those activities which, as a matter of common acceptance and universal experience, are 'ordinary' or usual as the direct accompaniment of business pursuits, on the one hand; and those which, though they may in some indirect and tenuous degree relate to the circumstances of a profitable occupation, are nevertheless personal in their nature, of a character applicable to human beings generally, and which exist on that plane regardless of the occupation, though not necessarily of the station in life, of the individuals concerned.

In the latter category, we think, fall payments made to servants or others occupied in looking to the personal wants of their employers. And we include in this group nursemaids retained to care for infant children.

Decision will be entered for the respondent.

PEVSNER v. COMMISSIONER
United States Court of Appeals, Fifth Circuit
628 F.2d 467 (1980), *reversing*, 38 T.C.M. (CCH) 1210 (1979)

SAM D. JOHNSON, CIRCUIT JUDGE: . . .

Since June 1973 Sandra J. Pevsner, taxpayer, has been employed as the manager of the Sakowitz Yves St. Laurent Rive Gauche Boutique located in Dallas, Texas. The boutique sells only women's clothes and accessories designed by Yves St. Laurent (YSL), one of the leading designers of women's apparel. Although the clothing is ready to wear, it is highly fashionable and expensively priced. Some customers of the boutique purchase and wear the YSL apparel for their daily activities and spend as much as $20,000 per year for such apparel.

As manager of the boutique, the taxpayer is expected by her employer to wear YSL clothes while at work. In her appearance, she is expected to project the image of an exclusive lifestyle and to demonstrate to her customers that she is aware of the YSL current fashion trends as well as trends generally. Because the boutique sells YSL clothes exclusively, taxpayer must be able, when a customer compliments her on her clothes, to say that they are designed by YSL. In addition to wearing YSL apparel while at the boutique, she wears them while commuting to and from work, to fashion shows sponsored by the boutique, and to business luncheons at which she represents the boutique. During 1975, the taxpayer bought, at an employee's discount, the following items: four blouses, three skirts, one pair of slacks, one trench coat, two sweaters, one jacket, one tunic, five scarves, six belts, two pairs of shoes and four necklaces. The total cost of this apparel was $1,381.91. In addition, the sum of $240 was expended for maintenance of these items.

Although the clothing and accessories purchased by the taxpayer were the type used for general purposes by the regular customers of the boutique, the taxpayer is not a normal purchaser of these clothes. The taxpayer and her husband, who is partially disabled because of a severe heart attack suffered in 1971, lead a simple life and their social activities are very limited and informal. Although taxpayer's employer has no objection to her wearing the apparel away from work, taxpayer stated that she did not wear the clothes during off-work hours because she felt that they were too expensive for her simple everyday lifestyle. Another reason why she did not wear the YSL clothes apart from work was to make them last longer. Taxpayer did admit at trial, however, that a number of the articles were things she could have worn off the job and in which she would have looked "nice." . . .

The principal issue on appeal is whether the taxpayer is entitled to deduct as an ordinary and necessary business expense the cost of purchasing and maintaining the YSL clothes and accessories worn by the taxpayer in her employment as the manager of the boutique. This determination requires an examination of the relationship between Section 162(a) of the Internal Revenue Code of 1954, which allows a deduction for ordinary and necessary expenses incurred in the conduct of a trade or business, and Section 262 of the Code, which bars a deduction for all "personal, living, or family expenses." Although many expenses are helpful or essential to one's business activities — such as commuting expenses and the cost of meals while at work — these expenditures are considered inherently personal and are disallowed under Section 262.

The generally accepted rule governing the deductibility of clothing expenses is that the cost of clothing is deductible as a business expense only if: (1) the clothing is of a type specifically required as a condition of employment, (2) it is not adaptable to general usage as ordinary clothing, and (3) it is not so worn.

In the present case, the Commissioner stipulated that the taxpayer was required by her employer to wear YSL clothing and that she did not wear such apparel apart from work. The Commissioner maintained, however, that a deduction should be denied because the YSL clothes and accessories purchased by the taxpayer were adaptable for general usage as ordinary clothing and she was not prohibited from using them as such. The tax court, in rejecting the Commissioner's argument for the application of an objective test, recognized that the test for deductibility was whether the clothing was "suitable for general or personal wear" but determined that the matter of suitability was to be judged subjectively, in light of the taxpayer's lifestyle. Although the court recognized that the YSL apparel "might be used by some members of society for general purposes," it felt that because the "wearing of YSL apparel outside work would be inconsistent with . . . (taxpayer's) lifestyle" sufficient reason was shown for allowing a deduction for the clothing expenditures. . . .

. . . [T]he Circuits that have addressed the issue have taken an objective, rather than subjective, approach. . . . Under an objective test, no reference is made to the individual taxpayer's lifestyle or personal taste. Instead, adaptability for personal or general use depends upon what is generally accepted for ordinary street wear.

The principal argument in support of an objective test is, of course, administrative necessity. The Commissioner argues that, as a practical matter, it is virtually impossible to determine at what point either price or style makes clothing inconsistent with or inappropriate to a taxpayer's lifestyle. Moreover, the Commissioner argues that the price one pays and the styles one selects are inherently personal choices governed by taste, fashion, and other unmeasurable values.

Indeed, the tax court has rejected the argument that a taxpayer's personal taste can dictate whether clothing is appropriate for general use. An objective test, although not perfect, provides a practical administrative approach that allows a taxpayer or revenue agent to look only to objective facts in determining whether clothing required as a condition of employment is adaptable to general use as ordinary streetwear. Conversely, the tax court's reliance on subjective factors provides no concrete guidelines in determining the deductibility of clothing purchased as a condition of employment.

In addition to achieving a practical administrative result, an objective test also tends to promote substantial fairness among the greatest number of taxpayers. As the Commissioner suggests, it apparently would be the tax court's position that two similarly situated YSL boutique managers with identical wardrobes would be subject to disparate tax consequences depending upon the particular manager's lifestyle and "socio-economic level." This result, however, is not consonant with a reasonable interpretation of Sections 162 and 262.

For the reasons stated above, the decision of the tax court upholding the deduction for taxpayer's purchase of YSL clothing is reversed. Consequently, the portion of the tax court's decision upholding the deduction for maintenance costs for the clothing is also reversed.

[B]   "But For" Tests

1. If a taxpayer says that "but for" clothes or health she *could* not work, your response is likely to be that the statement is true but that it misses the point. The point is that the taxpayer would have spent the money anyway, whether or not she worked. In the language of the court in *Pevsner* (involving work clothing), these expenses are "inherently personal." Is there any evidence in the *Smith* case that the taxpayer would have spent the money for child care anyway, even if she had not worked?

2. The "but for the expense, could not work" test is just one version of the "but for" test, however. If the taxpayer offers to prove that "but for" work, she *would* not have incurred the expense, she is making a different argument. The claim is that the work makes the expense necessary, not that the expense is necessary for work. This is what the taxpayer argued in *Pevsner*. So the issue is when can a taxpayer deduct expenses by proving that, "but for" work, she would not make the expenditure.

If you adopt the but-for-work-would-not-spend test, there remains the question whether you adopt a subjective test (what would this taxpayer do?) or an objective test (what is the general pattern of behavior?). The Court of Appeals in *Pevsner* adopted an objective test to discourage deduction of work clothing.

In *Mella v. Commissioner*, 52 T.C.M. (CCH) 1216 (1986), the court denied a professional tennis player a deduction for his tennis clothes and tennis shoes. The court refused to adopt a subjective test — did the taxpayer wear such clothing for personal use — and instead stressed that the clothing was "suitable for general or personal wear." The court noted that "it is relatively commonplace for Americans in all walks of life to wear warm-up clothes, shirts, and shoes of the type purchased by the [taxpayer] while engaged in a wide variety of casual or athletic activities."

QUESTION

How is the employee taxed (a) if the employer in *Pevsner* had given the clothing to the employee (would § 132(a)(3), (d) apply)? (b) If the employer had forbidden her from wearing the clothes off duty? (c) If the employer had taken the clothes back after work?

[C]   Origin Test

Satisfying the "but for work, would not spend" test might not be sufficient to justify a deduction. Although it might be true that, but for work, the taxpayer would not make an expenditure, it might also be true that, but for some personal reason, the taxpayer also would not make the same expenditure. Should such expenditures be considered to originate in the work or personal sphere of the taxpayer's activity? The following *Gilmore* case suggests that a deductible expense must satisfy an "origin" test — that is, the expense must not originate in the taxpayer's personal sphere of activity.

In the context of work clothing, an origin test might lead to the following analysis. Some of the expenditure originates in personal choice because something must be spent on clothing. But that observation would not necessarily result in denying the deduction. Just because something would be spent on clothing for personal reasons in any event does not mean that there should not be a deduction for any extra amount spent because of the business activity. And, if some amount should be deducted, the easiest rule to administer might be to permit all of the expense to be deducted; or would the easier-to-administer rule be to disallow the entire expense deduction?

In the context of child care, the origin test might lead to disallowing the entire deduction because — but for the child, no expenses would be incurred. The argument is that the child care expenses "originate" with having children, not with working. In other words — even if the taxpayer would not spend but for work, it is also true that, but for children, the taxpayer would not spend.

In *Gilmore*, the taxpayer claimed a deduction for legal fees paid to defend against a divorce action brought by his wife. The taxpayer claimed to be protecting his property and livelihood which were put in jeopardy by the divorce action. The deduction was claimed under an earlier 1939 Code version of § 212(2), which was § 23(a)(2).

UNITED STATES v. GILMORE
United States Supreme Court
372 U.S. 39 (1963)

Mr. Justice Harlan delivered the opinion of the Court. . . .

At the time of the divorce proceedings, instituted by the wife but in which the husband also cross-claimed for divorce, respondent's property consisted primarily of controlling stock interests in three corporations, each of which was a franchised General Motors automobile dealer. As president and principal managing officer of the three corporations, he received salaries from them aggregating about $66,800 annually, and in recent years his total annual dividends had averaged about $83,000. His total annual income derived from the corporations was thus approximately $150,000. His income from other sources was negligible.

As found by the Court of Claims, the husband's overriding concern in the divorce litigation was to protect these assets against the claims of his wife. Those claims had two aspects: first, that the earnings accumulated and retained by these three corporations during the Gilmores' marriage (representing an aggregate increase in corporate net worth of some $600,000) were the product of respondent's personal services, and not the result of accretion in capital values, thus rendering respondent's stockholdings in the enterprises pro tanto community property under California law; second, that to the extent that such stockholdings were community property, the wife, allegedly the innocent party in the divorce proceeding, was entitled under California law to more than a one-half interest in such property.

The respondent wished to defeat those claims for two important reasons. First, the loss of his controlling stock interests, particularly in the event of their transfer in substantial part to his hostile wife, might well cost him the loss of his corporate positions, his principal means of livelihood. Second, there was also danger that if he were found guilty of his wife's sensational and reputation-damaging charges of marital infidelity, General Motors Corporation might find it expedient to exercise its right to cancel these dealer franchises.

The end result of this bitterly fought divorce case was a complete victory for the husband. He, not the wife, was granted a divorce on his cross-claim; the wife's community property claims were denied in their entirety; and she was held entitled to no alimony.

Respondent's legal expenses in connection with this litigation amounted to $32,537.15 in 1953 and $8,074.21 in 1954 — a total of $40,611.36 for the two taxable years in question. The Commissioner of Internal Revenue found all of these expenditures 'personal' or 'family' expenses and as such none of them deductible. . . .

For income tax purposes Congress has seen fit to regard an individual as having two personalities: 'one is (as) a seeker after profit who can deduct the expenses incurred in that search; the other is (as) a creature satisfying his needs as a human and those of his family but who cannot deduct such consumption and related expenditures.' The Government regards [§ 212] as embodying a category of the expenses embraced in the first of these roles.

Initially, it may be observed that the wording of [§ 212] more readily fits the Government's view of the provision than that of the Court of Claims. For in context 'conservation of property' seems to refer to operations performed with respect to the property itself, such as safeguarding or upkeep, rather than to a taxpayer's retention of ownership in it. But more illuminating than the mere language of [the statute] is the history of the provision.

Prior to 1942 [the statute] allowed deductions only for expenses incurred 'in carrying on any trade or business,' the deduction presently authorized by [§ 162]. In *Higgins v. Commissioner*, 312 U.S. 212, this Court gave that provision a narrow construction, holding that the activities of an individual in supervising his own securities investments did not constitute the 'carrying on of trade or business', and hence that expenses incurred in connection with such activities were not tax deductible. . . . The Revenue Act of 1942, by adding what is now [§ 212], sought to remedy the inequity inherent in the disallowance of expense deductions in respect of such profit-seeking activities, the income from which was nonetheless taxable.

As noted in *McDonald v. Commissioner*, 323 U.S. 57, 62, the purpose of the 1942 amendment was merely to enlarge 'the category of incomes with reference to which expenses were deductible.' And committee reports make clear that deductions under the new section were subject to the same limitations and restrictions that are applicable to those allowable under [§ 162]. . . .

A basic restriction upon the availability of a [§ 162] deduction is that the expense item involved must be one that has a business origin. That restriction not only inheres in the language of [the statute] itself, confining such deductions to 'expenses . . . incurred . . . in carrying on any trade or business,' but also follows from [§ 262], expressly rendering nondeductible 'in any case . . . (p)ersonal, living, or family expenses.' In light of what has already been said with respect to the advent and thrust of [§ 212], it is clear that the '(p)ersonal . . . or family expenses' restriction of [§ 262] must impose the same limitation upon the reach of [§ 212] — in other words that the only kind of expenses deductible under [§ 212] are those that relate to a 'business,' that is, profit-seeking, purpose. The pivotal issue in this case then becomes: was this part of respondent's litigation costs a 'business' rather than a 'personal' or 'family' expense?

The answer to this question has already been indicated in prior cases. In *Lykes v. United States*, 343 U.S. 118, the Court rejected the contention that legal expenses incurred in contesting the assessment of a gift tax liability were deductible. The taxpayer argued that if he had been required to pay the original deficiency he would have been forced to liquidate his stockholdings, which were his main source of income, and that his legal expenses were therefore incurred in the 'conservation' of income-producing property and hence deductible under [§ 212(2)]. The Court first noted that the 'deductibility (of the expenses) turns wholly upon the nature of the activities to which they relate,' and then stated:

> Legal expenses do not become deductible merely because they are paid for services which relieve a taxpayer of liability. That argument would carry us too far. It would mean that the expense of defending almost any claim would be deductible by a taxpayer on the ground that such defense was made to help him keep clear of liens whatever income-producing property he might have. For example, it suggests that the expense of defending an action based upon personal injuries caused by a taxpayer's negligence while driving an automobile for pleasure should be deductible. Section [212] never has been so interpreted by us. . . .

> While the threatened deficiency assessment . . . added urgency to petitioner's resistance of it, neither its size nor its urgency determined its character. It related to the tax payable on petitioner's gifts . . . . The

expense of contesting the amount of the deficiency was thus at all times attributable to the gifts, as such, and accordingly was not deductible.

If, as suggested, the relative size of each claim, in proportion to the income-producing resources of a defendant, were to be a touchstone of the deductibility of the expense of resisting the claim, substantial uncertainty and inequity would inhere in the rule. . . . It is not a ground for (deduction) that the claim, if justified, will consume income-producing property of the defendant.

In *Kornhauser v. United States*, 276 U.S. 145, this Court considered the deductibility of legal expenses incurred by a taxpayer in defending against a claim by a former business partner that fees paid to the taxpayer were for services rendered during the existence of the partnership. In holding that these expenses were deductible even though the taxpayer was no longer a partner at the time of suit, the Court formulated the rule that 'where a suit or action against a taxpayer is directly connected with, or . . . proximately resulted from, his business, the expense incurred is a business expense . . . .' Similarly, in a case involving an expense incurred in satisfying an obligation (though not a litigation expense), it was said that 'it is the origin of the liability out of which the expense accrues' or 'the kind of transaction out of which the obligation arose . . . which (is) crucial and controlling.'

The principle we derive from these cases is that the characterization, as 'business' or 'personal,' of the litigation costs of resisting a claim depends on whether or not the claim arises in connection with the taxpayer's profit-seeking activities. It does not depend on the consequences that might result to a taxpayer's income-producing property from a failure to defeat the claim, for, as Lykes teaches, that 'would carry us too far' and would not be compatible with the basic lines of expense deductibility drawn by Congress. Moreover, such a rule would lead to capricious results. If two taxpayers are each sued for an automobile accident while driving for pleasure, deductibility of their litigation costs would turn on the mere circumstance of the character of the assets each happened to possess, that is, whether the judgments against them stood to be satisfied out of income- or nonincome-producing property. We should be slow to attribute to Congress a purpose producing such unequal treatment among taxpayers, resting on no rational foundation.

Confirmation of these conclusions is found in the incongruities that would follow from acceptance of the Court of Claims' reasoning in this case. Had this respondent taxpayer conducted his automobile-dealer business as a sole proprietorship, rather than in corporate form, and claimed a deduction under [§ 162], the potential impact of his wife's claims would have been no different than in the present situation. Yet it cannot well be supposed that [§ 162] would have afforded him a deduction, since his expenditures, made in connection with a marital litigation, could hardly be deemed 'expenses . . . incurred . . . in carrying on any trade or business.' Thus, under the Court of Claims' view expenses may be even less deductible if the taxpayer is carrying on a trade or business instead of some other income-producing activity. But it was manifestly Congress' purpose with respect to deductibility to place all income-producing activities on an equal footing. And it would surely be a surprising result were it now to turn out that a change designed to achieve equality of treatment in fact had served only to reverse the inequality of treatment.

For these reasons, we resolve the conflict among the lower courts on the question before us in favor of the view that the origin and character of the claim with respect to which an expense was incurred, rather than its potential consequences upon the fortunes of the taxpayer, is the controlling basic test of whether the expense was 'business' or 'personal' and hence whether it is deductible or not under [§ 212]. We find the reasoning underlying the cases taking the 'consequences' view unpersuasive.

QUESTIONS AND COMMENTS

1. How would the child care case be decided today? *Gilmore* purports to be a decision based on how to tax income fairly — identifying nondeductible personal expenses. But there is a strong undercurrent of nontax policy — the concern with a nonlevel litigation playing field if litigation expenses are deductible. This can be important because, despite the fact that the origin test sounds mechanical, it is not easy to apply. The fact is that many expenses have both a personal and business origin and the court might have to pick which "origin" best characterizes the expense for tax purposes. If policy considerations are relevant, perhaps a contemporary court would decide that child cares expenses are business deductions, at least if it were writing on a clean slate.

2. Can a spouse deduct attorneys' fees to obtain alimony under § 212(1)? (*Gilmore* had relied on § 212(2).) In *Wild v. Commissioner*, 42 T.C. 706 (1964), *acq.*, 1967-2 C.B. 4, the court allowed the deduction even though the expense originated from a marital dispute and even though it might create a nonlevel litigation playing field.

3. Can a lawyer deduct legal expenses to prevent disbarment based on incompetence to handle money, as evidenced by bouncing checks to buy personal consumption? Is this example (1) like *Gilmore*, or (2) is it more like a case in which General Motors might have tried to terminate Gilmore's franchise, based on his marital difficulties? Are the expenses deductible in the latter case?

4. Can a dancer accused of being a Communist deduct legal expenses in a libel action to preserve his reputation so that he can obtain work? *Draper v. Commissioner*, 26 T.C. 201 (1956).

5. An individual employer incurs legal expenses to defend against a charge that he personally engaged in sexual harassment in the workplace. Are these expenses nondeductible because they have a personal origin? Or does the fact that the activity becomes actionable *because* of the work environment make the expenses deductible? What if the lawsuit alleges both a state law battery and a federal cause of action for gender discrimination in the workplace?

6. In *Vitale v. Commissioner*, 77 T.C.M. (CCH) 1869 (1999), *affirmed*, 217 F.3d 843 (4th Cir. 2000), the taxpayer was researching a book on prostitution. The court held that this was a genuine business venture, attempting to make a profit. But deductions claimed for visits to prostitutes as a customer in Nevada were

disallowed, even though the taxpayer kept a journal detailing events at the brothel and personal information about the prostitutes. The court stated: "We find that the expenditures incurred by petitioner to visit prostitutes are so personal in nature as to preclude their deductibility."

§ 8.03   DEPENDENT CARE

[A]   Modern Statutory Rules

Child care expenses have become too important to leave to the general rules about deducting business expenses. The statute now provides a tax credit for a percentage of expenses to care for a "qualifying individual" (typically a dependent child under age 13 or a disabled dependent relative) in order to be "gainfully employed." Household care expenses are also included if they are in part for care of a qualifying individual; § 21(b)(2)(A). The expenses to which the credit percentage is applied cannot exceed the lesser of (1) the earnings of the lesser-earning spouse (§ 21(d)(1)(B)), or (2) a specific sum of money which varies with the number of children (§ 21(c)).

Full-time students can use the credit. They are presumed to earn income so that they can satisfy the requirement that creditable expenses not exceed earnings of the lesser-earning spouse. § 21(d)(2).

QUESTIONS AND COMMENTS

1. Why does the law provide a credit instead of a deduction?

2. How much credit does the following family receive?

a) The husband earns $20,000. The wife is a full-time student for nine months of the year. They have one child, age 3, whom they support. They pay $3,500 during the nine-month period for a babysitter who also cleans the house during the days when the wife is at school.

b) Would your answer be different: (i) if the wife was not a student but earned $5,000 in part-time afternoon work, and paid the baby sitter $3,500 for working all day; or (ii) if the wife earned $3,000 at a full-time job to pay the babysitter $3,500?

Your answer to this problem reflects some changes made by the 2001 Tax Bill. You will have noted that the maximum amount of eligible employment-related expenses is not adjusted for inflation. Nonetheless, the 2001 Tax Bill increased the maximums from $2,400 to $3,000, if there is one qualifying individual, and from $4,800 to $6,000, if there are two qualifying individuals. In addition, it raised the maximum credit from 30% to 35%; and began the partial phase-out of the credit at $15,000 of AGI (not $10,000). Consequently, the credit percentage is reduced to 20% for taxpayers with AGI over $43,000. These increased credit percentages and higher income limits were made permanent by ATRA.

3. The taxpayer took her child out of public school and sent him to private school so that she could work. While in public school, the threat of school violence had been so great that the taxpayer had to remain at home so that she could pick up

her child from school on short notice. Is the taxpayer allowed a credit for the private school expenses? Should the court use a subjective "but for" test — but for work, she would not incur the expense? Should the court permit a credit if work was just one motive or only if it was the dominant motive for the private school expenses? *Brown v. Commissioner*, 73 T.C. 156 (1979).

4. If the employer pays for child care or runs a child care center at work, is the value of the child care included in income? *See* § **129**, which permits the exclusion from income of benefits provided by an employer-funded child care plan, up to $5,000 per year. If the plan favors highly compensated employees, those employees are not entitled to the § **129** exclusion. The excluded benefit reduces the dollar ceiling on employment-related expenses eligible for the child care credit. § **21(c)(final paragraph)**. Consequently, an employee receiving child care as a tax-free fringe benefit is unlikely to have many expenses left over that would be eligible for the credit.

[B]   Modern Case Law Evolution

[1]   Canada

Canada recently revisited the question of deducting child care expenses as a business deduction in *Symes v. Canada*, [1993] 4 S.C.R. 695, [1994] 1 C.T.C. 40. A seven-to-two majority denied a business expense deduction to a law firm partner who employed a nanny to care for her children so that she could work. Much of what the Court said contains interesting parallels to United States law.

The Court expressed a willingness to reconsider an 1891 case that had denied a business expense deduction for the child care expenses. This willingness was based on "a significant social change in the late 1970s and into the 1980s, in terms of the influx of women of child-bearing age into business and into the workplace. This change post-dates the earlier cases dismissing nanny expenses as a legitimate business deduction and therefore it does not necessarily follow that the conditions which prevailed in society at the time of the those earlier decisions will prevail now." The Court went on to state that "[t]he decision to characterize child care expenses as personal expenses was made by judges. As part of our case law, it is susceptible to reexamination in an appropriate case." The Court argued for reexamining the prior decision with a quote from an earlier case affirming that "[j]udges can and should adapt the common law to reflect the changing social, moral and economic fabric of the country." (Is this a strange comment to make? The case concerned statutory interpretation, not the common law.)

On the merits, the Court took note of the Canadian government's "income-producing circle" test, which is reminiscent of Justice Harlan's reference to a "two personality" test in the *Gilmore* case. Under the "circle" test, a distinction is made between nondeductible expenses outside the income-producing circle (such as clothing and commuting) and those deductible expenses incurred within the circle. The Court considered this test of "limited help," simply restating the personal vs. business dichotomy.

At this point in the opinion, unlike the U.S. Tax Court in the 1939 *Smith* case, the Court seemed poised to seriously consider allowing the deduction. But there was more. The Canadian statute contained a detailed rule passed in 1972 allowing child care expenses to be deducted up to a specified limit and varying with the number of children. This provision was reminiscent in its detail of the rules found in the current United States tax credit for child case expenses. § 21. The Court concluded that this specific provision was the exclusive method by which a taxpayer could reduce taxes for child care expenses, leaving no room for application of the general business expense deduction rule.

The two dissenting Justices relied heavily on the fact that the specific statutory tax break for child care expenses was passed at an earlier time, before a change in the background values regarding working women, and at a time when child care expenses were still considered personal. The change in background values deprived the specific statutory provision of any negative implication regarding the applicability of the basic statutory authorization of business expense deductions. The dissenters also drew sustenance from the principles of the Canadian Constitutional Charter prohibiting gender discrimination.

[2]   Note on Statutory Interpretation — The Impact of a Detailed Statute

The Canadian court's reference to the "common law" when interpreting a statute is not quite as strange as it sounds. The criteria for distinguishing between personal and business expenses are not clearly set forth in the statutory text and are determined by fundamental and broad principles that are part of the statutory structure — much like a common law principle. Why, then, can't the content of that principle change over time, much like a common law principle? Indeed, the dissent in the Canadian case made a strong argument that the content of the principle should change to allow a deduction for child care expenses, because the circumstances of the working woman made the old interpretation obsolete.

There are three arguments against the dissent's approach, all relating to the adoption of a detailed legislative rule dealing with child care expenses. First, the adoption of legislation treating some child care expenses favorably was intended to pre-empt the field, leaving no room for judicial elaboration of the underlying principle. The difficulty with this argument is that legislatures often lack any such specific intent. This is especially likely when events have changed significantly after passage of the law, as was true in Canada (the Canadian child care legislation was adopted in 1972 and the large-scale entry of women into the workforce came after that date).

Second, the legislation suggests that the issue of tax breaks for child care is on the legislative agenda. One reason courts sometimes act boldly is that the issue is simply not being considered at all by the political branches. More subtly, the court might be concerned that the bias of political forces strongly disfavors one side of the political dispute — in this case, those who favor encouraging women to work. Tax breaks for child care indicate that legislative inertia is not an obstacle to further legislative evolution.

Third, the detailed statutory rules might educate the court regarding the technical complexity and politically controversial nature of the problem and suggest staying the judicial hand. Look, for example, at the detail of § 21. How does it deal with the following — payments to relatives who babysit; payments to dependent care facilities outside the home; who gets the tax break and how much; students?

How should these considerations affect a U.S. court in deciding whether to revisit tax breaks for child care?

§ 8.04 TRAVELING EXPENSES

Traveling expenses test the outer boundaries of the definition of deductible business expenses. The potential for deducting personal expenses should be obvious. Along with entertainment expenses, they present the potential for so-called expense account living. Our discussion of traveling expenses first deals with meals and lodging and then with transportation expenses.

[A] Meals and Lodging

Section 162(a)(2) and the introductory language to § 162 support an elaborate development of cases and rulings dealing with tax deductible expenses for business travelers.

[1] Statutory Structure

The *Rosenspan* case (below) is an excellent discussion of the current rules and their rationale. Here is an outline of the major factual settings in which the issues arise. Which of the following can deduct meals and lodging at the business destination?

1. The typical business traveler has a home and a permanent business location in one city and travels on business to another city for a week (a convention, for example).

2. The traveler lives in one city and travels to another city, where his principal place of business is located.

3. The temporary worker has a home but no work close to home. He takes jobs some distance from his home, for relatively short periods (a construction worker, for example).

4. A taxpayer with no home travels all the time. This is not unheard of — e.g., some traveling salesmen and actors.

ROSENSPAN v. UNITED STATES
United States Court of Appeals, Second Circuit
438 F.2d 905 (1971)

FRIENDLY, CIRCUIT JUDGE: . . .

Plaintiff, Robert Rosenspan, was a jewelry salesman who worked on a commission basis, paying his own traveling expenses without reimbursement. In 1962 he was employed by one and in 1964 by two New York City jewelry manufacturers. For some 300 days a year he traveled by automobile through an extensive sales territory in the Middle West, where he would stay at hotels and motels and eat at restaurants. Five or six times a year he would return to New York and spend several days at his employers' offices. There he would perform a variety of services essential to his work — cleaning up his sample case, checking orders, discussing customers' credit problems, recommending changes in stock, attending annual staff meetings, and the like.

Rosenspan had grown [up] in Brooklyn and during his marriage had maintained a family home there. After his wife [died], he used his brother's Brooklyn home as a personal residential address, keeping some clothing and other belongings there, and registering, voting, and filing his income tax returns from that address. The stipulation of facts states that, on his trips to New York City, 'out of a desire not to abuse his welcome at his brother's home, he stayed more often' at an inn near the John F. Kennedy Airport. It recites also that 'he generally spent his annual vacations in Brooklyn, where his children resided, and made an effort to return to Brooklyn whenever possible,' but affords no further indication where he stayed on such visits. . . . Rosenspan does not contend that he had a permanent abode or residence in Brooklyn or anywhere else.

The basis for the Commissioner's disallowance of a deduction for Rosenspan's meals and lodging while in his sales territory was that he had no 'home' to be 'away from' while traveling. Not denying that this would be true if the language of § 162(a)(2) were given its ordinary meaning, Rosenspan claimed that for tax purposes his home was his 'business headquarters,' to wit, New York City where his employers maintained their offices, and relied upon the Commissioner's long advocacy of this concept of a 'tax home.' The Commissioner responded that although in most circumstances 'home' means 'business headquarters,' it should be given its natural meaning of a permanent abode or residence for purposes of the problem here presented. Rosenspan says the Commissioner is thus trying to have it both ways.

The provision of the Internal Revenue Code applicable for 1962 reads:

§ 162. Trade or business expenses.

(a) In general. — There shall be allowed as a deduction all the ordinary and necessary expenses paid or incurred during the taxable year in carrying on any trade or business, including —

(2) traveling expenses (including the entire amount expended for meals and lodging) while away from home in the pursuit of a trade or business; . . . .

. . .

What is now § 162(a)(2) was brought into the tax structure by 214 of the Revenue Act of 1921, 42 Stat. 239. Prior to that date, 214 had permitted the deduction of 'ordinary and necessary expenses paid or incurred . . . in carrying on any trade or business,' Revenue Act of 1918, 40 Stat. 1066 (1918), without further specification. In a regulation, the Treasury interpreted the statute to allow deduction of 'traveling expenses, including railroad fares, and meals and lodging in an amount *in excess of any expenditures ordinarily required for such purposes when at home,* ' T.D. 3101, 3 Cum. Bull. 191 (1920) (emphasis supplied). A formula was provided for determining what expenditures were thus 'ordinarily required'; the taxpayer was to compute such items as rent, grocery bills, light, etc. and servant hire for the periods when he was away from home, and divide this by the number of members of his family. Mim. 2688, 4 Cum. Bull. 209–11 (1921). The puzzlement of the man without a home was dealt with in a cryptic pronouncement, O.D. 905, 4 Cum. Bull. 212 (1921):

> Living expenses paid by a single taxpayer who has no home and is continuously employed on the road may not be deducted in computing net income.

The 1921 amendment, inserting what is now § 162(a)(2)'s allowance of a deduction for the entire amount of qualified meals and lodging, stemmed from a request of the Treasury based on the difficulty of administering the 'excess' provision of its regulation. While the taxpayer cites statements of legislators in the 1921 Congress that the amendment would provide 'a measure of justice' to commercial travelers, there is nothing to indicate that the members making or hearing these remarks were thinking of the unusual situation of the traveler without a home. There is likewise nothing to indicate that the Treasury sought, or that Congress meant to require, any change in the ruling that disallowed deductions for living expenses in such a case. The objective was to eliminate the need for computing the expenses 'ordinarily required' at home by a taxpayer who had one, and the words used were appropriate to that end. If we were to make the unlikely assumption that the problem of the homeless commercial traveler ever entered the legislators' minds, the language they adopted was singularly inept to resolve it in the way for which plaintiff contends. Thus, if the literal words of the statute were decisive, the Government would clearly prevail on the simple ground that a taxpayer cannot be 'away from home' unless he has a home from which to be away. Although that is our ultimate conclusion, the Supreme Court has wisely admonished that 'More than a dictionary is thus required to understand the provision here involved, and no appeal to the 'plain language' of the section can obviate the need for further statutory construction.' We turn, therefore, in the first instance to the Court's decisions.

The initial Supreme Court decision bearing on our problem is *C.I.R. v. Flowers*, 326 U.S. 465 (1946). Flowers, a lawyer, had a 'home' in the conventional sense in Jackson, Mississippi, but his principal post of business was at the main office of his employer, the Gulf, Mobile & Ohio Railroad in Mobile, Alabama. Flowers sought to deduct the cost of transportation for his trips to Mobile and the meal and lodging expenses which he incurred in that city. In upholding the Commissioner's disallowance of these deductions, the Court said that 'three conditions must thus be satisfied before a traveling expense deduction may be made' under what was substantially the present statute. These were:

> (1) The expense must be a reasonable and necessary traveling expense, as that term is generally understood. This includes such items as transportation fares and food and lodging expenses incurred while traveling.

> (2) The expense must be incurred 'while away from home.'

(3) The expense must be incurred in pursuit of business. This means that there must be a direct connection between the expenditure and the carrying on of the trade or business of the taxpayer or of his employer. Moreover, such an expenditure must be necessary or appropriate to the development and pursuit of the business or trade.

It noted that 'The meaning of the word 'home' . . . with reference to a taxpayer residing in one city and working in another has engendered much difficulty and litigation,' with the Tax Court and the administrative officials having 'consistently defined it as the equivalent of the taxpayer's place of business' and two courts of appeals having rejected that view and 'confined the term to the taxpayer's actual residence.' The Court found it 'unnecessary here to enter into or to decide this conflict.' This was because the Tax Court had properly concluded 'that the necessary relationship between the expenditures and the railroad's business was lacking.' The railroad's interest was in having Mr. Flowers at its headquarters in Mobile; it 'gained nothing' from his decision to continue living in Jackson; hence, the third condition the Flowers Court had enunciated as a prerequisite to deductibility was absent. Mr. Justice Rutledge dissented. He did not believe that when Congress used the word 'home,' it meant 'business headquarters,' and thought the case presented no other question. The most that Rosenspan can extract from Flowers is that it did not decide against his contention that the employer's business headquarters is the employee's tax home.

The Court's next venture into this area was in *Peurifoy v. C.I.R.*, 358 U.S. 59 (1958). That case dealt with three construction workers employed at a site in Kinston, North Carolina, for periods of 20 ½, 12 ½, and 8 ½ months respectively, who maintained permanent residences elsewhere in the state. The Tax Court had allowed them deductions for board and lodging during the employment at Kinston and expenses in regaining their residences when they left, apparently of their own volition and before completion of the project. The Fourth Circuit had reversed. After having granted certiorari 'to consider certain questions as to the application of [the 1939 version of section 162(a)(2)] raised by the course of decisions in the lower courts since our decision in *Commissioner v. Flowers*,' the Court announced in a per curiam opinion that it had 'found it inappropriate to consider such questions.' It read *Flowers* as establishing that 'a taxpayer is entitled to deduct unreimbursed travel expenses . . . only when they are required by 'the exigencies of business,' a 'general rule' which the majority seemed to feel would mandate disallowance of the deductions under consideration. However, the Court went on to acknowledge an exception to this rule engrafted by the Tax Court, which would have allowed the claimed deductions if the taxpayer's employment were shown to be 'temporary' rather than 'indefinite' or 'indeterminate.' Nevertheless, even within this framework, the majority thought that the Court of Appeals had been justified in holding the Tax Court's finding of temporary employment to be clearly erroneous. Mr. Justice Douglas joined by Justices Black and Whittaker, dissented. Adopting Mr. Justice Rutledge's position in *Flowers*, they disagreed 'with the Commissioner's contention that 'home' is synonymous with the situs of the employer's business.' While adhering to 'the exigencies of business' test announced in *Flowers*, they thought this requirement was satisfied by the fact that, in view of the impracticability of construction workers' moving their homes from job to job, 'the expenses incurred were necessary, not to the business of the contractor for whom the taxpayers worked, but for the taxpayers themselves in order to carry on their chosen trade.' While the three dissenting Justices thus rejected the Commissioner's identification of 'home' with 'the situs of the employer's business,' the majority did not adopt it and, so far as our problem is concerned, that matter remained in the state of indecision where *Flowers* had left it. . . .

Proper analysis of the problem has been beclouded, and the Government's position in this case has been made more difficult than it need be, by the Commissioner's insistence that 'home' means 'business headquarters,' despite the Supreme Court's having . . . declined to endorse this, and its rejection by several courts of appeals. When Congress uses such a nontechnical word in a tax statute, presumably it wants administrators and courts to read it in the way that ordinary people would understand, and not 'to draw on some unexpressed spirit outside the bounds of the normal meaning of words,' *Addison v. Holly Hill Fruit Prods.*, Inc., 322 U.S. 607, 617 (1944). The construction which the Commissioner has long advocated not only violates this principle but is unnecessary for the protection of the revenue that he seeks. That purpose is served, without any such distortion of language, by the third condition laid down in *Flowers*, namely, 'that there must be a direct connection between the expenditure and the carrying on of the trade or business of the taxpayer or of his employer' and that 'such an expenditure must be necessary or appropriate to the development and pursuit of the business or trade.' These requirements were enough to rule out a deduction for Flowers' lodging and meals while in Mobile even if he was 'away from home' while there. The deduction would not have been available to his fellow workers living in that city who obtained similar amenities in their homes or even in the very restaurants that Flowers patronized, and Flowers was no more compelled by business to be away from his home while in Mobile than were other employees of the railroad who lived there.

Since the Commissioner's definition of 'home' as 'business headquarters' will produce the same result as the third *Flowers* condition in the overwhelming bulk of cases arising under 162(a)(2), courts have often fallen into the habit of referring to it as a ground or an alternate ground of decision. . . . But examination of the string of cases cited by plaintiff as endorsing the 'business headquarters' test has revealed almost none, . . . which cannot be explained on the basis that the taxpayer had no permanent residence, or was not away from it, or maintained it in a locale apart from where he regularly worked as a matter of personal choice rather than business necessity. This principle likewise affords a satisfactory rationale for the 'temporary' employment cases. When an assignment is truly temporary, it would be unreasonable to expect the taxpayer to move his home, and the expenses are thus compelled by the 'exigencies of business'; when the assignment is 'indefinite' or 'indeterminate,' the situation is different and, if the taxpayer decides to leave his home where it was, disallowance is appropriate, not because he has acquired a 'tax home' in some lodging house or hotel at the worksite but because his failure to move his home was for his personal convenience and not compelled by business necessity. Under the facts here presented, we need not decide whether in the case of a taxpayer who is not self-employed, the 'exigencies of business' which compel the traveling expenses away from home refer solely to the business of his employer or to the business of the taxpayer as well. We note only that the latter contention is surely not foreclosed by decisions to date. . . .

Shifting the thrust of analysis from the search for a fictional 'tax home' to a questioning of the business necessity for incurring the expense away from the taxpayer's permanent residence thus does not upset the basic structure of the decisions which have dealt with this problem. It merely adopts an approach that better effectuates the congressional intent in establishing the deduction and thus provides a sounder conceptual framework for analysis while following the ordinary meaning of language. We see no basis whatever for believing that when the 1921 Congress eliminated the requirement for determining the excess of the costs of meals and lodging while on the road over what they would have been at home, it meant to disallow a deduction to someone who had the expense of maintaining a home from which business took him away but possessed no business headquarters. By the same token we find it impossible to read the words 'away from home' out of the statute, as Rosenspan, in effect, would have us do and allow a deduction to a taxpayer who had no 'home' in the ordinary sense. The limitation reflects congressional recognition of the rational distinction between the taxpayer with a permanent residence — whose travel costs represent a duplication of expense or at least an incidence of expense which the existence of his permanent residence demonstrates he would not incur absent business compulsion — and the taxpayer without such a residence. We fail to see how Rosenspan's occasional trips to New York City, assuming for the sake of argument that his 'business headquarters' was in New York rather than in his sales territory, differentiate him economically from the homeless traveling salesman without even the modicum of a business headquarters Rosenspan is claimed to have possessed. Yet we approved disallowance of the deduction in such a case many years ago.

It is enough to decide this case that 'home' means 'home' and Rosenspan had none. He satisfied the first and third conditions of *Flowers*, but not, on our reading of the statute, the second. The judgment dismissing the complaint must therefore be affirmed.

[2]   Note on Statutory Interpretation — Ordinary Usage

The court in *Rosenspan* opted for the ordinary everyday meaning of the term "home," rather than giving it a special tax meaning. An earlier discussion of statutory interpretation suggested that ordinary meaning might sometimes yield to a more technical tax meaning when that was necessary to implement the underlying structure of the tax code. *See* Chapter 3.02[A–B] ("cost" as value of property received, not "purchase price"). However, courts do not like to reject "plain meaning" — a synonym for ordinary meaning — unless they have to, and Judge Friendly's opinion is in that tradition. There is no way to know whether Judge Friendly would have rejected the ordinary meaning if that was necessary to implement statutory purpose.

[3] Temporary Worker

The government does not always say that "home" means "principal place of business." In Rev. Rul. 75-432, 1975-2 C.B. 60, it states this to be the "general rule." However, "in the rare case in which the employee has no identifiable principal place of business, but does maintain a regular place of abode in a real or substantial sense in a particular city from which the taxpayer is sent on temporary assignments, the tax home will be regarded as being the place of abode."

The rule permitting deduction of living expenses at a temporary workplace requires us to define "temporary." In 1992, the statute was amended to specify that a period of employment lasting more than one year was not temporary. That test is easy enough to apply if someone works at a 15-month job. But suppose the taxpayer works temporarily in a job under a one year contract, which is then renewed for another three months. Is he temporarily away from home for any or all of the 15-month period? Rev. Rul. 93-86, 1993-2 C.B. 71 interprets the statute to refer to *expectations*. Thus, if the job is expected to last more than a year, the expenses are not deductible, even if it lasts less than a year. Conversely, when a job that is expected to last no more than a year is extended so that it is expected to last more than a year, the expenses are no longer deductible once that period is extended — e.g., if a nine-month job is extended at the end of month 8 by another seven months, there are no deductions beginning after month 8.

What of the taxpayer who returns annually to jobs that last less than one year in a particular area? For example, if the taxpayer takes temporary jobs in the same place every year because he wants to stay permanently as a resident in another location, where he has no job prospects, the deduction will be disallowed because the personal decision where to live is the dominant explanation for the expense. *Tucker v. Commissioner*, 55 T.C. 783 (1971).

The temporary worker may also have trouble establishing a residence back home. What about the case of an actress who signs a six-month contract to act in a New York play? Her home is in Denver with her husband. After the play is a hit, she signs a second six-month contract, but in the meantime her marriage begins to disintegrate and she is about to get a divorce. The work in New York may still be temporary, but her home may now be New York. Consequently, she is not entitled to a deduction for meals and lodging in New York. *Six v. United States*, 450 F.2d 66 (2d Cir. 1971).

In *Wilbert v. Commissioner*, 553 F.3d 544 (7th Cir. 2009), Judge Posner narrowly interprets the deduction for meals and lodging by a "temporary worker." The taxpayer was a laid-off airline mechanic who lived with his wife in Minneapolis. Pursuant to his contract, he had a right to bump a more junior mechanic employed by the airline, which he did by taking temporary jobs in Chicago (a few days), Alaska (three weeks), and New York (one week). At no point during this period did he have a justifiable expectation of being rehired in his Minneapolis job within a short period after the initial layoff. The court stated:

> The Tax Court, with some judicial support, has tried to resolve cases such as this by asking whether the taxpayer's work away from home is "temporary" or "indefinite," and allowing the deduction of traveling ex-

penses only if it is the former. The Internal Revenue Code does not explicitly adopt the distinction, but does provide (with an immaterial exception) that "the taxpayer shall not be treated as being temporarily away from home during any period of employment if such period exceeds 1 year." 26 U.S.C. § 162(a).

The problem with the Tax Court's distinction is that work can be, and usually is, both temporary and indefinite. . . . [For example, a lawyer who] is trying [a case] in London might settle on the second day, or last a month; his sojourn away from his office will therefore be both temporary and indefinite. Indeed all work is indefinite and much "permanent" work is really temporary. An academic lawyer might accept a five year appointment as an assistant professor with every expectation of obtaining tenure at the end of that period at that or another law school; yet one would not describe him as a "temporary" employee even if he left after six months and thus was not barred from claiming temporary status by the one year rule. . . .

So "temporary versus indefinite" does not work well as a test of deductibility and neither does "personal choice versus reasonable response to the employment situation," tempting as the latter formula is because of its realism. If no reasonable person would relocate to his new place of work because of uncertainty about the duration of the new job, his choice to stay where he is, unlike a choice to commute from a suburb to the city in which one's office is located rather than live in the city, is not an optional personal choice like deciding to stay at a Four Seasons or a Ritz Carlton, but a choice forced by circumstances. Wilbert when first notified that he was being laid off could foresee a series of temporary jobs all across the country and not even limited, as we know, to the lower 48 states, and the costs of moving his home to the location of each temporary job would have been prohibitive. It would have meant moving four times in one year on a mechanic's salary to cities hundreds or (in the case of Anchorage versus Minneapolis, Chicago, or New York) thousands of miles apart.

The problem with a test that focuses on the reasonableness of the taxpayer's decision not to move is that it is bound to prove nebulous in application. For it just asks the taxpayer to give a good reason for not moving his home when he gets a job in a different place, and if he gave a good reason then his traveling expenses would be deductible as the product of a reasonable balancing of personal and business considerations. In the oft cited case of *Hantzis v. Commissioner*, 638 F.2d 248 (1st Cir.1981), the question was whether a law student who lived in Boston with her husband during the school year could deduct her traveling expenses when she took a summer job in New York. Given the temporary nature of the job, it made perfectly good sense for her to retain her home in Boston and just camp out, as it were, in New York. What persuaded the court to reject the deduction was that she had no business reason to retain the house in Boston. . . .

If this seems rather a mechanical reading of the statute, it has the support . . . of the even more influential precedent of *Commissioner v.*

Flowers, 326 U.S. 465 (1946), where the Supreme Court said that "the exigencies of business rather than the personal conveniences and necessities of the traveler must be the motivating factors" in the decision to travel. The "business exigencies" rule, though harsh, is supported by compelling considerations of administrability. To apply a test of reasonableness the Internal Revenue Service would first have to decide whether the taxpayer should have moved to his new place of work. This might require answering such questions as whether the schools in the area of his new job were far worse than those his children currently attend, whether his elderly parents live near his existing home and require his attention, and whether his children have psychological problems that make it difficult for them to find new friends. . . .

We are sympathetic to Wilbert's plight and recognize the artificiality of supposing that, as the government argues, he made merely a personal choice to "commute" from Minneapolis to Anchorage, and Chicago, and New York, as if Minneapolis were a suburb of those cities. But the statutory language, the precedents, and the considerations of administrability that we have emphasized persuade us to reject the test of reasonableness. The "temporary versus indefinite" test is no better, so we fall back on the rule of Flowers and Hantzis that unless the taxpayer has a business rather than a personal reason to be living in two places he cannot deduct his traveling expenses if he decides not to move. Indeed, Wilbert's situation is really no different from the common case of the construction worker who works at different sites throughout the country, never certain how long each stint will last and reluctant therefore to relocate his home. The construction worker loses, as must Wilbert.

There are two problems with this decision from the perspective of precedent: The construction worker case cited by Posner involved an indefinite job; and the IRS applies the one-year rule based on the taxpayer's expectations, not the actual period of work. Nonetheless, is Posner correct that a "reasonableness" test is too hard to administer? In this respect, he sets himself against Judge Friendly's position in *Rosenspan* — that "[w]hen an assignment is truly temporary, it would be unreasonable to expect the taxpayer to move his home, and the expenses are thus compelled by the 'exigencies of business.' "

[4] Overnight

In *United States v. Correll*, 389 U.S. 299 (1967), the Court upheld a Treasury Regulation limiting the deduction of meals and lodging to cases where the traveler required "sleep or rest." This is usually called the "overnight" rule, because in most cases the requirement is satisfied by staying at the business destination overnight. The Court of Appeals thought that the "plain language of the statute" ("away from home") precluded a temporal requirement. The Supreme Court disagreed, noting that "meals and lodging" implied an overnight stay. It also cited some 1954 legislative history affirming the overnight rule. Finally, it appealed to the administrative law principle that "long continued [regulations] without substantial change, applying to unamended or substantially reenacted statutes, are deemed to have received congressional approval and have the effect of law."

The fact that an employee cannot deduct the expenses discussed in *Correll* will not as a practical matter, result in taxing these amounts, if they are reimbursed by the employer. The employee is unlikely to report the reimbursement, so collection of tax depends on withholding tax from the reimbursement. At one time, such reimbursements were not considered "wages" subject to income tax withholding. *Central Illinois Public Serv. Co. v. United States*, 435 U.S. 21 (1978). As of July 1, 1990, however, the Regulations have been rewritten to define such reimbursements as wages subject to withholding. **Treas. Reg. § 31.3121(a)-3.** These regulations incorporate the income tax deduction rules to decide whether the reimbursements are wages — that is, if the expense would not be deductible by the employee, the reimbursements are wages.. The 1990 rules were applied in *Jordan v. United States*, 490 F.3d 677 (8th Cir. 2007), to a pilot who had his residence in Minnesota but was based in Alaska. His employer paid his transportation to Alaska for each work assignment and gave him lodging and a per diem for meals in Alaska. The court applied the Regulations to require withholding of income tax from these payments, because the expenses would not have been deductible by the employee under the normal rules applicable to traveling expenses.

[5]   Introductory Language of § 162(a)

Meals. In *Christey v. United States*, 841 F.2d 809 (8th Cir. 1988), the court considered whether state troopers could deduct the expenses incurred for restaurant meals while on duty, even though not "away" overnight. The court stated:

> As a requirement of their job, troopers must comply with the rules and regulations contained in the General Orders of the Patrol. These orders address in detail the conduct required of troopers while on duty. General Order R77-20-008 ("the General Order") provides troopers with specific instructions concerning meal breaks while on duty. The General Order requires that troopers "eat their meals in a public restaurant adjacent to the highway whenever practical" and "report by radio when they eat and . . . advise the telephone number or the code number of the restaurant where they are eating." The restaurant must be open to the public and may not serve liquor. The Order prohibits troopers from eating meals at home during working hours and has been interpreted to prohibit troopers from bringing meals from home and eating in their patrol cars. The Order also details the time at which troopers may eat, the time allowed for a meal, and the number of troopers who may eat together. Failure to adhere to these instructions renders troopers subject to reprimand.

> As set forth in the General Order, the principal purpose of these requirements "is to promote public safety and obedience to the law through the physical presence of troopers in uniform and to facilitate, through availability to the public, the reporting of accidents and the dissemination of information with reference to the traffic and motor vehicle laws of the state." The Order also ensures that meal breaks taken by the troopers are designated and staggered in order to maintain maximum coverage of patrol areas with minimal call response time.

There was testimony that during meals troopers are subject to calls for emergencies and other Patrol business to which they must respond immediately. Troopers are also subject to interruptions from the general public who are seeking information about road conditions, weather, traffic laws, and other subjects relating to trooper responsibilities. Thus, troopers are frequently interrupted during their meals and are often unable to finish meals for which they have paid. . . .

The court upheld the deduction, as follows:

It is beyond question that the cost of one's meals is ordinarily a personal expense which is nondeductible under § 262. Treas. Reg. § 1.262-1(b)(5) (1987). However, under certain limited circumstances, such expenses may be deducted under the general provision of § 162(a); "that which may be a personal expense under some circumstances can when circumscribed by company regulations take on the color of a business expense," Sibla v. Commissioner, 611 F.2d 1260, 1262 (9th Cir. 1980). . . .

In light of the circumstances of this case, we believe the district court's conclusion that the meal expenses which the taxpayers incurred while on duty in 1981 and 1982 were deductible as ordinary and necessary expenses under § 162(a) is not clearly erroneous. Accordingly, the district court's judgment is affirmed.

Lodging. **Proposed Regulation § 1.162-31** deals with the deduction of expenses for lodging when *not* traveling away from home and the correlative exclusion of employer reimbursement for such expenses. An introductory comment (subsection (a)) states that "one factor is whether the taxpayer incurs the expense because of a bona fide condition or requirement of employment imposed by the taxpayer's employer." Subsection (b) provides a safe harbor for local lodging at business meetings and conferences, stating that a deduction or exclusion will be allowed if:

(1)   The lodging is necessary for the individual to participate fully in or be available for a bona fide business meeting, conference, training activity, or other business function;

(2)   The lodging is for a period that does not exceed five calendar days and does not recur more frequently than once per calendar quarter;

(3)   If the individual is an employee, the employee's employer requires the employee to remain at the activity or function overnight; and

(4)   The lodging is not lavish or extravagant under the circumstances and does not provide any significant element of personal pleasure, recreation, or benefit.

Subsection (c) gives some examples:

Example 1. (i) Employer conducts training for its employees at a hotel near Employer's main office. The training is directly connected with Employer's trade or business. Some employees attending the training are traveling away from home and some employees are not traveling away from home. Employer requires all employees attending the training to remain at the hotel overnight for the bona fide purpose of facilitating the training.

Employer pays the costs of the lodging at the hotel directly to the hotel and does not treat the value as compensation to the employees.

(ii) Employer has a noncompensatory business purpose for paying the lodging expenses. Employer is not paying the expenses primarily to provide a social or personal benefit to the employees. If the employees who are not traveling away from home had paid for their own lodging, the expenses would have been deductible under section 162(a) as ordinary and necessary business expenses of the employees. Therefore, the value of the lodging is excluded from the employees' income as a working condition fringe under section 132(a) and (d).

Example 3. (i) Employer is a professional sports team. Employer requires its employees (players and coaches) to stay at a local hotel the night before a home game to conduct last minute training and ensure the physical preparedness of the players. Employer pays the lodging expenses directly to the hotel and does not treat the value as compensation to the employees.

(ii) Employer has a noncompensatory business purpose for paying the lodging expenses. Employer is not paying the lodging expenses primarily to provide a social or personal benefit to the employees. If the employees had paid for their own lodging, the expenses would have been deductible by the employees under section 162(a) as ordinary and necessary business expenses. Therefore, the value of the lodging is excluded from the employees' income as a working condition fringe.

However, the regulation then provides two examples where the employee's lodging is taxable. Example 4 states that an employee who currently lives 500 miles from his new employer's business premises is taxed on employer reimbursements for temporary lodging near the employer's business premises while the employee searches for a residence after being hired by the employer; and Example 5 states that employer-provided lodging is taxable to an employee (who normally commutes two hours each way to her office), when the employee stays at a hotel near the office while working late hours on a project.

Finally, Example 6 provides *nontaxability* when the employer "requires an employee to be 'on duty' each night to respond quickly to emergencies that may occur outside of normal working hours. Employees who work daytime hours each serve a 'duty shift' once each month in addition to their normal work schedule. Emergencies that require the duty shift employee to respond occur regularly. Employer has no sleeping facilities on its business premises and pays for a hotel room nearby where the duty shift employee stays until called to respond to an emergency." In other words, the "on duty" example is treated more favorably than the "working late" example.

The proposed regulation states that "until these proposed regulations are published as final regulations in the Federal Register, taxpayers may apply the proposed regulations to local lodging expenses that are paid or incurred in taxable years for which the period of limitation on credit or refund under section 6511 has not expired."

[6] Two Permanent Businesses

The logic of deducting business travel expenses — that the taxpayer must incur extra expenses away from home — implies that expenses related to business travel at the second of two permanent business locations is deductible. Which expenses are deductible in the following example? An Indianapolis corporate lawyer is also a partner in a Miami, Florida, firm. He lives in Miami in January, February, and March, practicing law in Florida. The lawyer nets 55% of his total income as a lawyer from the Florida practice, which consists primarily of being a lawyer for estates of deceased former clients. *Markey v. Commissioner*, 490 F.2d 1249 (6th Cir. 1974). *See also Andrews v. Commissioner*, 931 F.2d 132 (1st Cir. 1991), where the Court of Appeals reversed the Tax Court's refusal to allow any deduction for traveling expense on the ground that the taxpayer had two "tax homes." The Court of Appeals stated that the length of time spent on the business should "ordinarily" be the determining factor as to which was the primary place of business.

Suppose two spouses work, but in different cities. The husband was just promoted and moved to Chicago from Toledo. The wife will move to Chicago when she can get a job commensurate with her training. She has a Ph.D. in Chemistry. Meanwhile, she is continuing in her old job as an Assistant Professor of Chemistry in Toledo, Ohio. She lives four days a week in Chicago with her husband, going to Toledo to meet classes and students for three days per week. *Daly v. Commissioner*, 631 F.2d 351 (4th Cir. 1980), *reversed on rehearing*, 662 F.2d 253 (4th Cir. 1981); *Felton v. Commissioner*, 43 T.C.M. (CCH) 278 (1982), *affirmed*, 723 F.2d 66 (7th Cir. 1983). Are any of this family's meals and lodging expenses deductible?

[7] Luxury Travel

The deduction for traveling expenses encourages taxpayers to live well and deduct the expenses. Taxpayers attend conventions at luxury resorts, stay at the best hotels, and spend lavishly on food. Limitations imposed by employers or by the taxpayer's own financial constraints may have some effect, but the tax law pushes taxpayers toward spending more. When the tax law allowed all meals and lodging to be deducted to avoid the administrative difficulty of separating out normal from extra expenses, it created an incentive to increase the extras. Today many taxpayers rely on the deduction to support a significant tax-free enhancement of their lifestyles.

At this point in the discussion, someone usually mentions the famous example of the prince's aide who lives in the palace, eats at the royal table, and attends opera with the prince, but who hates opera and rich food. H. SIMONS, PERSONAL INCOME TAXATION 53 (1938). How would you respond to a taxpayer who argues against taxing luxury travel expenses because he hates travel? Is a subjective test irrelevant or should you consider the probabilities of subjective enjoyment in framing an objective rule?

Several statutory provisions limit deductions for luxury travel. First, § 162(a)(2) (**parenthetical**) denies a deduction for expenses that are "lavish or extravagant under the circumstances." Second, special rules apply to expenditures outside the United States. The expenses related to foreign conventions outside of North

America are deductible only if the meeting is directly related to the active conduct of a trade or business and it is as reasonable to meet outside North America as within North America. § 274(h). Certain Caribbean countries are included in North America for these purposes. Cruise ship conventions are also subject to special limitations. § 274(h)(2),(5). Were these rules about foreign expenditures adopted to implement tax fairness or for other reasons? What lobbying group would have favored these rules?

[8] 50% of Meals Expenses Deductible

Only 50% of meal expenses are deductible. § 274(n)(1). The rule is primarily aimed at deductions for business meals (as well as entertainment expenses, discussed in Chapter 8.05), but it applies as well to traveling expense deductions for meals.

QUESTIONS AND COMMENTS

In the following cases, determine whether expenses for meals or lodging are deductible.

1. A professor permanently employed at a New York school visits at another school in California for 10 months, incurring meals and lodging expenses in California.

a. If the professor brings his family, the expenses allocable to the family are not deductible. **Treas. Reg. § 1.162-2(c).** Contrast this rule with the exclusion for the whole family under § 119(a).

b. Must the professor reduce any deduction to which he is entitled by any rent he receives for renting his residence back home? Apparently not, even though the rent reduces the amount of extra expenses incurred at the business destination. But how are the rental income and related expenses for his residence back home treated? The expenses should be treated as nonbusiness expenses in an activity without a profit-making motive under § 183, discussed later in this chapter. That section permits a below the line deduction for expenses up to the amount of the gross income received in the activity, subject to the 2% floor.

c. Is the meal deduction disallowed because the professor shops at the grocery store, incurring no added expense over what he would have incurred at home? See *Cass v. Commissioner*, 86 T.C. 1275 (1986), rejecting the Commissioner's argument that no deduction should be allowed for food because a professor who spent an academic year at another institution set up a family household at the business destination identical to that which he would have sustained at home.

d. Does the statutory treatment of Members of Congress — treating their residence in the location from which they are elected as their tax home but limiting the amount of traveling expense deductions, suggest how long-term travelers (like the professor in this example) should be treated? § 162(a) (**flush paragraph**). *See also* § 162(h) for a similar but elective approach to state legislators.

2. When does a taxpayer not have a "home"? Is the following decision correct? In *Henderson v. Commissioner*, 143 F.3d 497 (9th Cir. 1998), the taxpayer worked as a stage hand for Walt Disney's World of Ice, which traveled all over the country. When not working, he lived with his parents in Boise, Idaho. He did not work in Boise and his employment had no connection with Boise. The court noted that, in most cases in which a traveling expense deduction was allowed, the taxpayer had some business connection where he lived. (Is that true of the temporary worker?) In addition, he had no substantial living expenses in Boise (he paid no rent). The court held, on these facts, that Henderson lacked a "tax home" in Boise and could not deduct meals and lodging while traveling with World of Ice.

The dissent by Judge Kozinski stated that a business connection to a personal home was not required when the job had no fixed location (as in the case of the temporary worker). He also said that the deduction would clearly have been allowed if the parents gave the taxpayer $600 to rent his own place in Boise, rather than giving him free housing in their home, and that these two cases should be decided the same way. Kozinski concluded: "In the name of family values, I dissent."

3. A taxpayer lives in the suburbs and works in the city. One night he has to stay in the city at a hotel because of an unusual business problem that required late-night and early-morning attention. Is it unreasonable to expect this taxpayer to move to the city because of an occasional late night business obligation? *See Coombs v. Commissioner*, 608 F.2d 1269 (9th Cir. 1979) (due to the combination of the unavoidable distance between their homes at the closest habitable community and their place of work at a nuclear test facility and the employer's requirement of the performance of overtime work, it was "necessary" for taxpayers to sleep overnight at the test site; taxpayer was held to be away from home on business in these circumstances and entitled to deduct the cost of any meals and lodging incurred at such times).

4. An employee is away from home on business on Friday. To save plane fare, the employee stays overnight on Saturday, incurring an additional $250 hotel and meal expenses, and engaging solely in personal nonbusiness activities on the weekend. Without the Saturday stay, round trip plane fare is $900; with the Saturday stay it is $500. The employer reimburses the employee for the $250 additional Saturday expense. Does the reimbursement increase the employee's taxable income by $250? Letter Ruling 9237014.

[B] Transportation

The term "transportation" refers to the cost of getting from one place to the other, such as plane fare to a business destination or car expenses for a traveling salesman.

[1] Commuting

The IRS has long taken the position that commuting expenses in getting from home to a place of work are not deductible. One way to support this conclusion is to define "home" as principal place of business and decide that the commuter is not away from home. The Supreme Court in *Commissioner v. Flowers*, 326 U.S. 465 (1946), decided that the deduction could be disallowed by holding that the commuting expense was occasioned by the taxpayer's decision about where to live and that commuting was therefore a personal expense without regard to the definition of "home." This seems to be an application of the origin test, discussed in *Gilmore*; the expense originates in the personal decision of where to live rather than the decision to work.

Do you agree with the conclusion that the gap between work and home is a personal decision? Can a taxpayer realistically live very close to work in the modern city? In *United States v. Tauferner*, 407 F.2d 243 (10th Cir. 1969), the court disallowed a deduction for commuting expenses even though the taxpayer worked for a company testing solid fuel rocket engines at a site located some distance from any residential community because of the danger.

If a deduction were allowed for commuting expenses, who would benefit most — the inner city commuter or the suburbanite?

[2]   No Home

If a taxpayer is a traveling salesman like Rosenspan, but with no principal place of business and no residence, can he deduct his transportation expenses? Could Correll (who was not "away" overnight) deduct his transportation expenses? These expenses are deductible, even though the taxpayer is not "away from home." The statutory authority for this result is the introductory language of § 162(a).? *Turner v. Commissioner*, 56 T.C. 27 (1971).

[3]   Temporary Work

Can a temporary construction worker who travels to the worksite in the morning and back to his home that night deduct commuting expenses? The taxpayer argues that the temporary nature of the job justifies the deduction for the same reason that meals and lodging would be deductible if he were gone overnight. In 1976, the government sought to disallow the deduction, arguing that "commuting is commuting." Rev. Rul. 76-453, 1976-2 C.B. 86 (Example 5).

The latest rulings are Rev. Rul. 94-47, 1994-2 C.B. 18 and Rev. Rul. 99-7, 1999-1 C.B. 361. They allow the deduction of commuting expenses in cases in which the temporary work is outside the metropolitan area in which the taxpayer lives and normally works. The rulings also allow the deduction of commuting expenses: (1) if the taxpayer has a regular work location away from the taxpayer's residence and the taxpayer travels to a temporary work location in the same trade or business (an accountant goes to a company's office to audit its books); or (2) if the taxpayer's residence is his principal place of business and the taxpayer travels to another work location in the same trade or business, whether it is temporary or regular (a doctor whose office is in his home and who travels to the hospital).

[4] Two Jobs

If a taxpayer travels ten miles to a principal job, another two miles to a second job, and then back home, the cost of traveling two miles between jobs is deductible. Rev. Rul. 76-453, 1976-2 C.B. 86 (Example 8). Should this be true if the two-mile trip is directly on the way home so that it does not increase the normal commuting distance?

[5] Foreign Travel

Look at § 274(c). Roughly speaking, it prevents a taxpayer who spends some time at a foreign business destination on business and some time on vacation from deducting the entire transportation cost, if the entire trip exceeds one week. For example, if the taxpayer spends one week in Paris going to meetings and one week in Paris on vacation, only one-half of the round-trip transportation in getting from his home to Paris is deductible. This section provides the kind of allocation formula in separating out the taxable from the nontaxable portion of an expenditure that is so frequently lacking in the fringe benefit area.

The Regulations provide a good example of a difference in taxing employees depending on whether the expenses are reimbursed by the employer or financed by the taxpayer's own funds. **Treas. Reg. § 1.274-4(f)(5)(I).** When the foreign transportation expenses are reimbursed, the employer is presumed to have so much control over how the money is spent that § 274(c) does not apply, unless the employee is a manager or 10% owner — that is, unless the employee controls the spending decision.

If a New York taxpayer spends six weeks in Paris on vacation and one week on business, would any part of the cost of transportation to Paris be deductible under § 162(a)? Remember that § 274(c) limits the deduction of what would otherwise be a deductible business expense in the first place. Thus, one week at a Miami or Paris business convention and six weeks' vacation at the same place would probably result in disallowing the deduction for round trip transportation under § 162(a), without ever reaching § 274(c).

[6] Travel as Education

By now, it should be clear that the effort to deduct personal expenses produces a running gun battle between the taxpayer and the IRS and Congress. For example, § 274(m)(2) prohibits deduction of travel as a form of education. A teacher of French history and culture, for example, cannot simply argue that a trip to historic sites in France is deductible. But, in *Jorgensen v. Commissioner*, 79 T.C.M. (CCH) 1926 (2000), the taxpayer was allowed to deduct the cost of trips to Asian countries to take academically useful courses (which included writing a research paper). The courses were related to her teaching in a culturally diverse high school back in the United States with a predominantly Asian-American population. And she used the material learned abroad to enrich her curriculum.

[C] Moving Expenses

Suppose a taxpayer moves to a first job or moves between jobs. Are the moving expenses deductible? Prior to the adoption of §§ 82, 217, the taxpayer could take these deductions only by proving that they were business expenses. This would be difficult if it were the first job, for reasons discussed in Chapter 13 dealing with capital expenditures. In addition, some courts treated unreimbursed moving expenses as nondeductible personal expenses. The unequal treatment of different taxpayers and the mobility of our society led to allowing the deduction of moving expenses, whether or not for the first job and whether or not reimbursed.

Before tax year 1994, the deduction rules were quite generous, including not only the cost of moving the family and household goods, but also (subject to dollar limits) certain housing search costs and incidental housing sale expenses. The 1994 changes limit deductible moving expenses to moving household goods and the cost of traveling to the new destination (but not meals).

The 1994 changes are not all bad. The moving expense deduction is now an above the line deduction (since 1986, it had been an itemized deduction, subject to the 2% floor). And employer reimbursements of deductible moving expenses are excludible fringe benefits under § 132(a)(6), (g); the taxpayer does not have to report them as gross income and take a deduction.

To obtain a moving expense deduction, the new principal place of work must be at least 50 miles farther from the taxpayer's former residence than was the prior principal place of work. That is, the commute must increase by at least 50 miles as a result of the new job. If the taxpayer had no prior work, the new principal place of work must be at least 50 miles from the former residence.

§ 8.05 ENTERTAINMENT EXPENSES

[A] Statutory Rules

Tax-free expense account living may be a more serious problem with entertainment than with travel expenses because they are probably more economically wasteful, in addition to permitting tax-free personal consumption. The typical situation is one in which a business taxpayer entertains a client by taking him out for a meal, or to a nightclub, or by providing theater tickets.

You might at first wonder how there could be a deduction in the first place, at least for the meals. After all, the taxpayer must eat and is not away from home overnight. The IRS's position is that, technically, the taxpayer could not deduct the portion of her meal that does not exceed normal living expenses. However, the IRS states: "The Service practice has been to apply this rule largely to abuse cases where taxpayers claim deductions for substantial amounts of personal living expenses." Rev. Rul. 63-144, 1963-2 C.B. 129. As a practical matter, entertainment expenses are generally deductible in full under § 162(a).

Well, not always deductible. In *Moss v. Commissioner*, 758 F.2d 211 (7th Cir. 1985), the taxpayer was a partner in a small law firm, which met daily for lunch at a nearby restaurant where they discussed cases and litigation strategy. Lunch meetings were chosen because court was not in session; there was no suggestion that the lawyers "dawdled" over lunch; and the restaurant was not "luxurious." The court stated:

> Although an argument can be made for disallowing any deduction for business meals, on the theory that people have to eat whether they work or not, the result would be excessive taxation of people who spend more money on business meals because they are business meals than they would spend on their meals if they were not working. Suppose a theatrical agent takes his clients out to lunch at the expensive restaurants that the clients demand. Of course he can deduct the expense of their meals, from which he derives no pleasure or sustenance, but can he also deduct the expense of his own? He can, because he cannot eat more cheaply; he cannot munch surreptitiously on a peanut butter and jelly sandwich brought from home while his client is wolfing down tournedos Rossini followed by soufflé au grand marnier. No doubt our theatrical agent, unless concerned for his longevity, derives personal utility from his fancy meal, but probably less than the price of the meal. He would not pay for it if it were not for the business benefit; he would get more value from using the same money to buy something else; hence the meal confers on him less utility than the cash equivalent would. The law could require him to pay tax on the fair value of the meal to him; this would be (were it not for costs of administration) the economically correct solution. But the government does not attempt this difficult measurement; it once did, but gave up the attempt as not worth the cost. The taxpayer is permitted to deduct the whole price, provided the expense is "different from or in excess of that which would have been made for the taxpayer's personal purposes." Sutter v. Commissioner, 21 T.C. 170, 173 (1953).

> Because the law allows this generous deduction, which tempts people to have more (and costlier) business meals than are necessary, the Internal Revenue Service has every right to insist that the meal be shown to be a real business necessity. This condition is most easily satisfied when a client or customer or supplier or other outsider to the business is a guest. . . . [I]t is undeniable that eating together fosters camaraderie and makes business dealings friendlier and easier. It thus reduces the costs of transacting business, for these costs include the frictions and the failures of communication that are produced by suspicion and mutual misunderstanding, by differences in tastes and manners, and by lack of rapport. A meeting with a client or customer in an office is therefore not a perfect substitute for a lunch with him in a restaurant. But it is different when all the participants in the meal are coworkers, as essentially was the case here. . . . They know each other well already; they don't need the social lubrication that a meal with an outsider provides — at least don't need it daily. If a large firm had a monthly lunch to allow partners to get to know associates, the expense of the meal might well be necessary, and would be allowed by the Internal Revenue Service. But Moss's firm never had more than eight

lawyers (partners and associates), and did not need a daily lunch to cement relationships among them.

It is all a matter of degree and circumstance (the expense of a testimonial dinner, for example, would be deductible on a morale-building rationale); and particularly of frequency. Daily — for a full year — is too often, perhaps even for entertainment of clients, as implied by *Hankenson v. Commissioner*, 47 T.C.M. (CCH) 1567, 1569 (1984), where the Tax Court held nondeductible the cost of lunches consumed three or four days a week, 52 weeks a year, by a doctor who entertained other doctors who he hoped would refer patients to him, and other medical personnel.

We may assume it was necessary for Moss's firm to meet daily to coordinate the work of the firm, and also, as the Tax Court found, that lunch was the most convenient time. But it does not follow that the expense of the lunch was a necessary business expense. The members of the firm had to eat somewhere, and the Café Angelo was both convenient and not too expensive. They do not claim to have incurred a greater daily lunch expense than they would have incurred if there had been no lunch meetings. Although it saved time to combine lunch with work, the meal itself was not an organic part of the meeting, as in the examples we gave earlier where the business objective, to be fully achieved, required sharing a meal.

The case might be different if the location of the courts required the firm's members to eat each day either in a disagreeable restaurant, so that they derived less value from the meal than it cost them to buy it, or in a restaurant too expensive for their personal tastes, so that, again, they would have gotten less value than the cash equivalent. But so far as appears, they picked the restaurant they liked most. Although it must be pretty monotonous to eat lunch the same place every working day of the year, not all the lawyers attended all the lunch meetings and there was nothing to stop the firm from meeting occasionally at another restaurant proximate to their office in downtown Chicago; there are hundreds.

Because of the difficulty in finding that entertainment expenses are not business-related in most instances, the code was amended to place limits on such deductions. The statute is very convoluted, reflecting the sensitive political climate. **Section 274(a)(1)(A)** starts off with a bang, limiting deductions to "directly related" expenses. The idea is that business must actually be conducted during the entertainment period; purchasing business good will is not enough. But then the statute waffles — entertainment expenses "associated with" business are deductible if they precede or follow substantial business discussion. Purchasing good will is therefore sufficient to support a deduction for business meals and nightclub expenses, if business discussions occur soon before or after. The business meal deduction is also expressly conditioned on the taxpayer or its employee being present — *see* **§ 274(k)(1)(B)**.

In some respects, however, the section has teeth. First, expenses for entertainment *facilities* are not deductible at all (yachts, hunting lodges, etc.). **§ 274(a)(1)(B)**. Second, only 50% of the expenses for meals and entertainment are deductible. **§ 274(n)(1)**. Third, club dues are not deductible. **§ 274(a)(3)**. Fourth, the deductible price of tickets to entertainment events is usually limited to face value, not scalper's prices, and the deductible price of luxury skyboxes is usually limited to the cost of nonluxury box seats. § 274(l). There is more, but this gives you a flavor of the detailed attention to expense account living in the code.

[B] Reimbursements

We have discussed entertainment expenses without paying attention to whether they were reimbursed or not. Many taxpayers incur such expenses without reimbursement — a partner in a business or a sole proprietor. There is no problem applying the deduction limits to these taxpayers. But suppose you are an employee who incurs entertainment expenses that are reimbursed by the employer. There are two candidates for losing the deduction — the reimbursing employer and the reimbursed employee. Because the expenses seem wasteful and not just disguised personal expenses, it might make sense to disallow the employer's deduction or even to tax both employer and employee, rather than just disallow the employee's deduction.

In fact, the § 274 limits on entertainment expenses (e.g., the directly related, associated with, and 50% limits) apply to the employer, not the employee, unless the employer decides to report the reimbursements as taxable wages for tax withholding purposes to the federal government. §§ 274(e)(2),(3), 274(n)(2)(A). The employer is unlikely to treat reimbursements as wages, so the § 274 limits normally apply to reimbursing employers, not reimbursed employees.

Be sure you understand that the employee must still satisfy § 162 in order to exclude the expenses from his tax base in the more usual case in which the employer does not report the benefit as wages. For example, how would the following transactions be taxed? *Transaction 1*. The employee takes a client from out of town to a nightclub but does not engage in business discussion before or after. The employer reimburses the employee for the $250 expense. Can the employer and/or the employee deduct the expense? *Transaction 2*. Would your answer be different if the out of town visitor was not a client but a friend, who plans to reciprocate the entertainment when the taxpayer visits the client's home town?

§ 8.06 RECORDKEEPING

Many taxpayers do not keep good records of expenses. Taxpayers usually have the burden of proof in tax litigation and that could have justified disallowing deductions for unsubstantiated expenses. However, an early case held that the amount of deductible expenses could be estimated once a court was convinced that some of them were deductible. *Cohan v. Commissioner*, 39 F.2d 540 (2d Cir. 1930). Although the court could severely limit the deduction amount because the taxpayer's records were bad, the prospect of deductibility led taxpayers to make inflated claims as a prelude to advantageous settlement in the audit process.

In response, the statute now conditions deduction of traveling and entertainment expenses on keeping good records regarding their amount, time, place, and business purpose. § 274(d). The precise content of these records is specified in Regulations and numerous Revenue Rulings, which often simplify recordkeeping for smaller expenses.

[A] Application of Recordkeeping Requirements to Reimbursed Employees

Reimbursed employees not only can avoid the substantive limits of § 274, but are also not usually required to maintain their own records to substantiate deductible expenses, *if* they make an adequate accounting to their employer. The IRS has discretion to treat certain reimbursement arrangements or per diem, mileage, or other traveling allowances as an adequate accounting. **Treas. Reg. § 1.274-5(g)**. Employees who own 10% or more of the employer must, however, keep their own records. The overall pattern, therefore, is that employers who reimburse their employees for travel and entertainment are the taxpayers who are likely to lose the deduction, if they fail to maintain adequate records.

[B] Wage Withholding from Certain Reimbursements

The rules limiting deductions are hard to enforce, especially in the case of reimbursed expenses. **Section 62(c)** is supposed to improve enforcement. It states that failure to provide an adequate accounting to the employer will result in the reimbursements being deductible by an *employee*, if at all, *only as* itemized deductions. Therefore, if the employee fails to adequately account to the employer, the employee must affirmatively prove eligibility for such deductions by deducting them on the employee's return, in addition to exceeding the 2% floor on itemized employee business deductions.

Of course, an inadequate accounting should often result in a denial of the employee's deduction under § 274(d) in any event, so the real impact of § 62(c) is in the Regulation's requirement (backed up by a Committee Report) that reimbursements for which there is no adequate accounting must be treated like wages subject to withholding by the employer. **Treas. Reg. § 1.62-2**. This will make reimbursed expenses vulnerable to employer withholding, absent an adequate accounting.

§ 8.07 HOME OFFICES

By now it should be obvious that taxpayers try to convert personal expenses into deductible business expenses. One setting in which this occurred was home offices. Newspaper accounts and word of mouth made taxpayers aware of the potential to set up an office in some part of the home and thereby deduct an allocable portion of what would otherwise be personal expenses. This practice became widespread and almost certainly led to a lot of fraudulent claims. The code responded with § 280A.

Section 280A(a),(c)(1) permits a deduction if the home office satisfies the following tests. *First*, the home office must be exclusively used (no personal use allowed) on a regular basis for business.

An employee cannot, however, satisfy the "exclusive use" test unless the use of the home office is for the convenience of the employer. **§ 280A(c)(1) (next to last sentence)**. Professors have a problem with this test. *See Weissman v. Commissioner*, 751 F.2d 512 (2d Cir. 1984) (professor could deduct home office expenses when forced to share office at the university with several others). In *Cadwallader v. Commissioner*, 919 F.2d 1273 (7th Cir. 1990), Judge Posner stated:

> Research and writing are the principal work of most university (as distinct from college) professors, including Professor Cadwallader. If, therefore, the university failed to supply him with adequate office facilities, this would imply that it expected him to equip his home with a suitable office. If he did so, and used the home office exclusively and on a regular basis for his scholarly research and writing, then he would be entitled to the home office deduction. But if he is given adequate facilities on the campus to conduct the major part of his scholarly research and writing there, the fact that he chooses to work at home instead does not entitle him to a deduction. It is then not the convenience of the employer but the professor's own convenience, and perhaps his tax planning, that induces him to maintain a home office. The Tax Court found that the two and a half offices which the university furnishes Cadwallader are adequate, so he has no imperative need for a home office.

Second, one of following three conditions must also be met — either the office is used to meet patients, clients, etc. in the normal course of business; or it is in a separate structure (such as a converted garage); or it is the principal place of business for *any* trade or business of the taxpayer. The business does not have to be the taxpayer's primary business, as long as the office is that business's principal place of business.

Musicians have been able to establish that their apartment is their principal place of business, rather than the building where the symphony played concerts. *Drucker v. Commissioner*, 715 F.2d 67 (2d Cir. 1983). But, in *Commissioner v. Soliman*, 506 U.S. 168 (1993), a doctor was unable to prove that his home was a principal place of business (where he did his billing and professional reading), rather than the hospital where he cared for most of his patients and performed operations; the Court used both time spent and the relative importance of the activities to the business as the major criteria. The doctor lost even though the hospital did not provide the doctor with an office to perform his business activities. Congress then amended the law (**§ 280A(c)(1)(last sentence)**)so that the principal place of business requirement is satisfied if the home office is where the taxpayer performs administrative or managerial duties and there is no other fixed location where the taxpayer conducts those activities.

Finally, there is a limit on the deductions available for a home office. Deductions cannot exceed the gross income from the business activity minus the sum of (a) the deductions allocable to use of the home office that are deductible without regard to business use (such as property taxes and home mortgage interest); plus (b) the deductions attributable to the business activity that are not attributable to use of the home office (such as the cost of professional journals). **§ 280A(c)(5)**. In effect, net business losses from use of the home office cannot be used to shelter other income. However, they can be carried over to future years to offset gross income from the business carried on at the home office.

The computations necessary to take the home office deduction require filling out a 43-line form and many taxpayers have been discouraged from taking the deduction because they fear that a mistake will trigger an audit. Therefore, beginning in 2013, a taxpayer can opt to take the following deduction, if the expenses related to the home office are otherwise deductible: the square footage of property used as an eligible home office multiplied by $5, up to a maximum of $1,500. The taxpayer who exercises this option can continue to take an itemized deduction for the full amount of deductible interest and taxes attributable to a personal residence, part of which is used as an eligible home office. Rev. Proc. 2013-13, 2013-6 I.R.B. 478.

§ 8.08   ESTATE PLANNING AND TAX DETERMINATION EXPENSES

[A]   Expenses with Multiple Purposes

Estate planning and tax determination expenses provide an opportunity to review and expand the discussion of statutory provisions dealing with deductions. Here is a problem to raise the issue. A taxpayer pays a $5,000 bill to her lawyer for "estate planning." The will sets up trusts for children, some of whom are minors and others of whom cannot manage money very well. It also places certain real estate property in a trust to be managed by a bank, and other property (stocks and bonds) to be placed in a trust managed by relatives. Finally, it minimizes estate taxes, by arranging for the surviving spouse to have certain interests under the trust.

How many different types of expenses can you identify? I can spot three personal, investment, and tax planning):

1. Are any of the expenses deductible under § 212(2) and, if so, could they be above the line deductions under § 62(a)(4)?

2. Are any of the expenses nondeductible personal expenses, under the "origin" test? *Luman v. Commissioner*, 79 T.C. 846 (1982).

3. Some of the expenses might be deductible tax planning expenses, deductible under § 212(3). *Merians v. Commissioner*, 60 T.C. 187 (1973) (§ 212(3) applies to tax planning as well as tax litigation). Does the deductibility of tax planning expenses provide an opportunity for Mr. Gilmore, whose divorce litigation expenses are otherwise nondeductible personal expenses?

[B]   Burden of Proof

Until the passage of § 7491 in 1998, the taxpayer had the burden of proof in most routine tax cases. The theory was that the burden should rest on the persons with control over the information needed to prove the facts. Despite this burden, taxpayer could still rely on the *Cohan* case (*see* Chapter 8.06) to estimate deductions, unless the code made *Cohan* inapplicable (e.g., by imposing recordkeeping requirements on the taxpayer for most travel and entertainment expenses).

There is, however, a new burden of proof rule, found in **§ 7491**. The popular press made a big point of this statute, suggesting that it shifted the burden of proof to the government in the routine tax case and going so far as to say that the taxpayer was no longer presumed "guilty," as though a tax dispute was a criminal matter. Here is a stripped-down excerpt from **§ 7491**:

§ 7491 Burden of proof

(a) Burden shifts where taxpayer produces credible evidence.

(1) General rule. If, in any court proceeding, a taxpayer introduces credible evidence with respect to any factual issue relevant to ascertaining the liability of the taxpayer for any tax . . . , the Secretary shall have the burden of proof with respect to such issue.

(2) Limitations. Paragraph (1) shall apply with respect to an issue only if —

(A) the taxpayer has complied with the requirements under this title to substantiate any item;

(B) the taxpayer has maintained all records required under this title and has cooperated with reasonable requests by the Secretary for witnesses, information, documents, meetings, and interviews; and

(C) in the case of a partnership, corporation, or trust, the taxpayer [does not have net worth exceeding $7 million].

The actual impact of **§ 7491** is likely to prove a serious disappointment to taxpayers. First, it does not do away with the recordkeeping requirements of **§ 274(d)**. *See* **§ 7491(a)(2)(B)**.

Second, the taxpayer must still "cooperate with reasonable requests [for] information." **§ 7491(a)(2)(B)**. Thus, in the example of a taxpayer who paid a lawyer $5,000 for estate planning, it is still up to the taxpayer to provide evidence (perhaps in the form of the lawyer's time sheets) to support his allocation of the expenses. In this connection, consider a pre **§ 7491** decision. In *Wong v. C.I.R.*, 58 T.C.M. (CCH) 1073 (1989), the taxpayers asserted that 80% of the time spent by a law firm in preparing their estate plan was attributable to tax planning. The court accepted the assumption that some tax planning was inherent in the usual estate planning case, but the taxpayer lost for failure to prove his case. The court said that "[n]o time sheets were submitted or testimony given which would provide an itemization of the legal work on an hourly basis." Also: "[P]etitioners did not retain separate counsel for advice on the nontax aspects of the estate plan." My reading of **§ 7491** suggests that the result in *Wong* would not change under the "new" burden of proof rules because the taxpayer had not cooperated by providing important information.

In Philip N. Jones, *The Burden of Proof 10 Years After the Shift*, 121 TAX NOTES 287 (Oct. 20, 2008), the author concludes that the shift in the burden of proof was "dramatically oversold" to the public.

[C] Professional Ethics

If some of the $5,000 legal fees are deductible tax planning expenses, lawyers are under considerable pressure to help clients allocate their fees to tax planning, so as to improve client acceptance of high fees. Would you shade your itemized bill to show a larger portion allocable to tax planning? How would you respond to a client's request that you depart from your usual practice of itemizing your bill, so as not to show the percentage allocable to tax planning? Rule 1.2(d) of the American Bar Association's Model Rules of Professional Conduct states "A lawyer shall not . . . assist a client in conduct that the lawyer knows is criminal or fraudulent. . . . "

§ 8.09 BUSINESS AS PLEASURE

[A] In General

So far, the tax law divides an individual's activities into personal, business, and income-producing spheres. There is yet another activity, which is a kind of hybrid, often called a "hobby." These are activities that are not engaged in purely for pleasure or for profit. The taxpayer seems to be trying to break-even but not to make a net profit. Typically, a summer vacation home might double as a ranch. In such cases, the net losses from the activity are not deductible and cannot be carried over to another year (they are personal expenses). That was the case law, long before it was codified in § 183. That section now adds a pro-taxpayer presumption that an activity is not a "hobby" if it produces *taxable* income for three of the five consecutive years, ending with the tax year. § 183(d). Why is the pro-taxpayer presumption "two of seven" years for horse breeding?

COMMENTS AND QUESTIONS

1. Assume that a taxpayer is engaged in a ranching activity other than for profit, and generates $50,000 gross income and $60,000 expenses (consisting of $5,000 interest on a mortgage secured by the ranch; $10,000 property taxes on the ranch; and $45,000 depreciation and salary expenses to run the ranch). The taxes and (probably) the interest are deductible under §§ 163(a), (h)(2)(D), (h)(3), 164(a)(2), 183(b)(1). (The interest deduction is discussed in Chapter 16.) The $10,000 net loss is not deductible under § 183(a). How much of the $50,000 deduction is an itemized deduction? If it is an itemized deduction, is it subject to the 2% floor? §§ 67(b), 183(a).

2. Is the test in the hobby loss area subjective (what profits did this taxpayer expect?), or objective (what would a reasonable taxpayer expect?)? § 183(a).

3. Taxpayers who make most of their money from personal services are usually unable to sustain an argument that farming is a profit-seeking activity. However, in *Holmes v. Commissioner*, 184 F.3d 536 (6th Cir. 1999), *reversing*, 74 T.C.M. (CCH) 494 (1997), the taxpayer succeeded. He earned about $200,000 as a sales manager for an insurance company and also owned a farm. Although expecting to make money was "unreasonable and unrealistic," the effort to make money was "honest."

The taxpayer had childhood training in farming and attended a farming-technique seminar at Michigan State University. He also switched crops when an earlier crop proved unprofitable. The court also found little "entertainment or recreational" benefit from the farm.

4. In *Dennis v. Commissioner*, 100 T.C.M. (CCH) 308 (2010), the court held that the taxpayer's horse-breeding activity was "for-profit," in part because his wife's business was not enough to pay their living expenses after accounting for the losses from horse breeding. In addition, the taxpayer's losses were not attributable only to depreciation deductions, but actually affected the family's cash flow.

[B]   An Artist

Does the following situation differ from the typical "vacation-ranch" hobby?

CHURCHMAN v. COMMISSIONER
United States Tax Court
68 T.C. 696 (1977)

FORRESTER, JUDGE: . . .

Petitioner Gloria Churchman (hereinafter Gloria or petitioner) is an artist who has been involved in artistic activities for 20 years. She mainly paints but also sculpts, designs, draws, and builds; writes short stories, poems, and songs, performs in films, and has recently made a film. In addition to an undergraduate degree, she has 2 ½ years of graduate work in psychology and 2 ½ years of work in art school. She has taught courses at [several schools] as well as given numerous workshops independently of any institution. During the years in issue, petitioner devoted a substantial amount of her time to her artistic activities and she held no other job except as a housewife. Petitioner does her artwork in a home studio which was built for that purpose. . . .

During the 20 years that petitioner has pursued her artistic activities, the income from the sale of her artwork has not exceeded her expenses in any year. Petitioner reported no art-related income whatsoever for the taxable year 1970 and 1971, but she reported $250 of such income for 1972.

[Editor — The IRS denied taxpayer a deduction of net operating losses from this activity.]

Respondent argues that petitioner's artistic activities are not engaged in for profit so that section 183 applies and the claimed deduction of petitioner's art-related expenses is not allowable. Section 183 allows deductions for ordinary and necessary expenses arising from an activity not engaged in for profit only to the extent of the gross income derived from such activity less the amount of those deductions which are allowable regardless of whether or not the activity is engaged in for profit. Petitioner, on the other hand, argues that her artistic activities were engaged in for profit so that her art-related expenses are deductible in full under sections 162 and 165.

In order to prevail, petitioner must show that she pursued her artistic activities during the years in question with the objective of making a profit. Petitioner's expectation of profit need not be reasonable, but she must establish that she continued her activities with a bona fide intention of making a profit. . . .

Viewing the record as a whole, we believe that petitioner had a bona fide intention to derive a profit from her artwork. There are admittedly factors in this case which indicate the absence of a profit motive. Petitioner has a history of losses; she has never been dependent upon income from her artistic activities; and there is a significant recreational element inherent in her activities. However, such a history of losses is less persuasive in the art field than it might be in other fields because the archetypal 'struggling artist' must first achieve public acclaim before her serious work will command a price sufficient to provide her with a profit. . . .

While petitioner's artwork involved recreational and personal elements, her work did not stop at the creative stage but went into the marketing phase of the art business where the recreational element is minimal. Petitioner, designed an art gallery and ran it for 1 year, she maintained a mailing list and sent announcements of her shows to persons on such list, she went to galleries in San Francisco and New York attempting to have her work shown, and she published a book. Furthermore, when petitioner saw that her paintings and other works were not selling well, she adopted new techniques, such as making posters and writing books, in an effort to make her work more available and more salable to the public. Although she did not keep a complete set of books pertaining to her artistic activities, petitioner kept all of the receipts for her art expenses and kept a journal recording what she sold and to whom. These facts indicate that petitioner carried on her artistic activities in a businesslike manner for profit.

Moreover, petitioner studied art for 2 ½ years, she has taught at the college level and in workshops, articles about her have appeared in newspapers and magazines, her work is shown in commercial galleries at least once a year, some of her work has been sold, and she has been given a grant to make a film. Such facts indicate that petitioner has the requisite training to become a successful artist. The fact that petitioner devotes a substantial amount of time to her artistic activities also indicates that she has a profit motive.

It is abundantly clear from her testimony and from the objective evidence that petitioner is a most dedicated artist, craves personal recognition as an artist, and believes that selling her work for a profit represents the attainment of such recognition. Therefore, petitioner intends and expects to make a profit. For section 183 purposes, it seems to us irrelevant whether petitioner intends to make a profit because it symbolizes success in her chosen career or because it is the pathway to material wealth. In either case, the essential fact remains that petitioner does intend to make a profit from her artwork and she sincerely believes that if she continues to paint she will do so.

Petitioner has a relatively large inventory, she has considerable training, she devotes substantial time to her artwork, she has sold some paintings in the past, and is attempting to sell more. It is certainly conceivable, in our view, that she may someday sell enough of her paintings to enable her 'to recoup the losses which have meanwhile been sustained in the intervening years.' Accordingly, we hold that petitioner's artistic activities were engaged in for profit so that section 183 is inapplicable and petitioner is entitled to deductions for her art-related expenses. . . .

Chapter 9

PERSONAL INSURANCE PROTECTION AND PERSONAL LOSSES

Numerous variables affect how personal insurance and personal losses are taxed. The rules are not uniform among different types of insurance and losses and you should consider whether the differences are justified. Here are the variables.

1. *What is the loss insured against?* This chapter considers disability (the inability to work); medical expenses; and loss of life.

2. *Insurance or loss recovery?* There are two potential tax events involving personal losses — (a) when the taxpayer obtains insurance protection; and (b) when the taxpayer suffers the losses for which the taxpayer receives compensation.

3. *How is the insurance financed?* Taxpayers acquire insurance or insurance-like protection in various ways. They can buy it; an employer can buy it for them; their employer can promise to pay them money if a loss occurs; or the government can make a similar promise. The employer or government promise is not technically insurance but is often the economic equivalent. In addition, compensation for losses can be received not only from insurance, but also from tort defendants.

We first look at the taxation of insurance (or insurance-like) protection (Chapter 9.01) and then at the tax rules when a loss occurs (Chapter 9.02). A detailed discussion of tort recoveries is left to a separate concluding section (Chapter 9.03).

§ 9.01 INSURANCE PROTECTION

[A] Premiums Paid for Insurance

Premiums to buy insurance covering personal losses are nondeductible personal expenses, unless the code otherwise provides. The citation is simply § 262, which disallows the deduction of personal expenses. This section disallows the deduction of disability, medical, legal, and life insurance premiums, unless the risks against which they insure are solely business risks. For example, there is no doubt that legal malpractice insurance premiums would be deductible. And disability insurance premiums would be deductible business expenses if *only* business risks were covered (e.g., only risks from performing hazardous work). Rev. Rul. 75-149, 1975-1 C.B. 64. We assume in the remainder of this chapter that the insurance covers "personal" risks.

The code does "otherwise provide" a deduction in a number of situations. Medical insurance premiums are deductible as medical expenses, except that the percentage floor on deductible medical expenses often makes this provision useless.

§ 213(a). In addition, a self-employed taxpayer is allowed to deduct a percentage of medical insurance costs as an above the line deduction. § 162(l). That percentage was originally 25% but reached 100% in 2003.

[B] Employer-Purchased Insurance

Taxpayers can often exclude the value of premiums from their income when the employer buys the insurance for the employee-taxpayer. Why does the code do this? First, remember that the employer's promise to pay for losses is not itself taxed (the employees are cash basis taxpayers who do not report the value of promises). Second, the code wants to encourage employers to purchase these socially desirable benefits (they are "tax expenditures").

A tax expenditure perspective suggests looking for policy-oriented conditions — especially "nondiscrimination" rules, which are intended to assure that the insurance protection is not limited to only highly paid employees and employee-owners. As explained later, only some employer-purchased insurance discussed in this chapter is subject to nondiscrimination rules.

Here is a quick summary of the exclusion rules applicable to employer-purchased personal insurance.

[1] Life Insurance

Only *term* life insurance protection can be excluded from an employee's income. If the insurance has a cash value to the employee (analogous to a bank account that can be borrowed against or cashed in), there is no exclusion of the value of life insurance protection from the employee's income. In addition, the premium value of no more than $50,000 of term life insurance can be excluded. The exclusion is conditioned on not limiting benefits to highly-compensated employees. § 79.

[2] Medical and Disability Insurance

Medical and disability insurance and insurance-like protection can be excluded from an employee's income. § 106. This covers not only insurance protection but also amounts set aside by an employer in a fund to cover employee losses. This exclusion is *not* conditioned on nondiscrimination, probably because small businesses appear to have inordinate trouble complying with nondiscrimination rules. Consequently, highly compensated employees can be the sole beneficiaries of tax-free employer-funded medical and disability insurance or insurance-like protection. (If the only beneficiaries are employees who are also shareholders of a corporation, there is some case law denying the exclusion on the ground that the plan is for shareholders, not employees. *Larkin v. Commissioner*, 394 F.2d 494 (1st Cir. 1968); *Seidel v. Commissioner*, 30 T.C.M. (CCH) 1021 (1971).)

Although the exclusion of medical insurance benefits for employees is not conditioned on meeting a nondiscrimination requirement, the Patient Protection and Affordable Health Care Act (Obamacare) (Public Law 111-148) modifies that rule in a somewhat odd way. The Act applies nondiscrimination requirements to "group health plans" (other than grandfathered plans in effect on March 23, 2010 and not changed significantly after that date), but the sanction for not meeting this requirement is not the loss of tax exemption. The penalty for providing discriminatory benefits is a complex set of excise taxes on the employer under **§ 4980D**. The law also authorizes a civil action by affected participants and the Department of Labor to compel the provision of nondiscriminatory benefits. Finally, the IRS has stated (in Notice 2011-1) that compliance with the Act is not required until after the agency issues administrative guidance.

The 1996 tax law expanded the definition of medical and disability insurance (referred to in the code as accident and health insurance) to include certain "long-term care" insurance. **§ 7702B(a)(1)**. The value of the premiums paid by an employer for such insurance is therefore tax free under **§ 106** (as well as being deductible as medical expenses up to specified amounts (inflation-adjusted)). **§ 213(d)(1)(D), (10))**.

[3] Self-Employed

Excluding insurance protection from an employee's income is one reason to form a corporation. Owners of a corporation hire themselves as corporate employees and become eligible for tax-free insurance protection as employees. However, as noted earlier, **§ 162(l)** allows self-employed taxpayers to deduct medical insurance premiums, there are no similar provisions allowing a self-employed taxpayer to deduct disability or life insurance premiums.

Here is a chart summarizing (with some imprecision) the prior discussion. Do the overall results make sense?

TAX DEDUCTIBLE OR TAX-FREE PERSONAL INSURANCE
[ND = CANNOT DISCRIMINATE FOR HIGHLY COMPENSATED EMPLOYEES]

TYPE OF INSURANCE	HOW FINANCED		
	BUY OWN INSURANCE	EMPLOYER FUNDED *50,000 limit*	SELF-EMPLOYED BUYS
LIFE	No *§ 262*	Yes (term ins.-ND)	No *§ 262*
MEDICAL	Yes (over 10% *§213* AGI)	Yes *§ 106*	Yes *§ 162(l)*
DISABILITY	No *§ 262*	Yes *§ 106*	No

Non-discrimination rules

[4] Who Gets the Tax Benefit

You might assume that the exclusion of insurance protection from an employee's income helps employees. Don't be too sure. Here is a possible scenario. An employee in the 35% bracket receives life insurance protection that is worth $65 to the employee and costs the employer $65. The employer knows that the employee would require $100 of before-tax wages to get $65 after-tax to buy the insurance. In other words, the before-tax equivalent of the $65 is $100. So the employer lowers the employee's wages by $100, at a $65 cost to the employer. The employer captures the $35 economic benefit of the exclusion that the law provides to the employee.

What might prevent this from happening? Suppose the employer has a lot of employees in lower tax brackets. Because they have lower income, they do not value insurance at the $65 cost to the employer. They have other needs for the money. By how much could the employer lower *their* wages when he pays $65 per person to buy them insurance? For example, assume one employee in the 15% bracket who values the insurance at only $60. The before-tax equivalent is only $70.59 ($60/(1 - .15)). Thus, these employee's wages can only be reduced by $70.59. Can the employer separate employees into different wage pools, lowering some wages by $100 and others by $70.59? If not, the most that the employer can lower wages is $70.59 and the taxpayer in the 35% bracket gets an economic benefit, enjoying a tax-free $65 benefit with a reduction of only $70.59 in wages, rather than $100. This is the same mechanism that allowed high bracket taxpayers to enjoy some of the benefits of the tax exemption for interest on state and local bonds (Chapter 6.01[C][3]).

§ 9.02 PERSONAL LOSSES

[A] Background

Now assume that a loss occurs — someone dies; becomes disabled; or incurs medical expenses.

The tax treatment of personal losses has a long history. After some uncertainty, early agency rulings excluded recoveries for personal injuries, such as physical injuries to the body, or nonphysical personal injuries, such as libel. Sol. Mem. 1384, 1920-2 C.B. 71; Sol. Op. 132, I-1 C.B. 92. These rulings used some misleading language. One ruling said that "the human body is a kind of capital" and the proceeds compensating for the loss represented "a conversion of the capital lost through the injury." This makes it sound as though the body has a basis equal to the cash recovery, so there is no gain. But the body has no basis.

What fundamental principle(s) about the definition of taxable gain might underlie these rulings? Does any of the following language provide a clue? One ruling justified the absence of taxable gain in the following terms: the invaded right is "personal" and "in no way transferable;" "in the very nature of things, there can be no correct estimate of the money value of the invaded rights. The rights on the one hand and the money on the other are incomparable things which cannot be placed on opposite sides of an equation." In discussing money received for surrender of custody of a minor child, one ruling stated that taxing the proceeds would be like treating the child as chattels.

Even this language leaves you wondering. Neither nontransferability nor estimation difficulties necessarily preclude taxing benefits. Is there something else? (1) Does the compensation simply make up for a loss rather than provide gain? *Cf. Clark v. Commissioner,* 40 B.T.A. 333 (1939) (Chapter 3.06[A][4]; a tax advisor's compensation for excess taxes caused by the advisor's negligence is not income); (2) is there something inappropriate about taxing amounts received upon a forced sale of a personal right, because it commercializes something that should not be treated as a market commodity?

[B] Uncompensated Losses

One possible implication of excluding compensation for personal injuries from income is that *uncompensated* losses should reduce taxable income. If compensation brings someone back to a "zero" baseline (as in *Clark*), rather than produce taxable gain, an *uncompensated* taxpayer has fallen below some baseline norm. Should the tax law recognize the uncompensated loss by allowing deductions? How would it determine whether such a loss occurred? What dollar figure would it attach to the loss?

You might assume that disability or loss of life calls for no tax adjustment when there is an uncompensated loss, because the income lost is simply not taxed. But something could be done for the taxpayer. The decline in income could result in downward income averaging, to override the accounting year barrier. Or sympathy for individuals suffering such losses could result in some tax break for whatever income they have left. Indeed, the tax law does adjust for some personal losses, although it might seem arbitrary. One example is an added standard deduction for the blind; § 63(f). *See also* § 22 (permanently and totally disabled taxpayers with disability income are eligible for tax credits, although the credit is carefully restricted to people with low income). Generally speaking, except for medical expenses discussed below, uncompensated losses for personal injuries do not result in a tax break.

[1] Medical Expenses

Sometimes, a personal loss gives rise to expenses, not just lost income. In that case, a deduction for the expenses seems a plausible possibility, because the expenses fix the amount of the loss. And that is what the law has provided for medical expenses since 1942, with limitations.

The medical expense deduction is limited to amounts over 10% of adjusted gross income (raised from the prior 7.5% figure), unless the taxpayer or the taxpayer's spouse is at least 65 years of age. For the elderly, the figure remains at 7.5% from 2013-2016.

The medical expense deduction is an "itemized" deduction, but is not subject to the 2% floor. Drug expenses are medical expenses if they are for prescribed drugs or insulin. § 213(b).

Here are some examples of deductible medical expenses. They raise two policy issues:

> (1) Does the deduction accurately identify personal losses that should reduce taxable gain? Are there parallels here to the distinction between business and personal expenses?

> (2) Does the deduction make sense as a tax expenditure — that is, as sound national health care policy?

1. A hospital bill for a private room is deductible. There is no indication that the IRS will question deductions for somewhat more comfortable or perhaps even luxurious medical facilities. The problem is analogous to first class traveling

expenses for business, which are apparently not questioned (despite the parenthetical in § 162(a)(2) prohibiting deduction of lavish traveling expenses).

2. The Regulations do not permit deduction of expenses to maintain general well being, such as a decent diet and exercise. **Treas. Reg. § 1.213-1(e)(1)(ii).** The point is analogous to disallowing the deduction of food as a business expense even though food is necessary for the taxpayer to be in business.

In Rev. Rul. 2002-19, 2002-1 C.B. 778, the IRS dealt with two taxpayers. Taxpayer A was diagnosed by a physician as obese; A did not suffer from any other specific disease. Taxpayer B was not obese but suffered from hypertension; B was directed by a physician to lose weight as treatment for the hypertension. A and B both participated in the X weight-loss program, and incurred both an initial fee to join X and an additional fee to attend periodic meetings. At the meetings, participants develop a diet plan, receive diet menus and literature, and discuss problems encountered in dieting. A and B also purchased X brand reduced-calorie diet food items.

The ruling noted that obesity is medically accepted as a disease in its own right by the National Heart, Lung, and Blood Institute (which is part of the National Institutes of Health), as well as other agencies. Therefore, the cost of A's participation in the X weight-loss program as treatment for A's obesity is a deductible medical expense. B can also deduct these costs, because B's participation in X is part of the treatment for B's hypertension, even though B is not medically obese. The ruling distinguished Rev. Rul. 79-151, in which the taxpayer was not suffering from any specific disease or ailment and participated in a weight-loss program merely to improve the taxpayer's general health and appearance.

The government also concluded that A and B could not deduct any portion of the cost of purchasing reduced-calorie diet foods because the foods are substitutes for the food A and B normally consume and satisfy their nutritional requirements.

If an everyday expense is abnormally large because of a medical condition, however, the excess is deductible. *Randolph v. Commissioner*, 67 T.C. 481 (1976) (extra cost of health food over normal costs is deductible by a taxpayer whose allergies require eating such food); Rev. Rul. 62-189, 1962-2 C.B. 88 (wig deductible when purchased after loss of hair because of a medical problem and a doctor stated that a wigless appearance created a mental health problem); Rev. Rul. 80-340, 1980-2 C.B. 81 (deduction of cost of adapting TV to receive audio portion visually for a hearing impaired viewer); Rev. Rul. 70-606, 1970-2 C.B. 66 (deduction of extra cost of adapting car for person in wheelchair). *But see Murray v. Commissioner*, 43 T.C.M. (CCH) 1377 (1982) (no deduction for health spa costs to lose weight, because there is no special medical problem requiring weight loss).

3. Luxurious personal expenses are sometimes claimed as medical expenses. Swimming pools are a favorite. There is a preliminary question whether the pool is necessary for medical treatment. Rev. Rul. 83-33, 1983-1 C.B. 70 (swimming helped arthritic condition); *Evanoff v. Commissioner*, 44 T.C.M. (CCH) 1394 (1982) (expense of in-ground residential pool disallowed because of availability of local community pool for $250). If the pool is medically necessary, the amount spent on the pool might still be too large for the entire cost to be considered a medical

expense. Courts vary in their willingness to second-guess the amount spent on the pool. The cheapest facility is not required, but it is unclear just how much more can be spent and still be deductible. *Ferris v. Commissioner*, 582 F.2d 1112 (7th Cir. 1978), *reversing*, 36 T.C.M. (CCH) 765 (1977). In any event, the amount of the deduction is reduced by any increase in the residence's value from pool installation. **Treas. Reg. § 1.213-1(e)(1)(iii).**

In *Emanuel v. C.I.R.*, T.C. Summary Opinion 2002-127, 2002 Tax Ct. Summary LEXIS 127, the taxpayer's doctor recommended that he swim to develop his motor skills for medical reasons related to a disability. The pool had a depth from 3 to 5½ feet and had wide steps and a grab rail in the shallow end, but no diving board or slide; it was tailored for use by the disabled taxpayer, and was usable throughout the year. Taxpayer used the pool about once a day with his wife's assistance, but other family members did not use it for recreation. The court held that the swimming pool had medical care as its primary purpose. Consequently, maintenance expenses were deductible. The court also noted that generally, a taxpayer is required to keep records to establish the amount of his deductions, but that the court could estimate the amount of medical expenses and allow a deduction to that extent, notwithstanding the absence of substantiating documentary evidence in the record. *Cohan v. Commissioner*, 39 F.2d 540 (2d Cir. 1930). The court relied on "credible" testimony from the taxpayer that he incurred $1,200 in pool maintenance expenses.

4. Private school tuition falls somewhere between luxury items and everyday expenses. If the school's resources for alleviating a mental or physical handicap are a principal reason for spending the tuition, the entire tuition expense is a medical expense. Schools for students with neurologically verifiable learning disabilities are a typical case. Rev. Rul. 78-340, 1978-2 C.B. 124. A more difficult case is one where the child has at least average intelligence but still has a learning problem. In *Greisdorf v. Commissioner*, 54 T.C. 1684 (1970), the school was specially established to deal with emotional problems that interfered with learning, the teachers all had psychological training, and education was incidental to the elimination of the students' learning disabilities. The expenses were deductible. But in *Ripple v. Commissioner*, 54 T.C. 1442 (1970), the fact that the school had a remedial reading program for students who had emotional problems did not make it a special school for which tuition was deductible.

5. Medical expenses arising from particular lifestyle choices are deductible, whatever the lifestyle, Rev. Rul. 73-325, 1973-2 C.B. 75 (treatment for alcoholics), *unless* the expenditure is illegal. Rev. Rul. 73-201, 1973-1 C.B. 140 (cost of legal vasectomy or abortion is deductible). *See also* Rev. Rul. 99-28, 1999-1 Cum. Bull 1269 (revoking Rev. Rul. 79-162) (because nicotine is addictive, payments for participation in a smoking-cessation program and for prescribed drugs designed to alleviate nicotine withdrawal are deductible medical expenses; however, the cost of nicotine gum and patches available without a prescription is not deductible as a medical expense).

6. *Cosmetic surgery.* Medical procedures are deductible if they "affect any structure or function of the body," even if nonmedical reasons motivate the expenditure. Rev. Rul. 73-201, 1973-2 C.B. 140 (abortion and vasectomy).

Since 1991, the deduction of "cosmetic surgery" expenses is explicitly disallowed, unless they ameliorate deformity arising from a congenital abnormality, a personal injury from an accident, or a disfiguring disease. In addition, the definition of nondeductible "cosmetic surgery" must be consulted: it is surgery directed at appearance that does not "meaningfully promote the proper function of the body or prevent or treat illness or disease." § 213(d)(9). Would hair transplant expenses to prevent baldness be deductible? Can you think of any argument why expenses for a nose job might be deductible?

In Rev. Rul. 2003-57, 2003-1 C.B. 959, the government stated that the cost of breast reconstruction surgery after a mastectomy was a deductible medical expense because it ameliorated a deformity arising from a disfiguring disease; and that laser eye surgery to correct for defective vision was also deductible because it meaningfully promotes the proper function of the body. However, the expense to whiten teeth discolored by age was not a deductible medical expense.

Would the cost of a sex change operation be deductible? Does it "ameliorate a deformity arising from . . . a congenital abnormality . . . or disfiguring disease?" Does it "meaningfully promote the proper function of the body or prevent or treat illness or disease?" See Chief Counsel Advisory, IRS CCA 200603025, 2005 IRS CCA LEXIS 82 (IRS CCA) (Jan. 20, 2006), which states that the cost of the operation is not a deductible medical expense.

However, in *O'Donnabhain v. Commissioner*, 134 T.C. 34 (2010), the court held that the cost of sex-change surgery and related feminizing hormones were, on the facts, deductible medical expenses. Regulations under § 213 included mental illness as a disease for which the taxpayer could incur deductible medical expenses; and the taxpayer had what the Diagnostic and Statistical Manual of Mental Disorders labeled a "genetic identity disorder (GID)." The court rejected the government's argument that GID was a "social construction" and "not a significant psychiatric disorder." The exclusion from deductible medical care for cosmetic surgery did not apply to the taxpayer because the taxpayer's expenditures were to "treat illness or disease," as provided by § 213(d)(9)(B).

The latest version of the Diagnostic and Statistical Manual of Mental Disorders replaces GID with "Gender Dysphoria," to emphasize that not all transgender individuals experience distress that amounts to a mental disorder. This suggests that only some transgender individuals will incur deductible medical expenses for a sex change operation.

Query? Why was cosmetic surgery ever deductible? Was the deduction required by the disjunctive "*or* for the purpose of affecting any structure etc." in § 213(d)(1)(A)? Could you justify a narrower interpretation denying the deduction by reference to the personal origin of the expense, analogous to the *Gilmore* case distinguishing between personal and income-producing expenses?

7. *Business vs. medical expense.* Because the medical expense deduction is subject to a percentage floor and is an itemized deduction, taxpayers are often better off if the expense is a business expense. In Rev. Rul. 71-45, 1971-1 C.B. 51, a professional singer wanted to deduct the costs of having her throat specially treated by a doctor to keep it in top singing condition. The ruling permitted the

deduction only as a medical expense. In Rev. Rul. 58-382, 1958-2 C.B. 59, a pilot who was required to have annual physicals to keep his job was allowed a § 162 business expense deduction for the physicals, but only a medical expense deduction for any subsequent treatment needed to keep him fit to be a pilot.

Are these rulings correct? Wouldn't it make more sense to permit the singer and the pilot to take business expense deductions for treatment that goes beyond what most people would bother about, if they did not do that kind of work? *See also Denny v. Commissioner*, 33 B.T.A. 738 (1935) (actor lost his teeth while acting and was allowed a business expense deduction for the cost of replacement); Rev. Rul. 75-316, 1975-2 C.B. 54 (expenses paid by a blind taxpayer to a reader for services in connection with the taxpayer's work were deductible as business expenses, not medical expenses).

8. *Impact of insurance recovery.* No deduction is allowed if medical expenses are "compensated for by insurance or otherwise." Suppose a taxpayer collects an unallocated tax exempt lump sum § 104 recovery (discussed in Chapter 9.03, dealing with tort recoveries). The lump sum includes compensation for *future* medical expenses. Rev. Rul. 79-427, 1979-2 C.B. 120, disallowed a § 213 deduction for medical expenses paid after the § 104 recovery. However, in *Niles v. United States*, 710 F.2d 1391 (9th Cir. 1983), the court disagreed and allowed the medical expense deduction, in part because allocating the § 104 recovery to future medical expenses would be very difficult.

9. *Traveling expense as medical expense.* A taxpayer who lives in New England is advised by her doctor to go to a warm, dry climate during certain months of the year to obtain relief from asthma and allergies. Can the taxpayer deduct transportation to get there; or meals or lodging at the destination? She requires no medical treatment at the destination. *Commissioner v. Bilder*, 369 U.S. 499 (1962), held that the negative implication of the statutory permission to deduct transportation, combined with explicit legislative history denying a deduction for meals and lodging, meant that meals and lodging at a medical destination were not deductible. *See* § 213(d)(1)(B). This general rule has apparently been ratified by § 213(d)(2), which permits lodging expenses at a medical destination to be deducted up to $50 per night per individual, under certain circumstances.

[2] Medical Savings Accounts and Health Savings Accounts

The tax law has experimented with tax breaks for savings to pay for medical expenses. The law first provided a deduction for contributions to Medical Savings Accounts (Archer MSAs) in § 220. This provision helped only a limited number of people and covered only the self-employed and employees of small employers; and only if the plan provided for a high deductible. After 2003, no new contributions could be made to these plans except by individuals who previously made Archer MSA contributions or were employees covered by a participating employer.

A more significant tax break for medical expenses now appears in § 223, providing for Health Savings Accounts (HSAs). The tax breaks for HSAs appeared in the Medicare legislation (Public Law 108-173), which also adopted the much-publicized drug benefit for the elderly.

The government permits (1) "eligible individuals" covered by a (2) "high-deductible health plan" to deduct (above the line) contributions to an HSA and to exclude contributions to an HSA by an employer for such individuals, (3) up to a specified ceiling amount. The ceiling amount for people eligible for Medicare is zero — so they are, in effect, not eligible to participate in HSAs.

Amounts distributed from an HSA for medical expenses are tax free. One big advantage of an HSA is that unused amounts carry over to later years. (This differs from amounts set aside but not used in cafeteria plans under § 125, discussed in Chapter 7.02[E]. These amounts are lost to the employee if not used in the relevant tax year.)

Amounts distributed from an HSA and not used for medical expenses are not only taxed but are also subject to a penalty, unless distributed after the taxpayer is disabled, dies, or is eligible for Medicare. This means that the HSA can be used as a tax-deferred retirement benefit, subject to tax but with no penalty upon distribution. (Retirement benefits are discussed in Chapter 24.06.)

[C]   Compensated Losses

Here is the statutory pattern for taxing compensation for personal losses financed through insurance and employer payments, covering loss of life, medical expenses, and disability benefits, and for the now-expired legal cost fringe benefit. As noted earlier, some early rulings excluded such compensation from the tax base, but today, most of these situations are covered by an explicit statutory provision.

As you read about the statute, consider these questions. (1) Does the rationale for excluding compensation for personal injury losses under the early agency rulings, explain the statutory pattern? (2) Does the tax-free compensation replace lost income and, if so, why is it tax free? Remember that *Glenshaw Glass* taxed both compensatory damages to make up for lost profits, as well as punitive damages. (We leave a detailed discussion of tort damages to the following section.)

[1]   Loss of Life

Life insurance proceeds are tax free if paid on account of the death of the insured, whether the insured buys the insurance or the employer provides it as a tax-free fringe benefit to the employee, and whether it is term insurance or has a cash value. § 101(a). Here is some information about the difference between term and cash value life insurance that helps you decide whether the exclusion of life insurance proceeds makes sense. Term insurance is a pure gamble. The insurance company receives a premium each year; the older you are the higher the premium. As in a horse race, there are winners and losers at the end of the year. The "winners" collect; the losers get no money.

With cash value life insurance, the life insurance premiums include both term insurance elements and a savings feature ("cash value"). The savings feature earns interest. You can borrow based on the cash value and can also cash in the policy during your life. When you die, the payment includes a lot of interest that has accrued on the cash value. If you die when you are quite old, is the insurance payment likely to be mostly cash value plus interest, or an amount paid for winning the gamble on the term interest portion of the annual premium? Is the exclusion from income for the interest element justified?

What if a terminally ill individual draws down life insurance benefits in excess of cost? The 1996 tax law defines tax exempt "death" benefits to include amounts paid to terminally ill individuals, even though the amounts are not paid on account of the death of the insured. **§ 101(g)(1)(A)**. A terminally ill individual is one whose physician certifies that death is reasonably expected to occur within 24 months. **§ 101(g)(4)(A)**.

In addition, payments under a life insurance contract can be excluded if paid to a chronically ill individual, defined in a manner similar to the new rules dealing with long-term care insurance. **§ 101(g)(1)(B),(3),(4)(B)**.

[2] Medical Expenses

Medical insurance proceeds are tax free if the insured buys the insurance. **§ 104(a)(3)**.

If the employer buys the insurance as a tax-free fringe benefit for the employee, the insurance proceeds are still tax free to the employee. **§ 105(a), (b)**. There are no nondiscrimination requirements imposed as a condition of excluding the value of the insurance. However, if the employer pays the employee's medical expenses directly (rather than buying insurance for the employee), exclusion from the employee's income depends on satisfying nondiscrimination rules. **§ 105(h)**.

Tax-free payment of medical expenses under **§ 105(b)** is available not only for an employee, but also for an employee's spouse and dependents. A child under the age of 27 is *deemed* to be a dependent for purposes of the exclusion from income of employer-funded medical expenses under **§ 105(b)**. It is no longer necessary for this child to be a dependent, which means that the child can provide more than one-half of his or her support and earn more than the exemption amount.

As noted earlier, the 1996 tax law has expanded the category of tax-favored insurance to include long-term care insurance. The proceeds are therefore exempt under **§ 104**, if the insurance is purchased by an individual for his or her own benefit (**§ 7702B(a)(2)**); and under **§ 105**, if purchased by an employer for an employee (**§ 7702B(a)(3)**). The exempt amounts are, however, subject to maximums, too detailed to consider here. **§ 7702B(d)**.

[3] Disability Benefits

Disability insurance proceeds are tax free if the insured buys the insurance. **§ 104(a)(3)**.

If the employer buys the insurance as a tax-free fringe benefit or pays disability benefits to the employee, the proceeds are tax free only under the following narrowly defined circumstances: the proceeds must be paid without regard to the time spent out of work and must be for permanent loss or loss of use of a member or function of the body, or permanent disfigurement. **§ 105(a), (c)**. An exception is

Workers Compensation, which is government-mandated disability insurance funded by employers. Workers Compensation benefits are tax free to the employee in all situations. § 104(a)(1).

[4]   Looking at Insurance Protection and Compensation Together

Our discussion has looked at insurance protection and compensation for personal losses separately. Was the cost of insurance protection a personal expense? Did the compensation produce "gain?" Maybe you should look at insurance proceeds and compensation together. Here is the argument for doing so.

Insurance is a wealth transfer from "losers" to "winners." In that respect, it is like a gift. There should be only one tax on the income transfer. If both the insurance protection and the compensation are included in taxable income, more than the total income transfer is taxed. Consider this example. Assume the income transfer occurs without the insurance company charging anything for its services. Ten people buy insurance, for $10 each. One of them suffers a $100 loss, and receives $100. Thus, ten people have paid a total of $100, and one person receives $100. If the insurance protection *and* the compensation are taxed, much more than $100 is taxed.

If there should be only one tax, should it be on the value of the insurance protection or on the compensation when loss occurs? The time of loss is likely to be an unpopular time to tax people on the compensation (as with life insurance). In some cases, the recipients may be very strapped for cash (as with medical insurance). Consequently, the better time to impose a single tax is when the insurance protection is provided and to exempt the compensation.

But maybe more than $100 *should* be taxed. If ten people go to bed at night secure in the knowledge that they are protected from serious loss, does security itself produce taxable personal consumption? The nine who suffer no loss have security valued at $90, and the loser has a $100 benefit (or do you subtract the $10 premium from the $100?).

Reconsider the pattern of taxing insurance protection and compensation for personal losses discussed in this chapter. When is there one tax, on either the protection or compensation? When is the value of *both* protection and compensation excluded from income? Does "double exclusion" make sense as social policy, whether or not it makes sense as a definition of taxable "gain?"

QUESTIONS

Although many of the legal issues regarding the taxation of insurance protection and personal losses are answered explicitly by the code (even though the answers are complicated), there are some situations where the answers are not explicit.

1. Suppose an individual buys legal insurance to cover against *personal* legal expenses. Or suppose that an employer buys such a policy for an employee. Would the insurance *proceeds* be taxable?

2. Suppose an individual buys tax audit insurance, which compensates the taxpayer both for any increase in tax resulting from an audit, and for tax counsel expenses for representation during the audit. Is all or part of the premium deductible? Are all or part of the insurance proceeds exempt from tax? *A Report on Tax Audit Insurance*, 22 Tax Notes 53 (1984).

§ 9.03 TORT RECOVERIES

As noted earlier, the exclusion of recoveries for personal injuries is rooted in a fundamental conception of gain. The idea is that the recoveries do not provide "gain," but only compensate for loss. The statute has long contained an explicit rule excluding damages for personal injury. § 104(a)(2).

The statutory exclusion has spawned a number of issues.

[A] Physical and Nonphysical Injury

[1] Nonphysical Injuries

There had been considerable uncertainty about whether compensation for *nonphysical* personal injury was excluded from income by the statute. Most courts held that it was; thus, defamation damages were excluded. *Church v. Commissioner*, 80 T.C. 1104 (1983). The injury nonetheless had to be "tort-like," not "contract-like." Payments to a taxpayer for advance contractual waiver of potential personal injury claims were not excludable. A taxpayer, for example, could not exclude payments received in exchange for releasing right of privacy claims potentially arising from a movie production. *Roosevelt v. Commissioner*, 43 T.C. 77 (1964). And proceeds from the sale of blood by a taxpayer with a rare blood type were taxable. *United States v. Garber*, 589 F.2d 843 (5th Cir. 1979).

There was less certainty about business torts. The government argued against exclusion for business tort recoveries in personal injury cases (e.g., a business libel), on the ground that damages are generally taxed like the replaced income would have been taxed under *Glenshaw Glass*, 348 U.S. 426 (1955). Because business profits were taxable, damages replacing the lost profits were taxable. Rev. Rul. 85-143, 1985-2 C.B. 55. But the courts generally favored the taxpayer, *Threlkeld v. Commissioner*, 848 F.2d 81 (6th Cir. 1988), on the ground that § 104 is an exception to the rule taxing damages like the income they replace. The replacement of lost wages is exempt under that section in typical negligence cases, even though wages are otherwise taxable, and there was no reason to be less generous to business tort plaintiffs in personal injury cases.

These disputes were mooted by a 1996 amendment, which stated that the exclusion for damages applies only if it is on account of a personal *physical* injury or *physical* sickness; § 104(a)(2). The impetus for this statutory amendment was the proliferation of tort-like claims under Civil Rights statutes.

[2] Emotional Distress?

The 1996 statute adds, explicitly, that emotional distress is not a physical injury; § 104(a) (**next to last sentence**) ("For purposes of paragraph 104(a)(2), emotional distress shall not be treated as a physical injury or physical sickness."). And the Conference Committee Report to the 1996 law states that "emotional distress includes symptoms (e.g., insomnia, headaches, stomach disorders) which may result from such emotional distress."

The new law provides the following exception from the rule that disallows the exclusion of compensation arising from emotional distress: it excludes from income any compensation for medical expenses attributable to emotional distress arising from a nonphysical injury (e.g., medical treatment for mental anguish arising after a parent sues for emotional distress caused by witnessing an accident involving his or her child); § 104(a) (**last sentence**).

The new law also does not change prior law excluding damages for emotional distress *incident* to a physical injury. For example, pain and suffering damages incident to a car accident in which the plaintiff was physically injured are excluded. Such damages are on account of a physical injury, not on account of a nonphysical injury.

There remains a question whether damages can be excluded when they compensate for physical symptoms resulting from emotional distress, such as a stroke or heart attack. The government can be expected to deny an exclusion in such cases.

In *Sanford v. Commissioner*, T.C. Memo 2008-158 (2008), the taxpayer recovered damages arising from unlawful employment discrimination (sexual harassment). The court concluded that the damages were taxable, stating that it was "evident from the [agency] decision that none of the award was predicated on personal physical injury or physical sickness as the statute requires." Although "the emotional distress manifested itself in physical symptoms such as asthma, sleep deprivation, skin irritation, appetite loss, severe headaches, and depression[, t]hese physical symptoms were not the basis of the award petitioner received. [Taxpayer] sought, and was awarded, relief for sexual harassment, discrimination based on sex, and the failure of the [employer] to take appropriate corrective action. . . . Damages received on account of emotional distress, even when resultant physical symptoms occur, are not excludable from income under section 104(a)(2)."

Stadnyk v. Commissioner, 96 T.C.M. (CCH) 475 (2008), involved false imprisonment, but the taxpayer still lost. The taxpayer admitted that "she did not suffer physical harm during the course of her arrest and detention. She was not grabbed, jerked around, or bruised. Rather, [she] argue[d] that physical restraint and detention constitute a physical injury for purposes of section 104(a)(2). [She] contend[s] that a person does not have to be cut or bruised for physical injury to occur under tort law." The court concluded:

> Physical restraint and physical detention are not "physical injuries" for purposes of section 104(a)(2). Being subjected to police arrest procedures may cause physical discomfort. However, being handcuffed or searched is not a physical injury for purposes of section 104(a)(2). Nor is the depriva-

tion of personal freedom a physical injury for purposes of section 104(a)(2). Physical injury is not required for the tort of false imprisonment to occur. Kentucky courts define false imprisonment as "any deprivation of the liberty of one person by another or detention for however short a time without such person's consent and against his will, whether done by actual violence, threats or otherwise." The tort of false imprisonment protects personal interest in freedom from physical restraint; such an interest is "in a sense a mental one". . . . The alleged false imprisonment against petitioner wife did not cause her to suffer physical injury as required for relief under section 104(a)(2).

In its affirmance (367 Fed. Appx. 586 (6th Cir. 2010) (not selected for publication)), the Court of Appeals stated that "the mere fact that false imprisonment involves a physical act — restraining the victim's freedom — does not mean that the victim is *necessarily* physically injured as a *result* of that physical act."

But, in *Domeny v. Commissioner*, 99 T.C.M. (CCH) 1047 (2010), the taxpayer suffered a flare-up of her multiple sclerosis symptoms as a result of a hostile work environment — for which she received a damage settlement from her employer. The court excluded the damages, stating that they were for an exacerbation of an existing illness. The court did not refer to the legislative history, stating that physical manifestations of emotional distress, such as insomnia, headaches, and stomach disorders, are not to be treated as physical injuries. Is the court saying that compensation for aggravation of an existing physical sickness is exempt under § 104(a)(2)?

[B]   Telling the Jury that the Award Is Not Taxable?

In *Norfolk & Western Ry. Co. v. Liepelt*, 444 U.S. 490 (1980), the Court held that it was error for the trial judge not to tell the jury in a Federal Employers' Liability Act case that the jury award was tax free under § 104. The dissent thought that this would reduce damage awards and, therefore, reduce the disincentive effect of tort damages on the defendant's behavior. State courts remain free to decide what to tell their juries about claims made under state law.

[C]   Does an Unwanted Physical Touching Lead to a "Physical Injury?"

Suppose your client has been subject to sex discrimination on the job (a nonphysical injury), which included a physical touching. This violates federal civil rights law, but it may also be a battery under state law. Wouldn't damages for battery still be excluded under § 104? Remember that most cases are settled out of court. How would you draft the settlement agreement to favor your client?

The first letter ruling from the IRS on this issue, excerpted below, does not appear very generous to the taxpayer regarding a physical touching (a battery) that does not result in an identifiable physical injury, such as cuts or bruises. But, as you read the ruling, see whether it is susceptible of a more generous reading, so that a more careful allegation of the harms resulting from the touching might have resulted in tax-free compensation. For example, suppose the taxpayer received compensation for emotional distress after the physical touching *because* the touching led to extreme pain, headache, or digestive problems, any of which required medical attention. What does the ruling say about harms occurring after the "First Pain Incident" and before the "First Physical Injury?"

PRIVATE LETTER RULING 200041022
(July 17, 2000)

C and C's corporation employed A in various capacities from date 1 through date 4. From date 2 through date 3, A was C's full-time driver and accompanied C on many trips. Early in this period, C acted in a friendly manner toward A. After a while, however, C began a slow progression of attempts to make sexual contact with A and made several suggestive or lewd remarks in A's presence. Also, early in this period, C physically touched A but these contacts did not result in any observable bodily harm (e.g., cuts, bruises, etc.) to A's body or cause extreme pain to A. Later, while on a road trip, C assaulted A causing what A represents was extreme pain (the "First Pain Incident"). After the First Pain Incident, A began to have headache and digestive problems, but two doctors could not find anything physically wrong. Your ruling request does not assert that these problems were due to the First Pain Incident or prior events. On a subsequent road trip, C also assaulted A, cutting her and biting her (the "First Physical Injury"). . . .

A subsequently retained the services of a law firm, which presented C with a complaint. The complaint alleged that C inflicted emotional and physical harm on A. A's complaint asserted causes of action, including sex discrimination and reprisal under Statute, battery, and intentional infliction of emotional distress. . . . C executed the Settlement Agreement with A under which C agreed to pay $z to settle all claims of A. The Settlement Agreement did not allocate the proceeds to any of the claims.

Section 1605 of the Small Business Job Protection Act of 1996 (the "1996 Act") restricted the exclusion from gross income provided by sec. 104(a)(2) to amounts received on account of personal physical injuries or physical sickness. H.R. CONF. REP. No. 737, 104th Cong., 2d Sess. 301 (1996), provides the following explanation of the amendment made by the 1996 Act:

> The House bill also specifically provides that emotional distress is not considered a physical injury or physical sickness. Thus the exclusion from gross income does not apply to any damages received . . . based on a claim of employment discrimination or injury to reputation accompanied by a claim of emotional distress. Because all damages received on account of physical injury or physical sickness are excludable from gross income, the exclusion from gross income applies to any damages received based on a claim of emotional distress that is attributable to physical injury or physical sickness. . . .

Footnote 56 of the Conference Report states, "It is intended that the term emotional distress includes symptoms (e.g., insomnia, headaches, stomach disorders) which may result from such distress." H.R. CONF. REP. No. 737 at 301. . . .

The term "personal physical injuries" is not defined in either sec. 104(a)(2) or the legislative history of the 1996 Act. However, we believe that direct unwanted or uninvited physical contacts resulting in observable bodily harms such as bruises, cuts, swelling, and bleeding are personal physical injuries under sec. 104(a)(2). See *Black's Law Dictionary* 1304 (Rev. 4th ed. 1968) which defines the term "physical injury" as "bodily harm or hurt, excluding mental distress, fright, or emotional disturbance."

In this case, C's uninvited and unwanted physical contacts with A prior to the First Pain Incident did not result in any observable harms (e.g., bruises, cuts, etc.) to A's body or cause A pain. . . . Thus, any damages A received for events occurring prior the First Pain Incident are not received on account of personal physical injuries or physical sickness under sec. 104(a)(2).

However, according to the representations submitted, A suffered several physical injuries within a relatively short period of time commencing with the First Physical Injury. Thus, under the facts of this case, damages A received under the Settlement Agreement for pain, suffering, emotional distress and reimbursement of medical expenses that are properly allocable to the period beginning with the First Physical Injury are attributable to and linked to the physical injuries A suffered and were received on account of personal physical injuries or physical sickness under sec. 104(a)(2).

[D] Punitive Damages

[1] Current Law

Two things happened in 1996 regarding the taxation of punitive damages arising from personal injuries.

First, the code was amended in 1996 prospectively (**§ 104(a)(2)** (**first parenthetical**)) to tax punitive damages (with a minor exception).

Second, the Supreme Court held that the pre-1996 version of **§ 104(a)(2)** did not exclude punitive damages under any circumstances. *O'Gilvie v. United States*, 519 U.S. 79 (1996) (punitive damages where woman died of toxic shock). The Court relied on the "on account of" language in **§ 104(a)(2)**, concluding that punitive damages were not received on account of the personal injury; they were imposed to penalize the defendant.

[2] Note on Statutory Interpretation — Drafting History

Prior to the 1996 amendment and the 1996 *O'Gilvie* decision, the tax treatment of punitive damages in personal injury cases had been much disputed. Punitive damages are, of course, **§ 61** income. But were they excluded by **§ 104**? A 1989 amendment had stated that the exclusion from income provided in the statute "shall not apply to any punitive damages in connection with a case not involving physical injury or physical sickness." This might have suggested, by negative implication, that punitive damages in a case which *did* involve a physical injury were tax free — expressio unius est exclusio alterius. But an earlier draft of the 1989 amendment (which did not pass) had stated that the exclusion "shall not apply to any punitive damages unless such damages are in connection with a case involving physical injury or physical sickness." This drafting history — starting with a prior draft clearly taxing punitive damages in nonphysical injury cases and clearly exempting such damages in physical injury cases but ending up with a final draft clearly taxing such damages only in nonphysical injury cases — firmly established that Congress meant to leave open the question whether the exclusion *did* apply to punitive damages in a case that involved physical injury.

Drafting history is usually considered a more reliable form of legislative history, because it is not an explicit statement about legislative intent. Explicit statements of legislative intent by legislators may be an attempt to achieve a legal result that is too controversial to pass if it were explicitly put into the law. By contrast, drafting history is more likely to reflect an unselfconscious effort to get language that will achieve a legislative goal.

[E] Interest

Another issue is whether interest on an otherwise exempt tort recovery is exempt or is instead taxable because it is not received (as the statute requires in § 104(a)(2)) "on account of a personal injury. The judicial decisions favor inclusion in income. *Kovacs v. Commissioner*, 100 T.C. 124 (1993), *affirmed without published opinion*, 25 F.3d 1048 (6th Cir. 1994). *See also Forest v. Commissioner*, 70 T.C.M. (CCH) 349 (1995) ("Statutory interest imposed on tort judgments . . . must be included in gross income under section 61(a)(4), even under circumstances in which the underlying damages are excludable under section 104(a)(2)"; interest not received "on account of personal injuries"), *affirmed no opinion*, 104 F.3d 348 (1st Cir. 1996); *Brabson v. United States*, 73 F.3d 1040 (10th Cir. 1996) (prejudgment interest compensates for lost time value of money, not for the injury itself); *Rozpad v. Commissioner*, 154 F.3d 1 (1st Cir. 1998) (same).

[F] Wage Replacement

Why does the statute exclude not only amounts traceable to pain and suffering and to medical expenses, but also replacement of lost income in cases of personal physical injury? Why isn't wage replacement taxed like the wages would have been taxed, just as damages replacing business profits would be taxed in a case not involving personal injury (e.g., trademark infringement)?

Evaluate the following arguments for not taxing wage replacement.

1. *Sorting out settlements.* Most tort claims are settled. If the settlement consisted of both taxable and nontaxable income, fraudulent allocations by the negotiating parties would occur, and the agency would have considerable difficulty sorting out the correct amounts.

2. *Undercompensation.* Tort plaintiffs are undercompensated, especially after subtraction of attorneys' fees. Tax exclusion indirectly makes up for undercompensation. The risk of undercompensation increases if juries are told that tort recoveries are tax exempt.

3. *Double taxation of lump sum awards.* Perhaps we *should* tax wage replacement, but there is a problem if we tax the *lump sum* paid to the taxpayer as compensation in year 0. For example, if the injury to the taxpayer causes $20 lost wages per year for five years (years 1 through 5), payment to the taxpayer of $20 per year in those years should be taxed. But what will be the impact of taxing a lump sum payment in year 0?

To answer that, you must first figure out what the lump sum will be — by discounting the future lost wages to present value. That depends on the interest rate (we assume 20% in the following example). The lump sum will be the amount needed to buy an annuity which will pay the plaintiff $20 per year for five years. The $20 annuity payment will include some of the lump sum investment and some interest earned on that investment. After five years, the investment will be gone. The payments, broken down into annual payments of principal and interest, are as follows (some rounding occurs to force the totals).

$60 invested at 20% to produce 5-year $20 annuity

Year	Principal	Interest	Total
1	8	12	20
2	9.5	10.5	20
3	11.5	8.5	20
4	14	6	20
5	17	3	20
	60	40	100

If we tax the $60 lump sum in year 0, the plaintiff cannot purchase an annuity producing $20 per year. If the plaintiff is in the 28% bracket, taxing the $60 leaves him with only $43.20 to invest. That will produce a five-year annuity of only $14.40 per year. That is not surprising. $14.40 is 72% of $20. By taxing the $60 at a 28% rate, you leave 72% of $60 to invest, so it produces only 72% of what $60 would have produced annually.

Of course, $14.40 is exactly the right amount that the plaintiff should end up with every year, if wage replacement was taxed — it is the amount the plaintiff would be left with after paying a 28% tax on $20. The trouble is that some of the $14.40 received as an annuity is taxable interest on the $43.20 investment. After taxing the interest, the taxpayer ends up with less than $14.40 per year.

Will exempting the $60 lump sum payment produce the "correct" result — $14.40 per year after tax? No. The exemption is too generous. By exempting the $60 in year 0, rather than just *deferring* tax on the $60, we allow the taxpayer to use the $60 invested in year 0 as deductible basis. Only the 20% interest on the investment is taxed, not the full $20 annual payment. Consequently, the taxpayer who invests the $60 ends up with less than $20 but more than $14.40 in each of the following 5 years.

If we really wanted to equate the plaintiff with someone earning $20 per year, we would let the plaintiff *defer* tax on the $60, if it were invested to produce future annual payments. Then we would tax the $20 annual payments, yielding $14.40 after tax.

There are other ways to modify the generous results under current law and reach the "right" $14.40 answer. *First*, do not pay plaintiff a lump sum. Instead, pay the plaintiff annually an amount equal to the "correct" *after* tax wages (that is, $14.40); then exempt those annual payments.

That seems to be the impact of § 130(a), (c). This section deals with so-called "structured settlements," in which plaintiffs do not collect a lump sum, but arrange to have the lump sum paid to an insurance company, which then makes annual payments to the plaintiff. If the case involves a physical injury or physical sickness, the lump sum is not taxed upon receipt by the insurance company. The periodic payments can then be paid out as a tax-free annuity to the plaintiff. (See the exemption for "periodic payments" in the § 104(a)(2) parenthetical.) Using the prior figures, the expectation is that the insurance company will receive $43.20 tax free, which it will invest to produce exempt annual payments of $14.40. Of course, the actual payments will depend on bargaining over the settlement of the tort claim, so we cannot be sure of the final outcome. All we can do is be sure we know the tax rules in light of which the bargaining will occur.

Second, tax the $60 lump sum. That leaves $43.20 to be invested. Then, exempt the interest portion of the annuity when it is collected each year. $14.40 is therefore, collected each year without further tax.

[G] Allocation of Damage Awards

The prior discussion has suggested several situations requiring allocation of lump sum awards (including settlements) between taxable and nontaxable amounts — e.g., punitive damages and interest vs. compensatory awards for physical injuries; compensation for state law battery vs. compensation for nonphysical federal civil rights injuries.

1. The following case dealt with the allocation issue in a narrow context but has more general implications. Are there opportunities for fraud in negotiating tort settlements?

In *Delaney v. Commissioner*, 70 T.C.M. (CCH) 353 (1995), *affirmed*, 99 F.3d 20 (1st Cir. 1996), the jury in a tort action returned a verdict in favor of the petitioner in the amount of $287,000, consisting of $175,000 in nontaxable damages and $112,000 in taxable interest. During the appeal, the suit was settled for $250,000. The government allocated 39% of the settlement to taxable interest, based on the interest percentage in the jury's award (112/287). The court made the following general observations about how damage award allocations should be made, obviously leaving a lot to be worked out in future case-by-case litigation.

> We have often been asked to decide the proper allocation of the proceeds of a settlement agreement in the context of section 104(a)(2). In cases involving a settlement agreement which contains an express allocation, such allocation is generally the most important factor in deciding whether a payment was made on account of a tortious personal injury for purposes

of exclusion under section 104(a)(2). It is well settled that express allocations in a settlement agreement will be respected to the extent that the agreement is entered into by the parties at arm's length and in good faith. . . .

If no lawsuit was instituted by the taxpayer, then we must consider any relevant documents, letters, and testimony. If a lawsuit was filed but not settled, or if a lawsuit was settled but no express allocations were made in the settlement agreement, we must consider the pleadings, jury awards, or any court orders or judgments. If a taxpayer's claims were settled and express allocations are contained in the settlement agreement, we must carefully consider such allocations. As we stated above, however, we are not required to respect the express allocations unless they were negotiated at arm's length between adverse parties. . . .

In the instant case . . . the jury verdict identified statutory interest as a specific component of the sum awarded to petitioner. The jury awarded petitioner $287,000, which consisted of $175,000 in tort damages and $112,000 in statutory prejudgment interest. The parties later settled for $250,000. Although the stipulation expressly provided that the settlement amount did not include interest, the record in the instant case . . . is devoid of evidence that such provision of the stipulation was the product of arm's-length negotiations between the parties. The only evidence in the record is that the parties did not discuss the tax implications of such aspect of the stipulation. Accordingly, we conclude that petitioners have failed to establish that there was no interest component to the settlement.

Based on petitioners' failure to meet their burden of proof, we sustain respondent's determination in the notice of deficiency with respect to the inclusion of $97,561 as statutory prejudgment interest. [Editor — ($112,000/$287,000) * $250,000 = $97,561.]

See also *Francisco v. United States*, 267 F.3d 303 (3d Cir. 2001), dealing with "delay damages," which are similar to prejudgment interest. Such damages were taxable because they were not "on account of" the personal injury. In this case, the delay damages were part of a settlement entered into after trial and before the appeals process was completed. The settlement made no allocation among the elements of the plaintiff's recovery. The court identified the delay damages as the percentage of the settlement equal to the percentages of the damages attributable to delay damages which were awarded in the trial.

2. In *Rozpad v. Commissioner*, 154 F.3d 1 (1st Cir. 1998), the court drew a distinction between allocating settlement amounts involving interest depending on whether the settlement predated or postdated a judgment. It stated that allocation was required when "the interest component can be delineated with accuracy and ease — as when there has been a jury verdict and an ensuing judgment that contains separate itemizations of damages and interest. . . ." However, in a *pre*-judgment settlement, the "interest component is difficult to delineate" and it is sensible for the court to exempt the entire settlement (assuming the compensation is otherwise tax exempt). The settlement takes into account so many items — nature of injury, pain, economic loss, defendant's assets, costs of trial, etc. — to

which the "parties typically will not assign independent monetary values. . . ." The court concluded that "the absence of an allocation renders it too speculative for a court, in hindsight, to assign independent weight to each relevant factor and isolate a reliable figure representing prejudgment interest."

3. Frequently, there are no numbers available to help allocate income between exempt and nonexempt amounts — neither a jury award nor amounts reliably set forth in a complaint nor explicit statements in a settlement. In any event, the IRS is likely to be suspicious of self-serving statements in a complaint and in a settlement agreement. The settlement agreement, however, has one virtue that might make the figures reliable — they are the result of agreement between the payor and the payee. If the parties are adverse from a tax point of view — that is, if a taxable amount to a payee would be deductible by the payor and an exempt amount to the payee would be nondeductible by the payor, then it is likely that the exempt amounts have not been artificially inflated because that would cost the payor a deduction. But if both exempt and nonexempt amounts are taxed the same way by the payor — both deductible or nondeductible — then the parties are not adverse and the settlement agreement remains suspect.

Are payor-payee negotiations in the personal injury context likely to make the parties adverse regarding income taxes? No. First, assume that the defendant is insured. All of the insurance company's payments will be deductible costs of doing business, so the insurance company's tax is unaffected by the allocation. Second, assume that the defendant self-insures or owes more than the insurance company will pay. In such cases, there are three possibilities: (1) the payments would all be deductible above the line expenses if the defendant's tort arose from business; (2) they would all be miscellaneous itemized deductions if the defendant's tort arose from employment activities (except that the interest would be considered nondeductible personal interest (§ 163(h)(2)(A), discussed in Chapter 16); or (3) they would all be nondeductible personal expenses if the defendant's tort arose from personal activities.

4. In *Amos v. Commissioner*, 86 T.C.M. (CCH) 663 (2003), the court had to allocate amounts between tax-free compensation and taxable amounts paid to the plaintiff to assure the defendant that the plaintiff would keep the results of the settlement confidential. The taxpayer was a photographer who had been kicked in the groin by Dennis Rodman of the Chicago Bulls after Rodman landed on him during a professional basketball game. The photographer's tort suit against Rodman was settled for $200,000. The settlement provided that it covered both compensation for personal injury and a promise by the photographer not to reveal the terms of the settlement. Violation of the nondisclosure provision would result in a $200,000 payment to Rodman.

The court held that, if the settlement agreement lacks express language allocating payments, the intent of the payor is critical to that determination; the character of the settlement payment hinges on the dominant reason of the payor in making the payment. Based on that test, the court adopted a 60/40 tax-free/taxable allocation, because the dominant reason for the settlement was to provide compensation for personal injury. The $200,000 liquidated damages provision for violating the nondisclosure agreement did not reduce the compensation to a minimal amount.

Isn't the court's analysis questionable? Assertions about the payor's intent, when there is no adverse tax consequence to the payor from making any particular allocation, tell us nothing about what really happened. If the payor can successfully allocate most of a deductible payment to tax-free compensation for the payee, the payee might take less of a total payment from the payor, in effect sharing the tax savings with the payor.

[H]   Deduction of Plaintiff's Attorneys' Fees

Suits for personal injuries will result in attorneys' fees. They give rise to several tax problems.

[1]   Are the Attorneys' Fees Deductible at All?

First, the plaintiff's attorneys' fees might not be deductible at all if the lawsuit has a personal origin (e.g., a car accident on vacation). But the better view is that the legal expenses are a deductible § 212(1) expense to collect nonbusiness income (analogous to the deduction of a spouse's expenses to collect alimony; *Wild v. Commissioner*, 42 T.C. 706 (1964)), unless they are allocable to tax exempt income.

Second, expenses allocable to the production of *tax exempt* income are generally not deductible under § 265(a)(1), discussed later in Chapter 15. This means that attorneys' fees to produce tax exempt awards are not deductible, but the fees allocable to the taxable portion of the award are deductible.

The simplest way to make the allocation is on the basis of the amount of the taxable and nontaxable awards. That is what the government did in *Delaney v. Commissioner*, 70 T.C.M. (CCH) 353 (1995), *affirmed*, 99 F.3d 20 (1st Cir. 1996):

$$\text{total attorneys' fees} \quad \times \quad \frac{\text{nonexempt income}}{\text{total award}} \quad = \quad \text{deductible expenses}$$

But is that necessarily the best way to allocate expenses in all cases? Suppose most of the work, based on time spent, was done in connection with recovering the taxable or nontaxable damages; or suppose the really hard work was related to the taxable or nontaxable recovery. Is the dollar amount of recovery just a presumptive figure?

[2]   Are Deductible Attorneys' Fees Miscellaneous Itemized Deductions?

Assuming attorneys' fees are deductible, are they deductible in computing AGI or are they itemized deductions, subject to the 2% floor? If the damages are for employment discrimination and are taxable, the related attorneys' fees would be miscellaneous itemized deductions, originating in the trade or business of being an employee, and therefore subject to the 2% floor. *See Alexander v. IRS*, 72 F.3d 938 (1st Cir. 1995). Similarly, if the lawsuit arose from a personal activity (a car accident on vacation), the fees would be deductible only under § 212(1), which is a miscellaneous itemized deduction subject to the 2% floor.

The obvious way to avoid these problems is to demonstrate that the business origin of an expense is not an employment relationship. For example, in *Guill v. Commissioner*, 112 T.C. 325 (1999), the taxpayer was an independent contractor (not an employee) who recovered taxable compensatory and punitive damages in a lawsuit arising out of a business relationship with an insurance company. Because the origin of the claim was a business that was not employment, the attorneys' fees allocable to punitive as well as actual damages were deductible as nonitemized business expenses.

In addition to the 2% floor, the taxpayer must also be concerned with the fact that the itemized deductions would be reduced by § 68, at the rate of 3% of AGI above an inflation-adjusted threshold.

These reductions in the taxpayer's deductions are not a disaster, although they do not result in the deduction that the taxpayer might have anticipated. The taxpayer has more serious problems, however. Under the alternative minimum tax (explained in Chapter 18), the attorneys' fees would not be deductible at all, if they were miscellaneous itemized deductions, which are not deductible in computing the alternative minimum tax base.

Congress came to the rescue of some of these taxpayers. **Section 62(e)** now permits an above the line deduction for attorneys' fees and court costs incurred in lawsuits involving most civil rights claims. However, the amendment was prospective, so the legal issued remained important for transactions prior to the effective date of the amendment. Moreover, the amendment did not apply to claims not involving civil rights. For example, in a defamation claim arising out of the employment relationship, the contingent fees paid to a lawyer would still be an itemized deduction.

[3] Are the Attorneys' Fees the Plaintiff's Income in the First Place?

Another way for the plaintiff to avoid deductibility problems is for the attorneys' fees not to be the plaintiff's income in the first place. Defendants usually make out checks to the plaintiff and attorney jointly so that the attorney is sure to get paid. But that by itself does not prevent the amount from being the plaintiff's income followed by a payment to the attorney for tax purposes. Under conventional assignment of income doctrine, it is not unusual for the taxpayer to be unable to get his hands on money but still be taxed on an amount paid to someone else. In addition, the fact that the taxpayer owes a debt to the attorney is irrelevant; a taxpayer cannot avoid gross income by asking someone to pay his income to his creditor. After some uncertainty in lower court decisions, the Supreme Court held that collection of attorneys' fees by the lawyer did not deflect income from the tort plaintiff. *Commissioner v. Banks*, 543 U.S. 426 (2005).

[I] Recovery by Holocaust Victims

Suppose a victim of the World War II Holocaust sues to recover for his or her injuries. Would the recoveries be for physical or nonphysical injury, dealt with by § 104(a)(2)? Whether or not taxable under, could the taxpayer still argue that these recoveries were not § 61 income, based on the old rulings exempting recoveries for personal losses, noted in Chapter 9.02[A]? Apparently, yes. Rev. Rul. 56-518, 1956-2 C.B. 25, excluded payments to compensate for "persecution which resulted in damage to life, body, health, liberty, or to professional or economic advancement" because they were "in the nature of reimbursement for the deprivation of civil or personal rights." As to compensation for property, however, the ruling said that taxation depended on "the facts and circumstances."

The 2001 Tax Bill explicitly excludes from income restitution payments made to World War II Holocaust victims (including their heirs and estates), beginning in tax year 2001. The exclusion applies to any amounts received by an individual on account of persecution by the Nazis for reasons related to race, religion, disability, or sexual orientation. The exclusion also applies to amounts received by such individuals for assets stolen or hidden from, or lost to, such individuals before, during, or immediately after World War II. Interest on any funds established to make the above payments is also excluded. This provision is found in sec. 803 of the 2001 Tax Bill and is not codified in the Internal Revenue Code of 1986. The law states that this provision should not lead to any inference about the correct tax treatment of amounts received prior to 2001.

Chapter 10

CHARITY

§ 10.01 CHARITABLE DEDUCTIONS

[A] Rationale

The idea behind the charitable deduction is to allow taxpayers to exclude from their tax base whatever they give to charitable organizations. A nearly complete list of § 170(c) charitable donees includes organizations "organized and operated exclusively for religious, charitable, scientific, literary, or educational purposes," or to foster amateur sports competition, or prevent cruelty to animals. What language in this statutory text applies to the following: a hospital? a museum? a legal aid society serving the poor? a public interest law firm litigating issues of public interest where private interests are unlikely to provide effective advocacy (Rev. Proc. 71-39, 1971-1 C.B. 575)? In addition, tax deductible contributions can be made to the United States and state and local governments.

The most common justification for the charitable deduction is that the contributions help to defray costs the government would otherwise incur. This is clearly too broad a statement. The government is not likely to directly finance many of the activities covered by § 170(c). For example, universities are assisted by government funding but it is unlikely that public funding would be at the scale of charitable giving. Moreover, some types of activities would probably not get any government money, such as educational journals, especially those with an ideological slant. Finally, direct government funding of religious groups would violate the Establishment Clause of the Constitution. Perhaps we could reformulate the "substitute for government activity" rationale for charitable deductions by stating that the general activity is one which the government wants to foster, but in a pluralistic society the particular choices should be left to private decisions.

The charitable deduction, therefore, seems to be a tax expenditure, though one for which eligibility is very loosely defined. The outlays are an expression of the donor's preferences, which are not analogous to those personal expense deductions (such as medical expenses), which arguably do no more than maintain some benchmark standard of living.

Another possible justification for the deduction is that gifts do not provide the donor with taxable personal consumption, because enjoyment of the power and pleasure of giving is not taxable. But why is that enjoyment less taxable than any other use of money? Isn't all enjoyment intangible, however acquired?

What about the donees of the gift? Shouldn't they pay tax and, if so, wouldn't it be a good idea to *disallow* the donor's deduction as a proxy for taxing the donee? The force of this suggestion is diminished, however, when we look at who benefits from charitable giving. Either the poor benefit from the gift (and they should not pay tax on the gift) or the general public benefits from the charitable activities (and it is questionable whether anyone ought to be taxed on such widely dispersed benefits). The donor's deduction should, therefore, stand or fall on its own merits, uncomplicated by considerations related to the donee.

[B]   Deductions as the Incentive Mechanism

Any incentive provision invites the usual questions about whether a deduction is the proper method to encourage the activity. For example, why should the taxpayer in the 35% bracket save 35 cents for every one dollar given, while taxpayers in the 15% bracket save only 15 cents per dollar given? In effect, the 35% bracket taxpayer can give up 65 cents of after-tax income and force the government to match it with a 35 cent gift to the charity of his choice, while the 15% bracket taxpayer gives up 85 cents of after-tax income to force the government to contribute a 15 cent gift to his favorite charity. But that is always the effect of a deduction in a progressive tax rate structure. The question is whether it is needed as an incentive to engage in desirable behavior.

It is arguable that the well-off need the large benefits of a deduction to encourage them to give. Remember that charitable giving is likely to be low on the taxpayer's list of consumer preferences. The gift precludes other uses of the money, which is compounded if the donor must pay taxes out of other income on the amount of the gift. Lower income taxpayers might not need much of an incentive because they are more likely to give to the charity of their choice, such as a church. Consequently, the upside-down effects of a deduction in giving more dollar benefits to higher bracket taxpayers per dollar of expenditure is not necessarily inefficient as social policy, whatever its distributional effects.

[C]   Mechanics

Payment. Technically, a deduction requires a "payment." § 170(a)(1). "Payment" includes out-of-pocket expenses incurred by a taxpayer while helping a charity (for example, transportation to get to a charitable organization's meeting). However, depreciation is not a payment, which is why use of a car is not a deductible payment; Rev. Proc. 80-7, ¶ 3.02, 1980-1 C.B. 590.

Providing personal services without charge is also not a deductible payment — for example, a doctor volunteering some time in a local clinic. **Treas. Reg. § 1.170A-1(g).** The free service provider is not, however, disadvantaged because the value of the services is not included in income. In fact, one rationale for the charitable deduction is that it equates the free service provider (no income, no deduction) with someone who earns money and gives it to charity (income minus deduction).

Percentage limits on deduction. Taxpayers can deduct charitable contributions *to* certain organizations, up to 50% of their adjusted gross income (AGI). These 50% organizations (referred to a "public" charities) are listed in § 170(b)(1)(A), and include churches, schools, hospitals, a governmental unit, and organizations that receive a substantial part of their support from the government or the public.

Gifts to other charitable organizations can be deducted up to the lesser of: (1) 30% of AGI; or (2) 50% of AGI minus gifts to 50% organizations. **§ 170(b)(1)(B).** These "30% organizations" or "private" charities" may be private foundations that engage in charitable activities but do not receive a substantial part of their support from the government or the public. These private foundations can be huge — such as the Ford Foundation.

For example, a taxpayer with $100,000 AGI gives $40,000 to a university (a public charity), and $20,000 to a private charity — an educational organization that publishes historical studies. After deducting the $40,000 gift to the university, the donor has only 10% of AGI left over to support a deduction to the private charity — $10,000 in the example.

"To" or "for use of". A small statutory wrinkle with potentially large consequences imposes a 30%-of-AGI limit on gifts "for the use of" a charity (even for the use of a public charity). A gift in trust for a charity is "for the use of" the charity.

Carryover. Deductions that exceed the percentage ceilings can be carried forward for five years.

Itemized deduction. The charitable deduction is an itemized deduction, *not* subject to the 2% floor. There are proposals to make small dollar cash gifts above the line deductions (available even if the standard deduction is elected). For example, the House Ways and Means Committee reported out a bill in early June 2001 that would allow an above the line charitable deduction of $25 for single taxpayers and $50 for married taxpayers. The provision is referred to as "faith-based," because it is aimed primarily at contributions to churches.

Corporations. The above rules apply to individuals. Corporations are subject to different rules. They can deduct 10% of their taxable income as charitable gifts. The AGI and itemized deduction concepts are inapplicable to corporations. **§ 170(b)(2).**

No business deduction for gifts in excess of ceiling. Charitable deductions that exceed the percentage ceiling cannot be deducted as business expenses. **§ 162(b).**

Appreciated property. The deduction for charitable contributions of appreciated property is subject to limitations explained later in this chapter.

Procedure to obtain tax exemption. Requesting tax-exempt status from the IRS is usually a condition of becoming a tax-deductible organization. Once on the IRS published list, donors can take deductions for gifts to that organization unless they are aware of circumstances that would result in loss of exemption. Eligibility to receive tax deductible contributions is so important that it is one of the few situations in which disagreement with the IRS can be appealed to a court prior to paying tax or receiving a deficiency notice that tax is due. **§ 7428.**

Donor recordkeeping. The law requires the donor to keep records of charitable contributions. Section 170(f)(17) states:

> Recordkeeping.—No deduction shall be allowed under subsection (a) for any contribution of a cash, check, or other monetary gift unless the donor maintains as a record of such contribution a bank record or a written communication from the donee showing the name of the donee organization, the date of the contribution, and the amount of the contribution.

[D]   Working for Nothing

Some taxpayers are members of a religious order and take a vow of poverty. Although they have regular jobs, they direct that their entire pay checks be given to the religious order. In such cases, the taxpayer is the income earner and must include the earnings in gross income, even though all of the income is deflected to the charity. This is an application of the assignment of income rules discussed in Chapter 2. Examples include: a nurse-practitioner for the federal government (*Schuster v. Commissioner*, 84 T.C. 764 (1985), *affirmed*, 800 F.2d 672 (7th Cir. 1986)); Associate Professor of Religious Studies at Virginia University (*Fogarty v. United States*, 780 F.2d 1005 (Fed. Cir. 1986)); and a lawyer working for a law firm (Rev. Rul. 77-290, 1977-2 C.B. 26).

Sometimes the taxpayer acts as agent of the order and would not be taxed on the payment to the order. Rev. Rul. 77-290, 1977-2 C.B. 26. That is hardly a startling rule; no agent is taxed on the principal's money. For example, the order might provide one of its employees to perform services for the central business office of the church that supervises the order. When the taxpayer performs that task, payment to the order is not the taxpayer's income.

Rev. Rul. 74-581, 1974-2 C.B. 75, seems to be a closer case. Student clinics in a law school program handle criminal matters and faculty members are assigned as counsel, assisted by students whom the faculty supervise. The faculty member is sometimes entitled to payment for legal services under the provisions of the Criminal Justice Act of 1964. Each faculty member has agreed, as a condition of participation in the program, that any payments will be endorsed to the law school, because the time spent in supervising work of students on these cases and in the representation of the client is part of the faculty member's teaching duties for which the faculty member is already compensated by an annual salary. The ruling concludes that, in this situation, the faculty member is working solely as an agent of the law school, and realizes no personal gain from payments for services in representing the indigent defendants. It cites Rev. Rul. 65-282, 1965-2 C.B. 21, which holds that statutory legal fees received by attorneys for representing indigent defendants are not includible in gross income where the attorneys, pursuant to their employment contracts, immediately turn the fees over to their employer, a legal aid society; and Rev. Rul. 58-220, 1958-1 C.B. 26, which holds that the amount of the checks received by a physician from patients treated in the hospital by which he is employed full-time, which he is required to endorse over to the hospital, is not includible in his gross income.

The government cares whether a deductible contribution is first included in the taxpayer's gross income and then deducted, because of the 50%-of-AGI ceiling on charitable deductions. Does the 50% ceiling make sense for a taxpayer who takes a vow of poverty?

[E] Charitable Giving and the Assignment of Income Doctrine

A gift of property transfers the income from that property to the donee, charitable or otherwise. This is true even when the property is inventory, on which any gain would be ordinary income. *Campbell v. Prothro*, 209 F.2d 331 (5th Cir. 1954). By contrast, income accrued prior to the gift cannot be shifted to the donee. *Tatum v. Commissioner*, 400 F.2d 242 (5th Cir. 1968) (accrued rental income cannot be deflected to assignee).

Would the policy favoring charitable gifts tilt the decision against application of the assignment of income doctrine in a close case? Consider the following situations.

1. In *Commissioner v. Giannini*, 129 F.2d 638 (9th Cir. 1942), Mr. Giannini and his wife owned all the stock of a corporation. He was President of the corporation and was entitled to a large amount of compensation for services performed in 1927. When he learned how large the amount was for the first half of the year, he refused further compensation for that year. The refusal occurred before December 31, 1927. In February, 1928, the corporation donated what Giannini would have gotten as compensation for the rest of the year 1927 to a charity, responding to Mr. Gainnini's wishes that the money be used for charitable purposes. The court did not tax Mr. Giannini on the amount of the gift. Presumably, if Mr. Giannini had simply told his corporation to give his salary to charity, that salary would have been included in his gross income.

2. In Notice 2001-69, 2001-2 C.B. 491, the IRS discussed programs adopted by employers in the aftermath of the September 11, 2001 terrorist attacks, called "leave-based donation programs." Under these programs, an employee would forgo vacation, sick, or personal leave in exchange for employer contributions of amounts to tax-deductible organizations. The Service stated that it would not assert that such payments were gross income or wages to the employee, provided that the payments were made to such organizations before January 1, 2003. The government refused to extend this benefit beyond January 1, 2003. However, in 2005-40 I.R.B. 622, Notice 2005-68, the government did extend the same tax break for leave-based donation programs in the wake of Katrina, for payments made before January 1, 2007.

§ 10.02 TAX-EXEMPT ORGANIZATIONS

[A] In General

Tax-exempt organizations are a much broader category than the § 170(c) tax-deductible organizations. Many of them are listed in § 501(c). For example, labor unions, business leagues, and social clubs are exempt from income tax (except that social clubs are taxed on investment income). §§ 501(c)(5), (6), (7), 512(a)(3). Dues paid to these organizations are not deductible under § 170 and can only be deducted if they are business expenses. **Section 170(c)** and **§ 501(c)(3)** are almost identical, so people often refer to § 501(c)(3) tax-exempt organizations as those to whom tax deductible contributions can be made, even though § 170(c) is the accurate citation.

The § 501(c)(3) tax exemption for hospitals is now subject to additional requirements (§ 501(r)). The hospital must engage in a community health needs assessment every three years and adopt an implementation strategy to meet those needs; adopt and publicize a financial assistance policy and provide emergency medical treatment regardless of eligibility under the financial assistance policy; and withhold certain bill collection activities until it provides the patient with information about the financial assistance policy and determines the patient's eligibility under that policy.

Section 501(c)(4) provides tax exemption for organizations that promote social welfare, operated primarily to bring about civic betterments and social improvements, but contributions to such organizations are not deductible under § 170(c). The distinction between **(c)(4)** and **(c)(3)** organizations is murky. *Compare* Rev. Rul. 78-68, 1978-1 C.B. 149 (an organization formed to provide public transportation to isolated areas of town not served by existing city bus systems, thereby enabling low income residents to commute to work, is a **(c)(3)** organization); *with* Rev. Rul. 78-69, 1978-1 C.B. 156 (organization providing suburban residents with bus service during rush hours to supplement regular bus service to the city is a **(c)(4)** organization).

[B] Limits

[1] Profitmaking; Unrelated Business Income

[a] In General

There is no general rule prohibiting a tax-exempt charitable organization from making profits, as long as the profit-making activity does not undermine its charitable objective. It might undermine that objective if activities were conducted primarily with an eye to making profits, as in the case of a for-profit hospital or a blood bank organized to make money.

There is, however, a separate tax on the business income of otherwise tax-exempt charities when that income is unrelated to the purposes for which the exemption was granted. § 511–14. A famous example is a macaroni factory owned by New York University. A current example is some of the profits from running a museum gift shop. These shops sell some items that are related (reproductions) and others which are unrelated (souvenir items with a museum logo). See G.C.M. 38949, discussed in 18 TAX NOTES 287 (1983).

The existence of an unrelated business activity does not necessarily result in taxable profits. The organization's overhead, including depreciation on the building, must be allocated to the unrelated business activity. The result may be very little net income.

Unrelated business income is taxed only if it is "regularly carried on." One court held that this requirement prevented taxing advertising revenues from publishing the NCAA basketball program. The tournament lasted only a few weeks and was not serious competition for sports magazines. *NCAA v. Commissioner*, 914 F.2d 1417 (10th Cir. 1990).

The general idea behind taxing unrelated business income is that exempt organizations would otherwise have an unfair competitive advantage and would be encouraged to buy up for-profit businesses. These are empirical claims about the impact of the tax law that may or may not be true. A more important question may be whether some exempt organizations should be exempt in the first place. Some exempt organizations no longer need the exemption as an incentive to provide goods and services that would be under supplied (Are hospitals an example?); and some of the goods and services provided by tax-exempt organizations have a distinctly highbrow audience (Is public television TV an example?).

[b]   Advertising Income

Another example of unrelated business income is advertising revenue in an otherwise tax-exempt publication (such as National Geographic), if the ads are displayed on the basis of the advertiser's ability to pay rather than educating the public in accordance with the magazine's exempt purpose. *See United States v. American College of Physicians*, 475 U.S. 834 (1986).

Recent controversy has arisen over whether revenues received for football bowl sponsorship are unrelated business income (analogous to advertising revenue). A private business corporation, for example, pays to sponsor a bowl game and has its name prominently displayed on the playing field, scoreboard, and on player's uniforms. Public Television also receives contributions and then broadcasts acknowledgments that prominently display the donor's names, logos, and brief messages when the program begins. After considerable publicity, the government proposed regulations that virtually gave up trying to tax such income as unrelated business income. 58 FED. REG. 5687-02 (Jan. 22, 1993). As long as the contribution was not contingent on television ratings or attendance, there was no comparative information about a competitor's products, and no special treatment of the donor or its officials, the contributions were usually treated as tax-free "acknowledgment" income rather than taxable unrelated advertising business income.

Then Congress got into the act. The 1997 Tax Act (§ 513(i)) specifies that unrelated business income does not include "qualified sponsorship payments," which it defines to mean payments for which there is no arrangement or expectation of a "substantial return benefit," other than use or acknowledgment of the payor's name or logo or product lines. Moreover:

(1) the payee cannot provide messages containing qualitative or comparative language, price information, indications of savings or value, an endorsement, or an inducement to purchase, sell, or use the payor's products or services; and

(2) any payment cannot be conditioned on level of attendance at events, broadcast ratings, or other factors indicating public exposure.

[2] For the Benefit of an Individual

Even if the organization is not organized to make a profit, it is not exempt if the net earnings "inure to the benefit of any private shareholder or individual." § 70(c)(2)(c). Mail order churches often run afoul of this provision when the founder siphons off too much of the receipts for personal benefit. *See* Founding Church of Scientology v. United States, 412 F.2d 1197 (Ct. Cl. 1969).

In *United Cancer Council, Inc. v. Commissioner*, 165 F.3d 1173 (7th Cir. 1999), the court held that a charity (UCC) that paid about 90% of its funds as a fee to a professional fundraiser (W & H) was not one in which "the net earnings . . . inure[d] to the benefit of any private shareholder or individual," a statutory phrase interpreted to mean an "insider of the charity." The court noted that the IRS did not contend that any part of UCC's earnings found its way into the pockets of any members of the charity's board; the board members, who were medical professionals, lawyers, judges, and bankers, served without compensation. Nor did it contend that any members of the board were owners, managers, or employees of W & H, or relatives or even friends of any of W & H's owners, managers, or employees. The government conceded that the contract between charity and fundraiser was negotiated at arm's length, but argued that the contract was so advantageous to W & H and so disadvantageous to UCC that the charity must be deemed to have surrendered the control of its operations and earnings to the noncharitable enterprise that it hired to raise money for it.

The court explained the high ratio of payments to contributions on the ground that the charity had been on the brink of bankruptcy in 1984 because of defection by member societies to the American Cancer Society. It, therefore, negotiated a contract that provided a high ratio of expenses to net charitable receipts to a fund-raising specialist in order to survive. The court concluded that "the ratio of expenses to net charitable receipts is unrelated to the issue of inurement," noting that the inurement issue would not exist if "UCC had spent $26 million to raise $28 million but the $26 million had been scattered among a host of suppliers rather than concentrated on one."

Judge Posner's opinion explained that "[c]haritable organizations are plagued by incentive problems" because "[n]obody owns the right to the profits and, therefore, no one has the spur to efficient performance that the lure of profits creates"; donors "do not have a profit incentive to monitor the care with which the charity's funds are used." Posner hinted that tax law might have "a role to play in assuring the prudent management of charities" through application of the "operated for charitable purposes" test, but distinguished this from the "inurement" test.

[3] Political Activity

The charitable deduction is conditioned on the organization not engaging in certain political activities, discussed in Chapter 14.03[E].

[C] Section 501(c)(3) — Defining "Charitable"

[1] Public Policy

BOB JONES UNIVERSITY v. UNITED STATES
United States Supreme Court
461 U.S. 574 (1983)

CHIEF JUSTICE BURGER delivered the opinion of the Court. . . .

I

A

Until 1970, the Internal Revenue Service granted tax-exempt status to private schools, without regard to their racial admissions policies, under § 501(c)(3) of the Internal Revenue Code, and granted charitable deductions for contributions to such schools under § 170 of the Code. . . .

The [IRS'] revised policy on discrimination was formalized in Rev. Rul. 71-447, 1971-2 C.B. 230,

> "Both the courts and the Internal Revenue Service have long recognized that the statutory requirement of being 'organized and operated exclusively for religious, charitable, . . . or educational purposes' was intended to express the basic common law concept [of 'charity']. . . . All charitable trusts, educational or otherwise, are subject to the requirement that the purpose of the trust may not be illegal or contrary to public policy."

Based on the "national policy to discourage racial discrimination in education," the IRS ruled that "a private school not having a racially nondiscriminatory policy as to students is not 'charitable' within the common law concepts reflected in sections 170 and 501(c)(3) of the Code."

The application of the IRS construction of these provisions to petitioners, two private schools with racially discriminatory admissions policies, is now before us. . . .

[Editor — The Court noted that, until 1971, "Negroes were completely excluded from Bob Jones University; from 1971–1975, "Negroes" married within their race were accepted; and since mid-1975, students dating or married outside their race were expelled.]

II

A

Section 501(c)(3) provides that "[c]orporations . . . organized and operated exclusively for religious, charitable . . . or educational purposes" are entitled to tax exemption. Petitioners argue that the plain language of the statute guarantees them tax-exempt status. They emphasize the absence of any language in the statute expressly requiring all exempt organizations to be "charitable" in the common law sense, and they contend that the disjunctive "or" separating the categories in § 501(c)(3) precludes such a reading. Instead, they argue that if an institution falls within one or more of the specified categories it is automatically entitled to exemption, without regard to whether it also qualifies as "charitable." The Court of Appeals rejected that contention and concluded that petitioners' interpretation of the statute "tears section 501(c)(3) from its roots."

It is a well-established canon of statutory construction that a court should go beyond the literal language of a statute if reliance on that language would defeat the plain purpose of the statute:

> "The general words used in the clause . . . , taken by themselves, and literally construed, without regard to the object in view, would seem to sanction the claim of the plaintiff. But this mode of expounding a statute has never been adopted by any enlightened tribunal — because it is evident that in many cases it would defeat the object which the Legislature intended to accomplish. And it is well settled that, in interpreting a statute, the court will not look merely to a particular clause in which general words may be used, but will take in connection with it the whole statute . . . and the objects and policy of the law . . . ." Brown v. Duchesne, 15 L. Ed. 595, 19 How. 183, 194 (1857).

Section 501(c)(3), therefore, must be analyzed and construed within the framework of the Internal Revenue Code and against the background of the Congressional purposes. Such an examination reveals unmistakable evidence that, underlying all relevant parts of the Code, is the intent that entitlement to tax exemption depends on meeting certain common law standards of charity — namely, that an institution seeking tax-exempt status must serve a public purpose and not be contrary to established public policy.

This "charitable" concept appears explicitly in § 170 of the Code. That section contains a list of organizations virtually identical to that contained in § 501(c)(3). It is apparent that Congress intended that list to have the same meaning in both sections. In § 170, Congress used the list of organizations in defining the term "charitable contributions." On its face, therefore, § 170 reveals that Congress' intention was to provide tax benefits to organizations serving charitable purposes. The form of § 170 simply makes plain what common sense and history tell us: in enacting both § 170 and § 501(c)(3), Congress sought to provide tax benefits to charitable organizations, to encourage the development of private institutions that serve a useful public purpose or supplement or take the place of public institutions of the same kind.

Tax exemptions for certain institutions thought beneficial to the social order of the country as a whole, or to a particular community, are deeply rooted in our history, as in that of England. The origins of such exemptions lie in the special privileges that have long been extended to charitable trusts. . . .

What little floor debate occurred on the charitable exemption provision of the 1894 Act and similar sections of later statutes leaves no doubt that Congress deemed the specified organizations entitled to tax benefits because they served desirable public purposes. See, e.g., 26 Cong. Rec. 585–86 (1894); id., at 1727. In floor debate on a similar provision in 1917, for example, Senator Hollis articulated the rationale:

> "For every dollar that a man contributes to these public charities, educational, scientific, or otherwise, the public gets 100 percent." 55 id., at 6728 (1917). . . .

In enacting the Revenue Act of 1938, ch. 289, 52 Stat. 447 (1938), Congress expressly reconfirmed this view with respect to the charitable deduction provision:

> "The exemption from taxation of money and property devoted to charitable and other purposes is based on the theory that the Government is compensated for the loss of revenue by its relief from financial burdens which would otherwise have to be met by appropriations from other public funds, and by the benefits resulting from the promotion of the general welfare." H.R. REP. No. 1860, 75th Cong., 3d Sess. 19 (1938).

A corollary to the public benefit principle is the requirement, long recognized in the law of trusts, that the purpose of a charitable trust may not be illegal or violate established public policy. . . .

When the Government grants exemptions or allows deductions all taxpayers are affected; the very fact of the exemption or deduction for the donor means that other taxpayers can be said to be indirect and vicarious "donors." Charitable exemptions are justified on the basis that the exempt entity confers a public benefit — a benefit which the society or the community may not itself choose or be able to provide, or which supplements and advances the work of public institutions already supported by tax revenues. History buttresses logic to make clear that, to warrant exemption under § 501(c)(3), an institution must fall within a category specified in that section and must demonstrably serve and be in harmony with the public interest. The institution's purpose must not be so at odds with the common community conscience as to undermine any public benefit that might otherwise be conferred.

B

We are bound to approach these questions with full awareness that determinations of public benefit and public policy are sensitive matters with serious implications for the institutions affected; a declaration that a given institution is not "charitable" should be made only where there can be no doubt that the activity involved is contrary to a fundamental public policy. But there can no longer be any doubt that racial discrimination in education violates deeply and widely accepted views of elementary justice. Prior to 1954, public education in many places still was conducted under the pall of *Plessy v. Ferguson*, 163 U.S. 537 (1896); racial segregation in primary and secondary education prevailed in many parts of the country. This Court's decision in *Brown v. Board of Education*, 347 U.S. 483 (1954), signaled an end to that era. Over the past quarter of a century, every pronouncement of this Court and myriad Acts of Congress and Executive Orders attest a firm national policy to prohibit racial segregation and discrimination in public education.

[Editor — The Court then recounts the various cases, statutes, and executive orders implementing this policy.]

Few social or political issues in our history have been more vigorously debated and more extensively ventilated than the issue of racial discrimination, particularly in education. Given the stress and anguish of the history of efforts to escape from the shackles of the "separate but equal" doctrine of Plessy v. Ferguson, it cannot be said that educational institutions that, for whatever reasons, practice racial discrimination, are institutions exercising "beneficial and stabilizing influences in community life," or should be encouraged by having all taxpayers share in their support by way of special tax status.

There can, thus, be no question that the interpretation of § 170 and § 501(c)(3) announced by the IRS in 1970 was correct. . . . Racially discriminatory educational institutions cannot be viewed as conferring a public benefit within the "charitable" concept discussed earlier, or within the Congressional intent underlying § 170 and § 501(c)(3). . . .

D

The actions of Congress since 1970 leave no doubt that the IRS reached the correct conclusion in exercising its authority. It is, of course, not unknown for independent agencies or the Executive Branch to misconstrue the intent of a statute; Congress can and often does correct such misconceptions, if the courts have not done so. Yet for a dozen years Congress has been made aware — acutely aware — of the IRS rulings of 1970 and 1971. As we noted earlier, few issues have been the subject of more vigorous and widespread debate and discussion in and out of Congress than those related to racial segregation in education. Sincere adherents advocating contrary views have ventilated the subject for well over three decades. Failure of Congress to modify the IRS rulings of 1970 and 1971, of which Congress was, by its own studies and by public discourse, constantly reminded; and Congress' awareness of the denial of tax-exempt status for racially discriminatory schools when enacting other and related legislation make out an unusually strong case of legislative acquiescence in and ratification by implication of the 1970 and 1971 rulings.

Ordinarily, and quite appropriately, courts are slow to attribute significance to the failure of Congress to act on particular legislation. We have observed that "unsuccessful attempts at legislation are not the best of guides to legislative intent." Here, however, we do not have an ordinary claim of legislative acquiescence. Only one month after the IRS announced its position in 1970, Congress held its first hearings on this precise issue. Equal Educational Opportunity: Hearings Before the Senate Select Comm. on Equal Educational Opportunity, 91st Cong., 2d Sess. 1991

(1970). Exhaustive hearings have been held on the issue at various times since then. These include hearings in February 1982, after we granted review in this case.

Non-action by Congress is not often a useful guide, but the non-action here is significant. During the past 12 years there have been no fewer than 13 bills introduced to overturn the IRS interpretation of § 501(c)(3). Not one of these bills has emerged from any committee, although Congress has enacted numerous other amendments to § 501 during this same period, including an amendment to § 501(c)(3) itself. Tax Reform Act of 1976, Pub. L. 94-455, § 1313(a), 90 Stat. 1520, 1730 (1976). It is hardly conceivable that Congress — and in this setting, any Member of Congress — was not abundantly aware of what was going on. In view of its prolonged and acute awareness of so important an issue, Congress' failure to act on the bills proposed on this subject provides added support for concluding that Congress acquiesced in the IRS rulings of 1970 and 1971.

The evidence of Congressional approval of the policy embodied in Revenue Ruling 71-447 goes well beyond the failure of Congress to act on legislative proposals. Congress affirmatively manifested its acquiescence in the IRS policy when it enacted the present § 501(i) of the Code, Act of October 20, 1976, Pub. L. 94-568, 90 Stat. 2697 (1976). That provision denies tax-exempt status to social clubs whose charters or policy statements provide for "discrimination against any person on the basis of race, color, or religion." Both the House and Senate committee reports on that bill articulated the national policy against granting tax exemptions to racially discriminatory private clubs. S. REP. No. 1318, 94th Cong., 2d Sess., 8 (1976); H.R. REP. No. 1353, 94th Cong., 2d Sess., 8 (1976), U.S. Code Cong. & Admin. News 1976, p. 6051.

Even more significant is the fact that both reports focus on this Court's affirmance of *Green v. Connally*, 330 F. Supp. 1150 (DC 1971), affirmed sub nom., *Coit v. Green*, 404 U.S. 997 (1971), as having established that "discrimination on account of race is inconsistent with an educational institution's tax-exempt status." S. REP. No. 1318, supra, at 7–8 and n. 5; H.R. REP. No. 1353, supra, at 8 and n. 5, U.S. Code Cong. & Admin. News, p. 6058. These references in Congressional committee reports on an enactment denying tax exemptions to racially discriminatory private social clubs cannot be read other than as indicating approval of the standards applied to racially discriminatory private schools by the IRS subsequent to 1970, and specifically of Revenue Ruling 71-447.

[Editor — Portions of the opinion dealing with the taxpayer's free exercise of religion claim are omitted.]

The judgments of the Court of Appeals are, accordingly,

Affirmed.

QUESTIONS AND COMMENTS

1. The Supreme Court has held that it is unconstitutional for an all-male state-supported school (Virginia Military Academy) to deny admission on gender grounds. *United States v. Virginia*, 518 U.S. 515 (1996). Does this mean that gender discrimination is as violative of public policy as race discrimination for

purposes of the charitable deduction? An earlier Technical Advice Memorandum 7744007 held that the "Federal courts have not established that sex discrimination is clearly contrary to public policy" but is instead subject to a "rationality test." Is that what you learned in constitutional law?

2. Are schools exempt if admissions policies limit students to: all female; all African-American?

3. Would anyone have standing to force the government to tax someone on the ground that the school should not be tax-exempt?

[2] Note on Statutory Interpretation

[a] Literal Language vs. Plain Purpose

The critical interpretive step in the *Bob Jones* case was to find a statutory requirement that all tax-exempt organizations listed in § 501(c)(3) be "charitable," even though the statutory text already refers to both "charitable *or* educational" organizations. The Court finds that this "charitable" requirement is the "plain purpose" of the law. What justifies reading a general "charitable" requirement into the entire list of exempt organizations; is it the historical context of the statute?

This is not the first time you have seen a court read the statute in light of its "spirit" or "purpose." One criticism of doing so in this case is that the text posed the following problem. The statute already explicitly referred to a "charitable" institution in § 501(c)(3). By reading "charitable" into the statute, the Court seemed to make the explicit statutory reference superfluous. But that textual difficulty evaporates if the charitable "purpose" and the reference to "charitable" in the text serve different purposes. And they do. The "charitable purpose" assures that the exempt organizations do not violate public policy. The reference to "charitable" in the statutory text is a catch-all category that provides a tax exemption for activities not specifically listed. For example, the list includes educational, scientific, and religious organizations, but where does it identify a public interest law firm (which is a § 501(c)(3) "charitable" organization)?

[b] Historical Context and Evolving Meaning

Even if the Court can read into the statute a requirement that tax-deductible organizations be "charitable," based on historical context, how can nondiscrimination be one of those requirements? The statute was originally adopted (in 1894) when segregation was the law and practice of the land. One answer is that statutes, like the common law, can change meaning. But that is controversial. In the charitable context, however, it is not controversial. The concept of "charity" at common law had always evolved. In other words, the hard part was reading a common law requirement that the organization be "charitable" into the statute (in the sense of not violating public policy). Once that was done, the common law concept incorporated into the statute could evolve, just like any other common law concept. And, surely, the modern concept of "charity" was not satisfied by an organization that discriminated on the basis of race.

[c]   Legislative Inaction

We earlier discussed the reenactment doctrine in connection with the *Glenshaw Glass* case — Chapter 3.06[A][1]. We noted that, even assuming legislative awareness of an intervening case or agency rule that interprets a statute, the mere fact of reenacting the statute does not necessarily mean that the legislature ratifies the intervening interpretation. Sometimes courts go further and cite legislative inaction as evidence of approval of an intervening interpretation. The appeal to the inaction doctrine by the Court in *Bob Jones* — that inaction signified approval of the Revenue Rulings prohibiting discrimination — has proven to be even more controversial than its reading of "charitable" into the statute.

As a general matter, how can legislative inaction ratify a prior agency interpretation of a statute? First, inaction is not the constitutional route by which law is made. Even if the legislature is aware of the agency's interpretation — which is often not the case but was true in the *Bob Jones* case — inaction does not constitute passage of a law and signature by the President. At least a reenactment formally involves passage of a law; inaction does not even have that to recommend it.

Second, considering the way the legislative process works, there are many reasons for inaction that have nothing to do with approval. For example: legislatures are busy; or inaction may be the result of a committee bottling up proposals to reject the agency rule, rather than majority approval. In *Bob Jones*, it is quite possible that liberal committee chairs prevented bills overriding the Revenue Rulings from reaching the floor of Congress.

[d]   Legislative History

The Court also cites Committee Reports supporting the view that schools that practice racial discrimination are not tax-exempt. Legislative history is frequently relied on by courts, especially when the statute is unclear (as this one arguably was). The strongest case for relying on the legislative history is that it provides guidance about statutory meaning from people who are likely to know a lot about how to implement the legislative policy. In this respect, legislative history is similar to agency regulations, to which courts often defer.

The problem with relying on legislative history is both constitutional and institutional. Constitutionally, the text of legislative history has not been passed by Congress and signed by the President. This is less of an obstacle than it seems, however, because a court is not deferring to the history as it would to a statutory text; it is merely using it to help interpret legislation. After all, agency rules are also not passed by Congress but courts use them to interpret legislation.

Institutionally, the pragmatic objection to relying on legislative history is that it can be manipulated to achieve a result that is too controversial to pass. Or, somewhat less dramatically, legislative history can contain statements that are so politically controversial that they should only be legislated at the level of an explicit statutory text, not left to committee reports. An argument can be made that tax-exemption policy regarding organizations that engage in racial discrimination should not be made at the level of a legislative committee.

[e] Statutory Analogies

Yet another statutory interpretation issue in *Bob Jones* is raised by the citation to § 501(i). That section prohibited tax exemption for social clubs with written statements providing for discrimination on the basis of race. The Court appears to be making a statutory analogy argument, inferring a more general statutory policy against racial discrimination by tax-exempt organizations from the specific statutory rule about social clubs. This is not a legislative intent argument. It assumes that the court has some interpretive discretion and seeks guidance from any relevant source, including other statutory provisions. This is the common law method of analogical reasoning, applied to legislation.

But this reference to the statutory rule about social clubs raises some problems. First, why didn't the statutory rule call attention to a *failure* to adopt a similar policy regarding schools and other tax-exempt organizations, rather than provide support for a broad anti-discrimination policy? This is, of course, the expressio unius argument. In fact, it is unlikely that the rule about social clubs had any negative implications regarding other tax-exempt organizations.

Second, the argument by analogy must deal with the fact that the statutory text only deals with social clubs having *written* statements favoring discrimination. **Section 501(i)** is silent on discriminatory *practices*, which probably undermines the statute's effectiveness. It is plausible that the social club rule was a bit of legislative posturing, appearing to strike a blow against race discrimination, without actually doing so.

§ 10.03 DEFINING "GIFTS"

[A] The "Quid Pro Quo" Test

[1] What Is a Quid Pro Quo?

A deduction depends on more than just giving money to a charitable organization. You must also make a gift. If you buy a ticket to attend a symphony, you are purchasing taxable consumption, not making a deductible gift. What kinds of quid pro quo will prevent a payment from being a "gift"?

You have already encountered the rules exempting gifts from a donee's income and defining a "gift" as something proceeding from a "detached and disinterested generosity." *See* Chapter 4.02[A], discussing § 102. Despite an occasional case to the contrary, the definition of gift for the § 102 exclusion is not the same as the definition for deducting charitable contributions under § 170. Here is why. A payment for business publicity — to build up good will — is not made out of detached and disinterested generosity. But many deductible charitable contributions purchase good will. For example, corporations contribute to the local symphony, and expect a plaque with their name to be prominently displayed. And private business corporations support a bowl game or a public television program and expect a public acknowledgment. A "detached and disinterested" test would disallow § 170 deductions for such payments and that would discourage a lot of charitable giving.

QUESTIONS

1. The case of *Singer Co. v. United States*, 449 F.2d 413 (Ct. Cl. 1971), tries to draw the line between a charitable deduction and a nondeductible payment for a quid pro quo. A gift of Singer sewing machines to schools where people learned to sew was not a deductible gift. The expectation was that the users would become future purchasers. However, gifts of sewing machines to other groups were deductible gifts (for example, to a university theater that used sewing machines to make costumes).

Why might Singer want a charitable deduction? Couldn't it take a business deduction? The answer is that transferring property as a business expense is a realizable taxable event. Thus, if the value of the sewing machines was $100 and their basis was $80, their transfer as a deductible business expense results in $100 amount realized and a $20 taxable gain. Transfers of property as a charitable gift are not realizable taxable events.

2. Suppose a school solicits contributions from parents of enrolled children to support its educational functions. Under what circumstances are the contributions charitable deductions? How do the following facts influence your answer? Rev. Rul. 83-104, 1983-1 C.B. 46.

a. The contribution is a necessary condition of school admission.

b. The school admits a significantly larger percentage of applicants whose parents make contributions.

c. Suppose the school is a parochial school run by a church.

(i) No tuition is charged. Contributions by parents constitute the bulk of funds needed to run the school, although funds are solicited from church members and nonmembers, and no one whose parents do not contribute is denied admission.

(ii) Would your answer change if there was also a significant tuition charge in addition to the contributions, so that the contributions by parents did not constitute the bulk of the school's costs?

(iii) Suppose the church charges tuition to nonmembers but not to church members whose children attend the church school. Contributions are received from all church members, split about 50/50 between parents with children in school and other members.

Consider the decision in *Winters v. Commissioner*, 468 F.2d 778 (2d Cir. 1972), when answering these questions. The taxpayers were active members of a church that ran a school. They enrolled their four children in a school operated by the church, which established a fund for the exclusive purpose of supporting the school. The taxpayers were not required to pay tuition and were under no compulsion to contribute. But they were encouraged and expected to contribute and signed pledge cards for the amount they were expected to contribute. The court denied the deduction, noting that "the mere absence of a legal obligation to make a payment does not establish that such a payment constitutes a charitable contribution . . . ." It stated that "the appellants realized that they had to pay in order to keep the schools in operation and that the amount of their contributions to the education fund was determined, at least to some extent, by what they believed to be the cost of educating their children."

3. In exchange for a lighter sentence, a drug trafficker pleaded nolo contendere and agreed to pay $80,000 to the police department to finance a sting operation. Is this payment a "gift," which could be a charitable deduction? *Ruddel v. Commissioner*, 71 T.C.M. (CCH) 2419 (1996).

[2] Payment More Than Quid Pro Quo

Suppose payment is made for a quid pro quo, but the payment exceeds the "fair market value." Is some amount deductible or do you assume that the donor has a high preference for the purchased goods or services, which precludes any deduction? Consider the following examples:

a. Opera tickets, which usually sell for $80 are sold for $200, because the proceeds of this fundraising event go to the Red Cross (which is a § 170(c) organization).

b. In exchange for contributions of at least $25 to a public television station, the donor gets a free coffee mug or tee shirt with the station logo; for contributions of $100 or more, the donor gets a compact disk recording.The agency has issued a ruling disregarding certain quid pro quo received in exchange for contributions to tax-deductible organizations (including public television). Rev. Proc. 90-12, 1990-1 C.B. 471, sec. 3.01, paragraph 2, states that the agency will disregard the following:

(a) The fair market value of all of the benefits received in connection with the payment, which are not more than 2 percent of the payment, or $50, whichever is less; and

(b) If the payment is $25 (adjusted for inflation) or more, benefits received in connection with the payment that are token items (bookmarks, calendars, key chains, mugs, posters, tee shirts, etc.) bearing the organization's name or logo. . . .

c. Taxpayer contributes $1,000 to the university, which entitles him to purchase football tickets that would otherwise be very difficult to get. Is all or some part of this contribution deductible? § 170(l).

[B] Donor Control Over Gift; Donor Relation to Donee

1. Suppose a contributor to a university scholarship fund names the scholarship beneficiary. That is not a deductible gift to the charity because the donor retains too much control over how the money is spent.

2. A similar problem arose in *Davis v. United States*, 495 U.S. 472 (1990), where Mormon parents spent money to help their children finance their missionary work, which was the children's religious obligation. The parents transferred funds to the children's personal checking account to support them while they did missionary work. This example not only involves donor control but also a special family

relationship between donor and donee, so that the alleged gift finances a donor-relative's personal consumption.

There were two technical legal issues in the *Davis* case. First, the parents sought a deduction on the ground that the payments were "for the use of" the Church. The Court disagreed, limiting "for the use of" to gifts in trust. Second, the taxpayers argued that the expenses were deductible gifts "to" the Church, by analogy to the deduction for out-of-pocket expenses while performing charitable services. Again, the Court disagreed, limiting the out-of-pocket rule to cases where the taxpayer's expenses were incident to their own services, not someone else's services (their children's, in this case). Whatever the technical issues in the case, it seems clear that the result is intended to prevent a deduction when the donor has too much control over the gift and/or the benefit of the gift inures to the donor's benefit (other than merely enjoying the act of giving to charity).

3. Suppose the Church (not the parents) had taken the initiative in setting up a special fund to support the children's missionary work and the parents had paid the money directly to the Church. Now the donor has not exercised control over the charity's use of the gift, but the relationship between donor and donee is one fraught with the potential for providing tax-deductible personal consumption for the donor's family. Arguably, this is not a deductible gift when the money is paid by the parents, but would be a deductible gift if paid by someone not related to the missionary children. In general, there should be no obstacle to a charitable organization deciding on the specific uses for its money and then soliciting the general public to support those expenditures.

Query. Would there be a deductible contribution if a donor gave money to support a financially shaky symphony orchestra whose conductor was the donor's son? The money does not go specifically to the son, but helps to maintain the organization that pays his salary.

4. These examples should be distinguished from a situation in which the organization is established to help only a narrow group of people, rather than an organization that has a broader purpose but sets up a fund to aid specific people.

a. In some organizations that provide for only a narrow group of people, the organization is established to help the founder's relatives and would lose its exemption on the ground that the earnings inured to the benefit of a private individual. This would be true, for example, of an organization set up to help find organ transplants for people who included the child of the founder and controlling officer of the organization. *Wendy L. Parker Rehab. Found., Inc. v. Commissioner*, 52 T.C.M. (CCH) 51 (1986).

b. But suppose an organization was formed to help a single-named person finance an organ transplant, and the person is unrelated to the founder or officers of the organization or to the donors. For example, the organization might be formed solely to finance the medical bills for a child in the community suffering from a rare disease or a disabling accident. Would contributions to that organization be tax deductible?

[C] The Religious Quid Pro Quo

[1] The Church of Scientology

The following case held that a payment to a religious organization was not a deductible "gift."

HERNANDEZ v. COMMISSIONER
United States Supreme Court
490 U.S. 680 (1989)

JUSTICE MARSHALL delivered the opinion of the Court.

Section 170 of the Internal Revenue Code of 1954, permits a taxpayer to deduct from gross income the amount of a "charitable contribution." The Code defines that term as a "contribution or gift" to certain eligible donees, including entities organized and operated exclusively for religious purposes. We granted certiorari to determine whether taxpayers may deduct as charitable contributions payments made to branch churches of the Church of Scientology (Church) in order to receive services known as "auditing" and "training." We hold that such payments are not deductible. . . .

Scientologists believe that an immortal spiritual being exists in every person. A person becomes aware of this spiritual dimension through a process known as "auditing." Auditing involves a one-to-one encounter between a participant (known as a "preclear") and a Church official (known as an "auditor"). An electronic device, the E-meter, helps the auditor identify the preclear's areas of spiritual difficulty by measuring skin responses during a question and answer session. Although auditing sessions are conducted one-on-one, the content of each session is not individually tailored. The preclear gains spiritual awareness by progressing through sequential levels of auditing provided in short blocks of time known as "intensives."

The Church also offers members doctrinal courses known as "training." Participants in these sessions study the tenets of Scientology and seek to attain the qualifications necessary to serve as auditors. Training courses, like auditing sessions, are provided in sequential levels. Scientologists are taught that spiritual gains result from participation in such courses.

The Church charges a "fixed donation," also known as a "price" or a "fixed contribution," for participants to gain access to auditing and training sessions. These charges are set forth in schedules and prices vary with a session's length and level of sophistication. In 1972, for example, the general rates for auditing ranged from $625 for a 12 ½-hour auditing intensive, the shortest available, to $4,250 for a 100-hour intensive, the longest available. Specialized types of auditing required higher fixed donations: a 12 ½-hour "Integrity Processing" auditing intensive cost $750; a 12 ½ "Expanded Dianetics" auditing intensive cost $950. This system of mandatory fixed charges is based on a central tenet of Scientology known as the "doctrine of exchange," according to which any time a person receives something he must pay something back. In so doing, a Scientologist maintains "inflow" and "outflow" and avoids spiritual decline.

The proceeds generated from auditing and training sessions are the Church's primary source of income. The Church promotes these sessions not only through newspaper, magazine, and radio advertisements, but also through free lectures, free personality tests, and leaflets. The Church also encourages, and indeed rewards with a 5% discount, advance payment for these sessions. The Church often refunds unused portions of prepaid auditing or training fees, less an administrative charge. . . .

The legislative history of the "contribution or gift" limitation, though sparse, reveals that Congress intended to differentiate between unrequited payments to qualified recipients and payments made to such recipients in return for goods or services. Only the former were deemed deductible. . . . Using payments to hospitals as an example, both [Senate and House] Reports state that the gift characterization should not apply to "a payment by an individual to a hospital *in consideration of* a binding obligation to provide medical treatment for the individual's employees. It would apply only if there were no expectation of any quid pro quo from the hospital." . . .

In light of this understanding of § 170, it is readily apparent that petitioners' payments to the Church do not qualify as "contribution[s] or gift[s]." As the Tax Court found, these payments were part of a quintessential quid pro quo exchange: in return for their money, petitioners received an identifiable benefit, namely, auditing and training sessions. The Church established fixed price schedules for auditing and training sessions in each branch church; it calibrated particular prices to auditing or training sessions of particular lengths and levels of sophistication; it returned a refund if auditing and training services went unperformed; it distributed "account cards" on which persons who had paid money to the Church could monitor what prepaid services they had no yet claimed; and it categorically barred provision of auditing or training sessions for free. Each of these practices reveals the inherently reciprocal nature of the exchange.

Petitioners do not argue that such a structural analysis is inappropriate under § 170 or that the external features of the auditing and training transactions do not strongly suggest a quid pro quo exchange. Indeed, the petitioners . . . conceded at trial that they expected to receive specific amounts of auditing and training in return for their payments. Petitioners argue instead that they are entitled to deductions because a quid pro quo analysis is inappropriate under § 170 when the benefit a taxpayer receives is purely religious in nature. Along the same lines, petitioners claim that payments made for the right to participate in a religious service should be automatically deductible under § 170.

We cannot accept this statutory argument for several reasons. First, . . . [t]he Code makes no special preference for payments made in the expectation of gaining religious benefits or access to a religious service. . . .

Second, petitioners' deductibility proposal would expand the charitable contribution deduction far beyond what Congress has provided. Numerous forms of payments to eligible donees plausibly could be categorized as providing a religious benefit or as securing access to a religious service. For example, some taxpayers might regard their tuition payments to parochial schools as generating a religious benefit or as securing access to a religious service; such payments, however, have long been held not to be charitable contributions under § 170. Taxpayers might make similar claims about payments for church-sponsored counseling sessions or for medical care at church-affiliated hospitals that otherwise might not be deductible. . . .

Accordingly, we conclude that petitioners' payments to the Church for auditing and training sessions are not "contribution[s] or gift[s]" within the meaning of that statutory expression. . . .

The Court also rejected petitioners' argument that disallowing this deduction was inconsistent with the IRS' longstanding practice of permitting deductions to other religious institutions regarding religious practices. To support this argument, the taxpayer cited Rev. Rul. 70-47, 1970-1 C.B. 49, which stated: "Pew rents, building-fund assessments, and periodic dues paid to a church . . . are all methods of making contributions to the church, and such payments are deductible as charitable contributions within the limitations set out in section 170 of the Code." The Court also assumed for purposes of argument that the IRS also allows taxpayers to deduct "specified payments for attendance at High Holy Day services, for tithes, for torah readings and for memorial plaques." The Court stated that, on this record, there was no way to determine whether these decisions were correct for the other religions and whether they were inconsistent with disallowing the deduction for Scientologists. It noted the fact that there was no information about whether any or all of the services provided by other religions were generally provided whether or not the encouraged "mandatory" payments were made. The dissenters (Justices O'Connor and Scalia) could find no distinction between Scientologists and other (mainstream) religions and concluded that the distinction was, therefore, constitutionally impermissible.

COMMENTS AND QUESTIONS

1. The Court concedes that the quid pro quo received from the Church of Scientology was a noncommercial benefit, but seems worried that a deduction could open the way to deducting payments for benefits that are similar to commercially sold services — such as education and counseling services.

2. The dissent is convinced that the decision discriminates between traditional and nontraditional religions, based on the rulings permitting deductions for pew rents, high holy day tickets, etc. Could the majority have distinguished the Church of Scientology from traditional religions on the ground that, in a traditional religion, people worship in groups and the benefits are provided even if the payment is not made? The dissent argued that this was an invalid distinction, but doesn't the group setting and the fact that the contribution is not needed to finance the provision of benefits diminish the link between the payment and the benefit, and, therefore, make the payment less in exchange for a quid pro quo?

3. Two things happened in 1993 of relevance to the problem raised by *Hernandez*.

a. First, Congress conditioned a charitable deduction of $250 or more on taxpayer substantiation by written acknowledgment from the donee organization (§ 170(f)(8)), including a statement whether the organization has provided goods or services to the donor and a good faith valuation of those goods and services. But it exempted from this valuation requirement goods or services consisting solely of an "intangible religious benefit." This section does not, however, say anything about what constitutes a charitable deduction; it only requires substantiation of a charitable contribution claim.

b. Second, a closing agreement between the Church of Scientology and the IRS (Oct. 1, 1993) ended the IRS' 20-year effort to deny the Church its tax-exempt status and also allowed a deduction of the very payments that *Hernandez* had held were nondeductible. 97 TAX NOTES TODAY, 251-24 (Dec. 31, 1997) (the closing agreement was confidential, but it leaked to the public). *See also* Rev. Rul. 93-73, 1993-2 C.B. 75, which stated that Rev. Rul. 78-189, 1978-1 C.B. 68 was obsolete; Rev. Rul. 78-189 had previously disallowed a deduction of the *Hernandez*-type payments.

It was never made clear why the IRS gave up on its dispute with the Church of Scientology. A taxpayer had brought a post-*Hernandez* refund case claiming that the nondeductibility of his payments to the Church resulted in inconsistent administration, based on the conceded deductibility of payments for Jewish High Holy Day tickets, mandatory Mormon tithes, and stipends for special Catholic masses. In *Powell v. United States*, 945 F.2d 374 (11th Cir. 1991), the court held that the taxpayer had stated a cause of action, because it was illegal for the agency to treat similarly situated taxpayers differently, especially where religious affiliation was involved. After remand, the case disappears from the reports, suggesting that the IRS may have conceded the issue and that this case may have led to the 1993 closing agreement and Revenue Ruling.

[2] Religious School Tuition

It is generally believed that a taxpayer can deduct the tuition paid for "Sunday" school (or the like) where there is only religious training. But taxpayers have not fared so well with tuition for a religious (parochial) school that combines religious and secular education. *See* Rev. Rul. 83-104, 1983-1 C.B. 46

Taxpayers have argued that the exemption for intangible religious benefits from certain reporting requirements implies that a religious quid pro quo does not prevent a deduction. But the courts have held that the exemption applies only to the reporting requirements, not to the substantive law of deductibility.

As for the substantive issue, taxpayers have lost either on the grounds that a religious quid pro quo prevents the tuition from being a "gift" (citing *Hernandez*); or that the taxpayer did not prove that the tuition exceeded the value of the secular portion of the education. *See Sklar v. Commissioner*, 79 T.C.M. (CCH) 1815 (2000), *affirmed*, 282 F.3d 610 (9th Cir. 2002); *Sklar v. Commissioner*, 125 T.C. 281 (2005), affirmed, *Sklar v. Commissioner*, 549 F.3d 1252 (9th Cir. 2008); *De Jong v. Commissioner*, 309 F.2d 373, 376 (9th Cir. 1962), *affirming*, 36 T.C. 896 (1961).

§ 10.04 NONCASH GIFTS

[A] Appreciated Property

Absent any special limiting provision, §170(a)(1) authorizes the deduction of the fair market value of property given to an eligible charity. No gain is recognized to the donor even if property is transferred to discharge a pledge to the charity. Rev. Rul. 55-410, 1955-1 C.B. 297. Conversely, only the value of depreciated property is deductible and the taxpayer cannot deduct a loss when depreciated property is given to charity. *Withers v. Commissioner*, 69 T.C. 900 (1978).

The taxpayer who gives appreciated property to charity, therefore, has a "tax shelter," because income not given to charity is sheltered from tax by the deduction of the untaxed appreciated gain. For example, assume that the taxpayer owned inventory with a cost of $80 and a value of $100. It is fair to permit an $80 deduction because that equals the taxpayer's expenditure for the asset. But why should the untaxed $20 gain, which is tax deferred income, be deducted from other income (such as income from medical or legal fees)? That is inconsistent with the theory behind charitable deductions, which is to exclude otherwise taxable income from the tax base if it is given away, not to shelter other income from tax.

Section 170(e) is a limited response to this problem. When it applies, it reduces the charitable deduction otherwise allowable by the amount of income that would have been taxed if the property had been sold rather than given away.

PROBLEMS

The following problems illustrate the operation of § 170(e). Assume in all cases that the cost is $80 and the value is $100. Unless otherwise stated, disregard the possibility that the statute might provide an exception to § 170(e) to allow some or all of the entire value of the property to be deducted.

1. A dealer in stock gives stock to a university. Because the taxpayer is a dealer, the gain on a sale would have been ordinary income, not long-term capital gain.

2. An investor holds a capital asset two years (more than one year is long enough to be eligible for long-term capital gain) and then gives it to a private foundation, other than a private foundation listed in § 170(b)(1)(E). Does it matter whether the stock is publicly traded stock? *See* § 170(e)(5).

3. An investor in rare jewels holds them as a capital asset for five years and then gives them to a museum. Suppose the jewels had instead been given to a church.

4. An investor holds stock or land as a capital asset for five years and then gives it to a university.

You should see the fruits of some intense lobbying buried in the technical complexity of § 170(e). Which lobbying interests prevailed in getting a deduction for the value of appreciated property under certain circumstances?

These lobbying interests were not completely successful. If appreciated capital gain property is given to a "public" charity and the full value is deductible because § 170(e) does not apply, gifts of such appreciated property are deductible only up to 30% of adjusted gross income (not 50%). § 170(b)(1)(c). However, the 50% ceiling is reinstated if the taxpayer elects to deduct no more than the property's adjusted basis.

5. *Valuation.* The IRS is not bashful about challenging inflated valuation claims by donors (e.g., paintings by lesser known artists). In one case, the court found that the value was 20% of that claimed by the donor. *Skripak v. Commissioner*, 84 T.C. 285 (1985). Special penalties apply if the taxpayer's overvaluation is excessive. § 6662(b)(3), (e)(1)(A). AJCA (2004) adds a number of provisions to assure that the value of the deduction for certain noncash property is accurate (§ 170(f)(11)), which vary depending on whether the claimed value exceeds $500, $5,000, or $500,000. In addition, special rules apply to the donation of motor vehicles, boats, and planes worth more than $500. § 170(f)(12).

In *Herman v. U.S.*, 73 F. Supp. 2d 912 (E.D. Tenn. 1999), the taxpayer succeeded in proving a much higher value than the government was willing to concede. The $40,000 price paid for medical equipment at a bankruptcy sale by the taxpayer was not used to determine the value of the property later given to charity. The bankruptcy court was not a willing seller, but was compelled to sell the equipment, and the sale itself was made in haste, without objection from creditors and without a valuation hearing. In addition, the appraiser relied on by the taxpayer to establish a higher value was accredited in medical sales by a health industries association, had 30 years of experience in buying and selling new and used medical equipment, had regularly performed appraisals of hospital and medical equipment, did not know that his appraisal would be used for tax purposes, and was not paid for his services. The court upheld a $1 million value!

6. *Patents and other intellectual property.* A 2004 Tax Law changed the rules applicable to charitable gifts of patents and most other intellectual property. Even if the fair market value of a patent, copyright, trademark, trade secret, know-how, etc. would have been deductible in full — because it is intangible property given to a public charity and the gain on any sale would have been long-term capital gain — the deduction is reduced by the amount of the gain. § 170(e)(1)(B)(iii). This new rule prevents the taxpayer from making inflated claims about the future income potential of the donated asset. Instead, the taxpayer is allowed to deduct a percentage of the income earned by the donee from the donated property in years after the donation (to the extent that the income exceeds any deduction the donor already took for the donation), as long as the income is received within the lesser of the legal life of the property or 10 years. The percentage of the income that is deductible under this rule is 100% of the income for the first two years after the donation and declines in subsequent years. § 170(m).

7. *Relaxation of § 170(e) for certain property.* § 170(e)(3) relaxes the rule reducing value to basis for charitable gifts of food — extended through 2013 by ATRA. The statute provides a formula allowing more than basis but less than value to be deducted. Prior law (now expired) provided the same tax break for contributions of books and computers.

[B]   Bargain Sale to Charity

Suppose a taxpayer, who pays $80 for property now worth $100, sells the asset to the charity for $80. In effect, he has made a $20 gift to the charity. Does he recognize gain on the sale? How much of the $20 gift can he deduct? Absent a special provision, the proceeds of a bargain sale are first allocated to the basis. **Treas. Reg. § 1.1001-1(e).** If that rule applied to a bargain sale to charity, the taxpayer in the above example could eliminate taxable gain ($80 amount realized minus $80 basis), and still deduct $20, *if* **§ 170(e)** did not apply to the $20 gift.

Sections 170(e)(2), 1011(b) changed the way gain is computed on a bargain sale to charity. These sections require the basis to be allocated between the sale and the gift in the same proportion as the value of the sale and the gift. In the above example, the sale and gift are divided in an 80/20 ratio and the $80 basis is, therefore, allocated $64 to the sale and $16 to the gift. The taxpayer is treated as selling property with a $64 basis for $80, and as making a charitable gift of property with a $16 basis and a value of $20. Whether the taxpayer can deduct $16 or $20 in this example depends on whether **§ 170(e)** applies to reduce the deductible gift below fair market value.

[C]   Untaxed Property Given to Charity

In *Haverly v. United States*, 513 F.2d 224 (7th Cir. 1975), the taxpayer received unsolicited textbooks in 1967 and 1968, which he gave to the school's library in 1968. He claimed the gifts as a charitable deduction in 1968. Value at the time of receipt of the books and at the time of the gifts was $400. The government claimed that the taxpayer had $400 of income in 1968.

The court stated that, under *Glenshaw Glass*, "when the intent to exercise complete dominion over unsolicited samples is demonstrated by donating those samples to a charitable institution and taking a tax deduction, therefore, the value of the samples received constitutes gross income." It rejected the District Court's view that the "receipt of the property [was] indistinguishable from other acts unrelated to the tax laws which also evidence an intent to accept property as one's own, such as a school principal donating his sample texts to the library without claiming a deduction." The Court of Appeals refused to decide what the result would be if the taxpayer had not taken a deduction, but held "that when a tax deduction is taken for the donation of unsolicited samples the value of the samples received must be included in the taxpayer's gross income." It noted that its

> conclusion [wa]s consistent with Revenue Ruling 70-498, 1970-2 Cum. Bull. 6, in which the Internal Revenue Service held that a newspaper's book reviewer must include in his gross income the value of unsolicited books received from publishers which are donated to a charitable organization and for which a charitable deduction is taken. This ruling was issued to supersede an earlier ruling, Rev. Rul. 70-330, 1970-1 Cum. Bull. 14, that mere retention of unsolicited books was sufficient to cause them to be gross income.
>
> The Internal Revenue Service has apparently made an administrative decision to be concerned with the taxation of unsolicited samples only when

failure to tax those samples would provide taxpayers with double tax benefits. It is not for the courts to quarrel with an agency's rational allocation of its administrative resources.

COMMENTS AND QUESTIONS

1. *Haverly* was decided before passage of **§ 170(e)**. Under **§ 170(e)** today, would the taxpayer be able to deduct the fair market value of the property? Yes. The gift is to a public charity, is of tangible personal property related to the donee's charitable purposes, and any gain on sale would be capital gain (the asset is not held primarily for sale in the ordinary course of doing business, which would prevent it from being a capital asset; *see* **§ 1221(a)(1)**). Consequently, the same double benefit problem presented in *Haverly* (both an exclusion and a deduction) would arise today.

2. Apparently, the tax year in which to include the value of the donated books in income is the year of the charitable gift. Should it be the earlier year when the books were received by the taxpayer?

3. How much income would the donor have in the year of the gift if: (a) the books were worth $300 in 1967 when received and $400 in 1968 when donated; (b) the books were worth $400 in 1967 and had declined in value to $300 in 1968? If the problem to be avoided is a double tax break, shouldn't the answer be $300; that is, the lower of the value not taxed and the deduction taken?

4. The *Haverly* case presents a very difficult problem of statutory interpretation. The taxpayer was seeking the same advantage that is enjoyed by investors who give appreciated property to charity and use the untaxed appreciation to shelter other income. Why is the exclusion of the book's value from income in *Haverly* inconsistent with deducting the full value of the books as a gift, *if* exclusion of untaxed appreciation is not inconsistent with deducting the appreciation?

By analogy, assume the taxpayer had received a $100 as a tax-exempt gift or as tax-exempt interest and had given that cash to charity. In that case, the $100 charitable gift could shelter the donee's other income, even though the donee excluded the $100 from income under **§ 102** or **§ 103**. To deny that result would defeat the policy of the statute to exclude gifts or tax-exempt interest from income. How is the cash gift of tax-exempt income, which is given to charity, different from the *Haverly* case?

5. *Frequent flyer miles.* The gift of untaxed books may be an important tax issue for professors who get these books and give them to the library, but the frequent flyer example is of more general interest. Announcement 2002-18 gave the following reason for not taxing employees on frequent flyer benefits financed by employers:

> There are numerous technical and administrative issues relating to these benefits on which no official guidance has been provided, including issues relating to the timing and valuation of income inclusions and the basis for identifying personal use benefits attributable to business (or official)

expenditures versus those attributable to personal expenditures. Because of these unresolved issues, the IRS has not pursued a tax enforcement program with respect to promotional benefits such as frequent flyer miles.

This sounds as though administrative convenience is a major reason for the exclusion. And, as long as the exclusion is based on administrative convenience, the double benefit is as inappropriate in the frequent flyer example as in the professor's book case.

Does your answer change if you think that the frequent flyer miles were *de minimis* fringe benefits, excluded from the taxpayer's income by § 132(a)(4), (e)(1)? In other words, does the explicit statutory exemption preclude application of the principle adopted by the *Haverly* case, just as a tax-exempt gift or tax-exempt interest income can be used to make a deductible charitable contribution? Another similar example would be a charitable gift of property purchased at an employer-provided discount, where the discount was not taxable under § 132(a)(2), (c). For example, suppose the employee purchased an asset worth $5,000 at a 20% discount (for $4,000), and the $1,000 extra value was not taxed under § 132(a)(2), (c). Could that taxpayer deduct $5,000, if that property was given to charity (assuming § 170(e) would not apply to reduce the deduction)? Does your answer depend on whether the statutory exclusions are based on the same administrative concerns that led the agency not to bother taxing the books in *Haverly* in the first place, rather than on other considerations — such as a subsidy to the industries that provide such tax-free fringe benefits?

SAVINGS

Part I-B dealt primarily with the personal consumption component of income. Part I-C focuses on savings.

Savings are expenditures that provide value beyond the end of the tax year. Consequently, their deduction is usually deferred by adding the expenditure to basis, unless there are good administrative or policy reasons to permit a current deduction ("expensing").

The expenditure for savings will often be deductible in the future, either through depreciation (Chapter 11) or as a loss deduction (Chapter 12). Chapter 13 explains how to decide whether an expenditure is for savings added to basis or is instead a current expense.

Chapter 11

DEPRECIATION

§ 11.01 DEPRECIATION THEORY

[A] Depreciable Assets

An asset is depreciable for tax purposes if: (1) it is used for business or income production; and (2) has a determinable useful life (that is, it will eventually lose its usefulness). The depreciation deduction allocates the deduction of an asset's basis over its useful life, in accordance with some formula. Before you consider possible formulas, be sure you understand why some assets are depreciable.

If a taxpayer pays rent for a business building during its entire useful life, the rent is obviously a deductible business expense. A taxpayer who owns the building should be treated the same way — the periodic cost of the building should be deductible. The owner is like a renter, and the cost of the building is like prepaid rent, the deduction of which should be spread out over its useful life.

One implication of this analogy is that property held for personal use (a home, for example) is not depreciable. Rent on a home is a nondeductible personal expense, so the investment in the home is not depreciable.

The "determinable useful life" requirement serves a different function. It precludes depreciation of property whose usefulness persists, without time limit. Market value may fluctuate but will not inevitably disappear. Land and corporate stock are examples of nondepreciable assets, even though they are held for income production.

Depreciable assets can be tangible (buildings; machines), or intangible (covenants not to compete), as long as they have a determinable useful life. The term "amortization" is usually used for intangible property instead of depreciation.

Depreciation is not limited to property that physically wastes away. Depreciation is a financial concept dealing with investments, not a physics concept dealing with atoms and molecules. If business property is expected to become obsolete in 10 years, it has a 10-year life, even though it physically exists after 10 years.

[B] Computing Depreciation

The depreciation deduction should meet certain theoretical standards. It should "clearly reflect income" by matching deductions against the income generated by the asset. It should not include the asset's anticipated salvage value (e.g., the amount you could get by selling an obsolete computer after five years). In practice, these standards are administratively too difficult to meet. The percentage of basis allowed as a depreciation deduction each year is usually fixed by a formula that does not necessarily reflect how the asset is actually used up by the business in particular cases. And salvage value is usually disregarded.

Two other significant policy decisions must be made. (1) Should depreciation be based on historical cost (that is, original basis), or should it take account of inflation? Our tax system does not adjust depreciation basis for inflation. (2) Should depreciation be used to encourage investments as well as attempt to clearly reflect income? Our tax system does use the depreciation deduction to encourage investment.

With that background, here are some examples of two depreciation methods — (1) straight line and (2) the accelerated method known as double (200%) declining balance. The asset has a $60 cost, a five-year life, and no salvage value. The basis of the asset after the deduction of depreciation is in parentheses after the deduction amount. (We will discuss later whether any particular method of depreciation can be used.)

Depreciation — $60 Cost (post-depreciation basis in parentheses)

Year	Straight line	Accelerated method — 200% declining balance
1	12 (48)	24 (36)
2	12 (36)	14.40 (21.60)
3	12 (24)	8.64 (12.96)
4	12 (12)	6.48 (6.48)
5	12 (0)	6.48 (0)
	60	60

There are several things to notice about the accelerated method. (1) Straight line depreciation spreads the depreciation deduction evenly over the useful life. The straight line depreciation rate is always 1 divided by the number of years of useful life — in this example, 1/5th or 20%. The "double" in double declining balance (that is, 200%) refers to twice the straight line rate. Double the 20% straight line rate is 40%. (2) "Declining balance" refers to the application of the 40% depreciation rate to the basis remaining *after* deduction of prior depreciation. (3) When the application of the 40% depreciation rate to the declining basis produces depreciation less than straight line over the remaining life of the asset, switch to straight line (that occurs in years 4 and 5 in the example — 40% times 12.96 would be less than 12.96/2, which equals 6.48).

There are other methods of depreciation, based not on useful life, but on what the asset produces, or more precisely, is "expected to produce." One example is the unit of production method, which allocates total basis each year based on the amount produced as a percentage of total anticipated production. If a mine is expected to produce 100,000 tons of ore during its entire life and produces 8,000 tons in a particular year, 8% of the mine's basis is a depreciation deduction. This is often called "cost depletion," rather than depreciation, and is used to recover the basis of investments in natural resources. §§ **611, 612**. The idea behind cost depletion is the same as depreciation — a reasonable method of deducting basis over the life of the asset.

Percentage depletion. Cost depletion should not be confused with percentage depletion, which allows certain taxpayers to deduct a specified percentage of gross income. This deduction is available even if it exceeds normal depreciation and even though total percentage depletion deductions over time exceed cost basis. The benefit is available to producers of certain minerals, most famously oil and gas. However, after the huge spike in oil and gas prices in the 1970s, the largest producers of these minerals are no longer eligible for percentage depletion. **§§ 613, 613A.**

Percentage depletion deductions vary depending on the mineral. At present, the range is 5–22%. There are some limits on the deduction for percentage depletion. First, it is usually limited to 50% of taxable income (100% for oil and gas properties). Second, the gross income to which the percentage is applied is limited to the income derived primarily from extraction of the mineral, which requires separating out the income attributable to extraction during the earlier stages of the mining and exploration activity from the production and distribution process at the later stages.

[C] Basis Adjustment

When a taxpayer takes a depreciation (or amortization or cost depletion) deduction, some of the basis is deducted. Consequently, the basis must be reduced. When the statute refers to "adjusted basis," the adjustment is often for depreciation deductions. If the rule were otherwise and the basis were not reduced, the same basis could be deducted twice — for example, once through depreciation and again as a recovery of basis when the asset was sold. *See* **§§ 1011(a), 1016(a)(2).**

[D] Annuities — A Simple Example of Straight Line Depreciation

A simple example of straight line depreciation is the tax treatment of annuities. An annuity is an agreement to pay an annual sum of money to an investor (referred to as an annuitant). Generally, the payor of the annuity is a commercial enterprise, such as a life insurance company.

Consider, for example, a 60-year old taxpayer who pays $50,000 to a commercial annuity company in exchange for a promise of $5,000 per year for the rest of his life, beginning at age 65. How much of the $5,000 should be taxed each year? **Section 72** provides the answer. Technically, it provides an "exclusion" of some of the $5,000 from annual income. **§ 72(b).** In this example, the exclusion depends on life expectancy. If the purchaser is expected to live 15 years when the annual $5,000 payments begin, total expected income equals $75,000. (The Regulations provide gender neutral life expectancy tables; **Treas. Reg. § 1.72-9.**) The exclusion is two-thirds of each $5,000 (because the $50,000 investment is two thirds of the $75,000 expected income). Notice that this exclusion equals straight line depreciation of the $50,000 investment over 15 years:

$$\frac{5000}{(15 \times 5000)} \quad \times \quad 5000 \quad = \quad \text{excludible amount}$$

QUESTIONS

1. Why does the statute provide for an income exclusion rather than a deduction?

2. How is the $5,000 taxed if the taxpayer lives longer than expected (say, 20 years)? Is there a loss deduction if the taxpayer dies early (say, in 10 years)? § 72(b)(2),(3).

[E] Decelerated Depreciation

Straight line depreciation is always an acceptable depreciation method, if you cannot identify a better depreciation method to clearly reflect income. *See* **Treas. Reg. § 1.167(b)-1(a)**. One argument for this conclusion is that straight line depreciation would clearly reflect income, on the reasonable assumption that the property produces equal annual income. But that is wrong. Straight line depreciation does *not* clearly reflect income when the asset produces equal annual income.

Assume that a $60 investment with a five-year useful life produces $20 income per year, before depreciation. After five years, the property is used up. The $60 is the present value of $20 earned annually over the next five years, assuming a 20% discount rate. What annual depreciation of the $60 investment will produce *net* income (after depreciation) which equals a 20% annual rate of return on the asset's value at the beginning of each year? The following table gives the figures (rounded so that the totals add correctly). Notice that the depreciation is *decelerated* — less than straight line.

In the real world the only investors who routinely use this method are banks when they amortize their loans. When a bank makes a five-year $60 loan at 20% interest, its annual net income is reflected by the following chart, using decelerated depreciation. Notice that the net income in the early years is *larger* than it would be using straight line depreciation. This is, however, very good for the *borrower* financing purchase of a home, whose interest deduction equals the bank's annual net income on the loan. Larger interest deductions during the early years of repayment are better for the homeowner.

Decelerated depreciation
Asset cost = $60; 20% interest rate

Year	Value at beginning of year	Depreciation	Gross Income	Net Income
1	60	8	20	12
2	52	9.5	20	10.5
3	42.5	11.5	20	8.5
4	31	14	20	6
5	17	17	20	3
		60	100	40

[F] Property Purchased from a Spouse

Husband and wife are often treated as part of the same taxable unit — for example, filing joint returns under § 1; denying loss on sale between spouses under § 267(a)(1).

If spouses are truly part of a single economic unit, the following tax avoidance technique should not be allowed. Husband owns depreciable property with a $20 basis and a $100 value. The unrealized $80 gain would not be eligible for depreciation. The property is sold to the spouse for $100, often producing preferentially taxed capital gain. The buyer then depreciates the $100 cost, reducing ordinary income. **Section 1239** prevents this result by denying capital gain treatment for the selling spouse.

§ 11.02 DEPRECIATION UNDER THE STATUTE

The discussion has so far focused primarily on possible approaches to depreciation deductions, with limited attention to current statutory rules. There is a reason for this. The rules change frequently, often to provide economic incentives.

The amount of the depreciation deduction depends in theory on the answer to three questions. First, determine the basis used to compute depreciation. A major issue here is whether to disregard salvage value. Second, determine the time over which to depreciate. In the absence of any special provision, useful life depends on the business practice of the particular taxpayer, including consideration of technological obsolescence, not just the physical life of the asset. *Massey Motors, Inc. v. United States*, 364 U.S. 92 (1960). Third, determine the rate at which depreciation will be computed.

Statutory depreciation rules vary in accordance with the political judgments of Congress. The rules are very technical but the critical decisions often vary in accordance with the following: whether the property is a building; whether the property is tangible or intangible; whether the property is new or used; and the expected useful life of the property. Not every one of these variables has been important at all times, but each has been relevant in framing depreciation rules at some time or another.

Here is a brief summary of recent U.S. "tax depreciation" history. The general authority for deducting depreciation is § 167(a), but there are many other provisions permitting more generous deductions under certain circumstances.

[A] Before the Tax Reform Act of 1986

[1] Pre-1981

For about a decade before 1981, the useful life of assets was determined by the Asset Depreciation Range system (ADR). This system specified the useful life of classes of assets used in the same business activity, except that assets with common characteristics (like cars) had their own ADR life. The ADR system substantially shortened the useful lives previously employed for depreciation. Moreover, taxpayers could elect lives 20% shorter or longer than the ADR life.

When the ADR system was originally proposed by Treasury Regulation, a lawsuit challenging the agency's authority to adopt them was brought by Members of Congress, Common Cause, a business association whose members could not benefit from accelerated depreciation to the same extent as its competitors, and a real estate investor for whom there were no benefits. *Common Cause v. Connally*, Civil Action 1337-71 (D.D.C. 1971). Their standing to bring the lawsuit was doubtful but the issue was mooted when Congress adopted a specific statutory provision authorizing the ADR system. The list of litigants in this lawsuit suggests one of the major features of accelerated depreciation deductions; the benefits are skewed toward industries that are more capital- than labor-intensive.

The permissible rate of depreciation varied with the type of property. For example, tangible property (other than buildings) with a useful life of at least three years was eligible for 200% declining balance depreciation, if it was not used property. Buildings were not eligible for the 200% rate unless they were new residential realty. Other buildings were eligible for a 150% depreciation rate, except that the rates were lower if the buildings were not new.

Pre-1981 law also permitted the salvage value of "personal property" to be reduced by 10% of the original cost if the property had at least a three-year useful life. "Personal property" referred primarily to tangible and intangible property other than buildings.

[2] 1981; The ACRS System

The Economic Recovery Act of 1981 introduced the Accelerated Cost Recovery System (ACRS), applicable to depreciable tangible property. In most cases, it significantly increased depreciation deductions for tangible personal and real property, such as machines and buildings. Original cost (not reduced by salvage value) was the basis for depreciation, and both new property and used property were eligible for ACRS.

There were five categories of assets, with depreciable useful lives of 3, 5, 10, 15, and 19 years. The category into which an asset fell generally depended on the ADR life that the asset had under the prior ADR system, but the ACRS system shortened the depreciation period. Buildings had a 19-year life, much below the ADR life; low-income housing had a 15-year life.

In general, the ACRS depreciation rates for tangible property, other than buildings, were 150% declining balance. The rules for buildings were a little different. Tables published by the Treasury provided 175% declining balance over 19 years, except for low-income housing, for which the rates were 200% declining balance over 15 years.

[B]   Tax Reform Act of 1986, as Amended in 1993 (MACRS)

Significant revisions of the depreciation rates and recovery periods were made by the Tax Reform Act of 1986, producing a Modified Accelerated Cost Recovery system (MACRS). **§ 168(a), (b), (c), (e).** *Tangible personal property* generally falls into six recovery periods and depreciation rates — 3-year (200%); 5-year (200%); 7-year (200%); 10-year (200%); 15-year (150%); 20-year (150%). The new MACRS recovery periods are based on the old Asset Depreciation Range class life. Thus, 3-year MACRS property includes property with a 4-year or less ADR class life, except that cars have been moved to the 5-year MACRS category. **§ 168(e)(3)(B).**

Real property was the big loser in the 1986 Act. Residential rental property is eligible for straight-line depreciation over 27.5 years. Other realty, such as commercial real estate (e.g., shopping centers), became depreciable over 31.5 years, extended to 39 years by the 1993 Act.

Salvage value is still disregarded and the current rules apply to both new and used property.

The Tax Reform Act of 1986, like prior law, adopted conventions concerning when property is placed in use. Personal property is assumed to be placed in use at the midpoint of the year. However, if more than 40% of the taxpayer's personal property is placed in use in the last three months of the year, the property is assumed to be placed in service in the middle of the quarter in which it was acquired (that is, a mid-quarter convention). For realty, a mid-month, instead of a mid-year, convention is used. **§ 168(d).**

In addition, a few types of property are eligible for bonus 50%-in-the-first-year depreciation. This tax break expires after 2013. **§ 168(k).**

A different "alternative depreciation" system is used for certain property. **§ 168(g).** The alternative system uses straight-line depreciation over specified time periods that are longer than under MACRS. One type of property subject to these rules is business property, which can still be financed by tax-exempt Industrial Revenue Bonds (discussed in Chapter 6.01[C][4]). The idea is that the existing tax exemption for interest on loans incurred to make the investment provides sufficient investment incentives, which should not be augmented by favorable MACRS depreciation methods. Taxpayers can also opt to use the longer periods provided by the "alternative depreciation" system. **§ 168(g)(1)(E).**

Before the Tax Reform Act of 1986, lessees who constructed a building on property were allowed to use the leasehold period rather than the ACRS period to amortize the cost of the building, if the leasehold period was shorter. Lessees are no longer allowed to do this and must depreciate the building using MACRS lives. **§ 168(i)(8).**

Limitations on depreciation for "listed property." Specific rules limit the depreciation deduction for "listed property." (In addition, the property is not eligible for the favorable expensing under **§ 179**, explained below.) Listed property includes cars, property used for entertainment, computers. **§ 280F.** Cell phones were removed from the list in 2010; IRS Notice 2011-72.

> If depreciable listed property is used 50% or less for business purposes, depreciation of the cost attributable to business use is limited to straight-line under the alternative depreciation system with longer lives than MACRS. Employees are not treated as using listed property for business (and are therefore denied *any* depreciation deduction), unless such use is for the convenience of the employer and is required as a condition of employment.

A special rule favors use of computers. A computer is not "listed property" if it is used at a business establishment owned or leased by the taxpayer. Use in a residence satisfies this exception only if the computer is used in a "home office" that qualifies for deductions under **§§ 280A(c)(1).** (Recall how hard it is for an employee to obtain a deduction for home office expenses; Chapter 8.07). If property used in a business avoids "listed property" status, the taxpayer can use the favorable MACRS and **§ 179** rules.

Tax expenditure? The manipulation of depreciation rules has always been a very attractive political technique because it has the effect of lowering taxes, without explicitly changing the tax rates. For this reason the amount of depreciation in excess of straight-line depreciation has usually been included in the tax expenditure budgets. In a controversial move, the 1983 tax expenditure budget published by the Reagan administration did not include this item. Office of Management and Budget, The Budget of the United States Government, 1983 Special Analysis G, Tax Expenditures, 6–7. (1982) contains the following explanation:

> A further illustration of the definition of tax subsidies is provided by the Accelerated Cost Recovery System (ACRS) provisions enacted in the Economic Recovery Tax Act of 1981. Any income tax requires a set of rules for determining how the cost of depreciable assets is recovered. The ACRS provisions now constitute the general income tax rules for that purpose. To see this, one need only ask: If ACRS is "special," what is the "general" rule in the Internal Revenue Code governing the recovery of cost of depreciable property to which ACRS is an exception? The treatment of ACRS may be contrasted with that of the investment tax credit, which has very similar economic effects for machinery and equipment. The investment credit is considered a tax subsidy because, unlike ACRS, it does not deal with one of the basic structural elements of an income tax. Note further that the fact that the ACRS provisions are clearly a divergence from any measure of economic income is not relevant to the determination that they do not constitute a tax subsidy.

However, OMB later decided to report excess depreciation in its tax expenditure budget under the heading "pre-1983 budget method," making it clear that it did not approve of that method.

[C]   Reasonable Method of Depreciation

The accelerated methods discussed so far are available without regard to proof that early high depreciation deductions might reflect a reasonable method of depreciation under § 167(a). Some reasonable methods might, however, result in high early deductions without regard to MACRS. **Section 168(f)(1)** therefore permits the taxpayer to elect out of MACRS when depreciation is based on a method not tied to the number of years that the property will be useful. One example is the unit of production method. Under this method, depreciation in any given year is a percentage of depreciable cost equal to the percentage of total production to be derived from the property over its entire life that actually occurs during that year. This method can be used, for example, for equipment related to natural resources exploration.

Another reasonable method of depreciation is the income forecast method. This method is usually used for intangible assets, such as movies or patents. It allows depreciation by using a fraction in which the numerator is income in a given year and the denominator is total income expected from the asset, or some variation on that theme. Under current law, § 197 usually provides 15-year amortization for such intangible assets, but if that section does not apply, the income forecast method can be used.

The government has argued that the income forecast method is only available for intangible assets similar to movies. However, the court disagreed in *ABC Rentals of San Antonio, Inc. v. Commissioner*, 142 F.3d 1200 (10th Cir. 1998), *reversing*, 68 T.C.M. (CCH) 1362 (1994), and permitted use of that method for owners of rent-to-own property. Congress then responded in the 1997 Tax Act by disallowing the income forecast method for rent-to-own consumer durables. § 167(g)(6). However, the same law added a special three-year depreciation method for "qualified rent-to-own property." § 168(e)(3)(A)(iii), (i)(14)(D).

[D]   Intangibles; § 197

Prior to the 1993 tax law, the depreciation of intangibles was governed by the regular § 167(a) rules. The MACRS method does not apply to intangibles. Many intangibles, such as stock and good will, were not depreciable, because they had no determinable useful life. Other intangible assets, such as copyrights, patents, covenants not to compete, and advantageous contract rights to buy and sell certain assets, were depreciable under any reasonable method (as authorized by § 167(a)), assuming their useful life could be determined.

These rules spawned considerable litigation about whether assets "related" to good will were really depreciable. In 1993, the Supreme Court decided *Newark Morning Ledger Co. v. United States*, 507 U.S. 546 (1993). The taxpayer had purchased a newspaper business and allocated some of the cost to the value of the attachment of at-will subscribers. It argued that this value gradually disappeared and that it was therefore a depreciable asset, unlike good will. The Court agreed, concluding that the value of the "paid subscribers" diminished over an ascertainable period.

Congress addressed the problem of depreciating intangibles in 1993 by adopting a uniform 15-year depreciation period for all "section 197 intangibles." These rules, among other things, *permit* previously nondepreciable good will to be depreciated over 15 years; and *require* depreciable "customer-based intangibles," such as the subscriber's attachment to the business in Newark Ledger, to be depreciated over 15 years, even if prior law allowed a shorter period. **§ 197(a).**

The new **§ 197** does much more, however, than address the specific problem of good will and customer-based intangibles. It provides broadly for 15-year depreciation for a long list of section 197 intangibles. Where the new **§ 197** does not apply, **§ 167(a)** rules usually apply, permitting a reasonable method of depreciation if the property has an ascertainable useful life. However, some intangibles, excluded from "section 197 intangible" status, have special useful life periods — e.g., (1) computer software has a 36-month life, if it is readily available for purchase by the general public, subject to a nonexclusive license, and has not been substantially modified (that is, "off-the-shelf" software; **§§ 167(f)(1), 197(e)(3)**); and (2) **§ 197** does not apply to the premium a taxpayer pays for an existing indebtedness, based on the fact that the interest rate is higher than current market interest rates (**§ 197(e)(5)(B)**); that premium is generally amortizable under **§ 171.**

Here is an incomplete chart of the old and new rules applicable to selected intangibles, with some of the subtleties omitted. **Section 197(d)** contains the list of **§ 197** intangibles, and **§ 197(c)(2), (e)** contains exceptions. Reference in the chart to "§ 167 dep." refers to a reasonable method of depreciation.

Section 197 does *not* generally apply to *self-created* intangibles, unless they are described in **§ 197(d)(1)(D)–(F)** (e.g., a franchise, trademark, or trade-name); **§ 197(c)(2).**

	Old law	Current law
1. Stock	No dep.	No dep.
2. Good will	No dep.	§ 197-15 year
3. Customer-based intangibles (e.g., lists and favorable contracts)	§ 167 dep.	§ 197-15 year
4. Sports franchise	No dep.	§ 197-15 year
5. Covenant not to compete entered into in connection with acquiring a business	§ 167 dep.	§ 197-15 year
6. Patent and copyright		
(a) if created by business taxpayer	§ 167 dep.	§ 167 dep.
(b) purchased	§ 167 dep.	§ 197-15 year

Is it good or bad to avoid § 197? Suppose a business taxpayer self-creates a patent. It is probably good for the taxpayer that this is not a **§ 197** intangible. Depreciation is then available under normal depreciation rules, probably under the income-forecast method. **§ 167(g)(6); Treas. Reg. § 1.167(a)-14(c)(4).**

Favorable leases. A favorable lease is one where the obligation under the lease differs from the market rental rate in the absence of a lease. Payments for such a lease would include a premium. Lease premiums paid as part of the acquisition of property subject to a favorable lease (that is, with lease rents *more* than market rents) are added to the cost of the underlying property (e.g., lease premiums paid when buying a shopping center are part of the shopping center's cost). **§ 167(c)(2)**.

However, if a *lessee* acquires a favorable lease (with lease rents *less* than market rents), the rules permitting a reasonable method of depreciation apply. An example is a lessee acquiring a leasehold interest in using airport gates. *See* **§§ 178, 197(e)(5)(A)**.

Lease termination costs. Suppose the taxpayer-lessee pays a large sum to terminate a lease and then enters into a new lease for similar property with the same lessor — e.g., for a more modern computer. In *U.S. Bancorp v. Commissioner*, 111 T.C. 231 (1998), the issue was whether this sum could be deducted in the year it was paid or had to be amortized over the life of the new lease. (There was no doubt about the taxpayer's right to deduct the rental payments under the new lease.) The court described this situation as falling between two extremes.

> At one end [of the spectrum] is the case where a lessee pays a lessor to terminate a lease and no subsequent lease is entered into between the parties. In such a case the termination fee is clearly deductible in the year incurred, as there is no second lease raising the possibility that the lessee will realize significant future benefits beyond the current taxable year as a result of the termination payment. At the opposite end is the case of a lessee that cancels a lease and then immediately enters into another lease with the same lessor, covering the same property. In substance, the first lease is not canceled but continues in modified form, and any unrecovered costs of the first lease, or costs incurred to cancel the first lease, are not currently deductible but rather are costs of continuing the first lease in modified form.

> The case at hand lies between the two extremes. It is not a case of simply terminating a lease without entering into another lease. Neither is it a termination of one lease, immediately followed by entry into a second lease with the same lessor covering the same property, insofar as the two computers covered by the two leases are not identical. Along the range between the extremes presented by petitioner and respondent, we find the case at hand is both closer to and qualitatively more similar to the modification of lease case than to the simple termination.

Consequently, the lease termination cost had to be added to basis and amortized over the life of the second lease.

[E]   Critique of Accelerated Depreciation as Economic Incentive

Two major problems have plagued the depreciation system, one of which was partially corrected by the Tax Reform Act of 1986. First, tax incentives were not uniform. Of course, special favoritism for some investment activities might be purposeful, such as for oil exploration or building low-income housing. But many tax provisions could not be justified on this ground. Assets with different real economic lives were lumped together in the same useful life category. The five-year life category, for example, might contain assets with real economic lives of five or eight years. Even when the assets in a useful life category had the same economic life, the incentives varied *between* useful life categories, because the shortening of economic lives was not uniform in each category. For example, even if all five-year MACRS property had an economic eight-year life, and all 19-year MACRS property had an economic 40-year life, the shortening of lives would be more advantageous for the 19-year MACRS category.

[1]   Uniform Incentives?

The Tax Reform Act of 1986 moves in the direction of placing assets with similar economic lives in the same MACRS category and providing similar incentives for assets in all categories. It therefore comes closer to the ideal of providing uniform incentives to all investment. If you wanted to reach that ideal completely, here is how you would do it. The incentive can be quantified in terms of the familiar concept of present value. The full expensing of a deduction is the benchmark. The present value of expensing an outlay is the amount of the outlay. Thus, if $10,000 is spent today and deducted today, the present value of the deduction is $10,000 because the deduction is not postponed. Next, compute the present value of depreciation deductions using "correct" economic depreciation to accurately reflecting income. For this discussion, assume that straight-line depreciation provides the correct economic depreciation method. Thus, if the asset had a ten-year life, you would compute the present value of deductions of $1,000 per year over the next ten years. Assume for discussion that the present value is $6,000. If Congress wanted to give the taxpayer an incentive equal to one-half of what current expensing would give, it should raise the present value of the future depreciation deductions to $8,000.

[2]   Inflation

The second problem addressed by accelerated depreciation is inflation. As the cost of replacing assets increases above historical cost, higher depreciation rates might approximate the adjustment to depreciable cost that would be made for inflation. The trouble is that accelerated depreciation rates in the statute are not specifically designed to adjust for inflation. As we saw earlier, the correct method of dealing with inflation is to adjust basis upwards to account for changes in the cost of living. When ACRS was introduced in 1981, inflation was high and the tax benefits of accelerated depreciation approximated what the deductions would be if basis for depreciation had been adjusted for inflation. The solution, however, was fixed by statute without regard to any changes in future inflation rates. Declines in inflation made existing accelerated depreciation extraordinarily favorable, which is one reason the Tax Reform Act of 1986 cut back on depreciation deductions.

The Treasury has proposed dealing with inflation in an analytically straightforward manner, by multiplying the amount of depreciation available under the statutory schedule by the inflation rate. For example, assume that the depreciation deduction without inflation adjustment is $12.00 two years after the initial investment (that is, in year 2). If inflation had gone up after the year of investment by 5% per year, the depreciation deduction in year 2, adjusted for inflation, would be $12.00 times 1.05^2 (that is, $13.23).

The Tax Reform Act of 1986 does nothing to deal specifically with inflation, which could be its Achilles heel. If inflation increases again, the pressure to raise depreciation will increase and the tax laws may again provide incentives that will become obsolete if inflation declines. The better approach is to let accelerated depreciation rates directly address the incentive issue and provide separately for inflation adjustments to cost.

[F]   When Does Depreciation Begin

Assume land has been leased to a tenant for 20 years for $100,000 per year rent, and, in year 5, the tenant constructs a building for $350,000. In year 12, the taxpayer purchases the land with the right to acquire the building at the end of the lease. Market rents for land have declined to $90,000. Total purchase price is $1,250,000. Is any portion of the purchase price depreciable and, if so, when? *Geneva Drive In Theatre, Inc. v. Commissioner*, 622 F.2d 995 (9th Cir. 1980).

[G]   Collector-Antique Items Used in Business

It should be obvious that the depreciation rules are complex, varying with the type of property and subject to frequent legislative changes. Lawyers are not generally concerned with depreciation, which is the stuff of accounting work. But, occasionally, a "fun" issue arises that requires statutory interpretation skills. The depreciation of musical instruments is an example.

LIDDLE v. COMMISSIONER
United States Court of Appeals, Third Circuit
65 F.3d 329 (3d Cir. 1995), affirming, 103 T.C. 285 (1994)

McKEE, CIRCUIT JUDGE: . . .

In this appeal from a decision of the United States Tax Court we are asked to decide if a valuable bass violin can be depreciated under the Accelerated Cost Recovery System when used as a tool of trade by a professional musician even though the instrument actually increased in value while the musician owned it. We determine that, under the facts before us, the taxpayer properly depreciated the instrument and therefore affirm the decision of the Tax Court. . . .

In 1984, after a season with the Philadelphia Orchestra, [Liddle] purchased a 17th century bass violin made by Francesco Ruggeri (c. 1620–1695), a luthier who was active in Cremona, Italy. . . . Liddle paid $ 28,000 for the Ruggeri bass, almost as much as he earned in 1987 working for the Philadelphia Orchestra. The instrument was then in an excellent state of restoration and had no apparent cracks or other damage. . . . Liddle purchased the bass because he believed it would serve him throughout his professional career — anticipated to be 30 to 40 years.

Despite the anticipated longevity of this instrument, the rigors of Liddle's profession soon took their toll upon the bass and it began reflecting the normal wear and tear of daily use, including nicks, cracks, and accumulations of resin. . . . Moreover, as common sense would suggest, basses are more likely to become damaged when used as performance instruments than when displayed in a museum. Accordingly, professional musicians who use valuable instruments as their performance instruments are exposed to financial risks that do not threaten collectors who regard such instruments as works of art, and treat them accordingly.

There is a flourishing market among nonmusicians for Cremonese School instruments such as Mr. Liddle's bass. Many collectors seek primarily the "label", i.e., the maker's name on the instrument as verified by the certificate of authenticity. As nonplayers, they do not concern themselves with the physical condition of the instrument; they have their eye only on the market value of the instrument as a collectible. As the quantity of these instruments has declined through loss or destruction over the years, the value of the remaining instruments as collectibles has experienced a corresponding increase.

Eventually, Liddle felt the wear and tear had so deteriorated the tonal quality of his Ruggeri bass that he could no longer use it as a performance instrument. Rather than selling it, however, he traded it for a Domenico Busan 18th century bass in May of 1991. The Busan bass was appraised at $ 65,000 on the date of the exchange, but Liddle acquired it not for its superior value, but because of the greater tonal quality. Liddle . . . claimed a depreciation deduction of $ 3,170 for the Ruggeri bass under the Accelerated Cost Recovery System ("ACRS"), **I.R.C. § 168**.

The Commissioner originally argued that the ACRS deduction under § 168 is inappropriate here because the bass actually appreciated in value. However, the Commissioner has apparently abandoned that theory, presumably because an asset can appreciate in market value and still be subject to a depreciation deduction under tax law. . . .

Here, the Commissioner argues that the Liddles can claim the ACRS deduction only if they can establish that the bass has a determinable useful life. Since Mr. Liddle's bass is already over 300 years old, and still increasing in value, the Commissioner asserts that the Liddles can not establish a determinable useful life and therefore can not take a depreciation deduction. In addition, the Commissioner argues that this instrument is a "work of art" which has an indeterminable useful life and is therefore not depreciable. . . .

[Editor — The court then explains that the 1981 and 1986 changes in the tax rules for depreciation were intended to encourage investment and eliminate disputes about useful life.]

The Commissioner argues that . . . § 168 did not eliminate the [prior] § 167 requirement that tangible personalty used in a trade or business must also have a determinable useful life in order to qualify for the ACRS deduction. She argues that the phrase "of a character subject to the allowance for depreciation" demonstrates that the . . . § 167 requirement for a determinable useful life is the threshold criterion for claiming the § 168 ACRS deduction.

Much of the difficulty inherent in this case arises from two related problems. First, Congress left § 167 unmodified when it added § 168; second, § 168 contains no standards for determining when property is "of a character subject to the allowance for depreciation." In the absence of any express standards, logic and common sense would dictate that the phrase must have a reference point to some other section of the Internal Revenue Code. Section 167(a) would appear to be that section. As stated above, that section provides that "there shall be allowed as a depreciation deduction a reasonable allowance for the exhaustion, wear and tear . . . of property used in a trade or business . . . ." The Commissioner assumes that all of the depreciation regulations promulgated under § 167 must, of necessity, be imported into § 168. That importation would include the necessity that a taxpayer demonstrate that the asset have a demonstrable useful life, and (the argument continues) satisfy the phrase "tangible property of a character subject to the allowance for depreciation" in § 168.

However, we do not believe that Congress intended the wholesale importation of § 167 rules and regulations into § 168. Such an interpretation would negate one of the major reasons for enacting the Accelerated Cost Recovery System. Rather, we believe that the phrase "of a character subject to the allowance for depreciation" refers only to that portion of § 167(a) which allows a depreciation deduction for assets which are subject to exhaustion and wear and tear. Clearly, property that is not subject to such exhaustion does not depreciate. Thus, we hold that "property of a character subject to the allowance for depreciation" refers to property that is subject to exhaustion, wear and tear, and obsolescence. However, it does not follow that Congress intended to make the ACRS deduction subject to the § 167 useful life rules, and thereby breathe continued life into a regulatory scheme that was bewildering, and fraught with problems, and required "substantial restructuring."

We previously noted that Congress believed that prior depreciation rules and regulations did not provide the investment stimulus necessary for economic expansion. Further, Congress believed that the actual value of the depreciation deduction declined over the years because of inflationary pressures. In addition, Congress felt that prior depreciation rules governing the determination of useful lives were much too complex and caused unproductive disagreements between taxpayers and the Commissioner. Thus, Congress passed a statute which "de-emphasizes the concept of useful life." Accordingly, we decline the Commissioner's invitation to interpret § 168 in such a manner as to re-emphasize a concept which Congress has sought to "de-emphasize."

The Commissioner argues that de-emphasis of useful life is not synonymous with abrogation of useful life. As a general statement, that is true. However, the position of the Commissioner, if accepted, would reintroduce unproductive disputes over useful life between taxpayers and the Internal Revenue Service. Indeed, such is the plight of Mr. Liddle.

Congress de-emphasized the § 167 useful life rules by creating four short periods over which taxpayers can depreciate tangible personalty used in their trade or business. These statutory "recovery periods . . . are generally unrelated to, but shorter than, prior law useful lives." The four recovery periods are, in effect, the statutorily mandated useful lives of tangible personalty used in a trade or business. . . .

Thus, in order for the Liddles to claim an ACRS deduction, they must show that the bass is recovery property as defined in I.R.C. § 168(c)(1). . . . What is disputed is whether the bass is "property of a character subject to the allowance for depreciation." We hold that that phrase means that the Liddles must only show that the bass was subject to exhaustion and wear and tear. The Tax Court found as a fact that the instrument suffered wear and tear during the year in which the deduction was claimed. That finding was not clearly erroneous. Accordingly, the Liddles are entitled to claim the ACRS deduction for the tax year in question.

Similarly, we are not persuaded by the Commissioner's "work of art" theory, although there are similarities between Mr. Liddle's valuable bass, and a work of art. The bass is highly prized by collectors; and, ironically, it actually increases in value with age much like a rare painting. Cases that addressed the availability for depreciation deductions under § 167 clearly establish that works of art and/or collectibles were not depreciable because they lacked a determinable useful life. See, *Associated Obstetricians and Gynecologists, P.C. v. Commissioner*, 762 F.2d 38 (6th Cir. 1985) (works of art displayed on wall in medical office not depreciable); *Hawkins v. Commissioner*, 713 F.2d 347 (8th Cir.) (art displayed in law office not depreciable). See also, Rev. Rul. 68-232, 1968-1 C.B. 79 ("depreciation of works of art generally is not allowable" because '[a] valuable and treasured art piece does not have a determinable useful life.' "). [Editor — Does this mean that an antique desk used by a law firm partner is depreciable, but not the art work on the wall?]

. . . In Brian Liddle's professional hands, his bass viol was a tool of his trade, not a work of art. It was as valuable as the sound it could produce, and not for its looks. Normal wear and tear from Liddle's professional demands took a toll upon the instrument's tonal quality and he, therefore, had every right to avail himself of the depreciation provisions of the Internal Revenue Code as provided by Congress.

Accordingly, for the reasons set forth above, we will affirm the decision of the tax court.

COMMENTS AND QUESTIONS

1. Evaluate the following critique of the *Liddle* decision (and the decision in *Simon v. Commissioner*, 68 F.3d 41 (2d Cir. 1995), which reached the same result). The Commissioner nonacquiesces in the *Liddle* and *Simon* decisions; 1996-2 C.B. 2.

The "wear and tear" and "useful life" requirements for depreciation (which are imposed by § 167 and **Treas. Reg. § 1.167(a)-1**) serve the underlying purpose of "clearly reflecting income." When an asset's value will not decline, income cannot be clearly reflected by allowing depreciation and the tax law should be interpreted in light of that principle. It is true that the 1981/1986 laws allowed some departure from a "clearly reflect income" principle by eliminating a lot of the disputes about useful life, but the asset must still be the type of asset that could decline in value, determined without regard to any special tax rules shortening those lives in § 168.

Collector-antiques do not satisfy this condition. The court's emphasis on physical "wear and tear" obscures the fact that tax depreciation is concerned with financial rather than physical reality.

There are two possible responses to this critique. First, at least some types of (admittedly) depreciable assets are very unlikely to decline in value because of inflation (e.g., buildings). But collector-antiques are different. It is well known that inflation can prevent decline in value of some assets, and one major purpose of the favorable depreciation rules in § 168 was to be an explicit substitute for periodically adjusting the depreciable basis for inflation. Assets that maintain their value because of their special market characteristics as antiques are very different from those that maintain their value due to inflation.

Second, the depreciation rules usually disregard salvage value and, if a court takes account of an asset's retention of value, it is in effect considering salvage value. Again, collector-antiques are different. Salvage value should be disregarded only if the asset is depreciable in the first place. It is one thing to disregard the salvage value of depreciable assets and quite another matter to neglect the reality that "salvage value" is almost certain to equal or exceed original cost in deciding whether the asset is depreciable.

2. The Tax Court opinion in *Liddle* distinguished the musical instrument from a work of art on the ground that a work of art is a "passive object . . . displayed for admiration of its aesthetic qualities." But why does that distinguish artwork from the musical instrument, if they are both used actively as a tool of the trade? Doesn't displayed artwork also deteriorate *eventually* with light and atmospheric exposure? As long as the musical instrument and the artwork are used in the business, why should one be depreciable and the other not?

3. Suppose artwork costs $100,000 and, after six years, it is removed from the law firm where it is displayed and used for personal enjoyment in a home. Does the change in use result in taxable income? Can the IRS effectively tax such income? Does thinking about this question explain why artwork used in a business might not be depreciable but a musical instrument used in a business would be? *Cf.* § 179(d)(10).

4. Under the version of § 168 applicable to the tax years in this case, § 168 applied only if the property was "of a character subject to the allowance for depreciation." Current § 168(a) states that "the depreciation deduction provided by section 167(a) . . . shall be determined" as provided in § 168. Does the different wording of current § 168 produce a different result? The *Liddle* opinion emphasizes that § 168 does not import the "useful life" requirement imposed by § 167. Perhaps the explicit reference in the *current* version of § 168(a) to § 167 would import that requirement (although *Selig v. Commissioner*, 70 T.C.M. (CCH) 1125 (1995), held to the contrary).

5. At an auction of assets owned by Jacqueline Kennedy's estate, the owner of a well-known cigar magazine paid more than $500,000 for a humidor (for keeping cigars) owned by President Kennedy. Would that cost be depreciable if the asset were displayed in the magazine's business headquarters?

§ 11.03   OTHER INVESTMENT INCENTIVES

[A]   Expensing and Short-period Depreciation

The statute is filled with numerous rules permitting short-period depreciation (often 60 months) and expensing (a deduction in the year of the expenditure). Expensing is rapid depreciation carried to the extreme of allowing the expenditure to be deducted in full in the year it is incurred.

Sometimes these provisions are tax incentives. But sometimes expensing is explicitly permitted, not so much as an incentive, but to simplify administration. As explained in Chapter 13, expenditures producing assets with a life beyond the end of the tax year should theoretically be added to basis rather than deducted immediately. However, drawing the line between expenditures that should be added to basis and those that should be expensed is often very difficult because it is hard to tell whether the value extends beyond the end of the tax year. The statute sometimes responds to this administrative difficulty by explicitly permitting expensing.

The beneficiaries of these tax breaks are often specific industries (such as farmers, oil producers, or timber growers), a particular region (such as New Orleans after Katrina), or a political cause (such as environmental concerns).

[1]   In General

Here is a partial list of some statutory provisions permitting short-period depreciation (often called "amortization") or expensing. What is your best guess as to whether the provision is an incentive or simplifies administration?

Type of expenditure	Statutory section
farmer's soil/water conservation	§ 175 (expense)
farmer's fertilizer, etc. for land	§ 180 (expense)
research and development	§ 174 (expense or 60-month)
remove barriers to handicapped	§ 190 (expense)
pollution control facility	§ 169 (60-month)
intangible oil and gas drilling	§ 263(c) (expense)
newspaper circulation	§ 173 (expense)
exploration and development of mines	§§ 616, 617

What is the purpose of permitting amortization of the organization costs of a corporation or partnership? §§ 248, 709(b).

[2]   Section 179

Section 179 permits a taxpayer to expense the cost of depreciable tangible personal property used in an active trade or business, up to a ceiling. In addition, the amount that can be expensed is reduced dollar per dollar as total business investment in tangible personal property exceeds a threshold. The amount expensed cannot exceed income from an active trade or business, although unused

§ 179 deductions can be carried forward. This is a very big tax break for small businesses.

For 2010 and 2011, the ceiling on the amount that can be expensed under **§ 179** was $500,000 and the threshold above which the amount that can be expensed begins to disappear is $2,000,000 (as provided by the Small Business Jobs Act of 2010, Pub. L. 111-240). ATRA extended this benefit through 2013. After 2013, the law is scheduled to revert to much lower expensing and threshold amounts, but Congress has been very willing to extend this tax break for investment in the past. Stay tuned.

[B]   Tax Credits

Investment tax credit. At various times, the tax law has provided a tax incentive for business investment in the form of an investment tax credit for tangible personal property (not buildings or intangible property). A tax credit is a reduction of *tax*, not income, by some percentage of the investment. A 10% investment tax credit for investing in a $100,000 machine, for example, would reduce tax by $10,000.

The tax law, since the Tax Reform Act of 1986, does *not* provide a general business investment tax credit. When that credit was provided, the basic provisions were as follows: (1) a 10% credit, reduced to 6% for short-lived property; (2) one half of the credit reduced basis eligible for depreciation; (3) the credit was limited to $25,000 tax liability plus 75% of tax over $25,000; (4) investments in *used* property eligible for the credit were subject to a separate dollar ceiling; (5) the credit was not "refundable" if it exceeded tax liability; and (6) unused credits could be carried forward to later years.

Other business credits. The tax credit mechanism (as well as accelerated depreciation) remains popular for specific investments — on either a temporary or permanent basis. For example, there is now a credit for housing rehabilitation (§§ 38(b)(1), 46(1), 47) and investment in low-income housing (§ 42(a)). The orphan drug credit was extended by the 1996 Act and made permanent by the 1997 Act (§ 45C). The research credit (§ 41) has been extended by ATRA through 2013. And the Work Opportunity Credit provided by § 51 has been extended by ATRA through 2013. A particular favorite is credits for energy efficiency — such as for the purchase of energy-efficient homes and appliances (§§ 45L, 45M), extended by ATRA through 2013.

Adoption. The adoption credit (§ 23) and employee's income of employer-provided adoption benefits (§ 137) have been made permanent by ATRA. The 2013 figures are $12,970 of adoption expenses eligible for the credit and income exclusion; and a phase-out threshold of $194,580.

Employer-provided child care. The 2001 Tax Bill also adopted a credit for employers who provide child care to employees, beginning in tax year 2002. § 45F. The credit is 25% of qualified child care expenditures and 10% of qualified child care resource and referral expenditures. The credit is capped at $150,000. This tax break has been made permanent by ATRA.

§ 11.04   RECAPTURE OF PRIOR DEPRECIATION DEDUCTION

[A]   Basic Idea — Breaking Down Accounting Year Barriers

The basic idea behind statutory "recapture" rules is to reverse the effects of earlier deductions when, in a later year, the deduction turns out to be excessive. The prior deduction is "recaptured" in the later year by turning capital gain into ordinary income. The primary example of deductions that are recaptured are depreciation deductions. For example, if a taxpayer buys an asset for $100, takes $40 depreciation in year 1, and sells the asset for $75 in the year 2, the taxable gain is $15 ($75 minus the $60 basis). (The basis was adjusted downward for depreciation. 1016(a)(2).) The asset did not decline in value to $60, however, in the amount of the depreciation deduction. It only declined by $25 instead of the $40 reflected in the depreciation deduction. The $15 of excess depreciation must be recaptured as ordinary income; the gain is not capital gain.

The idea behind recapture of prior deductions as ordinary income is not as unfamiliar as it might seem. The earlier benefit (an ordinary depreciation deduction) justifies reduction of a later benefit (capital gains). The tax accounting year barrier is broken down so that events in an earlier tax year influence taxation in a later year. A similar idea underlay the decision in the *Haverly* case, where an earlier benefit (exclusion of a book from gross income) resulted in gross income in a later year when the taxpayer made a charitable contribution and claimed a deduction; Chapter 10.04[C]. And Chapter 5 dealt with the "tax benefit" and "tax detriment" rules, both of which broke down the tax accounting year barrier.

[B]   Statutory Rules

The basic recapture provision is § 1245, applicable primarily to assets other than buildings. It is illustrated by the following example. Suppose a corporate taxpayer pays $20,000 for a business machine and deducts $12,000 depreciation. The basis is adjusted downward to $8,000. § 1016(a)(2). If the taxpayer sells the property for $10,000, the gain is $2,000. How much gain is "recaptured" as ordinary income? All of it. *See* § 1245(a)(1).

If the asset was sold for $25,000 because it had gone up in value, the gain would be $17,000. Of that gain, $12,000 would be recaptured as ordinary income (recomputed basis of $20,000 minus $8,000 basis). The remaining $5,000 of gain would probably be capital gain (under § 1231, discussed in Chapter 20.03).

An additional consequence of converting capital gain to ordinary income is to deny a charitable donor a deduction for the gain that would be ordinary income. For example, if a chemical manufacturer paid $10,000 for a machine, and took $2,000 depreciation, a gift of the asset when it was worth $11,000 would result in only a $9,000 charitable deduction. § 170(e)(1)(A).

There are many other recapture rules in the statute. Earlier in this chapter we mentioned "expensing" provisions. Although expensing is not technically depreciation, the statute often provides for recapture of prior expenses if the taxpayer sells an asset created by an expenditure that has been expensed for tax purposes. § 1245(a)(2)(C).

[C]   Real Estate Gain and Recapture; Increasing the Capital Gains Rate

Under current law, none of the gain on real estate is recaptured as ordinary income. The fact that only straight-line depreciation is allowed over a fairly long period may be only a partial explanation for this rule. The more favorable rules for buildings may be a tax incentive, or (perhaps) recognition that the gain is more likely to be the result of inflation. Nonetheless, when the 1997 Tax Act lowered capital gains rates, it added a rule that the tax rate on amounts that would otherwise be recapture income on the sale of real estate would be capped at 25%, not a lower preferential rate. § 1(h)(1)(D).

For example, assume an individual buys a building for $100,000 and the taxpayer takes depreciation deductions on a straight-line basis equal to $40,000. Adjusted basis is $60,000. The building is sold for $110,000 after four years. The $50,000 gain is taxed as follows: $10,000 eligible for the preferential tax rate on long-term capital gains; $40,000 eligible for a 25% maximum tax rate.

[D]   Basis for Computing Gain

Suppose the taxpayer has a $100 cost for an asset. Proper depreciation is $20, but the taxpayer (erroneously) takes a $25 depreciation deduction. **Section 1016(a)(2)** says that the downward basis adjustment is the greater of the amount allow*ed* or allow*able*. The amount "allowed" is the greater $25 amount, so basis is $75. This means that recapture gain is greater than if the depreciation basis were computed "correctly." However, if the deduction of the amount allowed in excess of what is allowable ($5 in the example) does not result in a reduction of tax, basis is not reduced by the excess. **§ 1016(a)(2)(B)**. This statutory rule overrides *Virginian Hotel Corp. v. Helvering*, 319 U.S. 523 (1943). This is one aspect of a much broader problem — to what extent is the taxpayer bound in a later year by errors made in a prior year, rather than the government being required to go back to the earlier year to make a correction to the income computation in the earlier year?

What if the amount allowed is *less* than the amount allowable — e.g., the taxpayer deducted only $15 of depreciation when $20 was permitted. In that case, **§ 1245(a)(2)(B)** states that the amount recaptured as ordinary income will not exceed $15, if the taxpayer can prove that the amount allowed was less than the amount allowable. The taxable gain is $20, but only $15 is recaptured as ordinary income.

§ 11.05   BUYER vs. SELLER CONSISTENCY

A buyer obviously wants to allocate more of the purchase price of a business to assets that can be deducted as quickly as possible — that is, depreciable assets with the shortest lives. Sellers are interested in minimizing their taxes by allocating the sales price to preferentially taxed assets, such as capital gains rather than ordinary income. If the parties are adverse regarding taxes, the allocation is likely to be accepted by the government. For example, they are adverse in the following situation:

	Seller	Buyer
Asset 1	Bad Ordinary Income	Good Fast Depreciation
Asset 2	Good Long Term Capital Gain	Bad Slow or No Depreciation

Courts have used a variety of tests to determine how to allocate a purchase price to different elements of a transaction — (1) parties must stick to the values assigned in an agreement between the parties absent "strong proof" to the contrary (although the government can still question how those values were assigned); (2) parties must stick to the values assigned in an agreement if they reflect mutual intent, unless that intent does not reflect economic reality; and (3) parties must stick to the values assigned in an agreement, absent a showing of mistake, undue influence, fraud, or duress in forming the agreement (referred to as the *Danielson* rule, 378 F.2d 771 (3d Cir. 1967)).

In *Becker v. Commissioner*, 92 T.C.M. (CCH) 481 (2006), the court discussed the mutual intent and *Danielson* rule and found that the agreement unambiguously assigned all of the purchase price to nondepreciable stock and that the parties also had a mutual intent to reach that result (producing capital gain to the seller). None of the price was therefore allocated to a covenant not to compete (which would have resulted in depreciation to the buyer and ordinary income to the seller). Notice that the parties were probably adverse with respect to the allocation of the purchase price to stock and a covenant not to compete — the seller of the stock received capital gains and the buyer of the stock acquired a nondepreciable asset; the seller of the covenant not to compete received ordinary income and the buyer acquired a capital asset.

See also § 1060, which reduces the potential for taxpayers to manipulate the allocation of the purchase price of a trade or business among the business assets. It forces both the buyer and seller to use a specified method of allocating the sales price of such assets. It also states that a specific agreement between buyer and seller about allocating the purchase price is binding on both parties unless the IRS determines that the allocation is not appropriate.

Chapter 12

LOSSES

We have already discussed the recovery of basis through the computation of gain on disposition of an asset (§ 61) and through depreciation (§ 167). Those basis recovery rules deal with some but not all of the situations in which an asset with a basis can become useless to the taxpayer. For example, what are the tax consequences if an asset is sold at a loss (that is, for less than its basis), or is destroyed by fire when there is no insurance? The loss deduction rules cover such cases.

§ 12.01 REALIZATION

[A] Realizable Event vs. Market Fluctuation

Realization of a loss is a *necessary* condition for a deduction, but realization does not always mean that a loss is deductible. The following paragraphs discuss realization; later sections discuss whether a realized loss can be deducted, and, if so, how much.

Realized losses generally result from sale, casualty, or seizure of an asset. They can also result from total obsolescence or abandonment, as long as the taxpayer can fix such a loss by an identifiable event; *Dezendorf v. Commissioner*, 312 F.2d 95 (5th Cir. 1963) (intent to abandon and some act evidencing that intent are required). Market fluctuations do not produce a realized loss, any more than they produce a realized gain.

A number of cases have addressed whether loss of a monopoly position results in a realized loss — for example, when deregulation of airline routes permits free entry into airline markets. If the air carrier continues to fly the routes, though with fewer flights and with competition, the loss of monopoly position without explicit abandonment of a market is not a realized loss, even though value declines. Rev. Rul. 84-145, 1984-2 C.B. 47.

[B] Separating Realized Loss from Market Decline

When a realized casualty loss occurs, there is often an additional decline in value due to market resistance to buying an asset in a risk-prone area — e.g., after an avalanche or earthquake. *See Martin v. Commissioner*, 79 T.C.M. (CCH) 1534 (2000) (no deduction for market decline due to buyer fear of future earthquakes); *Lund v. United States*, 2000-1 U.S. Tax Cas. (CCH) ¶ 50,234 (D. Utah 2000) (same result; avalanche). In *Lund*, the court stated:

[Government] contends "a casualty loss is limited to the decline in a home's fair market value resulting from a natural disaster . . . that is directly linked to actual physical damage to the subject property or to its use and may not include any diminution in fair market value attributable to buyer resistance." On the other hand, plaintiffs assert that, because their home is in an avalanche zone, the use of the home is permanently restricted during winter months and the drop in the appraisal value of their home is not due to mere temporary buyer resistance. . . .

Section 165 has been interpreted by case authority as not being intended to cover loss in market value not due to physical damage directly caused by the casualty. For example, in Kamanski v. Commissioner, 477 F.2d 452 (9th Cir. 1973), it was found that a drop in the market value of the taxpayers' residence was due to buyer resistance rather than damage directly caused by the casualty, in that case a landslide. . . .

Where alleged losses result from a mere fluctuation in [market] value, there is no deductible loss. Thornton v. Commissioner, 47 T.C. 1 (1966); Peterson v. Commissioner, 30 T.C. 660 (1958). See also Pulvers v. Commissioner, 407 F.2d 838 (9th Cir. 1969), affirming, 48 T.C. 245 (1967) (no deduction allowed where landslide destroyed neighboring homes, but there was no actual physical damage to taxpayer's property; casualty loss depends upon actual physical damage, not hypothetical loss, mere fluctuation in value, or temporary buyer resistance). . . .

Here the basis of plaintiffs' deduction is . . . a lower appraisal value attributed to anticipated buyer resistance because of avalanche risk. In support of its position plaintiffs state that the Utah County Sheriff on occasion has closed access to their home, and at times discouraged them from visiting their home in winter months. Plaintiffs also state that their home cannot be completely protected from avalanche danger and that several homes in the area have been destroyed and may not be rebuilt. The court is of the opinion that those conditions are not [] permanent changes . . . entitling the taxpayer to a casualty loss deduction.

See also Chamales v. Commissioner, 79 T.C.M. (CCH) 1428 (2000); Caan v. United States, 99-1 U.S. Tax Cas. (CCH) ¶ 50,349 (C.D. Cal. 1999). Two neighbors of O.J.Simpson claimed that a decline in value of their homes after the death of Nicole Brown Simpson and Ronald Goldman on Simpson's property was a deductible casualty loss. Both cases denied the deduction on the ground that reductions in value due to "buyer resistance" do not produce a deductible casualty loss; the loss is unrealized.

[C] Possibility of Compensation

There is no deductible loss if a loss is compensated (e.g., by insurance), so the question becomes whether the possibility of compensation is sufficiently likely to postpone the deduction until that possibility is resolved.

Is it fair to postpone the taxpayer's loss deduction while the taxpayer argues with the insurance company? A $100,000 realized loss is postponed because of the prospect of recovering $100,000 at a future date, but the present value of that prospect is *less* than $100,000.

In *United States v. S.S. White Dental Mfg. Co.*, 274 U.S. 398 (1927), the Court dealt with a case in which property had been seized in 1918 by a government with which the United States was at war. There was a chance that some compensation would be recovered after the war, but it was a matter of "grace," not of right, and in any event depended on the hazards of the war in progress. The taxpayer took the deduction in 1918 and the Court agreed. The seizure created a loss "fixed by identifiable events," not mere market fluctuation. In addition, the taxpayer did not have to be "an incorrigible optimist" regarding recovery of the assets or later compensation. The loss therefore resulted from a "closed" transaction — a phrase the Court used as a synonym for "realization."

Sometimes, it is reasonably clear that only some compensation will be received. In that case, the remainder of the loss is realized. Thus, if the taxpayer has a $100,000 loss and will clearly receive $65,000 insurance, a $35,000 loss is realized. If it later turns out that the insurance company will pay another $35,000 (even though that prospect could only have been described as incorrigibly optimistic), the taxpayer has $35,000 income at that time, unless the prior $35,000 deduction was useless (that is, unless the tax benefit rule applies — Chapter 5.03).

[D] Failure to File Insurance Claim

Should a casualty loss deduction be contingent on filing an insurance claim? You can imagine a taxpayer deciding not to file out of fear that the policy might be cancelled. Case law held that the taxpayer who did not file a claim was like a taxpayer with no insurance — and was therefore entitled to the loss deduction. *Hills v. Commissioner*, 76 T.C. 484 (1981), *affirmed*, 691 F.2d 997 (11th Cir. 1982); *Miller v. Commissioner*, 733 F.2d 399 (6th Cir. 1984). The statute was then amended to prohibit the deduction for loss of *personal use* property unless an insured taxpayer filed a timely claim. § 165(h)(4)(E). Does that statutory amendment imply anything about the correct answer when the property is used for business or income production?

§ 12.02 PERSONAL ASSETS

[A] Casualty Loss

Should there ever be a deduction for losses of personal assets — that is, assets used for personal purposes, such as a home? Recall the discussion of depreciation, where we agreed that depreciation deductions for personal assets were not allowed because they were the equivalent of rent for personal consumption. If you buy a home for $60,000 and it is destroyed by fire (no insurance) the day after the purchase, what personal consumption have you enjoyed from your investment? None.

The tax law responds to this observation by allowing loss deductions of personal use property *only* when the loss arises from "fire, storm, shipwreck, or other casualty, or theft." § 165(c)(3). There is, therefore, no loss deduction on the sale or abandonment of personal use property. This result is based on the assumption that any such loss is the result of the property's personal use.

What is a casualty? The law needs some way to distinguish between the gradual wearing away of the asset, which is the equivalent of nondeductible depreciation, and casualties, where the loss is not the equivalent of personal consumption. The rulings draw some very fines lines, as the following questions indicate. The general rule is that a casualty occurs only when it is sudden, unexpected, and unusual. Rev. Rul. 72-592, 1972-2 C.B. 101.

QUESTIONS

Which of the following are deductible casualty losses of personal use property? To what extent do the rules accurately distinguish between what should and should not be deductible?

1. Losses due to a hurricane; due to the action of waves on the foundation of oceanfront property. Rev. Rul. 76-134, 1976-1 C.B. 54.

2. Loss of a rusty water heater which bursts; loss of a rug when the bursting water heater damages the rug. Rev. Rul. 70-91, 1970-1 C.B. 37.

3. Damage to a car due to the owner's negligence. **Treas. Reg. § 1.165-7(a)(3).** There is no casualty loss if the loss is the result of gross negligence or an intentional act. In *Blackman v. Commissioner*, 88 T.C. 677 (1987), *affirmed in unpublished opinion*, 867 F.2d 605 (1st Cir. 1988), a loss deduction was not allowed when the taxpayer burned his wife's clothes after a major argument and the fire spread to the entire house. According to the court, this was at least gross negligence.

4. Loss of a home in Saigon abandoned before the city fell to the North Vietnamese (*Popa v. Commissioner*, 73 T.C. 130 (1979)); abandoning a car which turns out to be a lemon.

5. Payment to an extortioner who kidnapped a relative. Rev. Rul. 72-112, 1972-1 C.B. 60.

6. Loss of ring that falls off while walking; loss of ring when a car door slammed on a finger. *Jones v. Commissioner*, 24 T.C. 525 (1955); *White v. Commissioner*, 48 T.C. 430 (1967).

[B] Deducting Personal Consumption from Use of Personal Assets?

In fact, taxpayers can sometimes deduct the value of the personal consumption they enjoy from personal use assets. Here is how.

Personal residence. Assume taxpayer pays $100,000 for a residence and lives there for one-half of its useful life. Due to inflation or changes in land use patterns the house is still worth $100,000 when he sells it. How much gross income does he have? Basis is not reduced to account for use of the residence, so there is no gain.

This "no gain" result could be avoided if the adjusted basis of the property were adjusted downward to reflect nondeductible depreciation. For example, if a taxpayer bought a home for $100,000 and lived there for one-half its useful life, the "adjusted basis" could be $50,000, and sale for $100,000 would produce $50,000 gain. This approach has not been adopted, however, in part for administrative reasons (individuals would have to keep track of basis adjustments of personal use property), and in part because the general public probably does not think of the $50,000 as gain.

Life insurance. Another context in which recovery of basis upon disposition of an asset might result in the deduction of personal consumption — besides sale of a home — is the sale of life insurance during the insured's life. For example, assume that the taxpayer has paid $500 per year for 10 years to purchase whole life insurance — that is, life insurance that has a savings feature that allows the taxpayer to cash in the policy before death. After 10 years, the contract is sold for $6,000. The question is whether the gain is only $1,000, because the taxpayer can deduct the $5,000 costs in computing gross income.

Deduction of $5,000 would result in deducting some personal consumption because the $500 per year premiums consisted of two parts (a term insurance amount that would not have been deductible if the taxpayer had purchased term life insurance and a deductible saving element that earned interest over the life of the policy). Assume that the total of the premiums attributable to term insurance was $1,500. From an economic perspective, the $3,500 of savings would have earned $2,500 of interest, resulting in a $6,000 cash value after 10 years. The correct computation of gross income would result from allowing the taxpayer to deduct only $3,500 of cost (not the $5,000 that he paid) from the $6,000 payment received from the insurance company.

In Rev. Rul. 2009-13, 2009-1 C.B. 1029, the government ruled that the taxpayer must reduce the cost basis of the insurance by an amount equal to the term insurance premium attributable to each yearly premium — in other words, the theoretically correct result. Because this result departed from what many taxpayers had previously thought was the law, the part of the ruling dealing with the sale of the insurance policy was made prospective.

Another part of the ruling dealt with the surrender of the life insurance contract to the insurance company. The ruling posits premiums of $64,000 and a $78,000 cash surrender value, which reflected the subtraction of $10,000 of "cost-of-insurance" charges collected by the insurance company for periods ending on or before the surrender of the contract. Because the cash value already reflected a reduction for the insurance portion of the premiums, the basis of the contract remained $64,000, resulting in a $14,000 taxable gain.

Finally, the ruling dealt with the sale of term insurance — hypothesizing a level premium 15-year term life insurance contract *without* cash surrender value in which the monthly prepaid premium was $500. Through June 15 of Year 8, the taxpayer paid premiums totaling $45,000 and, on June 15 of Year 8, taxpayer sold the life insurance contract for $20,000. The cost basis was $250, which was the amount of the premium attributable to the second half of June; that is, the period *after* the sale for which the taxpayer received no insurance protection. This portion of the ruling was also prospective.

§ 12.03 AMOUNT OF DEDUCTION

[A] Business and Income-Producing Assets

If there is a total loss of a business or income-producing asset, the adjusted basis of the asset is deductible. **§ 165(b); Treas. Reg. § 1.165-7(b)(1).** That makes sense — the adjusted basis reflects an after-tax investment (an accretion to wealth) on which tax has been paid and which can be used for personal consumption and savings. If that accretion to wealth is lost, that fact should be reflected in the tax base as a deduction to reverse the prior inclusion in the tax base.

If there is a partial loss, the deduction is the difference between pre-loss and post-loss value, but not more than the adjusted basis of the asset. The computation of pre-loss and post-loss value may be difficult, so the Regulations permit the taxpayer to use the cost of repairs as a proxy for computing the decline in value, if (1) the repairs are necessary to restore the property to pre-loss condition; (2) the amount spent is not excessive; (3) the repairs do not care for more than the damage suffered; and (4) the value of the property does not exceed pre-loss value as a result of the repairs. **Treas. Reg. § 1.165-7(a)(2)(ii).**

It is unclear why a partial loss deduction is not the adjusted basis times the percentage of pre-loss value that has been lost. Thus, if an asset has an adjusted basis of $12,000, a partial loss resulting in a decline in value from $14,000 to $7,000 produces a $7,000 deduction. Why not a $6,000 deduction, because the property declined in value by one-half? After all, if one half the property had been sold, only one-half the basis (that is, $6,000) would be deductible. Do you agree with the following statement, justifying the difference between the partial sale and partial loss cases? "[A] partial sale indicates that there is at least an economic divisibility of the property, and it seems reasonable to apportion the basis . . . according to what is kept and what is disposed of. A partial casualty loss indicates no such divisibility for frequently the entire damage must be restored before the whole is to have any productive value." *Alcoma Ass'n v. United States*, 239 F.2d 365, 370 (5th Cir. 1956).

[B] Personal Use Assets

[1] Rewriting the Statute

If the asset is used for personal purposes (such as a home), the deductible loss is limited by pre-loss value, rather than adjusted basis, as explained in the following case.

HELVERING v. OWENS
United States Supreme Court
305 U.S. 468 (1939)

Mr. Justice Roberts delivered the opinion of the Court.

The courts below have given opposing answers to the question whether the basis for determining the amount of a loss sustained during the taxable year through injury to property not used in a trade or business, and therefore not the subject of an annual depreciation allowance, should be original cost or value immediately before the casualty. To resolve this conflict we granted certiorari. . . .

. . . [T]he facts are that the respondent Donald H. Owens purchased an automobile at a date subsequent to March 1, 1913, and prior to 1934, for $1,825, and used it for pleasure until June 1934 when it was damaged in a collision. The car was not insured. Prior to the accident its fair market value was $225; after that event the fair market value was $190. The respondents filed a joint income tax return for the calendar year 1934 in which they claimed a deduction of $1635, the difference between cost and fair market value after the casualty. The Commissioner reduced the deduction to $35, the difference in market value before and after the collision. . . .

The income tax acts have consistently allowed deduction for exhaustion, wear and tear, or obsolescence only in the case of "property used in the trade or business." The taxpayers in these cases could not, therefore, have claimed any deduction on this account for years prior to that in which the casualty occurred. For this reason they claim they may deduct upon the unadjusted basis, — that is, — cost. As the income tax laws call for accounting on an annual basis; as they provide for deductions for "losses sustained during the taxable year"; as the taxpayer is not allowed annual deductions for depreciation of non-business property; as [§ 165(b)] requires that the deduction shall be on "the adjusted basis provided in [§ 1011]," thus contemplating an adjustment of value consequent on depreciation; and as the property involved was subject to depreciation and of less value in the taxable year, than its original cost, we think [§ 1011(a)] must be read as a limitation upon the amount of the deduction so that it may not exceed cost, and in the case of depreciable non-business property may not exceed the amount of the loss actually sustained in the taxable year, measured by the then depreciated value of the property. The Treasury rulings have not been consistent, but this construction is the one which has finally been adopted.

COMMENTS

1. *Rationale for the pre-loss value limitation.* The idea behind this decision is that pre-loss declines in value are assumed to be attributable to personal use and should not be deductible. The mechanics of the loss deduction for personal use property are therefore as follows:

(a)   partial loss — the difference between pre-loss and post-loss value, but not more than adjusted basis;

(b)   total loss — the pre-loss value, but not more than adjusted basis.

2. *Use of Pre-loss Value to Prevent "Depreciation" Deductions.* Sometimes it does not seem fair to use pre-loss value to limit the deduction of personal use assets, because the decline in value does not really measure the value of prior personal consumption. As soon as you put the ignition key into a new car, for example, the value goes way down. The "purer" rule, as noted earlier in connection with computing gain, would be to measure nondeductible depreciation on the asset, reduce its basis to adjust for that depreciation, and use that adjusted basis to measure the deductible casualty loss (rather than using pre-loss value). For example, if the taxpayer bought a car for $20,000 and held it for one-fourth of its useful life, adjusted basis for casualty loss purposes would be $15,000, using straight-line depreciation. A total loss of the car would produce a $15,000 loss deduction, even if the pre-loss value had declined to $12,000. Notice that this approach argues for a change in the law to allow loss deductions on the *sale* of personal use assets, as well as on casualties, whenever the sales price is less than adjusted basis.

One objection to allowing a deduction for the loss of a personal use asset when value is less than some adjusted basis is that it understates personal consumption for people whose lifestyle caused the asset to decline in value below adjusted basis — such as heavy personal use of a car.

[2] Note on Statutory Interpretation — Plain Meaning vs. Tax Term of Art

The limitation imposed by the *Owens* case on the loss deduction for personal use assets makes sense. If a taxpayer cannot deduct depreciation on personal use assets, the decline in value equivalent to personal use should not be deductible as a casualty loss deduction. But what statutory language produces this result?

The statute says that adjusted basis is deductible and adjusted basis equals original cost in the case of a personal asset. *Owens* is one of the clearest cases of statutory structure demanding an interpretation that goes beyond what the statute seems to say. Another example was the definition of the "cost" of property received as compensation as the fair market value at which the property was taken into income. Chapter 3.02[A]–[B].

[3] Further Limits on Loss Deduction of Personal Use Assets

The rules on deducting casualty losses of personal use assets contain additional limitations, which often prevent use of the deductible loss. After you compute the amount of the loss deduction in accordance with above rules (including a reduction for compensation), further limits apply. First, the first $100 of each casualty loss is not deductible. Second, the total losses of personal use property are deductible only if they exceed the sum of casualty gains plus 10% of adjusted gross income. § 165(h). In addition, the deduction is an itemized deduction, but is not subject to the 2% floor.

[C]   Convert from Personal to Business Use

There are many reasons why a taxpayer prefers property that is "lost" to be considered business or income-producing, rather than personal use property: the loss is deductible even if it does not result from a casualty; the loss deduction is not limited to pre-loss value; insurance claims (probably) do not have to be filed; and there is neither a 10% of adjusted gross income floor nor a $100 deductible. Taxpayers therefore may try to convert personal use property to income-producing property.

QUESTIONS AND COMMENTS

1. Suppose a taxpayer owns a home, for which she paid $100,000. The home is later converted to business or income-producing use when the building is worth $90,000. Thereafter, the building burns down (no insurance). How much deduction can the taxpayer take?

2. When does a taxpayer convert the property to business or income-producing use — by offering it for sale? Offering it for rent? Actually renting it? The cases are unclear and the statute is not much help.

The statute refers to losses incurred in "a transaction entered into for profit." **§ 165(c)(1), (2).** When is that requirement met? Some of the uncertainty regarding this issue is obvious in the following excerpt from *Martin v. Commissioner*, 79 T.C.M. (CCH) 1534 (2000). For example, is offering for rent enough or must the property actually be rented?

> Generally, taxpayers must do more than merely list their residential realty to convert its use from personal to one which would permit a loss under section 165 that is not subject to the limitation of section 165(h)(1) and (2). *See, e.g., Newcombe v. Commissioner*, 54 T.C. 1298, 1302–1303 (1970); *Rogers v. Commissioner*, T.C. Memo. 1965-8. Although petitioners had listed the property for sale and were continuing to make repairs to enhance the property, some of their furniture remained, and the property was listed for sale rather than for rent. Petitioners were able to lease the property just 4 days after the earthquake [causing the loss] occurred, but these events are not sufficient to place them over the threshold necessary to convert their personal residence into property for which section 165(c)(1) or (c)(2) losses would be available.

Does **Treas. Reg. § 1.165-9(b)** help answer this question? The Regulation refers to "rent[ing] or otherwise appropriat[ing property] to income-producing purposes" as a necessary condition to taking a loss deduction.

Compare **§ 167(a)(2)**, which allows depreciation deductions if property is "held for production of income." Perhaps that imposes a lower standard to qualify for a depreciation rather than a loss deduction, because the deductible amount is less. Thus, offering for rent might support a depreciation deduction but not a loss deduction.

[D] Government as Insurer?

There is no deduction for insurance premiums on assets used for personal purposes. That is considered a nondeductible personal expense. Should the government help taxpayers insure against losses by providing a casualty loss deduction when there is no deduction for the insurance premiums themselves? Does the loss deduction provide an incentive (1) against buying insurance; (2) toward purchasing somewhat less sturdy assets? Is the loss deduction nonetheless fair, notwithstanding its incentive effects?

§ 12.04 DISALLOWING THE LOSS DEDUCTION

[A] Wagering Losses

Can a taxpayer who has gambling losses deduct the losses? The statute says that gambling losses are only deductible up to gambling gains. § 165(d). The usual explanation is that the losses are presumed equal to personal enjoyment from gambling. They are personal expenses.

There may be other explanations. First, a deduction might encourage activity that should be discouraged. Second, gamblers might lie about their losses. The rule simplifies administration by reducing the need to check on the veracity of loss claims.

[B] Wash Sale

If an investor pays $100 for General Motors common stock, sells it for $90, and purchases substantially identical GM common stock for (a) $85 or (b) $95, within 30 days of the original sale, he cannot recognize the loss. § 1091. The investor's financial position has not changed enough to justify a loss deduction. What is the seller's basis in the stock he acquires within the 30-day period in the two examples given above?

[C] Sale between Related Parties

In an early case, the Supreme Court disallowed a loss deduction on a sale between a taxpayer and his wholly owned corporation. *Higgins v. Smith*, 308 U.S. 473 (1940). The Court found so much dominion and control over the asset sold to the corporation, resulting from 100% ownership, that no loss was "sustained."

The statute now specifically disallows a loss deduction on a sale between related parties, as defined in the statute. § 267(a)(1), (b). Related parties include a corporation and a more than 50% owner (by value); and certain specifically defined relatives. § 267(b)(1), (2), (c)(4).

§ 12.05   "MADOFF" LOSSES

Taxpayers who thought they were making investments managed by Madoff's Ponzi scheme found themselves out-of-pocket to the tune of $50 billion (or so). Rev. Rul. 2009-9, 2009-1 C.B. 735, takes some of the sting out of these losses by providing taxpayers with ordinary deductions in the year the loss was discovered (2008), based on the following analysis. The first issue is whether these losses are ordinary or capital. In a section not yet discussed in the course, the code requires worthlessness of stock to be a capital loss. § 165(g). The idea is that sale produces a capital loss and there should be no difference between a sale at a loss and the loss of a worthless security. But Madoff never invested the taxpayer's money. Therefore, the loss was a theft loss that results in an ordinary loss, not a loss from a worthless security.

The second issue is whether any of the limitations on deductions apply — the § 67 (2% floor) rules; the § 68 (overall limitation on itemized deduction) rules; and the excess-of-10% rule applicable to § 165(c)(3) personal casualty losses. Once again, the taxpayer is in luck. The taxpayer who opened a Madoff account entered into a transaction for profit, so any theft loss was deductible under § 165(c)(2), not § 165(c)(3). Investment losses deducted under § 165(c)(2) are not subject to any of these limitations — § 67(b)(3), § 68(c)(3), § 165(c)(3), (h)(2)(A), (4)(b).

What is the amount of the loss deduction in 2008? It obviously includes the amount invested. But it also includes the investment income that was reported as taxpayer income and was purportedly (but not actually) reinvested by Madoff; this is consistent with the idea that basis equals the amount included in gross income.

Another "amount of loss" issue is whether the possibility of recovery postpones the loss deduction until such time as any claims are resolved. Rev. Proc. 2009-20, 2009-1 C.B. 749, states that a taxpayer who is not seeking recovery of any of the theft loss from a third party can deduct 95% of the total theft loss; and a taxpayer who is seeking such recovery can deduct 75% of the total theft loss. Adjustments are required in later years (either additional deductions if the loss is total; or an income item if a recovery is for any amount previously deducted).

Finally, it gets even better. We earlier discussed the carryover of net operating loss (NOL) deductions for business losses (Chapter 5.02). It turns out that the Code treats § 165(c)(2) losses (which include theft losses related to an investment entered into for profit) as attributable to a trade or business for the NOL carryover rules; § 172(d)(4)(C). Consequently, the Madoff losses can be carried back and forward in the same manner as a business NOL. For 2008, these rules are especially advantageous — permitting a carryback for as many as five years.

Chapter 13

CAPITAL EXPENDITURE vs. CURRENT EXPENSE

§ 13.01 INTRODUCTION

Savings, at least in theory, are part of the income tax base. Despite numerous exceptions, this generalization is a valid starting point. The distinction between current expenses and capital expenditures implements the taxation of savings. A capital expenditure *is* savings. The expenditure is therefore added to basis (that is, "capitalized"), rather than being deducted when incurred (that is, "expensed").

How is the line drawn between current expenses and capital expenditures? The idea is that any expenditure producing value expected to last beyond the end of the taxable year is savings and should be added to basis. However, drawing that line can pose formidable administrative difficulties. Moreover, the difference between expensing and savings is "just" a matter of timing. If the tax timing differences are small or not necessary to "clearly reflect income," the taxpayer is sometimes allowed to expense a capital expenditure.

Chapter 13.02 discusses acquisition costs. Chapter 13.03 distinguishes maintenance expenses from improvements and acquisitions. Chapter 13.04 considers the tax treatment of education expenditures, which are sometimes current expenses and sometime capital expenditures.

Personal assets. The dominant perspective in this chapter is that of the taxpayer who prefers a current expense to adding an expenditure to basis. The assumption is that it is better to get a deduction now (as an expense) rather than later (through a deduction of basis). In fact, that is not always the case. Expenses related to personal use assets are not deductible, but their cost may be (in computing gain on sale or as a casualty loss). Taxpayers therefore prefer to add expenditures to the basis of personal use assets, rather than treat them as expenses.

Sometimes a court does not make clear whether a deduction is denied in the expenditure year because it is a capital expenditure or a personal expense. Recall the Supreme Court *Gilmore* case, applying the origin test to disallow litigation expenditures related to a divorce. A later case permitted Mr. Gilmore to add the expenditures to the basis of the stock he tried to protect from his wife. The court concluded that the denial of the deduction in the expenditure year by the Supreme Court was consistent with adding the expenditure to the stock's basis. *Gilmore v. United States*, 245 F. Supp. 383 (N.D. Cal. 1965).

Is the District Court opinion in *Gilmore* correct? If the activity originated in the taxpayer's personal sphere of life, should the basis of investment assets be increased? Suppose Gilmore had been trying to protect a bank account; what asset's basis would be increased?

§ 13.02   ACQUISITION COSTS

When a taxpayer buys land, a building, shares of stock, or a car, it is easy to conclude that the expenditure is a capital expenditure. The asset obviously lasts beyond the tax year of purchase and its cost should be added to basis, just like cash in a savings account. It is also easy to slip into the assumption that the tax concept of savings, recorded in basis, correlates with tangible property that you can see and touch. That is a mistake. The tax concept of savings is, fundamentally, a financial accounting concept, which records investments in basis because that is the best way to clearly reflect income. The "assets" acquired with tax savings are not limited to tangible assets.

The section of the code usually cited as authority for capitalizing expenditures is § 263, which disallows a deduction for amounts paid out for permanent improvements. A much better cite would be § 446(b), which insists that the taxpayer's accounting method (which includes the timing of deductions) clearly reflect income.

[A]   Prepaid Expenses

COMMISSIONER v. BOYLSTON MARKET ASS'N
United States Court of Appeals, First Circuit
131 F.2d 966 (1st Cir. 1942)

MAHONEY, CIRCUIT JUDGE. . . .

We are asked to determine whether a taxpayer who keeps his books and files his returns on a cash basis is limited to the deduction of the insurance premiums actually paid in any year or whether he should deduct for each tax year the pro rata portion of the prepaid insurance applicable to that year. . . .

. . . Advance rentals, payments of bonuses for acquisition and cancellation of leases, and commissions for negotiating leases are all matters which the taxpayer amortizes over the life of the lease. Whether we consider these payments to be the cost of the exhaustible asset, as in the case of advance rentals, or the cost of acquiring the asset, as in the case of bonuses, the payments are prorated primarily because the life of the asset extends beyond the taxable year. To permit the taxpayer to take a full deduction in the year of payment would distort his income. Prepaid insurance presents the same problem and should be solved in the same way. Prepaid insurance for a period of three years may be easily allocated. It is protection for the entire period and the taxpayer may, if he desires, at any time surrender the insurance policy. It thus is clearly an asset having a longer life than a single taxable year. The line to be drawn between capital expenditures and ordinary and necessary business expenses is not always an easy one, but we are satisfied that in treating prepaid insurance as a capital expense we are obtaining some degree of consistency in these matters. . . .

Notice that *Boylston* requires prepaid expenses to be capitalized and then depreciated (assuming the asset is depreciable), whether the taxpayer is a cash or accrual method taxpayer.

[1] Prepayment and Explicit Statutory Authority for Deduction

If the statute explicitly authorizes a deduction, does that provision override the more general rules requiring capitalization? For example, § 163(a), (h)(1), (2)(D), (3) allows a deduction for home loan interest under certain circumstances discussed in Chapter 16.01[C][1]. Does that provision permit a deduction for *prepaid* home loan interest in the year paid, when the prepayment covers more than one year's interest obligation? After some litigation, the statute was amended to require prepaid interest to be capitalized and amortized over the loan period. § 461(g).

There is an exception, however, for "points" on a home purchase or improvement mortgage (which is the economic equivalent of prepaid interest), if such payments are customary business practice. The permission to expense rather than amortize points is elective with the taxpayer. *See* Letter Ruling 199905033 (taxpayer was unable to take advantage of the deduction for points because of the standard deduction; instead, taxpayer added points to basis as prepaid interest and amortized the basis over future years).

[2] Prepayment and Dissolution of Business

In *Steger v. Commissioner*, 113 T.C. 227 (1999), the taxpayer had retired from the practice of law in 1993. That same year, he bought malpractice insurance coverage for the amount of $3,168, which covered him for an indefinite period of time after retirement but only for malpractice based on services rendered before retirement. The IRS argued that the taxpayer could not deduct the entire cost of the policy in 1993 because the policy had "a useful life of indefinite duration beyond one year." The court held for the taxpayer, as follows:

> . . . [I]t is a longstanding rule of law that if a taxpayer incurs a business expense, but is unable to deduct the cost of the same either as a current expense or through yearly depreciation deductions, the taxpayer is allowed to deduct the expense for the year in which the business ceases to operate. . . . [R]espondent contends that the cost of the Policy is not "ordinary" because it is a capital expenditure given its indefinite useful life. However, even if we assume that the Policy is a capital asset, petitioners are nevertheless entitled to deduct the cost of the Policy in the year in issue. The Policy has no ascertainable useful life but rather is an intangible asset providing petitioner with malpractice coverage for an indefinite term of years. Although as a capital asset with an indefinite useful life the Policy would not be currently deductible, it is deductible upon dissolution of petitioner's business. Thus, even if the Policy is a capital asset, because petitioner purchased the Policy in the same year that he ceased to operate his business, petitioners are entitled to deduct the cost of the Policy in that year.

Is the court correct? On the one hand — in favor of capitalizing — the insurance provides the taxpayer with a future benefit by protecting assets and future income from being seized by creditors. But, on the other hand — in favor of expensing — the future benefits test is itself an effort to clearly define income, which is the fundamental issue in determining when an expenditure should be deducted; and, once the business has been dissolved, there is no future business income to be protected, and therefore, the deduction should be allowed in the year of dissolution.

[B] Tangible Property — Acquisition and Production Costs

[1] Supreme Court

The Court discussed the capitalization of building costs in the following case.

COMMISSIONER v. IDAHO POWER CO.
United States Supreme Court
418 U.S. 1 (1974)

Mr. Justice Blackmun delivered the opinion of the Court.

[Editor — The taxpayer is a utility. It used cars and trucks to construct assets used to transmit electricity. Cars and trucks are depreciable assets and the taxpayer took depreciation deductions on those assets attributable to the period during which the construction occurred. The Court disallowed the deductions, as follows.]

Our primary concern is with the necessity to treat construction-related depreciation in a manner that comports with accounting and taxation realities. Over a period of time a capital asset is consumed and, correspondingly over that period, its theoretical value and utility are thereby reduced. Depreciation is an accounting device which recognizes that the physical consumption of a capital asset is a true cost, since the asset is being depleted. As the process of consumption continues, and depreciation is claimed and allowed, the asset's adjusted income tax basis is reduced to reflect the distribution of its cost over the accounting periods affected. . . . When the asset is used to further the taxpayer's day-to-day business operations, the periods of benefit usually correlate with the production of income. Thus, to the extent that equipment is used in such operations, a current depreciation deduction is an appropriate offset to gross income currently produced. It is clear, however, that different principles are implicated when the consumption of the asset takes place in the construction of other assets that, in the future, will produce income themselves. In this latter situation, the cost represented by depreciation does not correlate with production of current income. Rather, the cost, although certainly presently incurred, is related to the future and is appropriately allocated as part of the cost of acquiring an income-producing capital asset.

There can be little question that other construction-related expense items, such as tools, materials, and wages paid construction workers, are to be treated as part of the cost of acquisition of a capital asset. The taxpayer does not dispute this. Of course, reasonable wages paid in the carrying on of a trade or business qualify as a deduction from gross income. § 162(a)(1). But when wages are paid in connection with the construction or acquisition of a capital asset, they must be capitalized and are then entitled to be amortized over the life of the capital asset so acquired.

Construction-related depreciation is not unlike expenditures for wages for construction workers. The significant fact is that the exhaustion of construction equipment does not represent the final disposition of the taxpayer's investment in that equipment; rather, the investment in the equipment is assimilated into the cost of the capital asset constructed. Construction-related depreciation on the equipment is not an expense to the taxpayer of its day-to-day business. It is, however, appropriately recognized as a part of the taxpayer's cost or investment in the capital asset. The taxpayer's own accounting procedure reflects this treatment, for on its books the construction-related depreciation was capitalized by a credit to the equipment account and a debit to the capital facility account. By the same token, this capitalization prevents the distortion of income that would otherwise occur if depreciation properly allocable to asset acquisition were deducted from gross income currently realized. An additional pertinent factor is that capitalization of construction-related depreciation by the taxpayer who does its own construction work maintains tax parity with the taxpayer who has its construction work done by an independent contractor. The depreciation on the contractor's equipment incurred during the performance of the job will be an element of cost charged by the contractor for his construction services, and the entire cost; of course, must be capitalized by the taxpayer having the construction work performed. . . .

The presence of § 263(a)(1) in the Code is of significance. Its literal language denies a deduction for '(a)ny amount paid out' for construction or permanent improvement of facilities. The taxpayer contends, and the Court of Appeals held, that depreciation of construction equipment represents merely a decrease in value and is not an amount 'paid out,' within the meaning of § 263(a)(1). We disagree.

The purpose of § 263 is to reflect the basic principle that a capital expenditure may not be deducted from current income. It serves to prevent a taxpayer from utilizing currently a deduction properly attributable, through amortization, to later tax years when the capital asset becomes income producing. The regulations state that the capital expenditures to which § 263(a) extends include the 'cost of acquisition, construction, or erection of buildings.' Treas. Reg. § 1.263(a)-2(a). This manifests an administrative understanding that for purposes of § 263(a)(1), 'amount paid out' equates with 'cost incurred.' The Internal Revenue Service for some time has taken the position that construction-related depreciation is to be capitalized. Rev. Rul. 59-380, 1959-2 C.B. 87; Rev. Rul. 55-252, 1955-1 C.B. 319.

There is no question that the cost of the transportation equipment was 'paid out' in the same manner as the cost of supplies, materials, and other equipment, and the wages of construction workers. The taxpayer does not question the capitalization of these other items as elements of the cost of acquiring a capital asset. We see no reason to treat construction-related depreciation differently. In acquiring the transportation equipment, taxpayer 'paid out' the equipment's purchase price; depreciation is simply the means of allocating the payment over the various accounting periods affected. As the Tax Court stated in Brooks v. Commissioner, 50 T.C., at 935, 'depreciation — inasmuch as it represents a using up of capital — is as much an 'expenditure' as the using up of labor or other items of direct cost."

COMMENTS

1. *Statutory Interpretation — Consistent Usage.* The Court notes that depreciation is *not* a "payment" for purposes of the § 170 charitable deduction, but concludes that the charitable deduction rules are irrelevant for identifying when an amount "paid out" must be capitalized under § 263.

A familiar linguistic canon of interpretation presumes that words are used consistently throughout a statute. But modern statutes are often amended at different times and these amendments often have different policy implications, even if the statutory texts are similar. Consequently, it is not unusual to find that the different temporal or policy context in which statutory drafting occurs results in similar terms having different meanings, despite being codified in the same law.

2. *Equating Builder and Purchaser. Idaho Power* talks about putting the taxpayer who builds its own building on a par with the person who buys the building from a contractor who constructs the building. The decision means that even wages, which are usually deductible business expenses, would be capital expenditures if incurred in connection with an asset's construction. *Idaho Power* accomplishes this result because the depreciation on the equipment used to construct the building (and wages paid to construction workers) would be included in the contractor's costs and therefore in the sale price charged to the taxpayer. However, *Idaho Power* is powerless to completely equate the taxpayer who buys the building from a contractor with a taxpayer who constructs the building. If the taxpayer buys the building for $100,000, it will pay $100,000 out of after-tax income, which equals basis. If it builds the building for $90,000, including depreciation in the $90,000 cost, it has a basis of only $90,000. The taxpayer does not include the additional $10,000 of builder profit in income or basis, thereby deferring tax on the $10,000 until the lower depreciation ($90,000 instead of $100,000) results in higher income in later years.

[2] Regulations

Facilitate acquisition. Treasury Regulations flesh out the principles underlying the otherwise cryptic statutory language in § 263, which had been applied in *Idaho Power*. The latest version is **Treas. Reg. § 1.263(a)-2T**. Among other things, these regulations require capitalization of payments to facilitate the acquisition or production of tangible property (real or personal). This includes amounts paid to investigate an acquisition. However, there is an exception for the cost of investigating whether and which real estate to acquire; these costs can be expensed. **Section 263** does not require these payments to be capitalized.

Inherently facilitative. Some costs are considered inherently facilitative and must always be capitalized (even for real estate); these include the costs of appraisal, title evaluation, obtaining regulatory approval and licensing, and brokers' commissions. Treas. Reg. § 1.263(a)-2T(f). If it turns out that the property is not acquired, the taxpayer has a loss deduction when the effort to acquire the property is abandoned; § 165.

Internal costs. Amounts spent for employee compensation and overhead (that is, expenses internal to the business) are not considered facilitation costs. This means that these expenditures can be expensed but payments to a third-party provider must be capitalized.

[3] Defending Title

Treas. Reg. § 1.263(a)-2T(e) explicitly states that amounts paid to defend or perfect title must be capitalized. However, Example 2 of these regulations distinguishes a title defense from the following deductible expense — payments incurred to invalidate an ordinance that is adopted several years after the business was established and that would prohibit operation of the taxpayer's business.

[4] De Minimis Expenditures — Is Capitalizing Costs Worth the Trouble?

Sometimes it is not worth the administrative effort to argue about whether small expenditures should be deducted or added to basis. The Temporary Regulations now provide that some small expenditures (but not for land or inventory) do not have to be added to cost. **Treas. Reg. § 1.162-3T(g)**. To be eligible, the taxpayer must have expensed the item on a financial statement; and the total of such expenses must be less than or equal to .1 percent of gross receipts for the taxable year or 2 percent of total depreciation for the tax year. Amounts below this threshold can be expensed even if total expenses exceed the threshold. Moreover, this benefit is elective with the taxpayer on an item-by-item basis. This means that a taxpayer with total de minimis expenses over the threshold should elect to expense those costs with longer depreciation lives that are under the threshold and depreciate the shorter-lived assets over the threshold.

Disposition of property to which the de minimis rule is applied is not a disposition of a capital asset; the gain is ordinary income. This rule (found in the Regulations) is an application of a similar case law recapture rule adopted by the Supreme Court in *Hillsboro National Bank v. Commissioner*, 460 U.S. 370 (1983). The usual statutory recapture rules under § 1245 would not apply because the cost of the property had not been depreciated.

[5] Uniform Capitalization Rules

Even if an expenditure can be expensed under the rules discussed so far, the taxpayer must still worry about § 263A. When § 263A applies, it requires the capitalization of payments that would otherwise be deductible.

Here is the problem addressed by § 263A. Cases like *Idaho Power* deal with "direct" costs, which can be readily attributed to the production of a specific asset. There are, however, serious accounting problems with allocating "indirect" costs to the construction and production of property for use or sale, and to property purchased for resale. For example, should the salary paid to a manager or a business executive be allocated among various assets constructed, produced, or purchased by the taxpayer? How should interest on corporate loans used to finance construction, production, or purchase of various assets be allocated? Taxpayers were, for a long time, successfully expensing many of these indirect costs and even some direct costs. One example is the permission given to cash basis farmers to expense the direct cost of feeding cattle. **Treas. Reg. § 162-12(a)**.

The statute has now been explicitly amended to require both direct and indirect costs to be allocated to the basis of *real* property or *tangible* personal property produced by the taxpayer and real or personal property acquired for resale. **§ 263A** (uniform capitalization rules). ("Tangible personal property" includes a film, videotape, book, or similar property.) For example, in *PMT, Inc. v. Commissioner*, 72 T.C.M. (CCH) 5 (1996), 75% of the salary of the corporation's president was capitalized as a **§ 263A** inventory cost, because he was intimately involved in production design and development of the corporation's inventory.

There are, however, some explicit statutory exceptions: for example, **§ 263A** does *not* apply to *intangible* property produced by the taxpayer; or to purchasers for resale of any personal property with no more than $10 million gross receipts. **§ 263A(b)**.

Another important exception is for farmers under limited circumstances. **§ 263A(d)**. This means that some cash basis farmers who qualify under **§ 263A(d)** can still expense some direct costs, if they are permitted to use the cash method of accounting (**§ 447**) (discussed in Chapter 23.02)[A][2]).

Of special interest to creative authors and artists is **§ 263A(h)**, which exempts such individuals from the **§ 263A** capitalization requirements. Thus, periodically purchased writing materials and art supplies do not have to be added to the cost of the created product — at least as far as **§ 263A** is concerned. The basic accounting rules distinguishing current expenses from capital expenditures would still apply. *See generally Encyclopaedia Britannica, Inc. v. Commissioner*, 685 F.2d 212 (7th Cir. 1982) (discussing book publisher and author deductions).

Finally, **§ 263A** does not apply to a business engaged in providing services; it only applies to "property." **§ 263A(a)(1), (b)**.

Extensive regulations found in **Treas. Reg. § 1.263A-1 through -15** provide detailed guidance regarding the uniform capitalization rules.

[C]   Intangible Property — Acquisition and Production Costs

[1]   The *Indopco* Case

A separate set of regulations deals with expenditures related to intangible assets. These rules were adopted after the following Supreme Court decision.

INDOPCO, INC. v. COMMISSIONER
United States Supreme Court
503 U.S. 79 (1992)

Justice Blackmun delivered the opinion of the Court.

[Editor — A corporation was a target of a friendly takeover. The taxpayer, Indopco, Inc. (formerly named National Starch and Chemical Corporation) manufactures and sells adhesives, starches, and specialty chemical products. Representatives of Unilever United States, Inc., expressed interest in acquiring National Starch, which was one of its suppliers, through a friendly transaction. National Starch was a large publicly held corporation with more than 6,563,000 common shares held by approximately 3,700 shareholders. Frank and Anna Greenwall were the corporation's largest shareholders and owned approximately 14.5% of the common stock. The Greenwalls indicated that they would transfer their shares to Unilever only if a tax-free transaction could be arranged, which was done. National Starch's directors were told by Debevoise, Plimpton, Lyons & Gates, National Starch's counsel, that under Delaware law they had a fiduciary duty to ensure that the proposed transaction would be fair to the shareholders. National Starch thereupon engaged the investment banking firm of Morgan Stanley & Co., Inc., to evaluate its shares, to render a fairness opinion, and generally to assist in the event of the emergence of a hostile tender offer.

The tax issue was whether payments to Debevoise and Morgan Stanley related to the takeover, amounting to about $2,500,000, were capital expenditures. The Court dealt explicitly with its earlier decision in Commissioner v. Lincoln Savings & Loan *Ass'n*, 403 U.S. 345 (1971).]

National Starch contends that the decision in Lincoln Savings . . . announced an exclusive test for identifying capital expenditures, a test in which "creation or enhancement of an asset" is a prerequisite to capitalization, and deductibility under § 162(a) is the rule rather than the exception. We do not agree, for we conclude that National Starch has overread *Lincoln Savings*.

In Lincoln Savings, we were asked to decide whether certain premiums, required by federal statute to be paid by a savings and loan association to the Federal Savings and Loan Insurance Corporation (FSLIC), were ordinary and necessary expenses under § 162(a), as Lincoln Savings argued and the Court of Appeals had held, or capital expenditures under § 263, as the Commissioner contended. We found that the "additional" premiums, the purpose of which was to provide FSLIC with a secondary reserve fund in which each insured institution retained a pro rata interest recoverable in certain situations, "serv[e] to create or enhance for Lincoln what is essentially a separate and distinct additional asset." "[A]s an inevitable consequence," we concluded, "the payment is capital in nature and not an expense, let alone an ordinary expense, deductible under § 162(a)."

Lincoln Savings stands for the simple proposition that a taxpayer's expenditure that "serves to create or enhance . . . a separate and distinct" asset should be capitalized under § 263. It by no means follows, however, that only expenditures that create or enhance separate and distinct assets are to be capitalized under § 263. We had no occasion in *Lincoln Savings* to consider the tax treatment of expenditures that, unlike the additional premiums at issue there, did not create or enhance a specific asset, and thus the case cannot be read to preclude capitalization in other circumstances. In short, *Lincoln Savings* holds that the creation of a separate and distinct asset well may be a sufficient but not a necessary condition to classification as a capital expenditure. Nor does our statement in *Lincoln Savings* that "the presence of an ensuing benefit that may have some future aspect is not controlling" prohibit reliance on future benefit as a means of distinguishing an ordinary business expense from a capital expenditure. Although the mere presence of an incidental future benefit — "some future aspect" — may not warrant capitalization, a taxpayer's realization of benefits beyond the year in which the expenditure is incurred is undeniably important in determining whether the appropriate tax treatment is immediate deduction or capitalization. . . .

In applying the foregoing principles to the specific expenditures at issue in this case, we conclude that National Starch has not demonstrated that the investment banking, legal, and other costs it incurred in connection with Unilever's acquisition of its shares are deductible as ordinary and necessary business expenses under § 162(a).

Although petitioner attempts to dismiss the benefits that accrued to National Starch from the Unilever acquisition as "entirely speculative" or "merely incidental," the Tax Court's and the Court of Appeals' findings that the transaction produced significant benefits to National Starch that extended beyond the tax year in question are amply supported by the record. For example, in commenting on the merger with Unilever, National Starch's 1978 "Progress Report" observed that the company would "benefit greatly from the availability of Unilever's enormous resources, especially in the area of basic technology." . . .

In addition to these anticipated resource-related benefits, National Starch obtained benefits through its transformation from a publicly held, freestanding corporation into a wholly owned subsidiary of Unilever. . . .

Courts long have recognized that expenses such as these, " 'incurred for the purpose of changing the corporate structure for the benefit of future operations are not ordinary and necessary business expenses.' " Deductions for professional expenses thus have been disallowed in a wide variety of cases concerning changes in corporate structure. . . .

The expenses that National Starch incurred in Unilever's friendly takeover do not qualify for deduction as "ordinary and necessary" business expenses under § 162(a). The fact that the expenditures do not create or enhance a separate and distinct additional asset is not controlling; the acquisition-related expenses bear the indicia of capital expenditures and are to be treated as such.

[Editor — These costs do *not* acquire "section 197 intangibles" and therefore cannot be depreciated over 15 years. § 197(e)(8).]

[2]   The Reaction to *Indopco*; The New Regulations

[a]   Introduction

The "future benefits" test in the *Indopco* case caused major concerns for taxpayers, because it threatened to require the capitalization of many expenditures for self-created intangibles with the potential to produce future income. Actually, *Indopco* did not exactly adopt a "future benefits" test; it held that the creation of a "separate and distinct" asset was a sufficient but not necessary reason for capitalization and made "future benefits" a factor in requiring capitalization. But that was enough to worry taxpayers.

For several expenditures, the government put the taxpayer at ease:

1. Rev. Rul. 92-80, 1992-2 C.B. 57, stated that "[t]he *Indopco* decision does not affect the treatment of advertising costs under section 162(a) of the Code. These costs are generally deductible under that section even though advertising may have some future effect on business activities, as in the case of institutional or goodwill advertising."

2. In Rev. Rul. 96-62, 1996-2 C.B. 9, the IRS was similarly permissive of deductions for training costs: "The Indopco decision does not affect the treatment of training costs under § 162. Amounts paid or incurred for training, including the costs of trainers and routine updates of training materials, are generally deductible as business expenses under that section even though they may have some future benefit."

3. In Rev. Rul. 94-77, 1994-2 C.B. 19, the IRS also struck a pro-taxpayer note, permitting the deduction of severance pay even though it helped to lower costs and therefore increase future net income. This was an important ruling in light of the move toward downsizing the workforce in the 1990s. The ruling stated: "[A]lthough severance payments made by a taxpayer to its employees in connection with a business down-sizing may produce some future benefits, such as reducing operating costs and increasing operating efficiencies, these payments principally relate to previously rendered services of those employees. Therefore, such severance payments are generally deductible as business expenses. . . ."

4. In Rev. Rul. 95-32, 1995-1 C.B. 8, the IRS applied the severance payment ruling to a case involving expenditures incurred by a public utility for the implementation and operation of energy conservation programs. The utility paid contractors to install low-cost water heating and lighting systems in its customers' houses and to make energy-saving structural improvements to its customers' houses, without obligating customers to purchase power in the future. The expenditures were not capital expenditures even though they might reduce future operating and capital costs.

However, despite the pro-taxpayer tone of these rulings, the advertising and training cost rulings struck a cautious if limited pro-government note, stating that these costs must be capitalized in unusual circumstances — where advertising is directed toward obtaining future benefits significantly beyond those traditionally associated with ordinary product advertising or with institutional or goodwill advertising (citing *Cleveland Electric Illuminating Co. v. United States*, 7 Cl. Ct. 220 (Ct. Cl. 1985) (capitalization of advertising costs incurred to allay public opposition to the granting of a license to construct a nuclear power plant)); or where training is intended primarily to obtain future benefits significantly beyond those traditionally associated with training provided in the ordinary course of a taxpayer's trade or business (also citing the *Cleveland Electric* case). Moreover, in a later case, the IRS argued that expenditures to *create* an advertising campaign should be capitalized, unlike expenditures to *execute* the campaign (although the court rejected that argument — *RJR Nabisco Inc. v. Commissioner*, 76 T.C.M. (CCH) 71 (1998)).

In any event, neither taxpayers nor the government seemed content with the uncertainty spawned by the rulings and case law and the result was a new set of

Regulations that were generally pro-taxpayer. The Explanation and Summary of Comments to the Regulations state:

> [The Regulations] provide that an amount paid to acquire or create an intangible not otherwise required to be capitalized by the regulations is not required to be capitalized on the ground that it produces significant future benefits for the taxpayer, unless the IRS publishes guidance requiring capitalization of the expenditure. If the IRS publishes guidance requiring capitalization of an expenditure that produces future benefits for the taxpayer, such guidance will apply prospectively.

This means that taxpayers do not have to worry about the IRS relying on a future benefits test without further notice, except insofar as that test is embodied in the remainder of the new Regulations. One commentator has concluded that, instead of calling these the *Indopco* Regulations, they should be called the anti-*Indopco* Regulations, because they are so pro-taxpayer. Ethan Yale, *The Final INDOPCO Regulations*, 105 Tax Notes 435, 436 (Oct. 25, 2004) (Special Supplement).

In one respect, the cautious use of the "future benefits" standard in the regulations probably means that one issue which had been contentious prior to the *Indopco* regulations will now be decided for the taxpayer. Two pre-*Indopco* cases had allowed the deduction of costs to investigate business expansion — Briarcliff Candy Corp. v. Commissioner of Internal Revenue, 475 F.2d 775, 787 (2d Cir. 1973); NCNB Corp. v. United States, 684 F.2d 285 (4th Cir. 1982) (*en banc*), *reversing*, 651 F.2d 942 (4th Cir. 1981). But, in Norwest Corp. v. Commissioner, 112 T.C. 89 (1999), *reversed*, Wells Fargo & Co. v. Commissioner, 224 F.3d 874 (8th Cir. 2000), the Tax Court held that *Indopco* had overridden those cases. The regulations do not (in my reading) require that expenditures to produce this future benefit be capitalized, which means that they can be deducted.

[b]   *Indopco* Regulations

The structure of the new regulations is as follows: Treas. Reg. § 1.263(a)-4 sets forth the rules dealing with capitalization of amounts paid to acquire or create intangibles and amounts paid to facilitate the acquisition or creation of intangibles, with the following exception; Treas. Reg. § 1.263(a)-5 deals with amounts paid to facilitate an acquisition of a trade or business or a change in the capital structure of a business entity. The following discussion touches on selected highlights of these regulations; it makes no attempt to explain every rule or every exception to the rules. The detail should alert you to the fact that deciding whether or not to capitalize costs relating to intangibles is among the most difficult income tax issues. In addition, many of the examples relate to corporate merger activities, where the amounts at stake are significant.

[i]   Amounts Paid to Acquire or Create Intangibles; Treas. Reg. § 1.263(a)-4

Treas. Reg. § 1.263(a)-4 has several important subsections. *First*, **Treas. Reg. § 1.263(a)-4(b)(1)(iii)** repeats the pre-*Indopco* law — that an "amount paid to create or enhance a *separate and distinct* intangible asset within the meaning of paragraph (b)(3)" must be capitalized. This type of asset is defined in paragraph (b)(3) as follows:

> (i) Definition. The term separate and distinct intangible asset means a property interest of ascertainable and measurable value in money's worth that is subject to protection under applicable State, Federal or foreign law and the possession and control of which is intrinsically capable of being sold, transferred or pledged (ignoring any restrictions imposed on assignability) separate and apart from a trade or business.

Second, **Treas. Reg. § 1.263(a)-4(c)** deals with the *acquisition* of intangibles, such as the purchase of good will or customer lists when buying a business. This section often requires the acquisition costs for an intangible to be capitalized, even though expenditures to self-create the intangible might be expensed. This result runs contrary to the policy in the *Idaho Power* case (which involved the capitalization of expenditures to self-create *tangible* assets), where capitalization was justified because it treated acquisition and creation costs in a similar fashion.

Third, **Treas. Reg. § 1.263(a)-4(d)** deals with a variety of expenditures that create intangible value, some of which are noted here. Costs for the following must usually be capitalized: creation of a financial asset (such as a debt instrument or credit card agreement); prepaid expenses (such as prepaid insurance, as in the *Boylston* decision in Chapter 13.02[A]); membership or license fees (such as doctors' payments for hospital privileges, payments to join a trade association, and bar admission fees).

This section of the regulations also requires capitalization of amounts paid to another party to "create, originate, enter into, renew, or renegotiate" certain rights, subject to a de minimis exception; if the payment does not exceed $5,000, it can be expensed. Another exception to this capitalization requirement is an amount paid "with the mere hope or expectation of developing or maintaining a business relationship with that party and is not contingent on the origination, renewal or renegotiation of an agreement with that party." An example of an expenditure that must be capitalized under this paragraph is a signing bonus to an employee to come to work for the payor, unless the employee can leave the employer without any obligation to repay the bonus.

Termination payments are *not* generally capitalized, but there are three important exceptions. The following must be capitalized: (1) payments by a lessor to terminate a lease for real or personal tangible property; (2) payment to terminate an exclusive license or distribution agreement; and (3) payment to terminate a covenant not to compete. Payments to terminate a transaction involving the potential acquisition of a trade or business are dealt with by **Treas. Reg. § 1.263(a)-5**.

Fourth, **Treas. Reg. § 1.263(a)-4(e)** deals primarily with indirect costs incurred to facilitate the acquisition or creation of intangibles. These costs are generally required to be capitalized if the direct costs must be capitalized, but there are many exceptions. The regulations adopt what it calls simplifying assumptions, which are elective with the taxpayer, and which exclude from capitalized facilitation costs the following: employee compensation (including payments to people who are not employees of the taxpayer if they are for secretarial, clerical, or similar supports services); overhead; and de minimis costs (which do not exceed $5,000). There was some thought given to permitting these simplifying assumptions only if the taxpayer also expensed them for financial accounting, but this proposal did not make it into the final regulations.

[ii] Facilitating Acquisition of Trade or Business or Change in Capital Structure; Treas. Reg. § 1.263(a)-5

A different section of the regulations deals with amounts paid to facilitate transactions to acquire a trade or business or to change the capital structure of a business entity. The general rule is that these amounts must be capitalized, with exceptions.

1. *Termination payments.* An important issue arising in this context is how to deal with termination payments — e.g., when a taxpayer terminates someone's right to acquire its business. Treas. Reg. § 1.263(a)-5(b)(8) states:

> An amount paid to terminate (or facilitate the termination of) an agreement to enter into a transaction . . . constitutes an amount paid to facilitate a second transaction [and is therefore capitalized] . . . only if the transactions are mutually exclusive.

"Mutually exclusive" is explained in the following two examples: Treas. Reg. § 1.263(a)-5(*l*) (**examples 13 and 14**):

> *Example 13. Corporate acquisition; mutually exclusive costs.* (i) [Y, threatened with a hostile takeover by Z] finds W, a white knight. Y and W execute a letter of intent on March 10, 2005. Under the terms of the letter of intent, Y must pay W a $10,000,000 break-up fee if the merger with W does not occur. On April 1, 2005, Z significantly increases the amount of its offer, and Y decides to accept Z's offer instead of merging with W. . . .
>
> (iii) . . . [B]ecause Y could not merge with both W and Z, . . . the $10,000,000 termination payment facilitates the transaction between Y and Z. Accordingly, Y must capitalize the $10,000,000 termination payment as an amount that facilitates the transaction with Z.
>
> *Example 14. Break-up fee; transactions not mutually exclusive.* N corporation and U corporation enter into an agreement under which U would acquire all the stock or all the assets of N in exchange for U stock. Under the terms of the agreement, if either party terminates the agreement, the terminating party must pay the other party $10,000,000. U decides to terminate the agreement and pays N $10,000,000. Shortly thereafter, U acquires all the stock of V corporation, a competitor of N. U had the financial resources to have acquired both N and V. U's $10,000,000 payment does not facilitate U's acquisition of V. Accordingly, U is not required to capitalize the $10,000,000 payment under this section.

2. *Exploring the acquisition of a business.* The Regulations also deal with payments to investigate the acquisition of a trade or business. Treas. Reg.

§ 1.263(a)-5(e). They distinguish between pre-investigative payments (which can usually be expensed) and payments to facilitate acquisition of a business (which must be added to cost). Payments are pre-investigative (and can therefore usually be expensed) if they occur before the earlier of two specified events — (1) the date on which a letter of intent is executed by both acquirer and target, or (2) the date on which the material terms of the transaction as tentatively agreed to by both parties are authorized by taxpayer's appropriate officials (or, if authorization is not required, the date on which a binding contract is executed).

However, certain expenditures are "inherently facilitative" and must be capitalized regardless of when they occur — for example: for securing an appraisal or fairness opinion regarding an acquisition; obtaining tax advice regarding the structure of the transaction; and getting regulatory approval. This would probably result in capitalizing most of the expenditures in *Indopco*, which were incurred for tax advice, an appraisal, and a fairness opinion.

Moreover, the expensing of payments to explore the acquisition of a business is subject to an important qualification. The taxpayer must be in a trade or business, not entering into a business for the first time or exploring the acquisition of a business unrelated to the business in which he is currently engaged. The possibility of deducting these "start-up" expenditures is discussed later.

3. *Hostile mergers.* The following examples in the regulations (**Treas. Reg. § 1.263(a)-5(l)**) discuss whether expenditures to defend against a *hostile* takeover bid must be capitalized, when the bid is eventually successful. The detail in the regulations should alert you to the fact that large amounts of money with tax consequences are at stake in corporate takeovers.

> *Example 11. Corporate acquisition; defensive measures.* (i) On January 15, 2005, Y corporation, a publicly traded corporation, becomes the target of a hostile takeover attempt by Z corporation. In an effort to defend against the takeover, Y pays legal fees to seek an injunction against the takeover and investment banking fees to locate a potential "white knight" acquirer. Y also pays amounts to complete a defensive recapitalization, and pays $50,000 to an investment banker for a fairness opinion regarding the price contained in Z's initial offer. Y's efforts to enjoin the takeover and locate a white knight acquirer are unsuccessful, and on March 15, 2005, Y's board of directors decides to abandon its defense against the takeover and negotiate with Z in an effort to obtain the highest possible price for its shareholders. After Y abandons its defense against the takeover, Y pays an investment banker $1,000,000 for a second fairness opinion and for services rendered in negotiating with Z.
>
> (ii) The legal fees paid by Y to seek an injunction against the takeover are not amounts paid in the process of investigating or otherwise pursuing the transaction with Z. Accordingly, these legal fees are not required to be capitalized under this section.
>
> (iii) The investment banking fees paid to search for a white knight acquirer do not facilitate an acquisition of Y by a white knight because none of Y's costs with respect to a white knight were inherently facilitative amounts

and because Y did not reach the [critical date] with respect to a white knight. Accordingly, these amounts are not required to be capitalized under this section.

(iv) The amounts paid by Y to investigate and complete the recapitalization must be capitalized . . . . [Editor — **Treas. Reg. § 1.263(a)-5(a)(4).**]

(v) The $50,000 paid to the investment bankers for a fairness opinion during Y's defense against the takeover and the $1,000,000 paid to the investment bankers after Y abandons its defense against the takeover are inherently facilitative amounts with respect to the transaction with Z and must be capitalized . . . .

Example 12. Corporate acquisition; acquisition by white knight. (i) Assume the same facts as in Example 11, except that Y's investment bankers identify three potential white knight acquirers: U corporation, V corporation, and W corporation. Y pays its investment bankers to conduct due diligence on the financial condition of three potential white knight acquirers. On March 15, 2005, Y's board of directors approves a tentative acquisition agreement under which W agrees to acquire all of the stock of Y, and the investment bankers stop due diligence on U and V. On June 15, 2005, W acquires all of the stock of Y.

(ii) . . . [T]he amounts paid to conduct due diligence on U, V, and W prior to March 15, 2005 (the date of board of directors' approval) are not amounts paid to facilitate the acquisition of the stock of Y and are not required to be capitalized under this section. However, the amounts paid to conduct due diligence on W on and after March 15, 2005, facilitate the acquisition of the stock of Y and are required to be capitalized.

[3]   Start-Up Costs

[a]   In General

If a taxpayer enters business for the first time (or explores going into an unrelated business), the start-up costs would not be deductible because the taxpayer is not yet in business. The best known case is *Richmond Television Corp. v. United States*, 345 F.2d 901 (4th Cir. 1965) (concerning costs of training personnel prior to beginning business; even though taxpayer made a decision to enter into business and spent money in preparation for entering that business, he has not 'engaged in carrying on any trade or business' within § **162(a)** until the business has begun). If a taxpayer loses a case like *Richmond Television*, it is especially serious because the asset acquired usually has no ascertainable useful life and is therefore not depreciable under § **167**. Moreover, the value of a trained workforce is *not* usually a "section 197 intangible" (§ **197(d)(1)(C)(i)**), eligible for 15-year depreciation, if it is *self-created*. § **197(c)(2)**. A great deal therefore turns on defining when the business begins, after which many of these otherwise-capitalized start-up expenses could be deducted.

[b]   Elective Amortization — Section 195

Section 195, passed after *Richmond Television,* permits the taxpayer to elect to deduct "start-up expenditures" beginning in the year in which the active trade or business begins, as follows: (1) expensing the lesser of (a) the start-up expenditures or (b) $10,000 reduced by the excess of those expenditures over $60,000 and (2) the remainder of those expenditures over a 180-month period beginning with the month when the active trade or business begins. Disposition of the business before completion of the amortization period results in a loss deduction under § **165** for unrecovered basis. No deduction is allowed for start-up expenditures except as provided by § **195.** This provision takes some of the pressure off distinguishing start-up from post-start-up expenses. However, it is still much better to expense than to rely on § **195.**

Section 195 defines eligible start-up expenditures as either "investigation costs" or costs incurred in "creating" a business. Rev. Rul. 99-23, 1999-1 C.B. 998 (excerpted below) adopts a narrow definition of "investigation" costs. § **195(c)(1)(A)(i).** After reading this Revenue Ruling, do you think that the training expenses in *Richmond Television* would be eligible for § **195** deductions?

Rev. Rul. 99-23 first quotes from the legislative history, as follows:

> . . . [E]ligible expenses consist of investigatory costs incurred in reviewing a prospective business prior to reaching a final decision to acquire or to enter that business. These costs include expenses incurred for the analysis or survey of potential markets, products, labor supply, transportation facilities, etc. . . . [T]he amortization election for startup expenditures does not apply to amounts paid or incurred as part of the acquisition cost of a trade or business.

The ruling then asserts "that expenses incurred in the course of a general search for, or an investigation of, a business that relate to the decisions whether to purchase a business and which business to purchase are investigatory costs. However, once a taxpayer has focused on the acquisition of a specific business, expenses that are related to an attempt to acquire that business are capital in nature." The ruling gives the following example.

> In April 1998, corporation U hired an investment banker to evaluate the possibility of acquiring a trade or business unrelated to U's existing business. The investment banker conducted research on several industries and evaluated publicly available financial information relating to several businesses. Eventually, U narrowed its focus to one industry. The investment banker evaluated several businesses within the industry, including corporation V and several of V's competitors. The investment banker then commissioned appraisals of V's assets and an in-depth review of V's books and records in order to determine a fair acquisition price. On November 1, 1998, U entered into an acquisition agreement with V to purchase all the assets of V. U did not prepare and submit a letter of intent, or any other preliminary agreement or written document evidencing an intent to acquire V prior to executing the acquisition agreement.

The ruling concludes:

[In this example], an examination of the nature of the costs incurred indicates that U made its decision to acquire V after the investment banker conducted research on several industries and evaluated publicly available financial information. The costs incurred to conduct industry research and review public financial information are typical of the costs related to a general investigation. Accordingly, the costs incurred to conduct industry research and to evaluate publicly available financial information are investigatory costs eligible for amortization as start-up expenditures under sec. 195. However, the costs relating to the appraisals of V's assets and an in-depth review of V's books and records to establish the purchase price facilitate consummation of the acquisition, and thus, are capital acquisition costs. The costs incurred to evaluate V and V's competitors also may be investigatory costs, but only to the extent they were incurred to assist U in determining whether to acquire a business and which business to acquire. If the evaluation of V and V's competitors occurred after U had made its decision to acquire V (for example, in an effort to establish the purchase price for V), such evaluation costs are capital acquisition costs.

Rev. Rul 99-23 makes the "final decision" to acquire a trade or business the critical date before which an outlay can be eligible for § 195. In Wells Fargo & Co. v. Commissioner, 224 F.3d 874 (8th Cir. 2000), the court held that the taxpayer "made its 'final decision' regarding acquisition no later than July 22, 1991. On that date, [taxpayer] and Norwest entered into the Agreement and Plan of Reorganization [for taxpayer to merge with Norwest]." Consequently, legal fees to consummate the merger after the final decision had been made were not eligible "start-up expenditures."

The above ruling does *not* deal with § **195(c)(1(A)(ii)**, which covers "*creating* an active trade or business," rather than *investigating* the creation of a trade or business. Despite the agency's narrow reading of "investigation" costs, pre-business training costs appear to be amortizable "creation" costs. *See, e.g., Cleveland Electric Illuminating Co. v. United States*, 7 Cl. Ct. 220 (1985) (suggesting that pre-business training costs are covered by § **195**). *See also* Rev. Rul. 81-150, 1981-1 C.B. 119 (management fee paid to managing partner during oil rig construction was a "creation" cost covered by § **195**).

Section 248. There is one more section relevant to business "creation" expenditures, adopted in 1976 (four years before § **195** was adopted in 1980). **Section 248** permits a deduction of the costs "incident to the creation of a corporation" up to $5,000 (reduced by the excess of such costs over $50,000) and permits the remainder of such costs to be amortized over 180 months beginning with the month in which the business begins. A typical § **248** expenditure is the fee paid to a lawyer to organize a corporation.

[c]   Research and Development

In one situation, the code permits expensing of outlays before business has begun. **Section 174** permits expensing of research and experimental costs "in connection with a trade or business." Snow v. *Commissioner*, 416 U.S. 500 (1974), held that this language was broader than "carrying on a trade or business" and permitted preoperating outlays to be expensed. The Court was undoubtedly influenced by the fact that the provision was meant as an economic incentive and that any other interpretation would have favored existing businesses over businesses that were still getting started.

[4] Job Search Costs

An older ruling deals with a particular kind of outlay that is often for business expansion but could also be for getting started in business — job search costs (e.g., travel costs or an employment agency fee). Rev. Rul. 75-120, 1975-1 C.B. 55, held the following: (a) job search costs to successfully or unsuccessfully obtain new employment in the *same* trade or business are deductible expenses; (b) job search costs to obtain employment in a *new* trade or business are not deductible, whether or not the search is successful. Is this ruling correct, insofar as it prohibits deduction of unsuccessful search costs to obtain a job in a new trade or business?

It makes sense to distinguish expenditures to successfully acquire a job in the *same* trade or business vs. a *new* trade or business, on the ground that the latter involve the kind of expansion costs that should not be deducted. But why should there be no deduction for the unsuccessful costs of a job search for a *new* trade or business? Isn't there a deductible loss when the costs are unsuccessful?

Is a third-year law student taxed on reimbursements received from a law firm for interview travel costs? Presumably, the reimbursements are not a working condition fringe benefit under § 132(a)(3), (d), because the student is not an employee. But are the reimbursements § 61 income?

§ 13.03 TANGIBLE PROPERTY — REPAIR/MAINTENANCE EXPENSES vs. COSTS FOR IMPROVEMENTS AND ACQUISITIONS

Is an expenditure related to property a deductible repair (or maintenance) expense or a capital cost of improvement? Two issues arise. First, what is the unit of property with respect to which this decision is made? The larger the unit, the more likely the payment will be a deductible repair of the larger unit rather than a capital cost of a separate item. Second, once the unit is identified, what are the criteria for determining whether a payment is for a repair or an improvement? **Treas. Reg. § 1.263(a)-3T** address these issues in the context of tangible property. In general, the costs are capitalized if they better or restore the property or adapt it for a new use. The Regulations provide extensive examples. The "T" in the citation to the Regulations indicates that they are temporary and may still be amended. They are now scheduled to go into effect in 2014, but taxpayers can rely on these Regulations prior to their effective date.

[A] What Is the Unit?

The general rule adopted by the Regulations is that all components of property that are "functionally interdependent" are considered a single unit of property. A computer and printer are two units of property because they can be used separately. However, the engine of a truck is not a separate property because the truck cannot run without the engine.

There are some exceptions, of which buildings are an important example. Payments to improve the "building structure" or any one of eight building systems (e.g., heating and air-conditioning; elevators) are considered improvement costs that must be capitalized, even though the building itself is the unit of property. However, these costs are added to the cost of the building (and depreciated over the life of the building), not to the cost of the components of the building.

In addition, a taxpayer who treats a component as a separately depreciable asset must treat that component as a unit of property for applying the repair vs. improvement rules, even if those rules would not otherwise treat that component as a separate unit of property. For example, if the taxpayer treats tires as a unit of property separate from the vehicle, the replacement of the tires is not considered a repair of the vehicle. **Treas. Reg. § 1.263(a)-3T(e)(5)(i) and Example 16.**

[B] Criteria for Distinguishing Deductible Repair Expenses from Capital Improvement Costs

Earlier regulations required an expenditure to be capitalized if it added to a property's value, substantially prolonged its useful life, or adapted it to a new use. The new Regulations replace the first two tests. Expenditures must be capitalized if they better the property (a variation of the "add to value" test, which has been rejected because it is administratively too difficult to apply); or if the expenditures restore the property (a variation on the earlier "prolong useful life" test." The "adapt to new use" test is retained.

[1] Betterment

In general, an expenditure betters property (and is, therefore, a capital expenditure) if it:

(1) ameliorates a material condition or defect that either existed before taxpayer's acquisition or that arose during the production of the property;

(2) results in a material addition to the property, such as its enlargement or expansion, or

(3) results in a material increase in capacity, productivity, efficiency, strength, or quality of the property.

The examples under the Regulations address some typical problems. First, if replacement parts are unavailable (typically, for older property), purchase of an improved part does not in and of itself result in improvement of the property. For example, if wooden shingles are no longer available, replacement of storm-damaged shingles with asphalt shingles is not an improvement even though they add to the strength of the property. However, the cost of other better shingles may be a capital cost. **Treas. Reg. § 1.263(a)-3T(h), Examples 14-15.**

Second, when the taxpayer is correcting a defect in the property, such as a leaking underground storage tank, it does not matter whether the taxpayer knew of the defect when it acquired the property. This can seem unfair to the taxpayer, if the cost of the property was inflated because the taxpayer was unaware of the defect. The discovery of the defect will result in a nondeductible decline in the property's value, but the cost of fixing the defect will still be added to basis. The following examples illustrate this rule.

Example 1. Amelioration of pre-existing material condition or defect. In Year 1, X purchases a store located on a parcel of land that contained underground gasoline storage tanks left by prior occupants. Assume that the parcel of land is the unit of property. The tanks had leaked, causing soil contamination. X is not aware of the contamination at the time of purchase. In Year 2, X discovers the contamination and incurs costs to remediate the soil. The remediation costs result in a betterment to the land under paragraph (h)(1)(i) of this section because X incurred the costs to ameliorate a material condition or defect that existed prior to X's acquisition of the land.

Example 2. Not amelioration of pre-existing condition or defect. X owns a building that was constructed with insulation that contained asbestos. The health dangers of asbestos were not widely known when the building was constructed. X determines that certain areas of asbestos-containing insulation had begun to deteriorate and could eventually pose a health risk to employees. Therefore, X pays an amount to remove the asbestos-containing insulation from the building structure and replace it with new insulation that is safer to employees, but no more efficient or effective than the asbestos insulation. . . . Although the asbestos is determined to be unsafe under certain circumstances, the asbestos is not a preexisting or material defect of the building structure under paragraph (h)(1)(i) of this section. In addition, the removal and replacement of the asbestos does not result in a material addition to the building structure under paragraph (h)(1)(ii) of this section or result in a material increase in capacity, productivity, efficiency, strength, or quality of the building structure or the output of the building structure under paragraph (h)(1)(iii) of this section. Therefore, the amount paid to remove and replace the asbestos insulation does not result in a betterment to the building structure under paragraph (h) of this section.

Third, the Regulations specify how to make the comparisons to decide whether there has been an improvement. When there has been an event requiring maintenance, the betterment standard is applied by comparing the condition of the property *after* the expenditure with the condition immediately *before* the event. This is true whether or not the "event" is a law or regulation. If maintenance is needed because of normal wear and tear, the comparison is with the property's condition prior to the last time the taxpayer corrected the effects of wear and tear; or, if this is the first time the taxpayer dealt with wear and tear, the comparison is with the property's condition when it was acquired. The following example illustrates this rule.

Example 12. Not a betterment; regulatory requirement. X owns a meat processing plant. X discovers that oil is seeping through the concrete walls of the plant, creating a fire hazard. Federal meat inspectors advise X that it must correct the seepage problem or shut down its plant. To correct the problem, X pays an amount to add a concrete lining to the walls from the floor to a height of about four feet and also to add concrete to the floor of the plant. Under paragraph (e)(2)(ii) of this section, if the amount paid results in a betterment to the building structure or any building system, X must treat the amount as an improvement to the building. The event necessitating the expenditure was the seepage of the oil. Prior to the seepage, the plant did not leak and was functioning for its intended use. X is not required to treat the amount paid as a betterment under paragraph (h) of this section because it does not result in a material addition or material increase in capacity, productivity, efficiency, strength or quality of the building structure or its output compared to the condition of the structure prior to the seepage of the oil. The federal meat inspectors' requirement that X correct the seepage to continue operating the plant is not relevant in determining whether the amount paid improves the plant.

[2] Restoration

Here are some examples of expenditures that result in a capitalized cost of restoration: (1) they replace a component of property for which a loss deduction has properly been taken, whether or not the loss was the result of a casualty; (2) they return property to efficient operation after it has deteriorated so it was no longer functional; (3) they rebuild the property to "like-new condition after the end of its depreciable class life; or (4) they replace a part that is a "major component" of property. An "engine" would be a major component of a vehicle or boat. **Treas. Reg. § 1.263(a)-3T(i).**

The "major component" issue is addressed in the following examples:

Example 8: Replacement of major component or substantial structural part; personal property. X is a common carrier that owns a fleet of petroleum hauling trucks. X pays amounts to replace the existing engine, cab, and petroleum tank with a new engine, cab, and tank. Assume the tractor of the truck (which includes the cab and the engine) is a single unit of property, and that the trailer (which contains the petroleum tank) is a separate unit of property. The new engine and cab constitute parts or combinations of parts that comprise a major component or substantial structural part of X's tractor. Therefore, the amounts paid for the replacement of those components must be capitalized under paragraph (i)(1)(vi) of this section. The new petroleum tank constitutes a part or combination of parts that comprise a major component and a substantial structural part of the trailer. Accordingly, the amounts paid for the replacement of the tank also must be capitalized under paragraph (i)(1)(vi) of this section.

Example 12. Replacement of major component or substantial structural part; roof. X owns a large retail store. X discovers a leak in the roof of the store and hires a contractor to inspect and fix the roof. The contractor discovers that a major portion of the sheathing and rafters has rotted, and recommends the replacement of the entire roof. X pays the contractor to replace the entire roof with a new roof. Under paragraph (e)(2)(ii) of this section, if the amount paid results in a restoration of the building structure or any building system, X must treat the amount as an improvement to the building. The roof is part of the building structure under paragraph (e)(2)(ii)(A) of this section and comprises a major component or substantial structural part of X's building structure under paragraph (i)(4) of this section. Under paragraph (i)(1)(vi) of this section, X must treat the amount paid to replace the roof as a restoration because X paid the amount to replace a major component or substantial structural part of X's building structure. Therefore, in accordance with paragraph (e)(2)(ii) of this section, X must treat the amount paid to restore the building structure as an improvement to the building and must capitalize the amount paid under paragraph (d)(2) of this section. [Editor — Example 13 provides the same result as Example 12, if a substantial part of the roof is replaced.]

[3] Adapt to New Use

This portion of the Regulations is the same as prior regulations. For example, knocking out walls so that three retail salesrooms are converted to one large retail salesroom is not an adaptation to a different use. But amounts paid to convert a manufacturing building to a showroom are capital expenditures. **Treas. Reg. § 1.263(a)-3T(j) (Examples 1 and 2).**

[4] Routine Maintenance Safe Harbor

The Regulations provide a safe harbor deduction for expenditures that might otherwise be capitalized if they provide "routine maintenance" on property other than buildings. However, the Regulations do not allow use of the safe harbor if the amount is "paid for the replacement of a component of a unit of property and the taxpayer has properly deducted a loss for that component" or the amount is paid "to return a unit of property to its ordinarily efficient operating condition, if the property has deteriorated to a state of disrepair and is no longer functional for its intended use."

Treas. Reg. § 1.263(a)-3T(g) states:

An amount paid for routine maintenance performed on a unit of property other than a building or a structural component of a building is deemed not to improve that unit of property. Routine maintenance is the recurring activities that a taxpayer expects to perform as a result of the taxpayer's use of the unit of property to keep the unit of property in its ordinarily efficient operating condition. Routine maintenance activities include, for example, the inspection, cleaning, and testing of the unit of property, and the replacement of parts of the unit of property with comparable and commercially available and reasonable replacement parts. The activities are routine only if, at the time the unit of property is placed in service by the taxpayer, the taxpayer reasonably expects to perform the activities more than once during the class life [] of the unit of property. Among the factors to be considered in determining whether a taxpayer is performing routine maintenance are the recurring nature of the activity, industry practice, manufacturers' recommendations, the taxpayer's experience, and the taxpayer's treatment of the activity on its applicable financial statement. . . .

The Regulations provide the following example, which will be of great interest to the aviation industry. Prior rulings had left the industry unsure whether different types of periodic maintenance performed on the aircraft would be capitalized. This example gives them assurance that the payments for at least some of this maintenance can be expensed. Notice that the safe harbor applies even though the depreciable class life has expired. Early deductions through accelerated depreciation can combine with deductible expenses that keep the property going after the end of the class life.

> *Example 1. Routine maintenance on component.* (i) X is a commercial airline engaged in the business of transporting passengers and freight throughout the United States and abroad. To conduct its business, X owns or leases various types of aircraft. As a condition of maintaining its airworthiness certification for these aircraft, X is required by the Federal Aviation Administration (FAA) to establish and adhere to a continuous maintenance program for each aircraft within its fleet. These programs, which are designed by X and the aircraft's manufacturer and approved by the FAA, are incorporated into each aircraft's maintenance manual. The maintenance manuals require a variety of periodic maintenance visits at various intervals. One type of maintenance visit is an engine shop visit (ESV), which X expects to perform on its aircraft engines approximately every 4 years in order to keep its aircraft in its ordinarily efficient operating condition. In Year 1, X purchased a new aircraft, which included four new engines attached to the airframe. [] In Year 5, X performs its first ESV on the aircraft engines. The ESV includes disassembly, cleaning, inspection, repair, replacement, reassembly, and testing of the engine and its component parts. During the ESV, the engine is removed from the aircraft and shipped to an outside vendor who performs the ESV. If inspection or testing discloses a discrepancy in a part's conformity to the specifications in X's maintenance program, the part is repaired, or if necessary, replaced with a comparable and commercially available and reasonable replacement part. After the ESVs, the engines are returned to X to be reinstalled on another aircraft or stored for later installation. Assume that the unit of property for X's aircraft is the entire aircraft, including the aircraft engines, and that the class life for X's aircraft is 12 years. . . .

> (ii) Because the ESVs involve the recurring activities that X expects to perform as a result of its use of the aircraft to keep the aircraft in ordinarily efficient operating condition, and consist of maintenance activities that X expects to perform more than once during the 12 year class life of the aircraft, X's ESVs are within the routine maintenance safe harbor under paragraph (g) of this section. Accordingly, the amounts paid for the ESVs are deemed not to improve the aircraft and are not required to be capitalized under paragraph (d) of this section.

> *Example 2. Routine maintenance after class life.* Assume the same facts as in Example 1, except that in year 15, X pays amounts to perform an ESV

on one of the original aircraft engines, after the end of the class life of the aircraft. Because this ESV involves the same routine maintenance activities that were performed on aircraft engines in Example 1, this ESV also is within the routine maintenance safe harbor []. Accordingly, the amounts paid for this ESV, even though performed after the class life of the aircraft, are deemed not to improve the aircraft and are not required to be capitalized under paragraph (d) of this section.

§ 13.04 EDUCATION EXPENDITURES

[A] Trade or Business Expenses?

The deduction for education expenditures is analyzed using the same principles distinguishing personal from business expenses and current expenses from capital expenditures and personal from business expenses that we have discussed in Chapters 8 and 13.

[1] Getting Started?

In *Toner v. Commissioner*, 71 T.C. 772 (1979), *reversed*, 623 F.2d 315 (3d Cir. 1980), the Tax Court dealt with the educational expenses of a lay teacher (Mrs. Toner) at a Catholic elementary school. When she began teaching, she had a high school diploma and had completed two years of college. No parish required its elementary school teachers to have higher qualifications, but teachers in Catholic high schools and in public and nonreligious private schools had to have a bachelor's degree. Mrs. Toner incurred expenses for college courses after she began her elementary school teaching. In a confused opinion, the Tax Court held that Mrs. Toner could not deduct her expenses, applying both the "minimum educational requirement" and "new trade or business" sections of the regulations. **Treas. Reg. § 1.162-5(b)(2), (3).** The problem with this holding was that the Regulations stated that "all teaching and related duties shall be considered to involve the same general type of work." Consequently, Mrs. Toner would not have been entering a new trade or business if she taught outside of the Catholic elementary school system and she clearly met the minimum educational requirements for her elementary school duties. That is why the Court of Appeals reversed and held for the taxpayer.

The taxpayer in *Toner* is an example of someone who qualifies (just barely) to get started in a business but needs more training to get ahead. These taxpayers often fail to meet minimum qualifications because the job is not permanent and, in such cases, the Regulations disallow the deduction. That is how courts usually dispose of graduate assistants who try to deduct Ph.D. costs. *Jungreis v. Commissioner*, 55 T.C. 581 (1970). Toner, however, had a permanent job.

[2]   New Trade or Business

SHARON v. COMMISSIONER
United States Tax Court
66 T.C. 515 (1976), *affirmed per curiam* 591 F.2d 1273 (9th Cir. 1978)

SIMPSON, JUDGE: . . .

3. License to Practice Law in California

[Editor — The following excerpt deals with the deductibility of bar review course expenditures.]

It is clear that the amount the petitioner paid for the bar review course was an expenditure 'made by an individual for education' within the meaning of section 1.162-5(a) of the Income Tax Regulations. Although the petitioner was authorized to practice law in some jurisdictions when he took the California bar review course, such course was nevertheless educational in the same sense as the first bar review course. The deductibility of such educational expenses is governed by the rules of section 1.162-5 of the regulations. . . .

Educational expenses which are incurred to meet the minimum educational requirements for qualification in a taxpayer's trade or business or which qualify him for a new trade or business are 'personal expenditures or constitute an inseparable aggregate of personal and capital expenditures.' Sec. 1.162-5(b), Income Tax Regs. We find that the bar review course helped to qualify the petitioner for a new trade or business so that its costs are personal expenses.

We have previously adopted a 'commonsense approach' in determining whether an educational expenditure qualifies a taxpayer for a 'new trade or business.' If the education qualified the taxpayer to perform significantly different tasks and activities than he could perform prior to the education, then the education qualifies him for a new trade or business. Thus, we have held that a professor of social work is in a different trade or business than a social caseworker. A licensed public accountant is in a different trade or business than a certified public accountant. A registered pharmacist is in a different trade or business than an intern pharmacist, even though an intern performs many of the same tasks as a registered pharmacist, but under supervision.

Before taking the bar review course and passing the attorney's bar examination, the petitioner was an attorney licensed to practice law in New York. As an attorney for the Regional Counsel, he could represent the Commissioner in this Court. However, he could not appear in either the State courts of California, the Federal District Courts located there, nor otherwise act as an attorney outside the scope of his employment with the IRS. *See* Cal. Bus. & Prof. Code sec. 6125 (West 1974); 20 Op. Cal. Atty. Gen. 291 (1952). If he had done so, he would have been guilty of a misdemeanor. Cal. Bus. & Prof. Code sec. 6126 (West 1974). Yet, after receiving his license to practice law in California, he became a member of the State bar with all its accompanying privileges and obligations. He could appear and represent clients in all the courts of California. By comparing the tasks and activities that the petitioner was qualified to perform prior to receiving his license to practice in

California with the tasks and activities he was able to perform after receiving such license, it is clear that he has qualified for a new trade or business. Consequently, the expenses of his bar review course were personal and are not includable in the cost of his license to practice law in California.

It is true that even before he became a member of the bar of California, the petitioner was engaged in the business of practicing law. However, in applying the provisions of section 1.162-5 of the regulations to determine whether educational expenses are personal or business in nature, it is not enough to find that the petitioner was already engaged in some business — we must ascertain the particular business in which he was previously engaged and whether the education qualified him to engage in a different business. Before taking the bar review course and becoming a member of the bar of California, the petitioner could not generally engage in the practice of law in that State, but the bar review course helped to qualify him to engage in such business. . . .

COMMENTS

1. **Bar exam and court admission fees.** *Sharon* also discussed other expenses to become a member of the California bar — bar exam and court admission fees. Unlike the education expenses, these expenses were amortizable over the taxpayer's life expectancy. These deductions are probably small, but the same principle supports amortization of larger amounts, such as physicians' fees to acquire hospital privileges.

2. **MBA.** In *Allemeier v. Commissioner*, 90 T.C.M. (CCH) 197 (2005), the taxpayer worked as a salesman for a company (Selane Products) and, after holding that job for three years, paid tuition to obtain an M.B.A. The court held that the tuition was deductible because it did not qualify the taxpayer for a "new trade or business," stating:

We must next determine whether petitioner's MBA qualified him to perform a trade or business that he was unqualified to perform before he earned the MBA. Whether an education qualifies a taxpayer for a new trade or business depends upon the tasks and activities he or she was qualified to perform before the education and those that he or she was qualified to perform afterwards. The Court has repeatedly disallowed education expenses where the education qualifies the taxpayer to perform "significantly" different tasks and activities. The relevant inquiry is whether the taxpayer is objectively qualified in a new trade or business.

. . . Respondent argues that petitioner's trade or business before the MBA was principally sales related and involved only limited managerial and financial duties, but that once petitioner began the MBA program he advanced to numerous other jobs and was given advanced managerial, marketing, and financial duties, all of which were "significantly" different from the duties he performed before enrolling. In sum, respondent argues that the MBA qualified petitioner for the specific new trade or business of "advanced marketing and finance management."

Petitioner disagrees and argues that the MBA enhanced and maintained skills he already used in his job, but did not qualify him for a new trade or business or for any particular promotions. Petitioner argues that the MBA merely capitalized on his abilities that he had before beginning the program, giving him a better understanding of financials, costs analyses, marketing, and advertising. After careful consideration, we agree with petitioner.

Petitioner was hired by Selane Products for his experience in sports medicine, and he was hired, at first, to sell a sports-related product. Petitioner excelled in his duties and was rewarded with increased responsibility, including management, marketing, and finance-related tasks. The record establishes that he performed these myriad tasks before he enrolled in the MBA program. Once he enrolled, but before he finished the MBA program, he was promoted to new positions involving more complex tasks, but still involving the same marketing, finance, and management duties. . . .

Petitioner's business after enrolling in the MBA program did not significantly change. After completing the MBA program, petitioner established with testimony that his business involved the same general activities that he performed before enrolling in the program, activities involving sales, marketing, and management. While petitioner was awarded with new positions and titles after he enrolled in the program and while the MBA may have sped his advancement within Selane Products, the basic nature of his duties did not significantly change. The MBA rather improved preexisting skills that petitioner used before enrolling in the MBA program.

We also distinguish our facts from cases involving taxpayers embarking on a course of study that qualified them for a professional certification or license. . . . For instance, the Court denied taxpayers' deduction for law school expenses on four occasions because law was a field of study that led the taxpayers to qualify for the new trade or business of being an attorney. Petitioner's MBA was not a course of study leading him to qualify for a professional certification or license. Courts have found similarly where the course of study led taxpayers to qualify for professional certifications. For instance, the Court has found that a licensed public accountant is in a different trade or business from a certified public accountant. *See* Glenn v. Commissioner, 62 T.C. 270, 275 (1974). The Court has also found that a pharmacist intern is in a different trade or business from a registered pharmacist, even where they each perform many of the same tasks and activities. *See* Antzoulatos v. Commissioner, T.C. Memo. 1975-327 (1975).

[3] **Prebusiness Expenses**

If a taxpayer has not yet entered a trade or business, education expenses are not deductible, even if they would be deductible for someone in a trade or business. Thus, a taxpayer who has completed a J.D. degree and then immediately obtains an LL.M. degree, before joining a law firm, cannot deduct the cost of the LL.M. degree. *Randick v. Commissioner*, 35 T.C.M. (CCH) 195 (1976) (the fact that the taxpayer did some remunerative legal work while at law school did not make a difference).

In *Ruehmann v. Commissioner*, 30 T.C.M. (CCH) 675 (1971), however, the taxpayer studied law for three years in a state where two years of law school were sufficient to permit practice of law. He worked at a law firm between the second and third year of law school and again during the Christmas break of the third year. The firm made him an offer of permanent work during the third year. He worked with the firm in the summer after the third year and then studied for an LL.M. degree. He was permitted to deduct the cost of the LL.M. degree. The cost of the third year of law school was not deductible, however, because it was customary for law students to complete three years of law school before practice, and the J.D. was therefore a minimum qualification for being a lawyer.

[4] Amortization

Why can't a taxpayer amortize the cost of college, law school, or the bar review course? (1) Are they personal expenses, because they reflect a choice about what line of work the taxpayer will engage in during his life? (2) What would be the policy implications of permitting amortization? Recall the discussion of whether commuting expenses should be deductible business expenses in the case of the suburban commuter.

In *Duecaster v. C.I.R.*, 60 T.C.M. (CCH) 917 (1990), the taxpayer argued that expenditures to obtain a law school degree could be amortized as start-up expenses under § 195. The court held that this section only applied to an expenditure "that would have been allowable as a deduction if the taxpayer had been engaged in [a] trade or business when it was paid or incurred." In this respect, § 195 is like § 212, which does not create a deduction for an expenditure that would not have been a trade or business deduction under § 162. Just as a personal expenditure that is not deductible under § 162 does not become deductible under § 212, so expenditures to obtain a law school degree are presumed personal and are not eligible for § 195 amortization.

[5] Employer Fringe Benefit

Suppose an employer pays for an employee's education under circumstances that would not qualify as an *employee* deduction because it qualifies the employee for a new trade or business. The employee should in that case include the value of the education in taxable income. It is not a working condition fringe benefit because the expenditure is neither deductible nor depreciable; *see* § 132(d). Such on-the-job-training may be good for the economy, however — for example, a secretary training to be a paralegal. Moreover, as a practical matter, it is hard to know what is a new trade or business. To ease administrative problems and to encourage such training, § 127 was passed (and made permanent buy ATRA), excluding employer educational assistance program benefits from an employee's income. However, the excluded amount is capped — presently, at $5,250 (not inflation-adjusted). The tax-free fringe benefit is limited to programs where the employer does not discriminate in favor of highly compensated employees and the employer does not incur more than 5% of the expenditures for more-than-5% owners.

[B]   Scholarships

Scholarship income is excluded for degree candidates. § 117(a). Only amounts used for tuition, fees, books, supplies, and equipment are excluded. § 117(b). Amounts for food and lodging were excluded before 1986 but no longer. The idea behind repealing the living expense exclusion was that taxpayers with low incomes used for normal living expenses should rely on the personal exemption and standard deductions to lower their taxes. Students were no different from other lower income taxpayers.

[1]   Services Required as a Condition of Scholarship

The exclusion of scholarship income is withdrawn if the scholarship is a payment for services required as a condition for receiving the scholarship. § 117(c). The "no payment for services" rule is not easy to apply. It generally does not hurt recipients of college scholarships, because they are not required to do any work to get the scholarship. Graduate students who work as teaching and research assistants are vulnerable, however, as discussed below.

Private Ruling 9526020 dealt with a scholarship conditioned on the "recipient agree[ing] to practice on a full-time basis in a public service, not-for-profit, or lower-income sector of the legal profession for a specified period of time following completion of legal training. The areas of acceptable service [we]re within the selection option of the grantee, but [we]re restricted by compensation limitations intended to have the effect of requiring recipients to perform work of a public nature or benefit. Recipients [we]re not required to work for, or as directed by [the law school]." The ruling notes that "scholarships that represent payment for services are not excludable under current law, [but that] not all grants that are subject to conditions or limitations represent payment for services." It then concludes as follows:

> [This scholarship does] not represent compensation for services within the meaning of section 117(c) of the Code. The service commitment imposed upon participants . . . does not constitute the requirement of a substantial quid pro quo from the recipients; on the contrary, the grants are relatively disinterested grants of the [law school], designed to accomplish public rather than private or proprietary purposes. Recipients are free to take nearly any position of their choosing, anywhere, subject only to the compensation limitations prescribed. The service commitment is essentially a de minimis limitation designed to assure that [the] graduates practice in all income sectors of the legal profession, including public, lower-paying, and otherwise underserved areas or capacities, a public purpose for which the . . . scholarship program has been established by [the law school]. Any benefit inuring to the University-grantor appears remote, insubstantial, and inconsequential for purposes of section 117(c).

COMMENTS

1. *Athletic scholarship.* Rev. Rul. 77-263, 1977-2 C.B. 47 held that the value of an athletic scholarship was excludible under § 117, when the university expects but does not require the student to participate in a particular sport, requires no particular activity in lieu of participation, and does not cancel the scholarship if the student cannot participate.

2. *Certain government scholarships.* The 2001 Tax Law explicitly exempted amounts received under the National Health Services Corps Scholarship program and the Armed Forces Health Professions Scholarship and Financial Assistance program, without regard to any service obligation imposed on the recipient of the award. § 117(c)(2). This provision was made permanent by ATRA.

[2] Qualified Tuition Reduction

Another subsection excludes from gross income the value of tuition reduction provided to employees of educational institutions, primarily under two circumstances. § 117(d). *First*, it excludes the tuition reduction for family members of school employees (such as the child or spouse of a professor) who attend the employer's school or another school with whom the employer has a reciprocal relationship. It is a fringe benefit that often benefits the teacher of this course with children in school. *Second*, the exclusion also applies to tuition reduction for the school's employees, not just the employee's family. This often helps university staff members who can take courses at reduced tuition.

[3] A Closer Look at the Graduate Student

How does § 117(d) apply to the graduate student doing teaching and research in exchange for a tuition reduction? An initial observation, adverse to the graduate student, is that § 117(d) applies only to education below the graduate level (see the parentheses in (d)(2)). The counter observation, favorable to the graduate student, refers to § 117(d)(4), which permits graduate students who are teaching or research assistants to rely on the § 117(d) exclusion. But you are not home free. The § 117(d) exclusion for qualified tuition reduction is itself limited by the rule in § 117(c), which taxes scholarships *and* tuition reduction if the student is required to work as a condition of receiving the scholarship or tuition reduction. This leaves something of a puzzle. The tax break for graduate level tuition reduction requires that the graduate student be an employee performing teaching or research services. But tuition reduction *conditioned* on performing services is *not* excluded from income. How can the graduate student perform teaching or research services and still receive a tax free tuition reduction? Would tuition reduction be tax free in either of the following cases?

(1) The graduate student receives a $2,000 stipend for being a teaching assistant. She also receives a tuition reduction; instead of $5,000 tuition, she pays $1,000.

(2) All graduate students must teach as a condition of getting a degree — e.g., a Masters in Education degree. Some or all graduate students also get tuition reductions.

[C]   Education Tax Subsidies

The nondeductibility of many education expenses sometimes leads to the observation that the income tax law disfavors investment in human capital, in comparison to the tax breaks for physical capital (depreciation, expensing, etc.). But that may not be true. In addition to excluding scholarship income, the difference between tuition and the school's cost of education is not taxable income to the student, providing the economic equivalent of a deduction of some portion of expenses for education.

Moreover, the code contains a host of provisions favoring education, some of which were discussed previously in this course and some of which are noted below. *See generally* Joint Committee on Taxation, *Overview of Tax and Savings Incentives for Education* (JCX-1-01—Feb. 12, 2001), TAX NOTES TODAY, Feb. 13, 2001. This study concludes that "the variety and complexity of educational benefits afforded through the tax code, when coupled with expenditures that do not receive favorable tax treatment, make it difficult to determine the extent to which educational expenditures are subsidized by the tax code, relative to investments in physical capital."

Among the tax breaks for education discussed in other sections of this book are the following:

1. Exclusion of scholarship income. Chapter 13.04[B].

2. Parent's deduction for dependents can be available for children who are students even though they earn more than the exemption amount. Chapter 1.03.

3. Exclusion of employer educational assistance fringe benefit. Chapter 13.04[A][5].

4. Education loan forgiveness is not income if the student takes certain public interest jobs. Chapter 3.06[C][1][c].

5. An above-the-line deduction for interest on certain "qualified" higher education loans. Chapter 16.01[C][3].

6. The penalty on early withdrawal from retirement IRAs is waived if the withdrawal is spent for certain educational purposes. Chapter 24.06[B][1].

7. Exemption from tax on income earned on after-tax investments in qualified tuition programs. Chapter 7.04[C].

There are, in addition, the following minor tax breaks for education:

1. § 135 (gain on U.S. savings bonds excluded from income if the proceeds are used for "qualified education expenses" and if income is below a certain figure).

2. §§ 141(e)(1)(E), 144(b) (tax exemption for interest on certain student loan bonds, when the state or local government is a conduit for paying the interest).

The following important tax breaks for education are discussed in this section:

1. The Hope and Lifetime credits (§ 25A), added by the 1997 Tax Act.

2. Coverdell Education Savings Accounts (§ 530), added by the 1997 Act.

3. Deduction for qualified higher education expenses (§ 222), added by the 2001 Tax Law.

[1] Hope Scholarship and Lifetime Learning Credits; Section 25A

The 1997 law adopted a Hope scholarship credit (Hope) (now renamed the American Opportunity Tax Credit) and a Lifetime learning credit (Lifetime). The Lifetime credit is not available for any expenditures for which the Hope credit is claimed in that same year. The education must be provided at an "eligible educational institution" (generally, degree and certificate granting institutions, including some vocational institutions).

Both credits are available for the education expenditures of the taxpayer, the taxpayer's spouse, and the taxpayer's dependents. However, no credit is allowed to an individual for whom a dependent's deduction is "allowed" under § 151 to another taxpayer (e.g., a child of a parent). In such cases, the tuition paid by the dependent is treated as paid by the other taxpayer (e.g., the parent).

Hope credit. The Hope credit covers the first four years of the student's post-secondary education. (The student must carry at least one-half of a full-time course load.) The credit covers qualified tuition, books, and course materials. In 2013, the credit is 100% of the first $2,000 and 25% of the next $2,000 of eligible expenses (not inflation-adjusted). The maximum credit is therefore $2,500. Forty percent of the credit is refundable. ATRA extended this tax benefit through 2018. Thereafter the law will revert to the less generous rules applicable in earlier tax years, unless Congress changes its mind.

The Hope credit is phased out based on modified AGI over a $80,000-$90,000 range for single taxpayers and $160,000-$180,000 range for married taxpayers (thereby avoiding a marriage tax penalty). These figures are not adjusted for inflation.

Lifetime credit. The Lifetime credit equals 20% of up to $10,000 per year. The credit percentage is multiplied by the *total* expenditures that the taxpayer incurs for qualified students (the Hope credit is per student). The Lifetime credit (1) is available for an unlimited number of years of study, (2) applies to undergraduate *and* graduate schooling, and (3) does not require meeting half-time course load requirements, *if* the education improves job skills.

The Lifetime credit is phased out based on a modified AGI figure that is adjusted for inflation. For 2013, the range for single individuals is $53,000-$63,000 and for married taxpayers is $107,000-$127,000.

[2] Coverdell Education Savings Accounts; Section 530

The Hope/Lifetime credits are for current expenses. The Coverdell education savings account (made permanent by ATRA) provides another tax break for education expenses. It allows taxpayers to plan in advance by setting aside after-tax amounts that can accumulate income without tax and later distribute the money tax-free for the educational expenses of designated beneficiaries. No contribution qualifies if made after the beneficiary reaches age 18, except that contributions after age 18 are permitted for a "special needs" beneficiary, as defined by Treasury Regulations. The maximum amount that can be contributed to a Coverdell education savings account under this program is $2,000 per year per beneficiary; this amount is not indexed for inflation.

A distribution is tax free only if it is used exclusively to pay for the "qualified higher education expenses" of a designated beneficiary. (There is a 10% penalty on taxable distributions, which is waived if the distribution is made under certain circumstances — primarily on account of the death or disability of the beneficiary.) The definition of qualified higher education expenses is less restrictive than for the Hope/Lifetime credits. It covers tuition, books, and room and board (up to a limited amount) for a student attending at least half-time and enrolled in a degree or certificate program.

Beginning in tax year 2002, qualified education expenses include elementary and secondary school expenses. A tax break for elementary and secondary school expenses operates something like an educational voucher for parents because it provides a government subsidy for these expenses. This is an immensely controversial provision that did not receive much political attention. Arguably, it will defuse political support to improve public financing of public schools.

The $2,000 maximum amount is phased out as modified adjusted gross income rises above a threshold (which is not adjusted for inflation). The 2001 Tax Bill (effective for tax year 2002), provides a phase-out range of $95,000–110,000 for single taxpayers, and $190,000–220,000 for married couples.

Tax-free transfers (or rollovers) of account balances for one beneficiary to another beneficiary are allowed, if the new beneficiary is a family member (defined in the same way as for § 529).

Now that both § 529 (qualified tuition programs; discussed in Chapter 7.04[C]) and § 530 (Coverdell education savings account) provide for an exemption from income of future distributions for qualified education expenses, based on a prior after-tax investment, the differences between these two programs should be carefully noted. In some respects, § 529 is better and in some respects worse than § 530. For example, § 530 applies to elementary and secondary education, but § 529 still only applies to higher education; conversely, § 529 does *not* have a phase-out provision as AGI rises, but § 530 does.

There is no clear explanation in the statute of how to allocate distributions of amounts that qualify under both § 529 and § 530 to the educational expenses of a designated beneficiary.

[3] Deduction for Qualified Higher Education Expenses; Section 222

The 2001 Tax Law added a new tax break (beginning in tax year 2002) in the form of an above the line deduction for qualified higher education expenses (defined in the same way as for Hope/Lifetime credits). The deductible amounts are as follows:

AGI not exceed a dollar threshold		Deductible amount
Single	Married	
$65,000	$130,000	$4,000
$80,000	$160,000	$2,000

Sometimes the § 222 deduction would provide more of a tax break than a credit. First, the income thresholds are higher for the § 222 deduction. Second, in some instances, a deduction is worth more than the credit. Assume $3,000 of education expenses that would be eligible for both the Lifetime credit and the deduction under § 222. The credit is only 20% of the $3,000, but the deduction for someone in a tax bracket over 20% would receive a bigger tax reduction by taking a deduction.

This tax deduction has been extended through 2013.

[4] Preventing Multiple Tax Breaks

Given the number of tax provisions for education, there are (not surprisingly) complex rules for dealing with the potential for multiple tax benefits, most of which are too complex to be considered here. The general pattern is that only one of the tax breaks for current education expenses can be taken for a single student in the same tax year.

However, the 2001 Tax Bill provides that a taxpayer can take a Hope/Lifetime credit under § 25A and also receive tax free distributions under §§ 529/530 (the qualified tuition and Coverdell education savings account programs), as long as the credited expenses and tax-free distributions are not spent for the same expenses. Specifically, the education expenses eligible for the Hope/Lifetime credits reduce education expenses eligible for the tax exemption of distributions under §§ 529/530. For example, if a student incurs $7,000 of educational expenses and $5,000 is eligible for the Hope/Lifetime credits, $2,000 of exempt income can be received from a §§ 529/530 plan.

In addition, the Hope and Lifetime credits cannot be claimed based on expenditures for which another tax break is allowed (e.g., the exclusion of scholarships and the employer educational assistance fringe benefit), or for which a deduction is taken (e.g., as a business expense).

Finally, the § 222 deduction is an alternative to the Hope/Lifetime credits for current education expenses in any specific tax year. Thus, a taxpayer cannot claim both a deduction and a Hope/Lifetime credit with respect to the same student in the same tax year. Moreover, the expenses that qualify for the § 222 deduction are reduced by amounts excluded from income under §§ 529/530.

Part I-D

LIMITS ON DEDUCTIONS

Parts I-B and I-C discussed the basic structural provisions of the tax law permitting a deduction for certain expenses and losses. This Part is about limits on these deductions.

Chapter 14 discusses public policy limitations on deductions that would otherwise meet the statutory requirements for deductibility — whether an expense is "ordinary, necessary, reasonable, or lavish"; expenditures relating to illegal activity; and expenditures to influence politics.

Chapter 15 deals with limitations on the deduction of expenses to produce tax-exempt income. If such expenses were deductible, the exemption of gross income would result in related expenses reducing otherwise taxable income.

Chapter 16 deals with limitations on the interest deduction.

Chapter 17 discusses the inclusion of borrowed money in basis and the limitations on deductions that this rule has spawned. A primary concern in this chapter is tax shelters and how the case law and the statutory and ethical practice rules deal with this problem.

Chapter 14

PUBLIC POLICY

§ 14.01 ORDINARY, NECESSARY, REASONABLE, LAVISH

[A] "Ordinary and Necessary"

We considered § 162 without paying much attention to the requirement that the expenses be "ordinary and necessary." That was not an oversight. The words do not mean much. As the Court said in *Commissioner v. Tellier*, 383 U.S. 687 (1966):

> Our decisions have consistently construed the term "necessary" as imposing only the minimal requirement that the expense be 'appropriate and helpful' for 'the development of the (taxpayer's) business.' *Welch v. Helvering*, 290 U.S. 111, 113 (1933). The principal function of the term "ordinary" in § 162(a) is to clarify the distinction, often difficult, between those expenses that are currently deductible and those that are in the nature of capital expenditures, which, if deductible at all, must be amortized over the useful life of the asset.

[1] "Extraordinary" as an Independent Limitation

The *Welch* case, *infra*, is somewhat troublesome. It says that "ordinary" invokes the difference between current expenses and capital expenditures and that "necessary" means "appropriate and helpful," but it also says some other things that have proved distracting. Here is Justice Cardozo's opinion.

WELCH v. HELVERING
United States Supreme Court
290 U.S. 111 (1933)

Mr. Justice Cardozo delivered the opinion of the court.

The question to be determined is whether payments by a taxpayer, who is in business as a commission agent, are allowable deductions in the computation of his income if made to the creditors of a bankrupt corporation in an endeavor to strengthen his own standing and credit.

In 1922 petitioner was the secretary of the E. L. Welch Company, a Minnesota corporation, engaged in the grain business. The company was adjudged an involuntary bankrupt, and had a discharge from its debts. Thereafter the petitioner made a contract with the Kellogg Company to purchase grain for it on a commission. In order to re-establish his relations with customers whom he had known when acting for the Welch Company and to solidify his credit and standing, he decided to pay the debts of the Welch business so far as he was able. In fulfillment of that resolve, he made payments of substantial amounts during five successive years. . . .

We may assume that the payments to creditors of the Welch Company were necessary for the development of the petitioner's business, at least in the sense that they were appropriate and helpful. He certainly thought they were, and we should be slow to override his judgment. But the problem is not solved when the payments are characterized as necessary. Many necessary payments are charges upon capital. There is need to determine whether they are both necessary and ordinary. Now, what is ordinary, though there must always be a strain of constancy within it, is none the less a variable affected by time and place and circumstance. Ordinary in this context does not mean that the payments must be habitual or normal in the sense that the same taxpayer will have to make them often. A lawsuit affecting the safety of a business may happen once in a lifetime. The counsel fees may be so heavy that repetition is unlikely. None the less, the expense is an ordinary one because we know from experience that payments for such a purpose, whether the amount is large or small, are the common and accepted means of defense against attack. The situation is unique in the life of the individual affected, but not in the life of the group, the community, of which he is a part. At such times there are norms of conduct that help to stabilize our judgment, and make it certain and objective. The instance is not erratic, but is brought within a known type.

The line of demarcation is now visible between the case that is here and the one supposed for illustration. We try to classify this act as ordinary or the opposite, and the norms of conduct fail us. No longer can we have recourse to any fund of business experience, to any known business practice. Men do at times pay the debts of others without legal obligation or the lighter obligation imposed by the usages of trade or by neighborly amenities, but they do not do so ordinarily, not even though the result might be to heighten their reputation for generosity and opulence. Indeed, if language is to be read in its natural and common meaning, we should have to say that payment in such circumstances, instead of being ordinary is in a high degree extraordinary. There is nothing ordinary in the stimulus evoking it, and none in the response. Here, indeed, as so often in other branches of the law, the decisive distinctions are those of degree and not of kind. One struggles in vain for any verbal formula that will supply a ready touchstone. The standard set up by the statute is not a rule of law; it is rather a way of life. Life in all its fullness must supply the answer to the riddle.

The Commissioner of Internal Revenue resorted to that standard in assessing the petitioner's income, and found that the payments in controversy came closer to capital outlays than to ordinary and necessary expenses in the operation of a business. His ruling has the support of a presumption of correctness, and the petitioner has the burden of proving it to be wrong. Unless we can say from facts within our knowledge that these are ordinary and necessary expenses according to the ways of conduct and the forms of speech prevailing in the business world, the tax must be confirmed. But nothing told us by this record or within the sphere of our judicial notice permits us to give that extension to what is ordinary and necessary. Indeed, to do so would open the door to many bizarre analogies. One man has a family name that is clouded by thefts committed by an ancestor. To add to this own standing he repays the stolen money, wiping off, it may be, his income for the year. The payments figure in his tax return as ordinary expenses. Another man conceives the notion that he will be able to practice his vocation with greater ease and profit if he has an opportunity to enrich his culture. Forthwith the price of his education becomes an expense of the business, reducing the income subject to taxation. There is little difference between these expenses and those in controversy here. Reputation and learning are akin to capital assets, like the good will of an old partnership. For many, they are the only tools with which to hew a pathway to success. The money spent in acquiring them is well and wisely spent. It is not an ordinary expense of the operation of a business. . . .

COMMENT

Welch raises the question whether the "extraordinary" nature of the expense, apart from its being a capital expenditure, is a ground for disallowing the deduction. Some courts seemed to think so. For example, in *Friedman v. Delaney*, 171 F.2d 269 (1st Cir. 1948), a lawyer paid a client's bankruptcy debt because he had assured creditors that his client would be able to pay his debts. The court denied the deduction, stating that the taxpayer's payment originated in a "gratuitous assurance," and a "voluntary underwriting of the obligation of another." It concluded: "The emphasis placed by the [taxpayer] upon his moral obligation to keep his professional word should not obscure the fact that the transaction on his part was voluntary from the beginning"; and it is "no part of a lawyer's business to take on a personal obligation to make payments which should come from his client." All this is somewhat puzzling, because it does not focus on whether the lawyer's reputation-related payment was a deductible current expense or a capital expenditure. The "voluntariness" of the payment looms as a dispositive fact, without any explanation of why that should be so.

Later decisions have downplayed any implication that a voluntary or unusual expense is, on that account, not deductible. The cases are not easy, because it is always hard to draw the line between current expenses and capital expenditures when the outlay is related to intangible assets (like reputation). But the framework is the conventional one of current expense vs. capital expenditure analysis unencumbered by additional criteria limiting deductions. The following Revenue Ruling is a more up-to-date discussion of reputation-related expenses.

REVENUE RULING 76-203
1976-1 C.B. 45

The taxpayer is a furniture moving and storage company. During the taxable year a fire totally destroyed its warehouse, which contained household goods of many of the taxpayer's customers. Although some of the customers are insured under personal policies and some are insured under the taxpayer's general insurance policy, other customers have no insurance coverage. The taxpayer is in the process of rebuilding its warehouse, and is continuing its operations in temporary quarters. Some of the taxpayer's customers were unhappy over their losses and complained that they were not sufficiently informed about their insurance options. To preserve its goodwill among its customers, and to protect its business reputation, the taxpayer plans to make at least partial monetary restitutions to the uninsured customers. . . .

In *Dunn & McCarthy, Inc. v. Commissioner*, 139 F.2d 242 (2d Cir. 1943), the court held that a corporation's payment of personal debts owed by the corporation's insolvent deceased president, and due its salesmen, qualified as an ordinary and necessary business expense because such payment was paid to conserve its goodwill among its salesmen and customers. In its opinion, the court emphasized the payment was an outlay to retain existing goodwill rather than an outlay to acquire goodwill for a new business. . . .

In the present case, the sole purpose of the planned monetary restitutions by the taxpayer to its uninsured customers is to preserve the taxpayer's goodwill among its customers and to protect its business reputation.

Accordingly, the amounts to be expended by the taxpayer to preserve its goodwill and to protect its business reputation under the above circumstances are ordinary and necessary business expenses that are deductible under section 162(a) of the Code.

––––––––––

The following two cases probably have the effect of overruling the *Friedman v. Delaney* decision, which had disallowed the lawyer's deduction for voluntarily paying off his client's debts. *Jenkins v. Commissioner*, 47 T.C.M. (CCH) 238 (1983) (country music singer can deduct voluntary payments to investors in his defunct entertainment business, intended to preserve his business reputation); *Pepper v. Commissioner*, 36 T.C. 886 (1961) (lawyer can deduct payments to creditors of defrauding client when the lawyer had helped arrange the loans without knowing about the fraud).

This leaves *Friedman v. Delaney* out on a limb. Either it was wrong in emphasizing that a voluntary expense cannot be a deductible ordinary and necessary expense, or it was based on an unarticulated rationale, which was that a lawyer paying a client's debts violated public policy. We return to the "public policy" issue in Chapter 14.02.

Occasionally, a court invokes the "ordinary and necessary" standard to disallow a deduction. One suspects, however, that there are other reasons for the result. For example, in *Love Box Co., Inc. v. Commissioner*, 842 F.2d 1213 (10th Cir. 1988), the taxpayer paid a well-known free enterprise advocate to give seminars about economic history and comparative economics to employees, customers, and the general public. Most of those attending were neither employees nor customers. With a dissent, the court held that the business connection was too tenuous to justify the deduction, either as education for employees or promotional/goodwill as to others. The court stated:

> Whether and to what extent deductions shall be allowed depends upon legislative grace; and only as there is clear provision therefore can any particular deduction be allowed." *New Colonial Ice Co. v. Helvering*, 292

U.S. 435, 440 (1934). . . . The primary requirement for deductibility under section 162 is that the particular expense be an ordinary and necessary expense which bears a "proximate and direct relationship to the taxpayer's trade or business.

In my view, the expenses in *Love Box* were probably personal expenses, incurred to indulge the taxpayer's personal political preferences.

[2] Note on Statutory Interpretation — Substantive Canons of Interpretation

The court in *Love Box* refers to deductions being a matter of legislative grace. In effect, the court is applying a substantive canon of interpretation — bringing to the statute a presumption that a taxpayer's claim to a deduction has one or two strikes against it. This presumption is the opposite of the pro-taxpayer presumption referred to in *Irwin v. Gavit* (discussed in Chapter 4.05[A]).

The "legislative grace" canon is hard to justify. Like all substantive canons, it must rest on some principle in the legal landscape or on a reasonable guess about legislative intent. But it is hard to identify any such principle or any reason to think that Congress might want the court to be skeptical of a deduction claim. First, if the deduction implements the principle that only personal consumption and savings should be taxed, it is part of the warp and woof of the tax base, not a matter of legislative grace. At least that is true as long as the income tax is supposed to fall on *net* income. One way to make this point is that it makes no sense to have a canon against taxing gross income and a canon against deductions that define net income.

Second, if the deduction implements nontax policy (such as an economic incentive), it is arguable that the court should squint hard before deciding that the deduction is available. This would implement the principle that the income tax law should not be used too casually to provide tax preferences. The problem is that it is hard to infer any congressional reluctance to rely on deductions to implement policy goals, given the plethora of tax breaks that appear in the tax code. Moreover, there is no indication in the cases that the "legislative grace" canon is limited to situations where the deduction implements nontax policy.

[3] "Reasonable"

In *Kurzet v. Commissioner*, 222 F.3d 830 (10th Cir. 2000), the issue was whether an expense was so unreasonable that it was not "ordinary and necessary." The Court of Appeals reversed the Tax Court and held for the taxpayer. But the fact that the government and the Tax Court thought that the expense was unreasonable and therefore not deductible is a warning for taxpayers. The taxpayer had deducted the costs of a private Lear Jet to travel to a business destination. The Tax Court would have allowed the deduction of first-class travel ($1,600 per trip), but that is all.

The Court of Appeals was more generous to the taxpayer, as follows:

> For an expense to be considered ordinary and necessary, it must also be reasonable in amount. *See Harmon City, Inc. v. United States*, 733 F.2d 1381, 1383 (10th Cir. 1984) ("Although [§ 162] does not limit deduc-

tions . . . to a 'reasonable' amount, the reasonableness of such payments must be explored to determine whether they are 'ordinary and necessary' . . . ."); *see also* Treas. Reg. § 1.162-2(a) ("Only such traveling expenses as are reasonable and necessary in the conduct of the taxpayer's business and directly attributable to it may be deducted.").

The court considered the government's argument that the Lear Jet expenses were not reasonable because all they did was avoid the inconvenience of normal commercial air travel. The court disagreed with the government:

> The tax court made a factual finding that the average time for one-way commercial air travel between Orange, California and North Bend, Oregon was nine hours and involved two stops and at least one change of planes. The record reflects that this trip took less than three hours one way when using the Lear jet. Thus, our review of the record confirms the Kurzets' claim that they saved twelve hours round trip when flying from California to Oregon. Based on a twelve-hour savings, the Kurzets saved approximately 888 hours of travel time when making the 74 trips to Oregon in 1987, 1988, and 1989. . . .

The court computed the time saved by taking a private plane compared to commercial plane service, and converted that to a dollar figure based on a $200 per hour value for the taxpayer's time. The extra cost of the private plane over the $1,600 price of a first-class ticket on a regular commercial airline (which was accepted as a permissible deduction) was not more than the dollar value of the time saved. Therefore, the expenses were reasonable.

In reaching this decision, the court held that it was improper to consider the amount of depreciation claimed on the jet to decide whether the expenses were reasonable. It stated that depreciation is "not really an 'expenditure' but an allowance based on a presumed wasting of a previous capital investment," governed by § 168. It therefore did not "fall under the regulatory rubric of trade or business expense" and should not be included in the amount of business expense when assessing the reasonableness of that expense. That was an odd conclusion. Rent would be subject to the "reasonableness" requirement and depreciation is, in part, the financial equivalent of rent to an owner.

[4] Note on Statutory Interpretation — Statutory Surplusage

The cases strongly suggest that the statutory words "ordinary and necessary" do not mean much. Either they prevent deduction of capital expenditures and personal expenses, in which case other sections deal with the issue (§§ 162, 262, 263, 446), or the court will not rely on this statutory text to second-guess business judgment.

This violates one of the standard linguistic canons of statutory construction — that the statute should not contain surplusage. When this and other linguistic canons are violated, the courts usually fall back to the position that the canon is no more than a guide to determining statutory meaning, not a rigid rule.

[B]   Excessive Compensation — Reasonable Salary

[1]   Note on Statutory Interpretation — Legislative History and Statutory Language

Section 162(a)(1) allows a deduction for "a reasonable allowance for salaries or other compensation for personal services actually rendered." There is evidence in the legislative history of this section that it was never meant to limit deductions, but was instead meant to *allow* deductions. It was passed when there was a tax on excess profits. Under the excess profits tax, owners of an unincorporated business who did not draw down salary would have their profits overstated (and therefore subject to tax) unless some provision permitted the taxpayer to reduce profits by the value of the services. Griswold, *New Light on "A Reasonable Allowance for Salaries*, 59 HARV. L. REV. 286 (1945).

Knowing this legislative history might call attention to an ambiguity in the wording of § 162(a)(1) that would otherwise escape attention. Why, for example, would a section limiting a deduction refer to a reasonable *"allowance for salaries"* rather than a reasonable *"payment of salary"*? The "allowance" language makes sense, however, as permission to the taxpayer to reduce income by an amount that had not been paid.

[2]   Employees and Owners

Whatever the history, § 162(a)(1) now limits the deduction of salaries to a reasonable amount. In effect, this is one area where an expense must be more than just "appropriate and helpful." The statutory rule is usually applied to employees who are also major owners of the corporation. Shareholders of a corporation want to take out corporate income as salary rather than profits, because profit distributions (that is, dividends) are not deductible by the corporation.

However, § 162(a)(1) is not needed to achieve this result. Any unreasonable salary paid to a corporate owner would be recharacterized as a nondeductible dividend, even without that section. A dividend is simply not an "expense." This must be the correct interpretation of the statute or else an unreasonable rental payment or other excessive price paid to a shareholder would be deductible by the corporation, even though it was a disguised dividend. *See Safway Steel Scaffolds Co. v. United States*, 590 F.2d 1360 (5th Cir. 1979) (excessive rent to shareholder-lessor was a nondeductible dividend).

If the employee is not an owner, § 162(a)(1) will be considered when the employee has contracted for a percentage of profits and the business later flourishes. If the original contract for the profit percentage was a "free bargain," the profit payment will not be questioned, even though it exceeds the reasonable salary that would be paid if the salary were negotiated in the later payment year. If the original bargain was not "free," (as evidenced by family pressure on the payor to help an owner's relative, for example), the deductible amount will be limited to the reasonable value of services in the year of payment. *Harolds Club v. Commissioner*, 340 F.2d 861 (9th Cir. 1965).

[a]   Multi-Factor Test

The courts have had some difficulty identifying the test used to determine whether the salary is reasonable. In *Exacto Spring Corp. v. Commissioner*, 196 F.3d 833 (7th Cir. 1999), Judge Posner rejected the multi-factor test used by the Tax Court to determine whether a salary was reasonable. He stated:

> The factors [used by the Tax Court to determine reasonable compensation] are . . . "(1) the type and extent of the services rendered; (2) the scarcity of qualified employees; (3) the qualifications and prior earning capacity of the employee; (4) the contributions of the employee to the business venture; (5) the net earnings of the employer; (6) the prevailing compensation paid to employees with comparable jobs; and (7) the peculiar characteristics of the employer's business." 75 T.C.M. at 2525. It is apparent that this test, though it or variants of it (one of which has the astonishing total of 21 factors), are encountered in many cases, leaves much to be desired — being, like many other multi-factor tests, "redundant, incomplete, and unclear."

> To begin with, it is nondirective. No indication is given of how the factors are to be weighed in the event they don't all line up on one side. . . .

> Second, the factors do not bear a clear relation either to each other or to the primary purpose of section 162(a)(1), which is to prevent dividends (or in some cases gifts), which are not deductible from corporate income, from being disguised as salary. . . .

> Third, the seven-factor test invites the Tax Court to set itself up as a superpersonnel department for closely-held corporations . . . , a role unsuitable for courts. . . .

> Fourth, since the test cannot itself determine the outcome of a dispute because of its nondirective character, it invites the making of arbitrary decisions based on uncanalized discretion or unprincipled rules of thumb.

> Fifth, because the reaction of the Tax Court to a challenge to the deduction of executive compensation is unpredictable, corporations run unavoidable legal risks in determining a level of compensation that may be indispensable to the success of their business. . . .

Judge Posner concludes that the Tax Court test "does not provide adequate guidance to a rational decision." He further notes that the Courts of Appeals "owe no deference to the Tax Court's statutory interpretations, its relation to us being that of a district court to a court of appeals, not that of an administrative agency to a court of appeals. 26 U.S.C. § 7482(a)(1)." He then explains the rationale for limiting the salary deduction and argues for "an indirect market test," as follows:

> The Internal Revenue Code limits the amount of salary that a corporation can deduct from its income primarily in order to prevent the corporation from eluding the corporate income tax by paying dividends but calling them salary because salary is deductible and dividends are not. . . . In the case of a publicly held company, where the salaries of the highest executives are fixed by a board of directors that those executives do not control, the

danger of siphoning corporate earnings to executives in the form of salary is not acute. The danger is much greater in the case of a closely held corporation, in which ownership and management tend to coincide; unfortunately, as the opinion of the Tax Court in this case illustrates, judges are not competent to decide what business executives are worth.

There is, fortunately, an indirect market test, as recognized by the Internal Revenue Service's expert witness. A corporation can be conceptualized as a contract in which the owner of assets hires a person to manage them. The owner pays the manager a salary and in exchange the manager works to increase the value of the assets that have been entrusted to his management; that increase can be expressed as a rate of return to the owner's investment. The higher the rate of return (adjusted for risk) that a manager can generate, the greater the salary he can command. If the rate of return is extremely high, it will be difficult to prove that the manager is being overpaid, for it will be implausible that if he quit if his salary was cut, and he was replaced by a lower-paid manager, the owner would be better off; it would be killing the goose that lays the golden egg. . . .

. . . [However,] we can imagine cases in which the return, though very high, is not due to the CEO's exertions. Suppose Exacto had been an unprofitable company that suddenly learned that its factory was sitting on an oil field, and when oil revenues started to pour in its owner raised his salary from $50,000 a year to $1.3 million. The presumption of reasonableness would be rebutted. There is no suggestion of anything of that sort here and likewise no suggestion that Mr. Heitz was merely the titular chief executive and the company was actually run by someone else, which would be another basis for rebuttal. . . .

Not everyone accepts Judge Posner's analysis in the *Exacto* case. *See Haffner's Service Stations, Inc. v. Commissioner*, 326 F.3d 1 (1st Cir. 2003), holding that multiple factors may be relevant and noting that "[t]here is always a balance to be struck between simplifying doctrine and accuracy of result . . . ."

But, in *Menard, Inc. v. Commissioner*, 560 F.3d 620 (7th Cir. 2009), *reversing*, T.C. Memo 2004-207 (2004), Judge Posner again refused to characterize as unreasonable a large payment to an employee — the company's chief executive (who also owned all of the company's voting stock). Most of the executive's $20 million-plus salary was a 5%-of-net-income bonus equal to $17,467,800. Posner objected to the standard in the Regulations, as follows:

A difficult case — which is this case — is thus that of a corporation that pays a high salary to its CEO who works full time but is also the controlling shareholder. The Treasury regulation defines a "reasonable" salary as the amount that "would ordinarily be paid for like services by like enterprises under like circumstances," § 1.162 7(b)(3), but that is not an operational standard. No two enterprises are alike and no two chief executive officers are alike, and anyway the comparison should be between the total compensation package of the CEOs being compared, and that requires consideration of deferred compensation, including severance packages, the amount of risk in the executives' compensation, and perks.

Posner's opinion objected (among other things) to the Tax Court's "disregard[ing of the] differences in the full compensation packages of the three executives [of other companies] being compared, differences in whatever challenges faced the companies in 1998, and differences in the responsibilities and performance of the three CEOs."

[b]   Section 162(m)

Compensation paid by publicly held corporations has not been subjected to scrutiny under § 162(a)(1), because the shareholder-employee does not appear to have the kind of control that exists in a corporation owned by a few people or families. Consequently, the 1993 tax law added another limit on the deduction of salary, which prevents a publicly held corporation from deducting more than $1 million of compensation paid to any of five corporate officials — the chief executive officer and (in most cases) the four highest paid officers. § 162(m). There are two exceptions that make the rule ineffectual at limiting compensation — (1) commissions based on income generated directly by the officer's performance; and (2) amounts payable on account of meeting performance goals (such as stock price, market share, sales, or earnings), if the goals and related compensation package are determined by a committee of outside directors and by a shareholder majority vote.

[c]   Compensation Paid by Health Insurance Providers

The Patient Protection and Affordable Health Care Act (Obamacare) (Public Law 111-148) provides that the deduction for compensation paid by health insurance providers is limited to $500,000. The law applies to payments beginning in 2013 for services performed after 2009. The ceiling on the deduction applies to payment to employees and independent contractors and is not limited to top executives; and there is no exception for performance-based compensation. § 162(m)(6).

[C]   Lavish or Extravagant

Several statutory provisions disallow the deduction of "lavish or extravagant" meals, lodging, or entertainment. § 162(a)(2) (meals and lodging while traveling); § 274(k)(1)(A) (business meals). These phrases may be as ineffective in limiting deductions as the word "necessary" in the introductory language of § 162(a). However, the Committee Reports to the Tax Reform Act of 1986 state that the reference in § 274(k)(1)(A) was added, "thereby emphasizing an intent that this standard is to be enforced by the Internal Revenue Service and the courts."

In addition, a host of specific rules prevent deduction of business expenses that seem extravagant and wasteful, and that may provide personal consumption. *See, e.g.*, §§ 274(h) (certain cruise ships and foreign conventions); 274(l) (limit deduction to face value of entertainment tickets); 274(m) (luxury water transportation); 274(n) (50% of meals and entertainment); 280F (limit on luxury automobile depreciation). At least some of these deductions are probably disallowed to disadvantage foreign competitors of U.S. business (e.g., foreign cruises, conventions, and luxury automobiles).

§ 14.02　ILLEGAL ACTIVITY

[A]　"Tax Fines"

■ Policy

You have read about tax expenditures — tax provisions explicitly designed to encourage activities that Congress considers desirable. Now we consider the use of the tax law to discourage undesirable activities by disallowing deductions that would otherwise be allowed. If the analogy between tax expenditures and direct subsidies is apt, then disallowing deductions to achieve nontax policy should invite comparison between the use of the tax law to discourage the activity and the use of civil or criminal fines imposed by an agency or court charged with implementing that policy.

If we conceptualize disallowance of a deduction as a "tax fine," we are naturally led to ask whether tax fines make any sense in comparison with civil or criminal penalties. First, the tax fine varies with the tax rate, rather than with the rules relevant under the state or federal law imposing penalties on undesirable behavior. Second, it is not always clear that permitting the deduction has any effect on behavior.

In reading the cases dealing with expenses against public policy, you might be tempted to question whether they are ordinary and necessary business expenses in the first place. Perhaps you would like to think that taxpayers do not ordinarily make expenditures that violate public policy. But, of course, that is not true — e.g., a trucker might very well incur fines for weight overloads on the highway to beat out or simply match the competition.

■ Note on Statutory Interpretation — Judicial Competence

Even if a "tax fine" makes sense, should the courts have read this principle into the tax law? For courts to do this, they must decide about the strength or weakness of the public policy served by disallowing the deduction; the impact of the taxpayer's tax bracket; and whether the tax penalty ought to be added to any other penalties imposed by law. The courts might not be good at making that judgment. Indeed, the predominant reason for courts disallowing these deductions was symbolic — preventing the tax law from appearing to sanction the illegal behavior — rather than any well-thought out decision that a tax fine was a good way to enforce the law.

Concern about the judicial role led to the following evolution in the tax law in which judicially created rules gave way, in most situations, to statutory law.

[B]　Expenses — Case Law

In *Commissioner v. Tellier*, 383 U.S. 687 (1966), the taxpayer incurred legal expenses in the unsuccessful defense of a criminal prosecution originating in the securities business. The deduction was challenged on public policy grounds. The Court expressed a grudging acceptance of the public policy limitation on deductions, but found no policy against incurring legal expenses in criminal cases. The Court stated:

> . . . [W]here Congress has been wholly silent, it is only in extremely limited circumstances that the Court has countenanced exceptions to the general principle [of deductibility]. Only where the allowance of a deduction would 'frustrate sharply defined national or state policies proscribing particular types of conduct' have we upheld its disallowance. Further, the 'policies frustrated must be national or state policies evidenced by some governmental declaration of them.' Finally, the 'test of nondeductibility always is the severity and immediacy of the frustration resulting from allowance of the deduction.' *Tank Truck Rentals v. Commissioner*, 356 U.S. 30, 35. In that case, . . . we upheld the disallowance of deductions claimed by taxpayers for fines and penalties imposed upon them for violating state penal statutes; to allow a deduction in those circumstances would have directly and substantially diluted the actual punishment imposed.

> The present case falls far outside that sharply limited and carefully category. No public policy is offended when a man faced with serious criminal charges employs a lawyer to help in his defense. That is not 'proscribed conduct.' It is his constitutional right. In an adversary system of criminal justice, it is a basic of our public policy that a defendant in a criminal case have counsel to represent him.

> Congress has authorized the imposition of severe punishment upon those found guilty of the serious criminal offenses with which the respondent was charged and of which he was convicted. But we can find no warrant for attaching to that punishment an additional financial burden that Congress has neither expressly nor implicitly directed. To deny a deduction for expenses incurred in the unsuccessful defense of a criminal prosecution would impose such a burden in a measure dependent not on the seriousness of the offense or the actual sentence imposed by the court, but on the cost of the defense and the defendant's particular tax bracket. We decline to distort the income tax laws to serve a purpose for which they were neither intended nor designed by Congress.

[C]　1969 Legislation

Judicial impatience with disallowing a deduction on public policy grounds spilled over into Congress in 1969, when § 162 was amended to adopt § 162(c), (f), (g). The Senate Finance Committee Report for the 1969 Act stated that the "provision for the denial of the deduction of payments in these situations which are deemed to violate public policy is intended to be all inclusive. Public policy, in other circumstances, generally is not sufficiently clearly defined to justify the disallowance of deductions." S. Rept. No. 91-552, 91st Cong., 1st Sess. (1969), *reprinted in* 1969 U.S. CODE CONG. & AD. NEWS 2027, 2311.

In its present form, § 162(c), (f), (g) accomplishes the following.

[1]   Illegal Payments, Etc.

Section 162(c) is a catch-all for a variety of illegal payments. Illegal bribes and illegal kickbacks paid to government officials and government employees are not deductible, except that payments to foreign officials and foreign employees are not deductible only if the payments are illegal under the Foreign Corrupt Practices Act of 1977. **§ 162(c)(1)**. Bribes and kickbacks (even if not illegal) are not deductible when made to suppliers of services in connection with Medicaid and Medicare. **§ 162(c)(3)**.

Illegal bribes and illegal kickbacks (not already covered by **§ 162(c)(1)**), and other illegal payments, are also not deductible, *if* they would subject the taxpayer to a criminal penalty or loss of license or privilege to engage in business. **§ 162(c)(2)**. The "other illegal payment" rule is subject to an interesting qualification in the case of payments that are illegal under state law. The state law must be "generally enforced." Desuetude is therefore a legally relevant consideration in determining whether an expense is so contrary to state public policy that it should not be deductible. The Regulations state that a law is generally enforced unless it is never enforced or enforced only when the defendants are infamous or the violations are extraordinarily flagrant; in other words, it is not easy to prove that a law is not generally enforced. **Treas. Reg. § 1.162-18(b)**.

The 1969 statute might prevent deduction of some expenses previously permitted. In *Commissioner v. Sullivan*, 356 U.S. 27 (1958), the Court allowed a deduction for rent and wages paid by the operators of a gambling enterprise, even though both the business itself and the specific rent and wage payments were illegal under state law. Would these payments be nondeductible under **§ 162(c)**?

Under all of the provisions of **§ 162(c)**, the government has the burden of proof on the question of illegality.

COMMENTS AND QUESTIONS

1. In Rev. Rul. 74-323, 1974-2 C.B. 40, a taxpayer had incurred advertising expenses but the advertisement violated the law against sex discrimination. Because there was no criminal penalty or loss of a license or privilege to do business for violating the law, the expenses were deductible.

2. Can a taxpayer deduct a legal kickback — for example, a payment made by a record producer to a disc jockey (assuming it *is* legal)? *Raymond Bertolini Trucking Co. v. Commissioner*, 736 F.2d 1120 (6th Cir. 1984) (kickbacks deductible as "ordinary" expenses), *reversing* 45 T.C.M. (CCH) 44 (1982); *Car-Ron Asphalt Paving Co. v. Commissioner*, 758 F.2d 1132 (6th Cir. 1985) (kickbacks not deductible because they were not "necessary"; taxpayer obtained most of his contracts without kickbacks).

3. Suppose a lawyer advances court costs for the client. Assume further that, absent any public policy issues, the amounts are deductible. This assumption *may* be incorrect — the advances may be loans (*Badell v. Commissioner*, 80 T.C.M. (CCH) 422 (2000)). However, in *Boccardo v. Commissioner*, 56 F.3d 1016 (9th Cir.

1995), the court held that they were deductible expenses when there was no explicit client obligation to repay.

But there was another issue. These advances might have violated the rules of professional responsibility, adopted by the California Supreme Court. If they did, would they be nondeductible "illegal payments"? Is the Supreme Court rule a "state law"? In *Boccardo*, the court stated: "The Rules of Professional Conduct approved by the California Supreme Court and governing the legal profession might, in a pinch, be treated as 'state law,' although the characterization is arguable when there is a state statute regulating the same matters." In any event, the court found that no one ever lost a licence to practice law for this kind of behavior, so the expenses were deductible. *See also* **Treas. Reg. § 1.162-18(b)**, defining "state law" to be a statute of a state or District of Columbia for purposes of **§ 162(c)(2)**.

[2] Fines and Similar Penalties

Section 162(f) disallows the deduction of fines or similar penalties paid to a government. The Regulations include civil as well as criminal fines in the nondeductible category, but compensatory damages are deductible (assuming an income-producing origin for the expense). **Treas. Reg. § 1.162-21(b)**.

It is not always easy to identify a fine. A "fine or similar penalty" has a "punitive, as opposed to remedial, meaning." *Jerry Rossman Corp. v. Commissioner*, 175 F.2d 711 (2d Cir. 1949). But how do you draw the line between punitive and remedial? First, legislative intent is often considered relevant in drawing the line, but legislative intent is no easier to divine on this question than on any other. Second, courts may rely on their own model of what constitutes a punitive rather than a remedial payment — such as the method of computing the payments. Often, both considerations appear in an opinion.

One setting in which judges have grappled with this issue is a statute that provides for "liquidated damages," or some other fixed amount of compensation. Courts dealt with this problem when *excluding* damages under **§ 104(a)**. In *Commissioner v. Schleier*, 515 U.S. 323 (1995), the Court concluded that the liquidated damages provisions of the civil rights statute were punitive, which meant that they were not amounts received "on account of" personal injury. The same issue arises on the deduction side.

In *Hawronsky v. Commissioner*, 105 T.C. 94 (1995), the court held that the liquidated damages provisions of the statute were punitive "fines" rather than compensatory payments. The taxpayer had received a tax-exempt scholarship from the Indian Health Services Scholarship Program to attend medical school. The statute regulating the scholarship program required the taxpayer to sign a contract agreeing to serve in the Indian Health Service for four years. Failure to serve this term resulted (under the statute) in treble damages paid to the Department of Health and Human Services (HHS).

After completing about one year and eight months of the required four years of service with the Indian Health Service, taxpayer quit and paid $275,326.86 as treble damages to HHS. Taxpayer claimed a deduction for this amount as a business expense. Taxpayer argued that the treble damages payment was compensatory and not punitive, but the court held that Congress intended the treble damages under this statute to be an enforceable civil penalty. The court also noted that the treble damages had no demonstrated relationship to the Government's actual damages from the loss of petitioner's services — such as by taking into account the costs of finding a doctor to practice in an underserved area.

One implication of emphasizing legislative intent is that the characterization of liquidated damages can vary from statute to statute. If that is true, it is difficult to determine whether such damages are or are not nondeductible fines under § 162(f). *See, e.g., Colt Indus., Inc. v. United States*, 880 F.2d 1311 (Fed. Cir. 1989), in which the court looked at legislative history to find a legislative intent to punish.

In two rulings, the IRS could not find a legislative intent to punish. In Rev. Rul 80-334, 1980-2 C.B. 61, a taxpayer that engaged in the sale of petroleum products was allowed to deduct court-ordered payments to prior customers and to the Treasury for oil price violations when the taxpayer's violation was *unintentional*. As part of the consent order requiring the payments, the Department of Energy agreed that civil or criminal penalties would be inappropriate. And, in Rev. Rul. 88-46, 1988-1 C.B. 76, payments labeled as "performance penalties" were not fines because the legislative history showed that they were imposed to equalize the costs on those whose violations of environmental standards would otherwise give them a competitive advantage.

In *True v. United States*, 894 F.2d 1197 (10th Cir. 1990), *reversing*, 603 F. Supp. 1370 (D. Wyo. 1985), the method of computing the payment was important. The court disallowed the deduction, distinguishing between deductible compensatory/ remedial payments to the government and nondeductible punitive/retributive payments, under the Federal Water Pollution Control Act. The payments in this case were not deductible, in part because the amounts were determined by reference to the size of the payor's business and the effect on the payor continuing business, both of which bore no relation to compensating an injured party.

COMMENTS AND QUESTIONS

1. **Payment "to."** The fact that the payment is not technically made "to" the government is not dispositive. In *Waldman v. Commissioner*, 88 T.C. 1384 (1987), *affirmed*, 850 F.2d 611 (9th Cir. 1988), the court held that restitution paid to victims by order of the court to avoid execution of a sentence was a nondeductible fine. *See also* Rev. Rul. 79-148, 1979-1 C.B. 93 (the court ordered the taxpayer to pay money to a charity in lieu of a fine; the payment was not a deductible charitable gift because it was paid under compulsion, and was disallowed as a business deduction because of § 162(f)).

2. **Settlements.** Payments "in settlement of the taxpayer's actual or potential liability for a fine or penalty" are fines. **Treas. Reg. § 1.162-21(b)(1)(iii).** In *Allied-Signal v. Commissioner*, 63 T.C.M. (CCH) 2672 (1992), there was a lawsuit to determine whether the taxpayer had to pay a fine for environmental pollution. The case was settled before there was a finding of taxpayer responsibility. The settlement called for a payment by the taxpayer to a § 501(c)(4) organization that helped clean up the environment. Payments to this organization were not tax

deductible charitable contributions, but could be § 162(a) expenses. The taxpayer insisted that the payments were voluntary and therefore not fines or settlements in lieu of fines. The court disallowed the deduction on the ground that they were fines, placing little weight on the "voluntariness" of the payment.

The settlement cases remind us that nondeductibility may not always be desirable public policy because it will discourage settlement. For example, state governments sued cigarette manufacturers for damages on the ground that cigarettes caused health problems resulting in increased financial burdens on government-sponsored medical programs. In 1997, the case was settled for billions of dollars. Would that settlement have occurred if the payments had been in lieu of "fines?"

3. **Punitive damages.** Can punitive damages in a breach of contract action be deducted? Rev. Rul. 80-211, 1980-2 C.B. 57 permitted the deduction of punitive damages. What justifies that result? The fact that the payments are "to" the plaintiff, not the government, should not be dispositive, as long as the court orders the payment.

4. **Treble damages.** In civil anti-trust cases, a losing defendant must pay three times actual damages. **Section 162(g)** disallows a deduction for the two-thirds portion of the treble damages, if the taxpayer has been convicted or pleads guilty or nolo contendere in a criminal proceeding. What effect might this have on the taxpayer's willingness to plead guilty?

[D]   Costs — Defining "Gross Income"

The discussion so far has focused primarily on § 162 expense deductions, which are deductible in reducing § 61 gross income to taxable income. What happens if the expenditure that the taxpayer wants to deduct is a cost, which reduces amount realized (that is, gross receipts) to gross income? The authorities seem inconsistent.

Added to cost. A Committee Report, S. Rep. 97 494 (Vol.1) at 309 (1982), supports including in the cost of goods sold an amount that would not be deductible as an expense. The Report discusses the disallowance of deductions under **§ 280E** for expenses related to drug dealing, stating: "To preclude possible challenges on constitutional grounds, the adjustment to gross receipts with respect to effective costs of goods sold is not affected by [§ 280E]." In *Californians Helping to Alleviate Medical Problems, Inc. v. Commissioner*, 128 T.C. 173 (2007), the court noted that the government has conceded "that the disallowance of sec. 280E does not apply to costs of goods sold, a concession that is consistent with the case law on that subject and the legislative history underlying sec. 280E. *See Peyton v. Commissioner*, T.C. Memo. 2003-146 (2003); *Franklin v. Commissioner*, T.C. Memo. 1993-184 (1993); *Vasta v. Commissioner*, T.C. Memo. 1989-531 (1989)."

Presumably, the constitutional problem is that refusing to increase cost of goods sold would increase gross income, and that would result in taxing something that was not gross income without apportionment among the states according to population. But apportionment is required only for a direct tax, and the increase in tax based on illegal drug activity appears to be an indirect excise tax, not subject to the apportionment requirement.

Not added to cost. The current Regulations purport to give an answer to this question. (**Treas. Reg. § 1.471-3 (last sentence)**) state that outlays of a type for which a deduction would be disallowed under **§ 162(c), (f), (g)** cannot be added to cost. *See also* TAM 200629030, where the IRS insisted that a fine or penalty that would not be deductible cannot be added to cost pursuant to **§ 263A**. Surely, that is the right result. Cost is nothing but an expenditure that should be added to basis for future deduction, so the difference between an expense and a cost lies only in the timing of a deduction. How can the public policy doctrine have greater vitality when the deduction is claimed at the time the expenditure is made, rather than when the deduction is deferred?

[E]   Costs — Losses

In *Mazzei v. Commissioner*, 61 T.C. 497 (1974), two crooks demonstrated to the taxpayer a black box that appeared to print counterfeit money from real $10 bills. Tempted by this scheme, the taxpayer brought cash to the crooks, who staged a raid while "printing" the money and escaped with taxpayer's cash. Taxpayer claimed a loss deduction under **§ 165**, but the government denied the deduction on public policy grounds.

The court relied on *Richey v. Commissioner*, 33 T.C. 272 (1959), which disallowed a deduction to a conspirator in a counterfeiting scheme when his co-conspirators stole $15,000 of the money he had provided for use in the scheme. *Richey* held that a loss deduction "would constitute an immediate and severe frustration of the clearly defined policy against counterfeiting obligations of the United States." The court refused to follow *Edwards v. Bromberg*, 232 F.2d 107 (5th Cir. 1956), where the court allowed a deduction for a loss incurred by the taxpayer when money, which he thought was being bet on a fixed race, was stolen from him. The taxpayer never intended to participate in fixing the race.

The dissenters in *Mazzei* argued that disallowing the deduction violated the spirit (if not the letter) of the Senate Finance Committee report for the 1969 Tax Reform Act, which stated: "The provision for the denial of the deduction for payments in these situations which are deemed to violate public policy is intended to be all inclusive. Public policy, in other circumstances, generally is not sufficiently clearly defined to justify the disallowance of deductions." They added:

> Congress has authorized the imposition of severe punishment upon those found guilty of counterfeiting United States currency. It is designed to repress such criminal conduct. In the interest of uniform application of the Internal Revenue Code, where the frustration of State or national policy is neither severe nor immediate, we must not be tempted to impose a 'clean hands doctrine' as a prerequisite to deductibility. To hold otherwise, especially in light of the broad brush-stroke of public policy applied by the majority opinion, makes the taxing statute an unwarranted instrument of further punishment.

See also King v. United States, 152 F.3d 1200 (9th Cir. 1998), where the taxpayer had to forfeit to the government the proceeds from the illegal sale of drugs. The taxpayer was not allowed to deduct the forfeited proceeds under § **165** because the forfeiture was like a fine paid to the government. The government rejected the analogy of the embezzler who, as the Court stated in *James v. United States*, 366 U.S. 213 (1961), could deduct the repayment of embezzled funds to the victim of the embezzlement.

The loss deduction cases raise the question whether there is still life in the judicial version of the "public policy" doctrine. This issue could also arise in the following setting: can investors in low-income housing take advantage of the § **42** credit if they discriminate against tenants on the basis of race?

[F] Extramarital Relationships

An individual can be a dependent of a taxpayer if the individual fits the definition of a "qualifying relative," which includes an individual who has a principal place of abode in the taxpayer's household, receives more than one-half of the individual's support from the taxpayer, and earns less than the exemption amount. § **152(d)(1), (2)(H)**. In addition, the relationship of the individual to the taxpayer cannot be in violation of local law. § **152(f)(3)**. The original version of this law was aimed at preventing dependency deductions for "common law" spouses, when this relationship was not recognized under state law. *See Ochs v. Commissioner*, 52 T.C.M. (CCH) 1218 (1986); *Peacock v. Commissioner*, 37 T.C.M. (CCH) 177 (1978), denying dependency deductions in the case of adulterous and "open and notorious cohabitation." However, this issue is more likely to arise today in the context of same-sex households. The issue is important, not only for the dependency deduction, but also for head-of-household status (§ **2(b)(1)(A)(ii)**), and the exclusion of employer-funded fringe benefits for a taxpayer and the taxpayer's dependents (**Treas. Reg. § 1.106-1**).

QUESTIONS AND COMMENTS

1. *Federal constitutional law. Lawrence v. Texas*, 539 U.S. 558 (2003), held that it was a violation of Due Process for the government to criminalize intimate personal relationships between same-sex couples. Perhaps this decision makes it impossible for such relationships to be in violation of local law and thereby renders § **152(f)(3)** obsolete.

2. *State or local law permitting same-sex marriage or civil union.* Would a state or local law permitting same-sex couples to marry or to enter into a civil union make it clear that same-sex couples living together did not violate local law? Or would such a law indicate that same-sex couples could avoid violating local law only by taking advantage of the state or local law?

3. *State law prohibiting same-sex marriage or civil union.* Would such a state law indicate a public policy against same-sex couples and thereby make it impossible to satisfy § **152(f)(3)**? Or does the state law mean only that same-sex couples cannot obtain the advantages associated with marriage, such as alimony, child visitation, etc., without any further disability?

4. *Federal Defense of Marriage Act.* This Act (Pub. L. No. 104-199, 104th Cong., 2d Sess., 110 Stat. 2419), states that "marriage" means only the union of a man and a woman as husband and wife, for purposes of federal law. It should have no impact on whether a relationship has been declared in violation of local law.

5. *Is local law irrelevant in practice?* (1) Letter Ruling 9603011 stated that "domestic partners" could satisfy the dependency rules, but did not allude to any local law recognizing such a relationship. (2) Letter Ruling 200339001 stated that an employer could rely on the employee's certification that a domestic partner qualified as a dependent.

§ 14.03 POLITICAL EXPENDITURES

[A] Nondeductible Business Expenses

Many political expenditures are incurred for income-producing purposes. These include the cost of getting elected, lobbying legislators to obtain passage of a statute favorable to business, and grass-roots lobbying to get public support for such statutes. In 1918, Treasury Regulations stated that corporations could not deduct lobbying expenses and this rule was extended to individuals in 1938. The Supreme Court upheld the Regulations in *Cammarano v. United States*, 358 U.S. 498 (1959). The expense of getting elected and reelected is also not deductible. *McDonald v. Commissioner*, 323 U.S. 57 (1944).

Concerns about deducting political expenses are especially serious when applied, not to expenditures to advance a substantive political agenda, but to advance candidacy for office. Should a very rich person spending $600 million to get elected be allowed to deduct these expenditures, either currently or through depreciation, when political rivals cannot raise that much money to spend in opposition?

You should be conscious of the fact that the tax rules about political expenditures seem to be little more than tinkering with a very fundamental problem, which can only be addressed by more substantial measures, such as public financing of elections or spending limits. More substantial measures, however, raise serious political and legal issues about the relationship of government to political activity, not the least of which is their constitutionality. *Buckley v. Valeo*, 424 U.S. 1 (1976); *McConnell v. Federal Election Commission*, 540 U.S. 93 (2003); *Citizens United v. Federal Election Commission*, 558 U.S. 310 (2010).

[B] Getting Elected vs. Staying in Office

Since 1993, the statute explicitly states what the case law had previously established — that no deduction is allowed for expenses related to a political campaign on behalf of or in opposition to a candidate. § 162(e)(1)(B). The following ruling, however, distinguishes recall elections from the usual candidate elections.

REVENUE RULING 71-470
1971-2 C.B. 121

Advice has been requested whether the amounts paid by a taxpayer under the circumstances described below are deductible under section 162 of the Internal Revenue Code of 1954 as ordinary and necessary business expenses.

The taxpayer was elected to a public office, but shortly after he entered office, a special election was held wherein the voters were asked to vote whether he should be recalled from that office.

The taxpayer waged an active campaign in his defense, and successfully defeated the recall. He incurred and paid expenses in his campaign against recall. . . .

In *Michael F. McDonald v. Commissioner*, 323 U.S. 57 (1944), the Supreme Court of the United States held that the campaign expenditures of a taxpayer seeking election as a judge were not incurred in carrying on the taxpayer's business of 'judging.' The Court held that such expenditures were neither losses incurred in a transaction entered into for profit nor expenses incurred for the production or collection of income.

However, the taxpayer in the instant case was not a candidate for public office, and was not seeking a new term. He was merely defending his position for his current term, and the Supreme Court of the United States has held that the ordinary and necessary expenses of defending one's business are deductible. *Commissioner v. S. B. Heininger*, 320 U.S. 467 (1943), Ct. D. 1956, C.B. 1944, 484.

Accordingly, the amounts paid by the taxpayer in this case in defending his position as an elected public official are deductible as ordinary and necessary business expenses under section 162 of the Code.

COMMENTS AND QUESTIONS

1. You should find the distinction between retaining office (the facts of the Ruling) and seeking election (*McDonald*) very troublesome. The taxpayer in *McDonald* actually lost the election and, under normal tax principles, might therefore have been allowed a loss deduction. *McDonald* is usually thought to stand for the proposition that normal tax principles do *not* apply to political election expenses. *Cf. Levy v. United States*, 535 F.2d 47 (Ct. Cl. 1976) (taxpayer cannot add cost of getting elected to basis and depreciate the basis). Why then should "retaining office" expenses be deductible as ordinary and necessary expenses, as the IRS held in Rev. Rul. 71-470? Is such a deduction less likely to "corrupt" politics with money? Should a Revenue Ruling draw policy distinctions between recall and other elections?

2. A taxpayer unsuccessfully sought reelection as president of a large union. *Carey v. Commissioner*, 56 T.C. 477 (1971), *affirmed per curiam*, 460 F.2d 1259 (4th Cir. 1972), held that the expenses were *not* deductible, on the ground that the presidency of a large public union was analogous to public office.

3. President Ford nominated New York Governor Rockefeller to be Vice President to fill a vacancy after President Nixon's resignation elevated Vice-

President Ford to the Presidency (relying on the procedures in U.S. Const., Amendment 25). Could Rockefeller deduct expenses related to the nomination process? *Rockefeller v. Commissioner*, 83 T.C. 368 (1984), *affirmed*, 762 F.2d 264 (2d Cir. 1985). The court denied the deduction on the ground that the taxpayer was not in the business of being Vice-President. *See* Rev. Rul. 75-120, 1975-1 C.B. 55 (job search costs to successfully or unsuccessfully obtain employment in a new trade or business are not deductible expenses). There was, therefore, "no occasion to decide whether the 'policy' reasons underlying the decisions disallowing expenses incurred in elections apply to expenses incurred in seeking confirmation to an appointive office which would seem to be properly regarded as the same trade or business, or whether if they generally do not, there are special considerations for applying them to the unusual bicameral confirmation required by the Twenty-Fifth Amendment which the Commissioner characterizes as the equivalent of an election."

4. Are legal expenses to defend against a criminal charge of vote-buying deductible? Rev. Rul. 86-3, 1986-1 C.B. 81. Remember that legal fees were deductible in *Tellier*, where the criminal case arose from business activities. Does the political origin of the legal expenses prevent the deduction?

[C]   Doing Your Political Job vs. Getting Elected

In *Diggs v. Commissioner*, 715 F.2d 245 (6th Cir. 1983), the court drew a distinction between deductible expenses related to doing a political office-holder's job and nondeductible expenses to get elected. It held that a congressman's expenses to attend 10 meetings of the National Black Political Conference helped him to understand and further the goals of his constituents. However, costs of attending the Democratic National Convention were not deductible because they were "inextricably connected to his own election goals and to the election goals of the Democratic Party. . . . [H]is attendance was more directly related to his own personal political goals and to the goals of his party than it was to the goals of his constituents."

[D]   Lobbying

[1]   In General

In 1962, Congress decided that some *legislative* lobbying expenses should be deductible, if they were otherwise deductible expenses. Then, the 1993 tax law reversed course.

[a]   Legislative Lobbying

First, the 1993 law explicitly reinstated the pre-1962 prohibition on the deduction of expenses for *legislative* lobbying. § 162(e)(1)(A). However, the permission to deduct business-related legislative lobbying survives in one situation. The statute still allows a deduction for expenses directly connected to appearances and communications with a local council or similar body regarding legislation or proposed legislation of direct interest to the taxpayer and for communications with organizations of which the taxpayer is a member regarding such legislation. § **162(e)(2)**. The reason is that local legislation is often hard to distinguish from administrative rulemaking, and expenses to seek administrative rules are usually deductible.

[b]　　Grass Roots Lobbying

Second, the 1993 law codified the nondeductibility of expenses for *grass roots* lobbying to influence elections, legislative matters, or referendums. § **162(e)(1)(C)**.

In a referendum, the public is asked to vote on adopting a constitutional or statutory provision. An unusual referendum case is *Geary v. Commissioner*, 235 F.3d 1207 (9th Cir. 2000). A policeman began patrolling his beat with a ventriloquist dummy, whom he named Officer Brendan O'Smarty. He used the dummy to help break down language and cultural barriers with neighborhood residents. The police department ordered him to "[g]et rid of the dummy because it makes the department look stupid."

So Geary decided to seek an initiative at the next election that would allow him to use the dummy in his police work. It cost him more than $11,000 in petition circulation and promotion fees to place the initiative on the ballot ($9,000 of which went to a professional petition signature collector to obtain the necessary 10,000 signatures). He deducted these expenses on his tax return, but the government disallowed the deduction, based on § **162(e)(1)(C)**. The court agreed, rejecting the taxpayer's claim that he was not trying to influence the public, only informing them about the issue.

[c]　　Administrative Lobbying

Third, the 1993 law also added to the list of nondeductible lobbying expenses amounts paid to communicate with the President, Vice President and certain high executive officials in an attempt to influence *their official actions*. Previously, all administrative lobbying expenses were deductible. § **162(e)(1)(D), (6)**.

The rules about lobbying expenses related to executive officials and other administrators are now quite complex. (1) Payments to *all* such officials to influence their participation in the *legislative* process are not deductible under the § **162(e)(1)(A)** prohibition. (2) Payments to the President, Vice President, and certain high executive officials to influence *their official actions* are not deductible, as noted above. (3) Payments to other executive and administrative officials to influence their *official administrative (not legislative) actions* continue to be subject to the regular deduction rules and are not disallowed by § **162(e)(1)**.

[d]　　Internal Costs

There is an exception to the prohibition on deducting political expenditures for legislative and administrative lobbying, up to $2,000 of internal costs. Indirect overhead costs are not taken into account in determining whether the $2,000 amount has been exceeded. § **162(e)(5)(B)**.

[e]   Preventing Avoidance of Business Expense Deduction Limits Through Use of a Conduit

Can the taxpayer circumvent the disallowance of lobbying expense deductions by making a deductible payment of dues to a tax-exempt organization, such as a union or trade association? The statute explicitly *disallows* a business deduction for the percentage of dues paid to such organizations, which the organization notifies the taxpayer are allocable to nondeductible political expenses. **§ 162(e)(3)**. The dues are nonetheless deductible if the organization pays a "proxy" tax on its political expenses in lieu of providing notice to the dues-paying members. **§ 6033(e)(2)**. This proxy tax was upheld against a First Amendment challenge in *American Society of Ass'n Executives v. United States*, 23 F. Supp. 2d 64 (D.D.C. 1998), *affirmed*, 195 F.3d 47 (D.C. Cir. 1999).

[2]   What is Legislative Lobbying?

The code disallows deductions for influencing legislation, defined as "any attempt to influence any legislation through communication with any member or employee of a legislative body. . . ." **§ 162(e)(1)**, **(4)(A)**. Regulations define "influencing legislation" to mean "[a]ny attempt to influence any legislation through a lobbying communication" and define "lobbying communication" to be a communication that "[r]efers to specific legislation and reflects a view on that legislation." **Treas. Reg. § 1.162-29(b)(1, 3)**. The Regulation defines "specific legislation" to include "a specific legislative proposal that has not been introduced in a legislative body." **Treas. Reg. § 1.162-29(b)(5)**.

[E]   Charitable Deductions

A complete picture of the impact of the tax law on political expenditures requires considering the rules dealing with charitable deductions. If expenditures that are not deductible business expenses *are* charitable deductions, the policy against deducting political expenditures would obviously be circumvented. The business deduction rules broke down into two major categories — election-related and lobbying — and the same distinctions will be followed in discussing charitable deductions.

[1]   Election-Related

Section 170(c)(2)(D) prohibits charitable deductions to organizations that participate in a campaign for or against a candidate.

This prohibition was applied in *Branch Ministries, Inc. v. Rossotti*, 40 F. Supp. 2d 15 (D.D.C. 1999), *affirmed*, 211 F.3d 137 (D.C. Cir. 2000). On October 30, 1992, four days before the presidential election, the church expressed its concern about the moral character of Governor Clinton in a full page advertisement in the *Washington Times* and in *USA Today*. The advertisement proclaimed "Christians Beware. Do not put the economy ahead of the Ten Commandments." It asserted that Governor Clinton supported abortion on demand, homosexuality, and the distribution of condoms to teenagers in public schools. The advertisement cited various Biblical passages and stated that "Bill Clinton is promoting policies that are in rebellion to God's laws." It concluded with the question: "How then can we vote for Bill Clinton?" At the bottom of the advertisement, in fine print, was the following notice: "This advertisement was co-sponsored by The Church at Pierce Creek, Daniel J. Little, Senior Pastor, and by churches and concerned Christians nation-wide. Tax-deductible donations for this advertisement gladly accepted. Make donations to: The Church at Pierce Creek," at a specified mailing address.

[2] Lobbying

Most tax-deductible organizations listed in § 170(c) cannot engage in "substan-tial" lobbying (see the cross-reference in § 170(c)(2)(D) to § 501(c)(3)), and still retain tax-deductible status. The statutory phrase for "lobbying" is "attempting to influence legislation."

The "substantiality" test for lobbying produced a lot of criticism because a fixed dollar amount that was substantial for one organization might be insubstantial for another. Moreover, the government was reluctant to invoke the test because it was an all-or-nothing penalty; too much political lobbying cost the organization its status as a tax-deductible organization. The statute was therefore amended to permit (but not require) public charities to elect to be subject to a 25% excise tax on "excess" expenditures to influence legislation, broadly defined to include both influencing legislators and engaging in grass roots lobbying. "Excess" lobbying expenditures are, in general, those that exceed a certain percentage of the organization's total exempt purpose expenditures. The percentage declines as the expenditures by the organization increase, so that a smaller organization can spend a larger percentage of its expenditures on political activity without incurring an excise tax. § 4911.

If the charity elects to be subject to the excise tax, the "substantiality" test is not applied to determine whether the organization loses its tax-deductible status. Instead, that status is denied because of lobbying activities only if the lobbying expenditures exceed 150% of the amount above which an excise tax is imposed during a consecutive four-year period. § 501(h); Treas. Reg. § 1.501(h)-3(b), (c)(7).

Private foundations continue to be subject to the uncertainties of the "substan-tiality" test and are, in addition, subject to an excise tax on certain political expenditures. § 4945(d)(1), (2), (e).

Churches cannot elect to be subject to the excise tax on excess lobbying expenditures. § 501(h)(3)(B), (5)(A). Why not? Do they prefer to take their chances with the "substantiality" test?

[3] Defining "Grass Roots" Lobbying

Consider whether the definition of "grass roots" lobbying is the same for § 162 and § 170. "Grass roots lobbying," in the charity context, must express a view about specific legislation (including legislative proposals) and encourage action by the recipient of the communication. Treas. Reg. § 56.4911-2(b)(2); see 48 TAX NOTES 1305 (1990). Thus, an advertisement notifying the public of proposed legislation increasing the tax on social security benefits, without encouraging action, would *not* be grass roots lobbying. Encouraging action is defined as one of the following four steps: telling people to contact legislators; giving a legislator's address or phone contact; providing a petition, tear-off card or the like to reach a legislator; or identifying opposed or undecided legislators, the recipient's representative, or the relevant committee members. The rules are more lenient for "nonpartisan positions" (which contain a full and fair exposition of facts to enable an independent conclusion); **Treas. Reg. § 56.4911-2(c)(1)**. There is also a rebuttable presumption that advertising about the general subject of legislation in the mass media two weeks before a vote on highly publicized legislation will, under certain circumstances, be grass roots lobbying.

The definition of "grass roots" lobbying under **§ 162** may be *less* favorable to the taxpayer than under the rules applicable to charities — they are certainly more general and open-ended. **Treas. Reg. § 1.162-20(c)(4)** ("no deduction shall be allowed for any expenses incurred in connection with 'grassroot' campaigns or any other attempts to urge or encourage the public to contact members of a legislative body for the purpose of proposing, supporting, or opposing legislation").

[4] Charitable Deductions for Political Expenditures?

Do these rules about charitable deductions potentially allow taxpayers to deduct political expenditures, even though they would not be deductible business expenses? There must be some tax avoidance potential because the 1993 tax law prohibits a charitable deduction if a principal purpose of the contribution is to avoid taxes by obtaining a deduction for political expenses that would *not* have been deductible under **§ 162(e)(1)**, if the taxpayer had incurred the expenditures directly. **§ 170(f)(9)**.

Can you think of ways that a charitable deduction might indirectly permit the deduction of political expenditures, absent the **§ 170(f)(9)** prohibition? Suppose a charitable organization: (1) incurs lobbying expenses, but not in excessive amounts; (2) engages in grass roots lobbying that might be a nondeductible business expense but would not be considered "grass roots" lobbying by a charity; or (3) lobbies high executive officials to influence their official action.

[5] Advocacy and Action Organizations

The lobbying rules discussed so far are primarily aimed at organizations that are otherwise tax exempt but that engage in too much lobbying. However, the core activities of some organizations are so political that they should not be tax-deductible organizations in the first place. The "advocacy" and "action" organization regulations address this problem, preventing an otherwise "educational" organization from achieving tax-deductible status. The administration of these rules can be worrisome, because the government is looking closely at how the organization is getting its political ideas across to the public.

[a] Advocacy Groups

In *Big Mama Rag, Inc. v. United States*, 631 F.2d 1030 (D.C. Cir. 1980), the court dealt with the Regulations requiring "advocacy" groups to present a "full and fair exposition of the pertinent facts," as a condition to receiving deductible contributions. The court held that the definition of "advocacy" and a "full and fair exposition" were both so vague as to be unconstitutional. For example, there was a "full and fair exposition" if the organization allowed "an individual or the public to form an independent opinion or conclusion," but "mere presentation of unsupported opinion" did not meet the required standard. **Treas. Reg. § 1.501(c)(3)-1(d)(3).**

After the *Big Mama Rag* case, the IRS issued Rev. Proc. 86-43, 1986-2 C.B. 729, which explained in detail how the IRS would determine whether an advocacy group was too "political" for contributions to be charitable deductions. In the *The Nationalist Movement v. Commissioner*, 102 T.C. 558 (1994), the court held that the Revenue Procedure was not unconstitutional because it focused on the method rather than the content of the presentation.

[b]   Action Groups

Another Regulation prohibits "action" groups from being 501(c)(3) organizations; **Treas. Reg. § 1.501(c)(3)-1(c)(3).** In *Fund for the Study of Economic Growth and Tax Reform v. IRS*, 161 F.3d 755 (D.C. Cir. 1998), the court applied the "action" group Regulations to an organization advocating a flat tax. Some factual background gives you a sense of the political context.

On April 3, 1995, the Republican leadership in Congress — then-Senate Majority Leader, Robert Dole, and then-Speaker of the House of Representatives, Newt Gingrich — announced the formation of the National Commission on Economic Growth and Tax Reform which was charged with the task of designing a "flatter, fairer, and simpler" system of taxation. Dole and Gingrich appointed Jack Kemp as chair of the Commission, who in turn established the Fund — a charitable trust intended to be the legal entity providing the financial support (through solicited donations) for the activities of the Commission. Kemp eventually became the Republican Party's vice-presidential nominee for the 1996 election. Here is some of what the court said:

> An organization is an "action" organization if it has the following two characteristics: "(a) Its main or primary objective or objectives (as distinguished from its incidental or secondary objectives) may be attained only by legislation or a defeat of proposed legislation; and (b) it advocates, or campaigns for, the attainment of such main or primary objective or objectives as distinguished from engaging in nonpartisan analysis, study, or research, and making the results thereof available to the public." Treas. Reg. § 1.501(c)(3)-1(c)(3)(iv).

> The IRS determined that the Commission met both prongs of this "action" organization test because (a) it sought to encourage the implementation of a flat tax, a goal that could only be accomplished by legislation, and (b) it advocated for this goal. In finding that the Commission advocated, the IRS looked primarily to the final report issued by the Commission, noting that "[b]ecause the final report is virtually the only product of the Commission, the facts and circumstances that lead us to conclude that its predominate purpose is advocacy are centered in that document." With respect to the report, the IRS concluded that it "read . . . like a brief or manifesto in support of a particular list of tax law changes"; that it was drafted "to

present the most forceful arguments in favor of one point of view"; and that, "as a whole," it was "a document rooted in advocacy. . . ." The IRS's initial determination was therefore that the Fund did not qualify for § 501(c)(3) tax exemption because it constituted an "action" organization.

. . . While there is no bright line distinguishing an organization which advocates from an organization which engages in nonpartisan analysis, study or research — and we do not attempt to draw one here — we can in this case easily conclude that the district court did not clearly err in finding that the Fund crossed over the line into advocacy. The Commission existed for one year — the year before the 1996 Presidential elections. It studied one issue, an issue that was at the time a very central and controversial political one. With great fanfare, the Commission published a final report wherein it extolled the benefits of the flat tax and "recommend[ed] to the Congress and to the President of the United States that the current Internal Revenue Code be repealed in its entirety." Moreover, the district court did not clearly err in concluding that the Commission's activities were not mere "nonpartisan analysis, study, or research and making the results thereof available to the public." Based on the record before us, the court could reasonably conclude that the Commission had not set out to study tax reform generally and only later concluded that a flat tax was preferable to the present system of taxation. Rather, the indications are that the Commission assumed a conclusion — the preferability of a flat tax — and then tried to sell this conclusion both to Congress and the President, and to the public more broadly. . . .

[6] Exemption for Veterans Organization

Not every organization listed in § 170(c) is prohibited from engaging in political activity. There is an exception for veterans organizations. *See* § 170(c)(3). In *Regan v. Taxation with Representation*, 461 U.S. 540 (1983), the Court upheld the special rule permitting lobbying by veterans' organizations, making the following points. First, Congress can legitimately favor veterans. Second, there is no indication that any other group was denied tax exemption for political activity because of its unpopular ideas.

Third, other groups could set up a separate § 501(c)(4) tax exempt organization and carry on lobbying without losing § 501(c)(3) status for its other activities. For example, it is a common practice for organizations to set up § 501(c)(3)/§ 170(c) nonpolitical branches to receive deductible contributions, while maintaining separate sister organizations that lobby — the NAACP did that with the NAACP, Inc. Fund, and the Sierra Club split up into an organization that did lobbying and an organization that did not. Favorable § 501(c)(3) tax-deductible status was not therefore conditioned on abandoning its First Amendment right to lobby through another related group.

[F] Taxing Political Recipients and Organizations

[1] Gifts to Political Campaign

Gifts to a politician or her campaign are not taxable to the recipient unless converted to personal (nonpolitical) use. Rev. Rul. 75-103, 1975-1 C.B. 17. This rule developed as a gloss on the definition of § 61 income. Surely, the gifts are not excluded under § 102; there is not enough "detached and disinterested generosity." But the result makes sense, doesn't it? One tax is imposed on the contributions — on the donor, as in the case of intrafamily gifts.

Taxpayers who transfer appreciated property to a political organization must pay tax on the appreciation at the time of the contribution. § 84. This differs from the intrafamily gift, where the *donee* is taxed on appreciated gain.

[2] Taxing Political Organizations

[a] Section 527 Organizations

Political campaign organizations are not taxed on contributions they receive, as long as the contributions are devoted to the political process of selecting candidates (referred to in the statute as an "exempt function"). "Exempt function" is defined as "influencing or attempting to influence the selection, nomination, election, or appointment of any individual to any Federal, State, or local public office or office in a political organization, or the election of Presidential or Vice-Presidential electors. . . ." The organizations are taxed, however, on income from investing contributions (such as interest and dividends). § 527(a), (b), (e)(2).

COMMENT — Section 501(c) Organizations

A § 501(c) organization that is exempt from income tax under § 501(a) — including a social welfare organization, labor union, or business league (§ 501(c)(4–6)) — is nonetheless taxed on the amount it spends on an "exempt function" (but not in excess of its investment income). § 527(e)(2), (f).

[b] Defining "Exempt Function"

You cannot understand § 527 organizations without taking note of campaign finance law. Under campaign finance law an organization that is a political committee — that is, organized to help elect a candidate (usually known as a PAC) — cannot receive contributions in excess of a specific dollar ceiling. Organizations came to rely on a distinction between candidate-advocacy groups (PACs) and issue-advocacy groups, which could receive unlimited contributions. They understood candidate-advocacy to be narrowly defined to require "magic words," saying "Vote for [a named candidate]. It was not enough to say candidate Y was good or bad, without more. (It's silly, I know.)

But, if the issue- vs. candidate-advocacy line used to distinguish between what is and is not a PAC was used for organizations seeking § 527 status, these organizations might not be engaged in an "exempt function," which requires candidate advocacy. However, candidate advocacy for § 527 purposes might include activity that was considered issue advocacy under the PAC definition rules; and that is the assumption under which § 527 organizations have successfully operated.

Consequently, you need to draw a line between candidate-advocacy and issue-advocacy in two tax contexts: (1) making sure that § 527 organizations are not taxed on contributions used for an exempt purpose (involving candidate-advocacy); and (2) taxing exempt § 501(c) organizations on amounts spent for an exempt function. Rev. Rul. 2004-6, 2004-1 C.B 328, deals with this issue in the context of taxing § 501(c) organizations, providing extensive and non-exclusive lists of factors (with examples) that tend to show that an advocacy communication on a public policy issue is really for a candidate-related "exempt function."

Chapter 15

EXPENSES TO PRODUCE TAX EXEMPT INCOME

§ 15.01   GENERAL PRINCIPLE

An otherwise deductible expense is often not deductible if it is incurred to produce tax-exempt income. This rule makes sense on the theory that the real purpose of the income exemption is to exclude the *net* income produced by the exempt activity from the tax base. If expenses to produce tax-exempt income were deductible, the exemption would also permit a taxpayer to shelter nonexempt income from tax. For example, if the taxpayer spent $20 to earn $100 of tax-exempt income, and also had $20 of wages, his taxable income should be $20, not zero; only the $80 net income from the exempt activity should go untaxed. Disallowing the expense deduction assures that result.

The most common example of tax-exempt income is interest on state and local bonds (§ 103), but there are other examples: e.g., a portion of scholarships (§ 117); recoveries for personal physical injuries (§ 104(a)(2)); certain foreign personal service income (§ 911); parsonage allowances (§ 107).

The most important section dealing with expenses related to tax exempt income is **§ 265. Section 265(a)(1)** prohibits all deductions "allocable" to all categories of exempt income, *except* tax-exempt interest. Under **§ 265(a)(1)**, if an expense is "allocable to both a class of nonexempt income and a class of exempt income, a reasonable proportion thereof determined in the light of all the facts and circumstances in each case shall be allocated to each." **Treas. Reg. § 1.265-1(c).** For example, litigation expenses are deductible only to the extent allocable to taxable punitive damages, not personal injury recoveries exempt under **§ 104; Rev. Rul. 85-98, 1985-2 C.B. 51.**

When the exempt income is interest, however, **§ 265(a)(1)** only forbids the deduction of **§ 212**, not **§ 162** expenses. The major impact of this exception is that the deduction of business expenses is not prohibited by **§ 265(a)(1)** when they are incurred to produce tax-exempt interest income. Banks that invest in tax-exempt bonds obviously benefit from this provision. But individual investors can not deduct **§ 212** expenses allocable to **§ 103** income.

There is, however, another provision dealing with tax-exempt interest income. **Section 265(a)(2)** prohibits the deduction of *interest* expenses related to tax-exempt interest. **Section 265(a)(2)** is discussed in Chapter 16.02[A].

Section 264(a)(1) is a specific provision implementing the same idea that underlies **§ 265(a)(1)**. It deals with life insurance premiums paid by a business to cover the lives of key employees, with the proceeds payable to the business (not the employee's family). Such expenses would be deductible under § 162. The insurance proceeds are, however, exempt under § 101. To prevent a double benefit, § 264(a)(1) disallows the deduction of such premiums.

§ 15.02   IS DEPRECIATION AN "EXPENSE"?

[A]   Section 212 vs. Section 167

A taxpayer buys a depreciable interest in an intangible asset — specifically a life estate interest in a trust. The trust pays out tax-exempt interest. The taxpayer claims depreciation deductions under § 167(a)(2), because a life estate is a depreciable asset, and the depreciation expense is related to the production of income. In the following case, the government argued that the depreciation expense was essentially a § 212 expense to produce tax-exempt interest, whose deduction was disallowed by § 265(a)(1). The court held for the taxpayer and allowed the deduction, as follows.

MANUFACTURERS HANOVER TRUST CO. v. COMMISSIONER
United States Court of Appeals, Second Circuit
431 F.2d 664 (2d Cir. 1970)

WATERMAN, CIRCUIT JUDGE: . . .

. . . [I]t has been traditionally accepted that amortization does not fall within the usual meaning of 'expenses,' but is considered an exhaustion of a capital asset of limited income-producing duration. If amortization is an 'expense,' it follows that depreciation would also fall into that category, yet for a half-century Congress has deemed it necessary to provide for depreciation deductions separately from 'expense' deductions. Against this background the Commissioner's contention that, for the purpose of cases like the one at bar, 'amortization' and 'expenses incurred in the production of income' should merge in meaning must find support outside the language of the statute. . . .

The legislative history of the relevant enactments . . . is colorless. It does not indicate one way or the other why Congress chose to impose a limitation on § 212 expenses but chose not to impose the same limitation with regard to deductions for § 167(a) depreciation of non-business property. The Commissioner's argument on this point is at most one of policy. He argues in his brief that 'there appears to be no logical reason why Congress, on one hand, would have intended to prohibit the allowance of non-business expenses allocable to tax-exempt interest, and, yet, on the other, allow non-business amortization deductions allocable to tax-exempt interest income.' In urging us not to 'attribute irrationality to the drafters of the provision,' the Commissioner refers us to *J. C. Penney Co. v. C.I.R.*, 312 F.2d 65 (2d Cir. 1962) (Friendly, J.), a case in which our court held that Congress did not mean what it had said by a cross-reference in a section inserted in the 1954 Internal Revenue Code during a late stage of its passage. *J. C. Penney* is clearly inapposite to the case at bar, however, for in that case there was a wealth of legislative history that demonstrated that the drafters could not possibly have meant what they wrote.

When a statute is 'plain and unambiguous' and there is no evidence of a contrary purpose than the purpose appearing in the precise terms of the statute it 'transcends the judicial function' to rewrite the statute to conform to considerations of policy.

[B]   Note on Statutory Interpretation — Statutory Structure

The government seemed on very strong ground in arguing against the deduction. Depreciation allows a deduction for a part of the taxpayer's basis and basis is nothing but a deferred expense. There is no sound reason why a deferred expense should be treated differently from a current expense when disallowing deductions for expenses related to tax-exempt income. Apparently, the court insisted on clear legislative history to overcome what it thought was the clear language of the statute permitting the deduction. That approach raises several questions.

First, not everyone agrees that strong legislative history should be allowed to override a clear statutory text.

Second, was the statutory text so clear? Shouldn't the statutory text be interpreted sensibly in the light of the underlying structure of the code, whether or not there is legislative history.

Third, doesn't the statutory structure equate depreciation deductions (which are a portion of deferred expenses that are part of basis), with current expenses (that is, rent)? A § 212 deduction for rent would clearly be disallowed by § 265(a)(1). Why should depreciation deductions be treated differently?

Fourth, if the code did not provide explicitly for a depreciation expense deduction in § 167(a), wouldn't taxpayers be able to take such deductions under § 162 and § 212?

§ 15.03   "ALLOCABLE" TO EXEMPT INCOME

In the following case, the taxpayer earned foreign personal services income, which was exempt under § 911. At the time this case was decided, § 911(a) stated: "An individual shall not be allowed, as a deduction from his gross income, any deductions . . . properly allocable to or chargeable against amounts excluded from gross income under [§ 911]." The issue was whether some of the petitioner's moving expenses, otherwise deductible under § 217, must be disallowed because they are "properly allocable to" exempt foreign personal service income, earned at the new foreign principal place of employment.

HUGHES v. COMMISSIONER
United States Tax Court
65 T.C. 566 (1975)

STERRETT, JUDGE: . . .

Petitioner's primary argument is that his moving expenses are deductible in full because they are personal rather than business expenses, and as such they are not 'properly allocable to or chargeable against' his income exempted from tax under section 911(a). Petitioner in support of his position points to several elements included in the moving expense deduction which he claims are purely personal. Respondent's answer is that, although petitioner's moving expenses meet the requirements of section 217, the deduction is subject to the allocation provisions of section 911(a).

Before their deductibility was authorized by statute, moving expenses were considered by this Court to be nondeductible personal expenses. Section 217 now provides for their deductibility but only when they are incurred in connection with the commencement of work at a new principal place of employment. Such expenses then to be deductible must have a definite relationship to the production of gross income. It is in those situations where the relationship does not exist that moving expenses are purely personal and nondeductible.

We believe that this analysis is supported by the legislative history that accompanied the adoption of section 217. Before the enactment of section 217, an existing employee reimbursed for his moving expenses was not required to include such sum in his gross income because such expenses were considered to have been incurred 'in the interest of the employer.' The Congress believed that this discriminated against new employees and employees who were not reimbursed. One of the purposes of section 217 then was to equalize this latter group with those employees who were reimbursed. This appears to be a recognition that moving expenses could be incurred in the 'interest of the employee' and his trade or business. . . .

Furthermore, Congress placed moving expenses in the category of items deductible from gross income to reach adjusted gross income, giving further evidence of their view that such an expense is income-related.

[Editor — From 1986 to 1993, moving expenses were itemized deductions. If the case had come up then, should the result have been different?]

DAWSON, C.J., DISSENTING:

. . . Underlying [section 217] was a congressional desire to remove a deterrent to labor mobility, moving expenses, which would in turn assist in reducing local structural unemployment. H. REP. No. 749, 88th Cong., 1st Sess. (1963), 1964-1 C.B. (Part 2) 125, 183. Congress, not wanting to allow such a deduction to any taxpayer electing to move, limited this personal expense deduction to those moving for the purpose of living near their place of employment. . . .

. . . I think section 217 provides qualifying taxpayers with a deduction for personal expenses which are not related to the income from a trade or business, despite the language in section 217 which conditions its benefits on postmove employment. This language was included only to limit the section's coverage to taxpayers who are a part of the work force after their move. The overriding concern of Congress was to remove a hindrance to labor mobility. This conclusion does nothing to contravene the operation of section 911, which was enacted to promote foreign trade by encouraging American businessmen to venture overseas and sell American-made products. Any removal of a hindrance to mobility should complement section 911. . . .

Accordingly, I would hold that Mr. Hughes is entitled to deduct fully his moving expenses incurred under section 217.

COMMENTS

1. The basic issue in this case is whether the moving expense deduction is a subsidy for a particular activity and whether the subsidy would be undermined by disallowing the deduction when the subsidy relates to a business activity that produces tax-exempt income. This is a very difficult interpretive issue. It concerns the implications of legislation providing a tax subsidy in contexts where Congress never explicitly considered what those implications might be. The dissent in *Hughes* thought that disallowing the deduction when the taxpayer moved abroad and earned tax exempt personal service income would undermine the subsidy for moving expenses. The majority must have thought that this policy was not strong enough to override the rules disallowing the deduction of expenses allocable to tax-exempt income.

2. In 2006, § 911 was changed so that the "exempt" foreign personal service income pushed other income into a higher tax bracket. For example, if $80,000 personal services income was exempt and the taxpayer had no other income, there would be no U.S. tax. However, if the taxpayer also had $100,000 of nonexempt income, that $100,000 would be taxed as though it were in the tax bracket applicable to income higher than $80,000. What does this new law suggest about the disallowance of the deduction for expenses allocable to tax exempt § 911 income? For some taxpayers, that income is still exempt in the full sense of the term; it results in no increase in the income tax. But for other taxpayers the "exempt" income can result in a higher tax than would be the case if the income were fully exempt. Does this mean that, for the latter taxpayer, the income is not "exempt" and related expenses can be deducted? In this connection, remember that tax exempt interest is often included in modified AGI to determine whether a taxpayer is subject to a phantom tax rate; and no one suggests that the interest is, on that account, not exempt. Is pushing income into a higher tax bracket different from causing more taxes to be paid because of a phantom tax rate?

4. In Rev. Rul. 74-140, 1974-1 C.B. 50, the taxpayer received income exempt from federal income tax, but taxable under the state income tax. The taxpayer was not allowed to deduct all of the state income taxes that would normally have been deductible under § 164. The portion of the state income tax allocable to the income exempt at the federal level was not deductible under § 265(a)(1). Does this ruling interfere with the public policy underlying the deduction of state income taxes, which is to provide a form of revenue sharing to the states?

§ 15.04   EXEMPT REIMBURSEMENTS

MANOCCHIO v. COMMISSIONER
United States Tax Court
78 T.C. 989 (1982)

DAWSON, JUDGE: . . .

Petitioner is a veteran of the U.S. Air Force. During 1977, he was employed as an airline pilot with Hughes Air West. He attended flight-training classes approved by the Veterans' Administration (VA) at National Jet Industries in Santa Ana, Calif. . . . The classes cost a total of $4,162 and maintained and improved skills required in petitioner's trade or business.

As a veteran, petitioner was eligible for an educational assistance allowance from the VA pursuant to 38 U.S.C. sec. 1677 (1976), equal to 90 percent of the costs incurred. . . . The VA [] mailed petitioner a check for 90 percent of the amount specified, which he then endorsed over to the flight school. He paid the remaining 10 percent by personal check.

During 1977, petitioner received $3,742.88 from the VA as a direct reimbursement of his flight-training expenses. On his 1977 Federal income tax return, he excluded the VA payments from income pursuant to 38 U.S.C. sec. 3101(a) (1976). He also claimed a deduction of [$4,162]. . . .

It is respondent's position that the portion of the flight-training expenses reimbursed by the VA is allocable to a class of tax-exempt income and, therefore, nondeductible under section 265. . . .

We agree with respondent that section 265 bars the deduction of the reimbursed expenses. . . . Under this provision, an amount cannot be deducted if it is "allocable to" a class of tax-exempt income other than interest. . . . [T]he reimbursement received by petitioner clearly qualifies as a class of exempt income for purposes of section 265. The only issue, then, is whether the educational costs are allocable to the reimbursement.

Petitioner argues that the expenses are not allocable to the reimbursement, but rather to the income derived from his employment as a pilot. More specifically, his position is that section 265(1) was intended to apply only to expenses incurred in the production of exempt income, and should not be construed to apply to expenses which were merely paid out of exempt income. In support, he quotes from the committee reports accompanying section 24(a)(5) of the Revenue Act of 1934, ch. 277, 48 Stat. 680, 691 (the predecessor of sec. 265), which indicate that the purpose of the statute is to disallow deductions allocable "to the production" of exempt income.

Unquestionably, a principal target of the legislation was expenses incurred in connection with an ongoing trade or business or investment activity, the conduct of which generates exempt income. The committee reports give as examples expenses incurred in earning interest on State securities, salaries by State employees, and income from leases of State school property. Nevertheless, we do not infer from these examples that Congress intended to limit the application of the statute to such situations and preclude its application under the circumstances presented in this case. The words it selected to describe the necessary relationship between the expense and exempt income — "allocable to" — do not carry an inherently restrictive connotation. Certainly, if Congress had wanted to confine the reach of the statute to the standard situations referred to in the committee reports, it could have easily done so by using more precise definitional language. It did not take a narrow approach, however, and we think the language employed is broad enough, particularly when construed in light of the policy behind the statute, to embrace the reimbursement situation where, but for the expense, there would simply be no exempt income. The right to reimbursement for the flight-training expenses arises only when the VA receives a certification from the flight school, signed by both the veteran and a school official, of the actual training received by the veteran during the month and the cost of such training. The training allowance is then computed at 90 percent of the certified cost. Thus, there is a fundamental nexus between the reimbursement income and the expense which, in our opinion, falls within the scope of any reasonable interpretation of the "allocable to" requirement. . . .

Although it is true that petitioner is left in the identical situation, from the standpoint of tax consequences, as if he had received a taxable reimbursement, in which case section 265 would not bar his deduction, there will obviously be instances where the veteran's flight-training expenses will be nondeductible irrespective of section 265. For example, the expenses might not satisfy the conditions for deductibility imposed by section 1.162-5, Income Tax Regs., or assuming they do, the veteran might not have sufficient itemized deductions to take advantage of the deduction. In either of these situations, he would realize additional taxable income in the absence of the exemption provision.

In short, there is nothing in the legislative history of the relevant veterans' provisions to suggest that Congress intended for a veteran to have both an exemption and a tax deduction where his reimbursed flight-training expenses otherwise qualify as deductible business-related education. On the other hand, the legislative purpose behind section 265 is abundantly clear: Congress sought to prevent taxpayers from reaping a double tax benefit by using expenses attributable to tax-exempt income to offset other sources of taxable income. This is precisely what petitioner is attempting to do here, and in our judgment, the application of section 265(1) to disallow the reimbursed portion of the flight-training expense deduction is both reasonable and equitable.

COMMENTS AND QUESTIONS

1. The problem this case raises is whether the exemption of the reimbursement from income is meant to allow the taxpayer both an exclusion of the reimbursement and a deduction of the expense. Before you conclude too quickly that the answer must be "no," remember that a tax exempt gift and tax-exempt interest can be used to incur deductible business expenses. To deny the deduction would deny the tax exemption. In other words, the *Manocchio* case is another *Haverly*-type problem (which involved charitable gifts funded by tax-exempt income; Chapter 10.04[C]), where the issue was whether to combine an exclusion from tax with a later deduction. There is no way to resolve this issue without asking whether the double

benefit makes sense as a matter of statutory interpretation.

2. Why isn't an exempt reimbursement for veterans' education like an exempt gift or exempt interest income? The court must be concluding that it would stretch legislative intent too far in the case of veterans' benefits to provide both an exclusion and a deduction. It interprets the exclusion of in-kind veterans' educational benefits (in the penultimate paragraph of the opinion) to be an assurance of a tax-free educational benefit for all recipients, whether or not the expenses would be deductible if incurred out of the taxpayer's own pocket.

3. However, it is a little strained to reach that result through § 265(a)(1), because that section does not appear to prohibit deductions of an expenditure based on the fact that the expenditure is financed by tax-exempt reimbursements for a particular expenditure. The focus of § 265(a)(1) is on the exempt nature of the income, in connection with which the taxpayer incurs a *separate* expenditure, like attorneys' fees to collect tax-exempt personal injury recoveries. Still, perhaps an interpretation of § 265(a)(1) to disallow a double benefit is not too strained, if the result is satisfactory. The deeper question is where the court gets its understanding of legislative intent. The court in *Manocchio* says there was nothing in the legislative history to suggest allowing a double benefit (exclusion and deduction), but was there anything in the legislative history to deny it?

4. Another situation in which there could have been both an exclusion and a deduction arises from § 139A, which excludes from income federal subsidy payments made to a sponsor of a qualified retiree prescription drug plan. Beginning in 2013, any deduction allowable for payments related to this income is reduced by excludible subsidy payments. This result was achieved by deleting the second sentence of § 139A — which had stated: "This section shall not be taken into account for purposes of determining whether any deduction is allowable with respect to any cost taken into account in determining such payment."

Chapter 16

LIMITING THE INTEREST DEDUCTION

§ 16.01   PERSONAL LOANS

[A]   Background

Section 163(a) states that interest is deductible. This provision was included in the original Income Tax Act of 1913 without explanation in the legislative history. The original provision was very broad. It applied to interest on loans for personal use, whether for current consumption (like a vacation) or for personal use assets (like a home or car), and for income-producing purposes, even if the loan was used to make a capital expenditure. Over the years, limitations have been placed on the interest deduction. We have already encountered one — requiring most prepaid interest to be capitalized and later amortized (**§ 461(g)**).

The deduction of interest on loans incurred for personal purposes is usually said to be a tax expenditure, but there is a counterargument. Interest is unavailable to the taxpayer for consumption or savings. Admittedly, the interest payment enables the taxpayer to get the loan and thereby to accelerate personal consumption. But accelerating the date of personal consumption is not itself personal consumption. Remember that the code taxes the income earned at a later date to repay the loan, so the loan only enables the taxpayer to accelerate use of the money. Moreover, the interest deduction favors current over future consumption, which is an inherent feature of the income tax.

[B]   Loans to Buy Personal Assets

The above comments justifying the deduction of personal interest usually leave people unconvinced, but that is probably because there is another reason to be concerned about the interest deduction. The loan is often used to acquire personal-use property, like a home, which produces tax-exempt income in the form of the property's rental value. The interest expense is equal to some portion of that exempt income, and the uneasiness about the interest deduction arises from uneasiness about this exemption. The following paragraphs explain this problem.

[1]   Renter

The taxpayer who pays rent for his home does so out of *after-tax* income. The rent covers the landlord's costs, including: depreciation on the building; interest on any loan the landlord incurred for construction or acquisition of the building; and profit for the landlord. Assume that the rental amount is $10,000.

[2]   Homeowners Who Do Not Borrow

Someone who has the wealth to invest in a home enjoys a return on the investment, much like a landlord. Assume that the rental value of the home is $10,000, to parallel the renter. That enjoyment is personal consumption, but is any of it included in income? Most of it is not. Some of the $10,000 is taxed indirectly, because it includes nondeductible depreciation (assume it is $4,000). What about the $10,000 rental value in excess of depreciation — $6,000 in the example? The investor does not have to include that amount in income. It is "imputed income," which is not considered "realized" § 61 income. Some of the $10,000 rental value is, therefore, not taxed.

[3]   Homeowners Who Do Borrow

Now, assume that the investor borrows some of the money to buy the home, producing the same total $10,000 rental value. In addition to the $4,000 depreciation, the owner pays $4,500 interest. If you decide that the rental value ought to be taxed to the maximum amount possible, you could disallow the interest deduction. Then at least $8,500 of the $10,000 rental value would be taxed ($4,000 depreciation, plus $4,500 interest; the $1,500 "profit" would *not* be taxed). Moreover, if you think renters get a bum deal in the tax law, because they finance personal consumption out of after-tax income, you can get closer to equal treatment of renters and borrowers by disallowing the deduction of interest incurred to finance the purchase of personal-use assets.

[4]   Dilemma

Disallowing the interest deduction for home loans brings borrowers closer to renters, but introduces another inequity into the tax law. The wealthy investor who does not borrow, and the borrower who has paid off the loan, do not pay tax on the rental value in excess of depreciation. There is nothing you can do about this dilemma, unless you give renters a deduction for a portion of rent, and let borrowers deduct the interest. Barring that, you must choose which inequity to accept. Current law, as you will see, allows a deduction for most home loan interest, allowing the borrower to more closely approximate the nonborrowing investor. As we become a nation of renters, this may change and we may disallow the interest deduction to bring the borrower closer to the renter.

[5]   Tax Breaks for Renters and Co-op Owners?

Renters. Renters are disadvantaged under the tax law because they cannot deduct property taxes (as well as interest). A homeowner (borrower or otherwise) can deduct such taxes under § 164(a)(1). One state tried to design its law so that a portion of the rent would be considered to be a real property tax payment, and therefore a deductible tax, but the government did not allow the deduction. Rev. Rul. 79-180, 1979-1 C.B. 95.

Co-op owners. A co-op(erative) owner invests in stock of a corporation that owns an apartment building. Stock ownership entitles the investor to live in an apartment and to pay maintenance expenses to the corporation to cover various building costs, including interest and property taxes. **Section 216** entitles the co-op owner to deduct that portion of the maintenance expenses attributable to interest and property taxes.

[C] Statutory Rules

Prior to the Tax Reform Act of 1986, interest on personal loans was deductible. That has changed. Now only interest on *some* personal loans is deductible. **§ 163(h).** Notice that the statutory definition of nondeductible personal interest is *all* interest, except interest which is specifically listed.

[1] Qualified Residence Interest

Section 163(h)(2)(D) allows "qualified residence interest" to be deducted. The definition applies to certain loans related to the principal residence and one other residence, if the debt is secured by the residence. This means that vacation home loans, dear to the real estate industry, can qualify.

There are two categories of eligible "residence" loans. (1) Acquisition indebtedness covers acquiring, constructing, or substantially improving the residence. Eligible acquisition indebtedness cannot exceed $1 million. The acquisition debt on which the interest is deductible is reduced as the loan is paid off. (2) Interest on home equity indebtedness is the other category of qualified residence interest. It equals the value of a qualified residence minus unpaid acquisition indebtedness. The home equity loan can be used for any purpose, including a personal purpose. The maximum amount of home equity loans on which interest is deductible is $100,000. **§ 163(h)(3), (4).**

For example, assume a purchaser buys a home for $500,000, with a $400,000 debt, and pays off $50,000 of the debt. The value of the home goes up to $575,000. The interest on the acquisition loan (which is $350,000 after paying off $50,000 of debt) is deductible. Home equity equals $575,000 minus $350,000, or $225,000, but is subject to the $100,000 ceiling. The taxpayer could, therefore, borrow up to $100,000 secured by a second mortgage on the home to buy a car for personal use, and deduct the interest.

In Rev. Rul. 2010-25, 2010-2 C.B. 571, the IRS decided that indebtedness incurred by a taxpayer to acquire, construct, or substantially improve a qualified residence can constitute "home equity indebtedness" to the extent it exceeds $1 million. For example, if a taxpayer buys a principal residence for $1,500,000, paying $200,000 in cash and borrowing the remaining $1,300,000 through a loan that is secured by the residence, $1 million is "acquisition indebtedness" and another $100,000 is "home equity indebtedness." The agency rejected a Tax Court decision adverse to the taxpayer in *Catalano v. Commissioner*, 79 T.C.M. (CCH) 1632 (2000).

Qualified residence interest is an itemized deduction, *not* subject to the 2% floor on miscellaneous itemized deductions.

[2]   Business vs. Personal Loans

[a]   Education That is Personal

Interest on business loans continues to be deductible; the code exempts trade or business interest from the definition of personal interest. § 163(h)(2)(A). In *Keane v. Commissioner*, 75 T.C.M. (CCH) 2046 (1998), the taxpayer had received a government scholarship for medical school on condition that he fulfills a subsequent public service obligation. Taxpayer defaulted on this obligation because he wanted to devote more time to his medical practice business. A settlement with the government resulted in an interest payment by the taxpayer to the government. The taxpayer claimed that the interest had a business origin but the court held that the origin of the debt was the education scholarship, which was a personal expense under the rules applicable to education expenditures. Therefore, the interest was nondeductible personal interest.

[b]   Employee Business?

Although nondeductible personal interest does not include business interest, employment is not considered a business for this purpose. Thus, interest on a loan related to the business of being an employee is not deductible. § 163(h)(2)(A) **(parenthetical)**.

[c]   Interest on Income Tax Deficiencies

Is interest on an individual's income tax deficiency a nondeductible personal expense, if the tax dispute deals with a question involving the computation of business income? **Temp. Treas. Reg. §§ 1.163-8T, 1.163-9T(b)(2)(i)(A)** conclude that the interest is a personal expense, and therefore not deductible under the current law. The Tax Court, in *Redlark v. Commissioner*, 106 T.C. 31 (1996), held that the interest was a deductible business expense, but the Court of Appeals reversed — 141 F.3d 936 (9th Cir. 1998). Four other Courts of Appeals agreed with the government. And, in *Robinson v. Commissioner*, 119 T.C. 44 (2002) (reviewed by the court), a majority of the Tax Court abandoned its opinion in Redlark and deferred to the agency's regulation disallowing the deduction. The court was free to reach its own decision because an appeal did not lie to any of the Courts of Appeals that had sided with the government.

[3] Student Loans

Because the 1986 amendments defined all interest as personal, absent an explicit exception, the 1986 law disallowed a deduction for interest on student loans. But the 1997 Tax Act permits an above the line deduction for interest on certain "qualified" higher education loans. § 221.

The deduction is available on loans to pay for the "qualified" education expenses of the taxpayer, the taxpayer's spouse, or the taxpayer's dependent. Qualified expenses are defined broadly to include tuition, books, room, and board. The maximum interest deduction was $1,000, but is now to $2,500.

The deduction is phased out (adding yet another phantom tax rate) as modified adjusted gross income (AGI) exceeds a threshold (adjusted for inflation). For 2013, the threshold amounts are $60,000 for a single taxpayer and $125,000 for a married taxpayer.

The phase-out formula reduces the otherwise deductible amount by:

$$\frac{\text{modified AGI minus threshold amount}}{\$15,000 \text{ (single)};\$\,30,000 \text{ (married)}} \quad \times \quad \text{deductible amount}$$

This produces the following phase-out ranges for 2013: single taxpayer ($60,000–75,000); married taxpayer ($125,000–155,000).

In addition, there had been a 60-month limit on the number of months for which the interest was deductible, but this has been permanently repealed by ATRA.

§ 16.02   INTEREST EXPENSE TO EARN TAX-EXEMPT INTEREST

Taxpayers often borrow to invest in many types of tax-exempt activities, not just to acquire personal use assets. **Section 265(a)(1)**, discussed in Chapter 15, disallows the deduction of interest expenses "allocable" to tax-exempt income, with the major exception of interest expenses on loans related to tax-exempt bonds. When a taxpayer borrows to "purchase or carry" tax-exempt bonds, **§ 265(a)(2)** is the applicable provision disallowing the deduction.

The first issue is "tracing" — is the loan traceable to the purchasing or carrying of tax-exempt bonds? The second problem, assuming that the loan is so traced, is to decide how much of the interest deduction should be disallowed. Rev. Proc. 72-18, infra, deals with both of these issues. The rules discussed in the Revenue Procedure are applied *before* the rules dealing with personal interest under **§ 163(h)**. In other words, first you decide if the deduction of any interest is disallowed under **§ 265(a)(2)**. If **§ 265(a)(2)** does not disallow the deduction, then go to **§ 163(h)** to see whether *that* section disallows the deduction.

[A]   Section 265(a)(2)

Section 265(a)(2) prevents the deduction of "interest on indebtedness incurred or continued to carry or purchase obligations the interest on which is wholly tax exempt." If **§ 265(a)(2)** applies, the effect is to discriminate between borrowers and investors who use their own funds. The investor who uses his own funds can sell a taxable investment (e.g., stock), giving up the taxable dividend, and buy a tax exempt bond, thereby avoiding tax. The borrower, who pays interest, also foregoes use of a taxable dividend (in the amount equal to the interest payment). But the borrower does not avoid tax, because the interest on the loan traced to the tax-exempt bond is not deductible to offset the taxable dividend. *Denman v. Slayton*, 282 U.S. 514 (1931), held that such discrimination was constitutional.

REVENUE PROCEDURE 72-18
1972-1 C.B. 740

SECTION 1. PURPOSE.

The purpose of this Revenue Procedure is to set forth guidelines for taxpayers and field offices of the Internal Revenue Service for the application of section 265(2) of the Internal Revenue Code of 1954 [Editor — now § 265(a)(2)] to certain taxpayers holding state and local obligations the interest on which is wholly exempt from Federal income tax. . . .

SEC. 3. GENERAL RULES.

.01 Section 265(2) of the Code is only applicable where the indebtedness is incurred or continued for the purpose of purchasing or carrying tax-exempt securities. Accordingly, the application of section 265(2) of the Code requires a determination, based on all the facts and circumstances, as to the taxpayer's purpose in incurring or continuing each item of indebtedness. Such purpose may, however, be established either by direct evidence or by circumstantial evidence.

.02 Direct evidence of a purpose to purchase tax-exempt obligations exists where the proceeds of indebtedness are used for, and are directly traceable to, the purchase of tax-exempt obligations. Section 265(2) does not apply, however, where proceeds of a bona fide business indebtedness are temporarily invested in tax-exempt obligations. . . .

.03 Direct evidence of a purpose to carry tax-exempt obligations exists where tax-exempt obligations are used as collateral for indebtedness. '[O]ne who borrows to buy tax-exempts and one who borrows against tax-exempts already owned are in virtually the same economic position. Section 265(2) makes no distinction between them.' *Wisconsin Cheeseman v. United States*, 388 F.2d 420, at 422 (1968).

.04 In the absence of direct evidence linking indebtedness with the purchase or carrying of tax-exempt obligations as illustrated in paragraphs .02 and .03 above, section 265(2) of the Code will apply only if the totality of facts and circumstances supports a reasonable inference that the purpose to purchase or carry tax-exempt obligations exists. Stated alternatively, section 265(2) will apply only where the totality of facts and circumstances establishes a 'sufficiently direct relationship' between the borrowing and the investment in tax-exempt obligations. *See Wisconsin Cheeseman*, 388 F.2d 420, at 422. The guidelines set forth in [section 4] . . . shall be applied to determine whether such a relationship exists.

.05 Generally, where a taxpayer's investment in tax-exempt obligations is insubstantial, the purpose to purchase or carry tax-exempt obligations will not ordinarily be inferred in the absence of direct evidence as set forth in sections 3.02 and 3.03. In the case of an individual, investment in tax-exempt obligations shall be presumed insubstantial only where during the taxable year the average amount of the tax-exempt obligations (valued at their adjusted basis) does not exceed 2 percent of the average adjusted basis of his portfolio investments (as defined in section 4.04) and any assets held in the active conduct of a trade or business. . . .

SEC. 4. GUIDELINES FOR INDIVIDUALS.

.01 In the absence of direct evidence of the purpose to purchase or carry tax-exempt obligations (as set forth in sections 3.02 and 3.03), the rules set forth in this section shall apply.

.02 An individual taxpayer may incur a variety of indebtedness of a personal nature, ranging from short-term credit for purchases of goods and services for personal consumption to a mortgage incurred to purchase or improve a residence or other real property which is held for personal use. Generally, section 265(2) of the Code will not apply to indebtedness of this type, because the purpose to purchase or carry tax-exempt obligations cannot reasonably be inferred where a personal purpose unrelated to the tax-exempt obligations ordinarily dominates the transaction. For example, section 265(2) of the Code generally will not apply to an individual who holds salable municipal bonds and takes out a mortgage to buy a residence instead of selling his municipal bonds to finance the purchase price. Under such circumstances, the purpose of incurring the indebtedness is so directly related to the personal purpose of acquiring a residence that no sufficiently direct relationship between the borrowing and the investment in tax-exempt obligations may reasonably be inferred.

.03 The purpose to purchase or carry tax-exempt obligations generally does not exist with respect to indebtedness incurred or continued by an individual in connection with the active conduct of trade or business (other than a dealer in tax-exempt obligations) unless it is determined that the borrowing was in excess of business needs. However, there is a rebuttable presumption that the purpose to carry tax-exempt obligations exists where the taxpayer reasonably could have foreseen at the time of purchasing the tax-exempt obligations that indebtedness probably would have to be incurred to meet future economic needs of the business of an ordinary, recurrent variety. *See Wisconsin Cheeseman v. United States*, 388 F.2d 420, at 422. The presumption may be rebutted, however, if the taxpayer demonstrates that business reasons, unrelated to the purchase or carrying of tax-exempt obligations, dominated the transaction.

.04 Generally, a purpose to carry tax-exempt obligations will be inferred, unless rebutted by other evidence, wherever the taxpayer has outstanding indebtedness which is not directly connected with personal expenditures (see section 4.02) and is not incurred or continued in connection with the active conduct of a trade or business (see section 4.03) and the taxpayer owns tax-exempt obligations. This inference will be made even though the indebtedness is ostensibly incurred or continued to purchase or carry other portfolio investments.

Portfolio investment for the purposes of this Revenue Procedure includes transactions entered into for profit (including investment in real estate) which are not connected with the active conduct of a trade or business. Purchase and sale of securities shall not constitute the active conduct of a trade or business unless the taxpayer is a dealer in securities within the meaning of section 1.471-5 of the Income Tax Regulations. A substantial ownership interest in a corporation will not be considered a portfolio investment. For example, where a taxpayer owns at least 80 percent of the voting stock of a corporation that is engaged in the active conduct of a trade or business, the investment in such controlling interest shall not be considered to be a portfolio investment.

A sufficiently direct relationship between the incurring or continuing of indebtedness and the purchasing or carrying of tax-exempt obligations will generally exist where indebtedness is incurred to finance portfolio investment because the choice of whether to finance a new portfolio investment through borrowing or through the liquidation of an existing investment in tax-exempt obligations typically involves a purpose either to maximize profit or to maintain a diversified portfolio. This purpose necessarily involves a decision, whether articulated by the taxpayer or not, to incur (or continue) the indebtedness, at least in part, to purchase or carry the existing investment in tax-exempt obligations.

A taxpayer may rebut the presumption that section 265(2) of the Code applies in the above circumstances by establishing that he could not have liquidated his holdings of tax-exempt obligations in order to avoid incurring indebtedness. The presumption may be overcome where, for example, liquidation is not possible because the tax-exempt obligations cannot be sold. The presumption would not be rebutted, however, by a showing that the tax-exempt obligations could only have been liquidated with difficulty or at a loss; or that the taxpayer owned other investment assets such as common stock that could have been liquidated; or that an investment advisor recommended that a prudent man should maintain a particular percentage of assets in tax-exempt obligations. Similarly, the presumption would not be rebutted by a showing that liquidating the holdings of tax-exempt obligations would not have produced sufficient cash to equal the amount borrowed.

The provisions of this paragraph may be illustrated by the following example:

> Taxpayer A, an individual, owns common stock listed on a national securities exchange, having an adjusted basis of $200,000; he owns rental property having an adjusted basis of $200,000; he has cash of $10,000; and he owns readily marketable municipal bonds having an adjusted basis of $41,000. A borrows $100,000 to invest in a limited partnership interest in a real estate syndicate and pays $8,000 interest on the loan which he claims as an interest deduction for the taxable year. Under these facts and circumstances, there is a presumption that the $100,000 indebtedness which is incurred to, finance A's portfolio investment is also incurred to carry A's existing investment in tax-exempt bonds since there are no additional facts or circumstances to rebut the presumption. Accordingly, a portion of the $8,000 interest payment will be disallowed under section 265(2) of the Code. See section 7 concerning the amount to be disallowed.

SEC. 7. PROCEDURES.

.01 When there is direct evidence under sections 3.02 and 3.03 establishing a purpose to purchase or carry tax-exempt obligations (either because tax-exempt obligations were used as collateral for indebtedness or the proceeds of indebtedness were directly traceable to the holding of particular tax-exempt obligations), no part of the interest paid or incurred on such indebtedness may be deducted. However, if only a fractional part of the indebtedness is directly traceable to the holding of particular tax-exempt obligations, the same fractional part of the interest paid or incurred on such indebtedness will be disallowed. For example, if A borrows $100,000 from a bank and invests $75,000 of the proceeds in tax-exempt obligations, 75 percent of the interest paid on the bank borrowing would be disallowed as a deduction.

.02 In any other case where interest is to be disallowed in accordance with this Revenue Procedure, an allocable portion of the interest on such indebtedness will be disallowed. The amount of interest on such indebtedness to be disallowed shall be determined by multiplying the total interest on such indebtedness by a fraction, the numerator of which is the average amount during the taxable year of the taxpayer's tax-exempt obligations (valued at their adjusted basis) and the denominator of which is the average amount during the taxable year of the taxpayer's total assets (valued at their adjusted basis) minus the amount of any indebtedness the interest on which is not subject to disallowance to any extent under this Revenue Procedure.

QUESTIONS AND COMMENTS

1. The obvious pattern in this Revenue Procedure is to make it much harder for someone who already owns tax exempt bonds to deduct interest when the loan is used to make investments, rather than to acquire personal use property or to finance business needs.

2. On June 1 and June 20, your client buys $20,000 worth of tax exempt bonds. On June 10, he takes out a $20,000 home mortgage loan. Is the interest on this personal loan deductible? *Mariorenzi v. Commissioner*, 490 F.2d 92 (1st Cir. 1974).

3. Rev. Proc. 72-18 suggests how difficult it is to trace loans to particular asset acquisitions. The problem is that taxpayers can often choose whether to keep one asset (asset A) and borrow to buy another (asset B), *or* to sell asset A and use the cash to buy asset B. Given these options, it is hard to say which asset (A or B) the taxpayer is financing with the loan — the purchase of asset B or the retention of asset A. This difficulty is sometimes used as an argument for allowing all interest to be deducted.

But is it really so difficult to devise a system to trace interest deductions to particular assets? Consider the following two possibilities, using tax exempt bonds as an example: (1) All interest would be allocated between investments in tax exempt bonds and all other assets, based on their adjusted basis. Rev. Proc. 72-18 uses such an allocation formula to determine nondeductible interest, but only *after* the loan has first been traced to carrying tax exempt bonds; or (2) use a stacking procedure that assumes that interest is first allocated either: (a) to tax-exempt bonds; or (b) to assets producing other income.

4. Regardless of what system you use to identify assets related to loans, you should omit assets that are very hard to sell — unless the hard-to-sell assets have been purchased with or pledged as security for the loan — because the hard-to-sell assets are not available to the taxpayer to finance the purchase of alternative assets.

[B] Critique of Disallowing Interest Deduction

Interest is a peculiar kind of expense. It is the cost of capital and taxpayers can incur this cost either by disposing of an investment, thereby foregoing investment income, or by borrowing. There is nothing to stop a taxpayer in the 35% bracket, who earns 10% taxable interest (yielding 6.5% after tax), from selling his investment and buying a tax exempt bond (yielding 7.5% before and after tax), ending up with *no* taxable income. Why can't he borrow at 10% interest (keeping the taxable investment earning 10%), and invest in the 7.5% tax exempt bond, and *still* end up with *no* taxable income?

You can describe a taxpayer who makes either of these investment decisions as engaged in arbitrage. A taxpayer engaged in arbitrage gives up a return in one market, where he gets a lower after-tax return, and obtains a better after-tax return in another market. There are several reasons to discourage arbitrage, but they might not be very persuasive in the context of tax exempt bonds.

Shifting investments to obtain a tax-exempt return might be economically undesirable, because: (1) it might not create any new investment but only move investments around; (2) the exemption might encourage investment in activities with low real economic returns, but high after-tax returns; (3) it might encourage only well-off high-bracket investors to make the investment, and they are not necessarily the persons who know the most about good investing.

The trouble with these arguments is that they all seem to undercut the underlying congressional decision to allow tax-exempt interest on state and local bonds in the first place. Of course, the exemption does not encourage new investment. It was supposed to encourage shifting investment to state and local government bonds. Moreover, the possibility that the economic returns to the tax-exempt investment are low is another way of questioning whether the governmental activities financed by the bonds are necessarily desirable. Congress seems to have decided that they are deductible. Finally, it is true that the well-off control the investment decision, but those with wealth always control investment decisions. And they are probably pretty good at making the kind of investments that § 103 encourages. In sum, all of these arguments against the interest deduction on loans to invest in tax-exempt bonds seem to be attacks on the exemption itself. Does § 265(a)(2) persist because we are in fact uneasy about taxpayers borrowing to buy tax-exempt Industrial Revenue Bonds (*see* Chapter 6.04[C][4]), some of which are still afforded tax exemption even though they are not the traditional type of tax-exempt bond?

In Chapter 17, we will consider the problem of tax shelters more closely, where taxpayers borrow to invest in what are in effect tax-exempt (or partially tax-exempt) investments. The borrowing is often "nonrecourse," which means that the taxpayer is not personally liable to repay the loan except out of the asset purchased with the borrowed funds. In that context, the economic efficiency concerns about arbitrage by borrowing to invest in tax-preferred investments might be much stronger than in the case of borrowing to invest in tax-exempt bonds.

§ 16.03 LOANS FOR INVESTMENT PURPOSES

[A] Statutory Rules

The taxpayer who borrows to make an investment must worry not only about § 265(a)(2), if he owns tax-exempt bonds at the time of the loan, but also about § 163(d), whether or not he owns tax-exempt bonds. **Section 163(d)** limits the deduction of investment interest. The **§ 163(d)** limits are applied *after* applying § 265(a)(2). Therefore, a taxpayer who pays some investment interest not disallowed under § 265(a)(2) must then contend with § 163(d).

Here is an example where there are *no* tax-exempt bonds. A taxpayer borrows $100,000 to invest in appreciating investment property (land or speculative stock). The property will not produce much income until many years later, probably when the asset is sold. All the appreciated gain is "unrealized" income. The gain may even avoid tax altogether if the investor dies and there is a date-of-death-value basis. Rather than add the interest to the basis of specific assets, § **163(d)** disallows the deduction of investment interest, *to the extent it exceeds investment income.*

The problem at which § **163(d)** is aimed is the borrower whose wealth has not decreased, because of unrealized appreciation on investments, but who claims an interest deduction. For example, the taxpayer could incur $10,000 interest to acquire a technology stock that pays no dividends but goes up $10,000 in value; net wealth from this transaction is zero, but an interest deduction could shelter non-investment income. However, the rules disallowing the deduction of investment interest are not limited to cases in which the taxpayer actually has unrealized appreciation. That would be too difficult to administer.

Investment income, from which investment interest can be deducted, includes net income from interest. Before the 1993 Act, investment income also included the net gain from disposition of investment assets. At that time, the preferential tax rate on long-term capital gains was 28% and the top individual tax rate was 31%, not too much of a difference. Therefore, deducting investment interest in an amount equal to preferentially taxed capital gain was not too much of a tax break. The 1993 tax law, however, increased the gap between the top individual rate (39.6%) and the preferential capital gains rate of 28% at that time. (The gap is still substantial — 35% is the top individual rate, and the preferential rate on long-term capital gains is generally 15%.) Consequently, preferentially taxed capital gain is *no longer* considered investment income, except to the extent the taxpayer elects to report that gain as ordinary income. § 163(d)(4)(B). For example, assume the taxpayer incurs $20,000 investment interest and has $5,000 interest income and $15,000 preferentially taxed long-term capital gain. $15,000 of the investment interest cannot be deducted.

Before the 2003 Tax Law, investment income also included dividends from which investment interest could be deducted. Because the 2003 Tax Law provided that dividend income would be taxed at the same preferential rates as long-term capital gain, dividends are no longer investment income under § **163(d)**, unless the taxpayer elects to report the dividends as ordinary income subject to non-preferential tax rates.

The excess of investment interest over investment income can be carried forward to future years and deducted from later investment income, if any. § 163(d)(2).

The impact of these rules is that a taxpayer can shelter *existing* investment income taxed at ordinary rates by paying interest on loans to make new investments, even if those new investments do not produce current investment income. The taxpayer who is hurt by these rules is one who has inadequate investment income, but who borrows to invest in appreciating property, hoping to shelter non-investment income with the interest — e.g., a lawyer or doctor with a lot of personal service income. In effect, the statute makes a stacking decision, allocating all investment interest first to taxable investment income.

The investment interest deduction is an itemized deduction, which is *not* subject to the 2% floor on miscellaneous itemized deductions.

Section 163(d) only applies to *individuals*. Why doesn't it apply to corporate borrowers? By contrast, § 265(a)(2) applies to all taxpayers, both individuals and corporations.

[B] Tracing

The limits on the deduction of investment interest apply only to loans "properly allocable to property held for investment." § 163(d)(3)(A). In other words, the interest is disallowed only after the loan is "traced" to investment purposes. What tracing rules apply under § 163(d)? Is it the complex approach set forth in Rev. Proc. 72-18, applicable to carrying tax-exempt bonds, or is it a more direct "tracing" approach, requiring an actual tracing of borrowed funds to purchasing an investment?

Temporary Regulations (**Temp. Treas. Reg. § 1.163-8T(a)(3)**) define investment interest for **§ 163(d)** by reference to the *use* to which the loan is put. This means, for example, that pledging investment stock as security for a loan used to buy a personal car generates personal, not investment interest. The fact that investment property was pledged as security does *not* link the loan with investment property under **§ 163(d)**. This contrasts with the rules dealing with "carrying" tax-exempt bonds. If tax-exempt bonds had been pledged as security for a loan, the interest would be traced to carrying the tax-exempt bonds, not to the use to which the loan proceeds were put.

[C] Carryover Limits?

How should the rules governing carryover of undeducted investment interest apply in the following situation? Suppose a taxpayer has $25,000 investment interest, no investment income, and taxable income of $20,000 earnings in a particular year. Can he carry forward $20,000 or $25,000 of unused investment interest under **§ 163(d)**? Before adoption of **§ 163(d)**, the taxpayer could have deducted the $20,000 investment interest from the $20,000 of personal service income, but could not carry over the unused $5,000 deduction to another year. The general rules on carrying over net losses to another year do not allow the excess of investment interest over taxable income to be carried forward, because the excess is not a business net operating loss (see § 172). Now that § 163(d) prevents the deduction of investment interest against non-investment income, but permits a carry forward of undeducted investment interest to future years, does the carry forward include the full $25,000 in this example, or only the $20,000 (equal to the earned income)? In other words, is there a trade-off — the taxpayer gives up the old opportunity to reduce non-investment (personal service) income by investment interest, but increases the amount of the interest that can be carried over to another year?

After litigating this issue in numerous cases (*see, e.g., Beyer v. Commissioner*, 916 F.2d 153 (4th Cir. 1990), *reversing*, 92 T.C. 1304 (1989)), the IRS stopped arguing that the carryover of investment interest in excess of taxable income (that is, $5,000) was not allowed. Rev. Rul. 95-16, 1995-1 C.B. 9. Therefore, in the prior example, $25,000 of unused investment interest can be carried forward. The IRS noted that four federal appellate courts and the United States Tax Court (in a 1993 reviewed-by-the-court opinion) had rejected the Service's position.

Do not think this was an entirely altruistic move on the government's part. In *Allbritton v. Commissioner*, 37 F.3d 183 (5th Cir. 1994), involving the carryover of investment interest in excess of taxable income, the court had awarded litigation costs to the taxpayer in accordance with § 7430. The court stated:

> The government's assertion of deficiencies in the Taxpayers' income taxes, and its appeal based on the same statutory interpretation previously rejected by the Fourth Circuit, the Federal Circuit, and several district courts constitutes "circuit-shopping" at the Taxpayers' expense in the hopes of creating a circuit conflict. Under 26 U.S.C. § 7430, a taxpayer who establishes that "the position of the United States in the proceeding was not substantially justified" may recover the reasonable costs of litigation. The Commissioner's repeated losses on the identical issue establish beyond serious question that the government's actions in assessing the deficiencies, litigating again an issue so consistently lost, and appealing the grant of the Taxpayers' motion for summary judgment, were not "justified to a degree that could satisfy a reasonable person."

> We have previously ruled that, while the Commissioner is free by law to relitigate prior lost issues in other circuits, he does so at the risk of incurring the obligation to reimburse the taxpayer. Therefore, in continuing to litigate this issue despite constant jurisprudence to the contrary, the Commissioner is not substantially justified and should bear all reasonable costs of Taxpayers' litigation.

[D] Global vs. Schedular Tax?

The carryover of the disallowed investment interest deduction highlights a feature of the tax law that is becoming more prominent. It treats investment activities as a category of income different from business income. We no longer have what has been called a "global" income tax, in the sense that all income is treated alike, with net losses from one activity automatically reducing gains from unrelated activities, *if* they occur in the same tax year. Now, net losses from *certain* activities are "quarantined," and can only be carried over to reduce income from the same activity in another year. The term "schedular" is sometimes used to describe such a tax system, in which different types of income are subject to different tax rules (that is, taxed in accordance with different "schedules").

§ 16.04 ECONOMIC REALITY

[A] Case Law Limits

The following case discusses a case law limitation on the interest deduction, based on the economic reality of the underlying transaction. It is important to remember that these case law rules apply to all investors, whether corporations or individuals, but that some statutory limits on the interest deduction (like § 163(d)) do not apply to corporations.

Economic
Substance

GOLDSTEIN v. COMMISSIONER
United States Court of Appeals, Second Circuit
364 F.2d 734 (2d Cir. 1966)

WATERMAN, CIRCUIT JUDGE. . . .

During the latter part of 1958, petitioner received the good news that she held a winning Irish Sweepstakes ticket and would shortly receive $140,218.75. This windfall significantly improved petitioner's financial situation, for she was a housewife approximately 70 years old and her husband was a retired garment worker who received a $780 pension each year. In 1958, the couple's only income, aside from this pension and the unexpected Sweepstakes proceeds, was $124.75, which represented interest on several small savings bank accounts. The petitioner received the Sweepstakes proceeds in December 1958 and she deposited the money in a New York bank. She included this amount as gross income in the joint return she and her husband filed for 1958 on the cash receipts and disbursements basis.

Petitioner's son, Bernard Goldstein, was a certified public accountant, practicing in New York in 1958. In November of that year, Bernard either volunteered or was enlisted to assist petitioner in investing the Sweepstakes proceeds, and in minimizing the 1958 tax consequences to petitioner of the sudden increase in her income for that year. A series of consultations between Bernard and an attorney resulted in the adoption of a plan, which, as implemented, can be summarized as follows: During the latter part of December 1958, petitioner contacted several brokerage houses that bought and sold securities for clients and also arranged collateral loans. With the assistance of one of these brokerage houses, Garvin, Bantel & Co., petitioner borrowed $465,000 from the First National Bank of Jersey City. With the money thus acquired, and the active assistance of Garvin, Bantel, petitioner purchased $500,000 face amount of United States Treasury 1/2% notes, due to mature on October 1, 1962. Petitioner promptly pledged the Treasury notes so purchased as collateral to secure the loan with the Jersey City Bank. At approximately the same time in 1958, Bernard secured for petitioner a $480,000 loan from the Royal State Bank of New York. With the assistance of the Royal State Bank petitioner purchased a second block of $500,000 face amount of United States Treasury 1 1/2%

notes, due to mature on October 1, 1961. Again, the notes were pledged as collateral with this bank to secure the loan. Bernard testified that the petitioner purchased the Treasury notes because he believed 'the time was ripe' to invest in this kind of government obligation. Also, pursuant to the prearranged plan, petitioner prepaid to the First National Bank of Jersey City and to the Royal State Bank the interest that would be due on the loans she had received if they remained outstanding for 1 1/2 to 2 1/2 years. These interest prepayments, made in late December of 1958, totaled $81,396.61. Petitioner then claimed this sum as a Section 163(a) deduction on the 1958 income tax return she filed jointly with her husband.

[Editor — The Tax Court disallowed the deduction because the transactions were a "sham," with the prepayment of interest being compensation to the bank for setting up the transaction.]

There is a certain force to the foregoing analysis. Quite clearly, the First National Bank of Jersey City and the Royal State Bank of New York preferred to engage in the transactions they engaged in here rather than invest funds directly in Treasury notes because petitioner's loans bore interest at an appreciably higher rate than that yielded by the government obligations. This fact, combined with the impeccable property pledged as security for the loans, may have induced these banks to enter into these transactions without all the panoply that the court indicates usually accompanies loan transactions of such size. Indeed, while on its face purporting to be a debtor-creditor transaction between a taxpayer and a bank, in fact there can be a situation where the bank itself is, in effect, directly investing in the securities purportedly pledged by taxpayer as collateral to taxpayer's obligation; in such a transaction, the taxpayer truly can be said to have paid a certain sum to the bank in return for the 'facade' of a loan transaction. For Section 163(a) purposes, such transactions are properly described as 'shams' creating no 'genuine indebtedness' and no deduction for the payment of 'interest' to the bank should be allowed.

In our view, however, the facts of the two loan arrangements now before us fail in several significant respects to establish that these transactions were clearly shams. We agree with the dissent below that the record indicates these loan arrangements were ' . . . regular and, moreover, indistinguishable from any other legitimate loan transaction contracted for the purchase of Government securities.' In the first place, the Jersey City Bank and the Royal State Bank were independent financial institutions; it cannot be said that their sole function was to finance transactions such as those before us. Second, the two loan transactions here did not within a few days return all the parties to the position from which they had started. . . . Third, the independent financial institutions from which petitioner borrowed the funds she needed to acquire the Treasury obligations possessed significant control over the future of their respective loan arrangements: for example, the petitioner's promissory note to the Jersey City Bank explicitly gave either party the right to accelerate the maturity of the note after 30 days, and it was the Jersey City Bank's utilization of this clause that necessitated recourse to Gruntal; the Royal State Bank had the right at any time to demand that petitioner increase her collateral or liquidate the loan, and on several occasions it made such a demand. Fourth, the notes signed by petitioner in favor of both banks were signed with recourse. If either of the independent lending institutions here involved had lost money on these transactions because of the depreciation of the collateral pledged to secure the loans we are certain that, upon petitioner's default of payment, they would have without hesitation proceeded against petitioner to recover their losses. Moreover, all things being equal, the banks' chances of judgments in their favor would have been excellent. In view of this combination of facts, we think it was error for the Tax Court to conclude that these two transactions were 'shams' which created no genuine indebtedness. Were this the only ground on which the decision reached below could be supported we would be compelled to reverse. . . .

One ground advanced by the Tax Court seems capable of reasoned development to support the result reached in this case by that court. The Tax Court found as an ultimate fact that petitioner's purpose in entering into the Jersey City Bank and Royal State Bank transactions 'was not to derive any economic gain or to improve here beneficial interest; but was solely an attempt to obtain an interest deduction as an offset to her sweepstake winnings.' This finding of ultimate fact was based in part on a set of computations made by Bernard Goldstein shortly after the Jersey City Bank and Royal State Bank loan transactions had been concluded. These computations were introduced by the Commissioner below and they indicated that petitioner and her financial advisors then estimated that the transactions would produce an economic loss in excess of $18,500 inasmuch as petitioner was out of pocket the 4% interest she had prepaid and could expect to receive 1 1/2% interest on the Treasury obligations she had just purchased plus a modest capital gain when the obligations were sold. This computation also reflected Bernard's realization that if the plan was successful, this economic loss would be more than offset by the substantial reduction in petitioner's 1958 income tax liability due to the large deduction for interest 'paid or accrued' taken in that year. . . .

Before the Tax Court, and before us, petitioner has argued that she realistically anticipated an economic gain on the loan transactions due to anticipated appreciation in the value of the Treasury obligations, and that this gain would more than offset the loss that was bound to result because of the unfavorable interest rate differential. In support of this position, Bernard testified, and documentary evidence was introduced, to the effect that in December 1958, the market for Treasury obligations was unreasonably depressed, and that many investors at that time were favorably disposed toward their purchase. In short, petitioner argued that she intended a sophisticated, speculative, sortie into the market for government securities.

In holding that petitioner's sole purpose in entering into the Jersey City Bank and Royal State Bank transactions was to obtain an interest deduction, the Tax Court rejected this explanation of her purpose in entering into these transactions. For several reasons we, hold that this rejection was proper. First, petitioner's evidence tending to establish that she anticipated an economic profit on these transactions due to a rising market for Treasury obligations is flatly contradicted by the computations made by Bernard contemporaneously with the commencement of these transactions . . . . These computations almost conclusively establish that petitioner and her advisors from the outset anticipated an economic loss. Petitioner's answer to this damaging evidence is that the set of Bernard's computations introduced by the Commissioner was only one of several arithmetic projections made at the same time by Bernard, and that Bernard intended the computations introduced by the Commissioner to represent the worst that could befall the plan if prices for government obligations continued to decline. . . . [Editor — The court goes on to conclude that petitioner and her advisors could not have entertained a reasonable hope of economic profit.]

For all of the above reasons, the Tax Court was justified in concluding that petitioner entered into the Jersey City Bank and Royal State Bank transactions without any realistic expectation of economic profit and 'solely' in order to secure a large interest deduction in 1958 which could be deducted from her sweepstakes winnings in that year. This conclusion points the way to affirmance in the present case.

We hold, for reasons set forth hereinafter, that Section 163(a) of the 1954 Internal Revenue Code does not permit a deduction for interest paid or accrued in loan arrangements, like those now before us, that cannot with reason be said to have purpose, substance, or utility apart from their anticipated tax consequences. Although it is by no means certain that Congress constitutionally could tax gross income, it is frequently stated that deductions from 'gross income' are a matter of 'legislative grace.' There is at least this much truth in this oft-repeated maxim: a close question whether a particular Code provision authorizes the deduction of a certain item is best resolved by reference to the underlying Congressional purpose of the deduction provision in question.

Admittedly, the underlying purpose of Section 163(a) permitting the deduction of 'all interest paid or accrued within the taxable year on indebtedness' is difficult to articulate because this provision is extremely broad: There is no requirement that deductible interest serve a business purpose, that it be ordinary and necessary, or even that it be reasonable. Nevertheless, it is fair to say that Section 163(a) is not entirely unlimited in its application and that such limits as there are stem from the Section's underlying notion that if an individual or corporation desires to engage in purposive activity, there is no reason why a taxpayer who borrows for that purpose should fare worse from an income tax standpoint than one who finances the venture with capital that otherwise would have been yielding income.

In order fully to implement this Congressional policy of encouraging purposive activity to be financed through borrowing, Section 163(a) should be construed to permit the deductibility of interest when a taxpayer has borrowed funds and incurred an obligation to pay interest in order to engage in what with reason can be termed purposive activity, even though he decided to borrow in order to gain an interest deduction rather than to finance the activity in some other way. In other words, the interest deduction should be permitted whenever it can be said that the taxpayer's desire to secure an interest deduction is only one of mixed motives that prompts the taxpayer to borrow funds; or, put a third way, the deduction is proper if there is some substance to the loan arrangement beyond the taxpayer's desire to secure the deduction. After all, we are frequently told that a taxpayer has the right to decrease the amount of what otherwise would be his taxes, or altogether avoid them, by any means the law permits. E.g., Gregory v. Helvering, 293 U.S. 465 (1935). On the other hand, and notwithstanding Section 163(a)'s broad scope this provision should not be construed to permit an interest deduction when it objectively appears that a taxpayer has borrowed funds in order to engage in a transaction that has no substance or purpose aside from the taxpayer's desire to obtain the tax benefit of an interest deduction: and a good example of such purposeless activity is the borrowing of funds at 4% in order to purchase property that returns less than 2% and holds out no prospect of appreciation sufficient to counter the unfavorable interest rate differential. Certainly, the statutory provision's underlying purpose, as we understand it, does not require that a deduction be allowed in such a case. Indeed, to allow a deduction for interest paid on funds borrowed for no purposive reason, other than the securing of a deduction from income, would frustrate Section 163(a)'s purpose; allowing it would encourage transactions that have no economic utility and that would not be engaged in but for the system of taxes imposed by Congress. When it enacted Section 163(a), Congress could not have intended to permit a taxpayer to reduce his taxes by means of an interest deduction that arose from a transaction that had no substance, utility, or purpose beyond the tax deduction. . . .

[T]he Supreme Court cautions us . . . that in cases like the present 'the question for determination is whether what was done, apart from the tax motive, was the thing which the statute intended.' We here decide that Section 163(a) does not 'intend' that taxpayers should be permitted deductions for interest paid on debts that were entered into solely in order to obtain a deduction. It follows therefore from the foregoing, and from the Tax Court's finding as a matter of 'ultimate' fact that petitioner entered into the Jersey City Bank and Royal State Bank transactions without any expectation of profit and without any other purpose except to obtain an interest deduction, and that the Tax Court's disallowance of the deductions in this case must be affirmed.

COMMENT — OUT-OF-POCKET LOSS

A taxpayer like Goldstein is still out-of-pocket the difference between the interest expense and the gross income from the investment. Is that difference deductible under § 165(c)(2) as a loss in an income-producing transaction? *Knetsch v. United States*, 348 F.2d 932 (Ct. Cl. 1965) (no deduction).

In some cases in which an interest expense exceeds the return on the investment, the person who persuaded the taxpayer to make the investment lied to the taxpayer. He falsely stated that property had actually been purchased for the taxpayer with the borrowed funds. In such a case, can the taxpayer deduct the out-of-pocket investment as an embezzlement or theft loss? *Nichols v. Commissioner*, 43 T.C. 842 (1965) (deduction allowed for theft loss, because taxpayer deceived).

[B]   Note on Statutory Interpretation — Tax Avoidance

Goldstein is helpful in defining the issue of tax avoidance as one of statutory interpretation. This is not the first time this issue has arisen. Whether or not a couple is married for tax law purposes, even though divorced under state law, is an issue of statutory interpretation that arises in the context of tax avoidance (avoiding the tax on marriage).

Goldstein holds, as a matter of statutory interpretation, that the interest deduction is permitted only if the loan is incurred in a transaction that could produce an economic profit (or is it a subjective test — a transaction that the taxpayer thought could produce an economic profit?).

Less helpful is the court's statement that congressional intent is relevant. The court says that "Congress could not have intended to permit a taxpayer" a deduction in this case. This is a very common statement for judges to make, in order to claim a legislative intent pedigree for their conclusions about statutory meaning. But, in most of these cases, the legislature probably had no specific intent about the type of transaction at issue. Indeed, when a judge says that "Congress could not have intended" something, that is often a clear sign that the interpretation of the statute rests on something other than a good guess about legislative intent.

The general principle in *Goldstein* — the "economic profit apart from taxes" test — is difficult to apply, because it is not always clear how much of a profit motive is necessary and whether Congress intended tax benefits, even for tax-motivated transactions. In *Fox v. Commissioner*, 82 T.C. 1001, 1014–27 (1984), the court held that § 165(c)(2) (dealing with loss deductions in transactions "entered into for profit") required a "primary profit" motive. The statutory test under § 165(c)(2) seems to be a different (and stricter) requirement than the "case law" *Goldstein* test, which does not require a "primary" profit motive. But, in the process of applying § 165(c)(2), the court made a statement that is relevant to all tests based on potential economic profit. The court stated that it would relax the profit requirement "for those essentially tax-motivated transactions which are unmistakably within the contemplation of congressional intent." The court listed as examples of such congressionally sanctioned transactions an investment in tax-exempt securities and purchases motivated by a combination of accelerated depreciation, the investment tax credit, and the interest deduction.

Now you should see why the problem of tax avoidance is so difficult. How does a court decide which transactions with negligible economic purposes, apart from tax breaks, should be recognized for tax purposes? Which tax breaks does the code want the taxpayer to exploit, even if there are low pre-tax economic profits? We return to this issue in the context of tax shelters in Chapter 17.

[C]   Legislating the Economic Substance Rule

In 2010, Congress enacted an "economic substance" requirement in the Reconciliation Act amendments (Public Law 111-152) to the Patient Protection and Affordable Health Care Act. See § 7701(o), effective March 30, 2010. The statute requires a showing that a transaction changed the taxpayer's "economic position" in a "meaningful way (apart from federal income tax effects)" *and* that the taxpayers had "a substantial purpose (apart from Federal Income tax effects)" — in other words, both an objective and a subjective test. The law does not apply to a taxpayer's efforts to avoid state income taxes, federal estate taxes, and foreign taxes.

Prior case law regarding the economic substance doctrine was unclear. (*Goldstein* is only one example.) Some cases recognized a transaction if there was *either* economic substance or a business purpose. And the Federal Claims Court had suggested that judicial use of the doctrine violated separation of powers. *Coltec Industries, Inc. v. United States*, 62 Fed. Cl. 716 (2004), *vacated and remanded*, 454 F.3d 1340 (Fed. Cir. 2006).

Several features of the "economic substance" law cause concern:

First, the statutory terms "meaningful" and "substantial" are unclear.

Second, the statute is written in the conjunctive — requiring both economic substance and a business purpose.

Third, the penalties are substantial. Tax understatements resulting from transactions that fail the statutory test will be subject to a 40% strict liability penalty if they are not disclosed by the taxpayer, 20% if there is disclosure. § 6662(b)(6), (i). There is no reasonable-cause exception, so opinions given by tax advisors will not prevent the penalty. § 6664(c)(2),(d)(2).

Fourth, the method of determining the profit potential to prove economic substance and business purpose is unclear. The legislative history states that "if a taxpayer relies on a profit potential, the present value of the reasonably expected pre-tax profit must be substantial in relation to the present value of the expected net tax benefits that would be allowed if the transaction were respected. Fees and other transaction expenses are taken into account as expenses in determining pre-tax profit." An earlier draft of the law explicitly used the low risk-free rate of return as the discount rate used to compute present value, which was a pro-taxpayer provision. (The lower the discount rate, the higher the present value of the expected pre-tax profit.) The legislation that passed is silent regarding the discount rate.

Fifth, the statute states that the economic substance doctrine only applies when it is "relevant" and that "[t]he determination of whether the economic substance doctrine is relevant to a transaction shall be made in the same manner as if this subsection had never been enacted." § 7701(o)(1),(5). And § 7701(o)(5)(A) further states that "[t]he 'economic substance doctrine' means the common law doctrine under which tax benefits [] with respect to a transaction are not allowable if the transaction does not have economic substance or lacks a business purpose." This means that the applicability of the doctrine continues to depend on interpreting the tax law to decide whether tax breaks are intended to be available whether or not there is nontax economic substance. And the reference to "common law" in a statute that is decidedly not drawn from common law antecedents further implies that the doctrine will evolve in uncertain ways in accordance with principles developed by the courts.

The legislative history (Joint Committee on Taxation Report, JCX-18-10, Technical Explanation of the Revenue Provisions of the Reconciliation Act of 2010) tries to ease some taxpayer concern by stating that the new law is not meant to change the tax rules applicable to the choice between certain economic alternatives, such as a corporation's decision to issue debt or equity or a taxpayer's decision to use either a foreign or domestic corporation to make foreign investments. In addition, the legislative history states that a transaction is not suspect if there is a congressional purpose to allow the taxpayer to take advantage of certain tax breaks — "The doctrine of economic substance becomes applicable . . . where a taxpayer seeks to claim tax benefits, *unintended by Congress*, by means of transactions that serve no economic purpose other than tax savings (emphasis added)." In other words, the new law does not eliminate the statutory interpretation question whether Congress intended to permit transactions that achieve tax savings whether or not they have nontax economic substance.

The IRS (in a Directive issued by the agency's Large and Mid-Size Business Division) has also tried to put taxpayers at ease by explaining how the new law applies in general to various transactions. See 2011 LMSB Directive (issued July 15, 2011), extended to all field offices in April, 2012 by Chief Counsel Notice CC-2012-008, 2012 CCN Lexis 4. This Directive makes imposition of the economic substance doctrine and its related penalty more difficult than it might otherwise be, but the details are too complex to be reviewed here. As an example: the Directive considers relevant but not dispositive whether the transaction is promoted by tax advisors or involves a tax-indifferent counter-party (such as a tax-exempt organization that neither recognizes income nor takes deductions). Despite this Directive, however, the IRS will not issue letter rulings identifying whether or not the economic substance doctrine will be applied to specific transactions. Rev. Proc. 2012-3, §§ 1.01, 1.02(4), 3.02(1).

Although many tax avoidance transactions are too complex to be considered in a basic tax course, the next chapter will consider sale-leaseback transactions. The legislative history of the new law clearly states that "[l]easing transactions . . . will continue to be analyzed in light of all the facts and circumstances," indicating that such transactions will remain vulnerable under the economic substance test. You might also revisit the *Cottage Savings* decision (Chapter 3.03[D]), in which a taxpayer exchanged claims against one set of debtors for claims against other debtors without altering the credit risk. The taxpayer was trying to realize a tax loss, without recognizing the loss for banking regulation purposes. The Court held that there was a realized tax loss because the change in the debtors created a different legal situation for the taxpayer-creditor. But was the taxpayer's economic position changed in a "meaningful" way apart from taxes; was there a substantial business purpose apart from taxes?

You might wonder why Congress stepped in to codify the economic substance doctrine when courts had given the government several victories. One reason is that the added revenue from the statutory provision (as computed by the Congressional Budget Office when it "scores" the effect of federal legislation) can be used to offset additional expenditures in other federal legislation — thereby reducing any adverse impact on the stated federal budget deficit. As long as the doctrine was left to the vagaries of judicial implementation, its revenue consequences were uncertain and could not be taken into account in making budget calculations.

Chapter 17

LOANS, BASIS, AND TAX SHELTERS

§ 17.01 LOANS AND BASIS

[A] Debt Included in Basis

When can debt be included in a taxpayer's basis? For example, if a taxpayer buys a building with a $50,000 loan, is the building's basis $50,000?

Basis is usually the amount invested out of after-tax income. The tax issue raised by loans is whether a taxpayer is entitled to include debt in basis, even though the investment of after-tax income (by repaying the debt) will occur in the future. In effect, the taxpayer wants to accrue the debt and include it in basis before the debt is paid.

We have already seen that borrowing is not taxed at the time of the loan. You can think of the borrower's obligation as offsetting the receipt of the loan proceeds, thus preventing any increase in net wealth. The expectation of loan repayment arguably justifies the offset.

A corollary of this approach is that borrowed money that is used to purchase property is included in the property's basis. If the $50,000 loan used to buy a building were not included in basis (that is, if basis were zero), then when the taxpayer sold the building before repaying the loan, the taxpayer would have $50,000 gross income. In effect, the taxpayer would be taxed on the loan proceeds prior to the time of repayment. But that would be inconsistent with the fundamental rule postponing taxation until the loan is repaid out of after-tax income.

The full implications of this conclusion can only be appreciated by considering the use of borrowed money to make investments in depreciable and expensed property. Taxpayers can combine early deduction rules for investments with exclusion of loan proceeds from income, with startling results.

The *Crane* case, *infra*, is usually cited as the seminal authority for including debt in basis. Technically, the case held that inherited property has a basis equal to its gross value, including debt to which the property is subject. "Debt to which the property is subject" refers to situations in which the property is security for the debt but the debtor is *not* personally liable (often referred to as *nonrecourse* debt). The case was later extended to property acquired by *purchase* with borrowed money. *Mayerson v. Commissioner*, 47 T.C. 340 (1966). Consequently, unpaid debt is included in basis, both when the taxpayer is personally liable and when the debt is nonrecourse, and whether the property is inherited or purchased.

CRANE v. COMMISSIONER
United States Supreme Court
331 U.S. 1 (1947)

MR. CHIEF JUSTICE VINSON delivered the opinion of the court.

[Editor — Assume the following facts. Taxpayer inherited depreciable property worth $100,000, subject to a $100,000 debt (that is, the property was security for the debt). The owner was not personally liable. She treated the property as though it had a $100,000 basis and took $60,000 depreciation deductions over several years. She never paid off any of the debt. When she sold the property, the property's value had increased to $103,000, but she received only $3,000 cash, because the property was still encumbered by a $100,000 debt.

She argued that the basis of the sold property was zero, and that she had a $3,000 gain on the sale. She claimed that the original basis at inheritance was zero, because the net value (considering the $100,000 debt) was zero. She admitted that her claim of a zero basis was inconsistent with her prior depreciation deductions. The remedy for that, she said, was to go back to earlier tax years and disallow the depreciation. The government responded that the original basis was $100,000, including the debt, and that *therefore* the amount realized at the time of the sale included unpaid debt.

These issues arose under an earlier version of the code with different section numbers. The code references are deleted from the case but the statutory text is the same as under current law in all important respects, regarding the definition of "amount realized," "basis," and "adjusted basis."]

The question here is how a taxpayer who acquires depreciable property subject to an unassumed mortgage, holds it for a period, and finally sells it still so encumbered, must compute her taxable gain. . . .

The 1938 Act defines the gain from 'the sale or other disposition of property' as 'the excess of the amount realized therefrom over the adjusted basis. . . .' It proceeds to define 'the amount realized from the sale or other disposition of property' as 'the sum of any money received plus the fair market value of the property (other than money) received.' Further, . . . the 'adjusted basis for determining the gain or loss from the sale or other disposition of property' is declared to be 'the basis . . . adjusted . . . for exhaustion, wear and tear, obsolescence, amortization . . . to the extent allowed (but not less than the amount allowable). . . .' The basis . . . 'if the property was acquired by . . . devise . . . or by the decedent's estate from the decedent,' is 'the fair market value of such property at the time of such acquisition.'

Logically, the first step under this scheme is to determine the unadjusted basis of the property, and the dispute in this case is as to the construction to be given the term 'property.' If 'property,' as used in that provision, means the same thing as 'equity,' it would necessarily follow that the basis of petitioner's property was zero, as she contends. If, on the contrary, it means the land and building themselves, or the owner's legal rights in them, undiminished by the mortgage, the basis was [$100,000].

We think that the reasons for favoring one of the latter constructions are of overwhelming weight. . . . [T]he words of statutes — including revenue acts — should be interpreted where possible in their ordinary, everyday senses. The only relevant definitions of 'property' to be found in the principal standard dictionaries are the two favored by the Commissioner, i.e., either that 'property' is the physical thing which is a subject of ownership, or that it is the aggregate of the owner's rights to control and dispose of that thing. 'Equity' is not given as a synonym, nor do either of the foregoing definitions suggest that it could be correctly so used. Indeed, 'equity' is defined as 'the value of a property . . . above the total of the liens. . . . ' The contradistinction could hardly be more pointed. Strong counter-vailing considerations would be required to support a contention that Congress, in using the word 'property,' meant 'equity,' or that we should impute to it the intent to convey that meaning.

A further reason why the word 'property' in should not be construed to mean 'equity' is the bearing such construction would have on the allowance of deductions for depreciation and on the collateral adjustments of basis.

[The statute] permits deduction from gross income of 'a reasonable allowance for the exhaustion, wear and tear of property. . . .' [It] declare[s] that the 'basis upon which depletion exhaustion, wear and tear . . . are to be allowed' is the basis ' . . . for the purpose of determining the gain upon the sale' of the property, which is the basis 'adjusted . . . for exhaustion, wear and tear . . . to the extent allowed (but not less than the amount allowable). . . .'

Under these provisions, if the mortgagor's equity were the basis, it would also be the original basis from which depreciation allowances are deducted. If it is, and if the amount of the annual allowances were to be computed on that value, as would then seem to be required, they will represent only a fraction of the cost of the corresponding physical exhaustion, and any recoupment by the mortgagor of the remainder of that cost can be effected only by the reduction of his taxable gain in the year of sale. If, however, the amount of the annual allowances were to be computed on the value of the property, and then deducted from an equity basis, we would in some instances have to accept deductions from a minus basis or deny deductions altogether. The Commissioner also argues that taking the mortgagor's equity as the basis would require the basis to be changed with each payment on the mortgage, and that the attendant problem of repeatedly recomputing basis and annual allowances would be a tremendous accounting burden on both the Commissioner and the taxpayer. Moreover, the mortgagor would acquire control over the timing of his depreciation allowances.

Thus it appears that the applicable provisions of the Act expressly preclude an equity basis, and the use of it is contrary to certain implicit principles of income tax depreciation, and entails very great administrative difficulties. It may be added that the Treasury has never furnished a guide through the maze of problems that arise in connection with depreciating an equity basis, but, on the contrary, has consistently permitted the amount of depreciation allowances to be computed on the full value of the property, and subtracted from it as a basis. Surely, Congress' long-continued acceptance of this situation gives it full legislative endorsement.

We conclude that the proper basis is the value of the property, undiminished by mortgages thereon, and that the correct basis here was [$100,000]. The next step is to ascertain what [basis] adjustments are required. As the depreciation rate was stipulated, the only question at this point is whether the Commissioner was warranted in making any depreciation adjustments whatsoever.

Petitioner urges that she was not entitled to depreciation deductions, whatever the basis of the property, because the law allows them only to one who actually bears the capital loss, and here the loss was not hers but the mortgagee's. We do not see, however, that she has established her factual premise. There was no finding of the Tax Court to that effect, nor to the effect that the value of the property was ever less than the amount of the lien. Nor was there evidence in the record, or any indication that petitioner could produce evidence, that this was so. The facts that the value of the property was only equal to the lien in 1932 and that during the next six and one-half years the physical condition of the building deteriorated and the amount of the lien increased, are entirely inconclusive, particularly in the light of the buyer's willingness in 1938 to take subject to the increased lien and pay a substantial amount of cash to boot. Whatever may be the rule as to allowing depreciation to a mortgagor on property in his possession which is subject to an unassumed mortgage and clearly worth less than the lien, we are not faced with that problem and see no reason to decide it now.

At last we come to the problem of determining the 'amount realized' on the 1938 sale. [The statute], it will be recalled, defines the 'amount realized' from 'the sale . . . of property' as 'the sum of any money received plus the fair market value of the property (other than money) received,' and [the statute] defines the gain on 'the sale . . . of property' as the excess of the amount realized over the basis. Quite obviously, the word 'property,' used here with reference to a sale, must mean 'property' in the same ordinary sense intended by the use of the word with reference to acquisition and depreciation, both for certain of the reasons stated heretofore . . . , and also because the functional relation of the two sections requires that the word mean the same in one section that it does in the other. If the 'property' to be valued on the date of acquisition is the property free of liens, the 'property' to be priced on a subsequent sale must be the same thing.

Starting from this point, we could not accept petitioner's contention that the [$3,000] net cash was all she realized on the sale except on the absurdity that she sold a [valuable] property for roughly one per cent of its value, and took a 99 per cent loss. Actually, petitioner does not urge this. She argues, conversely, that because only [$3,000] was realized on the sale, the 'property' sold must have been the equity only, and that consequently we are forced to accept her contention as to the meaning of 'property' [for computing basis]. We adhere, however, to what we have already said on the meaning of 'property', and we find that the absurdity is avoided by our conclusion that the amount of the mortgage is properly included in the 'amount realized' on the sale.

Petitioner concedes that if she had been personally liable on the mortgage and the purchaser had either paid or assumed it, the amount so paid or assumed would be considered a part of the 'amount realized.' The cases so deciding have already repudiated the notion that there must be an actual receipt by the seller himself of 'money' or 'other property,' in their narrowest senses. It was thought to be decisive that one section of the Act must be construed so as not to defeat the intention of another or to frustrate the Act as a whole, and that the taxpayer was the 'beneficiary' of the payment in 'as real and substantial (a sense) as if the money had been paid it and then paid over by it to its creditors.'

Both these points apply to this case. The first has been mentioned already. As for the second, we think that a mortgagor, not personally liable on the debt, who sells the property subject to the mortgage for additional consideration, realizes a benefit in the amount of the mortgage as well as the boot.[1] If a purchaser pays boot, it is immaterial as to our problem whether the mortgagor is also to receive money from the purchaser to discharge the mortgage prior to sale, or whether he is merely to transfer subject to the mortgage — it may make a difference to the purchaser and to the mortgagee, but not to the mortgagor. Or put in another way, we are no more concerned with whether the mortgagor is, strictly speaking, a debtor on the mortgage, than we are with whether the benefit to him is, strictly speaking, a receipt of money or property. We are rather concerned with the reality that an owner of property, mortgaged at a figure less than that at which the property will sell, must and will treat the conditions of the mortgage exactly as if they were his personal obligations. If he transfers subject to the mortgage, the benefit to him is as real and substantial as if the mortgage were discharged, or as if a personal debt in an equal amount had been assumed by another.

Therefore we conclude that the Commissioner was right in determining that petitioner realized [$103,000] on the sale of this property. . . .

COMMENTS AND QUESTIONS

1. **Changing basis?** What was the Court in *Crane* worried about when it stated:

> The Commissioner also argues that taking the mortgagor's equity as the basis would require the basis to be changed with each payment on the mortgage, and that the attendant problem of repeatedly recomputing basis and annual allowances would be a tremendous accounting burden on both the Commissioner and the taxpayer. Moreover, the mortgagor would acquire control over the timing of his depreciation allowances.

Consider this example. The taxpayer pays $5,000 down in year 1 and promises to pay $185,000 for a building. It then pays $3,000 of the debt in year 1. What complications arise if the taxpayer cannot use $190,000 as the basis for depreciation. Assume the tax law provides for a 19-year useful life. Would you depreciate the $8,000 out-of-pocket investment in year 1 over 19 years? If $4,000 more principal on the debt were paid in year 2, would that be another investment, depreciable over 19 (or 18) years?

Isn't there any easy way to solve the problem of changing basis? Just compute depreciation using the $190,000 basis, but cap the deduction at the actual out-of-

---

[1] [37] [Editor — The bracketed numbers in the footnotes in this chapter refer to the numbers in the reported case.] Obviously, if the value of the property is less than the amount of the mortgage, a mortgagor who is not personally liable cannot realize a benefit equal to the mortgage. Consequently, a different problem might be encountered where a mortgagor abandoned the property or transferred it subject to the mortgage without receiving boot. That is not this case.

pocket investment. In the example, $10,000 depreciation in the first year would be capped at $8,000 ($5,000 down plus $3,000 debt paid). The unused $2,000 deduction would be carried forward to the next year, so a total of $12,000 potential depreciation would be allowed, *if* that much additional out-of-pocket investment were paid.

2. **Amount realized when basis includes debt.** Be sure you understand why the amount realized must include unpaid debt. Using the above example, how much debt does the taxpayer still owe after one year? The answer is $182,000 (only $3,000 of the $185,000 debt is paid). How much of the purchase price of the building has been deducted — $10,000. That $10,000 includes the $8,000 the taxpayer paid ($5,000 down plus $3,000 debt paid). The taxpayer has gotten a $10,000 deduction, for an $8,000 out-of-pocket investment.

What is wrong with this $10,000 deduction? After all, the taxpayer can deduct unpaid debt. But we allow the deduction of unpaid debt *because* the debt is going to be paid in the future. Once the taxpayer disposes of the property, what chance is there that the debt will be paid by the taxpayer? The answer is "none," if the taxpayer is not personally liable and, very little, even if he is personally liable. The taxpayer will therefore enjoy a $10,000 deduction but only pay $8,000. That is like borrowing $10,000 and paying back only $8,000.

What to do? Do the same thing that the tax law did in the case of debt forgiveness, discussed in Chapter 3.06[C]. Tax the $2,000 as income. The mechanical rule, which includes unpaid debt in amount realized, will always have that effect. For example, assume the property is worth $182,000. Because the debt equals value, no one will pay additional cash for the property. A transfer of the property for which the debt was security would result in $182,000 amount realized. The basis of the property is $180,000 ($190,000 minus the $10,000 depreciation deduction). The gain is therefore $2,000.

3. **Realizable taxable event.** The need for this rule is sufficiently strong that the tax law treats events as taxable dispositions that would not otherwise be taxable. For example, the transfer of property as a gift is not usually a taxable event. A gift of property subject to a debt is, however, a taxable event — the amount realized equals the unpaid debt. A gift to a child or a charity can therefore produce taxable gain to the donor. (There is an exception. If property subject to a liability in excess of basis is transferred to a spouse or former spouse pursuant to § 1041, there is *no* taxable gain to the transferor on the excess of liability over basis, and the transferee takes the transferor's basis in the property. § 1041(e); **Treas. Reg. § 1.1041-1T(d) (Q-12 and A-12).**)

Abandonment of property is also a realizable taxable event. This might sound fanciful. Why abandon property? Assume that the investment of $190,000 in the prior example was an investment in a partnership that has not been very productive. After some years the property is worth $130,000 but the unpaid debt is still quite high — say, $150,000. The partners are not personally liable and do not want to continue paying off the debt. The partnership therefore abandons the property to the creditor-bank. Unpaid debt minus basis is taxable gain.

L & C Springs Assocs. v. Commissioner, 188 F.3d 866 (7th Cir. 1999), dealt with the question of when an abandonment occurred. The taxpayer argued that "for there to be an abandonment of property creating a 'disposition' for purposes of I.R.C. § 1001, there must be both an intent to abandon and an unmistakable and overt act of abandonment." The court distinguished between gain and loss situations. "The weight given to various factors must depend on the economic realities of the situation. For instance, when a taxpayer seeks to take a beneficial [loss] deduction because of an abandonment, an affirmative act on the part of the taxpayer is entitled to great weight because it provides some objective measure of the taxpayer's intent. On the other hand, when the abandonment will result in the recognition of income, the taxpayer's unilateral activity is entitled to less weight because it might well be motivated by a desire to postpone the recognition of income. The proper test is whether, under the facts and circumstances, it is clear for all practical purposes that the taxpayer will not retain the property; an overt act of abandonment by the taxpayer is not necessary." The court concluded:

> The Tax Court was not clearly erroneous in its determination that L & C Springs had abandoned the property in 1990. L & C Springs had failed to make a balloon payment, had failed to claim any rental income from the property as of November 1, 1990, and had not paid its property taxes. Given that the land had not produced a profit in many years, it was extremely unlikely that L & C Springs would concern itself with the extinguishment of its leasehold interest. . . . The later passage of legal title by foreclosure sale was a mere formality. In these respects, this case is similar to *Cozzi*, 88 T.C. at 445–48, in which the Tax Court held that abandonment occurred when it was clear that a venture would not turn a profit and the taxpayer made no effort toward payment of a debt; a later formal agreement extinguishing the taxpayer's interest did not establish the time of abandonment.

Another example where taxing gain is obviously necessary when the property is abandoned is the case of a taxpayer with appreciated property who borrows cash, pledging the property as security. For example, assume a taxpayer owns stock with a $50,000 basis but a much higher value (at least $150,000). He then borrows $150,000 cash from a bank, pledging the stock as security. The cash is available in this case for any purpose, not just to buy the property (it is not a purchase-money debt). When the property declines in value to $130,000, still subject to the $150,000 debt, the taxpayer abandons the property to the bank. There is $150,000 amount realized and $100,000 taxable gain. *Woodsam Assocs., Inc. v. Commissioner*, 198 F.2d 357 (2d Cir. 1952).

4. **Property value less than unpaid debt.** For some time, there was doubt about whether amount realized included unpaid debt when the value of the property was *less* than nonrecourse debt at the time of gift or abandonment. *See* footnote 37 in the *Crane* case. This *Crane* footnote was based on a failure to understand the similarity between a discharge of indebtedness and a situation in which deductions exceed out-of-pocket investment. Thus, a taxpayer who takes a $10,000 deduction and pays only $8,000 should have $2,000 gain, even if the property is worthless at a later date. The Court revisited this issue in *Commissioner v. Tufts*, 461 U.S. 300 (1983), and got it right. Amount realized includes unpaid debt regardless of the value of the

property at the time the property is disposed of.

As a practical matter the government still has trouble finding the taxpayer who gives or abandons property that has declined in value. The law is clear but taxpayers often "forget" to report the gain, especially when no cash changes hands. Consequently, business creditors with a security interest in property must now report receipt or abandonment of the property, so that unpaid debt will not go unreported. **§ 6050J.**

5. **Discharge of indebtedness vs. sales income.** There is another issue to consider. When the taxpayer disposes of property secured by unpaid debt, should the income be gain from the sale or exchange of the property, or should it be discharge of indebtedness income under § 108? Which is better for the taxpayer or government — discharge of indebtedness income (remember the possibility of a § 108 election to defer tax), or sale or exchange treatment (remember the difference between capital gains and ordinary "recapture" income; and the possibility that there might be a loss on the sale or exchange, which might or might not be deductible)? In other words — you cannot generalize about whether a sale or discharge of debt is better without more information regarding the facts of the particular case.

The rules applicable to the taxation of the disposition of property secured by unpaid debt can be illustrated by this example. Assume an unpaid debt of $182,000; the value of the asset is $179,000 and basis is $180,000. *See* **Treas. Reg. § 1.1002.**

a. *If the taxpayer is not personally liable on the debt (nonrecourse debt)*, the unpaid debt is an amount realized on a sale of the asset and all gain is from sale of the property ($2,000 in this example), not discharge of indebtedness income. Rev. Rul. 76-111, 1976-1 C.B. 214; **§ 7701(g)** (fair market value treated as not less than nonrecourse debt to which the property is subject). This result often occurs on release of the property to a creditor-bank. The same result follows if the property is transferred to a third party who assumes or pays the debt in a transaction in which the creditor-bank also releases the debt. *2925 Briarpark, Ltd. v. Commissioner*, 163 F.3d 313 (5th Cir. 1999).

b. *If the taxpayer is personally liable (recourse debt)*, the answer is more complex. In the usual case, the property is released to the creditor (whether through foreclosure sale or otherwise) and the debt is forgiven. **Treas. Reg. § 1.1001-2(c) (example 8).** In that case, any gain resulting from the excess of unpaid debt over the value of the property is discharge of indebtedness income ($3,000 in the prior example — debt of $182,000 minus $179,000 of value). Then compute gain or loss from the sale of the asset, based on the difference between the value and basis (a loss of $1,000 in the example — $180,000 basis minus $179,000 value). The net result is still $2,000 gain, as it was in the nonrecourse example. However, it is divided differently — there is $3,000 discharge of indebtedness income minus a $1,000 loss, assuming the loss is deductible.

Is there any reason why the recourse and nonrecourse examples should be treated differently? The Court in *Commissioner v. Tufts*, 461 U.S. 300 (1983), acknowledged that the nonrecourse loan case should be treated like the personal liability case, but acquiesced in the government's treatment of the entire gain as gain on the sale of the asset ($2,000 in the example) when the debt is nonrecourse.

What happens if the debtor remains personally liable after the creditor takes the property? Does that postpone discharge of indebtedness income ($3,000 in the example)? The answer should turn on whether the debtor is likely to discharge his personal liability and the answer to that question should be "no." **Section 357(d)(1)(A)** does *not* postpone discharge of indebtedness income for a personally liable debtor under a limited set of circumstances involving corporate tax law, but the same principle ought to apply across-the-board.

But see Aizawa v. Commissioner, 99 T.C. 197 (1992), *affirmed in unpublished opinion*, 29 F.3d 630 (9th Cir. 1994). In *Aizawa*, the court held that, if the debtor remained personally liable after release of the property to the creditor, the discharge of indebtedness income based on the difference between the debt and the value of the property is *held in suspense* to see if the debtor will pay the debt in the future. This means that the taxpayer, in the example, takes a $1,000 loss and waits to see if he must report $3,000 of discharge of indebtedness income in the future. What chance is there that the debtor will report the discharge of indebtedness income, if the debt is not repaid? *See* Wolfman, *Foreclosure Sales and Recourse Debt*, 78 Tax Notes 221 (1998) (criticizing *Aizawa* decision).

[B]   Note on Statutory Interpretation — Dictionaries and Statutory Structure

The *Crane* case is awash in statutory interpretation issues — necessary to determine the meaning of the word "property." That word had to be defined because inherited property has a basis equal to "the fair market value of such property at the time of such acquisition," and the *Crane* taxpayer had inherited the property subject to the debt.

First, the Court looked at the dictionary. The dictionary is not usually a very good way to determine the meaning of a statutory term because it defines words out of context. It gives you possible meanings of a word but does not help you understand how the language is used in the broader linguistic and policy context of the legislation. If it made sense to define "property" as "equity" (value minus debt), surely the Court would have reached that conclusion, whatever the dictionary said.

Second, the Court cited the agency Regulation to support the view that basis included debt. The decision was long before the *Chevron* case but, when the statute is unclear, it makes sense to rely on the agency's Regulations. *See* Chapter 6.02[A].

Third, the Court also noted that, because the "relevant statutory provision has been repeatedly reenacted since [the adoption of the agency's Regulation] in substantially the same form, the [Regulation] may itself now be considered to have the force of law." The reenactment doctrine was criticized in Chapter 3.06[A][2][b], on the ground that legislative reenactment is often weak evidence of an intent to ratify an intervening interpretation.

Fourth, the Court took note of the administrative implications of *not* including debt in basis — specifically, the problem of a changing basis as debt is paid off. Now the Court is, sensibly, interpreting the statute in light of the policy implications of various approaches. As I suggested earlier, there is a solution to this problem but it is not a solution that the Court would feel comfortable adopting on its own, without agency support. (The problem of negative basis that the Court raises is not a problem at all. We have had negative numbers at least since Descartes. Most people today can compute gain in the following situation — amount realized is +10; basis is -10; +10 minus -10 = + 20).

What is missing from the opinion is a clear explanation of why the structure of the tax code requires including unpaid debt in basis even when the taxpayer is not personally liable. The answer is that the taxpayer is as likely to pay the debt as when he is personally liable, so that it makes sense to accrue the debt into basis and allow that basis to be used for depreciation and other deductions prior to actual repayment of the debt. At least it makes sense if the taxpayer is really likely to pay the debt. We will soon see an example where the taxpayer is not likely to pay the debt — where the value of the property is much less than the debt at the time the property is acquired and the taxpayer is not personally liable. The Court's failure to focus on this structural explanation for why basis includes unpaid debt is a major weakness in the opinion's effort to interpret the statute.

The most sensible part of the opinion is the conclusion that, once basis includes debt, amount realized must include unpaid debt. The Court stated: "Quite obviously, the word 'property,' used here with reference to a sale, must mean 'property' in the same ordinary sense intended by the use of the word with reference to acquisition and depreciation, . . . because the functional relation of the two sections requires that the word mean the same in one section that it does in the other. If the 'property' to be valued on the date of acquisition is the property free of liens, the 'property' to be priced on a subsequent sale must be the same thing." This "functional" symmetry produces the right statutory structure, because it prevents the permanent deduction of debt that will never be repaid — as explained earlier. You do not need the dictionary to get this answer.

§ 17.02 CRITIQUE OF INCLUDING BORROWED FUNDS IN BASIS

[A] Tax Exempt Bond Analogy

A taxpayer who deducts investments financed with loans gets the best of two worlds. The investment is eligible for the tax breaks that reduce the tax on savings (such as accelerated depreciation, expensing, or an investment tax credit). At the same time the interest is deductible. Recall the earlier discussion in Chapter 3.03[B], which explained how deducting savings (of which accelerated depreciation and expensing are examples) is like taxing the savings but exempting the income. In effect, some portion of the investment is analogous to buying tax exempt bonds. And yet interest on the loan to acquire that investment is deductible, a result that is denied in the tax exempt bond situation under § 265(a)(2).

You can understand this point by the following example. First, assume a taxpayer who invests $500, at a 10% rate of return, for one year. The $500 is expensed for tax purposes even though it has value beyond the year. In year 2, the taxpayer collects $550. The tax rate in all years is 28%. The after tax-income in year 2 is $396 (72% of $550). Notice that this is the equivalent of taxing the $500 in year 1, investing $360 after-tax (.72 times 500), and keeping the 10% return of $36 tax free.

Now assume that the taxpayer made this investment by borrowing $360 of its purchase price, with a 10% interest charge. Still, the entire $500 deduction is allowed, producing the equivalent of a $360 investment earning 10% tax free. But the interest on the $360 loan to produce this "exempt" income is deductible!

[B]   Tax Shelter Computations

Tax shelter materials (especially the computations) are rough going for everyone, not just law students. Tax shelter promoters count on people not understanding too much about what goes into a tax shelter, thereby discouraging efforts at tax reform. The reason for spending some time on this material in an introductory course is that an educated bar is essential to such efforts.

A mechanical but complete way of looking at the tax advantages of including debt in basis is to compute the rate of return that the taxpayer gets on his out-of-pocket investment when he borrows. For example, if a taxpayer invests $20,000 out-of-pocket and borrows $80,000 to invest a total of $100,000 in a business, his real concern is whether the return on the $20,000 in future years is a good rate of return. The following summary of factors will help you understand how that rate of return would be computed. It explains what goes into a tax shelter. You should pay close attention to whether the factors are tax rules or financial facts that exist independently of the tax rules. It is too common to focus on the desirable tax results without paying attention to the financial facts that might make the investment unwise, despite the tax advantages. Factors 1–5 deal with annual cash flows. Factors 6–7 deal with disposing of the property.

First, what is the gross income from the venture? This is a financial fact.

Second, what cash payments must be made each year? This is also a financial fact. The taxpayer might have expenses unrelated to debt, such as maintenance costs for the property. However, many tax shelters involve a taxpayer who owns property and leases it to a tenant; and, in a lease transaction, the tenant is often responsible for these costs (referred to as a "net lease"). The investor is likely to be a lawyer or doctor who never sees the property and does not want responsibility for managing it. The most significant payments by the taxpayer are for principal and interest on the debt. The period over which the debt will be paid determines how much principal and interest will be paid each year. If the payments in the early years are mostly interest (something that will look good to the taxpayer because the interest is deductible), the taxpayer must remember that he may have to raise money in the future to repay the debt. Sometimes all the payments in the early years are interest and the principal must be repaid in one year in the future (a balloon payment). Frequently, the debt and interest payments equal the gross income from the property.

Third, the tax deductions and credits must be computed for every year of the investment. If the investment is eligible for an investment credit, that usually has the effect of reducing the amount of out-of-pocket investment the taxpayer must incur. It may also reduce basis. The rate at which basis can be deducted must also be computed. This requires determining depreciation and amortization rates and deciding whether outlays can be expensed rather than capitalized. Every legal question you have encountered involving depreciation and amortization rates and the distinction between capital expenditures and current expenses becomes important at this point. To the extent that the tax deductions exceed the income from the venture, the sheltering effect comes into play and the taxpayer increases cash flow in the form of reduced taxes on other income.

In the early years of the venture there will be net operating losses. Most debts are paid off in level payments, with the interest being a large portion of the payment in the early years. Thus, repayment of an $80,000 debt will consist of a very small amount of debt repayment in the early years, with most of the payment being interest. However, the basis for depreciation deductions will include the full $80,000, and will be much more than the principal payments on the debt. Interest plus depreciation deductions will therefore exceed the gross income from the venture.

Fourth, the tax rate must be estimated. The value of the tax shelter usually depends on net losses being deducted from other income, the value of which depends on the tax rate.

Fifth, in the later years, the tax deductions will decline, as the depreciation is used up, and the taxable income from the venture becomes positive. The point in time when this occurs is usually called the crossover point. At that time the taxpayer must pay tax, often resulting in a negative cash flow. The debt payments are probably continuing unabated and the taxpayer must consider how to get the money to pay the tax. One way to deal with this possibility is to subtract from the earlier positive cash flow a sum of money (a sinking fund) and put it in a bank where it will accumulate interest sufficient to pay off the obligations that might arise in the future. For financial planning purposes, this sum of money is generally treated as a reduction of the positive cash flows in the early years of the tax shelter and reduces the net cash flow in those years.

Sixth, the taxpayer must think about the possibility that he will want to get out of the venture, often at the crossover point. In this connection, he must consider how easily he can sell the property. He must also consider what the value of the property is likely to be. Both of these facts are financial facts, not tax facts. If the value is high enough, he might sell the property and get cash over and above any unpaid debt. If the property has gone down in value, the taxpayer must worry about whether the debt is recourse or nonrecourse. If it is recourse, he must find the money to repay the debt unless the buyer will assume the debt. If the debt is nonrecourse, however, he can walk away from the property and let the creditor worry about collecting the debt out of the value of the property. It is too common for investors in tax shelters not to worry about the future, because they are blinded by the sheltering effects of the early deductions. In fact, the economic projections for a tax shelter may assume optimistic future values, without which the investment would be unwise.

Seventh, the tax consequences of disposition must also be considered. Any disposition (including a gift) triggers realization of unpaid debt as an amount realized. The government suspects that many taxpayers never report this amount. The tax treatment of the gain is also important. If recapture rules apply, converting capital gain to ordinary income, a great deal of the gain will be ordinary income.

A complex example in Chapter 17.07 (an Appendix to this chapter) illustrates how an investment in residential rental real estate might provide a tax shelter. Even without working out the numbers, however, it is apparent that certain changes in the tax law would reduce or increase the after-tax rate of return. The rate of return is reduced by: (1) slower depreciation; (2) a lower tax bracket; and (3) ending the preferential tax on capital gains at the time of disposition. The rate of return is increased by: (1) faster depreciation or expensing; and (2) a higher tax rate (because the value of a deduction increases).

[C]   Policy Concerns Specific to Tax Shelter Borrowing

There are several reasons why borrowing to make tax shelter investments might pose more serious policy concerns than borrowing for other activities.

1. The investments might not be economically desirable. Congress probably adopted many of the tax incentives, such as accelerated depreciation and credits, without expecting borrowers to package the tax breaks to produce unexpectedly large total benefits for activities producing a low economic return.

2. High-bracket borrowers might buy up property from those who cannot use the tax breaks. They do this because they are able to use the deductions and credits to offset not only the income from the activity financed with loans but also other income. They can, in other words, shelter other income, such as personal service and investment income with tax losses from the activity. This may cause a shift of ownership to urban dwellers, such as lawyers, doctors, and others who know little about the business in which they invest.

3. The investor is not taking much risk. Tax shelter borrowing is often nonrecourse so the creditor can foreclose only on property used as security, not other investments that the taxpayer may own. This is likely to produce a lot of excess speculation in property with low economic returns.

4. Another way to think about the tax shelter is that the ability to shelter income with the deductible loan allows the individual taxpayer to use the tax sheltered money for personal consumption purposes. In effect, the taxpayer is borrowing for personal consumption. It is true that taxpayers can usually borrow for personal consumption without current tax, but the typical consumer loan is usually short-term. The time gap between tax shelter borrowing and repayment might be quite large. Moreover, a lot of consumer interest is not deductible anymore and it would be anomalous to allow consumer interest to be deductible through a tax shelter vehicle.

These criticisms have not led Congress to prevent debt (not even nonrecourse debt) from being included in basis, but they have provided political support for modifications in the law applicable to investments generally — the slowing down of depreciation, cutting back on expensing, and requiring certain costs to be capitalized. Criticism of tax shelters is also sometimes used to justify lower tax rates, which reduce the tax break from deductions.

Congress has, moreover, responded specifically to the tax shelter problem in two ways — limiting the deductibility of net losses (1) created by nonrecourse debt, and (2) when the taxpayer does not materially participate in the business activity. These legislative provisions are discussed in Chapter 17.05. But first we turn our attention in Chapters 17.03 and 17.04 to several judicial doctrines (*not* explicit statutory rules) that directly limit the inclusion of debt in basis.

§ 17.03   DEBT NOT INCLUDED IN BASIS

The *Crane* case assumed that the taxpayer had a real financial commitment equal to the debt. Even if the debtor was not personally liable, the opportunity to acquire equity in the property, eventually ripening into full ownership, would result in payment of the debt. There was no hint in *Crane* that the debt was artificially inflated to exceed the value of the property. Nor was the debt contingent. Inflated or contingent debt provides insufficient likelihood of payment to justify inclusion in basis, as this section explains.

[A]   Contingent Debt

"Contingent debt" is not included in basis, even after *Crane*. "[N]o amount is to be included in cost with respect to those obligations which are so contingent and indefinite that they are not susceptible to present valuation, until such time as they become fixed and absolute and capable of determination with reasonable accuracy." Rev. Rul. 55-675, 1955-2 C.B. 567. In *Gibson Products Co. v. United States*, 460 F. Supp. 1109 (N.D. Tex. 1978), *affirmed*, 637 F.2d 1041 (5th Cir. 1981), the court summarized the cases dealing with contingent debt, as follows: "These cases hold that an obligation, which is too contingent and speculative, should not be included in cost basis, irrespective of the possible application of the *Crane* doctrine. In a sense, the nature of the inquiry is similar to the all-events test used for accrual tax accounting purposes, although none of the above-cited cases make reference to that test." *See also Redford v. Commissioner*, 28 T.C. 773 (1957) (purchaser agreed to pay the lesser of $25,000 or one-half of the profits from the resale of the purchased land; the obligation could not be included in basis).

[B]   Value Less Than Nonrecourse Debt

ESTATE OF FRANKLIN v. COMMISSIONER
United States Court of Appeals, Ninth Circuit
544 F.2d 1045 (9th Cir. 1976)

SNEED, CIRCUIT JUDGE: . . .

[Editor — In order to understand what the taxpayer was trying to do in this case, keep in mind that partners are able to deduct the losses incurred by a partnership in the year they arise. In other words, a partnership is a pass-through tax entity, unlike the typical corporation. Also keep in mind that the transaction is a two-party transaction, in which the seller is the creditor (not an independent third-party such as a bank or insurance company), and in which the buyer immediately leases the purchased property back to the seller. A later section discusses three-party transactions.]

This case involves another effort on the part of the Commissioner to curb the use of real estate tax shelters. In this instance he seeks to disallow deductions for the taxpayers' distributive share of losses reported by a limited partnership with respect to its acquisition of a motel and related property. These "losses" have their origin in deductions for depreciation and interest claimed with respect to the motel and related property. These deductions were disallowed by the Commissioner on the ground either that the acquisition was a sham or that the entire acquisition transaction was in substance the purchase by the partnership of an option to acquire the motel and related property on January 15, 1979. The Tax Court held that the transaction constituted an option exercisable in 1979 and disallowed the taxpayers' deductions. We affirm this disallowance although our approach differs somewhat from that of the Tax Court.

The interest and depreciation deductions were taken by Twenty-Fourth Property Associates (hereinafter referred to as Associates), a California limited partnership of which Charles T. Franklin and seven other doctors were the limited partners. The deductions flowed from the purported "purchase" by Associates of the Thunderbird Inn, an Arizona motel, from Wayne L. Romney and Joan E. Romney (hereinafter referred to as the Romneys) on November 15, 1968.

Under a document entitled "Sales Agreement," the Romneys agreed to "sell" the Thunderbird Inn to Associates for $1,224,000. The property would be paid for over a period of ten years, with interest on any unpaid balance of seven and one-half percent per annum. "Prepaid interest" in the amount of $75,000 was payable immediately; monthly principal and interest installments of $9,045.36 would be paid for approximately the first ten years, with Associates required to make a balloon payment at the end of the ten years of the difference between the remaining purchase price, forecast as $975,000, and any mortgages then outstanding against the property.

The purchase obligation of Associates to the Romneys was nonrecourse; the Romneys' only remedy in the event of default would be forfeiture of the partnership's interest. The sales agreement was recorded in the local county. A warranty deed was placed in an escrow account, along with a quitclaim deed from Associates to the Romneys, both documents to be delivered either to Associates upon full payment of the purchase price, or to the Romneys upon default.

The sale was combined with a leaseback of the property by Associates to the Romneys; Associates therefore never took physical possession. The lease payments were designed to approximate closely the principal and interest payments with the consequence that with the exception of the $75,000 prepaid interest payment no cash would cross between Associates and Romneys until the balloon payment. The lease was on a net basis; thus, the Romneys were responsible for all of the typical expenses of owning the motel property including all utility costs, taxes, assessments, rents, charges, and levies of "every name, nature and kind whatsoever." The Romneys also were to continue to be responsible for the first and second mortgages until the final purchase installment was made; the Romneys could, and indeed did, place additional mortgages on the property without the permission of Associates. Finally, the Romneys were allowed to propose new capital improvements which Associates would be required to either build themselves or allow the Romneys to construct with compensating modifications in rent or purchase price.

In holding that the transaction between Associates and the Romneys more nearly resembled an option than a sale, the Tax Court emphasized that Associates had the power at the end of ten years to walk away from the transaction and merely lose its $75,000 "prepaid interest payment." It also pointed out that a deed was never recorded and that the "benefits and burdens of ownership" appeared to remain with the Romneys. Thus, the sale was combined with a leaseback in which no cash would pass; the Romneys remained responsible under the mortgages, which they could increase; and the Romneys could make capital improvements. The Tax Court further justified its "option" characterization by reference to the nonrecourse nature of the purchase money debt and the nice balance between the rental and purchase money payments.

Our emphasis is different from that of the Tax Court. We believe the characteristics set out above can exist in a situation in which the sale imposes upon the purchaser a genuine indebtedness within the meaning of section 167(a), Internal Revenue Code of 1954, which will support both interest and depreciation deductions. . . .

In none of [the cases establishing a genuine indebtedness], however, did the taxpayer fail to demonstrate that the purchase price was at least approximately equivalent to the fair market value of the property. Just such a failure occurred here. The Tax Court explicitly found that on the basis of the facts before it the value of the property could not be estimated.[2] In our view this defect in the taxpayers' proof is fatal. [Editor — The seller in this case was the creditor. That is why the debt exceeded the value of the property. A third-party lender, such as a bank, is unlikely to lend more than value.]

Reason supports our perception. An acquisition such as that of Associates if at a price approximately equal to the fair market value of the property under ordinary circumstances would rather quickly yield an equity in the property which the purchaser could not prudently abandon. This is the stuff of substance. It meshes with the form of the transaction and constitutes a sale.

No such meshing occurs when the purchase price exceeds a demonstrably reasonable estimate of the fair market value. Payments on the principal of the purchase price yield no equity so long as the unpaid balance of the purchase price

---

[2] [4] The Tax Court found that appellants had "not shown that the purported sales price of $1,224,000 (or any other price) had any relationship to the actual market value of the motel property . . . . Petitioners spent a substantial amount of time at trial attempting to establish that, whatever the actual market value of the property, Associates acted in the good faith *belief* that the market value of the property approximated the selling price. However, this evidence only goes to the issue of sham and does not supply substance to this transaction. . . .

exceeds the then existing fair market value. Under these circumstances the purchaser by abandoning the transaction can lose no more than a mere chance to acquire an equity in the future should the value of the acquired property increase. While this chance undoubtedly influenced the Tax Court's determination that the transaction before us constitutes an option, we need only point out that its existence fails to supply the substance necessary to justify treating the transaction as a sale ab initio. It is not necessary to the disposition of this case to decide the tax consequences of a transaction such as that before us if in a subsequent year the fair market value of the property increases to an extent that permits the purchaser to acquire an equity.[3]

Authority also supports our perception. It is fundamental that "depreciation is not predicated upon ownership of property *but rather upon an investment in property*. In the transaction before us and during the taxable years in question the purchase price payments by Associates have not been shown to constitute an *investment in the property*. Depreciation was properly disallowed. Only the Romneys had an investment in the property.

Authority also supports disallowance of the interest deductions. This is said even though it has long been recognized that the absence of personal liability for the purchase money debt secured by a mortgage on the acquired property does not deprive the debt of its character as a bona fide debt obligation able to support an interest deduction. However, this is no longer true when it appears that the debt has economic significance only if the property substantially appreciates in value prior to the date at which a very large portion of the purchase price is to be discharged. Under these circumstances the purchaser has not secured "the use or forbearance of money." Nor has the seller advanced money or forborne its use. Prior to the date at which the balloon payment on the purchase price is required, and assuming no substantial increase in the fair market value of the property, the absence of personal liability on the debt reduces the transaction in economic terms to a mere chance that a genuine debt obligation may arise. This is not enough to justify an interest deduction. To justify the deduction the debt must exist; potential existence will not do. For debt to exist, the purchaser, in the absence of personal liability, must confront a situation in which it is presently reasonable from an economic point of view for him to make a capital investment in the amount of the unpaid purchase price. Associates during the taxable years in question, confronted no such situation. *Compare Crane v. Commissioner*, 331 U.S. 1 (1947).

Our focus on the relationship of the fair market value of the property to the unpaid purchase price should not be read as premised upon the belief that a sale is not a sale if the purchaser pays too much. Bad bargains from the buyer's point of view — as well as sensible bargains from buyer's, but exceptionally good from the seller's point of view — do not thereby cease to be sales. We intend our holding and explanation thereof to be understood as limited to transactions substantially similar to that now before us.

---

[3] [5] These consequences would include a determination of the proper basis of the acquired property at the date the increments to the purchaser's equity commenced.

COMMENTS AND QUESTIONS

1. *Estate of Franklin* does not technically decide whether some value *less* than the nonrecourse debt could be included in basis when the asset is purchased. In *Pleasant Summit Land Corp. v. Commissioner*, 863 F.2d 263 (3d Cir. 1988), the court held that the *value* of the property could be included in basis, where the nonrecourse debt exceeded value. The court reasoned that the taxpayer would be likely to pay off *that amount* to prevent the creditor from foreclosing. The government objected that this created significant valuation problems. And, indeed, most courts have disagreed with *Pleasant Summit* and have not allowed the taxpayer to include in basis any of the unpaid debt in an *Estate of Franklin* situation — that is, whenever unpaid nonrecourse debt is much greater than the purchased asset's value. *See Bergstrom v. United States*, 37 Fed. Cl. 164 (1996).

Evaluate the following critique of *Pleasant Summit*. *First*, if the taxpayer wants the property, he would be willing to pay its value. But does he want it? If not, we cannot be confident that even the property's value will be paid. Taxpayers who incur nonrecourse debt far in excess of value are after the tax breaks, not the property. Often, there is a balloon payment obligation (the debt is due only after 10 or 20 years). This is very different from nonrecourse buyers whose debt is *less* than value in a typical commercial purchase; these buyers want the property and will pay the debt. *Second*, it is hard to know what the value is. Why should the taxpayer be allowed to create difficult valuation problems for the government when the debt is much greater than value?

2. If basis does *not* include nonrecourse debt *or* value at the time of purchase, what if value later exceeds unpaid debt (an issue the court in *Estate of Franklin* explicitly leaves open) — e.g., either because debt is paid or value increases? Do you suddenly include the remaining unpaid debt in basis for the future?

3. If basis does not include debt or value, because unpaid debt far exceeds value, how should the taxpayer treat the annual debt payments that are in fact made? In *Estate of Franklin*, the borrower leased the property back to the seller for rent, and the buyer-borrower's "debt" and "interest" payments equaled the rent received. It was a financial washout. Shouldn't the tax law recognize these events as a washout by permitting a deduction of the "debt" and "interest" payments from the rent? On what theory — are they depreciation? *Cf. Holden Fuel Oil Co. v. Commissioner*, 479 F.2d 613, 616 (6th Cir. 1973) (depreciation based on annual payments made to purchase a customer list); **Treas. Reg. § 1.167(a)-14(c)(4)** (annual payment to purchase a copyright equals depreciation deduction).

§ 17.04 TAX OWNERSHIP

You have read the Court of Appeals decision in *Estate of Franklin*, which emphasized that the unpaid debt far exceeded the asset's value. The Tax Court had relied on a different theory to prevent including the unpaid debt in basis — that the taxpayer was not the tax owner of the property. The taxpayer was instead like the holder of an option to buy the property. If the taxpayer thought the investment was a good one, the "debt" would be paid and the property would then (and only then) belong to the taxpayer.

The material in this section discusses the concept of "tax ownership" — when a taxpayer is treated as the owner for tax purposes, whether or not he is the owner under state law. This inquiry is related to the question asked frequently in this course — when is a state law relationship recognized for tax purposes (e.g., what does "marriage" mean in the tax law)?

[A]   In General

The issue usually arises when three-party sale-leasebacks are used to finance construction of buildings or other property. The cast of characters includes an outside party who is the lender (often a bank or insurance company). The other two key players are the buyer and seller of the property. The buyer (who is the taxpayer) borrows money to buy the property and then leases the property to the seller — hence the phrase "sale-leaseback." Or at least that is how the parties want the transaction to be viewed for tax purposes.

In fact, the "buyer" may have little to gain from the transaction, other than tax breaks. The seller is very much like a borrower who obtains a loan to finance the construction. When the "seller" becomes a tenant, by taking back a lease from the buyer, the rent is like the principal and interest on the loan. The issue in these cases is whether the "seller" should be treated as the borrower and owner of the property, instead of the buyer.

The seller-tenant would probably have preferred to borrow directly and own the property. The seller-tenant is, however, unable to use the tax breaks (such as accelerated depreciation), or at least cannot use them as advantageously as the "buyer." The seller-tenant may already have net operating losses or be in a lower tax bracket than the buyer. So a "middleman" becomes the buyer, uses the tax breaks, and compensates the "seller-tenant" in some way — often through a lower rent charge.

The case law usually relies on the following criteria to decide whether the "middleman" is in fact the tax owner of the property.

1. Is the taxpayer a typical individual tax shelter investor who is trying to shelter otherwise taxable income so it is available for personal consumption?

2. Did the taxpayer invest a significant amount of money, and, if so, for what purpose was that money spent?

3. How likely is it that the taxpayer will own the property at the end of the lease period and thereby enjoy any increase in the property's economic value? In this connection, note whether the tenant has an option to purchase the property when the lease expires and whether the option price is low enough to make a purchase a virtual certainty.

[B]   Cases

In the following two cases, the taxpayer wins in *Frank Lyon Co.* and loses in *Hilton*. The decisions turn on a multi-factor analysis, where the weight of the factors is unclear and the application of the factors is very sensitive to the fact situations. What factors helped the taxpayer win in *Frank Lyon* and lose in *Hilton*?

FRANK LYON CO. v. UNITED STATES
United States Supreme Court
435 U.S. 561 (1978)

Mr. Justice Blackmun delivered the opinion of the court.

[Editor — Here is an abbreviated statement of the facts. Lyon (the taxpayer) is a closely held corporation. Worthen is a bank that wants a building for its offices. Frank Lyon is a majority shareholder in Lyon and serves on Worthen's board of directors. Federal regulations did not allow Worthen to invest directly in a new bank building. The deal to construct the building took shape in accordance with the State Bank Department's requirement that Worthen have an option to buy the building at the end of the fifteenth year of the lease and the Federal Reserve Board's requirement that the building be owned by an independent third party. It was arranged for Worthen to construct and Lyon to acquire the building and lease it to Worthen on a net lease basis. In a net lease, the tenant is responsible for all expenses related to the property such as insurance, taxes, and repairs. City Bank, first, and then New York Life Insurance Company would provide $7,140,000 to finance the construction and acquisition of the building. Lyon also paid $500,000 of its own funds to implement this plan. Lyon originally offered Worthen a reduced rental obligation. However, eventually it was agreed that the rent would be higher than this offer but that Lyon would pay more interest to Worthen on an unrelated loan from Worthen to Lyon.

[The primary term of the lease was 25 years. Rental payments from Worthen equaled the debt and interest due to the New York Life Insurance Company. Lyon was personally liable on the $7,140,000 debt. After 25 years Worthen could renew the lease for eight five-year terms, at $300,000 rent per year. The land on which the building sat was owned by Worthen and was rented to Lyon for 75 years, which was 10 years longer than the building lease period could run if all options to renew were exercised. The rent for the land (called "ground rent") was negligible for the first 25 years but substantial thereafter, except that it declined to $10,000 for the last 10 years. The net payments to Lyon resulting from any lease renewals after the first 25 years (equal to the building rent minus ground rent) were calculated to approximate payment to Lyon of the $500,000 it had invested plus 6% compound interest. Worthen had options to buy the building at 11, 15, 20, and 25 years after entry into the lease, with the price set to assure payment of the insurance company's loan and Lyon's $500,000 with 6% compound interest. The District Court found as a fact that the option prices were the negotiated estimate by the parties of the fair market value of the building at the option dates and that they were reasonable.]

. . . [T]he Government takes the position that the Worthen-Lyon transaction in its entirety should be regarded as a sham. The agreement as a whole, it is said, was only an elaborate financing scheme designed to provide economic benefits to Worthen and a guaranteed return to Lyon. The latter was but a conduit used to forward the mortgage payments, made under the guise of rent paid by Worthen to Lyon, on to New York Life as mortgagee. This, the Government claims, is the true substance of the transaction as viewed under the microscope of the tax laws. Although the arrangement was cast in sale-and-leaseback form, in substance it was only a financing transaction, and the terms of the repurchase options and lease renewals so indicate. It is said that Worthen could reacquire the building simply by satisfying the mortgage debt and paying Lyon its $500,000 advance plus interest, regardless of the fair market value of the building at the time; similarly, when the mortgage was paid off, Worthen could extend the lease at drastically reduced bargain rentals that likewise bore no relation to fair rental value but were simply calculated to pay Lyon its $500,000 plus interest over the extended term. Lyon's return on the arrangement in no event could exceed 6% compound interest (although the Government conceded it might well be less). Furthermore, the favorable option and lease renewal terms made it highly unlikely that Worthen would abandon the building after it in effect had "paid off" the mortgage. The Government implies that the arrangement was one of convenience which, if accepted on its face, would enable Worthen to deduct its payments to Lyon as rent and would allow Lyon to claim a deduction for depreciation, based on the cost of construction ultimately borne by Worthen, which Lyon could offset against other income, and to deduct mortgage interest that roughly would offset the inclusion of Worthen's rental payments in Lyon's income. If, however, the Government argues, the arrangement was only a financing transaction under which Worthen was the owner of the building, Worthen's payments would be deductible only to the extent that they represented mortgage interest, and Worthen would be entitled to claim depreciation; Lyon would not be entitled to deductions for either mortgage interest or depreciation and it would not have to include Worthen's "rent" payments in its income because its function with respect to those payments was that of a conduit between Worthen and New York Life. . . .

There is no simple device available to peel away the form of this transaction and to reveal its substance. The effects of the transaction on all the parties were obviously different from those that would have resulted had Worthen been able simply to make a mortgage agreement with New York Life and to receive a $500,000 loan from Lyon. . . .

[M]ost significantly, it was Lyon alone, and not Worthen, who was liable on the notes, first to City Bank, and then to New York Life. Despite the facts that Worthen had agreed to pay rent and that this rent equaled the amounts due from Lyon to New York Life, should anything go awry in the later years of the lease, Lyon was primarily liable. No matter how the transaction could have been devised otherwise, it remains a fact that as the agreements were placed in final form, the obligation on the notes fell squarely on Lyon. Lyon, an ongoing enterprise, exposed its very business well-being to this real and substantial risk.

The effect of this liability on Lyon is not just the abstract possibility that something will go wrong and that Worthen will not be able to make its payments. Lyon has disclosed this liability on its balance sheet for all the world to see. Its financial position was affected substantially by the presence of this long-term debt, despite the offsetting presence of the building as an asset. To the extent that Lyon has used its capital in this transaction, it is less able to obtain financing for other business needs. . . .

[Editor — The Court then discussed the government's treatment of Lyon's $500,000 investment as a loan which accrued original issue discount during the

11-year period prior to the first date on which Worthen could exercise an acquisition option. The original issue discount was computed on the assumption that the option price equaled the redemption price of the loan. The Court noted that there is no legal obligation between Lyon and Worthen representing the $500,000 "loan" extended under the Government's theory. And the assumed 6% return on this putative loan — required by the audit to be recognized in the taxable year in question — will be realized only when and if Worthen exercises its options.]

It is not inappropriate to note that the Government is likely to lose little revenue, if any, as a result of the shape given the transaction by the parties. No deduction was created that is not either matched by an item of income or that would not have been available to one of the parties if the transaction had been arranged differently. . . .

We recognize that the Government's position, and that taken by the Court of Appeals, is not without superficial appeal. One, indeed, may theorize that Frank Lyon's presence on the Worthen board of directors; Lyon's departure from its principal corporate activity into this unusual venture; the parallel between the payments under the building lease and the amounts due from Lyon on the New York Life mortgage; . . . the nature and presence of the several options available to Worthen; and the tax benefits, such as the use of double declining balance depreciation, that accrue to Lyon during the initial years of the arrangement, form the basis of an argument that Worthen should be regarded as the owner of the building and as the recipient of nothing more from Lyon than a $500,000 loan.

We however, as did the District Court, find this theorizing incompatible with the substance and economic realities of the transaction: . . . Worthen's undercapitalization; Worthen's consequent inability, as a matter of legal restraint, to carry its building plans into effect by a conventional mortgage and other borrowing; the additional barriers imposed by the state and federal regulators; the suggestion, forthcoming from the state regulator, that Worthen possess an option to purchase; the requirement, from the federal regulator, that the building be owned by an independent third party; the presence of several finance organizations seriously interested in participating in the transaction and in the resolution of Worthen's problem; the submission of formal proposals by several of those organizations; the bargaining process and period that ensued; the competitiveness of the bidding; the bona fide character of the negotiations; the three-party aspect of the transaction; Lyon's substantiality and its independence from Worthen; the fact that diversification was Lyon's principal motivation; Lyon's being liable alone on the successive notes to City Bank and New York Life; the reasonableness, as the District Court found, of the rentals and of the option prices; the substantiality of the purchase prices; Lyon's not being engaged generally in the business of financing; the presence of all building depreciation risks on Lyon; the risk borne by Lyon, that Worthen might default or fail, as other banks have failed; the facts that Worthen could "walk away" from the relationship at the end of the 25-year primary term, and probably would do so if the option price were more than the then-current worth of the building to Worthen; the inescapable fact that if the building lease were not extended, Lyon would be the full owner of the building, free to do with it as it chose; Lyon's liability for the substantial ground rent if Worthen decides not to exercise any of its options to extend; the absence of any understanding between Lyon and

Worthen that Worthen would exercise any of the purchase options; the nonfamily and nonprivate nature of the entire transaction; and the absence of any differential in tax rates and of special tax circumstances for one of the parties — all convince us that Lyon has far the better of the case.

In so concluding, we emphasize that we are not condoning manipulation by a taxpayer through arbitrary labels and dealings that have no economic significance. Such, however, has not happened in this case.

In short, we hold that where, as here, there is a genuine multiple-party transaction with economic substance which is compelled or encouraged by business or regulatory realities, is imbued with tax-independent considerations, and is not shaped solely by tax-avoidance features that have meaningless labels attached, the Government should honor the allocation of rights and duties effectuated by the parties. Expressed another way, so long as the lessor retains significant and genuine attributes of the traditional lessor status, the form of the transaction adopted by the parties governs for tax purposes. What those attributes are in any particular case will necessarily depend upon its facts. It suffices to say that, as here, a sale-and-leaseback, in and of itself, does not necessarily operate to deny a taxpayer's claim for deductions.

The judgment of the Court of Appeals, accordingly, is reversed.

————————

The taxpayer did not fare so well in *Hilton v. Commissioner*, 74 T.C. 305 (1980), *affirmed per curiam*, 671 F.2d 316 (9th Cir. 1982). In *Hilton*, Broadway constructed a department store with insurance company financing. The store was then sold to several limited partnerships, which leased the store back to Broadway, which ran the store.

The taxpayers were the partners who had invested $334,000 in the limited partnerships. Under partnership tax law, tax losses are passed through to partners. All of the partners' investment was used to pay the tax shelter promoters. The lease was a net lease. The lessee's rent during the first 30-year term was sufficient to pay 90% of the insurance company's nonrecourse construction loan. The remaining 10% was due at the end of the first 30-year term (hence the description "balloon payment"). Thereafter the lease could be renewed for consecutive terms of 23, 23, and 22 years. Rent under the first renewal term would more than cover any refinancing of the balloon payment.

The taxpayer's expert witness was unable to substantiate his claim that the department store would have a substantial residual value at the end of the various lease terms. It was also very likely that the tenant would renew the lease for one term (extending the 30-year term for another 23 years) because of the low rents. The court found that the taxpayers "would not at any time find it imprudent from an economic point of view to abandon the property."

The court, applying *Frank Lyon*, stated that "the transaction . . . will not stand or fall merely because it involved a sale-leaseback . . . , but rather must be tested to determine whether it (the transaction) (1) is genuinely multiple-party, (2) with economic substance, (3) compelled or encouraged by business realities (no "regulatory" realities are claimed), and (4) is imbued with tax-independent considerations which are not shaped solely by tax-avoidance features." The court added: "[W]e do not deem the existence of a net lease, a nonrecourse mortgage or rent during the initial lease term geared to the cost of interest and mortgage amortization to be, in and of themselves, much more than neutral commercial realities. Furthermore, the fact that the transaction was put together by an 'orchestrator' . . . would not alone prove fatal to the buyer-lessor's cause provided the result is economically meaningful on both sides of the equation."

The court concluded as follows:

Under the *Frank Lyon* test, petitioners must show not only that their participation in the sale-leaseback was not motivated or shaped solely by tax avoidance features that have meaningless labels attached, but also that there is economic substance to the transaction independent of the apparent tax shelter potential. Another way of stating the test is suggested by the Ninth Circuit's opinion in *Estate of Franklin v. Commissioner*, 544 F.2d 1045 (9th Cir. 1976), affg., 64 T.C. 752 (1975), to wit: Could the buyer-lessor's method of payment for the property be expected at the outset to rather quickly yield an equity which buyer-lessor could not prudently abandon? . . .

We recognize that the result in *Estate of Franklin* was predicated upon a finding that the purchase price of the property in question exceeded a demonstrably reasonable estimate of the fair market value. Nevertheless, we consider the imprudent abandonment test to be equally applicable to other fact patterns. For example, we find it appropriate to inquire, as we do in the instant case, whether the foreseeable value of the property *to the buyer-lessor* would ever make abandonment imprudent. This then requires an examination of the economics of the buyer-lessor's position to determine whether there has been, in fact, an investment in the property. . . .

[T]he potential sources of economic gain for the petitioners under the following categories:

(1) Net income or losses;

(2) Net proceeds resulting from: (a) mortgage refinancing; (b) condemnation; or (c) sale. . . .

. . . [W]e first address the following question: At what point, at what time, and under what conditions could it be presumed there would be net income to distribute, and in what amounts? Under the lease and deed of trust, all rent payments due under the lease for the first 30 years are to be used to service the mortgage notes, so no cash flow will be available to petitioners during the 30-year period. The lease rental is sufficient to amortize 90 percent of the principal amount of the mortgage notes, leaving $313,750 due in 1998.

At the end of the initial term of the lease, petitioners will have the option of either making capital contributions to cover the balloon payment or refinancing the balloon. Since there would be little incentive to do the former, in light of the rent provisions in the lease for subsequent option periods and the probability . . . that Broadway would continue its occupancy for 23 years (at least beyond 1998), it must be assumed that, if possible, refinancing will be sought.

Assuming refinancing at 5 1/8-percent interest (the rate in the original mortgage) over the 23-year period of the first lease extension, the annual financing cost would be approximately $23,000, to be paid out of the fixed rental of $47,062.50; thus leaving a total pre-tax cash flow for division among and distribution to all of the petitioners of approximately $23,000 per annum. It goes without saying that the opportunity to earn $23,000 annually, commencing 30 years from the inception of the transaction, would not in and of itself appear to justify the $334,000 original investment by the petitioners in the . . . partnerships.

The foregoing analysis assumes, of course, that Broadway would exercise its renewal option for the first 23-year period. Given the extremely favorable terms on which Broadway could renew, however, the only conceivable reason why it (or any corporate successor) would not renew would be that the property had lost its economic viability, in which event the property would also be worthless to the petitioners. . . .

We are, in summary, persuaded that an objective economic analysis of this transaction from the point of view of the buyer-lessor . . . should focus on the value of the cash flow derived from the rental payments and that little or no weight should be placed on the speculative possibility that the property will have a substantial residual value at such time, if ever, that Broadway abandons the lease. The low rents and almost nominal cash flow leave little room for doubt that, apart from tax benefits, the value of the interest acquired by the petitioners is substantially less than the amount they paid for it. In terms discussed above, the buyer-lessor would not at any time find it imprudent from an economic point of view to abandon the property. *Estate of Franklin v. Commissioner*, 544 F.2d 1045 (9th Cir. 1976), affg., 64 T.C. 752 (1975). There is thus no justification for the petitioners' participation in this transaction apart from its tax consequences.

Having so analyzed petitioners' lack of potential for economic gain, we must nevertheless confront the question of how petitioners' position differs, if it does, from that of the buyer-lessor in the *Frank Lyon* case. . . .

[Editor — The court distinguished *Frank Lyon* as follows: (1) The rent during the initial lease term was sufficient to completely amortize the underlying mortgage principal, whereas in the case before us, the rent will amortize only 90 percent of the note principal, leaving a sizable balloon at the end. (2) The rent in *Frank Lyon* was fair rental value for the property. . . . In the case before us, the rent is not based on fair rental value. . . . (3) The buyer-lessor in *Frank Lyon* paid $500,000 of its own funds to the seller-lessee; in the case before us none of petitioners' funds went to Broadway. (4) In *Frank Lyon*, the buyer-lessor stood to realize a substantial gain in the event the seller-lessee exercised its repurchase option; in the case before us, the petitioners cannot dispose of the property at a profit. (5) In *Frank Lyon*, the buyer-lessor was a substantial corporate entity which participated actively in negotiating the terms and conditions of the sale and leaseback, while in the instant case the entire "deal" was packaged as a financing transaction by the orchestrator and then marketed by him and his colleagues as a tax shelter. . . . (6) The fact that the buyer-lessor in *Frank Lyon* was personally liable on the mortgage was, of course, a significant factor supporting the bona fides of the sale-leaseback transaction in that case. Nevertheless, we regard personal liability on the mortgage as atypical in modern real estate transactions and, consequently, we consider the absence of personal liability as a neutral factor in the case before us.]

In summary, after considering all of the facts and circumstances in the case before us, we find that the petitioners have failed to show a genuine multiparty transaction with economic substance, compelled or encouraged by business realities and imbued with tax-independent considerations and not shaped solely by tax-avoidance features that have meaningless labels attached. . . .

COMMENT — Tax-Exempt Seller-Tenant

A question that should occur to someone examining a sale-leaseback arrangement is why the seller-tenant does not keep the property and use the deductions associated with owning the property (depreciation and interest), rather than selling the property to someone else who uses those deductions. The answer is that the seller-tenant is usually less able to use the deductions than the buyer-lessor — e.g., because it is in a lower tax bracket or has net operating losses.

In one situation, the tax law prohibits a buyer-lessor from taking a deduction for depreciation and interest in excess of rent where the seller-tenant is (obviously) unable to use the deductions — that is, when the seller-tenant is a tax-exempt entity (including a government). § 470.

[C] Critique of Sale-Leasebacks as Tax Expenditures

You should be accustomed by now to taxpayers shifting around tax breaks through economic bargaining. For example, much of the benefit of tax-exempt bond interest accrues to the state and local government debtor, not the taxpayer whose interest is exempt. Perhaps parties to sale-leaseback transactions shift tax breaks with favorable public policy results. Buildings get built that would not otherwise be built and renters enjoy lower rents. But there is some reason to doubt whether sale-leasebacks produce such favorable consequences. First, some of the investment by middleman-lessors goes to pay tax shelter promoters. Second, the renter does not capture all of the tax breaks through lower rent. The middleman keeps some of the tax benefits. A Joint Committee on Taxation study found that 21.5% of the tax benefits went to the middleman-lessor.

[D]   Note on Statutory Interpretation — Technical Tax Meaning and Tax Administration

The cases in this section separate the issue of tax ownership from property law ownership under certain circumstances. Just as marriage law or financial accounting rules might not be incorporated automatically into the tax law, so tax law and property law ownership might vary.

Administrative problems always temper the enthusiasm with which legal concepts imported from outside the tax law are modified to serve tax law purposes. Indeed, in Chapter 3.03[D], realization of losses when a bank exchanged one set of debtors for another depended on legal rather than economic substance; that was the administratively easy solution. But when tax shelters are involved — packaging fast depreciation, capital gains, tax deferral, and the interest deduction — the courts have been more willing to scrutinize the economic reality of the transaction to decide whether there are significant upside or downside economic risks accruing to the alleged "owner," despite the administrative difficulty of making those determinations. Perhaps the reason is that tax shelters undermine faith in the entire tax system, whereas the deduction of realized losses discussed in Chapter 3.03[D] was isolated to a specific industry (banking) and arose in the context of the savings and loan crisis.

§ 17.05   STATUTORY LIMITS ON A TAX OWNER'S TAX BENEFITS

The materials in the prior sections show how hard it is for courts to deal with tax shelter problems. Unless economic potential, regardless of taxes, is virtually nonexistent, the transaction is not likely to be recast to deny tax breaks or tax ownership to the apparent owner. The code has therefore been modified to limit the use of tax benefits under certain circumstances.

The major provisions deny deduction of *net losses* when there is either insufficient financial commitment (the at-risk rules) or insufficient participation in the business by the taxpayer (passive business activities). Remember that these rules apply only after the case law determines that the taxpayer is entitled to deductions in the first place.

These rules are a typical tax reform statute. Rather than alter the general rules about when basis includes debt, the code limits the impact of those rules with complex and finely tuned provisions, which make very difficult reading.

[A]   Limiting Deductible Net Losses to Financial Stake

There are several keys to achieving a tax shelter. One is to include debt in basis. Another is to use net losses from a business to offset other income, such as personal service income. Doctors and lawyers often invested in tax shelters to reduce tax on professional fees. **Section 465** is the code's initial direct response to this problem, adopted in 1976 and applied to real estate in 1986. As you go through the discussion, ask yourself whether the taxpayers in *Frank Lyon Co., Hilton,* or *Estate of Franklin* would be caught by **§ 465.**

The best way to understand § 465 is to keep in mind the issues to which it is addressed. (1) *What taxpayers* are affected? (2) *What activities* are affected? (3) *What deductions are disallowed*: (a) deductions attributable to all debt or only *nonrecourse* debt; (b) all deductions, including those which offset income from the business financed by the debt, or, less broadly, only the deduction of *net losses* from that business? Think of § 465 as a series of forks in the road that give answers to these questions.

(1) *What taxpayers* are affected? **Section 465** affects individuals, partnerships, and corporations with five or fewer shareholders owning more than 50% of the stock. Other corporations, including publicly held corporations, do not worry about § 465.

(2) *What activities* are affected? With two exceptions, all activities are covered. (Before 1986, real estate was *not* covered.) The exceptions are for corporations with five or fewer shareholders owning more than 50% of the stock. These corporations are *not covered*, *if* the activity is equipment leasing (a computer, for example), or is an "active business," with, among other things, at least three non-owner employees. § 465(c)(4), (7).

(3) *What deductions are disallowed?* The target of the section is nonrecourse debt that produces net losses, capable of reducing taxable income. The section does not prevent deductions that offset income arising from the specific activity in which the debt is incurred. That produces the following rules. § 465(a)(1), (b)(1), (2).

(a) *At-risk limitations.* First, net losses from the debt-financed activity are deductible only to the extent the taxpayer is "at risk." What does "at risk" mean? (1) It refers to out-of-pocket investment and debt for which the taxpayer is personally liable. (2) In addition, nonrecourse loans secured by real estate are treated as "at risk," if the lender is a typical business lender (like a bank or insurance company), or a party related to the borrower if the loan is similar to what a commercial lender would make. This is an obvious benefit for real estate investment and tends to confine the at-risk rules applicable to real estate transactions to two-party sale-leasebacks, as in the *Estate of Franklin* case. § 465(b)(6).

(b) *Only net losses affected.* Second, the at-risk limitation only applies to net losses, not deductions offsetting net income from the debt-financed activity itself.

These rules are illustrated by the following example. Assume an individual taxpayer pays $10,000 down and borrows nonrecourse $180,000 at 10% interest, to buy a business machine.

The *financial* facts are:

Receipts

rent		=	$19,000

Expenditures

interest		=	$18,000
debt principal repayment		=	2,000

The *tax* facts are:

Gross income

rent		=	$19,000

Deductions

interest		=	$18,000
depreciation		=	27,000
			45,000

Net tax loss   (26,000)

Imagine yourself as a tax policymaker confronted with the above example. Your *first* thought might be that $12,000 of the depreciation deduction ($27,000) should be deductible, because it is supported by the $12,000 out-of-pocket investment ($10,000 down and a $2,000 debt payment), but that the remaining $15,000 of depreciation should not be deducted, because it is supported only by nonrecourse debt. That might seem a bit harsh, however. In this example, the business income without depreciation is $1,000 (rent minus interest — $19,000 minus $18,000). You might therefore decide to take a *second* approach and let the nonrecourse debt support a deduction of basis equal to the net income from the investment financed by the nonrecourse debt (that is, $1,000), and only disallow the deduction of *net losses* from the business attributable to the nonrecourse debt.

The statute takes this *second* approach. It specifies that only $12,000 of the $26,000 net loss is deductible, available to shelter the taxpayer's other income. This means that the remaining $14,000 of net losses is not deductible, but is carried forward to later years. This means that the nonrecourse debt is available to support a deduction against the $1,000 net income from the activity.

Put somewhat differently, the $27,000 of depreciation is deductible, up to $13,000, as follows: $1,000 offsets net income from the activity financed by the loan; $12,000 of the net operating loss is deductible, because that is the amount at risk. The remaining $14,000 of the net operating loss is not deductible until a later year.

In later years, the previously undeducted net loss of $14,000 is deductible (1) when the taxpayer has sufficient net income in future years (either because basis has been used up or because unpaid debt has been included in income upon disposition of the asset under the *Crane* and *Tufts* cases, *supra*); or (2) when the taxpayer pays off the nonrecourse debt and therefore has placed sufficient assets at risk.

[B]   Limiting Deductible Net Losses if Losses are "Passive"

After § 465 was adopted, Congress continued to worry about the deduction of net business losses by certain taxpayers who were able to successfully negotiate the § 465 maze. Consequently, § 469 was adopted in 1986. The taxpayer first applies § 465 to see if some or all net losses are still deductible. If they are, the taxpayer considers whether § 469 applies.

[1]   General Idea

The general idea, not always worked out precisely in the statutory text, is that net losses from business should be available only if the taxpayer "materially participates" in the business. Even an at-risk investment is insufficient. The statutory term for a net loss arising from a business activity in which the taxpayer does not "materially participate" is a "passive activity loss."

More specifically, the statute generally prevents passive business activity losses from offsetting investment income, personal service income, and business income, except that a net loss from a passive business activity can offset gain from another passive business activity. For example, assume that a taxpayer covered by the passive business activity rules has a $100,000 loss from a passive business activity, $40,000 gain from a passive business activity, and $80,000 personal service income. $40,000 of the $100,000 passive business activity loss offsets the $40,000 of passive business activity gain; but $60,000 of the passive business activity loss is disallowed. The passive business activity rules are therefore like the investment interest rules — all passive business activity losses and gains are lumped together the way investment interest and investment income are lumped together, and the overall losses from these activities are disallowed. This is different from the at-risk rules, where deduction of the net losses from each individual investment is disallowed, regardless of what other income the taxpayer has. § 469(a)(1)(A), (d)(1).

If passive business activity losses are disallowed, they are carried forward to a later year and may end up being deducted in the future when the taxpayer has passive business activity income. In addition, any unused but carried-forward passive business activity losses are deductible in full when the taxpayer disposes of his entire interest in the passive business activity in a fully taxable transaction (e.g., sells the business), to the extent they exceed passive business activity gains in the sale year. For example, assume that a real estate activity had generated $50,000 of undeducted passive business activity losses in prior years, that a sale of the business produces a $10,000 taxable gain, and that there was $5,000 of other passive business activity gains in the sale year. The unused $35,000 of passive business activity losses becomes deductible in the year of sale. § 469(g)(1).

In addition, any unused passive business activity losses are deductible in full when the taxpayer dies, with one important modification. If the transferee of the property gets a stepped-up basis, the gain that disappears because of the stepped-up basis reduces the passive business activity loss that becomes available because of the disposition by death. For example, if the taxpayer dies with a $50,000 carryover of passive business activity losses, and the property has a value of $100,000 with a basis of $90,000 prior to death, the $10,000 step up in basis reduces the $50,000 deductible loss to $40,000. This explicit provision taking away the benefit of a stepped-up basis at death is unusual. **§ 469(g)(2)**.

[2]   Who Is Covered by Passive Activity Loss Rules?

Individuals, including partners, are covered by the passive business activity loss rules. Corporations are *not* covered, with some exceptions. *First*, a corporation principally engaged in earning personal service income attributable to an owner's services is usually covered. *Second*, a corporation with five or fewer shareholders owning more than 50% of the stock (based on value) cannot use passive business activity losses to offset investment income, but can use passive business activity losses to offset business income that does not arise from passive activities. Thus, a small family corporation could deduct passive losses from its "nonpassive" business income, but not from dividends and interest on its investments.

These rules leave most large corporations untouched. They can use net losses from passive activities to offset any income. Should General Electric be allowed to use passive losses to offset its income from sale of electric light bulbs or from interest and dividends?

[3]   Defining Passive Activity

The statute defines "material participation" (thereby avoiding "passive activity" status) to mean "regular, continuous, and substantial" involvement in the operations of the activity. That is some, but not much, help. Regulations provide an elaborate definition. **Temp. Treas. Reg. § 1.469-5T**. Limited partners usually lack "material participation."

Because the test is so difficult to administer, the statute treats some activities as automatically "passive." Rental activity is in that category. Then the statute gives back a little of what it took away — for example, a net loss from *real estate* rental activity is not from a passive business activity if an individual (but not a partnership) "actively" participates in the business, but only up to $25,000 per year (a boon that disappears as income rises over $100,000). This typically helps someone who owns a boarding house as a second source of income.

These rules will strike you as exceedingly complex and dry, but a lot of people care about them. In one State of the Union message, President Bush (the elder) advocated repeal of the passive business activity loss rules — to considerable applause. One can only wonder what the TV audience thought.

[4]   Defining "Passive Income" to Absorb "Passive Losses"

Section 469 is just one more example of the point-counterpoint between taxpayers attempting to obtain an advantage, met with a legislative response, followed by a taxpayer response, and so forth. Taxpayers took net loss deductions, to which Congress responded, first with **§ 465** and then **§ 469**. Taxpayers then sought ways to absorb passive business activity losses with passive business activity income, but Regulations denied passive business activity income status to certain types of income, followed by litigation over the validity of the Regulations, as in the following case.

SCHAEFER v. COMMISSIONER
United States Tax Court
105 T.C. 227 (1995)

RAUM, JUDGE: . . .

Under the provisions of section 469, a taxpayer's right to make use of passive activity losses in any year is limited to the amount of the taxpayer's passive activity income for that year. § 469(a), (d)(1). While it has been stated that "issues arising under section 469 typically focus on whether a loss is to be properly characterized as a 'passive' loss so that the taxpayer may utilize the loss to offset what the taxpayer and respondent agree is passive income", the issue here . . . is whether the taxpayer's income is passive so that it may be offset by the taxpayer's passive losses.

Section 1.469-2T(c)(7)(iv), Temporary Income Tax Regs., 53 Fed. Reg. 5686, 5716 (Feb. 25, 1988), provides that passive activity gross income does not include "Gross income of an individual from a covenant by such individual not to compete". The result of this provision is that income from a covenant not to compete may not be offset by passive losses. § 469(a), (d)(1). Petitioner argues that this regulation is invalid. We hold otherwise.

We begin by noting that a temporary regulation is entitled to the same weight as a final regulation. . . . Treasury regulations are entitled to a high degree of deference from the courts. A Treasury regulation must be upheld if it "implement[s] the congressional mandate in some reasonable manner". Put differently, Treasury regulations "must be sustained unless unreasonable and plainly inconsistent with the revenue statutes". Indeed, the Supreme Court has stated that the issue is not how the Court itself might construe the statute in the first instance, "but whether there is any reasonable basis for the resolution embodied in the Commissioner's Regulation." Our conclusion, hereinafter reached, is that [the Temporary Regulation] fairly implements the congressional purpose underlying section 469 and is a valid regulation. . . .

[C]ertain types of income are specifically excluded from the computation of passive income. These include so-called portfolio income, namely, interest, dividends, annuities, or royalties, as well as gain attributable to the disposition of property, and earned income; § 469(e). Further, the Secretary is specifically instructed to issue regulations "which provide that certain items of gross income will not be taken into account in determining income or loss from any activity", § 469(l)(2). Congress included these exceptions because these income sources "generally are positive income sources that do not bear deductible expenses to the same extent as passive investments. Since taxpayers commonly can rely upon salary and portfolio income to be positive . . . they are susceptible to sheltering by means of investments in activities that predictably give rise to tax losses." Staff of the Joint Comm. on Taxation, General Explanation of the Tax Reform Act of 1986, at 215 (J. Comm. Print 1987). It is with this understanding of the purpose behind section 469, and the specific types of income Congress meant to ensure were not sheltered by losses from passive activities, that we examine [the Temporary Regulations]. . . .

[Editor — The court then discusses a long line of cases holding that payments for a covenant not to compete are ordinary income, not capital gain, because they are a substitute for personal service income.] These cases are cited to show the long history of viewing payments under a covenant not to compete as similar to types of income specifically excluded from passive income by Congress itself under section 469(e)(3). In view of this history, the regulation at issue cannot be held unreasonable or contrary to Congress's intent. . . .

. . . Petitioner argues that compensation under a covenant not to compete is the polar opposite of earned income, because the point of a covenant not to compete is that services will not be rendered. . . .

Petitioner's point is superficially persuasive, but reflection will disclose that it is fallacious. It is fallacious because petitioner assumes that "services actually rendered" must involve some positive action, rather than affirmatively refraining from doing something. And it is that personal deliberate failure to act that the purchaser has bargained for in this case. Such personal refraining to engage in competition traditionally has been equated in the tax law with the rendition of personal services. . . . At most, the interpretation of the statutory language, "personal services actually rendered," is open to differing interpretations — precisely the kind of situation that is appropriate for a regulation to resolve.

In *Sidell v. Commissioner*, 225 F.3d 103 (1st Cir. 2000), the court deferred to government regulations denying passive activity status to rent, if the property "[i]s rented for use in a trade or business activity . . . in which the taxpayer materially participates. . . ." **Treas. Reg. § 1.469-2(f)(6)(i).** "Material participation" includes activity "conducted through C corporations that are subject to section 469, S corporations, and partnerships." **Treas. Reg. § 1.469-4(a).** C corporations are entities that are taxed on their profits and their shareholders are taxed on dividends; an S corporation is an entity whose profits are taxed to shareholders in the year they arise at the corporate level, but (usually) there is no tax on the corporation and no second tax on dividends; in other words, an S corporation is (roughly) taxed like a partnership.

The Regulation approved in the *Sidell* case prevents a taxpayer who owns a building used in his business from placing the business into a wholly owned corporation, while retaining ownership of the building, and then renting the building to his corporation to create passive business activity income. If this taxpayer had continued to own the business, including the realty used in the business, without forming a corporation, none of the income would have been passive business activity income.

[C] Vacation Homes

Vacation homes work like this. A taxpayer invests in a second home, but only lives there part of the year, renting it out for some portion of the remaining period. Any expenses allocable to personal use should, of course, not be deductible, except for interest and taxes that are deductible regardless of personal use. The net losses attributable to the rental period could, however, be substantial. Are they in effect personal expenses, tolerated by the taxpayer as an expense of taking vacations (like "hobby" losses; Chapter 8.09)?

The statute responds with one clear rule. Net losses on vacation homes are not deductible if the taxpayer lives there during the year for more than the greater of 14 days or 10% of the time the property is rented. Two weeks is the operative planning period because of rental uncertainties. § 280A(a), (b), (c)(3, 5)(d), (e). If the taxpayer lives in the vacation home for "too long," expenses related to the rental period are deductible only up to the rental income (computed after deduction of interest and taxes attributable to the rental property), but net losses are not deductible. These vacation home rules take priority over the passive business activity rules; § 469(j)(10).

Taxpayers who are covered by these rules will want to attribute as little interest and taxes as possible to the rental income, so that there is more income to absorb other deductions (such as depreciation). Remember that home interest and taxes *not* attributable to rental income are usually deductible anyway, even though they are personal expenses. Is the denominator for allocating interest and taxes the entire year or only the number of days the property is used for business and pleasure? The taxpayer wants to use the entire year (a large denominator means less interest and taxes attributed to the rental period). *McKinney v. Commissioner*, 732 F.2d 414 (10th Cir. 1983), agrees with the taxpayer.

[D] Profit-Making Purpose? — Section 183

If a taxpayer successfully avoids the limits on deducting net losses discussed in the prior paragraphs, the government has one more string to its bow. If the government can prove that the taxpayer never really expects to make an economic profit, it can invoke § 183 to disallow the net losses. Although § 183 is aimed primarily at hobby losses (Chapter 8.09), where the taxpayer's purpose is personal, the statutory text is written broadly to apply whenever the taxpayer lacks an income-producing purpose. It has therefore provided the government with a statutory basis to prevent net losses from tax shelters from being deducted against other income. *Brannen v. Commissioner*, 78 T.C. 471 (1982), *affirmed*, 722 F.2d 695 (11th Cir. 1984); *Estate of Baron v. Commissioner*, 798 F.2d 65 (2d Cir. 1986).

This has raised concerns among some investors who respond to specific tax incentives by engaging in activity without hope of economic profit apart from the tax benefit from deducting net losses. *See* Rev. Rul. 79-300, 1979-2 C.B. 112 (investors in low-income housing who regularly suffer economic losses computed without regard to the tax breaks targeted on these investments are *not* denied a deduction for the net losses). This ruling recognizes that the nonrecognition of net losses because the taxpayer is "avoiding taxes" is always a matter of statutory interpretation. Thus, there is nothing wrong with avoiding taxes if the statute targets certain activities — such a low income housing — for special tax breaks. The problem is knowing when an activity is specifically targeted for favorable tax treatment and when astute tax counsel is packaging tax breaks to provide a benefit not intentionally provided by Congress.

§ 17.06   NONSUBSTANTIVE LAW ATTACKS ON TAX SHELTERS

A detailed examination of the penalties and ethical rules aimed at discouraging tax shelters must be left to a course in tax administration. The following gives you some idea of the continuing (and perhaps futile) effort to adopt rules to achieve that goal.

[A]   Penalties, Etc.

The substantive law uncertainties regarding tax shelters led many taxpayers to take their chances, given the low risk of audit. The tax law has responded with several provisions.

Taxpayers who make tax shelter investments must worry not only about the usual fraud and negligence penalties, but also about a variety of other penalties. First, there is a 20% penalty on substantial understatements of tax. **§ 6662(b)(2), (d)**. In the case of non-tax shelter items, this penalty is avoided if the taxpayer's position is supported by "substantial authority" or there is "adequate disclosure" and a reasonable basis for the taxpayer's position. For a tax shelter, disclosure is unavailing, and the taxpayer must reasonably believe that his position was more likely than not to prevail.

Second, there are additional penalties for understatement of tax and for failure to report transactions defined as "reportable" or "listed" transactions (which are identified by the IRS as having tax avoidance or tax evasion potential). **§ 6662A, § 6707A**. In addition, **§ 163(m)** disallows the deduction of interest on underpayments of tax attributable to an understatement arising from a reportable or listed transaction that is not "adequately disclosed."

In addition, the statute imposes reporting obligations on tax shelter organizers and promoters and on business creditors with a security interest in property (so that unpaid debt will not go unreported).

We have been using the phrase "tax shelters" in this discussion as though it were self-defining — sort of "know it when you see it." The code attempts a definition of tax shelters in **§ 461(i)(3)** and **§ 6662(d)(2)(C)**, and the definitions differ.

[B]   Ethical Rules

[1]   American Bar Association

The American Bar Association has adopted ethical rules specifically aimed at lawyers who counsel about tax shelters. These rules recognize that the lawyer's role extends beyond responsibility to the client to include concern about the impact of his or her actions on the general investing public, when the public is likely to rely on the lawyer. In this respect, a lawyer is treated like an accountant whose financial audits are available to investors.

A.B.A. Formal Ethics Opinion 346 provides ethical standards for dealing with tax shelter opinions. The fact that investors are likely to rely on the contents of the opinion, insofar as they are directed to potential investors in offering materials or other forms of sales promotion, shapes the ethical rules. The opinion states that the lawyer who renders such an opinion functions more as an advisor than an advocate.

The critical requirement concerns gathering facts. If any of the facts given to the lawyer seem incomplete in any material respect, suspect, inconsistent, or open to question, the lawyer must make further inquiry. The extent of the inquiry depends on whether a prior relationship with the client indicates that trust is appropriate and whether the client seems reluctant to provide information. If the inquiry does not give the lawyer sufficient confidence regarding the facts, the lawyer should refuse to give an opinion. The A.B.A. Opinion gives as an example where an appraisal or financial projection that makes little common sense or where the appraiser's reputation or expertise is dubious. However, the opinion cautions that the lawyer is not required to "audit" the client's affairs or to assume that the client's statement of the facts is unreliable.

Once the facts are gathered, the lawyer must write an opinion that relates the law to the facts. The lawyer must not disclaim responsibility for inquiring as to the accuracy of the facts, analyze all critical facts, and refrain from discussing hypothetical facts.

The lawyer should, if possible, give an opinion as to the probable outcome of any litigation regarding each material tax issue. However, if the lawyer decides in good faith that it is not possible to judge the outcome of a material issue, the lawyer should state that conclusion with reasons. In other words, the lawyer is not required to give a conclusion regarding every issue. The lawyer may question the validity of an agency revenue ruling or a court opinion which the lawyer thinks is wrong, with reasons, but with an explanation of the government's likely position and the risks of any likely litigation.

Finally, the lawyer should make an evaluation of the extent to which the significant tax benefits are likely to be realized – that they probably will or will not be realized or that the probabilities are evenly divided. The lawyer may, in "rare" instances, conclude that it is not possible to judge whether the significant tax benefits will be realized — e.g., when the benefits depend on a new law for which there are not regulations or useful legislative history. But any such equivocal or negative opinion must be clearly stated and prominently noted in the materials offering the tax shelter to the public.

QUESTIONS

Based on A.B.A. Formal Ethics Opinion 346, consider how the lawyer should deal with the following:

1. The client tells the lawyer that the property subject to a $1 million debt is, in fact, worth $1 million (cf. *Estate of Franklin*).

2. The tenant in a sale-leaseback situation has an option to buy the property at the end of the lease for: (a) a sum fixed at the time of the sale-leaseback, which is

substantial but not necessarily its fair market value at the time of the exercise of the option; (b) for $1.

[2]   Treasury Rules; Updated Circular 230

A 2004 Tax Law gave the Treasury new authority to impose tax shelter opinion standards; according to the legislative history, this merely affirmed prior authority. In any event, the Treasury has responded as follows.

Effective June 20, 2005, a new set of rules applies to tax advisors who provide certain opinions related to tax avoidance schemes. A general and partial overview of these rules follows. These regulations do not provide examples and the meaning of many terms will have to be fleshed out. The 2004 Tax Law also attempts to put more teeth into enforcement of Circular 230 by adding censure and monetary penalties to the existing disbarment and suspension sanctions available to the Treasury. **31 U.S.C. § 330(b)**. Presumably, these lesser sanctions are more likely to be used than disbarment or suspension.

a. *Covered opinions.* The rules, set forth in 31 C.F.R. § 10.35, apply to "covered opinions." A "covered opinion" refers to "written advice" (including electronic communication) that concerns one or more "federal tax issues" arising from: . . .

> (2) an entity, plan, or arrangement *"the principal purpose"* of which is tax avoidance or evasion; or (3) an entity, plan or arrangement for which *"a significant" (rather than a principal) purpose* is tax avoidance or evasion, but only when the written advice is in the form of "a reliance opinion" or a "marketed opinion."

A "reliance opinion" is one that is meant to be used to prevent tax penalties, by giving the taxpayer a reasonable belief that the tax claim is more likely than not to succeed (more than 50%). "Reliance opinion" status can be avoided by prominently disclosing in the written advice that it was not intended to be used and cannot be used to avoid penalties.

An opinion is a "marketed opinion" if "the practitioner knows or has reason to know that the written advice will be used or referred to by a person other than the practitioner . . . in promoting, marketing or recommending a partnership or other entity, investment plan or arrangement to one or more taxpayer(s)." Marketed opinion status can be avoided by prominently disclosing that it was not intended and cannot be used to avoid penalties, that it was written to support marketing of the transaction, and that the taxpayer should seek advice based on the taxpayer's circumstances from an independent tax advisor.

"Prominent disclosure" means placement in a separate statement at the beginning of the written advice in boldface and in type larger than otherwise used in the written advice.

b. *Standards applicable to covered opinions.* The standards applicable to a "covered opinion" include the following: (1) the practitioner must use reasonable efforts to ascertain the facts (including future events) and to determine which facts are relevant, and must disclose these relevant facts in the opinion; (2) the practitioner must not rely on unreasonable assumptions or on unreasonable factual statements by the taxpayer, defined as assumptions or facts that the practitioner knows or should know are incorrect or incomplete or are prepared by an unqualified person; and all factual assumptions and statements relied on by the practitioner must be identified in a separate section of the written opinion; and (3) the opinion must relate the law to the relevant facts and must not assume a favorable resolution of any significant federal tax issue.

The opinion also must provide a conclusion as to the likelihood of success on the merits of all significant federal tax issues considered in the opinion or state why no conclusion can be reached, with a description of the reasons for these conclusions. If the conclusion is reached at a confidence level of less than "more likely than not," this must be disclosed in the opinion. (In addition, a "marketed opinion" for a "substantial tax avoidance" transaction must contain a "more likely than not" conclusion or else not be issued.) (*Query.* The disclosure requirement is *not* included in the ABA rules. Why the difference?)

The practitioner's evaluation of the issues cannot consider whether the return will be audited, whether the issue will be raised on audit, or whether the issue will be resolved through settlement.

c. *Penalties, etc.* Circular 230 specifies (in **31 C.F.R. § 10.52**) that penalties may be imposed only for "willfully violating" or for "recklessly or through gross incompetence (within the meaning of § 10.51(l)) violating . . . § 10.35. . . ."

In addition, **31 C.F.R. § 10.33** sets forth aspirational "best practices," that identify higher standards than those appearing elsewhere in Circular 230. Failure to follow these standards does not result in any sanction, but following them might mitigate the application of penalties for violating the rules for which a sanction can be imposed. The preamble to the regulations also states that adherence to "best practices" might reduce the risk of malpractice liability. (*Query*: Can federal regulations affect state malpractice rules?)

§ 17.07   APPENDIX; TAX SHELTER EXAMPLE

The text explaining tax shelters is illustrated by the following example.

Financial facts. We assume that residential rental real estate is purchased in year 0 for $20,000 down and an $80,000 nonrecourse 30-year loan, paying 10% interest. Debt payments and rent begin in year 1. The annual payments on the mortgage are $8,486.33, part interest, part principal. Annual rent is $10,607.92. This rent gives the taxpayer a real financial 10% rate of return on the $100,000 investment over 30 years, assuming that real financial depreciation (not tax depreciation) occurs on a decelerated depreciation basis. (The present value of year 30 rent is $607.92 ($10,607.92/1.1^{30}$); *real* depreciation in year 1 is therefore $607.92 and net income is $10,000.) We further assume that the taxpayer sells the asset after five years, and that the asset has sufficient value over unpaid debt for the taxpayer to collect $20,000 cash. This assumption is made to provide easy comparison between the rates of return for the tax shelter investor and for the investor who puts $20,000 into a bank account for five years; in each case the investor invests $20,000, which he gets back after a five-year period.

Tax facts. The taxpayer can deduct the interest and depreciate the $100,000 purchase price over a 27.5-year period ($100,000 divided by 27.5 = $3,636.36 per year — assume a full year's depreciation begins in year 1). Capital gains are taxed at 25%, because "recapture" income on sale of depreciable real estate is taxed at 25%. (In this example, the gain is less than prior depreciation, so the entire gain is "real estate recapture" income.) The taxpayer is in the 35% tax bracket. One would expect therefore that the after-tax return on the $20,000 investment for a taxpayer in the 35% bracket would be 6.5%, given the 10% before tax rate of return. The taxpayer, however, does better than that. Why?

(A) CASH FLOW WITHOUT TAX *BEFORE* SALE

YEAR	RENT	INTEREST	PRINCIPAL	TOTAL PAYMENTS	NET CASH FLOW
1	10607.92	8000.00	486.33	8486.33	2121.59
2	10607.92	7951.36	534.97	8486.33	2121.59
3	10607.92	7897.86	588.47	8486.33	2121.59
4	10607.92	7839.02	647.31	8486.33	2121.59
5	10607.92	7774.28	712.05	8486.33	2121.59
			2969.13		

Cash flow after sale, without tax. The sale in year 5 increases net cash flow IN YEAR 5 by $20,000, for a year 5 total of $22,121.59.

(B) TAX COMPUTATION BEFORE SALE

YEAR	RENT	INTEREST	DEPREC.	TOTAL DEDUCTION	TAXABLE INCOME	TAX REFUND
1	10607.92	8000.00	3636.36	11636.36	(1028.44)	359.95
2	10607.92	7951.36	3636.36	11587.72	(979.80)	342.93
3	10607.92	7897.86	3636.36	11534.22	(926.30)	324.21
4	10607.92	7839.02	3636.36	11475.38	(867.46)	303.61
5	10607.92	7774.28	3636.36	11410.64	(802.72)	280.95

(C) COMPUTATION OF TAX ON SALE

The sale in year 5 would produce gain, computed as follows:

1. AMOUNT REALIZED = UNPAID DEBT PLUS CASH.

The unpaid debt is the original $80,000 debt minus $2,969.13 of principal paid, which equals $77,030.87. Cash received equals $20,000. Amount realized is therefore $97,030.87.

2. BASIS = ORIGINAL COST MINUS DEPRECIATION.

The original cost is $100,000. Depreciation (5 times $3,636.36) equals $18,181.80. Basis is therefore $81,818.20.

3. GAIN = AMOUNT REALIZED MINUS BASIS = $15,212.67 ($97,030.87 MINUS $81,818.20).

4. TAX ON "RECAPTURE" CAPITAL GAIN = $3,803.17 (.25 TIMES $15,212.67).

The overall year 5 tax is therefore a *payment* (not a refund) of $3,522.22 ($3,803.17 MINUS the $280.95 refund before computing tax on the sale).

(D) CASH FLOW WITH TAXES

YEAR	NET CASH FLOW WITHOUT TAXES	TAX REFUND (+) OR PAYMENT (-)	TOTAL CASH FLOW
1	2121.59	+ 359.95	2481.54
2	2121.59	+ 342.93	2464.52
3	2121.59	+ 324.21	2445.79
4	2121.59	+ 303.61	2425.20
5	22121.59	-3522.22	18599.37

The total cash flow produces an after-tax rate of return on the original $20,000 of 9.06%, rather than 6.5%. You can see this by thinking of the annual cash flow as money you can draw down from a bank at a 9.06% interest rate (that is, $1,812 per year; 9.06% times $20,000). You may think the rate of return is higher than that, looking at annual total cash flows, but remember that you must not take all of the annual cash flow each year because you must save some money to pay taxes in year 5 (a sinking fund) and still have $20,000 left.

Whether this is a good enough rate of return to entice an investment is a function not merely of the rate of return, but also of the risk associated with the investment. A 9.06% rate of return on residential rental real estate may not be good enough when compared with a *safe* 6.5% return from a bank.

THE ALTERNATIVE MINIMUM TAX

Congress is aware of the criticism of many of the tax benefits discussed in prior chapters. Some have been repealed, but many remain, with the potential for lowering the effective tax rate. The problem first came dramatically to the public's attention when the Treasury published data showing that many rich taxpayers paid no tax at all. The alternative minimum tax was therefore adopted. Technically, § 55 imposes an alternative minimum tax (AMT) on an amount equal to the "tentative minimum tax" minus the "regular tax" — e.g., if the tentative minimum tax is $100 and the regular tax is $80, the AMT is $20. But people often refer to the $100 figure as the AMT.

This Part consists of only one chapter, dealing with the AMT. It explains the following: the general idea behind the AMT; its mechanics; and "traps" that subject taxpayers to the AMT when they never expected that result.

It is entirely possible that the AMT will disappear. There has been a lot of criticism that it has failed in its original purpose of taxing the wealthy (for reasons you will soon see) and has instead extended its reach down into the middle class. Its inadequacies in taxing the wealthy are likely to persist now that the regular tax rates have been raised in 2013 by ATRA. Its impact on the middle class is now unclear because amendments adopted by ATRA permit most tax credits under the regular tax to be available under the AMT, thereby reducing the situations in which the regular tax will be less than the AMT. Still, the AMT may persist as a major nuisance because of the inertia that surrounds a lot of legislation. Or, perhaps, recent proposals to revive a redesigned AMT in its original form — as a 30% tax on the wealthy — will gain some traction.

Chapter 18

ALTERNATIVE MINIMUM TAX

§ 18.01 THE GENERAL IDEA

The Alternative Minimum Tax (AMT) has the same general attributes as the regular tax — its own tax base, personal exemptions, and tax rates. The AMT tax rates are lower than the highest bracket regular rates found in § 1 (individuals) and § 11 (corporations) — only 26%/28% for individuals; 20% for corporations. The general idea is to define a broader more inclusive tax base than is found under the regular tax and to make sure that some minimum tax is paid on that amount. In effect, Congress has identified those tax expenditures that should not enable taxpayers to avoid paying tax at the minimum rate. However, the tax expenditures so characterized are not the complete list that appears in either the executive or congressional branches' tax expenditure budgets; Chapter 6.01[C]. Political factors still shape the definition of the alternative minimum tax base.

Some observers argue that tax breaks disallowed under the AMT should instead be slated for disallowance under the regular tax. And, indeed, in some instances AMT rules have ended up being adopted for the regular income tax — such as the 10% floor on medical expense deductions. But the more usual pattern is for the AMT to serve as a cop-out, allowing legislators to avoid reforming the regular tax.

Political factors also influence who is subject to the AMT. Small businesses were successful in the 1997 Tax Act in gaining an exemption from the AMT for "small corporations." A small corporation is one that has no more than $5,000,000 average gross receipts for the three tax years ending with the first tax year beginning after December 31, 1996. Once eligible, the corporation usually retains small corporation status as long as the prior three-year average of gross receipts does not exceed $7,500,000.

§ 18.02 MECHANICS

[A] Tax Rates

The alternative minimum tax rate for individuals is 26% on the first $179,500 of alternative minimum taxable income, and 28% on income over that amount (inflation-adjusted). A graduated rate structure was an innovation in 1993; before then the rate was a flat 24%. The alternative minimum tax rate on corporations is a flat 20% (this was unchanged in 1993). § 55(b)(1).

The increase in regular tax rates by ATRA (in 2013) reduces the situations in which wealthy taxpayers will be subject to the AMT because the AMT tax rates are significantly lower than the rates adopted by ATRA. Conversely, the fact that low tax rates apply to those with lower incomes increases the risk that lower income taxpayers will be unexpectedly subject to the AMT.

[B] Tax Base

Here is a small sampling of how the alternative minimum tax base differs from the regular tax base.

[1] Individuals and Corporations

AMT taxable income is regular taxable income, with adjustments and additions. § 55(b)(2). Most of the adjustments add back regular tax deductions. The pattern here should be obvious. Various items have long been targeted for "tax reform" elimination, but the political will to do so is lacking. As a compromise, these tax benefits are eliminated under the AMT, but not the regular tax.

1. For purposes of the AMT, the 200% declining balance method under the regular tax is modified so that taxpayers use a 150% rate. Beginning in tax year 1999, the depreciation period for the AMT is the same as for the regular tax (previously, the longer "alternative depreciation" periods provided by § 168(g) had to be used). § 56(a)(1)(A).

The AMT is really a parallel tax universe to the regular tax. Thus, slower depreciation produces a higher basis under the AMT than under the regular tax. Computation of gain under the AMT will therefore be different than under the regular tax. For example, if an asset costing $300,000 is entitled to $30,000 depreciation under the regular tax, its adjusted basis is $270,000. Under the AMT, slower depreciation (assume only $20,000) results in an adjusted basis for the AMT of $280,000. Sale of the asset for $350,000 produces less gain under the AMT than under the regular tax ($70,000, rather than $80,000).

2. A complete list of adjustments and additions common to individuals and corporations appears in §§ 56(a), 57. In addition to the rules modifying depreciation and expensing, a few adjustments add back exempt income; see § 57(a)(5) (interest on most "private activity" bonds — referred to as Industrial Revenue Bonds in Chapter 6.01[C][4] — is not exempt under the AMT).

3. The long-term capital gain that is deductible on certain gifts of appreciated property to charity (§ 170(e)) was once a tax preference item under the AMT, but not after the 1993 tax law. Consequently, the full value of artwork and stock (not just the basis) is deductible in computing alternative minimum taxable income. Museums and universities are obvious beneficiaries of this rule.

[2] Individuals

1. The AMT permits only certain itemized deductions that are allowed under the regular tax. § 56(b)(1). These include the casualty, charitable, and medical expense deductions. State income, sales, and property taxes are *not* deductible. In addition, miscellaneous itemized deductions are not deductible under the AMT. Therefore, employee business expense deductions that are *itemized* deductions (subject to the

2% floor) are not deductible in computing the AMT tax base. Loss of employee business expense deductions is one way that lower income taxpayers might find themselves subject to the AMT.

2. Personal interest deductions on home loans are also more narrowly defined for the AMT. The loan must be used to acquire, construct, or rehabilitate the residence. The opportunity afforded under the regular tax to deduct interest on a home equity loan is not permitted under the AMT. And the second residence, in connection with which interest can be deducted, is more narrowly defined for the AMT; e.g., boats cannot be included. § 56(b)(1)(C)(i), (e). The AMT rules on the deduction of personal interest are a good example of a provision that could be adopted by the regular tax to reduce current tax breaks.

3. The fact that below the line deductions are not generally available under the AMT puts a premium on finding that an activity is a trade or business eligible for above the line deductions. For example, gamblers try to prove that their activities are a significant effort to earn a livelihood and therefore amount to a business, because otherwise deductible gambling losses are below the line deductions. *See Commissioner v. Groetzinger*, 480 U.S. 23 (1987) (professional gambler entitled to above the line deductions).

4. As for business deductions, the permission to expense circulation expenditures (§ 173) under the regular tax is replaced by three-year amortization under the AMT; and the expensing of research and experimental expenditures (§ 174(a)) is often replaced by ten-year amortization unless the taxpayer materially participates in the activity (§ 56(b)(2)(A).

COMMENT

Under the AMT, no deduction is allowed for "for any [nonbusiness] taxes described in paragraph (1), (2), or (3) of section 164(a)," which includes property taxes paid by homeowners. § 56(b)(1)(A)(i), (ii). **Section 216** permits taxpayers in a cooperative apartment to deduct that portion of the rent they pay equal to their share of property taxes under the regular income tax. The taxpayer argued that the § 216 deduction was not disallowed under the AMT because the law did not disallow a deduction for taxes listed in § 216, only those listed in § 164(a). The court did not agree with the taxpayer, refusing to reach what it called the "anomalous result" of treating homeowners and tenant-shareholders in cooperative housing corporations differently. Similar treatment for homeowners and tenant-shareholders was the reason for allowing the deduction for tenant-shareholders under the regular income tax and the same equal treatment rationale should lead to *disallowance* under the AMT. *Ostrow v. Commissioner*, 122 T.C. 378 (2004), *affirmed*, 430 F.3d 581 (2d Cir. 2005).

[3] Corporations

The AMT taxable income for corporations is increased by 75% of the excess of a modified version of earnings and profits over what would otherwise be the tax base for the AMT. The earnings and profits figure is something like what accountants would compute as the economic profits of the business. It *includes* tax-exempt interest income from state and local bonds. § 56(c)(1), (g).

[4]   Net Operating Loss Carryovers

Under the AMT, the net operating loss deduction cannot exceed 90% of the AMT taxable income. § 56(d)(1).

[5]   Long-Term Capital Gains; Dividends

Section 55(b)(3) provides that the benefit of the preferential tax rates on long-term gains and dividends is applicable to taxpayers subject to the AMT. That is one reason the wealthy are often not burdened by the AMT.

[C]   Exemptions — Section 55(d)

[1]   Amounts

After computing the alternative minimum tax base, the individual taxpayer deducts an exempt amount. Prior to the 2001 Tax Bill, the exemption was $45,000 for married couples and $33,750 for single individuals. Thereafter, during the next decade, the exemption amount was periodically increased by legislation and not automatically adjusted for inflation.

ATRA now provides that the exemption amount for *individuals* in 2013 is $80,800 for married couples and $51,900 for a single individual. In addition, these amounts are now permanent and are indexed for inflation beginning in 2013. Notice that there is no attempt to make the exemption amount for married couples double the exemption amount for single taxpayers, resulting in a tax on marriage.

Corporations receive a $40,000 exemption.

[2]   Phase-Out

In 2013, the exemption amounts for individuals are phased out at the rate of 25 cents per dollar of alternative minimum taxable income above $153,900 for a married couple couple and above $115,400 for a single individual. This introduces a phantom tax rate into the AMT, above the 26/28% stated rate. The loss of $1 of deductions raises AMT taxable income to $1.25. If the taxpayer was subject to a 28% AMT, that results in an increase in tax of 35 cents (.28 times 1.25) — producing a 35% tax on the extra $1 of income (or a 7% phantom tax rate).

The phase-out thresholds for individuals are now inflation-adjusted.

The corporation's $40,000 exemption is phased out at the rate of 25 cents per dollar of income over $150,000.

[3]   Kiddie Tax

Recall the kiddie tax under the regular income tax (Chapter 1.03[A]), designed to prevent one member of the family from shifting investment income to a child. **Section 59(j)** provides that any child who would be subject to the kiddie tax under § 1(g) shall be entitled to no more than a reduced personal exemption amount under the AMT — specifically, earned income plus $5,000 (inflation-adjusted to $7,150 for 2013).

[D] Credits

The discussion has so far focused on how the AMT deals with deductions and exclusions that reduce the regular tax. Tax credits, however, can also reduce the regular tax. How does the AMT deal with tax credits?

The general pattern (prior to the 2001 Tax Bill) was that tax credits did not reduce the AMT (with a few exceptions for some business tax credits). Consequently, if the regular tax without credits was $100, and the AMT was $95, a $20 credit would reduce the regular tax to $80 and expose the taxpayer to a $15 AMT. This forced many taxpayers (unexpectedly) to pay an AMT.

ATRA changes this. It makes permanent the use of the nonrefundable portion of all personal credits to reduce the AMT. This includes the earned income credit, the credit for dependent care, the child tax credit, the adoption credit, and the American Opportunity tax credit (the old Hope Scholarship credit).

[E] Tax Planning

Can you generalize about when an individual taxpayer should start worrying about the alternative minimum tax? Only very tentatively. In most instances, a taxpayer will discover that he owes an AMT by consulting a tax preparer, running tax computation software, or getting a bill from the IRS.

[F] The Problem of Deferral Tax Preferences

The interaction of the alternative minimum and regular taxes creates a potential for double taxation of the same item when the AMT results from disallowing tax deferral (rather than tax exemption) available under the regular tax. The problem is illustrated by the following extreme example. Assume $500 of income taxable under both the regular and AMT in both years 1 and 2. Assume, in addition, a $100 expenditure in year 1, which is expensed under the regular income tax in year 1, but cannot be deducted at all in year 1 under the AMT. The expenditure is, however, deductible in full in year 2 under the AMT.

Year		Regular tax	AMT
1	Gross income =	500	500
	Deduction =	100	0
	Total =	400	500
2	Gross income =	500	500
	Deduction −	0	100
	Total =	500	400

The excess of the alternative minimum tax base over the regular tax base in year 1 is $100, and that same $100 is subject to regular tax in year 2.

The law addresses this problem by isolating how much of an AMT the taxpayer has to pay in year 1 as a result of *deferral* tax preferences (such as having to add back some fast depreciation or expensing). That additional AMT is then carried forward as a credit to later years and reduces the excess of the regular tax over the tentative minimum tax in a later year. § 53. Using the above figures, assume that the year 1 AMT resulting from adding back the $100 deduction was $26 (assuming a 26% rate). Assume further that in year 2, the regular tax on $500 now exceeds the tentative minimum tax on $400 by $35, assuming a 35% regular tax rate. The credit reduces the regular tax by $26 and only $9 regular tax is due in year 2, *attributable to the $100*. That produces a total of $35 tax over *both* years on the $100 ($26 in year 1, and $9 in year 2), which is the regular tax rate.

The complication raised by this solution is to limit the credit to the year 1 AMT attributable to *deferral* tax breaks. Some taxpayers may have AMT due to other disallowed tax breaks, such as losing an interest deduction. Thus, assume that the above taxpayer had an alternative minimum tax base in year 1 of $550 (more than the $500 in the above example), because $50 of home equity interest was attributable to a loan used to buy a personal car. The interest deduction is a *non*deferral tax break. The excess of the AMT over the regular tax attributable to the nondeferral tax break is *not* available as a credit in future years.

[G]   Impact on Incentives

One of the consequences of having parallel tax universes is that the incentive effects of deductions under the regular tax will be eliminated for someone subject to the AMT, *if* the deduction is unavailable under the AMT.

If the deduction is available under the AMT, what is the incentive effect of the deduction for someone subject to the AMT? The tax benefit of a deduction is often less under the AMT, because the tax rate is less (only 26% or 28%).

§ 18.03   AMT "TRAPS"

As noted earlier, the AMT has expanded down into the middle class, well beyond the well-off taxpayers at whom it was originally aimed. Here are some examples of AMT "traps" — in the sense that taxpayers do not expect to be subjected to the AMT. ATRA has reduced the number of "trapped" individuals by allowing nonrefundable credits under the regular tax to reduce the AMT as well.

1. *Combining personal exemption and miscellaneous itemized deductions.* Taxpayers may be unexpectedly exposed to the AMT if they have too many children. Assume that a taxpayer has ten children. The personal exemption deductions under § 151 are not allowed in computing the AMT tax base. There is an AMT $62,550 exemption deduction for married couples, but its impact is much reduced when netted out against the loss of personal exemption deductions for a large family.

For example, in *Klaassen v. Commissioner*, 76 T.C.M. (CCH) 20 (1998), *affirmed in unpublished opinion*, 182 F.3d 932 (10th Cir. 1999), the taxpayer had about $80,000 of adjusted gross income, which was reduced by itemized deductions. Many of these itemized deductions were not deductible in computing the AMT tax base —

e.g., state and local taxes are not deductible. Taxable income under the regular tax was also reduced by 12 personal exemption deductions, including those for 10 children. When the AMT tax base was computed, and the 26% tax rate applied, it produced a figure in excess of the regular tax rate times the taxable income computed under **§ 63**. (Notice that a lot of the income under the regular tax was subject to low tax rates under **§ 1**.) The court held that the taxpayer could not rely on the fact that the AMT "was not intended to apply to them." The statutory text was too clear to permit reliance on congressional intent to help the taxpayer. The Court of Appeals referred to the "high degree of specificity" in the statutory text.

2. *Employee business expenses.* In *Holly v. Commissioner*, 75 T.C.M. (CCH) 1752 (1998), the taxpayer had about $30,000 of unreimbursed employee business expenses, which were not deductible in computing the AMT tax base. The result was an AMT. The court turned a deaf ear to taxpayer's complaint that the AMT was aimed at "wealthier individuals." The statute was clear. Can you think of a reason why the teacher of this course might be concerned with the *Holly* case?

See also Ruggiero v. Commissioner, 74 T.C.M. (CCH) 662 (1997), in which a professor received a $60,000 fellowship but was denied sabbatical leave by his university. He then negotiated a leave with full pay in exchange for paying the university $30,000 of his fellowship. But the $30,000 was a below the line itemized employee business expense deduction that was not deductible in computing the alternative minimum tax base. Consequently, an AMT was due.

3. *Tort recoveries and contingent attorneys' fees.* Assume that the taxpayer recovers $5,000,000 in taxable damages in a tort case (either punitive damages or damages for a nonphysical personal injury). Pursuant to a contingency fee arrangement, $1,500,000 is paid to the lawyer. Under the AMT, miscellaneous itemized deductions are not deductible at all. The miscellaneous itemized deduction problem could be avoided if the expenses were nonemployee business expenses (above the line) and, therefore, deductible in computing both the regular and AMT tax base, but that argument was often unavailable — e.g., when the lawsuit arose from employment discrimination. *See* Chapter 9.03[H]. Taxpayers then argued that the attorneys' fees were not their income. Either *Lucas v. Earl* did not apply because the fees were generated by the lawyers' services or the lawyers were like partners for whom the fees were like a share of profits. The Supreme Court resolved this issue against the taxpayer in *Commissioner v. Banks*, 543 U.S. 426 (2005), holding that the contingent fees had to be included in income and deducted only as provided by the tax law. The Court did not reach an argument made in *Vincent v. Commissioner*, T.C. Memo 2005-95 (2005) — whether "sums awarded to an attorney under a fee shifting statute are includable in the client's gross income." The Tax Court held that these awards were includable in the client's income, relying on *Sinyard v. Commissioner*, 268 F.3d 756 (9th Cir. 2001).

Congress came to the rescue of some of these taxpayers. The 2004 Tax Law permitted an above the line deduction for attorneys' fees and court costs incurred in lawsuits involving most civil rights claims. **§ 62(e)**. However, this amendment did not completely resolve the problem. The amendment was prospective, so the legal issued remained important for transactions prior to the effective date of the amendment. Moreover, the amendment did not apply to claims not involving civil rights. For example, in a defamation claim arising out of the employment relationship, the contingent fees paid to a lawyer would not be deductible under the AMT.

QUESTION

What are the policy implications of the tax law? Will a lower tax on civil rights plaintiffs result in lower awards, especially if jurors are told that the taxpayer will not pay tax on the attorneys' fees?

Part I-F

APPRECIATION

The taxation of appreciation in the value of property has been a problem ever since the decision was reached not to tax unrealized gain. Nontaxation of unrealized gain creates the lock-in effect, which makes people reluctant to sell or exchange capital assets. The tax law has responded in a number of ways, which are dealt with in this Part — nonrecognition of gains and losses on certain transactions (Chapter 19); the capital gains preference (Chapter 20); and the deferral of tax on gain (Chapter 21). We also discuss the special problem of carved out income interests (Chapter 22).

Chapter 19

NONRECOGNITION OF REALIZED GAIN

§ 19.01 INTRODUCTION

One of the basic structural principles in the tax law is the requirement that gain be realized before it can be included in § 61 income. One important consequence of this rule is that appreciated gain is not taxed until some event other than mere appreciation. This creates a sharp distinction between retention of an asset and its sale for cash or exchange for another asset. This is often called the lock-in effect, because the tax burden on sale locks in the taxpayer's investment. One way to eliminate this effect would be to permit a nontaxable sale or exchange to occur, if the taxpayer replaced the sold property with qualified replacement property. Gain would technically be realized under § 61, but not recognized. Taxable gain would be deferred until such time as the taxpayer withdrew his investment from the qualified property. The tax law has a number of provisions like the general rule just proposed, but they are hedged with many conditions. This Chapter deals with the mechanics of these provisions and reviews some of the definitional problems encountered in determining which transactions are eligible.

§ 19.02 NONRECOGNITION — MECHANICS

There are many tax provisions that explicitly defer tax on realized gain. The statute usually states that the gain is not "recognized."

Work out the following problems under § 1031(a), (b), (d) to see how tax deferred exchanges are treated. Assume that § 1031, dealing with "like-kind" exchanges, applies. The same general pattern of nonrecognition mechanics prevails in other tax-deferred transactions, including the rules dealing with (1) corporate organizations and reorganizations (§§ 351, 354) and (2) reinvestment of the proceeds of an involuntary conversion in property which is similar or related in kind or use to the converted property (§ 1033).

PROBLEMS

It will help you to understand the mechanics of § 1031 if you remember (1) that a sale of property with a $40,000 basis for $60,000 cash cannot produce more than $20,000 recognized gain, and (2) that cash always has a basis equal to its face amount.

1. The taxpayer transfers Property A with a basis of $40,000 and a value of $60,000. The taxpayer receives in exchange like-kind property B worth $60,000. What gain, if any, is realized; what gain is recognized; and what is

the taxpayer's basis in Property B?

2. How would your answer change if (a) Property B was worth $50,000 and the taxpayer also received $10,000 cash or (b) Property B was worth $35,000 and the taxpayer received $25,000 cash?

3. Now change the example so that the value of Property A is $30,000 (there is a loss on the exchange); basis is still $40,000. The taxpayer receives Property B, worth $25,000 and $5,000 cash. What is taxpayer's basis in Property B?

4. Suppose the taxpayer owns Property A with a basis of $40,000, a gross value of $70,000, subject to a $10,000 debt. (a) Property A is exchanged for like-kind Property B worth $60,000. Does the taxpayer recognize any gain? Does it matter whether or not the transferee assumes a personal liability for the $10,000 debt? § 1031(d) (last sentence, including cross-reference to § 357(d)). (b) What if the Property B received by the taxpayer had a $90,000 gross value, subject to a $30,000 debt? Treas. Reg. § 1.1031(d)-2 (example 2).

§ 19.03 LIKE-KIND EXCHANGES

One major example of a nonrecognition transaction is a like-kind exchange, provided for by § 1031.

[A] Statutory Coverage

1. To be eligible, a taxpayer must exchange property held for investment or for productive use in a trade or business, for like-kind property held for investment or for productive use in a trade or business. Property held for personal use (such as a residence) is therefore ineligible for tax deferral under § 1031(a)(1). Property is characterized by the exchanging taxpayer's use, not by the use to which the property is put by the person from whom the property is received.

2. Property held "primarily for sale" (such as inventory) is also not eligible. § 1031(a)(2)(A). However, unproductive realty held for future use or for future realization of increment in its value is held for investment, not primarily for sale. Treas. Reg. § 1.1031(a)-1(b).

But suppose the taxpayer buys real estate with a current plan to subdivide the property into lots for sale. Is it held "primarily for sale" as that phrase is used in § 1031? The phrase "primarily for sale" also appears in § 1221(a)(1), where it is part of a broader phrase — "held by the taxpayer primarily for sale to customers in the ordinary course of his trade or business." The primary function of that phrase in § 1221(a)(1) is to distinguish capital assets from ordinary assets. Section 1031 has a different function. It deals with tax deferred exchanges and the question arises whether the phrase "primarily for sale" in § 1031 is broader than in § 1221(a)(1).

Neal T. Baker Enterprises, Inc. v. Commissioner, 76 T.C.M. (CCH) 301 (1998), held that "primarily for sale" in § 1031 has the broader meaning. The factual context involved a real estate developer who had purchased land with an as-yet unimplemented primary plan to subdivide the property for sale. As we will see in Chapter 20, such property is probably *not* an ordinary asset — that is, not held "primarily for sale to customers in the ordinary course of business." under § 1221(a)(1). But the court decided that it was property held "primarily for sale" and therefore ineligible for tax-deferred exchange treatment under § 1031.

3. Certain investment interests, such as stock and debt, are explicitly excluded from § 1031. Partnership interests are also excluded, even though exchange of the underlying business property might have qualified. § 1031(a)(2)(B), (D). The exclusion of partnership interests was adopted in 1984, in part to discourage the exchange of tax shelter partnership interests, but its scope is not limited to tax shelters.

QUESTIONS AND COMMENTS

1. Suppose Taxpayer A exchanges a farm used for business for a building in a rural area used and owned by Taxpayer B as a personal residence. Taxpayer A will convert B's former residence to a farm. Is either A or B eligible for like-kind exchange treatment under § 1031?

2. The reasons for deferring tax on like-kind exchanges and on the receipt of stock dividends (discussed in *Eisner v. Macomber*, Chapter 3.03[A]) are sometimes said to be similar — there is no cash received on the exchange, valuation is very difficult, and the taxpayer has not really changed his investment. Do these policies really explain tax deferral on like-kind exchanges? Can you have a tax deferred exchange and still receive cash? If you get cash, do you have to know the value of the assets exchanged? As for the "change of investment rationale," consider the following examples developed in the regulations.

[B] Administrative Rules

[1] In General

What is like-kind property? The Regulations state that like-kind refers to the "nature or character of the property and not to its grade or quality. . . ." **Treas. Reg. § 1.1031(a)-1(b)**.

If property is of like-kind: (a) property held for business use can be exchanged for property held for investment use and vice versa (**Treas. Reg. § 1.1031(a)-1(a)**); (b) new property can be exchanged for used property (**Treas. Reg. § 1.1031(a)-1(c)**); and (c) a lease of at least 30 years is "like" a fee interest (Rev. Rul. 78-72, 1978-1 C.B. 258; **Treas. Reg. § 1.1031(a)-1(c)**).

[2] Realty

The Regulations put some flesh on the definition of like-kind property in a way that is quite generous to real estate. Thus, "the fact that any real estate involved is improved or unimproved is not material, for that fact relates only to the grade or quality of the property and not its kind or class." **Treas. Reg. § 1.1031(a)-1(b)**. And, if taxpayer A owns farmland and buildings used for business purposes and taxpayer

B owns land and a building used for business in the city, they can swap properties, and both are eligible for § 1031. **Treas. Reg. § 1.1031(a)-1(c).**

Despite the pro-taxpayer breadth of the regulations, it is still necessary to analyze the nature of the underlying real property interests to determine whether they are of "like-kind." In *Wiechens v. United States*, 228 F. Supp. 2d 1080 (D. Ariz. 2002), the taxpayer who exchanged water rights (which was an interest in property) for a fee simple interest in farmland was unsuccessful in relying on § 1031. The court held that the "water rights were limited in priority, quantity, and duration, and they were not sufficiently similar to the fee simple interest . . . to qualify as like-kind property."

[3] Personalty

Regulations set forth rules about whether personal property is of a "like class," in which case it is considered "like-kind." **Treas. Reg. § 1.1031(a)-2.** Although failure to be of "like class" creates no negative inference about whether the assets are like-kind, the "like class" safe havens may operate to limit what a tax planner will consider "like-kind."

Intangible property. Specific rules apply to intangible property — for example, copyrights on different novels are of like-kind, but not copyrights on a song and a novel; good will of different businesses is not of like-kind. **Treas. Reg. § 1.1031(a)-2(c).**

Coins. Coins can be held for different purposes, such as: currency, collector's items, bullion for the value of their metal, or for industrial use. Each use differs from the other so that only an exchange within each category can qualify as a like-kind exchange. Rev. Rul. 79-143, 1979-1 C.B. 264 (numismatic-type gold coins are not like bullion-type gold coins); Rev. Rul. 82-166, 1982-2 C.B. 190 (gold and silver bullion held for investment are not like-kind, because silver is essentially an industrial commodity).

In *California Federal Life Ins. v. Commissioner*, 680 F.2d 85 (9th Cir. 1982), the court refused to treat gold franks and Swiss coins as like-kind, stating that gold franks "are exchanged in the marketplace only by numismatists, and are valued primarily for their rarity, as collector items. The Swiss francs, on the other hand, are currently circulating currency, and to their investors they represent investments in the Swiss national economy."

The Ninth Circuit said two important things in reaching this conclusion. First, "the interpretation of the Tax Court is entitled to respect because of its special expertise in the field. *Cruttenden v. Commissioner*, 644 F.2d 1368, 1374 (9th Cir. 1981); *Allstate Savings & Loan Ass'n v. Commissioner*, 600 F.2d 760, 762 (9th Cir. 1979)." Many observers suspect that courts continue to treat the Tax Court as an expert tribunal, despite § 7482(a) (discussed in Chapter 6.03[B]).

Second, "the Tax Court did not err in refusing to apply the lenient treatment of real estate exchanges to the exchange of personal property in the present case. Congress has suggested by an amendment to sec. 1031 that personal property is to be accorded different treatment; the amendment provides: '(L)ivestock of different sexes are not property of like-kind.' The legislative history of that amendment indicates that its proponents viewed it as declaratory of Congress' original intent in passing sec. 1031 and intended it to overcome too lenient interpretations of the 'like-kind' requirement." The use of one statutory provision to interpret another is an especially interesting analogical approach to statutory interpretation.

[C] Sale vs. Exchange

Section 1031 sharply distinguishes between (a) a taxable sale for cash followed by reinvestment of the proceeds in like-kind property and (b) a tax-deferred exchange of like-kind property. This produces a tax planning problem when the taxpayer wants like-kind property but wants cash from the buyer if such property cannot be found. The following case illustrates how taxpayers have tried to deal with the problem and the government's response.

CARLTON v. UNITED STATES
United States Court of Appeals, Fifth Circuit
385 F.2d 238 (5th Cir. 1967)

GEWIN, CIRCUIT JUDGE: . . .

[Editor — The taxpayer-appellant, Carlton, owned ranch property that he wanted to exchange for other ranch property. But, failing that, he wanted cash. Carlton gave General an option to buy the ranch property. The contract with General "also provided that the appellant could require General, by notifying it in writing, to acquire such other land as designated by the appellants for the purpose of exchange in lieu of a cash payment or mortgage." Carlton definitely wanted to obtain like-kind property for both business and tax reasons. Carlton then found two like-kind properties, conducted all the negotiations to obtain such property, and then (pursuant to the contract) notified General to purchase these like-kind properties to exchange with Carlton.]

. . . On May 11, 1959 General exercised its option to acquire the ranch property and arrangements were made to close the entire transaction around August 1, 1959. The closing of the several transactions actually occurred on August 3rd and 4th and in closing the appellants deviated from the original plan which resulted in the tax problem here in issue.

In order to avoid unnecessary duplication in title transfer, a procedure was adopted whereby title to the [like-kind] properties would be conveyed directly to the appellants instead of to General and then to the appellants. To accomplish this result, General, on August 3rd, assigned to the appellants its contracts to purchase the [like-kind properties] and paid the appellants, by check, the total amount it would have been required to pay if it had actually first purchased the [properties] in its own name and then conveyed the land to the appellants. Later that same day Carlton took the assignment of the contracts to purchase [the properties], using his personal check to close the sale. . . .

Both parties agree that had the appellants followed the original plan, whereby General would have acquired the legal title to the . . . properties and then transferred the title to such properties to the appellants for their ranch property, the appellants would have been entitled to postpone the recognition of the gain pursuant to 1031. However, instead of receiving the title to the . . . properties from General for their ranch property, the appellants received cash and an assignment of General's contract rights to those properties. Thus, the ultimate question becomes whether the receipt of cash by the appellants upon transferring their ranch property to General transformed the intended exchange into a sale. The Government asserts that it does, and under the facts and in the circumstances of this case, we agree.

Section 1031 was designed to postpone the recognition of gain or loss where property used in a business is exchanged for other property in the course of the continuing operation of a business. In those circumstances, the taxpayer has not received any gain or suffered any loss in a general and economic sense. Nor has the exchange of property resulted in the termination of one venture and assumption of another. The business venture operated before the exchange continues after the exchange without any real economic change or alteration, and without realization of any cash or readily liquefiable asset. The statute specifically limits the nonrecognition of gain or loss to exchanges of property, and it is well settled that a sale and repurchase do not qualify for nonrecognition treatment under the section. Thus, even though the appellants continued their ranching business after the transaction here in question, that does not control the tax consequences of the transfers. Rather, it is essential that the transfers constituted an exchange and not a sale and repurchase if the tax benefits of 1031 are to be applicable.

The appellants contend that the entire transaction must be viewed as a whole in determining whether a sale or an exchange has occurred. They argue that the transfer of the ranch property to General for the cash and assignments was part of a single unitary plan designed and intended to effect an exchange of their ranch property for other property suitable for ranching. Thus, they conclude, the transfers of property should be construed to be an exchange.

While it is true that the incidence of taxation is to be determined by viewing the entire transaction as a whole, that rule does not permit us to close our eyes to the realities of the transaction and merely look at the beginning and end of a transaction without observing the steps taken to reach that end. The requirement is that the transaction be viewed in its entirety in order to determine its reality and substance, for it is the substance of the transaction which decides the incidence of taxation. In the instant case, while elaborate plans were laid to exchange property, the substance of the transaction was that the appellants received cash for the deed to their ranch property and not another parcel of land. The very essence of an exchange is the transfer of property between owners, while the mark of a sale is the receipt of cash for the property. Where, as here, there is an immediate repurchase of other property with the proceeds of the sale, that distinction between a sale and exchange is crucial. Further, General was never in a position to exchange properties with the appellants because it never acquired the legal title to either the Lyons or the Fernandez property. Indeed, General was not personally obligated on either the notes or mortgages involved in these transaction. Thus it never had any property of like-kind to exchange. Finally, it can not be said that General paid for the [like-kind] properties and merely had the properties deeded directly to the appellants. The money received from General by the appellants for the ranch property was not earmarked by General to be used in purchasing the . . . properties. It was unrestricted and could be used by the appellants as they pleased. The fact that they did use it to pay for the . . . properties does not alter the fact that their use of the money was unfettered and unrestrained. It is an inescapable fact that the money received by appellants from General was money paid to them for a conveyance of their land. As a result, the separate transaction between General and the appellants must be construed to be a sale, and the transactions between the appellants and [the owners of the like-kind property] as a purchase of other property.

The appellants' intention and desire to execute an exchange does not alter the reality and substance of the situation. It is well established that the intention of a taxpayer to avail himself of the advantages of a particular provision of the tax laws does not determine the tax consequences of his action, but what was actually done is determinative of the tax treatment. Thus, the intention of the appellants to effect an exchange does not convert the transfer of property for cash into an exchange. . . .

Therefore, we are compelled to conclude that the transfer of the ranch property to General constituted a sale, and rendered the nonrecognition of gain provisions of 1031 inapplicable. Considering how close the appellants came to satisfying the requirements of that section and the stipulation that an exchange was intended, this result is obviously harsh. But there is no equity in tax law, and such must the result be if the limitation in 1031 to exchanges is to have any meaning.

The judgment of the district court is Affirmed.

QUESTION

Suppose the taxpayer in *Carlton* had found the like-kind property by contacting a third party and arranged to have it transferred directly to the taxpayer, without General taking title; and, further, General paid the third party for the like-kind property with cash, rather than paying the taxpayer. Is that a like-kind exchange? Rev. Rul. 90-34, 1990-1 C.B. 154.

[D] Note on Statutory Interpretation — Statutory Purpose; "Equity of the Statute"

The decision in *Carlton* makes one remarkable statement at the end of the opinion. The judge says that tax law has no "equity." What does that mean? It has nothing to do with whether the tax law is or is not harsh. In statutory interpretation lingo, the "equity" of a statute refers to its purpose. So understood, the court's statement that tax law has no "equity" is much too simplistic. We have already seen examples where purpose prevailed over a clear text — (1) the *Owens* case (Chapter 12.03[B][1]), which limited the deduction of personal losses to the value before the loss, not to the adjusted basis of the asset; and (2) the *Prophit* case (Chapter 1.03[C]), where a child was the dependent of the noncustodial father, not of the custodial nonresident alien mother.

The lack of "equity" in tax law might mean that form prevails over substance. But we know from prior discussion that this also is too simplistic. Substance has sometimes prevailed over the letter of the tax law, not only in the charitable organization context where there is a common law background (*Bob Jones* — Chapter 10.02[C][1]), but also when the issue originates solely in the tax law — (1) the *Hilton* case (Chapter 17.04[B]), where a property law owner with no economic prospects of gain was not considered the "tax owner"); and (2) the *Goldstein* case (Chapter 16.04[A]), where interest deductions were disallowed in a transaction in which there was no opportunity for economic gain apart from the impact of the tax law.

The better way to state the point in *Carlton* about lack of equity is to say that sometimes form *is* substance and that is why it prevails. Thus, in § 1031, a sale for cash is the "substance" of the transaction even though it is a formal step that is adopted as part of a plan to immediately purchase like-kind property with the cash.

All "form vs. substance" distinctions suffer from the same ambiguity. Form prevails over substance *when* that implements the statutory purpose. Judicial statements about statutory "substance" are always legal conclusions. The question in all cases is what does the statute mean. If § 1031 forbids receipt of cash, then receipt of cash is not an irrelevant formal step, to be disregarded in the interest of some broader statutory substance.

[E]   Deferred Receipt of Like-Kind Property

In *Starker v. United States*, 602 F.2d 1341 (9th Cir. 1979), the taxpayer entered into a "land exchange agreement" to convey 1843 acres of timberland in Oregon to the buyer. The buyer agreed to transfer other like-kind realty to the taxpayer within five years after the timberland was received, or to pay cash. The buyer added a 6% "growth factor" for each year it failed to convey land to the taxpayer. The government argued that simultaneity of exchange is a formal requirement of § 1031. However, the court declined to require simultaneity as a condition of qualifying for § 1031 deferral, but did insist that the 6% growth factor was taxable interest when received by the taxpayer.

Section 1031(a)(3) reverses the *Starker* decision and requires that the like-kind property be identified and transferred to the taxpayer within a specified period. The committee reports express concern with the indefinite deferral that *Starker* might permit. What is wrong with indefinite deferral of the gain? Perhaps the government is concerned with the deferral of tax on interest — what the taxpayer called the 6% growth factor in *Starker*. Although a growth factor is taxable interest (**Treas. Reg. § 1.1031(k)-1(h)**), it is apparently not original issue discount that must be accrued *prior* to receipt.

[F]   Losses

[1]   Sale-Leasebacks

Section 1031 defers recognition of losses as well as gains. This leads taxpayers with losses to try to *avoid* like-kind exchanges by receiving cash. Sale-leaseback arrangements are a common feature in cases where the taxpayer tries to recognize a loss. For example, assume the taxpayer owns property with a $4,000,000 basis, which is now worth $2,400,000. Taxpayer sells the property for cash, to recognize the loss, and leases it back from the buyer for 30 years. In such cases, the government argues that the primary purpose of § 1031 is to eliminate valuation problems and that any reciprocal exchange of like-kind property (here it is a fee interest for a 30-year lease) falls within the nonrecognition provisions. *Century Electric Co. v. Commissioner*, 192 F.2d 155 (8th Cir. 1951), agreed with the government and denied a loss deduction.

Other cases support the taxpayer. *Leslie Co. v. Commissioner*, 539 F.2d 943 (3d Cir. 1976); *Jordan Marsh Co. v. Commissioner*, 269 F.2d 453 (2d Cir. 1959). In *Leslie*, for example, the court emphasized that the rent paid when the seller leased the property back from the buyer was fair rental value, so that the taxpayer gave up a fee interest and received no property interest in return, other than the $2,400,000 cash. If the rents were below market value, then the taxpayer might have received a property interest in the form of a bargain-rental 30-year leasehold, in addition to the cash.

Courts finding for the taxpayer stress that the primary purpose of § 1031 is to eliminate recognition (either gain or loss) of paper gains and losses on property exchanges. A taxpayer receiving $2,400,000 for property whose value equals that amount does not have any paper gain or loss on a property exchange. The pro-taxpayer opinion in *Leslie* states that if the statute "intended to obviate the necessity of making difficult valuations, one would have expected them to provide for nonrecognition of gains and losses in all exchanges, whether the property received in exchanges were 'of like-kind' or *not* of a like-kind."

[2]   Sale or Loan

Not all receipts of cash are necessarily sales proceeds. This has led the government to try to recast some "loss" transactions in which the taxpayer receives cash as something other than a sale.

Who else gets cash besides a seller in a property transaction? Borrowers who pledge property as security as well as sellers get cash. So the government often tries to recast sale-leasebacks as secured loans in which the "seller-tenant" is more like a borrower. That would be true if the seller-tenant is very likely to own the property after the lease term. For example, suppose the "seller-tenant" has an option to buy the property after the 30-year lease expires for $1; or to renew the lease at a bargain rental, for most of the property's useful life.

Treating the sale as a loan because the "seller" is still the owner for tax purposes is based on the same type of analysis that we used in Chapter 17.04, when we discussed the issue of tax ownership in sale-leaseback situations. In those cases, a middleman purported to own the property but the tenant often had a very favorable economic opportunity to buy the property at the end of the lease or to keep renewing the lease. In those cases, the tenant might be the owner for tax purposes. Similarly, a seller for cash who leases the property back and becomes a tenant might be treated as the owner of the property for tax purposes. Any cash he gets from the "buyer" would then be treated as a loan and the "rent" would be a payment of principal and interest to the "buyer-lessor," who is really a lender.

§ 19.04 OTHER NONRECOGNITION PROVISIONS

Section 1031 is just one of many tax deferral provisions. In other situations where the statute allows tax deferral, a taxpayer can sometimes receive all cash, as long as the cash is reinvested in certain property. In some cases, gain is deferred but loss is not. Here are a few examples. What justifies the statutory rule permitting receipt of all cash, unlike § 1031, as long as it is "properly" reinvested?

[A] Sale of Principal Residence; Exemption vs. Deferral

Under an earlier law, § 1034 allowed taxpayers to sell a principal residence for cash and reinvest the proceeds in another principal residence on a tax deferred basis, recognizing only the gain up to the amount of unreinvested sales proceeds. In addition, an older version of § 121 *exempted* up to $125,000 of otherwise recognized gain on the sale of a principal residence by a taxpayer age 55 or older; this was a one-time exclusion.

Current law reflects the repeal of § 1034 and a greatly broadened exemption under § 121. The law now provides an exemption from gain on the sale of a principal residence equal to $250,000 ($500,000 for (a) a married couple filing a joint return and for (b) a surviving spouse if the sale occurs within two years of the spouse's death). The exemption applies regardless of the taxpayer's age. Moreover, the exclusion is no longer a one-time tax break; every sale is eligible as long as there is a two-year gap between sales. The benefits of § 121 are elective with the taxpayer.

To obtain the exemption, the home must have been owned and occupied as the principal residence in two of the five years prior to the sale. There are special rules allowing some portion of the gain to be excluded if the sale is due to unforeseen circumstances that prevent satisfaction of the time limit requirements. This two-out-of-five-year rule should minimize the nagging problem of deciding whether the taxpayer who rents out the residence for a period of time while looking for a buyer has maintained the abode as a principal residence.

The exemption does *not* apply to any depreciation adjustments provided by § 1250(b)(3) on the residence. Thus, if the taxpayer rents out the property and takes $10,000 depreciation, gain will not be exempt up to that $10,000 amount.

[B] Involuntary Conversions; Section 1033

In a § 1031 transaction, the taxpayer cannot get cash, but in a § 1033 the taxpayer can get cash.

Tax deferral under § 1033 generally applies in more narrow circumstances than § 1031 (except that it is not limited to business and investment property). (1) § 1033 applies only to *involuntary* conversions, not voluntary transfers. (2) The replacement property must be "similar or related in service or use" to the lost property, which is narrower than like-kind. (3) Reinvestment of cash in qualified replacement property must usually be within two years of the end of the tax year in which the forced sale occurs. A typical § 1033 transaction is the reinvestment of insurance proceeds in a new factory to replace a factory that burns down, or reinvestment in new land to replace condemned land.

The idea behind § 1033 seems to be that it is unfair to tax someone who reinvests in virtually the same asset after an involuntary conversion. The reinvestment shows that the taxpayer did not want to sell at all. If the taxpayer does not reinvest some part of the proceeds, that is "boot," taxable up to the amount of the gain on the transaction — just as in § 1031. Thus, assume a $40,000 cost and $60,000 insurance proceeds, only $50,000 of which is reinvested in § 1033 property. The $10,000 retained by the taxpayer is taxed; basis in the replacement property is $40,000. **§ 1033(a)(2)(A), (b).**

This rationale has led to a generous interpretation of what amounts to an involuntary conversion. In *Willamette Industries, Inc. v. C.I.R.*, 118 T.C. 126 (2002), some of the taxpayer's trees were partially damaged and the taxpayer was compelled to salvage the trees by harvesting them *before* the normal harvesting date, or they would have been lost through decay, insects, etc. Taxpayer did not sell the trees in their damaged state but processed them into the end products that it normally produces and then sold the end product. Taxpayer sought to defer tax only on the portion of the gain attributable to the difference between its basis and the fair market value of the damaged trees in place; it did not try to defer the part of the sales gain attributable to the processing of the trees or to the manufacturing of the end products.

The court acknowledged that the taxpayer's business circumstances were more favorable than might have been expected after the usual "casualty," because of the opportunity to process the trees into finished products for sale. But the court said that § 1033 was a relief provision, to be construed liberally. It refused to deny relief just because the taxpayer was *both* a grower of trees and also a manufacturer of products using trees, compared to a similarly situated grower of trees who did *not* use the damaged trees to make final products for sale. Consequently, the taxpayer could defer "the portion of the gain that it was compelled to realize on account of the damage to its trees," but not the gain from any further processing.

Because § 1033 is more of a taxpayer relief provision than § 1031, losses are recognized if there is an involuntary conversion, even if the taxpayer reinvests cash proceeds incident to the conversion. In addition, tax deferral of gain after money is reinvested in "similar" property is optional with the taxpayer. By contrast, § 1031 is mandatory and losses are not recognized. **§ 1031(c).**

The difference between §§ **1031 & 1033** is illustrated by Letter Ruling 9723032. The issue was whether a motel was similar or related in service or use to an apartment building destroyed by fire so that the realized gain from the insurance proceeds attributable to the apartment building could be deferred under **§ 1033(a).** The ruling denied tax deferral based on the fact that the taxpayer changed his relationship from a lessor of apartments to an operator of a motel, which substantially altered his relationship to the properties. As a lessor of apartment units, the essence of the taxpayer's investment was the generation of fixed, periodic rental income. Although the taxpayer provided certain services typical of a landlord, he was not required to be on the premises on a daily basis. As a landlord, the taxpayer was insulated from the day-to-day operating responsibilities and activities that are demanded by the operation of the motel. In contrast, the business of operating the motel required daily oversight. Taxpayer was responsible for furnishing the rooms, cleaning the rooms, and washing the linens — services that were not required as an apartment building landlord. By changing from an owner-lessor of property to an owner-operator, taxpayer's relationship to the properties changed substantially and the property was not similar or related in service or use. By contrast, the exchange of the apartment for the motel property would be a like-kind exchange under § 1031.

Section 1033(g) provides that, if business or investment *realty* is condemned, qualified replacement property includes both "like-kind" *and* "similar" property. Why isn't the same concession made for insurance proceeds, if a building burns down?

Section 1033(h) provides a special rule for the involuntary conversion of a principal residence and its contents, damaged by presidentially declared disasters. First, the insurance proceeds for the residence and scheduled property are treated as though they were received for a single item of property. (Scheduled property is valuable property, such as antiques, jewelry, silver, etc., that is separately listed, valued, and insured by the insurance company.) This means that the proceeds received for the scheduled property can be reinvested in a principal residence on a tax-deferred basis, even though it would otherwise not meet the "similar" property requirement. Second, the statute extends the § 1033 replacement period for property covered by § 1033(h) from two to four years. Third, no gain is recognized on receipt of insurance proceeds for "unscheduled" property — usually routine personal contents of the house.

[C] Corporation Organizations

Assume that a taxpayer doing business as a sole proprietorship or partnership wants to form a corporation to carry on the business. It is reasonable to say that not much has happened to the investment except to change the form of doing business — shifting from noncorporate to corporate form. Although technically there has been a realization event, the economics of doing business have not changed much. Moreover, it is economically desirable for the tax law to permit changing the form of doing business without any tax burden.

The tax law has long provided that the organization of a corporation does not result in recognized income on the asset transfers in exchange for stock to a controlling group of shareholders. Instead the shareholders and the corporation carry over the basis in the assets transferred to the corporation so that gain or loss will be recognized in the future. A major qualification to this generalization is that gain attributable to the receipt of property that does *not* provide continuity of investment interest (for example, cash, bonds, short-term debt, and (sometimes) preferred stock — referred to as "boot") will be taxable. §§ 351, 358, 362.

For example, assume a taxpayer owns a business. Basis in the assets equals $100, and their value is $300. The taxpayer transfers the assets to a corporation in exchange for 100% of its common stock plus $100 in bonds. This results in nonrecognition of gain on the receipt of the stock and a tax on the $100 of bonds (probably as capital gains). Basis in the stock remains $100; the corporation takes the $100 basis in the assets received from the taxpayer, increased by the $100 gain recognized on the distribution of the bonds to the shareholders. These are the same rules that apply to like-kind exchanges.

[D]   Miscellaneous

Tax deferral is a handy policy tool.

1. **Sections 1081–1083** provide tax deferral for gain and loss on exchanges of stocks and securities to obey orders of the Securities and Exchange Commission.

2. **Section 1043** allows public officials who must divest themselves of property when they take office to elect to defer gain on the sales proceeds if they reinvest within 60 days in "permitted" property (generally U.S. obligations or diversified investment funds).

3. **Section 1044** permits certain taxpayers who sell publicly traded stock to elect to defer a limited amount of gain, if the sales proceeds are reinvested in a "specialized small business investment company."

Chapter 20

CAPITAL GAINS AND LOSSES — DEFINITION

In Chapter 3.04[A], we discussed the tax preference for certain capital gains — primarily, a 20% maximum tax rate. You may want to review that discussion now, especially the determination of "net capital gain." The essential prerequisites for capital gains are "sale or exchange" of a "capital asset." To obtain the lower preferential tax rate, the asset has to be held for more than one year.

In this chapter we look closely at the definitions of the key terms — primarily "capital asset," but also "sale or exchange."

§ 20.01 PRIMARILY FOR SALE IN THE ORDINARY COURSE OF BUSINESS

The primary distinction between capital gain and ordinary income is between the gain attributable to property that produces income and the periodic income produced by that property. This distinction is implemented by the exclusion from the definition of a "capital asset" provided in § 1221(a)(1) (property held primarily for sale in the ordinary course of business). (Periodic rent, interest, etc. does not produce capital gain because it is not received in a sale or exchange.) As the following decision in the *Biedenharn* case illustrates, the application of that phrase depends on a close examination of the facts.

The very lengthy excerpt from *Biedenharn* is meant to alert you to the fact-specific nature of the inquiry when deciding whether property is held primarily for sale in the ordinary course of business. The opinion in *Biedenharn* does not refer to a lettered subsection of § 1221 — e.g. § 1221(a), etc. — because the letters were added to the statute later.

[A] Cases

BIEDENHARN REALTY CO. v. UNITED STATES
United States Court of Appeals, Fifth Circuit
526 F.2d 409 (5th Cir. 1976)

GOLDBERG, CIRCUIT JUDGE:

The taxpayer-plaintiff, Biedenharn Realty Company, Inc. (Biedenharn), filed suit against the United States in May, 1971, claiming a refund for the tax years 1964, 1965, and 1966. . . . In its present action, plaintiff asserts that the whole real estate profit represents gain from the sale of capital assets and consequently that the Government is indebted to taxpayer for $32,006.86 in overpaid taxes. Reviewing the facts of this case in the light of our previous holdings and the directions set forth in this opinion, we reject plaintiff's claim and in so doing reverse the opinion of the District Court.

I.

. . . [W]e believe it useful to set out in plentiful detail the case's background and circumstances as best they can be ascertained.

A. *The Realty Company.* Joseph Biedenharn organized the Biedenharn Realty Company in 1923 as a vehicle for holding and managing the Biedenharn family's numerous investments. The original stockholders were all family members. The investment company controls, among other interests, valuable commercial properties, a substantial stock portfolio, a motel, warehouses, a shopping center, residential real property, and farm property.

B. *Taxpayer's Real Property Sales — The Hardtimes Plantation.* Taxpayer's suit most directly involves its ownership and sale of lots from the 973 acre tract located near Monroe, Louisiana, known as the Hardtimes Plantation. The plaintiff purchased the estate in 1935 for $50,000.00. B. W. Biedenharn, the Realty Company's president, testified that taxpayer acquired Hardtimes as a 'good buy' for the purpose of farming and as a future investment. The plaintiff farmed the land for several years. Thereafter, Biedenharn rented part of the acreage to a farmer who Mr. Biedenharn suggested may presently be engaged in farming operations.

1. *The Three Basic Subdivisions.* Between 1939 and 1966, taxpayer carved three basic subdivisions from Hardtimes — Biedenharn Estates, Bayou DeSiard Country Club Addition, and Oak Park Addition — covering approximately 185 acres. During these years, Biedenharn sold 208 subdivided Hardtimes lots in 158 sales, making a profit in excess of $800,000.00. These three basic subdivisions are the source of the contested 37 sales of 38 lots. Their development and disposition are more fully discussed below.

a) Biedenharn Estates Unit 1, including 41.9 acres, was platted in 1938. Between 1939 and 1956, taxpayer apparently sold 21 lots in 9 sales. Unit 2, containing 8.91 acres, was sold in 9 transactions between 1960 and 1965 and involved 10 lots.

b) Bayou DeSiard Country Club Addition, covering 61 acres, was subdivided in 1951, with remaining lots resubdivided in 1964. Approximately 73 lots were purchased in 64 sales from 1951 to 1966.

c) Oak Park Units 1 and 2 encompassed 75 acres. After subdivision in 1955 and resubdivision in 1960, plaintiff sold approximately 104 lots in 76 sales. . . .

[Editor — The court then describes the sale of lots from non-Hardtimes property.] Unfortunately, the record does not unambiguously reveal the number of *sales* as opposed to the number of *lots* involved in these dispositions. Although some doubt exists as to the actual sales totals, even the most conservative reading of the figures convinces us of the frequency and abundance of the non-Hardtimes sales. For example, from 1925 to 1958, Biedenharn consummated from its subdivided Owens tract a minimum of 125, but perhaps upwards of 300, sales (338 lots). Eighteen sales accounted for 20 lots sold between 1923 and 1958 from Biedenharn's

Cornwall property. Taxpayer's disposition from 1927 to 1960 of its Corey and Cabeen property resulted in at least 50 sales. Plaintiff made 14 sales from its Thomas Street lots between 1937 and 1955. Moreover, Biedenharn has sold over 20 other properties, a few of them piecemeal, since 1923. . . .

D. *Real Property Improvements.* Before selling the Hardtimes lots, Biedenharn improved the land, adding in most instances streets, drainage, water, sewerage, and electricity. The total cost of bettering the Plantation acreage exceeded $200,000 and included $9,520.17 for Biedenharn Estates Unit 2, $56,879.12 for Bayou DeSiard Country Club Addition, and $141,579.25 for the Oak Park Addition.

E. *Sale of the Hardtimes Subdivisions.* Bernard Biedenharn testified that at the time of the Hardtimes purchase, no one foresaw that the land would be sold as residential property in the future. Accordingly, the District Court found, and we do not disagree, that Biedenharn bought Hardtimes for investment. Later, as the City of Monroe expanded northward, the Plantation became valuable residential property. The Realty Company staked off the Bayou DeSiard subdivision so that prospective purchasers could see what the lots 'looked like.' As demand increased, taxpayer opened the Oak Park and Biedenharn Estates Unit 2 subdivisions and resubdivided the Bayou DeSiard section. Taxpayer handled all Biedenharn Estates and Bayou DeSiard sales. Independent realtors disposed of many of the Oak Park lots. Mr. Herbert Rosenhein, a local broker, sold Oak Park Unit 1 lots. Gilbert Faulk, a real estate agent, sold from Oak Park Unit 2. Of the 37 sales consummated between 1964 and 1966, Henry Biedenharn handled at least nine transactions (Biedenharn Estates (2) and Bayou DeSiard (7)) while 'independent realtors' effected some, if not all, of the other 28 transactions (Oak Park Unit 2.). Taxpayer delegated significant responsibilities to these brokers. In its dealings with Faulk, Biedenharn set the prices, general credit terms, and signed the deeds. Details, including specific credit decisions and advertising, devolved to Faulk, who utilized on-site signs and newspapers to publicize the lots.

In contrast to these broker induced dispositions, plaintiff's non-brokered sales resulted after unsolicited individuals approached Realty Company employees with inquiries about prospective purchases. At no time did the plaintiff hire its own real state salesmen or engage in formal advertising. Apparently, the lands' prime location and plaintiff's subdivision activities constituted sufficient notice to interested persons of the availability of Hardtimes lots. Henry Biedenharn testified:

> (O)nce we started improving and putting roads and streets in people would call us up and ask you about buying a lot and we would sell a lot if they wanted it.

The Realty Company does not maintain a separate place of business but instead offices at the Biedenharn family's Ouachita Coca-Cola bottling plant. A telephone, listed in plaintiff's name, rings at the Coca-Cola building. Biedenharn has four employees: a camp caretaker, a tenant farmer, a bookkeeper and a manager. The manager, Henry Biedenharn, Jr., devotes approximately 10% of his time to the Realty Company, mostly collecting rents and overseeing the maintenance of various properties. The bookkeeper also works only part-time for plaintiff. Having set out these facts, we now discuss the relevant legal standard for resolving this controversy.

II.

The determination of gain as capital or ordinary is controlled by the language of the Internal Revenue Code. The Code defines capital asset, the profitable sale or exchange of which generally results in capital gains, as 'property held by the taxpayer.' 26 U.S.C. § 1221. Many exceptions limit the enormous breadth of this congressional description and consequently remove large numbers of transactions from the privileged realm of capital gains. In this case, we confront the question whether or not Biedenharn's real estate sales should be taxed at ordinary rates because they fall within the exception covering 'property held by the taxpayer primarily for sale to customers in the ordinary course of his trade or business.' 26 U.S.C. § 1221(1).[1]

The problem we struggle with here is not novel. We have become accustomed to the frequency with which taxpayers litigate this troublesome question. Chief Judge Brown appropriately described the real estate capital gains-ordinary income issue as 'old, familiar, recurring, vexing and ofttimes elusive.' The difficulty in large part stems from ad-hoc application of the numerous permissible criteria set forth in our multitudinous prior opinions. Over the past 40 years, this case by case approach with its concentration on the facts of each suit has resulted in a collection of decisions not always reconcilable. . . .

Assuredly, we would much prefer one or two clearly defined, easily employed tests which lead to predictable, perhaps automatic, conclusions. However, the nature of the congressional 'capital asset' definition and the myriad situations to which we must apply that standard make impossible any easy escape from the task before us. No one set of criteria is applicable to all economic structures. Moreover, within a collection of tests, individual factors have varying weights and magnitudes, depending on the facts of the case. The relationship among the factors and their mutual interaction is altered as each criteria increases or diminishes in strength, sometimes changing the controversy's outcome. As such, there can be no mathematical formula capable of finding the X of capital gains or ordinary income in this complicated field.

Yet our inability to proffer a panaceatic guide to the perplexed with respect to this subject does not preclude our setting forth some general, albeit inexact, guidelines for the resolution of many of the § 1221(1) cases we confront. This opinion does not purport to reconcile all past precedents or assure conflict free future decisions. Nor do we hereby obviate the need for ad-hoc adjustments when confronted with close cases and changing factual circumstances. Instead, with the hope of clarifying a few of the area's mysteries, we more precisely define and suggest points of emphasis for the major *Winthrop* delineated factors[2] as they

---

[1] [20] [Editor — The bracketed numbers in the footnotes in this chapter refer to the numbers in the reported case.] Neither party contends, nor do we find, that Internal Revenue Code sec. 1237, guaranteeing capital gains treatment to subdividing taxpayers in certain instances, is applicable to the facts of this suit.

[2] [22] *In United States v. Winthrop*, 5 Cir. 1969, 417 F.2d 905, 910, the Court enumerated the following factors:

(1) the nature and purpose of the acquisition of the property and the duration of the

appear in the instant controversy. In so doing, we devote particular attention to the Court's recent opinions in order that our analysis will reflect, insofar as possible, the Circuit's present trends.

III.

We begin our task by evaluating in the light of *Biedenharn's* facts the main *Winthrop* factors — substantiality and frequency of sales, improvements, solicitation and advertising efforts, and brokers' activities — as well as a few miscellaneous contentions. A separate section follows discussing the keenly contested role of prior investment intent. . . .

A. *Frequency and Substantiality of Sales*

Scrutinizing closely the record and briefs, we find that plaintiff's real property sales activities compel an ordinary income conclusion.[3] In arriving at this result, we examine first the most important of Winthrop's factors — the frequency and substantiality of taxpayer's sales. Although frequency and substantiality of sales are not usually conclusive, they occupy the preeminent ground in our analysis. The recent trend of Fifth Circuit decisions indicates that when dispositions of subdivided property extend over a long period of time and are especially numerous, the likelihood of capital gains is very slight indeed. Conversely, when sales are few and isolated, the taxpayer's claim to capital gain is accorded greater deference.

On the present facts, taxpayer could not claim 'isolated' sales or a passive and gradual liquidation. Although only three years and 37 sales (38 lots) are in controversy here, taxpayer's pre-1964 sales from the Hardtimes acreage as well as similar dispositions from other properties are probative of the existence of sales 'in the ordinary course of his trade or business.' . . . Biedenharn sold property, usually a substantial number of lots, in every year, save one, from 1923 to 1966. . . .

The frequency and substantiality of Biedenharn's sales go not only to its holding purpose and the existence of a trade or business but also support our finding of the ordinariness with which the Realty Company disposed of its lots. These sales easily meet the criteria of normalcy set forth in *Winthrop*. . . .

---

ownership; (2) the extent and nature of the taxpayer's efforts to sell the property; (3) the number, extent, continuity and substantiality of the sales; (4) the extent of subdividing, developing, and advertising to increase sales; (5) the use of a business office for the sale of the property; (6) the character and degree of supervision or control exercised by the taxpayer over any representative selling the property; and (7) the time and effort the taxpayer habitually devoted to the sales.

The numbering indicates no hierarchy of importance.

[3] [25] Our power to review the District Court's ultimate legal determination that taxpayer did not hold property 'primarily for sale to customers in the ordinary course of his trade or business' is plenary and not limited by the clearly erroneous rule. *See* United States v. Winthrop, 5 Cir. 1969, 417 F.2d 905, 910,.

B. *Improvements*

Although we place greatest emphasis on the frequency and substantiality of sales over an extended time period, our decision in this instance is aided by the presence of taxpayer activity — particularly improvements — in the other Winthrop areas. Biedenharn vigorously improved its subdivisions, generally adding streets, drainage, sewerage, and utilities. . . .

C. *Solicitation and Advertising Efforts*

Substantial, frequent sales and improvements such as we have encountered in this case will usually conclude the capital gains issue against taxpayer. Thus, on the basis of our analysis to this point, we would have little hesitation in finding that taxpayer held 'primarily for sale' in the 'ordinary course of (his) trade or business.' '(T)he flexing of commercial muscles with frequency and continuity, design and effect' of which Winthrop spoke, is here a reality. This reality is further buttressed by Biedenharn's sales efforts, including those carried on through brokers. Minimizing the importance of its own sales activities, taxpayer points repeatedly to its steady avoidance of advertising or other solicitation of customers. Plaintiff directs our attention to stipulations detailing the population growth of Monroe and testimony outlining the economic forces which made Hardtimes Plantation attractive residential property and presumably eliminated the need for sales exertions. We have no quarrel with plaintiff's description of this familiar process of suburban expansion, but we cannot accept the legal inferences which taxpayer would have us draw.

The Circuit's recent decisions . . . implicitly recognize that even one inarguably in the real estate business need not engage in promotional exertions in the fact of a favorable market. As such, we do not always require a showing of active solicitation where 'business . . . (is) good, indeed brisk,' and where other Winthrop factors make obvious taxpayer's ordinary trade or business status. Plainly, this represents a sensible approach. In cases such as Biedenharn, the sale of a few lots and the construction of the first homes . . . as well as the building of roads, addition of utilities, and staking off of the other subdivided parcels constitute a highly visible form of advertising. Prospective home buyers drive by the advantageously located property, see the development activities, and are as surely put on notice of the availability of lots as if the owner had erected large signs announcing 'residential property for sale.' We do not by this evaluation automatically neutralize advertising or solicitation as a factor in our analysis. . . . [I]nherent notice represents only one band of the solicitation spectrum. Media utilization and personal initiatives remain material components of this criterion. When present, they call for greater Government oriented emphasis on Winthrop's solicitation factor.

D. *Brokerage Activities*

In evaluating Biedenharn's solicitation activities, we need not confine ourselves to the . . . *Winthrop* theory of brisk sales without organizational efforts. Unlike in . . . Winthrop where no one undertook overt solicitation efforts, the Realty

Company hired brokers who, using media and on site advertising, worked vigorously on taxpayer's behalf. We do not believe that the employment of brokers should shield plaintiff from ordinary income treatment. Their activities should at least in discounted form be attributed to Biedenharn. . . . In [some cases], the taxpayer turned the entire property over to brokers, who, having been granted total responsibility, made all decisions including the setting of sales prices. In comparison, *Biedenharn* determined original prices and general credit policy. Moreover, the Realty Company did not make all the sales in question through brokers. . . .

IV.

The Government asserts that Biedenharn Realty Company did not merely 'liquidate' an investment but instead entered the real estate business in an effort to dispose of what was formerly investment property. Claiming that Biedenharn's activities would result in ordinary income if the Hardtimes Plantation had been purchased with the intent to divide and resell the property, and finding no reason why a different prior intent should influence this outcome,[4] the Government concludes that original investment purpose is irrelevant. Instead, the Government would have us focus exclusively on taxpayer's intent and the level of sales activity during the period commencing with subdivision and improvement and lasting through final sales. Under this theory, every individual who improves and frequently sells substantial numbers of land parcels would receive ordinary income.[5] While the facts of this case dictate our agreement with the Internal Revenue Service's ultimate conclusion of taxpayer liability, they do not require our acquiescence in the Government's entreated total elimination of *Winthrop*'s first criterion, 'the nature and purpose of the acquisition.' Undoubtedly, in most subdivided-improvement situations, an investment purpose of antecedent origin will not survive into a present era of intense retail selling. The antiquated purpose, when overborne by later, but substantial and frequent selling activity, will not prevent ordinary income from being visited upon the taxpayer. Generally, investment purpose has no built-in perpetuity nor a guarantee of capital gains forever more. Precedents, however, in certain circumstances have permitted landowners with earlier investment intent to sell subdivided property and remain subject to capital gains treatment. . . .

We reject the Government's sweeping contention that prior investment intent is always irrelevant. There will be instances where an initial investment purpose endures in controlling fashion notwithstanding continuing sales activity. We doubt that this aperture, where an active subdivider and improver receives capital gains, is very wide; yet we believe it exists. We would most generally find such an opening

---

[4] [38] The Government emphasizes the 'unfairness' of two taxpayers engaging in equal sales efforts with respect to similar tracts of land but receiving different tax treatment because of divergent initial motives.

[5] [39] The Government suggests that taxpayer can avoid ordinary income treatment by selling the undivided, unimproved tract to a controlled corporation which would then develop the land. However, this approach would in many instances create attribution problems with the Government arguing that the controlled corporation's sales are actually those of the taxpayer. Furthermore, we are not prepared to tell taxpayers that in all cases a single bulk sale provides the only road to capital gains.

where the change from investment holding to sales activity results from unanticipated, externally induced factors which make impossible the continued pre-existing use of the realty. *Barrios Estate v. Commissioner*, 5 Cir. 1959, 265 F.2d 517, is such a case. There the taxpayer farmed the land until drainage problems created by the newly completed intercoastal canal rendered the property agriculturally unfit. The Court found that taxpayer was 'dispossessed of the farming operation through no act of her own.' Similarly, Acts of God, condemnation of part of one's property, new and unfavorable zoning regulations, or other events forcing alteration of taxpayer's plans create situations making possible subdivision and improvement as a part of a capital gains disposition.[6] . . .

. . . [W]e caution that although permitting a land owner substantial sales flexibility where there is a forced change from original investment purpose, we do not absolutely shield the constrained taxpayer from ordinary income. That taxpayer is not granted carte blanche to undertake intensely all aspects of a full blown real estate business. Instead, in cases of forced change of purpose, we will continue to utilize the Winthrop analysis discussed earlier but will place unusually strong taxpayer-favored emphasis on Winthrop's first factor.

Clearly, under the facts in this case, the distinction just elaborated undermines Biedenharn's reliance on original investment purpose. Taxpayer's change of purpose was entirely voluntary and therefore does not fall within the protected area. Moreover, taxpayer's original investment intent, *even if* considered a factor sharply supporting capital gains treatment, is so overwhelmed by the other *Winthrop* factors discussed supra, that that element can have no decisive effect. However wide the capital gains passageway through which a subdivider with former investment intent could squeeze, the Biedenharn Realty Company will never fit. . . .

VI.

Having surveyed the Hardtimes terrain, we find no escape from ordinary income. The frequency and substantiality of sales over an extended time, the significant improvement of the basic subdivisions, the acquisition of additional properties, the use of brokers, and other less important factors persuasively combine to doom taxpayer's cause. Applying *Winthrop's* criteria, this case clearly falls within the ordinary income category delineated in that decision. . . .

We cannot write black letter law for all realty subdividers and for all times, but we do caution in words of red that once an investment does not mean always an investment. A simon-pure investor forty years ago could by his subsequent activities become a seller in the ordinary course four decades later. The period of Biedenharn's passivity is in the distant past; and the taxpayer has since undertaken the

---

[6] [40] A Boston University Law Review article canvassing factors inducing involuntary changes of purpose in subdivided realty cases enumerates among others the following: a pressing need for funds in general, illness or old age or both, the necessity for liquidating a partnership on the death of a partner, the threat of condemnation, and municipal zoning restrictions. Levin, *Capital Gains or Income Tax on Real Estate Sales*, 37 B.U. L. Rev. 1965, 194–95 (1957). Although we might not accept all of these events as sufficient to cause an outcome favorable to taxpayer, they are suggestive of the sort of change of purpose provoking events delineated above as worthy of special consideration.

role of real estate protagonist. The Hardtimes Plantation in its day may have been one thing, but as the plantation was developed and sold, Hardtimes became by the very fact of change and activity a different holding than it had been at its inception. No longer could resort to initial purpose preserve taxpayer's once upon a time opportunity for favored treatment. The opinion of the District Court is reversed.

QUESTIONS AND COMMENTS

1. Why is original investment purpose relevant? The decision in *Biedenharn* obviously downplays the relevance of this factor but is reluctant to give it up. Does it have anything to do with the fair treatment of an investor who holds property for a long time, during which it rises in value, and who then sells the asset in the ordinary course of business? Would it be fair to allocate the gain between capital gain (based on value when the shift to selling in the ordinary course of business occurs) and ordinary income? **Section 1237** achieves that result in a limited way under limited circumstances. *See also* footnote 39 in *Biedenharn*.

2. *Biedenharn* states that the taxpayer was primarily selling, not investing or holding with a dual investment/sale purpose. On reflection, that is a puzzling way to explain the distinction between capital gain and ordinary income. After all, many investors (including the core capital gain example of the stock investor) hold primarily for sale, but receive capital gains. When the court in *Biedenharn* contrasts *investing* with selling, it probably identifies investing to include *both* (1) holding an asset to produce periodic income, as when property is farmed or leased; *and* (2) holding an investment asset *for sale*, but *not* in the ordinary course of business. That would explain why most of the opinion, denying capital gain, is about *how* the taxpayer sold (that is, in the ordinary course of business), not whether sale was the primary motive.

3. This suggests a further question. Why can't investment property held to produce income (such as rent) also be held primarily for sale in the ordinary course of business? The following case deals with that issue.

INTERNATIONAL SHOE MACHINE CORP. v. UNITED STATES
United States Court of Appeals, First Circuit
491 F.2d 157 (1st Cir. 1974)

Coffin, Chief Judge. . . .

[Editor — The government argued that gain on the property was not taxable as capital gain because it was "held primarily for sale in the ordinary course of business."]

It is undisputed that during the years in question, 1964 through 1966, appellant's main source of income derived from the leases of its shoe machinery equipment, rather than from their sales. The revenue from sales of the leased machinery comprised, respectively, only 7 per cent, 2 per cent, and 2 per cent of appellant's gross revenues. In fact, because the appellant preferred the more profitable route of leasing its machines, it never developed a sales force, never solicited purchases, set prices high to make purchasing unattractive, and even attempted to dissuade customers from purchasing them.

Yet the district court found that, beginning in 1964, when the investment tax credit made it more attractive for shoe manufacturers to buy shoe machinery rather than to lease it, the selling of machinery became an accepted and predictable, albeit small, part of appellant's business. Since appellant's chief competitor was selling leased shoe machines, it was necessary for appellant to offer its customers the same option. During the years in issue, appellant never declined to quote a price, nor did it ever decline to make a sale if the customer was persistent. Unlike previous years, purchase inquiries were referred to the appellant's vice president for sales, normally charged with selling new, nonleased machines, whereupon a price was negotiated. A schedule was prepared, indicating the sales price of leased machines, based upon the number of years that the machines had been leased. In total, 271 machines were sold to customers who, at the time of the sales, had been leasing the machines for at least six months. . . .

In support of its contention that 'primarily' refers to a contrast between sales and leases, appellant relies upon *Malat v. Riddell*, 383 U.S. 569 (1966). There, the taxpayer purchased a parcel of land, with the alleged intention of developing an apartment project. When the taxpayer confronted zoning restrictions, he decided to terminate the venture, and sold his interest in the property, claiming a capital gain. The lower courts found, however, that the taxpayer had had a 'dual purpose' in acquiring the land, a 'substantial' one of which was to sell if that were to prove more profitable than development. Therefore, since the taxpayer had failed to establish that the property was not held primarily for sale to customers in the ordinary course of his business, his gain was treated as ordinary income. The Supreme Court vacated and remanded the case, stating that the lower courts had applied an incorrect legal standard when they defined 'primarily' as merely 'substantially' rather than using it in its ordinary, everyday sense of 'first importance' or 'principally'. . . .

We cannot agree that Malat is dispositive. Even if 'primarily' is defined as 'of first importance' or 'principally', the word may still invoke a contrast between sales made in the 'ordinary course of . . . business' and those made as liquidations of inventory, rather than between leases and sales. Malat itself concerned the dual purposes of developing an apartment complex on the land and selling the land. Although these two possible sources of income might be characterized as income from 'lease' or 'sale,' a more meaningful distinction could be made between on-going income generated in the ordinary course of business and income from the termination and sale of the venture. . . .

The real question, therefore, concerns whether or not the income from the sales of appellant's shoe machinery should have been characterized as having been generated in the 'ordinary course of . . . business.' Appellant contests the conclusion of the district court that selling was 'an accepted and predictable part of the business' by pointing out that sales were made only as a last resort, after attempts to dissuade the customer from purchasing had failed. We think that the district court was correct in its finding. While sales were made only as a last resort, it seems clear the after 1964 such sales were expected to occur, on an occasional basis, and policies and procedures were developed for handling them. Purchase inquiries were referred to the vice president for sales, a price schedule was drawn up, and discounts were offered to good customers. Appellant may not have desired such sales. It is likely that appellant would never have developed a sales policy for its leased machines had it not been forced to do so by the pressure of competition. But it was justifiable to find that such occasional sales were indeed 'accepted and predictable.'

Even 'accepted and predictable' sales might not, however, occur in the 'ordinary course of . . . business.' For example, a final liquidation of inventory, although accepted and predictable, would normally be eligible for capital gains treatment. Appellant's final contention, therefore, is that the sales in question represented the liquidation of an investment. Appellant points out that the machines were leased for an average of eight and one half years before they were sold, during which time depreciation was taken on them and repairs were made. Thus, appellant seeks to bring itself within the scope of the 'rental-obsolescence' decisions, which hold that the sale of rental equipment, no longer useful for renting, is taxable at capital gains rates.

In the 'rental obsolescence' decisions, however, equipment was sold only after its rental income-producing potential had ended and 'such sales were . . . the natural conclusion of a vehicle rental business cycle.' Moreover, the equipment was specifically manufactured to fit the requirements of lessees; it was sold only when lessees no longer found the equipment useful. In the present case, however, the shoe manufacturing equipment was sold, not as a final disposition of property that had ceased to produce rental income for the appellant, but, rather as property that still retained a rental income producing potential for the appellant. Had appellant chosen not to sell the shoe machinery, the machinery would have continued to generate ordinary income in the form of lease revenue. Thus, the sale of such machinery, for a price which included the present value of that future ordinary income, cannot be considered the liquidation of an investment outside the scope of the 'ordinary course of . . . business.'

COMMENTS

1. The actual decision in *International Shoe* should seem relatively unimportant because the asset was tangible personal property subject to depreciation and the recapture rules would turn the gain into ordinary income, except in the unlikely case of the gain exceeding prior depreciation. Under current law, however, gain on the sale of buildings does not produce recaptured ordinary income (and gain on land never did), so the decision is still important in identifying when gain on the sale of previously rented real property is capital gain or ordinary income.

2. As *Biedenharn* indicates, a developer who changes the way he conducts his real estate activities is usually switching from investing to selling in the ordinary course of business. *Olstein v. Commissioner*, 78 T.C.M. (CCH) 383 (1999), was unusual in that the developer did the opposite — he switched from selling homes in the ordinary course of business to liquidating an investment, thereby becoming eligible for capital gains treatment.

[B]   Note on Statutory Interpretation — Statutory Structure

In effect, the court in *International Shoe* rewrote the statute — moving the "for sale" text so that the statute read as follows — "held for sale primarily in the ordinary course of business." This way "primarily" relates to "ordinary course of business," rather than to the verb "sale." The statute is therefore concerned with how the sale occurs — primarily in the ordinary course of business vs. primarily in liquidation — rather than with whether the taxpayer's purpose in holding the property was primarily sale or something else. In other words, the meaning of the text followed from the statutory structure, which was to impose ordinary tax rates on sales occurring in the ordinary course of business.

§ 20.02   TAXPAYER'S PERSONAL EFFORTS CREATE PROPERTY

[A]   Copyright, Etc.

The tax law has long provided that self-created artistic and literary property and the copyright therein is not a capital asset. § 1221(a)(3). This has generally meant that authors and artists could not sell their work and be eligible for capital gains rates. It conforms the ordinary income treatment of personal service income to the taxation of gain on the sale of assets created by personal services. (Notice that a patent created by the taxpayer is not deprived of capital asset status by this code section, although the patent might be held primarily for sale in the ordinary course of business.)

A 2005 Tax Law changed this rule for self-created *musical* works. Sale of such works is now eligible for capital gains (at the election of the taxpayer). However, the taxpayer who self-creates a musical work is still not allowed to deduct the fair market value of these works as a charitable deduction. § 1221(b)(3).

[B]   Blood, Etc.

[1]   Service?

In the charitable deduction context, the government has argued that a blood donation is the rendition of a service and therefore cannot support a charitable deduction. Rev. Rul. 53-162, 1953-2 C.B. 127 (predating § 170(e)). If the service characterization in the charitable deduction context carries over to the capital gains setting, the sale of blood can never be a sale of property to support a preferential tax rate. In *United States v. Garber*, 589 F.2d 843 (5th Cir. 1979), the government argued that the "sale price" for blood was a payment for services, but the court did not resolve this dispute.

[2]   Property — Ordinary or Capital?

In *Green v. Commissioner*, 74 T.C. 1229 (1980), the court held that the sale of a rare blood type was not the sale of a capital asset, because the taxpayer sold her blood on a regular basis over a period of seven years; the property was therefore held primarily for sale in the ordinary course of business. Presumably, *some* sales of blood, on this reasoning, could be the sale of a capital asset. (The court also held that the taxpayer could take a business expense deduction for the extra cost of high-protein food necessary to make her blood plasma salable.)

COMMENTS AND QUESTIONS

Sale of body parts generally — e.g., kidneys, sperm, embryos — would presumably raise the same issues as the sale of blood. Would it matter in deciding whether the transaction was a sale of property or the provision of a service whether the taxpayer had made a significant investment to enhance the value of the body part — for example, by spending money on a special diet to make blood more valuable or on hormone injections to make an embryo's sale more likely? Would it matter if those expenditures had been deducted?

§ 20.03   SECTION 1231

Look at § 1221(a)(2). It excludes certain assets used in the trade or business from the definition of a capital asset. An example is a factory and the land on which it sits. But isn't the gain on these assets as deserving of preferential capital gain treatment as the typical investment in stock? Or should the business function of the asset prevent preferential tax treatment?

Until 1938, the gain on such assets was capital gain. Consequently, losses were capital losses, which meant that their deduction was limited. During the Depression, the loss limitation became a problem for businesses that wanted to dispose of their old business assets. The businesses claimed that they were discouraged from selling the assets by the loss limitation. Moreover, the losses were thought to be the functional equivalent of depreciation deductions that had not been taken but should have been taken. To respond to these concerns, certain business assets were removed from the capital asset definition. The losses were now ordinary. But that also meant that the gain was ordinary. By 1942, gains were common because values went up during the war.

The current statutory pattern, adopted in 1942, is found in § 1231. It is illustrated by the following problems. The statute treats *net* losses from § 1231 transactions as ordinary losses, but *net* gains as long-term capital gains. A net § 1231 gain goes into the § 1222 calculation pot, to be added to other capital gains and netted with capital losses under § 1222.

PROBLEMS

Assume all transactions occur in the same tax year unless otherwise specified; and that the factory has been held for more than one year. In doing this problem, you will encounter one of the pro-taxpayer results from not recapturing depreciation on buildings as ordinary income, but instead subjecting such "recapture" gain to a 25% maximum tax rate. The 25%-recapture rule leaves the gain attributable to prior depreciation as § 1231 gain; if the gain had been recaptured as ordinary income under § 1245, it would not be eligible for § 1231 treatment.

How much capital gain or ordinary loss does the taxpayer have in each of the following problems, assuming that the following assets are dealt with in the specified transactions.

	Asset	Cost	Proceeds	Transaction
1.	Factory	80	100	Sale
2.	Factory	100	70	Condemned under eminent domain
3.	Factory	100	55	Fire loss, covered by $55 insurance
4.	Factory	40	70	Fire loss, with $70 insurance reinvested in similar factory

Problem 1. Transactions 1 & 2. This illustrates the core example of a § 1231 transaction, which is the sale or compulsory or involuntary conversion of property used in the business and held for more than one year.

Problem 2. Transactions 1 & 3. This illustrates the operation of § 1231(a)(4)(C). The purpose of this provision is to treat taxpayers who deduct insurance premiums for business casualty insurance in the same way as taxpayers who do not insure (or who underinsure) their business property, but suffer losses.

Problem 3. Transactions 1, 3 & 4. This problem should remind you that § 1231 (and § 1221) do not create recognized gain or loss, but only operate on otherwise recognizable gains or losses.

Problem 4. Transaction 2 is followed four years later by transaction 1. This problem addresses the taxpayer's opportunity to obtain an ordinary loss deduction even though the taxpayer has unrealized § 1231 gains in the same tax year. **Section 1231(c)** reduces that opportunity.

§ 20.04   SALE OF ENTIRE BUSINESS

The distinction among sales of inventory, § 1231 assets, and certain investment property should now be apparent. This is important when a taxpayer sells an unincorporated business (a sole proprietorship, for example). In that case, sale of the business is treated as a sale of each item of business property. *Williams v. McGowan*, 152 F.2d 570 (2d Cir. 1945). Sales proceeds must therefore be allocated among the items sold.

However, when a taxpayer owns stock in a corporation that owns various properties, the tax differences among types of property are homogenized and the taxpayer simply sells stock, which is usually a capital asset.

Partnership interests are hybrids. Sale of a partnership interest is usually sale of a capital asset, except to the extent that the proceeds are attributable to (1) inventory and (2) unrealized receivables. **§§ 741, 751.**

§ 20.05   CAPITAL vs. ORDINARY LOSSES

Although we normally think that a capital transaction favors the taxpayer, an ordinary loss is better than a capital loss because capital losses are (generally) limited to capital gains. The Supreme Court has dealt with three efforts by taxpayers to obtain ordinary losses and, in every instance, rejected the taxpayer's argument (although, in the first case, it had to correct an earlier decision).

[A]   "Integral Part of the Business"?

Can stocks or bonds ever be ordinary rather than capital assets? Sure. If a taxpayer holds them for sale primarily in the ordinary course of business, they are not capital assets. Are there other examples?

Here is a hypothetical. A taxpayer needs raw materials to produce a product. To secure a steady supply, the taxpayer buys stock or bonds in a supplier. Variations on this theme are purchases of stock or bonds in a buyer of business output to assure steady sales.

Some interpretations of a Supreme Court case — *Corn Prods. Refining Co. v. Commissioner*, 350 U.S. 46 (1955) — seemed to support ordinary asset treatment on such stocks and bonds. The taxpayer in that case manufactured products made from grain corn. It had limited storage capacity — only three weeks' supply. So, to secure a steady supply of corn, it purchased options to acquire corn. If corn was scarce, the value of the options increased; if corn was plentiful, the value of the options declined. The taxpayer sold the unexercised options each year if they were not needed, sometimes realizing gain and sometimes loss. In *Corn Products*, gains far exceeded losses, so the taxpayer argued that they were capital gains.

The Supreme Court disagreed with the taxpayer, holding that the sales produced ordinary gain and loss. However, it used some language that later came back to haunt the government in cases like the earlier stock and bond examples, when the taxpayer had a *loss* on the investment. The Court buttressed its "ordinary income" holding in *Corn Products* with the observation that the options were "an integral part of its business designed to protect its manufacturing operation against a price increase in its principal raw material and to assure a ready supply for future manufacturing requirements." That observation seemed to describe stocks and bonds purchased in supplier-corporations to protect a source of supply, or, inferentially, in buyer-corporations to protect sales volume.

In *Arkansas Best Corp. v. Commissioner*, 485 U.S. 212 (1988), the Court corrected mistaken implications derived from the prior *Corn Products* decision. The taxpayer was a diversified holding company that invested in the stock of National Bank of Commerce (Bank). For some time, the Bank prospered and there was no doubt that the asset was a capital asset. Beginning in 1972, however, Bank suffered losses and the taxpayer's subsequent investments in Bank were meant (according to the Tax Court) to "preserve the [taxpayer's] business reputation," because the added capital was needed to keep Bank from failing. The Tax Court held that loss on the stock acquired from 1972 was an ordinary loss.

The Supreme Court disagreed with the Tax Court. It first reviewed the text of § 1221, noting that it defined a capital asset as "property," excluding five specific exceptions. It held that these five exceptions were exclusive, rejecting the view that there was some generalized exception for investments made for a business purpose beyond what the statute said. It then stated "that Corn Products is properly interpreted as involving an application of § 1221's inventory exception." The corn futures, although not actual inventory, were "substitutes for the corn inventory such that they came within a broad reading of 'property of a kind which would properly be included in the inventory of the taxpayer' in § 1221." The Court concluded that "*Corn Products* is properly interpreted as standing for the narrow proposition that hedging transactions that are an integral part of a business' inventory-purchase system fall within the inventory exclusion of § 1221. Arkansas Best, which is not a dealer in securities, has never suggested that the Bank stock falls within the inventory exclusion. *Corn Products* thus has no application to this case."

The Court added a note of concern about the tax avoidance potential of a contrary result, as follows:

> [I]f capital stock purchased and held for a business purpose is an ordinary asset, whereas the same stock purchase and held with an investment motive is a capital asset, a taxpayer such as Arkansas Best could have significant influence over whether the asset would receive capital or ordinary treatment. Because stock is most ordinarily viewed as a capital asset, the Internal Revenue Service would be hard pressed to challenge a taxpayer's claim that stock was therefore a capital gain. If the same stock is sold at a loss, however, the taxpayer may be able to garner ordinary-loss treatment by emphasizing the business purpose behind the stock's acquisition.

The statute now states that a "hedging transaction that is clearly identified as such before the close of the day on which it was acquired" is not a capital asset. § 1221(a)(7). Regulations define "a hedging transaction." **Treas. Reg. § 1.1221-2(b)**.

[B] Bad Debts

Worthless debts produce capital loss, *if* the debt is a capital asset, and *if* § **165(g)** treats worthlessness as a sale or exchange. This typically applies to bonds traded on an established securities market.

But § **165(g)** does not apply to debt without interest coupons or not in registered form, such as loans to a corporation on open account payable on demand. What is the tax treatment of worthless debts *not* covered by § **165(g)**? To answer that question, turn to § **166**. For corporations, the deduction is ordinary. § **166(a)**. For individuals, there is a distinction between business and nonbusiness bad debts. § **166(d)**. Business bad debts are ordinary losses; nonbusiness bad debts are short-term capital losses.

In *United States. v. Generes*, 405 U.S. 93 (1972), the Court dealt with the effort by the owner of a corporation to characterize a loan to the corporation as related to his business of being a corporate employee rather than related to his investment in the corporation, thereby obtaining a business bad debt deduction when the debt went bad (that is, an ordinary loss). The Court rejected the attempt. It acknowledged that, although the owner's status as a shareholder was a nonbusiness interest, its status as an employee was a business interest. It then discussed the Regulation's requirement that a business bad debt have a "proximate" relation to the lender's trade or business. "Proximate" required a "dominant" business motivation, rather than a "significant" business motivation, as the taxpayer had argued. The Court stated that by "making the dominant motivation the measure, . . . [it] prevents the mere presence of a business motive, however small and however insignificant, from controlling the tax result at the taxpayer's convenience." It went on to conclude that the loan by the owner-employee could not reasonably be ascribed to a dominant business motivation to preserve the taxpayer's salary.

[C]   Transactional Approach

In Chapter 5, we considered whether the events in one tax year should affect how later events are taxed — that is, break down the accounting year barrier. Here is another example, prompted by a repayment of money originally taxed preferentially as capital gains. The capital gain had occurred on the liquidation of a corporation. It later turned out that the corporation owed some money and the shareholders who had received the liquidation proceeds had to pay the corporate debt. In *Arrowsmith v. Commissioner*, 344 U.S. 6 (1952), the Court held that the repayment was a capital loss, but it had some trouble finding a rationale.

The Court said that § 1222 "treats losses from sales or exchanges of capital assets as 'capital losses' and § 331 requires that liquidation distributions be treated as exchanges. The losses here fall squarely within the definition of 'capital losses' contained in these sections." How squarely? A repayment is *not* a sale or exchange.

The Court was influenced by the fact that a repayment in the liquidation year would have reduced the proceeds eligible for capital gain and that, therefore, a repayment in a later year should also result in a capital loss, reducing capital gain. It was also influenced by the equitable argument that repayment of preferentially taxed income should not be deductible at ordinary rates.

QUESTIONS AND COMMENTS

1. The capital loss deduction limitation is intended to prevent taxpayers from choosing when losses are recognized, but the taxpayers in *Arrowsmith* were not choosing to take a loss. Does that suggest that the taxpayer should have been allowed an ordinary loss deduction?

2. One argument for the result in *Arrowsmith* is that a transaction producing no economic gain should not produce a gain after tax, which is what would happen if $1 was taxed at 15% (the preferential capital gains rate), costing the taxpayer 15 cents, but repayment produced an ordinary deduction (saving the taxpayer 35 cents, if he was in the 35% bracket). This leads to the following question — would the *Arrowsmith* principle apply if capital gains were not eligible for a preferential tax rate? In other words, would the repayment still be a capital loss, usually deductible only up to capital gains?

3. When is a repayment so closely linked to a prior receipt that *Arrowsmith* applies? Section 16(b) of the Securities Act of 1934 specifies that certain corporate shareholders must turn over profits from dealing in the corporation's stock *to the corporation*, if a purchase and sale of the stock occur within six months of each other. The corporate President buys stock for $80,000 and sells it one year later for $140,000 to another individual. He then buys it back two months after that, for $120,000 ($20,000 less than the sales price). He argues that the Securities Act does not apply but, to avoid bad publicity, he pays the $20,000 to the company. Should the $20,000 be a capital loss, an ordinary deduction, or (perhaps) added to the basis of the stock bought for $120,000? *Brown v. Commissioner*, 529 F.2d 609 (10th Cir. 1976) (not ordinary expense deduction), *reversing*, 32 T.C.M. (CCH) 1330 (1973); *Cummings v. Commissioner*, 506 F.2d 449 (2d Cir. 1974) (long-term capital loss). To decide this question, should the court consider the public policy implications of allowing an ordinary deduction?

4. Oil producers can sometimes deduct a percentage of their gross income in computing taxable income (the percentage depletion allowance), even though it exceeds regular depreciation deductions. Assume the deduction is 20% of oil gross income, in effect taxing only 80 cents per dollar received. If the taxpayer has to pay back $1 of prior oil income, can it deduct $1 or only 80 cents? Does *Arrowsmith* apply to reduce the deduction to 80 cents?

United States v. Skelly Oil Co., 394 U.S. 678 (1969), limited the deduction to 80 cents. The dissent perceived a congressional policy favoring oil exploration, so that the transactional approach should not be applied to limit the deduction of the $1 repayment.

5. You should see the *Arrowsmith* and *Skelly Oil* problem as yet another version of the statutory interpretation issue we have previously encountered — when should a tax break (e.g., the capital gains or percentage depletion deduction) override what might seem like a sensible implementation of the tax structure (that is, the transactional approach)? For example, should recapture as ordinary income apply when the recaptured expenses were deductible research expenses under § 174? Should a taxpayer be entitled to both exclusion of an item from income and a charitable deduction if that item is given to charity? Should a veteran be able to exclude reimbursement of educational expenses and also deduct those expenses? Similarly, should a taxpayer be able to enjoy the lower capital gains tax rate and/or the percentage depletion deduction and still take a full ordinary deduction of a repayment of income eligible for those tax breaks?

§ 20.06   CASE LAW LIMITS ON CAPITAL GAINS

The statutory language defining a "capital asset" is very expansive — all "property" is a capital asset, subject to exceptions. **Section 1221 (introductory language).** Courts have not been bashful, however, about interpreting the definition narrowly to make sure that capital gains preferences are not applied beyond their rationale. This does not mean that the courts always get it right, as the prior discussion of the history of the *Corn Products* doctrine suggests. This section evaluates some other judicial attempts at defining capital assets.

[A] Original Issue Discount/Market Discount

OID. Original issue discount was discussed earlier in the course. Chapter 3.05[B]. The statute now explicitly requires lenders to accrue interest attributable to original issue discount. Before that statute was passed, however, the Supreme Court held that gain attributable to this discount was ordinary income upon disposition of the asset. *United States v. Midland-Ross Corp.*, 381 U.S. 54 (1965). The Court noted its approach to the statute — "that the term 'capital asset' is to be construed narrowly in accordance with the purpose of Congress to afford capital-gains treatment only in situations typically involving the realization of appreciation in value accrued over a substantial period of time, and thus to ameliorate the hardship of taxation of the entire gain in one year." It then observed that original issue discount "serves the same function as stated interest, concededly ordinary income and not a capital asset; it is simply 'compensation for the use or forbearance of money.' Unlike the typical case of capital appreciation, the earning of discount to maturity is predictable and measurable, and is 'essentially a substitute for . . . payments which [the statute] expressly characterizes as gross income. . . .'" Original issue discount, like interest, compensated for the "mere passage of time."

Market discount arises when interest fluctuates *after* a loan is made. For example, a $100 loan earning 10% interest is worth $100, if market interest rates are 10%. If market interest rates rise to 12%, the investor can only sell the claim for less than $100 (say, $80). (Who would invest $100 to earn a 10% rate of interest when interest rates are 12%?) The difference between the buyer's $80 investment and the $100 face amount of the claim is market discount.

In *Midland-Ross*, the Court explicitly did "not reach the question of the tax treatment of 'market discount' arising from post-issue purchases at prices varying from issue price plus a ratable portion of the original issue discount . . . ." The statute now taxes market discount that is the equivalent of interest as ordinary income when the claim is disposed of. The interest equivalent is the ratable portion of the total market discount ($20 in the example), based on the number of days the investor owned the claim (a straight line method). This is different from the compound interest method used to tax original issue discount. For example, assume that the bond in the example has 10 years to go before collection after its purchase for $80, and is sold for $95 five years later (one half of the ten-year period). The sale produces $10 of ordinary income and $5 of capital gain. In lieu of this approach, the $80 investor can elect to use the compound interest computation method instead of straight line; and the investor can also elect to accrue the interest annually, rather than wait for disposition of the claim. §§ 1276(a)(1),(b)(1)–(2), 1278(b).

[B] Already Earned Income

Capital gain does not include periodic income accrued to property, like rent or interest. I.T. 3175, 1938-1 C.B. 200. Otherwise, a taxpayer could just delay collection of rent or interest, and convert it to capital gain by selling the claim to the accrued income. That is true even if the taxpayer sells the rented land or building along with the right to the accrued rent, or the bond with accrued interest.

(In that case, the taxpayer must allocate the sales price between the property, which is often a capital asset producing capital gain, and the right to the accrued income, the sale of which produces ordinary income.)

For example, assume a taxpayer has invested $80 in land on January 1. The land soon turns out to be much more valuable as rental property because rental values go way up. The land is therefore now worth $200. The taxpayer rents the property for $20 per year. Two years after the purchase, on December 20, almost an entire year's rent has accrued but is not yet collected. Assume the taxpayer sells the land and the accrued rent for $219.40. The capital gain is the difference between the value of the land ($200) and the original cost ($80), equal to $120. The sales price attributable to the accrued rental income produces $19.40 ordinary income.

The underlying idea is that the capital gains preference should reduce the tax burden *only* when the taxpayer realizes the present value of *future* income by selling property. In effect, the taxpayer has collapsed into the year of the sale the future income that would otherwise have been taxed in later years. The government gets its money early, so it seems fair to lower the tax rate. Moreover, if the tax is not lowered, the taxpayer is reluctant to sell and accelerate tax on the income, rather than wait for future collection. This rationale for the capital gains preference does not apply to the sale of past-accrued income.

There are borderline cases. For example, if past accrued interest income might not be collected, because the debtor has been defaulting on interest payments, should the original lender get capital gain even on the sales price attributable to the accrued interest? *Jaglom v. Commissioner*, 303 F.2d 847 (2d Cir. 1962), forced the lender to allocate some of the sales price to ordinary income (attributable to accrued interest). However, the purchaser of such a risky investment in accrued interest (not the original lender), who later sells the claim including the right to accrued defaulted interest, is entitled to capital gain on the entire gain. Rev. Rul. 60-284, 1960-2 C.B. 464. This is an example of a buyer getting capital gain on an asset, when he later sells the asset, even though there would be ordinary income to the original seller.

[C]   Contract Rights

Another case law qualification to the definition of a capital asset appears in the following case, dealing with sales of contract rights.

BISBEE-BALDWIN CORP. v. TOMLINSON
United States Court of Appeals, Fifth Circuit
320 F.2d 929 (5th Cir. 1963)

WISDOM, CIRCUIT JUDGE. . . .

Bisbee-Baldwin, the taxpayer, is in the mortgage banking business. Most of its loans are secured by mortgages on residential property in Jacksonville, Florida. After making a loan, the company invariably assigns the mortgage to an institutional investor. The essential profit-making element is the investor's agreement to employ the mortgage company as its agent to service the mortgages. The company receives no profit on the assignment of a mortgage but earns an annual commission of one-half of one per cent of the principal outstanding balance of the mortgages serviced. The servicing activities generate other business. For example, the company often writes fire insurance on the property mortgaged, acts as real estate broker when the property is sold, and serves as property manager when a mortgage is foreclosed. Escrow deposits by the mortgagors enhance its credit standing, a substantial benefit since the company must borrow large sums from the banks in the operation of its affairs. Thus the success of the mortgage servicing business depends upon the amount of mortgage indebtedness it services. . . .

During the fiscal year ending April 30, 1957, various investors cancelled servicing agreements with the taxpayer, and gave the business to other agents. When an investor cancels such an agreement without cause, it is customary for the investor to pay a termination fee equal to one per cent of the principal balance of the mortgages then being serviced by the mortgage company. In this case, . . . [t]he taxpayer received net termination fees of $206,454.63. . . .

The question is, what do the mortgage servicing rights under the contracts represent. If they represent the right to earn future income in the form of commissions for services rendered, then the sum received for the cancellation of the contracts and the transfer of rights is ordinary income. . . .

The line between contractual rights representing capital assets and those representing the right to receive future income is far from clear. Judge Friendly, for the Second Circuit, after an extremely able, thorough survey of all the relevant cases, reached the following conclusion:

> "One common characteristic of the group held to come within the capital gain provision is that the taxpayer had either what might be called an 'estate' in (*Golonsky, McCue, Metropolitan*), or an 'encumbrance' on (*Ray*), or an option to acquire an interest in (*Dorman*), property which, if itself held, would be a capital asset. In all these cases the taxpayer had something more than an opportunity, afforded by contract, to obtain periodic receipts of income, by dealing with another (*Starr, Leh, General Artists, Pittston*), or by vendering services (*Holt*), or by virtue of ownership of a larger 'estate' (*Hort, P. G. Lake*)." *Commissioner v. Ferrer*, 2nd Cir. 1962, 304 F.2d 125, 130–131.

In Judge Friendly's analysis, . . . some components of the 'bundle' of contractual rights held by a taxpayer are capital assets while others represent a substitute for future income. Thus in Ferrer the taxpayer's 'lease' of a play and his power, incident to the lease, to prevent a disposition of motion picture, radio, and television rights until after a certain date were capital assets. However, that part of the taxpayer's compensation for his contractual rights representing his right to forty per cent of the proceeds from the motion picture was taxable as ordinary income. We agree with this analysis. . . .

[Editor — The taxpayer in *Ferrer* held these contractual rights in a literary property, which eventually became the movie *Moulin Rouge*. Although his lease of the play entitled him to produce a play based on the literary property, he never produced a play based on these rights. Instead he released all of his rights back to the original author.]

Applying these principles to the factual situation before us, we find that the basic rights Bisbee-Baldwin sold were the annual servicing commissions on the principal balance outstanding on the mortgages. Indeed the termination fee of one per cent of the mortgages serviced by the taxpayer was equivalent to two years gross income in commissions and was, to our minds, a substitute for the income which would have been earned by Bisbee-Baldwin had the contracts not been transferred. . . .

Still, some parts of the 'bundle' of contractual rights transferred by Bisbee-Baldwin were capital assets. The mortgage correspondent relationships have value in addition to the rights to servicing commissions. It acts as a 'feeder' for related businesses, such as insurance and real estate, frequently engaged in by mortgage bankers. The monthly escrow deposits made by the mortgagors considerably enhance the servicing agent's credit standing. Moreover, . . . there *is* a sale of 'good will'. The mortgage portfolio of the mortgage banker tends to increase each year as both the mortgagors and the investors look to the mortgaging servicing agent for further funds and further outlets for investment. The taxpayer's extensive files and equipment are in the nature of capital assets. (Most of these were retained by the taxpayer.) These items are closely related to the everyday business operations of the taxpayer. They are not so integrally related, however, as to be insusceptible of separate valuation.

We summarize. Essentially, the contract was a management contract for the employment of personal services. The consideration received for the right to earn future servicing commissions must be regarded as a substitute for such future ordinary income. This important part of the bundle of rights sold or exchanged can be separated from the other parts and should be taxed for what it is — not for what it is not. . . .

[Editor — The court remanded to the District Court to allocate the purchase price between a sale of capital and ordinary assets.]

COMMENTS AND QUESTIONS

1. **Personal services contracts.** In *Bisbee-Baldwin* itself, the taxpayer's personal service relationship was "at will"; there was no binding contract to provide services. Perhaps the case should be limited to these facts, but the principle on which the decision relies is much broader. *Bisbee-Baldwin* is one of a larger group of cases denying capital gains on proceeds from disposition of personal service contracts. *See, e.g., Foxe v. Commissioner*, 53 T.C. 21 (1969); *Furrer v. Commissioner*, 566 F.2d 1115 (9th Cir. 1977); *Foote v. Commissioner*, 81 T.C. 930 (1983), *affirmed*, 751 F.2d 1257 (5th Cir. 1985) (damages received for improper denial of tenure). *But see Jones v. Corbyn*, 186 F.2d 450 (10th Cir. 1950) (capital gains on release of lifetime general insurance agency contract).

2. **Sale of contracts rights.** *Bisbee-Baldwin* is also one of a larger group of cases that denies capital gains when the taxpayer disposes of *any* contract right, not just for personal services. The quote in *Bisbee-Baldwin* from the *Ferrer* case is a good summary: "An opportunity, afforded by contract, to obtain periodic receipts of income, by dealing with another," is not a capital asset. Typical cases denying capital gains involve sale of the right to purchase raw materials (*Commercial*

Solvents Corp. v. United States, 427 F.2d 749 (Ct. Cl. 1970)), or to sell products to a particular customer (*Commissioner v. Starr Bros., Inc.*, 204 F.2d 673 (2d Cir. 1953)).

3. **Why not capital gain?** Why shouldn't the sale of a contract right produce capital gain? It is often said that capital gain is denied because the taxpayer is selling a right to future income. But that is an unsatisfactory explanation. The sale of stock is also a sale of a right to future income and that produces capital gain.

An argument in favor of capital gain when the taxpayer sells a contract right is that the taxpayer has taken a risk regarding future income. For example, if the taxpayer is committed to a 10-year obligation to buy or sell property at a given price, the taxpayer is taking a risk regarding which way prices will fluctuate in the future. Why shouldn't the taxpayer get capital gain if the prices move in his favor (e.g., a contract to sell at $100 for ten years when market prices decline to $80)?

Is capital gain denied when the taxpayer sells a contract right because the taxpayer has no out-of-pocket investment in the contract? *See Bellamy v. Commissioner*, 43 T.C. 487 (1965) (capital asset is something in which the taxpayer has an investment).

Letter Ruling 200215037 appears to struggle with these issues. The ruling allowed capital gains when the taxpayer received consideration "for rights to sell power to an electric utility at above-market rates" (an Exclusive Power Agreement) — even though the taxpayer had what looked like "an opportunity afforded by contract to obtain periodic receipts of income by dealing with another." The ruling relied (correctly) on the fact that capital gain usually arises from fluctuations in market prices (which is, of course, also true of the sale of contract rights). But it considered irrelevant (in my view, incorrectly) another factor usually associated with the *absence* of capital gains — that the "[t]axpayer had not acquired the Existing Power Agreement through purchase and had no basis in the contract. . . . " The ruling stressed that the benefits were created by governmental action, similar to other rights that have been treated as capital assets. *See, e.g.*, Rev. Rul. 66-58, 1966-1 C.B. 186 (cotton acreage allotments); Rev. Rul. 70-644, 1970-2 C.B. 167 (milk allocation rights) — which sounds a lot like the approach to defining a capital asset by reference to the asset's status as "property" under conventional property law notions.

4. **Why is good will a capital asset?** *Bisbee-Baldwin* also states the general rule that good will is a capital asset. Why should that be true, at least if the taxpayer has no independent investment in the purchase of good will and any expenditures to self-create good will have been deducted? To be sure, good will is a property interest under state law, not a contract right. But why should state law characterization as "property" be dispositive for tax law?

[D]   Note on Statutory Interpretation — Technical Tax Meaning vs. Meaning Borrowed from Property Law

Some of the cases in this section define "property" in the tax code's definition of a capital asset so that its meaning implements the underlying structure of the statute — to provide a preferential tax rate for risky investments that may produce income in the future.

These cases raise two important questions about statutory interpretation. First, have the courts been successful in deciding when taxpayers should be eligible for the capital gains tax preference? For example, the *Corn Products* decision is generally considered a wrong turn. But, in my judgment, the *Bisbee-Baldwin* line of cases (disallowing capital gains when there is no investment) makes sense. In any event, does your appraisal of how well the courts have dealt with these interpretive issues suggest anything more general about whether the courts should attempt to interpret the statute in light of the statutory structure? Remember that courts make mistakes in developing the common law, but you would not suggest (would you?) that they should therefore abandon their common law powers.

Second, many of the cases are older decisions, predating the contemporary view held by many judges and commentators that the courts should stick as closely as possible to the plain meaning of the statutory text. It is hard to be sure what modern courts would have done if these cases had come up today, for the first time, uncomplicated by existing precedent. It is also hard to be sure how creative the courts will (or should) be in applying these old cases to new fact situations. We previously encountered this problem when we discussed application of the old assignment of income doctrine to the modern problem of contingent attorneys' fees in the context of the alternative minimum tax (*see* Chapter 18.03). One approach the courts could take is to apply the old cases mechanically and let Congress respond. Thus, even if *Arrowsmith* was a wrong turn in relying on the transactional approach to deny an ordinary deduction for repayment of the proceeds of a liquidation, a court might simply apply the transactional approach to other situations (such as oil income), without worrying too much about how tax breaks and statutory structure interact.

[E] Sale of Lottery Winnings

In *United States v. Maginnis*, 356 F.3d 1179 (9th Cir. 2004), the taxpayer sold the right to collect future lottery winnings for a lump sum — *after* he had won the lottery. The court held that the right to the payments was not a capital asset for three reasons. First, there was no underlying capital investment. The purchase of the lottery ticket was not considered an investment because "[l]ottery prizes are treated by the tax code as gambling winnings, which are taxed as ordinary income." That analysis seems to be both a nonsequitur and questionable — the taxpayer took a chance with a small investment and it paid off.

Second, "treating the sale of Maginnis' lottery right as a capital gain would reward lottery winners who elect to receive periodic payments in lieu of a direct lump sum payment from the state, and then sell that payment right to a third party. Those who would do so would receive a tax advantage as compared to those taxpayers who would simply choose originally to accept their lottery winning in the form of a lump sum payment." But that reasoning also seems questionable. Some commentators argue that the capital gains preference compensates the taxpayer for accelerating the taxation of gain that would otherwise be deferred as future periodic payments. Moreover, the fact that collection of the lottery winnings in a lump sum would produce ordinary income — because there is no sale or exchange

— might not be a good reason to tax the sale; maybe the collection of the lump sum should result in capital gain. In other words, taxing the collection as ordinary income may be the wrong result, and it is a mistake to treat that result as a principle from which to reason. There are situations in which the tax law treats a collection as a sale or exchange, as noted in the next section (Chapter 20.07).

Third, the payment did not compensate for any increase in the value of the taxpayer's investment over time. But the payment did compensate for an increase in value that occurred after the purchase of the lottery ticket. If a taxpayer makes a small investment in land that turns out to contain uranium — resulting in a sudden increase in value — is the gain on the sale of the land not entitled to the preferential capital gains rate?

COMMENTS

1. *Sure thing; Already earned?* In *Lattera v. Commissioner*, 437 F.3d 399 (3d Cir. 2006), the court held that proceeds from the sale of lottery winnings were ordinary income. It adopted a "family resemblance" test — stocks clearly produced capital gains and interest/rental income was clearly ordinary income. For assets between these two poles, the court looked to the "character of the asset." It concluded that "[a]ssets that constitute a right to earn income merit capital-gains treatment, while those that are a right to earned income merit ordinary-income treatment." Because the lottery winnings had already been earned, the sale proceeds were ordinary income. Does this argument analogize the sale of the lottery winnings to the sale of interest or rent which has accrued on a bond or land? Maybe you are not entitled to capital gains once the future flow of income has become a sure thing.

Similarly, in *Prebola v. Commissioner*, 482 F.3d 610 (2d Cir. 2007), the court held that the sale of the right to future lottery winnings was ordinary income. It stressed that the winnings were "already earned," apparently by analogy to the sale of a right to accrued interest. The court rejected the argument that the value of the winnings depended in part on interest rates, which were beyond the taxpayer's control.

2. *Public policy?* In *Watkins v. Commissioner*, 447 F.3d 1269 (10th Cir. 2006), the court denied capital gains on the sale of a lottery winner's right to future payouts of lottery income. Following *Maginnis*, the court said that "[t]he purchase of a lottery ticket is no more an underlying investment of capital than is a dollar bet on the spin of a roulette wheel." Does this suggest that there a whiff of "public policy" in the decisions? The lottery ticket is just not the kind of investment that deserves the preferential tax rate.

3. *Investment by purchaser of the right to lottery winnings?* The courts have not decided whether the claim to lottery winnings is a capital asset in the hands of the person who purchases the right to the lottery payments from the original winner. That purchaser would have a substantial investment and the value of the future lottery winnings might appreciate if the lottery turned out to be a much better investment than stocks, bonds, etc.

§ 20.07   "SALE OR EXCHANGE"

[A]   In General

Capital gains arise only if there is a sale or exchange. § 1222. There can be gain or loss, however, even if there is no sale or exchange. For example, suppose the taxpayer has an $8,000 basis in a building that burns down and he collects $10,000 of insurance. Or suppose an investor buys a claim against a financially strapped debtor for $8,000, when the amount owed is $10,000; the debtor's fortunes improve and $10,000 is collected. In each case, the collection of the $10,000 liquidates the taxpayer's investment (there is a disposition), but the money is not (technically) received in a sale or exchange. Unless a specific section of the code treats the event as a sale or exchange (as many do), the gain is ordinary income.

The same question arises on the loss side. If a taxpayer with an $8,000 basis in good will abandons the business because it has no prospect of showing profit, the abandonment results in an ordinary loss deduction because there is no sale or exchange. Rev. Rul. 57-503, 1957-2 C.B. 139.

There are many code sections treating collection and worthlessness of an investment as a sale or exchange, but they do not cover every situation. Losses from the worthlessness of securities held as a capital asset produce a capital loss. § 165(g). Retirement of most debt will be treated as a sale or exchange (§ 1271(a)(1), (b)(1), § 1275(a)(1)). Liquidation of a corporation (§ 331) is usually treated as a sale or exchange. Collection of insurance is also treated as a sale or exchange (§ 1231), if the property was held for more than one year and was either used in a trade or business or was a capital asset held in a transaction entered into for profit (but not if it was personal use property).

Section 1234A, adopted in 1981, treats gain or loss attributable to the "cancellation, lapse, expiration, or other termination of a right or obligation with respect to property which is (or on acquisition would be) a capital asset in the hands of the taxpayer" as gain or loss from *sale* of a capital asset. This provision legislates the result in the *Ferrer* case (discussed in *Bisbee-Baldwin, supra*), as it applied to the termination of the taxpayer's right to produce a play by releasing that right back to the copyright owner.

There are two arguments that might justify at least some of the statutory provisions treating dispositions as sales or exchanges. First, when there is a loss, it is wrong to distinguish abandoning worthless property from a sale just prior to the abandonment. Unless the law treats these events the same, there is an artificial distinction between sellers, who get capital losses, and others, who would get ordinary losses. Moreover, unless worthlessness is treated as a sale, the taxpayer has an incentive to go through the motions of selling a worthless asset for a nominal price, forcing the government either to invoke a form over substance doctrine to deny "sale" treatment in such cases, or to treat sales and worthlessness differently.

Second, it is arguable that any liquidation of an investment deserves capital gains treatment, because its value accrues to an out-of-pocket investment and arises from market fluctuation. This argument stresses the tax incentive rationale for the preferential taxation of capital gains. If the liquidation is voluntary, the capital gains preference also reduces the lock-in effect that confronts an investor with gain.

[B]   Close Cases

In the following case the Tax Court and Court of Appeals struggled with whether settlement proceeds in a lawsuit resulted in ordinary income or capital gains. The facts were these: a corporation named Wehr had a claim in a lawsuit against Xerox for loss of profits; Wehr sold all of its assets (including the claim) to Nahey, the taxpayer; the taxpayer later settled the lawsuit. The issue was whether the proceeds of the settlement received by the buyer, Nahey, resulted in capital gains. Pay special attention to the court's discussion of the *Hudson* and *Fahey* cases, which we will revisit in Questions and Comments after the case.

You should be alert to whether any of the prior themes influenced the judicial decisions — such as (1) whether the asset provided a sure thing (analogous to already earned income); (2) whether the taxpayer had a significant investment; or (3) whether there are policy reasons for the result.

NAHEY v. COMMISSIONER
United States Tax Court
111 T.C. 256 (1998)

Jacobs, Judge: . . .

A sale or exchange is a prerequisite to the rendering of capital gain treatment. Sec. 1222. The phrase "sale or exchange" is not defined in section 1222, but we apply the ordinary meaning to those words.

It is well established that a compromise or collection of a debt is not considered a sale or exchange of property because no property or property rights passes to the debtor other than the discharge of the obligation. In this regard, whatever property or property rights might have existed vanish as a result of the compromise or collection.

On several occasions we have addressed the issue of whether a sale or exchange occurred on the payment of a judgment or the settlement of a claim. *Hudson v. Commissioner*, 20 T.C. 734 (1953), affirmed per curiam sub nom. *Ogilvie v. Commissioner*, 216 F.2d 748 (6th Cir.1954); *Fahey v. Commissioner*, 16 T.C. 105 (1951). In *Fahey v. Commissioner, supra*, we held that where an attorney was assigned an interest in a contingent lawsuit fee in exchange for a cash payment, settlement of the lawsuit and payment of the fee to the attorney did not give rise to capital gain treatment because no sale or exchange occurred. . . .

In *Hudson v. Commissioner, supra*, the taxpayers purchased a 50-percent interest in a judgment from the legatees of an estate, and subsequently the taxpayers settled the judgment with the debtor. The taxpayers reported the payment of the judgment as capital gain. We held that the payment should be characterized as ordinary income. . . .

[However, the taxpayer relies on] *Commissioner v. Ferrer*, 304 F.2d 125 (2d Cir.

1962), reversing in part and remanding 35 T.C. 617 (1961). In *Ferrer*, the taxpayer acquired from an author the right to produce a play (based on the author's book) which included the right to prevent the author's transfer of film rights. Subsequently, the taxpayer surrendered his rights (the "lease") in exchange for the leading role in a film production. The issue arose as to whether the surrendering of the taxpayer's rights constituted a sale or exchange for purposes of the capital gain provisions. In holding that a sale or exchange of the surrendered lease occurred, the Court of Appeals for the Second Circuit stated that Congress was disenchanted with the "formalistic distinction" between a sale of property rights to third parties (which would give rise to capital gain or loss) and the release of those rights that results in their extinguishment (and which would not give rise to capital gain or loss). The court continued:

> In the instant case we can see no sensible business basis for drawing a line between a release of Ferrer's rights . . . and a sale of them. . . . Tax law is concerned with the substance, here the voluntary passing of "property" rights allegedly constituting "capital assets," not with whether they are passed to a stranger or to a person already having a larger "estate." . . .

Petitioners have misread *Ferrer* and its import. *Ferrer* (and the cases cited therein) can be factually distinguished from the instant case because in *Ferrer* the taxpayer's interest (or lease) to produce the play and prevent the author's transfer of film rights did not disappear but instead reverted to the author after the taxpayer surrendered the lease; whereas in the instant case, . . . rights in the lawsuit vanished both in form and substance upon the receipt of the settlement proceeds.

. . . We find no discernible distinction between the situation herein and the situations discussed in *Fahey v. Commissioner, supra,* or *Hudson v. Commissioner, supra.* In each case, the debtor made payment to the creditor or an assignee of the original creditor in exchange for the extinguishment of the claim. Whether the claim is reduced to judgment before payment is not relevant; ultimately the debtor receives nothing in the form of property or property rights which can later be transferred. Consequently, we hold that the settlement of the lawsuit . . . does not constitute a sale or exchange and hence capital gain treatment is not warranted.

The Court of Appeals affirmed, *Nahey v. Commissioner,* 196 F.3d 866 (7th Cir. 1999) (Judge Posner), but took a different approach. The court emphasized that the proceeds of the settlement replaced ordinary income; it did *not* rely on the absence of a sale or exchange. The court noted the taxpayer's concession that if Wehr "had settled its suit against Xerox on the same terms that Nahey [the taxpayer] did, the entire settlement price of $6 million would have been taxed to Wehr [the seller] as ordinary income rather than as a capital gain because the amount received in the settlement would have replaced ordinary income of which Xerox had deprived Wehr" — specifically, lost profits. The court conceded that a "settlement, or equally a litigated judgment, resembles a sale because it extinguishes the plaintiff's claim." But it emphasized the "principle that 'the [tax] classification of amounts received in settlement of litigation is to be determined by the nature and basis of the action settled, and amounts received in compromise of a claim must be considered as having the same nature as the right compromised.' "

The court also could find no "practical reason for why the tax treatment of the proceeds of a suit should change merely because of an intervening change in ownership" — "Why should it make a difference that the assignment was packaged with a sale of other assets (the rest of Wehr's assets) as well?" Judge Posner also made a policy argument, stressing that "[i]t is desirable that rules of taxation be simple and that they be neutral, in the sense of not influencing business judgments except when the purpose of a particular provision of tax law is to influence behavior, which is not contended to be the case here. Judged by this twofold standard the Tax Court's decision is sound; a corporate acquisition should not affect the tax treatment of any claims that are transferred in the acquisition."

The concurring opinion by Judge Cudahy found the case more troubling. He called attention to the fact that an " 'intermediate transaction' generally changes the identity, circumstances and economic function of the taxpayer in ways that ought to be recognized in the analysis. For example, if a car appreciates in the hands of a car dealer, the gain is generally ordinary. 26 U.S.C. § 1221(1). If it appreciates in the hands of a customer to whom the car has been sold, the gain is generally capital." He also relied on the analogy of the junk bond that had been purchased by a transferee — "A junk bond might furnish a more helpful analogy. This is a bond that could be valued . . . far below par because of the risk of non-payment of interest or of non-recovery of capital. When the bond later is redeemed at face value in the hands of the transferee . . . [t]he increase in value of a junk bond when redeemed, reflecting a reward for the transferee's successful risk-taking, might be analogized to the settlement of the 'speculative' lawsuit in the instant case." However, Judge Cudahy concurred with the majority because "some deference is due the Tax Court, which deals regularly with the issues that trouble us."

QUESTIONS AND COMMENTS

1. *Treat as sale or exchange.* Under the current § **1234A**, adopted in 1981, would the taxpayer receive capital gains treatment in *Fahey* (where the taxpayer had purchased the right to collect a contingent attorneys' fee in a lawsuit), or *Hudson* (where the taxpayer had purchased a legatee's interest in a judgment owned by an estate)? The tax years in *Fahey* and *Hudson* all predated adoption of § **1234A**, which now states: "Gain or loss attributable to the cancellation, lapse, expiration, or other termination of — (1) a right or obligation . . . with respect to property which is (or on acquisition would be) a capital asset in the hands of the taxpayer . . . shall be treated as gain or loss from the sale of a capital asset. The preceding sentence shall not apply to the retirement of any debt instrument. . . ." Are the interests owned in *Fahey* and *Hudson* "property" that would be a "capital asset" within the meaning of § **1234A**?

2. *Relevance of investment.* The Court of Appeals majority in *Nahey* is convinced that there is no reason to treat the purchasing taxpayer any differently from the corporation which had sold the claim. But the taxpayer had an investment in the claim, not merely a right to recover lost profits. Is that a distinction that could justify a different result? Regarding the relevance of an investment, consider the following:

a. Under § 1241, adopted in 1958, a taxpayer's release of a distributorship *is* treated as a sale or exchange, if the taxpayer has a significant investment in the distributorship.

b. In *Martin v. Commissioner*, 50 T.C. 341 (1968), a theater producer owned the right to produce a play based on a book and to a percentage of future profits from a movie based on the book. He had invested in the play, which was produced. Unlike the disposition of the right to movie profits in the *Ferrer* case (which resulted in ordinary income), the sale of a claim to the movie profits in Martin resulted in capital gains.

3. *Sure thing; Already earned.* Maybe the best way to justify ordinary income in the *Nahey* case, although it was not mentioned in the opinions and it is not clear that the facts would support this analysis, is that the taxpayer bought a claim that was virtually certain to be collected. In such cases, the taxpayer is taking little risk and (arguably) should not be entitled to capital gain, by application of the principle that sale of a right to already-earned income (such as accrued interest) does not produce capital gain.

4. How should the following case be decided? Person X had a right to share in 12.5% of the proceeds from the sale of property P, at such time as property P is sold. Taxpayer T bought a percentage of whatever Person X had a right to collect. *Pounds v. United States*, 372 F.2d 342 (5th Cir. 1967).

(a) Taxpayer T sells the right he purchased from Person X to a third party (i) before the right to share in 12.5% of the proceeds had become a liquidated dollar amount (that is, a sum certain), or (ii) after the right had become a sum certain.

(b) Taxpayer collects his percentage share of the proceeds of the sale of property P, which he had purchased from Person X.

§ 20.08 HOLDING PERIOD

The capital gains preference requires a capital asset and a sale or exchange. It also requires holding the asset for more than one year. The determination of the taxpayer's holding period raises problems in two situations. First, the taxpayer might hold the property for less than the required period, but might have acquired the property as a gift or in a nonrecognition transaction. Arguably, in such cases, the taxpayer's holding period should be longer than the period during which he has actually held the property. Second, the taxpayer might have insulated himself from market fluctuations before expiration of the one year period, but (technically) held the asset for more than one year. In such cases, the taxpayer should not be entitled to the preference for long-term capital gain.

[A] Tacking

It seems easy enough to determine the holding period for determining eligibility for preferential rates on capital gains — just compare the purchase and sale dates. But what if the taxpayer has given the property to a relative or has disposed of the property in a nonrecognition transaction (e.g., § 1031). In these situations, there is a "substituted" basis ("transferred" in the gift case and "exchanged" in the nonrecognition case). § 7701(a)(42–44). In the gift case, the donor's holding period is tacked on to the donee's holding period. § 1223(2). In the nonrecognition case, the taxpayer's holding period of the property given up is tacked on to the holding period of the replacement property (e.g., property received in a like-kind exchange), if the property given up was a capital asset or § 1231 property. § 1223(1).

Inherited property with a date-of-death basis is treated as held for more than one year, even if it is sold within one year of the decedent's death. § 1223(9) (referring to property with a basis determined under the date-of-death rules in § 1014).

If a taxpayer buys an option to acquire property, the option period is *not* tacked on to the holding period of the property purchased by exercising the option. The purchase price for the property is a significant new investment and receives its own holding period. *Weir v. Commissioner*, 10 T.C. 996 (1948), *affirmed*, 173 F.2d 222 (3d Cir. 1949).

[B] Short Sales

Suppose a taxpayer has held stock for four months — e.g., since August 31, 1992 — and fears a decline in market value. He wants to freeze his gain, so he enters into the following arrangement on December 31, 1992. He finds someone interested in buying the stock and receives the sales price of the stock from the prospective buyer, but does not actually deliver the stock now. He agrees to deliver the stock nine months from now, on September 30, 1993. This is referred to as a "short sale." If the price of the stock goes up, the taxpayer can deliver the old stock to the buyer. However, the seller has insulated himself from downward fluctuations in the market as of December 31, 1992.

Before the law was amended in 1997, the code addressed this problem by treating the holding period as coming to an end when the risk of decline terminated — after four months, on December 31, 1992. But this resulted in short term-capital gain only when the property was eventually delivered on September 30, 1993. § 1233(b).

A 1997 amendment treats a short sale of stock and securities as a realizable taxable event, when the stock to be delivered is the same or substantially identical to the stock owned at the time of the sale, *and* the taxpayer has an unrealized gain in the stock he owns. Thus, in the prior example, the taxpayer would realize short term capital gain on December 31, 1992. Under prior law, the short sale did not produce realized gain until the delivery of the stock to the buyer (on September 30, 1993). § 1259.

Chapter 21

DEFERRED PAYMENTS

§ 21.01 TIMING OF GAIN

In prior chapters, we focused on what the taxpayer sold. In this chapter, we focus on what the taxpayer receives for the sale. We consider *when* gain is taxed, as well as whether it is capital gain or ordinary income. We start first with timing (*when* is gain taxed) and then discuss whether deferred gain is capital gain.

Assume that a taxpayer owns a capital asset with a $60,000 basis. The asset is now worth $100,000. He sells the asset in year 0 for $30,000 cash, payable in year 0 at the time of sale, and five annual installments of $14,000 cash, payable in years 1 to 5. Adequate interest is charged to compensate for deferral of the receipt of cash beyond year 0, the year of sale. In other words, the interest is sufficient to prevent application of the original issue discount rules. The promise to pay the $14,000 installments is in the form of five nonnegotiable notes. There is some market for these notes but it is not very well-developed. If the seller tried to sell all five notes, he would probably get a total of $35,000 cash, not their $70,000 face value.

The following chart describes four ways in which the $40,000 gain on the sale ($100,000 minus $60,000) might be reported. The choice of methods carries with it certain implications about whether the income is (or should be) ordinary income or capital gain. However, this section focuses on why the timing of gain is different in each column of the chart. The next section worries about whether the gain is ordinary income or capital gain. The text following the chart explains each column.

Timing of $40,000 Gain

Year	(1) Installment Method	(2) Closed Transaction — Equivalent of cash	(3) Open Transaction	(4) Closed Transaction— Regulation
0	$12,000	$5,000	0	$40,000
1	5,600	7,000	0	0
2	5,600	7,000	0	0
3	5,600	7,000	12,000	0
4	5,600	7,000	14,000	0
5	5,600	7,000	14,000	0
	40,000	40,000	40,000	40,000

[A] Installment Method

Column 1 is the installment method, allowed by § 453. When used by the taxpayer, it permits deferral of tax, by allowing the taxpayer to spread out his tax payments over the period in which the sales proceeds are collected. In general, this means that, as cash is collected, tax will be paid. Tax on gain is, therefore, deferred beyond the year of sale.

When the installment method is permitted by the statute, that is the method the taxpayer must use, unless the taxpayer elects out of the installment method. § 453(a), (b), (c), (d). If the installment method is used, other methods of reporting gain are irrelevant. Columns 2, 3, and 4 are, therefore, possible choices only if the installment method is not used.

[1] Mechanics

The mechanism for achieving tax deferral under the installment method is as follows. A percentage of each installment payment is taxable. The percentage is the gross profit on the entire transaction divided by the total contract price. § 453(c). Thus, if a taxpayer with a basis of $60,000 sells property worth $100,000 for $30,000 cash and five $14,000 annual installments, 4/10ths of each installment is taxable, because the total gross profit is $40,000 ($100,000 minus $60,000) and the total contract price is $100,000.

Another way of looking at the statutory mechanics is that the installment method allocates a portion of the basis of the property sold to each payment. When 3/10ths of the sales price is collected in year 0 (that is, $30,000), then 3/10ths of the $60,000 basis is allocated to the $30,000 (3/10 times $60,000 = $18,000. Gain equals $30,000 minus $18,000; which is $12,000, which is also 4/10ths of $30,000.

As a practical matter, the key provision is § 453(f)(3), (4), (5), which excludes evidences of indebtedness from the definition of "payment," unless the debt: (1) is payable on demand; or (2) is readily tradable on an established securities market. This means that a taxpayer can usually receive notes (even negotiable notes), but still defer tax under the installment method.

Debt to which the property is subject is included in the selling price, thereby increasing gross profit. But the debt is not included in the contract price, except to the extent that the debt exceeds basis. **Treas. Reg. § 15A.453-1(b)(2), -1(b)(5)(Example 2)** gives the following example. Selling price is $160,000, including $60,000 of debt encumbering the property. Basis is $90,000. Gross profit is $70,000 (the $160,000 selling price minus $90,000). The contract price is $100,000 (the selling price of $160,000 reduced by the $60,000 debt). The $100,000 contract price is paid in ten equal annual cash installments, with adequate interest. 7/10ths of each $10,000 is taxable gain (gross profit/contract price; $70,000/$100,000). In effect, the $60,000 debt reduces basis to $30,000 and the $100,000 of cash to be collected results in a total gain of $70,000, taxable in 10 equal annual installments.

[2] What Property Is Eligible?

The installment method is available for sales of property, but there are some important exceptions. First, dealer dispositions of real and personal property (e.g., a sale of inventory) are not usually eligible for the installment method. § 453(b)(2), (*l*)(1).

Second, sale of publicly traded stock or securities (and other property regularly traded on an established market, as determined by Treasury Regulations) is not eligible for the installment method. This rule was adopted by the Tax Reform Act of 1986 and is probably a reaction to corporate takeovers in which the sellers of publicly traded stock or securities used the installment method. § 453(k)(2). It also prevents using the installment method to defer the gain on December 31 sales of publicly traded securities until following payment year.

Third, any gain on the sold asset that is recapture (ordinary) income cannot be postponed by using the installment method. § 453(i). For example, if the taxpayer's original cost for tangible personal property was $75,000, but the basis is now $60,000, after $15,000 depreciation, an installment sale for $100,000 in year 0 (with all cash receipts deferred) would result in $15,000 ordinary income in year 0. Basis would then be $75,000 ($60,000 + $15,000) and the additional $25,000 gain would be taxable under the installment method, assuming no other disqualification, unless the taxpayer elected not to use the installment method.

There has been some litigation over whether the sale of a contract right, such as the mortgage servicing contracts in *Bisbee-Baldwin* (Chapter 20.06[C]), is eligible for the installment sales provisions. The contracts are not capital assets, but there is no reason why they should not be "property" within the meaning of § 453. The purposes of the capital gains and installment method provisions are different. The lack of an investment or the absence of a lock-in effect might justify denial of a preferential tax rate, but that has nothing to do with timing tax payments to coincide with the cash payments received in installments. The word "property" can mean different things in § 1221, § 1231 and § 453. *Realty Loan Corp. v. Commissioner*, 54 T.C. 1083 (1970), *aff'd*, 478 F.2d 1049 (9th Cir. 1973), agrees with this analysis, and permits deferral even though the asset is not a capital asset.

[3] Charge Interest for Tax Deferral

The problem of tax deferral by using the installment method has attracted considerable attention and the statute has sometimes responded by charging the taxpayer interest on deferred taxes. Thus, rather than eliminating the opportunity to defer taxes, the government charges the taxpayer a price for lending the taxpayer the use of the deferred tax. § 453A. This is a complication that cannot realistically be imposed on all taxpayers using the installment method. The statutory rules are too complex to consider here, except to note: (1) that the section does not apply to an obligation arising from a sale for $150,000 or less or to sales of personal-use property or farm property; and (2) does not apply unless there is more than $5 million of covered unpaid obligations that arise in and are still due at the end of the year.

[4] Sale to Related Party

There is also a provision that prevents a seller from deferring tax by an installment sale to a relative (for example, parent to child), followed by a sale of the asset by the related installment buyer. If these two sales occur, the first seller must report the amount realized at the time of the second sale by the related buyer, up to the first seller's sales price (minus payments already received by the first seller). § 453(e).

For example, an installment sale of property to the child in year 1 for $100,000, payable in year 5, followed by a sale of that property by the child in year 2 for $100,000, would result in the *parent* having $100,000 amount realized in year 2. This prevents the parent from deflecting the $100,000 amount realized to the child through an installment sale, before the parent has to pay tax on the $100,000. After all, if the parent had first sold the property to an outsider and assigned collection of the $100,000 sales proceeds to the child in year 2, the assignment of income doctrine would have taxed the parent on the $100,000 amount realized in year 2. The "related party" sale rule in § 453(e) reaches the same result.

There are exceptions to the application of the related party sale rule, which include the following. The rule does not apply to a sale by the related party buyer: (1) if the sale occurs two or more years after acquiring the property; (2) if the sale occurs after the death of the related party seller; or (3) if neither the seller nor the buyer had avoidance of federal income taxes as one of its principal purposes.

[5] Loans Secured by Installment Claims

If an installment claim creditor pledges an installment claim as security for a loan, and the installment sales price exceeds $150,000, the net proceeds of the loan are generally taxable as a payment received on the installment obligation. § 453A(b)(1), (d). Sometimes loans are taxable!

[B] Closed Transaction; Equivalent of Cash

1. Column 2 is the "closed transaction" method. The transaction is "closed" because the market value of the installment contract is treated as the "equivalent of cash" received as sales proceeds in the year of sale. In the chart, the value of the installment contract is $35,000. Therefore, if the closed transaction method is used, the amount realized in the sale year is $65,000 (that is, $30,000 cash plus $35,000 market value of the notes).

2. When *should* a contract be treated as having a market value that is the equivalent of cash? In *Cowden v. Commissioner*, 289 F.2d 20 (5th Cir. 1961), the court stated:

> A promissory note, negotiable in form, is not necessarily the equivalent of cash. Such an instrument may have been issued by a maker of doubtful solvency or for other reasons such paper might be denied a ready acceptance in the market place. We think the converse of this principle ought to be applicable. We are convinced that if a promise to pay of a solvent obligor is unconditional and assignable, not subject to set-offs, and is of a kind that is frequently transferred to lenders or investors at a discount not substantially greater than the generally prevailing premium for the use of money, such promise is the equivalent of cash and taxable in like manner as cash would have been taxable had it been received by the taxpayer rather than the obligation.

The case is unusual in suggesting that a mere promise will occasionally be the equivalent of cash. However, the Court of Appeals rejected the implication in the Tax Court's opinion that the debtor's willingness to pay cash upon execution of the contract was relevant in deciding whether the promise was the equivalent of cash.

3. By closing the transaction in the year of sale, the taxpayer recognizes gain or loss on the sale by including the value of the claim in amount realized. The collection of future proceeds on the claim is then a separate transaction.

4. The computation of gain on the collection of future proceeds is determined by recovering basis in the claim to future proceeds against the amount collected. The basis in the claim would be the value at which the claim was included in amount realized ($35,000 in the chart example). The chart assumes that this basis is amortized straight-line over the five-year collection period. Another way to recover basis would be to defer taxable gain until the amount collected on the notes exceeds the $35,000 amount realized in the year of sale (which would result in no income in years 1 and 2, and $7,000, $14,000, and $14,000 in years 3, 4, and 5 respectively). Occasionally, this latter deferral method is used when collection seems very doubtful. *See Phillips v. Frank*, 295 F.2d 629 (9th Cir. 1961).

[C] Open Transaction

Column 3 is the "open transaction" method. Under this method, no gain is recognized until sales proceeds exceed basis. In effect, all of the basis is allocated to the early collection of the sales proceeds.

The courts have taken varied positions on when the taxpayer can use the open transaction method upon receipt of fixed payment obligation, instead of treating the obligation as the equivalent of cash. In one case, the Fifth Circuit stated that the transaction would be closed for tax purposes only if the promise to pay did not sell at a discount that was "substantially greater than the generally prevailing premium for the use of money." *Cowden v. Commissioner*, 289 F.2d 20 (5th Cir. 1961). The Tax Court agreed with the Fifth Circuit in *Warren Jones Co. v. Commissioner*, 60 T.C. 663 (1973), *rev'd and remanded*, 524 F.2d 788 (9th Cir. 1975), but the Ninth Circuit reversed, treating the discounted value of the contract as the equivalent of cash in the year of sale, regardless of the discount.

[D] Regulation — Installment Method Not Used

Column 4 closes the transaction, but in a different way from Method 2 above, when the creditor receives a fixed payment obligation. It conclusively presumes that the value of the obligation is at least equal to the value of the property sold minus any other consideration received. In the chart example, that presumed value is $70,000 ($100,000 value of property minus $30,000 cash). The Regulation describing this method requires this valuation method whether or not the obligations have that value under the traditional "equivalent of cash" doctrine. **Treas. Reg. § 15a.453-1(d)(2)(i),(ii).**

The government takes the position in the above-cited Regulation that, if the taxpayer elects not to use the installment method, the taxpayer *must* use Method 4 to report gain on a fixed payment obligation. Excerpts from that Regulation appear below. The subparagraph (iii) referred to in the Regulation deals with *contingent payments*, such as sales proceeds that are based on profits. We return to contingent payments in a later section.

> (2) *Treatment of an installment sale when a taxpayer elects not to report on the installment method* — (i) In General. A taxpayer who elects not to report an installment sale on the installment method must recognize gain on the sale in accordance with the taxpayer's method of accounting. The fair market value of an installment obligation shall be determined in accordance with paragraph (d)(2)(ii) and (iii) of this section. In making such determination, any provision of contract or local law restricting the transferability of the installment obligation shall be disregarded. Receipt of an installment obligation shall be treated as a receipt of property, in an amount equal to the fair market value of the installment obligation, whether or not such obligation is the equivalent of cash. An installment obligation is considered to be property and is subject to valuation, as provided in paragraph (d)(2)(ii) and (iii) of this section, without regard to whether the obligation is embodied in a note, an executory contract, or any other instrument, or is an oral promise enforceable under local law.

> (ii) *Fixed amount obligations.* (A) A fixed amount obligation means an installment obligation the amount payable under which is fixed. A taxpayer using the cash receipts and disbursements method of accounting shall treat as an amount realized in the year of sale the fair market value of the installment obligation. . . . In no event will the fair market value of the installment obligation be considered to be less than the fair market value of the property sold (minus any other consideration received by the taxpayer on the sale). A taxpayer using the accrual method of accounting shall treat as an amount realized in the year of sale the total amount payable under the installment obligation. . . . Under no circumstances will an installment sale for a fixed amount obligation be considered an "open" transaction.

COMMENTS

1. The point of this Regulation is to preclude use of Method 2 (closed transaction at *discounted* value) and Method 3 (open transaction), if the installment method is not used by the taxpayer. The question is whether it is a valid regulation. You can answer this question better after considering whether gain under any of these methods is ordinary income or capital gain, as discussed in the next section.

2. Even if you conclude that the Regulation is valid in requiring Method 4 when the installment method is not elected, you have not wasted your time considering Methods 2 and 3. Method 2 (closed transaction) is a variation on the equivalent of cash doctrine, which is an application of the cash method of accounting. What counts as a taxable equivalent of cash will be relevant in other transactions taxable on the cash method, discussed in Chapter 24. And Method 3 (open transaction) is available, even for sales, when the consideration is contingent — discussed in Chapter 21.04 below.

§ 21.02   ORDINARY INCOME OR CAPITAL GAIN

Assume that the asset sold in the prior discussion is a capital asset or a § 1231 asset, with no recapture income. How much of the gain is capital gain and how much is ordinary income under each of the methods of reporting gain set forth in the chart? The answer is quite mechanical, following from the assumptions underlying the method used to report gain. Recall the four methods:

Method 1 — Installment method

Method 2 — Closed Transaction — Equivalent of Cash

Method 3 — Open Transaction

Method 4 — Closed Transaction — Treasury Regulation

Method 1 — Installment method. Under the installment method, the gain is capital gain. Under general statutory principles, sales proceeds are capital gain, unless the gain is recapture income. The logic of the installment method is that taxation of sales proceeds is deferred until cash is received, but they are still sales proceeds. Thus, the gain in years 0 through 5 is capital gain under Method 1.

Method 2 — Closed transaction — Equivalent of cash. Under the traditional version of the closed transaction method, the value of the obligations is treated as sales proceeds in the year of sale. Later collections of these obligations are an independent transaction, not referable to the original sale.

It is unclear whether the collection of the $14,000 notes in this example would be treated as the "sale" of a capital asset, or ordinary income. **Section 1271(a), (b)** treats retirement of debt as a sale or exchange, whether the debtor is a natural person or a corporation. But the market discount rules *appear* to apply when a taxpayer collects a debt that has previously been reported as an amount realized on a discounted basis; and market discount is taxable as ordinary income, overriding § 1271(a) treatment of collection as a sale or exchange. The relevant market discount rules are too complex to be reviewed here, but the citations are **§§ 1276(a)(1), (b), 1278(a)(1)(D)(i)–(ii), (a)(3), 1273(b)(4).**

In sum, under Method 2, there is capital gain (or perhaps loss) in year 0 (the year of sale). It is unclear whether any gain on collection of the debt in later years (years 1 through 5 in the Chart) would be ordinary income or capital gain.

Method 3 — Open transaction. The open transaction method also treats the cash received as sales proceeds, although basis is allocated differently. The taxable gain is capital gain, but it is deferred until years 3 through 5 in this example (year 3, $12,000; year 4, $14,000; year 5, $14,000). The taxpayer likes this a lot — deferral plus capital gain.

Method 4 — Closed transaction — Treasury Regulation. Under the government's version of the closed transaction method, in which the value of the property is an amount realized in the year of sale, the taxpayer would report gain as capital gain. There is unlikely to be any further gain on collection of the debt under these circumstances, because the cash collected will equal the face value of the debt previously reported as an amount realized.

Argument against Method 3 (open transaction). Is there anything anomalous about permitting both deferral and capital gain? If one of the major purposes of the capital gains preference is relief from bunching the future risky flow of income that is realized early (when an asset is sold), does it make sense to provide the capital gains preference if the sales proceeds are not bunched up in the year of sale (that is, if they are deferred)? What if the payments stretch out over five or ten years? This question is not academic. It has relevance in deciding whether the open transaction method (Method 3), which provides the maximum deferral combined with capital gains, should be permitted. If combining deferral and capital gains is anomalous, the open transaction method should not be encouraged in the context of a sale of a capital asset. This supports the government position prohibiting the open transaction method in fixed payment obligation situations and requiring Method 4 if the taxpayer does not use the installment method.

Argument against Method 2 (closed transaction — equivalent of cash). Should the taxpayer be allowed to use the Method 2 version of the closed transaction, if the taxpayer elects not to use the installment method? Under Method 2, the taxpayer reports the fair market value of the claim as the amount realized in the year of sale. Retirement of the debt might result in either capital gain or ordinary income. If some of the retirement-of-debt gain is capital gain, Method 2 (like Method 3) combines deferral and capital gain, which seems anomalous. In any event, Method 2 requires valuation of the installment claim in year 0, which arguably imposes an unreasonable burden on the tax administration. Consequently, there is a strong case against allowing the taxpayer to use Method 2 and requiring Method 4, if the taxpayer opts not to use the installment method.

§ 21.03 DISTINGUISHING SALES PROCEEDS FROM INTEREST

If a taxpayer defers receipt of sales proceeds *and* charges *inadequate* interest, some portion of the sales proceeds should be recharacterized as interest. This is another version of the original issue discount problem, except that the taxpayer (seller) is transferring property, not money to the borrower (buyer). The statute should be concerned with two issues: separating out the interest element from the sales proceeds; and whether the interest ought to be accrued annually or taxed only when the sales proceeds are collected.

For example, if a taxpayer sells an asset in year 0 for $600,000 without interest, due in year 5, the taxpayer has in effect loaned the asset's *present value* to the buyer. Some portion of the $600,000 ought to be interest, and some sales proceeds.

[A] Section 1274

[1] Actual Value

The analytically pure answer in these cases is to treat the asset's fair market value as sales proceeds, which are loaned back to the buyer, and which then accrue original issue discount annually. § 1274. That is, in fact, the rule in some cases, including sales where the property sold is publicly traded stock or securities, or the consideration for the sale is publicly traded securities. In such cases, valuing the property sold by reference to the public trading value is easy. § 1273(b)(3). Thus, a sale of land for publicly traded securities worth $350,000 would be treated as a $350,000 sale, followed by a $350,000 loan to the buyer. The lender would then accrue interest annually in accordance with the usual original issue discount rules, and a total of $250,000 interest would be taxed as ordinary income spread out over the five-year period. The $350,000 sales proceeds would be taxed in accordance with the accounting method used to report sales.

Another situation in which actual valuation of the sold property would probably be required is a nonrecourse loan in a sale-leaseback transaction (recall the *Estate of Franklin* situation — Chapter 17.03[B]). In those situations, the parties have an incentive to inflate the nonrecourse debt, which would overstate the sales price and understate the interest. Use of actual value would prevent the understatement of interest. § 1274(b)(3).

Remember to separate the treatment of gain from taxation of interest. Any gain on transactions in which actual value is used to determine the sales price will *not* be eligible for the installment method, *if* the property sold was stock or securities traded on an established exchange. § 453(k)(2). However, the gain could be reported on the installment method in the sale-leaseback example described in the *Estate of Franklin* case.

[2] Present Value Formula

Because valuation is difficult, the statute often does not require the taxpayer to determine the actual value of the property sold at the time of the sale. Instead, the sales proceeds and loan amount are identified by measuring the present value of the future payment ($600,000 in the prior example), using an interest rate measured by reference to the rate on federal bonds of similar maturity to the loan period. For example, if the appropriate interest rate were 9%, the $600,000 "sale" would include a $386,357 sale (the statute compounds interest semi-annually; $600,000/1.045^{10} = $386,357). The rest of the $600,000 is original issue discount. If the taxpayer uses the installment method, the gain on the sale would be reported in year 5; otherwise, the gain or loss would be recognized in year 0 in compliance with the Treasury Regulation (referred to earlier as Method 4). In any event, in years 1 through 5, interest would accrue periodically to the seller at the appropriate interest rate on a $386,357 loan.

[B] Section 483

This brief review of the division of "sales" proceeds into a sale and a loan is not complete. Sometimes § 1274 does not force a seller to accrue the interest annually (the exceptions appear in § 1274(c)(3)), but the statute still requires interest to be separated from sales proceeds. The mechanism to do this is specified by § 483. It is the older of the two sections imputing interest and a taxpayer exempted from § 1274 must examine § 483 to see if and how it applies. For example, § 483 (rather than § 1274), applies to sales of farms by individuals for no more than $1,000,000, sales of principal residences, and sales of anything for less than $250,000.

Section 483 taxes some portion of the sales proceeds as interest, *when the sales proceeds are collected.* The interest is *not* accrued annually, like original issue discount. The following example illustrates how the computations are made. Assume that the sale is for two $300,000 installments, payable in years 2 and 5. If the present value of the two installments is $400,000, then *total* interest is $200,000, which is *one third* of the total $600,000 "sales" proceeds. Consequently, one third of each $300,000 installment payment is interest taxed when collected in year 2 and year 5; each $300,000 payment consists of $100,000 interest and $200,000 sales proceeds.

§ 21.04 CONTINGENT PAYMENTS

The open transaction method (Method 3 in the earlier chart) is usually allowed when payments are "contingent" — e.g., sales proceeds based on gross receipts, gross income, or net income from a purchased business. This result is traced to the decision in *Burnet v. Logan*, 283 U.S. 404 (1931). The taxpayer sold stock in exchange for cash plus a promise of future payments contingent on the mining of ore. The cash received at the time the stock was sold was insufficient to recover the taxpayer's basis in the stock. The Court did not force the seller to value the contingent payments, allowing gain to be deferred until the payments exceeded basis.

The same 1981 Regulation dealing with fixed payment obligations, cited earlier, also deals with contingent payments. It permits the open transaction method when contingent payments are to be received "only in those rare and extraordinary cases in which the fair market value of the obligation . . . cannot reasonably be ascertained." **Treas. Reg. § 15a.453-1(d)(2)(iii).** This Regulation's bark is probably more severe than its bite. Transactions like the one in *Burnet v. Logan*, involving contingent payments, continue to be reported by taxpayers on the open transaction method.

[A] Contingent Payments and Installment Method

Does the following argument justify the government's stinginess in permitting tax deferral for contingent payments under the open transaction method? Before 1980, a court sympathetic with the taxpayer's desire to defer tax on contingent payments could only permit deferral through the open transaction method. In 1980, however, the statute for the first time explicitly *permitted* taxpayers to report contingent payment sales on the installment method. **§ 453(j)(2).** Before that, the government did not allow the installment method in contingent payment cases because it was too difficult to compute the gain when the amount realized was contingent. (What was the contract price, from which the gross profit percentage would be computed?) After 1980, that changed.

The Regulations now state that the maximum contract price, as stated in the contract, will be the amount realized for computing the gross profit percentage; if there is no maximum, but there is a set payment period, basis will be allocated evenly over the payment period; in all other cases, cost will generally be allocated over 15 years. **Treas. Reg. § 15a.453-1(c).** Now that the taxpayer has a way to defer tax without using the open transaction method, maybe there is less need to permit the open transaction method for contingent payment sales.

[B]   Contingent Payments and Capital Gain

Do contingent payments eligible for the open transaction method produce capital gain? In *Commissioner v. Carter*, 170 F.2d 911 (2d Cir. 1948), a taxpayer owned stock in a corporation that distributed all of its assets to its stockholders in liquidation. She received easy-to-value property that exceeded her stock basis by $20,000, *plus* oil brokerage contracts that everyone agreed had "no ascertainable market value when distributed." Each brokerage contract provided for payment of commissions on future deliveries of oil. Contingencies associated with earning commissions made the amount and time of payment uncertain. Thereafter, taxpayer collected about $35,000 in commissions. The court held that these commissions were capital gains, treating them as deferred proceeds from disposition of the stock. Because liquidations are treated like sales (§ 331), the deferred proceeds were treated as consideration received for the sale of the stock — that is, capital gain. The court stated that "no reason is apparent for taxing [the commissions] as ordinary income." Isn't there a "good reason" to deny capital gain when gain is deferred?

[C]   Contingent Payments and Imputed Interest

If deferred contingent payments are sales proceeds, the problem of distinguishing sales proceeds from interest recurs. Adequate interest *could* be charged on a contingent payment — for example, the seller could insist that the payment of 5% of the gross receipts received as payment for sale of a business must be supplemented by an added interest charge at some specified rate. Frequently, however, no such interest is charged. In that case, some portion of each contingent payment is usually converted to interest when the payment is collected. § 483(f)(1).

To determine the interest, the payment is discounted back to present value at the time of the sale; the difference between the later payment and present value is interest. The longer the deferral, therefore, the higher the portion of the later payment which is interest. For example, using a 10% interest rate, the present value of a payment 10 years from now on which no interest is charged contains a little more than 60% interest, assuming annual compounding. If there is a lot of interest, the opportunity to combine tax deferral and capital gain on contingent sales is significantly reduced.

§ 21.05   DEFERRAL, CAPITAL GAINS, AND PERSONAL SERVICE INCOME

Individuals who provide personal services are always seeking ways to defer personal service income and convert it into capital gains. This section discusses some of the ways that might be done.

[A] Restricted Property

One popular way to achieve deferral and capital gains on personal service income was to receive property from the employer, often stock of a corporate employer. There would be significant restrictions on the transferability of the stock or on its retention and, further, the property might be subject to a repurchase option at a value significantly below market value. The courts often held that the restrictions prevented the imposition of tax at the time the stock was received, under a generous (pro-taxpayer) reading of the "equivalent of cash" doctrine. Tax would be postponed until the restrictions lapsed, at which time the taxpayers received ordinary income. Moreover, when the restrictions lapsed, the employees were often allowed to report ordinary income equal to the value of the property when it was *originally* transferred to them. In the usual case, value had increased and the increase in value over the amount taxed as ordinary income would be capital gains when the property was sold.

Section 83 alters prior case law. How is the employee in the following problem taxed under § 83? An employee of a corporation received some of the corporation's stock as compensation without having to pay anything. The stock is forfeited back to the corporation if the employee changes employers at any time within five years of receiving the stock. Moreover, the forfeiture rule applies even if the stock has been transferred to another owner by the employee. For ten years, the corporation can repurchase the stock from the owner at the value of the stock on the date it was originally transferred to the employee. The value of the stock when transferred to the employee (year 0) is $10,000. It rises to $15,000 when the forfeiture condition is lifted five years later (year 5). In another seven years (year 12), the stock is sold for $23,000.

In general, the taxpayer must pay tax on the value of the stock as ordinary income, when a substantial risk of the forfeiture lapses (year 5 in the example). The value of the stock is discounted to account for a buy-back provision, only if that provision cannot lapse in the future. The taxpayer can avoid tax when the forfeiture lapses by electing to include as income in year 0 the value of the compensation.

QUESTIONS

1. How could the employee use § 83(b) in the above example? He could elect to include the $10,000 ordinary income in year 0, taking a $10,000 basis in the property. By accelerating tax (eliminating deferral), there is no tax when the forfeiture provisions expire in year 5 and future recognized gain is capital gain.

2. Suppose, in the prior example, the employee paid $10,000 for the restricted property in year 0 (that is, an amount equal to its value), instead of receiving it without charge. Would the employee have to report income in year 5 when the sale restriction lapsed and the property was worth $15,000? The taxpayer will argue that he received nothing in year 0 and should, therefore, not be taxed in year 5, because it is silly to make him elect to pay tax in year 0 on a zero net value ($10,000 minus $10,000). But how do we know whether there was any net value to the employee in year 0, without measuring value in year 0, which is administratively difficult? Arguably, the taxpayer's exclusion in year 5 should depend on electing to

report as income the "zero net value" in year 0 (even though that produces no tax), so as to alert the IRS to a valuation issue, as a condition of not paying tax in year 5 when the restrictions are removed. *Alves v. Commissioner*, 79 T.C. 864 (1982), *aff'd*, 734 F.2d 478 (9th Cir. 1984).

3. What effect does § 83(h) have on tax planning? It prohibits the employer's deduction until the employee has income under § 83(a). If the corporate tax rate is much higher than the individual's tax rate, will the corporation want to avoid losing the deduction and provide the employee only with compensation taxable in the year of receipt? Will a public corporation really care about the loss of a deduction when deciding how to compensate top executives?

[B] Options

Another way employers try to provide both deferral and capital gains to employees is by giving the employee an option to buy stock in the employer corporation (or, perhaps, other property owned by the corporation). **Section 83(e)(3), (4)** preserves the prior case law on this issue, as illustrated by this example. In year 0, a corporation grants an employee an option to buy stock for $100 for five years; in year 0, the stock is worth $100 and the option is worth $5. When the stock goes up in value to $120 in year 5, the employee buys it for $100. The case law held that, if the option had a reasonably ascertainable value, its value was taxable as ordinary income in year 0 (that is, $5 ordinary income), but there was no taxable event on the exercise of the option in year 5. This meant that any personal service income inherent in the $20 gain in year 5 was deferred. Moreover, the gain on the sale of the stock (assume a sale for $120 in year 12) was $15 capital gain, not ordinary income (that is, $120 amount realized, minus $105, which is the basis equal to the purchase price plus the taxed option value).

If the option did *not* have an ascertainable value, no tax would be imposed when the option was received in year 0, but then the exercise of the option in year 5 would result in ordinary income on the spread between the purchase price and the value of the stock at the time of exercise — $20 in the example. Because there was usually a significant gain in value between the time the option was granted and its exercise, the government usually found itself arguing that the option had *no* ascertainable value in year 0. This position is just the opposite of the government's argument in a *Commissioner v. Carter* or *Burnet v. Logan* type of case, concerning the potential for using the open transaction doctrine, where the government wants to argue that the value of contingent payments *can* be ascertained.

Taxpayers who get hard-to-value options can sometimes be stuck with a large tax bill and few assets if the stock they have purchased by exercising their options declines in value. Many employees in dot.com companies in recent years made the "mistake" of holding on to stock purchased pursuant to options received as compensation, after the free fall in stock prices. Prudence suggested selling immediately after purchasing the stock, but these taxpayers instead held on to the stock and sold it after the decline in value. For example, assume a hard-to-value option to buy 1,000 shares of gogo.com stock for $10 per share (that is, a total of $10,000); and that the value of the option was not taxed when received. The option is later exercised when the stock is worth $100,000 ($100 per share) and the stock is purchased for $10,000. Ordinary income at the time of exercise would be $90,000 ($100,000 value minus $10,000 basis). If the employee held on to the stock until it declined to $20 per share and then sold it for $20,000, that would produce an $80,000 capital loss at the time of the sale that would be deductible from ordinary income only up to $3,000.

[C] Incentive Stock Options

Finally, there is a statutory provision excluding from ordinary income *both* the value of stock options received from a corporate employer and the value of the spread between the option price and the value of the stock when the option is exercised, if certain requirements are met by the stock option plan. **§ 421, § 422; Treas. Reg. § 14a.422A-1**. Most important, the employee cannot own more than 10% of the corporation's voting stock; the option price must equal the value of the stock when the option is granted; and no disposition of the stock can occur within two years of granting the option or within one year of receipt of the stock. **§ 422(b)(4), (6)**. However, stockholders who own more than 10% of the corporation's voting stock are still eligible for the tax break if the option price is at least 110% of the value of the stock at the time the option is granted and the option is exercisable only within five years of its grant. **§ 422(c)(5)**. If the taxpayer qualifies under these sections, no gain is taxed until sale of the stock, and the gain is (almost certainly) capital gain. The employer cannot deduct any of the value of the shares transferred pursuant to an incentive stock option. **§ 421(a)(2)**.

Before you assume that the incentive stock option rules are as good as they look, keep the alternative minimum tax in mind. The difference between the option price and the value of the stock at the time the option is exercised is income under the AMT, unless recognition would be deferred under § 83 (e.g., because of a substantial risk of forfeiture). **§ 56(b)(3)**.

[D] Carried Interests

A "carried interest" typically works this way. A partnership has a general partner who manages the partnership. This way of doing business is used for private equity and venture capital firms that buy and sell stock in companies with growth potential. This stock is a capital asset that normally produces capital gain and loss. This kind of a partnership is not itself taxed (unlike a corporation), but its income (including capital gain) is passed through to its partners.

The general partner contributes approximately 1–5% of the partnership capital, but is entitled to 20% of the profits from the sale of securities (in addition to compensation for personal services). The general partner reports its 20% share of the gain as capital gain, even though a significant part of the gain appears to be compensation for personal services in managing the partnership — specifically, the amount of the 20% gain in excess of the 1–5% investment that the partner put at risk. Congress has considered but (so far) not passed a law taxing all or part of this excess gain as ordinary income, but it is high on the list of proposed tax reforms.

Chapter 22

CARVED OUT INCOME INTERESTS

§ 22.01 THE PROBLEM

The problem addressed by this chapter arises whenever there is a "carve out" of an income interest (often referred to as a term interest) from a remainder interest. Before you worry about why this causes a problem, be sure you understand what is meant by a carved out income interest. This was explained in Chapter 4.05 but is repeated here with more detail.

You are familiar with dividing property physically — 60% of the land to one person and 40% to another. Property can also be divided temporally. For example, assume that property is worth $100 because it will produce $20 per year forever before tax (e.g., rent from land), when the before-tax discount rate is 20%. This asset could be divided into two parts — a five-year income interest and a remainder interest, which vests in possession when the five years expire. Based on the income and interest rate assumptions just made, the present value of the five-year income interest is just about $60. (Discount $20 per year, using a 20% discount rate. The present value is just a few cents below $60, but we round up to $60.) The remainder interest is, therefore, worth $40 — it has to be worth $100 minus the value of the income interest. A carved out income interest is simply the *temporal* carving out of an income interest, leaving the remainder interest and income interests in different ownership.

To understand the tax avoidance potential from a carved out income interest, you must understand what happens *before* a carve out. Assume that the example above involves nondepreciable property, such as land or stock. It produces $20 income per year. *The benchmark for tax analysis is that $20 should be reported each year as taxable income.* When a carve out occurs, the $20 might not be reported annually. To see why, consider one type of carve out — the sale of a five-year income interest and retention of the remainder by the seller. The sale of the income interest is for $60, and the seller retains a remainder worth $40. First, we look at the buyer and then at the seller who retains the remainder interest. Assume also that the entire asset has a $100 basis, equal to its value.

The buyer. The buyer has bought a depreciable five-year asset for $60. How much income will the buyer report each year (using straight line depreciation)?

Year	Gross Income	Buyer of Income Interest	
		Depreciation	Net Income
1	20	12	8
2	20	12	8
3	20	12	8
4	20	12	8
5	20	12	8
	100	60	40

Something has gone wrong. There is only $8 taxable income per year and a $40 total for five years. Before the sale, there was $20 per year and $100 total for five years. Where is the missing $60 income over five years?

The seller. Now look at the seller, who sold a carved out income interest worth $60. Based on what we have learned so far (although it is not the law, as we will see in a later section), you would conclude the following. Any gain on the sale of the income interest would be taxed. But, because the income interest was worth 60% of the total asset and the basis of the entire asset was $100, the seller has a $60 basis in the income interest; $60 sales proceeds minus $60 basis = $0. *No gain!*

But the remaining $60 of income has not disappeared. Look at the owner of the remainder interest, who is also the seller in this example. What is the value of the retained remainder at the time of sale — $40 ($100 minus the $60 sales price of the carved out income interest). What happens to that value over the next five years? Before you try to answer that question, answer this one — what is the property worth to the owner of the remainder interest *after* five years, assuming interest rates stay the same and the property's expected income continues to be $20 per year? Be sure you understand that the answer *must be* $100. And, if you have property worth $40 today, which will be worth $100 in five years, you have $60 gain after five years have passed. There it is. The "missing" $60 gain accrues to the retained remainder interest.

Based on the assumptions in the example, how much income accrues to the remainder owner each year? As time passes, the value of the remainder increases annually by 20%, as follows (after rounding to the nearest half dollar):

Year	Value accruing to remainder
1	$8
2	9.5
3	11.5
4	14
5	17
	60

So there really *is* a total of $100 income over the five years earned by the owners of both income and remainder interests. No alchemy caused some income to disappear. What kind of income accrues to the remainder interest? Isn't it ordinary income, based on the *Midland-Ross* discussion of original issue discount? It seems to be income that is "predictable and measurable," arising due to the "mere passage of time." But the analogy to original issue discount is not precise. There is no fixed payment obligation due in five years, so the appreciation is not, technically, original issue discount.

The difficulties of taxing the remainder's $60 income should be obvious. Will the annual appreciation of value be taxed; will gain after five years be taxed? Will gain on sale be reported as capital gain? Will date-of-death value result in disappearance of tax on the $60?[1] How can we assure taxation of the remainder's $60 income? In the rest of this Chapter, we consider case law and statutory solutions to this problem in a variety of situations involving a carved out income interest. Note that a carve out can occur in many ways, including the prior example of a sale of an income interest with a retained remainder. Here are the most likely variations.

1. *Sell term/retain remainder.* A taxpayer could sell a term interest and keep the remainder, as in the prior example.

2. *Gift of term/gift of remainder.* A term and remainder interest could both be given away, either inter vivos or through inheritance, to a spouse and child of a deceased. *See Irwin v. Gavit*, Chapter 4.05[A].

3. *Gift of term/retain remainder.* A term interest could be given to a family remember, with the donor retaining the remainder. *See Helvering v. Horst*, Chapter 4.05[D][1].

4. *Buy term/buy remainder.* Two people could buy term and remainder interests from an owner or owners.

5. *Retain term/give or sell remainder.* A term interest could be retained, but the remainder interest given away or sold.

You will find that the *case law* has addressed some of these situations effectively, that *statutory* provisions have been adopted to deal with some situations, and that sometimes no specific solution has been reached in the case law or statutory text.

§ 22.02 THE SOLUTIONS

[A] Sale of Income Interest — Retained Remainder

There is a lot of case law dealing with the *sale* of a carved out income interest, with retained remainder. In the earlier discussion of this example, we concluded that general tax principles would result in no taxable gain on the sale of the term interest, because the $60 basis equaled the $60 proceeds of the sale. The case law, however, reaches a different result. Here is some of what the courts typically said.

In *Commissioner v. Gillette Motor Transport Inc.*, 364 U.S. 130 (1960), the government seized taxpayer's property for one year because it was needed during World War II. There was, in other words, a forced sale of a carved out income interest. The Court denied capital gains, as follows:

---

[1] For a suggestion that some of the gain accruing to the remainder might be ordinary income, analogous to original issue discount, see *Jones v. Commissioner*, 330 F.2d 302 (3d Cir. 1964).

While a capital asset is defined . . . as "property held by the taxpayer," it is evident that not everything which can be called property in the ordinary sense and which is outside the statutory exclusions qualifies as a capital asset. This Court has long held that the term 'capital asset' is to be construed narrowly in accordance with the purpose of Congress to afford capital-gains treatment only in situations typically involving the realization of appreciation in value accrued over a substantial period of time, and thus to ameliorate the hardship of taxation of the entire gain in one year. Burnet v. Harmel, 287 U.S. 103, 106. . . .

In *Commissioner v. P. G. Lake, Inc.*, 356 U.S. 260 (1958), the taxpayer sold three years of income from oil property. The Court denied capital gains:

The purpose of [the capital gains provision] was 'to relieve the taxpayer from . . . excessive tax burdens on gains resulting from a conversion of capital investments, and to remove the deterrent effect of those burdens on such conversions.' See Burnet v. Harmel, 287 U.S. 103, 106. And this exception has always been narrowly construed so as to protect the revenue against artful devices.

We do not see here any conversion of a capital investment. The lump sum consideration seems essentially a substitute for what would otherwise be received at a future time as ordinary income. The pay-out of these particular assigned oil payment rights could be ascertained with considerable accuracy. Such are the stipulations, findings, or clear inferences. In the O'Connor case, the pay-out of the assigned oil payment right was so assured that the purchaser obtained a $9,990,350 purchase money loan at 3 ½ percent interest without any security other than a deed of trust of the $10,000,000 oil payment right, he receiving 4 percent from the taxpayer. Only a fraction of the oil or sulphur rights were transferred, the balance being retained. . . . [C]ash was received which was equal to the amount of the income to accrue during the term of the assignment, the assignee being compensated by interest on his advance. The substance of what was assigned was the right to receive future income. The substance of what was received was the present value of income which the recipient would otherwise obtain in the future. In short, consideration was paid for the right to receive future income, not for an increase in the value of the income-producing property.

The language of *P. G. Lake* has given commentators fits because it states that sales proceeds are ordinary income if they are a substitute for future ordinary income. But capital gains *are* a substitute for future income. Capital gains result from realizing the present value of future income.

The *Gillette* case is also misleading. Selling one year's income can produce a bunching of gain into one year. If the taxpayer had bought the property in 1938 and sold one year's income in 1945, surely that right to one year's income would have gone up in value gradually as a result of wartime inflation and recovery from the Depression and past gain would be bunched in the sale year.

The actual holding of these cases, as opposed to the theory stated by the Court, is quite sensible. The holdings deny capital gains to the seller of the carved out income interest, but also do much more. Indeed, they would have to do more to deal with the tax avoidance problem, because denying capital gains treatment has no impact on the taxpayer if there is no gain to tax. Consequently, the cases also deny the seller of the carved out income interest any use of the basis attributable to the term interest. *Shafer v. United States*, 204 F. Supp. 473 (S.D. Ohio 1962), *aff'd*, 312 F.2d 747 (6th Cir. 1963). For example, reverting to our earlier example of the sale of a five-year interest, *the seller would have $60 ordinary income* under the *Gillette* and *P. G. Lake* rules (Amount realized = $60; Basis = $0). That means that the seller of the carved out income interest has $60 ordinary income at the time of sale and the buyer of the carved out income interest has $8 annual income for five years — a total of $40; $20 annual gross income, minus $12 annual depreciation. A total of $100 is taxed over the five-year period.

In chart form, this produces the following result, assuming that the sale occurs on January 1, year 1, and the annual income is earned in years 1–5.

Year	Buyer of Income Interest	Seller of Term Interest; Owner of Retained Remainder Interest	Total
1	8	$60	68
2	8	-	8
3	8	-	8
4	8	-	8
5	8	-	8
	40	60	100

Not a bad result. A total of $100 is reported over five years, which is the correct total. However, it is a little unfair to the taxpayer. Now, the income is reported *earlier* than if there had been no sale. $60 is accelerated as ordinary income to year 1. In effect, the case law taxes the $60 accruing to the retained remainder in year 1. (Notice that the seller who is taxed on the $60 ordinary income under *Gillette* and *P. G. Lake* is the same person who has income accruing to the remainder interest — the seller *is* the owner of the retained remainder.)

QUESTIONS AND COMMENTS

1. **Missing basis?** We have found the missing income, but now there is a missing basis problem. What happens to the $60 basis that the seller of the carved out income interest could not use? Remember that the cases dealt with the sale of the income interest. The courts did not have to decide what happens to the basis. Presumably it does not disappear, but is given to the remainder interest. Thus, assuming the seller's basis in the income interest is $60, the owner of the remainder interest should have a $100 basis after the sale of the carved out income interest.

2. **No capital gains preference?** Does the *Gillette* and *P. G. Lake* approach have a place in the law even if capital gains are not preferentially taxed? Sure. In the

example, the property did not even have a gain. Its total value was $100 and so was the basis. The problem is really about preventing tax avoidance on the $60 of income over the five-year period, regardless of whether capital gains are preferentially taxed.

3. **Sale as loan.** Suppose the "sale" for $60 in the prior example had been recast as a $60 loan. The so-called "seller" of the income interest would be treated as the continued owner of the *entire* property, who borrowed $60. During each of the five years after the "purchase," the so-called "buyer" would get $20, but not as a buyer; the "buyer" would be treated as a lender and the $20 would be treated as a loan repayment plus interest. That means that the so-called "seller" reports the $20 annual income from the property as the owner of the property and deducts the interest portion of the $20 that the "buyer" receives. The buyer reports the interest portion of the $20 as income, but not the portion attributable to the loan repayment.

Look at the tax result of loan treatment during the five-year loan period in the following chart. That is a sensible result, isn't it, taxing the "buyer" and the "seller" annually on some of the $20 income? Notice something else about this result. The computation of the buyer-lender's income is the result of the following computation — $20 received minus annual amortization of the loan. Thus, the year 1 interest income to the buyer-lender equals the $20 he received from the seller-borrower minus $8 amortization of the loan (not minus $12 of straight-line depreciation). We did not allow straight line depreciation, but instead used the decelerated depreciation method explained in Chapter 11.01[E]. But, as noted in the earlier discussion of depreciation, decelerated depreciation is often the theoretically correct method.

Moreover, look at the result to the seller-borrower. He is treated just like someone who retained a $40 remainder interest and accrued income as though it were *compound* interest — starting at the low $8 figure in year 1 and increasing in later years (20% times the $40 investment equal $8 in year 1). In fact, this is the theoretically correct way to deal with carved out income interests in all situations — using both decelerated depreciation and compound interest, rather than straight-line depreciation and straight-line income accrual each year.

Year		Seller-Borrower		Buyer-Lender
	Gross income	Interest Deduction	Taxable income	Interest Income
1	20	12	8	12
2	20	10.5	9.5	10.5
3	20	8.5	11.5	8.5
4	20	6	14	6
5	20	3	17	3
			60	40

Under current law, in the *P. G. Lake* situation itself (where the taxpayer sold a carved out income interest in oil), the statute now treats the sale as a loan. § **636.** In addition, there is case law treating sales of carved out income interests as loans when the "buyer" is virtually guaranteed payment of the "purchase price" plus interest. *Mapco, Inc. v. United States*, 556 F.2d 1107 (Ct. Cl. 1977). In other cases involving sale of a carved out income interest, the *P. G. Lake* and *Gillette* case law still applies, taxing the sales proceeds as ordinary income at the time of the sale without reduction of basis attributable to the sold property — e.g., sale of a carved out income interest in real estate or stock. *See Stranahan's Estate v. Commissioner*, 472 F.2d 867 (6th Cir. 1973) (sale of carved out interest in future dividends from stock).

[B] Income and Remainder Interests Acquired by Gift

Armed with this understanding of the underlying problem and a critique of the case law applicable to the sale or retention case, examine the rules applicable to other carved out income situations and critique the results.

Assume that someone dies leaving land to two individuals — L inherits a life estate and R inherits the remainder interest. The *total* value and basis of both L and R at death is $100. Under current law, the basis is allocated between L and R in accordance with life expectancy and an assumed interest rate. **Treas. Reg. § 1.1014-5(a); § 21.2031-7(f) (Table B)**. The Regulations specify that the basis is adjusted as L gets older — L's basis goes down and R's goes up. And those Regulations adjust basis using the theoretically correct decelerated depreciation and compound interest method. Thus, using the now familiar 60%/40% allocation for L and R, L's basis after one year is $52 (60 minus 8) and R's basis is $48 (40 plus 8). When L dies, R's basis will be $100.

Now, consider how L and R would be taxed (just as we did in the sale/retention case), *if* there were no special statutory rules. L owns a depreciating asset. The underlying land is not depreciable, but the life estate is. Assuming a five-year life expectancy (paralleling the prior sale/retention example), L reports net income *after* depreciation. The same problem of "disappearing income" encountered in the sale/retention case recurs.

[1] Depreciation of Income Interest?

The statute has a specific solution to this problem. L loses the depreciation deduction. § 273. People who receive term interests by gift or inheritance cannot depreciate their basis. (This was also the case law rule adopted by *Irwin v. Gavit*, Chapter 4.05[A].) Consequently, assuming $20 income per year, the full $20 is taxed each year to L. There is no "missing" income. There is no need to tax the owner of the remainder interest on the annual increase in the value of his interest. Because L and R are probably in the same family, it is not offensive to tax L on the entire $20, even the portion accruing to R.

[2] Sale of Income Interest

What happens if L sells the income interest that he has inherited for $60 on the day after the inheritance. Without any special statutory provision, the seller has a $60 basis, which reduces the gain to $0. In *McAllister v. Commissioner*, 157 F.2d 235 (2d Cir. 1946), the court held that L *could* use the $60 basis to compute gain.

Now the problem of missing income recurs as a result of the sale. The buyer from L for $60 has a depreciable asset, reporting only $8 income per year (assuming $12 annual straight-line depreciation). R, the remainder owner, has an asset worth $40 at the time of death which gradually increases in value to $100, but that gain is unlikely to be taxed.

Here is how the statute responds. **Section 1001(e)** denies L (the seller) the right to use the $60 basis at the time of sale, just as L could not take depreciation deductions. This denial of basis on sale occurs whenever L acquired the property by gift or inheritance. The seller, therefore, reports $60 *capital gain* at the time of sale. As in the *Gillette* and *P. G. Lake* cases, $60 is taxed at the time of sale, and the buyer is taxed on $8 annually during the five-year payout period ($20 gross income minus $12 straight-line depreciation per year = a total of $40 over five years). However, the $60 is capital gain. That makes good sense, however, because it lowers the tax in exchange for accelerating the taxable income.

[3] Why Give L and R a Basis?

You may be wondering why the Regulations bother to assign a basis to L and R, and then taking away L's basis. Look at § **1001(e)(3)** and consider this example. L and R get together and sell both their interests at the same time — L to B1 and R to B2. L and R can now use their basis to compute gain. The statute says so. L and R have no gain on the sale transaction. But now the "problem'" recurs. B1 depreciates his $60 basis and B2 is unlikely to report the gain accruing to the remainder interest for which he paid $40. The following paragraphs discuss whether the law has a response to this tax avoidance potential.

[C] Other Carve Out Situations

We earlier noted that carve outs are not limited to sale/retention or gift/gift situations. For example: (1) the term and remainder could be bought by two people (B1 and B2, as noted above); or (2) an owner might retain the term interest and give or sell the remainder. Does the case law or statute deal adequately with such cases?

[1] Statutory Provision — Section 167(e) (No Depreciation)

The carve out problem must have worried the Treasury and Congress, because in 1989, Congress passed § **167(e)**. It prohibits the owner of the carved out income interest from taking depreciation deductions, if the income and remainder owners are "related." "Related" is defined in the statute to include spouses, ancestors, and lineal descendants, and two corporations where one owns more than 50% of the other (determined by value). The statute makes § **167(e)** inapplicable when § **273** already applies (where L received the carved out income interest by gift or inheritance), because § **167(e)** would then be superfluous. However, § **167(e)** would apply if L sold his interest to B1 and R sold his interest to B2, who was B1's child.

Section 167(e) would also apply to the following case. A corporation owns land. It gives away a remainder interest in the land to a 100%-owned subsidiary corporation, retaining an income interest for a 40-year term. The transferor corporation tries to depreciate the income interest. There is one case prohibiting the depreciation deduction in this situation. *Lomas Santa Fe, Inc. v. Commissioner*, 74 T.C. 662 (1980), *aff'd*, 693 F.2d 71 (9th Cir. 1982). However, the government no longer has to rely on case law. **Section 167(e)** prevents depreciation.

What happens to the basis that is not depreciated because of **§ 167(e)**? As in the gift/gift case, the remainder owner's basis usually increases gradually as the income interest wastes away. See **§ 167(e)(3)**. Where applicable to the "related party" situation, this statutory basis rule overrides **Treas. Reg. § 1.1014-8(c)**, which states that there is no upward adjustment of a remainder's basis acquired by purchase. (The broader moral of these citations is that you must always check to see whether Regulations have been superseded by a more recent statutory provision.) Consequently, at the end of the term, the remainder's basis will equal the basis of the entire property when the property was split into income and remainder interests and **§ 167(e)** applied. The remainder's basis does not increase, however, if the income owner is a tax-exempt organization, because the denial of depreciation to a tax-exempt owner of the term interest does not increase taxable income. **§ 167(e)(4)(A)(i)**.

[2]   No Statutory Provision — Depreciation?

The statute and case law you have read do not specifically address every carve out problem. Assume, as before, a five-year income interest worth $60, and a remainder worth $40. (1) Suppose B1 and B2 buy the income and remainder interest from L and R respectively, who had originally inherited the property interests. B1 and B2 are *unrelated*. (2) Or suppose corporation X sells a remainder interest to Y for $40, an unrelated investor, and keeps a 40-year income interest, with a value and basis of $60. In such cases, there is no explicit statutory solution to the carve out problem.

Is there case law authority for denying depreciation deductions to the owner of the term interest? Why isn't *Irwin v. Gavit* authority for this result? That case was decided long before the passage of **§§ 167(e), 273** were passed, which deny the depreciation deduction to the owner of the term interest under certain circumstances. But the Supreme Court decision in *Irwin v. Gavit* reached the same result as these statutory provisions in order to prevent tax avoidance in the gift/gift situation. Why shouldn't that decision be extended by analogy to the case of a sale/sale to unrelated parties, and to a case where the taxpayer retains the term interest but sells the remainder to an unrelated party? Or would a modern court be reluctant to be so creative in devising a solution based on the statutory structure, especially in light of explicit congressional attention to selected versions of the carve-out problem?

In a private letter ruling, the government pays no attention to the *Irwin v. Gavit* analogy. It discusses the example of a sale of a term and remainder interest in land to two unrelated purchasers and asks whether the purchaser of the term interest can depreciate the purchase price of the term interest. PLR 200852013 states that the purchaser can take depreciation, which opens up a tax avoidance potential, although there is no discussion of how the remainderman is taxed. This favorable ruling is conditional on the purchase of the term interest not being funded by either the seller of the term or remainder interests.

There is one case that hints at taxing the gain accruing to the owner of the remainder interest as ordinary income in a carve out situation. In *Jones v. Commissioner*, 330 F.2d 302 (3d Cir. 1964), the court was "impressed" with the government's argument that the gain was "interest income" and remanded the case to the lower court "to determine what part, if any" was "the realization of interest discount."

[D] Gift of Income Interest — Retained Remainder

One carve-out example has not been discussed so far in this chapter — where the taxpayer gives away a carved out income interest and retains the remainder. As noted in Chapter 4.05[D][1], discussing the *Horst* case, the case law taxes the donor on all of income attributable to the carved out income interest. Thus, the owner of land cannot deflect one year's rent to a donee by giving away a carved out income interest. This "assignment of income" solution in the gift/retention situation obviates the need for taking away depreciation deductions from the owner of the term interest. The donor is treated as receiving the entire income ($20 in our example), and giving that income away to the donee.

[E] Section 1286

In one situation, the code treats the owners of a carved out income and remainder interest in accordance with the theoretically correct method of taxation, noted earlier in this section in connection with the discussion of sales taxed as loans; Chapter 22.02[A] (Questions and Comments #3). This situation is referred to by the statute as a "stripped bond." The statute applies to most debt when there is a separation in ownership between the income and remainder interests. It applies whether the separation occurs by sale or gift. § 1286.

The following example illustrates the operation of the section. A taxpayer pays $100 for a $100 bond, earning 10% interest ($10 per year). On December 31, 1993, the owner sells the following year's income from the bond. The basis in the income and remainder interest is $9.09 and $90.91 respectively. When the purchaser of the income interest collects $10 in 1994, he has $.91 taxable gain ($10 income minus $9.09 basis). The owner of the remainder interest accrues income in 1994 equal to $9.09 ($100 - $90.91). The seller and the purchaser have a total of $10 income, split between them.

Notice that § 1286 overrides the specific result in *Horst*, which involved a gift of a carved out income interest in a bond (even though § 1286 was not aimed at the family gift situation in *Horst*). The general principle of *Horst* is not overridden, however, because gifts of a carved out income interest in property other than a bond (land, for example) still cannot deflect any income to the donee.

§ 22.03   SELLING "LESS THAN ALL"

You have read a lot of cases in which the courts try to apply the theory underlying the capital gains rules without following the literal meaning of the text. Here is one last case that you can use to review the basic principles. The Court denies capital gains treatment. Does the result make sense?

HORT v. COMMISSIONER
United States Supreme Court
313 U.S. 28 (1941)

MR. JUSTICE MURPHY delivered the opinion of the Court.

We must determine whether the amount petitioner received as consideration for cancellation of a lease of realty in New York City was ordinary gross income as defined in [the predecessor of § 61]. . . .

Petitioner acquired the property, a lot and ten-story office building, by devise from his father in 1928. At the time he became owner, the premises were leased to a firm which had sublet the main floor to the Irving Trust Co. In 1927, five years before the head lease expired, the Irving Trust Co. and petitioner's father executed a contract in which the latter agreed to lease the main floor and basement to the former for a term of fifteen years at an annual rental of $25,000, the term to commence at the expiration of the head lease.

In 1933, the Irving Trust Co. found it unprofitable to maintain a branch in petitioner's building. After some negotiations, petitioner and the Trust Co. agreed to cancel the lease in consideration of a payment to petitioner of $140,000. Petitioner did not include this amount in gross income in his income tax return for 1933. . . . The Commissioner included the entire $140,000 in gross income. . . .

Petitioner apparently contends that the amount received for cancellation of the lease was capital rather than ordinary income and that it was therefore subject to [the rules] which govern capital gains and losses. . . .

The amount received by petitioner for cancellation of the lease must be included in his gross income in its entirety. [The predecessor of § 61] expressly defines gross income to include 'gains, profits, and income derived from . . . rent, . . . or gains or profits and income from any source whatever'. Plainly this definition reached the rent paid prior to cancellation just as it would have embraced subsequent payments if the lease had never been canceled. It would have included a prepayment of the discounted value of unmatured rental payments whether received at the inception of the lease or at any time thereafter. Similarly, it would have extended to the proceeds of a suit to recover damages had the Irving Trust Co. breached the lease instead of concluding a settlement. That the amount petitioner received resulted from negotiations ending in cancellation of the lease rather than from a suit to enforce it cannot alter the fact that basically the payment was merely a substitute for the rent reserved in the lease. . . .

. . . Where, as in this case, the disputed amount was essentially a substitute for rental payments which [the predecessor of § 61] expressly characterizes as gross income, it must be regarded as ordinary income, and it is immaterial that for some purposes the contract creating the right to such payments may be treated as 'property' or 'capital'. . . .

We conclude that petitioner must report as gross income the entire amount received for cancellation of the lease. . . .

COMMENTS AND QUESTIONS

Let us use *Hort* to review the issues discussed in this chapter.

1. Is the landlord-taxpayer in *Hort* selling a carved out income interest? No. He is a landlord who sold the premium value of a lease to the tenant (not to a third party). There was a premium value in the lease because the lease was entered into before the Depression and market rates plummeted during the Depression.

2. Recall that the taxpayer in *Hort* inherited the property in 1928. In other words, the taxpayer did not have an investment in the lease itself. Perhaps that argues against capital gains. But suppose the taxpayer had purchased the land, buildings, and the favorable lease in 1932, and had then been bought out by the tenant, Irving Trust Co. How would the proceeds received from the tenant be taxed in that case, where the taxpayer had an investment in the favorable lease?

3. Suppose an investor lends $10,000 at 15% interest and the market interest rate then drops to 10%. As a result, the value of the investor-creditor's claim increases to $12,000. The investor-creditor who sells the claim has $2,000 capital gain, even if he sells the claim back to the borrower — e.g., to a corporate borrower who buys back a corporate bond from the lender-creditor. How does this (creditor) investor differ from the landlord in *Hort*? In both cases, the underlying income-producing property reverts to the owner without the prior encumbrance — that is, the land reverts to the landlord without the lease after the tenant pays off the landlord in *Hort*, and the money goes back to the lender without an interest-bearing obligation when the debtor buys back a bond from the creditor.

4. A tenant who is bought out by a landlord when rents go *up* gets capital gain. *Commissioner v. McCue Bros.*, 210 F.2d 752 (2d Cir. 1954). However, a landlord who is bought out by the tenant when rents go down has ordinary income — that is the *Hort* case. Why does the tenant get capital gain, but Hort (the landlord) receive ordinary income?

5. In *Bell's Estate v. Commissioner*, 137 F.2d 454 (8th Cir. 1943), the owner of a life estate sold that interest to the remainderman. Relying on *Blair* (which permitted the owner of a life estate to assign the life estate income to an assignee — *see* Chapter 2.03[A]), the court held that the sale of the entire life estate (which is all that the taxpayer owned) resulted in sale of a capital asset. The dissenter thought that the *Hort* case required taxing the sale proceeds as ordinary income.

Part I-G

TIMING

We have been discussing timing issues throughout the course. For example: (1) realization is a timing issue, built into the definition of § 61 income; (2) so is the deferral of realized gain and loss through nonrecognition of income rules (*e.g.*, § 1031, discussed in Chapter 19.03); and so is the requirement that expenditures producing future benefit must be added to basis — that is, capitalized — to clearly reflect income (discussed in Chapter 13.02–.03). This Part discusses accounting methods — primarily the cash and accrual methods — which also specify when income and deductions should be reported.

We have given some attention to accounting methods in earlier chapters. The cash and accrual methods were described in Chapter 3.05[A], and the installment method was discussed in Chapter 21.01[A]. Some of the specifics of the cash method have also been considered — for example, is a property right taxable compensation (that is, the "equivalent of cash") if it is subject to a significant restriction (Chapter 21.05[A])?

This Part looks more closely at what the cash and accrual accounting methods mean and who can use these methods, and, more generally, at the technical and policy issues that different timing rules present.

Chapter 23 introduces the problem of accounting methods by reviewing the major legal issues — what is the cash and accrual method; who can use these methods; what transactions can or must be reported under these methods. In addition, this chapter explains what is at stake in how timing issues are resolved — does the "transactional" approach solve timing problems; what can be done about "mistakes" that accelerate or defer the timing of a taxable event? The chapter concludes with a discussion of the differences between tax and financial or regulatory accounting.

Chapters 24 and 25 present a detailed discussion of the cash and accrual methods respectively.

Chapter 23

INTRODUCTION TO ACCOUNTING METHODS; WHAT IS AT STAKE

§ 23.01 CASH AND ACCRUAL; CLEARLY REFLECT INCOME

There are two major accounting methods — the cash and accrual methods.

[A] Cash

Most taxpayers who perform personal services, such as doctors and lawyers, report income on the cash method — that is, when cash is received or paid. The critical issue is defining "cash." As we have seen in earlier discussions, "cash" includes the "equivalent of cash." These discussions explored some of the uncertainties in defining "equivalent of cash": (1) deeply discounted notes (Chapter 21.01[B]); (2) in-kind consumption (steamship ticket) (Chapter 3.07[A][1]); (3) property subject to restrictions (Chapter 21.05[A]). And we will say more about "equivalent of cash" in Chapter 24.

[B] Accrual — Accession to Wealth

The accrual method requires income and deductions to be reported when "all events" fixing the right to receive cash or pay a liability have occurred, except for the passage of time, and when the amount can be determined with reasonable accuracy. **Treas. Reg. § 1.446-1(c)(1)(ii).** Further refinements of the accrual method and the "all events" test are discussed in Chapter 25.

The significant feature of the accrual method is that income is reported *before* collection and deductions are taken *before* payment. The accrual method is often said to be the theoretically more sound accounting method, because it more accurately accounts for accessions to wealth. After all, if someone owes or has a right to $100, their wealth is likely to be altered by $100 (at least if adequate interest is charged). This principle is so fundamental that debt (which reduces wealth) is usually accrued into basis, whether or not the taxpayer is a cash or accrual basis taxpayer. The usual explanation for permitting the cash method is not that it accurately reflects income, but that it achieves administrative simplicity, both for the taxpayer computing income and for the government concerned with collection.

[C]   Clearly Reflect Income

A taxpayer cannot use any accounting method to the extent that it fails to "clearly reflect income," as determined by tax rather than financial or regulatory accounting considerations. Thus, the tax law may insist on accounting rules that produce administrative simplicity, permit ease of revenue collection, and prevent taxpayer manipulation — all in the name of "clearly reflecting income." This often results in a higher income figure for tax accounting, even though financial accounting would defer income so as not to mislead investors into thinking that a business is more profitable than it really is — for example, when an accrual basis taxpayer receives prepaid cash for services to be performed in the future or estimates expenses to be incurred at a later date.

§ 23.02   MANDATORY USE OF ACCRUAL ACCOUNTING

[A]   Which Taxpayers Must Accrue

[1]   In General

As noted above, the accrual method is supposed to reflect income more accurately. It usually records the taxpayer's net wealth, because accrued items are economic gains and losses (if interest charges are adequate). Moreover, it tends to match income with the expenses incurred to earn the income so as to reflect *net* accessions to wealth.

For this reason, the statute has restricted the taxpayers who are allowed to use the cash method. § 448. For example, the following can *not* use the cash method: (i) tax shelters (as defined in § 461(i)(3)); and (ii) corporations (other than personal service corporations) whose average annual gross receipts in the prior three years exceeded $5 million. Consequently, these taxpayers must use the accrual method. The exception for personal service corporations benefits professional corporations owned by lawyers, doctors, etc.

[2]   Farming

Farming corporations are not subject to the § 448 requirements summarized above, but to separate rules found in § 447. Farming corporations must use the accrual method, unless (i) their annual gross receipts in prior years did not exceed $1 million, or (ii) they are "family owned" and their prior annual gross receipts did not exceed $25 million (the "small family farm"). However, the raising or harvesting of trees (except fruit and nut trees) is not subject to mandatory accrual accounting. **§ 447(a) (last sentence)**. Why not?

Permitting some farmers to use the cash method is important because farmers are often allowed to deduct cash payments that are capital expenditures or inventory costs, even without any explicit statutory rules permitting the expensing of what would otherwise be added to basis. Thus, cash basis farmers have been allowed to expense some expenditures that would normally be added to basis, such as the cost of feed to raise livestock. **Treas. Reg. § 162-12(a)**.

Even if a taxpayer is allowed to use the cash method — e.g., the "small family farm" — the taxpayer might still not be allowed to rely on some of the more generous interpretations and applications of the cash method of accounting that allow costs to be expensed, because of § 263A (discussed in Chapter 13.02[B][5]). That section imposes "uniform capitalization rules," which require most inventory and capital costs to be added to basis. Even these rules have exceptions, however. For example, the "uniform capitalization rules" do not apply to cash method farmers who produce animals, or who produce plants with preproductive periods of two years or less. § 263A(d)(1)(A). And, once again, raising and harvesting certain trees are exempted. § 263A(c)(5). Consequently, if you work your way through this maze of statutes, you would find that some farmers can still use a very generous version of the cash method.

[3] Inventories

Taxpayers must use the accrual method to account for inventory, unless the IRS permits otherwise. **Treas. Reg. § 1.446-1(c)(2)(i)–(ii).** The pressure for an administrative exception based on record-keeping difficulties has been considerable, however. Consequently, the IRS issued a ruling allowing certain taxpayers with a relatively small amount of average annual gross receipts to use the cash method *See* Rev. Proc. 2000-22, 2000-1 C.B. 1008; Rev. Proc. 2001-10, 2001-1 C.B. 272; Rev. Proc. 2002-28, 2002-1 C.B. 815.

[B] Which Transactions Must Be Reported on the Accrual Method?

Sometimes, specific transactions (rather than a specific type of taxpayer) must be reported on the accrual method. We have already seen two examples in this course — (1) accrual of original issue discount, without regard to whether the creditor is a cash method taxpayer (§ 1272); and (2) the Regulation requiring a taxpayer who does not use the installment method to accrue the gain on sale of property for a fixed payment obligation; **Treas. Reg. § 15A.453-1(d)(2)(i)–(ii).**

§ 23.03   WHAT IS AT STAKE

There are two major reasons why taxpayers and the government care about timing issues, whether they are embodied in the definition of income (e.g., realization doctrine) or the use of particular accounting methods. First, tax rates may differ from year to year — either because of progressive tax rates, net operating losses, or changes in statutory rates. Second, the deferral or acceleration of tax is important, even when tax rates are constant.

There are various potential "solutions" to timing problems, critiqued in this section — (1) the use of the transactional method to break down the accounting year barrier; (2) charging interest to make up for tax deferral or acceleration; and (3) the separation of present value from unstated interest.

[A]   Transactional Approach as a Solution?

You might think that the "transactional" approach, which breaks down the accounting year barrier, eliminates issues of timing, by reducing the importance of the year in which an income or deduction item is reported. You have encountered many case law and statutory provisions applying the transactional approach. These included: (1) the "tax benefit" rule, eliminating tax on recovery of amounts attributable to useless deductions in a prior year (both in the case law and in § 111); (2) rules that selectively permit taxpayers to deduct repayments at rates applicable to the receipts in an earlier tax year (§ 1341); (3) recapture rules (§ 1245); and (4) characterizing repayments based on how the repaid income had previously been taxed — e.g., the *Arrowsmith* case (capital loss on repayment of proceeds of a corporate liquidation; Chapter 20.05[C]).

It would be a mistake to conclude, however, that the transactional approach is a substitute for adopting accurate timing rules in the first place.

First, there are many instances in the code where there is no adjustment to account for different tax rates in different years or for the existence of a preferential or disadvantageous tax rate on one of the two parts of the transaction. Thus, if a deduction is useful when the taxpayer is in the 15% bracket, the recovery of the deductible amount can be taxed at the top marginal rate in the recovery year. The only way the taxpayer can avoid this result is by treating the amount deducted as a capital expenditure, so that the deduction occurs in the recovery year (amount realized minus basis), rather than in the earlier year. Similarly, not all deductions for depreciation are recaptured as ordinary income. Thus, the maximum tax on real estate "recapture" gain is 25%, not the regular rates on ordinary income.

Second, even if tax rates are the same in all years, or the transactional approach breaks down accounting year barriers, timing rules can still accelerate or defer tax, with advantages to the government or taxpayer. Thus, allowing capital expenditures to be expensed is not "corrected" by later including recovery of the prior deduction in ordinary income. Early deductions permit tax deferral, whether or not recapture rules in a later year take away the capital gains preference. The only way the government can deal with this problem is either (1) to deny the early deductions (e.g., by limiting depreciation or by adding an expenditure to basis); or (2) by charging interest for tax deferral.

Conversely, early reporting of income deprives the taxpayer of the use of the income tax payment made in the earlier year, even if repayment is deductible at the tax rates applicable in the earlier year.

[B]   Interest Charges When "Mistakes" Accelerate or Defer Tax?

One way to "correct" prior "mistakes" that produce deferral or acceleration of tax is to charge interest on an early tax break, or, conversely, for the government to pay interest if an item was taxed too early. The taxpayer usually gets an early tax break for one of the following reasons: the taxpayer is allowed to use the cash method or installment method for reporting income and thereby defers the income; the taxpayer can take early deductions through accelerated depreciation or expensing; or the taxpayer underestimates accrued income or overestimates accrued deductions.

Conversely, the government can tax too early if, for example, it overestimates income reported on the accrual basis — e.g., by not taking account of the need to incur expenses in the future to earn money received at an earlier date (discussed later in Chapter 25.01[B]).

It is administratively difficult, however, to charge interest on these kinds of timing "mistakes." Moreover, some of these events may not even be "mistakes." A "wrong" estimate of income for a particular year, for example, might still accurately reflect the taxpayer's wealth, if it is the best guess about what is likely to happen. The statute, therefore, has only a few interest-charging provisions — for example:

(1) when large amounts of installment sales arise and are outstanding at the end of the tax year, the taxpayer owes interest on the deferred tax resulting from use of the installment method (§ 453A — noted in Chapter 21.01[A][3]);

(2) § 1260(b) (interest due on deferred tax in certain financial transactions involving puts, calls, futures, etc.); and

(3) § 460(a)(2), (b)(3) provides in most cases for an interest payment from either the taxpayer or the government, if the percentage of completion of contract method of accounting is used (discussed in Chapter 3.05[A][6][a]) and the estimated contract profits reported as income during the early years of contract performance turn out to be larger or smaller than expected. This method of accounting is often used to report income from the production and sale of large-ticket items — such as planes, ships, and dams. For example, reporting $15 million profits after one half of the contract has been completed, based on expectations of a $30 million total profit, will overstate income if total profits turn out to be less than $30 million, and will understate income if profits exceed $30 million.

[C] The Problem of Separating Unstated Interest from Present Value

The earlier discussion suggested that the accrual method might be preferred because it more accurately records accession to wealth. But the accrual method will *not* accurately reflect accession to wealth if the creditor charges inadequate interest to account for deferral of payment. This can be unfair to either the taxpayer or the government, depending on whether the claim is being accrued into income or is claimed as a deduction. For example, a taxpayer who accrues $100,000 income in year 1 when the $100,000 is due in year 5 is treated unfairly, if the present value of the claim is less than $100,000, because inadequate interest is charged. Conversely, early deduction of a $100,000 debt, without interest, is unfair to the government because the debt's present value is less than $100,000.

In other words, it is important to separate out the amount that should be reported as an income or deduction item from the interest accruing to the present value of that amount. For example, recall the discussion of the installment method of reporting when the taxpayer had a right to $600,000 sale proceeds in five years, without charging adequate interest; Chapter 21.03[A]. Assume the present value of the claim was $350,000. Whether or not the taxpayer can defer the tax on $350,000, it is important to make sure that the $250,000 is correctly taxed as original issue discount (that is, interest). These computations are also important to the buyer, because the buyer should have only a $350,000 basis in the asset, for computing depreciation and gain or loss on disposition of the asset; and should be able to accrue an interest deduction annually based on the original issue discount. In sum, separating interest from present value is important for addressing two timing issues — the correct treatment of the interest and the correct treatment of the present value.

There are three ways to deal with the problem of separating present value from interest — (1) do nothing about separating the interest from the present value; (2) separate present value from interest, but require accrual of only one of these components of total value; or (3) separate present value from interest and require accrual of both of these items in order to clearly reflect income. The remainder of this section considers how the code deals with this problem in different situations. A fourth solution — postponing the accrual of future expenses — is discussed in Chapter 25.02[B][3].

[1] Sale

We have already seen one situation in which present value and interest are separated — in connection with the gain realized on the sale of property discussed in Chapter 21.03. Before the adoption of § 1274, taxpayers could defer both the present value of sales proceeds and interest, although § 483 often required the separation of the deferred sales proceeds from interest (so that the deferred interest would not be taxed as capital gain). Under current law, when § 1274 applies, interest must be separated from present value and accrued in accordance with the original issue discount rules. However, the present value can be deferred if the taxpayer can use the installment method. In other words, the interest is correctly taxed but the problem of deferring tax on the present value might remain, depending on whether the taxpayer can use the installment method.

[2] Use of Property

Similar issues arise whenever the taxpayer postpones receipt of cash for anything of value, even if it is not for the sale of property. For example, § 467(d) deals with postponed payments for use of property (that is, rent). When the total rental payments exceed $250,000 and at least one payment occurs after the year in which the property is used, the present value of the postponed payment must be accrued in the year of use, whether or not the person providing the property is a cash or accrual method taxpayer. In addition, any interest representing the difference between the actual payment and present value must be accrued annually in accordance with the original issue discount rules. In other words, both unstated interest and present value must be separately accounted for, and both the problem of accurately reporting the present value as accrued income and the problem of accurately reporting the interest are correctly solved.

If this section does not apply, the *entire* payment (without separation of the interest and present value) is reported in accordance with the taxpayer's accounting method: for an accrual method taxpayer, in the year the property is used and all events giving rise to the right to payment for the use have occurred; for a cash method taxpayer, when the payment is collected. In other words, neither the present value nor the interest element is "correctly" taxed.

For example, if collection of $300,000 of rent payable for use of property in year 0 is deferred until year 2, the owner must accrue the present value of the $300,000 in income in year 0, and then periodically accrue interest thereafter ($300,000 minus the present value of $300,000). If the rent had been only $200,000, § **467(d)** does not apply; a cash basis taxpayer would report $200,000 in year 2, and an accrual basis taxpayer would report $200,000 in year 0.

[3]   Personal Services

The rules for personal service income are both similar to and dissimilar to the rules for reporting income from the use of property. When the total consideration exceeds $250,000 for personal services, § **467(g)** authorizes the Treasury to separate the present value of future payments from interest and accrue the *interest* annually in accordance with original issue discount rules. However, the present value itself is still either accrued or deferred, depending on whether the taxpayer is an accrual or cash method taxpayer. In other words, the interest element is accurately reported, but the present value of the claim for personal services may be deferred, depending on the taxpayer's accounting method. Chapter 24.03 discusses the deferral of personal service income by a cash method taxpayer.

§ 23.04   CLEARLY REFLECT INCOME — RELATION OF TAX TO FINANCIAL ACCOUNTING

As noted earlier, all of the accounting methods used by the taxpayer are subject to an overarching requirement that they "clearly reflect income." § **446(b)**.

For example, even a cash method taxpayer cannot usually deduct a capital expenditure because that would distort income by allowing a deduction for savings. Conversely, some accounting conventions may be followed if they clearly reflect income, even if they appear to violate some technical rule about deductibility. An example was the deduction for de minimis expenses, discussed in (Chapter 13.02[B][4].

When the code requires that a method of accounting clearly reflect income, it invokes tax accounting concepts, not financial accounting or an accounting method used to meet the requirements of a regulatory agency. The differences in accounting systems result from a difference in their purposes. Tax accounting is not only concerned with accurately identifying accretions to net wealth, but also with preventing taxpayer manipulation, simplifying tax administration, and collecting revenue in an expeditious manner. Consequently, tax accounting might not even measure accretion to wealth in the most accurate manner — e.g., it may require reporting income earlier than a wealth accretion standard suggests.

By contrast, financial accounting is concerned that taxpayers do not overstate income, which would allow them to give the investing public the appearance of more profits than is actually the case. Consequently, financial accounting often defers income or accrues deductions more readily than income tax accounting.

In other words, income tax computations can follow a different logic from financial and regulatory accounting methods, just as nontax law is often not incorporated into tax law — e.g., marriage and property law do not necessarily determine the meaning of the tax code's definition of these terms. The dictates of income tax policy determine what accounting method to use for tax purposes.

The Supreme Court explained the difference between tax and nontax accounting in the following case.

THOR POWER TOOL CO. v. COMMISSIONER
United States Supreme Court
439 U.S. 522 (1979)

The taxpayer's major argument . . . is based on the Tax Court's clear finding that the [deduction] conformed to "generally accepted accounting principles." [Taxpayer] points to language in Treas. Reg. § 1.446-1(a)(2), to the effect that "[a] method of accounting which reflects the consistent application of generally accepted accounting principles . . . *will ordinarily be regarded* as clearly reflecting income" (emphasis added). . . . These provisions, [taxpayer] contends, created a *presumption* that an inventory practice conformable to "generally accepted accounting principles" is valid for income tax purposes. Once a taxpayer has established this conformity, the argument runs, the burden shifts to the Commissioner affirmatively to demonstrate that the taxpayer's method does not reflect income clearly. Unless the Commissioner can show that a generally accepted method "demonstrably distorts income," or that the taxpayer's adoption of such method was "motivated by tax avoidance," the presumption in the taxpayer's favor will carry the day. . . .

We believe . . . that no such presumption is present. Its existence is insupportable in light of the statute, the Court's past decisions, and the differing objectives of tax and financial accounting.

First, . . . § 1.446-1(a)(2) of the Regulations states categorically that "*no* method of accounting is acceptable unless, in the opinion of the Commissioner, it clearly reflects income" (emphasis added). Most importantly, the Code and Regulations give the Commissioner broad discretion to set aside the taxpayer's method if, "in [his] opinion," it does not reflect income clearly. This language is completely at odds with the notion of a "presumption" in the taxpayer's favor. The Regulations embody no presumption; they say merely that, in most cases, generally accepted accounting practices will pass muster for tax purposes. And in most cases, they will. But if the Commissioner, in the exercise of his discretion, determines that they do not, he may prescribe a different practice without having to rebut any presumption running against the Treasury.

Second, the presumption [taxpayer] postulates finds no support in this Court's prior decisions. . . . "[W]e are mindful that the characterization of a transaction for financial accounting purposes, on the one hand, and for tax purposes, on the other, need not necessarily be the same." *Frank Lyon Co. v. United States*, 435 U.S. 561, 577 (1978). *See Commissioner of Internal Revenue v. Idaho Power Co.*, 418 U.S. 1, 15 (1974). Indeed, the Court's cases demonstrate that divergence between tax and financial accounting is especially common when a taxpayer seeks a current deduction for estimated future expenses or losses. *E.g.*, *Commissioner of Internal Revenue v. Hansen*, 360 U.S. 446 (1959) (reserve to cover contingent liability in event of nonperformance of guarantee); *Brown v. Helvering*, 291 U.S. 193 (1934) (reserve to cover expected liability for unearned commissions on anticipated insurance policy cancellations). . . .

Third, the presumption petitioner postulates is insupportable in light of the vastly different objectives that financial and tax accounting have. The primary goal of financial accounting is to provide useful information to management, shareholders, creditors, and others properly interested; the major responsibility of the accountant is to protect these parties from being misled. The primary goal of the income tax system, in contrast, is the equitable collection of revenue; the major responsibility of the Internal Revenue Service is to protect the public fisc. Consistent with its goals and responsibilities, financial accounting has, as its foundation, the principle of conservatism, with its corollary that "possible errors in measurement [should] be in the direction of understatement rather than overstatement of net income and net assets." In view of the Treasury's markedly different goals and responsibilities, understatement of income is not destined to be its guiding light. Given this diversity, even contrariety, of objectives, any presumptive equivalency between tax and financial accounting would be unacceptable.

This difference in objectives is mirrored in numerous differences of treatment. Where the tax law requires that a deduction be deferred until "all the events" have occurred that will make it fixed and certain, *United States v. Anderson*, 269 U.S. 422, 441 (1926), accounting principles typically require that a liability be accrued as soon as it can reasonably be estimated. Conversely, where the tax law requires that income be recognized currently under "claim of right," "ability to pay," and "control" rationales, accounting principles may defer accrual until a later year so that revenues and expenses may be better matched. Financial accounting, in short, is hospitable to estimates, probabilities, and reasonable certainties; the tax law, with its mandate to preserve the revenue, can give no quarter to uncertainty. This is as it should be. Reasonable estimates may be useful, even essential, in giving shareholders and creditors an accurate picture of a firm's overall financial health; but the accountant's conservatism cannot bind the Commissioner in his efforts to collect taxes. "Only a few reserves voluntarily established as a matter of conservative accounting," Mr. Justice Brandeis wrote for the Court, "are authorized by the Revenue Acts." *Brown v. Helvering*, 291 U.S. at 201–202.

Finally, a presumptive equivalency between tax and financial accounting would create insurmountable difficulties of tax administration. Accountants long have recognized that "generally accepted accounting principles" are far from being a canonical set of rules that will ensure identical accounting treatment of identical transactions. "Generally accepted accounting principles," rather, tolerate a range of "reasonable" treatments, leaving the choice among alternatives to management. . . . Variances of this sort may be tolerable in financial reporting, but they are questionable in a tax system designed to ensure as far as possible that similarly situated taxpayers pay the same tax. If management's election among "acceptable" options were dispositive for tax purposes, a firm, indeed, could decide unilaterally — within limits dictated only by its accountants — the tax it wished to pay. Such unilateral decisions would not just make the Code inequitable; they would make it unenforceable.

QUESTIONS

The next two chapters discuss the cash and accrual methods in detail. Much of the discussion is technical, but you should try to figure out what problem(s) the court or code is attempting to solve (or is failing to resolve adequately).

1. Is there an improper deferral or acceleration of an income or deduction item?

2. What is causing the improper deferral or acceleration?

a. Is it the failure to use a particular method of accounting (e.g., by using the cash method instead of the accrual method)?

b. Is it a defect in the tax accounting rules (e.g., failure to separate present value and interest; tolerating wrong estimates of income or deduction items)?

3. What principle of tax accounting helps to explain the law — administrative simplicity, permitting ease of revenue collection, and/or preventing taxpayer manipulation?

4. What case law, agency rules, or statutory provisions are available to deal with these problems?

Chapter 24

CASH METHOD

The opportunity to use the cash method has been significantly narrowed by the code (as explained in Chapter 23.02), so many of the older cases defining cash and its equivalent have only limited current application. Nonetheless, some taxpayers still care a lot about the cash method, especially taxpayers who render personal services. This section discusses when cash or its equivalent has been received or paid.

The cash method certainly has attractions from the point of view of administrative simplicity for those taxpayers who do not keep financial records on the accrual method. It also allows revenue collection at a convenient time — when the taxpayer has cash. (Of course, if the taxpayer already maintains records on an accrual method, it will be administratively easier to use the accrual method for tax purposes as well, to avoid requiring two sets of books.)

The major concern for the government in implementing the cash method is to prevent taxpayer manipulation through the definition of "cash." To that end, the agency and courts have developed the doctrines of "equivalent of cash" and "constructive receipt" (discussed in Chapters 24.01, 24.02) — primarily to prevent the taxpayer from turning his back on what is conventionally considered cash. As we will see, these doctrines are not always effective in achieving this result.

§ 24.01 CASH OR ITS EQUIVALENT

[A] Embodiments of a Promise

[1] In General

A mere promise is not the equivalent of cash. If it were, there would be no difference between the cash and accrual methods. Promises are, however, often embodied in something that has a marketable value. What happens when a taxpayer receives a note, or the promise is embodied in a contract or other instrument that is commonly sold for a price? Here are some decisions addressing these questions. *Western Oaks Building Corp. v. Commissioner*, 49 T.C. 365 (1968) (value of the note or contract must be reported if it is "easily negotiable and freely exchangeable in commerce"); *Cowden v. Commissioner*, 289 F.2d 20 (5th Cir. 1961) (claim need not be negotiable to be cash equivalent, as long as market value is not discounted substantially more than is indicated by the prevailing interest rate). Rev. Rul. 68-606, 1968-2 C.B. 42 (contract right "freely transferable and readily salable" is equivalent of cash); Rev. Rul. 76-135, 1976-1 C.B. 114 (notes with $50 face value have $47 market value; $47 taxed when notes received).

Some cases explicitly state that a note or contract is the equivalent of cash, even if its market value is discounted substantially below face value. *Warren Jones v. Commissioner*, 524 F.2d 788 (9th Cir. 1975) (face = $133,000; market value = $76,980), *reversing*, 60 T.C. 663 (1973).

[2] Checks

Checks are usually "cash" in their face amount, regardless of what they would sell for. That makes sense in a society where checks typically pass as cash and are recorded that way in a taxpayer's records. *Kahler v. Commissioner*, 18 T.C. 31 (1952) (check's face amount taxed in 1982, even though received after banking hours on December 31). If the check, which was taxable in an earlier year, is not paid in a later year because the debtor does not have the funds, there is a loss deduction in the later year.

However, a check is not income when received if the debtor is insolvent. The court applied this principle in *Premji v. Commissioner*, 72 T.C.M. (CCH) 16 (1996), where the debtor had insufficient bank funds to pay the check and the check was dated the same day as the debtor filed for bankruptcy.

Walter v. United States, 148 F.3d 1027 (8th Cir. 1998), carries the principle that a check is income in the year received to the extreme. The taxpayer received a check in 1986 but it was never deposited, because it was lost when the taxpayer mailed it to the bank for deposit. In 1988, a new check was issued. Held — taxable in 1986. The court relied on the general rule that checks are taxable when received, unless the debtor is insolvent or imposes substantial restrictions or conditions that prevent the taxpayer from receiving the funds.

The rationale of these cases suggests that a check post-dated to a later year would only be taxable in the later year by a cash basis taxpayer. Post-dated checks do not commonly pass as cash in our commercial practice, and post-dating also suggests the possibility that the debtor may lack sufficient funds.

[B] Property Other than Embodiments of Promises; Economic Benefit

A cash method taxpayer who receives property, such as ownership of a home or an interest in a fund set aside to pay a debt, normally receives a taxable "equivalent of cash." This is usually referred to as the "economic benefit" branch of the "equivalent of cash" doctrine.

[1] Restricted Use

Property subject to significant restrictions on enjoyment or transfer is not the equivalent of cash. You have already encountered this issue in the context of taxpayers who render personal services, which is now dealt with by § 83. That section determines whether a property interest is subject to sufficient restrictions to prevent cash equivalence and how to value such interests (Chapter 21.05[A]).

If there is no specific statutory provision dealing with substantial restrictions (such as § 83), a property interest subject to restrictions might be taxable at a discounted value. *See United States v. Drescher*, 179 F.2d 863 (2d Cir. 1950), where a *nontransferable* annuity was taxable to the recipient of the annuity at less than its cost to the provider. This was an application of the "subjective discount" approach that we encountered in the case of the steamship ticket prize, discussed in Chapter 3.07[A][1].

[2]　Establishment of a Fund

[a]　In General

A common setting in which application of the equivalent of cash doctrine is at issue is the establishment of a fund to make future payments to the taxpayer. In *Thomas v. United States*, 213 F.3d 927 (6th Cir. 2000), the court said that the cash method "provides for the taxation of financial benefits that are: (1) fixed; (2) located in an irrevocable fund; and (3) not subject to the payor's debtors." The taxpayer in this case was not taxed in the year he claimed a lottery prize because payment to the winner had to await a verification process and the funds were not beyond the reach of the payor's creditors.

[b]　Escrow Accounts

There is case law holding that the taxpayer has not received an economic benefit that is the "equivalent of cash" when amounts are set aside in an escrow account, even though the escrow arrangement put the amount beyond the control of the payor. For example, in *Reed v. Commissioner*, 723 F.2d 138 (1st Cir. 1983), Cvengros had an option to buy stock from the taxpayer (Reed), which was exercised on November 23, 1973. Reed used the cash method to report income. The closing date for the sale was December 27, 1973. However, for tax reasons, Reed wanted to postpone tax until the next year. In early December 1973, Reed and Cvengros modified the sale agreement so that the purchase price of a little more than $800,000 would be placed with a third party in escrow. The taxpayer deferred reporting the gain until 1974 and the court agreed, even though all of the conditions entitling the payee to the escrow amount had been fulfilled except the passage of time. The court stressed the fact that the taxpayer was not entitled to receive any interest or investment income earned on the funds that were held in escrow.

Is this case correct? Why isn't the present value of the amounts placed in escrow taxed when the escrow account is established (in 1973)? Lack of entitlement to any income earned on the investment should affect the computation of the taxable present value, not defer tax on all of the escrowed amount.

§ 24.02　CONSTRUCTIVE RECEIPT

Cash or its equivalent is "received," not only in the conventional sense of "receipt," but also if it is "constructively" received. The core example of constructive receipt is interest on a bank account that the taxpayer is free to withdraw in year 1 but leaves with the bank. The interest is taxed in year 1. The general idea behind this rule is plain enough. A taxpayer cannot have the *legal* right to property, but turn his back on it to defer tax.

In Letter Ruling 200031031, the government explained the constructive receipt doctrine, as follows: "The courts have determined that the following conditions are necessary to tax an amount under the doctrine of constructive receipt: (1) the amount must be due; (2) the amount must be appropriated on the books of the obligor; (3) the obligor must be willing to pay; (4) the obligor must be solvent and able to pay; and (5) the obligee must have knowledge of the foregoing facts. In essence, the obligee's demand for payment must be the only thing that would be necessary for payment."

The "constructive receipt" doctrine does not wipe out the distinction between accrual and cash method taxpayers, which makes for some very artificial distinctions from the perspective of economic reality. There is nothing in the constructive receipt doctrine to stop a taxpayer in year 1 from negotiating a contract that defers income until year 2, even if the taxpayer had the *economic* power to contract for a year 1 payment. In that case, there is no *legal* right to the payment in year 1. In the bank interest case, there is constructive receipt because the taxpayer has a *legal* right to the property that matured in year 1.

The constructive receipt doctrine has some features in common with the "equivalent of cash" doctrine, but also differs from that doctrine. For example, both doctrines do not require a cash basis taxpayer to report income if it is subject to "substantial restrictions." Thus, if a taxpayer who invests in a certificate of deposit with a bank can withdraw interest prior to the date when the certificate of deposit comes due, but will thereby lose almost half the interest, the interest is neither the equivalent of cash nor constructively received. The penalty is a substantial limitation, postponing tax on the interest until the certificate of deposit comes due or the right to the interest is otherwise unrestricted. **Treas. Reg. § 1.451-2(a)(2);** Rev. Rul. 80-157, 1980-1 C.B. 186.

But, unlike the equivalent of cash doctrine, the constructive receipt doctrine is not concerned with whether the payor's creditors can gain access to the funds used to make the payment; thus, a creditor-depositor who has access to bank interest on December 31 has constructive receipt of that interest income, even if bank creditors could seize the funds needed to pay the interest.

One constructive receipt problem has been mooted by **§ 451(h)**, passed in 1998. Under that section, a cash basis winner of a contest, lottery, jackpot, game, or other similar arrangement can avoid application of the constructive receipt doctrine based on the taxpayer having a choice between a single cash payment and future payments, if (1) the future payments are spread out over at least ten years, (2) the payments are not for past services, and (3) the taxpayer does not have to perform substantial future services. Presumably, this provision was added because states wanted to encourage lottery prize winners to defer collection.

§ 24.03   DEFERRED COMPENSATION; PERSONAL SERVICE CONTRACTS

In Rev. Rul. 60-31, 1960-1 C.B. 174, the government dealt with the following arrangement to pay deferred personal service income to a football player:

> In June 1957, the taxpayer, a football player, entered into a two-year standard player's contract with a football club in which he agreed to play football and engage in activities related to football during the two-year term only for the club. In addition to a specified salary for the two-year term, it was mutually agreed that as an inducement for signing the contract the taxpayer would be paid a bonus of 150x dollars. The taxpayer could have demanded and received payment of this bonus at the time of signing the contract, but at his suggestion there was added to the standard contract form a paragraph providing substantially as follows:

> The player shall receive the sum of 150x dollars upon signing of this contract, contingent upon the payment of this 150x dollars to an escrow agent designated by him. The escrow agreement shall be subject to approval by the legal representatives of the player, the Club, and the escrow agent.

> Pursuant to this added provision, an escrow agreement was executed on June 25, 1957, in which the club agreed to pay 150x dollars on that date to the Y bank, as escrow and the escrow agent agreed to pay this amount, plus interest, to the taxpayer in installments over a period of five years. The escrow agreement also provides that the account established by the escrow agent is to bear the taxpayer's name; that payments from such account may be made only in accordance with the terms of the agreement; that the agreement is binding upon the parties thereto and their successors or assigns; and that in the event of the taxpayer's death during the escrow period the balance due will become part of his estate.

The ruling then noted that the constructive receipt doctrine was sparingly applied:

> . . . [U]nder the doctrine of constructive receipt, a taxpayer may not deliberately turn his back upon income and thereby select the year for which he will report it. Nor may a taxpayer, by a private agreement, postpone receipt of income from one taxable year to another. . . .

> However, the statute cannot be administered by speculating whether the payor would have been willing to agree to an earlier payment. See, for example, *J. D. Amend, et ux. v. Commissioner*, 13 T.C. 178, *acquiescence*, C.B. 1950-1, 1, in which the court, citing a number of authorities for its holding, stated:

> It is clear that the doctrine of constructive receipt is to be sparingly used; that amounts due from a corporation but unpaid, are not to be included in the income of an individual reporting his income on a cash receipts basis unless it appears that the money was available to him, that the corporation

was able and ready to pay him, that his right to receive was not restricted, and that his failure to receive resulted from exercise of his own choice.

Consequently, it seems clear that in each case involving a deferral of compensation a determination of whether the doctrine of constructive receipt is applicable must be made upon the basis of the specific factual situation involved.

But the ruling went on to distinguish this situation from others in which the taxpayer was allowed to defer tax:

In Revenue Ruling 55-727, the taxpayer, a professional baseball player, entered into a contract in 1953 in which he agreed to render services for a baseball club and to refrain from playing baseball for any other club during the term of the contract. In addition to specified compensation, the contract provided for a bonus to the player or his estate, payable one-half in January 1954 and one-half in January 1955, whether or not he was able to render services. . . . [The ruling held] that the bonus payments constituted ordinary income [and] were taxable for the year in which received by the player. However, under the facts set forth in Revenue Ruling 55-727 there was no arrangement, as here, for placing the amount of the bonus in escrow. Consequently, the instant situation is distinguishable from that considered in Revenue Ruling 55-727.

In *E. T. Sproull v. Commissioner*, 16 T.C. 244, *affirmed*, 194 F.2d 541 (6th Cir. 1952), the petitioner's employer in 1945 transferred in trust for the petitioner the amount of $10,500. The trustee was directed to pay out of principal to the petitioner the sum of $5,250 in 1945 and the balance, including income, in 1947. In the event of the petitioner's prior death, the amounts were to be paid to his administrator, executor, or heirs. The petitioner contended that the Commissioner erred in including the sum of $10,500 in his taxable income for 1945. In this connection, the court stated:

. . . It is undoubtedly true that the amount which the Commissioner has included in petitioner's income for 1945 was used in that year for his benefit . . . in setting up the trust of which petitioner, or, in the event of his death then his estate, was the sole beneficiary . . . .

The question then becomes . . . was "any economic or financial benefit conferred on the employee as compensation' in the taxable year. If so, it was taxable to him in that year. This question we must answer in the affirmative. The employer's part of the transaction terminated in 1945. It was then that the amount of the compensation was fixed at $10,500 and irrevocably paid out for petitioner's sole benefit. . . . ."

Applying the principles stated in the *Sproull* decision to the facts here, it is concluded that the 150x-dollar bonus is includible in the gross income of the football player concerned in 1957, the year in which the club unconditionally paid such amount to the escrow agent.

COMMENTS

1. **Assignment of income analogy.** Rev. Rul. 60-31 is about taxpayers deferring income by contract. Such deferral could be analogized to assigning earned income to a relative. If a taxpayer *cannot* assign earned income to another person for tax purposes — to reduce tax rates — why can the taxpayer assign it to another tax year for the same purpose?

2. **Renegotiating receipt of earned income.** In *Oates v. Commissioner*, 18 T.C. 570 (1952), *acquiesced in* 1960-2 C.B. 3, *affirmed*, 207 F.2d 711 (7th Cir. 1953), a taxpayer was entitled to renewal commissions on insurance contracts, but he renegotiated the payment dates to defer the income. The government cited the assignment of income cases (*Earl, Eubank,* and *Horst*) to prohibit deferral, but the court held for the taxpayer. *See also Veit v. Commissioner*, 8 T.C. 809 (1947), where an employee-taxpayer had a right to a share of 1940 business profits, payable in 1941. The taxpayer, as part of plan to move to another state and reduce his work for the employer, renegotiated his profit share in 1941, and deferred payment until 1942. The government was unsuccessful in arguing that the payment was constructively received in 1941. The court said that the contract was not a "mere subterfuge and a sham for the purpose of . . . postpon[ing] his income tax."

Should there be a difference in result depending on whether the deferral of a right to income is negotiated at the same time as the original contract for personal services, as in Situation 3 in Rev. Rul. 60-31; or whether the contract is renegotiated after the income has been earned as appeared to be the situation in the *Oates* and *Veit* cases, *supra*?

3. **Legislative blocking of proposed Regulations.** In 1978, the government proposed a regulation (43 Fed. Reg. 4638, 4639 (1978)), stating that "the amount of a taxpayer's basic or regular compensation fixed by contract, statute, or otherwise" cannot at the taxpayer's option be deferred beyond the year it would be paid but for the taxpayer's renegotiation of the timing of receipt. The government stated that it would reconsider Rev. Rul. 60-31 (example 3) and its acquiescence in *Oates* after the Regulation was adopted.

The government was, however, stopped in its tracks. The Revenue Act of 1978 stated that inclusion in income of amounts under private deferred compensation arrangements would be determined "in accordance with the principles set forth in regulations, rulings, and judicial decisions . . . which were in effect on February 1, 1978 [prior to the effective date of the Proposed Regulation]."

4. **Statutory limits on deferral.** The code has now been amended to make it harder for cash basis taxpayers to defer compensation. The new rules are found in § 409A, adopted in (2004). In general, § 409A prevents deferral pursuant to nonqualified deferred compensation plans, unless they meet several requirements. (Rev. Rul. 60-31 deals with nonqualified deferred compensation plans; qualified plans are discussed in Chapter 24.06.)

First, the plan cannot permit acceleration of the payments. Second, any election to defer compensation under the plan must be made in a year *prior* to earning that compensation (which was *not* true in the *Oates* and *Veit* cases, *supra.*). Third, the compensation may not be distributed earlier than: separation from service;

disability; death; a time specified at the date of deferral; change in ownership or control of the employer; *or* the occurrence of an unforeseeable emergency (such as illness or accident of the employee or employee's spouse or dependent, or casualty loss of the employee's property). Failure to meet these conditions will result in accrual of compensation under a nonqualified deferred compensation plan prior to receipt of payment.

5. **Present value vs. accrued interest.** Some unfunded deferred compensation arrangements can still defer compensation — for example, pursuant to an actor's or athlete's contract to receive a bonus two years after signing the contract, assuming the arrangement does not run afoul of § **409A**. In that case, some of the deferred personal service income might still be original issue discount, which must be accrued annually. Deferred personal service income is bifurcated into present value and original issue discount interest, if the amounts deferred exceed $250,000, and the interest is then accrued under the original issue discount rules. § **467(g)**. However, the present value of the claim to future personal service income can still be deferred under the usual rules applicable to cash basis taxpayers.

§ 24.04 INDIRECTLY TAXING CASH METHOD PAYEES ON ACCRUED INCOME

[A] Mechanics

The most important policy issue in this chapter is whether cash method taxpayers should be allowed to defer tax on accrued income until they receive cash. For example, if a cash method taxpayer has an accrued claim in year 0 to collect $100 in year 2, should the tax on the $100 be deferred? The accrued income is an increase in wealth, at least in an amount equal to its present value. If adequate interest is charged on the $100 to account for deferred receipt, then wealth is increased in year 0 by the full $100.

One way to deal with this problem is to force cash method taxpayers to accrue income. Sometimes the code does require accrual, as explained earlier. But the code is not always so hard on cash method taxpayers, especially regarding deferred compensation. The statutory rules about *qualified* retirement plans (discussed in Chapter 24.06) even allow tax deferral when the employee has a property interest that is the equivalent of cash and the employee's retirement fund earns interest.

[1] Disallow Payor's Deduction Until Payee is Taxed

There is a way to *indirectly* tax the cash method taxpayer with accrued income, without forcing the taxpayer to use the accrual method — which is to overtax the accrual method *payor* by disallowing a deduction until the payee is taxed. The following example illustrates how.

Assume the following. (Sorry, the arithmetic can be daunting.). The payor is willing to pay the payee $121 in year 2. It is now year 0, two years earlier. Both payor and payee are in the 30% tax bracket. If we do not want the *payee* to defer tax, then the payee *should* pay tax in year 0 on the present value of the $121.

Assuming a 10% interest rate, that amount is $100 ($121/1.1^2), and the tax on the accrued $100 is $30. If the taxpayer had actually received $70 after tax in year 0 and earned 7% interest after tax , he or she would end up with $80.143 in year 2 ($70 times 1.07^2). Therefore, the benchmark for deciding if we have indirectly taxed the payee is whether we can simulate that result, leaving the payee with $80.143.

Now look at the *payor*. How much could the accrual method payor deduct in years 0, 1, and 2? In year 0, the accrual method payor should deduct $100, the present value of the future payment; in the next two years the payor should also deduct the 10% interest accruing on the $100 owed to the payee. Indeed, the payor might actually set aside the $100 in year 0 and earn interest sufficient to produce $121 in year 2, two years later, as in the typical retirement plan arrangement.

Now — *disallow the payor's accrued deductions*. If the payor in the 30% bracket is not allowed to deduct $100 (the present value of $121), that leaves the payor with $70, which it is willing to commit to the payee. Assume that the payor deposits the $70 in the bank and earns 7% interest after tax (there is still no accrued deduction for the payor), yielding $80.143 at the end of year 2 (70 times 1.07^2). How much will the payor pay the payee in year 2, at which point the entire payment *will be* deductible by the payor (because the payee is taxed)? Because the payment is deductible, the payor will pay much more than $80.143 — in fact, an additional amount that equals the value of the deduction. For those of you who are arithmetically inclined, that payment will be $80.143 divided by .7 (.7 = 1 minus the 30% tax rate); and that equals $114.49. The cash basis pay*ee* in the 30% bracket will then pay tax equal to 30% of $114.49 in year 2 and have $80.143 left (70% times $114.49 = $80.143). *That is the amount the payee would have had if she had been on the accrual method in the first place.*

So, disallowing the *payor*'s accrued deduction for both present value and interest, until the pay*ee* reports the income, leaves the cash method employee in the same position as an accrual method employee. Or does it? Suppose the payor is the employer of the teacher of this course. Will loss of an accrued deduction lead it to reduce the $100 commitment to the payee to $70 in year 0? No. The equivalence only works if the payor and payee are in the same tax bracket. When the payor is in a lower tax bracket, bargaining between the payor and payee will determine who gets the economic benefit from the tax not imposed on the payor ($30 in the above example).

[2] The Statute

The code in fact postpones deductions by the payor until the payee is taxed in several circumstances, including those covered by Revenue Ruling 60-31, dealing with nonqualified deferred compensation. The fact that the corporate tax rate is close to the top individual tax rate usually makes deferral of the deduction a meaningful restraint on the payor, assuming the payor is a taxable entity and assuming someone is monitoring the impact on the payor of tax deferral for the employees.

1. § 404(a)(5) (no deduction for payor until payee reports deferred compensation, unless the payments are to a "qualified retirement" plan).

2. § 83(h) (no deduction for payor until payee rendering personal services includes the restricted property in gross income). This has been interpreted by the government to allow the payor a deduction for amounts "includ*ible*" in the personal service provider's income, as long as the payor complies with certain reporting requirements. **Treas. Reg. § 1.83-6(a)(1), (2).**

3. § 404(b)(2)(A) (no deduction for most deferred employee benefits until the payee reports the item or would report it if it were taxable — for example, an employer's commitment to provide medical benefits to an employee in a later year).

[B] Note on Statutory Interpretation — Statutory Structure

The meaning of § 404(a)(5) — deferring the payor's deduction until the payee reports deferred compensation — was litigated in *Albertson's Inc. v. Commissioner*, 42 F.3d 537 (9th Cir. 1994) (on rehearing). The payor identified part of a deferred payment as deferred compensation (the part equal to present value) and the remainder of the deferred payment as interest to account for the deferral of payment. It argued that the deferral-of-deduction rule applied only to the portion equal to the compensation (that is, the present value) and did *not* apply to the interest portion.

The court initially agreed with the taxpayer but then changed its mind. It stressed "that, notwithstanding the statutory language on which Albertson's relies, to hold the additional amounts to be deductible would contravene the clear purpose of the taxation scheme Congress created to govern deferred compensation plans. As the Supreme Court noted in *Bob Jones University v. United States*, 461 U.S. 574 (1983), a term in the Code 'must be analyzed and construed within the framework of the Internal Revenue Code and against the background of the congressional purposes.' " The relevant framework was the distinction between the treatment of *qualified* plans (discussed in Chapter 24.06 below) and *nonqualified* plans. Under a qualified plan, the payor can accrue deductions before payments are made to the employee. However, a qualified plan must satisfy numerous requirements to protect the employee — such as nondiscrimination in favor of highly compensated employees, minimum participation and coverage standards, restrictions on amounts that can be contributed, and guarantees to assure future payment. Nonqualified plans lacked these safeguards and permitting the deduction of accrued interest, as requested by Albertson's Inc., would seriously undermine the effort in the tax law to favor qualified plans. The court rejected the payor's argument, as follows:

> Albertson's has not been able to refute the argument that its interpretation of section 404 undercuts the provision's central purpose. Equally important, it offers us no reason why Congress would have wanted to treat the "interest" part of the deferred compensation package differently from the basic amounts for tax purposes.

> Instead, Albertson's rests its argument upon its contention that, because the plain language of § 404 only refers to "compensation" rather than "interest," the employers have a statutory right to deduct the additional amounts as interest under § 163. In this connection, Albertson's points out

that section 404 prohibits deduction under sections 162 and 212 but not under section 163, and it is the latter section that governs the deduction of interest. Albertson's argument as to the plain language of the statute is a strong one. We certainly agree that the additional payments resemble "interest" and that, under a literal reading of the statutory language, the deduction of interest is not affected by section 404. However, holding such payments to be deductible "interest" under section 404 would lead to an anomalous result: a taxation scheme designed to make nonqualified plans less attractive would in many cases provide incentives for adopting such plans, and a provision intended to apply the matching principle to nonqualified deferred compensation agreements would exempt substantial portions of [the employee's payments] from its application.

In the end we are forced, therefore, to reject Albertson's approach. We may not adopt a plain language interpretation of a statutory provision that directly undercuts the clear purpose of the statute. . . . In reaching our conclusion, we followed the Supreme Court's approach in *United States v. American Trucking Ass'ns*, 310 U.S. 534 (1940). There the Court noted that "when [a given] meaning has led to absurd results . . . this Court has looked beyond the words to the purpose of the act. Frequently, however, even when the plain meaning did not produce absurd results but merely an unreasonable one 'plainly at variance with the policy of the legislation as a whole,' this Court has followed that purpose, rather than the literal words." . . .

In rejecting Albertson's appeal, we take heed of the Supreme Court's instructions concerning the proper interpretation of the Internal Revenue Code when the plain language of the provision leads to an unreasonable result and directly contradicts its underlying purpose: the provision "must be analyzed and construed within the framework of the Internal Revenue Code and against the background of the congressional purposes." For the reasons we have expressed, we conclude that, despite the literal wording of the statute, Congress could not have intended to exclude interest payments, a substantial part of the deferred compensation package, from the rule prohibiting deductions until such time as the employee receives the benefits. Indeed, the matching principle would not be much of a principle if so substantial a part of the deferred compensation package were excluded from its operation.

The court also made the following striking observation about the judicial process:

We have now changed our minds about the result we reached in our original opinion and conclude that our initial decision was incorrect. The question is not an easy one, however. We have struggled with it unsuccessfully at least once, and it may, indeed, ultimately turn out that the United States Supreme Court will tell us that it is this opinion which is in error. This is simply one of those cases — and there are more of them than judges generally like to admit — in which the answer is far from clear and in which there are conflicting rules and principles that we are forced to try to apply simultaneously. Such accommodation sometimes proves to be impossible.

In some cases, as here, convincing arguments can be made for both possible results, and the court's decision will depend on which of the two competing legal principles it chooses to give greater weight to in the particular circumstance. Law, even statutory construction, is not a science. It is merely an effort by human beings, albeit judges, to do their best with imperfect tools to arrive at a correct result.

The court's approach in *Albertson's Inc.* is in the purpose-over-text tradition that we have seen explicitly in the *Bob Jones* case (Chapter 10.02[C][1]). The reliance on statutory structure and purpose was also a feature of several Justice Holmes decisions (preventing assignment of income in *Lucas v. Earl* — Chapter 2.02; preventing tax free gifts of income in *Irwin v. Gavit* — Chapter 4.05[A]). There are, however, two differences between these Justice Holmes decisions and the issue in *Albertson's, Inc.* First, Holmes did not have the same problem with the statutory text. The statute was arguably silent regarding who has income after an assignment to a family relative; and the statute exempting gifts contained text supporting a distinction between gifts of property and gifts of income. By contrast, the court had to overcome the plain meaning of the statutory text in *Albertson's Inc.*

The second and more fundamental difference may be that Holmes wrote in an earlier period when the courts seemed more willing to interpret the tax statute to preserve its underlying structure and purpose. A modern court might be less willing to rely on purpose, especially in an area as technical and as frequently amended as the taxation of deferred employee benefits.

Query. Does § 467(g) (adopted in 2004), which taxes interest as it accrues to the payee, change the statutory structure so that there is no longer any need to defer the employer's deduction of the interest?

§ 24.05 DEDUCTIBLE PAYMENTS

The definition of "cash *payments*" that can support a deduction is not symmetrical with the rules defining "cash *receipts*," which support inclusion.

[A] Constructive Payment?

For example, making cash available to a payee does not in itself constitute a "payment," just because the payee would constructively receive the money. *Vander Poel, Francis & Co., Inc. v. Commissioner*, 8 T.C. 407 (1947). Any one of the following reasons supports this conclusion: the likelihood of payment is still too uncertain to justify a deduction; a deduction would eradicate the distinction between accrual and cash basis taxpayers; or the taxpayer has too much control over when to make the payment available and can therefore manipulate the year of deduction.

[B] Equivalent of Cash?

[1] Notes

Giving a note is not the equivalent of a cash payment, even if the recipient of the note would receive the equivalent of cash. *Helvering v. Price*, 309 U.S. 409 (1940); Rev. Rul. 76-135, 1976-1 C.B. 114; *Don E. Williams Co. v. Commissioner*, 429 U.S. 569, 578 (1977) (no deduction for giving a note because "the note may never be paid. . .").

[2] Notes to Pay for Capital Costs

Suppose a taxpayer pays to improve property with a promissory note. Remember that debt is included in basis on the *purchase* of property. Is a debt, at least if embodied in a note, added to the basis of property when the cost is incurred to *improve* the property? *Owen v. United States*, 34 F. Supp. 2d 1071 (D. Tenn. 1999), did *not* allow the cost to be added to basis. The court was acutely aware of the treatment of purchase price debt, but noted that adding the improvement cost to basis would eliminate the distinction between accrual and cash basis taxpayers and allow the taxpayer a basis prior to paying the debt. (Why does that matter? Cash basis taxpayers can use basis prior to paying debt, just like an accrual basis taxpayer, if the taxpayer *purchases* the property with debt.)

The court in *Owen* observed that the note had been given to a creditor-corporation controlled by the taxpayer. Isn't *that* an independent reason to disallow the inclusion of the note in basis? The taxpayer in effect retained considerable control over whether and when the payment would be made to the creditor, unlike the usual case of debt due to an outsider that finances property improvement. Perhaps the result would be different if an unrelated creditor demanded a note in the ordinary course of business to pay for improving the taxpayer's property. A note given to an unrelated business creditor might be considered analogous to the taxpayer borrowing cash from a bank to pay for the improvement, in which case there is no doubt that the cash payment would increase basis.

[3] Credit Card Payments

Suppose a taxpayer makes a payment with a credit card. Is the amount deductible as a cash payment before the credit card bill is paid? Is it like borrowing cash from a bank and making a deductible payment, or like a nondeductible promise to pay in the future? Rev. Rul. 78-38, 1978-1 C.B. 67 (government accepts analogy of credit card payment to bank loan, reversing a prior Revenue Ruling; payment by credit card is deductible as a cash payment). This makes sense in a commercial world where credit card payments are considered the equivalent of cash payments.

[C] Checks

Checks, unlike notes, are payments by a cash method taxpayer when the check is delivered. Rev. Rul. 54-465, 1954-2 C.B. 93.

§ 24.06   QUALIFIED RETIREMENT PLANS

[A]   Introduction

The examples in this chapter often deal with deferred compensation. A common method of providing deferred compensation is through qualified employer retirement plans. How does the prior discussion apply to these plans?

A mere promise to pay the employee a retirement benefit as compensation for personal services is usually tax free at the time the promise was made to a cash basis taxpayer. But many retirement plans provide more than a promise to the employee, because employees are unwilling to rely on the employer's good faith and solvency. In the typical case, money is put into a trust fund or paid to an insurance company to be distributed to the employee as an annuity or lump sum at a future date, along with the investment income earned over time. Under usual principles of cash equivalence, the employer's contribution would be taxable to the employee as an economic benefit when it is paid to the trust fund or the insurance company.

The earliest statutory tax breaks for retirement plans provided that the employee would *not* be taxed, if the contributions were made to a "qualified" retirement plan. In addition, the plan was not taxed on its annual investment income. This permitted the employee to defer tax on plan contributions and annual income earned on the investment until the employee received a distribution from the plan (usually cash). At the same time, employers could deduct contributions to these plans without waiting until the employee was taxed. Unlike § 83, deferral for the employee did not come at the price of a deferred deduction for the employer. Since these original tax breaks were passed, the tax law has added a host of refinements and new provisions that expand the availability of tax preferences for retirement plans.

The remainder of this section provides a survey of the principal rules dealing with retirement plans (funded by both an employer and through contributions made by an individual taxpayer). The tax rules applicable to these plans are a sub-specialty that consumes the entire professional lives of some practitioners and we do little more than suggest the complexity of the rules; important detail is omitted. For example, the specific rules vary depending on whether the plan is a defined benefit or defined contribution plan (e.g., a defined benefit plan might pay out the average of the last five years' salary; a defined contribution plan might pay out whatever is earned by investing 10% of salary each year that the employee works); whether the employer is or is not a tax-exempt organization; and whether the fund is financed by the employer, the employee, or a self-employed individual.

The survey should nonetheless leave you with one clear impression — once a tax break appears in the law, it tends to expand and proliferate in ways that might not have been foreseen when the original rules were adopted.

[B]   No Tax Now; Taxable Later

[1]   Qualified Retirement Plans

The code first provided tax deferral for qualified retirement plans in the 1920s, although many of the conditions required for qualification came later. Under current law, a "qualified" retirement plan must not discriminate in favor of highly compensated employees regarding coverage and participation, and must meet certain funding and vesting requirements. In addition, there are maximums on amounts that can be contributed to a defined contribution plan, and on total retirement benefits that can be paid by a defined benefit plan. Special nondiscrimination, funding, and vesting rules apply in the case of "top heavy" plans (which favor key employees). *See generally* **§§ 401 et seq.**

Since 1962, self-employed individuals (including partners in a partnership) have been able to adopt a qualified retirement plan for themselves and their employees, without having to incorporate to become employees.

Payments from the retirement plan *must* usually begin in the year in which (1) the taxpayer reaches age 70½ or (2) retires, whichever comes later. (However, a 5% owner cannot defer commencement of the distribution until the later retirement date.) The employee can (and usually will) elect to receive the retirement benefit in annual amounts and thereby postpone taxation until the periodic payments are actually received. Payments *cannot* begin (unless the taxpayer pays a 10% penalty on early withdrawal) before death, disability, or the year in which the taxpayer reaches age 59½ (although there are a few additional exceptions permitting earlier distribution — for example, for medical and certain education expenses). There are also rules requiring an annual minimum distribution, which discourages using a retirement plan as an estate planning technique.

Distributions of tax-deferred retirement benefits are taxable in full as income in respect of decedent under **§ 691**, although the survivor(s) can often defer collection until a later date (e.g., as an annuity over the life of the decedent's surviving spouse or children). The fact that the retirement fund could be subject to the estate tax (as well as the income tax) might make retention of funds in the plan a bad estate planning technique, but high estate tax exemptions often eliminate this concern.

There are separate rules dealing with tax deferral for qualified retirement plans of employees who work for tax-exempt organizations and state and local governments. **§§ 403(b), 457.**

[2]   Traditional IRAs

Not a participant in a qualified plan. In 1974, the code provided that a taxpayer who is *not* a participant in a qualified retirement plan could defer tax by *deducting* contributions to an Individual Retirement Account (IRA). The deduction is "above the line" — that is, not an itemized deduction. The contribution and the income it earns are both tax deferred (as in a qualified plan) until payment is received. **§ 219.** Rules similar but not identical to those applicable to qualified retirement plans restrict early distributions from IRAs and specify when distributions must begin.

The maximum annual deduction was, originally, the lesser of $2,000 or the taxpayer's personal service income. In addition, the taxpayer's spouse was also allowed to deduct up to $2,000, based on the taxpayer's personal service income (if *neither* spouse was a participant in a qualified retirement plan). This $2,000 figure has been gradually raised; for 2013, it is $5,500.

The law has also increased the deductible amounts even further for individuals age 50 or older (a catch-up provision) on the theory that these taxpayers got a late start saving for retirement; $6,500 in 2013. One of the arguments for these catch-up provisions is that it will help women who entered the labor force late in life, even though the tax breaks are not gender-specific.

Participant in a qualified plan. The IRA tax break for contributions to IRAs was extended to taxpayers who were participants in qualified retirement plans. The idea was to encourage savings, but many people simply shifted income from a savings account into an IRA. A huge revenue loss ensued and the law was changed to put an income threshold on eligibility to make deductible contributions to an IRA by taxpayers who were already participants in a qualified retirement plan. The income phase-out range has gradually increased until, after adjustment for inflation in 2013, it is $59,000–$69,000 of AGI for single individuals and $95,000–$115,000 of AGI for married couples.

Suppose one spouse is a homemaker who is not a participant in a qualified retirement plan and is married to a wage earner who is a participant in a qualified retirement plan. Before the 1997 Tax Act, the homemaker-spouse could also take advantage of deductions for contributions to an IRA, relying on the earned income of the wage-earning spouse, but was subject to the low phase-out range rules noted above. The 1997 law relaxed the phase-out rules so that a homemaker can make contributions relying on a wage-earning spouse's earnings, subject to a higher inflation-adjusted phase-out range for the married unit (for 2013, $178,000–$188,000 of *modified* AGI). This will allow many individuals who work at home and earn no wages, but have wage-earning spouses, to take deductions for contributions to an IRA, even though the wage earning spouse might not (as a plan participant) make such contributions.

[3] Cash or Deferred Arrangement (CODA)

The law also allows an employee to elect that *some* of his salary be contributed to a qualified retirement plan on a tax-deferred basis if the employer has not contributed the maximum amount allowable — referred to as a cash or deferred salary arrangement (CODA). Absent this law, the cash amounts contributed to the plan would be constructively received and therefore taxed to the employee in the election year.

[4] Medical Savings Accounts (MSAs)

Recall MSAs provided by § 220 (discussed in Chapter 9.02[B][2]). Amounts paid to such accounts are deductible or excludible from an employee's income. Any portion of the amounts paid to such accounts can be carried over to future years. Amounts not used for medical expenses can be drawn down for nonmedical uses subject to a penalty, but there is no penalty if the taxpayer is disabled, dies, or is eligible for Medicare. Consequently, MSAs can be used as retirement plans *without an income limit.*

[5] Qualified Charitable Distributions from IRAs

Congress has grown fond of the following rule. A taxpayer aged 70 1/2 or older can distribute up to $100,000 from an IRA to a charitable organization without recognizing income and without taking a charitable deduction (thereby not using up the percentage limitation on charitable deductions). Moreover, the distribution counts toward the required minimum distribution from an IRA. This tax break was scheduled to expire after 2007 but has been extended through 2013 by ATRA. § 408(d)(8).

[C] Nondeductible Now; Exempt Later

[1] Roth IRAs

Beginning with the 1997 Tax Act, the code permits certain taxpayers to make *nondeductible* contributions out of earned income up to a specified annual amount (reduced by any amounts contributed to a traditional IRA). The nondeductible contributions accumulate income tax-free, *and* the distribution is tax-free under circumstances described below. § 408A. These accounts are referred to as Roth IRAs. The amount that can be contributed has increased over the years by the same amounts as the traditional IRA contributions have been permitted to increase. Thus, for 2013, $5,500 of after-tax earnings can be contributed to a Roth IRA. ("Catch-up" rules increase this amount to $6,500, as in the case of traditional IRAs.)

The Roth IRA is different from the typical retirement plan, where the contributions and income accumulations are tax-deferred, but taxable when collected at some future date. This should remind you of the earlier discussion about how to measure the value of deferral, where we noted that deferral of an amount is the equivalent of taxing that amount and earning tax-free income on the after-tax investment; Chapter 3.03[B]. An after-tax investment producing tax-free income under a Roth IRA is therefore the equivalent of investing a *larger* amount on a tax-deferred basis, assuming that tax-rates and rates of return are constant over the years. The larger amount depends on the tax rate. Assuming a 33⅓ % tax rate (to simplify arithmetic), a $5,000 after tax Roth IRA investment is the equivalent of a $7,500 tax-deferred investment. The Roth after-tax IRA contribution limits are therefore more generous than the deduction ceilings for traditional IRAs, even though the contribution ceilings are the same. Moreover, because the distribution is tax exempt, the recipient does not have to worry about paying tax on income in respect of a decedent under § 691.

A taxpayer can invest in a Roth IRA even if he or she participates in a qualified retirement plan. However, the contribution limits for Roth IRAs are phased out with rising income. The inflation-adjusted figures for 2013 are: for single taxpayers, between AGI of $112,000 and $127,000; and, for married couples, between AGI of $178,000 and $188,000.

Tax-free distributions from a Roth IRA are subject to the following rules. The distribution cannot be made within the five-year period beginning with the first taxable year for which a contribution is made to the Roth IRA; *and* the distribution can only be made on or after the individual attains age 59½ (except that earlier distribution is permitted tax-free if made on account of death, disability, or a limited amount to be used for first-time homebuyer expenses). If the distribution is not tax exempt under the above rules, the distribution comes first out of after-tax contributions, as a nontaxable return of capital, so there is no tax until distributions exceed contributions.

There are two other advantages of a Roth IRA. First, distributions do not have to begin at any particular age. Second, the estate tax implications for a Roth IRA are different than for tax-deductible plans. When someone dies with unpaid Roth IRA benefits, the tax paid to make nondeductible contributions during the decedent's lifetime are excluded from the taxpayer's estate for estate tax purposes (assuming the estate tax is an issue). By contrast, the estate tax falls on the full amount of tax-deductible retirement benefits paid out after the decedent's death, including the income tax due when those benefits are paid.

A final consideration is the tax rates in the contribution and distribution years. After retirement, the taxpayer may be in a lower tax bracket, as income declines — which favors tax deferral instead of a Roth IRA. However, you will make a different calculation if you expect a future increase in income tax rates.

[2] Rollovers into Roth IRA

Taxpayers have a lot of before-tax income salted away in qualified retirement plans and traditional IRAs. Before 2008, taxpayers had the option of shifting a traditional IRA into a Roth IRA by paying tax on the amounts rolled over. Beginning in 2008, the rollover option has been expanded to include qualified retirement plans.

Chapter 25

ACCRUAL METHOD

Recall the basic rule about when income (and deductions) accrue for income tax purposes — accrual occurs when all events have occurred fixing the right or liability (except for the passage of time), and the amount can be determined with reasonable accuracy, and the promisor is solvent (the "all events" test). **Treas. Reg. § 1.446-1(c)(1)(ii)**. And, recall further that any method of accounting must "clearly reflect income."

1. This chapter addresses the following technical questions regarding accrual:

a. When are all events "fixed"?

b. When are the amounts determined with "reasonable accuracy"?

c. How does the "clearly reflect income" standard apply to the transaction?

d. Special attention is paid to the following problems:

i. What happens when cash is received or paid *before* a liability would otherwise have accrued (Chapters 25.01[B], 25.02[A])?

ii. How does the tax law respond when the accrued amount of a deduction would not accurately reflect the present value of the debt that will eventually be paid (Chapter 25.02[B][3])? The distinction between accrued amounts and present value has already been discussed in the income context in Chapter 21.03 (sales proceeds) and Chapter 23.03[C] (sales, use of property, personal services).

2. Consider what policies the courts use to decide whether accrual has occurred:

a. Administrative simplicity

b. Ease of revenue collection

c. Preventing manipulation by a taxpayer

d. Implementing a fundamental objective of accrual accounting, which is to accurately measure accessions to wealth (e.g., by matching income and expenses)

§ 25.01   INCOME

[A]   Before Cash Is Received

In the following cases you are almost certain to have trouble coming up with a clear rule about how the "all events" test is applied to accrue income items. The *Continental* case requires accrual and the *Globe Corp.* case does not.

CONTINENTAL TIE & LUMBER CO. v. UNITED STATES
United States Supreme Court
286 U.S. 290 (1932)

Mr. Justice Roberts delivered the opinion of the Court.

. . . The railway company [petitioner] is a short-line carrier whose road was in possession and control of the United States and operated by the Director General of Railroads from December 28, 1917 to June 3, 1918, when it was relinquished, and thereafter throughout the remainder of the period of federal control operated by its owner. Approximately $25,000 of the additional income determined by the Commissioner consisted of a payment to the railway pursuant to an award of the Interstate Commerce Commission under the terms of section 204 of the Transportation Act 1920. . . .

The petitioner kept its accounts upon the accrual basis. The government insists, and the Court of Claims held, that the right to payment . . . ripened in 1920 [and] the taxpayer should have returned the estimated award under section 204 as income for that year. The petitioner replies that a determination whether it would receive any award under the section and, if so, the amount of it, depended on so many contingencies that no reasonable estimate could have been made in 1920, and that the sum ultimately ascertained should be deemed income for 1923, the year of the award and payment.

The Transportation Act took effect on February 28, 1920. On June 10, the Interstate Commerce Commission issued general instructions governing the compilation and submission of data by carriers entitled to awards under section 204. The petitioner correctly states that at the date of the act's adoption no railroad had a vested right in any amount; until the Commission made an award nothing could be paid, no proceeding was available to compel an allowance, or to determine the elements which should enter into the calculation. In short, says the petitioner, the carrier had no rights, but was dependent solely upon the Commission's exercise of an unrestrained discretion, and until an award was made nothing accrued. But we think that the function of the Commission under the act was ministerial, to ascertain the facts with respect to the carrier's operating income by a comparison of the experience during the test period with that during the term of federal control. The right to the award was fixed by the passage of the Transportation Act. What remained was mere administrative procedure to ascertain the amount to be paid. Petitioner's right to payment ripened when the act became law. What sum of money that right represented is, of course, a different matter.

The petitioner says that at the date of the passage of the act it was impossible to predict that any award would be made to the railway, and, assuming one would eventuate, its amount could not be estimated, for the reason that the principles upon which awards were to be made had to be settled by the Commission and were not finally formulated until 1923. The government insists that, while adjustments or settlement of principles by the Commission might vary the amount to be awarded, the petitioner's case presented problems not differing from those confronting many business concerns which keep accounts on an accrual basis and have to estimate for the tax year the amount to be received on transactions undoubtedly allocable to such year. Admitting there might be differences and discrepancies between the railway's estimate and the amount awarded by the Commission, these, says the government, could, as in similar cases, have been adjusted by an additional assessment or a claim for refund after final determination of the amount due.

The case does not fall within the principle that, where the liability is undetermined in the tax year, the taxpayer is not called upon to accrue any sum (*Lucas v. American Code Co.*, 280 U.S. 445, 50 S. Ct. 202, 74 L. Ed. 538), but presents the problem whether the taxpayer had in its own books and accounts data to which it could apply the calculations required by the statute and ascertain the quantum of the award within reasonable limits.

The carriers kept their accounts according to standards prescribed by the Commission; and these necessarily were the source of information requisite for ascertainment of the results of operation in the two periods to be compared. . . . As might have been expected, the general principles thus formulated did not cover in detail questions of fact, the solution of which required is some degree the exercise of opinion and judgment. . . . The petitioner points to the fact that [various computation] questions were raised by the railroads [], that the Commission gave extended consideration to them, and that, as respects sundry of them, the applicable principles were not settled until 1921, 1922, and 1923. Petitioner might have added that the Commission, while attempting as far as possible to formulate general principles applicable to large groups of carriers, found it necessary in addition to consider the peculiar conditions and special circumstances affecting individual carriers in order in each case to do justice to the carrier and to the United States. But in spite of these inherent difficulties, we think it was possible for a carrier to ascertain with reasonable accuracy the amount of the award to be paid by the Government. Subsequent to its order of June 10, 1920, the Commission made no amendment or alteration of the rules with respect to the information to be furnished under section 204. Obviously, the data had to be obtained from the railway's books and accounts and from entries therein all made prior to March 1, 1920. These accounts contained all the information that could ever be available touching relevant expenditures. The petitioner was promptly informed by the terms of section 209 . . . It does not appear that a proper effort would not have obtained a result approximately in accord with that the Commission ultimately found.

Much is made by the petitioner of the fact that, as a result of representations by the carriers, the Commission from time to time during 1921, 1922, and 1923 promulgated rulings respecting the method of adjusting book charges to actual experience, and it is asserted that petitioner could not in 1920 have known what these rulings were to be. But it is not clear that, if the taxpayer had acted promptly, an award could not have been made during 1920, or at least the principles upon which the Commission would adjust the railway's accounts to reflect true income have been settled during that year sufficiently to enable the railway to ascertain with reasonable accuracy the amount of the probable award. . . .

GLOBE CORPORATION v. COMMISSIONER
United States Tax Court
20 T.C. 299 (1953)

[Editor — Taxpayer manufactured aerial target assemblies for the government. The price paid for packaging and preservation services was to be negotiated after delivery, with provision for appeal to the head of the government department if negotiations failed. Items were delivered in 1945, and taxpayer submitted a $165,893.07 bill for services, which was questioned by the government. A settlement was reached in 1946 for $75,525.92, attributable to the 1945 deliveries. The court does not accrue the income in 1945.]

BRUCE, JUDGE: . . .

. . . Petitioner kept its books and filed its income tax returns on the calendar year basis and the accrual method of accounting. The sole question presented therefore is whether the income in question accrued within the year 1945 as contended by respondent, or in 1946 as contended by petitioner. . . .

. . . [The] *Continental Tie & Lumber Co.* case [is] distinguishable from the situation before us in that here more than a mere calculation or computation was required to fix the amount to be accrued. Rather there remained a negotiation between the parties upon terms not as yet agreed upon. There was no formula, method, or particular data which both could accept as the basis of the final agreement. . . .

Thus we conclude from the whole record that petitioner was not able to ascertain with reasonable accuracy the amount to accrue until 1946 when the negotiations were completed and the change orders or amendments were executed. That amount was, therefore, not fixed and definite until 1946, at which time it was properly accrued. Such accrual is not precluded by the fact that the items of cost, representing labor, material, and overhead, pertaining to these items were accrued by petitioner in 1945 and reflected in the computation of taxable income for that year. As to such amounts, liability and amount were fixed in that year.

COMMENTS AND QUESTIONS

1. *Continental Tie vs. Globe Corp.* How do these two cases compare on the basis of the policy criteria used to decide whether income should be accrued: administrative simplicity, ease of revenue collection, preventing taxpayer manipulation, and accurately measuring accession to wealth?

a. *Administrative simplicity.* The cases appear similar regarding administrative simplicity. In neither case was there a specific event that could easily be identified to accrue the liability. In both cases, the criteria to determine the amount of the liability had to be developed in a later year — in *Continental Tie*, there were still criteria to be adopted after 1920 (the accrual year) on the basis of which the Interstate Commerce Commission award would be computed, just as in *Globe Corp.* there were terms to be negotiated between the taxpayer and the government after 1945 to determine the amount of the liability.

b. *Revenue collection.* The cases sometimes appear to be concerned with revenue collection in the sense of taxing income in a high tax rate year. Continental Tie accrued income in the year 1920, before higher tax rates applicable during World War I had been reduced. Opportunistic judicial results designed to shift income to the higher tax rate year seem hard to defend on principle, but that may nonetheless help to explain some of the decisions. This criterion does not, however, explain the decision in *Globe Corp.*, which deferred accrual until 1946, when higher World War II rates had been reduced.

c. *Taxpayer manipulation.* Perhaps the difference between *Continental Tie* and *Globe Corp.* can be gleaned from a comment at the end of the *Continental Tie* decision, where the Court suggests that the taxpayer could control the timing and had postponed the payment. By contrast, in the *Globe Corp.* case, the government raised questions that postponed the settlement, which led to a payment in 1946 much less than the taxpayer's 1945 claim. Taxpayer manipulation would therefore be a greater problem in *Continental Tie.*

d. *Accession to wealth.* The accrual method is supposed to accurately measure accessions to wealth. Usually, this calls for matching expenses against income. That is not an issue in *Continental Tie*, where the accrued item was net income. In *Globe Corp.*, however, the court seems to disregard the matching criterion — the fact that the costs were incurred in 1945 but the related income was not accrued prior to 1946. But, in *Globe Corp.*, there was a large difference between the taxpayer's bill for services in 1945 and the amount actually determined in 1946, which suggests that an early accrual would not come close to measuring the taxpayer's accession to wealth.

2. Uncertainty regarding liability

a. In *Lucas v. North Texas Lumber Co.*, 281 U.S. 11 (1930), distinguished by the Court in *Continental Tie*, the seller and buyer entered into an executory contract to sell timber land on December 30, 1916. The buyer declared itself ready to close the transaction and pay the purchase price "as soon as the papers were prepared." The seller-taxpayer did not prepare the papers necessary to effect the transfer or make tender of title or possession or demand the purchase price in 1916. The Court refused to allow the taxpayer to accrue the income in 1916, stating:

> The title and right of possession remained in [the seller] until the transaction was closed. Consequently, unconditional liability of vendee for the purchase price was not created in that year. The entry of the purchase price in respondent's accounts as income in that year was not warranted. [The taxpayer] was not entitled to make return or have the tax computed on that basis, as clearly it did not reflect 1916 income.

The Court's acceptance of the taxpayer's argument for deferral is usually explained on the ground that the case involves uncertainty about liability, rather than uncertainty about the amount owed. But that distinction seems very mechanical. Policy arguments pull in opposite directions. "Waiting until title passage" is an *administratively simple* rule, but it nonetheless allows the taxpayer to *manipulate* the time of accrual.

On the facts of this case, early accrual in 1916 would have resulted in *lower revenue* for the government, because tax rates rose in 1917 after the United States entered Word War I. That is why the taxpayer in *North Texas Lumber* (unusually) wanted to report income in an earlier year.

b. *Schlumberger Technology Corp. v. United States*, 195 F.3d 216 (5th Cir. 1999), considered when a legal liability becomes sufficiently fixed that income accrues as litigation involving legal liability moves through the judicial process. The case held that a foreign arbitration award in Switzerland did not accrue until the time to appeal judicial confirmation of the award had expired in the jurisdiction in which enforcement was sought (France). The court noted that a domestic judgment in the United States is considered an accruable unconditional, fixed right to receive the award, despite the potential for collateral attack at the time of enforcement. But it distinguished foreign from domestic judgment, based on the following: domestic judgments are subject to full faith and credit and, unlike the foreign judgment, are not subject to a "roving public policy" exception to enforcing the judgment; and an arbitration award was not self-executing but had to be confirmed by a judicial judgment. The court stated that "[t]he lack of such enforcement for a bare arbitral award is [] a decisive distinction. Drawing the line at the existence of an unappealable judicial confirmation is also a rule that is easy to follow and apply. Furthermore, in the context of international arbitration, it makes sense to give the Taxpayer the benefit of the doubt given the inherent difficulties associated with collecting foreign awards in foreign countries."

> For these reasons, we hold that a fixed right to receive does not exist with respect to a foreign arbitral award until the award is judicially confirmed and no longer subject to appeal in the jurisdiction in which enforcement is sought.

3. **Statute does not require accrual of some personal service income.** In one situation, the statute provides a specific rule about accrual of income. **Section 448(d)(5)** prevents accrual of any portion of personal service income which experience indicates will not be collected, regardless of whether all events have otherwise occurred, *but only if* there is no interest or penalty for untimely payment.

The 2002 Tax Law narrows this opportunity for tax deferral by the income recipient so that it applies only to certain types of personal service income (health, law, engineering, accounting, actuarial science, performing arts, and consulting), or if the taxpayer has no more than an average of $5 million gross receipts in all prior years. § 448(d)(5).

[B]   When Cash Is Received

The receipt of cash is an administratively easy time to identify an income item; it is also a good time to collect revenue. Moreover, deferral of taxation on cash receipts on the ground that the income is not yet earned — because the taxpayer must incur expenses in the future to retain the money — opens a window for taxpayer manipulation that the government might want to avoid.

It is true that cash receipt of a loan is not taxable, regardless of accounting method, but in such cases the obligation to repay the entire amount of the cash received is clearly fixed, usually in a normal business transaction. There is much greater uncertainty associated with deferring prepaid cash income than in the case of loan. Assume a taxpayer receives $100 in year 1, and expects to incur related expenses of $40 in both years 1 and 2 to earn the money. How would the taxpayer compute deferred income? Would it estimate total expenses and use that to allocate income over future years (e.g., incurring one half the expenses annually would cause one half of the $100 to be reported annually)? Does this estimation approach give the taxpayer too much opportunity to defer tax based on numbers that are too speculative and too likely to be manipulated by the taxpayer?

Consequently, even though financial accounting routinely defers income that is not earned until future taxpayer performance — on the ground that there is no accession to wealth equal to the cash received when future expenses must be matched against previously received cash payments — deferral of cash receipts might not "clearly reflect income" under tax accounting standards. The following material deals with this issue.

[1]   Case Law

AMERICAN AUTOMOBILE ASS'N v. UNITED STATES
United States Supreme Court
367 U.S. 687 (1961)

MR. JUSTICE CLARK delivered the opinion of the Court.

In this suit for refund of federal income taxes the petitioner, American Automobile Association, seeks determination of its tax liability for the years 1952 and 1953. Returns filed for its taxable calendar years were prepared on the basis of the same accrual method of accounting as was used in keeping its books. The Association reported as gross income only that portion of the total prepaid annual membership dues, actually received or collected in the calendar year, which ratably corresponded with the number of membership months covered by those dues and occurring within the same taxable calendar year. The balance was reserved for ratable monthly accrual over the remaining membership period in the following calendar year as deferred or unearned income reflecting an estimated future service expense to members. The Commissioner contends that petitioner should have reported in its gross income for each year the entire amount of membership dues actually received in the taxable calendar year without regard to expected future service expense in the subsequent year. The sole point at issue, therefore, is in what year the prepaid dues are taxable as income.

In auditing the Association's returns for the years 1952 through 1954, the Commissioner, in the exercise of his discretion under § 41 of the Internal Revenue Code of 1939 [Editor — Now § 446], determined not to accept the taxpayer's accounting system. As a result, adjustments were made for those years principally by adding to gross income for each taxable year the amount of prepaid dues which the Association had received but not recognized as income, and subtracting from gross income amounts recognized in the year although actually received in the prior year.

. . . For many years, the association has employed an accrual method of accounting and the calendar year as its taxable year. It is admitted that for its purposes the method used is in accord with generally accepted commercial accounting principles. The membership dues, as received, were deposited in the Association's bank accounts without restriction as to their use for any of its corporate purposes. However, for the Association's own accounting purposes, the dues were treated in its books as income received ratably over the 12-month membership period. The portions thereof ratably attributable to membership months occurring beyond the year of receipt, i.e., in a second calendar year, were reflected in the Association's books at the close of the first year as unearned or deferred income. Certain operating expenses were chargeable as prepaid membership cost and deducted ratably over the same periods of time as those over which dues were recognized as income.

[Editor — The Court stated that an accounting method that is "in accord with generally accepted commercial accounting principles and practices" does not mean that "for income tax purposes it so clearly reflects income as to be binding on the Treasury." It went on to defer to the government's insistence that reporting the prepaid membership dues in the year of receipt was required to clearly reflect income. It also added the following observation about a 1954 statutory amendment.]

. . . [Moreover, since 1954,] Congress has authorized the desired accounting only in the instance of prepaid subscription income, which, as was pointed out in Michigan, is ratably earned by performance on "publication dates after the tax year." It has refused to enlarge § 455 to include prepaid membership dues. At the very least, this background indicates congressional recognition of the complications inherent in the problem and its seriousness to the general revenue. We must leave to the Congress the fashioning of a rule which, in any event, must have wide ramifications. The Committees of the Congress have standing committees expertly grounded in tax problems, with jurisdiction covering the whole field of taxation and facilities for studying considerations of policy as between the various taxpayers and the necessities of the general revenues. The validity of the long-established policy of the Court in deferring, where possible, to congressional procedures in the tax field is clearly indicated in this case. Finding only that, in light of existing provisions not specifically authorizing it, the exercise of the Commissioner's discretion in rejecting the Association's accounting system was not unsound, we need not anticipate what will be the product of further "study of this entire problem."

Affirmed.

[2] Post-*AAA* Developments

The *AAA* case has not been the last word on deferring prepaid income.

[a]   Case Law

In *Artnell v. Commissioner*, 400 F.2d 981 (7th Cir. 1968), advance payments for baseball tickets could be deferred because, unlike *AAA*, the performances had to occur on fixed future dates. And, in *Tampa Bay Devil Rays, Ltd. v. Commissioner*, 84 T.C.M. (CCH) 394 (2002), the court followed *Artnell*. It allowed deferral of prepayments for advance ticket sales to baseball games to the year when the games were played, where play occurred according to a fixed and definite schedule and where the major expenses of operating the team were incurred in the year when the games were played.

[b]   Statute

A number of statutory provisions permit accrual method taxpayers to defer prepaid income. In addition to § 455 dealing with publishers (noted in the *AAA* case), *see* § 456 (defer prepaid membership dues, overruling *AAA* on its facts beginning in 1960); § 458 (defer prepaid sales proceeds of certain returnable items). Notice that the deferral period permitted by statute is usually short, thereby reducing any negative revenue impact from the taxpayer manipulating the rules — §§ 456(e)(2) (not to exceed 36 months); § 458(b)(7) (2½ or 4½ months). There is, however, no requirement that deferral be for a short period under § 455 (publishers).

[c]   Agency Rules

In a number of situations, the IRS gives up the advantage it won in *AAA*, and permits deferral of prepaid income. Thus, **Treas. Reg.** § **1.451-5** allows an accrual method taxpayer to defer tax on prepaid income received for inventory sales, if the taxpayer also uses that accounting method for financial accounting purposes.

[i]   Personal Services

Two Revenue Procedures deal with personal services. Assume that the taxpayer receives a prepayment in year 0 for services to be performed in a later year. For financial accounting purposes, the income is properly deferred. The taxpayer is allowed to defer the income in accordance with financial accounting, but (in no event) later than the year following the receipt of the prepayment. In other words, the deferral can extend to year 1, but not year 2. This method is allowed even if the services can be performed after year 1. Rev. Proc. 71-21, 1971-2 C.B. 549; Rev. Proc. 2004-34, 2004-1 C.B. 991.

For example, a taxpayer receives payment in year 0 for 96 dance lessons, to be provided over years 0, 1, and 2. If eight lessons are provided in year 0, 1/16th of the prepayment must be reported in year 0, assuming that is the method used for financial reporting. The remaining 15/16ths must be reported in year 1, regardless of how many lessons are provided in that year.

[ii] Other Prepaid Income

In Rev. Proc. 2004-34, the government also added significantly to the situations in which the taxpayer can defer income, well-beyond what is specified in **Treas. Reg. § 1.451-5** and Rev. Proc. 71-21. The deferral rules are, in general, the same as under Rev. Proc. 71-21 and Rev. Proc. 2004-34 — no deferral beyond the year next succeeding the year in which a prepayment is received (that is, for a year 0 prepayment, no later than year 1).

The issuance of this Revenue Procedure was unusual because it followed a public notice and comment procedure that is usually used only for regulations.

The stated rationale for Rev. Proc. 2004-34 was that "[c]onsiderable controversy exists about the scope of Rev. Proc. 71-21. In particular, advance payments for non-services (and, often, for combinations of services and non-services) do not qualify for deferral under Rev. Proc. 71-21, and taxpayers and the Internal Revenue Service frequently disagree about whether advance payments are, in fact, for 'services.' . . . In the interest of reducing the controversy surrounding these issues, the Service has determined that it is appropriate to expand the scope of Rev. Proc. 71-21 to include advance payments for certain non-services and combinations of services and non-services."

Only certain payments are covered by Rev. Proc. 2004-34, among which are the following: for the use of intellectual property; for the occupancy or use of property if the occupancy or use is ancillary to the provision of services (for example, advance payments for the use of rooms or other quarters in a hotel, booth space at a trade show, campsite space at a mobile home park, and recreational or banquet facilities); for the sale, lease, or license of computer software; for warranty contracts ancillary to the above items; for subscriptions (other than subscriptions for which an election under § **455** is in effect), whether or not provided in a tangible or intangible format; for memberships in an organization (other than memberships for which an election under § **456** is in effect).

Payments that are *not* covered include the following: rents for real or personal property, except where ancillary to the provision of services; insurance premiums.

COMMENTS AND QUESTIONS

1. **Payments for services or something else.** The definition of "services" has arisen in connection with bank credit card fees (which are not covered by Rev. Proc. 2004-34). In *American Express Co. v. United States*, 262 F.3d 1376 (Fed. Cir. 2001), the taxpayer argued that bank credit card fees were for services, even though they were paid for an extension of credit, but the court disagreed. (Rev. Proc. 2004-34 did not apply specifically to credit card fees so the taxpayer had to rely on the rules applicable to service income to defer income.) The taxpayer had refused to argue that *some* of the fees could be allocated to "services" other than credit extension; in other words, the taxpayer was trying to win a favorable decision on the broadest possible grounds. The court emphasized that a General Counsel Memorandum (G.C.M.) interpreting Rev. Proc. 71-21 had refused to include credit extension in the definition of services. Although an agency

interpretation of a Revenue Procedure is not entitled to deference under the *Chevron* case, the court nonetheless concluded that "substantial deference" to a G.C.M. was appropriate. Presumably, the taxpayer is still free in another case to argue that an allocable portion of the credit card fees was, in fact, for services.

The court in the *American Express* case refused to follow *Barnett Banks of Florida, Inc. v. Commissioner*, 106 T.C. 103 (1996), in which the court held that payment for a bank credit card was for services, eligible for deferral under Rev. Proc. 71-21. In *Barnett Banks*, when a card issuer canceled the card, the taxpayer was refunded the annual fee on a pro rata basis for the remaining months in the one-year contract period. In rejecting the reasoning of the *Barnett Banks* decision, the court in *American Express* stated: "Whether or not credit provided to the cardholder is a "service" under Rev. Proc. 71-21 cannot hinge on such factual distinctions as whether or not the fee is refundable or on statements made in the cardholder agreement."

2. **Deposits.** Is a deposit more like a loan or prepaid income? In *C.I.R. v. Indianapolis Power & Light Company*, 493 U.S. 203 (1990), an electric utility company received deposits in year 1, if the customer could not meet credit standards. The company paid 6% interest on deposits held for one year or more. If the customer did not pay the bill, the deposit was used to meet the customer's obligation. The Court did not tax the deposit when received, distinguishing a deposit from an advance prepayment, as follows:

> An advance payment, like the deposits at issue here, concededly protects the seller against the risk that it would be unable to collect money owed it after it has furnished goods or services. But an advance payment does much more: it protects against the risk that the purchaser will back out of the deal before the seller performs. From the moment an advance payment is made, the seller is assured that, so long as it fulfills its contractual obligation, the money is its to keep. Here, in contrast, a customer submitting a deposit made no commitment to purchase a specified quantity of electricity, or indeed to purchase any electricity at all. IPL's right to keep the money depends upon the customer's purchase of electricity, and upon his later decision to have the deposit applied to future bills, not merely upon the utility's adherence to its contractual duties. Under these circumstances, IPL's dominion over the fund is far less complete than is ordinarily the case in an advance-payment situation.

In *Houston Industries Inc. v. United States*, 125 F.3d 1442 (Fed. Cir. 1997), the court applied the *Indianapolis Power & Light* case to a situation in which an electric utility charged customers based on estimated use of electricity and later reconciled this prepayment with accurate usage figures. Any overpayments were either credited against future bills or repaid, in each case with interest. The court held that the taxpayer had no guarantee of being able to keep the overpayments and that they were, therefore, not income in the earlier year of receipt, because the customers in *Houston Industries* had not contracted to buy electricity in the future.

3. **Advance trade discounts**. In *Westpac Pacific Food v. Commissioner*, 451 F.3d 970 (9th Cir. 2006), the court held that "advance trade discounts" were not income when they were received but were properly treated as downward adjustments to

the cost of goods sold for products purchased after receipt of such discounts. The court gave the following simplified example:

> The facts outlined below sound more complicated than they are, so imagine a simple hypothetical. Harry Homeowner goes to the furniture store, spots just the right dining room chairs for $500 each, and says "I'll take four, if you give me a discount." Negotiating a 25% discount, he pays only $1,500 for the chairs. He has not made $500, he has spent $1,500. Now suppose Harry Homeowner is short on cash, and negotiates a deal where the furniture store gives him a 20% discount as a cash advance instead of the 25% off. This means the store gives him $400 "cash back" today, and he pays $2,000 for the four chairs when they are delivered shortly after the first of the year. Harry cannot go home and say "I made $400 today" unless he plans to skip out on his obligation to pay for the four chairs. Even though he receives the cash, he has not made money by buying the chairs. He has to sell the chairs for more than $1,600 if he wants to make money on them. The reason why the $400 "cash back" is not income is that, like a loan, the money is encumbered with a repayment obligation to the furniture store and the "cash back" must be repaid if Harry does not perform his obligation.

In other words, the taxpayer could use the cash discount to reduce the cost of goods sold rather than report it as income when received, by analogy to the deposits in the *Indianapolis Power* case. The analogy was apt because the taxpayer had to return the discount if it did not meet its commitment to purchase goods in large volume.

The IRS has agreed to follow the *Westpac* case in Rev. Proc. 2007 53, 2007-2 C.B. 233, even though the government won a case disagreeing with *Westpac* (*Karns Prime & Fancy Food, Ltd. v. Commissioner*, 494 F.3d 404 (3d Cir. 2007)).

4. **Taxing the payee to get at the payor.** There *is* something troublesome about taxing prepaid income, because it is similar to a loan in that future expenses must be incurred to keep the money. Maybe one reason for taxing prepaid income has more to do with the *payor* than the *payee*. We earlier discussed prepayment for tuition (and other personal consumption items). We noted that there was likely to be a hidden interest-like element accruing to the *payor* in the prepayment arrangement that would not be taxed. Would taxing the *payee* on prepaid income indirectly tax the *payor* on such interest-like income? Let us see (with some complex arithmetic).

Assume that the *payor* prepays $100 in year 0 for services to be provided in year 2, two years later. Assuming a 10% interest rate, the interest element in the transaction is $10 and $11 in the two successive years (years 1 and 2). If the payor is in the 30% tax bracket, the payor should be taxed on that interest so that there is only a 7% return on the $100 investment. That should yield services worth only $114.49 to the payor ($100 times 1.07^2).

Will taxing the pay*ee* produce that result for the *payor* indirectly? Put yourself in the *payee's* position. You have received $100 in year 0, prepaid for services due in year 2 (e.g., for a car repair service contract). Assuming that the pay*ee* is also in the 30% bracket, that leaves the pay*ee* $70 after tax to fund whatever benefit the payee will provide to the payor in year 2. Of course, that $70 will earn 7% after-tax interest, producing $80.143 in year 2. What is the value of services the payee will provide to the payor, assuming that the payee has $80.143 of after-tax money, committed to the payor? Remember that the payor gets a deduction in year 2 for its costs in providing benefits to the payor. The payee will provide $114.49 worth of services, at an after-tax cost of $80.143 (.70 times 114.49 = 80.143). And that is the right result. As usual, this works only if the payor and payee are in the same tax bracket.

§ 25.02 DEDUCTIONS

[A] When Cash Is Paid

In *United States v. Consolidated Edison Co.*, 366 U.S. 380 (1961), an accrual basis taxpayer paid New York property taxes but contested the obligation. Payment was necessary to avoid seizure of property. The Court denied the deduction because the debt had not accrued under the all events test, analogizing the payment to a deposit.

After *Consolidated Edison*, the code was amended to override the decision in that case and permit deduction of payments, despite a contest over whether the obligation is due, if the payment would have been deductible in the absence of a contest. **§ 461(f); Treas. Reg. § 1.461-2(e)**.

COMMENT

Is the statutory amendment in **§ 461(f)**, which permits a deduction, a sensible rule? I think so. First, one argument against the deduction is that loans are not deductible. But loans are not deductible because of the likelihood of repayment. Isn't a taxpayer who makes a contested payment *less* likely to be repaid than in the case of a loan? Second, which rule creates the greatest opportunity for taxpayer manipulation — a deduction in the year of payment or the year in which the disputed liability is settled? It seems unlikely that a taxpayer would pay more taxes than he thinks he owes, simply to get an early deduction.

[B] Before Cash Is Paid

[1] Case Law

The accrual of deductions prior to payment, like the accrual of income, is also determined by the "all events" test. Indeed, the "all events" test was created in *United States v. Anderson*, 269 U.S. 422 (1926), which involved a deduction. An accrual basis taxpayer had an accrued obligation to pay taxes in 1916 but wanted to deduct them in 1917, the year of payment. The government successfully argued for 1916 accrual. (Why was the government arguing for an *earlier* deduction in *Anderson*?)

Applying the "all events" test to deductions is as difficult as applying that test to determine when income accrues, especially when there are doubts about whether and how much the taxpayer will owe. Many cases were very tolerant of the taxpayer's claim that the legal liability was fixed and the amount determinable with reasonable accuracy. Some of these cases, allowing a deduction, dealt with obligations to a group of employees, even though the ultimate payee was in doubt: *see, e.g., Lukens Steel Co. v. Commissioner*, 442 F.2d 1131 (3d Cir. 1971) (employer's obligation to contribute to Supplemental Unemployment Compensation plan, which would eventually be paid to some employees); *Kaiser Steel Corp. v. United States*, 717 F.2d 1304 (9th Cir. 1983) (estimated reserve to pay Workers Compensation claims to employees after injury occurred but before a claim had been filed).

Then the Supreme Court decided the *General Dynamics* case, which appeared to make it more difficult to find that the "legal liability" prong of the all events test had been satisfied.

UNITED STATES v. GENERAL DYNAMICS CORP.
United States Supreme Court
481 U.S. 239 (1987)

MR. JUSTICE MARSHALL delivered the opinion of the Court.

Beginning in October 1972, General Dynamics became a self-insurer with regard to its medical care plans. Instead of continuing to purchase insurance from outside carriers, it undertook to pay medical claims out of its own funds, while continuing to employ private carriers to administer the medical care plans.

To receive reimbursement of expenses for covered medical services, respondent's employees submit claims forms to employee benefits personnel, who verify that the treated persons were eligible under the applicable plan as of the time of treatment. Eligible claims are then forwarded to the plan's administrators. Claims processors review the claims and approve for payment those expenses that are covered under the plan.

Because the processing of claims takes time, and because employees do not always file their claims immediately, there is a delay between the provision of medical services and payment by General Dynamics. To account for this time lag, General Dynamics established reserve accounts to reflect its liability for medical care received, but still not paid for, as of December 31, 1972. It estimated the amount of those reserves with the assistance of its former insurance carriers. . . .

It is fundamental to the "all events" test that, although expenses may be deductible before they have become due and payable, liability must first be firmly established. . . .

We think that this case . . . involves a mere estimate of liability based on events that have not occurred before the close of the taxable year, and therefore the proposed deduction does not pass the "all events" test. We disagree with the legal conclusion of the courts below that the last event necessary to fix the taxpayer's liability was the receipt of medical care by covered individuals. A person covered by a plan could only obtain payment for medical services by filling out and submitting a health expense benefits claim form. Employees were informed that submission of satisfactory proof of the charges claimed would be necessary to obtain payment under the plans. General Dynamics was thus liable to pay for covered medical services only if properly documented claims forms were filed. Some covered individuals, through oversight, procrastination, confusion over the coverage provided, or fear of disclosure to the employer of the extent or nature of the services received, might not file claims for reimbursement to which they are plainly entitled. Such filing is not a mere technicality. It is crucial to the establishment of liability on the part of the taxpayer. . . .

This is not to say that the taxpayer was unable to forecast how many claims would be filed for medical care received during this period, and estimate the liability that would arise from those claims. Based on actuarial data, General Dynamics may have been able to make a reasonable estimate of how many claims would be filed for the last quarter of 1972. But that alone does not justify a deduction. . . .

General Dynamics did not show that its liability as to any medical care claims was firmly established as of the close of the 1972 tax year, and is therefore entitled to no deduction. The judgment of the Court of Appeals is reversed.

COMMENT

The dissent argued that this case was indistinguishable from *United States v. Hughes Properties, Inc.*, 476 U.S. 593 (1986), where an accrual method casino operator was allowed to deduct amounts guaranteed for payment on "progressive" slot machines but not yet won by a playing patron. The jackpot on a progressive slot machine increases as more money is gambled and, under Nevada law, a casino operator is prohibited from reducing the jackpot amount. The Court held that all events had occurred to determine the liability despite the fact that the jackpot might not be won for as long as four years. The fact that the casino might go out of business, lose its license, or go bankrupt was irrelevant, because these occurrences are always potential threats to payment of an accrued debt and do not prevent accrual.

The dissent also dismissed the majority's emphasis on the fact that no liability arose until the employee filed a medical claim, viewing the failure to file a claim as a " 'merely formal contingenc[y], or [one] highly improbable under the known facts,' that this Court has viewed as insufficient to preclude accrual and deductibility." Indeed, in *Anderson*, the deductible tax accrued prior to assessment; and in *Continental Tie*, income accrued when "what remained was mere administrative procedure to ascertain the amount to be paid." Similarly, in *General Dynamics*, the dissenters argued that "the filing and processing of a claim is purely routine and ministerial, and in the nature of a formal contingency. . . ."

[2]   The Problem and Possible Solutions

We could dwell on accrued deduction cases dealing with when liability for an obligation is fixed and when the amount can be determined with reasonable accuracy, but statutory changes in 1984 have dramatically reduced the significance of the dispute. The legislative action was prompted by two concerns.

1. *Estimation errors.* First, there were administrative difficulties in estimating accrued deductions.

2. *Deduction exceeds present value.* Second, absent specific legislation, accrued amounts do not have to be discounted to present value. *See Burnham Corp. v. Commissioner*, 90 T.C. 953 (1988), *aff'd*, 878 F.2d 86 (2d Cir. 1989) (government concedes that the "clearly reflect income" requirement in § **446(b)** does not require discounting to present value).

Occasionally, courts held that a large payment due far in the future could not be accrued prior to payment, relying on the requirement that an accounting method must "clearly reflect income." These courts were undoubtedly influenced by concern over the difference between face amount and present value. *See Mooney Aircraft, Inc. v. United States*, 420 F.2d 400 (5th Cir. 1969) (no current accrual of debt due 15 years later, because it would create a mismatch between income and expenses and might never be paid, despite the fixed liability); *Ford Motor Co. v. Commissioner*, 102 T.C. 87 (1994) (taxpayer cannot, in 1980, deduct $504,000 due 42 years later; the present value of the obligation is only $141,124; the current value of the deduction, assuming a 40% tax rate, was $201,600, an amount in excess of the present value).

There are also a few specific statutory provisions separately identifying present value, not only for reporting income but also for limiting deductions. *See, e.g.*, § **467(d)** (deduction of deferred rental obligations over $250,000 limited to present value). However, these specific provisions do not deal with the general problem of accruing deductions when the estimates of future payment are excessive and are not discounted for present value.

———

Before you read about the 1984 statutory "solution" to the general problem of accruing debts paid in the future, consider the different times at which future obligations might be deducted. Assume an obligation to pay $121 in year 2, and 10% interest rates. Financially, present value in year 0 is $100, with $10 and $11 interest accruing in years 1 and 2. Here are three deduction possibilities:

	Year 0	Year 1	Year 2
Method 1	-121		
Method 2			-121
Method 3	-100	-10	-11

Method 1 is too generous. It allows a future debt to be deducted in year 0, without discounting.

Method 3 is the theoretically accurate method. It discounts the future debt to present value, deducting present value in year 0, and deducting interest as it accrues annually. But there is still the administrative problem of accurately estimating the future debt on which to compute present value.

Method 2 defers the deduction until year 2, the year of payment. This is too severe, compared to method 3, but the statute (discussed below) often adopts this approach. By waiting until payment, the law solves the administrative and taxpayer manipulation problems that arise when estimating future expenses. But it defers the deduction for too long, compared to the correct method 3.

[3] Statutory and Regulatory Solutions — Economic Performance

The 1984 statutory solution specifies that the all events test is not satisfied any *earlier* than "*economic performance.*" § 461(h). This will moot most disputes about whether "all events" have occurred, because economic performance usually takes place *after* all events could possibly have occurred to justify the deduction.

1. *Payment to creditor.* For many liabilities, economic performance occurs only when payment is made to the person to whom the liability is owed. The code so states for Workers Compensation and tort liability. § 461(h)(2)(C) (overriding the *Kaiser Steel* case, *supra*, which permitted accrual of an estimated reserve for Workers Compensation liability). The Regulations expand the payment require- ment to include many other liabilities, including those for breach of contract, violation of law, rebates, awards, prizes, taxes, and jackpots (overriding *Hughes Properties* regarding jackpots, discussed in *General Dynamics*, *supra*). **Treas. Reg. § 1.461-4(g)(2-8)**.

"Payment" generally occurs only when: (1) the payor has made the kind of cash payment that would support a deduction by a cash basis taxpayer (this excludes giving a note); *and* (2) the *payee* has actually or constructively received the payment. **Treas. Reg. § 1.461-4(g)(1)(i), (ii)(A-B)**.

This "payment" rule is Method 2, above — postponing the deduction until $121 is paid in year 2.

2. *Payment to third party.* Under the rules outlined so far, economic performance does *not* occur when a taxpayer makes a payment to a third party to be held for future payment to the creditor. Such third parties might include a trust, escrow holder, or court-administered fund. **Treas. Reg. § 1.461-4(g)(1)(i)**. This is a puzzling rule. If the debtor has irrevocably committed the present value of the future debt by making payment to a third party, there is no uncertainty regarding either the amount or fact of payment. Consequently, the amount paid (and therefore the deduction) is not likely to exceed present value. Why shouldn't that present value be deductible when paid to a third party?

This question also occurred to Congress and has produced § 468B. Payments to "designated settlement funds" — defined as *court*-established funds to extinguish tort liabilities — are deductible at the time of the payment. In addition, the Regulations under § 468B define as economic performance (and therefore allow a deduction for) payments to "qualified settlement funds," which are a broader category than the statutorily defined "designated settlement funds" in three respects. First, these qualified funds include those created by government order (not limited to court-established funds) — e.g., they would include judicially enforceable arbitration awards and administrative awards. Second, these qualified funds can extinguish liabilities for breach of contract or for violations of law (including environmental laws), not just tort liability. **Treas. Reg. § 1.468B-1(a), (c)(1, 2), (e)**. Third, unlike "designated settlement" funds, "qualified settlement funds" can be used when liabilities are contested.

Both types of fund are taxable on their investment income at § 1(e) rates.

Notice that the deduction for payments to these funds is not as generous as Method 3, discussed earlier, where the taxpayer with a $121 year-2 obligation could accrue a deduction for the present value of $100 in year 0 and the $10 and $11 interest obligations in years 1 and 2. Unlike Method 3, the fund is taxed on its investment income. If a taxpayer wants to fund a year 2 payment of $121 with a year-0 deductible payment, it must contribute more than $100 to produce $121 in year 2 because the investment income is taxed each year.

3. *Structured settlements.* The rules about payments to a third party do not eliminate the favorable treatment of certain "structured settlements," in which money is paid to an insurance company to fund future payments to discharge a tort liability. If the money is paid to the insurance company to finance the discharge of a tort liability arising from physical injury or physical sickness, a debtor is (in effect) allowed to use Method 3 (deduction for $100 in year 0 and deduction for $10 interest in years 1 and 2). The mechanism producing this result is the treatment of the tort defendant's payment to an insurance company as "economic performance," *and* the insurance company's deduction of the income earned on the structured settlement fund that is committed to paying off the plaintiff's tort claim. § 130; **Treas. Reg. § 1.461-6(a)**.

4. *Exception for recurring items.* **Section 461(h)(3)** permits the deduction of debt in the accrual year (without waiting for economic performance), if: (1) the debt is a "recurring item" paid "soon" after the end of the accrual year; *and* if: (2) the item is: (a) not "material"; or (b) accrual would more properly match expenses and income. ("Soon" refers to the earlier of a "reasonable period" after the close of the accrual year or 8½ months after the close of that year.) The Regulations give this example: the deduction in year 1 of an obligation accrued that year to refund the purchase price to dissatisfied consumers who register their claims before the end of the year, as long as they receive the refund before September 15 of year 2. **Treas. Reg. § 1.461-5(e) (Example 1)**.

5. *Remember — Other accounting rules still apply.* These rules about economic performance state that a deduction will not occur any *earlier* than economic performance. They do not supersede other rules postponing deductions, such as a requirement that an expenditure be added to basis. Economic performance regarding accrued debt will not support deduction of a capital expenditure or inventory cost prior to the time when such capital expenditures or inventory costs are deductible.

TAXES OTHER THAN INDIVIDUAL INCOME TAXES

Part I dealt with the income tax on individuals, which has until recently been considered the fairest United States tax. But the individual income tax has become riddled with so many special tax breaks that it has lost whatever coherence it once had as a fair method of raising revenue. In addition, the tax administration is viewed as either too burdensome on taxpayers or too easy on the rich, both of which undermine faith in how the tax law is applied. These doubts about the income tax justify taking a closer look at other taxes in an introductory tax course. In addition, the beginning student should have an awareness of some of the income tax problems that arise in more complex settings — such as entity and international taxation.

This Part deals with the following:

— Part II-A: Taxation of property
  — Property tax
  — Estate and gift tax
— Part II-B: Payroll taxes
  — Social security taxes
— Part II-C: Taxes on consumption
  — Sales tax
  — Tax on value added
  — Consumption tax
— Part II-D: Entity taxation
  — Pass-through entities: Partnerships, Trusts, and Estates
  — Corporate income tax

— Part II-E: Multi-jurisdictional issues
  — International taxation
  — Interstate taxation

Consideration of these issues in an introductory course cannot substitute for the more intensive study that occurs in courses devoted to these revenue sources — viz., state and local taxation (sales and property taxes; and interstate taxation issues); a specialized estate and gift tax course; one or more specialized courses in corporate and partnership taxation; and one or more specialized international tax courses. But an introductory course can explore the basic themes that underlie these taxes and lay the groundwork for further study.

Part II-A

TAXATION OF PROPERTY

This Part discusses the taxation of property in the United States. Chapter 26 deals with the property tax, which is now primarily a local tax on real property. Chapter 27 deals with the estate and gift tax, which is imposed on the transfer of all types of wealth.

Chapter 26

PROPERTY TAX

§ 26.01 HISTORICAL NOTE

At one time, a tax on property seemed the fairest and the easiest to administer, because land and buildings were the dominant forms of wealth. Property taxes reached a tax base that was owned by the most well-off part of the society and tax assessors did not have trouble locating the property. Consequently, most states in the nineteenth century relied heavily on the property tax.

However, nineteenth-century state property taxes applied to all property — real and personal, tangible and intangible. At least that was what the law usually said. And, as personal property became a more significant part of personal wealth, the property tax became harder to administer fairly. Personal property was harder to locate than real estate, especially in the case of intangible property (such as stocks and bonds), which was becoming an increasingly important source of wealth.

Consequently, the states yielded the property tax base to local governments and the property tax on individuals became almost exclusively a tax on real property. The property tax has gone from being the major state tax around 1900 (more than 50% of state tax revenue) to providing around 2% of state revenues today. At the local level, the property tax produces about 60% of tax revenues. There are now only two major categories of personal property subject to a property tax — tangible personal property owned by businesses, and consumer durables whose ownership by individuals must be registered (such as cars and boats).

There is some state-to-state variation; a few states rely more heavily on state property taxes. For example, in Montana, Washington and Wyoming, which do not have income or sales taxes, a state property tax produces more than 10% of state revenue.

The property tax has retained its position in local taxation for two major reasons: (1) it is easy for local tax administrators to find taxable real property; and (2) it is hard for the taxpayer to move the property out of the jurisdiction (although businesses and individuals can often choose where to locate and might consider property taxes in making that decision). Property taxes also seem to have a closer link to benefits for local residents — for example, schools — although property taxpayers in the jurisdiction will not routinely get fair value for taxes paid.

In recent years, polls indicate that a substantial minority of individuals consider the property tax to be the most unfair of all taxes. One possible reason is that, unlike sales and income taxes, which are collected periodically, property taxpayers receive a large bill once a year. Many states have therefore provided some relief: (1) limiting the growth of local property taxes; (2) providing localities with assistance in the form of state financial aid to replace lost property tax revenue (often financed by an increase in sales taxes); and/or (3) taking over some services that had been provided at the local level.

Property taxes have never been a major feature of the federal tax landscape because they are direct taxes and the federal government is required to apportion direct taxes by population. This requirement usually imposes insuperable political obstacles to their passage, although property taxes were occasionally used by the federal government in the late eighteenth and early nineteenth centuries.

§ 26.02 COMPUTING THE TAX

Tax equals the tax base times the tax rate. The property tax rate, however, is a misleading figure. It is determined *after* deciding how much revenue the taxing jurisdiction needs, based on property values. Once you know two of the three items in the taxing formula (tax = tax rate times tax base), the third item is a residual figure. Thus, if the taxing jurisdiction has a budget requiring $1 million in revenue and the property value equals $10 million, the tax rate is 10%. Lower values necessarily result in higher rates — for example, $5 million in value requires a 20% rate to produce $1 million in revenue. In other words, a high tax rate does not necessarily mean a higher tax payment.

The fact that the tax rate is a residual figure masks the potential for unequal treatment. Two taxpayers with equal real property values that are assessed at different percentages of real value will be treated unequally. For example, if two taxpayers own property worth $6 million, but are assessed at $3 million and $4.5 million, a 10% tax rate on these two properties results in an effective tax rate of 5% and 7.5% respectively ($300,000/$6,000,000 and $450,000/$6,000,000). As we will see, unequal valuation can occur between types of property (for example, homeowners, commercial and industrial property, and farmers), or within classes of property (for example, some homeowners are taxed at 50% of fair market value and others at 75%). These inequalities can be the result of legislation or administrative action.

The potential for tax rates to mislead also arises under the income tax. For example, if two income taxpayers have $100,000 taxable income and pay a $25,000 tax, their effective tax rates vary if their "real" incomes are $100,000 and $200,000 — their effective tax rates are 25% and 12.5%, respectively. As with the property tax, these disparities can be the result of conscious legislative choice or administrative shortcomings. Usually, disparities in the income tax are the result of explicit (if not well-publicized) legislative choices — for example, percentage depletion for the oil and gas industry; faster depreciation or expensing for timber and other industries; and exclusion of certain employee fringe benefits. Disparities arising from administrative choices are less common, although they exist. The administrative practice of not taxing the value of bargain purchases by employees favored the retail industry long before it was ratified by legislation; and the administrative decision not to tax frequent flyer benefits helps employees who can keep those benefits when they fly on business paid for by employers — *see* Chapter 7.02[C][8].

§ 26.03   VALUATION DISPARITIES

[A]   Full Value vs. Fractional Assessment

Many state constitutions and statutes specify that property should be assessed at fair market value, although this requirement is widely disregarded. Other states require assessment at some specified fractional percentage of fair market value. Yet another group of states specify only that the assessment of property tax shall be "uniform," which implies permission to vary from full value assessment while adhering to some unspecified but uniform fractional assessment.

[B]   Fractional Assessment Varies Among and Within Classes

Some state constitutions and statutes explicitly permit variation in the assessment percentage among classes of property, such as homes, farms, and commercial or industrial property. Sometimes, the state constitution permits the legislature to adopt "exemptions," but does not specify which classes of property are eligible; homeowners and farmers are frequent beneficiaries of these legislative provisions. Inter-class disparity can also be the result of administrative practice, without explicit legal sanction.

Valuation disparities also occur within classes. These variations can be more or less systematic — among identifiable subclasses, such as overvaluing homes in poor areas or undervaluing homes in older residential neighborhoods. Or it can occur because of administrative difficulties, such as the lag time in the revaluation of property or the inherent difficulty in determining value.

[C]   Why Is Fractional Assessment So Common?

Fractional assessment is common for a number of reasons.

[1]   Intra-Unit Variation

Local assessors sometimes undervalue property when they work for a smaller government unit than the one that fixes the tax rate in an effort to shift tax burdens to other government units. For example, assume that the taxing county requires $1 million in revenue. The value in each of two townships within the county is $10 million but their assessed value is $6 and $4 million respectively. A 10% tax rate will yield $600,000 and $400,000 revenue from each township, even though real values are equal.

[2]   Increased State Aid

States often provide financial aid to poorer local communities (such as school districts) based on assessed property values; lower value therefore increases state aid. This gives local taxing districts an incentive to understate value. States usually respond to this ploy by setting up Equalization Boards to identify the assessment ratios used in each taxing district and adjust their aid formulas accordingly. Taxpayers who challenge unequal tax assessment practices that depart from state equalization standards are sometimes permitted to use those standards as evidence of nonuniform taxation, but this evidence is not conclusive.

[3] Tax Preferences

Fractional assessment might implement social or economic policy, by encouraging homeownership or business investment or by helping farmers — as long as other property is not assessed at the same percentage of value. These policies not only influence legislatures, but also the tax administration.

Somewhat more invidiously, taxpayers with political clout but without sound policy support might be underassessed — for example, tax assessors might favor permanent residents over vacationers with a second home. In addition, assessors might distinguish among racial, ethnic, or poorer neighborhoods — for example, it is rumored that the Irish community in Boston is underassessed.

A more explicit way to encourage local business is a legislatively sanctioned tax abatement program for a period of time after a taxpayer starts a business. Sometimes, the tax break must be used to finance development of the new business property — referred to as "tax increment" financing. These tax breaks are often inefficient, especially if the taxpayer ends up closing the business when the property comes on the tax rolls, without having to reimburse the local taxing district.

[4] Inertia

Low assessment ratios are often the result of inertia — the inability of the tax administration to catch up with out-of-date results. First, in the early years of property tax assessment, assessors took it upon themselves to compensate for the fact that a lot of personal property (bonds, stock, tangible household goods) was not taxed as a practical matter. Lower valuation of real estate injected some rough-and-ready fairness into the system.

Second, there is a lag time in updating assessments. Inadequate funding makes it extremely difficult for the tax assessors to keep valuation current and, in a rising market, this results in overassessment of property that has recently been sold. In addition, the tendency for politically popular tax breaks to persist prevents these old assessments from being raised too much.

[5] Who Are the Assessors?

Tax assessors often lack sufficient training and adequate compensation. Given the difficulty of valuing property (discussed in Chapter 26.06 below), it is unreasonable to expect too much. States sometimes try to make up for this shortcoming by using equalization boards to fix assessment discrepancies (not just to assure fairness in the distribution of state financial aid), but the impact of these boards has been mixed. Some states hire professional appraisers to do the job — again, with mixed results.

[6] Difficulty in Getting a Taxpayer Remedy

Taxpayers are often unaware of valuation discrepancies, especially when they are already taxed at less than full value — albeit at a higher percentage of real value than other properties. It is also very costly for taxpayers to make the case that assessment rates are nonuniform. A lot of data about the assessment of other properties must be gathered and it is hard to prove the correct value in order to show that the taxpayer's property has been overtaxed.

Some states reject a taxpayer remedy, unless the assessment error is more than a certain minimum percentage of the average assessment ratio for the taxing unit; for example, if the average assessment ratio for the unit is 50%, an overassessment might have to be more than 10% over that ratio (that is, over 60%).

Some states insisted that the only remedy for unequal valuation was raising the value of undervalued property, not lowering the value of the taxpayer's excess valuation. However, the U.S. Supreme Court held that limiting the remedy to raising the value of undervalued property was unconstitutional. *Hillsborough v. Cromwell*, 326 U.S. 620 (1946); *Sioux City Bridge Co. v. Dakota County*, 260 U.S. 441 (1923).

A recent technique to encourage fairer assessments (adopted in New Orleans) allows property owners to access information over the Internet about the property taxes owed by other taxpayers. This may not be enough to encourage people to go to court, but it may have a chastening effect on administrators when they assess taxes.

§ 26.04 STATE LAW ABOUT NONUNIFORM TAXATION

[A] Full Value

New York was not unusual in its legal requirement of assessment at full value. But it was unusual in trying to judicially enforce that requirement. In the following case, the taxpayer made a direct assault on the system of fractional valuation, refusing to claim either overvaluation or unequal treatment in the assessment of her property. She relied only on the state's legal mandate that "[a]ll real property in each assessing unit shall be assessed at the full value thereof."

HELLERSTEIN v. ASSESSOR OF THE TOWN OF ISLIP
New York Court of Appeals
332 N.E.2d 279 (N.Y. 1975)

WACHTLER, J.: . . .

[Editor — The court first notes the "ancient lineage" of the state property tax law.]

Section 306 of the Real Property Tax Law has an ancient lineage. In 1788 the New York Legislature directed "the assessors of each respective city, town, and place in every county of this State (to) make out a true and exact list of the names of all the freeholders and inhabitants and opposite the name of every such person shall set down the real value of all his or her whole estate real and personal as near as they can discover the same". . . . The term "full value" first appeared in [an 1829 law]: "All real and personal estate liable to taxation, the value of which shall not have been specified by affidavit of the person taxed, shall be estimated by the assessor at its full value, as they would themselves be willing to receive the same in payment of a just debt due from a solvent debtor. . . ."

Although the statute is one of the oldest in the State there does not appear to be any extant legislative history indicating what the full value requirement was intended to accomplish. And despite the fact that the custom of fractional assessments appears to be at least as old as the statute; it has prompted very little litigation. . . .

[Editor — The court then rejected the lower court's reliance on cases that had permitted fractional assessments — specifically, *C. H. O. B. Assocs. v. Board of Assessors of County of Nassau*, 209 N.E.2d 820 (N.Y. 1965), and its progeny — stating that fractional assessment had not been sanctioned by longstanding practice.]

One of the most peculiar aspects of the township's case is the narrowness of their defense of the practice of fractional assessments. They are satisfied to rest on the theory "thus it has been, thus it always must be", without making any effort to explain how the custom began, whether it serves any useful purpose, and what would happen if the assessors complied, or were made to comply, with the strict letter of the law. Our own cases do not discuss these points; but they have been extensively reviewed and debated by scholarly commentators and by the courts in other jurisdictions.

The vast majority of States require assessors, either by statute or constitutional prescription, to assess at full value, true value, market value, or some equivalent standard. Two States have expressly provided by statute that this requires assessment at 100% of value (see 13 Ariz. Rev. Stat. Ann., § 42-227; California Revenue & Taxation Code, §§ 401, 408). Several States have specifically authorized fractional assessments, and this seems to be the modern trend. In 1917, there were four States in this latter category; and, as of 1962, 15 States had enacted legislation providing for fractional assessments, either at a fixed percentage or according to local option (Note, 75 Harvard L. Rev. 1374, 1377, n.28).

Where full value is required, the standard has been almost universally disregarded. A 1957 study by the United States Census Bureau placed the average assessment ratio in the country at 30% of actual value.

No one seems to know exactly how the practice of fractional assessment began. In an early case the Supreme Court suggested that: "If we look for the reason for this common consent to substitute a custom for the positive rule of the statute, it will probably be found in the difficulty of subjecting personal property, and especially invested capital, to the inspection of the assessor and the grasp of the collector. The effort of the land-owner, whose property lies open to view, which can be subjected to the lien of a tax not to be escaped by removal, or hiding, to produce something like actual equality of burden by an underevaluation of his land, has led to this result" (*Cummings v. National Bank*, 101 U.S. 153, 163, 25 L. Ed. 903 (1880)).

This may well explain the origin of the rule, but it does not account for its remarkable powers of endurance, especially in a State like New York, which has removed personal property from the tax rolls. Its survival depends on other factors none of which are particularly commendable.

Bonbright, in his treatise (Valuation of Property), lists "several reasons for the persistence of partial valuation. Gullible taxpayers associate a larger valuation with a larger tax, or at any rate are less contentious about a relatively excessive assessment if it does not exceed their estimate of true value. The ability to maintain a stable rate and to increase revenue by tampering with the tax base — a change which calls for less publicity and less opposition — is naturally desired by the party in power. Occasionally, partial valuation is intended as a substitute for a varied system of rates; i.e., different forms of property, while nominally taxed at the same rate, are in fact taxed at differing rates by being assessed at different proportions of full values. Undervaluation of realty is sometimes justified as compensating for the elusiveness of personalty; but even if the latter is assessed fully when caught, experience has shown that the net result is to furnish an additional incentive for evasion. Another inducement to undervaluation has been that, since the state relies on the property tax for part of its revenue, the county assessors seek to lighten their constituents' burden at the expense of the rest of the state by assessing the local property at a lower percentage than is applied elsewhere. This process has often resulted in a competition between counties as to which could most nearly approach the limit of nominal valuation. With the increasing trend in some states toward reserving the property tax for the support of the local communities, and in other states toward the creation of state boards of equalization, the enthusiasm for percentage valuation has been dampened."

Most of these considerations have probably served to perpetuate the custom in New York; but there may be other factors at work. This State, of course, does not depend on real property taxes as a source of State revenue. However, the State does supply financial aid to communities based primarily on assessed valuation, and this undoubtedly furnishes "another inducement to undervaluation." The activities of the State Equalization Board are meant to correct this problem but as one commentator observes "possibly local tax officials believe that there is no harm in trying."

[Editor — The court then notes that one of the major vices of fractional assessment is that the percentage of undervaluation is rarely known, which makes it difficult to determine whether there is uniformity in the proportion or whether, through incompetence, favoritism, or corruption of the assessors, some portions of the taxpaying body are bearing the others' burdens, as between either individuals or local groups.]

In sum, for nearly 200 years our statutes have required assessments to be made at full value and for nearly 200 years assessments have been made on a percentage basis throughout the State. The practice has time on its side and nothing else. It has been tolerated by the Legislature, criticized by the commentators and found by our own court to involve a flagrant violation of the statute. Nevertheless, the practice has become so widespread and been so consistently followed that it has acquired an aura of assumed legality. . . .

[Editor — But the court insisted on enforcing the full value mandate and refused to "indorse th[is] practice or withhold relief insofar as future assessments are concerned." Still, it refused to create "disorder and confusion" by striking down *past* assessments, stating as follows.]

Future compliance with the full value requirement will undoubtedly cause some disruption of existing procedures, but time should cure the problem. The difficulty of transition is sufficient reason to defer relief, but not to deny it. The petitioner thus is entitled to an order directing the township to make future assessments at full value as required by section 306 of the Real Property Tax Law. The order, however, should not go into effect immediately. To make this transition, the township should be allowed a reasonable time, but not later than December 31, 1976. In the interim assessments may be made in accordance with the existing practice and any tax levies, liens, foreclosures, or transfers based on such assessments shall not be subject to challenge for failing to comply with section 306 of the Real Property Tax Law.

The politics of property taxation eventually undermined the *Hellerstein* decision. The lower courts and later legislation extended the time for compliance. And, eventually, the legislature permitted variation among types of properties and prevented a shifting of the tax burden to homeowners, who had been routinely undertaxed. No wonder taxpayers are reluctant to challenge assessment practices in court. (The petitioner in the *Hellerstein* case was a close relative of the authors of a casebook dealing with state and local taxation.)

[B]   Unequal Fractional Assessments and State Uniformity Clauses

In *Hellerstein*, the objection to fractional assessment was broad — the failure to assess at full value. The taxpayer did not object to unequal fractional assessments of different classes of property, such as residential, farm, commercial, and industrial property. The more common complaint is about inequality rather than fractional assessment. State constitutions vary as to whether they forbid or permit nonuniform taxation. In addition, some state legislation or judicial indifference to assessment practices permit unequal assessments (sometimes despite what the state constitution says) as a way of providing economic incentives or preferences for certain types of property ownership. Farms and residential housing are frequent beneficiaries of nonuniform taxation.

[1]   An Example

In *Anderson's Red & White Store v. Kootenai County*, 215 P.2d 815 (Idaho 1950), a complaint by 165 merchants stated that their merchandise had been assessed at 20% of value and all other property at 10% of value. The taxpayers got the court's attention, but it should be apparent how costly and time-consuming the legal victory must have been, requiring determination of the respective assessment ratios of merchandise in different businesses (as well as engaging in more litigation after a remand). Notice also that the discrepancy was not between large classes of property owners who might be expected to make strong policy arguments in favor of preferential treatment or at least to have the political clout to get such treatment from the legislature — such as homeowners and farmers. The court stated:

> While the courts will not attempt to correct mere mistakes or errors of judgment on the part of the assessor or board of equalization, where intentional, systematic discrimination occurs, either through undervaluation or through over-valuation of one property or class of property as compared to other property in the county, the courts will grant relief. . . .

> . . . [Under certain circumstances, the assessor] must assess all property at the same proportion of its market or other actual current value. . . . Without explanation the [taxpayers'] assessments were fixed at 20% of [] value, while according to the testimony of those who qualified as experts other property was assessed at 10% of current market values. If this disparity is not reasonably justified, then the constitutional requirement of uniformity has been violated. . . .

> The trial court did not determine upon what relative basis property, other than merchandise, was assessed. This finding is essential to a determination of the ultimate question of discrimination and the extent thereof. Accordingly, the judgment is reversed and the cause remanded with directions to the court to find upon what relative basis other property in the county was assessed, and, if found to be systematically undervalued as compared to appellants' property, or if appellants' property is found to be systematically overvalued, compared to the other property, to reduce appellants' assessments by such amounts as will equalize them with the assessments on other property, or as nearly so as the evidence will permit.

[2] Doing the Math

One way to get a court's attention is to use a mathematical measure of the variation of assessed property values around the median assessment — known as the coefficient of dispersion. The larger the coefficient of dispersion the more of a red flag to the court that something is not working right.

For example, the numbers 2,5,8 and 4,5,6 have the same median (that is, 5)[1], but the former set of numbers has a much greater dispersion. Here is the formula:

[1] add the differences from the median for the numbers in the group;

[2] then divide that sum by the number of examples in the group; and

[3] then divide the result in [2] by the median.

In the two examples, the coefficients of dispersion are, respectively:

For the 2,5,8 example: .4, because [6/3 = 2.0; 2.0/5 = .4]; and

For the 4,5,6 example: .133, because [2/3 = .667; .667/5 = .133].

---

[1] The median is the midpoint of all the numbers, not the average. The median is the preferred figure because it avoids the distortion caused by extremes. For example, a tall basketball player entering the room can significantly change the average, but will have little effect on the median height of the group.

Obviously, the 2,5,8 pattern has a higher coefficient of dispersion.

As will often be the case, the issue will not be whether or not to use the coefficient of dispersion, but whether the correct data have been used. In *Waccubuc Construction Corp. v. Assessor of the Town of Lewisboro*, 166 A.D.2d 523 (N.Y. App. Div. 2d 1990), the court stated:

> Generally, a coefficient of dispersion is a statistical comparison of "the closeness of assessment ratios of individual parcels to each other." A high coefficient of dispersion indicates a high degree of variance with respect to the assessment ratios under consideration. A low coefficient of dispersion indicates a low degree of variance. In other words, a low coefficient of dispersion indicates that the parcels under consideration are being assessed at close to an equal rate.

> [The taxpayer's expert] opined that in 1983, the coefficient of dispersion with respect to the defendant's assessment roll was "too high". However, the defendant's assessor [], using essentially the same raw data used by [the taxpayer's expert], arrived at a coefficient of dispersion that was considerably less than the [taxpayer's] number.

> The [lower court] credited [the assessor's] testimony and discredited [taxpayer's expert.] We agree. . . . [Taxpayer's expert] arbitrarily eliminated from his calculations those assessment ratios that he felt were "out of gear". Additionally, [he] did not factor the effect of a volatile real estate market into his calculations, even though he acknowledged that this failure could have impacted upon the correctness of his result. . . .

Apparently, the expert ("arbitrarily") left out some assessments that should have been included and failed to omit some assessments that reflected a volatile market. What is an example of volatility that produces unreliable information — bank foreclosure during a credit crunch? A recent natural catastrophe? What else?

COMMENT

Another way of to compute whether assessments are too far off-base is the use of a "common level ratio." *See Keebler Co.* v. Board of Revision of Taxes of Phila., 436 A.2d 583 (Pa. 1981). Divide total assessed value by total real value and see whether a significant number of properties diverge from that ratio. For example, assume 100 parcels, each worth $100; total real value is $10,000. Ninety parcels are assessed at 60% of value (90 x 60 = a total of $5,400); 10 parcels are assessed at 20% of value (10 x 20 = a total of $200). Total assessed value is $5,600, or 56% of total real value. The property taxed at 20% of value diverges significantly from the common level ratio of 56%. (Another way of identifying the common level ratio is to average the 60% and 20% ratios, which equals 40%, but that does not take account of the greater number of properties taxed at 60% of value.)

[C]   Permitting Some Nonuniform Tax Preferences — Low Income Taxpayers, Homeowners, and Farmers

[1]   Progressivity; Circuit Breakers

A substantial minority of states legislate what are called "circuit breakers" to help taxpayers with lower incomes, analogous to tax breaks for low income taxpayers under the income tax. A circuit breaker is explicitly tied to the taxpayer's income and is often targeted at farm and residential property. When the tax bill on eligible property exceeds a certain percentage of income, the excess will often be refunded — usually through a credit against income taxes or by direct payment from the state. Some type of circuit breaker may also be available to renters on the theory that the property tax is passed on to them in the form of higher rent. Lower income taxpayers benefit from the circuit breaker because their property taxes (or the percentage of rent deemed equal to property taxes) are more likely to exceed the income threshold.

Sometimes, state courts have to work hard to uphold circuit breakers against the argument that they violate the state constitution's uniformity requirement for property taxes. *State ex rel. Harvey v. Morgan*, 139 N.W.2d 585 (Wis. 1966), upheld a credit with the following characteristics: it was "refundable" — that is, if the credit exceeded the income tax, the taxpayer received money equal to the excess; it was financed from general revenue appropriations; it was only available to persons 65 years of age or over and with income no greater than $3,000; and it was also available to renters as well as property owners.

The doctrinal peg on which the Wisconsin decision relied was that the circuit breaker was not a tax law, but a "relief" law. Therefore, the tax uniformity clause was inapplicable. The court stressed the introductory statutory language — "to provide relief to certain persons 65 years of age and over." This language replaced the introductory language of a statute passed earlier in the session and then repealed — "to provide property tax relief."

The Court's conclusion stressed several factors that were more cogent than the introductory statutory language. These factors related to the overbreadth and underbreadth of the tax breaks in relation to property ownership. First, the tax break was overbroad in helping renters as well as property owners. Second, the tax break was underbroad in helping only aged taxpayers with property interests who had low income (an income redistribution policy). Third, the court stressed the use of general revenue financing, which made property tax relief vulnerable to competing political claims on general revenues and therefore made it less likely that the tax relief was simply a way of shifting property tax burdens to other taxpayers.

[2]   Homestead Exemption or Credit

The tax burden on homeowners is often reduced by exempting some portion of residential value from the tax base or, as in the following Ohio case, giving a credit for some portion of the property tax. Some type of homestead tax break is provided in almost all states. A fixed dollar exemption has the effect of excluding from the tax base a declining percentage of property value as those values increase (that is,

$40,000 is 40% of $100,000 but only 10% of $400,000).

The Ohio credit (equal to 2.5% of the property tax) was upheld in *State ex rel. Swetland v. Kinney*, 402 N.E.2d 542 (Ohio 1980). The Constitution provided:

> Art. XII, § 2 — Land and improvements thereon shall be taxed by uniform rule according to value, except that laws may be passed to reduce taxes by providing for a reduction in value of the homestead of permanently and totally disabled residents and residents sixty-five years of age or older . . . .

However, the state's statutory homestead exemption was not limited to the disabled or the aged, as specified in the Constitution.

The Court stated that "the constitutional requirement of uniformity mandates uniformity in the valuation of the real property and uniformity in the percentage of value which would constitute the property tax base." But it went on to hold that the uniformity clause did not apply to exemptions or partial exemptions (of which this credit was considered an example)! Exemptions were subject only to Article I of the State Constitution, requiring equal protection of the laws. The equal protection standard is a notoriously weak standard when applied to state property taxation. Nonetheless, the court added that a *total* exemption for homestead property might be struck down, because that would place an unreasonable burden on other taxpayers. If you find these doctrinal twists and turns hard to follow, that may be because the court is determined to let popular property tax relief stand, despite what the law might say.

Not every court is so determined to find a way to permit legislation to lower taxes on residential property. In *Hoffman v. Lehnhausen*, 269 N.E.2d 465 (Ill. 1971), the Illinois Supreme Court struck down a tax break for homesteads in the form of a $1,500 reduction in the value of residences owned by taxpayers 65 years or older. This violated a constitutional provision that stated (Art. IX, § 1): "Every person and corporation shall pay a tax in proportion to the value of his, her, or its property." The Illinois Constitution was then changed to permit counties with a population of more than 200,000 to adopt reasonable property tax classifications (Illinois Const., § 4).

§ 26.05 FEDERAL CONSTITUTIONAL RULES

[A] Interstate Issues

When a state tries to prefer its own businesses or residents over those of another state, the federal Due Process and Commerce Clauses are implicated. These issues are discussed in Chapter 35.

[B] Federal Uniformity Clause

Article I, § 8, cl. 1 of the federal Constitution requires that federal taxes be uniform throughout the United States. But this requires only geographic uniformity, not inter- or intra-class uniformity. *United States v. Ptasynski*, 462 U.S. 74 (1983). Moreover, the federal uniformity clause does not apply to state and local taxation. Consequently, federal constitutional protection from unequal property taxation depends on proving a violation of Equal Protection.

[C]   Equal Protection

An Equal Protection claim is very hard to sustain because the courts apply the lax "rationality" standard. For example, in *Lehnhausen v. Lake Shore Auto Parts Co.*, 410 U.S. 356 (1973), the Court held that a state constitutional provision prohibiting a tax on an individual's personal property, but permitting such a tax on corporations, did not violate Equal Protection.

In *Nordlinger v. Hahn*, 505 U.S. 1 (1992). The Supreme Court upheld California's Proposition 13, which was a 1978 ballot initiative amending the California Constitution to impose strict limits on the rate at which real property was taxed and on the rate at which real property assessments could be increased from year to year. The discrimination occurred because these limits did not apply to newly purchased property. In effect, Proposition 13 adopted an "acquisition value" system of taxation rather than "current value" taxation; real property would be assessed at values related to the time of acquisition rather than current market value. The Proposition was labeled, sarcastically, a "welcome stranger" approach, because the newcomer is welcomed to a community with the expectation that he will contribute a larger percentage of support for local government than his settled neighbor who owns a comparable home.

A California court had previously upheld Proposition 13, distinguishing the U.S. Supreme Court's decision in *Allegheny Pittsburgh Coal Co. v. County Comm'n of Webster Cty.*, 488 U.S. 336 (1989), in which the Court had struck down a West Virginia assessor's method of assessment. The West Virginia assessor had assessed recently purchased property on the basis of its purchase price, while making only minor modifications to raise valuation in assessing property that had *not* recently been sold. Recently purchased properties were reassessed and taxed at values between 8 and 35 times the value of properties that had not been sold. The California court concluded that the West Virginia practice was unconstitutional because the assessor had violated a state constitutional requirement of uniform taxation based on current value. By contrast, California voters had explicitly adopted the acquisition cost method of assessment; there was no arbitrary administrative action. The U.S. Supreme Court went on to uphold Proposition 13.

NORDLINGER v. HAHN
United States Supreme Court
505 U.S. 1 (1992)

Mr. Justice Blackmun delivered the opinion of the Court. . . .

The appropriate standard of review is whether the difference in treatment between newer and older owners rationally furthers a legitimate state interest. In general, the Equal Protection Clause is satisfied so long as there is a plausible policy reason for the classification, the legislative facts on which the classification is apparently based rationally may have been considered to be true by the governmental decisionmaker, and the relationship of the classification to its goal is not so attenuated as to render the distinction arbitrary or irrational. This standard is especially deferential in the context of classifications made by complex tax laws. . . .

We have no difficulty in ascertaining at least two rational or reasonable considerations of difference or policy that justify denying petitioner the benefits of her neighbors' lower assessments. First, the State has a legitimate interest in local neighborhood preservation, continuity, and stability. The State, therefore, legitimately can decide to structure its tax system to discourage rapid turnover in ownership of homes and businesses, for example, in order to inhibit displacement of lower income families by the forces of gentrification or of established, "mom-and-pop" businesses by newer chain operations. By permitting older owners to pay progressively less in taxes than new owners of comparable property, the [] assessment scheme rationally furthers this interest.

Second, the State legitimately can conclude that a new owner at the time of acquiring his property does not have the same reliance interest warranting protection against higher taxes as does an existing owner. The State may deny a new owner at the point of purchase the right to "lock in" to the same assessed value as is enjoyed by an existing owner of comparable property, because an existing owner rationally may be thought to have vested expectations in his property or home that are more deserving of protection than the anticipatory expectations of a new owner at the point of purchase. A new owner has full information about the scope of future tax liability before acquiring the property, and if he thinks the future tax burden is too demanding, he can decide not to complete the purchase at all. By contrast, the existing owner, already saddled with his purchase, does not have the option of deciding not to buy his home if taxes become prohibitively high. To meet his tax obligations, he might be forced to sell his home or to divert his income away from the purchase of food, clothing, and other necessities. . . .

Petitioner argues that [Proposition 13] cannot be distinguished from the tax assessment practice found to violate the Equal Protection Clause in *Allegheny Pittsburgh*. . . . But an obvious and critical factual difference between this case and *Allegheny Pittsburgh* is the absence of any indication in *Allegheny Pittsburgh* that the policies underlying an acquisition-value taxation scheme could conceivably have been the purpose for the Webster County tax assessor's unequal assessment scheme. In the first place, Webster County argued that "its assessment scheme is rationally related to its purpose of assessing properties at true current value." Moreover, the West Virginia "Constitution and laws provide that all property of the kind held by petitioners shall be taxed at a rate uniform throughout the State according to its estimated market value," and the Court found "no suggestion" that "the State may have adopted a different system in practice from that specified by statute." . . .

To be sure, the Equal Protection Clause does not demand for purposes of rational-basis review that a legislature or governing decisionmaker actually articulate at any time the purpose or rationale supporting its classification. Nevertheless, this Court's review does require that a purpose may conceivably or "may reasonably have been the purpose and policy" of the relevant governmental decisionmaker. *Allegheny Pittsburgh* was the rare case where the facts precluded any plausible inference that the reason for the unequal assessment practice was to achieve the benefits of an acquisition-value tax scheme. By contrast, [Proposition 13] was enacted precisely to achieve the benefits of an acquisition-value system.

[Editor — In a footnote, the Court insisted that "[i]n finding *Allegheny Pittsburgh* distinguishable, we do not suggest that the protections of the Equal Protection Clause are any less when the classification is drawn by legislative mandate, as in this case, than by administrative action, as in *Allegheny Pittsburgh*. Nor do we suggest that the Equal Protection Clause constrains administrators, as in *Allegheny Pittsburgh*, from violating state law requiring uniformity of taxation of property." In separate opinions, Justices Thomas and Stevens concluded that the *Allegheny Pittsburgh* decision could not be distinguished.]

COMMENTS

1. *State court approaches to "welcome stranger" laws.* States have also addressed the constitutionality of "welcome stranger" laws under their own constitutions. Some states equate their uniformity requirement with the lax Equal Protection standard and uphold such laws. *See In re Property of One Church Street, City of Burlington*, 565 A.2d 1349, 1352 (Vt. 1989); *American Mobilehome Ass'n v. Dolan*, 553 P.2d 758, 762 (Colo. 1976); *State ex rel. Jones v. Nolte*, 165 S.W.2d 632, 636 (Mo. 1942).

But the state of Washington held that a "welcome stranger" law violated the state constitution's uniformity requirement; *Belas v. Kiga*, 959 P.2d 1037 (Wash. 1998). The Washington court refused to read a rational basis exception into the uniformity requirement of the state constitution (analogous to the federal Equal Protection standard), stating: "The only discrepancies in uniformity that will be tolerated are those required by the practical necessities of revaluing property when the program is carried out in an orderly manner and pursuant to a regular plan, and if it is not done in an arbitrary, capricious, or intentionally discriminatory manner."

2. *Revenue stability.* In *USGen New England, Inc. v. Town of Rockingham*, 838 A.2d 927 (Vt. 2003), the owner of hydroelectric power plants challenged a statutory freeze in its property tax values at the 1997 level for tax years 1998-2000. The freeze occurred following the deregulation of the electrical power markets, which (arguably) lowered real property values. The court upheld the freeze, as follows:

> We find that our decision in [an earlier case] controls here. That case involved a taxpayer challenge to a "rolling reappraisal" method of assessment in which every two years the town would reassess only that class of property determined by the State Tax Department to be "most in need" — i.e., where on average there was the greatest percentage discrepancy between the listed value of the properties in the class and their fair market value. The taxpayers argued [] that this "rolling reappraisal" method violated the Proportional Contribution Clause [which imposed the same standard as the federal Equal Protection Clause]. . . . [W]e concluded that the town's actions had a rational basis —"keeping appraisals as

current as possible within the resources available by attacking the worst underassessment problem areas." . . .

The appropriate standard of review is whether the difference in treatment between newer and older owners rationally furthers a legitimate state interest [citing *Nordlinger v. Hahn*, 505 U.S. 1 (1992)]. In general, the Equal Protection Clause is satisfied so long as there is a plausible policy reason for the classification, the legislative facts on which the classification is apparently based rationally may have been considered to be true by the governmental decisionmaker, and the relationship of the classification to its goal is not so attenuated as to render the distinction arbitrary or irrational. This standard is especially deferential in the context of classifications made by complex tax laws. [I]n structuring internal taxation schemes the States have large leeway in making classifications and drawing lines which in their judgment produce reasonable systems of taxation. Based on this deferential standard, we have no problem concluding that the freeze is constitutional. . . .

Here, the State argues that the freeze has a rational basis: ensuring temporary stability of tax revenues in a number of small Vermont towns, in the face of difficulties in determining the fair market value of hydroelectric facilities brought about by the "changing and deregulated utility market." We agree with the trial court that this purpose "is certainly legitimate and important, and is arguably compelling."

3. *Indefinite duration of assessment and varying rates of changes in value; Impact on the poor.* In *Clifton v. Allegheny County*, 969 A.2d 1197 (Pa. 2009), the court dealt with a county's indefinite use of a "stagnant" out-of-date base year market value to assess real property. The court first noted that "absolute equality and perfect uniformity are not required" and that a classification "related to any legitimate state purpose" is permissible. It also stated that the state constitution's Uniformity Clause was generally analyzed in the same way as the Equal Protection Clause of the U.S. Constitution. It then held that the use of a base year did not violate the state constitution's Uniformity Clause "on its face." Consequently, annual reassessments were not required. However, the base market year method, as applied by Allegheny County, did violate the Uniformity Clause because of its indefinite duration and because the municipalities in the county experienced varying rates of appreciation and depreciation over a prolonged period. The court also noted that "lower-value neighborhoods where property values often appreciate at a lower rate than in higher-value neighborhoods" were at a special disadvantage.

§ 26.06 VALUATION METHODS

There are three basic methods of valuing property: (1) sales price; (2) replacement cost minus depreciation; and (3) capitalization of income. Different methods are often considered to be more useful for different types of property. However, it is common for all three methods of valuation to be offered by the litigants, which gives the fact finder a great deal of leeway.

[A]   Sales Price

[1]   Comparable Sales

The "comparable sales" method of valuation is usually used for homes. The problem is to identify comparable property, and then to adjust value up or down for characteristics that make the comparable property less or more valuable than the assessed property — for example, number of bathrooms, floor size, financing of sale, age, and condition, etc. Often, the appraiser uses the median figure of comparable sales to avoid the skewing of results from the impact of outliers on the average or mean value.

Comparable sales are also used as evidence of value for property other than homes. Appellate courts are likely to be very tolerant of how the trial court relies on such evidence. For example, in *Ford Motor Co. v. Township of Edison*, 604 A.2d 580 (N.J. 1992), dealing with an auto assembly plant, the Tax Court had rejected certain evidence of comparable sales. The appellate court thought that this was a mistake, but harmless error. It stated:

> The four excluded sales were of large industrial properties that ranged in size from 819,000 to 1,020,000 square feet; indeed, several were industrial properties in the same geographic area as Ford's property. . . . Ford proffers that the four offered comparables, although not used as automobile-assembly plants, were similar in that they were all large industrial facilities. Its expert had adjusted the comparables for land-to-building ratio, size, time, and condition.

> Had this case been tried to a jury, we would be hard pressed to sustain the exclusion of those comparables from consideration by a jury. Generally speaking, comparable sales include all sales that will lend logical, coherent support if they show "comparable building density ratios, functional similarities, proximity of sale dates to assessing dates, similarity of age, construction, and condition, and in some cases, size." . . .

> In this case, however, although the issue is posed in terms of rejection of the comparables, the qualitative issue is really what weight should have been given to the sales. Although the Tax Court did not extensively review in its opinion the specifics of each sale, the parties did, in the course of the trial. Were we to remand this matter to the Tax Court to consider the weight it might give to those four sales as part of its overall analysis of the market approach as determinative of value, we doubt that the Tax Court's disposition would be altered.

> There were many problems with those sales that would have limited their value to the Tax Court in using the market-data approach. [Editor — The court commented as follows on two of the four sales. (1) The Lily-Tulip sale had substantially more warehouse and less manufacturing space than the Ford property; Lily's electrical capacity was substantially less; its sewage treatment was an on-site package treatment plant, versus Ford's extensively developed pretreatment facilities, including access to public sewers; the Lily facility had two wells, rather than a public water supply; and it had

substantially inferior road access. (2) The property in the Owens-Illinois to Hartz Mountain sale had been a glass-manufacturing facility, had no heating capacity other than from the industrial furnaces, and was severely depreciated.]

In short, the asserted functional dissimilarities and the differences in construction and market conditions lead us to believe that whatever mistake of law might have been made in not considering the sales was for all practical purposes harmless in the context of this litigation.

[2] Highest and Best Use

The relevant comparable sales price is usually for the property at its highest and best use. If an owner is not fully utilizing property, that does not reduce its value to someone else, who will pay for exploiting its full potential. This is not only an equity issue (because the taxpayer could realize the value of the highest and best use through a sale), but is also an economically desirable result because it discourages underutilization of property.

A few states do not follow the highest best use rule. For example, Indiana assesses market value "in use." 2002 Real Property Assessment Manual, p. 2, based on authority granted by **I.C. § 6-1.1-31-6(c)**.

More generally, farms are (by law) often an exception to the highest and best use rule. If farmers want to continue farming the property, the property's value will not be determined based on its use as a shopping center, even if that is its highest and best commercial use. But who is a "farmer"? Florida requires "good faith commercial agricultural use"; *see Roden v. K & K Land Mgt., Inc.*, 368 So. 2d 588 (Fla. 1978). A bona fide farming business is also an issue under the income tax — when farming is alleged to be a hobby — so that net operating losses are not deductible (Chapter 8.09); and when farmers are permitted to use favorable accounting methods (Chapter 23.02[A][2]).

[B] Replacement Cost Minus Depreciation?

[1] "Specialty" Property

The "comparable sales" approach assumes that the goal of the property tax is to rely on market value to determine the property tax base. However, market value is not used as the tax base when property has little or no value on the market because its use is special to its owner and is not readily adaptable to other uses by prospective purchasers. Such property is called a "specialty." In such cases, courts use replacement (or, sometimes, reproduction) cost minus depreciation.

This type of property poses a challenge to the property tax system. It suggests that the property tax is not only concerned with the objective market value of real estate, but with something else as well. The idea seems to be that a taxpayer should not be able to use economic resources to construct real property that retains significant economic value to the taxpayer and then avoid a property tax because no one else will buy it.

The New York Stock Exchange is usually presented as the typical "specialty" property. Its value for property tax purposes was at issue in *People ex rel. New York Stock Exchange Bldg. Co. v. Cantor*, 221 A.D. 193 (N.Y. App. Div. 1927). The taxpayer contended "that the building did not enhance the value of the land," because the "building can only be adequately used by the New York Stock Exchange and not by any one else, not even the other exchanges, therefore, there is no actual market value, and hence the building adds nothing to the value of the land." The court stated:

> . . . [S]ection 6 of the Tax Law provides: "All real and personal property subject to taxation shall be assessed at the full value thereof. . . . " The [taxpayer] makes no reference to this provision of the Tax Law, but relies solely on the language of section 889 of the Greater New York Charter, requiring deputy tax commissioners to assess all taxable property and to furnish to the board of taxes and assessments "the sum for which, in their judgment, each separately assessed parcel of real estate under ordinary circumstances would sell."

> Under the principle which requires that statutes in pari materia must be read together, real property must be assessed at its full value, whether or not there is an ascertainable market value. . . . I do not understand that, under the provisions of the charter, simply because the property cannot be sold under ordinary circumstances, it is therefore to escape taxation. It seems to me that, if the building is of such a character that it cannot be sold except under extraordinary circumstances, it is still the duty of the deputy tax commissioner in the first instance in ascertaining the value of the property, and of the commissioners of taxes in imposing the assessment, to determine its actual value from such material as the circumstances of the case afford.

[2] When to Use Replacement or Reproduction Cost

The court in the *New York Stock Exchange* case goes on to adopt the reproduction-cost-less-depreciation method of valuation, stating:

> If here we take the reproduction cost of the building on the tax day, namely, October 1, 1920, and allow for depreciation, we reach the result that the value of the building was at least the amount for which the tax commissioners have assessed the building, namely, $2,050,000.

The use of reproduction cost is often the wrong figure because no one would spend the money to reproduce an older building with the same materials originally used. More modern and less expensive materials would be used to replace the function of the older building; *replacement* cost is, therefore, the more common standard.

In *American Express Financial Advisors, Inc. v. County of Carver*, 573 N.W.2d 651 (Minn. 1998), however, the court argued that reproduction cost does not necessarily overstate value if the depreciation allowance takes account of functional obsolescence.

American Express also attacks the tax court's use of reproduction cost, rather than replacement cost, in making its cost approach valuation. Replacement cost is the estimated cost to construct a building with an equivalent utility to the building being appraised, at current prices, using modern materials, standards, design, and layout. Reproduction cost, on the other hand, is the estimated cost to construct an exact replica of the subject property using the same materials, standards, design, and layout and embodying all the deficiencies and obsolescence of the subject building. Replacement cost is generally lower and may provide a better indication of current value than reproduction cost because it does not embody obsolescent features which would not be constructed in a new building. However, reproduction cost can be adjusted to account for functional obsolescence through appropriate deductions. Both methods have been used to build cost approaches to value in our courts. Provided that proper deductions for functional obsolescence are made, it is not error to use reproduction cost in estimating value under the cost approach.

[3] "Quirky" Residence

In *Turnley v. City of Elizabeth*, 68 A. 1094 (N.J. 1908), the court struggled with a situation in which a residence contained a number of features that were very costly to the taxpayer but of little value to prospective buyers. The court stated that neither original cost nor the estimated cost of reproduction was the correct standard for valuing this property, but went on to say:

> We are not disposed, however, to give much force to the argument that, because there are very few actual buyers for so costly a residence, the valuation to be placed upon it under the statutory criterion should be correspondingly depreciated. The criterion established by the statute is a hypothetical sale; hence the buyers therein referred to are hypothetical buyers, not actual and existing purchasers. If this be not so, a citizen by the erection of a residence so costly that no one could buy it would escape all taxation, which is obviously not the intent of the Legislature, or the proper interpretation of its statute. Taxation normally bears some relation both to the degree of protection required by the taxpayer and to his ability to contribute to such public burden, as manifested by the permanent improvement of his real property. Mere costliness, therefore, cannot rationally be made the basis of exemption from taxation.

It then reduced the valuation of the residence from $60,000 to $37,500, without explaining how it reached that figure — giving some discount from replacement cost but not fully reducing the value to account for a very small sales market. This suggests that there is some truth to the suggestion that the property tax lacks any clear conceptual foundation. *See generally* Youngman, *Defining and Valuing the Base of the Property Tax*, 58 WASH. L. REV. 713 (1983).

COMMENTS AND QUESTIONS

1. Newspapers reported that the owner of Dell Computers had his eight-bedroom, 21-bathroom, 22,000-square-foot Texas home, with conference room and gym, assessed at around $22 million (its construction cost), even though (he claimed) it would sell for no more than $6. One article described the home as "Bauhaus-meets-spaceship-meets-community-college," set on 22 acres. The taxpayer appealed the assessment but the case was (according to a newspaper report) settled for a $12 million value (N.Y. TIMES, Sept. 4, 2000, p.A10).

2. The examples of the idiosyncratically expensive residence might find a parallel in a more common and more modest example — the residential swimming pool that costs a lot more than will be reflected in the market price of the home. Some people find the pool a nuisance so the resident who spends $30,000 on its construction might not be able to recoup that cost in a sale. Should the property tax value reflect the cost or the market value of the pool?

[4] Prestige Buildings

A building might provide intangible prestige value to an owner-tenant that is not attributable to the real property. This issue has arisen in connection with buildings with a distinctive architectural style that provide favorable publicity for its owner-tenant. In *Matter of Joseph E. Seagram & Sons, Inc. v. The Tax Comm'n of New York*, 18 A.D.2d 109 (N.Y. App. Div. 1963), *affirmed*, 200 N.E.2d 447 (N.Y. 1964), the court dealt with such a case, where the construction cost of the building (only a few years before the assessment year) far exceeded the value based on capitalization of rental value. The court described the building as follows:

> . . . [The building is] an unusual one in its nature, though not unique. It has these distinctive features which are the hallmarks of its class: It is generally known by its name (having relationship to the owner) instead of a street address; it is constructed of unusual and striking materials; its architecture is noteworthy; and it is well set back from the streets on which it fronts, the space involved being employed in distinctive decorative effects. The net effect is that this building, and the limited number that resemble it, gives up a substantial fraction of the land that might be built upon, with a consequent diminution of the rentable space, and its construction involves a cost materially in excess of utilitarian standards.

> These buildings serve their owners in a fourfold way: 1. They house their activities; 2. They provide income from the rental of the space not used by the owner; 3. They advertise the owner's business; and 4. They contribute to the owner's prestige.

The taxpayer failed in its effort to reduce value below the original construction cost. But the court did not rely on the possibility that the building was like a "specialty," having special use value to the owner-occupant — which would have supported taxation based on replacement cost (presumably equal to the original cost of a relatively new building). The court did address the fact that capitalization of actual rents paid by tenants who were not the taxpayer seemed to produce a value much lower than original cost. (Capitalization of property income is another way to value property, discussed below.) But it suggested that this discrepancy could be overcome because the hypothetical rent that would be paid by the owner-tenant was substantially more than would normally be paid in rent, because of the prestige factor. Capitalization of rental value could therefore support a considerably higher value than would be the case if usual rental values were considered. In future years (the court hinted), the hypothetical rental value attributed to the prestige factor might be expected to depreciate at a much greater rate than value based on actual rents.

[C] Capitalize Income

Capitalizing income is commonly used for commercial and other business buildings. Thus, if rental income is $1 million and the appropriate interest rate is 5%, capitalizing the rent results in a $20 million value. (The capitalization rate is 100 divided by the interest rate; $100/5 = 20$.)

This method of determining value encounters two obvious problems — what is the proper measure of income and what is the correct capitalization rate? First, the difficulty in measuring income arises because only income from property should be considered. The fact that the taxpayer successfully or unsuccessfully engages in business on the land or in the building should be separated from the income from the property itself. For example, both the entrepreneurial success enjoyed by the taxpayer and the wastefulness of certain expenditures should be disregarded. Separating out business profits from property income can, however, be extremely difficult, especially when rents are typically measured by the tenant's profits. *See F. W. Woolworth Co. v. Commission of Taxation & Assessment*, 26 A.D.2d 759 (N.Y. App. Div. 1966), *affirmed*, 200 N.E.2d 447 (1964):

> Assuming that the custom throughout the nation is generally to base long term leases for national chain variety stores on annual gross sales figures, it seems reasonable to permit an owner-occupied national chain variety store to offer in evidence its annual gross sales figures and suggest a property valuation for real property tax assessment purposes by applying a capitalization percentage rate to such figures. However, such a valuation may not be conclusive in determining the value of the property . . . .

Second, the proper capitalization rate is a function of the risk associated with earning income from the property. The income tax routinely avoids this issue by fixing a discount rate in the statute, but property tax rules are not so clear.

[D] Property Subject to Burdens

[1] Leases and Mortgages

There are a variety of restrictions to which property can be subject. First, the property might be burdened with an unfavorable long-term lease (that is, with rentals below current market value). The general pattern in the cases is to disregard the low-rent lease and to value the property based on current market rentals, even though the property would sell for less than if it were not burdened by an unfavorable lease. These cases are influenced by the analogy to property burdened by a mortgage, which does *not* reduce the assessed property tax value (although some states provide a mortgage exemption that reduces assessed value by a modest amount). The point is that the property tax is supposed to reach the value of property; and property of equal value should be taxed equally, regardless of the financial burdens placed on the property.

A more practical point is that a taxpayer has voluntarily entered into a mortgage or a lease and such voluntary action should not reduce property values, or else the tax could be too easily avoided. Tax avoidance might seem far-fetched in the case of an unfavorable lease. However, taxpayers might be tempted to enter into reciprocal low-rent leases to lower property tax values or to lease the property at a low value and receive a compensating side payment from the tenant, if low-rent leases lowered property tax values.

[2] Government Regulations

Property values are usually reduced when the burden on the property results from government regulation, such as zoning or rent control. This suggests that the operative principle is concern with tax avoidance, because the government regulation carries no taint of voluntary taxpayer action.

Low-income housing for which low rents are required has raised difficult issues. On the one hand, the government appears to be limiting the rent. On the other hand, the taxpayer will often obtain financial benefits for providing low and moderate income housing, such as tax breaks and low interest loans, and will have negotiated the terms of eligibility for these benefits. This suggests that the lower rents are "voluntary." *Compare Knickerbocker Village, Inc. v. Boyland*, 16 A.D.2d 223 (N.Y. App. Div. 1962) (no reduction in value to account for low rents), *affirmed*, 190 N.E.2d 239 (N.Y. 1963), *with Kargman v. Jacobs*, 411 A.2d 1326 (R.I. 1980) (value adjusted to account for low rents).

[3] Easements

Easements burden property — for example, by permitting someone to cross the land or by prohibiting construction which would block sunlight. One approach to the taxation of property subject to an easement is to assume that the easement lowers the value of the burdened property, but raises the value of the property entitled to the easement in equal amounts — referred to as the "additive" approach. There is therefore no need to worry about a low value for the burdened property. *People ex rel. Poor v. O'Donnel*, 139 A.D. 83 (N.Y. App. Div. 1910), *aff'd mem. sub nom., People ex rel. Poor v. Wells*, 93 N.E. 1129 (N.Y. 1910) (Gramercy Park in New York City).

One problem with the "additive" approach is that an easement does not necessarily result in equal increases and decreases in the value of the related properties. One commentator cites Bonbright's example of an easement of light that provides little added value to buildings for whom the sunlight is not blocked, but a large decline in the value of property on which construction is now forbidden; and an easement of passage over forest land might dramatically raise the value of the land enjoying the easement of passage without lowering the forest land's value very much; Youngman, 58 Wash. L. Rev. at 777.

[4] Common Properties in Planned Communities

The "additive" approach has been used to justify the conclusion that a park or golf course has little or no value when it is part of a planned community whose residential owners (and no one else) can benefit from the surrounding park or golf course amenities. *See Tualatin Dev. Co. v. Department of Revenue*, 473 P.2d 660 (Or. 1970); *Twin Lakes Golf & Country Club v. King County*, 548 P.2d 538 (Wash. 1976).

Similarly, in *Breezy Knoll Association, Inc. v. Town of Morris*, 946 A.2d 215 (Conn. 2008), the court seemed willing to deny any more than a nominal value to property owned by a homeowners association — specifically, common areas consisting of tennis courts, a parking lot, and a lakefront strip, adjacent to homes owned by the association's resident members — because the value of the adjacent homes was increased by the ability to use the common areas. The court relied on a similar result reached in *Lake Monticello Owners' Assn. v. Ritter*, 327 S.E.2d 117 (Va. 1985), and *Waterville Estates Assn. v. Campton*, 446 A.2d 1167 (N.H. 1982).

But not all courts agree. In *Lake County Bd. of Review v. Property Tax Appeal Bd.*, 414 N.E.2d 173 (Ill. App. Ct. 1980), a lake was owned by a homeowner's association under a deed that restricted its use to those who owned residences surrounding the lake. The court refused to find that the lake was worth nothing just because neighboring houses were worth more due to their proximity to the golf course. It noted, by analogy, that low-rent long-term leases do not lower the property tax value of the landlord's property. The court stated:

> It is apparent that property adjoining or in close proximity to a body of water, a park, golf course, or other scenic view may well have an increased value because of its location. However, there is no assessment principle in Illinois which provides that the assessed value of the scenic property may itself be correspondingly reduced because of its effect on surrounding property.

And, in *Sahalee Country Club, Inc. v. State Bd. of Tax Appeals*, 735 P.2d 1320 (Wash. 1987), the court distinguished the *Twin Lake* decision (which had found no value in a golf course that was part of a planned community). The court refused to find that a golf course had no value, as follows:

> [Taxpayer argues] that *Twin Lakes* is based on the theories of "shifting value" and "double taxation". [Taxpayer] argues that its golf course increased the property values of neighboring residential lots by a total of $13 million, an amount far in excess of the cost of building the golf course. [Taxpayer] contends that $13 million in value has shifted from the course to the residential lots, which would leave the golf course without value. [Taxpayer] argues that taxing the golf course as well as taxing the residences for the additional $13 million would amount to double taxation. Under this argument, [taxpayer] focuses on the dollar amount of the benefit that accrues to the neighboring lot owners, not the dollar amount of the burden that this relationship places on the golf course.
>
> This argument, however, misinterprets *Twin Lakes*. *Twin Lakes* did not mention the concepts of "shifting value" or "double taxation" in its analysis. Rather, this court's analysis focused on the extent to which the golf course

retained any market value, not on the extent to which neighboring properties were increased in value. While we agree that value sometimes is transferred from burdened to benefited properties, there is no necessary dollar-for-dollar correlation between the decrease in value of the burdened property and the increase in value of the benefited property.

One should note that there is no necessary equivalence between the damage a landowner suffers by being subjected to an easement and the benefit other land obtains from that easement. An easement of passage over A's forest land to the road may greatly enhance the value of B's hotel property without correspondingly depreciating A's land; while on the other hand an easement of light over C's lot may merely make D's backyard slightly pleasanter while preventing C from building an apartment house.

Chapter 27

ESTATE AND GIFT TAX

§ 27.01   A BRIEF EXPLANATION[1]

[A]   History

A federal tax on property at the time of death has come in and out of the law at various times, usually associated with wartime or the prospect of war — for example: at the end of the eighteenth century (when war with France was a possibility); during the Civil War; and at the end of the nineteenth century (associated with the Spanish-American War). However, these taxes did not survive the end of the hostilities.

Some of these laws were inheritance rather than estate taxes. The difference is this. An estate tax is imposed on the value of the decedent's property at a uniform tax rate. An inheritance tax (sometimes called as "accessions tax") is imposed on the receipt of property by individual beneficiaries and the rates vary with the beneficiary — with lower rates usually applying to bequests to closer relatives. Today, states often rely on inheritance rather than estate taxes, but the federal government imposes an estate tax.

Wartime was not the only motive for an estate or inheritance tax. Toward the end of the nineteenth century, the same concern that led to advocating a tax on income earned by wealthier individuals led to proposals for an estate tax on large aggregations of wealth. Although we might assume that the wealthy would generally oppose an estate tax that has not always been the case. For example, Andrew Carnegie in the late nineteenth century argued that inherited wealth was not good for either the recipient (whose initiative would be dampened) or the society (which would be better served by spending the wealth for the public good).

The first modern estate tax was adopted by the United States in 1916, in part to satisfy the need to finance military expenditures on the eve of our entry into World War I. But the estate tax was not repealed after the war (although rates were lowered), because the tax was also viewed as a way to modify wealth inequality and to place some limits on the economic and political power associated with large concentrations of wealth. Tax rates were increased during the Depression, and the top rate reached 77% in 1954; the top rate is now 40% (in 2013). The 2001 Tax Law

---

[1] The historical and statistical material in this chapter relies heavily on Johnson & Eller, *Internal Revenue Service, Federal Taxation of Inheritance and Wealth Transfer*, http://www.irs.gov/pub/irs-soi/ inhwlttr.pdf, and GRAETZ & SHAPIRO, DEATH BY A THOUSAND CUTS (2005).

provided that the estate tax would expire in 2010, but that later law reinstated the tax for subsequent years.

The gift tax has a more complex history. A temporary gift tax was adopted in 1924 to prevent taxpayers from making lifetime gifts to reduce their taxable estates, but was repealed in 1926. The gift tax was made permanent in 1932.

Recent data indicate the limited coverage of the current estate and gift tax. In 2004, taxable estate tax returns were filed for about 8/10ths of 1% of deaths. (In 2002, the percentage was 2.12%; the peak was 7.65% in 1977.) The estate and gift tax produced $27.8 billion in 2006, which equaled 1.2% of federal revenue; the highest percent after WWII was 2.6% in 1972. *See generally* Staff of the Joint Committee on Taxation History, Present Law, and Analysis of the Federal Wealth Transfer System, JCX-108-07 (Nov. 13, 2007).

[B] Exemptions

Before 1981, the estate tax exemption was relatively low — $60,000. Consequently, the tax was not limited to the very rich, especially after inflation had increased the value of property. Estates of farmers and small business owners without liquid assets were especially hard hit by the tax. In 1981, the exemption was increased to $600,000.

In 2001, Congress increased the exemption for the estate tax in phases, starting at $1 million in 2002 and reaching $3.5 million in 2009. ATRA sets the exception at $5 million, inflation-adjusted to $5,250,000 in 2013.

The actual mechanism for providing an exemption is to compute a tax on the entire value of taxable property and to subtract the tax on the exemption amount computed at the *bottom* of the estate tax rate scale. This means that the exemption does not operate like the personal exemption deduction in the income tax. In the income tax, the deduction lowers taxable income; the tax rates then apply to that lower income. Under the estate tax, the "exempt amount" pushes the rest of the property into a higher bracket, because of the way the credit works. For example, assume a $100 exemption; and assume a 10% tax rate on $100, and a 20% tax rate on property over $100. A taxpayer with $300 of property has a *pre-credit* tax of $50 (10% times $100; plus 20% times $200 = $40). A $10 credit eliminates the tax on the first $100 (assuming the exempt amount is $100), but the remaining $200 is subject to the higher 20% rate; that is, $40. If the $100 exempt amounts were a deduction from the top of the estate tax rate scale (analogous to the income tax personal exemption), the remaining $200 would result in a $30 tax, computed as follows: 10% on the first $100, and 20% on the next $100.

[C] Marital Deduction

Transfers to a surviving spouse are generally deductible in full in computing the estate tax base, as explained below (Chapter 27.03[D][1]).

[D]   Politics of Estate Tax Repeal

The politics swirling around the estate tax are complex. First, the estate tax produces a small percentage of federal revenue — generally no more than 2%. This small percentage suggests that repeal of the estate tax might be uncontroversial. However, the dollar amounts produced by the estate tax are significant, especially when compared to the budgets of certain agencies, so repeal might impose a selective burden.

Second, you might think that the estate tax would be popular because it falls on only a small percentage of estates, primarily the very wealthy. Although opponents of the tax often cite the burden that the estate tax places on small businesses and farmers, nearly two-thirds of the assets taxed are liquid assets, such as traded stocks and bonds. Moreover, the tax law provides several tax breaks for farmers and small businesses. First, valuation of real property used for farming or other business purposes is based on current use rather than the highest and best use, if such property constitutes 50% or more of the estate's value (and if certain other conditions are met). However, the code provides that the decrease in value cannot exceed a specified amount, which is inflation-adjusted — equal to $1,070,000 in 2013). Moreover, disposition of the property or cessation of an eligible use within a specified period after the decedent's death can result in an additional estate tax. **§ 2032A.** Second, there is an extended period to pay the estate tax to reduce the liquidity problems that might otherwise exist for an estate with a closely held business, if the value of the eligible property is a significant part of the taxable estate. **§ 6166.**

In any event, the estate tax is not politically popular. About three-quarters of the people think that the estate tax affects all Americans; and about one-third think that it will affect them, despite the high exemption levels. Perhaps Americans are forever optimistic that they will acquire enough wealth to be subject to the tax.

[E]   Tax on Property Transfer

The estate tax is, technically, a tax on the transfer of property, not a tax on property. As such, it is an indirect tax (like the sales tax), which avoids the U.S. constitutional requirement of apportionment by population. *New York Trust Co. v. Eisner*, 256 U.S. 345 (1921) (estate tax has "always [] been regarded as the antithesis of a direct tax"; Justice Holmes stated that "a page of history is worth a volume of logic").

An interesting example of the distinction between a property tax and a tax on the transfer of property arose in *United States v. Wells Fargo Bank*, 485 U.S. 351 (1988). The Court unanimously held that the following statutory language did *not* grant an exemption from the estate tax: "[Certain property] . . . shall be exempt from all taxation now or hereafter imposed." How could this language *not* apply to an estate tax? The Court stated: "Well before [this Act] was passed, an exemption of property from all taxation had an understood meaning: the property was exempt from *direct* taxation, but certain privileges of ownership, such as the right to transfer property, could be taxed." The property was therefore subject to estate tax, which was a tax on the transfer of property, not a "direct" tax on property.

§ 27.02 GIFT TAX

[A] Purpose

The gift tax protects the estate tax. If there were no tax on gifts, a taxpayer could give away property during his or her lifetime and avoid the estate tax. As noted earlier, a temporary gift tax was adopted from 1924 to 1926, and Congress adopted a permanent gift tax in 1932.

The gift tax also protects against shifting income from property to lower income taxpayers, who are likely to be subject to lower tax rates than the donor. The concern with income shifting is evident from the fact that there was a gift tax in 2010, when there was no estate tax.

[B] Unified Rate Structure

Beginning in 1976, the estate and gift tax rate structures were unified. Consequently, lifetime gifts count against the estate tax exemption. For example, using simplified numbers,if there is a $1 million estate tax exemption, a lifetime gift of $400,000 counts against the decedent's total $1 million estate tax exemption.

There is still one advantage to making a lifetime rather than a testamentary gift. Payment of the gift tax reduces the taxable estate. By contrast, a decedent's estate is not reduced by the amount of any estate tax which must be paid by the estate; the value of the estate includes the estate tax. For this reason, § 2035 addresses the special case of a gift made within three years of death in order to prevent tax avoidance by gifts in contemplation of death; any gift tax paid by the decedent on such gifts is included in the taxable estate.

[C] Exclusions

The gift tax exemption is not the only way to give away a lot of property free of gift tax during the donor's lifetime. *First*, gifts to a spouse are not usually subject to the gift tax. *Second*, a donor can make annual gifts to any number of donees without gift tax up to a specified amount to each donee — $14,000 in 2013 (inflation adjusted). This is called an "exclusion," not an exemption. (Do not confuse the gift tax exclusion with the exclusion of gifts from the income tax base; Chapter 4.01.)

The donor's spouse can join with the donor to double the exclusion amount. This means that a taxpayer and spouse can give $28,000 per year to each donee. If the donees include a child, the child's spouse, and two grandchildren, a total of $112,000 can be given by a married couple free of gift tax in 2013. This $14,000 *exclusion* is over and above the *exemption* from gift and estate tax. There is no requirement that the taxpayer file to take advantage of the annual per donee exclusion.

Third, lifetime gifts that pay tuition or medical expenses directly to a donee's service provider are not subject to the gift tax, without dollar limit — for example, payment to a university for a child's tuition.

The annual exclusion is not available for gifts of future interests (typically, gifts in trust), with one exception. A transfer for the benefit of a minor qualifies for the exclusion: (a) if the income and principal may be expended for the minor before reaching age 21, and (b) to the extent not so expended, will pass to the minor (i) upon reaching age 21, or (ii) if the child dies before age 21, to the child's estate or as directed by the child acting under a general power of appointment.

§ 27.03 ESTATE TAX BASE

[A] Ownership

Ownership of property, which determines inclusion in a taxable estate, is determined by state law, but that is more complicated than it sounds. The general point is obvious — there is no federal property law, so ownership depends on state law. But how should a federal court determine state law in a particular case?

In *Commissioner v. Bosch's Estate*, 387 U.S. 456 (1967), the Court dealt with a lower state court decision that was clearly the result of a lawsuit brought for the purpose of directly affecting federal estate tax liability by fixing ownership of property interests most favorably for the taxpayer. The Court stated:

> This is not a diversity case but the same principle [as in *Erie v. Tompkins*] may be applied for the same reasons, viz., the underlying substantive rule involved is based on state law and the State's highest court is the best authority on its own law. If there be no decision by that court then federal authorities must apply what they find to be the state law after giving "proper regard" to relevant rulings of other courts of the State. In this respect, it may be said to be, in effect, sitting as a state court.

The Court rejected several other tests to determine state law — specifically: (1) defer to a state court judgment if it is binding upon the parties regarding their property rights; or (2) defer to a state trial court adjudication only when the judgment is the result of an adversary proceeding in the state court.

[B] Retaining Control

For a long time, it was possible to give away property during a taxpayer's lifetime to avoid estate tax, while still retaining dominion and control that amounted to effective ownership until the time of death (thereby also avoiding a gift tax). The law has since been amended to include in a taxable estate many arrangements in which a donor has retained enjoyment or control during his lifetime. (Chapter 2.03[B][1] noted that a similar issue arises under the income tax — where a trust grantor might be taxed on the income earned by the trust if the grantor retained too much control over the trust.)

The following is an incomplete list of situations that the code identifies as involving "too much" control.

— retained possession or enjoyment of the property, or the right to the income from the property: for example, a retained life estate (§ 2036(a)(1)).

— retained control during lifetime: specifically, "the right, either alone or in conjunction with any person, to designate the persons who shall possess or enjoy the property or income therefrom" (§ 2036(a)(2)).

— revocable transfers: for example, a trust subject to revocation by the grantor (§ 2038).

Strangi v. Commissioner, 417 F.3d 468 (5th Cir. 2005), illustrates that the determination of retained enjoyment or control depends on more than legal arrangements; it also requires a consideration of the reality of personal relationships, especially among family members. This case involved the application of § 2036(a)(1), dealing with retained beneficial ownership. The taxpayer had transferred property prior to his death to a family-limited partnership controlled by his children. The court explained the standard for the retention of possession or enjoyment under the statute, as the retention of a "substantial present economic benefit" from the property, as opposed to "a speculative contingent benefit which may or may not be realized." It also cited Treasury Regulations that required that there be an "express or implied" agreement "at the time of the transfer" that the transferor will retain possession or enjoyment of the property. **Treas. Reg. § 20.2036-1(a)**. The court concluded that the taxpayer retained substantial, present, and nonspeculative benefits, as follows: periodic payments made for his benefit prior to his death; the continued use of a house that had been transferred to the partnership; and the post-death payment of some of the taxpayer's debts and expenses. These benefits were clearly "substantial" and "present," as opposed to "speculative" or "contingent." Consequently, the only issue was whether there was "an express or implied agreement that [the taxpayer] would retain de facto control and/or enjoyment of the transferred assets."

The court affirmed the Tax Court's conclusion that an *implied* agreement existed, noting the following facts. First, the government relied on the various disbursements of funds to the taxpayer or his estate. As for the estate's response that most of the payments occurred after the taxpayer's death, the court said that this missed the point. "Possession or enjoyment" of assets includes the assurance that they will be available to pay debts and expenses at death. Here, the partnership paid more than $100,000 from 1994 to 1996 for funeral expenses, estate administration expenses, specific bequests, and various personal debts. The court said that "[t]hese repeated distributions provide[d] strong circumstantial evidence of an understanding between [the taxpayer] and his children that 'partnership' assets would be used to meet [taxpayer's] expenses."

Second, the Tax Court found "highly probative" [the taxpayer's] "continued physical possession of his residence after its transfer" to the partnership. Although rent was paid by the taxpayer, the rental payments did not occur until several years after occupancy. "Even assuming that the belated rent payment was not a post hoc attempt to recast [the taxpayer's] use of the house, such a deferral, in itself, provides a substantial economic benefit."

Third, the taxpayer retained very few liquid assets of his own after transferring 98% of his property to the partnership, which implied some arrangement to meet the taxpayer's expenses.

The court may have been influenced in reaching its decision by the fact that the taxpayer had been in failing health since 1990 and that his estate advisor and friend had attended a seminar suggesting that estate taxes could be reduced by establishing a family-limited partnership.

[C] Valuation

[1] The Relevant Date

Since 1935, the estate has been allowed to elect as the valuation date either the date of death or some date thereafter — currently, six months after death. This option cannot be made selectively for different property. The difference in dates can have a dramatic effect. Assume ownership of a copyright interest in a play to open on Broadway two months after the decedent's death. The play is a big hit but its value on the date of death is probably very low, given the uncertainties in the industry.

[2] Determining Value

Administration of the estate and gift tax encounters the usual problems of determining value — for example, is the best indicator of value the capitalization of income or the sales price of comparable property? What is the highest and best use of the property (assuming that is the proper standard; *see* Chapter 26.06[A][2])?

In the context of a family owned business — whether a corporation or a partnership — there is often an additional problem. The deceased will have shared ownership during his or her lifetime with another member of the family, often as a result of a lifetime conveyance by the founder of the business to his or her children. This often makes good business sense by passing control of the business to a younger generation. But there is also a tax angle, resulting from the possible discount of the value of the decedent's interest in the business when he or she dies. The discount might arise in several ways: there is a buy-out arrangement between owners on the death of one of the owners at a price well below market value at the time of death; it is difficult to sell the decedent's interest to a buyer who must deal with surviving family members (a marketability discount); and the decedent may lack a controlling interest in the business (a minority discount).

The following *Godley* case deals with the relevance of a buy-out price, and the marketability and minority ownership discounts.

[a] Buy-out Option

The code now deals explicitly with buy-out arrangements entered into or substantially modified after October 8, 1900 (§ **2703**), as follows:

(a) General rule. — For purposes of this subtitle, the value of any property shall be determined without regard to:

(1) any option, agreement, or other right to acquire or use the property at a price less than the fair market value of the property (without regard to such option, agreement, or right), or

(2) any restriction on the right to sell or use such property.

(b) Exceptions. — Subsection (a) shall not apply to any option, agreement, right, or restriction which meets each of the following requirements:

(1) It is a bona fide business arrangement.

(2) It is not a device to transfer such property to members of the decedent's family for less than full and adequate consideration in money or money's worth.

(3) Its terms are comparable to similar arrangements entered into by persons in an arms' length transaction.

The following case discussed whether there was a bona fide business arrangement and whether the buy-out arrangement was simply a device to transfer property for inadequate consideration under § 2703(b)(1–2).

ESTATE OF GODLEY v. COMMISSIONER
United States Tax Court
80 T.C.M. (CCH) 158 (2000), *affirmed*, 286 F.3d 210 (4th Cir. 2002)

GALE, J.:

[Editor — In this case, the business was conducted by several partnerships, which owned housing projects. The decedent, Godley, was one of the partners. The opinion explained that, at the time of the decedent-Godley's death, partnership agreements for each housing project contained a provision granting the decedent's son the option to purchase the decedent's interest in each partnership for the sum of $10,000. The son, who was the managing partner, exercised these options after the decedent died. The taxpayer claimed that the fair market value of the partnership interest was limited to the $10,000 option price, or, in the alternative, that the option provision at least reduced the value to some extent. The government took the position that the option provision should be disregarded in determining the fair market value of the decedent's interest and the court agreed, as follows:]

It is well settled that an option agreement may fix the value of a business interest for Federal estate tax purposes if the following conditions are met: (i) The price must be fixed and determinable under the agreement; (ii) the agreement must be binding on the parties both during life and after death; and (iii) the agreement must have a bona fide business purpose and must not be a substitute for a testamentary disposition. [The government] does not dispute that [the taxpayer] meets the first two conditions but challenges whether the option provision had a bona fide business purpose and whether it was a substitute for testamentary disposition. According to taxpayer, the option provision was inserted in each of the partnership agreements for the purpose of allowing [the taxpayer's son] to maintain control of the businesses without the possibility of interference from other family members. The maintenance of family ownership and control constitutes a bona fide business purpose. However, even if we find that the option had a bona fide business purpose, it will be disregarded if it served as a device to pass decedent's interest to the natural objects of his bounty and to convey that interest for less than full and adequate consideration. We find that the option provision in each of the partnership agreements represents a testamentary device to convey decedent's interest to his son for less than full and adequate consideration, and therefore we disregard it in determining the value of those interests.

Taxpayer argues that the options were not a testamentary device because they were exchanged for full and adequate consideration. [Editor — The consideration was claimed to be the son's contribution of services to the partnership that far outweighed the value of the decedent's services to the partnership.] . . .

When both parties to the agreement are members of the same family and circumstances indicate that testamentary considerations influenced the creation of the option agreement, we do not assume that the price as stated in the agreement was a fair one. We first note that the fixed price of the option, without any adjustment mechanism to reflect changing conditions, invites close scrutiny. If decedent and [his son] really engaged in an arm's-length transaction in which it was decided that [the son's] greater contribution required decedent to give an option, we believe the price of the option would have included an adjustment mechanism to account for future appreciation. The fact that the price was set at $10,000, combined with the fact that the agreement was between a father and son, strongly suggests that there was no arm's-length bargain for the option price, but rather that the option was a testamentary device designed to pass decedent's interest for less than adequate consideration.

[Editor — The court went on to discount the son's claim of adequate consideration for the lowered option price as "self-serving."]

On balance, we believe the evidence that the options were a substitute for a testamentary device outweighs any evidence of their bona fide business purpose. . . .

[b] Marketability Discount

The Tax Court in *Godley* did find that there should be a 20% marketability discount. It noted that decedent's interests would not be readily marketable, because there was an irrevocable designation of the son as managing partner. Furthermore, the partnership agreements provided that, if one partner wanted to sell his interest, the other partners had a right of first refusal that gave them 60 days to purchase that interest, thereby resulting in a forced period of illiquidity on the selling partner.

[c] Minority Discount

ESTATE OF GODLEY v. COMMISSIONER
United States Court of Appeals, Fourth Circuit
286 F.3d 210 (4th Cir. 2002)

WILKINSON, CHIEF JUDGE: . . .

[Editor — The Tax Court in *Godley* rejected a minority discount and the Court of Appeals affirmed this finding of fact. The Court of Appeals noted that, at the time of the decedent's death, he owned a 50 percent interest in various partnerships that owned and/or managed housing projects for elderly tenants. It described the business as follows:]

The Housing Partnerships held multifamily rental housing projects [for elderly tenants] operated under Housing Assistance Payments contracts ("HAP contracts") with the United States Department of Housing and Urban Development. Pursuant to the HAP contracts, Housing Assistance payments are made to the Housing Partnerships to cover the difference between the rental rates agreed to under the HAP contracts and the portion of the rent paid by eligible families. In addition, in the event of a vacancy, the HAP contracts entitled the owner to payments in the amount of eighty percent of the contract rent for up to sixty days. If the vacancy period exceeded sixty days, the owner could request additional payments. The term of the HAP contracts [varied between 20 and 30 years].

[Decedent's son] was the managing partner for the Housing Partnerships. This gave him control over the overall management of the partnerships. [He] likewise took care of the day-to-day management of the Housing Partnerships. He would pay bills, set aside reserves for replacement of assets or to cover contingencies, and acquire those properties that the partnership had decided upon. However, [he] could not make any "major decision" without the affirmative vote of seventy-five percent of the partnership shares. "Major decisions" included buying or selling land or partnership property, securing financing, spending in excess of $2,500, entering into major contracts, or taking any other action "which materially affects the Partnership or the assets or operation thereof." . . .

During valuation a fact finder must decide whether the value should be increased or discounted for any reason. A minority discount may be appropriate if the block of stock does not enjoy the rights associated with control of the enterprise. The application of such a discount is only appropriate if, as a factual matter, the minority status of the interest would affect the value that a willing buyer would pay. Thus, the question of whether a discount for a lack of control is warranted depends, like the question of valuation generally, on the facts and circumstances of the case.

Control has been defined as an interest which allows the shareholder to "unilaterally direct corporate action, select management, decide the amount of distribution, rearrange the corporation's capital structure, and decide whether to liquidate, merge, or sell assets." These various powers support applying a control premium to a controlling block of shares in order to reflect the inherent value of that controlling interest. On the other hand, a minority discount is applied to reflect the lack of power and risks a minority interest poses. And like a corporate minority shareholder, "a limited partner generally has no voice in the management of the partnership and cannot control investment policies or partnership distribution," so a minority discount may apply to the value of that interest as well.

A premium for control or discount for lack of control may be appropriate as a factual matter for several reasons. First, an investor who believes a business may be improved by better management or other changes may be willing to pay more for a controlling interest. "Investors often pay a premium when they believe that they have unearthed an undervalued corporation." An investor purchasing a minority interest, however, may recognize that he will be unable to make any changes and will, therefore, want to pay less than fair market value. Second, control over a business may decrease the risk a particular investment poses to the investor, increasing the value of that interest. And an investor will also recognize that the increased risks a minority shareholder faces may decrease the value of an interest. Third, with control over the business, an investor may be able to pay himself an excessive salary or to otherwise self-deal. While courts would be unlikely to recognize any such prospect as the basis for a control premium, the minority shareholder may risk falling victim to such self-dealing. Thus, the rights conveyed by corporate control, "the ability to determine management, distributions, and corporate structure," enhance the value of the corporation and command a premium. "Conversely, in recognition of the potential exploitation of minority shareholders, stock lacking control generally receives a minority discount." Any of these rationales may support a factual finding that control warrants a premium, or that the lack thereof warrants a discount. Absent some explanation of why control has economic value, however, no premium or discount is warranted.

It is true that in a closely-held corporation, a minority interest in stock is ordinarily discounted to reflect lack of control. However, the mere presumption that a discount may exist does not lead to the conclusion that a discount must be applied as a matter of law whenever a shareholder owns less than fifty-one percent of a corporation. Our view that the question of whether to apply a minority discount is factual in nature is one that is widely shared. We thus turn to the facts of the case at hand.

In this case, the Tax Court determined that the value of the partnership interests was subject to a discount for lack of marketability, but not for the alleged lack of control. This finding was not clearly erroneous. As the evidence demonstrates, there was little to be gained by having control of these partnerships and little risk in holding a minority interest.

Here, the Housing Partnerships were guaranteed a long-term, steady income stream under the HUD contracts. The Housing Partnerships had little risk of losing the HUD contracts and the management of the properties did not require particular expertise. Indeed, the HUD contracts allowed the Housing Partnerships to collect above-market rents, and there was no other use for the partnerships that would increase their profits. Therefore, control of the Housing Partnerships did not carry with it any appreciable economic value. Nor did a lack of control reduce the value of a fifty percent interest such that a minority discount was required.

The Estate argues that a minority discount was required because "the record supports a finding that the managing partner had significant latitude in determining the extent of partnership distributions and the amounts set aside in reserve." However, each partnership agreement required the partnership to distribute its "net cash flow" annually and set forth a specific calculation of that net cash flow. There was no risk that [the decedent], a fifty percent partner, would not realize an annual payout. Although the agreements also granted the managing partner the power to set aside reserves, that power was characterized as one of "day-to-day management." It appears unlikely that this "set aside" power could be used to defeat the requirement of an annual distribution. At a minimum, [the decedent] could exercise his power under the partnership agreements to prevent any change to the guarantee of an annual distribution. Thus, as the Tax Court determined, [the decedent] was effectively guaranteed a reasonable annual distribution of partnership income. And while an inability to force a distribution of income may under other circumstances warrant a discount for lack of control, the Tax Court correctly found that this factor was not relevant in this case.

Similarly, the Estate contends that [the decedent's] fifty percent interest made it impossible for him to compel liquidation or sell partnership assets. However, neither [the decedent nor his son] could compel liquidation or make any "major decision" without the affirmative vote of seventy-five percent of the partnership shares. Moreover, given the passive nature of the business and the almost certain prospect of steady profits, the ability to liquidate or sell assets was of little practical import. Thus, as the Tax Court reasoned, the guarantee of above-market rents and other factors unique to the Housing Partnerships meant that the power to liquidate the partnership or to sell partnership assets would have minimal value to an investor. . . .

The Tax Court carefully considered the expert testimony, the expert valuations of the partnerships, and the unique nature of the rent-controlled housing business in reaching its decision not to apply a minority discount to [the decedent's] fifty percent interest. . . . We are satisfied that the Tax Court's valuation determinations were not clearly erroneous.

[d]   Estate "Freezes"

Suppose a taxpayer who owns a family corporate business wants to keep control and some income during his life but also transfer the opportunity to enjoy appreciation in the value of the business to a future generation. One way to do this is to retain voting stock with a limited profit interest (such as 6% voting preferred stock), and transfer common stock with minority voting control to his children. Any future appreciation of the corporation's value will accrue to the common stock. This looks a lot like the kind of retained control of property that might result in inclusion of the corporation's stock (both preferred and common) in the taxpayer's estate under § 2036, and Congress provided for this result in 1987. But, in 1990, Congress decided that this provision was both overbroad and unclear in operation and it was retroactively repealed.

Congress instead adopted a different technique to prevent tax avoidance. It requires a more realistic valuation of the gift of the common stock, which is subject to a gift tax. In general, the value of the common stock equals the value of the corporation minus the present value of the retained preferred stock, but the value of the preferred stock is deemed to be zero unless it is entitled to a cumulative right to dividend payments at a fixed rate (analogous to interest payments for which a debtor would be obligated). These future dividend payments are discounted at a market rate to determine present value of the preferred stock. Failure to pay these dividends on the preferred stock can result in an additional gift tax. §§ 2701–2704.

[D] Deductions

[1] Marital Deduction

The estate is entitled to a deduction for property given to a surviving spouse. § 2056. Although the marital deduction does not usually apply to a terminable interest in the surviving spouse (such as a life estate), there are two important exceptions, which are critical for estate planning:

— (1) A life estate to the surviving spouse with a general power of appointment in the spouse is eligible for the marital deduction. (A general power of appointment is a power exercisable in favor of any of the following — the decedent, the decedent's estate, or the creditors of the above.)

— (2) A life estate to the surviving spouse, with remainder to anyone specified by the decedent (such as a child), or (if the decedent wishes) to the surviving spouse with a special power of appointment (which is more limited than a general power) — as long as an election is made by the decedent's executor to include the entire value of the property in the surviving spouse's estate. This is known as QTIP, or qualified terminable interest property. Because the QTIP limits the surviving spouse's ability to transfer property away from the decedent's children, it is much more popular than the general power of appointment option, especially in the second-marriage context.

This leads to the following technique, which allows both spouses to take advantage of the full amount of the estate tax exemption. (Assume a $3 million exemption, for ease of computation. Assume further that the decedent has a $6 million estate and that the surviving spouse has no other assets.) The decedent does *not* simply give all of the decedent's $6 million of property to the surviving spouse; such an outright transfer is eligible for the marital deduction but would mean that, upon the surviving spouse's death, only $3 million would be exempt out of the inherited $6 million.

Instead, the decedent leaves the $6 million in two parts. First, property equal to the $3 million exempt amount is left in trust for the spouse's life, remainder to the children, in such a way that this trust amount is *not* included in the surviving spouse's estate on his or her death (for example, by giving the surviving spouse only a special power of appointment limited to the children); the *decedent's estate* takes advantage of the $3 million estate tax exemption on this amount in computing the decedent's taxable estate, rather than the marital deduction. Second, the remaining $3 million of the decedent's property is left to the spouse for life, remainder to the children, in such a way that it is included in the surviving spouse's estate (usually a QTIP, with an election by the decedent's executor to include the trust property in the surviving spouse's estate); this amount is eligible for the marital deduction when the decedent dies. When the surviving spouse dies, the $3 million QTIP that had been eligible for the decedent's marital deduction will now be included in the surviving spouse's estate and be eligible for the $3 million estate tax exemption in the *spouse's estate*; no estate tax will be due on the surviving spouse's estate. This means that $6 million (not just $3 million) will pass to the children without estate tax. Under 2013 law, this total amount equals $10,500,000 (two times the $5,250,000 exemption.)

[2] Charitable Deduction

Another important technique for reducing estate tax is the charitable deduction. The income tax deduction is limited to a percentage of adjusted gross income. The estate tax exemption, however, is unlimited. Opponents of estate tax repeal often emphasize the potential loss of an incentive to leave property to charity, which is provided by the current estate tax. Charitable bequests currently hover around 10% of the value of taxable estates.

§ 27.04 GENERATION-SKIPPING TAX

One complication in the current estate tax is the generation-skipping tax. Its adoption in 1986 closed the following loophole. The decedent could create a trust for A's life (A is the surviving spouse), and then for the life of B (A's child), and then to C (A's grandchild), etc. Prior to 1986, there was no estate tax as the property skipped from generation to generation under these arrangements. The 1986 law imposed a generation-skipping tax.

In the typical case, a generation-skipping transfer results in a potential tax when there is a "taxable termination" (usually the death of someone with a life estate), which results in the passing of an interest in the property to a person, two or more generations below the decedent. Thus, in the prior example, there is a potential for a generation-skipping tax after the death of A (the surviving spouse) and the death of B (the decedent's child), when a grandchild becomes the beneficiary. Generally speaking, this means that the decedent can use the estate tax exemption to leave property to his or her children, but that passage of the property to the grandchildren is subject to a generation-skipping tax, with its own set of exemptions. Further discussion of the complexities of the generation-skipping tax must be left to a course on the estate tax.

§ 27.05 A TAX ON NET WEALTH?

Another way to tax wealth — besides an annual property tax and a one-time estate tax — is an *annual* tax on net wealth. In theory, a tax on net wealth is like an income tax in one respect; it is imposed annually on value owned by an individual and can therefore be readily adjusted to individual and family circumstances. In practice, a net wealth tax has enjoyed limited and declining popularity. Although it was a staple in some European countries at one time, it has been repealed in many of those countries. *See* Isaacs, *Do We Want a Wealth Tax in America?*, 32 U. MIAMI L. REV. 23 (1977); Cooper, *Taking Wealth Tax Seriously*, 34 REC. OF ASS'N OF THE BAR OF THE CITY OF N.Y. 24 (1979). *See also Colloquium on Wealth Transfer Taxation*, Parts I and II, 51 TAX LAW REV. (1996); 53 TAX LAW REV. 499 (2000).

Several rationales have been advanced for a net wealth tax:

— property ownership gives rise to imputed income in the form of security and power;

— loopholes in the income tax permit wealth to accumulate;

— administration of an income tax would benefit from information gathered from imposing a net wealth tax (by exposing the use of unreported income to accumulate wealth);

— taxpayers with property yielding inadequate income would be motivated to put the property to its best economic use (the usual example being the maharajah whose wealth consists in large part of jewels, yielding no annual income).

In the United States, a tax on net wealth would probably be a direct tax and therefore politically impossible to adopt, unless it was considered an income tax that did not have to be apportioned among the states by population. It might look more like an income tax if, instead of a tax on net wealth, some hypothetical amount of income from net wealth were imputed to the taxpayer and added to the income tax base.

A more practical concern about adopting a *net* wealth tax is the deduction for debt, so that the tax is only on net wealth. If some wealth is exempt from the net wealth tax, the problem of allocating debt to taxable and nontaxable wealth arises, so that the debt allocable to exempt property is not deductible. This is similar to the problem under the income tax in deciding how to allocate interest on debts to taxable and tax-exempt property income; see Chapter 16.02. For example, if the taxpayer owns exempt property (such as a home) and borrows money to buy investments subject to the wealth tax, is the debt allocable to the home because it is incurred to carry the tax-exempt property, even though the funds were not used to buy the home?

PAYROLL TAXES

A payroll tax is imposed on *gross* compensation from personal services. Unlike an income tax, there are no deductions in computing the tax base and no adjustment for family size.

Payroll taxes fund various social insurance programs for employees and others who perform personal services. The federal government adopted two such programs in 1935 during the Depression — Unemployment Insurance and Social Security.

Unemployment Insurance for employees is funded by a federal payroll tax imposed on employers (with minimal contributions by employees in a few states). This tax is, in large part, reduced by a credit for state taxes imposed to fund state unemployment insurance programs that meet federal guidelines for providing financial assistance to the unemployed. This model of a federal tax which is forgiven if states fund their own programs meeting federal standards is not widely followed outside of the unemployment insurance setting, but it deserves closer attention as a public policy tool in a federal system.

The Social Security program is funded entirely by federal taxes; there is no state involvement. The percentage contribution of Social Security taxes to total federal revenue has increased dramatically over the years — gradually rising from under 10% prior to 1958 to 33% in 2013.

In contrast to the United States, European Union countries impose much higher payroll taxes, averaging about 35% for the combined employer-employee portions (which is about double the U.S. tax rate). However, these European taxes fund a broader range of employee welfare benefits than in the United States.

Social Security is the best known of the U.S. social insurance programs funded by payroll taxes. For that reason, this Part contains only one chapter which deals with the Social Security tax.

Chapter 28

SOCIAL SECURITY TAX

§ 28.01 IN GENERAL

The modern Social Security tax finances three programs — for the aged, the disabled, and Medicare (hospital and doctors' costs) — with limited contributions from general revenue. The program for the aged was a feature of the original federal program adopted in 1935; the disability portion began in 1956; and Medicare was adopted in 1965. Post-1935 amendments expanded Social Security benefits to include the worker's relatives — such as an aged spouse and minor children. Since 1975, benefit levels have been adjusted for inflation.

In 1940, the Social Security tax rate was 2% of employee payroll. In 2013, the tax rate has risen to 7.65%, with an extra amount added to the Medicare tax beginning in 2013 (explained below). The maximum taxable earnings, after statutory and inflation adjustments, is $113,700 in 2013 for the aged and disability portion of the tax; there is no earnings cap on the 1.45% portion of the tax imposed to fund Medicare. Employers must contribute a matching sum equal to the employee's tax. Thus, in 2013, the employer-employee contributions equaled 15.3% of taxable payroll. It is generally believed that the economic burden of the employer's contribution falls on the employee in the form of lower wages.

People who earn personal service self-employment income (as independent contractors) must pay a Social Security tax at the rate of 15.3% on net earnings up to $113,700 (in 2013). Net earnings above that amount are subject only to the Medicare portion of the tax (2.9%). A typical self-employed taxpayer is a lawyer who is a partner in a law firm.

The Patient Protection and Affordable Health Care Act (Obamacare) (Public Law 111-148) increases the Medicare tax by 0.9% beginning in 2013 on an employee's wages and on the earned income of a self-employed individual above a threshold of $200,000 (for an individual) and $250,000 (for a married couple). The earned income of a married couple in excess of $250,000 that is subject to the additional 0.9% tax refers to the combined earnings of both spouses. This is a departure from the usual practice of imposing Social Security taxes based on the separate earnings of each spouse. These thresholds are not indexed for inflation.

Obamacare also provides a tax on "unearned income" to help fund Medicare, beginning in 2013. "Unearned income" refers to investment income, such as interest (not counting the tax exempt interest on state and local bonds), dividends, capital gains, royalties and rents, unless any of these items is derived from a trade or business. The tax is 3.8% of the lesser of (1) net investment income or (2) modified adjusted gross income in excess of $200,000 for an individual and $250,000 for a married couple. These threshold amounts reflect President Obama's pledge not to raise taxes on individuals with lesser amounts of income. For example, assume an individual has $180,000 of wages, $45,000 of unearned income, and modified adjusted gross income of $215,000. The 3.8% tax would be imposed on $15,000 (the lesser of $215,000 minus $200,000; and $45,000).

For lower income employees, the Social Security tax is often the highest tax that they pay, especially if the employer's portion is taken into account. The earned income tax credit is intended to reduce the Social Security tax burden on the payroll of lower-income workers. See Chapter 1.05.

As the ratio of younger workers to retirees decreases with an aging population, there is likely to be one or more of the following responses — the Social Security tax will increase; benefits will be reduced; and/or there will be a greater infusion of general revenue financing. Several moves in this direction have already occurred, including the following. First, the age at which a person can retire and get full benefits has gone up.

Second, some portion of Social Security benefits for the aged is now subject to an income tax, unless the taxpayer has low income (for a single taxpayer, no more than $25,000; for married taxpayers, no more than $32,000).

Third, insured individuals pay premiums for some portion of the Medicare Part B program (for outpatient doctor care) out of their own pocket — although the amount is collected somewhat painlessly by withholding from Social Security cash benefits. Moreover, some portion of these Medicare Part B premiums is now income-tested. In addition, individuals pay income-tested premiums to cover a small part of the cost of Medicare Part D (prescription drug coverage). The government computes the premium amount from income tax returns previously filed; the taxpayer does not have to make any computations or file new forms.

As benefits become less generous and more politically uncertain, there will be greater resistance to increasing the payroll tax, because the "insurance" analogy will seem less apt, and there will be a greater need for (and resistance to) general revenues to make up any shortfall.

The key to the successful administration of the Social Security program (and any program financed from payroll taxes) is wage withholding from employees, which leads to the following questions: What are wages? Who is an "employee" rather than an independent contractor?

§ 28.02   "WAGES"

[A]   In-Kind Remuneration

In *Rowan Companies, Inc. v. United States*, 452 U.S. 247 (1981), the issue was whether meals and lodging provided to the employee for the convenience of the employer on the business premises were "wages" under the Social Security tax, even though they were not income (let alone wages) for purposes of the income tax (§ 119). The government invoked a regulation treating these benefits as wages subject to withholding under the Social Security tax. **Treas. Reg. § 31.3121(a)- 1(f)**.

The Court in *Rowan* concluded that "wages" under the Social Security tax had the same meaning as "wages" under the income tax, in order to provide simplicity of administration. Because the item was not included in the income tax base, it could not be wages under either the income tax or the Social Security tax. In this pre-*Chevron* decision, the Treasury Regulation treating these benefits as Social Security wages was not entitled to substantial weight, because the agency had not consistently followed a rule of inclusion in wages. (*See* Chapter 6.02[A] for a discussion of the *Chevron* doctrine.)

Congress reacted to the *Rowan* decision in two ways. First, it concluded that the purposes of the Social Security tax justified a broader definition of "wages" than under the income tax. It explicitly gave the Treasury the power to adopt regulations that made that distinction. Second, Congress also specified that certain benefits would *not* be "wages" for Social Security purposes, including the § 119 benefits at issue in *Rowan*; § 3121(a)(19). Thus, despite the grant of regulatory power to broadly define wages for the Social Security tax, Congress blocked such efforts in specific situations. Indeed, when the Treasury suggested that it might treat the gain on the exercise of statutory stock options as wages under the Social Security tax, Congress amended the law in 2004 to prevent that result; § 3121(a)(22)(A).

QUESTIONS AND COMMENTS

1. *Consistent meaning?* When the same word appears more than once in legislation — such as the term "wages" in the Social Security and income tax law — courts sometimes say that they should have the same meaning. But there are reasons to be skeptical of that conclusion.

First, although a good drafter uses words consistently, authors of statutes do not always follow that practice, in part because they are rushed. Second, legislative texts with the same language may have been written at different times and/or by different legislators, in which case the assumption that the real legislative authors used similar language with the same meaning is not necessarily true. Indeed, as the post-*Rowan* legislation indicates, the Social Security and income tax laws might have very different purposes leading to different definitions of the term "wages," even if it is administratively simpler to adopt a common definition.

2. *Later legislation and statutory interpretation.* Does the post-*Rowan* legislation — indicating that wages could have a broader meaning under the Social Security tax — mean that the Court made a mistake in interpreting the Social Security law when it held that wages meant the same thing for both income and Social Security taxes?

How can a later law determine the meaning of prior legislation? The Court had decided that the policy of administrative simplicity made the most sense but Congress later decided that this policy was not as important as the Court thought. That does not mean that the Court was wrong, only that (on reflection and at a later date) Congress decided that a different approach made more sense.

[B]   Severance Payments for Teachers

APPOLONI v. UNITED STATES
United States Court of Appeals, Sixth Circuit
450 F.3d 185 (6th Cir. 2006)

KENNEDY, J., delivered the opinion of the court.

[Editor — This case involved whether severance payments made to public school teachers were "wages." The payments were received after the teachers resigned from their positions and relinquished their statutory tenure rights. The reference in the case to "FICA" is to the Federal Insurance Contribution Act, which is the name of the law imposing the Social Security tax. "ESP" refers to an "employee severance plan." The court holds that the payments were "wages," over a dissent. Another case — *North Dakota State University v. United States*, 255 F.3d 599 (8th Cir. 2001) — concludes that these payments are *not* wages.]

We begin by examining the definition of "wages" for purposes of FICA. Section 3121(a) of the Internal Revenue Code defines "wages" as "all remuneration for employment . . . " Congress, by enacting FICA, intended to impose FICA taxes on a broad range of remuneration in order to accomplish the remedial purposes of the Social Security Act. See H.R. Rep. No. 74-615, at 3 (1935) (describing the aims of the Social Security Act).

Both the Supreme Court and this circuit have emphasized the broad, inclusive nature of this definition. For example, in *Soc. Sec. Bd. v. Nierotko*, 327 U.S. 358, 365–66 (1946), the Supreme Court held that back pay awarded to wrongfully discharged employees under the National Labor Relations Act constituted "wages" for purposes of the Social Security Act of 1935. The Court specifically rejected the argument that "service" as used in the Act should be limited to "only productive activity" and emphasized the broad nature of the definition of FICA "wages". . . .

. . . The dissent indicates that our result is "largely ordained" by our choice to define this statute broadly. While we maintain such a construction of this statute is proper, we find a broad construction is not necessary, as we hold the facts presented easily fit within the definition of "wages," for the following reasons.

First, the eligibility requirements for qualifying for a payment — that a teacher served a minimum number of years — indicate the payments were for services performed rather than for the relinquishment of tenure rights. . . . We have consistently held that where a payment arises out of the employment relationship, and is conditioned on a minimum number of years of service, such a payment constitutes FICA wages. . . .

In this case, the severance payments were conditioned upon a teacher having served a certain number of years — exceeding that of obtaining tenure under Michigan law — with the school district. . . . Plaintiffs necessarily had to have tenure to be eligible for the buyout. However, longevity — not tenure — was the key factor for determining eligibility because these early retirement payments were offered to encourage teachers at a high pay rate to retire. Thus, the payments at issue in this case . . . arose out of the employment relationship, and were conditioned on a minimum number of years of service.

Plaintiffs make much of the fact that they gave up their rights as tenured teachers to continued employment absent just cause for termination. They argue that because the payments were in exchange for the relinquishment of that right, the payments are not "wages" taxable under FICA. This leads us to our next point: just because a teacher relinquishes a right when accepting early retirement does not convert what would be FICA wages into something else.

Plaintiffs maintain that the school districts were "buying" their tenure rights. This point also greatly influences the dissent. Yet, a court must not look simply at what is being relinquished at the point a severance payment is offered, but rather, how the right relinquished was earned. Thus, we cannot understate the importance of the fact that a teacher earns tenure by successfully completing a probationary period. In other words, a teacher does not obtain tenure at the onset of employment; it is a right that is earned like any other job benefit. Admittedly, the grant of this right is guaranteed and protected by statute. But we fail to see how the fact that this right is protected by statute takes away from the point that it still must be earned through services to the employer.

In any event, the payments at issue were not in exchange solely for the tenure rights; they were in exchange for the teachers' early retirement, and, as such, were essentially severance payments.

In this case, the school district's motivation was not to buy tenure rights — the motivation was to induce those teachers at the highest pay scales to retire early. Relinquishment of tenure rights was simply a necessary and incidental part of accepting the buyout. . . .

Griffin, J., concurring and dissenting in part:

I would follow the persuasive authority of *North Dakota State University v. United States*, 255 F.3d 599 (8th Cir. 2001). In doing so, I would hold that the payments at issue . . . do not constitute "wages" for purposes of the Federal Insurance Contributions Act ("FICA"). . . .

These cases present an issue of statutory construction. In this regard, the inquiry begins with the fundamental purpose of judicial construction of statutes, which is to ascertain and give effect to the original meaning of the words used by Congress:

> [W]e begin with the understanding that Congress "says in a statute what it means and means in a statute what it says there." As we have previously noted . . . , when "the statute's language is plain, the sole function of the courts — at least where the disposition required by the text is not absurd — is to enforce it according to its terms." *United States v. Ron Pair Enterprises, Inc.*, 489 U.S. 235, 241 (1989) (quoting *Caminetti v. United States*, 242 U.S. 470, 485 (1917)).

As Justice Scalia has further elaborated:

> The text is the law, and it is the text that must be observed. I agree with Justice Holmes's remark, quoted approvingly by Justice Frankfurter in his

article on the construction of statutes: "Only a day or two ago — when counsel talked of the intention of a legislature, I was indiscreet enough to say I don't care what their intention was. I only want to know what the words mean." And I agree with Holmes's other remark, quoted approvingly by Justice Jackson: "We do not inquire what the legislature meant; we ask only what the statute means."

The FICA defines "wages" as "all remuneration for employment . . . " 26 U.S.C. § 3121(a). "Employment" is further defined as "any service, of whatever nature, performed . . . by an employee for the person employing him. . . ." Id. at § 3121(b). Thus, the statute's plain language raises the issue of whether the plaintiffs received their ESP remuneration for "any service" performed by them for their employer.

Where, as here, no statutory definitions exist, courts may refer to dictionary definitions for guidance in discerning the plain meaning of a statute's language.

The ordinary, common meaning of the word "services" is "[a]n act or a variety of work done for others, especially for pay." AMERICAN HERITAGE DICTIONARY OF THE ENGLISH LANGUAGE 222 (4th ed. 2000). Other major English language dictionaries are to the same effect . . . .

. . . I conclude . . . that the ESP payments were made in exchange for the relinquishment of plaintiffs' statutory and constitutionally-protected tenure rights, rather than remuneration for "services" to the school districts. . . .

. . . Relying on *Nierotko* . . . , the majority reaches a result which is largely ordained by its choice of a rule of statutory construction — [that "wages" should be "broadly construed"].

In my view, the statute at issue, like all statutes, should not be construed "broadly," "narrowly," "strictly," or "liberally," but rather fairly and reasonably. In this regard, I agree with Justice Scalia that "[a] text should not be construed strictly, and it should not be construed leniently; it should be construed reasonably, to contain all that it fairly means." Scalia, A Matter of Interpretation at 23. . . .

. . . [T]here is no question that the severance payments would not have been paid had plaintiffs not relinquished their tenure rights. Were it not for their statutory tenure rights, plaintiffs would be at-will employees, subject to discharge without cause or consideration. Indeed, this is evidenced by similarly situated employees who worked the same number of years and were entitled to the same salary levels as plaintiffs, who did not receive the ESP payments. The ESP payments therefore were not made in exchange for any "service" that plaintiffs performed or were wrongfully prevented from performing, but, rather, in exchange for the relinquishment of a separate statutory right. Accordingly, the majority's conclusion that any damages arising from a lawsuit following the illegal deprivation of the tenure right would be taxable under Gerbec is not correct.

The uniformity in the amount of the ESP payments is further evidence that this consideration was not the sum of each individual teacher's loss of actual wages. The ESP payments are neither tailored, on a case-by-case basis, to the recipient's employment record nor to the recipient's current wage rate. Moreover, the ESP payments are not equivalent to each teacher's loss of earning capacity because the age of each teacher varies considerably. In sum, there is no correlation between the amount of the ESP payments and the teachers' individual employment circumstances that would lend support to the majority's theory that the ESP payments constitute discretely earned wages for purposes of income tax withholding and the FICA. As Gerbec holds, remuneration for actual wage loss, past and future, is subject to FICA taxation. However, payment in exchange for the relinquishment of other vested and bona fide claims such as tort and statutory rights are not subject to FICA taxation.

. . . The majority's rationale that the ESP payments were made in consideration of the plaintiffs' past years of service is belied by the fact that similarly situated employees who did not relinquish their tenure rights received nothing. The majority further ignores the critical fact that the rights relinquished by plaintiffs stemmed from the entirely separate grant of authority created by state statute and, thus, required specific relinquishment of statutorily protected tenure rights. For these reasons, I would hold that it was this relinquishment, not the years of service, for which the school districts paid.

COMMENTS AND QUESTIONS

1. It is tempting to look for analogies to the income tax law when deciding whether the severance payments are nonetheless "wages." The closest analogy concerns whether a property interest is a capital asset. The general income tax rule is that property created by the taxpayer's personal services is not usually a capital asset (for example, a copyright interest in a book created by the author). By the same token, the relinquishment of tenure rights might be characterized as wages (attributable to personal services) under the Social Security law. *See, e.g.,* *Foote v. Commissioner,* 81 T.C. 930 (1983) (tenure rights are not a capital asset), *aff'd,* 751 F.2d 1257 (5th Cir. 1985).

The problem with drawing such analogies is that — as the *Rowan* case indicated — the income tax and Social Security tax do not have to be interpreted the same way. An interest might be similar to wages for the income tax (and therefore not a capital asset), but might not be "wages" for the Social Security tax.

2. The dissent says two things that are questionable. First, the citation to the dictionary does not get us very far. The facts in the case are such that the payments could easily be viewed as for services or for a property right, and the code might be interpreted either way. The payments depend on serving a certain number of years (more than what is necessary for tenure) — implying "wages"; but the payments do not vary with the number of years worked (as the dissent stressed) — implying "not wages."

Second, by stressing that the taxpayer relinquished a property interest, the dissent seems to be equating property law with Social Security law. The Social Security law does not have to incorporate property law definitions, any more than the income tax law is required to take that approach.

3. The Third Circuit has followed the Sixth Circuit decision in *Appoloni* and held that early retirement payments to tenured faculty are wages subject to FICA

taxation. *University of Pittsburgh v. U.S.*, 507 F.3d 165 (3d Cir. 2007). There was a dissent.

§ 28.03 "EMPLOYEE"

[A] Common Law Standard

A payroll tax requires a definition of "employee," because employers are required to withhold the Social Security tax from an employee's wages. Employee status is critical to the administration of social insurance programs because it is often very difficult to get an individual who renders personal services as an independent contractor to disclose the income and pay taxes. Payors are supposed to file a Form 1099 with the government disclosing payments to independent contractors, but compliance with this requirement is also lax. One study showed that 99% of salary income was reported to the government when the worker was classified as an employee; the comparable figure for independent contractors was 77% when a Form 1099 was filed and 27% when no Form 1099 was filed. *See* Joint Committee on Taxation, Present Law and Background Relating to Worker Classifications for Federal Tax Purposes (JCX-26-07), May 7, 2007, p. 10 (hereafter referred to as "JCX").

For a time, the Supreme Court and Treasury Regulations toyed with a definition of "employee" for purposes of the social security law that was somewhat more expansive than the common law definition. As the court explained in *United States v. Thorson*, 282 F.2d 157 (1st Cir. 1960), the Court had adopted a purposive approach to defining "employee," as follows:

> [In] *United States v. Silk*, 331 U.S. 704 (1947), the Court adopted a broad definition of the term "employee" to effectuate as it thought the broadly remedial purposes of the [Social Security] Act. Saying that "the generality of the employment definitions indicates that the terms 'employment' and 'employee,' are to be construed to accomplish the purpose of the legislation," the Court said . . . : "As the federal social security legislation is an attack on recognized evils in our national economy, a constricted interpretation of the phrasing by the courts would not comport with its purpose. Such an interpretation would only make for a continuance, to a considerable degree, of the difficulties for which the remedy was devised and would invite adroit schemes by some employers and employees to avoid the immediate burdens at the expense of the benefits sought by the legislation." The Court accordingly rejected the common-law test of control in favor of the test of "economic reality."

But Congress rejected these efforts by adding paragraph (2) to § 3121(d) (definition of "employee"), as follows:

> The term "employee" means-

> (1) any officer of a corporation; or (2) any individual who, under the usual common law rules applicable in determining the employer-employee relationship, has the status of an employee. . . .

In effect, Congress mandated an approach to determining the meaning of "employee" that imported into the Social Security law the technical usage of that term from the common law. (Treasury Regulations apply the same common law test for defining an employee subject to income tax withholding from wages under § 3401.)

[1] 20 Factors

In the following Revenue Ruling, the IRS tried to give content to the common law definition with a 20-part (!) test. You may recall Judge Posner's broadside in *Exacto Spring Corp. v. Commissioner*, 196 F.3d 833 (7th Cir. 1999) (Chapter 14.01[B][2][a]), which railed against the usefulness of multi-factor tests — "It is apparent that this test, though it or variants of it (one of which has the astonishing total of 21 factors . . .), are encountered in many cases, . . . leaves much to be desired — being, like many other multi-factor tests, 'redundant, incomplete, and unclear.' "

REVENUE RULING 87-41
1987-1 C.B. 296

[The tax Regulations] provide that generally the relationship of employer and employee exists when the person or persons for whom the services are performed have the right to control and direct the individual who performs the services, not only as to the result to be accomplished by the work but also as to the details and means by which that result is accomplished. That is, an employee is subject to the will and control of the employer not only as to what shall be done but as to how it shall be done. In this connection, it is not necessary that the employer actually direct or control the manner in which the services are performed; it is sufficient if the employer has the right to do so.

Conversely, these sections provide, in part, that individuals (such as physicians, lawyers, dentists, contractors, and subcontractors) who follow an independent trade, business, or profession, in which they offer their services to the public, generally are not employees.

Finally, if the relationship of employer and employee exists, the designation or description of the relationship by the parties as anything other than that of employer and employee is immaterial. Thus, if such a relationship exists, it is of no consequence that the employee is designated as a partner, coadventurer, agent, independent contractor, or the like.

As an aid to determining whether an individual is an employee under the common law rules, twenty factors or elements have been identified as indicating whether sufficient control is present to establish an employer-employee relationship. The twenty factors have been developed based on an examination of cases and rulings considering whether an individual is an employee. The degree of importance of each factor varies depending on the occupation and the factual context in which the services are performed. The twenty factors are designed only as guides for determining whether an individual is an employee; special scrutiny is required in applying the twenty factors to assure that formalistic aspects of an arrangement designed to achieve a particular status do not obscure the substance of the arrangement (that is, whether the person or persons for whom the services are performed exercise sufficient control over the individual for the individual to be classified as an employee). The twenty factors are described below:

1. INSTRUCTIONS. A worker who is required to comply with other persons' instructions about when, where, and how he or she is to work is ordinarily an employee. This control factor is present if the person or persons for whom the services are performed have the RIGHT to require compliance with instructions.

2. TRAINING. Training a worker by requiring an experienced employee to work with the worker, by corresponding with the worker, by requiring the worker to attend meetings, or by using other methods, indicates that the person or persons for whom the services are performed want the services performed in a particular method or manner.

3. INTEGRATION. Integration of the worker's services into the business operations generally shows that the worker is subject to direction and control. When the success or continuation of a business depends to an appreciable degree upon the performance of certain services, the workers who perform those services must necessarily be subject to a certain amount of control by the owner of the business.

4. SERVICES RENDERED PERSONALLY. If the Services must be rendered personally, presumably the person or persons for whom the services are performed are interested in the methods used to accomplish the work as well as in the results.

5. HIRING, SUPERVISING, AND PAYING ASSISTANTS. If the person or persons for whom the services are performed hire, supervise, and pay assistants, that factor generally shows control over the workers on the job. However, if one worker hires, supervises, and pays the other assistants pursuant to a contract under which the worker agrees to provide materials and labor and under which the worker is responsible only for the attainment of a result, this factor indicates an independent contractor status.

6. CONTINUING RELATIONSHIP. A continuing relationship between the worker and the person or persons for whom the services are performed indicates that an employer-employee relationship exists. . . .

7. SET HOURS OF WORK. The establishment of set hours of work by the person or persons for whom the services are performed is a factor indicating control.

8. FULL TIME REQUIRED. If the worker must devote substantially full time to the business of the person or persons for whom the services are performed, such person or persons have control over the amount of time the worker spends working and impliedly restrict the worker from doing other gainful work. An independent contractor on the other hand, is free to work when and for whom he or she chooses.

9. DOING WORK ON EMPLOYER'S PREMISES. If the work is performed on the premises of the person or persons for whom the services are performed, that factor suggests control over the worker, especially if the work could be done elsewhere. Work done off the premises of the person or persons receiving the services, such as at the office of the worker, indicates some freedom from control. However, this fact by itself does not mean that the worker is not an employee. The importance of this factor depends on the nature of the service involved and the

extent to which an employer generally would require that employees perform such services on the employer's premises. Control over the place of work is indicated when the person or persons for whom the services are performed have the right to compel the worker to travel a designated route, to canvass a territory within a certain time, or to work at specific places as required.

10. ORDER OR SEQUENCE SET. If a worker must perform services in the order or sequence set by the person or persons for whom the services are performed, that factor shows that the worker is not free to follow the worker's own pattern of work but must follow the established routines and schedules of the person or persons for whom the services are performed. . . .

11. ORAL OR WRITTEN REPORTS. A requirement that the worker submit regular or written reports to the person or persons for whom the services are performed indicates a degree of control.

12. PAYMENT BY HOUR, WEEK, MONTH. Payment by the hour, week, or month generally points to an employer-employee relationship, provided that this method of payment is not just a convenient way of paying a lump sum agreed upon as the cost of a job. Payment made by the job or on a straight commission generally indicates that the worker is an independent contractor.

13. PAYMENT OF BUSINESS AND/OR TRAVELING EXPENSES. If the person or persons for whom the services are performed ordinarily pay the worker's business and/or traveling expenses, the worker is ordinarily an employee. An employer, to be able to control expenses, generally retains the right to regulate and direct the worker's business activities.

14. FURNISHING OF TOOLS AND MATERIALS. The fact that the person or persons for whom the services are performed furnish significant tools, materials, and other equipment tends to show the existence of an employer-employee relationship.

15. SIGNIFICANT INVESTMENT. If the worker invests in facilities that are used by the worker in performing services and are not typically maintained by employees (such as the maintenance of an office rented at fair value from an unrelated party), that factor tends to indicate that the worker is an independent contractor. . . . Special scrutiny is required with respect to certain types of facilities, such as home offices.

16. REALIZATION OF PROFIT OR LOSS. A worker who can realize a profit or suffer a loss as a result of the worker's services (in addition to the profit or loss ordinarily realized by employees) is generally an independent contractor, but the worker who cannot is an employee. For example, if the worker is subject to a real risk of economic loss due to significant investments or a bona fide liability for expenses, such as salary payments to unrelated employees, that factor indicates that the worker is an independent contractor. The risk that a worker will not receive payment for his or her services, however, is common to both independent contractors and employees and thus does not constitute a sufficient economic risk to support treatment as an independent contractor.

17. WORKING FOR MORE THAN ONE FIRM AT A TIME. If a worker performs

more than de minimis services for a multiple of unrelated persons or firms at the same time, that factor generally indicates that the worker is an independent contractor. However, a worker who performs services for more than one person may be an employee of each of the persons, especially where such persons are part of the same service arrangement.

18. MAKING SERVICE AVAILABLE TO GENERAL PUBLIC. The fact that a worker makes his or her services available to the general public on a regular and consistent basis indicates an independent contractor relationship.

19. RIGHT TO DISCHARGE. The right to discharge a worker is a factor indicating that the worker is an employee and the person possessing the right is an employer. An employer exercises control through the threat of dismissal, which causes the worker to obey the employer's instructions. An independent contractor, on the other hand, cannot be fired so long as the independent contractor produces a result that meets the contract specifications.

20. RIGHT TO TERMINATE. If the worker has the right to end his or her relationship with the person for whom the services are performed at any time he or she wishes without incurring liability, that factor indicates an employer-employee relationship.

[2]　Applying the Factors

These factors seem to cluster around two primary themes — whether the "employer" has the right to control the "employee"; and whether the "employee" is taking any financial risks.

Even if the taxpayer is an employee, there is a further issue. When an individual is sent out on jobs by an agency that provides services to individuals and businesses and retains some say in how the work is performed, is the individual an employee of the agency or of the person to whom he or she is sent to work? For example, when a nurse, babysitter, or secretary is sent to work in someone's home or office, is the employer the agency that provides the worker or the person in whose home or office the work is performed?

[a]　Secretaries

[i]　Employee of Law Firm

PRIVATE LETTER RULING 8606030
(Nov. 8, 1985)

You are an individual who operates a law office as a sole proprietor. In the conduct of your business you hired the Worker . . . to provide part-time services as a secretary.

The terms of the oral agreement provide that the Worker will work for you for an indefinite period on an as needed basis if allowed by the Worker's schedule. The Worker will be paid an hourly wage for services performed. . . .

The Worker reports to work at your office at irregular intervals. When the

Worker does work at your office, the Worker works 1 to 5 hours a day. The Worker types letters and documents and answers your telephone. You instruct the Worker concerning the format of letters and documents to be typed. You review the Worker's work for the purpose of making adjustments to work in progress and corrections on work completed.

You provide a typewriter and accessories such as paper, pens, and pencils for the Worker's services. The Worker does not furnish equipment, supplies, or materials for the Worker's services. You also occasionally reimburse the Worker for gasoline the Worker uses in performing services for you.

The Worker performs the services personally without the aid of assistants. You identify the Worker as your typist, or sometimes, as your secretary. The Worker does not maintain a business listing, represent to the public as being in business to perform similar services, or maintain a separate office. Furthermore, the Worker has no financial investment in your business and cannot incur a loss in the performance of services for you. Either you or the Worker may terminate the services of the Worker without obligation to the other. . . .

Generally, the relationship of employer and employee exists when the person for whom the services are performed has the right to control and direct the individual who performs the services not only as to the result to be accomplished by the work but also as to the details and means by which that result is accomplished. That means an employee is subject to the will and control of the employer not only as to what shall be done but as to how it shall be done. In this connection, it is not necessary that the employer actually direct or control the manner in which the services are performed: it is sufficient if he has the right to do so. The right to discharge is also an important factor indicating that the person possessing that right is the employer. Other factors characteristic of an employer but not necessarily present in every case, are the furnishing of tools and the furnishing of a place to work to the individual who performs the services. Furthermore, the parties' description of their relationship is not determinative where the facts prove otherwise. . . .

[The factors in this case] indicate you have a right to exercise control over the Worker and that you exercise that right. Consequently . . . we conclude that the relationship of employer and employee exists between you and the Worker. . . . Accordingly, for federal employment tax purposes, the Worker is an employee with respect to secretarial services the Worker performs for you. Secretaries can, however, be under the control of an employment agency, who is then their employer [under certain circumstances].

[ii]   Employee of Agency

In Rev. Rul. 75-41, 1975-1 C.B. 323, a corporation that provided secretaries to professional companies under the following circumstances was the employer.

[The corporation] enters into contracts with the subscribers under which the subscribers specify the services to be provided and the fee to be paid to the corporation for each individual furnished. Subscribers have the right to require that an individual furnished by the corporation cease providing services to them, and they have the further right to have such individual replaced by the corporation within a reasonable period of time, but the subscribers have no right to affect the contract between the individual and the corporation. The contracts also provide that the corporation has the right to remove or reassign any personnel furnished to subscribers but that it will, in such cases, either furnish a replacement promptly or adjust the fee to compensate for the vacancy created.

The individuals who are to perform the services are recruited by the corporation and given various tests to determine their qualifications and degrees of skill. The corporation hires the personnel, pays their wages, and provides them with liability and unemployment insurance, workmen's compensation, and other benefits. Under the contract with the corporation, the individuals agree to be available to perform services for any subscribers to which they are assigned. The contract sets forth the amounts to be paid to the individuals. The fee that the corporation charges to the subscribers is based on a predetermined mark up formula. The corporation has the right, under the contract, to evaluate the performance of the individuals and to discharge them if the evaluation shows that they are failing to satisfactorily perform the services contracted for by the subscribers. Individuals who enter into contracts with the corporation agree that they will not contract directly with any subscriber to which they are assigned for at least three months after cessation of their contracts with the corporation.

When the corporation considers an individual qualified to meet a subscriber's request, the corporation assigns the individual to the subscriber to work on the subscriber's premises with the subscriber's equipment. The corporation instructs the individual as to his work hours and the nature of his duties, based on the subscriber's request for that particular type of individual and the hours he is to work. Subscribers rely on the corporation to see that the individual meets the qualifications they require and give the individual no further tests.

[b]   Nurses

[i]   Licensed or Registered Nurse as Independent Contractor

In Rev. Rul. 61-196, 1961-2 C.B. 155, the government concluded that licensed practical nurses and registered nurses were (on the facts of the ruling) independent contractors when they engaged in private duty nursing — typically working temporarily for a patient in the hospital or at home during an illness. Both their training and their exercise of discretion were important factors in reaching this conclusion. However, when such nurses work for a hospital or doctor, they are employees.

[ii]   Unlicensed Nurse's Aides as Employee

1. Rev. Rul. 61-196, 1961-2 C.B. 155, also discusses unlicensed nurse's aides (who called themselves "practical nurses") and concludes that they are employees of the person to whom they provided services. These aides normally perform services expected of maids and servants — for example, bathing, combing hair, reading, and giving medication. Like domestics, these individuals are usually employees because they are subject to complete direction and control in the performance of their services.

2. In *Youngken v. United States*, 407 F.2d 836 (3d Cir. 1969), a son employed an unlicensed practical nurse, without formal medical training, to look after his aged mother after she returned to his home from the hospital. The nurse worked exclusively in this job for about 11 years. Her primary responsibility was to attend to the mother during the daytime in the event of an emergency. During this period, the nurse made her own Social Security tax payments. However, when she applied for Social Security benefits, she was told that she was not self-employed, had erroneously made the payments, and was given a refund. The son was then assessed for the Social Security tax payments as her employer.

The son argued that the nurse was not under his "direction and control," because how she cared for his mother was "completely within her discretion and not subject to the [son's] control." The court disagreed. It concluded that, "[c]onsidering the rather routine nature of the services rendered, we do not consider the 'how' aspect of particular importance. We think the only reasonable inference from the record is that plaintiff possessed the right of control, and the fact that the right may not have been exercised here in some particular aspect does not alter this conclusion." The fact that the nurse had paid her own Social Security taxes was not dispositive, "in view of the pertinent policy considerations and the nature of the services performed."

QUESTION

Suppose the mother returned to her own home, not the son's home, and the son lived in another state from which he exercised no actual control. Would the "routine" nature of the job still constitute the nurse as an employee, rather than an independent contractor? Suppose the mother was not mentally competent at the time?

[iii]   Licensed Nurse as Employee of Referring Agency

REVENUE RULING 75-101
1975-1 C.B. 318

A company, that is in the business of furnishing the services of licensed practical nurses, engages such nurses pursuant to oral contracts. The company requires each licensed practical nurse desiring to be placed on its register to complete an application form on which she must list her training and previous experience. The company reviews each application prior to assigning a nurse to one of its clients to insure that the nurse is fully trained, has passed the state board examination for licensed practical nurses, and has a current professional license. The nurse is expected to maintain her own license and certification. The company issues instructions to the nurse regarding her professional appearance and conduct while on assignment, and periodically checks with each client to determine if the nurse's services are satisfactory. In addition, the company employs a visiting registered nurse, on a full time basis, to make periodic on-the-job visits to evaluate the professional competence of the practical nurse. When appropriate, the visiting nurse has the authority to make recommendations to the practical nurse regarding the care of the patient. It is understood that the practical nurse will follow these recommendations.

The oral contract between the company and the nurse contemplates that substantially all services will be performed personally, under the company's name, for a predetermined hourly rate and that an assignment will be completed. In the event a nurse is unable to complete an assignment she will receive remuneration for the number of hours that she performed services. The nurse may terminate her relationship with the company at any time. The company may terminate her services for repeated failure to report on assignments, theft, habitual tardiness, indulgence in alcoholic beverages, or failure to perform satisfactory services. The nurse is not eligible for sick pay or bonuses.

A prospective client contracts the company regarding his particular need for nursing services. The company secures the pertinent information regarding the request, such as, time, place, length, and nature of the services. The company contacts one of its nurses and relays the information regarding the client. The nurse is free to accept or decline any assignment. If the assignment is accepted the nurse is expected to arrive at the time and place specified and is expected to report to the company by telephone on a weekly basis regarding the assignment. The nurse is paid by the company on a weekly basis as the services are performed. The company bills the client monthly or at the completion of the assignment.

An individual is an employee for Federal employment tax purposes if he has the status of an employee under the usual common law rules applicable in determining the employer-employee relationship. . . . Generally, the relationship of employer and employee exists when the person for whom the services are performed has the right to control and direct the individual who performs the services not only as to the result to be accomplished by the work but also as to the details and means by which that result is accomplished. That is, an employee is subject to the will and control of the employer not only as to what shall be done but as to how it shall be done. In this connection, it is not necessary that the employer actually direct or control the manner in which the services are performed; it is sufficient if he has the right to do so. The right to discharge is also an important factor indicating that the person possessing that right is the employer. . . .

Rev. Rul. 61-196, 1961-2 C.B. 155, states that whether a nurse is self-employed or an employee depends on the facts and circumstances of each case. Generally speaking, licensed practical nurses and registered nurses are considered to be self-employed. However, when such nurses are on the regular staff of a hospital, clinic, nursing home, or physician, work for a salary, follow prescribed routines during fixed hours, and are subject to the direction and control of those engaging them, they are employees. . . .

In this case, the nurse performs professional nursing services as a licensed practical nurse for the clients of the company. The nurse represents the company, her services are periodically checked by the company, she is issued instructions, paid on a weekly basis, and her services may be terminated by the company. The nurse is not engaged in an independent enterprise in which she assumes the risk of profit and loss. Since she is a skilled worker, she does not require constant supervision.

Accordingly, it is held that the company retains the right to exercise over the nurse the degree of control and direction necessary to establish the relationship of employer and employee, and, therefore, the nurse is an employee of the company. . . .

[Editor — However, in Letter Ruling 8822039, the company acted merely as a placement agency and the registered nurse therefore retained status as an independent contractor.]

[c]   Models — As Independent Contractors; or as Employees of Referring Agency

In Rev. Rul. 71-144, 1971-1 C.B. 285, the models were independent contractors. They held themselves out to the public through a referring agency; worked for numerous photographic illustrators; varied their working hours; had no permanent relationship with the people for whom they worked; fixed their own rates based on their ability, experience, and popularity; provided most of their own wearing apparel; and had the right to decline engagements.

However, in Rev. Rul. 74-332, 1974-2 C.B. 327, the models were employees of the referring agency. The agency was a training school for models as well as a modeling agency. After graduation the models are free to accept or reject modeling assignments, but are prohibited from performing freelance modeling even if the client contacts them. The models perform services under the agency's name and do not hold themselves out to the general public as being available for similar services, although they provide their own cosmetics. The models may be dropped by the agency if they refuse too many jobs or if there are too many complaints by clients. A representative of the agency periodically visits with the clients to review the models' services. *Query:* How important was the fact that the agency also trained the models?

[d]   Babysitters

[i]   Is the Babysitter an Employee of the Parents?

In Rev. Rul. 77-279, 1977-2 C.B. 12, the agency ruled that the babysitter was not the parents' employee. The facts were as follows:

> An individual takes care of a child whose parents work during the day. . . . The parents leave the child at the individual's home in the

morning before going to work and call for the child in the evening upon returning from work. The parents rely upon the individual's judgment in caring for the child and issue no instructions other than relative to diet, health and rest, and occasionally relative to special foods, medicines, etc., that the child may require from time to time. The individual is told whom to contract in case of emergency. The individual personally determines the amount of attention the child requires, the types of meals to be served, and the manner in which to cope with any situation likely to arise in rendering child care services. The individual is free to perform household chores at any time during which the child does not require personal attention, such as, while the child is taking an afternoon nap. The individual receives a fixed weekly fee from the parents for these services. However, the individual is not held out to the public as engaging in day care work, and is not required to obtain a license for such work under state law.

The government concluded that "there does not exist a sufficient right of control on the part of the parents to establish, for employment tax purposes, the relationship of employer and employee between the parents and the individual who cares for the child. Thus, the individual is not engaged to perform services as an employee, but is engaged in an independent trade or business."

Query: Would the answer be different if the babysitter worked in the parents' home, the child was very young and the parents left very clear instructions about feeding and bedtime, and the babysitter was paid on a per-hour basis? The following regulation indicates that the parents will often be the employer. *See* **Treas. Reg. § 31.3506-1(e) (Example 3):**

> As a service to the community a neighborhood association maintains a list of individuals who are available to babysit. Parents in need of a sitter contact the association and are provided with a list of names and telephone numbers. The association charges no fee for the service and takes no action other than compiling the list of sitters and making it available to members of the community. Issues such as hours of work, amount of payment, and the method by which the services are performed are all resolved between the sitter and parent. A, a parent, used the list to hire B to sit for A's child. B performs the services four days a week in A's home and follows specific instructions given by A. . . . Consequently, . . . B remains the employee of A.

[ii] Is the Babysitter an Employee of the Referring Agency?

In Rev. Rul. 80-365, 1980-2 C.B. 300, revoking Rev. Rul. 74-414, 1974-2 C.B. 334, the government dealt with the situation where an agency furnished babysitting services to customers. The 1980 ruling noted that Rev. Rul. 74-414, 1974-2 C.B. 334, had held "that individuals performing babysitting services for customers of a babysitting agency . . . are employees of the agency for federal employment tax purposes, since the agency has retained the primary right to direct and control them. That agency furnishes instructions regarding conduct, requires semimonthly reports, prohibits the individuals from engaging assistants or substitutes or securing work with a client other than through the agency, and determines the fee to be charged. The babysitters collect the total fee for the services from the clients and pay a fixed percentage to the agency."

However, the 1980 ruling went on to explain a change in the law as of 1974:

> Effective with respect to remuneration received after December 31, 1974, section 3506(a) of the Code provides that, for federal employment tax purposes, a person engaged in the trade or business of putting sitters in touch with individuals who wish to employ them shall not be treated as the employer of such sitters (and such sitters shall not be treated as employees of such person) if such person does not pay or receive the salary or wages of the sitters and such person is compensated by the sitters or the persons who employ them on a fee basis. Section 3506(b) provides that the term "sitters" means individuals who furnish personal attendance, companionship, or household care services to children or to individuals who are elderly or disabled.

Presumably, these agencies will now avoid employer status by making sure that the customers pay the babysitter directly for services performed.

[e]   Adult entertainment booth performers

In *303 West 42nd Street Enterprises, Inc. v. I.R.S.*, 916 F.Supp. 349 (S.D.N.Y. 1996), the court rejected the claim that booth performers in an adult entertainment establishment were independent contractors. It stated that "the retention by [the taxpayer] of 60% of revenues received for time spent in the booth by the patron [] is more usual with respect to employees than to independent contractors. Furthermore, as to the monies not retained, we conclude that the 40% coin money is akin to wages and the 100% cash money is akin to a tip. On its most basic level, a tip is a payment made by a person who has received a personal service. Like the waiter who is paid a salary and receives tips, it is the Court's understanding that the booth performer is paid a salary of 40% of the coin deposits and receives a tip of the cash for her personal performance."

[B]   Employer's Consistent and Reasonable Treatment as Non-Employee

It should be obvious that a worker's status can be easily be misclassified. One study found that almost 15% of employers wrongly classified employees as independent contractors; JCX, p. 10. To relieve the pressure on employers, the statute provides a safe harbor, as follows:

> A taxpayer who pays others for services is shielded from employment tax liability if the taxpayer has consistently treated them as other-than-employees unless the taxpayer had no reasonable basis for doing so. Revenue Act of 1978, § 530, as amended, 26 U.S.C.A. § 3401 note.

There are a number of interesting aspects to the safe harbor. First, the legislative history says that it is to be "construed liberally in favor of taxpayers." Second, it does not apply to certain types of workers — including a computer programmer, systems analyst or other similarly skilled worker in a similar line of work — thereby leaving the common law test in place for these workers.

In *Greco v. United States*, 380 F. Supp. 2d 598 (M.D. Pa. 2005), the court discussed the "reasonable basis" requirement in response to a motion for summary judgment. The court first noted that the taxpayer could establish a "reasonable basis" by relying on any of the following: (1) judicial precedent, published ruling, technical advice with respect to the taxpayer, or a letter ruling to the taxpayer; (2) a past IRS audit of the taxpayer in which there was no assessment attributable to the treatment (for employment tax purposes) of the individuals holding positions substantially similar to the position held by this individual; or (3) long-standing recognized practice of a significant segment of the industry in which such individual was engaged.

The court rejected all three arguments. First, the record did not compel a finding of reliance on an agency or court ruling or on technical advice because the taxpayer "was already classifying the workers as independent contractors prior to receiving such advice." Second, it was unclear whether any prior audit favorable to the taxpayer dealt with workers who performed under conditions similar to those of the workers at issue in this case. Third, there was a factual dispute about what the industry standard was regarding classification of the workers. Summary judgment was denied.

[C]   Are Medical Residents Eligible for "Student" Exception?

In *Mayo Foundation for Medical Education and Research v. United States*, 131 S. Ct. 704 (2011), the Court dealt with a Treasury Department rule interpreting the Social Security Act. That Act exempted from taxation "service performed in the employ of . . . a school, college, or university . . . if such service is performed by a student who is enrolled and regularly attending classes at such school, college, or university." The Treasury regulations exempted students whose work was "incident to and for the purposes of pursuing a course of study." In 2004, the Treasury replaced its case-by-case application of this standard with a rule that categorically excludes from the student exemption a "full-time employee," defined in all events as an employee "normally scheduled to work 40 hours or more per week." The issue was whether this regulation could be applied to deny an exemption for medical residents who have graduated from medical school and train for a specialty. These doctors are required to engage in formal educational activities but spend most of their time (50 to 80 hours per week) caring for patients. The Court concluded that Congress had not directly addressed this precise question because it did not define "student" or consider how to deal with medical residents. Consequently, it deferred to the Treasury regulation under the *Chevron* case (discussed in Chapter 6.02[A]).

TAXES ON CONSUMPTION

Before the income tax became the primary federal tax, taxes on personal consumption provided most of the federal tax revenue. Tariffs on imported goods were the dominant tax in the nineteenth century (about 90% of the revenue until the Civil War and usually over 50% during the remainder of the nineteenth century). Tariffs were supplemented by excise taxes on high demand products such as tobacco and alcohol, usually producing a bit under 50% of federal revenue after the Civil War. Excise taxes on specific products still provide a significant amount of federal tax (about 4%, primarily on tobacco, alcohol, airline transportation, and transportation fuel), but most federal internal revenue now comes from income taxes on individuals and corporations. Tariffs are primarily a factor in trade, not tax policy.

States began to tax personal consumption in a big way in the 1930s, and it is now the highest source of state revenue (about 50%), as well as a significant portion of local government revenue. Beginning in 1969, state tax revenues from a general sales tax on personal consumption (imposed on the sale of most tangible personal property) exceeded revenue from state excise taxes on specific items.

In theory, U.S. sales taxes are supposed to fall on personal consumption, but they do not come close to taxing all of a taxpayer's personal consumption because state sales taxes are imposed primarily on the sale of *tangible personal property*. Services, intangible personal property, and real estate are often exempt from the sales tax.

States usually impose sales taxes at a single point in the production-distribution chain — on retail sales. However, a sales tax can be imposed on every sale as goods move down the production or distribution chain to the final consumer. At one time, European countries taxed the full value of each sale (for example, by the producer, wholesaler, and retailer), leading to multiple tax burdens depending on how many sales occurred on the way to the final sale. This encouraged mergers to avoid multiple taxes as well as distorting the sales prices for goods depending on how many taxes were imposed. These inefficiencies led Europe to adopt a value added tax (referred to as a VAT) as its "sales" tax. In practice, a VAT tends to have a more expansive tax base than U.S. sales taxes, because it is not limited to the sale of tangible personal property.

There is yet one more way of taxing personal consumption, which relies on the equation: Income = Consumption + Savings. (The "Savings" in the equation refers to the increase in savings during the tax year.) A consumption tax records income and then allows a deduction for any increase in savings during the year (or increases the tax base when previously deducted savings are withdrawn for personal consumption). It is therefore likely to reach most personal consumption, unlike sales taxes or even a VAT. The modern policy justification for a consumption tax is usually a desire to encourage savings. A consumption tax can also make adjustments for different levels of spending and family size, because the tax base is income minus savings. This distinguishes the consumption tax from the typical sales tax and VAT, which cannot adjust for family size and can be progressive only through a clumsy effort to overburden purchases that are more likely to be made by higher income taxpayers (such as yachts) or by exempting purchases that are disproportionately purchased by lower income taxpayers (such as groceries).

India and Sri Lanka tried their hand at a consumption tax but did not enjoy much success. An effort by Bolivia to adopt a consumption tax failed when the United States ruled that it was not an income tax eligible for the foreign tax credit (discussed in Chapter 34.01[B]). There have also been serious proposals to adopt a consumption tax in the United States, on the theory that our greater experience with an income tax would make the consumption tax easier to administer, but nothing has come of it.

This Part examines taxes on consumption, as follows: Chapter 29 (sales taxes); Chapter 30 (the VAT); and Chapter 31 (a consumption tax).

Chapter 29

SALES TAX

§ 29.01 THE TAXPAYER AND TAX RATES

A sales tax is imposed on a sales transaction. Technically, the retail seller is usually the taxpayer, but it is expected that the tax will be passed on to the consumer as part of the purchase price. However, this expectation is often defeated because of the failure to tax all personal consumption uniformly — especially the failure to tax many *services* and the sale of *intangible personal property* and *real estate*. Sellers of taxed sales are therefore less able to charge higher prices, as buyers are attracted to untaxed products.

The U.S. sales tax is usually imposed at significantly less than a 10% rate, which reduces but does not eliminate the distortions resulting from the failure to impose a tax at a uniform rate on personal consumption.

The sales tax in the United States is usually (by law) stated separately on the purchaser's bill. This requirement is a political choice, so as not to make taxes too painless and too politically palatable. Still, the sales tax comes in small packets associated with individual purchases, which tends to reduce the pain. (Income tax withholding has a similar "soothing" effect on taxpayers.)

§ 29.02 TAXING JURISDICTION

Today, the sales tax is commonly used at the state and local levels in the United States, not by the federal government. Proposals to adopt a sales tax at the federal level are met with two important political objections — that it falls too heavily on those with lower incomes (leading F.D.R. to vigorously oppose its adoption in the 1930s); and that a federal tax might displace state reliance on the tax. Advocating a sales tax is not as much of a political third rail as modifying social security, but it has come close. Some prominent politicians who advocated a federal sales tax have been defeated and this has scared off other potential supporters.

There are additional technical objections to adopting a federal sales tax as a replacement of the federal income tax. *First*, states obtain revenue by piggybacking on the federal income tax and would insist that some way be found to make up the shortfall. *Second*, many taxpayers benefit from tax breaks provided under the income tax, especially credits for lower income taxpayers (some of which are refundable, such as the EIC and the child tax credit). Some way would have to be found to help these taxpayers if a sales tax replaced the income tax. *Third*, charities who benefit from an income tax deduction might suffer, although the tax break probably does not have a significant impact on behavior at lower income levels.

Consequently, any federal sales tax would probably supplement, not replace, the income tax.

§ 29.03   TAX BASE

[A]   Primarily Tangible Personal Property

As noted earlier, the sales tax falls primarily on the sale of tangible personal property, not on the sale of services, intangible property, and real estate. Casual sales of tangible personal property (such as garage sales) are generally exempt.

However, the reality is more complex than this oversimplified picture. There is a wide variety in the coverage of sales tax laws and the following discussion only hints at the complexity of state statutes, regulations, and judicial interpretations of the law. A thorough canvassing and critique of these rules can be found in JEROME R. HELLERSTEIN AND WALTER HELLERSTEIN, STATE TAXATION (Warren Gorham & Lamont).

[1]   Real Estate

The omission of real estate sales from state sales tax is often justified on the ground that property taxes have already been imposed. Another likely explanation is that the housing industry is influential in preserving the exemption. This does not mean that real estate avoids sales tax altogether; the purchase of materials used to construct buildings is often treated as a taxable sale.

[2]   Services

The omission of services from the sales tax was originally meant to avoid taxing labor. In today's modern service-oriented economy, however, this omission is a major gap in U.S. sales taxes. For example, lawyers' services, personal insurance, financial services, advertising, and laundry services are usually exempt. Some services might be exempt for policy reasons — for example, education and hospital stays.

Not all services are exempt in all states. Many states tax telecommunications services. And some services, often involving entertainment, are likely to be taxed — for example, tickets to movies and amusement parks. Hotel services are usually taxed, often at higher-than-normal tax rates; this allows the taxing jurisdiction to export the tax to out-of-staters who are visiting the state, assuming that high tax rates do not discourage tourists.

More broadly, many states have expanded their sales tax base to include selected services, largely as a result of services becoming a greater percentage of personal consumption — for example, repair and installation services. However, a 1987 Florida law taxing services generally — including lawyers and advertising services — lasted six months before being repealed.

[3] Intangibles

The omission of intangible personal property from the sales tax base has also come under pressure from the evolution of the modern economy. For example, after an Illinois court held that computer software was not taxable because it was intangible property (*First Nat'l Bank of Springfield v. Department of Revenue*, 421 N.E.2d 175 (Ill. 1981)), the state statute was amended to provide that computer software was "tangible personal property." This should remind you that, whatever the cases may say when applying a general sales tax statute, some specific situations may now be the subject of explicit legislation that resolves any doubts that the cases may reveal.

[4] Lease or Rental

Sales tax laws usually treat the lease or rental of tangible personal property as a taxable transaction. Otherwise, it would be too easy to disguise a sale as the rental of property.

[5] Progressivity?

Some sales of tangible personal property are not taxed in order to reduce the burden of the sales tax on those with lower income, although everyone gets the tax break. Thus, groceries are usually exempt, but restaurant meals are taxed.

In *Sparks Nugget, Inc. v. State ex rel. Dept. of Taxation*, 179 P.3d 570 (Nev. 2008), however, the food exemption was extended well beyond any policy of helping lower income taxpayers. The court was asked to decide whether the state constitution's exemption for "food for human consumption" applied to the purchase of *uncooked* food by a Nevada casino followed by its preparation and complimentary provision to selected customers and employees. The court held that "the constitution's plain language clearly and broadly exempts *all* food for human consumption (unless that food is 'prepared food intended for immediate consumption' at the time it is sold)." It contrasted the Nevada exemption with an Arizona provision that explicitly limited its food exemption to sale of food for home consumption. The court rejected the government's argument that the food was subject to the tax as "prepared food intended for immediate consumption," because the taxpayer prepared the uncooked food; it did not purchase food already prepared.

States also vary in the extent to which they tax utility services, such as gas and electricity. Exemption of residential utility services is often defended as a way of reducing the tax on people with low income.

[B] Business Inputs

A sales tax is not (in theory) supposed to fall on business inputs because these purchases are not for personal consumption. If the value of business inputs *and* final personal consumption sales are both taxed, the value of the product is overtaxed. The exemption for business inputs is implemented by the purchaser registering as a business and providing the seller with a registration number so that the sale will not be taxed. An exemption for business inputs is sometimes unavailable, however, because of the way the laws are written or interpreted.

First, a sale is usually exempt if the product is purchased for resale — the typical wholesaler's sale to a retailer.

Second, there is usually an exemption for sales of property used as an "ingredient" or "component" of tangible personal property. However, the narrow scope of this exception means that the purchase of a machine used to manufacture a product is subject to tax, because the machine is used up in the manufacturing process rather than becoming an ingredient of a product for later sale. Of course, this does not make sense from the point of view of sales tax theory, which is to tax personal consumption. Consequently, some states have passed laws explicitly exempting machinery used directly in the manufacture of goods. However, the "used directly" requirement often means that some inputs that are not so used are taxed, such as the purchase of delivery trucks used to transport a product.

The "ingredient/component" test may also be hard to apply. States use various tests — such as whether the property was "essential" to producing the final product, whether the purchased product has as its "primary purpose" its incorporation into the final product, or whether it is a "substantial ingredient" of the final product. *See American Distilling Co. v. Department of Revenue*, 368 N.E.2d 541 (Ill. App. Ct. 1977), which concluded that the purchase of barrels used to age whiskey was not taxable because wood extracts from the barrels became part of the final product. Although the wood extract was only a small part of the final product, the barrels were "vital to the production of the whiskey" — an "essentiality" test. *But see American Stores Packing Co. v. Peters*, 277 N.W.2d 544 (Neb. 1979) (purchase of casings into which frankfurter meat was stuffed and which were discarded after the manufacturing process was complete *was* taxable, even though some glycerine from the casing remained on the frankfurters; the glycerine was "incidental").

One major reason why these legal tests are very difficult to apply is that there is no clear rationale for deciding which business inputs should or should not be taxed. They all *should* be exempt if the tax base is personal consumption.

The failure to exempt business inputs is *not necessarily* an imperfection in the tax law, *if* the final personal consumption sale is not taxed. For example, if the sale of a residence is not taxed but business inputs for the builder are taxed, at least some of the personal consumption from housing is included in the tax base. Or, if the final consumption of personal services is not taxed — for example, lawyers' or dentists' services — taxing an intermediate input to the provider of those personal services (such as office supplies or dentures) does not lead to overtaxation.

[C] Fringe Benefits

If a business buys a product that can be used to supply personal consumption to an employee (for example, a fringe benefit such as a car), exemption of the purchase by the business is likely to result in exclusion of personal consumption from the tax base, because it is too hard to tax the employee on the receipt or use of the product. In other words, the problems we encountered in the income tax law regarding fringe benefits (in Chapters 7.01–.02) are replicated in a sales tax, if the cost of the fringe benefit is exempt as a business input. The higher the sales tax rate, the greater the incentive to enjoy personal consumption in the form of a tax-free fringe benefit provided by an employer. To prevent this tax avoidance, some items (such as cars) might be taxed when bought by a business, whether or not they would otherwise be taxable. (Frequently, these business purchases will be taxed in any event because they are not purchased for resale, are not an ingredient or component of tangible personal property, and are not used to manufacture a product.)

[D]   Consumer Durables

How should consumer durables be taxed under a sales tax? We will use a car as an example.

[1]   Present Value of Future Consumption

Personal consumption occurs over the life of the car, not in the year of purchase. However, the purchase price is the present value of the estimated annual rental value, so a sales tax on the present value at the time of purchase is an acceptable proxy for the tax that would have been imposed on future annual consumption. Because the sales tax rates are not progressive, the fact that the purchase price is much larger than the annual rental value does not distort the tax burden.

[2]   Casualty Loss

What happens if there is a casualty loss? Under the income tax, there is a deduction; Chapter 12.02[A]. However, no adjustment is made for casualties under a sales tax to account for unused consumption that has previously been taxed.

[3]   Trade-In

Suppose car 1 was bought when it was new but is now a used car, which is traded in for new car 2. As in the casualty loss situation, some portion of the prior sales tax on the purchase of car 1 has fallen on the value of car 1 that was not consumed. However, the purchase price of the new car 2 should be taxed. A fair result can be achieved by imposing a sales tax on the purchaser of new car 2 on the value of the new car 2, net of the trade-in value — that is, the value of the new car 2 minus the value of the trade-in of the used car 1. For example, assume a purchase of car 1 for $20,000, with a $12,000 trade-in of that car for new car 2 worth $25,000 (resulting in a $13,000 cash payment). This should result in a total of $33,000 being taxed — which is the $8,000 of car 1 that was consumed prior to the trade-in plus the $25,000 value of the new car. This result is achieved by imposing a tax on the $13,000 cash payment when car 2 is acquired ($25,000 minus the $12,000 trade-in). A total of $33,000 is taxed because $20,000 is taxed when car 1 is purchased and $13,000 is taxed when car 2 is acquired with a trade-in.

In *Department of Revenue v. Beyer*, 193 S.W.3d 755 (Ky. Ct. App. 2006), the court considered whether Kentucky law violated equal protection because it reduced the taxable sales price of a used car by a trade-in allowance, but not the taxable sales price of a new car. The court stated:

By permitting the retail price of a used motor vehicle to be setoff by the trade-in allowance, the legislature effectively lessened the tax burden upon used vehicle purchasers and thus, made the purchase of a used motor vehicle more economically attractive. By lowering the use tax upon a used motor vehicle, the used car industry undoubtedly benefited by a reduction in the total purchase price of a used car. We observe that economic growth is a legitimate governmental interest. Hence, we believe the difference in treatment between a "used motor vehicle" and a "new motor vehicle" . . . rationally furthers the goal of stimulating the used car industry. As there exists a legitimate state interest rationally related to the difference in treatment between a "used motor vehicle" and a "new motor vehicle," we are of the opinion that [the law does] not violate the equal protection clause and the Fourteenth Amendment of the United States Constitution [or the State Constitution] and the district court erred by so concluding.

[E]   Interstate Problems

Variations in state sales tax rates can encourage travel from a residence state to a lower tax jurisdiction to reduce tax on the sale. This sometimes occurs when a taxpayer crosses the border to purchase lower-taxed goods. (The taxpayer cannot do this successfully with a car, because a tax will be due when it is registered in the residence state.) In addition, a taxpayer who is already traveling on a trip may be tempted to avoid a sales tax by shipping the product back home to the state of residence, because exported goods are usually tax-exempt in the state of sale. (If an in-state resident gives an out-of-state address to which a product should be shipped, that is simply fraud.) Finally, taxpayers do not have to travel to buy goods from out-of-state. They can mail order the goods or (in recent years) use the Internet to purchase or download the product.

The problem of avoiding tax on goods imported into the state by whatever means is usually addressed by the residence state imposing a "use tax" on the resident's out-of-state purchases. Some statutes specify that the purchase must be for the *purpose* of "storage, use, or consumption" within the residence state, but others require only that the use occur in the residence state, whatever the original purpose. This distinction is important when property is brought into the state sometime after its original purchase. *Compare Atlantic Gulf & Pac. Co. v. Gerosa*, 209 N.E.2d 86 (N.Y. 1965) (taxable when brought into the state for six weeks of use eight years after purchase), *with Morrison-Knudsen Co. v. State Tax Comm'n*, 44 N.W.2d 449 (Iowa 1950) (property not purchased for use in the state but brought into state after eight years for one year's in-state use; not taxable). When a use tax is imposed on property brought into the state some time after purchase, the taxable amount is sometimes discounted from the original purchase price to account for prior out-of-state use.

Whatever the statutory rule, it is notoriously difficult to get the taxpayer to report out-of-state purchases, especially when the purchase is for retail use. This has been true of mail order sales for some time, and sales concluded over the Internet are an increasing problem, with the potential for severely reducing state sales tax revenues. States have tried to get out-of-state sellers to collect the tax on such sales and pay it to the residence jurisdiction, but there are constitutional obstacles to this result, discussed in Chapter 29.05[B]. Tax collection problems will be even more serious as delivery itself occurs over the Internet (for example, downloaded books and movies).

§ 29.04 TAXABLE SALES OF TANGIBLE PERSONAL PROPERTY

How does state law decide whether there is a taxable sale of tangible personal property or a nontaxable sale of services or intangible property?

[A] Tangible Personal Property vs. Services

If services are not taxed, how should a distinction be drawn between the sale of goods and the sale of services?

[1] Some Tests

[a] True Object; Dominant Purpose; Essence of Transaction

State courts use a variety of tests to decide whether tangible personal property whose value is derived primarily from services (such as artwork) is a taxable or nontaxable sale. Some states adopt a "true object" or "dominant purpose" or "essence of transaction" test by case law, regulation, or legislation — that is, if the true object or dominant purpose or essential nature of the transaction is to acquire the value of the services, the transaction is not taxable. This test is hard to apply, however, for the same reason that it is often hard to know which business inputs are exempt — because the distinction has nothing to do with the theoretical basis for the tax, which is to identify taxable personal consumption.

Some courts rely on a "primary purpose" of the purchaser test, which is presumably the same as the "dominant purpose" or "true object" test. In *Qualcomm, Inc. v. Dep't of Revenue*, 249 P.3d 167 (Wash. 2011), the court applied this test to distinguish between two types of services that were taxed at different rates — specifically, "information services" and "network telephone services." The case involved the sale of hardware, software, and a service that collected, manipulated, and transmitted data from trucks to trucking dispatch centers — referred to as the "OmniTRACS system." The court held that the primary purpose of the OmniTRACS system was to obtain data and that therefore it should be taxed as an "information service." It stated: "We adopt the 'primary purpose of the purchaser' rule when a service involves both the collection and processing of data and the transmission of data to determine whether the 'network telephone service' or 'information service' rate should apply." It further acknowledged that applying this test was more difficult when the facts involved two different types of services, rather than the more common situation of distinguishing between a good and a service.

[b]   Inconsequential Materials

Some cases say that a sale of tangible personal property has not occurred if tangible materials are only an "inconsequential" part of the total. *See, e.g., Washington Times-Herald, Inc. v. District of Columbia*, 213 F.2d 23 (D.C. Cir. 1954) (comic strip provided to newspaper was a nontaxable sale of services, disregarding the tangible medium used to transfer the comic strip). But this test is not likely to be applied to prevent a taxable sale of artwork created by a highly paid artist, just because the canvas and paints were an insignificant part of the total price.

[c]   Common Understanding

Given the artificiality of some of the tests distinguishing between a taxable sale and nontaxable services, some courts fall back on a "common understanding" test. The idea is that the best way to interpret the taxing statute is to rely on how people are most likely to characterize the transaction, however uncertain that test might be.

The court in *Qwest Dex, Inc. v. Arizona Dep't of Revenue*, 109 P.3d 118 (Ariz. Ct. App. 2005), applied the common understanding test. The taxpayer published telephone directories. To that end, it engaged the services of an out-of-state printer. The taxpayer was required to supply the paper on which the directories were printed, although the printer paid for the paper on the taxpayer's behalf and obtained reimbursement. The printer delivered the directories to the taxpayer and the state imposed a use tax on the full value of the directories — based on both the paper and printing services components. The taxpayer conceded a tax only on the value of the paper, but not on the printing services component of the directories. The court agreed with the taxpayer, applying the "common understanding" test. It stated:

> . . . [W]hether a transaction qualifies as the sale of tangible personal property or the sale of a service is determined by the parties' common understanding of the particular trade, business, or occupation. For example, in *Dun & Bradstreet, Inc. v. City of New York*, 11 N.E.2d 728 (N.Y. 1937), the New York court determined that books containing credit ratings constituted a service and not tangible personal property pursuant to the common understanding test. . . .

> [Editor — The court added a footnote citing two cases that supported its reliance on the common understanding test: *Community Telecasting Serv. v. Johnson*, 220 A.2d 500 (Me. 1966) (pamphlets sold to television station containing results of market surveys, which indicated which programs the audience was watching, represented the performance of a service, so that the transaction was not subject to a use tax); *Fingerhut Prods. Co. v. Commissioner of Revenue*, 258 N.W.2d 606, 610 (Minn. 1977) (typed mailing lists used by direct-mail merchandiser were not subject to use tax; the use of the tangible medium of the lists is merely incidental to the use of the information contained in those lists).]

Applying the common understanding test, we determine that Taxpayer does not owe a use tax on the printing of the directories. Few would dispute that the Printers provided a service to Taxpayer in agreeing to print the directories. Indeed, the very nature of the term "printing" denotes a service and not a tangible item. Moreover, case law has articulated that printers who print specific material on paper for a customer are not engaged in the business of selling tangible personal property, but are instead engaged in a service. The reasoning is that the paper is of no use to anyone except the customer for whom the printing is done.

[2]   Some Factual Settings

[a]   Relevance of Custom-Made?

Some states draw a distinction between a product that is made in bulk in advance and then sold to multiple purchasers (which is a taxable sale of tangible personal property), and a product that is custom-made for the purchaser and not adaptable for another's use (which is a nontaxable service). This distinction often has the undesirable effect of giving some taxpayers a competitive edge. For example, exempting custom-made computer software as a nontaxable service (or, perhaps, as a nontaxable sale of intangible property), tends to favor large business sellers who are more likely to provide a customized product.

The following case grapples with this variation on this issue.

SOUTHERN BELL TEL. & TEL. CO. v. DEPARTMENT OF REVENUE
Florida Court of Appeal, First District
366 So. 2d 30 (Fla. Dist. Ct. App. 1978)

BOYTER, JUDGE. . . .

The art work which Southern Bell acquired for use in the yellow pages fell into three different categories: (1) stock art, (2) speculative art, and (3) finished art. Southern Bell conceded in the proceedings below that it purchased stock art as tangible personal property and that those purchases were subject to the sales tax. However, Southern Bell contends that its transactions with artists who created speculative art and finished art were personal service transactions which involved sales as inconsequential elements for which no separate charges were made and thus, were exempt from sales tax by virtue of F.S. 212.08(7)(e).

. . . Stock art is previously created art work which is inventoried by dealers who publish catalogues describing the stock art. When Southern Bell purchases stock art, it acquires possession of papers bearing reproductions of previously prepared drawings, designs, or other representations of objects which are created by the company that sells the stock art, and are reproduced in quantity. Speculative art and finished art are created by artists with whom Southern Bell contracts. Speculative art refers to rough drawings created by artists at the specific request of the yellow pages salesperson. After a salesperson investigates the general nature of a prospective advertiser's business he gives this information to the artist who by himself or in collaboration with the salesperson creates an artistic design to show how an advertisement for the business might appear in the yellow pages. The design may be accepted or rejected by the prospective advertiser. If it is accepted, Southern Bell gives it back to the same or another artist with the request that finished art be created. Southern Bell becomes obligated to pay the artist who created the speculative art whether or not the design is accepted or rejected. The amount of the fee is measured by the size of the design and is not affected by whether or not the artist's work is used by Southern Bell. The fee is not broken down into separate amounts for the services performed and the tangible personal property transferred to Southern Bell. Finished art refers to designs which are actually photographed for use in particular yellow pages advertisements. While speculative art is a mock-up of the entire design of the advertisement, including the lettering, finished art consists of only the artistic design or illustration. Finished art is precisely drawn as opposed to being merely sketched as in the case of speculative art. Southern Bell photographs the finished art and it is the photograph not the finished art itself which is placed in the yellow pages advertisement. The fee for finished art is either a flat fee or based upon the amount of time spent by the artist and is not affected by the use which Southern Bell makes of finished art. The artists who prepare either speculative art or finished art furnish all the materials used in the creation of the design and the relative value of the materials used ranges from 1% to 6% of the amount paid by Southern Bell to the artist.

It is Southern Bell's position that theoretically, the artists could perform the services for which they are engaged without transferring any property to Southern Bell. In the case of speculative art, the artist could accompany the yellow pages salesperson on a visit to a prospective advertiser or the prospective advertiser could accompany the salesperson to the artist's studio. In the case of finished art, Southern Bell could photograph the finished art at the studio of the artist. However, Southern Bell contends both of those methods are economically impractical.

It is the Department's contention that Southern Bell purchased title and exclusive possession to the art work, since that is the only way Southern Bell could obtain the benefit of the product.

The Administrative Hearing Officer found that the transactions involved the furnishing of personal services and that no separate charge was made for the tangible personal property which was transferred. However, the Officer concluded that since it would not be economically feasible for Southern Bell to avail itself of the artist's services without taking possession of the material on which the services were performed the transfer of tangible personal property was not an inconsequential element of the transaction. Accordingly, the Officer concluded that the personal service exemption did not apply in this case. . . .

We agree with petitioner that the exemption set forth in F.S. 212.08(7)(e) applies to the transactions involved. When Southern Bell buys speculative and finished art, it is really purchasing the artist's idea and the fact that the idea is transmitted on tangible personal property is an inconsequential element of the transaction.

We reach this decision after considering several factors, viz:

(1) Whether or not the property to be transferred as a result of the transaction is already in existence or whether it is produced in the course of the services rendered.

(2) The value of the individual effort involved in the transaction as compared to the value of the property transferred.

(3) Finally, whether or not it is essential to the transaction that the specific tangible personal property be created.

Applying those factors to this case, we find that the art work (not stock art) transferred to Southern Bell was created solely in the context of the particular transactions and not prior to them. The value of the services performed for Southern Bell was much greater than the value of the tangible personal property transferred to Southern Bell. Finally, taking possession of the material on which the services were rendered was not essential to Southern Bell's realization of the value of the artist's services because the designs created by the artist could be disassociated from the tangible personal property even though it might not have been economically feasible to do so.

SMITH, JUDGE, dissenting: . . .

The majority's view will command respect from philosophers who hold that all things palpable are but shadows of some ideal. In a sense every work of art, indeed every wheel and lever, is a design separable from the tangible property in which it is embodied. But as the question is what Southern Bell has purchased — the image in the artist's mind or the one he drew with ink on paper. I cannot believe that the thing acquired is "the artist's idea and the fact that the idea is transmitted on tangible personal property is an inconsequential element of the transaction." If it were true that "the designs created by the artist could be disassociated from the tangible personal property" in which the designs are manifested, a Caruso record would be sold as wax and a Tolstoy novel as wood pulp, inconsequential elements of the artistry which created them, and hence nontaxable.

The hearing officer found as a fact that the end purpose of Southern Bell's transactions with artists is the acquisition of drawings, rough or finished, to show to prospective advertisers or to reproduce in the yellow pages. In my view, our inquiry ends when we have found substantial competent evidence to support that finding. I cannot grasp the majority's distinction between the taxable sale of stock art and the nontaxable sale of speculative or finished art. In either case, Southern Bell has characterized the transaction by specifying what is useful to it, and in either case, the thing specified is a tangible drawing, valuable in itself, which Southern Bell uses and discards or retains as its own. . . .

A different case might be presented if Southern Bell's artists licensed the use of their skill for particular purposes on particular occasions, as by drawing in chalk upon an advertiser's blackboard, then reclaiming their proprietary images by erasure.

COMMENTS

1. The prior case says that it is using the "inconsequential" test — is the tangible personal property an inconsequential feature of the transaction? But it does not apply that test by looking exclusively at whether the tangible personal property is a small percentage of the value of the final product. Instead, it applies three factors: (1) whether the product was custom-made; (2) whether the tangible personal property was an inconsequential part of the total (1%–6% was inconsequential); and (3) whether getting tangible personal property was essential to the transaction. All three factors favored the service exemption, rather than a taxable transfer of tangible personal property. Does this suggest that the court is really applying something like either the true object or dominant purpose or essence of the transaction test, even though it articulates an "inconsequential" test?

2. The dissent concluded that the transaction was a taxable sale of tangible personal property, comparing the taxable sale of paintings and books or records to the sale of the speculative or finished art. But isn't there a difference? Paintings, books, and records are not usually custom-made, and the transfer of the tangible personal property in these situations is essential to the transaction.

[b]   Services and Product Separate

In the prior examples, there was a sale of a product whose value incorporated personal services (for example, artwork). When a transaction can be bifurcated into a sale and service element, because the services are not embodied in the product, their respective values should be separated and the sales element taxed — for example, car repairs distinguished from car parts. The "true object" or "dominant purpose" or "essence of the transaction" test should not be used in such cases. *See Swain Nelson & Sons Co. v. Department of Finance*, 6 N.E.2d 632 (Ill. 1937) (landscaping services not taxed, but separately stated sale of trees is taxable).

Nonetheless, some states use these tests even when the services and product elements of the transaction are clearly separate. For example, there were cases that exempted the sale of eyeglasses by an *ophthalmologist* because the dominant purpose of the transaction was medical services; however, the sale of eyeglasses by an *optician* was taxable. Optometrists' sales fell in between these extremes; *compare Babcock v. Nudelman*, 12 N.E.2d 635 (Ill. 1937) (eyeglasses not taxable), *with Rice v. Evatt*, 59 N.E.2d 927 (Ohio 1945) (eyeglasses taxable). In any event, taxing one seller and not the other clearly violates the principle that the tax law should not give one taxpayer a competitive edge, and most states have passed statutes eliminating the distinction in the case of eyeglasses — to exempt the sale in all three situations.

The contents of the invoice should not matter. States should separate the taxable sale of tangible personal property from the nontaxable sale of services whether or not the seller has separately invoiced these two items. In *California Bd. of Equalization v. Advance Schools, Inc.*, 2 B.R. 231 (Bankr. N.D. Ill. 1980), the taxpayer was a correspondence school that provided both educational services (such as grading students' exams and monitoring their progress) and books.

Although the property and services were not separately invoiced, a tax was imposed on the "deemed retail prices" of the books. The court stated that reliance on the "true object test was misplaced." That test was considered appropriate when the services rendered were inseparable from the property transferred — that is, where the services found their way into the property, as in the case of a painting. The court concluded that where the services and property were separable, the separate tangible personal property should be taxed, unless it was "inconsequential." The value of the books was about 20% of the total, which was not inconsequential.

See also Rylander v. San Antonio SMSA Ltd. Partnership, 11 S.W.3d 484 (Tex. App. 2000) (when both services and telecommunications equipment are readily separable and of significant value in a transaction, the taxable and nontaxable values must be separately identified, even though not separately invoiced); *Dell, Inc. v. Superior Court*, 159 Cal. App. 4th 911 (Cal. Ct. App. 2008) (a nontaxable service should be separated from a taxable sale even when the invoice did not make that separation, as long as the sale was of a "mixed product" (separately identifiable), not a "bundled" product (involving inextricably intertwined values, as in the case of tax advice that may include some furnishing of tangible forms, etc.); the case involved the sale of a separable and nontaxable warranty service along with a taxable sale of a computer).

[B] Tangible or Intangible Personal Property

Distinguishing between sales of tangible and intangible property is as difficult as distinguishing between the sale of property and services. Frequently, the same "true object," "dominant purpose," "essence of the transaction," or "inconsequential value" tests are used to distinguish sales of tangible and intangible property. For example, in *Bullock v. Statistical Tabulating Corp.*, 549 S.W.2d 166 (Tex. 1977), the court held that the purpose of buying keypunch cards on which data was stored so that it could be read by a computer was to obtain the intangible data, not the tangible *But see, e.g., Navistar Int'l Transp. Corp. v. State Bd. of Equalization*, 884 P.2d 108 (Cal. 1994) (drawings, designs, and manuals were *not* exempt intangible property).

Computer software has been a frequent source of litigation. A distinction is often made between *canned software* and *custom-made-to-order software* — with the former treated as a taxable sale of tangible personal property and the latter as a sale of nontaxable intangible property (or as a nontaxable sale of services). Another distinction, which could become more important with the growing use of the internet to transfer items of value, is whether the product is conveyed in a *tangible medium* (such as a computer disc) or through an *electronic medium* (downloaded through a modem).

The following two cases deal with these issues The following Louisiana court decision in *South Central Bell* refused to make these distinctions, but (as subsequent discussion explains) this is far from a unanimous view. You should consider to what extent a court might be considering the revenue implications of exempting the sale of a product that is a growing part of the economy.

SOUTH CENTRAL BELL TELEPHONE CO. v.
BARTHELEMY

Louisiana Supreme Court
643 So. 2d 1240 (La. 1994)

HALL, JUSTICE. . . .

[Editor — The taxpayer Bell, which operated a telephone system, licensed two types of computer software for use in its central offices — switching software and data processing software. The former was delivered on magnetic tape and the latter was transmitted electronically via telephone lines through Bell's modem. The court discussed the taxation of this computer software, as follows:]

The taxation of computer software has . . . been considered by numerous courts across the country. These courts have split on the [whether the software was tangible or intangible] and have employed various analyses in reaching their decisions. The first case generally recognized as addressing the tangibility of computer software for tax purposes was *District of Columbia v. Universal Computer Assocs., Inc.*, 465 F.2d 615 (D.C. Cir. 1972), which held computer software to be intangible, and therefore, not taxable. The cases following soon thereafter, likewise held computer software to be intangible for sales, use and property tax purposes. However, as computer software became more prevalent in society, and as courts' knowledge and understanding of computer software grew, later cases saw a shift in courts' attitudes towards the taxability of computer software, and courts began holding computer software to be tangible for sales, use and property tax purposes [although] the trend was not uniform. The issue has also been the subject of numerous articles in various legal periodicals. Most commentators agree that computer software is tangible. . . .

To correctly categorize software, it is necessary to first understand its basic characteristics. In its broadest scope, software encompasses all parts of the computer system other than the hardware, i.e., the machine; and the primary non-hardware component of a computer system is the program. In its narrowest scope, software is synonymous with program, which, in turn, is defined as "a complete set of instructions that tells a computer how to do something." Thus, another definition of software is "a set of instructions" or "a body of information."

When stored on magnetic tape, disc, or computer chip, this software, or set of instructions, is physically manifested in machine readable form by arranging electrons, by use of an electric current, to create either a magnetized or unmagnetized space. The computer reads the pattern of magnetized and unmagnetized spaces with a read/write head as "on" and "off", or to put it another way, "0" and "1". This machine readable language or code is the physical manifestation of the information in binary form. . . .

South Central Bell argues that the software is merely "knowledge" or "intelligence," and as such, is not corporeal and thus, not taxable. We disagree with South Central Bell's characterization. The software at issue is not merely knowledge, but rather is knowledge recorded in a physical form which has physical existence, takes up space on the tape, disc, or hard drive, makes physical things happen, and can be perceived by the senses. . . . That we use a read/write head to read the magnetic or unmagnetic spaces is no different than any other machine that humans use to perceive those corporeal things which our naked senses cannot perceive.

The software itself, i.e., the physical copy, is not merely a right or an idea to be comprehended by the understanding. The purchaser of computer software neither desires nor receives mere knowledge, but rather receives a certain arrangement of matter that will make his or her computer perform a desired function. This arrangement of matter, physically recorded on some tangible medium, constitutes a corporeal body.

We agree with Bell and the court of appeal that the form of the delivery of the software — magnetic tape or electronic transfer via a modem — is of no relevance. However, we disagree with Bell . . . that the essence or real object of the transaction was intangible property. That the software can be transferred to various media, i.e., from tape to disk, or tape to hard drive, or even that it can be transferred over the telephone lines, does not take away from the fact that the software was ultimately recorded and stored in physical form upon a physical object. As . . . Bell readily admits, the programs cannot be utilized by Bell until they have been recorded into the memory of the electronic telephone switch. The essence of the transaction was not merely to obtain the intangible "knowledge" or "information", but rather, was to obtain recorded knowledge stored in some sort of physical form that Bell's computers could use. Recorded as such, the software is not merely an incorporeal idea to be comprehended, and would be of no use if it were. Rather, the software is given physical existence to make certain desired physical things happen.

One cannot escape the fact that software, recorded in physical form, becomes inextricably intertwined with, or part and parcel of the corporeal object upon which it is recorded, be that a disk, tape, hard drive, or other device. That the information can be transferred and then physically recorded on another medium is of no moment, and does not make computer software any different than any other type of recorded information that can be transferred to another medium such as film, video tape, audio tape, or books.

The court of appeal rejected the analogy of computer software to such media as motion pictures, books, video tape, audio tape, etc. . . . , which are taxable. Like the court of appeal, the earlier jurisprudence from other states uniformly rejected the analogy to such other artistic works, finding computer software distinguishable in several respects. More recent jurisprudence from other states, however, has recognized the appropriateness of such analogy, as have numerous commentators. The court of appeal distinguished the purchase of these types of storage devices, such as books, films, video and audio tapes, etc. . . . , which hold stories, ideas, information and knowledge in physical form, by reasoning that the true essence of such transactions is the purchase of the tangible medium, not the intangible property (the artist's expressions) contained in that medium, and that without the specific tangible medium, the artist's expressions are useless, whereas computer software is separable from the tangible object upon which it is recorded. This distinction simply does not exist. . . .

That the information, knowledge, story, or idea, physically manifested in recorded form, can be transferred from one medium to another does not affect the nature of that physical manifestation as corporeal, or tangible. Likewise, that the software can be transferred from one type of physical recordation, e.g., tape, to another type, e.g., disk or hard drive, does not alter the nature of the software, it still has corporeal qualities and is inextricably intertwined with a corporeal object. The software must be stored in physical form on some tangible object somewhere. The software was reduced to physical form and recorded on a tangible object prior to delivery to Bell, and Bell maintained the software in physical form on a tangible object — the computer hard drive. . . .

When the magnetic tapes, upon which the switching software was physically recorded, came to rest in the City of New Orleans, or alternatively, when the software was physically recorded into the memory of the electronic telephone switch, the use tax attached. Likewise, once the data processing software was transmitted via telephone line and then physically recorded into the memory of Bell's computer, the software came to rest in corporeal or tangible form in the City of New Orleans and the use tax attached. . . .

We . . . decline to adopt the canned versus custom distinction invoked by a few state legislatures, commentators and courts. "Canned" software is software which has been pre-written to be used by more than one customer, or mass marketed; "custom" software is specially designed for exclusive use by one particular customer. Under the canned versus custom distinction, canned programs are classified as taxable on the theory that the buyer acquires an end product; whereas, custom programs are classified as non-taxable services on the theory that the buyer acquires professional services.

While the Louisiana Department of Taxation's current sales tax regulation regarding software adopts the "custom" versus "canned" distinction, it has been observed that this distinction departs entirely from the general Louisiana property law concepts applicable for making the tangible versus intangible distinction. To put it simply, whether the software is custom or canned, the nature of the software is the same.

Another problem with the custom/canned distinction, as illustrated by the facts in this case, is that often the software at issue is mixed, i.e., canned software is modified to the buyer's specifications, and fits neatly into neither category. As the court of appeal commented, "the uncontroverted facts in this case tend to establish that the programs at issue were a combination of canned and custom programs. The programs were pre-made but apparently significant adaptations were required before [Bell] could use them."

As one commentator aptly articulated, several problems arise when the canned versus custom distinction is substituted for the tangible versus intangible distinction, including the following:

> [T]here is an element of delusion in categorizing any but the simplest and most standard types of software as "canned." In many of the decided cases, both those holding software programs non-taxable, as well as in those in which software was held taxable, some modification in the programs was needed in order to adapt them to the taxpayer's requirements. It seems probable that a substantial part of even standardized software that is

purchased by larger businesses is modified in some respects. Consequently, the line between customized and canned programs is so vague and imprecise that a rule that taxes canned, but not customized, software is difficult to administer and tends to encourage tax avoidance through minor adaptive modifications.

For the foregoing reasons we reject the canned versus custom distinction, particularly where there is nothing in the ordinance to indicate that such a distinction was intended to be applicable.

In sum, once the "information" or "knowledge" is transformed into physical existence and recorded in physical form, it is corporeal property. The physical recordation of this software is not an incorporeal right to be comprehended. Therefore we hold that the switching system software and the data processing software involved here is tangible personal property and thus is taxable by the City of New Orleans.

GILREATH v. GENERAL ELECTRIC CO.
Florida App. Ct., Fifth District
751 So. 2d 705 (Fla. Dist. Ct. App. 2000)

Dauksch, J.

. . . To be frank, the nature of software is not easy to categorize. The plaintiffs suggest that it is simply a series of electrons and binary instructions representing intellectual property, and having no intrinsic value. The defendants argue that the source codes for such programs are reduced to paper, the papers may be manually handled, and the end product is inherently extremely valuable. Both sides make valid points, and both positions have been most ably articulated by counsel for the respective parties. The Court, however, after considerable reflection concludes that the plaintiffs' position is more viable. . . .

While no appellate court in Florida has addressed the issue, the courts of our sister states have spoken with some frequency. The vast majority of cases cited by the parties and located by the Court have concluded that software is not tangible personal property. *See, e.g., District of Columbia v. Universal Computer Associates, Inc.,* 465 F.2d 615 (D.C. Cir. 1972); *Computer Associates International, Inc. v. City of East Providence,* 615 A.2d 467 (R.I. 1992); *Northeast Datacom v. City of Wallingford,* 563 A.2d 688 (Conn. 1989); *Protest of Strayer,* 716 P.2d 588 (Kan. 1986).

The court in *Dallas Central Appraisal District v. Tech Data Corp.,* 930 S.W.2d 119 (Tex. App. 1996), nicely summarizes the theory. In holding that computer application software was not tangible personal property subject to local taxation, the appellate court noted that "the 'imperceptible binary impulses' that make up computer application software are not capable of being 'seen, weighed, measured, felt or otherwise perceived by the senses.' " It noted that the essence of the property is the software itself, and not the tangible medium on which the software might be stored. . . .

The most significant case holding to the contrary comes out of the State of Louisiana. In *South Central Bell v. Barthelemy,* 643 So.2d 1240 (La. 1994), the

Supreme Court of Louisiana held that software was tangible personal property, and therefore subject to local taxation. Unlike the Florida Legislature and the other courts cited above that have considered the issue, the view of the Louisiana court was that under its civil law system software consisted of knowledge recorded in a physical form. As those physical forms — discs, tapes, hard drives, etc. — have a physical existence, take up space, and make things happen, they are tangible and taxable.

The court disagrees, and concludes that the views expressed in the other cited cases are more persuasive. Perhaps the Supreme Court of Connecticut stated it most succinctly. In *Northeast Datacom, Inc. v. City of Wallingford*, 563 A.2d 688 (Conn. 1989), the court determined that the physical components of software — the same discs, tapes, hard drives, etc. — discussed by the Louisiana court, are only "tangential incidents" of the program. It noted that "the fact that tangible property is used to store or transmit the software's binary instructions does not change the character of what is fundamentally a classic form of intellectual property."

COMMENT — DISK vs. MODEM

1. *The distinction does matter.* A dissent in *South Central Bell* stated:

> The software at issue was transmitted by two methods: (1) encoded on magnetic tape; or (2) electronically transferred via telephone wires and modems. The ordinary definition or generally prevailing meaning of "tangible personal property" would not cover either type of software.

> However, state jurisprudence gives the phrase an altered meaning which may be extended to cover the taped software. Applying the expansive reasoning of the jurisprudence, the lynch pin of holding the software to be tangible personal property seems to be that it is on a floppy disc, a tape or a compact disc and the value of the software is included in the price of the disc, tape or CD. The simplest example of this type of taxation is the purchase of a software program (such as WordPerfect, Windows, or Excel) at a local computer store. Who can argue that only the value of the floppy discs and the manual may be taxed and not the program?

> On the other hand, subscribers to "bulletin boards" can use modems and telephone connections to download software programs without being taxed. The analysis of software being taxed because it is bought on a tape or disc cannot be stretched logically to include data transmitted by modems and telephone wires.

> I respectfully concur on taxing the South Central Bell software purchased on tapes, but dissent as to software received electronically.

And a South Carolina court agreed that the mode of transfer matters. In *Citizens & S. Sys., Inc. v. S. Carolina Tax Comm'n*, 311 S.E.2d 717 (S.C. 1984), the court stated:

> [Taxpayer] asserts [that] the instructions could have been introduced into the computer through intangible means, telephone transmission or personal programming, and that only because the instructions were introduced

by tangible means, magnetic tape, is the sale taxed, and contends the medium of transmission is not what should be taxed. We agree with the Supreme Court of Vermont in *Chittenden Trust Company v. King*, Vt., 465 A.2d 1100, 1102 (1983), which held the bank had to accept the consequences of its choice to purchase the computer program in the form of a magnetic tape, finding that "[t]o base the tax consequences of a transaction on how it could have been structured would require rejection of the established tax principle that a transaction is to be given its tax effect in accord with what actually occurred and not in accord with what might have occurred."

2.   *The distinction doesn't matter.* But, in *Graham Packaging Co. v. Commonwealth*, 882 A.2d 1076 (Pa. Commw. Ct. 2005), the court applied the essence of the transaction or true object test to decide whether the transfer of software was a taxable transaction. It agreed with the Louisiana court in *South Central* Bell that a taxable transaction occurs whether the software is embodied in a disk or transmitted over telephone lines.

COMMENT — CANNED vs. CUSTOM-MADE SOFTWARE

The disagreement between the Louisiana and Florida courts is repeated in other cases. Some cases use the "essence of the transaction" approach to treat the sale of *canned* software as a *nontaxable* transfer of *intangible* property (*e.g.*, *First National Bank of Fort Worth v. Bullock*, 584 S.W.2d 548 (Tex. App. 1979)), although the decision was overridden by statute in Tex. Tax Code § 151.009 (tangible personal property defined to include computer programs for sales tax provisions). Other cases apply the "essence of the transaction" doctrine to reach the opposite result — that the canned software is tangible personal property; *e.g.*, *Graham Packaging Co. v. Commonwealth*, 882 A.2d 1076 (Pa. Commw. Ct. 2005).

The revenue implications of exempting canned software from the property tax has been apparent to some state legislatures. Statutes in Connecticut, Illinois, Wisconsin Texas, and Utah (and perhaps other states) have explicitly amended their tax law to define canned software to be tangible personal property.

See also Note, *Sales and Use Tax of Computer Software — Is Software Tangible Personal Property?* 27 WAYNE L. REV. 1503, 1531–36 (1981) (claiming that the majority of states with a sales and use tax treat *both* custom and canned software as taxable tangible personal property).

And don't forget that custom-made software might be considered a service, exempt from the sales tax. *See Measurex Sys., Inc. v. State Tax Assessor*, 490 A.2d 1192 (Me. 1985).

COMMENT — STATUTORY INTERPRETATION AND CHANGE

In *Graham Packaging Co. v. Commonwealth*, 882 A.2d 1076 (Pa. Commw. Ct. 2005), the court asked: "When the General Assembly defined tangible personal property as 'corporeal personal property,' did it have in mind the traditional sense of that term, i.e., only those items of physical matter that one can see with the naked eye and hold in one's hand?"

1. *Statutory list illustrative or exclusive?* To answer that question, the court in *Graham* observed that "[i]t would appear from the list of items included in the definition, such as electricity, cable, video programming, and telecommunications services, that the legislature did not intend to limit the taxable subject to such a narrow construct." Could the court have used the list differently — to infer that the failure to include computer software on the list meant that it was excluded from the definition of tangible personal property? What is the strongest argument against that inference? Does it matter what year the statutory list was adopted?

2. *Change?* If the computer software (or its transmission by modem) was a new technology (after passage of the law), should the court leave it to the legislature to decide whether to update the statute to include this technology within the definition of taxable tangible personal property, or should the court do the best it can to apply the historical statutory purpose to the new technology?

COMMENT — "COMMON UNDERSTANDING"

In *City of Boulder v. Leanin' Tree, Inc.*, 72 P.3d 361 (Colo. 2003), the taxpayer (Leanin' Tree) manufactured and sold greeting cards and other gift products that contained images of original artwork created by independent artists. The taxpayer entered into license agreements with the artists, borrowing their original artwork or its photographic or digital image and receiving the exclusive right to reproduce and publish the images. The taxpayer then transformed the image from its original size into a product usable size for its greeting cards or other products and routinely added borders or verse or both, changed the contrast of the image, often changed the composition of the image by adding or deleting elements in the image, and frequently cropped the image to best fit the product. The derivative image was then burned onto metal plates, after which the original artwork was returned to the artist. The court applied the "common understanding" test in concluding that the taxpayer was acquiring intangible property, as follows:

> Whether couched in terms of the true object, dominant purpose, or essence of the transaction, or of the consequential or incidental nature of the transfer of tangible property, the rationales of most courts attempting to characterize inseparably mixed transactions acknowledge, either explicitly or implicitly, that they are not reducible to a single, dispositive factor. While there has been no clear emergence of a comprehensive and consistent theory that more expressly articulates the goals of the analysis, a veritable plethora of factors have been relied on under the circumstances of individual cases. . . .

> Varied as these analyses may be, they largely share in common some attempt to identify characteristics of the transaction at issue that make it either more analogous to what is reasonably and commonly understood to be a sale of goods, or more analogous to what is generally understood to be the purchase of a service or intangible right. Perhaps the quintessential transaction for the purchase of an intangible right is the marketing of

literary works, in which the clear object, around which the entire transaction is structured, is the right to publish the author's work. Although the transactions by Leanin' Tree may superficially appear to be akin to the purchase of artwork, which is normally considered to be the sale of a tangible object, upon closer examination the transactions between Leanin' Tree and its artists have much more in common with a transaction for the right to publish.

However, in *Cinemark USA, Inc. v. Seest*, 190 P.3d 793 (Colo. Ct. App. 2008), the court interpreted the state's use tax on tangible personal property to apply to a movie theater's acquisition of the right to exhibit motion picture films to the public. Unlike in *Leanin' Tree*, the product was used by the movie theater in precisely the form in which it was received and was not an idea that could be used in a different form than conveyed. The transaction was more like the purchase of a work of art (clearly a taxable event) than payment for the intangible component of the film. And the copyright in the movie was of little value without the film reels. Consequently, "the totality of circumstances show[ed] that the essence of [the] transaction [was] the use of motion picture reels, tangible final products, for exhibition in [the taxpayer's] movie theater."

QUESTION — ELECTRICITY

How would a "common understanding" approach deal with the following case — involving electricity? In *Exelon Corp. v. Illinois Dept. of Revenue*, 917 N.E.2d 899 (Ill. 2009), the court held that sale of electricity was the sale of tangible personal property. It relied heavily on how scientists understood electricity, stating:

> The record in the present case contains the unrebutted affidavit and report of Dr. Fajans, entitled "The Physical Nature of Electricity." He defined electricity as the flow of electrons in a circuit. Dr. Fajans explained: "Electricity is physical and material because, microscopically, it consists of the flow and 'pressure' of a material entity, namely electrons, and macroscopically, it can be sensed (felt, tasted, seen, and heard), measured, weighed, and stored, and is subject to universal laws of nature." Dr. Fajans elaborated as follows: "Without electrons, electricity cannot be transmitted. Though electrons themselves are very small and lightweight, they are one of the basic constituents of matter; common matter like hydrogen or ion consists of electrons, protons, and neutrons in roughly equal number. Recently, scientists have been able to see electrons, or more precisely, the density of electrons, with devices called Scanning Tunneling Microscopes. . . . There is nothing more physical and material than an electron. Since electricity itself consists of the flow of a material object, electricity is physical and material." . . .

> We now join the several courts that have expressly held in varying contexts that electricity constitutes Atangible personal property." *See, e.g., Searles Valley Minerals Operations, Inc. v. State Board of Equalization*, 160 Cal. App. 4th 514, 521, 72 Cal. Rptr. 3d 857, 862 (2008); *Narragansett Electric Co. v. Carbone*, 898 A.2d 87, 97–98 (R.I. 2006); *Davis v. Gulf Power Corp.*, 799 So. 2d 298, 300 (Fla. Dist. Ct. App. 2001); *Curry v. Alabama*

Power Co., 243 Ala. 53, 59–60, 8 So. 2d 521, 526 (1942).

Because this decision departed from some obiter dictum in a prior case, it was made prospective.

§ 29.05   USE TAX AND CONSTITUTIONAL LAW

[A]   Avoiding Double Taxation

As noted earlier, states routinely impose a use tax on property purchased outside the state but brought or shipped into a destination state for use in that state. Although the state in which a sale originates usually does not impose tax on goods exported out of the state, it is possible that a tax will be paid to an origin state under certain circumstances and a use tax later imposed on the same item in the destination state. This is most likely to happen when property has been used in one state and later transported to another state for further use.

States that impose a use tax typically deal with this problem by giving the buyer a credit against the use tax for the tax previously paid to another state, up to the amount of the destination state's tax; or by exempting from the use tax any transaction already taxed in another state. Whether the use tax state *must* make some accommodation when taxes have been paid to another state has never been explicitly decided by the U.S. Supreme Court, but there are strong hints that this would be required under the Commerce Clause, which the Court interprets to require "fair apportionment" of taxes among the states. *See Oklahoma Tax Comm'n v. Jefferson Lines, Inc.*, 514 U.S. 175 (1995).

[B]   Collection Problems — Interstate Issues

[1]   In General

Collection of a use tax on personal consumption is extremely difficult because, as a practical matter, it requires the help of an out-of-state seller. States have tried to force out-of-state sellers to collect the tax and remit the revenue to the destination state, but there are constitutional obstacles to this approach. The destination state must have jurisdiction over the seller and that requires some level of business activity in the destination state. Two clauses of the U.S. Constitution — the Due Process and Commerce Clauses — raise potential obstacles.

In *Quill Corp. v. North Dakota*, 504 U.S. 298 (1992), the Supreme Court held that the Due Process Clause is satisfied by a minimal amount of activity in the destination state, which is usually satisfied by the seller's efforts to appeal to a destination state buyer through targeted advertising. However, the Court also held that the Commerce Clause required a much closer nexus between the seller's business activity and the destination state — such as an office. Reliance on the Commerce Clause is significant because it allows Congress to regulate use tax collection by extending the destination state's power to force origin state collection beyond what is allowed in the absence of legislation. In effect, the Court in *Quill* was insisting on a legislative solution to this growing problem, although it is more likely that a decision requiring out-of-state sellers to collect the tax would have goaded Congress into action.

As a result of the Court's decision in *Quill*, the use tax can realistically be collected from a buyer in only two situations. First, when a buyer must register the property in the destination state, as is usually true of cars and boats, the use tax can be collected at the time of registration. Second, it is also possible to collect a use tax when a business is subject to the tax and the business taxpayer is likely to be audited by the state tax administration in any event.

The following decision in *Quill* is interesting not only for what it says about state jurisdiction over taxpayers but also for its observations about whether to adopt a formalist or pragmatic approach to deciding cases. The decision suggests that the Court will usually avoid formalist bright-line rules in deciding when state taxes violate the Constitution, except when a bright-line rule serves important policy objectives.

The Court in *Quill* also reaffirms the four-part test for applying the Commerce Clause, which it had earlier adopted in *Complete Auto*, although it did little to explain how that test would be applied across the broad spectrum of state taxation. Indeed, the Court indicates that the rules applicable to sales or use taxes are not necessarily the same as for the income tax and other taxes. Chapter 35 deals with interstate taxation issues in more detail.

QUILL CORP. v. NORTH DAKOTA
United States Supreme Court
504 U.S. 298 (1992)

JUSTICE STEVENS delivered the opinion of the Court.

This case, like *National Bellas Hess, Inc. v. Department of Revenue of Ill.*, 386 U.S. 753 (1967), involves [North Dakota's] attempt to require an out-of-state mail-order house that has neither outlets nor sales representatives in the State to collect and pay a use tax on goods purchased for use within the State. In *Bellas Hess*, we held that a similar Illinois statute violated the Due Process Clause of the Fourteenth Amendment and created an unconstitutional burden on interstate commerce. In particular, we ruled that a "seller whose only connection with customers in the State is by common carrier or the United States mail" lacked the requisite minimum contacts with the State. . . .

I

Quill is a Delaware corporation with offices and warehouses in Illinois, California, and Georgia. None of its employees work or reside in North Dakota, and its ownership of tangible property in that State is either insignificant or nonexistent. Quill sells office equipment and supplies; it solicits business through catalogs and flyers, advertisements in national periodicals, and telephone calls. Its annual national sales exceed $200 million, of which almost $1 million are made to about 3,000 customers in North Dakota. It is the sixth largest vendor of office supplies in the State. It delivers all of its merchandise to its North Dakota customers by mail or common carrier from out-of-state locations. As a corollary to its sales tax, North Dakota imposes a use tax upon property purchased for storage, use, or consumption within the State. North Dakota requires every "retailer maintaining a place of business in" the State to collect the tax from the consumer and remit it to the State. North Dakota amended the statutory definition of the term "retailer" to include "every person who engages in regular or systematic solicitation of a consumer market in th[e] state." State regulations in turn define "regular or systematic solicitation" to mean three or more advertisements within a 12-month period. Thus, since 1987, mail-order companies that engage in such solicitation have been subject to the tax even if they maintain no property or personnel in North Dakota. . . .

Quill has taken the position that North Dakota does not have the power to compel it to collect a use tax from its North Dakota customers. . . . [But t]he North Dakota Supreme Court [concluded] that "wholesale changes" in both the economy and the law made it inappropriate to follow *Bellas Hess* today. The principal economic change noted by the court was the remarkable growth of the mail-order business "from a relatively inconsequential market niche" in 1967 to a "goliath" with annual sales that reached "the staggering figure of $183.3 billion in 1989." Moreover, the court observed, advances in computer technology greatly eased the burden of compliance with a " 'welter of complicated obligations' " imposed by state and local taxing authorities.

Equally important, in the court's view, were the changes in the "legal landscape." With respect to the Commerce Clause, the court emphasized that *Complete Auto Transit, Inc. v. Brady*, 430 U.S. 274 (1977), rejected the line of cases holding that the direct taxation of interstate commerce was impermissible and adopted instead a "consistent and rational method of inquiry [that focused on] the practical effect of [the] challenged tax." *Mobil Oil Corp. v. Commissioner of Taxes of Vt.*, 445 U.S. 425, 443 (1980). This and subsequent rulings, the court maintained, indicated that the Commerce Clause no longer mandated the sort of physical-presence nexus suggested in *Bellas Hess*.

Similarly, with respect to the Due Process Clause, the North Dakota court observed that cases following *Bellas Hess* had not construed "minimum contacts" to require physical presence within a State as a prerequisite to the legitimate exercise of state power. The state court then concluded that "the Due Process requirement of a 'minimal connection' to establish nexus is encompassed within the Complete Auto test" and that the relevant inquiry under the latter test was whether "the state has provided some protection, opportunities, or benefit for which it can expect a return."

Turning to the case at hand, the state court emphasized that North Dakota had created "an economic climate that fosters demand for" Quill's products, maintained a legal infrastructure that protected that market, and disposed of 24 tons of catalogs and flyers mailed by Quill into the State every year. Based on these facts, the court concluded that Quill's "economic presence" in North Dakota depended on services and benefits provided by the State and therefore, generated "a constitutionally sufficient nexus to justify imposition of the purely administrative duty of collecting and remitting the use tax."

II

The [Due Process and Commerce Clause] requirements differ fundamentally, in several ways . . . . [W]hile Congress has plenary power to regulate commerce among the States and thus, may authorize state actions that burden interstate commerce, it does not similarly have the power to authorize violations of the Due Process Clause. Thus, although we have not always been precise in distinguishing between the two, the Due Process Clause and the Commerce Clause are analytically distinct. . . . [T]hough overlapping, the two conceptions are not identical. There may be more than sufficient factual connections, with economic and legal effects, between the transaction and the taxing state to sustain the tax as against due process objections. Yet, it may fall because of its burdening effect upon the commerce. And, although the two notions cannot always be separated, clarity of consideration and of decision would be promoted if the two issues are approached, where they are presented, at least tentatively as if they were separate and distinct, not intermingled ones.

The Due Process Clause "requires some definite link, some minimum connection, between a state and the person, property, or transaction it seeks to tax," *Miller Brothers Co. v. Maryland*, 347 U.S. 340, 344–345 (1954), and that the "income attributed to the State for tax purposes must be rationally related to 'values connected with the taxing State,'" *Moorman Mfg. Co. v. Bair*, 437 U.S. 267, 273 (1978). Here, we are concerned primarily with the first of these requirements. Prior to *Bellas Hess*, we had held that that requirement was satisfied in a variety of circumstances involving use taxes. For example, the presence of sales personnel in the State or the maintenance of local retail stores in the State justified the exercise of that power because the seller's local activities were "plainly accorded the protection and services of the taxing State." The furthest extension of that power was recognized in *Scripto, Inc. v. Carson*, 362 U.S. 207 (1960), in which the Court upheld a use tax despite the fact that all of the seller's in-state solicitation was performed by independent contractors. These cases all involved some sort of physical presence within the State, and in *Bellas Hess*, the Court suggested that such presence was not only sufficient for jurisdiction under the Due Process Clause, but also necessary. We expressly declined to obliterate the "sharp distinction . . . between mail-order sellers with retail outlets, solicitors, or property within a State, and those who do no more than communicate with customers in the State by mail or common carrier as a part of a general interstate business."

Our due process jurisprudence has evolved substantially in the 25 years since *Bellas Hess*, particularly in the area of judicial jurisdiction. [Editor — Discussion of judicial jurisdiction cases is omitted.]

Comparable reasoning justifies the imposition of the collection duty on a mail-order house that is engaged in continuous and widespread solicitation of business within a State. . . . In "modern commercial life" it matters little that such solicitation is accomplished by a deluge of catalogs rather than a phalanx of drummers: The requirements of due process are met irrespective of a corporation's lack of physical presence in the taxing State. Thus, to the extent that our decisions have indicated that the Due Process Clause requires physical presence in a State for the imposition of duty to collect a use tax, we overrule those holdings as superseded by developments in the law of due process.

In this case, there is no question that Quill has purposefully directed its activities at North Dakota residents, that the magnitude of those contacts is more than sufficient for due process purposes, and that the use tax is related to the benefits Quill receives from access to the State. We therefore agree with the North Dakota Supreme Court's conclusion that the Due Process Clause does not bar enforcement of that State's use tax against Quill.

Editor — III is omitted.]

IV

Article I, § 8, cl. 3, of the Constitution expressly authorizes Congress to "regulate Commerce with foreign Nations, and among the several States." It says nothing about the protection of interstate commerce in the absence of any action by Congress. Nevertheless, as Justice Johnson suggested in his concurring opinion in *Gibbons v. Ogden*, 9 Wheat. 1, 231–232, 239 (1824), the Commerce Clause is more than an affirmative grant of power; it has a negative sweep as well. The Clause, in Justice Stone's phrasing, "by its own force" prohibits certain state actions that interfere with interstate commerce.

Our interpretation of the "negative" or "dormant" Commerce Clause has evolved substantially over the years, particularly as that Clause concerns limitations on state taxation powers. Our early cases . . . swept broadly, and . . . we declared that "no State has the right to lay a tax on interstate commerce in any form." We later narrowed that rule and distinguished between direct burdens on interstate commerce, which were prohibited, and indirect burdens, which generally were not. *Western Live Stock v. Bureau of Revenue*, 303 U.S. 250, 256–258 (1938), and subsequent decisions rejected this formal, categorical analysis and adopted a "multiple-taxation doctrine" that focused not on whether a tax was "direct" or "indirect" but rather on whether a tax subjected interstate commerce to a risk of multiple taxation. However, in *Freeman v. Hewit*, 329 U.S. 249, 256 (1946), we embraced again the formal distinction between direct and indirect taxation. . . . Most recently, in *Complete Auto Transit, Inc. v. Brady*, 430 U.S. at 285, we renounced the Freeman approach as "attaching constitutional significance to a semantic difference." We expressly overruled one of *Freeman*'s progeny, *Spector Motor Service, Inc. v. O'Connor*, 340 U.S. 602 (1951), which held that a tax on "the privilege of doing interstate business" was unconstitutional, while recognizing that a differently denominated tax with the same economic effect would not be unconstitutional. Spector . . . created a situation in which "magic words or labels" could "disable an otherwise constitutional levy." Complete Auto emphasized the importance of looking past "the formal language of the tax statute [to] its practical effect," and set forth a four-part test that continues to govern the validity of state taxes under the Commerce Clause.

Bellas Hess was decided in 1967, in the middle of this latest rally between formalism and pragmatism. Contrary to the suggestion of the North Dakota Supreme Court, this timing does not mean that *Complete Auto* rendered *Bellas Hess* "obsolete." *Complete Auto* rejected *Freeman* and *Spector*'s formal distinction between "direct" and "indirect" taxes on interstate commerce because that formalism allowed the validity of statutes to hinge on "legal terminology," "drafts-manship and phraseology." *Bellas Hess* did not rely on any such labeling of taxes and therefore, did not automatically fall with *Freeman* and its progeny.

While contemporary Commerce Clause jurisprudence might not dictate the same result were the issue to arise for the first time today, *Bellas Hess* is not inconsistent with *Complete Auto* and our recent cases. Under *Complete Auto*'s four-part test, we will sustain a tax against a Commerce Clause challenge so long as the "tax [1] is applied to an activity with a substantial nexus with the taxing State, [2] is fairly apportioned, [3] does not discriminate against interstate commerce, and [4] is fairly related to the services provided by the State." *Bellas Hess* concerns the first of these tests and stands for the proposition that a vendor whose only contacts with the taxing State are by mail or common carrier lacks the "substantial nexus" required by the Commerce Clause. . . .

The State of North Dakota relies less on *Complete Auto* and more on the evolution of our due process jurisprudence. The State contends that the nexus requirements imposed by the Due Process and Commerce Clauses are equivalent and that if, as we concluded above, a mail-order house that lacks a physical presence in the taxing State nonetheless satisfies the due process "minimum contacts" test, then that corporation also meets the Commerce Clause "substantial nexus" test. We disagree. Despite the similarity in phrasing, the nexus requirements of the Due Process and Commerce Clauses are not identical. The two standards are animated by different constitutional concerns and policies.

Due process centrally concerns the fundamental fairness of governmental activity. Thus, at the most general level, the due process nexus analysis requires that we ask whether an individual's connections with a State are substantial enough to legitimate the State's exercise of power over him. . . . In contrast, the Commerce Clause and its nexus requirement are informed not so much by concerns about fairness for the individual defendant as by structural concerns about the effects of state regulation on the national economy. . . .

The *Complete Auto* analysis reflects these concerns about the national economy. The second and third parts of that analysis, which require fair apportionment and non-discrimination, prohibit taxes that pass an unfair share of the tax burden onto interstate commerce. The first and fourth prongs, which require a substantial nexus and a relationship between the tax and state-provided services, limit the reach of state taxing authority so as to ensure that state taxation does not unduly burden interstate commerce. Thus, the "substantial nexus" requirement is not, like due process "minimum contacts" requirement, a proxy for notice, but rather a means for limiting state burdens on interstate commerce. Accordingly, contrary to the State's suggestion, a corporation may have the "minimum contacts" with a taxing State as required by the Due Process Clause, and yet lack the "substantial nexus" with that State as required by the Commerce Clause.

[Editor — In footnote 6, the Court states: "North Dakota's use tax illustrates well how a state tax might unduly burden interstate commerce. On its face, North Dakota law imposes a collection duty on every vendor who advertises in the State three times in a single year. Thus, absent the *Bellas Hess* rule, a publisher who included a subscription card in three issues of its magazine, a vendor whose radio advertisements were heard in North Dakota on three occasions, and a corporation whose telephone sales force made three calls into the State, all would be subject to the collection duty. What is more significant, similar obligations might be imposed by the Nation's 6,000-plus taxing jurisdictions.]

. . .

Complete Auto, it is true, renounced *Freeman* and its progeny as "formalistic." But not all formalism is alike. *Spector*'s formal distinction between taxes on the "privilege of doing business" and all other taxes served no purpose within our Commerce Clause jurisprudence, but stood "only as a trap for the unwary draftsman." In contrast, the bright-line rule of *Bellas Hess* furthers the ends of the dormant Commerce Clause. Undue burdens on interstate commerce may be avoided not only by a case-by-case evaluation of the actual burdens imposed by particular regulations or taxes, but also, in some situations, by the demarcation of a discrete realm of commercial activity that is free from interstate taxation. *Bellas Hess* followed the latter approach and created a safe harbor for vendors "whose only connection with customers in the [taxing] State is by common carrier or the United States mail." Under *Bellas Hess*, such vendors are free from state-imposed duties to collect sales and use taxes.

. . . [A] bright-line rule in the area of sales and use taxes [] encourages settled expectations and, in doing so, fosters investment by businesses and individuals. Indeed, it is not unlikely that the mail-order industry's dramatic growth over the last quarter century is due in part to the bright-line exemption from state taxation created in *Bellas Hess*.

Notwithstanding the benefits of bright-line tests, we have, in some situations, decided to replace such tests with more contextual balancing inquiries. . . . [Nonetheless], although in our cases subsequent to *Bellas Hess* and concerning other types of taxes we have not adopted a similar bright-line, physical-presence requirement, our reasoning in those cases does not compel that we now reject the rule that *Bellas Hess* established in the area of sales and use taxes. To the contrary, the continuing value of a bright-line rule in this area and the doctrine and principles of stare decisis indicate that the *Bellas Hess* rule remains good law. For these reasons, we disagree with the North Dakota Supreme Court's conclusion that the time has come to renounce the bright-line test of *Bellas Hess*.

This aspect of our decision is made easier by the fact that the underlying issue is not only one that Congress may be better qualified to resolve, but also one that Congress has the ultimate power to resolve. No matter how we evaluate the burdens that use taxes impose on interstate commerce, Congress remains free to disagree with our conclusions. . . . Congress is now free to decide whether, when, and to what extent the States may burden interstate mail-order concerns with a duty to collect use taxes.

[2] Use of Independent Contractors

Some out-of-state sellers have tried to avoid a "substantial nexus" with the purchaser's state by authorizing independent contractors to handle some of their online sales. New York passed a law requiring the out-of-state seller to collect a use tax in this type of situation (if New York gross receipts from such sales exceeded $10,000). The law stated that

> a person making sales of tangible personal property or services taxable under this article ("seller") shall be presumed to be soliciting business through an independent contractor or other representative if the seller enters into an agreement with a resident of this state under which the resident, for a commission or other consideration, directly or indirectly refers potential customers, whether by a link on an internet website or otherwise, to the seller. . . . This presumption may be rebutted by proof that the resident with whom the seller has an agreement did not engage in any solicitation in the state on behalf of the seller that would satisfy the nexus requirement of the United States constitution during the four quarterly periods in question.

The New York law specifies that the out-of-state seller is not subject to this law if it includes in its agreement a condition that in-state commissioned representatives are prohibited from engaging in solicitation activities in New York on its behalf.

Amazon entered into the following arrangement between Amazon and the independent contractors in New York as follows:

> Amazon created an "Associates Program," which allows participants ("Associates") to maintain links to Amazon.com on their own websites and compensates them by paying "a percentage of the proceeds of the sale." Amazon also offers incentives to Associates that "directly refer" customers to its Amazon Prime program through website links, paying them a "$12 bounty" for each new enrollee. Prospective Associates must apply to join the program. Assuming that Amazon accepts the application, the parties enter into an Operating Agreement, which makes clear that the "Relationship of [the] Parties" is that of "independent contractors." Associates are granted "a revocable, non-exclusive, worldwide, royalty-free license . . . solely for purposes of facilitating referrals from [their sites] to the Amazon Site." Amazon authorizes Associates to place different types of links from their websites to its own. For example, Associates can set up a "product link," generally allowing them to "select one or more Products [on Amazon's site] to list on [their own] site," a "search box link," which permits visitors to the Associate's site to view Amazon merchandise related to their queries, or a "cart link," which "when clicked will allow visitors [of the Associate's site] to add products to their shopping cart and/or purchase products via [Amazon's] 1-Click feature."

> . . . The Operating Agreement [] sets forth that Associates will be paid through a "referral fee" and can elect between the "Classic Fee Structure" (generally 4% of qualifying revenues from sales of products sold through special links) or the "Performance Fee Structure" (a percentage of

qualifying revenues set forth in a table that varies with the number of total items shipped). Amazon has hundreds of thousands of Associates. Thousands "of them have provided Amazon with addresses in New York." Sales to New York customers originating from New York-based Associate referrals constitute less than 1.5% of Amazon's New York sales. Without disclosing the dollar amount of those sales, Amazon simply acknowledges that its "Associates Program generates more than $10,000 per year in sales to customers located in New York."

A lower court held that New York could constitutionally require Amazon to collect use tax on sales to New York purchasers.

AMAZON.COM LLC v. NEW YORK STATE DEPT. OF TAXATION AND FINANCE
Supreme Court of New York
877 N.Y.S.2d 842 (N.Y. App. Div. 2009)

EILEEN BRANSTEN, J. . . .

In Scripto v. Carson, 362 U.S. 207 (1960) [] the United States Supreme Court held that a State could require tax collection by an out-of-state company that had contracts with 10 in-state residents-deemed "independent contractors" — who solicited orders for products on its behalf. The agreement with the contractors provided that they were to be paid by commission and salespeople sent orders out of state for fulfillment. In contrast, if the only connection with the State is solicitation from out of State — through catalogs, flyers, advertisements in national periodicals or telephone calls-and delivery of merchandise to customers by common carrier or use of mail, there is an insufficient nexus for taxation purposes (*see Quill Corp. v. North Dakota*, 504 U.S. 298 (1992). So long as there is a "substantial nexus" with the taxing State, the taxes that must be collected need not derive from the seller's in-state activity (*National Geographic Society v. California Board of Equalization*, 430 U.S. 551 (1977) [nonprofit society required to collect taxes from California mail-order customers based on maintenance of two offices in California from which advertising was solicited for its monthly magazine]). . . .

Amazon urges that the statute would bring within its ambit "simple advertising by in-state advertisers." The Commission-Agreement Provision, however, does no such thing. It imposes a tax-collection obligation on sellers who contractually agree to compensate New York residents for business that they generate and not simply for publicity. Amazon has not come close to refuting the Tax Law's presumed constitutionality and the statute must be upheld.

Amazon maintains that it lacks a substantial nexus with New York and that its Associates' activities are insufficient to justify imposition of New York tax-collection obligations. It argues that it has no physical presence in New York and that its Associates have no role in its sales transactions, which are completed out-of-state. Amazon emphasizes that its Associates "are mere advertisers who do not solicit sales at Amazon's behest" and that they are not "traveling salesmen" — they do not necessarily personally solicit sales from New York residents. It asserts that all its

Operating Agreements provide for is placement of links on Associates' websites.

Amazon further states that Associates' referrals to New York customers are not significantly associated with its ability to establish and maintain a market for sales in New York because they account for less than 1.5% of its New York sales. Amazon complains that "it is practically impossible" for it to determine with certainty which of its Associates are New York residents and then to disprove solicitation.

None of these allegations, however, sufficiently state a claim for violation of the Commerce Clause. Amazon contracts with thousands of Associates that provided it with a New York address. Certainly, if Amazon were to have a dispute with any of them, it could easily ascertain New York residency for purposes of a lawsuit. All of the information is publicly available. Indeed, there is no reason that the Associates application, which Amazon may accept or reject, cannot inquire about New York resident status.

It does not matter, moreover, that Associates do not solicit New York business at Amazon's direct behest or that Amazon contractually prohibits them from engaging in certain limited specified conduct such as offering its customers money back for Amazon purchases made through Associate links. Amazon chooses to benefit from New York Associates that are free to target New Yorkers and encourage Amazon sales, all the while earning money for Amazon in return for which Amazon pays them commissions. Amazon does not discourage its Associates from reaching out to customers or contributors and pressing Amazon sales.

Amazon has not contested that it contracts with thousands of New Yorkers and that as a result of New York referrals to New York residents it obtains the benefit of more than $10,000 annually. Amazon should not be permitted to escape tax collection indirectly, through use of an incentivized New York sales force to generate revenue, when it would not be able to achieve tax avoidance directly through use of New York employees engaged in the very same activities.

The *Amazon.com* decision was affirmed on appeal with a modification. 81 A.D.3d 183 (N.Y. App. Div. 2010). The court held that the law did not violate the Commerce Clause on its face, but remanded for further discovery on whether the law violated the Commerce Clause as applied. The court stated:

> The first of the "as applied" arguments to be addressed is the claim that the statute violates the Commerce Clause. Plaintiffs argue that since their representatives do nothing more than advertise on New York based Web sites, the statute cannot be applied in a constitutional manner. Inasmuch as there has been limited, if non existent, discovery on this issue we are unable to conclude as a matter of law that plaintiffs' in state representatives are engaged in sufficiently meaningful activity so as to implicate the State's taxing powers, and thus find that they should be given the opportunity to develop a record which establishes, actually, rather than theoretically, whether their in state representatives are soliciting business or merely advertising on their behalf. Although, as noted above, the advisory memoranda describe a process by which the representatives can certify that they do not solicit, the possibility remains that many of the in state represen-

tatives could certify that they are not soliciting, and, yet, the Department
of Taxation and Finance (DTF) could find that the activities in which they
are engaged do constitute solicitation. Additionally, it is within the realm of
possibility that the DTF could find that purported out of state representatives are actually located in state by virtue of misrepresenting their
address. It would also afford plaintiffs the opportunity to establish the bona
fides of their other claims, such as whether it is impossible to identify who
their in state representatives are (even though plaintiffs presumably need
an address to which to send, inter alia, any commission checks).

We are also unable to determine on this record whether the in state
representatives are engaged in activities which are "significantly associated" with the out of state retailer's ability to do business in the state, as
addressed in *Tyler Pipe Indus., Inc. v. Washington State Dept. of Revenue*,
483 U.S. 232, 250 (1987). In an affidavit from its vice president, Amazon
represents that, in 2007, its sales to New York State residents referred by
Associates which provided Amazon with New York addresses upon registration constituted less than 1.5% of its total sales to New York State
residents. It argues that this revenue is not "significantly associated" with
its ability to do business in New York. Whether plaintiffs can meet their
burden on this issue remains to be seen, but we cannot, on this record,
make a determination.

Possible Congressional action. As of July 2013, the Senate has passed (but the
House has not yet acted) on the Marketplace Fairness Act of 2013. (The bill is S.
743, passed by the Senate on May 6, 2013.) This Act would permit states to require
sellers (other than certain "small" sellers) to collect sales and use taxes on "remote"
sales – such as a sale over the internet to an out-of-state buyer. If enacted, New York
would not have to worry about whether its requirement that Amazon collect a use
tax on sales to New York buyers would violate the Constitution in the circumstances
described in the above case.

Chapter 30

VALUE ADDED TAX

§ 30.01   THE TAXPAYER AND THE TAX BASE

The value added tax (VAT), like the sales tax, is supposed to be a tax on personal consumption. The mechanics, however, are different from a sales tax. Instead of taxing a single transaction at the end of the distribution chain, the VAT is imposed on each sale as the product or service passes down the production or distribution chain until it reaches final consumption.

For example, assume a product sells for $100 to the final consumer and passes through two production stages and a wholesale and retail stage. Production stage 1 removes the raw material from the earth (to simplify the example, assume the producer does this without cost — that is, solely by personal services) and produces a $20 machine which is sold to a manufacturer. The second stage manufacturer uses the machine with some other personal services to produce the widget, which is then sold to a wholesaler for $45. The wholesaler markets the widgets to a retail store for $60, and the retail store sells the widgets for $100 to the final consumer. The value added (VA) at each stage of the four stages and the VAT (assuming a tax rate of 20%) is as follows:

	(1) 0→20;	(2) 20 → 45;	(3) 45 → 60;	(4) 60 → 100
VA =	20	25	15	40
VAT =	4	5	3	8

Total tax is $20, but instead of collecting $20 on the $100 retail sale, the tax is collected in bits and pieces at each stage.

§ 30.02   A BRIEF HISTORY OF THE VAT

The origin of the VAT in Europe and the failure of the VAT to take hold in the United States provides an interesting lesson in how public finance ideas translate into practice. Before adoption of the VAT, many European countries imposed a sales tax at every stage of production and distribution (referred to as a turnover tax). This led to considerable inefficiency, because the total tax depended on the number of taxable entities down the chain toward final consumption. It also provided an incentive for businesses to integrate (because a producer who was also the distributor who sold to the final consumer would have to pay only one tax). The VAT, which is also a tax at multiple stages, seemed to be a small step away from the turnover tax and a vast improvement in economic efficiency.

For example, if a product had a $20, $50, and $100 value as it moved down to the final consumer, a 10% turnover tax would be imposed on $170 (or more, if the tax was included in the sales tax base). But a different mix of sales prior to final consumption would produce a different tax, even though the products had the same value to the consumer. Thus, the total tax would be different if the value added on a $100 product at the various stages of production and distribution was $10, $80, $100; or if the goods were produced and sold by a fully integrated producer-wholesaler-retailer whose only sale was for $100 to the final consumer. Under a VAT, taxes are imposed only on the value added as the product moves down to the final consumer (in the three prior examples: $20 + $30 + $50; $10 + $70 + $20; and $100).

By contrast, the United States did not have turnover taxes so the VAT now seems more of a novelty. In addition, Europe has many more small businesses who sell to the final consumer and it is difficult to get them to collect a sales tax. Larger retailers in the United States are an easier target for the one-stage final-consumption retail sales tax adopted by the U.S. states.

European VAT tax rates are generally in the 10–20% range, much higher than U.S. state sales taxes. (However, unlike state sales taxes in the United States, the value added tax is included in the sales price — it is not separately stated.) Proposals to adopt a federal VAT in that range are even more likely to attract opposition from those who argue that a tax on personal consumption does not place a heavy enough burden on higher income taxpayers. A recent proposal would address this issue by eliminating the current income tax on people with low and moderate incomes (for example, up to $100,000) and adopting a VAT at higher European-level tax rates. *See* Graetz, *100 Million Unnecessary Returns: A Fresh Start for the U.S. Tax System*, 112 YALE L.J. 261 (2002).

From its origins in Europe, the VAT has spread to many other countries, such as Israel (1976), New Zealand (1986), Japan (1989), Canada (1991), and South Africa (1991), as well as many other nations in South America, Asia, and Africa. As of 2005, 145 countries used a VAT.

See generally ALAN SCHENK & OLIVER OLDMAN, VALUE ADDED TAX: A COMPARATIVE APPROACH (2006); "Report of a Special Committee on the Value-Added Tax of the Section of Taxation, American Bar Association," published in *Technical Problems in Designing a Broad-Based Value-Added Tax for the United States*, 28 TAX LAW. 193 (1974–1975).

§ 30.03   METHODS OF COMPUTING THE TAX

[A]   Credit Method

Most countries use a credit approach to collecting the VAT at each stage of production or distribution. This means that a tax is computed by the seller on the full sales price with a credit for the tax that the seller paid on the prior purchase. For example, assume the same numbers as in the initial example — successive sales for $20, $45, $60, and $100. The first stage producer would charge 20% times $20, or a $4 tax. The next seller for $45 would charge 20% times $45, or $9, but would take a $4 credit, for a net $5 tax obligation; and so forth.

[1]   Credit Method Helps Administration?

The credit method is the most popular, because it is supposed to keep the sellers honest. The idea is that each seller will report the tax paid to the prior seller from whom it made a taxable purchase in order to obtain the credit. If the prior seller has not reported that tax, that will become apparent to the taxing authorities, who will track down the sales for which a credit is claimed. For example, the taxpayer who bought the product for $20 and sold it for $45 had to report the $4 tax paid to its seller to reduce the $9 tax on the $45 sale. This cross-checking is usually administered by requiring the seller who claims a credit to maintain invoices provided by the person from whom the seller bought the creditable product.

Optimism about the self-correcting mechanics of a VAT should not be exaggerated. For example, an invoice stating that a $4 tax has been paid does not necessarily mean that the $4 tax was paid. This is, of course, fraud but that has been known to happen in most tax systems, especially when tax rates are high and the agency lacks the staff to track down delinquent taxpayers. *See* Keen & Smith, *VAT Fraud and Evasion: What Do We Know and What Can Be Done?*, 59 Nat'l Tax J. 861 (2006).

Another potential for fraud under a VAT is the concealment of a sale to the final consumer ($100 in the initial example). Although the seller for $100 will thereby forego the $12 credit on its $60 purchase, that $12 tax will still be included in the sales price to the final consumer. The incentive to conceal final sales will be greater when the value added at the last stage is significant, which is often true when the taxpayer provides personal services.

[2]   Refund for Excess Payments?

Under the credit method, a refund should be allowed if the credit exceeds the tax due on the later sale. Thus, if the second stage manufacturer sells the product for only $15 (instead of $45), the $3 tax (at a 20% rate) should be credited with the $4 tax paid to the first stage producer and the taxpayer should receive a $1 refund. Fearing fraud, some nations only permit excess tax credits to be carried over to future years to offset future VAT payments or, after some period of time, against other tax obligations (such as the income tax). However, a refund of credits on exports is routinely allowed without deferral — that is, when the goods are exported.

A refund claim is often suspect when the taxes are paid prior to beginning business. In such cases, the credit might be deferred until business begins or might depend on satisfactory evidence that the taxpayer is really planning to enter a business.

[B]   Subtraction Method

Another method of computing the VAT tax base is the subtraction method. Under this method, the tax base is total taxable sales minus total taxable purchases. Using the numbers in the prior example, the first stage producer would pay a $4 tax [20% times (20 minus 0)]; the second stage manufacturer would pay a $5 tax [20% times (45 minus 20)]; and so forth.

This method is sometimes used for selected industries in which the business inputs are not acquired from registered sellers (which means that there is no creditable tax as a result of paying for the inputs). For example, a gambling establishment pays winners who are not registered businesses, but those winnings are the cost (that is, inputs) of producing gambling gross receipts. The value added equals the gross receipts minus the amount paid to the winning gamblers. A similar approach might be used for insurance companies, who collect premiums (gross receipts) and incur costs in the form of payments to people with insured losses, which are not subject to tax. (Insurance is, however, usually exempt from the VAT).

[C]   Addition Method — Michigan

Another method of computing the VAT tax base is the addition method. The tax base equals the economic factors of production — wages, rent, interest, and profit — which equals the value added.

Michigan's Single Business Tax has been the only example of a value added tax in the United States but it has been repealed as of January 1, 2008, as a result of a voter initiative approved by the legislature. It used the addition method of computing the tax base.

§ 30.04   TAX BASE ISSUES

[A]   Capital Goods

If the VAT is the equivalent of a tax on personal consumption, business purchases of capital goods (such as a machine) should result in a credit for the tax paid on such investments (thereby keeping savings out of the overall tax base). This result is illustrated in the prior example by giving a credit for the $4 tax on the purchase of the $20 machine by the second manufacturer.

It is possible for a VAT to be the equivalent of an income tax, but that introduces some familiar complications. First, the credit would be limited to the tax due on the amount of the investment in capital goods equal to depreciation. In the prior example (using straight line depreciation and assuming a ten-year life for the $20 machine), the second stage producer would take a credit as though he paid only $2 in the particular year — similar to rent on the machine for that year. (A $20 cost over ten years results in $2 per year straight line depreciation.) A credit for a tax of 20% on $2 would equal an annual 40-cent credit over ten years, instead of a $4 credit in the year of purchase. This approach would require a depreciation schedule to be part of the VAT system. *See* Chapter 11.02 (income tax depreciation).

Second, limiting the credit to the tax on the depreciation portion of capital expenditures introduces into the VAT yet another issue that we encountered under the income tax — the difference between a capital expenditure and a repair. *See* Chapter 13.03. If repairs are either not taxed at all or their cost is credited in full, there is a difference between how the VAT would deal with capital costs and repairs.

[B]   Personal Consumption

Taxation is an intensely practical government activity and something that is theoretically part of the tax base will often be disregarded if it is too hard to tax. The de minimis principle used to identify nontaxable fringe benefits under the income tax is an example. *See* Chapter 7.02[C][7]. Conversely, when an item looms large in a particular tax, there is considerable pressure on the taxpayers to avoid the tax on that item and on the government to prevent this from happening. Consequently, a high tax rate on personal consumption, which is common under a VAT, will make the taxation of personal consumption items more important than it might otherwise be. Unlike an income tax that also taxes savings, and the typical state sales taxes that use single-digit tax rates, countries relying on a VAT typically impose double-digit tax rates on personal consumption. Some issues that seem less important for U.S. sales taxes are therefore likely to be more significant in a VAT.

For example, the value of self-produced items that are personally consumed are not likely to be reported to the taxing authorities. Food produced and consumed by a farmer will therefore not be taxed and the farmer is likely to take a credit for the tax on inputs used to produce the self-consumed product. (Under an income tax, this problem often takes the form of a deduction by the farmer for the cost of producing food, even though it is used for personal consumption.)

Another example, familiar from the income tax (Chapter 8.02[A]), is the purchase of work clothing by a self-employed taxpayer subject to the VAT. Can the tax paid on the clothing be credited against the tax on future sales or services or is it a personal consumption item? An example is an English barrister's purchase of a wig and dark suit.

[1]   Fringe Benefits

With a high tax rate on personal consumption, fringe benefits provided by an employer are likely to be a problem. The VAT might therefore deny businesses a credit or reduce the credit on the purchase of cars and entertainment-related purchases (such as club dues) on the theory that they can readily be used to provide personal consumption as a fringe benefit to employees, which would be difficult to tax.

The sale of items to employees must also be monitored so that the full fair market value of the items is reported by the employer, even though market value exceeds the bargain sales price (Cf. Chapter 7.02[C][1,5], dealing with bargain sales to employees.).

[2]   Hobbies

What if a taxpayer engages in a business with a personal consumption component — what is called a hobby in the income tax? *See* Chapter 8.09. (A typical example would be a ranch that was used as a vacation location and that also produced some products for sale.) Under the income tax, net losses cannot be deducted, but the expenses can reduce gross income. What should happen under a VAT? Either a credit should be denied for prior taxes on the theory that the entire activity provides personal consumption; or a refund should be denied if the credits exceed the tax on a sale of products by the "hobby" taxpayer? The latter approach seems the best analogy to what occurs under the income tax in the United States, where a deduction of net operating losses is disallowed.

[3] Interest — Current Personal Consumption

Interest on loans for current personal consumption (for example, travel) should not be taxed. The value of personal consumption is itself taxed, whether or not financed by a loan, and there is no further need to tax the interest. This implements a fundamental feature of a tax on personal consumption, which is its neutrality between current and future consumption.Taxing the interest would disturb that neutrality by overburdening current consumption. (Interest on loans to buy homes and consumer durables is discussed below.)

[C] Residential Use

[1] The Income Tax

Chapter 16.01[B] compared the taxation of homeowners (both those who borrow and those who self-finance the purchase of their homes with their own funds) and renters. Typically, the renter is disadvantaged, the self-financing homeowner is treated the best, and the borrower falls somewhere in between. Similar issues arise under the VAT. Consider the following hypothetical in order to understand how the VAT might treat the personal consumption derived from a residence. The home is constructed for $160,000; the value of the home is $200,000; the annual rental value is $30,000.

[2] VAT Rules?

In theory, a VAT that taxed personal consumption would tax the rental value of a residence each year. For the renter, this could be accomplished by imposing the tax on rent. A similar result could be obtained for the homeowner by taxing the $200,000 value of the home. Remember that the purchase price is the present value of the estimated future rental value so that a VAT on $200,000 is a good proxy for taxing future rental value. The fact that there is a large $200,000 amount subject to tax does not unfairly bunch consumption into one year because the VAT is not imposed at progressive rates. A shortcoming of this approach, for the government, is that present value might not accurately anticipate fluctuations in future rents; and a shortcoming for the taxpayer is the need to make a very large tax payment in the year of purchase. However, determining rental value each year is administratively difficult so taxing present value is an acceptable proxy.

What if the homeowner did not purchase the home for $200,000, but instead built it for $160,000? How can the additional $40,000 of value added become part of the tax base? We encountered a similar problem in the income tax when we discussed depreciation of self-constructed real property, noting that the purchase of a structure resulted in using a higher figure for depreciation than when the taxpayer built the structure. *See* Chapter 13.02[B]. The only way to equalize the two taxpayers is to subject the additional $40,000 to the VAT. This is, however, difficult to do because it requires valuing the new home.

These complexities usually lead to the following approach to taxing residential property. A VAT is imposed on the value added through the construction stage ($160,000), whether the taxpayer builds the home for $160,000 or buys it for $200,000. There is no tax on the purchase of the home for $200,000, but neither is there a credit for tax paid on the $160,000 construction cost; the additional $40,000 of value is exempt from the VAT.

As with the income tax, this would mean that the VAT discriminates against the renter, if rents are subject to tax. Consequently, a VAT is not likely to tax residential rent (except insofar as the $160,000 construction cost has already been taxed). That leaves only the $160,000 construction cost subject to tax for both homeowners and residential rental property.

What about the interest on loans to acquire a home? This interest is not likely to be taxed under the VAT for three reasons. First, it will be politically unpopular, given the preference for home ownership. Second, if rental value is not taxed to the self-financing homeowner, excluding interest treats borrowers and self-financers alike. Third, a tax on the construction cost prepays the tax on a significant portion of future rental value, which includes an interest factor (along with depreciation and profit).

[D]   Consumer Durables

The same questions that arise in connection with homes arise with any consumer durable, such as a car. The politics, however, are likely to be different because there is less concern for subsidizing the purchase of consumer durables and for the equal treatment of owners and renters. Moreover, not many people will pay to construct their own car, so there will be few taxpayers incurring construction costs less than fair market value.

The purchase price of the consumer durable, such as a car, would serve as a proxy for future rental value enjoyed by the owner and could therefore be subject to the VAT. Similarly, rental payments for use of a car would be subject to the VAT.

What about the treatment of interest on loans to buy a consumer durable? As long as the present value of the consumer durable has been taxed as a proxy for taxing the value of future personal consumption, there is no need to tax the interest, which is a component of the future use value of the asset.

[E]   Trade-Ins and Sales to Dealers

1. *Trade-in.* Suppose a consumer had paid a VAT when purchasing a $20,000 car. The car is now worth $12,000 and the consumer trades in the older car for a new car worth $25,000 (resulting in a $13,000 cash payment). The tax already paid on the $12,000 of trade-in value for the older car should not be taxed again when the taxpayer acquires the $25,000 car. Consequently, the acquisition of the new car in a

trade-in should result (on these facts) in a VAT on the $13,000 payment. This is the same result suggested for a sales tax in Chapter 29.03[D][3]. The dealer should be required to obtain an invoice from the person who traded in the car to verify the tax paid previously paid on the $20,000 purchase.

2. *Sales to dealers.* Suppose a car owner sells a used car to a dealer for cash and the dealer then sells the car to a new customer. (Assume that the original cost of the car when it was new was $25,000 and that, some years later, that car is sold as a used car to a dealer for $12,000.) If the car owner originally paid tax on the $25,000 purchase price of the new car, then the unused value representing the $12,000 sales price of the used car to the dealer should not be taxed again. If the dealer sells the car to a new customer for $15,000, the dealer should pay tax on $3,000 (in effect, using the subtraction method to compute the tax base).

§ 30.05 ZERO-RATING AND EXEMPTIONS

In practice, a VAT is complicated by the fact that not every purchase is subject to a uniform tax rate (such as 20%). There are two major ways this can occur — zero-rating and exemption. Zero-rating means that there is no tax on a sale but a credit is still provided to the purchaser who resells the zero-rated product. Exemption means that a taxpayer or product is not subject to the VAT. Zero-rating and exemption have very different impacts.

[A] Zero-Rating (And Multiple Rates)

Zero rating is one example of using multiple tax rates in a VAT system. For example, there can be more than one positive tax rate. Thus, if the usual tax rate is 20%, there might be a lower 5% tax rate on some transactions and a higher 25% rate on others. The higher and lower tax rates are one way to make the VAT more progressive. Thus, the sale of food can be taxed at a zero rate or at less than the usual rate (except at restaurants or for catering), and luxury items could be taxed at a higher rate. Zero rating can also be used to implement public policy (for example, by zero-rating educational services or pharmaceutical drugs).

Distinctions between zero-rated and taxable sales may be hard to draw. For example, paan leaves chewed for digestion and in some Hindu ceremonies were not considered zero-rated "food" by a Canadian court. However, prepared food sold in a grocery store to be heated at home was zero-rated "food," not analogous to restaurant purchases. And a court held that zero-rated books did not include a blank diary, in which the purchaser would record information; books contained material to be read when they were purchased. *See* Turnier, *Designing an Efficient Value Added Tax*, 39 TAX L. REV. 435 (1984) (a study of the British value added tax).

Zero rating is used for exports, which means that the VAT is imposed on a destination basis. The exporting country refunds prior VAT taxes to the exporter and the destination country is expected to impose its own VAT at its own tax rate, usually beginning at the import stage.

[B] Exemptions

[1] Scope of Exemptions

An exemption from VAT means that a sale is exempt from tax.

[a]   Product or Service

An exemption can be provided for particular goods or services, such as educational or medical services. This can lead to the usual problems of separating taxable and tax exempt sales — such as exempt eye doctor services and taxable eyeglasses sales.

[b]   Entity

Nonprofit institutions and governments are often tax-exempt providers. However, if they engage in activities that are unrelated to their exempt function, those activities should not be exempt.

New Zealand is unusual in having a very broad-based VAT, which includes goods and services provided by nonprofit entities and governments. For example, the provision of hospital and government services is often covered by the VAT. (This does not mean that tax is imposed; some sales of *specific* government goods and services by these taxpayers are zero-rated.)

[c]   Size of Provider

Exemption is sometimes provided to businesses based on small gross receipts, such as small farmers or small businesses. When exemption is based on size, it is necessary to have rules that prevent taxpayers seeking exemption from splitting up into smaller units to remain under the exemption threshold.

Another way in which taxpayers might reduce their gross receipts is to claim that people who provide them with personal services are self-employed, not employees whose gross receipts would be attributed to the employer. For example, a hairdresser who works in an establishment might receive payments from customers and pay a fee to the owner of the establishment. If these workers are employees, the payments from customers are included in the owner's gross receipts and those payments, net of the fee paid to the owner, constitute the employees' wages. However, if the workers are independent contractors, the owner's gross receipts include only the fee paid to the owner by the workers.

[2] Impact of Exemptions

An exemption does not necessarily result in preventing the imposition of a VAT. Quite the contrary; there is a risk of over-taxation because there is no credit given for prior taxes paid in the production-distribution chain. The exemption takes the transaction out of the VAT system.

[a]   Exemption Before Taxable Sales

If the exemption occurs before any sale is taxed, the VAT will be imposed on the value of final consumption and there will be no over-taxation. For example, exemption of the first sale for $20 in the initial example in this chapter will still result in the $100 in the $100 of final consumption being subject to tax.

[b]   Exemption Between Taxable Sales

There is a problem when an exempt sale occurs *between* sales subject to the VAT. This can create the problem of over-taxation and an incentive to merge that existed under the turnover tax system that the VAT was meant to replace.

For example, using the numbers in our prior example, assume that the first $20 sale was subject to a 20% tax (that is, $4) but that the later $45 sale to a wholesaler was exempt. When the wholesaler sells to the retailer for $60, there is a $12 tax, but no credit for the prior $4 tax, which occurred prior to the exempt sale. (Actually, because there is no credit, the price is likely to be increased above $60, which is what causes the economic distortion from multiple taxes, but the numbers in the example are not adjusted to take account of this effect.) The retailer who sells for $100 pays a $20 tax minus a $12 credit, which equals a net $8 tax. The total tax is therefore $24, not $20 (4 + 12 + 8).

The wholesaler in this example can avoid the loss of a tax credit by purchasing the exempt seller. In that case, the tax on any prior sale will be credited. For example, if the wholesaler purchases the second manufacturer from whom it previously made the exempt $45 purchase, there would be a taxable $20 sale (with a $4 tax) from the first manufacturer to the second manufacturer-wholesaler, followed by a taxable $60 sale (with a $12 tax minus a $4 credit), resulting in a second tax of $8. The last sale for $100 would be taxed at $20 minus $12, for an $8 tax, yielding a total of $20 tax (4 + 8 + 8).

There are two possible solutions to the problem of the exempt seller. First, exempt taxpayers could be permitted to register under the VAT, (that is, subject themselves to the VAT), so that their sales would be subject to creditable taxes. Second, a purchaser from an exempt seller might be given a credit at some statutorily specified rate to make up for the lack of the usual VAT credit (for example, when a wholesale food seller buys from an exempt farmer whose inputs have been taxed).

A less obvious example of an exemption between two taxable sales arises from the fact that employees are not subject to the VAT. If the employee makes a taxable purchase (such as for tools), no credit will be allowed for that tax when the employer sells the final product whose value includes the wages paid to the employee. This provides an incentive for the employer to make a creditable purchase of the tools that are then provided for the employee's use.

[c]   Exemption of the Last Taxable Sale

There is also an incentive to merge (but no over-taxation) when the only exempt seller is the last seller in the production or distribution chain. For example, if a bank provides exempt services to its customers, but legal services are (normally) subject to tax, the bank has an incentive to provide its own in-house legal services. The in-house performance of legal services by an exempt seller eliminates the tax on the sale of legal services.

[C]   Accounting Allocations

Zero-rating and exemptions often require accounting allocations.

[1]   Inputs

Exemptions and multiple tax rates require a business buyer to allocate purchases related to the production of products or services for later sale when those sales are subject to different tax rules. For example, assume that a taxpayer makes a purchase of an input for $20, which is taxable at 20%, and then makes two sales — one of which is taxable at the usual 20% rate and the other of which is exempt. The $20 input incurred a $4 tax but how should that tax be allocated — either to be credited against the tax on the sale taxed at 20%, or not to be credited at all on the exempt sale, or to be allocated between the two sales? This is likely to occur with the cost of capital goods that are used to produce products whose sale is subject to different tax rules. The taxpayer has an incentive (whether innocently or fraudulently) to allocate as much of the cost as possible to the sale of the taxable (nonexempt) item, so that the credit for prior taxes can be maximized.

[2]   Sales Price

The sale of an item with two components that are taxed differently can be troublesome. For example, some food sold at retail may be exempt or zero-rated but the fancy container in which the food is sold may be taxed at the regular VAT rate. Allocation of the sales price among these items is necessary for accurate taxation and, once again, there is an incentive to allocate the sales price to maximize the credit for taxes previously paid — exempt sale (no credit); zero-rated sale (credit for prior taxes and no further tax); taxed sale (credit for prior tax against tax on sale).

Similar allocation problems were encountered under United States sales tax regimes where the issue was to distinguish between taxable sales and nontaxable services or between the taxable sale of tangible property and the nontaxable sale of intangible property. *See* Chapter 29.04. VAT jurisdictions vary in the tests they use to separate taxable and nontaxable transactions. They may look to the dominant or major purpose of the transaction, giving no tax significance to "incidental" features of the transaction (such as tax-exempt incidental installation services); or instead work very hard to separate a transaction into multiple components, as in the case of package tours (where the value is attributable to both exempt transportation services and taxable meals and lodging).

§ 30.06 TIMING

The VAT is usually imposed on an accrual method except that the tax will be due earlier if payments are made to the seller prior to accrual. Deposits, however, are not considered taxable payments, leading to the same distinction we encountered in the income tax (Chapter 25.01[B][2][c][ii]).

Small business taxpayers are sometimes allowed to report taxable sales on the cash method. When this happens, there can be a serious mismatching of the tax on the seller and the buyer. The seller might defer tax until cash is received but the accrual method buyer who purchases from the cash method seller might be eligible for an immediate credit for the tax paid on the purchase price when the product is resold.

There are several responses to this mismatching problem. First, deferral of the VAT by a seller might be disallowed on sales between related parties. Second, transactions entered into for tax avoidance might not be reportable on the cash method. For example, a taxpayer who fractured the business into small units so as to be eligible for the cash method might have to use the accrual method for reporting taxable sales.

§ 30.07 FINANCIAL SERVICES

In developed economies, a significant portion of the gross domestic product results from providing financial services (including insurance). Typically, the value of most of these services is exempt from the VAT, but countries that have recently adopted a VAT have included at least some of these services in the tax base. Exemption of these services raises a number of problems.

First, what are exempt financial services? For example: credit card services; investment advice; custody of securities; ATM charges; safe deposit boxes; currency exchange?

Second, if the taxpayer makes both taxable and tax exempt sales, they must allocate input credits between the sale of taxable and tax exempt services; and they must separately account for the provision of both taxable and exempt services. To avoid these problems, some countries give taxpayers the option to be taxed on the provision of all financial services.

Third, an exemption gives taxpayers an incentive to self-produce inputs so that there is no tax on their purchase. Smaller taxpayers who cannot afford to integrate vertically will then be at a disadvantage. For example, if legal or cleaning services are taxable when their value is acquired from outside suppliers, the tax can be avoided by hiring house counsel or cleaning personnel as employees. This distortion can be avoided in several ways: giving the exempt taxpayer a credit for purchased inputs (even though that is not the usual rule); or imposing a VAT on the value of self-produced services (although this is administratively difficult).

Fourth, people who provide services in taxable transactions are at a disadvantage if the financial institution can provide them without tax. For example, banks sometimes provide estate planning services, most of which is likely to be for personal family planning. This value should be taxed, especially if lawyers' services to provide the same value are taxed. It is important not to distort consumer choices by making the same services taxable and nontaxable, depending on the service provider.

A major problem in trying to solve these issues is that it is difficult to identify the value of financial services because they are often buried in some other payment (such as interest). Lower interest rates are paid to *lenders*, who then receive some "free" services as compensation for accepting a lower interest rate. Free checking is one example. Instead of getting 4% interest and paying 1% for the checking account services (which could be subject to a VAT), the consumer gets 3% interest. Some valuation rule-of-thumb would have to be adopted to make taxation of these services administratively feasible — for example, by assuming that one-third of the lowered interest rate equals an amount "paid" for taxable services. Similarly, higher interest rates paid by *borrowers* may purchase some "free" services from a lender that should be taxed, such as financial advisory services from a lending bank.

Chapter 31

CONSUMPTION TAX

§ 31.01 BACKGROUND

The sales tax and the VAT use personal consumption as the tax base, but they are typically both overbroad (taxing some business inputs) and underbroad (omitting some services). Another way to tax personal consumption is a consumption tax, whose tax base is expected to be a more accurate measure of personal consumption. It does this by relying on the accounting reality that income equals consumption plus savings that occurs during the accounting period. The consumption tax imposes a tax on income minus savings.

In 1974, an important article by William Andrews revived an older proposal for a consumption tax (which had been advanced by Nicholas Kaldor in *An Expenditure Tax* (1955), and earlier by Thomas Hobbes and John Stuart Mill in the seventeenth and nineteenth centuries respectively); Andrews, *A Consumption-Type or Cash Flow Personal Income Tax*, 87 Harv. L. Rev. 1113 (1974). One of his arguments was that the income tax now contains so many preferences for savings (for example — exemption of unrealized gain; rapid depreciation and expensing; deduction of retirement savings) that we already have a hybrid income-consumption tax, and that it would be more practical to move in the direction of a consumption tax rather than a "purer" income tax. The current income tax is even more dotted with savings preferences than in 1974 (for example, for education expenditures) and some observers think that legislators have been surreptitiously moving toward a consumption tax without its explicit adoption.

Andrews also made the more controversial argument that a consumption tax was fairer than an income tax, because it taxed what the individual took out of the economy (consumption), rather than what the taxpayer left in the economy (savings).

One advantage of a consumption tax over a sales tax and a VAT is that it can take account of individual and family variations in the same manner as the current income tax, because it starts with income as the tax base. For example, the consumption tax base could provide personal exemptions, earned income and child tax credits, charitable deductions, and other tax breaks that exist under the current income tax law. It could also vary the tax rate for married couples and individual taxpayers and adopt progressive rates.

Moreover, a consumption tax will arguably have a more favorable impact on encouraging savings than the current income tax. A tax incentive for savings and investment is often considered an important economic policy goal for the United States.

However, a major obstacle to adopting a consumption tax in this country is that it is viewed as less progressive than an income tax, because lower income taxpayers are thought to consume a larger percentage of their income than those with higher incomes. For a low income taxpayer who consumes all of his income, a tax on consumption is already a tax on income. Progressive tax rates on consumption might not compensate for the tax impact of these spending patterns. *But see* Bankman & Weisbach, *The Superiority of an Ideal Consumption Tax Over an Ideal Income Tax*, 58 STAN. L. REV. 1413 (2006) (arguing that equity and economic efficiency considerations favor a consumption tax, but that its Achilles' heel is its implementation).

In the remainder of this chapter, we discuss some of the important issues that would arise in implementing a consumption tax. *See generally* Graetz, *Implementing a Progressive Consumption Tax*, 92 HARV. L. REV. 1575 (1979). One of the lessons to be learned is that a new tax that at first sounds attractive will often turn out to have complexities at least as great as our current income tax system.

§ 31.02   EX ANTE OR EX POST?

[A]   Ex Ante Might Equal Ex Post

The deduction of investments in the year they are made is the preferred method of treating savings under a consumption tax. When the investment is cashed in, the entire proceeds would be included in the tax base (unless reinvested). In effect, the taxpayer has a zero basis in the investment because it has been completely expensed. For example, a $1,000 deposit in a bank account in year 1 would be deductible and it would be taken into income in year 2 if it were withdrawn from the bank in that year. Whether or not this would result in tax depends on what the taxpayer did with the money in year 2. This is referred to as the cash flow method of taxation because deductions and inclusions in the tax base occur when cash flows in and out.

An alternative approach would not allow the taxpayer to deduct the savings but would instead permit the taxpayer to exclude the income from the after-tax investment. This proposal builds on an equivalence between a "pure" ex post consumption tax and an ex ante approach with an exemption from tax on the income earned on the after-tax investment, discussed in Chapter 3.03[B]. For example, assume a 50% tax rate and a $100 investment yielding a 10% annual rate of return. If the investment of $100 in year 1 is deductible and yields $110 in year 2, the taxpayer pays $55 tax when it is cashed in for personal consumption in year 2 and the taxpayer has $55 left — the ex post approach. Without a deduction — the ex ante approach — the taxpayer invests $50 but can earn a $5 (10%) tax exempt return on the investment, which also equals $55. The mathematical link between deducting savings and excluding the income from after-tax investments under a consumption tax is why the consumption tax is sometimes referred to as a tax on personal service income or a "wage tax" (that is, a tax on income other than investment income).

(I am following the practice of stating the consumption tax rate as a percentage of income used to finance personal consumption — that is, 50%. In the prior example, that avoids stating the consumption tax rate as 100% of consumption. 100% of the $55 of consumption financed out of $110 of income in year 2 equals $55. If the consumption tax rate were stated as a percentage of consumption, the high tax rates would be politically forbidding. The 50% rate would in any event be the withholding tax rate and the estimated tax rate applied to income to assist with the collection of the consumption tax.)

There are, however, several problems with relying on the equivalence between an ex ante and ex post approach. First, some taxpayers will do much better than the 10% rate of return and some will do worse, but they would be treated the same under an ex ante approach to applying a consumption tax. A taxpayer taxed on an ex ante basis, who gets a 20% return, will end up with $60, but a taxpayer whose investment earns nothing has only $50. Most conceptions of tax equity consider these two taxpayers to be in different positions regarding the opportunity for personal consumption, whatever may have been their equivalence prior to making the investment.

Second, the equivalence of an ex post and ex ante approach breaks down when tax rates are progressive — as would probably be the case in any consumption tax (especially if it replaced all or part of the income tax). For example, assume a 40% tax on $100, and a 50% tax on higher amounts. If the taxpayer had $100 of income, the taxpayer would have $60 to invest under an ex ante approach (after a $40 tax). If the investment doubles to $120, there is no further tax on the $120 available for personal consumption. If tax was imposed on an ex post basis, the $100 investment is not taxed. When that investment doubles to $200, there is a $90 tax — $40 (on $100) and $50 (on another $100). That leaves the taxpayer in an ex post tax regime with only $110 available for personal consumption. (The same discrepancy could exist if there were a change in the applicable *statutory* tax rates in different tax years.)

[B] Sometimes Ex Ante is Best — Homes and Consumer Durables

Many assets are acquired for personal use — for example, homes and consumer durables, such as cars. In theory, a consumption tax should permit a deduction for their cost and require annual inclusion of their fair rental value. However, estimating rental value is difficult for these assets and taxing such "imputed income" may seem unfair to taxpayers. The simplest method of taxing these assets is to disallow a deduction for their purchase price on the assumption that the present value (that is, the current purchase price) will be a good proxy for future rental value — the ex ante approach. (Loans to finance the purchase of homes and consumer durables are discussed in Chapter 31.05.)

[1] Gain

One question that arises from ex ante taxation is how to tax any gain on disposition of the asset. The ex ante approach, in effect, provides the asset with a basis on which gain could be computed (as under an income tax). But should there be recognized gain under a consumption tax? If the purchase price is an adequate proxy for future income — whether in the form of personal use or investment return — no gain should be recognized.

But gain on some personal use assets is likely to be very large, as in the case of antiques and artwork. For example, a $10,000 investment in a painting that hangs in a residence might appreciate to $45,000 (a $35,000 gain). (By contrast, the typical car is not likely to produce gain over original cost.) There is even a risk that the asset will be labeled personal by the taxpayer (such as artwork) to obtain ex ante taxation, in the hope that future investment gain might go untaxed. Consequently, the best way to treat the gain on such assets is to include the gain in the tax base — probably in excess of some pre-set interest rate of return. (Recall that the income tax treats "collectibles" differently from other capital assets — with a maximum 28% rate; Chapter 3.04[B].) For example, if we assume a 10% rate of return on the $10,000 investment in the prior example, that would yield $12,100 in two years with annual compounding of interest; the taxable gain under this approach would then be $32,900 ($35,000 minus $2,100).

[2] Depreciable Personal Use Property

The analysis in the case of depreciable personal use property (such as a home) is more complex. For example, assume that the taxpayer purchased a home for $200,000 and used it for one quarter of its useful life. Assume further that depreciation attributable to personal use occurs on a straight line basis, so that the basis would be $150,000. A sale for $200,000 should result in $50,000 gain, because (in effect) the taxpayer has received cash for that amount of personal consumption. However, a downward adjustment of basis for personal use is not required under the regular income tax and the same approach is likely to be followed under a consumption tax (especially when the asset is politically favored, like a home). *See* Chapter 19.04[A]. Consequently, there would probably be no gain in this example on the sale for $200,000.

Query: Would any gain in excess of $200,000 be taxed by analogy to the gain on artwork?

[3] Reinvestment

In most instances, reinvestment of the sales proceeds of investment property poses no problems under a consumption tax because the asset had a zero basis (its cost was expensed). The entire sales proceeds are included in income and deducted if reinvested.

However, ex ante taxation on the acquisition of personal use property presents some complexities. If the taxpayer reinvested the proceeds of the sale of personal use property that had a basis, the newly acquired asset should have a basis equal to the basis of the property sold (or, perhaps, equal to the proceeds of the sale if those proceeds were less than the basis of the property sold). The assumption would be that this basis is an amount on which tax has already been paid and which was either not used up in personal consumption or which was a tax-preferred item, such as a home; and that, therefore, this amount should not be taxed again. Rules would be required to decide which newly acquired property should take the carryover basis — such as a new home that replaces a residence that has burned down or been condemned, or like-kind investment property, or whatever property the taxpayer designates.

[4] Casualty Loss

If there is a casualty loss of an asset used for personal purposes on which an ex ante tax has been prepaid (for example, a house burned down and there was no insurance), a deduction might be allowed for the amount of the original cost not already used up in personal consumption — that is, the lowest of the following figures: original cost; or a basis adjusted downward for depreciation reflecting personal use; or the lower value at the time of loss (which is the income tax rule). *See* Chapter 12.03[B].

§ 31.03 AVERAGING

An ex ante approach taxes the present value of a future flow of personal consumption in the year of purchase. That amount is likely to be large and, if the tax rates are progressive, that will force the taxpayer into a higher tax bracket than would be the case if consumption were periodically included in the tax base in future years.

The income tax has occasionally dealt with the problem of including large income items in a single year in various ways. The only current example is farm income (*see* Chapter 5.05), but there have been other examples in the past. One conceptual difficulty with averaging consumption when there is a prepayment is that there is no way to know the taxpayer's tax bracket in future years. (Under the income tax, the averaging is based on a comparison of the current year's income to the income reported in *prior* years.)

The simplest solution under a consumption tax is illustrated by the following example. Assume a prepayment of $50,000 on which there is a consumption tax. Divide that amount by some statutorily-determined number — assume five in the example. Then compute the consumption tax in the year of purchase on $10,000 and multiply that result by five to get the total consumption tax due on the $50,000 purchase.

§ 31.04 BUSINESS vs. PERSONAL USE

[A] Fringe Benefits; Personal Expenses

The difficulty in distinguishing between business and personal consumption, which exists under the income tax, would be exaggerated under a consumption tax because the tax base is personal consumption and the tax rates on that component of income are likely to be higher than under the income tax. Identifying taxable fringe benefits and drawing a line between deductible business and nondeductible personal expenses is just as daunting a task as under an income tax, but the pressure on the tax administration to get it right would be greater.

[B] Dual Personal and Business or Investment Assets

An asset can be used separately for business and personal purposes. This might occur, for example, when a car is used for both business and pleasure or a home includes a home office. The cost allocable to business use would be deductible as an investment and the portion allocable to personal use would probably not be deductible, but would be taxed on an ex ante basis.

§ 31.05 LOANS

Loans should be included in income under a consumption tax. Thus, a $100 loan would be included in income and, if invested, would be deducted — a zero impact in the year of borrowing with investment. Because loans are included in income, the interest would be deductible, as would repayment of the loan.

However, this theoretically correct approach is not likely to be applied to loans incurred for personal purposes. Loans to purchase homes and consumer durables would not be treated as income and no deduction would be allowed for the investment. In the future, neither the principal nor the interest would be deductible. This has the result of including most of the future personal use value of the property in the tax base when debt and interest is repaid — everything except the excess of rental value over the debt-plus-interest payments. For example, assume a taxpayer borrows $200,000 to buy a home for $200,000; annual payments of interest and principal equal $24,000. If the tax rate on personal consumption is 20%, the taxpayer needs $30,000 of income to make the $24,000 payments — that is, a $6,000 tax payment plus the $24,000 of nondeductible interest and debt repayments equal $30,000. Any rental value in excess of $24,000 would not be taxed.

The same rule would apply to loans for current personal consumption (such as vacations) — the loan would not be included in income, and the interest and principal repayment would not be deductible. The justification for this result is that the consumption tax, unlike the income tax, does not change the ratio of current to future consumption that would exist without a tax, and the nondeductibility of consumer interest achieves that equivalence when the loan has not been included in the tax base. For example, assume that the taxpayer had $100 of income in year 1, that the rate of return on an investment is 10%, and that the tax rate is 50%. The taxpayer can either consume $50 in year 1 or $55 in year 2; that is a 10/11 ratio of current to future consumption. Now assume that the taxpayer borrows $50 in year 1 and pays 10% interest in year 2 (that is, $5) when the loan is repaid. Because the loan and interest are not deductible in year 2, the taxpayer needs $110 of income before tax in year 2 to repay the $55 of loan plus interest. The taxpayer thus has a choice of $50 in year 1 or, if he or she does not borrow, $55 in year 2 (50% of $110). That is the same 10/11 ratio that existed without the consumption tax.

The nondeductibility of the principal and interest as the loan is repaid usually allows the taxpayer to avoid the burden of progressive tax rates that would occur if the tax were imposed on the full amount of the loan at the time of purchase. However, it also allows the tax to be deferred until after the time of personal consumption, if the creditor is willing to defer the loan repayment beyond the personal consumption years.

If personal loans are not included in the tax base, forgiveness of these loans would have to be included in income without any offsetting deduction so that personal consumption would be taxed.

§ 31.06   GIFTS

One issue that is familiar in the current income tax might look different in a consumption tax — the treatment of gifts. The fact that the donee enjoys the personal consumption might suggest allowing the donor a deduction and taxing the donee on any consumption financed from cash gifts. (Under the income tax, the donor is taxed on the income used to make a nondeductible gift and the donee excludes the gift from income.) However, if tax rates on consumption should not be lowered by intra-family transfers, the better result is to preserve the income tax approach of taxing the donor and not the donee in the case of cash gifts.

In the case of gifts of investment assets, however, the donee would step into the donor's shoes (with a zero basis) and pay any tax that is due on the sales proceeds. Similarly, if the donor had paid tax on the purchase of property used for personal purposes (such as a home or consumer durable), a gift of that property would result in a carryover of basis to the donee and gain on any later sale would be included in the donee's income to the extent that this would have occurred for the original investor.

§ 31.07   PRESERVING TAX INCENTIVES

Income tax law provides many tax incentives and a consumption tax must decide whether to provide similar tax breaks. In some instances no further tax breaks seem appropriate. For example, the income tax law now provides consumption tax treatment for retirement savings — either by allowing a deduction for savings and imposing a tax when the savings plus the investment returns are drawn down (ex post), or by permitting after-tax savings to be invested without any further tax when the investment is withdrawn for current use (ex ante). *See* Chapter 24.06. Similarly, after-tax income can sometimes be invested for education without any further tax when the investment is drawn down for educational purposes (ex ante). *See* Chapter 7.04[C].

But the fact that savings are already deducted in a consumption tax does not *necessarily* mean the end of tax incentives for specific business or investment activities. Beneficiaries of income tax breaks for these activities might also receive special treatment under the consumption tax, even though the pressure to provide tax reductions might be reduced. Moreover, tax breaks for personal expenditures (such as medical expenses and charitable contributions) are likely to continue under a consumption tax.

[A]   Business or Investment Activities

The easiest way to consider how a consumption tax might provide incentives for business or investment activities is to look first at tax-exempt income and then at situations where the income might be entitled to a preferential tax rate.

[1] Exempt Income

Suppose the consumption tax continued the tax break for investments in tax-exempt bonds that existed under the income tax. For example, assume two sources of income — $100 wages and $100 tax exempt interest on state and local bonds. Assume further that the taxpayer spends $200 on personal consumption. The tax break in year 1 would be preserved by giving the taxpayer a tax deduction in year 1 for the $100 spent out of tax-preferred income. The result would be only $100 subject to the consumption tax.

Suppose that the taxpayer *saved* all of the income received in year 1, instead of purchasing personal consumption. The savings out of $100 of taxable income would wipe out any tax on that amount under the regular consumption tax rules. The question then arises whether and how to provide a tax break for the savings incurred out of the $100 of tax exempt income. A tax break could be provided *in year 1* by giving the taxpayer a refundable tax credit at a specified tax rate times the tax-exempt income, in addition to the savings deduction. But, the better approach is to carry forward the tax-exempt income that has been saved to offset otherwise taxable personal expenditures in a later year. Thus, if the taxpayer had $100 of income in year 2 that he used for personal consumption, the carryover of the $100 of exempt income from year 1 would eliminate any tax in year 2.

If the $100 of taxable income and $100 of tax-exempt income is used for both personal consumption and savings in year 1, the tax law would need a rule to allocate the savings and personal consumption to each type of income. For example, assume that $100 is saved and $100 is used for personal consumption in year 1. These expenditures could be allocated in a number of ways:

First, the $100 of personal consumption expenditures could be allocated entirely to the $100 of tax-exempt income, resulting in no tax in year 1. Second, the $100 of savings could be allocated to the $100 of tax-exempt income and carried forward to reduce otherwise taxable personal consumption in year 2. Third, the $100 of personal consumption expenditures and $100 of savings could be allocated 50/50 to both types of income because the $200 of income was derived from 50% taxable and 50% tax exempt income.

Tax breaks for particular industries that are currently in the form of favorable deductions are sometimes the equivalent of tax-exempt income to the extent of the deductions. The percentage depletion allowance for the income from various mining activities is one example. Thus, a 20% percentage depletion allowance means that $100 of mining income results in $80 taxable and $20 tax-exempt income. The taxable and tax-exempt income could then be allocated between savings and personal consumption in whatever manner the statute provides, as indicated in the prior examples.

It is administratively more difficult to convert faster-than-normal depreciation (including expensing) enjoyed by selected industries into an exempt income figure. Current income tax law conceptualizes these tax breaks as tax deferral, not as tax exemption, even though deferred income can be converted into an exemption for the income on an after-tax investment. *See* Chapter 3.03[B]. A consumption tax (which already provides for expensing investments) has the advantage of forcing the legislature to make any tax break that it wants to provide to a particular industry explicit in the form of tax-exempt income, so that it will be more transparent to policy makers than accelerated deductions for investments.

[2] Credits?

An alternative way to provide tax breaks under the consumption tax — rather than identifying tax exempt income — is to permit the taxpayer to take a credit against the consumption tax. For example, if a taxpayer earned $10,000 income and was entitled to a 10% earned income credit, $1,000 would reduce the tax on personal consumption. Moreover, the credit could disappear with rising income and could be refunded if it exceeded the consumption tax (both of which occur under current income tax law. *See* Chapter 1.05, dealing with the earned income credit).

[B] Tax-preferred Personal Expenses

Tax breaks for personal expenditures would usually be easy to provide under a consumption tax — by not treating them as taxable personal consumption. That would mean deducting them from income, like savings. For example, $100 of income spent on $100 of medical expenses would result in zero taxable personal consumption. The same approach could be taken for charitable contributions made in cash. If the taxpayer had tax-exempt income (as defined under the consumption tax), some method will be required to allocate the otherwise deductible personal expense between taxable and tax-exempt income.

Under the current income tax, a charitable deduction is often allowed for the value of property given to a charity, including the untaxed appreciated gain. *See* Chapter 10.04[A]. How would that tax break be provided in a consumption tax? Under the income tax, the deduction for appreciated gain, in effect, creates exempt income to the extent of the deductible gain. If that incentive is to be preserved under a consumption tax, personal consumption out of that gain would have to be eligible for the same tax breaks provided to personal consumption financed out of any other type of tax-exempt income.

For example, assume that the following occurs in year 1: the taxpayer has $100 of taxable income, which is invested in stock; the stock then appreciates to $150; there is another $50 of taxable wages; and the $150 of stock is given to charity; all this occurs in year 1. Under the income tax, there would be no taxable income, assuming no percentage limits on the charitable deduction — $150 of income and a $150 deduction. The $50 of wages could be used for personal consumption without being subject to an income tax — in effect, the wages are tax-exempt. Under a consumption tax, the $100 *cost* of the appreciated property would be deductible like a charitable contribution made in cash, and would not result in taxable personal consumption. But the $50 of *appreciated* gain given to charity would also reduce otherwise taxable income, converting the $50 of wages into tax-exempt income, available for tax-free personal consumption in year 1.

§ 31.08   CORPORATE TAXATION

What is the place of a corporate tax in a consumption tax regime? Corporate earnings are savings from the point of view of the investor. A "pure" consumption tax would therefore result in repeal of the corporate income tax. Such repeal is unlikely, however, because of the loss of revenue. Although the contribution of the corporate tax to total federal tax revenue has not returned to the 25–30% level that prevailed in the decade after World War II, it still hovers at about 10% (which is a substantial sum). Moreover, without a corporate tax, the regressive nature of the consumption tax might be too apparent.

If the corporate income tax is retained, many of the administrative advantages that are supposed to arise from exempting savings under a consumption tax are lost. For example, favorable depreciation schedules and selective expensing of desirable investments are still necessary, with all the attending complexities. This includes the recapture of prior depreciation as ordinary income, as long as corporate capital losses are deductible only up to corporate capital gains (which is the current law). And the distinction between deductible interest and nondeductible dividends persists, because it is necessary to compute the corporation's taxable income. Chapter 33 discusses the corporate tax in greater detail.

§ 31.09   TRANSITION

The transition to a consumption tax can be problematic because of the risk of double taxing the savings that were taxed prior to adopting the consumption tax. To see how this can occur, consider the mechanics of a consumption tax.

The consumption tax would be administered by computing income minus any annual change in savings. If a taxpayer was a net saver in any accounting period, the savings would reduce income to compute taxable personal consumption. But if the taxpayer drew down savings during that period — that is, a negative savings figure — the savings would show up in the consumption tax base. A taxpayer with $100,000 income who spent that $100,000 on personal consumption and also drew down $50,000 in prior savings for additional personal consumption would have a $150,000 tax base. This result makes sense because a consumption tax is supposed to defer the tax on savings until it is used for personal consumption.

But suppose the taxpayer had previously taxed savings under the prior income tax; it might seem unfair to add a negative savings figure to the consumption tax base when it had already been taxed. There are problems, however, with trying to avoid this unfairness. First, it would be difficult to determine whether the prior savings had been taxed. A lot of savings escapes the federal income tax under the current law. Second, some method would have to be devised to trace current negative savings to previously taxed savings as opposed to savings that arose after the consumption tax had been adopted.

Notice that a new sales tax or VAT presents the same "double taxation" problem, especially if the tax rates are significant. However, this objection is not usually heard when a new state sales tax is adopted, because the rates are relatively low. Moreover, a new state sales tax is not usually viewed politically as a double tax on savings previously subject to income tax at the federal level. Nonetheless, adoption of a *federal* VAT with a high tax rate might require some transition adjustment to prevent a consumption tax on previously taxed income.

The effort to provide a transition to a new consumption tax from the income tax will probably result in its introduction at gradually increasing tax rates each year. This means that the tax administration must administer both the old income tax and the new consumption tax for some period, which will place a heavy burden on the tax agency. The same burden exists if a consumption tax supplements rather than replaces the income tax.

ENTITY TAXATION

The discussion of the income tax in Part I made several references to the taxation of entities — for example, dealing with assignment of income by a shareholder to a corporation under his or her control (Chapter 2.05); and passing losses through to partners in a tax shelter (Chapter 17.04–.05). Part II-D looks more closely at the various ways entities can be and are taxed in the United States — including partnerships, trusts and estates, and corporations.

There are four general approaches to the taxation of entities.

First, the entity can be a pass-through entity. This means that the entity itself does not pay tax. Instead, the entity computes its income, which is then taxed to the beneficial owners in the year it is earned; taxation of the owners is not deferred until distribution. This is the method generally used for partnerships and some corporations in the United States (known as Subchapter S corporations). In addition, trusts and estates that distribute income arising in a particular year do not pay tax on that income and the income characteristics pass-through to the beneficiaries. To that extent, trusts and estates are pass-through entities.

Second, the entity can pay a tax on its income in the year it is earned, but this tax can then be credited against the beneficial owner's tax when the profits are distributed, thereby avoiding double taxation of the entity's profits. It also allows deferral of the tax on the owner until the year of distribution (as well as overtaxing the owner if the withholding rate exceeds the owner's tax). Something like this approach has (on occasions) been used for the taxation of trusts and their beneficiaries in the United States (when the income was distributed out of income accumulated from a prior year) and for corporations and shareholders in some foreign countries. The general idea is that the entity does not have an independent taxpaying capacity; the tax it pays is treated as a withholding tax.

713

Third, the entity has an independent taxpaying capacity, leading to a tax on the entity's income and another tax when the profits are distributed to the beneficial owner; there is a double tax on the entity's income. This is how corporations have traditionally been taxed in the United States (although the maximum tax on dividends is now 20%).

Fourth, the entity pays a tax in the year the income is earned, but there is no further tax when the income is distributed to the beneficiaries. This approach makes the most sense when the entity is taxed at a high tax rate so that there is no incentive to earn income through the entity to avoid higher individual tax rates. The entity tax can therefore be understood as an advance payment of the beneficiary's tax, avoiding the potential for tax avoidance by earning or retaining income at the entity level. This is the method now used for most domestic trusts on any income that they accumulate.

This Part deals with how these various approaches are applied to the taxation of entities and their owners. Chapter 32 discusses partnership and trust or estate taxation. Chapter 33 deals with the corporate tax.

Chapter 32

PARTNERSHIPS, TRUSTS AND ESTATES

§ 32.01 PARTNERSHIPS

This chapter relies heavily on the discussion of partnership taxation in Laura Cunningham & Noel Cunningham, The Logic of Subchapter K (3d ed. 2006).

[A] Organization

The organization of a partnership is usually a nonrecognition event, similar to a like-kind exchange, discussed in Chapter 19.03. The partners do not recognize gain or loss. The partners' basis in the transferred property carries over into the partnership (referred to as the partnership's "*inside basis*") and the partners' partnership interest retains the basis they had in the transferred property (referred to as the partners' "*outside basis*"). **§§ 721–723.**

These nonrecognition rules do not apply if the partner receives a partnership interest for past or future services. In that case, the partner's receipt of a partnership *capital* interest in exchange for the services results in taxing the partner on the value of that interest at the time it is received. **Treas. Reg. § 1.721-1(b); Prop. Reg. § 1.83-3(*l*).** The partners value the partnership interest by using the "liquidation method" — which refers to the cash payment the partner would receive if the partnership sold all of its assets and distributed cash in accordance with the partnership agreement. Taxation of this interest can be deferred if the interest is subject to forfeiture or (in some instances) limits on transferability, except that the partner can elect not to defer tax and instead to be taxed at the time of receiving the interest under **§ 83(b).**

If the partner receives only an interest in future profits (not a capital interest) in exchange for services to the partnership in his or her capacity as a partner, tax is *not* imposed when the partnership interest is received. Rev. Proc. 93-27, 1993-2 C.B. 343. **Prop. Reg. § 1.83-3(*l*)** provides a similar result by taxing the partner on the liquidation value of the interest, which is zero if there is only a profit interest.

[B] Pass-Through Entity

Partnerships are pass-through entities. There is no tax imposed on the entity. The income (and losses) are attributed to the partners in the year they are earned, without waiting for a distribution. These rules apply to traditional partnerships where all partners are personally liable for each other's debts (as in a typical law partnership); to limited partnerships (in which most of the partners are not liable for more than their investment in the partnership, just like a corporate shareholder); and to limited liability companies (a relative newcomer to state law).

[1] Character of Items, Including Capital Gains

The character of the partnership's income and deductions carries through to the partners — including ordinary income, short and long term capital gains and losses, tax-exempt interest, and charitable contributions. The pass-through of capital gains is especially important. Corporations do not enjoy a preferential tax rate on long term capital gains, but the pass-through of these gains to individual partners usually results in taxing the partners at the maximum 20% tax rate. These principles have special interest for private equity partnerships. The managing general partner of these partnerships typically contributes 1%-5% of the partnership's capital but is entitled to 20% of the profits from the sale of the partnership's securities (usually stock). The expectation is that the 20% (minus a small percentage as compensation for management services) will be capital gains passed through to the general partner, even though all of the excess of 20% over the 1%-5% capital contribution looks a lot like personal service compensation. Presumably there is no tax when the partnership is formed because the partner has only an interest in future profits, not a capital interest.

[2] Basis Adjustments

The partners' basis in their partnership interests is increased by the amount of income attributed to the partner (both taxable income and tax-exempt income, such as interest on state and local bonds); and decreased by distributions to the partner, by including charitable contributions, by partnership losses, and by expenses that are not deductible by the partnership (such as expenses that violate public policy).

[3] Contributed Property with Inherent Gain or Loss

If a partner contributed property with an inherent gain or loss at the time of the contribution, that gain or loss will usually be attributed to that partner when the property is sold by the partnership. § 704(c). For example, if two individuals (A and B) each contribute $100 worth of property, but A contributes cash and B contributes land with a basis of $80 and a value of $100, sale of the land by the partnership for $100 will result in taxing B on $20, even though the partners share partnership profits and losses equally.

This is a simple example of a discrepancy between how partners share the value of partnership assets (their book value) and how they share tax attributes in partnership property. Each partner has an equal share of the partnership's book value (reflecting their equal contributions); but each partner has a different share of the partnership's inside basis (which reflects the basis of the assets contributed by each partner to the partnership). The $20 gain that B had in the land was not recognized when the partnership was created, but is recognized by B when the partnership sells the asset. This prevents A from having to pay tax on one half of the recognized $20 gain when A does not enjoy any increase in the book value of A's partnership interest. (The sale for $100 still leaves a total of $200 of partnership assets, with A and B each sharing the book value equally — that is, each has a $100 share.)

If the land had been sold for $95, B would recognize only $15 gain, because there is a ceiling on B's gain equal to the gain recognized by the partnership on the sale. However, this is unfair to A, who has suffered a book loss — that is, the value of the partnership has declined to $195, of which A's share is $97.50. Various techniques are used to help A in this situation, the simplest of which is to reduce A's recognized gain on the sale of other partnership property by his share of the partnership's book loss (that is, $2.50).

More complicated computations are required if the property is depreciable. Permitting A and B to take the same depreciation deductions each year would mean that B would not recognize the $20 gain in the property. In general, the solution is to give a larger share of the depreciation deduction to A and a lesser share to B, so that B will pay tax on more income each year until B recognizes the $20 gain.

There are other situations where there can be a discrepancy between a partner's share of inside basis for tax purposes and the partnership's book value requiring adjustments similar to those just discussed — such as the contribution of money by a new partner for a partnership interest, followed by a revaluation of the book value of the assets to reflect a change in value between the time when the partnership was formed and the contribution by the new partner. For example, assume that each of two partners (A and B) organize a partnership with $80 cash contributions that are used to buy property. Thereafter, the property rises in value from $160 to $200 (shared equally by A and B). A new third partner contributes $100 cash for a one-third interest in the partnership and A and B revise their share of partnership book value to $100 each, even though their share of inside basis is only $80 each.

[4] Allocation of Income and Deductions Among Partners

One feature of partnership taxation that has made it attractive to taxpayers is the ability to allocate the partnership's income and deductions among the partners, as long as the allocation has "substantial economic effect." **§ 704(b)**. The most important of the rules to determine "substantial economic effect" requires that any allocation of deductions to a partner (often designed to give deductions to the partner who can use them to the best tax advantage) must be accompanied by that partner suffering the economic loss from the event giving rise to the deduction. For example, assume a partnership with two equal partners (50% each), reflecting equal capital contributions of $1 million each. If depreciation deductions are allocated entirely to one partner — for example, $100,000 — that partner must reduce his capital account in the partnership to reflect the deduction allocation — which results in a $900,000 capital account. If there is a total liquidating distribution of $1,900,000, because value declined at the same rate as depreciation, the partner receiving the depreciation deductions would receive only $900,000, thereby assuring that the depreciation allocation had substantial economic effect. Regulations provide more complex examples in this very complex corner of partnership tax law.

[5] Net Operating Losses

The ability to allocate net operating losses among partners presents opportunities for tax avoidance for tax shelter partnerships. It is also important in the context of start-up businesses that realize losses in the early business years. Although the pass-through of losses is limited to the partner's *outside* basis in the partnership, that basis includes debt incurred *by* the partnership — including nonrecourse debt incurred to purchase partnership assets, such as real estate. This rule is especially attractive for *limited* partners — who, like shareholders, are not liable beyond the amount of their investment in the entity.

This situation poses serious problems for the tax law because there is no way to allocate the losses created by *nonrecourse* debt based on substantial economic effect. None of the partners bears the loss on such property, which is suffered by the lender. The Regulations under § 704 give the partners a great deal of flexibility in allocating these losses, as long as there is a partnership agreement to allocate *gains* on the disposition of the property in the same manner as the losses were deducted. As you will recall (*see* Chapter 17.01[A]), gain will often arise because unpaid nonrecourse liability is an amount realized when the taxpayer disposes of property encumbered by the debt.

A partner's ability to deduct the partnership's net operating losses is limited by the anti-tax shelter rules discussed in Chapter 17.05 (§§ 465, 469). These rules prohibit a partner from deducting net operating losses (1) unless the partner has an at-risk investment (with an important exception for nonrecourse loans financing the purchase of real property); and (2) unless the partner materially participates in the partnership's business (which usually excludes limited partners).

[6]   Distribution of Inventory

There is a potential for tax avoidance when the partnership distributes property to a partner that is inventory to the partnership but is a capital asset in the hands of a partner. **Section 735(a)(2)** closes this loophole by treating the sale of such property by a partner as generating ordinary income or loss, if the distributed inventory is sold by the partner within five years of the distribution.

[7]   Publicly Traded Partnerships

The pass-through taxation rules do *not* apply to a "publicly traded partnership," which is taxed under the regular corporate tax rules. § 7704 (partnerships whose ownership interests are traded on an established securities market or a secondary market). However, publicly traded partnerships are exempt from the rule taxing them as corporations, if 90% or more of their income is investment income (such as interest or dividends), real property rents, income from mining and natural resources, or capital gains from selling property used to produce any of the above income.

[C]   Accounting Issues

[1]   Taxable Year

The partnership's gains and losses are passed through to the partners when the partnership's taxable year ends. For example, a partnership with a taxable year ending on June 30, 2013, passes through income to a partner who computes income on a calendar year basis in the year 2013. Generally, a partnership must use the taxable year of its principal partners, but a business purpose can justify using a different taxable year. § **706(b)**.

[2] Accounting Methods — Partnership Not Always a Conduit

Section 703(b) states that elections "affecting the computation of taxable income derived from a partnership" must usually be made at the partnership level, which can lead to differences in how income is computed depending on whether business is conducted in partnership form or by an individual as a sole proprietorship. In this respect, a partnership is *not* a pass-through entity. For example, the use of the installment method under **§ 453** is determined at the partnership level. Similarly, the election to use **§ 179** to expense the cost of certain property is made by the partnership. Partners cannot make their own elections.

Partnerships are generally allowed to elect whether to use a cash or accrual method of accounting, with two major exceptions. First, a partnership with a C corporation as a partner cannot use the cash method. However, this limitation on the use of the cash method does not apply if the C corporation is a personal service corporation (for example, providing law or medical services); or the partnership or corporation has average annual gross receipts for the prior three years of $5 million or less. ("C corporation" refers to a corporation that has not elected to be taxed as a pass-through entity under Subchapter S; pass-through Subchapter S corporations are discussed in the next chapter.) **§ 448(a)(2), (b)**.

Second, a "tax shelter" partnership is not allowed to use the cash method; **§ 448(d)(3)**. The definition of a tax shelter appears in **§ 461(i)(3)**.

[D] Partner Dealing with Partnership

[1] Nonpartner Capacity

[a]   In General

A partner can deal with the partnership *in a nonpartner capacity*, such as an employee or lender. In that case, the payments to the partner are generally treated in the same way as any payment to an outsider — for example, salary is deductible by the partnership (unless it is a capital expenditure) and is taxable as salary to the partner. **§ 707(a)**.

A partnership on the accrual method would normally accrue salary owed to an employee in year 1, even though it was not included in a cash basis employee's income until it was paid in year 2. However, **§ 267(a), (e)** requires the partnership to defer the deduction of such income when owed to a partner until the year it is included in a partner's income to prevent the parties from reducing taxes by taking deductions before income is reported.

[b]   Employee Fringe Benefits

A partner is not considered an "employee" of the partnership just because he or she is a partner. However, because § 707(a) specifies that a partner *can* be an employee of a partnership, an employee-partner can take advantage of various tax breaks for employees — such as §§ 79, 106, 132 (dealing with term life insurance, medical insurance, and certain other fringe benefits, respectively).

There are also explicit statutory rules allowing partners to take advantage of tax breaks for retirement savings on the same basis as qualified retirement plans for employees. And health insurance premiums can be fully deducted (100%) by a self-employed taxpayer, including partners (§ 162(*l*)). Consequently, a partnership does not have to convert to a corporation (so that "partners" can become employee-owners) in order to take advantage of the important tax breaks for retirement savings and medical insurance. *See also* **Treas. Reg. § 1.132-1(b)(2)(ii)**, treating a partner as an employee for purposes of excluding working condition fringe benefits from income.

[2]   Partner Capacity — Guaranteed Payments

If the partner receives a guaranteed payment *as a partner* and the guaranteed payment is not contingent on partnership income, the payment is treated like a § 707(a) payment (for example, as salary), except that the timing is the same as if the payment were a share of the partnership income. § 707(c). Consequently, the guaranteed payment does not take on the characteristics of the partnership income (such as tax-exempt interest or capital gains) in the hands of the partner receiving the guaranteed payment, as would have been the case if profits had been distributed to the partner. And the tax on the partner is deferred until the close of the partnership's tax year.

For example, assume a guaranteed payment for services equal to $30,000, payable on December 31, 2012. The partnership's accounting year ends on June 30, 2013. The $30,000 is (probably) deductible salary by the partnership but is included in the partner's *2013* income, because that is the timing rule for passing through partnership income to the partners. This differs from a § 707(a) payment of salary, which would be taxed in accordance with the partner's taxable year (which probably ends on December 31, 2012).

The line between a partner acting in a partner or nonpartner capacity is unclear, but the difference is probably between providing technical skills (acting in a nonpartner capacity) and compensation for managing the partnership (acting in a partner capacity).

[E]   Income Shifting

A partner who conveys a partnership interest to another person must report a reasonable amount to compensate for personal services rendered by the donor-partner. § 704(e). This is a statutory version of the *Lucas v. Earl* decision; Chapter 2.02. By contrast, a shareholder who gives away stock in a typical C corporation is not required to report the fair market value of his or her services as income, but is permitted to work for inadequate compensation without income attribution. (The rules applicable to a Subchapter S corporation are discussed in Chapter 33.03[B].)

[F]   Disposition of a Partnership Interest

[1]   Sale

The sale of a partnership interest is normally the sale of a capital asset. However, the sale produces ordinary gain or loss to the extent that it is attributable to the partnership's unrealized receivables and inventory. **§§ 741, 751(a), (c).** By contrast, the sale of stock in a corporation usually results in capital gain or loss.

"Unrealized receivables" includes the right to payment for services rendered or to be rendered — that is, to the gain in a typical personal service partnership — and the right to collect proceeds from the sale of inventory. It also includes gain that would be ordinary income under recapture rules (discussed in Chapter 11.04). In addition, partnership items that would not fit the definition of inventory when held by the partnership are considered "inventory," if they would be inventory in the hands of the selling partner. For example, assume that a partnership holds land as a **§ 1231** asset, but a partner deals in land as inventory. The partner's gain on sale of his or her partnership interest, which is attributable to the partnership's gain on the land, is ordinary income. **§ 751(d).**

In general, gain on the sale of a partnership interest can be reported under the installment method (discussed in Chapter 21.01[A]), except for **§ 751(a)** gain on unrealized receivables and inventory.

[2]   Like-Kind Exchange

Non-recognition of a like-kind exchange is not available for the exchange of a partnership interest (**§ 1031(a)(2)(D)**), even though the underlying assets could be exchanged without recognition of gain or loss. This rule was intended to make tax shelters less attractive. In this respect partnerships are not pass-through entities.

[3]   Distributions in Liquidation of a Partner's Interest

In general, there is no recognized gain or loss to either the partnership or the partners on a distribution of property in exchange for liquidating a partner's interest in the partnership. **§ 731.** Instead the distributee usually allocates his or her *outside* basis in the partnership to the asset(s) received in the distribution. **§ 732(b), (c), § 733.** The rules for making this allocation are complex when (as might be true) there is a variation in the partner's inside and outside basis and when some of the property received is ordinary income property. In general, the outside basis is first reduced by any cash received; it is then allocated to **§ 751(a)** property (unrealized receivables and inventory) in an amount equal to the *partnership's inside* basis in such assets; and the remaining outside basis, if any, is allocated to any other property.

The general rule that there is no recognized gain or loss on a liquidating distribution is subject to some exceptions. *Gain.* If the distributee receives cash (or marketable securities) in *excess* of his or her outside basis in the partnership, any gain is taxed as though received in an exchange, probably as capital gain. If the cash distribution is received in annual installments, the tax treatment is more favorable than under the installment method — no interest is attributable to deferred payments; and recognition of gain can be deferred until the cash exceeds the distributee's basis. **Treas. Reg. § 1.736-1(b)(7)(example 1)**. *Loss*. A partner who receives a liquidating distribution can deduct a loss if the partner receives only money and unrealized receivables and inventory, and the basis of such property is less than the partner's *outside* basis in the partnership.

[4] Abandonment or Worthless Interest

The loss of a partnership interest resulting from abandonment or worthlessness will often result in an ordinary loss — because there is no sale or exchange. However, a partner's share of a partnership's nonrecourse liabilities is treated as the distribution of cash to the partner when the partnership becomes worthless, and such distributions are treated as an amount realized on the sale or exchange of the partnership interest. Consequently, if total distributions (including the partner's share of nonrecourse liabilities) exceeds the partner's outside basis, the partner must recognize gain (instead of a loss). In contrast to the partnership rules, worthless stock is usually treated as a sale or exchange of the stock, producing only a capital loss; **§ 165(g)**.

§ 32.02 TRUSTS AND ESTATES

In Chapter 2.03[B][1] we noted that a trust grantor might be taxed on the income earned by the trust if the grantor retained too much control over the trust. This approach was first applied in the case law, was later developed in regulations, and was eventually codified in the statute. This section assumes that the grantor is *not* taxed, in which case there are two candidates for taxation — the trust and its beneficiaries. In the case of an estate, the decedent is out of the picture and the estate and its beneficiaries are the only possible taxpayers.

[A] Computing Trust and Estate Income

Trust and estate income is generally determined in the same manner as for an individual, with one important exception. **§ 67(e)**. Costs arising in connection with the administration of a trust or estate, which would not have been incurred if the property had not been held in the trust or estate, are deductible in arriving at adjusted gross income (that is, above the line). An above the line deduction avoids the 2% floor on deductions and is deductible under the alternative minimum tax.

A typical example of an above the line administration cost is the trustee's and executor's fee. The treatment of payments to financial advisers is more uncertain. As we discussed in Chapter 8.01, the Court in *Knight v. C.I.R.*, 552 U.S. 181 (2008), held that investment advisory fees are not above the line deductions, unless the investment advisor imposed a "special, additional charge applicable only to its fiduciary accounts," or the trust had "an unusual investment objective" that required "a specialized balancing of the interests of various parties, such that a reasonable comparison with individual investors would be improper."

Trusts and estates are entitled to a small personal exemption deduction (a trust that is required to distribute all of its income, $300; other trusts, $100; estates, $600), but no standard deduction. **§ 165(g)**. These amounts are not inflation-adjusted and there is no phase-out as income rises.

[B]   Tax Rates

Tax rates on trust and estate income reach a high marginal tax rate much faster than they do for individuals. **§ 1(e)**. In tax year 2013, the rates range from 15% to 39.6%, with the highest tax rate applicable to income over $11,950 (which is significantly lower than for individuals). The income brackets are indexed for inflation, as they are for individuals. These progressive tax rates are a response to two problems. First, the grantor might establish multiple trusts to reduce the impact of progressive tax rates. One method to deal with multiple trusts was to force their aggregation into a single trust for tax computation purposes. Some case law as well as **§ 643(e)** treated multiple trusts as a single trust under certain circumstances, but the high marginal tax rates at lower income levels (adopted in 1986) were a simpler solution that eliminated the incentive to split trust income among different trusts for tax purposes. Second, these higher tax rates reduce the tax incentive to retain income in a trust or estate for future distribution to a high income beneficiary, because the entity's retained income is no longer taxed at a low tax rate.

The 3.8% Medicare tax on investment income also applies to trusts and estates. It is imposed on the lesser of (a) investment income or (b) AGI minus the top bracket income level ($11,950 for 2013).

[C]   Taxing Beneficiaries on Distributions

[1]   Trusts

[a]   "Simple Trusts"

"Simple trusts" are those that are required to distribute all of their income and that do not distribute any of their corpus. A simple trust can still have taxable income, usually in the form of capital gains, which are added to corpus pursuant to state law or the governing instrument, and are not distributed to the income beneficiaries. **§§ 651, 652**. A trust is not a simple trust in the year of termination when it distributes corpus. **Treas. Reg. § 1.651(a)(3)**.

Simple trusts are tax conduits with respect to trust income, with the income retaining its characteristics in the hands of the beneficiaries. The code uses the concept of distributable net income (DNI) to implement this approach. (Trust distributions come first out of DNI and are deductible by the trust.) This result is achieved by defining DNI as taxable income with modifications — such as the addition of tax-exempt interest. Generally, each beneficiary reports his or her pro-rata share of DNI (for example, taxable and tax-exempt income). However, an allocation of particular types of income to different beneficiaries will be recognized for tax purposes, if the trust instrument or local law makes such a specific allocation and the allocation has economic effect independent of the income tax consequences. §§ 643(a), 651, 652. If the trustee has *discretion* to allocate different classes of income among beneficiaries, the allocation is not recognized for tax purposes; **Treas. Reg. § 1.652(b)-2(b)**.

For example, assume that a simple trust with two equal beneficiaries (A and B) has $50,000 of taxable interest, $50,000 of taxable dividends, $100,000 of tax-exempt interest, and $25,000 of long-term capital gains (which are allocated to trust corpus and are not paid, credited, or required to be distributed to a beneficiary during the taxable year). Each beneficiary receives a $100,000 distribution, consisting of $25,000 of taxable interest, $25,000 of dividends (taxable at a maximum 20% rate), and $50,000 of tax-exempt interest. The $200,000 distribution carries out the taxable income from the trust, except for the retained capital gains. If the trust instrument provides that A (in a higher bracket than B) gets all of the tax-exempt interest, A's $100,000 share of DNI is tax-exempt.

Trust deductions that enter into the computation of DNI must be allocated among income items. A deduction that is directly attributable to a particular type of income, such as repairs on rental property, is attributable to the rental income. **Treas. Reg. § 1.652(b)-3**. Deductions that are not attributable to a particular type of income, such as trustee's commissions, can be allocated to any item of income, except that a pro-rata portion must be allocated to exempt income (such as tax-exempt interest). The remaining deductions can be allocated as the trustee elects, which means that deductions can be allocated to taxable rent or interest rather than preferentially taxed dividends. The regulations give the following example:

> (b) The deductions which are not directly attributable to a specific class of income may be allocated to any item of income . . . included in computing distributable net income, but a portion must be allocated to nontaxable income . . . pursuant to section 265 and the regulations thereunder. For example, if the income of a trust is $30,000 (after direct expenses), consisting equally of $10,000 of dividends, tax-exempt interest, and rents, and income commissions amount to $3,000, one-third ($1,000) of such commissions should be allocated to tax-exempt interest, but the balance of $2,000 may be allocated to the rents or dividends in such proportions as the trustee may elect.

Trusts are not tax conduits with respect to expenses in excess of income and net losses, except that such expenses and losses carry through to beneficiaries in the year of termination. § 642(h)(2); *Treas. Reg. § 1.642(h)-1(a-b), -2(a)*. For example, capital losses and net operating losses during the years when the trust is in operation are only available to the trust, except in the year of termination (when previously unused losses are available to the beneficiaries with the same characteristics as for the trust — for example, as short- or long term capital losses). Other expenses in excess of trust income (such as trustee's commissions) are also carried through to the beneficiaries in the termination year.

[b] "Complex Trusts"

A "complex trust" is one that is not required to distribute income each year or that distributes trust corpus as well as trust income (usually capital gains). §§ 661–668. In general, distributions by a complex trust to a beneficiary shall consist "of the same proportion of each class of items entering into the computation of distributable net income as the total of each class bears to the total distributable net income of the estate or trust unless the terms of the governing instrument specifically allocate different classes of income to different beneficiaries." For example, if a trust has $100 of tax-exempt interest income and $100 of taxable interest, and the trust distributes $100 to a beneficiary, the beneficiary has $50 of tax-exempt interest and $50 of taxable interest (unless the trust instrument allocates a specific type of income to the beneficiary). The undistributed income is taxed to the trust (in this example, $50 of taxable interest).

Complex trusts are subject to the following exception to the rule that a distribution from a trust with DNI will carry out DNI. A distribution of a gift of a specific sum of money (or of specific property) that is paid in three or fewer installments, and that does not have to be paid out of trust income, does not carry out DNI and is not taxable to the beneficiary. § 663(a)(1). It is, in effect, a tax-exempt gift.

Frequently, a complex trust accumulates income for future distribution ("undistributed net income"). In that case, the trust will have paid tax on its income. Prior to mid-1997, income accumulated in a prior year and distributed in a later year (an "accumulation distribution"), was taxed to beneficiaries under a "throwback" rule, with the trust tax included in the beneficiaries' income (like any withholding tax). In general, the throwback rule traced the later trust distribution to a specific earlier year when the income arose and applied the beneficiaries' tax rate from the earlier year to the distribution of the previously undistributed net income. Today, accumulation distributions are *not* taxed again at the beneficiary level for domestic trusts (except for some trusts created before March 1, 1984). Consequently, the trust is usually the only taxpayer on previously undistributed income. However, the throwback rules continue to apply to foreign trusts (§ 665(c)), presumably because the higher tax rates applicable to a domestic trust might not apply to the income of a foreign trust.

For example, assume that a trust had $100,000 taxable income in 2010 on which the trust paid $25,000 tax. If the $75,000 of after-tax income from 2010 was distributed in 2013 by a domestic trust to a beneficiary, there would be no further tax to the beneficiary on that income.

A trust distribution of income to a charity is carried through as a charitable deduction to the beneficiaries. Each beneficiary adds his or her share of these charitable contributions to any other charitable contributions made by the taxpayer and takes a charitable deduction subject to the percentage of AGI limitations applicable to each beneficiary; *see* Chapter 10.01[C]. The trust's charitable contributions do not carry out DNI from the trust or estate. § 663(a)(2).

[2] Estates

The "complex trust" rules apply to estates. Distributions carry out DNI to the beneficiaries, as explained in the prior paragraphs.

Of special note is the rule that specific bequests of money or property are not usually treated as income distributions by the estate if paid out in three or fewer installments. This permits a decedent to provide for cash payments to relatives who need the money soon after the decedent has died without taxing the beneficiary. It also means that specific property distributed to a beneficiary does not carry out estate taxable income, but instead leaves that income to be taxed to the estate. For this reason, the decedent's will should provide for a specific bequest of tangible personal property that the decedent wants to go to specific individuals, so that the distribution of such property does not carry out taxable DNI to the recipients.

Chapter 33

CORPORATE INCOME TAX

§ 33.01   COMPUTING THE CORPORATE TAX

[A]   Taxable Income

Corporations, like individuals, must compute taxable income. But the computation of taxable income for a corporation is not always the same as for an individual. For example:

1. There is no distinction between above the line and below the line deductions for corporations. Deductions reduce gross income to taxable income, without adjusted gross income as an in-between stopping point.

2. Charitable deductions are capped at 10% of taxable income.

3. Corporations owned by many individuals are not usually subject to the anti-tax shelter rules (which require that the taxpayer be at-risk and not be a passive investor). *See* Chapter 17.05. The exception for these corporations may rest on the theory that the tax-sheltered money retained by the corporation is not available for personal consumption.

4. Corporations with large amounts of income are often required to use the accrual method of accounting. *See* Chapter 23.02[A][1].

5. Dividends are not deductible. This rule produces the double tax on corporate profits and draws a sharp distinction between nondeductible profit distributions to shareholders (that is, dividends), and deductible payments to someone in a nonshareholder capacity — such as wages to an employee, interest to a lender, or rent to a lessor. The impact of this distinction is discussed later in this chapter.

6. If an ongoing corporation distributes an asset that has appreciated in value to its shareholders as a dividend, the appreciated gain must be recognized as income to the corporation (but the loss is not recognized). § 311(b)(1). This statutory rule reverses the decision in *General Utilities Co. v. Helvering*, 296 U.S. 200 (1935). Consequently, the corporation cannot avoid the double tax on the corporation's gain in the distributed property by distributing the appreciated property as a dividend, rather than selling the asset at a gain and distributing the sales proceeds. If there is a liquidating distribution (because the corporation is terminating its activities), gain *and* loss are usually recognized to the corporation when its assets are distributed. § 336.

7. A corporation is not taxed on the issuance of its stock; § 1032. This rule is intuitively obvious when the corporation is organized and property is transferred

by controlling shareholders to the corporation in a tax-deferred transaction; see Chapter 19.04[C]. But the same result follows when an ongoing corporation receives cash for issuing stock. In effect, the issuance of stock is treated the same way as the issuance of a bond (that is, indebtedness). The receipt of value for the stock is not taxable, because the prospect of future payment of dividends and the payment to redeem the stock is analogous to the future payment of interest and the repayment of a debt.

8. The purchase of property by an ongoing corporation in exchange for its stock results in the corporation having a basis in the property equal to the value of the stock. It is as though the corporation issued the stock for cash and then purchased the property with the cash. Similarly, payment for services with stock of an ongoing corporation is treated the same as a payment of cash by the corporation and will usually result in a deductible business expense.

[B] Tax Rates

Current U.S. law provides progressive tax rates for corporations — 15% (up to $50,000), 25% (over $50,000 up to $75,000), 34% (more than $75,000 up to $10 million), and 35% (over $10 million). Bracket sizes are *not* indexed for inflation.

Section 11(b) provides that the benefit of the lower brackets disappears as income rises above a certain income level. This creates a phantom tax rate, which means that the stated tax rates (above) can be lower than the effective rates. The law state as follows:

> In the case of a corporation which has taxable income in excess of $100,000 for any taxable year, the amount of tax . . . for such taxable year shall be increased by the lesser of (i) 5 percent of such excess, or (ii) $11,750. In the case of a corporation which has taxable income in excess of $15,000,000, the amount of the tax determined under the foregoing provisions of this paragraph shall be increased by an additional amount equal to the lesser of (i) 3 percent of such excess, or (ii) $100,000.

The "lesser of" dollar figures in the statutory text — $11,750 and $100,000 — are not plucked out of thin air. They equal the reduction in tax resulting from application of lower tax rates on lower income brackets.

At one time, the benefit of lower tax rates on individuals disappeared as income rose (as it now does for corporations), but that provision has been repealed.

[C] Alternative Minimum Tax

The alternative minimum tax (AMT) originally applied only to individuals to prevent wealthy taxpayers from paying little or no tax, but it now applies to corporations as well. The AMT tax rate on corporations is 20% (compared to 26/28% for individuals).

There are some differences in how the AMT tax base is computed for corporations in contrast to individuals. The major difference is that the corporation's AMT tax base is increased by 75% of the excess of a modified version of earnings and profits over what would otherwise be the tax base for the AMT.

The earnings and profits figure is something like what accountants would compute as the economic profits of the business — for example, it *includes* tax-exempt bond income. § **56(c)(1), (g)(1)**. Thus, if modified earnings and profits are $500 and the tax base for the AMT would otherwise be $300, that tax base is increased by $150 — so that it equals $450.

However, "small corporations" are exempt from the AMT. A small corporation is one that has no more than $5,000,000 average gross receipts for the three tax years ending with the first tax year beginning after December 31, 1996. Once eligible, the corporation usually retains small corporation status as long as the prior three-year average of gross receipts does not exceed $7,500,000. § **55(e)**.

[D]   Effective U.S. Corporate Tax Rates

There is a significant difference between the statutory tax rates and the effective tax rates on corporations (depending on how you compute effective tax rates). One estimate fixes the effective corporate tax rate during the 1990s at about 25% (compared to more than 49% in the 1950s, 38% in the 1960s, and 33% in the 1970s). However, the effective tax rates vary widely (and wildly) by industry — one study showing a variation between 27.7% and 1.6%. This means that any effort to eliminate tax breaks and raise statutory tax rates will meet intense opposition from industries targeted for loss of their current tax advantages.

This data is reflected in a significant decline in corporate tax revenues as a percentage of federal revenue — hovering around 10% in the early 2010s, down from about 28% in the 1950s. A lot of the reduction in corporate taxes is the result of tax breaks that especially favor corporations — such as accelerated depreciation and expensing of investments, a credit for research and experimentation expenditures, and the availability of tax shelters (which are denied to individual taxpayers; *see* Chapter 17.05[A–B]). Some of this reduction, however, results from tax breaks that are either very popular and/or unlikely to be repealed — such as the exemption of interest on state and local bonds and the deferral of tax on profits earned by controlled foreign corporations (discussed in Chapter 34.01[C][2]).

§ 33.02   DOUBLE TAXATION OF DISTRIBUTED PROFITS

The major issue in the taxation of corporate income is whether distributed profits should be taxed twice — once as corporate income and again as dividends (without a deduction for the corporation).

[A]   An Example

In the United States, the corporate income tax is a separate tax on corporate income, resulting in a double tax on corporate profits — one tax when the income is earned by the corporation and another when the income is distributed as a dividend. For example, assume that there is $100 of corporate income in year 1 subject to a 34% tax in year 1; the shareholder is in the 28% bracket. How much of a burden is the double tax, assuming a distribution of all after-tax corporate profits in year 1? For comparison, assume that the individual could have done business as a sole proprietorship — in which case the $100 would be subject to a $28 tax.

The corporation would pay a $34 tax on the $100, leaving $66 for distribution. Assume that the shareholder pays tax on the dividend at the current 20% maximum rate (which reduces the double tax below what it would be if the 28% rate applied). The total tax is $47.20 ($34 plus $13.20), much more than $28. (I have disregarded the 3.8% Medicare tax on the investment income of high income taxpayers.)

Because dividends are not deductible, the tax results vary depending on whether an expenditure is deductible (such as wages, interest, or rent), or a nondeductible dividend. For example, the corporation can deduct a wage expense in computing taxable income (unless it is a capital expenditure) and the wage would be taxed at regular rates to the employee (plus social security taxes). By contrast, a dividend would not be deductible by the corporation, but the shareholder would be taxed at the maximum 20% rate. That is why excessive payments to shareholders in their capacity as employees are recharacterized as dividends; see Chapter 14.01[B].[1]

[B]   Some Further Complexities

A moment's reflection suggests that the analysis is more complicated than the prior example in several respects. The "double tax" critique uses as its baseline for comparison a shareholder tax on corporate dividends in the year the income is earned by the corporation. But that is not necessarily what will happen.

First, a dividend may not be paid for several years. Computation of the double tax burden therefore requires discounting the future tax on the individual shareholder's dividend back to year 1 (that is, back to the year when the corporation earns the income).

Second, the corporate tax may be less than the stated statutory rate because corporations may get tax breaks unavailable to individuals. For example, if corporate income is only $40 rather than $100 because of tax breaks available only to corporations, a 35% tax is only $14, which is the equivalent of a 14% tax on $100. A 20% tax on $86 of after-tax profits distributed as a dividend equals $17.20, for a total of $31.20. That is less than the higher tax rates on $100 applicable to individuals.

Third, individuals usually receive a basis at the time of death equal to the value of the inherited stock, and the gain on disposition of those shares might therefore be zero. In effect, the shareholder can enjoy the corporate profits in the amount of the gain on the stock *without* tax. The purchaser of the stock can then liquidate the corporation and receive corporate profits in a transaction that is treated as a sale or exchange of the stock — either no gain or capital gain.

---

[1] It is possible for the double tax to be less that the single tax imposed by sec. 1, if the corporate tax is low enough. For example, a 25% corporate tax ($25), followed by a 20% tax on $75 ($15) equals $40; with a 3.8% tax on high amounts of investment income, the total is $43.80. That might be less than a 39.6% tax on salary, when we also add an additional Social Security tax.

[C]　Does the Corporation Have a Taxpaying Capacity?

Calling the current system of taxing corporate profits a double tax assumes that the corporation does not have taxpaying capacity separate from its shareholders. But perhaps, corporations are centers of wealth and power receiving government protection and legal advantages that would justify paying some tax in exchange for the benefits. On this view, a corporation is subject to a single tax on this taxpaying capacity.

[D]　Corporate Shareholders

U.S. law prevents more than "double" taxation when the shareholder is a corporation — by reducing the amount of the taxable dividend. It provides for three categories of corporate shareholders, based on percentage of corporate ownership:

% of distributing corporation owned by corporate shareholder	% of dividend taxed to corporate shareholder
less than 20%	30%
20% to less than 80%	20%
80% or more	none

[E]　Accumulated Earnings Tax

If dividends are taxable, the corporation has an incentive to avoid the tax on shareholders by retaining profits beyond the needs of the business. Consequently, the code imposes an accumulated earning tax on undistributed profits if they exceed reasonable business needs. As a practical matter, this tax only applies to corporations owned by a few people or families, not publicly owned corporations. § 531. ATRA raised the accumulated earnings tax rate to 20% —which equals the maximum tax rate on capital gains.

[F]　Identifying a Dividend

The measure of corporate profits out of which a taxable dividend can be paid is broader than taxable income — it is "earnings and profits." This figure includes exempt income, such as tax-exempt interest and life insurance. The idea is that earnings and profits are closer to a financial definition of earnings than the code's definition of taxable income and should support dividend taxation to the shareholders. In effect, corporate tax exemption for certain types of income are *not* carried through to the shareholders when they receive dividends.

Accumulated earnings and profits will support a dividend — for example, if the corporation has negative $100 earnings and profits in year 1, positive earnings and profits of $150 in year 2, and no earnings and profits in year 3, a distribution of $50 to a shareholder in year 3 is taxed as a dividend. Earnings and profits *in the year of distribution* will also support a dividend even if accumulated earnings and profits are negative. For example, assume negative $100 of earnings and profits in year 1 and positive earnings and profits of $50 in year 2. A $50 distribution to a shareholder in year 2 is a dividend, even though accumulated earnings and profits are negative. This latter rule was adopted during the Depression so that there would be a tax on dividends when a corporation had some profits in a particular year even though it had overall losses because of the economic slowdown.

Although the computation of earnings and profits usually tracks the corporation's accounting method, there are exceptions. Some gains that are deferred in computing taxable income are not deferred in computing corporate earnings and profits. One example is the deferral of gain on installment sales, which is not permitted in computing earnings and profits. § 312(n)(5). Moreover, some accelerated deductions (whether through fast depreciation or expensing), which are allowed in computing taxable income, are not allowed when computing earnings and profits. § 312(k), (n)(1–2).

[G] Providing Use of an Asset

The double taxation of corporate profits has a somewhat surprising impact when an individual shareholder enjoys the use of an asset provided by a corporation — for example, when a corporation provides a shareholder with the tax-free use of a home or consumer durable (such as a car). Individuals who own such assets do not report the fair rental value of the property as income. However, when they receive use of such property from a corporation, the fair rental value is income. (Usually the rental value exceeds the expenses incurred by the corporation.)

In *Dean v. Commissioner*, 187 F.2d 1019 (3d Cir. 1951), the taxpayer and his wife were the sole shareholders of a corporation, with the wife owning 80% of the stock. The shareholders conveyed their home to the corporation and continued to occupy it. The court included the fair rental value of the residence property in the taxpayer's gross income, stating that the decision was "not based upon any thought that there is in this case any suggestion of tax evasion or avoidance. It is instead based upon taxpayer's valuable occupation of the corporation real estate." In addition, because the value of the house was a dividend, the corporation was not allowed to deduct the expenses it incurred relating to the house. (A similar arrangement for an employee would have resulted in taxing the fair market value to the employee as wages and a deduction of the expenses attributable to the asset by the corporation.)

§ 33.03 PREVENTING DOUBLE TAXATION

[A] Self-Help — Shareholders Receive Deductible Payments

Before considering statutory techniques to prevent double taxation, you should consider ways that corporate owners can achieve those results on their own. A single tax at individual tax rates can often be achieved by receiving distributions from a corporation that is controlled by the owners, as long as the distributions are received in a nonshareholder capacity — such as an employee or renter. The corporation can deduct the salary or rent, and the shareholders are taxed on the payments they receive. This technique is always vulnerable to an argument that the payments are excessive — different from what an outsider nonshareholder would receive from the corporation — in which case, the excess will be recharacterized as nondeductible dividends.

Another common way shareholders try to disguise a dividend as something other than a dividend is for a major shareholder to lend money to the corporation under circumstances where an independent lender would not assume a similar risk. The hope is that the annual payments received will be treated as deductible interest and the loan repayment as a nontaxable return of the investment in the loan. For example, if a taxpayer lends $100 to the corporation, interest is deductible by the corporation and taxable to the lender, and the $100 repayment is not taxed (no gain). If the loan had been treated as equity (that is, stock), the "interest" would be a nondeductible dividend. Moreover, if the loan had been treated as stock, the "repayment" would be a redemption of the stock and the redemption price will be treated as a dividend if it is similar to a dividend — for example, if the "lender" also owns 100% of the corporation's stock (Chapter 33.05[B][1] discusses when a redemption is "essentially equivalent to a dividend.").

SUMMARY OF DEBT vs. EQUITY TREATMENT

Debt	Equity
Annual interest —	Annual dividend —
Corporation deduct;	Corporation not deduct;
Lender taxed at ordinary rates	20% maximum on s/h
Loan repayment —	Redemption proceeds —
No gain	Might be taxed as dividend

Congress passed a law authorizing the adoption of regulations that would draw the line between debt and equity (§ 385), but no regulations ever became effective, despite several attempts. The code still contains the authorization, which says that the Treasury "may" consider the following factors in drawing the debt/equity distinction:

(1) whether there is a written unconditional promise to pay on demand or on a specified date a sum certain in money in return for an adequate consideration in money or money's worth, and to pay a fixed rate of interest;

(2) whether there is subordination to or preference over any indebtedness of the corporation;

(3) the ratio of debt to equity of the corporation;

(4) whether there is convertibility into the stock of the corporation; and

(5) the relationship between holdings of stock in the corporation and holdings of the interest in question.

A typical example of debt that would probably be treated as equity is a $50,000 loan by a shareholder who owns 100% of the corporation when the equity interest is worth only $5,000. The 10:1 ratio of debt to equity is extreme and it would probably be unusual for an outside lender (such as a bank) to make such a loan. This inference is accurate even if the loan has none of the other "equity" features listed in the regulations (such as convertibility into stock).

The broader point raised by trying to draw a line between debt and equity is that the world is more complex than the income tax law. The income tax law divides the world into two dichotomous categories — debt and equity. In fact, there is a spectrum of investment risk ranging from the least risky debt to the most risky shareholder equity, and drawing a sharp tax line is artificial from the perspective of financial reality. Taxpayers will try to stay on the "good side" of the tax line, while shaping the transaction to provide the desired financial results — e.g., tax treatment as a loan with as many "equity" characteristics as can be managed (perhaps, interest varying with the profits).

[B] Subchapter S Election

Current U.S. tax law allows some corporations to elect to be taxed as pass-through entities, with some exceptions. They are labeled Subchapter S corporations, after the subchapter of the tax code where the rules are found. The election results in a single tax on corporate profits at the shareholder's tax rate each year as the income is earned. There is no deferral of tax until the time of distribution. The shareholder's basis is increased by any corporate income taxed to the shareholder and reduced when the income is distributed.

Corporations eligible to make the Subchapter S election must meet certain criteria (§ 1361), including:

— no more than 100 shareholders (with certain members of a family aggregated as one shareholder);

— no shareholder who is not an individual (except for an estate and certain trusts);

— no nonresident alien shareholders; and

— no more than 1 class of stock, except that different voting rights among common stockholders and certain "straight" debt do not create more than one class of stock. ("Straight" debt means that payments of interest are not contingent on profits or on the borrower's discretion, the debt is not convertible into stock, and the creditor is an individual, an estate, certain trusts, or is actively and regularly engaged in the business of lending money.)

Although it is often said that a Subchapter S corporation is like a partnership, there are differences. The most important difference is that the pass-through of corporate losses cannot exceed the shareholder's basis in his or her stock and debt. This differs from the partnership rules, which permit the partner to increase his or her basis by the amount of the partner's share of the partnership debt. For example, a Subchapter S corporation's debt to purchase real estate is not included in the shareholder's basis. A partnership is therefore more useful as a tax shelter.

Subchapter S corporations (unlike regular corporations) are also not useful for obtaining the tax break for many fringe benefits available to employees. A more-than-2% shareholder is treated as a partner for the purpose of determining whether fringe benefits are excludible from an employee's income, which means that they cannot take advantage of the exclusion for employee fringe benefits; **§ 1372**.

However, although the more-than-2% shareholder-employee in a Subchapter S corporation cannot exclude medical insurance premiums from income, this shareholder is treated as a partner. Consequently, this shareholder can take advantage of the 100% deduction for such premiums available to partners under **§ 162(l)(1)(A)**. The shareholder reports the amount of the premium paid by the S corporation as *wage* income and then deducts the premium in computing adjusted gross income. *See* Notice 2008 1, 2008-1 C.B. 251.

The fact that the shareholder is not an employee is not all bad. If payments to the owner are not personal service income, they are not subject to Social Security taxes. This leads to the following attempt at avoiding taxes. A person whose income is derived from personal services (such as a lawyer) organizes a Subchapter S corporation and receives a portion of the profits as salary, subject to Social Security tax (which has no wage limit for the 1.45% portion attributable to Medicare). The rest of the income will be distributed by the corporation as a "dividend" and, the taxpayer hopes, this will not be considered wages. This technique (that is, inadequate wages) can always be reviewed to recharacterize the dividend distribution as wages, which is the opposite of the usual situation where the government tries to recharacterize excessive wages as a dividend. In *Watson, P.C. v. United States*, 714 F. Supp. 2d 954 (S.D. Iowa 2010), involving an accountant, the court recharacterized the entire distribution as wages.

In addition, there are rules to prevent use of a Subchapter S corporation to provide conduit treatment for passive investment income, if the corporation was once a regular C corporation. First, a corporation that has more than 25% "passive investment income" can be subject to a tax on some of that income, if it has any accumulated earnings and profits from a time when it was a regular Subchapter C corporation. **§ 1375**. Second, a Subchapter S election terminates if the corporation has too much passive investment income over three consecutive years and has accumulated earnings and profits from a time when it was a regular Subchapter C corporation. **§ 1362(d)(3)**. Third, a Subchapter S corporation that was once a C corporation is sometimes taxed on the built-in capital gains resulting from the sale of assets transferred to it by a shareholder, if those gains are recognized within ten years after the corporation acquired Subchapter S status. This prevents taxpayers from turning a C corporation into an S corporation to secure only one tax on capital gains. **§ 1374**.

Finally, an individual who is a family member of a shareholder of a Subchapter S corporation cannot work for inadequate compensation or provide capital to the corporation without adequate compensation. The government is authorized to include the value of the services or capital in the family member's income. **§ 1366(e)**.

[C] Proposals to Relieve Double Taxation

Many countries other than the United States provide some relief from double taxation in one of two ways — either treat part or all of the corporate tax as a credit against the shareholder's tax when the dividends are distributed; or permit the corporation to deduct part or all of the dividend distribution. The credit system in effect treats the corporate tax as a withholding tax on the shareholder's dividends. This approach does not treat corporations as pass-through entities because the tax relief is provided only when there is a distribution. Shareholders therefore enjoy deferring some of the tax (if their tax rates are higher than those imposed on the corporation) and pay some tax too early (if shareholder rates are lower than the corporate rate).

Both the credit and deduction techniques are flexible because they can provide either partial or complete relief from double taxation. However, the credit technique is usually preferred because it makes it easy to deny relief from double taxation for tax-exempt or foreign shareholders. Consequently, the following example deals only with the credit technique.

For example, assume that *one-half* of the dividend is not subject to double taxation. For ease of computation, assume a 40% tax rate at the corporate level and a 30% tax rate at the individual shareholder level. The corporation earns $60 income in year 1, and pays a $24 tax, leaving $36 after tax. It distributes the $36 as a cash dividend in year 1. Under a credit technique, the taxpayer would receive $36 in cash and would also be treated as receiving *one-half* of the corporate tax, or $12 (just like any withholding tax, which is included in income). The shareholder reports $48 dividend income ($36 plus the $12 withholding tax), on which it computes a 30% tax, or $14.40. After a credit of $12, the shareholder pays a tax of $2.40. Total tax is $26.40.

In effect, one-half of the corporate profits, or $30, has been taxed at the individual's tax rate of 30% (with no double tax) — equal to a $9 tax. The other one-half of corporate profits, or $30, is double taxed — a 40% corporate tax equals a $12 tax to the corporation; the remaining $18 is taxable to the shareholder upon distribution at a 30% tax rate, which equals a $5.40 tax on the shareholder (30% times $18). Again, the total tax is $26.40 ($9 plus $12 plus $5.40).

If there had been relief from double tax on the *entire* dividend, there would be a total tax of $18. The corporation would pay a $24 tax — 40% times $60; and the shareholder would get a $6 refund. The refund would equal the shareholder's $18 tax (30% times $60) minus the corporation's "withholding" $24 tax.

If there was no relief from double taxation, there would be a total tax of $34.80 — a $24 tax on the corporation, and a $10.80 tax (30% times $36) on the shareholder.

In sum, the total tax would vary as follows:

Double tax relief	Corporate tax	Individual tax	Total tax
100% relief	24	(6 refund)	18
50% relief	24	2.40	26.40
No relief	24	10.80	34.80

This simple example can also be used to illustrate some of the potential complexities of providing relief from double taxation on corporate profits. First, we assumed a constant corporate tax rate. If tax rates vary from year to year (e.g., because they are progressive or because statutory tax rates are changed), the corporate distribution must be attributed to a particular year to determine the amount of the credit. For example, if the distribution had occurred in year 2 when the corporate tax rate was higher or lower than 40%, a different set of computations would be required to compute the total tax obligation, *if* the distribution was presumed to come out of year 2 rather than year 1 profits.

Second, what should be done about preferentially taxed income? To take a simple example, assume that some corporate income is exempt and some corporate income is taxed at the full 40% corporate tax rate. Is a distribution to a shareholder out of exempt income, for which there would be no credit, or is it out of taxable income, or some pro rata proportion thereof?

Third, suppose an audit of a corporation's income ends up imposing a tax on more income than the corporation previously reported and this puts the corporation into a higher tax bracket. For example, assume a 30% corporate tax rate in year 1, which is imposed on $100 of corporate profits, resulting in a $70 distribution; and, further, that the shareholder's tax rate is 30%. The shareholder would assume that the $70 resulted in $100 of shareholder income (including all of the $30 corporate tax) and a $30 credit, resulting in no additional tax. Now suppose that a later audit of year 1 income results in $200 of corporate income on which an $80 corporate tax is imposed (40%) — because the corporate tax rates are progressive. The $70 distribution now includes a distribution of $46.66 out of the $80 corporate tax (that is, $70/$120 times $80); this produces total shareholder income of $116.66, on which there would be a $34.99 tax on the shareholder (assuming a 30% tax rate) and a $46.66 credit. Would numerous shareholders (who are often owners of public corporations) be expected to redo their computations for their year 1 tax returns?

Exempting dividends. Another proposal to relieve double taxation of dividends is exempting the dividend from tax at the shareholder level. This approach obviously does nothing to assure that the shareholder's tax rate applies to the distributed profits (which is one of the goals of the credit mechanism). It also does not avoid the problem of preferentially taxed income. A recent United States proposal to exempt dividends was dropped because the exemption would not have extended to preferentially taxed corporate income, and allocating the distribution between fully and preferentially taxed income was considered too daunting.

The U.S. 20% tax rate on dividends. A recent U.S. "solution" to double taxation lowers the tax on dividends to the same maximum 20% tax rate that applies to capital gains. However, the lower tax rate on dividends is a clumsy way of relieving the taxpayer of the double tax because it applies regardless of the effective tax rate on corporate and individual income. For example, even if the corporation pays no tax, the shareholder's tax rate is still lowered to a 20% maximum. Similarly, the tax is lowered to the same rate regardless of the shareholder's tax bracket. Consequently, the lower 20% shareholder tax rate does nothing to assure that one tax is paid on corporate profits at the regular tax rate applicable to individual shareholders.

§ 33.04 DEFINING A "CORPORATION" vs. A PASS-THROUGH ENTITY

Because a corporation in the United States is not usually a pass-through entity, the corporation's losses are not immediately deductible by the shareholder-owners. By contrast, a major tax advantage from using a pass-through entity is that losses are attributed to owners in the year they are realized by the entity. In addition, the preferential tax rate on capital gains is not available to corporations, but a partner's share of partnership capital gains would be taxed at the preferential rate. These considerations led taxpayers to set up entities that gave them many of the business advantages of a corporation (limited liability, easy transferability of ownership, etc.) while still maintaining pass-through entity status for tax purposes. The government often attacked these efforts by alleging that the entities were really taxable as corporations, but then issued Regulations that made it relatively easy (though not without some effort) to avoid corporate status.

The regulations identifying entities taxed as corporations have been eclipsed now that the government has agreed to a procedure that allows most unincorporated domestic businesses to elect corporate status — the so-called check-a-box procedure. Absent such an election, the entity is not a corporation for tax purposes. For example, this election is available to regular partnerships, limited partnerships, and limited liability companies (LLCs). LLCs are unincorporated entities created under state law with virtually all of the legal attributes of a corporation. LLCs offer far greater flexibility than a Subchapter S corporation — for example: there is no limit on the number of owners; there is no one-class-of-stock rule; and income and losses can be more easily allocated among owners. The check-a-box technique can also be used by a single-owner business. A noncorporate business with a single-owner that does not elect corporate status is taxed as a sole proprietorship (referred to as a "disregarded entity" — DRE). The election option does not work the other way — that is, a domestic corporation organized under state law cannot elect to be taxed as a partnership or sole proprietorship. **Treas. Reg. § 301.7701-3.**

§ 33.05 CONVERTING DIVIDENDS TO CAPITAL GAINS

Taxpayers have traditionally tried to turn dividends into capital gains on the liquidation of a corporation or the redemption of corporate stock, both of which are treated as a sale or exchange of the stock. That effort might seem unnecessary now that the maximum tax on capital gains and dividends is the same, but that would be a mistake. A shareholder is taxed on a dividend regardless of the basis in the stock on which the dividend is paid, as long as earnings and profits equal or exceed the dividend distribution. Thus, even if the taxpayer recently purchased stock of a profitable corporation for $100, a large dividend out of profits earned prior to the time of purchase is taxable in full, despite the reduction in stock value below the $100 purchase price. By contrast, a sale of the stock for $100 results in no gain (because amount realized equals basis). Moreover, capital gains are better than dividends in another respect: capital gains can be reduced by capital losses (*see* Chapter 3.04[C]), but dividends cannot be reduced by capital losses.

[A] Complete Liquidation

A complete liquidation of a corporation — even one with significant earnings and profits — is usually treated as a sale or exchange of the stock. There is a capital gain or loss and the earnings and profits of the corporation disappear. **§ 331(a)**.

[B] Redemption of Stock

[1] Similar to a Dividend

A shareholder might receive a distribution in redemption of the stock in a continuing corporation. (A redemption occurs when the shareholder gives up stock in exchange for corporate assets, other than in a complete liquidation of the corporation.) It should be obvious that there is a potential for tax avoidance if all redemptions are treated as a sale or exchange on which the amount realized is reduced by basis to compute taxable gain. Assume a 100% shareholder who has 10% of the stock redeemed. The shareholder still owns all of the corporation, but has received a corporate distribution — obviously a dividend.

The statute treats redemptions as dividends, if they are like a dividend. **§ 302**. However, the redemption is *not* treated as a dividend if it is substantially disproportionate. The most extreme example of a substantially disproportionate distribution is the complete redemption of all of the stock owned by a shareholder. A redemption is also treated as a sale or exchange if the reduction in ownership is significant — generally leaving the shareholder with less than 80% of *prior* ownership (based on vote and value) *and* less than 50% of the *total* voting power in the corporation.

There are attribution of ownership rules to make sure that retention of stock by a shareholder's family members (as well as by entities in which the shareholder or his family has an interest) does not result in the redeemed shareholder retaining, in practice, a significant ownership interest. Attribution rules are too complex to be explained here in any detail, except to note the following. If the taxpayer whose stock is redeemed has a spouse or child who still retains stock in the corporation, the taxpayer will be deemed to own the stock owned by the spouse or child, *unless* the redemption is a *complete* redemption and certain other conditions are met. If the shareholder's stock is completely redeemed, the family attribution rules are, in general, waived if the shareholder does not retain an interest in the corporation as an officer, director, or employee; has not received stock in the corporation from, or conveyed stock in the corporation to, certain relatives ten years before the redemption; and does not acquire stock in the corporation within ten years after the redemption.

A complete redemption often occurs after a shareholder has died, which usually results in the shareholder having a cost basis equal to a high date-of-death value. In such cases, the successor shareholder is often the estate of a deceased shareholder. Frequently, the purchase of the stock by the corporation from the estate is incident to a buy-out arrangement in which the corporation has an agreement (or an option) to purchase the stock to avoid a sale of the stock to someone outside of the decedent's family. If the redemption is treated as a sale or exchange of the stock by the estate to the purchasing corporation, dividend treatment is avoided and there is often no taxable gain. Once again, complex attribution rules determine whether the estate is treated as retaining a significant interest in the corporation after the redemption, based on the actual ownership of stock by beneficiaries of the estate.

For example, if the decedent's will provides for distribution of the estate's assets to a trust whose beneficiaries include persons who own stock in the corporation, the beneficiaries' stock is usually constructively attributed to the trust and the trust's constructively owned stock is then attributed to the estate, preventing a complete redemption from the estate. § 301(a)(3), (5)(A). However, if a person who owns stock in the corporation is entitled only to a cash bequest — e.g., to help a spouse or child after the decedent's death with household expenses — that person is *not* a beneficiary *after* the cash has been distributed; consequently, in order to avoid attribution of that person's stock to the estate, the redemption from the estate should occur after distribution of the cash bequest; **Treas. Reg. § 1.318-3(a)**.

[2]   Dividend to Non-Redeemed Shareholder

Redemption of stock by a corporation from one shareholder might be a dividend to another shareholder whose stock is *not* redeemed, if the other shareholder has an obligation to purchase the redeemed stock. This is an application of the familiar rule that payment of someone's debt is treated as a payment to the debtor; *see* Chapter 3.06[C][2].The following Revenue Ruling 69-608 explains when this can occur and how this result can be avoided. Notice how important it is to plan properly to achieve the desired result.

Rev. Rul. 69-608, 1969-2 C.B. 43 states the law as follows:

> Where a corporation redeems stock from a retiring shareholder, the fact that the corporation in purchasing the shares satisfies the continuing shareholder's executory contractual obligation to purchase the redeemed shares does not result in a distribution to the continuing shareholder provided that the continuing shareholder is not subject to an existing primary and unconditional obligation to perform the contract. . . . On the other hand, if the continuing shareholder, at the time of the assignment to the corporation of his contract to purchase the retiring shareholder's stock, is subject to an unconditional obligation to purchase the retiring sharehold-er's stock, the satisfaction by the corporation of his obligation results in a constructive distribution to him.

The ruling then gives some examples.

Situation 2

> A and B are unrelated individuals who own all of the outstanding stock of corporation X. An agreement between them provides unconditionally that within ninety days of the death of either A or B, the survivor will purchase the decedent's stock of X from his estate. Following the death of B, A causes X to assume the contract and redeem the stock from B's estate. The assignment of the contract to X followed by the redemption by X of the stock owned by B's estate will result in a constructive distribution to A because immediately on the death of B, A had a primary and unconditional obligation to perform the contract.

Situation 4

> A and B owned all of the outstanding stock of X corporation. A and B entered into a contract under which, if B desired to sell his X stock, A agreed to purchase the stock or to cause such stock to be purchased. If B chose to sell his X stock to any person other than A, he could do so at any time. In accordance with the terms of the contract, A caused X to redeem all of B's stock in X. At the time of the redemption, B was free to sell his stock to A or to any other person, and A had no unconditional obligation to purchase the stock and no fixed liability to pay for the stock. Accordingly, the redemption by X did not result in a constructive distribution to A.

Situation 7

> A and B owned all of the outstanding stock of X corporation. An agreement between the shareholders provided that upon the death of either, the survivor would purchase the decedent's shares from his estate at a price provided in the agreement. Subsequently, the agreement was rescinded and a new agreement entered into which provided that upon the death of either A or B, X would redeem all of the decedent's shares of X stock from his estate. The cancellation of the original contract between the parties in favor of the new contract did not result in a constructive distribution to either A or B. At the time X agreed to purchase the stock pursuant to the terms of the new agreement, neither A nor B had an unconditional obligation to purchase shares of X stock. The subsequent redemption of the stock from the estate of either pursuant to the terms of the new agreement will not constitute a constructive distribution to the surviving shareholder.

§ 33.06   CONTRIBUTIONS TO CAPITAL

Chapter 19.04[C] discussed the treatment of corporate organizations as tax-deferred events, analogous to like-kind exchanges. For example, an individual organizes a corporation by conveying land and buildings to a corporation for all of the stock. The land has $20 basis and the buildings have a $50 basis. That basis carries over to the corporation and the shareholder has a $70 basis in the stock.

This section looks more closely at contributions to the capital of an *ongoing* corporation. **§§ 118, 362.**

[A] Contribution as Shareholder

If a contribution to corporate capital is made by a shareholder acting in a shareholder capacity, the general rule is that there is no recognized income to the corporation. The contributed property's basis is carried over to the corporation and the shareholder's basis is increased by the basis in the contributed property. For example, if a 100% or 10% shareholder contributes land with a basis of $20 and a value of $100 to the corporation, the corporation takes the land with a $20 basis and the shareholder's basis in the stock is increased by $20.

[B] Contribution in Nonshareholder Capacity

Contributions to a corporation in a nonshareholder capacity can be taxable or nontaxable.

[1] Taxable vs. Nontaxable

Property contributed to the corporation by someone *not acting in a shareholder capacity* is taxable if it is *not* a contribution to capital — for example, if the contribution is "in aid of construction or any other contribution as a customer or potential customer." The Regulations give the following example: "any money or property transferred to the corporation in consideration for goods or services rendered," and "subsidies paid for the purpose of inducing the [corporate] taxpayer to limit production." **Treas. Reg. § 1.118-1.**

In *AT & T, Inc. v. United States*, 629 F.3d 505 (5th Cir. 2011), the court held that "the plaintiff taxpayer, AT&T Inc., an interstate telecommunications company, must pay income taxes on the funds it received from federal and state governmental entities for providing 'universal service' — viz., affordable telephone service mainly for lower income consumers and those in high cost rural, remote or isolated areas. . . " The payments were not exempt as nonshareholder contributions to capital under the Internal Revenue Code.

The court quoted from the Supreme Court's complex multi-factor test for identifying a nontaxable contribution to capital in *United States v. Chicago, Burlington & Quincy Railroad Co. (CB&Q)*, 412 U.S. 401 (1973).

> [1] [The payment] must become a permanent part of the transferee's working capital structure. [2] It may not be compensation, such as a direct payment for a specific, quantifiable service provided for the transferor by the transferee. [3] It must be bargained for. [4] The asset transferred foreseeably must result in benefit to the transferee in an amount commensurate with its value. [5] And the asset ordinarily, if not always, will be employed in or contribute to the production of additional income and its value assured in that respect.

And, from a review of Supreme Court cases, it derived the following principles:

> (1) Whether a payment to a corporation by a non shareholder is income or a capital contribution is controlled by the intention or motive of the transferor. (2) When the transferor is a governmental entity, its intent may

be manifested by the laws or regulations that authorize and effectuate its payment to the corporation. (3) Also, a court can determine that a transfer was not a capital contribution if it does not possess each of the first four, and ordinarily the fifth, characteristics of capital contributions that the Supreme Court distilled from its jurisprudence in CB&Q Applying these principles to the facts of this case, we conclude that, either by construing the controlling statutes and regulations or by applying the CB&Q five factor test, the governmental entities in making universal service payments to AT&T did not intend to make capital contributions to AT&T and thus, that the payments were income to AT&T.

The court concluded (1) that AT&T had failed to show that it had bargained for the payments "rather than simply having accepted the unilaterally imposed law and regulations determining the [] payments"; (2) that the payments "were paid to AT&T to compensate it for providing certain specific services"; and (3) that "AT&T fail[ed] to demonstrate that the payments it received from the federal and state [governments] became a permanent part of AT&T's working capital structure. . . . "

See also Sprint Nextel Corp. v. United States, 779 F. Supp. 2d 1184 (D. Kan. 2011), which dealt with "high-cost support payments" received by the corporate taxpayer from the Federal Communications Commission. These payments were intended to limit local telephone rates in high-cost areas so that lower-income telephone users could afford the service. The court held that these payments were *not* exempt nonshareholder contributions to capital because they were intended as supplements to gross income and were computed primarily by reference to the taxpayer's expenses.

It is obviously very difficult to make the fact-specific judgments to draw the line between payments in a nonshareholder capacity that are taxable income and nontaxable contributions to capital.

[2] Nontaxable

Nontaxability as a contribution to capital in a nonshareholder capacity comes at a price. These nontaxable contributions of property to corporate capital take a zero basis — that is, the gain equal to the amount of the contribution is deferred (not exempt). If money is received, property purchased by the corporation within twelve months of receipt of the money receives a zero basis; if no such property is acquired, the basis of other corporate property is reduced by the money received. The regulations give as an example of the zero basis approach "the value of land or other property contributed to a corporation by a governmental unit or by a civic group for the purpose of inducing the corporation to locate its business in a particular community, or for the purpose of enabling the corporation to expand its operating facilities." If the contribution had been made by a shareholder acting *in a shareholder capacity*, the transferor's basis in the land would have been carried over to the corporation.

§ 33.07 CORPORATE REORGANIZATIONS

[A] In General

The taxation of corporate reorganizations is often the subject of an entire tax course, but this introduction will help you understand the issues. There are two basic types of reorganizations. One type is the acquisitive reorganization — for example, when one corporation acquires all of the stock or assets of another corporation in exchange for the acquiring corporation's stock. The second type is the rearrangement of a single corporation — such as a division of corporate assets, or the shifting of the corporate charter to another state, or a recapitalization (such as an exchange by shareholders of common for preferred stock or vice versa). The basic idea in the taxation of a reorganization is that the parties deserve the same tax-deferred treatment as in a like-kind exchange — either because there is a continuity of investment interest or because the business rearrangements are good for the economy.

Reorganizations eligible for tax-deferred treatment are defined in § 368. Eligible transactions result in the corporate assets retaining their old basis at the corporate level and in the stock retaining its old basis at the shareholder level. Here are some examples of tax-deferred reorganizations. Nonrecognition and tax deferral are provided by §§ 354, 358, 361, 362.

Acquisitive — Asset acquisition. A taxpayer has a $100 basis in 100% of the stock of Corporation T; the stock is worth $300. Corporation T transfers substantially all of its assets (with a $100 basis and a $300 value) to Corporation A in exchange for voting stock of Corporation A, and Corporation T then distributes the voting stock of Corporation A to its shareholders in a liquidation of Corporation T. The shareholder-taxpayer and Corporation T pay no tax on this exchange; the taxpayer takes a $100 basis in the Corporation A voting stock which it received on the liquidation of the target Corporation T; and Corporation A acquires the assets of Corporation T with a $100 basis. (This result will often be achieved through a statutory merger of Corporation T into Corporation A.)

Acquisitive — Stock acquisition. A shareholder-taxpayer transfers 80% of the voting stock in Corporation T to Corporation A in exchange for Corporation A voting stock and Corporation T becomes a subsidiary of Corporation A. If we assume the same numbers as in the prior example, the shareholder-taxpayer's basis in the Corporation A stock would still be $100 and Corporation A would also have a $100 basis in the stock of Corporation T which it acquired. Asset basis stays the same because Corporation T remains in existence as a subsidiary of Corporation A. (This sometimes occurs through a newspaper advertising campaign in which Corporation A solicits the purchase of Corporation T stock.)

Rearrangement — Divisive. Corporation D conducts two businesses and has two shareholders (A and B), who do not get along and who each own 50% of Corporation D. Corporation D transfers one business to a new Corporation S1 for all of its stock and the other business to a new Corporation S2 in exchange for all of its stock. Corporation D then liquidates and distributes the Corporation S1 stock to A and the Corporate S2 stock to B, so that A owns 100% of the Corporation S1 stock and B owns 100% of the Corporation S2 stock. The business partners have split up the corporation and each now owns 100% of a separate business instead of 50% of two businesses. The basis of the assets at the corporate level (in S1 and S2) remains the same. Corporation D pays no tax. A and B receive the stock of S1 and S2, respectively, in a tax-deferred transaction — carrying over their old basis in their stock of Corporation D into the stock they receive in S1 and S2. **§ 355.**

[B] Acquisitive Reorganization

Consideration received. The most critical tax issues in deciding whether an acquisitive reorganization is a tax-deferred transaction are the following: (1) define the *type* of consideration that constitutes a continuity of investment interest; and (2) specify the *percentage* of the consideration received by the transferor, which must consist of property with the requisite continuity of interest. Regarding the type of consideration, the question is what stock constitutes continuity of interest (for example, must it be voting stock? Can it be preferred rather than common stock?). Regarding the amount of "continuity" consideration received in the transaction, the percentage can vary (for example: 100%, 80%, or 50%). This corner of the tax law is complex because there are many ways in which an acquisition can occur and the eligible property that provides sufficient continuity of interest is defined differently in each situation. These differences are not rational and are the result of the unstructured historical evolution of the law. The following simplified chart describes the rules defining a tax-deferred reorganization. In common tax jargon, a merger is referred to as an "A" reorganization, a stock acquisition as a "B" reorganization, and an asset reorganization as a "C" reorganization, after the subparagraphs in **§ 368(a)(1)** that describe these transactions.

ACQUISITION	CONTINUITY STOCK	% OF TOTAL CONSIDERATION
Statutory merger	Any stock; including nonvoting and preferred	50%
Stock acquisition	Voting stock	100%
Asset acquisition	Voting stock	80%

One of the more puzzling features of acquisitive reorganizations is that there is no requirement that the stock that constitutes tax-deferred continuity of interest also provide the transferring shareholders with a significant percentage ownership interest in the acquiring corporation. For example, the stock received as consideration in a tax-deferred reorganization can be 1% of the acquiring corporation's stock. Thus, a corporate whale can swallow up a corporate minnow (often a family corporation), with the result that the transferring shareholders can convert illiquid stock in a family corporation into easy-to-sell stock in a corporation listed on a major stock exchange, and they can do this in a tax-deferred exchange.

Reverse merger. Another acquisition technique is for the acquiring corporation to form a subsidiary, which is then merged into the target corporation (a so-called "reverse merger"). The end result is that the shareholders of the target corporation get voting stock of the acquiring corporation and the target corporation ends up as a subsidiary of the acquiring corporation. For no apparent reason, the eligible stock consideration must be voting stock (as in a stock acquisition), but only has to be 80% of the consideration received by the shareholders in a "reverse merger." In other words, although only voting stock can be received in a stock acquisition (a "B' reorganization), shareholders can receive 20% cash and 80% voting stock in a reverse merger — even though the target corporation ends up as a subsidiary of the acquiring corporation in both instances.

Elective, in effect. Another important feature of the acquisitive reorganization rules is that they are, in effect, elective — because the consideration in the transaction can be altered in ways that are not economically very significant but with dramatically different tax consequences. For example, a small amount of cash in a stock acquisition means that the acquisition is taxable, not tax-deferred. By contrast, some cash can be received in a tax-deferred reverse merger, and quite a bit of cash (up to 50% of the consideration) can be received in a tax-deferred asset acquisition achieved through a statutory merger. The elective nature of the reorganization rules is very important because the transferring and acquiring owners may have very different interests in which tax rule applies. In a tax-deferred transaction, the transferor's old basis (usually less than value) is retained by the acquiring corporation and the shareholders of the transferring corporation get tax deferral, rather than pay tax on any gain in the transferred stock. However, in a taxable transaction, the acquiring corporation basis equals the value of the property used to make the purchase (as would be the case in any taxable purchase), and that basis is usually higher than the transferor's basis. (A higher basis to the acquiring corporation often means higher depreciation deductions.) For example, if the consideration paid by an acquiring corporation in a statutory merger equals 51% cash and 49% stock of the acquiring corporation, the event is a taxable acquisition and the acquiring corporation's basis in the target's property equals the fair market value of the consideration paid in the acquisition; but the transferring corporation and its shareholders will pay tax on any gain.

Boot; Effect of a dividend. If a transaction *is* a tax-deferred acquisitive reorganization but the shareholders of the transferred corporation receive some consideration that lacks continuity of interest (such as cash or a bond — referred to as "boot"), that boot will be taxed as a dividend (if it has the "effect" of a dividend), up to the amount of gain on the transaction. **§ 356(a)**. It is unclear why the income taxed as a dividend does not exceed the gain when it is received in a tax-deferred reorganization. A taxable dividend is usually measured without regard to the taxpayer's gain in the stock on which the dividend is paid.

In any event, the "effect of a dividend" test is very pro-taxpayer after the Supreme Court's decision in *Commissioner v. Clark*, 489 U.S. 726 (1989), in which a 100% shareholder in a corporation received stock and cash in the acquiring corporation. This decision assumes (hypothetically) that the taxpayer received only stock of the acquiring corporation in the reorganization and then had some of the acquiring corporation's stock redeemed for cash. Under the rules applicable to redemptions, this will look like a sale of stock (not having the effect of a dividend), if the cash received equals more than 20% of the consideration received from the acquiring corporation (so that ownership appears to be reduced to less than 80% of prior ownership). **§ 302(b)(2)**. (In *Clark*, the taxpayer was assumed to receive 1.3%

of the acquiring corporation and to retain 0.9% interest after the cash consideration was taken into account.)

[C] Divisive Reorganization

The most important issue in a divisive reorganization is to make sure that the assets transferred by the corporation are business assets. Otherwise, there is a potential for converting an ordinary dividend of nonbusiness corporate assets (such as cash or investment stock) into capital gains. For example, a corporation (CO) conveys cash to a subsidiary (SUB) in exchange for all of SUB's stock; and then distributes the SUB stock to CO's sole shareholder. The shareholder then sells the SUB stock and receives capital gain.

The classic example of this tax avoidance technique occurred in the case of *Helvering v. Gregory*, 69 F.2d 809 (2d Cir. 1934), *affirmed*, 293 U.S. 465 (1935). The Learned Hand opinion in the Court of Appeals prevented the taxpayer from manipulating the tax law to achieve capital gains instead of a dividend and is one of the landmarks of statutory interpretation, not just in the field of corporate taxation. Although the code has long since been amended to prevent Mrs. Gregory from succeeding in converting dividends to capital gains, we will first read Learned Hand's opinion and then take note of the current statute. You should also remember that this tax avoidance scheme is not obsolete just because dividends and capital gains are now taxed at 20%. A capital gain is still better because it can absorb capital losses and because basis of the assets can be recovered against the amount realized on the transaction.

[1] Business Purpose; Tax Avoidance

HELVERING v. GREGORY
United States Court of Appeals, Second Circuit
69 F.2d 809 (2d Cir. 1934), *affirmed*, 293 U.S. 465 (1935)

L. HAND, CIRCUIT JUDGE.

The taxpayer owned all the shares of the United Mortgage Corporation, among whose assets were some of the shares of another company, the Monitor Securities Corporation. In 1928, it became possible to sell the Monitor shares at a large profit, but if this had been done directly, the United Mortgage Corporation would have been obliged to pay a normal tax on the resulting gain, and the taxpayer, if she wished to touch her profit, must do so in the form of a dividend, on which a [tax] would have been assessed against her personally. To reduce these taxes as much as possible, the following plan was conceived and put through: The taxpayer incorporated in Delaware a new company . . . and called [it] the Averill Corporation, to which the United Mortgage Corporation transferred all its shares in the Monitor Securities Corporation, under an agreement by which the Averill Corporation issued all its shares to the taxpayer. Being so possessed of all the Averill shares, she wound up the Averill company three days later, receiving as a liquidating dividend the Monitor shares, which she thereupon sold. It is not disputed that all these steps were part of one purpose to reduce taxes, and that the Averill Corporation, which was in existence for only a few days, conducted none, except to act as conduit for the Monitor shares in the way we have described. The taxpayer's return for the year 1928 was made on the theory that the transfer of the Monitor shares to the Averill Corporation was a 'reorganization' under [the predecessor of § 368(a)(1)(D)].

[Editor — Learned Hand then noted that, in a reorganization, the distribution of the stock of a party to the reorganization — the Averill stock — is not recognized as a taxable event. Further, Hand explained that the distribution of the assets of Averill Corp. — which were the Monitor stock — was treated by the taxpayer as a distribution in complete liquidation of Averill, and that a complete liquidation is normally treated as a sale or exchange of the stock of the liquidating corporation, producing capital gain.]

The Commissioner assessed a deficiency taxed upon the theory that the transfer of the Monitor shares to the Averill Corporation was not a true 'reorganization' . . . being intended only to avoid taxes. He treated as nullities that transfer, the transfer of the Averill shares to the taxpayer, and the winding up of the Averill Corporation ending in the receipt by her of the Monitor shares; and he ruled that the whole transaction was merely the declaration of a dividend by the United Mortgage Corporation consisting of the Monitor shares [], on which the taxpayer must pay a [tax] calculated at their full value. The taxpayer appealed and the Board held that the Averill Corporation had been in fact organized and was indubitably a corporation, that the United Mortgage Corporation had with equal certainty transferred to it the Monitor shares, and that the taxpayer had got the Averill shares as part of the transaction. All these transactions being real, their purpose was irrelevant, and [the reorganization rules were applicable], especially since it was part of a statute of such small mesh as the Revenue Act of 1928; the finer the reticulation, the less room for inference. . . .

We agree with the Board and the taxpayer that a transaction, otherwise, within an exception of the tax law, does not lose its immunity, because it is actuated by a desire to avoid, or, if one choose, to evade, taxation. Any one may so arrange his affairs that his taxes shall be as low as possible; he is not bound to choose that pattern which will best pay the Treasury; there is not even a patriotic duty to increase one's taxes. Therefore, if what was done here, was what was intended by [the statute], it is of no consequence that it was all an elaborate scheme to get rid of income taxes, as it certainly was. Nevertheless, it does not follow that Congress meant to cover such a transaction, not even though the facts answer the dictionary definitions of each term used in the statutory definition. It is quite true, as the Board has very well said, that as the articulation of a statute increases, the room for interpretation must contract; but the meaning of a sentence may be more than that of the separate words, as a melody is more than the notes, and no degree of particularity can ever obviate recourse to the setting in which all appear, and which all collectively create. The purpose of the section is plain enough; men engaged in enterprises — industrial, commercial, financial, or any other — might wish to consolidate, or divide, to add to, or subtract from, their holdings. Such transactions were not to be considered as 'realizing' any profit, because the collective interests still remained in solution. But the underlying presupposition is plain that the readjustment shall be undertaken for reasons germane to the conduct of the venture in hand, not as an ephemeral incident, egregious to its prosecution. To dodge the shareholders' taxes is not one of the transactions contemplated as corporate 'reorganizations.' . . .

We do not indeed agree fully with the way in which the Commissioner treated the transaction; we cannot treat as inoperative the transfer of the Monitor shares by the United Mortgage Corporation, the issue by the Averill Corporation of its own shares to the taxpayer, and her acquisition of the Monitor shares by winding up that company. The Averill Corporation held a juristic personality, whatever the purpose of its organization; the transfer passed title to the Monitor shares and the taxpayer became a shareholder in the transferee. All these steps were real, and their only defect was that they were not what the statute means by a 'reorganization,' because the transactions were no part of the conduct of the business of either or both companies; so viewed they were a sham, though all the proceedings had their usual effect. But the result is the same whether the tax be calculated as the Commissioner calculated it, or upon the value of the Averill shares as a dividend, and the only question that can arise is whether the deficiency must be expunged, though right in result, if it was computed by a method, partly wrong. Although this is argued with some warmth, it is plain that the taxpayer may not avoid her just taxes because the reasoning of the assessing officials has not been entirely our own.

COMMENTS

1. Although Hand's opinion has been quoted for the proposition that taxpayers can avoid taxes if the law allows it, the case has had much more growing power in the other direction. It has been cited for the view that transactions are entitled to favorable tax treatment only if they have a "business purpose" and are "not engaged in for a tax avoidance purpose." Exactly when either or both of these standards apply has never been entirely clear, especially because the tax law might want to provide a tax advantage for certain transactions even though they are not profitable without regard to the tax break. Sometimes, the statute explicitly imposes one or both of these standards — *see, for example*, § 357(b)(1) (requiring that the principal purpose of the transaction not be tax avoidance and not lack a business purpose); § 7701(o) (a transaction must change the taxpayer's economic position in a meaningful way apart from federal income tax effects *and* the taxpayer must have a substantial purpose apart from federal income tax effects).

2. Hand's insistence on the "melody" over the "notes" is one of the most famous judicial statements about statutory interpretation. It focuses attention on what the statute is trying to achieve, rather than on the dictionary meaning of a specific word. In effect, it looks at "statutory intent," which is a much better phrase than "legislative intent," because the legislature often has no specific intent regarding the facts of a particular case.

3. The *Gregory* decision can also be understood as an effort to determine the meaning of the statutory term "reorganization," rather than suggesting that the judge go behind the text to identify and apply the statute's intent or purpose. A rearrangement of corporate assets that does not serve a business purpose is not a "reorganization" as that term is used in the tax law.

4. In its affirmance of the Court of Appeals decision, the Supreme Court stated: "It is quite true that if a reorganization in reality was effected within the meaning of [the law], the ulterior purpose mentioned will be disregarded. The legal right of a taxpayer to decrease the amount of what otherwise would be his taxes, or altogether avoid them, by means which the law permits, cannot be doubted. But the question for determination is whether what was done, apart from the tax motive, was the thing which the statute intended. The reasoning of the court below in justification of a negative answer leaves little to be said."

[2]   The Modern Statute — The Divisive "D" Reorganization

The code section defining a tax-deferred divisive reorganization is § 368(a)(1)(D) — hence the reference to a "D" reorganization.

The modern statute deals with the tax avoidance potential of dividing assets of a corporation (as in the *Gregory* case) by eliminating the tax-free distribution of stock when there is a division of corporate assets, if either the distributing corporation or the corporation to which assets have been transferred do not possess assets of an active business that has been conducted for at least five years. § 355(b). The idea is that the value of the stock in either the distributing or transferee corporation should not consist of liquid nonbusiness assets that would be taxed as a dividend if distributed by the corporation; otherwise, the taxpayer can sell the stock of the corporation owning the liquid assets and pay capital gains tax on any gain. This rule would obviously prevent the distribution of Averill stock in the *Gregory* case from being tax-free (it would be a dividend from the United Corporation).

The current law requires defining what is an "active trade or business," which is not always obvious. One situation that has been a special concern is the transfer of land on which the corporation has conducted business. *See* **Treas. Reg. § 1.355-3(b)(2)(ii)** ("Separations of real property all or substantially all of which is occupied prior to the distribution by the distributing or the controlled corporation . . . will be carefully scrutinized with respect to the [active trade or business requirement]."). The Regulations in **Treas. Reg. § 1.355-3(c)** provide the following Example 3, in which the taxpayer failed the active trade or business test:

> Corporation X owns land on which it conducts a ranching business. Oil has been discovered in the area, and it is apparent that oil may be found under the land on which the ranching business is conducted. X has engaged in no significant activities in connection with its mineral rights. X transfers its mineral rights to new subsidiary Y and distributes the stock of Y to X's shareholders. Y will actively pursue the development of the oil producing potential of the property. Y does not satisfy the requirements of section 355(b) because X engaged in no significant exploitation activities with respect to the mineral rights during the five-year period ending on the date of the distribution.

Another situation of potential concern is the expansion of a business less than five years before the divisive reorganization. However, the following Example 7 from the above-cited Regulation does not seem worried about the tax avoidance potential of a business expansion:

> For the past nine years, corporation X has owned and operated a department store in the downtown area of the City of G. Three years ago, X acquired a parcel of land in a suburban area of G and constructed a new department store on it. X transfers the suburban store and related business assets to new subsidiary Y and distributes the stock of Y to X's shareholders. After the distribution, each store has its own manager and is operated independently of the other store. X and Y both satisfy the requirements of section 355(b).

Taxpayers who satisfy the active trade or business test cannot rest easy, however. The tax avoidance potential of divisive reorganizations is so great that the statute provides the government with a back-up — "the transaction [cannot be] used principally as a device for the distribution of the earnings and profits of the distributing corporation or the controlled corporation or both"; **§ 355(a)(1)(B)**.

The Regulations put some flesh on this rule, but are somewhat opaque; **Treas. Reg. § 1.355-2(d)**. The weight attributed to the following "device" factors depends on the "facts and circumstances";

(1) pro-rata distribution (in contrast to a split-up where two 50/50 shareholders end up each owning 100% of two separate corporations);

(2) sale of a substantial percentage of the stock soon after the distribution;

(3) a substantial amount of assets are not used in a trade or business (such as cash not needed in the business); and

(4) assets constitute a "secondary" business that serve the active trade or business (such as providing property or services to the business) and these assets can be sold without adversely affecting the conduct of the active trade or business — for example, where a taxpayer transfers an operation that supplies raw materials to a business but there is a long-term contract that insulates the taxpayer from any adverse consequences of disposing of the supply business.

In addition, the Regulations dealing with an "active trade or business" sometimes contain cryptic warnings that a transaction that satisfies the active trade or business test might run afoul of the "device" standard. This often occurs when the business is functionally related to the taxpayer's primary business. An example in **Treas. Reg. § 1.355-3(c)** states:

> Example (9). For the past eight years, corporation X has engaged in the manufacture and sale of household products. Throughout this period, X has maintained a research department for use in connection with its manufacturing activities. The research department has 30 employees actively engaged in the development of new products. X transfers the research department to new subsidiary Y and distributes the stock of Y to X's shareholders. After the distribution, Y continues its research operations on a contractual basis with several corporations, including X. X and Y both satisfy the [active business] requirements of section 355(b). The result in this example is the same if, after the distribution, Y continues its research operations but furnishes its services only to X. However, see § 1.355-2

(d)(2)(iv)(c) (related function device factor) for possible evidence of device.

MULTI-JURISDICTIONAL ISSUES

Multi-jurisdictional tax issues arise both in the international context across national borders and in the interstate domestic context within the United States. In the international context, the rules are found primarily in domestic law and treaties. The relevant treaties are bilateral, because multi-lateral treaties are not yet a reality. However, there are model treaties proposed by the U.S. Treasury, by the European-based Organization for Economic Cooperation and Development (OECD), and by the United Nations, the last of which is more friendly to economically less-developed nations than the other model treaties. Chapter 34 — the first of the two chapters in this Part — deals with the rules applicable to taxes on income in an international context.

In the interstate context, the rules are found primarily in state law and the federal constitution. Chapter 35 deals with these rules. Regarding state law, we look at how states allocate income among jurisdictions for the purpose of taxing income. Regarding the constitution, we look at the law applicable to more than just the income tax — primarily: gross receipts taxes, sales and use taxes, and severance taxes (on natural resources).

Chapter 34

INTERNATIONAL TAXATION

Countries make claims to tax income on two different grounds. First, residents are taxed on worldwide income. (The United States is unusual in also taxing its citizens on their worldwide income.) Second, countries tax a nonresident's income arising from business and investment activities within the jurisdiction. We first look at taxing the worldwide income of residents and then at taxing nonresidents on activities within the taxing jurisdiction. Finally, we examine efforts to prevent tax avoidance by locating income in countries that impose little or no tax ("tax havens). Emphasis is placed on U.S. law, with occasional references to the way other countries typically handle these issues.

§ 34.01 TAXING THE WORLDWIDE INCOME OF "RESIDENTS"

International tax regimes generally pursue one of two approaches. Export neutrality imposes the same income tax whether the investor invests at home or abroad; foreign income is not at an advantage or a disadvantage compared to investing in domestic enterprises. The foreign tax credit, discussed below, is an attempt at providing export neutrality.

Import neutrality imposes the same tax on income, regardless of where the taxpayer resides. This is often achieved by exempting residents from tax when business income is earned by a foreign permanent establishment. The effect is that the prevailing tax is imposed by the country with the permanent establishment, not the country of residence.

The United States follows the export neutrality model, relying on the foreign tax credit to prevent double taxation. Many European countries rely on the import neutrality approach for business conducted in another country through a permanent establishment. The United States, despite its ostensible reliance on the export neutrality model, comes closer to the import neutrality approach in one respect — it does not tax the income of foreign corporate subsidiaries (except for certain tax haven corporations) until the income returns to the United States.

[A] Who Is a Resident?

Different countries might have different definitions of a resident. United States tax law uses multiple alternative tests to define an individual's residence, including the following: green card status; or "substantial presence," based on complex rules about how long the taxpayer is present in the United States over a three-year period. § 7701(b). Treaties usually provide ways to resolve rival national definitions of a resident, although bilateral treaties do not exist between all nations. Typically, treaties provide tie-breaker rules for determining residence based on where the taxpayer has a permanent home, and then move on to other tests if that standard is inconclusive.

For corporations, the United States defines "residence" based on the place of incorporation. Other countries rely on the place of "effective management." Again, treaties provide tie-breakers in the event countries use different tests to identify a corporation's place of residence. The fact that the United States defines corporate residence as the place of incorporation means that, absent a special provision (of which there are many — discussed in Chapter 34.03[C]), the income of a foreign subsidiary corporation is deferred until it is distributed to the U.S. shareholders.

The difference in defining corporate residence is one of the ways businesses can avoid taxation. A typical example involves Ireland, which uses the "effective management" definition of corporate residence. A U.S. business organizes a subsidiary in Ireland, with its place of effective management in the United States. Under U.S. law, this subsidiary is an Irish resident and (as we will see) there is no U.S. tax on its income until the profits are brought back to the United States, unless a U.S. tax avoidance rule prevents this type of tax deferral (and these U.S. tax avoidance rules are often ineffective). However, because Ireland uses the "effective management" test for corporate residence and, because the effective management of this subsidiary is in the U.S., Ireland will not tax its worldwide income.

This example can also be used to alert you to what is to come in our discussion of international taxation. I already mentioned that U.S. tax rules intended to prevent deferral of tax on the income of a corporate subsidiary organized in a foreign country are not very effective. This is discussed later in Chapter 34.03[C].

A low Irish tax rate insures that whatever income is earned in Ireland (that is, has its "source" in Ireland) will be taxed at a low rate. This income is often royalty income charged to related businesses for use of intangible property owned by the Irish corporation (such as copyrights, patents, and trademarks) for use by related businesses throughout Europe and the rest of the world. Typically, the Irish corporation will charge a royalty at an excessive rate, thereby siphoning off income from higher-tax jurisdictions. As we will also see (in Chapter 34.03[B]), efforts to monitor intercompany pricing to make sure the price charged by related businesses is a fair price are not very effective.

[B] Avoiding Double Tax; Foreign Tax Credit (FTC)

Multiple taxation often arises from the claims of both a residence state and a state in whose jurisdiction the taxpayer engages in business or investment activity. Treaties usually mandate some form of relief from double taxation, but residence countries may provide such relief unilaterally. For example, the U.S. domestic tax law allows its residents (and citizens) to take a foreign tax credit (FTC) for income taxes imposed by a foreign country under circumstances described below, which reduces the tax imposed by the residence country. § 901. The FTC implements export neutrality by confronting the U.S. taxpayer with the same tax rate, whether or not the investment is made at home or abroad. However, as we will see, the mechanics of the FTC do not provide *complete* export neutrality, because a foreign tax in excess of the United States tax on foreign income does not result in a refund by the United States.

[1] Mechanics; Limitation on FTC

[a] Limitation Fraction

There is a limit on the FTC so that foreign tax rates higher than the U.S. tax rate do not reduce U.S. tax on U.S. income. **§ 904**. Export neutrality has its limits.

The mechanics of the FTC limit under U.S. law are illustrated by the following two examples. For both examples, assume that the taxpayer has $100 U.S. income and $200 foreign income; and that the U.S. tax rate is 30%, so that the U.S. tax (before the FTC) is $90 (30% times $300).

Example 1. In the first example, assume that the $200 foreign income comes from one country, F, which taxes income at 25%. The foreign tax is therefore $50. The limit on the FTC is the U.S. tax on the foreign income. More specifically, the formula for the limit on the foreign tax credit is:

$$\frac{\text{foreign source income}}{\text{worldwide income}} \quad \times \quad \text{U.S. income tax}$$

Applying that formula to the example, the limit on the foreign tax credit is ($200/ $300) times $90 = $60. The foreign tax of $50 (at a 25% rate) is less than the FTC limitation, so the entire foreign tax is credited against the $90 U.S. tax. The taxpayer pays $50 to the foreign country and $40 to the United States (that is, the U.S. tax equals a $30 tax on U.S. income and a $10 tax on foreign income).

An important wrinkle in computing the FTC limit is that the foreign source of the income is determined by U.S. law. Source rules are discussed later in this chapter, but it is possible for the United States and the foreign country to have different source rules. Consequently, the foreign country might tax certain income that U.S. law would consider to have a U.S. source. If that happened to all of the "foreign" income in the prior example, there would be no FTC, because the numerator of the FTC limitation fraction would be zero.

Example 2. In the second example, assume that the $200 of foreign income comes from two foreign countries — $100 from Country A, which exempts that income under Country A law, and $100 from Country B, which taxes that income at 50%. The total foreign tax is therefore $50. As noted, the U.S. tax rate is 30% times $300 — that is, $90. Notice that the Country B tax rate is higher than the U.S. tax rate so you might think that the FTC limitation would apply. However, the FTC limitation is computed on a global basis rather than on a per country basis. This means that the United States will give a credit for foreign taxes on foreign income from a specific country that exceeds the U.S. tax on that income, if the averaging of the high and low foreign tax rates works out to less than the U.S. tax on total foreign income. In this example, the total foreign tax is $50, which is only 25% of the $200 total foreign income, even though the Country B tax rate is 50%. The FTC limit is still $60 (as in the first example), which is more than the total foreign tax imposed by Countries A and B together.

The computation of the FTC limit on a global basis means that U.S. taxpayers will try to manipulate the source of income so that it arises in a low-tax foreign country. This will allow the U.S. taxpayer to average the foreign taxes in the high and low tax foreign jurisdictions, so that the overall foreign tax rate is less than the U.S. tax rate on foreign income. A per country limitation, adopted at various times by the United States in the past, prevents the taxpayer from averaging high and low taxed foreign income. However, a per country limitation would permit a taxpayer with no overall foreign income because of losses in one foreign country offsetting gains in another foreign country to use a credit for taxes paid to the "gain" country.

One common technique used by U.S. taxpayers to average income from high and low tax rate foreign countries is to source sales income in a foreign country by having title pass outside the United States in a low tax rate country — which is usually easy to do. That will be the result of applying the U.S. source rules, if a taxpayer *purchases* inventory outside the United States for sale outside the United States. If a U.S. taxpayer *produces* inventory in the United States and sells it to a foreign destination, there is less opportunity to manipulate the FTC limitation, but that opportunity is not completely eliminated. The producing-selling taxpayer must allocate the income to the two activities — production and sale. Regulations usually provide for this allocation on a 50/50 basis. The production activity is sourced where the production assets are located (in the United States) and the sales income arises where title passes (usually in a foreign country). The Regulations say that the title-passage source rule will not be followed if the transaction is structured for tax avoidance, but that admonition does not seem to be effective.

[b]   Different Baskets

Some attempts to average high and low taxed foreign income are prevented by putting the foreign income into different "baskets," each of which has its own FTC limitation:

$$\frac{\text{foreign source income for that basket}}{\text{worldwide income}} \quad \times \quad \text{U.S. income tax}$$

In other words, the FTC limitation fraction is not as simple as in our first example, which disregarded the different baskets.

FTC basket rules have varied over time. As of 2007, there are (usually) only two baskets for determining the FTC limitation — a general basket (typically, business income) and a passive income basket (typically, nonbusiness investment income). The passive income basket consists of income that is easy to shift to low tax jurisdictions — such as interest, dividends, rents, and royalties. However, financial services income (e.g., income earned by banks and insurance companies) and rents and royalties earned from an active trade or business are placed in the general basket. The idea is to prevent the taxpayer from averaging high-taxed business income with low-taxed passive income in order to reduce the foreign tax on foreign income to less than the U.S. tax on foreign income. For example, a 40% foreign tax on $100 of foreign business income and a 10% foreign tax on $100 of foreign passive interest income averages out to a 25% foreign tax on $200 of foreign income ($50/$200). That is likely to be less than the U.S. corporate tax rate. By having separate business and passive income baskets, U.S. law assures that the 40% foreign tax rate on business income exceeds the U.S. corporate tax rate and some FTC is denied.

United States law has a number of additional provisions to prevent circumvention of the FTC limitation. First, there is a "high-tax kickout," which places highly taxed passive income into the general basket. Absent this provision, the U.S. taxpayer could average low-taxed passive income with high-taxed passive income and bring the total foreign tax rate on foreign passive income below the U.S. tax rate. A common example of income subject to the high-tax kickout is rent, which is taxed on a net income basis by the United States but is sometimes taxed on a gross basis by the foreign country. For example, assume $100 gross rent, $50 expenses to produce the rent, and a 25% foreign tax on the $100 of *gross* rent. The foreign tax is $25, which equals 50% of the $50 of net income, as calculated under U.S. law. The high-tax kickout prevents the 50% foreign tax from being averaged with a low foreign tax on foreign interest and dividends.

The same rationale (preventing the averaging of high- and low-taxed foreign income) explains the rule that places income that is taxed by a foreign country but that is not considered income under U.S. law into the general basket. § 904(d)(2)(H). (In this instance, the foreign tax appears to be very high because there is no income that is also subject to U.S. tax.) An example is a distribution by a foreign corporation that is not taxable to its U.S. shareholders by the United States because the corporation lacks earnings and profits, but which is taxable as a dividend by the foreign country in which the distributing corporation resides for tax purposes.

There is more. Effective for tax years beginning after August 10, 2010, there is a new separate FTC basket for income that would be U.S. source income under U.S. statutory law but is resourced as foreign income under a tax treaty ☞ § 904(d)(6). Typically, this would occur by shifting interest or dividend income to a foreign branch. The idea is to prevent use of the tax treaty to inflate the foreign income numerator used to compute the foreign tax credit limitation.

In determining the character of foreign income for purposes of allocation to different baskets, the code sometimes uses "look-through" rules, which (in this respect) equate a foreign subsidiary to a foreign branch. If a controlled foreign corporation (defined, in general, as having U.S. ownership over 50% in vote or value) distributes dividends, interest, rents, or royalties to a 10% or more U.S. taxpayer, those distributions must be attributed to the distributing corporation's underlying income for allocation to a particular basket. Thus, if the distributing corporation has only trade or business income, the entire dividend, interest, rent, or royalty payment will be allocated to the basket containing trade or business income (that is, the general basket). If the distributing corporation has some passive income, then a pro-rata share of the payment would be attributable to that income basket.

[c]Allocation of Deductions

The FTC limitation fraction applies to net income. Consequently, U.S. taxpayers prefer to allocate deductions to U.S. source income to increase foreign *net* income so that more of the FTC will be available. The allocation of interest expenses and expenditures for research and development (R&D) raise special allocation problems and are the subject of complex statutory and regulations provisions, not discussed in this chapter. But you can see the problem. Very large R&D expenses to develop products sold around the world can, if used to reduce primarily U.S. income, allow foreign income to be larger than would be the case if some of those expenses reduced foreign income. *See, e.g.,* § 864(e) (interest expense); **Treas. Reg.** § 1.861-17 (providing alternative formulas for allocating the deduction of research and development expenditures).

[2]More Mechanics

[a]Carryovers

If the FTC is unavailable in a particular year because of the FTC limits, unused tax credits can be carried over to other years — currently, back one and forward ten years. § 904(c).

[b]Deductible Foreign Taxes; FTC is Elective

Foreign income taxes are usually deductible business or investment expenses (under § 162), except that the taxpayer cannot take both a deduction and a credit. The FTC is, however, elective. If the taxpayer has no total foreign income because a loss in one country offsets income in another country, a deduction of the foreign tax might be the preferable alternative. The ability to carryover unused tax credits to other tax years, however, might make the tax credit preferable to a deduction.

[c]Foreign and U.S. Losses

Assume that in year 1, a taxpayer has $100 U.S. income and a $100 foreign loss, so that total income is zero. In the following year 2, foreign income is $100. Absent a special rule, the foreign tax on the year 2 foreign income would be eligible for the foreign tax credit, even though total foreign income over the two-year period was zero. To prevent this result, the foreign income in year 2 is converted into U.S. income for computing the FTC limitation. But, in a concession to the taxpayer, the "conversion" does not exceed the lesser of the year 1 foreign loss or 50% of the year 2 foreign income. § 904(f)(1). For example, if the taxpayer has a $100 year 1 foreign loss and $150 year 2 foreign income, the amount of year 2 foreign income that is converted to U.S. income equals $75. The taxpayer still has $75 of year 2 foreign income.

In addition, the law now provides a tax break in the converse of the situation just discussed. Instead of having U.S. income and a foreign loss in year 1, assume a $100 U.S. loss and $100 of foreign income in year 1 (subject to a $25 foreign tax). In that case, there is no FTC in year 1 because there is no U.S. tax against which to apply the credit, despite having paid a foreign tax. In year 2, the taxpayer has $100 of U.S. income subject to U.S. tax and no foreign income. Over the two-year period, total U.S. income is zero and foreign income equals $100. **Section 904(g)(1)** allows this taxpayer to treat 50% of the U.S. income in year 2 as foreign income (equal to $50), thereby using some of the unused $25 FTC carried forward from year 1. Assuming a 30% U.S. tax, the FTC limitation in year 2 would be $15 (50/100 times 30).

[d]   Alternative Minimum Tax

The FTC can also offset the alternative minimum tax (AMT). **§ 904(a)**.

[3]   What Taxes Are Eligible for the FTC?

The FTC is available only for income taxes paid to a foreign country. This simple statement masks numerous issues.

[a]   Is it a Tax?

First, because a tax is a compulsory payment, the IRS will look to see whether a payment to a foreign government is voluntary — in which case it is *not* eligible for the FTC. This means that the taxpayer must make a reasonable attempt to litigate the foreign tax obligation in the foreign country as a condition of getting an FTC.

Second, is the payment for a benefit, rather than a tax? For example, some countries own their natural resources (such as oil) and a payment to the foreign country might be a royalty paid in exchange for permitting oil exploration, rather than a tax.

Third, a payment is not a creditable tax if the foreign country will return the payment as a subsidy. For example, Brazil imposes a 30% withholding tax on interest paid by its borrower-residents to a U.S. lender. It then rebates the 30% withheld to the Brazilian borrower. By this arrangement — in effect, reducing the U.S. tax by a creditable 30% withholding tax — Brazil hopes to keep interest rates down for the Brazilian borrower. Because the taxpayer does not really bear 30% tax in this situation, there will be no FTC for the 30% Brazilian "tax." **§ 901(i)**.

[b]   Is it an "Income" Tax?

Is the tax on income? The United States uses net income as its measure of taxable income and a foreign tax must generally follow that pattern to be considered an income tax, with two exceptions. First, if there is a reasonable effort to estimate a net income figure, the tax on the estimated amount will still be considered an income tax. Second, if the foreign country taxes gross receipts, that will still be considered an income tax if the income is not likely to have related expenses — as is often true of wages.

There was a split in the Courts of Appeals about whether the United Kingdom Windfall Profits Tax on certain utilities is an "income tax" eligible for the foreign tax credit. The Regulations state that a foreign levy is an income tax if and only if the predominant character of the tax is an income tax in the U.S. sense, which requires that it is likely to reach net gain in the normal circumstances in which it applies; and this requirement is satisfied only if the tax reaches realized gain. **Treas. Reg. § 1.901-2(a),(b).**

The Windfall Profits tax was intended to capture some profits enjoyed by utility companies which had to been sold to private companies and had enjoyed higher-than-expected profits, well in excess of what had been anticipated when the sales price had been determined. The tax fell on the difference between (1) the company's "profit-making value" (defined as its average annual profit per day over an earlier four-year period) multiplied by an imputed price-to-earnings ratio of 9 and (2) the price at which it had been sold to private companies. The government (and the Third Circuit) adopted a "text-bound approach," relying on the fact that the tax was levied on the difference between two values; it was therefore imposed on unrealized gain, which means that it is not an income tax under United States tax principles. The taxpayers argued (and the Tax Court and Fifth Circuit agreed) that the tax was based on prior revenues from the ordinary operation of the utility business, which were realized income; moreover, the tax could only reach utilities that had realized a profit. Consequently, the tax was an income tax eligible for the foreign tax credit.

The Supreme Court (in a unanimous opinion) held that the United Kingdom Windfall Profits Tax is eligible for the foreign tax credit. *PPL Corp. v. Commissioner*, 133 S.Ct. 1897 (2013).

[c] "In Lieu of" Income Taxes

A tax "in lieu of" an income tax is also creditable. **§ 903.** An "in lieu" tax must be a substitute for a general income tax that the country otherwise imposes. A tax on gross nonbusiness investment income of foreign investors — for example, a 30% tax on interest or dividends — fits this definition, assuming that it is a *substitute* for the (not an addition to) country's general income tax.

[d] Soak-Up Tax

An FTC is not allowed if the imposition of the foreign tax is conditioned on its reducing U.S. tax through the tax credit mechanism (referred to as a "soak-up" tax). Thus, if a country taxes the business income of U.S. residents at 20% but imposes no such tax on a resident of another country, which exempts the foreign income of a foreign permanent establishment (instead of providing a foreign tax credit), the 20% tax is not creditable. In such cases, the tax is not a generally applicable levy but is only selectively applied, depending on whether the law of the residence country provides a foreign tax credit. **Treas. Reg. § 903-1(b)(2).**

[4] Indirect FTC

Suppose a U.S. corporation owns 100% of a foreign corporation. The foreign corporation pays a 25% tax on its income to a foreign country. The U.S. taxpayer usually pays no tax to the United States until dividends are distributed. However, when the dividend is distributed, the corporate shareholder is eligible for an *indirect* FTC for foreign taxes paid by the subsidiary on the profits out of which the dividend is paid. (The example assumes a 100% owned subsidiary, but the indirect FTC is available to corporations owning at least 10% of the foreign corporation.) § 902.

The mechanics of the indirect credit require the credited tax to be included in the corporate shareholder's income (it is "grossed up"). For example, assume that the foreign corporation has $100 taxable income (which also equals its earnings and profits), that it pays $25 in foreign income tax on that income, and that it distributes the remaining $75 to its 100% parent corporation. The parent has $100 of income on which it pays U.S. tax and is entitled to a $25 FTC, subject to the rules limiting the FTC. In effect, the foreign tax paid by the distributing corporation is treated as a withholding tax. The numbers are more complicated if the shareholder owns less than 100% of the stock or the foreign corporation distributes less than all of its after-tax income, but the idea is the same.

Note that the taxpayer must be a shareholder to be eligible for the indirect FTC. In *Hewlett-Packard Co. v. Commissioner*, 103 T.C.M. (CCH) 1736 (2012), the government took the unusual position that an investment was a loan rather than an equity investment. In the domestic corporation context, taxpayers usually want an investment to be characterized as a loan to avoid dividend treatment of repayments from the corporation and the government argues that repayment is sufficiently uncertain that the investment should be considered equity. But, in the indirect FTC context, characterization as a loan deprives the investor of a FTC. In *Hewlett-Packard*, the government won its argument that the investment was a loan, because repayment was very likely.

[5]   Check-a-Box and the Foreign Tax Credit

The check-a-box regulations (Chapter § 33.04) provide an opportunity for U.S. taxpayers who would not otherwise be eligible for the indirect foreign tax credit to obtain a foreign tax credit. For example, assume a U.S. corporation owns less than 10% of the stock of a foreign business entity; 10% ownership is required for the U.S. corporation to obtain the indirect foreign tax credit provided by § 902. If the foreign entity is not considered a "per se" corporation under U.S. law, it can elect pass-through status. Its foreign taxes will therefore be treated as directly paid by its shareholders (including an 8% shareholder) and will be eligible for the direct foreign tax credit. At the same time, the foreign country may treat the entity as a corporation, eligible for whatever legal and tax advantages that might provide under foreign law. These entities are known as "hybrid entities" — treated one way under U.S. law and another way under foreign law.

[C]   Avoiding Double Tax; Exempting Foreign Income

[1]   European Practice

European countries often use the exemption method to prevent double taxation of business income, *if* the business income is earned abroad by a permanent establishment. (About one half of the European countries use the worldwide system used in the United States; and the other half use the territorial system exempting business income earned by a permanent establishment doing business in a foreign country.) The exemption approach provides import neutrality. Thus, if a French corporation does business in the United States through a permanent establishment, U.S. tax rates would apply to that business income (not French tax rates); and that same tax rate would be applicable to a U.S. resident doing business in the United States.

[2]   U.S. Practice; Foreign Subsidiaries

Although the United States does not exempt the income of U.S. taxpayers when it is earned by a foreign permanent establishment located in a foreign country, it provides something close to that result by not routinely taxing the income of a foreign subsidiary corporation owned by a U.S. person at the time the income is earned. Consequently, many U.S. corporations carry on business in foreign countries through foreign subsidiaries. (In certain tax avoidance situations, discussed later in Chapter 34.03[C], the undistributed profits of a foreign corporation are taxed to the U.S. shareholder.)

Proposals are sometimes made to end deferral of U.S. taxation on the income of foreign subsidiaries of U.S. corporations. In other words, a subsidiary would be taxed like a branch of a U.S. corporation doing business abroad. These proposals are often linked to the populist argument that tax deferral encourages U.S. corporations to take jobs abroad to foreign countries.

The argument *against* ending tax deferral is that it would put U.S. business at a competitive disadvantage. If other countries do not tax the income earned in a foreign country or defer tax until the profits are brought back to the "home" country, U.S. taxpayers doing business in foreign countries would pay more taxes than foreign taxpayers doing business in the same foreign countries. This would either require U.S. taxpayer to raise prices or leave the business with less money to reinvest, thereby giving an advantage to businesses that do not face this tax burden.

[3]   U.S. Practice; Exemption

The United States uses the exemption method in one situation — it exempts personal service income earned abroad under certain circumstances, up to a dollar ceiling; and also excludes from an employee's income "excessive" foreign housing costs (as defined in the law). The rationale advanced for this provision is that it lowers the cost of doing business abroad by U.S. employers, by reducing the pressure for higher wages. § 911.

[4]   Preventing U.S. corporations from "migrating" abroad

The current U.S. tax system (taxing worldwide income of U.S. resident corporations and deferring U.S. tax on income earned by foreign subsidiaries) has encouraged some U.S. corporations to "migrate" to foreign jurisdictions by shifting control of worldwide operations to a foreign subsidiary (referred to an "inversion" transaction). § 7874 is an effort to deal with that problem. In effect, it treats such newly-migrated foreign corporations as U.S. corporations for U.S. tax purposes (notwithstanding any treaty to the contrary). There is an important exception to this rule for foreign corporations that have "substantial business activities in the foreign country" in which they are organized. It turns out that § 7874 has numerous potential loopholes (too complex for present discussion) that probably make it ineffective as a technique for preventing tax avoidance.

You should also be aware that there is a possibility that European countries will abandon the territorial approach and, at the same time, not adopt tax deferral (as now practiced in the U.S.). European countries might instead tax the worldwide income of business enterprises when that income is earned. If that occurs, the U.S. could abandon deferral without fear of putting its businesses at a competitive disadvantage. Of course, there still remains the question of how U.S. and foreign corporate tax rates compare and the impact of any difference on business competition.

§ 34.02 TAXING NONRESIDENTS ON INCOME ARISING WITHIN THE TAXING JURISDICTION

The U.S. taxation of a nonresident's income arising within the United States distinguishes between income effectively connected with a U.S. trade or business and nonbusiness investment income. The law dealing with these issues identifies the source of the income (that is, whether or not the income arises from a U.S. source), but source is only sometimes the critical factor in deciding whether or not the U.S. taxes the income. Source rules are usually more important for the taxation of nonbusiness investment income, so most of the technical discussion of source is deferred until we discuss the taxation of nonbusiness investment income.

Determining U.S. statutory law is not always the final step in deciding whether a nonresident is taxed on income arising in the United States. Treaties usually make it more difficult to tax a nonresident on income arising within a jurisdiction.

We look first at business income and then at nonbusiness investment income.

[A] Effectively Connected with a U.S. Trade or Business

If a taxpayer has income effectively connected with a U.S. trade or business, the net income is generally taxed by the United States at the regular progressive tax rates applicable to U.S. taxpayers (*absent a treaty exception*). This contrasts with nonbusiness investment income (such as dividends and interest), which is taxed at 30% of gross income (absent a treaty exemption). The 30%-of-gross-income tax can be a higher tax than would be imposed by the regular tax rates on net income.

[1] U.S. Trade or Business

The first issue is whether the taxpayer is conducting a U.S. trade or business.

[a] Sale of Inventory

Sale of inventory resulting from "regular and sustained" activity in the United States is a U.S. trade or business. The IRS has ruled that demonstrating products in the United States for the purpose of soliciting orders satisfies this test. Rev. Rul.

56-165, 1956-1 C.B. 849. However, advertising in a U.S. newspaper or magazine would probably not constitute a U.S. trade or business without more U.S. activity.

[b]   Agent

The most contentious issue in determining whether a taxpayer conducts a U.S. trade or business arises when the business is conducted through an agent. Continuous and regular activities in the United States conducted by an agent who works primarily for the taxpayer and can only act with the principal's approval will likely constitute a U.S. trade or business by the foreign principal. Anything short of that level of activity through an agent may or may not constitute a U.S. trade or business by the principal.

Trading in stocks and securities are, by statute, subject to a special rule intended to encourage investment activity in U.S. markets by foreigners. § 864(b)(2). The general pattern is to make it much more difficult for an agent's activity to amount to a U.S. trade or business by the foreign investor.

[2]   Effectively Connected

When is income "effectively connected" to a U.S. trade or business? Historically, the taxation of U.S. business income that was effectively connected with a U.S. trade or business was conditioned on the income being from a U.S. source; and, for many years, this source rule was both mechanical and easily avoided. For example, title passage was the exclusive method for determining the source of inventory sales income (and still is for the foreign income tax credit limitation rules).

[a]   U.S. Office

Today, inventory sales are also sourced in the United States when the income is attributable to a U.S. office or fixed place of business, regardless of where title passes. This would typically mean that the sale of inventory has a U.S. source, if the sale is arranged by a U.S. branch of a foreign corporation; however, this source rule does not apply if the property is sold for use outside the United States with the material participation of a foreign-based office, even if arranged by a U.S. branch. § 865(e)(2). The "U.S. office" rule is similar to the accounting method used to locate the income of a permanent establishment under the laws of many European countries.

Determining whether the foreign taxpayer has a U.S. office is difficult when the U.S. activities occur through an agent. An agent's office will constitute the office of a foreign taxpayer in the United States under certain circumstances — for example, if the agent regularly exercises authority to make contracts or maintains a stock of merchandise from which he regularly fills orders for the principal, and is not an "independent" agent. (An agent who is an employee of the foreign taxpayer is not an "independent" agent.)

[b]   "Force of Attraction"

In addition, if a taxpayer is engaged in a U.S. trade or business, any U.S. source business income of a foreign taxpayer (other than periodical income, such as interest, dividends, and royalties) is automatically treated as effectively connected with the U.S. trade or business, in order to avoid arguments about exactly what income is really connected to the business (the so-called "force of attraction" rule). This avoids an argument about whether inventory sales income of a foreign corporation, in which title passes in the United States, is actually connected to the activities of a U.S. branch of the foreign taxpayer.

[c]   Investment-Type Business Income

When the *business* income consists of royalties, interest, or other (typically) investment income, the rules are similar to those for inventory sales, but the mechanics are different. Even if the income is still technically from a foreign source (for example, because a royalty arises from the business of licensing trademarks or patents for use outside the United States), it is taxed by the United States as effectively connected to a U.S. trade or business, if it is attributable to the activities of a U.S. office. § 864(c)(4)(B)(i)–(ii). Another example of investment-type income effectively connected to a U.S. trade or business is interest earned by a bank through its U.S. office. Such income is taxed as U.S. business income, rather than being subject to the rules applicable to nonbusiness investment income (discussed below), even though the interest is technically sourced in a foreign country because the debtor is a resident of a foreign country.

[3]   Real Estate

Sale of U.S. real estate is automatically treated as effectively connected with a U.S. trade or business. § 897(a)(1).

Real estate rental income is subject to a special rule. Renting U.S. real property may or may not be a U.S. business under domestic U.S. law. However, foreign taxpayers can elect to treat such rental income as derived from a U.S. trade or business, thereby paying tax at a graduated tax rate on net income, rather than paying a tax on 30% of gross income. § 871(d).

[4]   Personal Services

Performing personal services in the United States is a U.S. trade or business sourced at the place of performance. Although withholding is not usually required on trade or business income, someone who pays a foreign taxpayer for personal services performed in the United States must withhold at the 30% rate. However, the actual tax burden is likely to be less than 30% of gross personal service income because of the deduction of business expenses and the imposition of graduated tax rates. Taxpayers who pay personal service income to nonresident taxpayers can therefore enter into agreements with the U.S. government to reduce the amount of withholding.

U.S. legislation provides a de minimis exception to taxing foreign personal service income — the taxpayer must be present not more than 90 days, earn less than $3,000, and work for an employer who has no U.S. trade or business. § 864(b)(1).

When an individual's personal services create intangible property, such as a copyright, it is often difficult to decide whether a payment is for the services or is a royalty for use of the copyright (which has a different source rule, discussed later). *See Boulez v. Commissioner*, 83 T.C. 584 (1984) (orchestra conductor contracted to make recordings in the United States; payments to conductor were services income, not royalty income). Sometimes the dispute concerns whether the income is personal service or sales income — for example, when a taxpayer sells artwork. Similar issues arise under state sales taxes, which are not routinely imposed on services; Chapter 29.04[A].

[5]   Treaties

[a]   Business Income; Permanent Establishment

Treaties usually require that a trade or business be carried on through a "permanent establishment" before a country has the power to tax the business income of a foreign taxpayer. The definition of a permanent establishment varies from treaty to treaty, but a permanent establishment usually refers to a fixed place of business, a construction site, and to the activities of certain agents (usually an agent who is "dependent" on the taxpayer-principal — such as an employee or other agent whose financial livelihood depends primarily on working for the principal). The treaties usually exclude certain activities from being a "permanent establishment" — such as maintaining a stock of goods for storage, display, or delivery; or maintaining a fixed place of business to *purchase* goods (an export incentive). In addition, treaties usually prohibit the U.S. from applying its "force of attraction" rule, discussed above.

A capital-importing country may rely on a more expansive definition of a permanent establishment than would be true for the United States or Europe — in order to tax more income earned by foreign branches of a U.S. business than might otherwise be the case. For example, India has indicated that leasing tangible or intangible property for use in India might (under certain circumstances) constitute a permanent establishment. This diverges from the position taken in the model tax treaty adopted by the European-based Organization for Economic Cooperation and Development (OECD). *See* Tax Notes Int'l, pp. 238-39 (Jan. 19, 2009).

Another important issue concerns whether the location of high-speed servers to conduct very fast investment trading transactions in a particular country constitutes a permanent establishment (PE). Under the OECD Model Tax Treaty, the issue is whether the server is a "fixed place of business." The Commentary to the OECD Treaty says that, if the server is "at [the taxpayer's] own disposal," the server *could* be a PE. The National Tax Authority of Japan has stated that a foreign investor using a server located in Japan does not have PE in Japan because the investor does *not* have the "right to dispose of" or have "virtual control over" the server beyond "receiving and enjoying an environment for high-speed placement of orders." *See* Tax Notes Int'l, p. 485 (Nov. 14, 2011). Before a taxpayer is too comforted by this ruling, it must take note of the ruling's numerous qualifications — for example: the investor does not own or lease the server; the investor can only use the server to execute high-speed transactions; and the investor cannot enter the space where the server is installed.

[b] Personal Services

Treaties usually provide that independent personal services (that is, by a nonemployee) are taxable only in the country of residence, unless the income is attributable to a fixed base where the services are performed (for example, an architect from France working out of an office in the United States). Regarding employees, treaties usually require a greater U.S. personal service connection before the United States can impose a tax than is provided under U.S. domestic law — for example, the taxpayer must be present more than 183 days, unless the compensation is paid by a resident of the United States or a U.S. permanent establishment.

Treaties sometimes exempt the income of entertainers and athletes, usually if their income is not large. The recent United States Model Income Tax Convention of November 15, 2006 (Article 16) states that such income is exempt if the gross receipts (including expense reimbursements) do not exceed $20,000. The Canadian-U.S. treaty has an unusual provision (think professional sports). It states that athletes participating in team sports in leagues with regularly scheduled games in the United States and Canada are exempt, regardless of how much income they earn.

[B] Nonbusiness Investment Income

Nonresidents are generally taxed at a 30% tax rate on gross nonbusiness investment income, if the income has a U.S. source. § 871(a)(1). The tax is routinely collected through withholding by the payor, such as interest paid by a U.S. debtor. Remember that these rules do not apply to investment income that is effectively connected with a U.S. trade or business.

[1] Interest Income

Interest is sourced where the individual debtor resides or the debtor corporation is organized. However, the United States does not impose the 30% tax on investment interest from a U.S. source if it is "portfolio" interest — often interest paid on bonds issued to European lenders by U.S. debtors. This exemption from U.S. tax is intended to keep interest payments lower than they would otherwise be if the lender's receipt of interest were subject to U.S. source taxation. To prevent tax avoidance, this exemption does not apply if the lender is "related" to the borrower, or if the interest is really a disguised dividend. § 871(b)(1).

Interest on U.S. bank deposits is also not subject to the 30% tax as long as it is not effectively connected to a U.S. trade or business — which encourages foreign taxpayers to place deposits in U.S. banks. §§ 871(i)(2)(A); 881(d).

[2] Dividends

Dividends are usually sourced where the corporation is organized.

This place-of-corporate-organization source rule for dividends led to the following problem. Because dividends paid by a U.S. subsidiary of a foreign corporation are U.S. source income, foreign corporations would do business in the United States through a U.S. branch, rather than do business through a U.S. subsidiary corporation. United States law responded to this problem by imposing a "branch profits" tax, which taxes the repatriation to a foreign country of the profits of a U.S. branch at the same 30% tax rate that applies to dividends. § 884.

[3] Rents and Royalties

Rents and royalties from the lease of tangible property are sourced where the property is located. If the property is intangible, the source is where the property is used. This makes the distinction between personal services and royalty income important, because the source rules differ — services are sourced where performed and royalties are sourced where the intangible property is used. *See Boulez v. Commissioner supra*, involving the orchestra conductor who made recordings (service vs. not royalty income).

Sales income contingent on the productivity or use of an intangible asset — such as a percentage of profits paid to the owner of a patent — is considered royalty income. § 865(d)(1).

[4] Treaties

Treaties typically reduce the source country tax on nonbusiness investment income below 30%. Interest is often not taxed by the source country or taxed at 10%. The tax rate on dividends is often reduced to 15% (or to 5%, if the payee owns at least 10% of the dividend payor's voting stock). Royalties are often not taxed by the source country or are taxed at a reduced rate.

Developing nations want the option of withholding tax at a significant rate on investment income, because they are net importers of capital. The United Nations Model Tax Treaty reflects those concerns by permitting higher withholding rates than are typical in older treaties between economically developed nations.

[5] Income from Sale of Intangible Property

The source of sales income from the sale of an intangible held as an investment (that is, not effectively connected with a U.S. trade or business) is usually the seller's residence. (But, remember that sales contingent on productivity, use, or disposition of an asset are sourced as royalties.)

"Residence" is defined differently for the source rules applicable to the sale of intangible investment property than for determining whether the taxpayer is taxed on worldwide income. United States law looks to the taxpayer's "tax home" to define the source of investment sales income, and defines the "tax home" as a location at or near the taxpayer's principal place of business. §§ 865(g)(1)(A)(i); 911(d)(3). Still, a nonresident is unlikely to be taxed on such income (always assuming that it is not effectively connected with a U.S. trade or business). Not only is the income unlikely to be sourced in the United States (because the taxpayer lacks a U.S. tax home), but capital gains unconnected to a U.S. trade or business are not taxed by the United States even if they have a U.S. source, unless the nonresident taxpayer is present in the United States at least 183 days in the tax year. § 871(a)(2).

[6] Scholarships

Scholarships are neither business income nor investment income, but could be taxed by the United States if they have a U.S. source. They are sourced at the payor's location (for example — foreign source, if paid by a foreign government; or U.S. source, if paid by a U.S. foundation). Treaties usually exempt this type of income.

§ 34.03 UNDERTAXING INTERNATIONAL INCOME

In the current business environment in which taxpayers engage in worldwide business activities, there is at least as great a risk that income will be undertaxed as overtaxed.

[A] Treaty Shopping

Assume taxpayers in Country X do not have a favorable tax treaty with the United States, but there is a favorable treaty between the United States and Country A. Country X taxpayers organize a corporation in Country A in the hopes of gaining the advantages of the U.S. treaty with Country A, thereby reducing or eliminating their tax obligation to the United States. Some recent U.S. treaties deny the benefits normally available to Country A residents if more than 50% of the corporation's stock is owned by shareholders resident in Country X (unless the stock of the Country A corporation is publicly traded on an established securities market in Country A). For example, if dividends paid to Country A residents by a U.S. corporation are normally taxed at 15% pursuant to the U.S. treaty with Country A, that reduction below 30% might not apply to payments to the corporation organized in Country A, which is wholly owned by Country X shareholders.

[B] Intercompany Pricing

One way undertaxation can occur is through manipulation of intercompany pricing. For example, U.S. taxpayers who control a foreign business entity might sell manufactured products at a low price to its foreign subsidiary for resale in a foreign country. If the foreign country has a lower tax rate than the United States, some of the profits from this business are being siphoned off to a low-tax foreign country.

Reallocate income. United States domestic law provides that the government can reallocate the sales price (as well as other intercompany prices) between taxpayers subject to common control, in order to properly reflect the economic reality of the transaction. § 482. This is an extraordinarily difficult and contentious undertaking. No attempt will be made here to describe the variety of tests that can be used to make this judgment, except to note the need for "comparable" transactions to identify a fair intercompany price. (You should recall how difficult it was to identify "comparable" property transactions in order to value property for property tax purposes. Chapter 26.06[A][1].)

The effort to identify "comparable" transactions when you are dealing with controlled entities is theoretically flawed, because there are gains that result from integrated businesses that do not exist in transactions between unrelated businesses. Nonetheless, the United States rules (as well as the OECD Guidelines) require a comparison of transactions between related and unrelated parties to determine the "correct" pricing. Two broad approaches are taken: methods based on specific transactions; and methods that allocate the total profits of the controlled entities. The methods based on specific transactions include: the comparable uncontrolled price method (CUP) (focusing on the price charged by one related entity to another related entity, compared to prices between unrelated parties); the resale price method (RPM) (comparing the gross profit margin earned in sales of products between related parties with the gross profit margin on sales of products between unrelated parties);the cost plus method (comparing gross profit margins in transactions between related and unrelated business).

The Regulations (somewhat unhelpfully) require the taxpayer to use the best method, and then specify that this method will be determined by the degree of comparability between the transactions and the quality of the data. Comparability is judged by (among other things) the functions performed by the businesses engaged in the transactions; the contractual terms; the risks undertaken; and the economic conditions. When transactions are not comparable, an effort is often made to adjust the price arrived at by a particular method to account for whatever feature is not comparable, such as the existence of bulk sales in one but not the other situation.

Impact on FTC. A common result of reallocating prices is to allocate more income to a U.S. rather than to a foreign source, with a potential loss of the foreign tax credit, because of the way the FTC limitation is computed (discussed in Chapter 34.01[B][1][a]). At the same time, the foreign taxing country might not recognize the reallocation of the income away from its taxing jurisdiction and its taxes might not be reduced. Most tax treaties provide an administrative procedure to help resolve conflicting claims, but they do not always resolve issues to a taxpayer's satisfaction.

Intangibles. Income from intangible property (such as copyrights, patents, trade names, and business methods) are a common source of difficulty. Thus, licensing arrangements that attempt to siphon off profits from intangibles to a low tax country are subject to close scrutiny. Two code sections explicitly state that the royalties paid between two related businesses — often after a transfer of the intangible to a foreign country — shall be adjusted so that they are commensurate with the actual income attributable to the intangible. §§ 367(d), 482 (last sentence). This prevents a U.S. taxpayer from reducing taxes by transferring an intangible to a related foreign corporation in a low-tax jurisdiction, and charging a low royalty payable to the U.S. taxpayer, followed by significant profits generated by the intangible in the foreign country. The cited sections force a recasting of the royalty payment in light of *actual* income generated after the transfer of the intangible, so that the income of the U.S. taxpayer is more than the amount specified in the royalty contract.

Advanced pricing agreement. The uncertainties in applying § 482 are so great that the government is now willing to enter into advance pricing agreements (an APA) to avoid potential disputes about intercompany pricing; Rev. Proc. 96-53, 1996-2 C.B. 375. In an unusual turn of events, GlaxoSmithKline argued that the IRS illegally discriminated by denying it an APA when it had entered into an APA with a competitor. In September 2006, GlaxoSmithKline and the government agreed to the largest settlement ever reached with the IRS ($3.4 billion) to resolve transfer pricing claims. As part of the settlement, the taxpayer also withdrew its discrimination claim.

Form disclosure. Disputes about transfer pricing are (obviously) very controversial, uncertain in outcome, and involve a lot of money. The IRS has recently issued Schedule UTP (Uncertain Tax Position) (Announcement 2010-75), requiring business taxpayers with assets exceeding $100 million to report UTPs with their tax returns beginning in 2010. This requires businesses to report income tax positions to the IRS for which businesses have recorded a reserve in a financial statement audited by their accountants. Transfer pricing issues must be separately highlighted by the letter "T" on the Schedule UTP.

[C]   Tax Havens

Another technique for avoiding tax in the international context is to siphon off income into "tax havens," which refer to countries that impose little or no tax and in which little or no business activity is carried on. The following summary only scratches the surface of the U.S. rules designed to close this loophole, but it is a start.

[1]   Taxing Shareholders of Controlled Foreign Corporations (CFCs) on Imputed Dividend Income

U.S. domestic tax law addressed this problem in 1962 by ending the deferral of tax on the "tax haven" income of a "controlled foreign corporation" (CFC). A CFC is a foreign corporation that has U.S. shareholders (defined as shareholders who own 10% of the corporation's voting stock) and whose U.S. shareholders together control the foreign corporation (control is defined as either more than 50% of the vote or value of the stock).

The U.S. shareholder has to include the tax haven income of the CFC in income even though that income has not been distributed as a dividend — it is a "deemed dividend distribution." The shareholder increases its basis in the stock of the CFC as though the dividend had been contributed back to the CFC as a contribution to capital.[1]

---

[1] *Rodriguez v. Commissioner*, 137 T.C. 174 (2011), holds that the "deemed dividend" is not a dividend

The deemed dividend distribution carries with it an indirect foreign tax credit (FTC) resulting from any foreign taxes paid by the foreign subsidiary. In general, the imputed income of the CFC is placed in FTC baskets by the look-through method — that is, if the CFC has business income, the imputed income is (to that extent) business income; if the CFC has passive income, the imputed income is (to that extent) placed in the passive income basket.

[2] Typical Tax Haven Income

The U.S. tax law uses the following terminology to identify tax haven income. It is called "Subpart F" income (so described because it is in "Subpart F" of the tax law). The categories of Subpart F income discussed in this summary fall within the broad classification of "foreign base company income" (FBCI). FBCI includes: "foreign base company sales income"; "foreign base company services income"; and "foreign personal holding company income." There are other categories of income to which the imputed income rules apply but we only address these three categories in this summary.

[a]   Foreign Base Company Sales Income

A typical foreign tax haven might operate this way. A United States corporation (USC) establishes a wholly owned subsidiary corporation in Country X (Corp. X), which imposes no tax on corporations. USC sells products that it manufactures in the United States to the related Corp. X for resale to unrelated parties outside of Country X. Corp. X is typically a corporation that sells products throughout the continent in which it is located.

The general definition of foreign base company sale income, which includes this example, is a situation in which the property is purchased from a related party by a CFC and sold to an unrelated party, if the property is manufactured *and* sold for use outside the CFC country. The idea is that there is no value added in the CFC country. If the CFC manufactured the property in the CFC country or sold the property manufactured in the United States for use in the CFC country, the income would not be tax haven income. (Foreign base company sales income can also arise if the purchase is from an unrelated person and the sale is to a related person.) A related party is typically a corporation which controls or is controlled by a CFC — often a parent-subsidiary situation. Control is defined as either more than 50% of the vote or value of the stock.

It is important to define what counts as "manufacture" in the CFC country — so that the income can avoid classification as foreign base company sales income. **Treas. Reg. § 1.954-3(a)(4)(iii)** states as follows:

> If purchased property is used as a component part of personal property which is sold, the sale of the property will be treated as the sale of a manufactured product, rather than the sale of component parts, if the operations conducted by the selling corporation in connection with the property purchased and sold are substantial in nature and are generally

under § 1(h)(11) and is therefore not eligible for the maximum 20% tax rate on dividends. The case was argued before a Court of Appeals on April 3, 2013.

considered to constitute the manufacture, production, or construction of property. Without limiting this substantive test, which is dependent on the facts and circumstances of each case, the operations of the selling corporation in connection with the use of the purchased property as a component part of the personal property which is sold will be considered to constitute the manufacture of a product if in connection with such property conversion costs (direct labor and factory burden) of such corporation account for 20 percent or more of the total cost of goods sold. In no event, however, will packaging, repackaging, labeling, or minor assembly operations constitute the manufacture, production, or construction of property.

In the initial example, a U.S. corporation (USC) sold goods that it manufactured to a CFC (Corp. X — a related party), but there is no requirement that the manufacturing occur in the United States. For example, a manufacturing corporation organized and operating in European Country A (Corp. A) can sell to a CFC, which is a related party, organized in European Country B (Corp. B) for resale in Europe outside of country B; in that case, the income of Corp. B can be foreign base company sales income. The idea is that deferral of U.S. tax on corporate income should not be available if the income is shifted around to minimize taxes, rather than reflecting business activity.

Treasury Regulations effective July 1, 2009 expand the situations in which a CFC will be considered to have participated in the "manufacture, production or construction" of a product for sale, thereby expanding the situations in which a CFC will *not* have foreign base company sales income (FBCSI). The Regulations include situations in which employees of the CFC make a "substantial contribution" to the manufacture, production, or construction of the product; they also seek to accommodate the growing practice of producing goods through use of a contract manufacturer. **Treas. Reg. § 1.954 3(a)(4)(iv).** Examples flesh out the new rules.

One example (Example 10) deals with situations in which the CFC purchases raw materials and designs the products manufactured by a contract manufacturer, and manages manufacturing costs and capacities. Although the products "can be manufactured from the raw materials to [the CFC's] design specifications without significant oversight and direction, quality control, or control of manufacturing related logistics," the CFC has sufficient participation through its employees for the sales income to avoid FBCSI characterization.

Recall that European countries often exempt the income of a foreign branch. A branch activity in Country B, conducted by a corporation organized in Country A, can therefore have the same tax impact in reducing taxes as a corporation organized in Country B. For example, a manufacturing corporation in Country A (which is a CFC) sets up a selling branch in Country B, which is exempt from tax by Country A. Country B has a very low tax on sales income. United States law will therefore treat the branch in Country B like a related corporate subsidiary formed in Country B for purposes of determining whether there is a tax haven from which income will be imputed to a U.S. shareholder. **§ 954(d)(2); Treas. Reg. § 1.954-3(b)(1).**

[b]   Foreign Base Company Services Income

Another situation in which there is no value added in the CFC country occurs when Corp. X (which is organized in foreign Country X and is a CFC) performs services for its U.S. parent throughout the continent in which Country X is located, but the services are performed outside of Country X — such as warranty services on products sold by the U.S. parent. This type of income derived by Corp. X for performing services is referred to as "foreign base company services income," and is another category of foreign base company income.

[c]   Foreign Personal Holding Company Income

Another example of FBCI, which can result in a deemed dividend distribution from a CFC, is foreign personal holding company income — specifically, passive investment income such as dividends, interest, rents, and royalties. § 954(c). FBCI does not include investment income that results from the active conduct of a trade or business, such as the following: (1) banking income, and (2) rents and royalties from an active trade or business that are *not* received from a related party. § 954(c)(2)(A).

In addition, foreign personal holding company income does not include certain investment income from a related party when the income is generated within the *same* country in which the CFC is organized — specifically: rents and royalties received from a related party for the use of property in the country where the CFC is organized; and dividends and interest from a related party organized in the same country as the CFC, if the related party was engaged in a trade or business in the same country as the CFC. § 954(c)(3).

Finally, through 2013 (as extended by ATRA), a look-through rule sometimes applies in identifying foreign personal holding company income. § 954(c)(6). That section provides that dividends, interest, rents, and royalties received or accrued from a controlled foreign corporation that is a related person shall not be treated as foreign personal holding company income as long as the source of these payments is not Subpart F income. This allows a foreign corporation to transfer business profits to a related corporation (e.g., by paying interest or dividends) without the payments being treated as foreign personal holding company income.

Another way that foreign businesses can (sometimes) avoid Subpart F income is through use of the check-a-box option, discussed earlier. Foreign businesses which are not "pre se" corporations (and Treasury rules identify these corporations on a country-by-country basis) can elect to be disregarded entities by checking a box on their tax returns. If they make that election, payments between the disregarded entity and a related foreign corporation cannot be Subpart F income because there is no "payment." In effect, the money is being transferred from one pocket to another pocket.

[D]   None or All Income Treated as Tax Haven Income

The definition of foreign base company income is subject to de minimis rules. If the foreign base company income is less than the lower of 5% of the CFC's gross income or $1 million, the CFC has *no* FBCI. § 954(b)(3)(A). Conversely, if foreign base company income is more than 70% of the CFC's gross income, all of the CFC's gross income is FBCI. **§ 954(b)(3)(B)**.

Foreign base company income also does not include income that has been subject to foreign income taxes equal to at least 90% of the top tax rate applicable to U.S. corporations (currently 35%; so 90% times 35% = 31.5%). **§ 954(b)(4)**.

[E]   More on Investment Income

Another provision in the tax law aimed at preventing tax avoidance on investment income through ownership of foreign corporations appears in **§§ 1291–1298**. It deals with a foreign investment company owned by numerous individuals — a passive foreign investment company. These sections are not discussed in this chapter.

[F]   "Foreign Tax Credit Splitting Event"

Public Law 111-226, effective beginning in 2011, adds a new **§ 909** to prevent taxpayers from taking a foreign tax credit before they take the income into account, *if* there is "a foreign tax credit splitting event."

Here are two examples of the impact of § 909. First, a U.S. corporation controls two businesses organized in foreign Country X. One business is a "disregarded entity" under the U.S. law — such as a partnership in Country X; another business in Country X is a controlled foreign corporation (CFC). The CFC has $100 of income subject to a $30 foreign income tax. Under the laws of Country X, the disregarded entity is liable for the tax. This means that, under U.S. law, the $30 foreign tax would be treated as having been paid by the U.S. corporation which controls the partnership, even though the income in the CFC had not been distributed to the U.S. corporation. **Section 909** disallows the foreign tax credit for this $30 payment until the related income is distributed to the U.S. corporation.

Second, a foreign corporation is wholly owned by a U.S. corporation, such that the foreign corporation's income tax payments would be attributable to the U.S. corporation when the U.S. corporation receives a dividend. However, the foreign corporation is a "reverse hybrid" — that is, an entity that is considered a pass—through entity under the laws of the foreign country but a corporation under U.S. law. Consequently, the income of the foreign entity is attributed to the U.S. corporation that controls the foreign entity and a tax is imposed *by that foreign country* on the U.S. corporation, even though the foreign entity is considered a U.S. corporation under U.S. law and, consequently, none of the foreign entity's undistributed income is attributed to the U.S. corporation under U.S. law. The foreign tax paid by the U.S. corporation is not eligible for the foreign tax credit until the foreign entity's income is taxed to the U.S. corporation under U.S. tax law (e.g., when it is distributed as a dividend).

Chapter 35

INTERSTATE TAXATION

Interstate taxation raises two general issues — (1) the legislative framework used by the states to impose tax, and (2) the U.S. constitutional limits on state taxation.

The discussion of the first issue — the state's legal framework — focuses on the income tax and, more particularly, the taxation of business income. The second issue — constitutional limits on state taxation — deals with a wider range of taxes: specifically, income taxes, gross receipts taxes, sales or use taxes, and severance taxes (on natural resources).

§ 35.01 STATE LEGISLATIVE FRAMEWORK — INCOME TAX

[A] Allocation/Apportionment

State tax rules usually rely on one of two approaches to taxing income — "allocation" and "apportionment."

"Allocation" refers to the approach used in the international tax context to locate the source (or geographical nexus) of particular items of income — for example, sales income arises where title passes or where a business office is located to which the sales are attributable; interest arises at the debtor's residence; etc. States generally use the allocation method only for *nonbusiness* income.

"Apportionment" looks at inputs that contribute to producing income. State taxation of business income generally uses the apportionment method, which is a significant departure from the source approach used by the United States in the international tax context. Apportionment of income to a state is based on the state's percentage of several economic factors that contribute to earning the income. States usually use the Uniform Division of Income for Tax Purposes (UDITPA) formula, approved by the National Conference of Commissioners on Uniform State Laws in 1957. UDITPA adopts a three-factor formula — property, payroll, and sales, with each factor equally weighted.

[B] Apportionment Formula

The arithmetic of an equally-weighted three-factor formula is easy to describe; the problem lies in the details. Assume the following: the taxpayer's *total* income is $240; total sales, property, and payroll equals $200, $100, and $50, respectively. The input figures for the *origin* state (State-OR, where manufacturing occurs) are sales

($10), property ($90), and payroll ($50). The formula locates $112 of the $240 of total income to the *origin* State, as follows:

$$\frac{Sales;\ \dfrac{10}{200}\ +\ Property;\ \dfrac{90}{100}\ +\ Payroll;\ \dfrac{50}{50}}{3}\ \times\ 240\ =\ 156$$

[C] Overtaxation Potential

Overtaxation is possible for the following reasons: not every state uses the same formula (some might even use a one-factor formula); not every state uses an equal weighting for each factor; and the criteria for locating and measuring each criteria can vary.

For example, overtaxation will occur if the destination state in which the sales occur (State-D) uses a one-factor sales formula and, under State-D law, locates all of the sales in the destination state. In that case, all of the income ($240 in the prior example) is taxed by State-D. Total income taxed by State-OR and State-D equals $396. Whether or not this is a serious burden depends on the tax rates in the respective jurisdictions. If tax rates are low, a bit of "overtaxation" is no big deal, which may be one reason why the U.S. constitutional law dealing with this problem (discussed later in this chapter) is both uncertain and tolerant of state practices.

[D] Applying the Apportionment Factors

It is not always easy to apply each of the apportionment factors. A few of the uncertainties are noted below.

[1] Sales

The sales factor usually locates sales in the destination state, which is different from U.S. international tax rules. An uncertainty in applying state law arises when goods are shipped to dockside for further retransmission to a purchaser in another state. Is the destination where the dock is located or where the final purchaser receives the goods?

[2] Property

The property factor can be very difficult to administer. First, states try to simplify the task of valuing property by excluding some property (such as intangibles) and, in most states, by using original cost rather than fair market value to measure value. Second, most states include rented property, usually valued at eight times the rent. Third, states vary as to whether they include property available for use but not yet used in the business. Fourth, property that moves among states, such as trucks and construction equipment, is often apportioned among the states by a mileage or time-of-use factor.

[3] Payroll

The payroll factor is usually located at the place of performance. When performance occurs in more than one state, the payroll is usually located at the base of operations from which the services are controlled. Executive pay is often omitted because it is large and might skew application of the payroll factor.

[E] Undertaxation; Throwback and Throwout Rules

Undertaxation can occur if the destination state does not impose a tax on income and the other states attribute some income to the destination state. One reason this can occur is a federal statute (Public Law 86-272), which denies a state the power to tax net income from interstate commerce when the only in-state activity is solicitation of sales — specifically, when there is a "solicitation of orders . . . for sales of tangible personal property, which orders are sent outside the State for approval or rejection, and, if approved, are filled by shipment or delivery from a point outside the State. . . ." This law was passed after the U.S. Supreme Court interpreted the Constitution to permit a state to tax a business based on in-state solicitation activities. *See Northwestern States Portland Cement Co. v. Minnesota*, 358 U.S. 450 (1959). (Constitutional issues are discussed later in Chapter 35.02.)

There are two approaches to preventing this source of tax leakage — throwback and throwout rules. UDITPA recommends the throwback rule.

A *throwback* rule attributes a sale to the state of origin (often the state of manufacture from which the goods are shipped), if the destination state lacks the *power* to tax (not simply because it does not exercise a power to tax). Some states that otherwise rely on the UDITPA formula do *not* adopt a throwback rule.

A *throwout* rule removes such sales from the numerator and denominator of the sales factor rather than attributing the sale to the origin state — in effect, using a two-factor property or payroll formula.

The difference between the throwback and throwout rules is illustrated by the following example. Assume that 100% of the sales occur in a destination state; the property and payroll factors are both distributed 75/25 between the manufacturing and destination states. The destination state lacks the power to tax the income. The three factors are equally weighted. The total percentage of income that is attributed to the two states under the throwback and throwout rules is as follows:

	THROWBACK		THROWOUT	
	MANUF.	DEST.	MANUF.	DEST.
SALES	100%	—	—	—
PROP	75%	25%	75%	25%
PAYROLL	75%	25%	75%	25%
TOTAL	83.33%	16.67%	75%	25%

[F] Discretion to Depart from Apportionment Formula

States sometimes allow the tax administration to depart from its apportionment formula if it does not fairly represent the business activity in the state. There are two typical techniques: (1) use a separate accounting approach for the business activity in the state (similar to branch accounting for an office or permanent establishment under the income tax law); or (2) modify the way a factor is used in the apportionment formula if it appears to distort the apportionment of income in the particular case (for example, (a) take account of intangible property of a business that relies heavily on royalties from copyrights, even though intangible property is usually excluded from the formula; or (b) take account of the *value* of older property with a low cost but a high contemporary value that is the major contributor to producing income, even though property is usually taken into account at cost).

§ 35.02 FEDERAL CONSTITUTIONAL LIMITS

[A] Introduction; The Due Process/Commerce Clause Framework

[1] Congressional Power

State taxation is subject to constitutional limitations — primarily the Due Process and Commerce Clauses of the U.S. Constitution. Congress could legislate under its Commerce Clause power to *limit* a lot of state taxation that the Court permits under its interpretation of the Commerce Clause. We have already seen the example of Public Law 86-272, which denies a state the power it retains under the Constitution to tax *net income* from interstate commerce when the only in-state activity is solicitation of sales. Congress could also *expand* state taxing power. For example, the Court held in *Quill* (discussed below and, earlier, in Chapter 29.05[B]) that the Commerce Clause prohibited a sales destination state from forcing collection of a use tax by an out-of-state mail order seller to an in-state resident, unless the out-of-state seller has an in-state office. However, Congress could grant the resident state this collection power, even though it has so far failed to do so.

[2] Constitutional Requirements — Connection/Nexus; Nondiscrimination

[a] The *Quill* and *Complete Auto* Cases

The federal constitutional rules have been very hard to pin down, as the Supreme Court has shifted from one approach to another. Two basic issues arise — (1) is there a *sufficient connection* between the taxpayer's activities and the state to permit the state to impose tax; and (2) does the state's tax impermissibly *discriminate* against interstate commerce?

[i]   Connection; Sales vs. Income Tax

The *Quill* case, which dealt with *sales or use* taxes, makes a clear distinction between the Due Process and Commerce Clauses, regarding the connection required before a state can impose a tax. The *Due Process Clause* makes it relatively easy for the taxpayer to have a taxable connection to a state. For example, an out-of-state seller who targeted an in-state resident buyer has a sufficient connection to the resident state to satisfy Due Process standards. The *Quill* decision applies the weak Due Process "connection" standard adopted in an earlier income tax case — *Container Corp. of America v. Franchise Tax Bd.*, 463 U.S. 159 (1983) (there must be (1) a "minimal connection" or "nexus" between the interstate business and the taxing jurisdiction and (2) a "rational relationship between the income attributed to the State and the intrastate values of the enterprise".)

But the *Quill* case also held that the *Commerce Clause* (not the Due Process Clause) imposed a higher "connection" (or "nexus") standard — in effect, a physical presence test. Consequently, the out-of-state seller in *Quill*, who did not have an office in the resident state, did not satisfy the Commerce Clause. In reaching this conclusion, *Quill* relied on the four-part test under the Commerce Clause (adopted by *Complete Auto Transit, Inc. v. Brady*, 430 U.S. 274 (1977)), *Prong 1* of which required that there be a "substantial nexus" with the taxing state. In effect, the Court held that the Prong 1 "connection" standard under the Commerce Clause required a closer nexus to the state than under the Due Process Clause.

Although there is nothing in the *Quill* decision that explicitly limits its application to sales and use taxes, there are lower court cases that do not apply the "physical presence" version of Prong 1 (the connection/nexus requirement) to an income tax. A number of courts have considered whether a state can impose an income tax on royalties paid to an out-of-state taxpayer for the use of trademarks in the taxing state. For example, suppose Corporation A in a high-tax State A conveys an intangible trademark to a subsidiary Corporation B in a low-tax State B and then pays a royalty to Corporation B for use of the intangible in State A. Can State A tax the royalty received by Corporation B even though Corporation B does not have a physical presence in State A? Most of these courts have held that the physical presence requirement adopted by the Supreme Court in *Quill* under the Commerce Clause applied only to sales and use taxes and not to income taxation. Consequently, the tax on royalties received by the out-of-state taxpayer was upheld, even though the out-of-state taxpayer did not have the physical connection to the taxing state specified by *Quill*. See, e.g., *Capital One F.S.B. v. Commissioner of Revenue*, 899 N.E.2d 76 (Mass. 2009), *cert. denied*, 557 U.S. 919 (2009); *Geoffrey, Inc. v. Commissioner*, 899 N.E.2d 87 (Mass. 2009) (same), *cert. denied*, 557 U.S. 920 (2009). So far, the Supreme Court has refused to review these cases.[1]

---

[1] Another technique for taxing royalties paid to a low-taxed out-of-state related corporation is to add back the royalty payment to the income of the high-taxed corporation that had transferred the intangible to the corporation in the low-tax state. See *Surtees v. VFJ Ventures, Inc.*, 8 So. 3d 950 (Ala. Civ. App. 2008), aff'd, *Ex parte VFJ Ventures, Inc.*, 8 So. 3d 983 (Ala. 2008). It is unclear why Alabama did not choose to tax the royalty received by the out-of-state corporation, although it may have thought that its

In the royalty cases just cited, the income was paid to an out-of-state corporation that was affiliated with the payor (such as a parent or subsidiary). But a West Virginia court went further. It held that *Quill* did not apply to prevent West Virginia from imposing an income tax on an out-of-state corporation's credit card business that resulted from successfully soliciting business in West Virginia, even though the corporation had no physical presence in West Virginia and payments were not made between related parties. It was sufficient that the corporation had a "substantial economic presence" in West Virginia. *Tax Commissioner of State v. MBNA America Bank, N.A.*, 640 S.E.2d 226 (W. Va. 2006). The court stressed "that the [] physical-presence test, articulated in 1967, makes little sense in today's world. In the previous almost forty years, business practices have changed dramatically. [At one time,] it was generally necessary that an entity have a physical presence of some sort, such as a warehouse, office, or salesperson, in a state in order to generate substantial business in that state. This is no longer true. The development and proliferation of communication technology exhibited, for example, by the growth of electronic commerce now makes it possible for an entity to have a significant economic presence in a state absent any physical presence there. For this reason, we believe that the mechanical application of a physical-presence standard to franchise and income taxes is a poor measuring stick of an entity's true nexus with a state."

See also KFC v. Iowa Department of Revenue, 792 N.W.2d 308 (Iowa 2010), where the court held that the licensing of intangible property for use in Iowa by an out-of-state corporation (specifically, the use of KFC's trademark) constituted a sufficient connection to Iowa to permit Iowa to impose an income tax on royalties received by the out-of-state corporation for use of the trademark. The court emphasized the "demise of formalism in favor of a multifactor test" in the Supreme Court's decision in *Complete Auto*, especially the "substantial nexus" standard. It stressed that "physical presence" in today's world is not "a meaningful surrogate for the economic presence sufficient to make a seller the subject of taxation."

[ii]   Three More Prongs

The remaining three prongs of the *Complete Auto* test are — *Prong 2*: that the state tax be fairly apportioned; *Prong 3*: that the state does not discriminate against interstate commerce; and *Prong 4*: that the tax be "fairly related to the services provided by the State."

In the remainder of this chapter, we pay primary attention to Prong 2 and Prong 3 of the *Complete Auto* test. *Prong 2* asks whether the tax base is fairly apportioned. This Prong, in effect, imposes an additional "connection" test to the Prong 1 "substantial nexus" requirement. Not only must the taxpayer's activities have a substantial nexus with the taxing jurisdiction, but the tax base itself must be sufficiently connected to the taxing state. *Prong 3* is a nondiscrimination

---

power to do so was unclear as long as the U.S. Supreme Court has not held that the physical presence requirement in *Quill* was limited to sales and use taxes. In any event, the Alabama court upheld the add-back on the ground that "the evidence did not demonstrate that the application of the add back statute has resulted in taxation [by Alabama] that is out of proportion to [the Alabama corporation's] activities in [Alabama]."

requirement, which is harder to apply than it sounds.

We do not focus on Prong 4 of the *Complete Auto* test — "fairly related to services" — because it is very easy to satisfy. In *Commonwealth Edison Co. v. Montana*, 453 U.S. 609 (1981), the Court dealt with a severance tax on all of the coal mined in the state. The Court refused to look at whether the tax was related to the benefits provided by the State as measured by the costs the state incurred because of the taxpayer's activities. The only question under Prong 4 was whether the taxpayer shouldered its fair share of supporting the provision of various services, such as police and fire protection, a trained work force, and even a civilized society. A tax base measured by the value of the coal taken out of the ground satisfied this test.

[b]   Judicial Power — Practical Limits and the Dormant Commerce Clause

As you read the cases dealing with the constitutional limits on state taxation — dealing with fair apportionment and discrimination — you should ask whether the Court is biting off more than it can chew in trying to police state taxing practices, except when there are obvious cases of discrimination against interstate commerce. The decisions often have multiple opinions and are not consistent across different taxes. If you come away with a clear understanding of the law, you are missing something.

One reason for the confusion is that the cases dealing with the Commerce Clause are all examples of what is called the "dormant Commerce Clause." All the Constitution says is that Congress shall have power to regulate commerce among the states, but the Supreme Court has interpreted congressional *silence* as an intent to keep commerce free of excessive and discriminatory burdens. As the cases illustrate, this has required judges to exercise considerable discretion in adopting and applying legal standards. Justice Scalia, ever on the watch for excessive exercises of judicial power and for reducing legal uncertainty, would reject judicial application of the dormant Commerce Clause. He argues that the Court should only ask whether the tax "facially discriminates against interstate commerce" and whether it is "indistinguishable from a type of law previously held unconstitutional by this Court." *West Lynn Creamery, Inc. v. Healy*, 512 U.S. 186, 210 (1994) (concurring in the judgment). In *Oklahoma Tax Commission v. Jefferson Lines, Inc.*, 514 U.S. 175, 201 (1995) (Scalia, J., concurring in the judgment), Justice Scalia stated his view that the "negative" Commerce Clause is negative "not only because it negates state regulation of commerce, but also because it does not appear in the Constitution." He would reject the "unhelpful" four-part *Complete Auto* test and relegate it to "its rightful place . . . among other useless and discarded tools of our negative-Commerce Clause jurisprudence."

[B]   Fair Apportionment; Internal and External Consistency

The fair apportionment test is Prong 2 of *Complete Auto*.

[1] Income Tax

Many of the income tax cases involving fair apportionment of the tax base arise when a taxpayer carries on more than one business, sometimes through a parent or subsidiary relationship. The question is whether the businesses can be aggregated to apply the apportionment formula. The standard is whether there is a "unitary" business. The following *Container Corp.* case deals with this issue.

Container Corp. also explains the difference between the two components of the "fair apportionment" test — "internal" and "external" consistency. Internal consistency requires that, if all states used the same taxing rule, no more than 100% of the business income would be taxed. External consistency prohibits an apportionment formula that attributes income to a taxing jurisdiction that is "out of all proportion to the business transacted in that State." Generally, a one-, two-, or three-factor formula will pass both tests.

CONTAINER CORP. OF AMERICA v. FRANCHISE TAX BD.
United States Supreme Court
463 U.S. 159 (1983)

Justice Brennan delivered the opinion of the Court.

[Editor — California taxed a portion of the net income of a corporation that does in business in the State, using a three-factor equally-weighted formula. The issue was whether the State satisfied the "fair apportionment" prong of the *Complete Auto* test. The specific issue was whether it was proper to determine the income apportioned to California by treating the corporation and its controlled subsidiaries as a "unitary business." The unitary business approach would result in aggregating the income of the corporation and its subsidiaries, as well as the sales, property, and payroll factors of all of the corporations to determine California's portion of the total income of the corporate group to California. The Court held that aggregation was proper in this case, and it reached this conclusion even though the subsidiaries were foreign corporations.]

. . . California imposes a corporate franchise tax geared to income. In common with a large number of other States, it employs the "unitary business" principle and formula apportionment in applying that tax to corporations doing business both inside and outside the State. Appellant is a Delaware corporation headquartered in Illinois and doing business in California and elsewhere. It also has a number of overseas subsidiaries incorporated in the countries in which they operate. Appellee is the California authority charged with administering the state's franchise tax. This appeal presents three questions for review: (1) Was it improper for appellee and the state courts to find that appellant and its overseas subsidiaries constituted a "unitary business" for purposes of the state tax? (2) Even if the unitary business finding was proper, do certain salient differences among national economies render the standard three-factor apportionment formula used by California so inaccurate as applied to the multinational enterprise consisting of appellant and its subsidiaries as to violate the constitutional requirement of "fair apportionment"? (3) In any event, did California have an obligation under the Foreign Commerce Clause, U.S. Const., Art. I, § 8, cl. 3, to employ the "arm's-length" analysis used by the federal government and most foreign nations in evaluating the tax consequences of inter-corporate relationships?

I

Various aspects of state tax systems based on the "unitary business" principle and formula apportionment have provoked repeated constitutional litigation in this Court.

. . . In the case of a more-or-less integrated business enterprise operating in more than one State, arriving at precise territorial allocations of "value" is often an elusive goal, both in theory and in practice. For this reason and others, we have long held that the Constitution imposes no single formula on the States, and that the taxpayer has the "distinct burden of showing by 'clear and cogent evidence' that [the state tax] results in extraterritorial values being taxed. . . . "

One way of deriving locally taxable income is on the basis of formal geographical or transactional accounting. [Editor — This allocation on income method is used under the federal income tax law.] The problem with this method is that formal accounting is subject to manipulation and imprecision, and often ignores or captures inadequately the many subtle and largely unquantifiable transfers of value that take place among the components of a single enterprise. The unitary business/formula apportionment method is a very different approach to the problem of taxing businesses operating in more than one jurisdiction. It rejects geographical or transactional accounting, and instead calculates the local tax base by first defining the scope of the "unitary business" of which the taxed enterprise's activities in the taxing jurisdiction form one part, and then apportioning the total income of that "unitary business" between the taxing jurisdiction and the rest of the world on the basis of a formula taking into account objective measures of the corporation's activities within and without the jurisdiction. This Court long ago upheld the constitutionality of the unitary business/formula apportionment method, although subject to certain constraints. The method has now gained wide acceptance. . . .

B

Two aspects of the unitary business/formula apportionment method have traditionally attracted judicial attention. These are, as one might easily guess, the notions of "unitary business" and "formula apportionment," respectively.

. . . At the very least, . . . a State [can]not tax a purported "unitary business" unless at least some part of it is conducted in the State. It also requires that there be some bond of ownership or control uniting the purported "unitary business."

In addition, . . . [the] activities of the purported "unitary business" [must] be related in some concrete way to the in-State activities. The functional meaning of this requirement is that there be some sharing or exchange of value not capable of precise identification or measurement — beyond the mere flow of funds arising out of a passive investment or a distinct business operation — which renders formula apportionment a reasonable method of taxation. In *Underwood Typewriter Co. v. Chamberlain*, 254 U.S. 113 (1920), we held that a State could tax on an apportioned basis the combined income of a vertically integrated business whose various components (manufacturing, sales, etc.) operated in different States. . . . In *Butler Bros. v. McColgan*, 315 U.S. 501 (1942), we recognized that the unitary business principle could apply, not only to vertically integrated enterprises, but also to a series of similar enterprises operating separately in various jurisdictions but linked by common managerial or operational resources that produced economies of scale and transfers of value. . . .

A final point that needs to be made about the unitary business concept is that it is not, so to speak, unitary: there are variations on the theme, and any number of them are logically consistent with the underlying principles motivating the approach. For example, a State might decide to respect formal corporate lines and treat the ownership of a corporate subsidiary as per se a passive investment. In *Mobil Oil Corp.*, 445 U.S. 425, 440–441 (1980), however, we made clear that, as a general matter, such a per se rule is not constitutionally required. . . .

Having determined that a certain set of activities constitute a "unitary business," a State must then apply a formula apportioning the income of that business within and without the State. Such an apportionment formula must . . . be fair. The first, and again obvious, component of fairness in an apportionment formula is what might be called internal consistency — that is the formula must be such that, if applied by every jurisdiction, it would result in no more than all of the unitary business's income being taxed. The second and more difficult requirement is what might be called external consistency — the factor or factors used in the apportionment formula must actually reflect a reasonable sense of how income is generated. The Constitution does not "invalidat[e] an apportionment formula whenever it may result in taxation of some income that did not have its source in the taxing State. . . ." Nevertheless, we will strike down the application of an apportionment formula if the taxpayer can prove "by 'clear and cogent evidence' that the income attributed to the State is in fact 'out of all appropriate proportions to the business transacted in that State'. . . ."

California and the other States that have adopted the Uniform Act use a formula — commonly called the "three-factor" formula — which is based, in equal parts, on the proportion of a unitary business's total payroll, property, and sales which are located in the taxing State. We [have] approved the three-factor formula. . . . Indeed, not only has the three-factor formula met our approval, but it has become, for reasons we discuss in more detail infra, something of a benchmark against which other apportionment formulas are judged.

. . . [However, in *Moorman Mfg. Co. v. Bair*, 437 U.S. 267 (1978)], we explained that eliminating all overlapping taxation would require this Court to establish not only a single constitutionally mandated method of taxation, but also rules regarding the application of that method in particular cases. Because that task was thought to be essentially legislative, we declined to undertake it, and held that a fairly apportioned tax would not be found invalid simply because it differed from the prevailing approach adopted by the States. . . .

II

Appellant is in the business of manufacturing custom-ordered paperboard packaging. Its operation is vertically integrated, and includes the production of paperboard from raw timber and wastepaper as well as its composition into the finished products ordered by customers. The operation is also largely domestic. During the years at issue in this case — 1963, 1964, and 1965 — appellant controlled 20 foreign subsidiaries located in four Latin American and four European countries. Its percentage ownership of the subsidiaries (either directly or through other subsidiaries) ranged between 66.7% and 100%. In those instances (about half) in which appellant did not own a 100% interest in the subsidiary, the remainder was owned by local nationals. . . .

. . . Sales of materials from appellant to its subsidiaries accounted for only about 1% of the subsidiaries' total purchases. The subsidiaries were also relatively autonomous with respect to matters of personnel and day-to-day management. For example, transfers of personnel from appellant to its subsidiaries were rare, and occurred only when a subsidiary could not fill a position locally. There was no formal United States training program for the subsidiaries' employees, although groups of foreign employees occasionally visited the United States for 2–6 week periods to familiarize themselves with appellant's methods of operation. Appellant charged one senior vice-president and four other officers with the task of overseeing the operations of the subsidiaries. These officers established general standards of professionalism, profitability, and ethical practices and dealt with major problems and long-term decisions; day-to-day management of the subsidiaries, however, was left in the hands of local executives who were always citizens of the host country. Although local decisions regarding capital expenditures were subject to review by appellant, problems were generally worked out by consensus rather than outright domination. Appellant also had a number of its directors and officers on the boards of directors of the subsidiaries, but they did not generally play an active role in management decisions.

Nevertheless, in certain respects, the relationship between appellant and its subsidiaries was decidedly close. For example, approximately half of the subsidiaries' long-term debt was either held directly, or guaranteed, by appellant. Appellant also provided advice and consultation regarding manufacturing techniques, engineering, design, architecture, insurance, and cost accounting to a number of its subsidiaries, either by entering into technical service agreements with them or by informal arrangement. Finally, appellant occasionally assisted its subsidiaries in their procurement of equipment, either by selling them used equipment of its own or by employing its own purchasing department to act as an agent for the subsidiaries.

[Editor — A footnote states: There was also a certain spill-over of goodwill between appellant and its subsidiaries; that is, appellant's customers who had overseas needs would on occasion ask appellant's sales representatives to recommend foreign firms, and where possible, the representatives would refer the customers to appellant's subsidiaries. In at least one instance, appellant became involved in the actual negotiation of a contract between a customer and a foreign subsidiary.]

[Editor — The Court then concluded in Part III of the opinion that the California court's conclusion that there was a unitary business was "within the realm of permissible judgment."]

IV

We turn now to the question of fair apportionment. [Editor — specifically, the external consistency branch of the fair apportionment requirement]. . . . Appellant challenges the application of California's three-factor formula to its business on two related grounds, both arising as a practical (although not a theoretical) matter out of the international character of the enterprise. First, appellant argues that its foreign subsidiaries are significantly more profitable than it is, and that the three-factor formula, by ignoring that fact and relying instead on indirect measures of income such as payroll, property, and sales, systematically distorts the true allocation of income between appellant and the subsidiaries. The problem with this argument is obvious: the profit figures relied on by appellant are based on precisely the sort of formal geographical accounting whose basic theoretical weaknesses justify resort to formula apportionment in the first place. . . . Although separate geographical accounting may be useful for internal auditing, for purposes of state taxation it is not constitutionally required."

Appellant's second argument is related, and can be answered in the same way. Appellant contends that: "The costs of production in foreign countries are generally significantly lower than in the United States, primarily as a result of the lower wage rates of workers in countries other than the United States. Because wages are one of the three factors used in formulary apportionment, the use of the formula unfairly inflates the amount of income apportioned to United States operations, where wages are higher."

Appellant supports this argument with various statistics that appear to demonstrate, not only that wage rates are generally lower in the foreign countries in which its subsidiaries operate, but also that those lower wages are not offset by lower levels of productivity. Indeed, it is able to show that at least one foreign plant had labor costs per thousand square feet of corrugated container that were approximately 40% of the same costs in appellant's California plants.

The problem with all this evidence, however, is that it does not by itself come close to impeaching the basic rationale behind the three-factor formula. Appellant and its foreign subsidiaries have been determined to be a unitary business. It therefore may well be that in addition to the foreign payroll going into the production of any given corrugated container by a foreign subsidiary, there is also California payroll, as well as other California factors, contributing — albeit more indirectly — to the same production. The mere fact that this possibility is not reflected in appellant's accounting does not disturb the underlying premises of the formula apportionment method.

Both geographical accounting and formula apportionment are imperfect proxies for an ideal which is not only difficult to achieve in practice, but also difficult to describe in theory. Some methods of formula apportionment are particularly problematic because they focus on only a small part of the spectrum of activities by which value is generated. Although we have generally upheld the use of such formulas, we have on occasion found the distortive effect of focusing on only one factor so outrageous in a particular case as to require reversal. In *Hans Rees' Sons, Inc. v. North Carolina ex rel. Maxwell*, 283 U.S. 123 (1931), for example, an apportionment method based entirely on ownership of tangible property resulted in an attribution to North Carolina of between 66% and 85% of the taxpayer's income over the course of a number of years, while a separate accounting analysis purposely skewed to resolve all doubts in favor of the State resulted in an attribution of no more than 21.7%. We struck down the application of the one-factor formula to that particular business, holding that the method, "albeit fair on its face, operates so as to reach profits which are in no just sense attributable to transactions within its jurisdiction."

The three-factor formula used by California has gained wide approval precisely because payroll, property, and sales appear in combination to reflect a very large share of the activities by which value is generated. It is therefore able to avoid the sorts of distortions that were present in *Hans Rees' Sons, Inc.*

Of course, even the three-factor formula is necessarily imperfect. But we have seen no evidence demonstrating that the margin of error (systematic or not) inherent in the three-factor formula is greater than the margin of error (systematic or not) inherent in the sort of separate accounting urged upon us by appellant. . . .

V

For the reasons we have just outlined, we conclude that California's application of the unitary business principle to appellant and its foreign subsidiaries was proper, and that its use of the standard three-factor formula to apportion the income of that unitary business was fair. This proper and fair method of taxation happens, however, to be quite different from the method employed both by the Federal Government in taxing appellant's business, and by each of the relevant foreign jurisdictions in taxing the business of appellant's subsidiaries. Each of these other taxing jurisdictions has adopted a qualified separate accounting approach — often referred to as the "arm's-length" approach — to the taxation of related corporations. Under the arm's-length approach, every corporation, even if closely tied to other corporations, is treated for most — but decidedly not all — purposes as if it were an independent entity dealing at arm's length with its affiliated corporations, and subject to taxation only by the jurisdictions in which it operates and only for the income it realizes on its own books.

If the unitary business consisting of appellant and its subsidiaries were entirely domestic, the fact that different jurisdictions applied different methods of taxation to it would probably make little constitutional difference . . . Given that it is international, however, we must subject this case to the additional scrutiny required by the Foreign Commerce Clause.

[Editor — Although agreeing that the Foreign Commerce Clause imposes a higher standard than the domestic Commerce Clause, the Court declined to find any violation of the Foreign Commerce Clause in this case. Further discussion of the Foreign Commerce Clause omitted.]

COMMENTS ON UNITARY BUSINESS

1. *Lack of a unitary business; Allied-Signal, Inc. v. Director, Division of Taxation*, 504 U.S. 768 (1992), involved a State's attempt to include gain on the sale of stock by Bendix Corporation in another corporation (ASARCO) as subject to its apportionment formula. The Court did not find a unitary business, such that Bendix's gain on the sale of its 20.6% interest in ASARCO corporation could be included in apportioned income. It stated that functional integration and economies of scale could not exist because the companies were unrelated business enterprises. Nor was there centralization of management, because Bendix did not own enough ASARCO stock to have the potential to operate ASARCO as an integrated division of a single unitary business and because potential control was insufficient. The fact that the sales transaction was undertaken for a business purpose did not make the corporation whose stock was sold part of a unitary business.

The *Allied-Signal* case relied on the Court's decision in *ASARCO, Inc. v. Idaho Tax Comm'n*, 458 U.S. 307 (1982), in which the Court had struck down a state's attempt to include dividends received from other corporations in the apportioned income tax base. The Court found that the payor and payee corporations were not part of a unitary business. Although the dividend-payee owned 51.5% of the payor's stock, an agreement with the other shareholders prevented ASARCO from dominating the payee's board of directors.

More recently, in *Meadwestvaco Corp. v. Illinois Dept. of Revenue*, 553 U.S. 16 (2008), the Court repeated that the hallmarks of a unitary business are: functional integration, centralized management, and economies of scale. By those standards, the gain realized by Mead Corporation on the sale of its wholly owned Lexis/Nexis business could not be taxed by Illinois because Mead and the Lexis/Nexis business were not part of a unitary business. Only Justice Thomas wrote separately to assert that he would overrule cases relying on the negative Commerce Clause.

2. *Unitary business; Dividends, capital gains, and the apportionment factors?* In the *Allied Signal* and *ASARCO* cases, noted above, the context in which the unitary business issue arose was an effort by the state to include the following in apportionable income: a capital gain on the sale of stock in a corporation that was allegedly part of the unitary business; and a dividend received from such a corporation. This contrasts with *Container Corp.*, in which the income the state wanted to apportion was the income of both the parent and subsidiary corporations, not just the portion of that income that was paid out in dividends or that could be attributed to the capital gains on the sale of stock. Although the Court rejected the unitary business characterization in *Allied Signal* and *ASARCO*, the question arises: How should dividends and capital gains be treated *if* the corporations are part of a unitary business?

Here are two possibilities.

(a) Count only the capital gain or dividend in income and use only the apportionment factors of the taxpayer who received that income. This seems like an odd result because the apportionment factors of one corporation are being applied to income derived from business engaged in by another corporation (that is, the business income that supported the capital gain or the dividend). One case used this "odd" approach to apportioning dividend income, but the Court noted that there was no legal challenge to the apportionment formula, which relied only on the factors of the dividend-receiving corporation; *Mobil Oil Corp. v. Commissioner of Taxes*, 445 U.S. 425 (1980).

(b) Include the capital gain or dividend in the income to be apportioned but also include in the apportionment formula the factors of the corporation whose business created the capital gain or dividend income. But this raises the following question. If the corporation realizing capital gain or receiving a dividend owns less than 100% of the other corporation, should the apportionment formula be applied by counting only a percentage of the other corporation's sales, services, or property factors? (The same question arises when the income of several corporations is combined because they are part of a unitary business, but one or more of these corporations is not wholly owned by a parent corporation.)

COMMENTS ON APPORTIONMENT

1. *One-factor formulas?* As the Court noted in *Container Corp.*, *Moorman Mfg. Co. v. Bair*, 437 U.S. 267 (1978), permit the state to use a one-factor sales formula, thereby leaving in place a system in which states as a group are likely to tax more than 100% of the taxpayer's income. The Court in *Moorman* made the following two points in accepting Iowa's one-factor sales formula. First, the Court rejected the argument that Iowa was at fault in a constitutional sense. Other states could avoid a risk of duplication in taxing income by adopting Iowa's one-factor formula. In other words, there was no violation of the internal consistency requirement, as long as more than 100% of the tax base would not be taxed *if* every state adopted a particular taxing formula. Second, the Court refused to interpret the Commerce Clause to prohibit any overlap in the computation of taxable income. That would require the Court to adopt a uniform formula for all states, along with a uniform definition of each category in that formula, which only Congress could do. The judicial requirement of external consistency was not that robust.

But, in *Hans Rees' Sons, Inc. v. North Carolina ex rel. Maxwell*, 283 U.S. 123 (1931), the Court struck down an apportionment-of-income method based entirely on ownership of tangible personal property which resulted in an attribution to North Carolina of between 66% and 85% of the taxpayer's income over the course of a number of years. By contrast, a separate accounting analysis skewed to resolve all doubts in favor of the State resulted in an attribution of no more than 21.7% to North Carolina. ("Separate accounting" is analogous to branch accounting used in the international tax setting to attribute income to a fixed office or permanent establishment.)

2. *Tax on value-added.* In *Trinova Corp. v. Michigan Dep't of Treasury*, 498 U.S. 358 (1991), the Court upheld the use of an equally-weighted three-factor formula in Michigan's (now-defunct) tax on value added. The Court concluded that the theory behind the three-factor formula applied just as much to a tax on value added as to an income tax — that the contributions of the payroll, property, and sales factors to the tax base were inexorably intertwined and could not be disaggregated, absent a showing by "clear and cogent evidence" that the formula allocates the tax base in a way that is "out of all proportions to the business

transacted" in the State. The Court also noted that a business could have value added even though it was unprofitable — because valued added equals revenue minus cost of materials; which equals cost of labor plus depreciation plus interest plus profit; which means that profit can be negative even though value added is positive.

3. *Flat tax on trucking.* In *American Trucking Associations v. Scheiner*, 483 U.S. 266 (1987), the Court struck down Pennsylvania's "flat" lump-sum annual tax on the operation of trucks in the state. This flat tax was not apportioned by road use, which seemed to violate the internal consistency standard because more than 100% of road use would be taxed if every state imposed the same lump sum tax. This case evoked a strong dissent from Justice O'Connor. She argued that many earlier cases had upheld unapportioned taxes on interstate transportation and that the state of Pennsylvania had relied on these cases in imposing its flat tax, which produced substantial revenue. In addition, Congress had not seen fit to override the cases upholding these taxes and it was Congress's role to decide how to deal with the potential tax burdens on interstate transportation. She then addressed the argument that changing circumstances — in the form of "the growth of the interstate trucking industry and the increased reliance on mileage apportioned taxes in our time" — might "make an older rule, defensible when formulated, inappropriate." But she concluded "that the evolutionary changes we have seen in the trucking industry are [not] substantial enough to defeat the strong stare decisis concerns, and the resulting reliance interests of the States . . . ."

The more recent decision in *American Trucking Associations v. Michigan Public Service Commission*, 545 U.S. 429 (2005), suggests that the Court may have come around to O'Connor's conclusion. In this case, the Court upheld a flat $100 fee imposed by Michigan on trucks that engaged in some intrastate trucking. The taxpayers argued that this tax violated the Commerce Clause. Based on the earlier 1987 *Scheiner* case, the taxpayers argued that they did not have to demonstrate empirically the existence of a burdensome or discriminatory impact upon interstate trucking, but the Court disagreed, stating:

> Petitioners [state] add that Michigan's fee fails the "internal consistency" test — a test that we have typically used where taxation of interstate transactions is at issue. Generally speaking, that test asks, "What would happen if all States did the same?" We must concede that here, as petitioners argue, if all States did the same, an interstate truck would have to pay fees totaling several hundred dollars, or even several thousand dollars, were it to "top off" its business by carrying local loads in many (or even all) other States. But it would have to do so only because it engages in local business in all those States. An interstate firm with local outlets normally expects to pay local fees that are uniformly assessed upon all those who engage in local business, interstate and domestic firms alike. A motor carrier is not special in this respect.

The trucking cases suggest that an initial question in applying the internal consistency test is to determine the relevant tax base. In the income tax cases, it is obvious that income is the tax base. In the trucking cases, the internal consistency test is violated only if the relevant tax base for applying the internal consistency test is mileage usage. The Court in the later 2005 Michigan case suggests that the tax base was "local business," implying that a flat tax on local business does not violate internal consistency.

Another point made by the Michigan case is less clear. The Court stated that there was empirical proof in the earlier Pennsylvania case that the fees imposed a cost per mile on interstate trucks that was approximately "five times as heavy as the cost per mile borne by local trucks." No such proof existed in the later Michigan case. This may be an application of Prong 4 of *Complete Auto* — that the tax be fairly related to state services.

COMMENT ON THROWOUT RULE AND EXTERNAL CONSISTENCY

In *Whirlpool Properties, Inc. v. Director*, 26 A.3d 446 (N.J. 2011), the court had this to say about when use of the throw-out rule might violate external consistency.

> The Throw–Out Rule's external consistency depends on the rationale for throwing out the receipts. Throwing out receipts because another state does not have an income tax will not result in an externally consistent outcome because a state's decision to have an income tax is independent of a taxpayer's business activity. By way of example, [assume] . . . that the company was [] based in a non-taxing state such as Nevada and sold 90 widgets in Nevada and 10 in New Jersey. Without the Throw–Out Rule, the sales factor would be 10/100=10%. With the Throw–Out Rule, the sales factor would be 10/(100–90)= 100% to New Jersey. That result is neither just nor fair, considering how much more Nevada must have contributed to the production of income than New Jersey.

> On the other hand, the Throw–Out Rule is arguably externally consistent when the untaxed receipts are thrown out due to a state's lack of jurisdiction to tax. The Throw–Out Rule still operates to increase New Jersey's share, but in this situation New Jersey also may have contributed more to the production of a sale than the sales factor, without the Throw–Out Rule, would suggest. Again, assume that the Nevada company from the earlier example relocated to New Jersey while maintaining the same 90 sales to Nevada and 10 sales to New Jersey proportionality. The company's only dealings with Nevada would be shipping the product to Nevada, which is insufficient for taxation in Nevada under P.L. 86-272, even if Nevada had an income tax, because the factory and all operations are in New Jersey. Without the Throw–Out Rule the sales factor would be 10%, and with the Throw–Out Rule the sales factor would be 100% to New Jersey. In that circumstance, allocating 100% to New Jersey may be reasonable. Nevada contributed relatively little compared to New Jersey and application of the Throw–Out Rule may more closely reflect the economic reality of New Jersey's contributions to the Nevada sales. Although Nevada provided some benefits, such as a market, because those benefits were not enough to give Nevada jurisdiction to tax, they would be constitutionally insignificant in terms of apportionment. The minor distor-

tion likely would fall within the zone of permissible inaccuracy when using an apportionment formula. That is not to assert that this interpretation of the Throw–Out Rule would lead to a fair outcome in every case, but only that the systematic distortion would not render the rule facially unconstitutional. And, importantly, there would be further opportunity to eliminate unfairness to the corporation, such as if multiple states were using a Throw–Out Rule in identical fashion in respect of such results, through an as-applied challenge by the entity.

In a footnote 12, the court gave the following example to illustrate how the throw-out rule might be unconstitutional under the external consistency test — on an as-applied basis.

> By way of example, assume a corporate taxpayer that has business activity in all fifty states; however, its activity in two states is insufficient to support, constitutionally, the imposition of any income tax by those taxing states and therefore none is imposed on the receipts generated in those states. Assume further that the remaining forty-eight states all have throw-out rules identical to New Jersey's. If all forty-eight states seek to apply their respective throw-out rules to the untaxed receipts from the two other aforementioned states, and thereby swell the taxpayer's tax liability in every state, there may well be unfairness from a reflexive application of the Rule. In such circumstances, the taxpayer should be permitted to seek relief from an unfair application of New Jersey's Throw–Out Rule through an as-applied challenge. Additionally, there may be untold other circumstances that pose fact-sensitive, unfair applications of the Throw–Out Rule. They also are best addressed through the vehicle of an as-applied challenge seeking relief from the unique unfairness that is posed to a particular taxpayer.

[2] Gross Receipts and Sales Taxes

In the following case, the Court dealt with (and upheld) an *unapportioned sales tax* on a bus ticket purchased in Oklahoma for interstate travel. The Court noted that the "difficult question in this case is whether the tax is properly apportioned within the meaning of the second prong of *Complete Auto*'s test. . . . " Its decision contrasted with *Central Greyhound Lines, Inc. v. Mealey*, 334 U.S. 653 (1948), where the Court held that New York's taxation of an interstate bus line's *gross receipts* could be imposed only on the portion reflecting miles traveled within the taxing jurisdiction. Gross receipts taxes, like a sales tax, are imposed on the gross sales price. But, unlike a sales tax, they are not imposed on individual transactions. They are instead imposed on a seller's total gross receipts, in much the same way that a taxpayer's total net income might be subject to tax (except that there are no deductions).

OKLAHOMA TAX COMM'N v. JEFFERSON LINES, INC.
United States Supreme Court
514 U.S. 175 (1995)

JUSTICE SOUTER delivered the opinion of the Court. . . .

External consistency looks . . . to the economic justification for the State's claim upon the value taxed, to discover whether a State's tax reaches beyond that portion of value that is fairly attributable to economic activity within the taxing State. Here, the threat of real multiple taxation (though not by literally identical statutes) may indicate a State's impermissible overreaching. It is to this less tidy world of real taxation that we turn now, and at length.

The very term "apportionment" tends to conjure up allocation by percentages, and where taxation of income from interstate business is in issue, apportionment disputes have often centered around specific formulas for slicing a taxable pie among several States in which the taxpayer's activities contributed to taxable value. . . . [For example,] in *Central Greyhound Lines, Inc. v. Mealey*, 334 U.S. 653 (1948), we held that New York's taxation of an interstate bus line's gross receipts was constitutionally limited to that portion reflecting miles traveled within the taxing jurisdiction.

In reviewing sales taxes for fair share, however, we have had to set a different course. A sale of goods is most readily viewed as a discrete event facilitated by the laws and amenities of the place of sale, and the transaction itself does not readily reveal the extent to which completed or anticipated interstate activity affects the value on which a buyer is taxed. We have therefore consistently approved taxation of sales without any division of the tax base among different States, and have instead held such taxes properly measurable by the gross charge for the purchase, regardless of any activity outside the taxing jurisdiction that might have preceded the sale or might occur in the future.

Such has been the rule even when the parties to a sales contract specifically contemplated interstate movement of the goods either immediately before, or after, the transfer of ownership. . . .

In deriving this rule covering taxation to a buyer on sales of goods we were not, of course, oblivious to the possibility of successive taxation of related events up and down the stream of commerce, and our cases are implicit with the understanding that the Commerce Clause does not forbid the actual assessment of a succession of taxes by different States on distinct events as the same tangible object flows along. Thus, it is a truism that a sales tax to the buyer does not preclude a tax to the seller upon the income earned from a sale, and there is no constitutional trouble inherent in the imposition of a sales tax in the State of delivery to the customer, even though the State of origin of the thing sold may have assessed a property or severance tax on it. In light of this settled treatment of taxes on sales of goods and other successive taxes related through the stream of commerce, it is fair to say that because the taxable event of the consummated sale of goods has been found to be properly treated as unique, an internally consistent, conventional sales tax has long been held to be externally consistent as well.

A sale of services can ordinarily be treated as a local state event just as readily as a sale of tangible goods can be located solely within the State of delivery. . . .

Cases on gross receipts from sales of services include one falling into quite a different category, however, and it is on this decision that the taxpayer relies for an analogy said to control the resolution of the case before us. In 1948, the Court decided *Central Greyhound Lines, Inc. v. Mealey*, 334 U.S. 653, striking down New York's gross receipts tax on transportation services imposed without further apportionment on the total receipts from New York sales of bus services, almost half of which were actually provided by carriage through neighboring New Jersey and Pennsylvania. The Court held the statute fatally flawed by the failure to apportion taxable receipts in the same proportions that miles traveled through the various States bore to the total. The similarity of Central Greyhound to this case is, of course, striking, and on the assumption that the economic significance of a gross receipts tax is indistinguishable from a tax on sales the Court of Appeals held that a similar mileage apportionment is required here, as the taxpayer now argues.

We, however, think that Central Greyhound provides the wrong analogy for answering the sales tax apportionment question here. To be sure, the two cases involve the identical services, and apportionment by mileage per State is equally feasible in each. But the two diverge crucially in the identity of the taxpayers and the consequent opportunities that are understood to exist for multiple taxation of the same taxpayer. Central Greyhound did not rest simply on the mathematical and administrative feasibility of a mileage apportionment, but on the Court's express understanding that the seller-taxpayer was exposed to taxation by New Jersey and Pennsylvania on portions of the same receipts that New York was taxing in their entirety. The Court thus understood the gross receipts tax to be simply a variety of tax on income, which was required to be apportioned to reflect the location of the various interstate activities by which it was earned. This understanding is presumably the reason that the Central Greyhound Court said nothing about the arguably local character of the levy on the sales transaction. . . .

Here, in contrast, the tax falls on the buyer of the services, who is no more subject to double taxation on the sale of these services than the buyer of goods would be. The taxable event comprises agreement, payment, and delivery of some of the services in the taxing State; no other State can claim to be the site of the same combination. . . . The analysis should not lose touch with the common understanding of a sale; the combined events of payment for a ticket and its delivery for present commencement of a trip are commonly understood to suffice for a sale.

In sum, the sales taxation here is not open to the double taxation analysis on which Central Greyhound turned, and that decision does not control.

[Editor — The Court then considered the "possibility of successive taxation so closely related to the transaction as to indicate potential unfairness of Oklahoma's tax on the full amount of sale," suggesting that a tax imposed on interstate travel by another state would have to provide a credit for the tax on such travel by Oklahoma. The Court stated:]

[Although] it is not Oklahoma that has offered to provide a credit for related taxes paid elsewhere, . . . in taxing sales Oklahoma may rely upon use-taxing

States to do so. This is merely a practical consequence of the structure of use taxes as generally based upon the primacy of taxes on sales, in that use of goods is taxed only to the extent that their prior sale has escaped taxation. Indeed, the District of Columbia and 44 of the 45 States that impose sales and use taxes permit such a credit or exemption for similar taxes paid to other States. *See* 2 Hellerstein & Hellerstein ¶ 18.08, p. 18-48; 1 All States Tax Guide ¶ 256 (1994). As one state court summarized the provisions in force:

> "These credit provisions create a national system under which the first state of purchase or use imposes the tax. Thereafter, no other state taxes the transaction unless there has been no prior tax imposed . . . or if the tax rate of the prior taxing state is less, in which case the subsequent taxing state imposes a tax measured only by the differential rate." *KSS Transportation Corp. v. Baldwin*, 9 N.J. Tax 273, 285 (1987).

[The Court concluded that the taxpayer had failed] to show that Oklahoma's tax on the sale of transportation imputes economic activity to the State of sale in any way substantially different from that imputed by the garden-variety sales tax, which we have perennially sustained, even though levied on goods that have traveled in interstate commerce to the point of sale or that will move across state lines thereafter. . . . We accordingly conclude that Oklahoma's tax on ticket sales for travel originating in Oklahoma is externally consistent, as reaching only the activity taking place within the taxing State, that is, the sale of the service.

COMMENTS AND QUESTIONS

1. Justice Breyer's dissent was unable to distinguish the *Central Greyhound* decision dealing with gross receipts taxes, except on "purely formal differences in terminology." As for the suggestion that a mandatory credit mechanism would reduce the chances of unfair apportionment, Breyer stated:

> The Court creates an ingenious set of constitutionally based taxing rules . . . designed to show that any other State that imposes, say, a gross receipts tax on its share of bus ticket sales would likely have to grant a credit for the Oklahoma sales tax (unless it forced its own citizens to pay both a sales tax and a gross receipts tax). . . . The difficulties with this approach lie in its complexity and our own inability to foresee all the ways in which other States might effectively tax their own portion of the journey now (also) taxed by Oklahoma.

2. Is the distinction between the Court's approach to gross receipts and sales taxes (and the related analogy of the gross receipts tax to an income tax) an example of the kind of formalism that has been rejected in other contexts? Does the Court's insistence that sales are a "local activity" sound like the conclusion that intrastate trucking is local (*American Trucking Associations v. Michigan Public Service Commission*, 545 U.S. 429 (2005)), and, if so, is that yet another example of "formalism"?

3. Does the Court's suggestion that the use tax state can be relied on to give a credit for taxes imposed in the sales tax state come close to requiring that the states take a particular approach to apportioning the tax base? Recall that, in the income

tax context, the Court has refused to insist on any particular apportionment formula.

[C] Discrimination

Prong 3 of *Complete Auto* prohibits discrimination against interstate commerce. The following cases apply that standard.

[1] Gross Receipts Tax

TYLER PIPE INDUS. v. WASHINGTON STATE DEP'T OF REVENUE
United States Supreme Court
483 U.S. 232 (1987)

JUSTICE STEVENS delivered the opinion of the Court.

The principal question in these consolidated appeals is whether Washington's manufacturing tax [] violates the Commerce Clause of the Constitution because it is assessed only on those products manufactured within Washington that are sold to out-of-state purchasers. We conclude that [it does.]

I

For over half a century Washington has imposed a business and occupation (B & O) tax on "the act or privilege of engaging in business activities" in the State. The tax applies to the activities of extracting raw materials in the State, manufacturing in the State, making wholesale sales in the State, and making retail sales in the State. The State has typically applied the same tax rates to these different activities. The measure of the selling tax is the "gross proceeds of sales," and the measure of the manufacturing tax is the value of the manufactured products.

Prior to 1950, the B & O tax contained a provision that exempted persons who were subject to either the extraction tax or the manufacturing tax from any liability for either the wholesale tax or the retail tax on products extracted or manufactured in the State. Thus, the wholesale tax applied to out-of-state manufacturers but not to local manufacturers. In 1948, the Washington Supreme Court held that this wholesale tax exemption for local manufacturers discriminated against interstate commerce and therefore violated the Commerce Clause of the Federal Constitution. The State Supreme Court rejected the State's argument that the taxpayer had not suffered from discrimination against interstate commerce because it had not proved that it paid manufacturing tax to another State. The Washington Supreme Court also dismissed the State's contention that if the State in which a good was manufactured did not impose a manufacturing tax, the seller of the good would have a competitive advantage over Washington manufacturers. . . .

Two years later, in 1950, the Washington Legislature responded to this ruling by turning the B & O tax exemption scheme inside out. The legislature removed the wholesale tax exemption for local manufacturers and replaced it with an exemption from the manufacturing tax for the portion of manufacturers' output that is subject to the wholesale tax. The result, as before 1950, is that local manufacturers pay the manufacturing tax on their interstate sales and out-of-state manufacturers pay the wholesale tax on their sales in Washington. Local manufacturer-wholesalers continue to pay only one gross receipts tax, but it is now applied to the activity of wholesaling rather than the activity of manufacturing. . . .

III

A person subject to Washington's wholesale tax for an item is not subject to the State's manufacturing tax for the same item. This statutory exemption for manufacturers that sell their products within the State [is] facially discriminatory [because there is no similar exemption for out-of-state manufacturers]. . . .

. . . [O]ur conclusion that a tax facially discriminates against interstate commerce need not be confirmed by an examination of the tax burdens imposed by other States. . . . We conclude that Washington's multiple activities exemption discriminates against interstate commerce as did the tax struck down by the Washington Supreme Court in 1948. . . . The current B & O tax exposes manufacturing or selling activity outside the State to a multiple burden from which only the activity of manufacturing in-state and selling in-state is exempt. The fact that the B & O tax "has the advantage of appearing nondiscriminatory," does not save it from invalidation. . . .

IV

[Editor — The Court noted that compliance with the holding regarding discrimination was possible either by "a repeal of the manufacturing tax or an expansion of the multiple activities exemption to provide out-of-state manufacturers with a credit for manufacturing taxes paid to other States."]

QUESTIONS AND COMMENTS

1. *Applicability of the internal consistency test?* In commenting on *Tyler*, Hellerstein notes that the Washington tax law at issue in the *Tyler* case failed the internal consistency branch of the fair apportionment test. *See* Hellerstein, *Is "Internal Consistency" Foolish?: Reflections on an Emerging Commerce Clause Restraint on State Taxation*, 87 MICH. L. REV. 138 (1988):

> . . . [T]he interstate manufacturer/wholesaler in [Tyler] was put at a competitive disadvantage to the intrastate manufacturer/wholesaler on the assumption that every state had adopted [Washington's] taxing scheme. . . . [T]he interstate manufacturer/wholesaler would pay both a manufacturing tax to the state of manufacture and a wholesaling tax to the state of sale, whereas the intrastate manufacturer/wholesaler would pay but one tax — . . . a wholesaling tax under [Washington's law].

This suggests that a state tax that fails the internal consistency test will, in some instances, be considered discriminatory.

Justice Scalia's dissent in *Tyler* argued that the internal consistency test should have no place outside of the income tax context:

> [Except for dictum in one case,] the internal consistency test was applied only in cases involving apportionment of the net income of businesses that more than one State sought to tax. That was the issue in Container Corp., . . . and there is no reason automatically to require internal consistency in other contexts. A business can of course earn net income in more than one State, but the total amount of income is a unitary figure. Hence, when more than one State has taxing jurisdiction over a multistate enterprise, an inconsistent apportionment scheme could result in taxation of more than 100% of that firm's net income. Where, however, tax is assessed not on unitary income but on discrete events such as sale, manufacture, and delivery, which can occur in a single State or in different States, that apportionment principle is not applicable; there is simply no unitary figure or event to apportion.

2. *Is Washington's tax facially discriminatory?* Justice O'Connor's concurrence argued that the Washington law was *facially* discriminatory.

> I join the Court's opinion holding that "[i]n light of the facially discriminatory nature of the multiple activities exemption," the Washington taxpayers need not prove actual discriminatory impact "by an examination of the tax burdens imposed by other States."

Justice Scalia's dissent in *Tyler* stated that the Washington tax was not facially discriminatory, as follows:

> . . . [T]he Washington B & O tax is valid. It is not facially discriminatory. . . . Washington's selling tax is imposed on all goods, whether produced in-state or out-of-state. No manufacturing tax is (or could be) imposed on out-of-state manufacturers, so no discrimination is present (or possible) there. All the State does is to relieve local producer/sellers from the burden of double taxation by declining to assess a manufacturing tax on local businesses with respect to goods on which a selling tax is paid. Nor does this arrangement, notwithstanding its nondiscriminatory appearance, have discriminatory effects in and of itself. An in-state manufacturer selling in-state pays one tax to Washington; an in-state manufacturer selling out-of-state pays one tax to Washington; and an out-of-state manufacturer selling in-state pays one tax to Washington. The State collects the same tax whether interstate or intrastate commerce is involved. The tax can be considered to have discriminatory effects only if one consults what other States are in fact doing (a case-by-case inquiry that appeals to no one) or unless one adopts an assumption as to what other States are doing. It is the latter course that the internal consistency rule adopts, assuming for purposes of our Commerce Clause determination that other States have the same tax as the tax under scrutiny. As noted earlier, I see no basis for that assumption in the tradition of our cases; and I see little basis for it in logic as well. Specifically, I see no reason why the fact that other States, by adopting a similar tax, might cause Washington's tax to have a discriminatory effect on interstate commerce, is of any more significance than the fact

that other States, by adopting a dissimilar tax, might produce such a result. The latter, of course, does not suffice to invalidate a tax. To take the simplest example: A tax on manufacturing (without a tax on wholesaling) will have a discriminatory effect upon interstate commerce if another State adopts a tax on wholesaling (without a tax on manufacturing) — for then a company manufacturing and selling in the former State would pay only a single tax, while a company manufacturing in the former State but selling in the latter State would pay two taxes.

Justice O'Connor agreed with Scalia that the internal consistency test should not be extended outside the income tax context. However, as noted above, she insisted (unlike Scalia) that the Washington tax system was facially discriminatory.

3.   *Upholding facially discriminatory tax.* In *Department of Revenue v. Davis,* 553 U.S. 328 (2008), the Court *upheld* a facially discriminatory state law which excluded from its income tax base the interest on state and local bonds issued by Kentucky and its political subdivisions but taxed interest on bonds issued by other jurisdictions. The Court relied on the fact that the bonds were issued for a traditional government function, which the state could subsidize.

[2]   Severance Taxes

In *Commonwealth Edison Co. v. Montana,* 453 U.S. 609 (1981), the Court dealt with a severance tax imposed by Montana on each ton of coal mined in the State at varying rates; actual tax rates varied, depending on the value, energy content, and method of extraction of the coal. The maximum tax rate was 30% of the "contract sales price." The Court first stated that the fact that the tax was imposed on goods prior to their entering the stream of interstate commerce did not immunize it from Commerce Clause scrutiny.

The Court held that the connection/nexus and apportionment requirements of the *Complete Auto* test were satisfied. The mining activity had an obvious nexus to Montana; and there was no question regarding apportionment or potential multiple taxation because "the severance can occur in no other state" and "no other state can tax the severance." This sounds a bit like the argument in the *Jefferson Lines* case that a sale is a local activity that can be subject to an unappportioned tax.

The Court then held that the Montana tax did not discriminate against interstate commerce — Prong 3 of the *Complete Auto* test. Just because 90% of the coal is shipped to other States under contracts that shift the tax burden primarily to out-of-state buyers did not constitute discrimination against out-of-state consumers. The Court stated that it was not confronted with the type of differential tax treatment of interstate and intrastate commerce that the Court has found in other "discrimination" cases. There was no discrimination because the Montana tax was computed at the same rate regardless of the final destination of the coal, and there was no suggestion that the administration of the tax departed from that even-handed formula. There was, moreover, nothing in the Commerce Clause to prevent a state from exploiting its monopoly position with respect to the production of a particular product.

[3] Sales/Use Taxes

HALLIBURTON OIL WELL CEMENTING CO. v. REILY
United States Supreme Court
373 U.S. 64 (1963)

Mr. Chief Justice Warren delivered the opinion of the Court.

The sole issue before us is whether the Louisiana use tax, as applied to the appellant, discriminates against interstate commerce in violation of the Commerce Clause of the Constitution.

The Louisiana sales and use taxes . . . provides for [a 2% tax on] the sales price of each item or article of tangible personal property when sold at retail in this state. . . . It imposes another [2% tax on] the cost prices of each item or article of tangible personal property when the same is not sold but is used . . . in this state. . . . This latter tax, commonly known as a use tax, is to be reduced by the amount of any similar sales or use tax paid on the item in a different State. As noted by the Louisiana Supreme Court below . . . , the purpose of such a sales-use tax scheme is to make all tangible property used or consumed in the State subject to a uniform tax burden irrespective of whether it is acquired within the State, making it subject to the sales tax, or from without the State, making it subject to a use tax at the same rate. The appellant admits the validity of such a scheme. It contends, however, that in this case, Louisiana has departed from the norm of tax equality and imposes on the appellant a greater tax burden solely because the property it uses in Louisiana is brought from out-of-state. The difference in tax burden is admitted by the appellee.

 . . . The appellant is engaged in the business of servicing oil wells in a number of oil producing States, including Louisiana. Its business requires the use of specialized equipment including oil well cementing trucks and electrical well logging trucks. These trucks and their equipment are not generally available on the retail market, but are manufactured by the appellant at its principal place of business in Duncan, Oklahoma. The raw materials and semifinished and finished articles necessary for the manufacture of these units are acquired on the open market by the appellant and assembled by its employees. The completed units are tested at Duncan and then assigned to specific field camps maintained by the appellant. The assignment is permanent unless better use of the unit can be made at another camp. None of these units is manufactured or held for sale to third parties.

Between January 1, 1952, and May 31, 1955, the appellant shipped new and used units of its specialized equipment to field camps in Louisiana. In its Louisiana tax returns filed for these years, the appellant calculated and paid use taxes upon the value of the raw materials and semifinished and finished articles used in manufacturing the units. The appellant did not include in its calculations the value of labor and shop overhead attributable to assembling the units. It is admitted that this cost factor would not have been taxed had the appellant assembled its units in Louisiana rather than in Oklahoma. . . . [Editor — The State challenged the taxpayer's failure to include the value of labor and shop overhead in the use tax base. These amounts were part of the cost of the property shipped from Oklahoma to Louisiana.] . . .

The inequality of the Louisiana tax burden between in-state and out-of-state manufacturer-users is admitted. Although the rate is the same, the appellant's tax base is increased through the inclusion of its product's labor and shop overhead. The Louisiana Supreme Court characterized this discrepancy as incidental. However, equality for the purposes of competition and the flow of commerce is measured in dollars and cents, not legal abstractions. In this case, the 'incidental discrepancy' — the labor and shop overhead for the units in dispute — amounts to $1,547,109.70. The use tax rate in Louisiana is 2% and has risen in some States to 4%. The resulting tax inequality is clearly substantial.

But even accepting this, the Louisiana Supreme Court concluded that the comparison between in-state and out-of-state manufacturer-users is not the proper way to frame the issue of equality. It stated: "The proper comparison would be between the use tax on the assembled equipment and a sales tax on the same equipment if it were sold." On the basis of such a comparison, the out-of-state manufacturer-user is on the same tax footing with respect to the item used as the retailer of a similar item, or the competitor who buys from the retailer rather than manufacture his own. However, such a comparison excludes from consideration, without any explanation, the very in-state taxpayer who is most similarly situated to the appellant, the local manufacturer-user. . . .

While the inequality in question may have been an accident of statutory drafting, it does in fact strike at a significant segment of economic activity and carries economic effects of a type proscribed by many previous cases. The appellant manufactures equipment specially adapted to its oil servicing business. The equipment is expensive; because of its limited and custom production, the labor and shop overhead is necessarily a significant cost factor. Activity of this character is often on the forefront of economic development where equipment and methods have yet to reach the standardization and acceptance necessary for mass production. If Louisiana were the only State to impose an additional tax burden for such out-of-state operations, the disparate treatment would be an incentive to locate within Louisiana; it would tend "to neutralize advantages belonging to the place of origin." Disapproval of such a result is implicit in all cases dealing with tax discrimination since a tax which is "discriminatory in favor of the local merchant," also encourages an out-of-state operator to become a resident in order to compete on equal terms. If similar unequal tax structures were adopted in other States, a not unlikely result of affirming here, the effects would be more widespread. The economic advantages of a single assembly plant for the appellant's multistate activities would be decreased for units sent to every State other than the State of residence. At best, this would encourage the appellant to locate his assembly operations in the State of largest use for the units. At worst, it would encourage their actual fractionalization or discontinuance. Clearly, approval of the Louisiana use tax in this case would "invite a multiplication of preferential trade areas destructive of the very purpose of the Commerce Clause."

In light of these considerations . . . , we conclude that the Louisiana use tax as applied to the appellant's specialized equipment discriminates against interstate commerce.

COMMENT

Justice Brennan's concurrence in the *Halliburton Oil* case dealt with the dissent's claim that the Louisiana tax law provided equality of treatment by providing the in-state user with a credit for taxes paid to other States. Brennan argued that this equality was "wholly fortuitous," stating that the "credit for prior sales or use taxes will avert discrimination in the taxation of casual sales only if the out-of-state purchaser has already paid a sales or use tax equal to or greater than Louisiana's use tax, so that the credit is fully effective. If the purchaser abroad has paid no prior tax, or one of smaller amount, then upon his first use of the article in Louisiana, he incurs a tax liability which he would clearly have escaped had he made the identical purchase at an exempted casual sale within the State."

[4] Individual Income Tax, Personal Deductions, and Privileges and Immunities

The prior discussion of income taxes has focused on state taxation of businesses. However, states often impose an income tax on individuals and usually provide different rules for computing the taxable income of residents and nonresidents — often with regard to personal deductions. The U.S. Constitution does not allow states to discriminate against nonresidents in providing these deductions, but it is not always easy to decide when the Constitution has been violated. The U.S. constitutional provision that forbids discrimination against nonresidents in this situation is the Privileges and Immunities Clause, U.S. Const., Art. IV, § 2; it provides that "[t]he Citizens of each State shall be entitled to all Privileges and Immunities of Citizens in the several States."

The most recent U.S. Supreme Court case on this issue is *Lunding v. New York Tax Appeals Tribunal*, 522 U.S. 287 (1998). The case dealt with a provision of New York law that permitted New York residents but denied nonresidents a state income tax deduction for alimony. A Connecticut resident who derived taxable income from a legal practice in New York challenged this provision. In general, New York measures the income of nonresidents subject to New York tax as the percentage which New York income is of total income; and total income is defined as the adjusted gross income under the federal income tax, which permits an alimony deduction. However, the New York income of a nonresident (in the numerator of the fraction) does *not* include an alimony deduction, which has the effect of taxing the New York income of nonresidents without the benefit of an alimony deduction.

The highest court in New York state upheld the disallowance of the deduction, relying on *Goodwin v. State Tax Comm'n*, 286 A.D. 694 (N.Y. App. Div 1955), *aff'd*, 133 N.E.2d 711 (N.Y. 1956), for the proposition that personal expenses are attributable to the state of residence. In *Goodwin*, a New Jersey resident was *not* successful in challenging New York's denial of tax deductions respecting New Jersey real estate taxes, mortgage interest payments, medical expenses, and life insurance premiums.

The U.S. Supreme Court agreed that the state could disallow the deduction of expenses related to the production of out-of-state income citing two cases. First, *Shaffer v. Carter*, 252 U.S. 37 (1920), upheld a State's denial of business-related deductions for out-of-state losses. Second, in *Travis v. Yale & Towne Mfg. Co.*, 252 U.S. 60 (1920), the Court upheld the principle that a state may "limit nonresidents' deductions of business expenses and nonbusiness deductions based on the relationship between those expenses and in-state property or income."

However, the Court also noted two situations in which the state tax law had impermissibly discriminated against nonresidents. First, in *Travis*, the Court struck down a provision of New York law that denied nonresidents an exemption from tax on a certain level of income when that exemption was available to New York residents — in effect, a zero tax bracket. Second, in *Austin v. New Hampshire*, 420 U.S. 656 (1975), the Court struck down a commuter tax imposed by New Hampshire, which had the effect of taxing only nonresidents working in that State. The Court summarized these precedents, as follows:

> *Travis* and *Austin* make clear that the Privileges and Immunities Clause prohibits a State from denying nonresidents a general tax exemption provided to residents, while *Shaffer* and *Travis* establish that States may limit nonresidents' deductions of business expenses and nonbusiness deductions based on the relationship between those expenses and in-state property or income. While the latter decisions provide States a considerable amount of leeway in aligning the tax burden of nonresidents to in-state activities, neither they nor *Austin* can be fairly read as holding that the Privileges and Immunities Clause permits States to categorically deny personal deductions to a nonresident taxpayer, without a substantial justification for the difference in treatment.

In other words, a connection between an expense and New York income was *sufficient* to require allowing the deduction, but it was *not* a *necessary* condition. The Court went on to insist that New York had to have a legitimate policy rationale for denying the deduction of alimony paid by a nonresident that did not just consider the connection of expenses to income-production. And it was unable to find such a rationale, stating:

> Looking first at the rationale the New York Court of Appeals adopted in upholding [the tax], we do not find in the court's decision any reasonable explanation or substantial justification for the discriminatory provision. [The Court of Appeals relied] on rationales borrowed from another case, *Goodwin v. State Tax Comm'n*, 146 N.Y.S.2d 172, 1955 N.Y. App. Div. LEXIS 4121, *aff'd*, 133 N.E.2d 711 (1956). There, a New Jersey resident challenged New York's denial of deductions for . . . his medical expenses and life insurance premiums. . . . Although the *Goodwin* court's rationale concerning New York's disallowance of nonresidents' deduction of life insurance premiums and medical expenses assumed that such expenses, "made by [the taxpayer] in the course of his personal activities, . . . must be regarded as having taken place in . . . the state of his residence," the court also found that those expenses "embodie[d] a governmental policy designed to serve a legitimate social end," namely, "to encourage [New

York] citizens to obtain life insurance protection and . . . to help [New York] citizens bear the burden of an extraordinary illness or accident." In this case, the New York Court of Appeals . . . did not articulate any policy basis for [its law]. . . ." Quite possibly, [there is no such policy], given that, at the time *Goodwin* was decided, New York appears to have allowed nonresidents a deduction for alimony paid as long as the recipient was a New York resident required to include the alimony in income. And for several years preceding [the law's] enactment, New York law permitted nonresidents to claim a pro rata deduction of alimony paid regardless of the recipient's residence.

The Court also seemed influenced by the fact that "[i]n the context of New York's overall scheme of nonresident taxation, [disallowing the alimony deduction] is an anomaly. New York tax law currently permits nonresidents to avail themselves of what amounts to a pro rata deduction for other tax-deductible personal expenses besides alimony.

The Court also noted that "alimony payments [] differ from other types of personal deductions, such as mortgage interest and property tax payments, whose situs can be determined based on the location of the underlying property. . . . [Alimony payments] reflect an obligation of some duration that is determined in large measure by an individual's income generally, wherever it is earned. The alimony obligation may be of a 'personal' nature, but it cannot be viewed as geographically fixed in the manner that other expenses, such as business losses, mortgage interest payments, or real estate taxes, might be."

The Court concluded:

> . . . [W]e do not propose that States are required to allow nonresidents a deduction for all manner of personal expenses, such as taxes paid to other States or mortgage interest relating to an out-of-state residence. . . . [However,] we find that respondents have not presented a substantial justification for the categorical denial of alimony deductions to nonresidents. The State's failure to provide more than a cursory justification for [its tax law] smacks of an effort to "penaliz[e] the citizens of other States by subjecting them to heavier taxation merely because they are such citizens," We thus hold that [the New York tax law] is an unwarranted denial to the citizens of other States of the privileges and immunities enjoyed by the citizens of New York.

There were three dissenters — in an opinion by Justice Ginsburg, joined by Chief Justice Rehnquist and Justice Kennedy. They stressed two points. First, they questioned whether alimony should be considered an expense at all. They noted that the scheme for taxing alimony in the federal and state income tax law is best "seen as a determination with respect to choice of taxable person rather than as rules relating to the definition of income or expense. In effect, the [alimony payor] is treated as a conduit for gross income that legally belongs to the [alimony recipient] under the divorce decree." New York implemented this approach by providing its payor-residents with a deduction and taxing its payee-residents on the receipt of alimony. This led Justice Ginsburg to make the following observations about the resulting pattern when payor and payee lived in different states:

The Court's condemnation of New York's law seems to me unwarranted. As applied to a universe of former marital partners who, like Lunding and his former spouse, reside in the same State, New York's attribution of income to someone (either payer or recipient) is hardly unfair. True, an occasional New York resident will be afforded a deduction though his former spouse, because she resides elsewhere, will not be chased by New York's tax collector. And an occasional New York alimony recipient will be taxed despite the nonresidence of her former spouse. But New York could legitimately assume that in most cases, as in the Lundings' case, payer and recipient will reside in the same State. Moreover, in cases in which the State's system is overly generous (New York payer, nonresident recipient) or insufficiently generous (nonresident payer, New York recipient), there is no systematic discrimination discretely against nonresidents, for the pairs of former spouses in both cases include a resident and a nonresident.

The argument that a Connecticut resident with New York income who paid alimony to a Connecticut resident was entitled to a deduction in computing New York taxable income, seemed (to the dissenters) to be asking for "a windfall," leading to a total exemption from New York's tax for the alimony income. (There also happened to be no tax in Connecticut on the alimony payment to the former spouse because Connecticut had no income tax in the year at issue.)

The dissenter's second major point was that, if alimony was characterized as an expense, it should be linked to the residence state — in this case, Connecticut rather than New York. They stated:

> Alimony payments (if properly treated as an expense at all) are a personal expense, as the Court acknowledges. They "ste[m] entirely from the marital relationship," *United States v. Gilmore*, 372 U.S. 39, 51 (1963), and, like other incidents of marital and family life, are principally connected to the State of residence. Unlike donations to New York-based charities or mortgage and tax payments for second homes in the State, Lunding's alimony payments cannot be said to take place in New York, nor do they inure to New York's benefit. They are payments particularly personal in character, made by one Connecticut resident to another Connecticut resident pursuant to a decree issued by a Connecticut state court. Those payments "must be deemed to take place in" Connecticut, "the state of [Lunding's] residence, the state in which his life is centered." New York is not constitutionally compelled to subsidize them.

TABLE OF CASES

[References are to pages]

[References are to pages]

[References are to pages]

[References are to pages]

TABLE OF STATUTES

[References are to pages]

[References are to pages]

TABLE OF AGENCY DECISIONS

[References are to pages]

INDEX

[References are to sections.]

[References are to sections.]

[References are to sections.]

C

CAPITAL EXPENDITURE VERSUS CURRENT EXPENSE

Generally . . . 13.01
Acquisition costs (See ACQUISITION COSTS)
Betterment . . . 13.03[B][1]
Education expenditures (See EDUCATION COSTS)
Improvement costs versus maintenance expenses
   (See subhead: Maintenance expenses versus improvement costs)
Maintenance expenses versus improvement costs
     Generally . . . 13.03; 13.03[A]
       Deductible repair expenses versus capital improvement costs
         Generally . . . 13.03[B]
         Adaption to new use . . . 13.03[B][3]
         Betterment . . . 13.03[B][1]
         Restoration . . . 13.03[B][2]
         Routine maintenance safe harbor
           . . . 13.03[B][4]
Restoration . . . 13.03[B][2]

CAPITAL GAINS

Generally . . . 3.04
Blood donations
     Property . . . 20.02[B][2]
     Service . . . 20.02[B][1]
Business, sale of integral part of . . . 20.04
Carried interests . . . 21.05[D]
Contingent payments and . . . 21.04[B]
Contract rights . . . 20.06[C]
Copyrights . . . 20.02[A]
Employee stock options . . . 21.05[B]
History of preferential treatment . . . 3.04[B]
Holding period
     Generally . . . 20.08
     Short sales . . . 20.08[B]
     Tacking . . . 20.08[A]
Incentive stock options . . . 21.05[C]
Limits imposed by case law
     Generally . . . 20.06
     Contract rights . . . 20.06[C]
     Earned income, already . . . 20.06[B]
     Lottery winnings, sale of . . . 20.06[E]
     Original issue discount . . . 20.06[A]
     Sale of lottery winnings . . . 20.06[E]
     Statutory interpretation . . . 20.06[D]
Long-term capital gains
     Alternative minimum tax (AMT), subject to
       . . . 18.02[B][5]
     Section 1231 transactions . . . 20.03
Losses, capital
     Current law . . . 3.04[C][3]
     History of . . . 3.04[C][1]
     Rationale . . . 3.04[C][2]
Lottery winnings, sale of . . . 20.06[E]
Ordinary course of business, sales made in
     Generally . . . 20.01
     Cases . . . 20.01[A]
     Statutory interpretation . . . 20.01[B]
Original issue discount . . . 20.06[A]
Partnerships . . . 32.01[B][1]

CAPITAL GAINS—Cont.

Preferential rate on capital gains
     Generally . . . 3.04[D]
     Future income, bunching . . . 3.04[D][5]
     Incentive . . . 3.04[D][4]
     Inflation . . . 3.04[D][3]
     Lock-in . . . 3.04[D][2]
     Past income, bunching . . . 3.04[D][1]
Preferential treatment . . . 3.04[B]
Sale of lottery winnings . . . 20.06[E]
Sale or exchange
     Generally . . . 20.07[A]
     Cases . . . 20.07[B]
Statutory interpretation . . . 20.06[D]
Statutory structure . . . 3.04[A]
Taxpayer's personal efforts create property
     Blood donations
       Property . . . 20.02[B][2]
       Service . . . 20.02[B][1]
     Copyrights . . . 20.02[A]

CARVED OUT INCOME INTERESTS

Generally . . . 22.01
Economic reality . . . 4.05[B]
Gifts
     Income and remainder interests acquired by
       Generally . . . 22.02[B], [D]
       Depreciation of income interest
         . . . 22.02[B][1]
       L and R basis . . . 22.02[B][3]
       Sale of income interest . . . 22.02[B][2]
     Retained remainder
       Generally . . . 4.05[A]
       Horst decision . . . 4.05[D][1]
       Horst versus *Blair* . . . 4.05[D][2]
       Interest free loans . . . 4.05[D][4]
       Property versus personal services
         . . . 4.05[D][3]
"Less than all," selling . . . 22.03
No statutory provision . . . 22.02[C][2]
Other carve out situations
     Generally . . . 22.02[C]
     No statutory provision . . . 22.02[C][2]
     Statutory provision . . . 22.02[C][1]
Retained remainder . . . 22.02[D]
Sale of, with retained remainder . . . 22.02[A]
Section 1286 . . . 22.02[E]
Statutory interpretation
     Generally . . . 4.05[C][1]
     Substantive canons of interpretation
       . . . 4.05[C][2]
Statutory provision . . . 22.02[C][1]

CASH GIFTS

Generally . . . 4.01

CASH METHOD OF ACCOUNTING

Generally . . . 3.05[A][1]; 23.01[A]
Accrued income, indirect taxation of payees on
     Mechanics
       Generally . . . 24.04[A]
       Payor's deduction until payee is taxed,
         disallow . . . 24.04[A][1]
       Statute . . . 24.04[A][2]

[References are to sections.]

[References are to sections.]

[References are to sections.]

[References are to sections.]

[References are to sections.]

[References are to sections.]

[References are to sections.]